ENGLISH THESAURUS

ENGLISH THESAURUS

GEDDES&
GROSSET

Published by Geddes & Grosset,
David Dale House, New Lanark ML11 9DJ Scotland

© 2005 Geddes & Grosset

First published 2005

ISBN 1 84205 526 7

Printed and bound in Poland, EU

Contents

Contents

A

aback *adv* back, backward, rearward, regressively.

abaft *prep* (*naut*) aft, astern, back of, behind.

abandon *vb* abdicate, abjure, desert, drop, evacuate, forsake, forswear, leave, quit, relinquish, yield; cede, forgo, give up, let go, renounce, resign, surrender, vacate, waive. * *n* careless freedom, dash, impetuosity, impulse, wildness.

abandoned *adj* depraved, derelict, deserted, discarded, dropped, forsaken, left, outcast, rejected, relinquished; corrupt, demoralized, depraved, dissolute, graceless, impenitent, irreclaimable, lost, obdurate, profligate, reprobate, shameless, sinful, unprincipled, vicious, wicked.

abandonment *n* desertion, dereliction, giving up, leaving, relinquishment, renunciation, surrender.

abase *vb* depress, drop, lower, reduce, sink; debase, degrade, disgrace, humble, humiliate.

abasement *n* abjection, debasement, degradation, disgrace, humbleness, humiliation, shame.

abash *vb* affront, bewilder, confound, confuse, dash, discompose, disconcert, embarrass, humiliate, humble, shame, snub.

abashment *n* confusion, embarrassment, humiliation, mortification, shame.

abate *vb* diminish, decrease, lessen, lower, moderate, reduce, relax, remove, slacken; allow, bate, deduct, mitigate, rebate, remit; allay, alleviate, appease, assuage, blunt, calm, compose, dull, mitigate, moderate, mollify, pacify, qualify, quiet, quell, soften, soothe, tranquillize.

abatement *n* alleviation, assuagement, decrement, decrease, extenuation, mitigation, moderation, remission; cessation, decline, diminution, ebb, fading, lowering, sinking, settlement; allowance, deduction, rebate, reduction.

abbey *n* convent, monastery, priory.

abbreviate *vb* abridge, compress, condense, contract, cut, curtail, epitomize, reduce, retrench, shorten.

abbreviation *n* abridgment, compression, condensation, contraction, curtailment, cutting, reduction, shortening.

abdicate *vb* abandon, cede, forgo, forsake, give up, quit, relinquish, renounce, resign, retire, surrender.

abdication *n* abandonment, abdicating, relinquishment, renunciation, resignation, surrender.

abdomen *n* belly, gut, paunch, stomach.

abduct *vb* carry off, kidnap, spirit away, take away.

abduction *n* carrying off, kidnapping, removal, seizure, withdrawal.

aberrant *adj* deviating, devious, divergent, diverging, erratic, rambling, wandering; abnormal, anomalistic, anomalous, disconnected, eccentric, erratic, exceptional, inconsequent, peculiar, irregular, preternatural, singular, strange, unnatural, unusual.

aberration *n* departure, deviation, divergence, rambling, wandering; abnormality, anomaly, eccentricity, irregularity, peculiarity, singularity, unconformity; delusion, disorder, hallucination, illusion, instability.

abet *vb* aid, assist, back, help, support, sustain, uphold; advocate, condone, countenance, encourage, favour, incite, sanction.

abettor *n* ally, assistant; adviser, advocate, promoter; accessory, accomplice, associate, confederate.

abeyance *n* anticipation, calculation, expectancy, waiting; dormancy, inactivity, intermission, quiescence, remission, reservation, suppression, suspension.

abhor *vb* abominate, detest, dislike intensely, execrate, hate, loathe, nauseate, view with horror.

abhorrence *n* abomination, antipathy, aversion, detestation, disgust, hatred, horror, loathing.

abhorrent *adj* abominating, detesting, hating, loathing; hateful, horrifying, horrible, loathsome, nauseating, odious, offensive, repellent, repugnant, repulsive, revolting, shocking.

abide *vb* lodge, rest, sojourn, stay, wait; dwell, inhabit, live, reside; bear, continue, persevere, persist, remain; endure, last, suffer, tolerate; (*with* **by**) act up to, conform to, discharge, fulfil, keep, persist in.

abiding *adj* changeless, constant, continuing, durable, enduring, immutable, lasting, permanent, stable, unchangeable.

ability *n* ableness, adroitness, aptitude, aptness, cleverness, dexterity, efficacy, efficiency, facility, might, ingenuity, knack, power, readiness, skill, strength, talent, vigour; competency, qualification; calibre, capability, capacity, expertness, faculty, gift, parts.

abject *adj* base, beggarly, contemptible, cringing, degraded, despicable, dirty, grovelling, ignoble, low, mean, menial, miserable, paltry, pitiful, poor, servile, sneaking, slavish, vile, worthless, wretched.

abjectness *n* abasement, abjection, baseness, contemptibleness, meanness, pitifulness, servility, vileness.

abjuration *n* abandonment, abnegation, discarding, disowning, rejection, relinquishment, renunciation, repudiation; disavowal, disclaimer, disclaiming, recall, recantation, repeal, retraction, reversal, revocation.

abjure *vb* abandon, discard, disclaim, disown, forgo, forswear, give up, reject, relinquish, renounce, repudiate; disavow, disclaim, recall, recant, renounce, repeal, retract, revoke, withdraw.

able *adj* accomplished, adroit, apt, clever, expert, ingenious, practical, proficient, qualified, quick, skilful, talented, versed; competent, effective, efficient, fitted, quick; capable, gifted, mighty, powerful, talented; athletic, brawny, muscular, robust, stalwart, strong, vigorous.

ablution *n* baptism, bathing, cleansing, lavation, purification, washing.

abnegation *n* abandonment, denial, renunciation, surrender.

abnormal *adj* aberrant, anomalous, divergent, eccentric, exceptional, peculiar, odd, singular, strange, uncomfortable, unnatural, unusual, weird.

abnormality *n* abnormity, anomaly, deformity, idiosyncrasy, irregularity, monstrosity, peculiarity, oddity, singularity, unconformity.

aboard *adv* inside, within, on.

abode *n* domicile, dwelling, habitation, home, house, lodging, quarters, residence, residency, seat.

abolish *vb* abrogate, annul, cancel, eliminate, invalidate, nullify, quash, repeal, rescind, revoke; annihilate, destroy, end, eradicate, extirpate, extinguish, obliterate, overthrow, suppress, terminate.

abolition *n* abrogation, annulling, annulment, cancellation, cancelling, nullification, repeal, rescinding, rescission, revocation; annihilation, destruction, eradication, extinction, extinguishment, extirpation, obliteration, overthrow, subversion, suppression.

abominable *adj* accursed, contemptible, cursed, damnable, detestable, execrable, hellish, horrid, nefarious, odious; abhorrent, detestable, disgusting, foul, hateful, loathsome, nauseous, obnoxious, shocking, revolting, repugnant, repulsive; shabby, vile, wretched.

abominate *vb* abhor, detest, execrate, hate, loathe, recoil from, revolt at, shrink from, shudder at.

abomination *n* abhorrence, antipathy, aversion, detestation, disgust, execration, hatred, loathing, nauseation; contamination, corruption, corruptness, defilement, foulness, impurity, loathsomeness, odiousness, pollution, taint, uncleanness; annoyance, curse, evil, infliction, nuisance, plague, torment.

aboriginal *adj* autochthonal, autochthonous, first, indigenous, native, original, primary, prime, primeval, primitive, pristine.

abortion *n* miscarriage, premature labour; disappointment, failure.

abortive *adj* immature, incomplete, rudimental, rudimentary, stunted, untimely; futile, fruitless, idle, ineffectual, inoperative, nugatory, profitless, unavailing, unsuccessful, useless, vain.

abound *vb* flow, flourish, increase, swarm, swell; exuberate, luxuriate, overflow, proliferate, swarm, teem.

about *prep* around, encircling, surrounding, round; near; concerning, referring to, regarding, relating to, relative to, respecting, touching, with regard to, with respect to; all over, over, through. * *adv* around, before; approximately, near, nearly.

above *adj* above-mentioned, aforementioned, aforesaid, foregoing, preceding, previous, prior. * *adv* aloft, overhead; before, previously; of a higher rank. * *prep* higher than, on top of; exceeding, greater than, more than, over; beyond, superior to.

above-board *adj* candid, frank, honest, open, straightforward, truthful, upright. * *adv* candidly, fairly, openly, sincerely.

abrade *vb* erase, erode, rub off, scrape out, wear away.

abrasion *n* attrition, disintegration, friction, wearing down; scrape, scratch.

abreast *adv* aligned, alongside.

abridge *vb* abbreviate, condense, compress, shorten, summarize; contract, diminish, lessen, reduce.

abridgment *n* compression, condensation, contraction, curtailment, diminution, epitomizing, reduction, shortening; abstract, brief, compendium, digest, epitome, outline, précis, summary, syllabus, synopsis; deprivation, limitation, restriction.

abroad *adv* expansively, unrestrainedly, ubiquitously, widely; forth, out of doors; overseas; extensively, publicly.

abrogate *vb* abolish, annul, cancel, invalidate, nullify, overrule, quash, repeal, rescind, revoke, set aside, vacate, void.

abrogation *n* abolition, annulling, annulment, cancellation, cancelling, repeal rescinding, rescission, revocation, voidance, voiding.

abrupt *adj* broken, craggy, jagged, rough, rugged; acclivous, acclivitous, precipitous, steep; hasty, ill-timed, precipitate, sudden, unanticipated, unexpected; blunt, brusque, curt, discourteous; cramped, harsh, jerky, stiff.

abscess *n* boil, fester, pustule, sore, ulcer.

abscond *vb* bolt, decamp, elope, escape, flee, fly, retreat, run off, sneak away, steal away, withdraw.

absence *n* nonappearance, nonattendance; abstraction, distraction, inattention, musing, preoccupation, reverie; default, defect, deficiency, lack, privation.

absent *adj* abroad, away, elsewhere, gone, not present, otherwhere; abstracted, dreaming, inattentive, lost, musing, napping, preoccupied.

absolute *adj* complete, ideal, independent, perfect, supreme, unconditional, unconditioned, unlimited, unqualified, unrestricted; arbitrary, authoritative, autocratic, despotic, dictatorial, imperious, irresponsible, tyrannical, tyrannous; actual, categorical, certain, decided, determinate, genuine, positive, real, unequivocal, unquestionable, veritable.

absolutely *adv* completely, definitely, unconditionally; actually, downright, indeed, indubitably, infallibly, positively, really, truly, unquestionably.

absoluteness *n* actuality, completeness, ideality, perfection, positiveness, reality, supremeness; absolutism, arbitrariness, despotism, tyranny.

absolution *n* acquittal, clearance, deliverance, discharge, forgiveness, liberation, pardon, release, remission, shrift, shriving.

absolutism *n* absoluteness, arbitrariness, autocracy, despotism, tyranny.

absolve *vb* acquit, clear, deliver, discharge, exculpate, excuse, exonerate, forgive, free, liberate, loose, pardon, release, set free, shrive.

absorb *vb* appropriate, assimilate, drink in, imbibe, soak up; consume, destroy, devour, engorge, engulf, exhaust, swallow up, take up; arrest, engage, engross, fix, immerse, occupy, rivet.

absorbent *adj* absorbing, imbibing, penetrable, porous, receptive.

absorption *adj* appropriation, assimilation, imbibing, osmosis, soaking up; consumption, destroying, devouring, engorgement, engulfing, exhaustion, swallowing up; concentration, engagement, engrossment, immersion, occupation, preoccupation.

abstain *vb* avoid, cease, deny oneself, desist, forbear, refrain, refuse, stop, withhold.

abstemious *adj* abstinent, frugal, moderate, self-denying, sober, temperate.

abstinence *n* abstemiousness, avoidance, forbearance, moderation, self-restraint, soberness, sobriety, teetotalism, temperance.

abstinent *adj* abstaining, fasting; abstemious, restraining, self-denying, self-restraining, sober, temperate.

abstract *vb* detach, disengage, disjoin, dissociate, disunite, isolate, separate; appropriate, purloin, seize, steal, take; abbreviate, abridge, epitomize. * *adj* isolated, separate, simple, unrelated; abstracted, occult, recondite, refined, subtle, vague; nonobjective, nonrepresentational. * *n* abridgment, condensation, digest, excerpt, extract, précis, selection, summary, synopsis.

abstracted *adj* absent, absent-minded, dreaming, inattentive, lost, musing, preoccupied; abstruse, refined, subtle.

abstraction *n* absence, absent-mindedness, brown study, inattention, muse, musing, preoccupation, reverie; disconnection, disjunction, isolation, separation; abduction, appropriation, pilfering, purloining, seizure, stealing, taking.

abstruse *adj* abstract, attenuated, dark, difficult, enigmatic, hidden, indefinite, mysterious, mystic, mystical, obscure, occult, profound, recondite, remote, subtle, transcendental, vague.

absurd *adj* egregious, fantastic, foolish, incongruous, ill-advised, ill-judged, irrational, ludicrous, nonsensical, nugatory, preposterous, ridiculous, self-annulling, senseless, silly, stupid, unreasonable.

absurdity *n* drivel, extravagance, fatuity, folly, foolery, foolishness, idiocy, nonsense.

abundance *n* affluence, amplitude, ampleness, copiousness, exuberance, fertility, flow, flood, largeness, luxuriance, opulence, overflow, plenitude, profusion, richness, store, wealth.

abundant *adj* abounding, ample, bountiful, copious, exuberant, flowing, full, good, large, lavish, rich, liberal, much, overflowing, plentiful, plenteous, replete, teeming, thick.

abuse *vb* betray, cajole, deceive, desecrate, dishonour, misapply, misemploy, misuse, pervert, pollute, profane, prostitute, violate, wrong; harm, hurt, ill-use, ill-treat, injure, maltreat, mishandle; asperse, berate, blacken, calumniate, defame, disparage, lampoon, lash, malign, revile, reproach, satirize, slander, traduce, upbraid, vilify. * *n* desecration, dishonour, ill-use, misuse, perversion, pollution, profanation; ill-treatment, maltreatment, outrage; malfeasance, malversation; aspersion, defamation, disparagement, insult, invective, obloquy, opprobrium, railing, rating, reviling, ribaldry, rudeness, scurrility, upbraiding, vilification, vituperation.

abusive *adj* calumnious, carping, condemnatory, contumelious, damnatory, denunciatory, injurious, insolent, insulting, offensive, opprobrious, reproachful, reviling, ribald, rude, scurrilous, vilificatory, vituperative.

abut *vb* adjoin, border, impinge, meet, project.

abutment *n* bank, bulwark, buttress, embankment, fortification; abutting, abuttal, adjacency, contiguity, juxtaposition.

abuttal *n* adjacency, boundary, contiguity, juxtaposition, nearness, next, terminus.

abyss *n* abysm, chasm, gorge, gulf, pit.

academic *adj* collegiate, lettered, scholastic. * *n* academician, classicist, doctor, fellow, pundit, savant, scholar, student, teacher.

academy *n* college, high school, institute, school.

accede *vb* accept, acquiesce, agree, assent to, comply with, concur, consent, yield.

accelerate *vb* dispatch, expedite, forward, hasten, hurry, precipitate, press on, quicken, speed, urge on.

acceleration *n* expedition, hastening, hurrying, quickening, pickup, precipitation, speeding up, stepping up.

accent *vb* accentuate, emphasize, stress. * *n* cadence, inflection, intonation, tone; beat, emphasis, ictus.

accentuate *vb* accent, emphasize, mark, point up, punctuate, stress; highlight, overemphasize, overstress, underline, underscore.

accept *vb* acquire, derive, get, gain, obtain, receive, take; accede to, acknowledge, acquiesce in, admit, agree to, approve, assent to, avow, embrace; estimate, construe, interpret, regard, value.

acceptable *adj* agreeable, gratifying, pleasant, pleasing, pleasurable, welcome.

acceptance *n* accepting, acknowledgment, receipt, reception, taking; approbation, approval, gratification, satisfaction.

acceptation *n* construction, import, interpretation, meaning, sense, significance, signification, understanding; adoption, approval, currency, vogue.

access *vb* broach, enter, open, open up. * *n* approach, avenue, entrance, entry, passage, way; admission, admittance, audience, interview; addition, accession, aggrandizement, enlargement, gain, increase, increment; (*med*) attack, fit, onset, recurrence.

accession *n* addition, augmentation, enlargement, extension, increase; succession.

accessory *adj* abetting, additional, additive, adjunct, aiding, ancillary, assisting, contributory, helping, subsidiary, subordinate, supplemental. * *n* abettor, accomplice, assistant, associate, confederate, helper; accompaniment, attendant, concomitant, detail, subsidiary.

accident *n* calamity, casualty, condition, contingency, disaster, fortuity, incident, misadventure, miscarriage, mischance, misfortune, mishap; affection, alteration, chance, contingency, mode, modification, property, quality, state.

accidental *adj* casual, chance, contingent, fortuitous, undesigned, unintended; adventitious, dispensable, immaterial, incidental, nonessential.

acclamation *n* acclaim, applause, cheer, cry, plaudit, outcry, salutation, shouting.

acclimatization, acclimation *n* adaptation, adjustment, conditioning, familiarization, habituation, inurement, naturalization.

acclimatize, acclimate *vb* accustom, adapt, adjust, condition, familiarize, habituate, inure, naturalize, season.

acclivity *n* ascent, height, hill, rising ground, steep, upward slope.

accommodate *vb* contain, furnish, hold, oblige, serve, supply; adapt, fit, suit; adjust, compose, harmonize, reconcile, settle.

accommodation *n* advantage, convenience, privilege; adaptation, agreement, conformity, fitness, suitableness; adjustment, harmonization, harmony, pacification, reconciliation, settlement.

accompaniment *n* adjunct, appendage, attachment, attendant, concomitant.

accompany *vb* attend, chaperon, convoy, escort, follow, go with.

accomplice *n* abettor, accessory, ally, assistant, associate, confederate, partner.

accomplish *vb* achieve, bring about, carry, carry through, complete, compass, consummate, do, effect, execute, perform, perfect; conclude, end, finish, terminate.

accomplished *adj* achieved, completed, done, effected, executed, finished, fulfilled, realized; able, adroit, apt, consummate, educated, experienced, expert, finished, instructed, practised, proficient, qualified, ripe, skilful, versed; elegant, fashionable, fine, polished, polite, refined.

accomplishment *n* achievement, acquirement, attainment, qualification; completion, fulfilment.

accord *vb* admit, allow, concede, deign, give, grant, vouchsafe, yield; agree, assent, concur, correspond, harmonize, quadrate, tally. * *n* accordance, agreement, concord, concurrence, conformity, consensus, harmony, unanimity, unison.

accordant *adj* agreeable, agreeing, congruous, consonant, harmonious, suitable, symphonious.

accordingly *adv* agreeably, conformably, consistently, suitably; consequently, hence, so, thence, therefore, thus, whence, wherefore.

accost *vb* address, confront, greet, hail, salute, speak to, stop.

account *vb* assess, appraise, estimate, evaluate, judge, rate; (*with* for) assign, attribute, explain, expound, justify, rationalize, vindicate. * *n* inventory, record, register, score; bill, book, charge; calculation, computation, count, reckoning, score, tale, tally; chronicle, detail, description, narration, narrative, portrayal, recital, rehearsal, relation, report, statement, tidings, word; elucidation, explanation, exposition; consideration, ground, motive, reason, regard, sake; consequence, consideration, dignity, distinction, importance, note, repute, reputation, worth.

accountable *adj* amenable, answerable, duty-bound, liable, responsible.

accoutre *vb* arm, dress, equip, fit out, furnish.

accredit *vb* authorize, depute, empower, entrust.

accrue *vb* arise, come, follow, flow, inure, issue, proceed, result.

accumulate *vb* agglomerate, aggregate, amass, bring together, collect, gather, grow, hoard, increase, pile, store.

accumulation *n* agglomeration, aggregation, collection, heap, hoard, mass, pile, store.

accuracy *n* carefulness, correctness, exactness, fidelity, precision, strictness.

accurate *adj* close, correct, exact, faithful, nice, precise, regular, strict, true, truthful.

accusation *n* arraignment, charge, incrimination, impeachment, indictment.

accuse *vb* arraign, charge, censure, impeach, indict, tax.

accustom *vb* discipline, drill, familiarize, habituate, harden, inure, train, use.

ace *n* (*cards, dice*) one spot, single pip, single point; atom, bit, grain, iota, jot, particle, single, unit, whit; expert, master, virtuoso. * *adj* best, expert, fine, outstanding, superb.

acerbity *n* acidity, acridity, acridness, astringency, bitterness, roughness, sourness, tartness; acrimony, bitterness, harshness, severity, venom.

achieve *vb* accomplish, attain, complete, do, effect,

execute, finish, fulfil, perform, realize; acquire, gain, get, obtain, win.

achievement *n* accomplishment, acquirement, attainment, completion, consummation, performance, realization; deed, exploit, feat, work.

acid *adj* pungent, sharp, sour, stinging, tart, vinegary.

acknowledge *vb* recognize; accept, admit, accept, allow, concede, grant; avow, confess, own, profess.

acme *n* apex, climax, height, peak, pinnacle, summit, top, vertex, zenith.

acquaint *vb* familiarize; announce, apprise, communicate, enlighten, disclose, inform, make aware, make known, notify, tell.

acquaintance *n* companionship, familiarity, fellowship, intimacy, knowledge; associate, companion, comrade, friend.

acquiesce *vb* bow, comply, consent, give way, rest, submit, yield; agree, assent, concur, consent.

acquire *vb* achieve, attain, earn, gain, get, have, obtain, procure, realize, secure, win; learn thoroughly, master.

acquirement *n* acquiring, gaining, gathering, mastery; acquisition, accomplishment, attainment.

acquit *vb* absolve, clear, discharge, exculpate, excuse, exonerate, forgive, liberate, pardon, pay, quit, release, set free, settle.

acquittal *n* absolution, acquittance, clearance, deliverance, discharge, exoneration, liberation, release.

acquittance *n* discharge; quittance, receipt.

acrid *adj* biting, bitter, caustic, pungent, sharp.

acrimonious *adj* acrid, bitter, caustic, censorious, crabbed, harsh, malignant, petulant, sarcastic, severe, testy, virulent.

acrimony *n* causticity, causticness, corrosiveness, sharpness; abusiveness, acridity, asperity, bitterness, churlishness, harshness, rancour, severity, spite, venom.

act *vb* do, execute, function, make, operate, work; enact, feign, perform, play. * *n* achievement, deed, exploit, feat, performance, proceeding, turn; bill, decree, enactment, law, ordinance, statute; actuality, existence, fact, reality.

acting *adj* interim, provisional, substitute, temporary. * *n* enacting, impersonation, performance, portrayal, theatre; counterfeiting, dissimulation, imitation, pretence.

action *n* achievement, activity, agency, deed, exertion, exploit, feat; battle, combat, conflict, contest, encounter, engagement, operation; lawsuit, prosecution.

active *adj* effective, efficient, influential, living, operative; assiduous, bustling, busy, diligent, industrious, restless; agile, alert, brisk, energetic, lively, nimble, prompt, quick, smart, spirited, sprightly, supple; animated, ebullient, fervent, vigorous.

actual *adj* certain, decided, genuine, objective, real, substantial, tangible, true, veritable; perceptible, present, sensible, tangible; absolute, categorical, positive.

actuate *vb* impel, incite, induce, instigate, move, persuade, prompt.

acumen *n* acuteness, astuteness, discernment, ingenuity, keenness, penetration, sagacity, sharpness, shrewdness.

acute *adj* pointed, sharp; astute, bright, discerning, ingenious, intelligent, keen, quick, penetrating, piercing, sagacious, sage, sharp, shrewd, smart, subtle; distressing, fierce, intense, piercing, pungent, poignant, severe, violent; high, high-toned, sharp, shrill; (*med*) sudden, temporary, violent.

adage *n* aphorism, dictum, maxim, proverb, saw, saying.

adapt *vb* accommodate, adjust, conform, coordinate, fit, qualify, proportion, suit, temper.

add *vb* adjoin, affix, annex, append, attach, join, tag; sum, sum up, total.

addict *vb* accustom, apply, dedicate, devote, habituate. * *n* devotee, enthusiast, fan; head, junkie, user.

addicted *adj* attached, devoted, given up to, inclined, prone, wedded.

addition *n* augmentation, accession, enlargement, extension, increase, supplement; adjunct, appendage, appendix, extra.

address *vb* accost, apply to, court, direct. * *n* appeal, application, entreaty, invocation, memorial, petition, request, solicitation, suit; discourse, oration, lecture, sermon, speech; ability, adroitness, art, dexterity, expertness, skill; courtesy, deportment, demeanour, tact.

adduce *vb* advance, allege, assign, offer, present; cite, mention, name.

adept *adj* accomplished, experienced, practised, proficient, skilled. * *n* expert, master, virtuoso.

adequate *adj* able, adapted, capable, competent, equal, fit, requisite, satisfactory, sufficient, suitable.

adhere *vb* cling, cleave, cohere, hold, stick; appertain, belong, pertain.

adherent *adj* adhering, clinging, sticking. * *n* acolyte, dependant, disciple, follower, partisan, supporter, vassal.

adhesion *n* adherence, attachment, clinging, coherence, sticking.

adhesive *adj* clinging, sticking; glutinous, gummy, sticky, tenacious, viscous. * *n* binder, cement, glue, paste.

adieu *n* farewell, goodbye, parting, valediction.

adipose *adj* fat, fatty, greasy, oily, oleaginous, sebaceous.

adjacent *adj* adjoining, bordering, conterminous, contiguous, near, near to, neighbouring, touching.

adjoin *vb* abut, add, annex, append, border, combine, neighbour, unite, verge.

adjourn *vb* defer, delay, postpone, procrastinate; close, dissolve, end, interrupt, prorogue, suspend.

adjudge *vb* allot, assign, award; decide, decree, determine, settle.

adjunct *n* addition, advantage, appendage, appurtenance, attachment, attribute, auxiliary, dependency, help.

adjure *vb* beg, beseech, entreat, pray, supplicate.

adjust *vb* adapt, arrange, dispose, rectify; regulate, set right, settle, suit; compose, harmonize, pacify, reconcile, settle; accommodate, adapt, fit, suit.

administer *vb* contribute, deal out, dispense, supply; conduct, control, direct, govern, manage, oversee, superintend; conduce, contribute.

admirable *adj* astonishing, striking, surprising, wonderful; excellent, fine, rare, superb.

admiration *n* affection, approbation, approval, astonishment, delight, esteem, pleasure, regard.

admirer *n* beau, gallant, suitor, sweetheart; fan, follower, supporter.

admissible *adj* allowable, lawful, permissible, possible.

admission *n* access, admittance, entrance, introduction; acceptance, acknowledgement, allowance, assent, avowal, concession.

admit *vb* give access to, let in, receive; agree to, accept, acknowledge, concede, confess; allow, bear, permit, suffer, tolerate.

admonish *vb* censure, rebuke, reprove; advise caution, counsel, enjoin, forewarn, warn; acquaint, apprise, inform, instruct, notify, remind.

admonition *n* censure, rebuke, remonstrance; advice, caution, chiding, counsel, instruction, monition.

adolescence *n* minority, nonage, teens, youth.

adolescent *adj* juvenile, young, youthful. * *n* minor, teenager, youth.

adopt *vb* appropriate, assume; accept, approve, avow, espouse, maintain, support; affiliate, father, foster.

adore *vb* worship; esteem, honour, idolize, love, revere, venerate.

adorn *vb* beautify, decorate, embellish, enrich, garnish, gild, grace, ornament.

adroit *adj* apt, dextrous, expert, handy, ingenious, ready, skilful.

adulation *n* blandishment, cajolery, fawning, flattery, flummery, praise, sycophancy.

adult *adj* grown-up, mature, ripe, ripened. * *n* grown-up person.

adulterate *vb* alloy, contaminate, corrupt, debase, deteriorate, vitiate.

advance *adj* beforehand, forward, leading. * *vb* propel, push, send forward; aggrandize, dignify, elevate, exalt, promote; benefit, forward, further, improve, promote; adduce, allege, assign, offer, propose, propound; augment, increase; proceed, progress; grow, improve, prosper, thrive. * *n* march, progress; advancement, enhancement, growth, promotion, rise; offer, overture, proffering, proposal, proposition, tender; appreciation, rise.

advancement *n* advance, benefit, gain, growth, improvement, profit.

advantage *n* ascendancy, precedence, pre-eminence, superiority, upper-hand; benefit, blessing, emolument, gain, profit, return; account, behalf, interest; accommodation, convenience, prerogative, privilege.

advantageous *adj* beneficial, favourable, profitable.

advent *n* accession, approach, arrival, coming, visitation.

adventitious *adj* accidental, extraneous, extrinsic, foreign, fortuitous, nonessential.

adventure *vb* dare, hazard, imperil, peril, risk, venture. * *n* chance, contingency, experiment, fortuity, hazard, risk, venture; crisis, contingency, event, incident, occurrence, transaction.

adventurous *adj* bold, chivalrous, courageous, daring, doughty; foolhardy, headlong, precipitate, rash, reckless; dangerous, hazardous, perilous.

adversary *n* antagonist, enemy, foe, opponent.

adverse *adj* conflicting, contrary, opposing; antagonistic, harmful, hostile, hurtful, inimical, unfavourable, unpropitious; calamitous, disastrous, unfortunate, unlucky, untoward.

adversity *n* affliction, calamity, disaster, distress, misery, misfortune, sorrow, suffering, woe.

advertise *vb* advise, announce, declare, inform, placard, proclaim, publish.

advertisement *n* announcement, information, notice, proclamation.

advice *n* admonition, caution, counsel, exhortation, persuasion, suggestion, recommendation; information, intelligence, notice, notification; care, counsel, deliberation, forethought.

advisable *adj* advantageous, desirable, expedient, prudent.

advise *vb* admonish, counsel, commend, recommend, suggest, urge; acquaint, apprise, inform, notify; confer, consult, deliberate.

adviser *n* counsellor, director, guide, instructor.

advocate *vb* countenance, defend, favour, justify, maintain, support, uphold, vindicate. * *n* apologist, counsellor, defender, maintainer, patron, pleader, supporter; attorney, barrister, counsel, lawyer, solicitor.

aegis *n* defence, protection, safeguard, shelter.

aesthetic *adj* appropriate, beautiful, tasteful.

affable *adj* accessible, approachable, communicative, conversable, cordial, easy, familiar, frank, free, sociable, social; complaisant, courteous, civil, obliging, polite, urbane.

affair *n* business, circumstance, concern, matter, office, question; event, incident, occurrence, performance, proceeding, transaction; battle, combat, conflict, encounter, engagement, skirmish.

affairs *npl* administration, relations; business, estate, finances, property.

affect *vb* act upon, alter, change, influence, modify, transform; concern, interest, regard, relate; improve, melt, move, overcome, subdue, touch;

aim at, aspire to, crave, yearn for; adopt, assume, feign.

affectation *n* affectedness, airs, artificiality, foppery, pretension, simulation.

affected *adj* artificial, assumed, feigned, insincere, theatrical; assuming, conceited, foppish, vain.

affection *n* bent, bias, feeling, inclination, passion, proclivity, propensity; accident, attribute, character, mark, modification, mode, note, property; attachment, endearment, fondness, goodwill, kindness, partiality, love.

affectionate *adj* attached, devoted, fond, kind, loving, sympathetic, tender.

affiliate *vb* ally, annex, associate, connect, incorporate, join, unite. * *n* ally, associate, confederate.

affinity *n* connection, propinquity, relationship; analogy, attraction, correspondence, likeness, relation, resemblance, similarity, sympathy.

affirm *vb* allege, assert, asseverate, aver, declare, state; approve, confirm, establish, ratify.

affix *vb* annex, attach, connect, fasten, join, subjoin, tack.

afflict *vb* agonize, distress, grieve, pain, persecute, plague, torment, trouble, try, wound.

affliction *n* adversity, calamity, disaster, misfortune, stroke, visitation; bitterness, depression, distress, grief, misery, plague, scourge, sorrow, trial, tribulation, wretchedness, woe.

affluent *adj* abounding, abundant, bounteous, plenteous; moneyed, opulent, rich, wealthy.

afford *vb* furnish, produce, supply, yield; bestow, communicate, confer, give, grant, impart, offer; bear, endure, support.

affray *n* brawl, conflict, disturbance, feud, fight, quarrel, scuffle, struggle.

affright *vb* affray, alarm, appal, confound, dismay, shock, startle. * *n* alarm, consternation, fear, fright, panic, terror.

affront *vb* abuse, insult, outrage; annoy, chafe, displease, fret, irritate, offend, pique, provoke, vex. * *n* abuse, contumely, insult, outrage, vexation, wrong.

afraid *adj* aghast, alarmed, anxious, apprehensive, frightened, scared, timid.

after *prep* later than, subsequent to; behind, following; about, according to; because of, in imitation of. * *adj* behind, consecutive, ensuing, following, later, succeeding, successive, subsequent; aft, back, hind, rear, rearmost, tail.* *adv* afterwards, later, next, since, subsequently, then, thereafter.

again *adv* afresh, anew, another time, once more; besides, further, in addition, moreover.

against *prep* adverse to, contrary to, in opposition to, resisting; abutting, close up to, facing, fronting, off, opposite to, over; in anticipation of, for, in expectation of; in compensation for, to counterbalance, to match.

age *vb* decline, grow old, mature. * *n* aeon, date, epoch, period, time; decline, old age, senility; antiquity, oldness.

agency *n* action, force, intervention, means, mediation, operation, procurement; charge, direction, management, superintendence, supervision.

agent *n* actor, doer, executor, operator, performer; active element, cause, force; attorney, broker, commissioner, deputy, factor, intermediary, manager, middleman.

agglomeration *n* accumulation, aggregation, conglomeration, heap, lump, pile.

agglutinate *vb* cement, fasten, glue, unite.

aggrandize *vb* advance, dignify, elevate, enrich, exalt, promote.

aggravate *vb* heighten, increase, worsen; colour, exaggerate, magnify, overstate; enrage, irritate, provoke, tease.

aggravation *n* exaggeration, heightening, irritation.

aggregate *vb* accumulate, amass, collect, heap, pile. * *adj* collected, total. * *n* amount, gross, total, whole.

aggressive *adj* assailing, assailant, assaulting, attacking, invading, offensive; pushing, self-assertive.

aggressor *n* assailant, assaulter, attacker, invader.

aggrieve *vb* afflict, grieve, pain; abuse, ill-treat, impose, injure, oppress, wrong.

aghast *adj* appalled, dismayed, frightened, horrified, horror-struck, panic-stricken, terrified; amazed, astonished, startled, thunderstruck.

agile *adj* active, alert, brisk, lively, nimble, prompt, smart, ready.

agitate *vb* disturb, jar, rock, shake, trouble; disquiet, excite, ferment, rouse, trouble; confuse, discontent, flurry, fluster, flutter; canvass, debate, discuss, dispute, investigate.

agitation *n* concussion, shake, shaking; commotion, convulsion, disturbance, ferment, jarring, storm, tumult, turmoil; discomposure, distraction, emotion, excitement, flutter, perturbation, ruffle, tremor, trepidation; controversy, debate, discussion.

agnostic *n* doubter, empiricist, sceptic.

agonize *vb* distress, excruciate, rack, torment, torture.

agony *n* anguish, distress, pangs.

agree *vb* accord, concur, harmonize, unite; accede, acquiesce, assent, comply, concur, subscribe; bargain, contract, covenant, engage, promise, undertake; compound, compromise; chime, cohere, conform, correspond, match, suit, tally.

agreeable *adj* charming, pleasant, pleasing.

agreement *n* accordance, compliance, concord, harmony, union; bargain, compact, contract, pact, treaty.

agriculture *n* cultivation, culture, farming, geoponics, husbandry, tillage.

aid *vb* assist, help, serve, support; relieve, succour; advance, facilitate, further, promote. * *n* assistance, cooperation, help, patronage; alms, subsidy, succour, relief.

ailment *n* disease, illness, sickness.

aim *vb* direct, level, point, train; design, intend,

mean, purpose, seek. * n bearing, course, direction, tendency; design, object, view, reason.

air vb expose, display, ventilate. * n atmosphere, breeze; appearance, aspect, manner; melody, tune.

aisle n passage, walk.

akin adj allied, kin, related; analogous, cognate, congenial, connected.

alacrity n agility, alertness, activity, eagerness, promptitude; cheerfulness, gaiety, hilarity, liveliness, vivacity.

alarm vb daunt, frighten, scare, startle, terrify. * n alarm-bell, tocsin, warning; apprehension, fear, fright, terror.

alert adj awake, circumspect, vigilant, watchful, wary; active, brisk, lively, nimble, quick, prompt, ready, sprightly. * vb alarm, arouse, caution, forewarn, signal, warn. * n alarm, signal, warning.

alertness n circumspection, vigilance, watchfulness, wariness; activity, briskness, nimbleness, promptness, readiness, spryness.

alien adj foreign, not native; differing, estranged, inappropriate, remote, unallied, separated. * n foreigner, stranger.

alienate vb (legal) assign, demise, transfer; disaffect, estrange, wean, withdraw.

alienation n (legal) assignment, conveyance, transfer; breach, disaffection, division, estrangement, rupture; (med) aberration, delusion, derangement, hallucination, insanity, madness.

alike adj akin, analogous, duplicate, identical, resembling, similar. * adv equally.

aliment n diet, fare, meat, nutriment, provision, rations, sustenance.

alive adj animate, breathing, live; aware, responsive, sensitive, susceptible; brisk, cheerful, lively, sprightly.

allay vb appease, calm, check, compose; alleviate, assuage, lessen, moderate, solace, temper.

allege vb affirm, assert, declare, maintain, say; adduce, advance, assign, cite, plead, produce, quote.

allegiance n duty, homage, fealty, fidelity, loyalty, obligation.

allegory n apologue, fable, myth, parable, story, tale.

alleviate vb assuage, lighten, mitigate, mollify, moderate, quell, quiet, quieten, soften, soothe.

alliance n affinity, intermarriage, relation; coalition, combination, confederacy, league, treaty, union; affiliation, connection, relationship, similarity.

allot vb divide, dispense, distribute; assign, fix, prescribe, specify.

allow vb acknowledge, admit, concede, confess, grant, own; authorize, grant, let, permit; bear, endure, suffer, tolerate; grant, yield, relinquish, spare; approve, justify, sanction; abate, bate, deduct, remit.

allude vb glance, hint, mention, imply, insinuate, intimate, refer, suggest, touch.

allure vb attract, beguile, cajole, coax, entice, lure, persuade, seduce, tempt. * n appeal, attraction, lure, temptation.

allusion n hint, implication, intimation, insinuation, mention, reference, suggestion.

ally vb combine, connect, join, league, marry, unite. * n aider, assistant, associate, coadjutor, colleague, friend, partner.

almighty adj all-powerful, omnipotent.

alms npl benefaction, bounty, charity, dole, gift, gratuity.

alone adj companionless, deserted, forsaken, isolated, lonely, only, single, sole, solitary.

along adv lengthways, lengthwise; forward, onward; beside, together, simultaneously.

aloud adv audibly, loudly, sonorously, vociferously.

alter vb change, conform, modify, shift, turn, transform, transmit, vary.

altercation n bickering, contention, controversy, dispute, dissension, strife, wrangling.

alternating adj intermittent, interrupted.

alternative adj another, different, second, substitute. * n choice, option, preference.

although conj albeit, even if, for all that, notwithstanding, though.

altitude n elevation, height, loftiness.

altogether adv completely, entirely, totally, utterly.

always adv continually, eternally, ever, evermore, perpetually, unceasingly.

amalgamate vb blend, combine, commingle, compound, incorporate, mix.

amass vb accumulate, aggregate, collect, gather, heap, scrape together.

amateur n dilettante, nonprofessional.

amaze vb astonish, astound, bewilder, confound, confuse, dumbfound, perplex, stagger, stupefy.

amazement n astonishment, bewilderment, confusion, marvel, surprise, wonder.

ambassador n deputy, envoy, legate, minister, plenipotentiary.

ambiguous adj dubious, doubtful, enigmatic, equivocal, uncertain, indefinite, indistinct, obscure, vague.

ambition n aspiration, emulation, longing, yearning.

ambitious adj aspiring, avid, eager, intent.

ameliorate vb amend, benefit, better, elevate, improve, mend.

amenability n amenableness, responsiveness; accountability, liability, responsibility.

amenable adj acquiescent, agreeable, persuadable, responsive, susceptible; accountable, liable, responsible.

amend vb better, correct, improve, mend, redress, reform.

amends npl atonement, compensation, expiation, indemnification, recompense, reparation, restitution.

amenity n agreeableness, mildness, pleasantness, softness; affability, civility, courtesy, geniality, graciousness, urbanity.

amiable adj attractive, benign, charming, genial,

good-natured, harmonious, kind, lovable, lovely, pleasant, pleasing, sweet, winning, winsome.

amicable *adj* amiable, cordial, friendly, harmonious, kind, kindly, peaceable.

amiss *adj* erroneous, inaccurate, incorrect, faulty, improper, wrong. * *adv* erroneously, inaccurately, incorrectly, wrongly.

amnesty *n* absolution, condonation, dispensation, forgiveness, oblivion.

amorous *adj* ardent, enamoured, fond, longing, loving, passionate, tender; erotic, impassioned.

amorphous *adj* formless, irregular, shapeless, unshapen; noncrystalline, structureless; chaotic, characterless, clumsy, disorganized, misshapen, unorganized, vague.

amount *n* aggregate, sum, total.

ample *adj* broad, capacious, extended, extensive, great, large, roomy, spacious; abounding, abundant, copious, generous, liberal, plentiful; diffusive, unrestricted.

amputate *vb* clip, curtail, prune, lop, remove, separate, sever.

amuse *vb* charm, cheer, divert, enliven, entertain, gladden, relax, solace; beguile, cheat, deceive, delude, mislead.

amusement *n* diversion, entertainment, frolic, fun, merriment, pleasure.

analeptic *adj* comforting, invigorating, restorative.

analogy *n* correspondence, likeness, parallelism, parity, resemblance, similarity.

analysis *n* decomposition, dissection, resolution, separation.

anarchy *n* chaos, confusion, disorder, misrule, lawlessness, riot.

anathema *n* ban, curse, denunciation, excommunication, execration, malediction, proscription.

anatomy *n* dissection; form, skeleton, structure.

ancestor *n* father, forebear, forefather, progenitor.

ancestry *n* family, house, line, lineage; descent, genealogy, parentage, pedigree, stock.

anchor *vb* fasten, fix, secure; cast anchor, take firm hold. * *n* (*naut*) ground tackle; defence, hold, security, stay.

ancient *adj* old, primitive, pristine; antiquated, antique, archaic, obsolete.

ancillary *adj* accessory, auxiliary, contributory, helpful, instrumental.

angelic *adj* adorable, celestial, cherubic, heavenly, saintly, seraphic; entrancing, enrapturing, rapturous, ravishing.

anger *vb* chafe, displease, enrage, gall, infuriate, irritate, madden. * *n* choler, exasperation, fury, gall, indignation, ire, passion, rage, resentment, spleen, wrath.

angle *vb* fish. * *n* divergence, flare, opening; bend, corner, crotch, cusp, point; fish-hook, hook.

angry *adj* chafed, exasperated, furious, galled, incensed, irritated, nettled, piqued, provoked, resentful.

anguish *n* agony, distress, grief, pang, rack, torment, torture.

anile *adj* aged, decrepit, doting, imbecile, senile.

animadversion *n* comment, notice, observation, remark; blame, censure, condemnation, reproof, stricture.

animate *vb* inform, quicken, vitalize, vivify; fortify, invigorate, revive; activate, enliven, excite, heat, impel, kindle, rouse, stimulate, stir, waken; elate, embolden, encourage, exhilarate, gladden, hearten. * *adj* alive, breathing, live, living, organic, quick.

animosity *n* bitterness, enmity, grudge, hatred, hostility, rancour, rankling, spleen, virulence.

annals *npl* archives, chronicles, records, registers, rolls.

annex *vb* affix, append, attach, subjoin, tag, tack; connect, join, unite.

annihilate *vb* abolish, annul, destroy, dissolve, exterminate, extinguish, kill, obliterate, raze, ruin.

annotation *n* comment, explanation, illustration, note, observation, remark.

announce *vb* advertise, communicate, declare, disclose, proclaim, promulgate, publish, report, reveal, trumpet.

announcement *n* advertisement, annunciation, bulletin, declaration, manifesto, notice, notification, proclamation.

annoy *vb* badger, chafe, disquiet, disturb, fret, hector, irk, irritate, molest, pain, pester, plague, trouble, vex, worry, wound.

annul *vb* abolish, abrogate, cancel, countermand, nullify, overrule, quash, repeal, recall, reverse, revoke.

anoint *vb* consecrate, oil, sanctify, smear.

anonymous *adj* nameless, unacknowledged, unsigned.

answer *vb* fulfil, rejoin, reply, respond, satisfy. * *n* rejoinder, reply, response, retort; confutation, rebuttal, refutation.

answerable *adj* accountable, amenable, correspondent, liable, responsible, suited.

antagonism *n* contradiction, discordance, disharmony, dissonant, incompatibility, opposition.

antecedent *adj* anterior, foregoing, forerunning, precedent, preceding, previous. * *n* forerunner, precursor.

anterior *adj* antecedent, foregoing, preceding, previous, prior; fore, front.

anticipate *vb* antedate, forestall, foretaste, prevent; count upon, expect, forecast, foresee.

anticipation *n* apprehension, contemplation, expectation, hope, prospect, trust; expectancy, forecast, foresight, foretaste, preconception, presentiment.

antidote *n* corrective, counteractive, counter-poison; cure, remedy, restorative, specific.

antipathy *n* abhorrence, aversion, disgust, detestation, hate, hatred, horror, loathing, repugnance.

antique *adj* ancient, archaic, bygone, old, old-fashioned.

anxiety *n* apprehension, care, concern, disquiet, fear, foreboding, misgiving, perplexity, trouble, uneasiness, vexation, worry.

anxious *adj* apprehensive, restless, solicitous, uneasy, unquiet, worried.

apart *adv* aloof, aside, separately; asunder.

apathetic *adj* cold, dull, impassive, inert, listless, obtuse, passionless, sluggish, torpid, unfeeling.

ape *vb* counterfeit, imitate, mimic; affect. * *n* simian, troglodyte; imitator, mimic; image, imitation, likeness, type.

aperture *n* chasm, cleft, eye, gap, opening, hole, orifice, passage.

aphorism *n* adage, apothegm, byword, maxim, proverb, saw, saying.

apish *adj* imitative, mimicking; affected, foppish, trifling.

aplomb *n* composure, confidence, equanimity, self-confidence.

apocryphal *adj* doubtful, fabulous, false, legendary, spurious, uncanonical.

apologetic *adj* exculpatory, excusatory; defensive, vindictive.

apology *n* defence, justification, vindication; acknowledgement, excuse, explanation, plea, reparation.

apostate *adj* backsliding, disloyal, faithless, false, perfidious, recreant, traitorous, untrue. * *n* backslider, deserter, pervert, renegade, turncoat.

apostle *n* angel, herald, messenger, missionary, preacher; advocate, follower, supporter.

apothegm *n* aphorism, byword, dictum, maxim, proverb, saw, saying.

appal *vb* affright, alarm, daunt, dismay, frighten, horrify, scare, shock.

apparel *n* attire, array, clothes, clothing, dress, garments, habit, raiment, robes, suit, trappings, vestments.

apparent *adj* discernible, perceptible, visible; conspicuous, evident, legible, manifest, obvious, open, patent, plain, unmistakable; external, ostensible, seeming, superficial.

apparition *n* appearance, appearing, epiphany, manifestation; being, form; ghost, phantom, spectre, spirit, vision.

appeal *vb* address, entreat, implore, invoke, refer, request, solicit. * *n* application, entreaty, invocation, solicitation, suit.

appear *vb* emerge, loom; break, open; arise, occur, offer; look, seem, show.

appearance *n* advent, arrival, apparition, coming; form, shape; colour, face, fashion, feature, guise, pretence, pretext; air, aspect, complexion, demeanour, manner, mien.

appease *vb* abate, allay, assuage, calm, ease, lessen, mitigate, pacify, placate, quell, soothe, temper, tranquillize.

appellation *n* address, cognomen, denomination, epithet, style, title.

append *vb* attach, fasten, hang; add, annex, subjoin, tack, tag.

appendix *n* addition, adjunct, appurtenance, codicil; excursus, supplement.

appetite *n* craving, desire, longing, lust, passion; gusto, relish, stomach, zest; hunger.

applaud *vb* acclaim, cheer, clap, compliment, encourage, extol, magnify.

applause *n* acclamation, approval, cheers, commendation, plaudit.

applicable *adj* adapted, appropriate, apt, befitting, fitting, germane, pertinent, proper, relevant.

application *n* emollient, lotion, ointment, poultice, wash; appliance, exercise, practice, use; appeal, petition, request, solicitation, suit; assiduity, constancy, diligence, effort, industry.

apply *vb* bestow, lay upon; appropriate, convert, employ, exercise, use; addict, address, dedicate, devote, direct, engage.

appoint *vb* determine, establish, fix, prescribe; bid, command, decree, direct, order, require; allot, assign, delegate, depute, detail, destine, settle; constitute, create, name, nominate; equip, furnish, supply.

apportion *vb* allocate, allot, allow, assign, deal, dispense, divide, share.

apposite *adj* apt, fit, germane, pertinent, relevant, suitable, pertinent.

appraise *vb* appreciate, estimate, prize, rate, value.

appreciate *vb* appreciate, esteem, estimate, rate, realize, value.

apprehend *vb* arrest, catch, detain, seize, take; conceive, imagine, regard, view; appreciate, perceive, realize, see, take in; fear, forebode; conceive, fancy, hold, imagine, presume, understand.

apprehension *n* arrest, capture, seizure; intellect, intelligence, mind, reason; discernment, intellect, knowledge, perception, sense; belief, fancy, idea, notion, sentiment, view; alarm, care, dread, distrust, fear, misgiving, suspicion.

apprise *vb* acquaint, inform, notify, tell.

approach *vb* advance, approximate, come close; broach; resemble. * *n* advance, advent; approximation, convergence, nearing, tendency; entrance, path, way.

approbation *n* approval, commendation, liking, praise; assent, concurrence, consent, endorsement, ratification, sanction.

appropriate *vb* adopt, arrogate, assume, set apart; allot, apportion, assign, devote; apply, convert, employ, use. * *adj* adapted, apt, befitting, fit, opportune, seemly, suitable.

approve *vb* appreciate, commend, like, praise, recommend, value; confirm, countenance, justify, ratify, sustain, uphold.

approximate *vb* approach, resemble. * *adj* approaching, proximate; almost exact, inexact, rough.

apt *adj* applicable, apposite, appropriate, befitting, fit, felicitous, germane; disposed, inclined, liable, prone, subject; able, adroit, clever, dextrous, expert, handy, happy, prompt, ready, skilful.

aptitude *n* applicability, appropriateness, felicity, fitness, pertinence, suitability; inclination, tendency, turn; ability, address, adroitness, quickness, readiness, tact.

arbitrary *adj* absolute, autocratic, despotic, domineering, imperious, overbearing, unlimited; capricious, discretionary, fanciful, voluntary, whimsical.

arcade *n* colonnade, loggia.

arch[1] *adj* cunning, knowing, frolicsome, merry, mirthful, playful, roguish, shrewd, sly; consummate, chief, leading, pre-eminent, prime, primary, principal.

arch[2] *vb* span, vault; bend, curve. * *n* archway, span, vault.

archaic *adj* ancient, antiquated, antique, bygone, obsolete, old.

archives *npl* documents, muniments, records, registers, rolls.

ardent *adj* burning, fiery, hot; eager, earnest, fervent, impassioned, keen, passionate, warm, zealous.

ardour *n* glow, heat, warmth; eagerness, enthusiasm, fervour, heat, passion, soul, spirit, warmth, zeal.

arduous *adj* high, lofty, steep, uphill; difficult, fatiguing, hard, laborious, onerous, tiresome, toilsome, wearisome.

area *n* circle, circuit, district, domain, field, range, realm, region, tract.

argue *vb* plead, reason upon; debate, dispute; denote, evince, imply, indicate, mean, prove; contest, debate, discuss, sift.

arid *adj* barren, dry, parched, sterile, unfertile; dry, dull, jejune, pointless, uninteresting.

aright *adv* correctly, justly, rightly, truly.

arise *vb* ascend, mount, soar, tower; appear, emerge, rise, spring; begin, originate; rebel, revolt, rise; accrue, come, emanate, ensue, flow, issue, originate, proceed, result.

aristocracy *n* gentry, nobility, noblesse, peerage.

arm[1] *n* bough, branch, limb, protection; cove, creek, estuary, firth, fjord, frith, inlet.

arm[2] *vb* array, equip, furnish; clothe, cover, fortify, guard, protect, strengthen.

arms *npl* accoutrements, armour, array, harness, mail, panoply, weapons; crest, escutcheon.

army *n* battalions, force, host, legions, troops; host, multitude, throng, vast assemblage.

around *prep* about, encircling, encompassing, round, surrounding. * *adv* about, approximately, generally, near, nearly, practically, round, thereabouts.

arouse *vb* animate, awaken, excite, incite, kindle, provoke, rouse, stimulate, warm, whet.

arraign *vb* accuse, censure, charge, denounce, impeach, indict, prosecute, tax.

arrange *vb* array, class, classify, dispose, distribute, group, range, rank; adjust, determine, fix upon, settle; concoct, construct, devise, plan, prepare, project.

arrant *adj* bad, consummate, downright, gross, notorious, rank, utter.

array *vb* arrange, dispose, place, range, rank; accoutre, adorn, attire, decorate, dress, enrobe, embellish, equip, garnish, habit, invest. * *n* arrangement, collection, disposition, marshalling, order; apparel, attire, clothes, dress, garments; army, battalions, soldiery, troops.

arrest *vb* check, delay, detain, hinder, hold, interrupt, obstruct, restrain, stay, stop, withhold; apprehend, capture, catch, seize, take; catch, engage, engross, fix, occupy, secure, rivet. * *n* check, checking, detention, hindrance, interruption, obstruction, restraining, stay, staying, stopping; apprehension, capture, detention, seizure.

arrive *vb* attain, come, get to, reach.

arrogance *n* assumption, assurance, disdain, effrontery, haughtiness, loftiness, lordliness, presumption, pride, scornfulness, superciliousness.

arrogate *vb* assume, claim unduly, demand, usurp.

arrow *n* bolt, dart, reed, shaft.

art *n* business, craft, employment, trade; address, adroitness, aptitude, dexterity, ingenuity, knack, readiness, sagacity, skill; artfulness, artifice, astuteness, craft, deceit, duplicity, finesse, subtlety.

artful *adj* crafty, cunning, disingenuous, insincere, sly, tricky, wily.

article *n* branch, clause, division, head, item, member, paragraph, part, point, portion; essay, paper, piece; commodity, substance, thing.

artifice *n* art, chicanery, contrivance, cunning, deception, deceit, duplicity, effort, finesse, fraud, imposture, invention, stratagem, subterfuge, trick, trickery.

artificial *adj* counterfeit, sham, spurious; assumed, affected, constrained, fictitious, forced, laboured, strained.

artless *adj* ignorant, rude, unskilful, untaught; natural, plain, simple; candid, fair, frank, guileless, honest, plain, unaffected, simple, sincere, truthful, unsuspicious.

ascend *vb* arise, aspire, climb, mount, soar, tower.

ascendancy, ascendency *n* authority, control, domination, mastery, power, predominance, sovereignty, superiority, sway.

ascertain *vb* certify, define, determine, establish, fix, settle, verify; discover, find out, get at.

ashamed *adj* abashed, confused.

ask *vb* interrogate, inquire, question; adjure, beg, conjure, crave, desire, dun, entreat, implore, invite, inquire, petition, request, solicit, supplicate, seek, sue.

aspect *n* air, bearing, countenance, expression, feature, look, mien, visage; appearance, attitude, condition, light, phase, position, posture, situation, state, view; angle, direction, outlook, prospect.

asperity *n* ruggedness, roughness, unevenness; acrimony, causticity, corrosiveness, sharpness, sourness, tartness; acerbity, bitterness, churlishness, harshness, sternness, sullenness, severity, virulence.

aspersion *n* abuse, backbiting, calumny, censure, defamation, detraction, slander, vituperation, reflection, reproach.

aspiration *n* aim, ambition, craving, hankering, hope, longing.

aspire *vb* desire, hope, long, yearn; ascend, mount, rise, soar, tower.

assail *vb* assault, attack, invade, oppugn; impugn, malign, maltreat; ply, storm.

assassinate *vb* dispatch, kill, murder, slay.

assault *vb* assail, attack, charge, invade. * *n* aggression, attack, charge, incursion, invasion, onset, onslaught; storm.

assemble *vb* call, collect, congregate, convene, convoke, gather, levy, muster; converge, forgather.

assembly *n* company, collection, concourse, congregation, gathering, meeting, rout, throng; caucus, congress, conclave, convention, convocation, diet, legislature, meeting, parliament, synod.

assent *vb* accede, acquiesce, agree, concur, subscribe, yield. * *n* accord, acquiescence, allowance, approval, approbation, consent.

assert *vb* affirm, allege, aver, asseverate, declare, express, maintain, predicate, pronounce, protest; claim, defend, emphasize, maintain, press, uphold, vindicate.

assertion *n* affirmation, allegation, asseveration, averment, declaration, position, predication, remark, statement, word; defence, emphasis, maintenance, pressing, support, vindication.

assess *vb* appraise, compute, estimate, rate, value; assign, determine, fix, impose, levy.

asseverate *vb* affirm, aver, avow, declare, maintain, protest.

assiduous *adj* active, busy, careful, constant, diligent, devoted, indefatigable, industrious, sedulous, unremitting, untiring.

assign *vb* allot, appoint, apportion, appropriate; fix, designate, determine, specify; adduce, advance, allege, give, grant, offer, present, show.

assist *vb* abet, aid, befriend, further, help, patronize, promote, second, speed, support, sustain; aid, relieve, succour; alternate with, relieve, spell.

associate *vb* affiliate, combine, conjoin, couple, join, link, relate, yoke; consort, fraternize, mingle, sort. * *n* chum, companion, comrade, familiar, follower, mate; ally, confederate, friend, partner, fellow.

association *n* combination, company, confederation, connection, partnership, society.

assort *vb* arrange, class, classify, distribute, group, rank, sort; agree, be adapted, consort, suit.

assuage *vb* allay, alleviate, appease, calm, ease, lessen, mitigate, moderate, mollify, pacify, quell, relieve, soothe, tranquillize.

assume *vb* take, undertake; affect, counterfeit, feign, pretend, sham; arrogate, usurp; beg, hypothesize, imply, postulate, posit, presuppose, suppose, simulate.

assurance *n* assuredness, certainty, conviction, persuasion, pledge, security, surety, warrant; engagement, pledge, promise; averment, assertion, protestation; audacity, confidence, courage, firmness, intrepidity; arrogance, brass, boldness, effrontery, face, front, impudence.

assure *vb* encourage, embolden, hearten; certify, insure, secure against loss, vouch for.

astonish *vb* amaze, astound, confound, daze, dumbfound, overwhelm, startle, stun, stupefy, surprise.

astute *adj* acute, cunning, deep, discerning, ingenious, intelligent, penetrating, perspicacious, quick, sagacious, sharp, shrewd.

asylum *n* refuge, retreat, sanctuary, shelter.

athletic *adj* brawny, lusty, muscular, powerful, robust, sinewy, stalwart, stout, strapping, strong, sturdy.

athletics *npl* aerobics, eurythmics, exercise, exercising, gymnastics, sports, track and field, workout.

atom *n* bit, molecule, monad, particle, scintilla.

atone *vb* answer, compensate, expiate, satisfy.

atonement *n* amends, expiation, propitiation, reparation, satisfaction.

atrocity *n* depravity, enormity, flagrancy, ferocity, savagery, villainy.

attach *vb* affix, annex, connect, fasten, join, hitch, tie; charm, captivate, enamour, endear, engage, win; (*legal*) distress, distrain, seize, take.

attack *vb* assail, assault, charge, encounter, invade, set upon, storm, tackle; censure, criticise, impugn. * *n* aggression, assault, charge, offence, onset, onslaught, raid, thrust.

attain *vb* accomplish, achieve, acquire, get, obtain, secure; arrive at, come to, reach.

attempt *vb* assail, assault, attack; aim, endeavour, seek, strive, try. * *n* effort, endeavour, enterprise, experiment, undertaking, venture; assault, attack, onset.

attend *vb* accompany, escort, follow; guard, protect, watch; minister to, serve, wait on; give heed, hear, harken, listen; be attendant, serve, tend, wait.

attention *n* care, circumspection, heed, mindfulness, observation, regard, watch, watchfulness; application, reflection, study; civility, courtesy, deference, politeness, regard, respect; addresses, courtship, devotion, suit, wooing.

attentive *adj* alive, awake, careful, civil, considerate, courteous, heedful, mindful, observant, watchful.

attenuate *vb* contract, dilute, diminish, elongate, lengthen, lessen, rarefy, reduce, slim, thin, weaken.

attest *vb* authenticate, certify, corroborate, confirm, ratify, seal, vouch; adjure, call to witness, invoke; confess, display, exhibit, manifest, prove, show, witness.

attic *n* garret, loft, upper storey.

Attic *adj* delicate, subtle, penetrating, pointed, pungent; chaste, classic, correct, elegant, polished, pure.

attire *vb* accoutre, apparel, array, clothe, dress, enrobe, equip, rig, robe. * *n* clothes, clothing, costume, dress, garb, gear, habiliment, outfit, toilet, trapping, vestment, vesture, wardrobe.

attitude *n* pose, position, posture; aspect, conjuncture, condition, phase, prediction, situation, standing, state.

attract *vb* draw, pull; allure, captivate, charm, decoy, enamour, endear, entice, engage, fascinate, invite, win.

attraction *n* affinity, drawing, pull; allurement, charm, enticement, fascination, magnetism, lure, seduction, witchery.

attribute *vb* ascribe, assign, impute, refer. * *n* characteristic, mark, note, peculiarity, predicate, property, quality.

attrition *n* abrasion, friction, rubbing.

attune *vb* accord, harmonize, modulate, tune; accommodate, adapt, adjust, attempt.

audacity *n* boldness, courage, daring, fearlessness, intrepidity; assurance, brass, effrontery, face, front, impudence, insolence, presumption, sauciness.

audience *n* assemblage, congregation; hearing, interview, reception.

augment *vb* add to, enhance, enlarge, increase, magnify, multiply, swell.

augmentation *n* accession, addition, enlargement, extension, increase.

augury *n* prediction, prognostication, prophecy, soothsaying; auspice, forerunner, harbinger, herald, omen, precursor, portent, sign.

august *adj* awe-inspiring, awful, dignified, grand, imposing, kingly, majestic, noble, princely, regal, solemn, stately, venerable.

auspicious *adj* fortunate, happy, lucky, prosperous, successful; bright, favourable, golden, opportune, promising, prosperous.

austere *adj* ascetic, difficult, formal, hard, harsh, morose, relentless, rigid, rigorous, severe, stern, stiff, strict, uncompromising, unrelenting.

authentic *adj* genuine, pure, real, true, unadulterated, uncorrupted, veritable; accurate, authoritative, reliable, true, trustworthy.

authority *n* dominion, empire, government, jurisdiction, power, sovereignty; ascendency, control, influence, rule, supremacy, sway; authorization, liberty, order, permit, precept, sanction, warranty; testimony, witness; connoisseur, expert, master.

authorize *vb* empower, enable, entitle; allow, approve, confirm, countenance, permit, ratify, sanction.

auxiliary *adj* aiding, ancillary, assisting, helpful, subsidiary. * *n* ally, assistant, confederate, help.

avail *vb* assist, benefit, help, profit, use, service.

available *adj* accessible, advantageous, applicable, beneficial, profitable, serviceable, useful.

avarice *n* acquisitiveness, covetousness, greediness, penuriousness, rapacity.

avaricious *adj* grasping, miserly, niggardly, parsimonious.

avenge *vb* punish, retaliate, revenge, vindicate.

avenue *n* access, entrance, entry, passage; alley, path, road, street, walk; channel, pass, route, way.

aver *vb* allege, assert, asseverate, avouch, declare, pronounce, protest, say.

averse *adj* adverse, backward, disinclined, indisposed, opposed, unwilling.

aversion *n* abhorrence, antipathy, disgust, dislike, hate, hatred, loathing, reluctance, repugnance.

avid *adj* eager, greedy, voracious.

avocation *n* business, calling, employment, occupation, trade, vocation; distraction, hindrance, interruption.

avoid *vb* dodge, elude, escape, eschew, shun; forebear, refrain from.

avouch *vb* allege, assert, declare, maintain, say.

avow *vb* admit, acknowledge, confess, own.

awaken *vb* arouse, excite, incite, kindle, provoke, spur, stimulate; wake, waken; begin, be excited.

award *vb* adjudge, allot, assign, bestow, decree, grant. * *n* adjudication, allotment, assignment, decision, decree, determination, gift, judgement.

aware *adj* acquainted, apprised, conscious, conversant, informed, knowing, mindful, sensible.

away *adv* absent, not present. * *adj* at a distance; elsewhere; out of the way.

awe *vb* cow, daunt, intimidate, overawe. * *n* abashment, fear, reverence; dread, fear, fearfulness, terror.

awful *adj* august, awesome, dread, grand, inspired; abashed, alarming, appalled, dire, frightful, portentous, tremendous.

awkward *adj* bungling, clumsy, inept, maladroit, unskilful; lumbering, unfit, ungainly, unmanageable; boorish; inconvenient, unsuitable.

axiom *n* adage, aphorism, apothegm, maxim, postulation, truism.

axis *n* axle, shaft, spindle.

azure *adj* blue, cerulean, sky-coloured.

B

babble *vb* blather, chatter, gibber, jabber, prate, prattle. * *n* chat, gossip, palaver, prate, tattle.

babel *n* clamour, confusion, din, discord, disorder, hubbub, jargon, pother.

baby *vb* coddle, cosset, indulge, mollycoddle, pamper, spoil. * *adj* babyish, childish, infantile, puerile; diminutive, doll-like, miniature, pocket, pocket-sized, small-scale. * *n* babe, brat, child, infant, suckling, nursling; chicken, coward, milksop, namby-pamby, sad sack, weakling; miniature; innocent.

bacchanal *n* carouse, debauchery, drunkenness, revelry, roisterousness.

back *vb* abet, aid, countenance, favour, second, support, sustain; go back, move back, retreat, withdraw. * *adj* hindmost. * *adv* in return, in consideration; ago, gone, since; aside, away, behind, by; abaft, astern, backwards, hindwards, rearwards. * *n* end, hind part, posterior, rear.

backbite *vb* abuse, asperse, blacken, defame, libel, malign, revile, scandalize, slander, traduce, vilify.

backbone *n* chine, spine; constancy, courage, decision, firmness, nerve, pluck, resolution, steadfastness.

backslider *n* apostate, deserter, renegade.

backward *adj* disinclined, hesitating, indisposed, loath, reluctant, unwilling, wavering; dull, slow, sluggish, stolid, stupid. * *adv* aback, behind, rearward.

bad *adj* baleful, baneful, detrimental, evil, harmful, hurtful, injurious, noxious, pernicious, unwholesome, vicious; abandoned, corrupt, depraved, immoral, sinful, unfair, unprincipled, wicked; unfortunate, unhappy, unlucky, miserable; disappointing, discouraging, distressing, sad, unwelcoming; abominable, mean, shabby, scurvy, vile, wretched; defective, inferior, imperfect, incompetent, poor, unsuitable; hard, heavy, serious, severe.

badge *n* brand, emblem, mark, sign, symbol, token.

badger *vb* annoy, bait, bother, hector, harry, pester, persecute, tease, torment, trouble, vex, worry.

baffle *vb* balk, block, check, circumvent, defeat, foil, frustrate, mar, thwart, undermine, upset; bewilder, confound, disconcert, perplex.

bait *vb* harry, tease, worry. * *n* allurement, decoy, enticement, lure, temptation.

balance *vb* equilibrate, pose, (*naut*) trim; compare, weigh; compensate, counteract, estimate; adjust, clear, equalize, square. * *n* equilibrium, liberation; excess, remainder, residue, surplus.

bald *adj* bare, naked, uncovered, treeless; dull, inelegant, meagre, prosaic, tame, unadorned, vapid.

baleful *adj* baneful, deadly, calamitous, hurtful, injurious, mischievous, noxious, pernicious, ruinous.

balk *vb* baffle, defeat, disappoint, disconcert, foil, frustrate, thwart.

ball *n* drop, globe, orb, pellet, marble, sphere; bullet, missile, projectile, shot; assembly, dance.

balmy *adj* aromatic, fragrant, healing, odorous, perfumed.

ban *vb* anathematize, curse, execrate; interdict, outlaw. * *n* edict, proclamation; anathema, curse, denunciation, execration; interdiction, outlawry, penalty, prohibition

band[1] *vb* belt, bind, cinch, encircle, gird, girdle; ally, associate, combine, connect, join, league; bar, marble, streak, stripe, striate, vein. * *n* crew, gang, horde, society, troop; ensemble, group, orchestra.

band[2] *n* ligament, ligature, tie; bond, chain, cord, fetter, manacle, shackle, trammel; bandage, belt, binding, cincture, girth, tourniquet.

bandit *n* brigand, freebooter, footpad, gangster, highwayman, outlaw, robber.

baneful *adj* poisonous, venomous; deadly, destructive, hurtful, mischievous, noxious, pernicious.

bang *vb* beat, knock, maul, pommel, pound, strike, thrash, thump; slam; clatter, rattle, resound, ring. * *n* clang, clangour, whang; blow, knock, lick, thump, thwack, whack.

banish *vb* exile, expatriate, ostracize; dismiss, exclude, expel.

bank[1] *vb* incline, slope, tilt; embank. * *n* dike, embankment, escarpment, heap, knoll, mound; border, bound, brim, brink, margin, rim, strand; course, row, tier.

bank[2] *vb* deposit, keep, save. * *n* depository, fund, reserve, savings, stockpile.

banner *n* colours, ensign, flag, standard, pennon, standard, streamer.

banter *vb* chaff, deride, jeer, joke, mock, quiz, rally, ridicule. * *n* badinage, chaff, derision, jesting, joking, mockery, quizzing, raillery, ridicule.

bar *vb* exclude, hinder, obstruct, prevent, prohibit, restrain, stop. * *n* grating, pole, rail, rod; barricade, hindrance, impediment, obstacle, obstruction, stop; bank, sand bar, shallow, shoal, spit; (*legal*) barristers, counsel, court, judgement, tribunal.

barbarian *adj* brutal, cruel, ferocious, fierce, fell, inhuman, ruthless, savage, truculent, unfeeling. * *n* brute, ruffian, savage.

barbaric *adj* barbarous, rude, savage, uncivilized, untamed; capricious, coarse, gaudy, riotous, showy, outlandish, uncouth, untamed, wild.

bare *vb* denude, depilate, divest, strip, unsheathe; disclose, manifest, open, reveal, show. * *adj* denuded, exposed, naked, nude, stripped, unclothed, uncovered, undressed, unsheltered; alone, mere, sheer, simple; bald, meagre, plain, unadorned, uncovered, unfurnished; empty, destitute, indigent, poor.

bargain *vb* agree, contract, covenant, stipulate; convey, sell, transfer. * *n* agreement, compact, contract, covenant, convention, indenture, transaction, stipulation, treaty; proceeds, purchase, result.

barren *adj* childless, infecund, sterile; (*bot*) acarpous, sterile; bare, infertile, poor, sterile, unproductive; ineffectual, unfruitful, uninstructive.

barricade *vb* block up, fortify, protect, obstruct. * *n* barrier, obstruction, palisade, stockade.

barrier *n* bar, barricade, hindrance, impediment, obstacle, obstruction, stop.

barter *vb* bargain, exchange, sell, trade, traffic.

base[1] *adj* cheap, inferior, worthless; counterfeit, debased, false, spurious; baseborn, humble, lowly, mean, nameless, plebeian, unknown, untitled, vulgar; abject, beggarly, contemptible, degraded, despicable, low, menial, pitiful, servile, sordid, sorry, worthless.

base[2] *vb* establish, found, ground. * *n* foundation, fundament, substructure, underpinning; pedestal, plinth, stand; centre, headquarters, HQ, seat; starting point; basis, cause, grounds, reason, standpoint; bottom, foot, foundation, ground.

bashful *adj* coy, diffident, shy, timid.

basis **n** base, bottom, foundation, fundament, ground, groundwork.

bastard *adj* adulterated, baseborn, counterfeit, false, illegitimate, sham. * *n* love child.

batch *vb* assemble, bunch, bundle, collect, gather, group. * *n* amount, collection, crowd, lot, quantity.

bathe *vb* immerse, lave, wash; cover, enfold, enwrap, drench, flood, infold, suffuse. * *n* bath, shower, swim.

batter[1] *vb* beat, pelt, smite; break, bruise, demolish, destroy, shatter, shiver, smash; abrade, deface, disfigure, indent, mar; incline, recede, retreat, slope. * *n* batsman, striker.

batter[2] *n* dough, goo, goop, gunk, paste, pulp.

battle *vb* contend, contest, engage, fight, strive, struggle. * *n* action, affair, brush, combat, conflict, contest, engagement, fight, fray.

bauble *n* gewgaw, gimcrack, knick-knack, plaything, toy, trifle, trinket.

bawdy *adj* obscene, filthy, impure, indecent, lascivious, lewd, smutty, unchaste.

bawl *vb* clamour, cry, hoot, howl, roar, shout, squall, vociferate, yell.

bay[1] *vb* bark, howl, wail, yell, yelp.

bay[2] *n* alcove, compartment, niche, nook, opening, recess.

bay[3] *n* bight, cove, gulf, inlet.

bays *npl* applause, chaplet, fame, garland, glory, honour, plaudits, praise, renown.

beach *vb* ground, maroon, strand. * *n* coast, margin, rim, sands, seashore, seaside, shore, shoreline, strand, waterfront.

beacon *vb* brighten, flame, shine, signal; enlighten, illuminate, illumine, guide, light, signal. * *n* lighthouse, pharos, watchtower; sign, signal.

beadle *n* apparitor, church officer, crier, servitor, summoner.

beak *n* bill, mandible, (*sl*) nose; (*naut*) bow, prow, stem.

beam *vb* beacon, gleam, glisten, glitter, shine. * *n* balk, girder, joist, scantling, stud; gleam, pencil, ray, streak.

bear *vb* support, sustain, uphold; carry, convey, deport, transport, waft; abide, brook, endure, stand, suffer, tolerate, undergo; carry on, keep up, maintain; cherish, entertain, harbour; produce; cast, drop, sustain; endure, submit, suffer; act, operate, work. * *n* growler, grumbler, moaner, snarler; speculator.

bearable *adj* endurable, sufferable, supportable, tolerable.

bearing *n* air, behaviour, demeanour, deportment, conduct, carriage, conduct, mien, port; connection, dependency, relation; endurance, patience, suffering; aim, course, direction; bringing forth, producing; bed, receptacle, socket.

beastly *adj* abominable, brutish, ignoble, low, sensual, vile.

beat *vb* bang, baste, belabour, buffet, cane, cudgel, drub, hammer, hit, knock, maul, pound, pummel, punch, strike, thrash, thump, thwack, whack, whip; bray, bruise, pound, pulverize; batter, pelt; conquer, defeat, overcome, rout, subdue, surpass, vanquish; pulsate, throb; dash, strike. * *adj* baffled, bamboozled, confounded, mystified, nonplused, perplexed, puzzled, stumped; done, dog-tired, exhausted, tired out, worn out; beaten, defeated, licked, worsted. * *n* blow, striking, stroke; beating, pulsation, throb; accent, metre, rhythm; circuit, course, round.

beatific *adj* ecstatic, enchanting, enraptured, ravishing, rapt.

beatitude *n* blessing, ecstasy, felicity, happiness.

beau *n* coxcomb, dandy, exquisite, fop, popinjay; admirer, lover, suitor, sweetheart.

beautiful *adj* charming, comely, fair, fine, exquisite, handsome, lovely, pretty.

beautify *vb* adorn, array, bedeck, deck, decorate, embellish, emblazon, garnish, gild, grace, ornament, set.

beauty *n* elegance, grace, symmetry; attractiveness, comeliness, fairness, loveliness, seemliness; belle.

become *vb* change to, get, go, wax; adorn, befit, set off, suit.

becoming *adj* appropriate, apt, congruous, decent, decorous, due, fit, proper, right, seemly, suitable; comely, graceful, neat, pretty.

bed *vb* embed, establish, imbed, implant, infix, inset, plant; harbour, house, lodge. * *n* berth, bunk, cot, couch; channel, depression, hollow; base, foundation, receptacle, support, underlay; accumulation, layer, seam, stratum, vein.

bedim *vb* cloud, darken, dim, obscure.

befall *vb* betide, overtake; chance, happen, occur, supervene.

befitting *adj* appropriate, apt, becoming, decorous, fit, proper, right, suitable, seemly.

befool *vb* bamboozle, beguile, cheat, circumvent, delude, deceive, dupe, fool, hoax, hoodwink, infatuate, stupefy, trick.

befriend *vb* aid, benefit, countenance, encourage, favour, help, patronize.

beg *vb* adjure, ask, beseech, conjure, crave, entreat, implore, importune, petition, pray, request, solicit, supplicate.

beggarly *adj* destitute, needy, poor; abject, base, despicable, grovelling, low, mean, miserable, miserly, paltry, pitiful, scant, servile, shabby, sorry, stingy, vile, wretched.

begin *vb* arise, commence, enter, open; inaugurate, institute, originate, start.

beginning *n* arising, commencement, dawn, emergence, inauguration, inception, initiation, opening, outset, start, rise; origin, source.

beguile *vb* cheat, deceive, delude; amuse, cheer, divert, entertain, solace.

behaviour *n* air, bearing, carriage, comportment, conduct, demeanour, deportment, manner, manners, mien.

behest *n* bidding, charge, command, commandment, direction, hest, injunction, mandate, order, precept.

behind *prep* abaft, after, following. * *adv* abaft, aft, astern, rearward. * *adj* arrested, backward, checked, detained, retarded; after, behind. * *n* afterpart, rear, stern, tail; back, back side, reverse; bottom, buttocks, posterior, rump.

behold *vb* consider, contemplate, eye, observe, regard, see, survey, view.

behoove *vb* become, befit, suit; be binding, be obligatory.

being *n* actuality, existence, reality, subsistence; core, essence, heart, root.

beleaguer *vb* besiege, blockade, invest; beset, block, encumber, encompass, encounter, obstruct, surround.

belief *n* assurance, confidence, conviction, persuasion, trust; acceptance, assent, credence, credit, currency; creed, doctrine, dogma, faith, opinion, tenet.

bellow *vb* bawl, clamour, cry, howl, vociferate, yell.

belt *n* band, cincture, girdle, girth, zone; region, stretch, strip.

bemoan *vb* bewail, deplore, lament, mourn.

bemused *adj* bewildered, confused, fuddled, muddled, muzzy, stupefied, tipsy.

bend *vb* bow, crook, curve, deflect, draw; direct, incline, turn; bend, dispose, influence, mould, persuade, subdue; (*naut*) fasten, make fast; crook, deflect, deviate, diverge, swerve; bow, lower, stoop; condescend, deign. * *n* angle, arc, arcuation, crook, curvature, curve, elbow, flexure, turn.

beneath *prep* below, under, underneath; unbecoming, unbefitting, unworthy. * *adv* below, underneath.

benediction *n* beatitude, benefit, benison, blessing, boon, grace, favour.

benefaction *n* alms, boon, charity, contribution, donation, favour, gift, grant, gratuity, offering, present.

beneficent *adj* benevolent, bounteous, bountiful, charitable, generous, kind, liberal.

beneficial *adj* advantageous, favourable, helpful, profitable, salutary, serviceable, useful, wholesome.

benefit *vb* befriend, help, serve; advantage, avail, profit. * *n* favour, good turn, kindness, service; account, advantage, behalf, gain, good, interest, profit, utility.

benevolence *n* beneficence, benignity, generosity, goodwill, humanity, kindliness, kindness.

benevolent *adj* altruistic, benign, charitable, generous, humane, kind, kind-hearted, liberal, obliging, philanthropic, tender, unselfish.

benign *adj* amiable, amicable, beneficent, benevolent, complaisant, friendly, gentle, good, gracious, humane, kind, kindly, obliging.

bent *adj* angled, angular, bowed, crooked, curved, deflected, embowed, flexed, hooked, twisted; disposed, inclined, prone, minded; (*with* **on**) determined, fixed on, resolved, set on. * *n* bias, inclination, leaning, partiality, penchant, predilection, prepossession, proclivity, propensity.

bequeath *vb* devise, give, grant, leave, will; impart, transmit.

berate *vb* chide, rate, reprimand, reprove, scold.

bereave *vb* afflict, deprive of, despoil, dispossess, divest, rob, spoil, strip.

beseech *vb* beg, conjure, entreat, implore, importune, petition, supplicate; ask, beg, crave, solicit.

beset *vb* besiege, encompass, enclose, environ, encircle, hem in, surround; decorate, embarrass, embellish, entangle, garnish, ornament, perplex, set.

beside[1] *prep* at the side of, by the side of, close to, near; aside from, not according to, out of the course of, out of the way of; not in possession of, out of.

besides[1] *prep* barring, distinct from, excluding, except, excepting, in addition to, other than, over and above, save.

beside[2], **besides**[2] *adv* additionally, also, further, furthermore, in addition, more, moreover, over and above, too, yet.

besiege *vb* beset, blockade, encircle, encompass, environ, invest, surround.

besot *vb* drench, intoxicate, soak, steep; befool, delude, infatuate, stultify, stupefy.

bespatter *vb* bedaub, befoul, besmirch, smear, spatter.

bespeak *vb* accost, address, declare, evince, forestall, imply, indicate, prearrange, predict, proclaim, solicit.

best *vb* better, exceed, excel, predominate, rival, surpass; beat, defeat, outdo, worst. * *adj* chief, first, foremost, highest, leading, utmost. * *adv* advantageously, excellently; extremely, greatly. * *n* choice, cream, flower, pick.

bestial *adj* beast-like, beastly, brutal, degraded, depraved, irrational, low, vile; sensual.

bestow *vb* deposit, dispose, put, place, store, stow; accord, give, grant, impart.

bet *vb* gamble, hazard, lay, pledge, stake, wage, wager. * *n* gamble, hazard, stake, wager.

bethink *vb* cogitate, consider, ponder, recall, recollect, reflect, remember.

betide *vb* befall, happen, occur, overtake.

betimes *adv* beforehand, early, forward, soon.

betoken *vb* argue, betray, denote, evince, imply, indicate, prove, represent, show, signify, typify.

betray *vb* be false to, break, violate; blab, discover, divulge, expose, reveal, show, tell; argue, betoken, display, evince, expose, exhibit, imply, indicate, manifest, reveal; beguile, delude, ensnare, lure, mislead; corrupt, ruin, seduce, undo.

betroth *vb* affiance, engage to marry, pledge in marriage, plight.

better *vb* advance, amend, correct, exceed, improve, promote, rectify, reform. * *adj* bigger, fitter, greater, larger, less ill, preferable. * *n* advantage, superiority, upper hand, victory; improvement, greater good.

between *prep* amidst, among, betwixt.

bewail *vb* bemoan, deplore, express, lament, mourn over, rue, sorrow.

beware *vb* avoid, heed, look out, mind.

bewilder *vb* confound, confuse, daze, distract, embarrass, entangle, muddle, mystify, nonplus, perplex, pose, puzzle, stagger.

bewitch *vb* captivate, charm, enchant, enrapture, entrance, fascinate, spellbind, transport.

beyond *prep* above, before, farther, over, past, remote, yonder.

bias *vb* bend, dispose, incline, influence, predispose, prejudice. * *n* bent, inclination, leaning, partiality, penchant, predilection, prepossession, proclivity, propensity, slant, tendency, turn.

bicker *vb* argue, dispute, jangle, quarrel, spar, spat, squabble, wrangle.

bid *vb* charge, command, direct, enjoin, order, require, summon; ask, call, invite, pray, request, solicit; offer, propose, proffer, tender. * *n* bidding, offer, proposal.

big *adj* bumper, bulking, bulky, great, huge, large, massive, monstrous; important, imposing; distended, inflated, full, swollen, tumid; fecund, fruitful, productive, teeming.

bigoted *adj* dogmatic, hidebound, intolerant, obstinate, narrow-minded, opinionated, prejudiced.

bill[1] *vb* charge, dun, invoice; programme, schedule; advertise, boost, plug, promote, publicize. * *n* account, charges, reckoning, score; advertisement, banner, hoarding, placard, poster; playbill, programme, schedule; bill of exchange, certificate, money; account, reckoning, statement.

bill[2] *n* beak, mandible, (*sl*) nose; billhook, brushcutter, hedge-bill, hedging knife; caress, fondle, kiss, toy.

billet *vb* allot, apportion, assign, distribute, quarter, station. * *n* accommodation, lodgings, quarters.

billow *vb* surge, wave; heave, roll; bag, baloon, bulge, dilate, swell. * *n* roller, surge, swell, wave.

bin *n* box, bunker, crib, frame, receptacle.

bind *vb* confine, enchain, fetter, restrain, restrict; bandage, tie up, wrap; fasten, lash, pinion, secure, tie, truss; engage, hold, oblige, obligate, pledge; contract, harden, shrink, stiffen.

birth *n* ancestry, blood, descent, extraction, lineage, race; being, creation, creature, offspring, production, progeny.

bit *n* crumb, fragment, morsel, mouthful, piece, scrap; atom, grain, jot, mite, particle, tittle, whit; instant, minute, moment, second.

bite *vb* champ, chew, crunch, gnaw; burn, make smart, sting; catch, clutch, grapple, grasp, grip; bamboozle, cheat, cozen, deceive, defraud, dupe, gull, mislead, outwit, overreach, trick. * *n* grasp, hold; punch, relish, spice, pungency, tang, zest; lick, morsel, sip, taste; crick, nip, pain, pang, prick, sting.

bitter *adj* acrid; dire, fell, merciless, relentless, ruthless; harsh, severe, stern; afflictive, calamitous, distressing, galling, grievous, painful, poignant, sore, sorrowful.

black *adj* dark, ebony, inky, jet, sable, swarthy; dingy, dusky, lowering, murky, pitchy; calamitous, dark, depressing, disastrous, dismal, doleful, forbidding, gloomy, melancholy, mournful, sombre, sullen.

blacken *vb* darken; deface, defile, soil, stain, sully; asperse, besmirch, calumniate, defame, malign, revile, slander, traduce, vilify.

blamable *adj* blameable, blameworthy, censurable, culpable, delinquent. faulty, remiss, reprehensible.

blame *vb* accuse, censure, condemn, disapprove, reflect upon, reprehend, reproach, reprove, upbraid. * *n* animadversion, censure, condemnation, disapproval, dispraise, disapprobation, reprehension, reproach, reproof; defect, demerit, fault, guilt, misdeed, shortcoming, sin, wrong.

blameless *adj* faultless, guiltless, inculpable, innocent, irreproachable, unblemished, undefiled, unimpeachable, unspotted, unsullied, spotless, stainless.

blanch *vb* bleach, fade, etiolate, whiten.

bland *adj* balmy, demulcent, gentle, mild, soothing, soft; affable, amiable, complaisant, kindly, mild, suave.

blandishment *n* cajolery, coaxing, compliment, fascination, fawning, flattery, wheedling

blank *adj* bare, empty, vacuous, void; amazed, astonished, confounded, confused, dumbfounded, nonplussed; absolute, complete, entire, mere, perfect, pure, simple, unabated, unadulterated, unmitigated, unmixed, utter, perfect.

blare *vb* blazon, blow, peal, proclaim, trumpet. * *n* blast, clang, clangour, peal.

blasphemy *n* impiousness, sacrilege; cursing, profanity, swearing.

blast *vb* annihilate, blight, destroy, kill, ruin, shrivel, wither; burst, explode, kill. * *n* blow, gust, squall; blare, clang, peal; burst, discharge, explosion.

blaze *vb* blazon, proclaim, publish; burn, flame, glow. * *n* flame, flare, flash, glow, light.

bleach *vb* blanch, etiolate, render white, whiten.

bleak *adj* bare, exposed, unprotected, unsheltered, storm-beaten, windswept; biting, chill, cold, piercing, raw; cheerless, comfortless, desolate, dreary, uncongenial,

blemish *vb* blur, injure, mar, spot, stain, sully, taint, tarnish; asperse, calumniate, defame, malign, revile, slander, traduce, vilify. * *n* blot, blur, defect, disfigurement, fault, flaw, imperfection, soil, speck, spot, stain, tarnish; disgrace, dishonour, reproach, stain, taint.

blend *vb* amalgamate, coalesce, combine, commingle, fuse, mingle, mix, unite. * *n* amalgamation, combination, compound, fusion, mix, mixture, union.

bless *vb* beatify, delight, gladden; adore, celebrate, exalt, extol, glorify, magnify, praise.

blessedness *n* beatitude, bliss, blissfulness, felicity, happiness, joy.

blight *vb* blast, destroy, kill, ruin, shrivel, wither; annihilate, annul, crush, disappoint, frustrate. * *n* blast, mildew, pestilence.

blind *vb* blear, darken, deprive of sight; blindfold, hoodwink. * *adj* eyeless, sightless, stone-blind, unseeing; benighted, ignorant, injudicious, purblind, undiscerning, unenlightened; concealed, confused, dark, dim, hidden, intricate, involved, labyrinthine, obscure, private, remote; careless, headlong, heedless, inconsiderate, indiscriminate, thoughtless; blank, closed, shut. * *n* cover, curtain, screen, shade, shutter; blinker; concealment, disguise, feint, pretence, pretext, ruse, stratagem, subterfuge.

blink *vb* nictate, nictitate, wink; flicker, flutter, gleam, glitter, intermit, twinkle; avoid, disregard, evade, gloss over, ignore, overlook, pass over. * *n* glance, glimpse, sight, view, wink; gleam, glimmer, sheen, shimmer, twinkle.

bliss *n* beatification, beatitude, blessedness, blissfulness, ecstasy, felicity, happiness, heaven, joy, rapture, transport.

blithe *adj* airy, animated, blithesome, buoyant, cheerful, debonair, elated, happy, jocund, joyful, joyous, lively, mirthful, sprightly, vivacious.

bloat *vb* dilate, distend, inflate, swell.

block *vb* arrest, bar, blockade, check, choke, close, hinder, impede, jam, obstruct, stop; form, mould, shape; brace, stiffen. * *n* lump, mass; blockhead, dunce, fool, simpleton; pulley, tackle; execution, scaffold; jam, obstruction, pack, stoppage.

blood *n* children, descendants, offspring, posterity, progeny; family, house, kin, kindred, line, relations; consanguinity, descent, kinship, lineage, relationship; courage, disposition, feelings, mettle, passion, spirit, temper.

bloom *vb* blossom, blow, flower; thrive, prosper. * *n* blossom, blossoming, blow, efflorescence, florescence, flowering; delicacy, delicateness, flush, freshness, heyday, prime, vigour; flush, glow, rose.

blossom *vb* bloom, blow, flower. * *n* bloom, blow, efflorescence, flower.

blot *vb* cancel, efface, erase, expunge, obliterate, rub out; blur, deface, disfigure, obscure, spot, stain, sully; disgrace, dishonour, tarnish. * *n* blemish, blur, erasure, spot, obliteration, stain; disgrace, dishonour, stigma.

blow[1] *n* bang, beat, buffet, dab, impact, knock, pat, punch, rap, slam, stroke, thump, wallop, buffet, impact; affliction, calamity, disaster, misfortune, setback.

blow[2] *vb* breathe, gasp, pant, puff; flow, move, scud, stream, waft. * *n* blast, gale, gust, squall, storm, wind.

blue *adj* azure, cerulean, cobalt, indigo, sapphire, ultramarine; ghastly, livid, pallid; dejected, depressed, dispirited, downcast, gloomy, glum, mopey, melancholic, melancholy, sad.

bluff[1] *adj* abrupt, blunt, blustering, coarse, frank, good-natured, open, outspoken; abrupt, precipitous, sheer, steep. * *n* cliff, headland, height.

bluff[2] *vb* deceive, defraud, lie, mislead. * *n* deceit, deception, feint, fraud, lie.

blunder *vb* err, flounder, mistake: stumble. * *n* error, fault, howler, mistake, solecism.

blunt *adj* dull, edgeless, obtuse, pointless, unsharpened; insensible, stolid, thick-witted; abrupt, bluff, downright, plain-spoken, outspoken, unceremonious, uncourtly. * *vb* deaden, dull, numb, weaken.

blur *vb* bedim, darken, dim, obscure; blemish, blot, spot, stain, sully, tarnish. * *n* blemish, blot, soil, spot, stain, tarnish; disgrace, smear.

blush *vb* colour, flush, glow, redden. * *n* bloom, flush, glow, colour, reddening, suffusion.

bluster *vb* boast, brag, bully, domineer, roar, swagger, swell, vaunt. * *n* boisterousness, noise, tumult, turbulence; braggadocio, bravado, boasting, gasconade, swaggering.

board *n* deal, panel, plank; diet, entertainment, fare, food, meals, provision, victuals; cabinet, conclave, committee, council; directorate; panel.

boast *vb* bluster, brag, crack, flourish, crow, vaunt. * *n* blustering, boasting, bombast, brag, braggadocio, bravado, bombast, swaggering, vaunt.

bode *vb* augur, betoken, forebode, foreshadow, foretell, portend, predict, prefigure, presage, prophesy.

bodily *adj* carnal, corporeal, fleshly, physical. * *adv* altogether, completely, entirely, wholly.

body *n* carcass, corpse, remains; stem, torso, trunk; aggregate, bulk, corpus, mass; being, individual, mortal creature, person; assemblage, association, band, company, corporation, corps, coterie, force, party, society, troop; consistency, substance, thickness.

boggle *vb* demur, falter, hang fire, hesitate, shrink, vacillate, waver.

boil[1] *vb* agitate, bubble, foam, froth, rage, seethe, simmer. * *n* ebullience, ebullition.

boil[2] (*med*) gathering, pimple, pustule, swelling, tumour.

boisterous *adj* loud, roaring, stormy; clamouring, loud, noisy, obstreperous, tumultuous, turbulent.

bold *adj* adventurous, audacious, courageous; brave, daring, dauntless, doughty, fearless, gallant, hardy, heroic, intrepid, mettlesome, manful, manly, spirited, stouthearted, undaunted, valiant, valorous; assured, confident, self-reliant; assuming, forward, impertinent, impudent, insolent, push, rude, saucy; conspicuous, projecting, prominent, striking; abrupt, precipitous, prominent, steep.

bolster *vb* aid, assist, defend, help, maintain, prop, stay, support. * *n* cushion, pillow; prop, support.

bolt *vb* abscond, flee, fly. * *n* arrow, dart, missile; shaft; thunderbolt.

bombast *n* bluster, brag, braggadocio, fustian, gasconade, mouthing, pomposity, rant.

bond *vb* bind, connect, fuse, glue, join. * *adj* captive, enslaved, enthralled, subjugated. * *n* band, cord, fastening, ligament, ligature, link, nexus; bondage, captivity, chains, constraint, fetters, prison, shackle; attachment, attraction, connection, coupling, link, tie, union; compact, obligation, pledge, promise.

bondage *n* captivity, confinement, enslavement, enthralment, peonage, serfdom, servitude, slavery, thraldom, vassalage.

bonny *adj* beautiful, handsome, fair, fine, pretty; airy, blithe, buoyant, buxom, cheerful, jolly, joyous, merry. playful, sporty, sprightly, winsome.

bonus *n* gift, honorarium, premium, reward, subsidy.

booby *n* blockhead, dunce, fool, idiot, simpleton.

book *vb* bespeak, engage, reserve; programme, schedule; list, log, record, register. * *n* booklet, brochure, compendium, handbook, manual, monograph, pamphlet, textbook, tract, treatise, volume, work.

bookish *adj* erudite, learned, literary, scholarly, studious.

boon *adj* convivial, jolly, jovial, hearty; close, intimate. * *n* benefaction, favour, grant, gift, present; advantage, benefit, blessing, good, privilege.

boor *n* bumpkin, clodhopper, clown, lout, lubber, peasant, rustic, swain.

boorish *adj* awkward, bearish, clownish, course, gruff, ill-bred, loutish, lubberly, rude, rustic, uncivilized, uncouth, uneducated.

bootless *adj* abortive, fruitless, futile, profitless, vain, worthless, useless.

booty *n* loot, pillage, plunder, spoil.

border *vb* bound, edge, fringe, line, march, rim, skirt, verge; abut, adjoin, butt, conjoin, connect, neighbour. * *n* brim, brink, edge, fringe, hem, margin, rim, skirt, verge; boundary, confine, frontier, limit, march, outskirts.

bore[1] *vb* annoy, fatigue, plague, tire, trouble, vex, weary, worry. * *n* bother, nuisance, pest, worry.

bore[2] *vb* drill, perforate, pierce, sink, tunnel. * *n* calibre, hole, shaft, tunnel.

borrow *vb* take and return, use temporarily; adopt, appropriate, imitate; dissemble, feign, simulate.

boss[1] *vb* emboss, stud; * *n* knob, protuberance, stud.

boss[2] *vb* command, direct, employ, run. * *n* employer, foreman, master, overseer, superintendent.

botch *vb* blunder, bungle, cobble, mar, mend, mess, patch, spoil. * *n* blotch, pustule, sore; failure, miscarriage.

bother *vb* annoy, disturb, harass, molest, perplex, pester, plague, tease, trouble, vex, worry. * *n* annoyance, perplexity, plague, trouble, vexation.

bottom *vb* build, establish, found. * *adj* base, basic, ground, lowermost, lowest, nethermost, undermost. * *n* base, basis, foot, foundation, groundwork; dale, meadow, valley; buttocks, fundament, seat; dregs, grounds, lees, sediment.

bounce *vb* bound, jump, leap, rebound, recoil, spring. * *n* knock, thump; bound, jump, leap, spring, vault.

bound[1] *adj* assured, certain, decided, determined, resolute, resolved; confined, hampered, restricted, restrained; committed, contracted, engaged, pledged, promised; beholden, dutybound, obligated, obliged.

bound[2] *vb* border, delimit, circumscribe, confine, demarcate, limit, restrict, terminate. * *n* boundary, confine, edge, limit, march, margin, periphery, term, verge.

bound[3] *vb* jump, leap, spring. * *n* bounce, jump, leap, spring, vault.

boundary *n* border, bourn, circuit, circumference, confine, limit, march, periphery, term, verge.

boundless *adj* endless, immeasurable, infinite, limitless, unbounded, unconfined, undefined, unlimited, vast.

bountiful *adj* beneficent, bounteous, generous, liberal, munificent, princely.

bounty *n* beneficence, benevolence, charity, donation, generosity, gift, kindness, premium, present, reward.

bourn *n* border, boundary, confine, limit; brook, burn, rill, rivulet, stream, torrent.

bow[1] *n* (*naut*) beak, prow, stem.

bow[2] *vb* arc, bend, buckle, crook, curve, droop, flex, yield; crush, depress, subdue; curtsy, genuflect, kowtow, submit. * *n* arc, bend, bilge, bulge, convex, curve, flexion; bob, curtsy, genuflection, greeting, homage, obeisance; coming out, debut, introduction; curtain call, encore.

bowels *npl* entrails, guts, insides, viscera; compassion, mercy, pity, sympathy, tenderness.

box[1] *vb* fight, hit, mill, spar. * *n* blow, buffet, fight, hit, spar.

box[2] *vb* barrel, crate, pack, parcel. * *n* case, chest, container, crate, portmanteau, trunk.

boy *n* lad, stripling, youth.

brace *vb* make tight, tighten; buttress, fortify, reinforce, shore, strengthen, support, truss. * *n* couple, pair; clamp, girder, prop, shore, stay, support, tie, truss.

brag *vb* bluster, boast, flourish, gasconade, vaunt.

branch *vb* diverge, fork, bifurcate, ramify, spread. * *n* bough, offset, limb, shoot, sprig, twig; arm, fork, ramification, spur; article, department, member, part, portion, section, subdivision.

brand *vb* denounce, stigmatize, mark. * *n* firebrand, torch; bolt, lightning flash; cachet, mark, stamp, tally; blot, reproach, stain, stigma.

brave *vb* dare, defy. * *adj* bold, courageous, fearless, heroic, intrepid, stalwart.

bravery *n* courage, daring, fearlessness, gallantry, valour.

brawl *vb* bicker, dispute, jangle, quarrel, squabble. * *n* broil, dispute, feud, fracas, fray, jangle, quarrel, row, scuffle, squabble, uproar, wrangle.

brawny *adj* athletic, lusty, muscular, powerful, robust, sinewy, stalwart, strapping, strong, sturdy.

bray *vb* clamour, hoot, roar, trumpet, vociferate. * *n* blare, crash, roar, shout.

breach *n* break, chasm, crack, disruption, fissure, flaw, fracture, opening, rent, rift, rupture; alienation, difference, disaffection, disagreement, split.

bread *n* aliment, diet, fare, food, nourishment, nutriment, provisions, regimen, victuals.

break *vb* crack, disrupt, fracture, part, rend, rive, sever; batter, burst, crush, shatter, smash, splinter; cashier, degrade, discard, discharge, dismiss; disobey, infringe, transgress, violate; intermit, interrupt, stop; disclose, open, unfold. * *n* aperture, breach, chasm, fissure, gap, rent, rip, rupture; break-up, crash, debacle.

breast *vb* face, oppose, resist, stem, withstand. * *n* bosom, chest, thorax; affections, conscience, heart; mammary gland, mammary organ, pap, udder.

breath *n* exhaling, inhaling, pant, sigh, respiration, whiff; animation, existence, life; pause, respite, rest; breathing space, instant, moment.

breathe *vb* live, exist; emit, exhale, give out; diffuse, express, indicate, manifest, show.

breed *vb* bear, beget, engender, hatch, produce; bring up, foster, nourish, nurture, raise, rear; discipline, educate, instruct, nurture, rear, school, teach, train; generate, originate. * *n* extraction, family, lineage, pedigree, progeny, race, strain.

brevity *n* briefness, compression, conciseness, curtness, pithiness, shortness, terseness, transiency.

brew *vb* concoct, contrive, devise, excite, foment, instigate, plot. * *n* beverage, concoction, drink, liquor, mixture, potation.

bribe *vb* buy, corrupt, influence, pay off, suborn. * *n* allurement, corruption, enticement, graft, pay-off, subornation.

bridle *vb* check, curb, control, govern, restrain. * *n* check, control, curb.

brief *vb* direct, give directions, instruct; capsulate, summarize, delineate, describe, draft, outline, sketch; (*law*) retain. * *adj* concise, curt, inconsiderable, laconic, pithy, short, succinct, terse; fleeting, momentary, short, temporary, transient. * *n* abstract, breviary, briefing, epitome, compendium, summary, syllabus; (*law*) precept, writ.

brigand *n* bandit, footpad, freebooter, gangster, highwayman, marauder, outlaw, robber, thug.

bright *adj* blazing, brilliant, dazzling, gleaming, glowing, light, luminous, radiant, shining, sparkling, sunny; clear, cloudless, lambent, lucid, transparent; famous, glorious, illustrious; acute, discerning, ingenious, intelligent, keen; auspicious, cheering, encouraging, exhilarating, favourable, inspiring, promising, propitious; cheerful, genial, happy, lively, merry, pleasant, smiling, vivacious.

brilliant *adj* beaming, bright, effulgent, gleaming, glistening, glittering, lustrous, radiant, resplendent, shining, sparkling splendid; admirable, celebrated, distinguished, famous, glorious, illustrious, renowned; dazzling, decided, prominent, signal, striking, unusual.

brim *n* border, brink, edge, rim, margin, skirt, verge; bank, border, coast, margin, shore.

bring *vb* bear, convey, fetch; accompany, attend, conduct, convey, convoy, guide, lead; gain, get, obtain, procure, produce.

brisk *adj* active, alert, agile, lively, nimble, perky, quick, smart, spirited, spry.

brittle *adj* brash, breakable, crisp, crumbling, fragile, frangible, frail, shivery.

broach *vb* open, pierce, set; approach, break, hint, suggest; proclaim, publish, utter.

broad *adj* ample, expansive, extensive, large, spacious, sweeping, vast, wide; enlarged, hospitable, liberal, tolerant; diffused, open, spread;

coarse, gross, indecent, indelicate, unrefined, vulgar.

broaden *vb* augment, enlarge, expand, extend, increase, spread, stretch, widen.

broken *adj* fractured, rent, ruptured, separated, severed, shattered, shivered, torn; exhausted, feeble, impaired, shaken, shattered, spent, wasted; defective, halting, hesitating, imperfect, stammering, stumbling; contrite, humble, lowly, penitent; abrupt, craggy, precipitous, rough.

broker *n* agent, factor, go-between, middleman.

brood *vb* incubate, sit. * *n* issue, offspring, progeny; breed, kind, line, lineage, sort, strain.

brook *vb* abide, bear, endure, suffer, tolerate. * *n* burn, beck, creek, rill, rivulet, run, streamlet.

brotherhood *n* association, clan, clique, coterie, fraternity, junta, society.

brotherly *adj* affectionate, amicable, cordial, friendly, kind.

browbeat *vb* bully, intimidate, overawe, overbear.

bruise *vb* contuse, crunch, squeeze; batter, break, maul, pound, pulverize; batter, deface, indent. * *n* blemish, contusion, swelling.

brush[1] *n* brushwood, bush, scrub, scrubwood, shrubs, thicket, wilderness.

brush[2] *vb* buff, clean, polish, swab, sweep, wipe; curry, groom, rub down; caress, flick, glance, graze, scrape, skim, touch. * *n* besom, broom; action, affair, collision, contest, conflict, encounter, engagement, fight, skirmish.

brutal *adj* barbaric, barbarous, brutish, cruel, ferocious, inhuman, ruthless, savage; bearish, brusque, churlish, gruff, impolite, harsh, rude, rough, truculent, uncivil.

brute *n* barbarian, beast, monster, ogre, savage; animal, beast, creature. * *adj* carnal, mindless, physical; bestial, coarse, gross.

bubble *vb* boil, effervesce, foam. * *n* bead, blob, fluid, globule; bagatelle, trifle; cheat, delusion, hoax.

buccaneer *n* corsair, freebooter, pirate.

buck *vb* jump, leap. * *n* beau, blade, blood, dandy, fop, gallant, spark; male.

bud *vb* burgeon, germinate, push, shoot, sprout, vegetate. * *n* burgeon, gem, germ, gemmule, shoot, sprout.

budget *vb* allocate, cost, estimate. * *n* account, estimate, financial statement; assets, finances, funds, means, resources; bag, bundle, pack, packet, parcel, roll; assortment, batch, collection, lot, set, store.

buffet[1] *vb* beat, box, cuff, slap, smite, strike; resist, struggle against, * *n* blow, box, cuff, slap, strike;

buffet[2] *n* cupboard, sideboard; refreshment counter.

buffoon *n* antic, clown, droll, fool, harlequin, jester, mountebank.

build *vb* construct, erect, establish, fabricate, fashion, model, raise, rear. * *n* body, figure, form, frame, physique; construction, shape, structure.

building *n* construction, erection, fabrication; edifice, fabric, house, pile, substructure, structure,

bulk *n* dimension, magnitude, mass, size, volume; amplitude, bulkiness, massiveness; body, majority, mass.

bully *vb* browbeat, bulldoze, domineer, haze, hector, intimidate, overbear. * *n* blusterer, browbeater, bulldozer, hector, swaggerer, roisterer, tyrant.

bulwark *n* barrier, fortification, parapet, rampart, wall; palladium, safeguard, security.

bump *vb* collide, knock, strike, thump. * *n* blow, jar, jolt, knock, shock, thump; lump, protuberance, swelling.

bunch *vb* assemble, collect, crowd, group, herd, pack. * *n* bulge, bump, bundle, hump, knob, lump, protuberance; cluster, hand, fascicle; assortment, batch, collection, group, lot, parcel, set; knot, tuft.

bundle *vb* bale, pack, package, parcel, truss, wrap. * *n* bale, batch, bunch, collection, heap, pack, package, packet, parcel, pile, roll, truss.

bungler *n* botcher, duffer, fumbler, lout, lubber, mis-manager, muddler.

burden *vb* encumber, grieve, load, oppress, overlay, overload, saddle, surcharge, try. * *n* capacity, cargo, freight, lading, load, tonnage, weight; affliction, charge, clog, encumbrance, impediment, grievance, sorrow, trial, trouble; drift, point, substance, tenor, surcharge.

bureau *n* chest of drawers, dresser; counting room, office.

burial *n* burying, entombment, inhumation, interment, sepulture.

burlesque *vb* ape, imitate, lampoon, mock, ridicule, satirize. * *n* caricature, extravaganza, parody, send-up, take-off, travesty.

burn[1] *n* beck, brook, gill, rill, rivulet, runnel, runlet, stream. water

burn[2] *vb* blaze, conflagrate, enflame, fire, flame, ignite, kindle, light, smoulder; cremate, incinerate; scald, scorch, singe; boil, broil, cook, roast, seethe, simmer, stew, swelter, toast; bronze, brown, sunburn, suntan, tan; bake, desiccate, dry, parch, sear, shrivel, wither; glow, incandesce, tingle, warm. * *n* scald, scorch, singe; sunburn.

burning *adj* aflame, fiery, hot, scorching; ardent, earnest, fervent, fervid, impassioned, intense.

burnish *vb* brighten, buff, furbish, polish, shine. * *n* glaze, gloss, patina, polish, shine.

burst *vb* break open, be rent, explode, shatter, split open. * *adj* broken, kaput, punctured, ruptured, shattered, split. * *n* break, breakage, breach, fracture, rupture; blast, blowout, blowup, discharge, detonation, explosion; spurt; blaze, flare, flash; cloudburst, downpour; bang, crack, crash, report, sound; fusillade, salvo, spray, volley, outburst, outbreak flare-up, blaze, eruption.

bury *vb* entomb, inearth, inhume, inter; conceal, hide, secrete, shroud.

business *n* calling, employment, occupation, profession, pursuit, vocation; commerce, dealing, trade, traffic; affair, concern, engagement, matter, transaction, undertaking; duty, function, office, task, work.

bustle *vb* fuss, hurry, scurry. * *n* ado, commotion, flurry, fuss, hurry, hustle, pother, stir, tumult.

busy *vb* devote, employ, engage, occupy, spend, work. * *adj* employed, engaged, occupied; active, assiduous, diligent, engrossed, industrious, sedulous, working; agile, brisk, nimble, spry, stirring; meddling, officious.

but *conj* except, excepting, further, howbeit, moreover, still, unless, yet. * *adv* all the same, even, notwithstanding, still, yet.

butchery *n* massacre, murder, slaughter.

butt[1] *vb* bunt, push, shove, shunt, strike; encroach, impose, interfere, intrude, invade, obtrude. * *n* buck, bunt, push, shove, shunt, thrust.

butt[2] *n* barrel, cask.

butt[3] *n* aim, goal, mark, object, point, target; dupe, gull, victim.

butt[4] *vb* abut, adjoin, conjoin, connect, neighbour. * *n* end, piece, remainder, stub, stump; buttocks, posterior, rump.

buttonhole *vb* bore, catch, detain in conversation, importune.

buttress *vb* brace, prop, shore, stay, support. * *n* brace, bulwark, prop, stay, support.

buxom *adj* comely, fresh, healthy, hearty, plump, rosy, ruddy, vigorous.

byword *n* adage, aphorism, apothegm, dictum, maxim, proverb, saying, saw.

C

cabal *vb* conspire, intrigue, machinate, plot. * *n* clique, combination, confederacy, coterie, faction, gang, junta, league, party, set; conspiracy, intrigue, machination, plot.

cabbalistic, cabalistic *adj* dark, fanciful, mysterious, mystic, occult, secret.

cabaret *n* tavern, inn, public house, wine shop.

cabin *n* berth, bunk, cot, cottage, crib, dwelling, hovel, hut, shack, shanty, shed.

cabinet *n* apartment, boudoir, chamber, closet; case, davenport, desk, escritoire; council, ministry.

cachinnation *n* guffaw, laugh, laughter.

cackle *vb* giggle, laugh, snicker, titter; babble, chatter, gabble, palaver, prate, prattle, titter. * *n* babble, chatter, giggle, prate, prattle, snigger, titter.

cacophonous *adj* discordant, grating, harsh, inharmonious, jarring, raucous.

cadaverous *adj* bloodless, deathlike, ghastly, pale, pallid, wan.

cage *vb* confine, immure, imprison, incarcerate. * *n* coop, pen, pound.

caitiff *adj* base, craven, pusillanimous, rascally, recreant. * *n* coward, knave, miscreant, rascal, rogue, scoundrel, sneak, traitor, vagabond, villain, wretch.

cajole *vb* blandish, coax, flatter, jolly, wheedle; beguile, deceive, delude, entrap, inveigle, tempt.

calamity *n* adversity, affliction, blow, casualty, cataclysm, catastrophe, disaster, distress, downfall, evil, hardship, mischance, misery, misfortune, mishap, reverse, ruin, stroke, trial, visitation.

calculate *vb* cast, compute, count, estimate, figure, rate, reckon, weigh; tell.

calculating *adj* crafty, designing, scheming, selfish; careful, cautious, circumspect, far-sighted, politic, sagacious, wary.

calefaction *n* heating, warming; hotness, incandescence, warmth.

calendar *n* almanac, ephemeris, register; catalogue, list, schedule.

calibre *n* bore, capacity, diameter, gauge; ability, capacity, endowment, faculty, gifts, parts, scope, talent.

call *vb* christen, denominate, designate, dub, entitle, name, phrase, style, term; bid, invite, summons; assemble, convene, convoke, muster; cry, exclaim; arouse, awaken, proclaim, rouse, shout, waken; appoint, elect, ordain. * *n* cry, outcry, voice; appeal, invitation, summons; claim, demand, summons; appointment, election, invitation.

calling *n* business, craft, employment, occupation, profession, pursuit, trade.

callous *adj* hard, hardened, indurated; apathetic, dull, indifferent, insensible, inured, obdurate, obtuse, sluggish, torpid, unfeeling, unsusceptible.

callow *adj* naked, unfeathered, unfledged; green, immature, inexperienced, sappy, silly, soft, unfledged, unsophisticated.

calm *vb* allay, becalm, compose, hush, lull, smooth, still, tranquillize; alleviate, appease, assuage, moderate, mollify, pacify, quiet, soften, soothe, tranquillize. * *adj* halcyon, mild, peaceful, placid, quiet, reposeful, serene, smooth, still, tranquil, unruffled; collected, cool, composed, controlled, impassive, imperturbable, sedate, self-possessed, undisturbed, unperturbed, unruffled, untroubled. * *n* lull; equanimity, peace, placidity, quiet, repose, serenity, stillness, tranquillity.

calorific *adj* heat, heat-producing.

calumniate *vb* abuse, asperse, backbite, blacken, blemish, defame, discredit, disparage, lampoon, libel, malign, revile, slander, traduce, vilify.

calumny *n* abuses, aspersion, backbiting, defamation, detraction, evil-speaking, insult, libel, lying, obloquy, slander, vilification, vituperation.

camarilla *n* cabal, clique, junta, ring.

camber *vb* arch, bend, curve. * *n* arch, arching, convexity.

camp[1] *vb* bivouac, encamp, lodge, pitch, tent. * *n* bivouac, cantonment, encampment, laager; cabal, circle, clique, coterie, faction, group, junta, party, ring, set.

camp[2] *adj* affected, artificial, effeminate, exaggerated, mannered, theatrical.

canaille *n* mob, populace, proletariat, rabble, ragbag, riffraff, scum.

canal *n* channel, duct, pipe, tube.

cancel *vb* blot, efface, erase, expunge, obliterate; abrogate, annul, countermand, nullify, quash, repeal, rescind, revoke.

candelabrum *n* candlestick, chandelier, lustre.

candid *adj* fair, impartial, just, unbiased, unprejudiced; artless, frank, free, guileless, honest, honourable, ingenuous, naive, open, plain, sincere, straightforward.

candidate *n* applicant, aspirant, claimant, competitor, probationer.

candour *n* fairness, impartiality, justice; artlessness, frankness, guilelessness, honesty, ingenuousness, openness, simplicity, sincerity, straightforwardness, truthfulness.

canker *vb* corrode, erode, rot, rust, waste; blight, consume, corrupt, embitter, envenom, infect, poison, sour. * *n* gangrene, rot; bale, bane, blight, corruption, infection, irritation.

canon *n* catalogue, criterion, formula, formulary, law, regulation, rule, standard, statute.

canorous *adj* musical, tuneful.

cant[1] *vb* whine. * *adj* current, partisan, popular, rote, routine, set; argotic, slangy. * *n* hypocrisy; argot, jargon, lingo, slang.

cant[2] *vb* bevel, incline, list, slant, tilt, turn. * *n* bevel, inclination, leaning, list, pitch, slant, tilt, turn.

cantankerous *adj* contumacious, crabbed, cross-grained, dogged, headstrong, heady, intractable, obdurate, obstinate, perverse, refractory, stiff, stubborn, wilful, unyielding.

canting *adj* affected, pious, sanctimonious, whining.

canvas *n* burlap, scrim, tarpaulin.

canvass *vb* discuss, dispute; analyze, consider, examine, investigate, review, scrutinize, sift, study; campaign, electioneer, solicit votes. * *n* debate, discussion, dispute; examination, scrutiny, sifting.

canyon *n* gorge, gulch, ravine.

cap *vb* cover, surmount; complete, crown, finish; exceed, overtop, surpass, transcend; match, parallel, pattern. * *n* beret, head-cover, head-dress; acme, chief, crown, head, peak, perfection, pitch, summit, top.

capability *n* ability, brains, calibre, capableness, capacity, competency, efficiency, faculty, force, power, scope, skill.

capable *adj* adapted, fitted, qualified, suited; able, accomplished, clever, competent, efficient, gifted, ingenious, intelligent, sagacious, skilful.

capacious *adj* ample, broad, comprehensive, expanded, extensive, large, roomy, spacious, wide.

capacitate *vb* enable, qualify.

capacity *n* amplitude, dimensions, magnitude, volume; aptitude, aptness, brains, calibre, discernment, faculty, forte, genius, gift, parts, power, talent, turn, wit; ability, capability, calibre, cleverness, competency, efficiency, skill; character, charge, function, office, position, post, province, service, sphere.

caparison *vb* accoutre, costume, equip, outfit, rig out. * *n* accoutrements, armour, get-up, harness, housing, livery, outfit, panoply, tack, tackle, trappings, turnout .

caper *vb* bound, caracole, frisk, gambol, hop, leap, prank, romp, skip, spring. * *n* bound, dance, gambol, frisk, hop, jump, leap, prance, romp, skip.

capillary *adj* delicate, fine, minute, slender.

capital *adj* cardinal, chief, essential, important, leading, main, major, pre-eminent, principal, prominent; fatal; excellent, first-class, first-rate, good, prime, splendid. * *n* chief city, metropolis, seat; money, estate, investments, shares, stock.

caprice *n* crotchet, fancy, fickleness, freak, humour, inconstancy, maggot, phantasy, quirk, vagary, whim, whimsy.

capricious *adj* changeable, crotchety, fanciful, fantastical, fickle, fitful, freakish, humoursome, odd, puckish, queer, uncertain, variable, wayward, whimsical.

capsize *vb* overturn, upset.

capsule *n* case, covering, envelope, sheath, shell, wrapper: pericarp, pod, seed-vessel.

captain *vb* command, direct, head, lead, manage, officer, preside. * *n* chief, chieftain, commander, leader, master, officer, soldier, warrior.

captious *adj* carping, caviling, censorious, critical, fault-finding, hypercritical; acrimonious, cantankerous, contentious, crabbed, cross, snappish, snarling, splenetic, testy, touchy, waspish; ensnaring, insidious.

captivate *vb* allure, attract, bewitch, catch, capture, charm, enamour, enchant, enthral, fascinate, gain, hypnotize, infatuate, win.

captivity *n* confinement, durance, duress, imprisonment; bondage, enthralment, servitude, slavery, subjection, thraldom, vassalage.

capture *vb* apprehend, arrest, catch, seize. * *n* apprehension, arrest, catch, catching, imprisonment, seizure; bag, prize.

carcass *n* body, cadaver, corpse, corse, remains.

cardinal *adj* capital, central, chief, essential, first, important, leading, main, pre-eminent, primary, principal, vital.

care *n* anxiety, concern, perplexity, trouble, solicitude, worry; attention, carefulness, caution, circumspection, heed, regard, vigilance, wariness, watchfulness; charge, custody, guardianship, keep, oversight, superintendence, ward; burden, charge, concern, responsibility.

careful *adj* anxious, solicitous, concerned, troubled, uneasy; attentive, heedful, mindful, regardful, thoughtful; cautious, canny, circumspect, discreet, leery, vigilant, watchful.

careless *adj* carefree, nonchalant, unapprehensive, undisturbed, unperplexed, unsolicitous, untroubled; disregardful, heedless, inattentive, incautious, inconsiderate, neglectful, negligent, regardless, remiss, thoughtless, unobservant, unconcerned, unconsidered, unmindful, unthinking.

carelessness *n* heedlessness, inadvertence, inattention, inconsiderateness, neglect, negligence, remissness, slackness, thoughtlessness, unconcern.

caress *vb* coddle, cuddle, cosset, embrace, fondle, hug, kiss, pet. * *n* cuddle, embrace, fondling, hug, kiss.

caressing *n* blandishment, dalliance, endearment, fondling.

cargo *n* freight, lading. load.

caricature *vb* burlesque, parody, send-up, take-off, travesty. * *n* burlesque, farce, ludicrous, parody, representation, take-off, travesty.

carious *adj* decayed, mortified, putrid, rotten, ulcerated.

cark *vb* annoy, fret, grieve, harass, perplex, worry.

carnage *n* bloodshed, butchery, havoc, massacre, murder, slaughter.

carnal *adj* animal, concupiscent, fleshly, lascivious, lecherous, lewd, libidinous, lubricous, lustful, salacious, sensual, voluptuous; bodily, earthy, mundane. natural, secular, temporal, unregenerate, unspiritual.

carol *vb* chant, hum, sing, warble. * *n* canticle, chorus, ditty, hymn, lay, song, warble.

carousal *n* banquet, entertainment, feast, festival, merry-making, regale; bacchanal, carouse, debauch, jamboree, jollification, orgy, revel, revelling, revelry, saturnalia, spree, wassail.

carp *vb* cavil, censure, criticize, fault.

carping *adj* captious, cavilling, censorious, hypercritical. * *n* cavil, censure, fault-finding, hypercriticism.

carriage *n* conveyance, vehicle; air, bearing, behaviour, conduct, demeanour, deportment, front, mien, port.

carry *vb* bear, convey, transfer, transmit, transport; impel, push forward, urge; accomplish, compass, effect, gain, secure; bear up, support, sustain; infer, involve, imply, import, signify.

cart *n* conveyance, tumbril, van, vehicle, wagon.

carte-blanche *n* authority, power.

carve *vb* chisel, cut, divide, engrave, grave, hack, hew, indent, incise, sculpt, sculpture; fashion, form, mould, shape.

cascade *vb* cataract, descend, drop, engulf, fall, inundate, overflow, plunge, tumble. * *n* cataract, fall, falls, force, linn, waterfall.

case[1] *vb* cover, encase, enclose, envelop, protect, wrap; box, pack. * *n* capsule, covering, sheathe; box, cabinet, container, holder, receptacle.

case[2] *n* condition, plight, predicament, situation, state; example, instance, occurrence; circumstance, condition, contingency, event; action, argument, cause, lawsuit, process, suit, trial.

case-hardened *adj* hardened, indurated, steeled; brazen, brazen-faced, obdurate, reprobate.

cash *n* banknotes, bullion, coin, currency, money, payment, specie.

cashier *vb* break, discard, discharge, dismiss.

cast *vb* fling, hurl, pitch, send, shy, sling, throw, toss; drive, force, impel, thrust; lay aside, put off, shed; calculate, compute, reckon; communicate, diffuse, impart, shed, throw. * *n* fling, throw, toss; shade, tinge, tint, touch; air, character, look, manner, mien, style, tone, turn; form, mould.

castaway *adj* abandoned, cast-off, discarded, rejected. * *n* derelict, outcast, reprobate, vagabond.

caste *n* class, grade, lineage, order, race, rank, species, status.

castigate *vb* beat, chastise, flog, lambaste, lash, thrash, whip; chaste, correct, discipline, punish; criticize, flagellate, upbraid.

castle *n* citadel, fortress, stronghold.

castrate *vb* caponize, emasculate, geld; mortify, subdue, suppress, weaken.

casual *adj* accidental, contingent, fortuitous, incidental, irregular, occasional, random, uncertain, unforeseen, unintentional, unpremeditated; informal, relaxed.

casualty *n* chance, contingency, fortuity, mishap; accident, catastrophe, disaster, mischance, misfortune.

cat *n* grimalkin, kitten, puss, tabby, tomcat.

cataclysm *n* deluge, flood, inundation; disaster, upheaval.

catacomb *n* crypt, tomb, vault.

catalogue *vb* alphabetize, categorize, chronicle, class, classify, codify, file, index, list, record, tabulate. * *n* enumeration, index, inventory, invoice, list, record, register, roll, schedule.

cataract *n* cascade, fall, waterfall.

catastrophe *n* conclusion, consummation, denouement, end, finale, issue, termination, upshot; adversity, blow, calamity, cataclysm, debacle, disaster, ill, misfortune, mischance, mishap, trial, trouble.

catch *vb* clutch, grasp, gripe, nab, seize, snatch; apprehend, arrest, capture; overtake; enmesh, ensnare, entangle, entrap, lime, net; bewitch, captivate, charm, enchant, fascinate, win; surprise, take unawares. * *n* arrest, capture, seizure; bag, find, haul, plum, prize; drawback, fault, hitch, obstacle, rub, snag; captive, conquest.

catching *adj* communicable, contagious, infectious, pestiferous, pestilential; attractive, captivating, charming, enchanting, fascinating, taking, winning, winsome.

catechize *adj* examine, interrogate, question, quiz.

catechumen *n* convert, disciple, learner, neophyte, novice, proselyte, pupil, tyro.

categorical *adj* absolute, direct, downright, emphatic, explicit, express, positive, unconditional, unqualified, unreserved, utter.

category *n* class, division, head, heading, list, order, rank, sort.

catenation *n* conjunction, connection, union.

cater *vb* feed, provide, purvey.

cathartic *adj* abstergent, aperient, cleansing, evacuant, laxative, purgative. * *n* aperient, laxative, physic, purgative, purge.

catholic *adj* general, universal, world-wide; charitable, liberal, tolerant, unbigoted, unexclusive, unsectarian.

cause *vb* breed, create, originate, produce; effect, effectuate, occasion, produce. * *n* agent, creator, mainspring, origin, original, producer, source, spring; account, agency, consideration, ground, incentive, incitement, inducement, motive, reason; aim, end, object, purpose; action, case, suit, trial.

caustic *adj* acrid, cathartic, consuming, corroding, corrosive, eating, erosive, mordant, virulent; biting, bitter, burning, cutting, sarcastic, satirical, scalding, scathing, severe, sharp, stinging.

caution *vb* admonish, forewarn, warn. * *n* care, carefulness, circumspection, discretion, forethought, heed, heedfulness, providence, prudence, wariness, vigilance, watchfulness; admonition, advice, counsel,injunction, warning.

cautious *adj* careful, chary, circumspect, discreet, heedful, prudent, wary, vigilant, wary, watchful.

cavalier *adj* arrogant, curt, disdainful, haughty, insolent, scornful, supercilious; debonair, gallant, gay. * *n* chevalier, equestrian, horseman, horse-soldier, knight.

cave *n* cavern, cavity, den, grot, grotto.

cavil *vb* carp, censure, hypercriticize, object.

cavilling *adj* captious, carping, censorious, critical, hypercritical.

cavity *n* hollow, pocket, vacuole, void.

cease *vb* desist, intermit, pause, refrain, stay, stop; fail; discontinue, end, quit, terminate.

ceaseless *adj* continual, continuous, incessant, unceasing, unintermitting, uninterrupted, unremitting; endless, eternal, everlasting, perpetual.

cede *vb* abandon, abdicate, relinquish, resign, surrender, transfer, yield; convey, grant.

celebrate *vb* applaud, bless, commend, emblazon, extol, glorify, laud, magnify, praise, trumpet; commemorate, honour, keep, observe; solemnize.

celebrated *adj* distinguished, eminent, famed, famous, glorious, illustrious, notable, renowned.

celebrity *n* credit, distinction, eminence, fame, glory, honour, renown, reputation, repute; lion, notable, star.

celerity *n* fleetness, haste, quickness, rapidity, speed, swiftness, velocity.

celestial *adj* empyreal, empyrean; angelic, divine, god-like, heavenly, seraphic, supernal, supernatural.

celibate *adj* single, unmarried. * *n* bachelor, single, virgin.

cellular *adj* alveolate, honeycombed.

cement *vb* attach, bind, join, combine, connect, solder, unite, weld; cohere, stick. * *n* glue, paste, mortar, solder.

cemetery *n* burial-ground, burying-ground, churchyard, god's acre, graveyard, necropolis.

censor *vb* blue-pencil, bowdlerize, cut, edit, expurgate; classify, kill, quash, squash, suppress. * *n* caviller, censurer, faultfinder.

censorious *adj* captious, carping, caviling, condemnatory, faultfinding, hypercritical, severe.

censure *vb* abuse, blame, chide, condemn, rebuke, reprehend, reprimand, reproach, reprobate, reprove, scold, upbraid. *n* animadversion, blame, condemnation, criticism, disapprobation, disapproval, rebuke, remonstrance, reprehension, reproach, reproof, stricture.

ceremonious *adj* civil, courtly, lofty, stately; formal, studied; exact, formal, punctilious, precise, starched, stiff.

ceremony *n* ceremonial, etiquette, form, formality, observance, solemnity, rite; parade, pomp, show, stateliness.

certain *adj* absolute, incontestable, incontrovertible, indisputable, indubitable, positive, undeniable, undisputed, unquestionable, unquestioned; assured, confident, sure, undoubting; infallible, never-failing, unfailing; actual, existing, real; constant, determinate, fixed, settled, stated.

certainty *n* indubitability, indubitableness, inevitableness, inevitability, surety, unquestionability, unquestionableness; assurance, assuredness, certitude, confidence, conviction, surety.

certify *vb* attest, notify, testify, vouch; ascertain, determine, verify, show.

cerulean *adj* azure, blue, sky-blue.

cessation *n* ceasing, discontinuance, intermission, pause, remission, respite, rest, stop, stoppage, suspension.

cession *n* abandonment, capitulation, ceding, concession, conveyance, grant, relinquishement, renunciation, surrender, yielding.

chafe *vb* rub; anger, annoy, chagrin, enrage, exasperate, fret, gall, incense, irritate, nettle, offend, provoke, ruffle, tease, vex; fret, fume, rage.

chaff *vb* banter, deride, jeer, mock, rally, ridicule, scoff. * *n* glumes, hulls, husks; refuse, rubbish, trash, waste.

chaffer *n* bargain, haggle, higgle, negotiate.

chagrin *vb* annoy, chafe, displease, irritate, mortify, provoke, vex. * *n* annoyance, displeasure, disquiet, dissatisfaction, fretfulness, humiliation, ill-humour, irritation, mortification, spleen, vexation.

chain *vb* bind, confine, fetter, manacle, restrain, shackle, trammel; enslave. * *n* bond, fetter, manacle, shackle, union.

chalice *n* bowl, cup, goblet.

challenge *vb* brave, call out, dare, defy, dispute; demand, require. * *n* defiance, interrogation, question; exception, objection.

chamber *n* apartment, hall, room; cavity, hollow.

champion *vb* advocate, defend, uphold. * *n* defender, promoter, protector, vindicator; belt-holder, hero, victor, warrior, winner.

chance *vb* befall, betide, happen, occur. * *adj* accidental, adventitious, casual, fortuitous, incidental, unexpected, unforeseen. * *n* accident, cast, fortuity, fortune, hap, luck; contingency, possibility; occasion, opening, opportunity; contingency, fortuity, gamble, peradventure, uncertainty; hazard, jeopardy, peril, risk.

change *vb* alter, fluctuate, modify, vary; displace, remove, replace, shift, substitute; barter, commute, exchange. * *n* alteration, mutation, revolution, transition, transmutation, turning, variance, variation; innovation, novelty, variety, vicissitude.

changeable *adj* alterable, inconstant, modifiable, mutable, uncertain, unsettled, unstable, unsteadfast, unsteady, variable, variant; capricious, fickle, fitful, flighty, giddy, mercurial, vacillating, volatile, wavering.

changeless *adj* abiding, consistent, constant, fixed,

immutable, permanent, regular, reliable, resolute, settled, stationary, unalterable, unchanging.

channel *vb* chamfer, cut, flute, groove. * *n* canal, conduit, duct, passage; aqueduct, canal, chute, drain, flume, furrow; chamfer, groove, fluting, furrow, gutter.

chant *vb* carol, sing, warble; intone, recite; canticle, song.

chaos *n* anarchy, confusion, disorder.

chapfallen *adj* blue, crest-fallen, dejected, depressed, despondent, discouraged, disheartened, dispirited, downcast, downhearted, low-spirited, melancholy, sad.

chaplet *n* coronal, garland, wreath.

char *vb* burn, scorch.

character *n* emblem, figure, hieroglyph, ideograph, letter, mark, sign, symbol; bent, constitution, cast, disposition, nature, quality; individual, original, person, personage; reputation, repute; nature, traits; eccentric, trait.

characteristic *adj* distinctive, peculiar, singular, special, specific, typical. * *n* attribute, feature, idiosyncrasy, lineament, mark, peculiarity, quality, trait.

charge *vb* burden, encumber, freight, lade, load; entrust; ascribe, impute, lay; accuse, arraign, blame, criminate, impeach, inculpate, indict, involve; bid, command, exhort, enjoin, order, require, tax; assault, attack bear down. * *n* burden, cargo, freight, lading, load; care, custody, keeping, management, ward; commission, duty, employment, office, trust; responsibility, trust; command, direction, injunction, mandate, order, precept; exhortation, instruction; cost, debit, expense, expenditure, outlay; price, sum; assault, attack, encounter, onset, onslaught.

charger *n* dish, platter; mount, steed, war-horse.

charily *adv* carefully, cautiously, distrustfully, prudently, sparingly, suspiciously, warily.

charitable *adj* beneficial, beneficent, benignant, bountiful, generous, kind, liberal, open-handed; candid, considerate, lenient, mild.

charity *n* benevolence, benignity, fellow-feeling, good-nature, goodwill, kind-heartedness, kindness, tenderheartedness; beneficence, bounty, generosity, humanity, philanthropy. liberality.

charlatan *n* cheat, empiric, impostor, mountebank, pretender, quack.

charm *vb* allure, attract, becharm, bewitch, captivate, catch, delight, enamour, enchain, enchant, enrapture, enravish, fascinate, transport, win. * *n* enchantment, incantation, magic, necromancy, sorcery, spell, witchery; amulet, talisman; allurement, attraction, attractiveness, fascination.

charming *adj* bewitching, captivating, delightful, enchanting, enrapturing, fascinating, lovely.

charter *vb* incorporate; hire, let. * *n* franchise, immunity, liberty, prerogation, privilege, right; bond, deed, indenture, instrument, prerogative.

chary *adj* careful, cautious, circumspect, shy, wary; abstemious, careful, choice, economical, frugal, provident, saving, sparing, temperate, thrifty, unwasteful.

chase *vb* follow, hunt, pursue, track; emboss. * *n* course, field-sport, hunt, hunting.

chasm *n* cavity, cleft, fissure, gap, hollow, hiatus, opening.

chaste *adj* clean, continent, innocent, modest, pure, pure-minded, undefiled, virtuous; chastened, pure, simple, unaffected, uncorrupt.

chasten *vb* correct, humble; purify, refine, render, subdue.

chastening *n* chastisement, correction, discipline, humbling.

chastise *vb* castigate, correct, flog, lash, punish, whip; chasten, correct, discipline, humble, punish, subdue.

chastity *n* abstinence, celibacy, continence, innocence, modesty, pure-mindedness, purity, virtue; cleanness, decency; chasteness, refinement, restrainedness, simplicity, sobriety, unaffectedness.

chat *vb* babble, chatter, confabulate, gossip, prate, prattle. * *n* chit-chat, confabulation, conversation, gossip, prattle.

chatter *vb* babble, chat, confabulate, gossip, prate, prattle. * *n* babble, chat, gabble, jabber, patter, prattle.

cheap *adj* inexpensive, low-priced; common, indifferent, inferior, mean, meretricious, paltry, poor.

cheapen *vb* belittle, depreciate.

cheat *vb* cozen, deceive, dissemble, juggle, shuffle; bamboozle, befool, beguile, cajole, circumvent, deceive, defraud, chouse, delude, dupe, ensnare, entrap, fool, gammon, gull, hoax, hoodwink, inveigle, jockey, mislead, outwit, overreach, trick. * *n* artifice, beguilement, blind, catch, chouse, deceit, deception, fraud, imposition, imposture, juggle, pitfall, snare, stratagem, swindle, trap, trick, wile; counterfeit, deception, delusion, illusion, mockery, paste, sham, tinsel; beguiler, charlatan, cheater, cozener, impostor, jockey, knave, mountebank, trickster, rogue, render, sharper, seizer, shuffler, swindler, taker, tearer.

check *vb* block, bridle, control, counteract, curb, hinder, obstruct, repress, restrain; chide, rebuke, reprimand, reprove. * *n* bar, barrier, block, brake, bridle, clog, control, curb, damper, hindrance, impediment, interference, obstacle, obstruction, rebuff, repression, restraint, stop, stopper.

cheep *vb* chirp, creak, peep, pipe, squeak.

cheer *vb* animate, encourage, enliven, exhilarate, gladden, incite, inspirit; comfort, console, solace; applaud, clap. * *n* cheerfulness, gaiety, gladness, glee, hilarity, jollity, joy, merriment, mirth; entertainment, food, provision, repast, viands, victuals; acclamation, hurrah, huzza.

cheerful *adj* animated, airy, blithe, buoyant, cheery, gay, glad, gleeful, happy, joyful, jocund, jolly, joyous, light-hearted, lightsome, lively, merry, mirthful, sprightly, sunny; animating, cheering, cheery, encouraging, enlivening, glad, gladdening, gladsome, grateful, inspiriting, jocund, pleasant.

cheerless *adj* dark, dejected, desolate, despondent, disconsolate, discouraged, dismal, doleful, dreary, forlorn, gloomy, joyless, low-spirited, lugubrious, melancholy, mournful, rueful, sad, sombre, spiritless, woe-begone.

cherish *vb* comfort, foster, nourish, nurse, nurture, support, sustain; treasure; encourage, entertain, indulge, harbour.

chest *n* box, case, coffer; breast, thorax, trunk.

chew *vb* crunch, manducate, masticate, munch; bite, champ, gnaw; meditate, ruminate.

chicanery *n* chicane, deception, duplicity, intrigue, intriguing, sophistication, sophistry, stratagems, tergiversation, trickery, wiles, wire-pulling.

chide *vb* admonish, blame, censure, rebuke, reprimand, reprove, scold, upbraid; chafe, clamour, fret, fume, scold.

chief *adj* first, foremost, headmost, leading, master, supereminent, supreme, top; capital, cardinal, especial, essential, grand, great, main, master, paramount, prime, principal, supreme, vital. * *n* chieftain, commander; head, leader.

chiffonier *n* cabinet, sideboard.

child *n* babe, baby, bairn, bantling, brat, chit, infant, nursling, suckling, wean; issue, offspring, progeny.

childbirth *n* child-bearing, delivery, labour, parturition, travail.

childish *adj* infantile, juvenile, puerile, tender, young; foolish, frivolous, silly, trifling, weak.

childlike *adj* docile, dutiful, gentle, meek, obedient, submissive; confiding, guileless, ingenuous, innocent, simple, trustful, uncrafty.

chill *vb* dampen, depress, deject, discourage, dishearten. * *adj* bleak, chilly, cold, frigid, gelid. * *n* chilliness, cold, coldness, frigidity; ague, rigour, shiver; damp, depression.

chime *vb* accord, harmonize. * *n* accord, consonance.

chimera *n* crochet, delusion, dream, fantasy, hallucination, illusion, phantom.

chimerical *adj* delusive, fanciful, fantastic, illusory, imaginary, quixotic, shadowy, unfounded, visionary, wild.

chink[1] *vb* cleave, crack, fissure, crevasse, incise, split, slit. * *n* aperture, cleft, crack, cranny, crevice, fissure, gap, opening, slit.

chink[2] *vb, n* jingle, clink, ring, ting, tink, tinkle.

chip *vb* flake, fragment, hew, pare, scrape. * *n* flake, fragment, paring, scrap.

chirp *vb* cheep, chirrup, peep, twitter.

chirrup *vb* animate, cheer, encourage, inspirit.

chisel *vb* carve, cut, gouge, sculpt, sculpture.

chivalrous *adj* adventurous, bold, brave, chivalric, gallant, knightly, valiant, warlike; gallant, generous, high-minded, magnanimous.

chivalry *n* knighthood, knight-errantry; courtesy, gallantry, politeness; courage, valour.

choice *adj* excellent, exquisite, precious, rare, select, superior, uncommon, unusual, valuable; careful, chary, frugal, sparing. * *n* alternative, election, option, selection; favourite, pick, preference.

choke *vb* gag, smother, stifle, strangle, suffocate, throttle; overcome, overpower, smother, suppress; bar, block, close, obstruct, stop.

choleric *adj* angry, fiery, hasty, hot, fiery, irascible, irritable, passionate, petulant, testy, touchy, waspish.

choose *vb* adopt, co-opt, cull, designate, elect, pick, predestine, prefer, select.

chop *vb* cut, hack, hew; mince; shift, veer. * *n* slice; brand, quality; chap, jaw.

chouse *vb* bamboozle, beguile, cheat, circumvent, cozen, deceive, defraud, delude, dupe, gull, hoodwink, overreach, swindle, trick, victimize. * *n* cully, dupe, gull, simpleton, tool; artifice, cheat, circumvention, deceit, deception, delusion, double-dealing, fraud, imposition, imposture, ruse, stratagem, trick, wile.

christen *vb* baptize; call, dub, denominate, designate, entitle, name, style, term, title.

chronic *adj* confirmed, continuing, deep-seated, inveterate, rooted.

chronicle *vb* narrate, record, register. * *n* diary, journal, register; account, annals, history, narration, recital, record.

chuckle *vb* crow, exult, giggle, laugh, snigger, titter. * *n* giggle, laughter, snigger, titter.

chum *n* buddy, companion, comrade, crony, friend, mate, pal.

churl *n* boor, bumpkin, clodhopper, clown, countryman, lout, peasant, ploughman, rustic; curmudgeon, hunks, miser, niggard, scrimp, skinflint.

churlish *adj* brusque, brutish, cynical, harsh, impolite, rough, rude, snappish, snarling, surly, uncivil, waspish; crabbed, ill-tempered, morose, sullen; close, close-fisted, illiberal, mean, miserly, niggardly, penurious, stingy.

churn *vb* agitate, jostle.

cicatrice *n* cicatrix, mark, scar, seam.

cicesbeo *n* beau, escort, gallant, gigolo.

cincture *n* band, belt, cestos, cestus, girdle.

cipher *n* naught, nothing, zero; character, device, monogram, symbol; nobody, nonentity.

circle *vb* compass, encircle, encompass, gird, girdle, ring; gyrate, revolve, rotate, round, turn. * *n* circlet, corona, gyre, hoop, ring, rondure; circumference, cordon, periphery; ball, globe, orb, sphere; compass, enclosure; class, clique, company, coterie, fraternity, set, society; bounds, circuit, compass, field, province, range, region, sphere.

circuit *n* ambit, circumambience, circumambiency, cycle, revolution, turn; bounds, district, field, province, range, region, space, sphere, tract; boundary, compass; course, detour, perambulation, round, tour.

circuitous *adj* ambiguous, devious, indirect, roundabout, tortuous, turning, winding.

circulate *vb* diffuse, disseminate, promulgate, propagate, publish, spread.

circumference *n* bound, boundary, circuit, girth, outline, perimeter, periphery.

circumlocution *n* circuitousness, obliqueness, periphrase, periphrasis, verbosity, wordiness.

circumscribe *vb* bound, define, encircle, enclose, encompass, limit, surround; confine, restrict.

circumspect *adj* attentive, careful, cautious, considerate, discreet, heedful, judicious, observant, prudent, vigilant, wary, watchful.

circumstance *n* accident, incident; condition, detail, event, fact, happening, occurrence, position, situation.

circumstantial *adj* detailed, particular; indirect, inferential, presumptive.

circumvent *vb* check, checkmate, outgeneral, thwart; bamboozle, beguile, cheat, chouse, cozen, deceive, defraud, delude, dupe, gull, hoodwink, inveigle, mislead, outwit, overreach, trick.

circumvention *n* cheat, cheating, chicanery, deceit, deception, duplicity, fraud, guile, imposition, imposture, indirection, trickery, wiles.

cistern *n* basin, pond, reservoir, tank.

citation *n* excerpt, extract, quotation; enumeration, mention, quotation, quoting.

cite *vb* adduce, enumerate, extract, mention, name, quote; call, summon.

citizen *n* burgess, burgher, denizen, dweller, freeman, inhabitant, resident, subject, townsman.

civil *adj* civic, municipal, political; domestic; accommodating, affable, civilized, complaisant, courteous, courtly, debonair, easy, gracious, obliging, polished, polite, refined, suave, urbane, well-bred, well-mannered.

civility *n* affability, amiability, complaisance, courteousness, courtesy, good-breeding, politeness, suavity, urbanity.

civilize *vb* cultivate, educate, enlighten, humanize, improve, polish, refine.

claim *vb* ask, assert, challenge, demand, exact, require. * *n* call, demand, lien, requisition; pretension, privilege, right, title.

clammy *adj* adhesive, dauby, glutinous, gummy, ropy, smeary, sticky, viscid, viscous; close, damp, dank, moist, sticky, sweaty.

clamour *vb* shout, vociferate. * *n* blare, din, exclamation, hullabaloo, noise, outcry, uproar, vociferation.

clan *n* family, phratry, race, sect, tribe; band, brotherhood, clique, coterie, fraternity, gang, set, society, sodality.

clandestine *adj* concealed, covert, fraudulent, furtive, hidden, private, secret, sly, stealthy, surreptitious, underhand.

clap *vb* pat, slap, strike; force, slam; applaud, cheer. * *n* blow, knock, slap; bang, burst, explosion, peal, slam.

clarify *vb* cleanse, clear, depurate, purify, strain.

clash *vb* collide, crash, strike; clang, clank, clatter, crash, rattle; contend, disagree, interfere. * *n* collision; clang, clangour, clank, clashing, clatter, crash, rattle; contradiction, disagreement, interference, jar, jarring, opposition.

clasp *vb* clutch, entwine, grasp, grapple, grip, seize; embrace, enfold, fold, hug. * *n* buckle, catch, hasp, hook; embrace, hug.

class *vb* arrange, classify, dispose, distribute, range, rank. * *n* form, grade, order, rank, status; group, seminar; breed, kind, sort; category, collection, denomination, division, group, head.

classical *adj* first-rate, master, masterly, model, standard; Greek, Latin, Roman; Attic, chaste, elegant, polished, pure, refined.

classify *vb* arrange, assort, categorize, class, dispose, distribute, group, pigeonhole, rank, systematize, tabulate.

clatter *vb* clash, rattle; babble, clack, gabble, jabber, prate, prattle. * *n* clattering, clutter, rattling.

clause *n* article, condition, provision, stipulation.

claw *vb* lacerate, scratch, tear. * *n* talon, ungula.

clean *vb* cleanse, clear, purge, purify, rinse, scour, scrub, wash, wipe. * *adj* immaculate, spotless, unsmirched, unsoiled, unspotted, unstained, unsullied, white; clarified, pure, purified, unadulterated, unmixed; adroit, delicate, dextrous, graceful, light, neat, shapely; complete, entire, flawless, faultless, perfect, unabated, unblemished, unimpaired, whole; chaste, innocent, moral, pure, undefiled. * *adv* altogether, completely, entirely, perfectly, quite, thoroughly, wholly.

cleanse *vb* clean, clear, elutriate, purge, purify, rinse, scour, scrub, wash, wipe.

clear *vb* clarify, cleanse, purify, refine; emancipate, disenthral, free, liberate, loose; absolve, acquit, discharge, exonerate, justify, vindicate; disembarrass, disengage, disentangle, extricate, loosen, rid; clean up, scour, sweep; balance; emancipate, free, liberate. * *adj* bright, crystalline, light, limpid, luminous, pellucid, transparent; pure, unadulterated, unmixed; free, open, unencumbered, unobstructed; cloudless, fair, serene, sunny, unclouded, undimmed, unobscured; net; distinct, intelligible, lucid, luminous, perspicuous; apparent, conspicuous, distinct, evident, indisputable, manifest, obvious, palpable, unambiguous, undeniable, unequivocal, unmistakable, unquestionable, visible; clean, guiltless, immaculate, innocent, irreproachable, sinless, spotless, unblemished, undefiled, unspotted, unsullied; unhampered, unimpeded, unobstructed; euphonious, fluty, liquid, mellifluous, musical, silvery, sonorous.

cleave[1] *vb* crack, divide, open, part, rend, rive, sever, split, sunder.

cleave[2] *vb* adhere, cling, cohere, hold, stick.

cleft *adj* bifurcated, cloven, forked. * *n* breach, break, chasm, chink, cranny, crevice, fissure, fracture, gap, interstice, opening, rent, rift.

clemency *n* mildness, softness; compassion, fellow-feeling, forgivingness, gentleness, kindness, lenience, leniency, lenity, mercifulness, mercy, mildness, tenderness.

clement *adj* compassionate, forgiving, gentle, humane, indulgent, kind, kind-hearted, lenient, merciful, mild, tender, tender-hearted.

clench *vb* close tightly, grip; fasten, fix, rivet, secure.

clergy *n* clergymen, the cloth, ministers.

clever *adj* able, apt, gifted, talented; adroit, capable, dextrous, discerning, expert, handy, ingenious, knowing, quick, ready, skilful, smart, talented.

click *vb* beat, clack, clink, tick. * *n* beat, clack, clink, tick; catch, detent, pawl, ratchet.

cliff *n* crag, palisade, precipice, scar, steep.

climate *n* clime, temperature, weather; country, region.

climax *vb* consummate, crown, culminate, peak. * *n* acme, consummation, crown, culmination, head, peak, summit, top, zenith.

clinch *vb* clasp, clench, clutch, grapple, grasp, grip; fasten, secure; confirm, establish, fix. * *n* catch, clutch, grasp, grip; clincher, clamp, cramp, holdfast.

cling *vb* adhere, clear, stick; clasp, embrace, entwine.

clink *vb, n* chink, jingle, ring, tinkle; chime, rhyme.

clip *vb* cut, shear, snip; curtail, cut, dock, pare, prune, trim. * *n* cutting, shearing; blow, knock, lick, rap, thump, thwack, thump.

clique *n* association, brotherhood, cabal, camarilla, clan, club, coterie, gang, junta, party, ring, set, sodality.

cloak *vb* conceal, cover, dissemble, hide, mask, veil. * *n* mantle, surcoat; blind, cover, mask, pretext, veil.

clock *vb* mark time, measure, stopwatch; clock up, record, register. * *n* chronometer, horologue, timekeeper, timepiece, timer, watch.

clog *vb* fetter, hamper, shackle, trammel; choke, obstruct; burden, cumber, embarrass, encumber, hamper, hinder, impede, load, restrain, trammel. * *n* dead-weight, drag-weight, fetter, shackle, trammel; check, drawback, encumbrance, hindrance, impediment, obstacle, obstruction.

cloister *n* abbey, convent, monastery, nunnery, priory; arcade, colonnade, piazza.

close¹ *adj* closed, confined, snug, tight; hidden, private, secret; incommunicative, reserved, reticent, secretive, taciturn; concealed, retired, secluded, withdrawn; confined, motionless, stagnant; airless, oppressive, stale, stifling, stuffy, sultry; compact, compressed, dense, form, solid, thick; adjacent, adjoining, approaching, immediately, near, nearly, neighbouring; attached, dear, confidential, devoted, intimate; assiduous, earnest, fixed, intense, intent, unremitting; accurate, exact, faithful, nice, precise, strict; churlish, close-fisted, curmudgeonly, mean, illiberal, miserly,

niggardly, parsimonious, penurious, stingy, ungenerous. * *n* courtyard, enclosure, grounds, precinct, yard.

close² *vb* occlude, seal, shut; choke, clog, estop, obstruct, stop; cease, complete, concede, end, finish, terminate; coalesce, unite; cease, conclude, finish, terminate; clinch, grapple; agree. * *n* cessation, conclusion, end, finish, termination.

closet *n* cabinet, retiring-room; press, store-room.

clot *vb* coagulate, concrete. * *n* coagulation, concretion, lump.

clothe *vb* array, attire, deck, dress, rig; cover, endow, envelop, enwrap, invest with, swathe.

clothes *n* apparel, array, attire, clothing, costume, dress, garb, garments, gear, habiliments, habits, raiment, rig, vestments, vesture.

cloud *vb* becloud, obnubilate, overcast, overspread; befog, darken, dim, obscure, shade, shadow. * *n* cirrus, cumulus, fog, haze, mist, nebulosity, scud, stratus, vapour; army, crowd, horde, host, multitude, swarm, throng; darkness, eclipse, gloom, obscuration, obscurity.

cloudy *adj* clouded, filmy, foggy, hazy, lowering, lurid, murky, overcast; confused, dark, dim, obscure; depressing, dismal, gloomy, sullen; clouded, mottled; blurred, dimmed, lustreless, muddy.

clown *n* churl, clod-breaker, clodhopper, hind, husbandman, lubber; boor, bumpkin, churl, fellow, lout; blockhead, dolt, clodpoll, dunce, dunderhead, numbskull, simpleton, thickhead; buffoon, droll, farceur, fool, harlequin, jack-a-dandy, jack-pudding, jester, merry-andrew, mime, pantaloon, pickle-herring, punch, scaramouch, zany.

clownish *adj* awkward, boorish, clumsy, coarse, loutish, ungainly, rough, rustic; churlish, ill-bred, ill-mannered, impolite, rude, uncivil.

cloy *vb* glut, pall, sate, satiate, surfeit.

club *vb* combine, unite; beat, bludgeon, cudgel. * *n* bat, bludgeon, cosh, cudgel, hickory, shillelagh, stick, truncheon; association, company, coterie, fraternity, set, society, sodality.

clump *vb* assemble, batch, bunch, cluster, group, lump; lumber, stamp, stomp, stump, trudge. * *n* assemblage, bunch, cluster, collection, group, patch, tuft.

clumsy *adj* botched, cumbrous, heavy, ill-made, ill-shaped, lumbering, ponderous, unwieldy; awkward, blundering, bungling, elephantine, heavy-handed, inapt, mal adroit, unhandy, unskilled.

cluster *vb* assemble, batch, bunch, clump, collect, gather, group, lump, throng. * *n* agglomeration, assemblage, batch, bunch, clump, collection, gathering, group, throng.

clutch¹ *vb* catch, clasp, clench, clinch, grab, grapple, grasp, grip, hold, seize, snatch, squeeze. * *n* clasp, clench, clinch, grasp, grip, hold, seizure, squeeze.

clutch² *n* aerie, brood, hatching, nest.

clutches *npl* claws, paws, talons; hands, power.

clutter *vb* confuse, disarrange, disarray, disorder, jumble, litter, mess, muss; clatter. * *n* bustle, clatter, clattering, racket; confusion, disarray, disorder, jumble, litter, mess, muss.

coadjutor *n* abettor, accomplice, aider, ally, assistant, associate, auxiliary, collaborator, colleague, cooperator, fellow-helper, helper, helpmate, partner.

coagulate *vb* clot, congeal, concrete, curdle, thicken.

coalesce *vb* amalgamate, blend, cohere, combine, commix, incorporate, mix, unite; concur, fraternize.

coalition *n* alliance, association, combination, compact, confederacy, confederation, conjunction, conspiracy, co-partnership, federation, league, union.

coarse *adj* crude, impure, rough, unpurified; broad, gross, indecent, indelicate, ribald, vulgar; bearish, bluff, boorish, brutish, churlish, clownish, gruff, impolite, loutish, rude, unpolished; crass, inelegant.

coast *vb* flow, glide, roll, skim, sail, slide, sweep. * *n* littoral, seaboard, sea-coast, seaside, shore, strand; border.

coat *vb* cover, spread. * *n* cut-away, frock, jacket; coating, cover, covering; layer.

coax *vb* allure, beguile, cajole, cog, entice, flatter, persuade, soothe, wheedle.

cobble *vb* botch, bungle; mend, patch, repair, tinker.

cobweb *adj* flimsy, gauzy, slight, thin, worthless. * *n* entanglement, meshes, snare, toils.

cochleate *adj* cochlear, cochleary, cochleous, cochleated, spiral, spiry.

cockle *vb* corrugate, pucker, wrinkle.

coddle *vb* caress, cocker, fondle, humour, indulge, nurse, pamper, pet.

codger *n* churl, curmudgeon, hunks, lick-penny, miser, niggard, screw, scrimp, skinflint.

codify *vb* condense, digest, summarize, systematize, tabulate.

coerce *vb* check, curb, repress, restrain, subdue; compel, constrain, drive, force, urge.

coercion *n* check, curb, repression, restraint; compulsion, constraint, force.

coeval *adj* coetaneous, coexistent, contemporaneous, contemporary, synchronous.

coexistent *adj* coetaneous, coeval, simultaneous, synchronous.

coffer *n* box, casket, chest, trunk; money-chest, safe, strongbox; caisson.

cogent *adj* compelling, conclusive, convincing, effective, forcible, influential, irresistible, persuasive, potent, powerful, resistless, strong, trenchant, urgent.

cogitate *vb* consider, deliberate, meditate, ponder, reflect, ruminate, muse, think, weigh.

cognate *adj* affiliated, affined, akin, allied, alike, analogous, connected, kindred, related, similar.

cognizance *n* cognition, knowing, knowledge, notice, observation.

cohere *vb* agree, coincide, conform, fit, square, suit.

coherence *n* coalition, cohesion, connection, dependence, union; agreement, congruity, consistency, correspondence, harmony, intelligibility, intelligible, meaning, rationality, unity.

coherent *adj* adherent, connected, united; congruous, consistent, intelligible, logical.

cohort *n* band, battalion, line, squadron.

coil *vb* curl, twine, twirl, twist, wind. * *n* convolution, curlicue, helix, knot, roll, spiral, tendril, twirl, volute, whorl; bustle, care, clamour, confusion, entanglements, perplexities, tumult, turmoil, uproar.

coin *vb* counterfeit, create, devise, fabricate, forge, form, invent, mint, originate, mould, stamp. * *n* coign, corner, quoin; key, plug, prop, wedge; cash, money, specie.

coincide *vb* cohere, correspond, square, tally; acquiesce, agree, harmonize, concur.

coincidence *n* corresponding, squaring, tallying; agreeing, concurrent, concurring.

cold *adj* arctic, biting, bleak, boreal, chill, chilly, cutting, frosty, gelid, glacial, icy, nipping, polar, raw, wintry; frost-bitten, shivering; apathetic, cold-blooded, dead, freezing, frigid, indifferent, lukewarm, passionless, phlegmatic, sluggish, stoical, stony, torpid, unconcerned, unfeeling, unimpressible, unresponsive, unsusceptible, unsympathetic; dead, dull, spiritless, unaffecting, uninspiring, uninteresting. * *n* chill, chilliness, coldness.

collapse *vb* break down, fail, fall. * *n* depression, exhaustion, failure, faint, prostration, sinking, subsidence.

collar *vb* apprehend, arrest, capture, grab, nab, seize. * *n* collarette, gorget, neckband, ruff, torque; band, belt, fillet, guard, ring, yoke.

collate *vb* adduce, collect, compare, compose.

collateral *adj* contingent, indirect, secondary, subordinate; concurrent, parallel; confirmatory, corroborative; accessory, accompanying, additional, ancillary, auxiliary, concomitant, contributory, simultaneous, supernumerary; consanguineous, related. * *n* guarantee, guaranty, security, surety, warranty; accessory, extra, nonessential, unessential; consanguinean, relative.

collation *n* luncheon, repast, meal.

colleague *n* aider, ally, assistant, associate, auxiliary, coadjutor, collaborator, companion, confederate, confrere, cooperator, helper, partner.

collect *vb* assemble, compile, gather, muster; accumulate, aggregate, amass, garner.

collected *adj* calm, composed, cool, placid, self-possessed, serene, unperturbed.

collection *n* aggregation, assemblage, cluster, crowd, drove, gathering, group, pack; accumulation, congeries, conglomeration, heap, hoard, lot, mass, pile, store; alms, contribution, offering, offertory.

colligate *vb* bind, combine, fasten, unite.

collision *n* clash, concussion, crash, encounter, impact, impingement, shock; conflict, crashing, interference, opposition.

collocate *vb* arrange, dispose, place, set.

colloquy *n* conference, conversation, dialogue, discourse, talk.

collude *vb* concert, connive, conspire.

collusion *n* connivance, conspiracy, coven, craft, deceit.

collusive *adj* conniving, conspiratorial, , dishonest, deceitful, deceptive, fraudulent.

colossal *adj* Cyclopean, enormous, gigantic, Herculean, huge, immense, monstrous, prodigious, vast.

colour *vb* discolour, dye, paint, stain, tinge, tint; disguise, varnish; disguise, distort, garble, misrepresent, pervert; blush, flush, redden, show. * *n* hue, shade, tinge, tint, tone; paint, pigment, stain; redness, rosiness, ruddiness; complexion; appearance, disguise, excuse, guise, plea, pretence, pretext, semblance.

colourless *adj* achromatic, uncoloured, untinged; blanched, hueless, livid, pale, pallid; blank, characterless, dull, expressionless, inexpressive, monotonous.

colours *n* banner, ensign, flag, standard.

column *n* pillar, pilaster; file, line, row.

coma *n* drowsiness, lethargy, somnolence, stupor, torpor; bunch, clump, cluster, tuft.

comatose *adj* drowsy, lethargic, sleepy, somnolent, stupefied.

comb *vb* card, curry, dress, groom, rake, unknot, untangle; rake, ransack, rummage, scour, search. * *n* card, hatchel, ripple; harrow, rake.

combat *vb* contend, contest, fight, struggle, war; battle, oppose, resist, struggle, withstand. * *n* action, affair, battle, brush, conflict, contest, encounter, fight, skirmish.

combative *adj* belligerent, contentious, militant, pugnacious, quarrelsome.

combination *n* association, conjunction, connection, union; alliance, cartel, coalition, confederacy, consolidation, league, merger, syndicate; cabal, clique, conspiracy, faction, junta, ring; amalgamation, compound, mixture.

combine *vb* cooperate, merge, pool, unite; amalgamate, blend, incorporate, mix.

combustible *adj* consumable, inflammable.

come *vb* advance, approach; arise, ensue, flow, follow, issue, originate, proceed, result; befall, betide, happen, occur.

comely *adj* becoming, decent, decorous, fitting, seemly, suitable; beautiful, fair, graceful, handsome, personable, pretty, symmetrical.

comfort *vb* alleviate, animate, cheer, console, encourage, enliven, gladden, inspirit, invigorate, refresh, revive, solace, soothe, strengthen. * *n* aid, assistance, countenance, help, support, succour; consolation, solace, encouragement, relief; ease, enjoyment, peace, satisfaction.

comfortable *adj* acceptable, agreeable, delightful, enjoyable, grateful, gratifying, happy, pleasant, pleasurable, welcome; commodious, convenient, easeful, snug; painless.

comfortless *adj* bleak, cheerless, desolate, drear, dreary, forlorn, miserable, wretched; brokenhearted, desolate, disconsolate, forlorn, heartbroken, inconsolable, miserable, woe-begone, wretched.

comical *adj* amusing, burlesque, comic, diverting, droll, farcical, funny, humorous, laughable, ludicrous, sportive, whimsical.

coming *adj* approaching, arising, arriving, ensuing, eventual, expected, forthcoming, future, imminent, issuing, looming, nearing, prospective, ultimate; emergent, emerging, successful; due, owed, owing. * *n* advent, approach, arrival; imminence, imminency, nearness; apparition, appearance, disclosure, emergence, manifestation, materialization, occurrence, presentation, revelation, rising.

comity *n* affability, amenity, civility, courtesy, politeness, suavity, urbanity.

command *vb* bid, charge, direct, enjoin, order, require; control, dominate, govern, lead, rule, sway; claim, challenge, compel, demand, exact. * *n* behest, bidding, charge, commandment, direction, hest, injunction, mandate, order, requirement, requisition; ascendency, authority, dominion, control, government, power, rule, sway, supremacy.

commander *n* captain, chief, chieftain, commandment, head, leader.

commemorate *vb* celebrate, keep, observe, solemnize.

commence *vb* begin, inaugurate, initiate, institute, open, originate, start.

commend *vb* assign, bespeak, confide, recommend, remit; commit, entrust, yield; applaud, approve, eulogize, extol, laud, praise.

commendation *n* approbation, approval, good opinion, recommendation; praise, encomium, eulogy, panegyric.

commensurate *adj* commeasurable, commensurable; co-extensive, conterminous, equal; adequate, appropriate, corresponding, due, proportionate, proportioned, sufficient.

comment *vb* animadvert, annotate, criticize, explain, interpret, note, remark. * *n* annotation, elucidation, explanation, exposition, illustration, commentary, note, gloss; animadversion, observation, remark.

commentator *n* annotator, commentator, critic, expositor, expounder, interpreter.

commerce *n* business, exchange, dealing, trade, traffic; communication, communion, intercourse.

commercial *adj* mercantile, trading.

commination *n* denunciation, menace, threat, threatening.

commingle *vb* amalgamate, blend, combine,

commix, intermingle, intermix, join, mingle, mix, unite.

comminute *vb* bray, bruise, grind, levigate, powder, pulverize, triturate.

commiserate *vb* compassionate, condole, pity, sympathize.

commiseration *n* compassion, pitying; condolence, pity, sympathy.

commission *vb* authorize, empower; delegate, depute. * *n* doing, perpetration; care, charge, duty, employment, errand, office, task, trust; allowance, compensation, fee, rake-off.

commissioner *n* agent, delegate, deputy.

commit *vb* confide, consign, delegate, entrust, remand; consign, deposit, lay, place, put, relegate, resign; do, enact, perform, perpetrate; imprison; engage, implicate, pledge.

commix *vb* amalgamate, blend, combine, commingle, compound, intermingle, mingle, mix, unite.

commodious *adj* advantageous, ample, comfortable, convenient, fit, proper, roomy, spacious, suitable, useful.

commodity *n* goods, merchandise, produce, wares.

common *adj* collective, public; general, useful; common-place, customary, everyday, familiar, frequent, habitual, usual; banal, hackneyed, stale, threadbare, trite; indifferent, inferior, low, ordinary, plebeian, popular, undistinguished, vulgar.

commonplace *adj* common, hackneyed, ordinary, stale, threadbare, trite. * *n* banality, cliché, platitude; jotting, memoir, memorandum, note, reminder.

common-sense, common-sensical *adj* practical, sagacious, sensible, sober.

commotion *n* agitation, disturbance, ferment, perturbation, welter; ado, bustle, disorder, disturbance, hurly-burly, pother, tumult, turbulence, turmoil.

communicate *vb* bestow, confer, convey, give, impart, transmit; acquaint, announce, declare, disclose, divulge, publish, reveal, unfold; commune, converse, correspond.

communication *n* conveyance, disclosure, giving, imparting, transmittal; commence, conference, conversation, converse, correspondence, intercourse; announcement, dispatch, information, message, news.

communicative *adj* affable, chatty, conversable, free, open, sociable, unreserved.

communion *n* converse, fellowship, intercourse, participation; Eucharist, holy communion, Lord's Supper, sacrament.

community *n* commonwealth, people, public, society; association, brotherhood, college, society; likeness, participancy, sameness, similarity.

compact[1] *n* agreement, arrangement, bargain, concordant, contract, covenant, convention, pact, stipulation, treaty.

compact[2] *vb* compress, condense, pack, press; bind, consolidate, unite. * *adj* close, compressed, condensed, dense, firm, solid; brief, compendious, concise, laconic, pithy, pointed, sententious, short, succinct, terse.

companion *n* accomplice, ally, associate, comrade, compeer, confederate, consort, crony, friend, fellow, mate; partaker, participant, participator, partner, sharer.

companionable *adj* affable, conversable, familiar, friendly, genial, neighbourly, sociable.

companionship *n* association, fellowship, friendship, intercourse, society.

company *n* assemblage, assembly, band, bevy, body, circle, collection, communication, concourse, congregation, coterie, crew, crowd, flock, gang, gathering, group, herd, rout, set, syndicate, troop; party; companionship, fellowship, guests, society, visitor, visitors; association, copartnership, corporation, firm, house, partnership.

compare *vb* assimilate, balance, collate, parallel; liken, resemble.

comparison *n* collation, compare, estimate; simile, similitude.

compartment *n* bay, cell, division, pigeonhole, section.

compass *vb* embrace, encompass, enclose, encircle, environ, surround; beleaguer, beset, besiege, block, blockade, invest; accomplish, achieve, attain, carry, consummate, effect, obtain, perform, procure, realize; contrive, devise, intend, meditate, plot, purpose. * *n* bound, boundary, extent, gamut, limit, range, reach, register, scope, stretch; circuit, round.

compassion *n* clemency, commiseration, condolence, fellow-feeling, heart, humanity, kindheartedness, kindness, kindliness, mercy, pity, rue, ruth, sorrow, sympathy, tenderheartedness, tenderness.

compassionate *adj* benignant, clement, commiserative, gracious, kind, merciful, pitying, ruthful, sympathetic, tender.

compatible *adj* accordant, agreeable to, congruous, consistent, consonant, reconcilable, suitable.

compeer *n* associate, comrade, companion, equal, fellow, mate, peer.

compel *vb* constrain, force, coerce, drive, necessitate, oblige; bend, bow, subdue, subject.

compend *n* abbreviation, abridgement, abstract, breviary, brief, compendium, conspectus, digest, epitome, précis, summary, syllabus, synopsis.

compendious *adj* abbreviated, abridged, brief, comprehensive, concise, short, succinct, summary.

compensate *vb* counterbalance, counterpoise, countervail; guerdon, recompense, reimburse, remunerate, reward; indemnify, reimburse, repay, requite; atone.

compensation *n* pay, payment, recompense, remuneration, reward, salary; amends, atonement, indemnification, indemnity, reparation, requital, satisfaction; balance, counterpoise, equalization, offset.

compete *vb* contend, contest, cope, emulate, rival, strive, struggle, vie.

competence *n* ability, capability, capacity, fitness, qualification, suitableness; adequacy, adequateness, enough, sufficiency.

competent *adj* able, capable, clever, equal, endowed, qualified; adapted, adequate, convenient, fit, sufficient, suitable.

competition *n* contest, emulation, rivalry, rivals.

competitor *n* adversary, antagonist, contestant, emulator, opponent.

compile *vb* compose, prepare, write; arrange, collect, select.

complacency *n* content, contentment, gratification, pleasure, satisfaction; affability, civility, complaisance, courtesy, politeness.

complacent *adj* contented, gratified, pleased, satisfied; affable, civil, complaisant, courteous, easy, gracious, grateful, obliging, polite, urbane.

complain *vb* bemoan, bewail, deplore, grieve, groan, grouch, grumble, lament, moan, murmur, repine, whine.

complainant *n* accuser, plaintiff.

complaining *adj* fault-finding, murmuring, querulous.

complaint *n* grievance, gripe, grumble, lament, lamentation, plaint, murmur, wail; ail, ailment, annoyance, disease, disorder, illness, indisposition, malady, sickness; accusation, charge, information.

complete *vb* accomplish, achieve, conclude, consummate, do, effect, effectuate, end, execute, finish, fulfil, perfect, perform, realize, terminate. * *adj* clean, consummate, faultless, full, perfect, perform, thorough; all, entire, integral, total, unbroken, undiminished, undivided, unimpaired, whole; accomplished, achieved, completed, concluded, consummated, ended, finished.

completion *n* accomplishing, accomplishment, achieving, conclusion, consummation, effecting, effectuation, ending, execution, finishing, perfecting, performance, termination.

complex *adj* composite, compound, compounded, manifold, mingled, mixed; complicate, complicated, entangled, intricate, involved, knotty, mazy, tangled. * *n* complexus, complication, involute, skein, tangle; entirety, integration, network, totality, whole; compulsion, fixation, obsession, preoccupation, prepossession; prejudice.

complexion *n* colour, hue, tint.

complexity *n* complication, entanglement, intricacy, involution.

compliance *n* concession, obedience, submission; acquiescence, agreement, assent, concurrence, consent; compliancy, yieldingness.

complicate *vb* confuse, entangle, interweave, involve.

complication *n* complexity, confusion, entanglement, intricacy; combination, complexus, mixture.

compliment *vb* commend, congratulate, eulogize, extol, flatter, laud, praise. * *n* admiration, commendation, courtesy, encomium, eulogy, favour, flattery, honour, laudation, praise, tribute.

complimentary *adj* commendatory, congratulatory, encomiastic, eulogistic, flattering, laudatory, panegyrical.

comply *vb* adhere to, complete, discharge, fulfil, meet, observe, perform, satisfy; accede, accord, acquiesce, agree to, assent, consent to, yield.

component *adj* composing, constituent, constituting. * *n* constituent, element, ingredient, part.

comport *vb* accord, agree, coincide, correspond, fit, harmonize, square, suit, tally.

compose *vb* build, compact, compound, constitute, form, make, synthesize; contrive, create, frame, imagine, indite, invent, write; adjust, arrange, regulate, settle; appease, assuage, calm, pacify, quell, quiet, soothe, still, tranquillize.

composed *adj* calm, collected, cool, imperturbable, placid, quiet, sedate, self-possessed, tranquil, undisturbed, unmoved, unruffled.

composite *adj* amalgamated, combined, complex, compounded, mixed; integrated, unitary. * *n* admixture, amalgam, blend, combination, composition, compound, mixture, unification.

composition *n* constitution, construction, formation, framing, making; compound, mixture; arrangement, combination, conjunction, make-up, synthesize, union; invention, opus, piece, production, writing; agreement, arrangement, compromise.

compost *n* fertilizer, fertilizing, manure, mixture.

composure *n* calmness, coolness, equanimity, placidity, sedateness, quiet, self-possession, serenity, tranquillity.

compotation *n* conviviality, frolicking, jollification, revelling, revelry, rousing, wassailling; bacchanal, carousal, carouse, debauch, orgy, revel, saturnalia, wassail.

compound[1] *vb* amalgamate, blend, combine, intermingle, intermix, mingle, mix, unite; adjust, arrange, compose, compromise, settle. * *adj* complex, composite. * *n* combination, composition, mixture; farrago, hodgepodge, jumble, medley, mess, olio.

compound[2] *n* enclosure, garden, yard.

comprehend *vb* comprise, contain, embrace, embody, enclose, include, involve; apprehend, conceive, discern, grasp, know, imagine, master, perceive, see, understand.

comprehension *n* comprising, embracing, inclusion; compass, domain, embrace, field, limits, province, range, reach, scope, sphere, sweep; connotation, depth, force, intention; conception, grasp, intelligence, understanding; intellect, intelligence, mind, reason, understanding.

comprehensive *adj* all-embracing, ample, broad, capacious, compendious, extensive, full, inclusive, large, sweeping, wide.

compress *vb* abbreviate, condense, constrict, contract, crowd, press, shorten, squeeze, summarize.

compression *n* condensation, confining, pinching, pressing, squeezing; brevity, pithiness, succinctness, terseness.

comprise *vb* comprehend, contain, embody, embrace, enclose, include, involve.

compromise *vb* adjust, arbitrate, arrange, compose, compound, settle; imperil, jeopardize, prejudice; commit, engage, implicate, pledge; agree, compound. * *n* adjustment, agreement, composition, settlement.

compulsion *n* coercion, constraint, force, forcing, pressure, urgency.

compulsory *adj* coercive, compelling, constraining; binding, enforced, imperative, necessary, obligatory, unavoidable.

compunction *n* contrition, misgiving, penitence, qualm, regret, reluctance, remorse, repentance, sorrow.

computable *adj* calculable, numerable, reckonable.

computation *n* account, calculation, estimate, reckoning, score, tally.

compute *vb* calculate, count, enumerate, estimate, figure, measure, number, rate, reckon, sum.

comrade *n* accomplice, ally, associate, chum, companion, compatriot, compeer, crony, fellow, mate, pal.

concatenate *vb* connect, join, link, unite.

concatenation *n* connection; chain, congeries, linking, series, sequence, succession.

concave *adj* depressed, excavated, hollow, hollowed, scooped.

conceal *vb* bury, cover, screen, secrete; disguise, dissemble, mask.

concede *vb* grant, surrender, yield; acknowledge, admit, allow, confess, grant.

conceit *n* belief, conception, fancy, idea, image, imagination, notion, thought; caprice, illusion, vagary, whim; estimate, estimation, impression, judgement, opinion; conceitedness, egoism, self-complacency, priggishness, priggery, self-conceit, self-esteem, self-sufficiency, vanity; crotchet, point, quip, quirk.

conceited *adj* egotistical, opinionated, opinionative, overweening, self-conceited, vain.

conceivable *adj* imaginable, picturable; cogitable, comprehensible, intelligible, rational, thinkable.

conceive *vb* create, contrive, devise, form, plan, purpose; fancy, imagine; comprehend, fathom, think, understand; assume, imagine, suppose; bear, become pregnant.

concern *vb* affect, belong to, interest, pertain to, regard, relate to, touch; disquiet, disturb, trouble. * *n* affair, business, matter, transaction; concernment, consequence, importance, interest, moment, weight; anxiety, care, carefulness, solicitude, worry; business, company, establishment, firm, house.

concert *vb* combine, concoct, contrive, design, devise, invent, plan, plot, project. * *n* agreement,

concord, concordance, cooperation, harmony, union, unison.

concession *n* acquiescence, assent, cessation, compliance, surrender, yielding; acknowledgement, allowance, boon, confession, grant, privilege.

conciliate *vb* appease, pacify, placate, propitiate, reconcile; engage, gain, secure, win, win over.

concise *adj* brief, compact, compendious, comprehensive, compressed, condensed, crisp, laconic, pithy, pointed, pregnant, sententious, short, succinct, summary, terse.

conclave *n* assembly, cabinet, council.

conclude *vb* close, end, finish, terminate; deduce, gather, infer, judge; decide, determine, judge; arrange, complete, settle; bar, hinder, restrain, stop; decide, determine, resolve.

conclusion *n* deduction, inference; decision, determination, judgement; close, completion, end, event, finale, issue, termination, upshot; arrangement, closing, effecting, establishing, settlement.

conclusive *adj* clinching, convincing, decisive, irrefutable, unanswerable; final, ultimate.

concoct *vb* brew, contrive, design, devise, frame, hatch, invent, mature, plan, plot, prepare, project.

concomitant *adj* accessory, accompanying, attendant, attending, coincident, concurrent, conjoined. * *n* accessory, accompaniment, attendant.

concord *n* agreement, amity, friendship, harmony, peace, unanimity, union, unison, unity; accord, adaptation, concordance, consonance, harmony.

concordant *adj* accordant, agreeable, agreeing, harmonious.

concordat *n* agreement, bargain, compact, convention, covenant, stipulation, treaty.

concourse *n* confluence, conflux, congress; assemblage, assembly, collection, crowd, gathering, meeting, multitude, throng.

concrete *vb* cake, congeal, coagulate, harden, solidify, thicken. * *adj* compact, consolidated, firm, solid, solidified; agglomerated, complex, conglomerated, compound, concreted; completely, entire, individualized, total. * *n* compound, concretion, mixture; cement.

concubine *n* hetaera, hetaira, mistress, paramour.

concupiscence *n* lasciviousness, lechery, lewdness, lust, pruriency.

concupiscent *adj* carnal, lascivious, lecherous, lewd, libidinous, lustful, prurient, rampant, salacious, sensual.

concur *vb* accede, acquiesce, agree, approve, assent, coincide, consent, harmonize; combine, conspire, cooperate, help.

concurrent *adj* agreeing, coincident, harmonizing, meeting, uniting; associate, associated, attendant, concomitant, conjoined, united.

concussion *n* agitation, shaking; clash, crash, shock.

condemn *vb* adjudge, convict, doom, sentence; disapprove, proscribe, reprobate; blame, censure, damn, deprecate, disapprove, reprehend, reprove, upbraid.

condemnation *n* conviction, doom, judgement, penalty, sentence; banning, disapproval, proscription; guilt, sin, wrong; blame, censure, disapprobation, disapproval, reprobation, reproof.

condemnatory *adj* blaming, censuring, damnatory, deprecatory, disapproving, reproachful.

condense *vb* compress, concentrate, consolidate, densify, thicken; abbreviate, abridge, contract, curtail, diminish, epitomize, reduce, shorten, summarize; liquefy.

condescend *vb* deign, vouchsafe; descend, stoop, submit.

condescension *n* affability, civility, courtesy, deference, favour, graciousness, obeisance.

condign *adj* adequate, deserved, just, merited, suitable.

condiment *n* appetizer, relish, sauce, seasoning.

condition *vb* postulate, specify, stipulate; groom, prepare, qualify, ready, train; acclimatize, accustom, adapt, adjust, familiarize, habituate, naturalize; attune, commission, fix, overhaul, prepare, recondition, repair, service, tune. * *n* case, circumstances, plight, predicament, situation, state; class, estate, grade, rank, station; arrangement, consideration, provision, proviso, stipulation; attendant, necessity, postulate, precondition, prerequisite.

condole *vb* commiserate, compassionate, console, sympathize.

condonation *n* forgiveness, overlooking, pardon.

condone *vb* excuse, forgive, pardon.

conduce *vb* contribute, lead, tend; advance, aid.

conducive *adj* conducting, contributing, instrumental, promotive, subservient, subsidiary.

conduct *vb* convoy, direct, escort, lead; administer, command, govern, lead, preside, superintend; manage, operate, regulate; direct, lead. * *n* administration, direction, guidance, leadership, management; convoy, escort, guard; actions, bearing, behaviour, career, carriage, demeanour, deportment, manners.

conductor *n* guide, lead; director, leader, manager; propagator, transmitter.

conduit *n* canal, channel, duct, passage, pipe, tube.

confederacy *n* alliance, coalition, compact, confederation, covenant, federation, league, union.

confer *vb* advise, consult, converse, deliberate, discourse, parley, talk; bestow, give, grant, vouchsafe.

confess *vb* acknowledge, admit, avow, own; admit, concede, grant, recognize; attest, exhibit, manifest, prove, show; shrive.

confession *n* acknowledgement, admission, avowal.

confide *vb* commit, consign, entrust, trust.

confidence *n* belief, certitude, dependence, faith, reliance, trust; aplomb, assurance, boldness, cocksureness, courage, firmness, intrepidity, self-reliance; secrecy.

confident *adj* assured, certain, cocksure, positive, sure: bold, presumptuous. sanguine, undaunted.

confidential *adj* intimate, private, secret; faithful, trustworthy.

configuration *n* conformation, contour, figure, form, gestalt, outline, shape.

confine *vb* restrain, shut in, shut up; immure, imprison, incarcerate, impound, jail, mew; bound, circumscribe, limit, restrict. * *n* border, boundary, frontier, limit.

confinement *n* restraint; captivity, duress, durance, immurement, imprisonment, incarceration; childbed, childbirth, delivery, lying-in, parturition.

confines *npl* borders, boundaries, edges, frontiers, limits, marches, precincts.

confirm *vb* assure, establish, fix, settle; strengthen; authenticate, avouch, corroborate, countersign, endorse, substantiate, verify; bind, ratify, sanction.

confirmation *n* establishment, settlement; corroboration, proof, substantiation, verification.

confiscate *vb* appropriate, forfeit, seize.

conflict *vb* clash, combat, contend, contest, disagree, fight, interfere, strive, struggle. * *n* battle, collision, combat, contention, contest, encounter, fight, struggle; antagonism, clashing, disagreement, discord, disharmony, inconsistency, interference, opposition.

confluence *n* conflux, junction, meeting, union; army, assemblage, assembly, concourse, crowd, collection, horde, host, multitude, swarm.

confluent *adj* blending, concurring, flowing, joining, meeting, merging, uniting.

conform *vb* accommodate, adapt, adjust; agree, comport, correspond, harmonize, square, tally.

conformation *n* accordance, agreement, compliance, conformity; configuration, figure, form, manner, shape, structure.

confound *vb* confuse; baffle, bewilder, embarrass, flurry, mystify, nonplus, perplex, pose; amaze, astonish, astound, bewilder, dumfound, paralyse, petrify, startle, stun, stupefy, surprise; annihilate, demolish, destroy, overthrow, overwhelm, ruin; abash, confuse, discompose, disconcert, mortify, shame.

confront *vb* face; challenge, contrapose, encounter, oppose, threaten.

confuse *vb* blend, confound, intermingle, mingle, mix; derange, disarrange, disorder, jumble, mess, muddle; darken, obscure, perplex; befuddle, bewilder, embarrass, flabbergast, flurry, fluster, mystify, nonplus, pose; abash, confound, discompose, disconcert, mortify, shame.

confusion *n* anarchy, chaos, clutter, confusedness, derangement, disarrangement, disarray, disorder, jumble, muddle; agitation, commotion, ferment, stir, tumult, turmoil; astonishment, bewilderment, distraction, embarrassment, fluster, fuddle, perplexity; abashment, discomfiture, mortification, shame; annihilation, defeat, demolition, destruction, overthrow, ruin.

confute *vb* disprove, oppugn, overthrow, refute, silence.

congeal *vb* benumb, condense, curdle, freeze, stiffen, thicken.

congenial adj kindred, similar, sympathetic; adapted, agreeable, natural, suitable, suited; agreeable, favourable, genial.

congenital adj connate, connatural, inborn.

congeries n accumulation, agglomeration, aggregate, aggregation, collection, conglomeration, crowd, cluster, heap, mass.

congratulate vb compliment, felicitate, gratulate, greet, hail, salute.

congregate vb assemble, collect, convene, convoke, gather, muster; gather, meet, swarm, throng.

congregation n assemblage, assembly, collection, gathering, meeting.

congress n assembly, conclave, conference, convention, convocation, council, diet, meeting.

congruity n agreement, conformity, consistency, fitness, suitableness.

congruous adj accordant, agreeing, compatible, consistent, consonant, suitable; appropriate, befitting, fit, meet, proper, seemly.

conjecture vb assume, guess, hypothesize, imagine, suppose. surmise, suspect; dare say, fancy, presume. * n assumption, guess, hypothesis, supposition, surmise, theory.

conjoin vb associate, combine, connect, join, unite.

conjugal adj bridal, connubial, hymeneal, matrimonial, nuptial.

conjuncture n combination, concurrence, connection; crisis, emergency, exigency, juncture.

conjure vb adjure, beg, beseech, crave, entreat, implore, invoke, pray, supplicate; bewitch, charm, enchant, fascinate; juggle.

connect vb associate, conjoin, combine, couple, hyphenate, interlink, join, link, unite; cohere, interlock.

connected adj associated, coupled, joined, united; akin, allied, related; communicating.

connection n alliance, association, dependence, junction, union; commerce, communication, intercourse; affinity, relationship; kindred, kinsman, relation, relative.

connive vb collude, conspire, plot, scheme.

connoisseur n critic, expert, virtuoso.

connotation n comprehension, depth, force, intent, intention, meaning.

connubial adj bridal, conjugal, hymeneal, matrimonial, nuptial.

conquer vb beat, checkmate, crush, defeat, discomfit, humble, master, overcome, overpower, overthrow, prevail, quell, reduce, rout, subdue, subjugate, vanquish; overcome, surmount.

conqueror n humbler, subduer, subjugator, vanquisher; superior, victor, winner.

conquest n defeat, discomfiture, mastery, overthrow, reduction, subjection, subjugation; triumph, victor; winning.

consanguinity n affinity, kinship, blood-relationship, kin, kindred, relationship.

conscientious adj careful, exact, fair, faithful, high-principled, honest, honourable, incorruptible, just, scrupulous, straightforward, uncorrupt, upright.

conscious adj intelligent, knowing, percipient, sentient; intellectual, rational, reasoning, reflecting, self-conscious, thinking; apprised, awake, aware, cognizant, percipient, sensible; self-admitted, self-accusing.

consecrate vb dedicate, devote, ordain; hallow, sanctify, venerate.

consecutive adj following, succeeding.

consent vb agree, allow, assent, concur, permit, yield; accede, acquiesce, comply. * n approval, assent, concurrence, permission; accord, agreement, consensus, concord, cooperation, harmony, unison; acquiescence, compliance.

consequence n effect, end, event, issue, result; conclusion, deduction, inference; concatenation, connection, consecution; concern, distinction, importance, influence, interest, moment, standing, weight.

consequential adj consequent, following, resulting, sequential; arrogant, conceited, inflated, pompous, pretentious, self-important, self-sufficient, vainglorious.

conservation n guardianship, maintenance, preservation, protection.

conservative adj conservatory, moderate, moderationist; preservative; reactionary, unprogressive. * n die-hard, reactionary, redneck, rightist, right-winger; moderate; preservative.

conserve vb keep, maintain, preserve, protect, save, sustain, uphold. * n confit, confection, jam, preserve, sweetmeat.

consider vb attend, brood, contemplate, examine, heed, mark, mind, ponder, reflect, revolve, study, weigh; care for, consult, envisage, regard, respect; cogitate, deliberate, mediate, muse, ponder, reflect, ruminate, think; account, believe, deem, hold, judge, opine.

considerate adj circumspect, deliberate, discrete, judicious, provident, prudent, serious, sober, staid, thoughtful; charitable, forbearing, patient.

consideration n attention, cogitation, contemplation, deliberation, notice, heed, meditation, pondering, reflection, regard; consequence, importance, important, moment, significant, weight; account, cause, ground, motive, reason, sake, score.

consign vb deliver, hand over, remand, resign, transfer, transmit; commit, entrust; ship.

consignor n sender, shipper, transmitter.

consistency n compactness, consistence, density, thickness; agreement, compatibility, conformableness, congruity, consonance, correspondence, harmony.

consistent adj accordant, agreeing, comfortable, compatible, congruous, consonant, correspondent, harmonious, logical.

consolation n alleviation, comfort, condolence, encouragement, relief, solace.

console vb assuage, calm, cheer, comfort, encourage, solace, relieve, soothe.

consolidate *vb* cement, compact, compress, condense, conduce, harden, solidify, thicken; combine, conjoin, fuse, unite.

consolidation *n* solidification; combination, union.

consonance *n* accord, concord, conformity, harmony; accord, accordance, agreement, congruence, congruity, consistency, unison.

consonant *adj* accordant, according, harmonious; compatible, congruous, consistent. * *n* articulation, letter-sound.

consort *vb* associate, fraternize. * *n* associate, companion, fellow, husband, spouse, partner.

conspectus *n* abstract, brief, breviary, compend, compendium, digest, epitome, outline, precis, summary, syllabus, synopsis.

conspicuous *adj* apparent, clear, discernible, glaring, manifest, noticeable, perceptible, plain, striking, visible; celebrated, distinguished, eminent, famed, famous, illustrious, marked, noted, outstanding, pre-eminent, prominent, remarkable, signal.

conspiracy *n* cabal, collusion, confederation, intrigue, league, machination, plot, scheme.

conspire *vb* concur, conduce, cooperate; combine, compass, contrive, devise, project; confederate, contrive, hatch, plot, scheme.

constancy *n* immutability, permanence, stability, unchangeableness; regularity, unchangeableness; decision, determination, firmness, inflexibility, resolution, steadfastness, steadiness; devotion, faithfulness, fidelity, loyalty, trustiness, truth.

constant *adj* abiding, enduring, fixed, immutable, invariable, invariant, permanent, perpetual, stable, unalterable, unchanging, unvaried; certain, regular, stated, uniform; determined, firm, resolute, stanch, steadfast, steady, unanswering, undeviating, unmoved, unshaken, unwavering; assiduous, diligent, persevering, sedulous, tenacious, unremitting; continual, continuous, incessant, perpetual, sustained, unbroken, uninterrupted; devoted, faithful, loyal, true, trusty.

consternation *n* alarm, amazement, awe, bewilderment, dread, fear, fright, horror, panic, terror.

constituent *adj* component, composing, constituting, forming; appointing, electoral. * *n* component, element, ingredient, principal; elector, voter.

constitute *vb* compose, form, make; appoint, delegate, depute, empower; enact, establish, fix, set up.

constitution *n* establishment, formation, make-up, organization, structure; character, characteristic, disposition, form, habit, humour, peculiarity, physique, quality, spirit, temper, temperament.

constitutional *adj* congenital, connate, inborn, inbred, inherent, innate, natural, organic; lawful, legal, legitimate. * *n* airing, exercise, promenade, stretch, walk.

constrain *vb* coerce, compel, drive, force; chain, confine, curb, enthral, hold, restrain; draw, impel, urge.

constriction *n* compression, constraint, contraction.

construct *vb* build, fabricate, erect, raise, set up; arrange, establish, form, found, frame, institute, invent, make, organize, originate.

construction *n* building, erection, fabrication; configuration, conformation, figure, form, formation, made, shape, structure; explanation, interpretation, rendering, version.

construe *vb* analyse, explain, expound, interpret, parse, render, translate.

consult *vb* advise, ask, confer, counsel, deliberate, interrogate, question; consider, regard.

consume *vb* absorb, decay, destroy, devour, dissipate, exhaust, expend, lavish, lessen, spend, squander, vanish, waste.

consummate[1] *vb* accomplish, achieve, compass, complete, conclude, crown, effect, effectuate, end, execute, finish, perfect, perform.

consummate[2] *adj* complete, done, effected, finished, fulfilled, perfect, supreme.

consumption *n* decay, decline, decrease, destruction, diminution, expenditure, use, waste; atrophy, emaciation.

contact *vb* hit, impinge, touch; approach, be heard, communicate with, reach. * *n* approximation, contiguity, junction, juxtaposition, taction, tangency, touch.

contagion *n* infection; contamination, corruption, infection, taint.

contagious *adj* catching, epidemic, infectious; deadly, pestiferous, pestilential, poisonous.

contain *vb* accommodate, comprehend, comprise, embody, embrace, enclose, include; check, restrain.

contaminate *vb* corrupt, defile, deprave, infect, poison, pollute, soil, stain, sully, taint, tarnish, vitiate.

contamination *n* contaminating, defilement, defiling, polluting, pollution; abomination, defilement, impurity, foulness, infection, pollution, stain, taint, uncleanness.

contemn *vb* despise, disdain, disregard, neglect, scorn, scout, slight, spurn.

contemplate *vb* behold, gaze upon, observe, survey; consider, dwell on, meditate on, muse on, ponder, reflect upon, study, survey, think about; design, intend, mean, plan, purpose.

contemplation *n* cogitation, deliberation, meditation, pondering, reflection, speculation, study, thought; prospect, prospective, view; expectation.

contemporaneous *adj* coetaneous, coeval, coexistent, coexisting, coincident, concomitant, contemporary, simultaneous, synchronous.

contemporary *adj* coetaneous, coeval, coexistent, coexisting, coincident, concomitant, concurrent, contemporaneous, current, present, simultaneous, synchronous; advanced, modern, modernistic, progressive, up-to-date. * *n* coeval, coexistent, compeer, fellow.

contempt *n* contumely, derision, despite, disdain, disregard, misprision, mockery, scorn, slight.

contemptible *adj* abject, base, despicable, haughty, insolent, insulting, low, mean, paltry, pitiful, scurvy, sorry, supercilious, vile, worthless.

contemptuous *adj* arrogant, contumelious, disdainful, haughty, insolent, insulting, scornful, sneering, supercilious.

contend *vb* battle, combat, compete, contest, fight, strive, struggle, vie; argue, debate, dispute, litigate; affirm, assert, contest, maintain.

content[1] *n* essence, gist, meaning, meat, stuff, substance; capacity, measure, space, volume.

content[2] *vb* appease, delight, gladden, gratify, humour, indulge, please, satisfy, suffice. * *adj* agreeable, contented, happy, pleased, satisfied. * *n* contentment, ease, peace, satisfaction.

contention *n* discord, dissension, feud, squabble, strife, quarrel, rapture, wrangle, wrangling; altercation, bickering, contest, controversy, debate, dispute, litigation, logomachy.

contentious *adj* belligerent, cross, litigious, peevish, perverse, petulant, pugnacious, quarrelsome, wrangling; captious, caviling, disputatious.

conterminous *adj* adjacent, adjoining, contiguous; co-extensive, coincident, commensurate.

contest *vb* argue, contend, controvert, debate, dispute, litigate, question; strive, struggle; compete, cope, fight, vie. * *n* altercation, contention, controversy, difference, dispute, debate, quarrel; affray, battle, bout, combat, conflict, encounter, fight, match, scrimmage, struggle, tussle; competition, contention, rivalry.

contexture *n* composition, constitution, framework, structure, texture.

contiguous *adj* abutting, adjacent, adjoining, beside, bordering, conterminous, meeting, near, neighbouring, touching.

continent[1] *n* mainland, mass, tract.

continent[2] *adj* abstemious, abstinent, chaste, restrained, self-commanding, self-controlled, moderate, sober, temperate.

contingency *n* accidentalness, chance, fortuity, uncertainty; accident, casualty, event, incident, occurrence.

contingent *adj* accidental, adventitious, casual, fortuitous, incidental; conditional, dependent, uncertain. * *n* proportion, quota, share.

continual *adj* constant, constant, perpetual, unceasing, uninterrupted, unremitting; endless, eternal, everlasting, interminable, perennial, permanent, perpetual, unending; constant, oft-repeated.

continuance *n* abiding, continuation, duration, endurance, lasting, persistence, stay; continuation, extension, perpetuation, prolongation, protraction; concatenation, connection, sequence, succession; constancy, endurance, perseverance, persistence.

continue *vb* endure, last, remain; abide, linger, remain, stay, tarry; endure, persevere, persist, stick; extend, prolong, perpetuate, protract.

continuous *adj* connected, continued, extended, prolonged, unbroken, unintermitted, uninterrupted.

contour *n* outline, profile.

contraband *adj* banned, forbidden, illegal, illicit, interdicted, prohibited, smuggled, unlawful.

contract *vb* abbreviate, abridge, condense, confine, curtail, diminish, epitomize, lessen, narrow, reduce, shorten; absorb, catch, incur, get, make, take; constrict, shrink, shrivel, wrinkle; agree, bargain, covenant, engage, pledge, stipulate. * *n* agreement, arrangement, bargain, bond, compact, concordat, covenant, convention, engagement, pact, stipulation, treaty.

contradict *vb* assail, challenge, controvert, deny, dispute, gainsay, impugn, traverse; abrogate, annul, belie, counter, disallow, negative, contravene, counteract, oppose, thwart.

contradiction *n* controversion, denial, gainsaying; antinomy, clashing, contrariety, incongruity, opposition.

contradictory *adj* antagonistic, contrary, incompatible, inconsistent, negating, opposed, opposite, repugnant.

contrariety *n* antagonism, clashing, contradiction, contrast, opposition, repugnance.

contrary *adj* adverse, counter, discordant, opposed, opposing, opposite; antagonistic, conflicting, contradictory, repugnant, retroactive; forward, headstrong, obstinate, refractory, stubborn, unruly, wayward, perverse. * *n* antithesis, converse, obverse, opposite, reverse.

contrast *vb* compare, differentiate, distinguish, oppose. * *n* contrariety, difference, opposition; comparison, distinction.

contravene *vb* abrogate, annul, contradict, counteract, countervail, cross, go against, hinder, interfere, nullify, oppose, set aside, thwart.

contravention *n* abrogation, contradiction, interference, opposition, transgression, traversal, violation.

contretemps *n* accident, mischance, mishap.

contribute *vb* bestow, donate, give, grant, subscribe; afford, aid, furnish, supply; concur, conduce, conspire, cooperate, minister, serve, tend.

contribution *n* bestowal, bestowment, grant; donation, gift, offering, subscription.

contrite *adj* humble, penitent, repentant, sorrowful.

contrition *n* compunction, humiliation, penitence, regret, remorse, repentance, self-condemnation, self-reproach, sorrow.

contrivance *n* design, inventive, inventiveness; contraption, device, gadget, invention, machine; artifice, device, fabrication, machination, plan, plot, scheme, shift, stratagem.

contrive *vb* arrange, brew, concoct, design, devise, effect, form, frame, hatch, invent, plan, project; consider, plan, plot, scheme; manage, make out.

control *vb* command, direct, dominate, govern, manage, oversee, sway, regulate, rule, superintend; bridle, check, counteract, curb, check, hinder, repress, restrain. * *n* ascendency, command, direction, disposition, dominion, government, guidance, mastery, oversight, regiment, regulation, rule, superintendence, supremacy, sway.

controversy *n* altercation, argument, contention, debate, discussion, disputation, dispute, logomachy, polemics, quarrel, strife; lawsuit.

contumacious *adj* disobedient, cross-grained, disrespectful, haughty, headstrong, intractable, obdurate, obstinate, pertinacious, perverse, rebellious, refractory, stiff-necked, stubborn.

contumacy *n* doggedness, haughtiness, headiness, obduracy, obstinacy, pertinacity, perverseness, stubbornness; contempt, disobedience, disrespect, insolence, insubordination, rebelliousness.

contumelious *adj* abusive, arrogant, calumnious, contemptuous, disdainful, insolent, insulting, opprobrious, overbearing, rude, scornful, supercilious.

contumely *n* abuse, affront, arrogance, contempt, contemptuousness, disdain, indignity, insolence, insult, obloquy, opprobrium, reproach, rudeness, scorn, superciliousness.

contuse *vb* bruise, crush, injure, knock, squeeze, wound.

contusion *n* bruise, crush, injury, knock, squeeze, wound.

convalescence *n* recovery, recuperation.

convene *vb* assemble, congregate, gather, meet, muster; assemble, call, collect, convoke, muster, summon.

convenience *n* fitness, propriety, suitableness; accessibility, accommodation, comfort, commodiousness, ease, handiness, satisfaction, serviceability, serviceableness.

convenient *adj* adapted, appropriate, fit, fitted, proper, suitable, suited; advantageous, beneficial, comfortable, commodious, favourable, handy, helpful, serviceable, timely, useful.

convent *n* abbey, cloister, monastery, priory.

convention *n* assembly, congress, convocation, meeting; agreement, bargain, compact, contract, pact, stipulation, treaty; custom, formality, usage.

conventional *adj* agreed on, bargained for, stipulated; accustomed, approved, common, customary, everyday, habitual, ordinary, orthodox, regular, standard, traditional, usual, wonted.

conversable *adj* affable, communicative, free, open, sociable, social, unreversed.

conversation *n* chat, colloquy, communion, confabulation, conference, converse, dialogue, discourse, intercourse, interlocution, parley, talk.

converse[1] *vb* commune; chat, confabulate, discourse, gossip, parley, talk. * *n* commerce, communication, intercourse; colloquy, conversation, talk.

converse[2] *adj* adverse, contradictory, contrary, counter, opposed, opposing, opposite; *n* antithesis, contrary, opposite, reverse.

conversion *n* change, reduction, resolution, transformation, transmutation; interchange, reversal, transposition.

convert *vb* alter, change, transform, transmute; interchange, reverse, transpose; apply, appropriate, convince. * *n* catechumen, disciple, neophyte, proselyte.

convey *vb* bear, bring, carry, fetch, transmit, transport, waft; abalienate, alienate, cede, consign, deliver, demise, devise, devolve, grant, sell, transfer.

conveyance *n* alienation, cession, transfer, transference, transmission; carriage, carrying, conveying, transfer, transmission.

convict *vb* condemn, confute, convince, imprison, sentence. * *n* criminal, culprit, felon, malefactor, prisoner.

convivial *adj* festal, festive, gay, jolly, jovial, merry, mirthful, social.

convocation *n* assembling, convening, convoking, gathering, summoning; assembly, congress, convention, council, diet, meeting, synod.

convoke *vb* assemble, convene, muster, summon.

convoy *vb* accompany, attend, escort, guard, protect. * *n* attendance, attendant, escort, guard, protection.

convulse *vb* agitate, derange, disorder, disturb, shake, shatter.

convulsion *n* cramp, fit, spasm; agitation, commotion, disturbance, shaking, tumult.

cook *vb* bake, boil, broil, fry, grill, microwave, roast, spit-roast, steam, stir-fry; falsify, garble.

cool *vb* chill, ice, refrigerate; abate, allay, calm, damp, moderate, quiet, temper. * *adj* calm, collected, composed, dispassionate, placid, sedate, self-possessed, quiet, staid, unexcited, unimpassioned, undisturbed, unruffled; cold-blooded, indifferent, lukewarm, unconcerned; apathetic, chilling, freezing, frigid, repellent; bold, impertinent, impudent, self-possessed, shameless. * *n* chill, chilliness, coolness; calmness, composure, coolheadedness, countenance, equanimity, poise, self-possession, self-restraint.

coop *vb* cage, confine, encage, immure, imprison. * *n* barrel, box, cage, pen.

cooperate *vb* abet, aid, assist, co-act, collaborate, combine, concur, conduce, conspire, contribute, help, unite.

cooperation *n* aid, assistance, co-action, concert, concurrence, collaboration, synergy.

coordinate *vb* accord, agree, arrange, equalize, harmonize, integrate, methodize, organize, regulate, synchronize, systematize. * *adj* coequal, equal, equivalent, tantamount; coincident, synchronous. * *n* complement, counterpart, like, pendant; companion, fellow, match, mate.

copartnership *n* association, fraternity, partnership; company, concern, establishment, firm, house.

cope *vb* combat, compete, contend, encounter, engage, strive, struggle, vie.

copious *adj* abundant, ample, exuberant, full, overflowing, plenteous, plentiful, profuse, rich.

copiousness *n* abundance, exuberance, fullness, plenty, profusion, richness.

copse *n* coppice, grove, thicket.

copulation *n* coition, congress, coupling.

copy *vb* duplicate, reproduce, trace, transcribe; follow, imitate, pattern. * *n* counterscript, duplicate, facsimile, off-print, replica, reproduction, transcript; archetype, model, original, pattern; manuscript, typescript.

cord *n* braid, gimp, line, string.

cordate *adj* cordiform, heart-shaped.

cordial *adj* affectionate, ardent, earnest, heartfelt, hearty, sincere, warm, warm-hearted; grateful, invigorating, restorative, pleasant, refreshing. * *n* balm, balsam, elixir, tisane, tonic; liqueur.

core *n* centre, essence, heart, kernel.

corner *vb* confound, confuse, nonplus, perplex, pose, puzzle. * *n* angle, bend, crutch, cusp, elbow, joint, knee; niche, nook, recess, retreat.

corollary *n* conclusion, consequence, deduction, induction, inference.

coronal *n* bays, chaplet, crown, garland, laurel, wreath.

corporal *adj* bodily; corporeal, material, physical.

corporeal *adj* bodily, fleshly, substantial; corporal, material, nonspiritual, physical.

corps *n* band, body, company, contingent, division, platoon, regiment, squad, squadron, troop.

corpse *n* body, carcass, corse, remains; ashes, dust.

corpulent *adj* big, burly, fat, fleshy, large, lusty, obese, plump, portly, pursy, rotund, stout.

corpuscle *n* atom, bit, grain, iota, jot, mite, molecule, monad, particle, scintilla, scrap, whit.

correct *vb* adjust, amend, cure, improve, mend, reclaim, rectify, redress, reform, regulate, remedy; chasten, discipline, punish. * *adj* accurate, equitable, exact, faultless, just, precise, proper, regular, right, true, upright.

correction *n* amendment, improvement, redress; chastening, discipline, punishment.

corrective *adj* alternative, correctory, counteractive, emendatory, improving, modifying, rectifying, reformative, reformatory.

correctness *n* accuracy, exactness, faultlessness, nicety, precision, propriety, rectitude, regularity, rightness, truth.

correlate *n* complement, correlative, counterpart.

correspond *vb* accord, agree, answer, comport, conform, fit, harmonize, match, square, suit, tally; answer, belong, correlate; communicate.

correspondence *n* accord, agreement, coincidence, concurrence, conformity, congruity, fitness, harmony, match; correlation, counterposition; communication, letters, writing.

corroborate *vb* confirm, establish, ratify, substantiate, support, sustain, strengthen.

corrode *vb* canker, erode, gnaw; consume, deteriorate, rust, waste; blight, embitter, envenom, poison.

corrosive *adj* acrid, biting, consuming, cathartic, caustic, corroding, eroding, erosive, violent; consuming, corroding, gnawing, mordant, wasting, wearing; blighting, cankerous, carking, embittering, envenoming, poisoning.

corrugate *vb* cockle, crease, furrow, groove, pucker, rumple, wrinkle.

corrupt *vb* putrefy, putrid, render; contaminate, defile, infect, pollute, spoil, taint, vitiate; degrade, demoralize, deprave, pervert; adulterate, debase, falsify, sophisticate; bribe, entice. * *adj* contaminated, corrupted, impure, infected, putrid, rotten, spoiled, tainted, unsound; abandoned, debauched, depraved, dissolute, profligate, reprobate, vicious, wicked; bribable, buyable.

corruption *n* putrefaction, putrescence, rottenness; adulteration, contamination, debasement, defilement, infection, perversion, pollution, vitiation; demoralization, depravation, depravity, immorality, laxity, sinfulness, wickedness; bribery, dishonesty.

corsair *n* buccaneer, picaroon, pirate, rover, sea-robber, sea-rover.

corset *n* bodice, girdle, stays.

cosmonaut *n* astronaut, spaceman.

cosmos *n* creation, macrocosm, universe, world; harmony, order, structure.

cost *vb* absorb, consume, require. * *n* amount, charge, expenditure, expense, outlay, price; costliness, preciousness, richness, splendour, sumptuousness; damage, detriment, loss, pain, sacrifice, suffering.

costly *adj* dear, expensive, high-priced; gorgeous, luxurious, precious, rich, splendid, sumptuous, valuable.

costume *n* apparel, attire, dress, robes, uniform.

cosy, cozy *adj* comfortable, easy, snug; chatty, conversable, social, talkative.

coterie *n* association, brotherhood, circle, club, set, society, sodality.

cottage *n* cabin, chalet, cot, hut, lodge, shack, shanty.

couch *vb* lie, recline; crouch, squat; bend down, stoop; conceal, cover up, hide; lay, level. * *n* bed, davenport, divan, lounge, seat, settee, settle, sofa.

council *n* advisers, cabinet, ministry; assembly, congress, conclave, convention, convocation, diet, husting, meeting, parliament, synod.

counsel *vb* admonish, advise, caution, recommend, warm. * *n* admonition, advice, caution, instruction, opinion, recommendation, suggestion; deliberation, forethought; advocate, barrister, counsellor, lawyer.

count *vb* enumerate, number, score; calculate, cast, compute, estimate, reckon; account, consider, deem, esteem, hold, judge, regard, think; tell. * *n* reckoning, tally.

countenance *vb* abet, aid, approve, assist, befriend, encourage, favour, patronize, sanction, support. * *n* aspect, look, men; aid, approbation, approval, assistance, encouragement, favour, patronage, sanction, support.

counter[1] *n* abacus, calculator, computer, meter, reckoner, tabulator, totalizator; bar, buffet, shopboard, table; (*naut*) end, poop, stern, tail; chip, token.

counter[2] *vb* contradict, contravene, counteract, oppose, retaliate. * *adj* adverse, against, contrary, opposed, opposite. * *adv* contrariwise, contrary. * *n* antithesis, contrary, converse, opposite, reverse; counterblast, counterblow, retaliation.

counteract *vb* check, contrapose, contravene, cross, counter, counterpose, defeat, foil, frustrate, hinder, oppose, resist, thwart, traverse; annul, countervail, counterbalance, destroy, neutralize, offset.

counteractive *adj* antidote, corrective, counteragent, medicine, remedy, restorative.

counterbalance *vb* balance, counterpoise; compensate, countervail.

counterfeit *vb* forge, imitate; fake, feign, pretend, sham, simulate; copy, imitate. * *adj* fake, forged, fraudulent, spurious, supposititious; false, feigned, hypocritical, mock, sham, simulated, spurious; copied, imitated, resembling. * *n* copy, fake, forgery, sham.

countermand *vb* abrogate, annul, cancel, recall, repeal, rescind, revoke.

counterpane *n* coverlet, duvet, quilt.

counterpart *n* copy, duplicate; complement, correlate, correlative, reverse, supplement; fellow, mate, match, tally, twin.

counterpoise *vb* balance, counteract, countervail, counterbalance, equilibrate, offset. * *n* balance, counterweight.

countersign *n* password, watchword.

countervail *vb* balance, compensate, counterbalance.

country *n* land, region; countryside; fatherland, home, kingdom, state, territory; nation, people, population. * *adj* rural, rustic; countrified, rough, rude, uncultivated, unpolished, unrefined.

countryman *n* compatriot, fellow-citizen; boor, clown, farmer, hind, husbandman, peasant, rustic, swain.

couple *vb* pair, unite; copulate, embrace; buckle, clasp, conjoin, connect, join, link, pair, yoke. * *n* brace, pair, twain, two; bond, coupling, lea, link, tie.

courage *n* audaciousness, audacity, boldness, bravery, daring, derring-do, dauntlessness, fearlessness, firmness, fortitude, gallantry, hardihood, heroism, intrepidity, manhood, mettle, nerve, pluck, prowess, resolution, spirit, spunk, valorousness, valour.

courageous *adj* audacious, brave, bold, chivalrous, daring, dauntless, fearless, gallant, hardy, heroic, intrepid, lion-hearted, mettlesome, plucky, reso-lute, reliant, staunch, stout, undismayed, valiant, valorous.

course *vb* chase, follow, hunt, pursue, race, run. * *n* career, circuit, race, run; road, route, track, way; bearing, direction, path, tremor, track; ambit, beat, orbit, round; process, progress, sequence; order, regularity, succession, turn; behaviour, conduct, deportment; arrangement, series, system.

court *vb* coddle, fawn, flatter, ingratiate; address, woo; seek; invite, solicit. * *n* area, courtyard, patio, quadrangle; addresses, civilities, homage, respects, solicitations; retinue, palace, tribunal.

courteous *adj* affable, attentive, ceremonious, civil, complaisant, courtly, debonair, elegant, gracious, obliging, polished, polite, refined, respected, urbane, well-bred, well-mannered.

courtesan *n* harlot, prostitute, strumpet, vamp, wanton, wench, whore.

courtesy *n* affability, civility, complaisance, courteousness, elegance, good-breeding, graciousness, polish, politeness, refine, urbanity.

courtly *adj* affable, ceremonious, civil, elegant, flattering, lordly, obliging, polished, polite, refined, urbane.

courtyard *n* area, court, patio, quadrangle, yard.

cove[1] *n* anchorage, bay, bight, creek, firth, fjord, inlet.

cove[2] *n* bloke, chap, character, customer, fellow, type.

covenant *vb* agree, bargain, contract, stipulate. * *n* bond, deed; arrangement, bargain, compact, concordat, contract, convention, pact, stipulation, treaty.

cover *vb* overlay, overspread; cloak, conceal, curtain, disguise, hide, mask, screen, secrete, shroud, veil; defend, guard, protect, shelter, shield; case, clothe, envelop, invest, jacket, sheathe; comprehend, comprise, contain, embody, embrace, include. * *n* capsule, case, covering, integument, tegument, top; cloak, disguise, screen, veil; guard, defence, protection, safeguard, shelter, shield; shrubbery, thicket, underbrush, undergrowth, underwood, woods.

covert *adj* clandestine, concealed, disguised, hidden, insidious, private, secret, sly, stealthy, underhand. * *n* coppice, shade, shrubbery, thicket, underwood; asylum; defence, harbour, hiding-place, refuge, retreat, sanctuary, shelter.

covet *vb* aim after, desire, long for, yearn for; hanker after, lust after.

covetous *adj* acquisitive, avaricious, close-fisted, grasping, greedy, miserly, niggardly, parsimonious, penurious, rapacious.

cow[1] *n* bovine, heifer.

cow[2] *vb* abash, break, daunt, discourage, dishearten, frighten, intimidate, overawe, subdue.

coward *adj* cowardly, timid. * *n* caitiff, craven, dastard, milksop, poltroon, recreant, skulker, sneak, wheyface.

cowardly *adj* base, chicken-hearted, coward, craven, dastardly, faint-hearted, fearful, lily-livered, mean, pusillanimous, timid, timorous, white-livered, yellow.

cower *vb* bend, cringe, crouch, fawn, shrink, squat, stoop.

coxcomb *n* beau, dandy, dude, exquisite, fop, jackanapes, popinjay, prig.

coy *adj* backward, bashful, demure, diffident, distant, modest, reserved, retiring, self-effacing, shrinking, shy, timid.

coyness *n* affectation, archness, backwardness, bashfulness, coquettishness, demureness, diffidence, evasiveness, modesty, primness, reserve, shrinking, shyness, timidity.

cozen *vb* beguile, cheat, chouse, circumvent, deceive, defraud, diddle, dupe, gull, overreach, swindle, trick, victimize.

cozy *see* **cosy**.

crabbed *adj* acrid, rough, sore, tart; acrimonious, cantankerous, captious, caustic, censorious, churlish, cross, growling, harsh, ill-tempered, morose, peevish, petulant, snappish, snarling, splenetic, surly, testy, touchy, waspish; difficult, intractable, perplexing, tough, trying, unmanageable.

crabbedness *n* acridity, acridness, roughness, sourness, tartness; acerbity, acrimonious, asperity, churlishness, harshness, ill-tempered, moodiness, moroseness, sullenness; difficulty, intractability, perplexity.

crack *vb* break; chop, cleave, split; snap; craze, madden; boast, brag, bluster, crow, gasconade, vapour, vaunt. * *adj* capital, excellent, first-class, first-rate, tip-top. * *n* breach, break, chink, cleft, cranny, crevice, fissure, fracture, opening, rent, rift, split; burst, clap, explosion, pop, report; snap.

cracked *adj* broken, crackled, split; crack-brained, crazed, crazy, demented, deranged, flighty, insane.

crackle *vb* crepitate, decrepitate, snap.

craft *n* ability, aptitude, cleverness, dexterity, expertness, power, readiness, skill, tact, talent; artifice, artfulness, cunning, craftiness, deceitfulness, deception, guile, shrewdness, subtlety; art, avocation, business, calling, employment, handicraft, trade, vocation; vessel.

crafty *adj* arch, artful, astute, cunning, crooked, deceitful, designing, fraudulent, guileful, insidious, intriguing, scheming, shrewd, sly, subtle, tricky, wily.

crag *n* rock; neck, throat.

craggy *adj* broken, cragged, jagged, rough, rugged, scraggy, uneven.

cram *vb* fill, glut, gorge, satiate, stuff; compress, crowd, overcrowd, press, squeeze; coach, grind.

cramp *vb* convulse; check, clog, confine, hamper, hinder, impede, obstruct, restrain, restrict. * *n* convulsion, crick, spasm; check, restraint, restriction, obstruction.

crank *vb* bend, crankle, crinkle, turn, twist, wind. * *n* bend, quirk, turn, twist, winding.

cranny *n* breach, break, chink, cleft, crack, crevice, fissure, gap, hole, interstice, nook, opening, rift.

crapulous *adj* crapulent, drunk, drunken, inebriated, intoxicated, tipsy.

crash *vb* break, shatter, shiver, smash, splinter. * *adj* emergency, fast, intensive, rushed, speeded-up. * *n* clang, clash, collision concussion, jar.

crass *adj* coarse, gross, raw, thick, unabated, unrefined.

cravat *n* neckcloth, neckerchief, necktie.

crave *vb* ask, beg, beseech, entreat, implore, petition, solicit, supplicate; desire, hanker after, long for, need, want, yearn for.

craven *n* coward, dastard, milk-sop, poltroon, recreant. *adj* cowardly, chicken-hearted, lily-livered, pusillanimous, yellow.

craving *n* hankering, hungering, longing, yearning.

craw *n* crop, gullet, stomach, throat.

craze *vb* bewilder, confuse, dement, derange, madden; disorder, impair, weaken. * *n* fashion, mania, mode, novelty.

crazy *adj* broken, crank, rickety, shaky, shattered, tottering; crack-brained, delirious, demented, deranged, distracted, idiotic, insane, lunatic, mad, silly.

create *vb* originate, procreate; cause, design, fashion, form, invent, occasion, produce; appoint, constitute, make.

creation *n* formation, invention, origination, production; cosmos, universe; appointment, constitution, establishment, nomination.

creator *n* author, designer, inventor, fashioner, maker, originator; god.

creature *n* animal, beast, being, body, brute, man, person; dependant, hanger-on, minion, parasite, retainer, vassal; miscreant, wretch.

credence *n* acceptance, belief, confidence, credit, faith, reliance, trust.

credentials *npl* certificate, diploma, missive, passport, recommendation, testament, testimonial, title, voucher, warrant.

credibility *n* believability, plausibility, tenability, , trustworthiness.

credit *vb* accept, believe, trust; loan, trust. * *n* belief, confidence, credence, faith, reliance, trust; esteem, regard, reputableness, reputation; influence, power; honour, merit; loan, trust.

creditable *adj* estimable, honourable, meritorious, praiseworthy, reputable, respectable.

credulity *n* credulousness, gullibility, silliness, simplicity, stupidity.

credulous *adj* dupable, green, gullible, naive, over-trusting, trustful, uncritical, unsuspecting, unsuspicious.

creed *n* belief, confession, doctrine, dogma, opinion, profession, tenet.

creek *n* bay, bight, cove, fjord, inlet; rivulet, streamlet.

creep *vb* crawl; steal upon; cringe, fawn, grovel, insinuate. * *n* crawl, scrabble, scramble; fawner, groveller, sycophant, toady.

crenate *adj* indented, notched, scalloped.

crepitate *vb* crack, crackle, decrepitate, snap.

crest *n* comb, plume, topknot, tuft; apex, crown, head, ridge, summit, top; arms, badge, bearings.

crestfallen *adj* chap-fallen, dejected, depressed, despondent, discouraged, disheartened, dispirited, downcast, down-hearted, low-spirited, melancholy, sad.

crevice *n* chink, cleft, crack, cranny, fissure, fracture, gap, hole, interstice, opening, rent, rift.

crew *n* company, complement, hands; company, corps, gang, horde, mob, party, posse, set, squad, team, throng.

crib *vb* cage, confine, encage, enclose, imprison; pilfer, purloin. * *n* manger, rack; bin, bunker; plagiarism, plunder, theft.

crick *vb* jar, rick, wrench, wrick. * *n* convulsion, cramp, jarring, spasm, rick, wrench, wrick.

crime *n* felony, misdeed, misdemeanour, offence, violation; delinquency, fault, guilt, iniquity, sin, transgression, unrighteousness, wickedness, wrong.

criminal *adj* culpable, felonious, flagitious, guilty, illegal, immoral, iniquitous, nefarious, unlawful, vicious, wicked, wrong. * *n* convict, culprit, delinquent, felon, malefactor, offender, sinner, transgressor.

criminate *vb* accuse, arraign, charge, convict, impeach, indict; implicate, involve.

crimp *vb* crisp, curl.

cringe *vb* bend, bow, cower, crouch, fawn, grovel, kneel, sneak, stoop, truckle.

cripple *vb* cramp, destroy, disable, enfeeble, impair, lame, maim, mutilate, paralyse, ruin, weaken.

crisis *n* acme, climax, height; conjuncture, emergency, exigency, juncture, pass, pinch, push, rub, strait, urgency.

crisp *adj* brittle, curled, friable, frizzled.

criterion *n* canon, gauge, measure, principle, proof, rule, standard, test, touchstone.

critic *n* arbiter, caviller, censor, connoisseur, judge, nit-picker, reviewer.

critical *adj* accurate, exact, nice; captious, carping, caviling, censorious, exacting; crucial, decisive, determining, important, turning: dangerous, dubious, exigent, hazardous, imminent, momentous, precarious, ticklish.

criticism *n* analysis, animadversion, appreciation, comment, critique, evaluation, judgement, review, strictures.

criticize *vb* appraise, evaluate, examine, judge.

croak *vb* complain, groan, grumble, moan, mumble, repine; die.

crone *n* hag, witch.

crony *n* ally, associate, chum, friend, mate, mucker, pal.

crook *vb* bend, bow, curve, incurvate, turn, wind. * *n* bend, curvature, flexion, turn; artifice, machination, trick; criminal, thief, villain

crooked *adj* angular, bent, bowed, curved, winding, zigzag; askew, aslant, awry, deformed, disfigured, distorted, twisted, wry; crafty, deceitful, devious, dishonest, dishonourable, fraudulent, insidious, intriguing, knavish, tricky, underhanded, unfair, unscrupulous.

crop *vb* gather, mow, pick, pluck, reap; browse, nibble; clip, curtail, lop, reduce, shorten. * *n* harvest, produce, yield.

cross *vb* intersect, pass over, traverse; hinder, interfere, obstruct, thwart; interbred, intermix. * *adj* transverse; cantankerous, captious, crabbed, churlish, crusty, cynical, fractious, fretful, grouchy, ill-natured, ill-tempered, irascible, irritable, morose, peevish, pettish, petulant, snappish, snarling, sour, spleeny, splenetic, sulky, sullen, surly, testy, touchy, waspish. * *n* crucifix, gibbet, rood; affliction, misfortune, trial, trouble, vexation; cross-breeding, hybrid, intermixture.

cross-grained *adj* cantankerous, headstrong, obdurate, peevish, perverse, refractory, stubborn, untractable, wayward.

crossing *n* intersection, overpass, traversing, under-pass.

crossways, crosswise *adv* across, over, transversely.

crotchet *n* caprice, fad, fancy, freak, quirk, vagary, whim, whimsy.

crouch *vb* cower, cringe, fawn, truckle; crouch, kneel, stoop, squat; bow, curtsy, genuflect.

croup *n* buttocks, crupper, rump.

crow *vb* bluster, boast, brag, chuckle, exult, flourish, gasconade, swagger, triumph, vapour, vaunt.

crowd *vb* compress, cram, jam, pack, press; collect, congregate, flock, herd, huddle, swarm. * *n* assembly, company, concourse, flock, herd, horde, host, jam, multitude, press, throng; mob, pack, populace, rabble, rout.

crown *vb* adorn, dignify, honour; recompense, requite, reward; cap, complete, consummate, finish, perfect. * *n* bays, chaplet, coronal, coronet, garland, diadem, laurel, wreath; monarchy, royalty, sovereignty; diadem; dignity, honour, recompense, reward; apex, crest, summit, top.

crowning *adj* completing, consummating, dignifying, finishing, perfecting.

crucial *adj* intersecting, transverse; critical, decisive, searching, severe, testing, trying.

crude *adj* raw, uncooked, undressed, unworked; harsh, immature, rough, unripe; crass, coarse, unrefined; awkward, immature, indigestible, rude, uncouth, unpolished, unpremeditated.

cruel *adj* barbarous, blood-thirsty, dire, fell, ferocious, inexorable, hard-hearted, inhuman, merciless, pitiless, relentless, ruthless, sanguinary, savage, truculent, uncompassionate, unfeeling, unmerciful, unrelenting; bitter, cold, hard, severe, sharp, unfeeling.

crumble *vb* bruise, crush, decay, disintegrate, perish, pound, pulverize, triturate.

crumple *vb* rumple, wrinkle.

crush *vb* bruise, compress, contuse, squash, squeeze; bray, comminute, crumble, disintegrate, mash; demolish, raze, shatter; conquer, overcome, overpower, overwhelm, quell, subdue.

crust *n* coat, coating, incrustation, outside, shell, surface.

crusty *adj* churlish, crabbed, cross, cynical, fretful, forward, morose, peevish, pettish, petulant, snappish, snarling, surly, testy, touchy, waspish; friable, hard, short.

cry *vb* call, clamour, exclaim; blubber, snivel, sob, wail, weep, whimper; bawl, bellow, hoot, roar, shout, vociferate, scream, screech, squawk, squall, squeal, yell; announce, blazon, proclaim, publish. * *n* acclamation, clamour, ejaculation, exclamation, outcry; crying, lament, lamentation, plaint, weeping; bawl, bellow, howl, roar, scream, screech, shriek, yell; announcement, proclamation, publication.

crypt *n* catacomb, tomb, vault.

cuddle *vb* cosset, nestle, snuggle, squat; caress, embrace, fondle, hug, pet. * *n* caress, embrace, hug.

cudgel *vb* bang, baste, batter, beat, cane, drub, thrash, thump. * *n* bastinado, baton, bludgeon, club, shillelagh, stick, truncheon.

cue *vb* intimate, prompt, remind, sign, signal. * *n* catchword, hint, intimation, nod, prompting, sign, signal, suggestion.

cuff *vb* beat, box, buffet, knock, pummel, punch, slap, smack, strike, thump. * *n* blow, box, punch, slap, smack, strike, thump.

cul-de-sac *n* alley, dead end, impasse, pocket.

cull *vb* choose, elect, pick, select; collect, gather, glean, pluck.

culmination *n* acme, apex, climax, completion, consummation, crown, summit, top, zenith.

culpability *n* blame, blameworthiness, criminality, culpableness, guilt, remissness, sinfulness.

culpable *adj* blameable, blameworthy, censurable, faulty, guilty, reprehensible, sinful, transgressive, wrong.

culprit *n* delinquent, criminal, evil-doer, felon, malefactor, offender.

cultivate *vb* farm, fertilize, till, work; civilize, develop, discipline, elevate, improve, meliorate, refine, train; investigate, prosecute, pursue, search, study; cherish, foster, nourish, patronize, promote.

culture *n* agriculture, cultivation, farming, husbandry, tillage; cultivation, elevation, improvement, refinement.

cumber *vb* burden, clog, encumber, hamper, impede, obstruct, oppress, overload; annoy, distract, embarrass, harass, perplex, plague, torment, trouble, worry.

cumbersome *adj* burdensome, clumsy, cumbrous, embarrassing, heavy, inconvenient, oppressive, troublesome, unmanageable, unwieldy, vexatious.

cuneiform *adj* cuneate, wedge-shaped.

cunning *adj* artful, astute, crafty, crooked, deceitful, designing, diplomatic, foxy, guileful, intriguing, machiavellian, sharp, shrewd, sly, subtle, tricky, wily; curious, ingenious. * *n* art, artfulness, artifice, astuteness, craft, shrewdness, subtlety; craftiness, chicane, chicanery, deceit, deception, intrigue, slyness.

cup *n* beaker, bowl, chalice, goblet, mug; cupful, draught, potion.

cupboard *n* buffet, cabinet, closet.

cupidity *n* avidity, greed, hankering, longing, lust; acquisitiveness, avarice, covetousness, greediness, stinginess.

curative *adj* healing, medicinal, remedial, restorative.

curator *n* custodian, guardian, keeper, superintendent.

curb *vb* bridle, check, control, hinder, moderate, repress, restrain. * *n* bridle, check, control, hindrance, rein, restraint.

cure *vb* alleviate, correct, heal, mend, remedy, restore; kipper, pickle, preserve. * *n* antidote, corrective, help, remedy, reparative, restorative, specific; alleviation, healing, restorative.

curiosity *n* interest, inquiringness, inquisitiveness; celebrity, curio, marvel, novelty, oddity, phenomenon, rarity, sight, spectacle, wonder.

curious *adj* interested, inquiring, inquisitive, meddling, peering, prying, scrutinizing; extraordinary, marvellous, novel, queer, rare, singular, strange, unique, unusual; cunning, elegant, fine, finished, neat, skilful, well-wrought.

curl *vb* coil, twist, wind, writhe; bend, buckle, ripple, wave. * *n* curlicue, lovelock, ringlet; flexure, sinuosity, undulation, wave, waving, winding.

curmudgeon *n* churl, lick-penny, miser, niggard, screw, scrimp, skinflint.

currency *n* publicity; acceptance, circulation, transmission; bills, coins, money, notes.

current *adj* common, general, popular, rife; circulating, passing; existing, instant, present, prevalent, widespread. * *n* course, progression, river, stream, tide, undertow. * *adv* commonly, generally, popularly, publicly.

curry *vb* comb, dress; beat, cudgel, drub, thrash.

curse *vb* anathematize, damn, denounce, execrate, imprecate, invoke, maledict; blast, blight, destroy, doom; afflict, annoy, harass, injure, plague, scourge, torment, vex; blaspheme, swear. * *n* anathema, ban, denunciation, execration, fulmination, imprecation, malediction, malison; affliction, annoyance, plague, scourge, torment, trouble, vexation; ban, condemnation, penalty, sentence.

cursed *adj* accursed, banned, blighted, curse-laden, unholy; abominable, detestable, execrable, hateful, villainous; annoying, confounded, plaguing, scourging, tormenting, troublesome, vexatious.

cursory *adj* brief, careless, desultory, hasty, passing, rapid, slight, summary, superficial, transient, transitory.

curt *adj* brief, concise, laconic, short, terse; crusty, rude, snappish, tart.

curtail *vb* abridge, dock, lop, retrench, shorten; abbreviate, contract, decrease, diminish, lessen.

curtain *vb* cloak, cover, drape, mantle, screen, shade, shield, veil. * *n* arras, drape, drop, portière, screen, shade.

curvature *n* arcuation, bend, bending, camber, crook, curve, flexure, incurvation.

curve *vb* bend, crook, inflect, turn, twist, wind. * *n* arcuation, bend, bending, camber, crook, flexure, incurvation.

curvet *vb* bound, leap, vault; caper, frisk.

cushion *vb* absorb, damp, dampen, deaden, dull, muffle, mute, soften, subdue, suppress; cradle, pillow, support. * *n* bolster, hassock, pad, pillow, woolsack.

cusp *n* angle, horn, point.

custodian *n* curator, guardian, keeper, sacristan, superintendent, warden.

custody *n* care, charge, guardianship, keeping, safe-keeping, protection, watch, ward; confinement, durance, duress, imprisonment, prison.

custom *n* consuetude, convention, fashion, habit, manner, mode, practice, rule, usage, use, way; form, formality, observation; patronage; duty, impost, tax, toll, tribute.

customary *adj* accustomed, common, consuetudinary, conventional, familiar, fashionable, general, habitual, gnomic, prescriptive, regular, usual, wonted.

cut *vb* chop, cleave, divide, gash, incise, lance, sever, slice, slit, wound; carve, chisel, sculpture; hurt, move, pierce, touch; ignore, slight; abbreviate, abridge, curtail, shorten. * *n* gash, groove, incision, nick, slash, slice, slit; channel, passage; piece, slice; fling, sarcasm, taunt; fashion, form, mode, shape, style.

cutthroat *adj* barbarous, cruel, ferocious, murderous; competitive, exacting, exorbitant, extortionate, rivalling, ruthless, usurious, vying.* *n* assassin, murderer, ruffian.

cutting *adj* keen, sharp; acid, biting, bitter, caustic, piercing, sarcastic, sardonic, satirical, severe, trenchant, wounding.

cycle *n* age, circle, era, period, revolution, round.

Cyclopean *adj* colossal, enormous, gigantic, Herculean, immense, vast.

cynical *adj* captious, carping, censorious, churlish, crabbed, cross, crusty, fretful, ill-natured, ill-tempered, morose, peevish, pettish, petulant, sarcastic, satirical, snappish, snarling, surly, testy, touchy, waspish; contemptuous, derisive, misanthropic, pessimistic, scornful.

cynosure *n* attraction, centre.

cyst *n* pouch, sac.

D

dab *vb* box, rap, slap, strike, tap touch; coat, daub, smear. * *adj* adept, expert, proficient; pat. * *n* lump, mass, pat.

dabble *vb* dip, moisten, soak, spatter, splash, sprinkle, wet; meddle, tamper, trifle.

daft *adj* absurd, delirious, foolish, giddy, idiotic, insane, silly, simple, stupid, witless; frolicsome, merry, mirthful, playful, sportive.

dagger *n* bayonet, dirk, poniard, stiletto.

dainty *adj* delicate, delicious, luscious, nice, palatable, savoury, tender, toothsome; beautiful, charming, choice, delicate, elegant, exquisite, fine, neat; fastidious, finical, finicky, over-nice, particular, scrupulous, squeamish. * *n* delicacy, titbit, treat.

dale *n* bottom, dell, dingle, glen, vale, valley.

dalliance *n* caressing, endearments, flirtation, fondling.

dally *vb* dawdle, fritter, idle, trifle, waste time; flirt, fondle, toy.

damage *vb* harm, hurt, impair, injure, mar. * *n* detriment, harm, hurt, injury, loss, mischief.

damages *npl* compensation, fine, forfeiture, indemnity, reparation, satisfaction.

dame *n* babe, baby, broad, doll, girl; lady, madam, matron, mistress.

damn *vb* condemn, doom, kill, ruin. * *n* bean, curse, fig, hoot, rap, sou, straw, whit.

damnable *adj* abominable, accursed, atrocious, cursed, detestable, hateful, execrable, odious, outrageous.

damp *vb* dampen, moisten; allay, abate, check, discourage, moderate, repress, restrain; chill, cool, deaden, deject, depress, dispirit. * *adj* dank, humid, moist, wet. * *n* dampness, dank, fog, mist, moisture, vapour; chill, dejection, depression.

damper *n* check, hindrance, impediment, obstacle; damp, depression, discouragement, wet blanket.

dandle *vb* amuse, caress, fondle, pet, toss; dance.

danger *n* jeopardy, insecurity, hazard, peril, risk, venture.

dangerous *adj* critical, hazardous, insecure, perilous, risky, ticklish, unsafe.

dangle *vb* drape, hang, pend, sway, swing; fawn.

dank *adj* damp, humid, moist, wet.

dapper *adj* active, agile, alert, brisk, lively, nimble, quick, ready, smart, spry; neat, nice, pretty, spruce, trim.

dapple *vb* diversify, spot, variegate. * *adj* dappled, spotted, variegated.

dare *vb* challenge, defy, endanger, hazard, provoke, risk. * *n* challenge, defiance, gage.

daring *adj* adventurous, bold, brave, chivalrous, courageous, dauntless, doughty, fearless, gallant, heroic, intrepid, valiant, valorous. * *n* adventurousness, boldness, bravery, courage, dauntlessness, doughtiness, fearlessness, intrepidity, undauntedness, valour.

dark *adj* black, cloudy, darksome, dusky, ebon, inky, lightless, lurid, moonless, murky, opaque, overcast, pitchy, rayless, shady, shadowy, starless, sunless, swart, tenebrous, umbrageous, unenlightened, unilluminated; abstruse, cabbalistic, enigmatical, incomprehensible, mysterious, mystic, mystical, obscure, occult, opaque, recondite, transcendental, unillumined, unintelligible; cheerless, discouraging, dismal, disheartening, funereal, gloomy; benighted, darkened, ignorant, rude, unlettered, untaught; atrocious, damnable, infamous, flagitious, foul, horrible, infernal, nefarious, vile, wicked. * *n* darkness, dusk, murkiness, obscurity; concealment, privacy, secrecy; blindness, ignorance.

darken *vb* cloud, dim, eclipse, obscure, shade, shadow; chill, damp, depress, gloom, sadden; benight, stultify, stupefy; obscure, perplex; defile, dim, dull, stain, sully.

darkness *n* blackness, dimness, gloom, obscurity; blindness, ignorance; cheerlessness, despondency, gloom, joylessness; privacy, secrecy.

darling *adj* beloved, cherished, dear, loved, precious, treasured. * *n* dear, favourite, idol, love, sweetheart.

dart *vb* ejaculate, hurl, launch, propel, sling, throw; emit, shoot; dash, rush, scoot, spring.

dash *vb* break, destroy, disappoint, frustrate, ruin, shatter, spoil, thwart; abash, confound, disappoint, surprise; bolt, dart, fly, run, speed, rush. * *n* blow, stroke; advance, onset, rush; infusion, smack, spice, sprinkling, tincture, tinge, touch; flourish, show.

dashing *adj* headlong, impetuous, precipitate, rushing; brilliant, gay, showy, spirited.

dastardly *adj* base, cowardly, coward, cowering, craven, pusillanimous, recreant. * *n* coward, craven, milksop, poltroon, recreant.

data *npl* conditions, facts, information, premises.

date *n* age, cycle, day, generation, time; epoch, era, period; appointment, arrangement, assignation, engagement, interview, rendezvous, tryst; catch, steady, sweetheart.

daub *vb* bedaub, begrime, besmear, blur, cover, deface, defile, grime, plaster, smear, smudge, soil, sully. * *n* smear, smirch, smudge.

daunt *vb* alarm, appal, check, cow, deter, discourage, frighten, intimate, scare, subdue, tame, terrify, thwart.

dauntless *adj* bold, brave, chivalrous, courageous, daring, doughty, gallant, heroic, indomitable, intrepid, unaffrighted, unconquerable, undaunted, undismayed, valiant, valorous.

dawdle *vb* dally, delay, fiddle, idle, lag, loiter, potter, trifle.

dawn *vb* appear, begin, break, gleam, glimmer, open, rise. * *n* daybreak, dawning, cockcrow, sunrise, sun-up.

day *n* daylight, sunlight, sunshine; age, epoch, generation, lifetime, time.

daze *vb* blind, dazzle; bewilder, confound, confuse, perplex, stun, stupefy. * *n* bewilderment, confusion, discomposure, perturbation, pother; coma, stupor, swoon, trance.

dazzle *vb* blind, daze; astonish, confound, overpower, surprise. * *n* brightness, brilliance, splendour.

dead *adj* breathless, deceased, defunct, departed, gone, inanimate, lifeless; apathetic, callous, cold, dull, frigid, indifferent, inert, lukewarm, numb, obtuse, spiritless, torpid, unfeeling; flat, insipid, stagnant, tasteless, vapid; barren, inactive, sterile, unemployed, unprofitable, useless. * *adv* absolutely, completely, downright, fundamentally, quite; direct, directly, due, exactly, just, right, squarely, straight. * *n* depth, midst; hush, peace, quietude, silence, stillness.

deaden *vb* abate, damp, dampen, dull, impair, muffle, mute, restrain, retard, smother, weaken; benumb, blunt, hebetate, obtund, paralyse.

deadly *adj* deleterious, destructive, fatal, lethal, malignant, mortal, murderous, noxious, pernicious, poisonous, venomous; implacable, mortal, rancorous, sanguinary.

deal *vb* allot, apportion, assign, bestow, dispense, distribute, divide, give, reward, share; bargain, trade, traffic, treat with. * *n* amount, degree, distribution, extent, lot, portion, quantity, share; bargain, transaction.

dear *adj* costly, expensive, high-priced; beloved, cherished, darling, esteemed, precious, treasured. * *n* beloved, darling, deary, honey, love, precious, sweet, sweetie, sweetheart.

dearth *n* deficiency, insufficiency, scarcity; famine, lack, need, shortage, want.

death *n* cessation, decease, demise, departure, destruction, dissolution, dying, end, exit, mortality, passing.

deathless *adj* eternal, everlasting, immortal, imperishable, undying; boring, dull, turgid.

debacle *n* breakdown, cataclysm, collapse; rout, stampede.

debar *vb* blackball, deny, exclude, hinder, prevent, prohibit, restrain, shut out, stop, withhold.

debase *vb* adulterate, alloy, depress, deteriorate, impair, injure, lower, pervert, reduce, vitiate; abase, degrade, disgrace, dishonour, humble, humiliate, mortify, shame; befoul, contaminate, corrupt, defile, foul, pollute, soil, taint.

debate *vb* argue, canvass, contest, discuss, dispute; contend, deliberate, wrangle. * *n* controversy, discussion, disputation; altercation, contention, contest, dispute, logomachy.

debauch *vb* corrupt, deprave, pollute, vitiate; deflower, ravish, seduce, violate. * *n* carousal, orgy, revel, saturnalia.

debauchery *n* dissipation, dissoluteness, excesses, intemperance; debauch, excess, intemperance, lewdness, licentiousness, lust; bacchanal, carousal, compotation, indulgence, orgies, potation, revelry, revels, saturnalia, spree.

debilitate *vb* enervate, enfeeble, exhaust, prostrate, relax, weaken.

debility *n* enervation, exhaustion, faintness, feebleness, frailty, imbecility, infirmity, languor, prostration, weakness.

debonair *adj* affable, civil, complaisant, courteous, easy, gracious, kind, obliging, polite, refined, urbane, well-bred.

debris *n* detritus, fragments, remains, rubbish, rubble, ruins, wreck, wreckage.

debt *n* arrears, debit, due, liability, obligation; fault, misdoing, offence, shortcoming, sin, transgression, trespass.

decadence *n* caducity, decay, declension, decline, degeneracy, degeneration, deterioration, fall, retrogression.

decamp *vb* abscond, bolt, escape, flee, fly.

decapitate *vb* behead, decollate, guillotine.

decay *vb* decline, deteriorate, disintegrate, fail, perish, wane, waste, wither; decompose, putrefy, rot. * *n* caducity, decadence, declension, decline, decomposition, decrepitude, degeneracy, degeneration, deterioration, dilapidation, disintegration, fading, failing, perishing, putrefaction, ruin, wasting, withering.

deceased *adj* dead, defunct, departed, gone, late, lost.

deceit *n* artifice, cheating, chicanery, cozenage, craftiness, deceitfulness, deception, double-dealing, duplicity, finesse, fraud, guile, hypocrisy, imposition, imposture, pretence, sham, treachery, tricky, underhandedness, wile.

deceitful *adj* counterfeit, deceptive, delusive, fallacious, hollow, illusive, illusory, insidious, misleading; circumventive, cunning, designing, dissembling, dodgy, double-dealing, evasive, false, fraudulent, guileful, hypocritical, insincere, tricky, underhanded, wily.

deceive *vb* befool, beguile, betray, cheat, chouse, circumvent, cozen, defraud, delude, disappoint, double-cross, dupe, ensnare, entrap, fool, gull, hoax, hoodwink, humbug, mislead, outwit, overreach, trick.

deceiver *n* charlatan, cheat, humbug, hypocrite,

knave, impostor, pretender, rogue, sharper, trickster.

decent *adj* appropriate, becoming, befitting, comely, seemly, decorous, fit, proper, seemly; chaste, delicate, modest, pure; moderate, passable, respectable, tolerable.

deception *n* artifice, cheating, chicanery, cozenage, craftiness, deceitfulness, deception, double-dealing, duplicity, finesse, fraud, guile, hoax, hypocrisy, imposition, imposture, pretence, sham, treachery, trick, underhandedness, wile; cheat, chouse, ruse, stratagem, wile.

deceptive *adj* deceitful, deceiving, delusive, disingenuous, fallacious, false, illusive, illusory, misleading.

decide *vb* close, conclude, determine, end, settle, terminate; resolve; adjudge, adjudicate, award.

decided *adj* determined, firm, resolute, unhesitating, unwavering; absolute, categorical, positive, unequivocal; certain, clear, indisputable, undeniable, unmistakable, unquestionable.

deciduous *adj* caducous, nonperennial, temporary.

decipher *vb* explain, expound, interpret, reveal, solve, unfold, unravel; read.

decision *n* conclusion, determination, judgement, settlement; adjudication, award, decree, pronouncement, sentence; firmness, resolution.

decisive *adj* conclusive, determinative, final.

deck *vb* adorn, array, beautify, decorate, embellish, grace, ornament; apparel, attire, bedeck, clothe, dress, robe.

declaim *vb* harangue, mouth, rant, speak, spout.

declamation *n* declaiming, haranguing, mouthing, ranting, spouting.

declamatory *adj* bombastic, discursive, fustian, grandiloquent, high-flown, high-sounding, incoherent, inflated, pompous, pretentious, rhetorical, swelling, turgid.

declaration *n* affirmation, assertion, asseveration, averment, avowal, protestation, statement; announcement, proclamation, publication.

declaratory *adj* affirmative, annunciatory, assertive, declarative, definite, enunciative, enunciatory, expressive; explanatory, expository.

declare *vb* advertise, affirm, announce, assert, asseverate, aver, blazon, bruit, proclaim, promulgate, pronounce, publish, state, utter.

declension *n* decadence, decay, decline, degeneracy, deterioration, diminution; inflection, variation; declination, nonacceptance, refusal.

declination *n* bending, descent, inclination; decadence, decay, decline, degeneracy, degeneration, degradation, deterioration, diminution; aberration, departure, deviation, digression, divagation, divergence; declinature, nonacceptance, refusal.

decline *vb* incline, lean, slope; decay, droop, fail, flag, languish, pine, sink; degenerate, depreciate, deteriorate; decrease, diminish, dwindle, fade, ebb, lapse, lessen, wane; avoid, refuse, reject; inflect, vary. * *n* decadence, decay, declension, dec-

lination, degeneracy, deterioration, diminution, wane; atrophy, consumption, marasmus, phthisis; declivity, hill, incline, slope.

declivity *n* declination, descent, incline, slope.

decompose *vb* analyse, disintegrate, dissolve, distil, resolve, separate; corrupt, decay, putrefy, rot.

decomposition *n* analysis, break-up, disintegration, resolution; caries, corruption, crumbling, decay, disintegration, dissolution, putrescence, rotting.

decorate *vb* adorn, beautify, bedeck, deck, embellish, enrich, garnish, grace, ornament.

decoration *n* adorning, beautifying, bedecking, decking, enriching, garnishing, ornamentation, ornamenting; adornment, enrichment, embellishment, ornament.

decorous *adj* appropriate, becoming, befitting, comely, decent, fit, suitable, proper, sedate, seemly, staid.

decorum *n* appropriate behaviour, courtliness, decency, deportment, dignity, gravity, politeness, propriety, sedateness, seemliness.

decoy *vb* allure, deceive, ensnare, entice, entrap, inveigle, lure, seduce, tempt. * *n* allurement, lure, enticement.

decrease *vb* abate, contract, decline, diminish, dwindle, ebb, lessen, subside, wane; curtail, diminish, lessen, lower, reduce, retrench. * *n* abatement, contraction, declension, decline, decrement, diminishing, diminution, ebb, ebbing, lessening, reduction, subsidence, waning.

decree *vb* adjudge, appoint, command, decide, determine, enact, enjoin, order, ordain. * *n* act, command, edict, enactment, fiat, law, mandate, order, ordinance, precept, regulation, statute.

decrement *n* decrease, diminution, lessening, loss, waste.

decrepit *adj* feeble, effete, shattered, wasted, weak; aged, crippled, superannuated.

decry *vb* abuse, belittle, blame, condemn, denounce, depreciate, detract, discredit, disparage, run down, traduce, underrate, undervalue.

dedicate *vb* consecrate, devote, hallow, sanctify; address, inscribe.

deduce *vb* conclude, derive, draw, gather, infer.

deducible *adj* derivable, inferable.

deduct *vb* remove, subtract, withdraw; abate, detract.

deduction *n* removal, subtraction, withdrawal; abatement, allowance, defalcation, discount, rebate, reduction, reprise; conclusion, consequence, corollary, inference.

deed *n* achievement, act, action, derring-do, exploit, feat, performance; fact, truth, reality; charter, contract, document, indenture, instrument, transfer.

deem *vb* account, believe, conceive, consider, count, estimate, hold, imagine, judge, regard, suppose, think; fancy, opine.

deep *adj* abysmal, extensive, great, profound; abstruse, difficult, hard, intricate, knotty, mysterious, recondite, unfathomable; astute, cunning, designing, discerning, intelligent, insidious, penetrating, sagacious, shrewd; absorbed, engrossed; bass, grave, low; entire, great, heartfelt, thorough. * *n* main, ocean, water, sea; abyss, depth, profundity; enigma, mystery, riddle; silence, stillness.

deeply *adv* profoundly; completely, entirely, extensively, greatly, thoroughly; affectingly, distressingly, feelingly, mournfully, sadly.

deface *vb* blotch, deform, disfigure, injure, mar, mutilate, obliterate, soil, spoil, sully, tarnish.

de facto *adj* actual, real. * *adv* actually, in effect, in fact, really, truly.

defalcate *vb* abate, curtail, retrench, lop.

defalcation *n* abatement, deduction, diminution, discount, reduction; default, deficiency, deficit, shortage, shortcoming; embezzlement, fraud.

defamation *n* abuse, aspersion, back-biting, calumny, detraction, disparagement, libel, obloquy, opprobrium, scandal, slander.

defamatory *adj* abusive, calumnious, libellous, slanderous.

defame *vb* abuse, asperse, blacken, belie, besmirch, blemish, calumniate, detract, disgrace, dishonour, libel, malign, revile, slander, smirch, traduce, vilify.

default *vb* defalcate, dishonour, fail, repudiate, welsh. * *n* defalcation, failure, lapse, neglect, offence, omission, oversight, shortcoming ; defect, deficiency, deficit, delinquency, destitution, fault, lack, want.

defaulter *n* delinquent, embezzler, offender, peculator.

defeat *vb* beat, checkmate, conquer, discomfit, overcome, overpower, overthrow, repulse, rout, ruin, vanquish; baffle, balk, block, disappoint, disconcert, foil, frustrate, thwart. * *n* discomfiture, downfall, overthrow, repulse, rout, vanquishment; bafflement, checkmate, frustration.

defect *vb* abandon, desert, rebel, revolt. * *n* default, deficiency, destitution, lack, shortcoming, spot, taint, want; blemish, blotch, error, flaw, imperfection, mistake; failing, fault, foible.

defection *n* abandonment, desertion, rebellion, revolt; apostasy, backsliding, dereliction.

defective *adj* deficient, inadequate, incomplete, insufficient, scant, short; faulty, imperfect, marred.

defence *n* defending, guarding, holding, maintaining, maintenance, protection; buckler, bulwark, fortification, guard, protection, rampart, resistance, shield; apology, excuse, justification, plea, vindication.

defenceless *adj* exposed, helpless, unarmed, unprotected, unguarded, unshielded, weak.

defend *vb* cover, fortify, guard, preserve, protect, safeguard, screen, secure, shelter, shield; assert, espouse, justify, maintain, plead, uphold, vindicate.

defender *n* asserter, maintainer, pleader, upholder; champion, protector, vindicator.

defer[1] *vb* adjourn, delay, pigeonhole, procrastinate, postpone, prorogue, protract, shelve, table.

defer[2] *vb* abide by, acknowledge, bow to, give way, submit, yield; admire, esteem, honour, regard, respect.

deference *n* esteem, homage, honour, obeisance, regard, respect, reverence, veneration; complaisance, consideration; obedience, submission.

deferential *adj* respectful, reverential.

defiance *n* challenge, daring; contempt, despite, disobedience, disregard, opposition, spite.

defiant *adj* contumacious, recalcitrant, resistant; bold, courageous, resistant.

deficiency *n* dearth, default, deficit, insufficiency, lack, meagreness, scantiness, scarcity, shortage, shortness, want; defect, error, failing, falling, fault, foible, frailty, imperfection, infirmity, weakness.

deficient *adj* defective, faulty, imperfect, inadequate, incomplete, insufficient, lacking, scant, scanty, scarce, short, unsatisfactory, wanting.

deficit *n* deficiency, lack, scarcity, shortage, shortness.

defile[1] *vb* dirty, foul, soil, stain, tarnish; contaminate, debase, poison, pollute, sully, taint, vitiate; corrupt, debauch, deflower, ravish, seduce, violate.

defile[2] *vb* file, march, parade, promenade. * *n* col, gorge, pass, passage, ravine, strait.

define *vb* bound, circumscribe, designate, delimit, demarcate, determine, explain, limit, specify.

definite *adj* defined, determinate, determined, fixed, restricted; assured, certain, clear, exact, explicit, positive, precise, specific, unequivocal.

definitive *adj* categorical, determinate, explicit, express, positive, unconditional; conclusive, decisive, final.

deflect *vb* bend, deviate, diverge, swerve, turn, twist, waver, wind.

deflower *vb* corrupt, debauch, defile, seduce.

deform *vb* deface, disfigure, distort, injure, mar, misshape, ruin, spoil.

deformity *n* abnormality, crookedness, defect, disfigurement, distortion, inelegance, irregularity, malformation, misproportion, misshapenness, monstrosity, ugliness.

defraud *vb* beguile, cheat, chouse, circumvent, cozen, deceive, delude, diddle, dupe, embezzle, gull, overreach, outwit, pilfer, rob, swindle, trick.

defray *vb* bear, discharge, liquidate, meet, pay, settle.

deft *adj* adroit, apt, clever, dab, dextrous, expert, handy, ready, skilful.

defunct *adj* dead, deceased, departed, extinct, gone; abrogated, annulled, cancelled, inoperative.

defy *vb* challenge, dare; brave, contemn, despise, disregard, face, flout, provoke, scorn, slight, spurn.

degeneracy *n* abasement, caducity, corruption, debasement, decadence, decay, declension, decline, decrease, degenerateness, degeneration, degradation, depravation, deterioration; inferiority, meanness, poorness.

degenerate *vb* decay, decline, decrease, deteriorate, retrograde, sink. * *adj* base, corrupt, decayed, degenerated, deteriorated, fallen, inferior, low, mean, perverted.

degeneration *n* debasement, decline, degeneracy, deterioration.

degradation *n* deposition, disgrace, dishonour, humiliation, ignominy; abasement, caducity, corruption, debasement, decadence, decline, degeneracy, degeneration, deterioration, perversion, vitiation.

degrade *vb* abase, alloy, break, cashier, corrupt, debase, demote, discredit, disgrace, dishonour, disparage, downgrade, humiliate, humble, lower, pervert, vitiate; deteriorate, impair, lower, sink.

degree *n* stage, step; class, grade, order, quality, rank, standing, station; extent, measure; division, interval, space.

deify *vb* apotheosize, idolize, glorify, revere; elevate, ennoble, exalt.

deign *vb* accord, condescend, grant, vouchsafe.

deject *vb* depress, discourage, dishearten, dispirit, sadden.

dejected *adj* blue, chapfallen, crestfallen, depressed, despondent, disheartened, dispirited, doleful, downcast, down-hearted, gloomy, low-spirited, miserable, sad, wretched.

delay *vb* defer, postpone, procrastinate; arrest, detain, check, hinder, impede, retard, stay, stop; prolong, protract; dawdle, linger, loiter, tarry. * *n* deferment, postponement, procrastination; check, detention, hindrance, impediment, retardation, stoppage; prolonging, protraction; dallying, dawdling, lingering, tarrying, stay, stop.

delectable *adj* agreeable, charming, delightful, enjoyable, gratifying, pleasant, pleasing.

delectation *n* delight, ecstasy, gladness, joy, rapture, ravishment, transport.

delegate *vb* appoint, authorize, mission, depute, deputize, transfer; commit, entrust. * *n* ambassador, commissioner, delegate, deputy, envoy, representative.

delete *vb* cancel, efface, erase, expunge, obliterate, remove.

deleterious *adj* deadly, destructive, lethal, noxious, poisonous; harmful, hurtful, injurious, pernicious, unwholesome.

deliberate *vb* cogitate, consider, consult, meditate, muse, ponder, reflect, ruminate, think, weigh. * *adj* careful, cautious, circumspect, considerate, heedful, purposeful, methodical, thoughtful, wary; well-advised, well-considered; aforethought, intentional, premeditated, purposed, studied.

deliberation *n* caution, circumspection, cogitation, consideration, coolness, meditation, prudence, reflection, thought, thoughtfulness, wariness; purpose.

delicacy *n* agreeableness, daintiness, deliciousness, pleasantness, relish, savouriness; bonne bouche, dainty, tidbit; elegance, fitness, lightness, niceness, nicety, smoothness, softness, tenderness; fragility, frailty, slenderness, slightness, tenderness, weakness; carefulness, discrimination, fastidiousness, finesse, nicety, scrupulousness, sensitivity, subtlety, tact; purity, refinement, sensibility.

delicate *adj* agreeable, delicious, pleasant, pleasing, palatable, savoury; elegant, exquisite, fine, nice; careful, dainty, discriminating, fastidious, scrupulous; fragile, frail, slender, slight, tender, delicate; pure, refined.

delicious *adj* dainty, delicate, luscious, nice, palatable, savory; agreeable, charming, choice, delightful, exquisite, grateful, pleasant.

delight *vb* charm, enchant, enrapture, gratify, please, ravish, rejoice, satisfy, transport. * *n* charm, delectation, ecstasy, enjoyment, gladness, gratification, happiness, joy, pleasure, rapture, ravishment, satisfaction, transport.

delightful *adj* agreeable, captivating, charming, delectable, enchanting, enjoyable, enrapturing, rapturous, ravishing, transporting.

delineate *vb* design, draw, figure, paint, sketch, trace; depict, describe, picture, portray.

delineation *n* design, draught, drawing, figure, outline, sketch; account, description, picture, portrayal.

delinquency *n* crime, fault, misdeed, misdemeanour, offence, wrong-doing.

delinquent *adj* negligent, offending. * *n* criminal, culprit, defaulter, malefactor, miscreant, misdoer, offender, transgressor, wrong-doer.

delirious *adj* crazy, demented, deranged, frantic, frenzied, light-headed, mad, insane, raving, wandering.

delirium *n* aberration, derangement, frenzy, hallucination, incoherence, insanity, lunacy, madness, raving, wandering.

deliver *vb* emancipate, free, liberate, release; extricate, redeem, rescue, save; commit, give, impart, transfer; cede, grant, relinquish, resign, yield; declare, emit, promulgate, pronounce, speak, utter; deal, discharge.

deliverance *n* emancipation, escape, liberation, redemption, release.

delivery *n* conveyance, surrender; commitment, giving, rendering, transference, transferral, transmission; elocution, enunciation, pronunciation, speech, utterance; childbirth, confinement, labour, parturition, travail.

dell *n* dale, dingle, glen, valley, ravine.

delude *vb* beguile, cheat, chouse, circumvent, cozen, deceive, dupe, gull, misguide, mislead, overreach, trick.

deluge *vb* drown, inundate, overflow, overwhelm, submerge. * *n* cataclysm, downpour, flood, inundation, overflow, rush.

delusion *n* artifice, cheat, clap-trap, deceit, dodge,

fetch, fraud, imposition, imposture, ruse, snare, trick, wile; deception, error, fallacy, fancy, hallucination, illusion, mistake, mockery, phantasm.

delusive *adj* deceitful, deceiving, deceptive, fallacious, illusional, illusionary, illusive.

demand *vb* challenge, exact, require; claim, necessitate, require; ask, inquire. * *n* claim, draft, exaction, requirement, requisition; call, want; inquiry, interrogation, question.

demarcation *n* bound, boundary, confine, distinction, division, enclosure, limit, separation.

demeanour *n* air, bearing, behaviour, carriage, deportment, manner, mien.

demented *adj* crack-brained, crazed, crazy, daft, deranged, dotty, foolish, idiotic, infatuated, insane, lunatic.

dementia *n* idiocy, insanity, lunacy.

demerit *n* delinquency, fault, ill-desert.

demise *vb* alienate, consign, convey, devolve, grant, transfer; bequeath, devise, leave, will. * *n* alienation, conveyance, transfer, transference, transmission; death, decease.

demolish *vb* annihilate, destroy, dismantle, level, over-throw, overturn, pulverize, raze, ruin.

demon *n* devil, fiend, kelpie, goblin, troll.

demoniac, demoniacal *adj* demonic, demonical, devilish, diabolic, diabolical, fiendish, hellish, infernal, Mephistophelean, Mephistophelian, satanic; delirious, distracted, frantic, frenzied, feverish, hysterical, mad, overwrought, rabid.

demonstrate *vb* establish, exhibit, illustrate, indicate, manifest, prove, show.

demonstration *n* display, exhibition, manifestation, show.

demonstrative *adj* affectionate, communicative, effusive, emotional, expansive, expressive, extroverted, open, outgoing, passionate, sentimental, suggestive, talkative, unreserved; absolute, apodictic, certain, conclusive, probative; exemplificative, illustrative.

demoralize *vb* corrupt, debase, debauch, deprave, vitiate; depress, discourage, dishearten, weaken.

demulcent *adj* emollient, lenitive, mild, mollifying, sedative, soothing.

demur *vb* halt, hesitate, pause, stop, waver; doubt, object, scruple. * *n* demurral, hesitance, hesitancy, hesitation, objection, pause, qualm, scruple.

demure *adj* prudish; coy, decorous, grave, modest, priggish, prudish, sedate, sober, staid.

den *n* cavern, cave; haunt, lair, resort, retreat.

denial *n* contradiction, controverting, negation; abjuration, disavowal, disclaimer, disowning; disallowance, refusal, rejection.

denizen *n* citizen, dweller, inhabitant, resident.

denominate *vb* call, christen, designate, dub, entitle, name, phrase, style, term.

denomination *n* appellation, designation, name, style, term, title; class, kind, sort; body, persuasion, school, sect.

denote *vb* betoken, connote, designate, imply, indicate, mark, mean, note, show, signify, typify.

dénouement *n* catastrophe, unravelling; consummation, issue, finale, upshot, conclusion, termination.

denounce *vb* menace, threaten; arraign, attack, brand, censure, condemn, proscribe, stigmatize, upbraid; accuse, inform, denunciate.

dense *adj* close, compact, compressed, condensed, thick; dull, slow, stupid.

dent *vb* depress, dint, indent, pit. * *n* depression, dint, indentation, nick, notch.

dentate *adj* notched, serrate, toothed.

denude *vb* bare, divest, strip.

denunciation *n* menace, threat; arraignment, censure, fulmination, invective; exposure.

deny *vb* contradict, gainsay, oppose, refute, traverse; abjure, abnegate, disavow, disclaim, disown, renounce; disallow, refuse, reject, withhold.

depart *vb* absent, disappear, vanish; abandon, decamp, go, leave, migrate, quit, remove, withdraw; decease, die; deviate, diverge, vary.

department *n* district, division, part, portion, province; bureau, function, office, province, sphere, station; branch, division, subdivision.

departure *n* exit, leaving, parting, removal, recession, removal, retirement, withdrawal; abandonment, forsaking; death, decease, demise, deviation, exit.

depend *vb* hang, hinge, turn.

dependant *n* client, hanger-on, henchman, minion, retainer, subordinate, vassal; attendant, circumstance, concomitant, consequence, corollary.

dependence *n* concatenation, connection, interdependence; confidence, reliance, trust; buttress, prop, staff, stay, support, supporter; contingency, need, subjection, subordination.

dependency *n* adjunct, appurtenance; colony, province.

dependent *adj* hanging, pendant; conditioned, contingent, relying, subject, subordinate.

depict *vb* delineate, limn, outline, paint, pencil, portray, sketch; describe, render, represent.

deplete *vb* drain, empty, evacuate, exhaust, reduce.

deplorable *adj* calamitous, distressful, distressing, grievous, lamentable, melancholy, miserable, mournful, pitiable, regrettable, sad, wretched.

deplore *vb* bemoan, bewail, grieve for, lament, mourn, regret.

deploy *vb* display, expand, extend, open, unfold.

deportment *n* air, bearing, behaviour, breeding, carriage, comportment, conduct, demeanour, manner, mien, port.

depose *vb* break, cashier, degrade, dethrone, dismiss, displace, oust, reduce; avouch, declare, depone, testify.

deposit *vb* drop, dump, precipitate; lay, put; bank, hoard, lodge, put, save, store; commit, entrust. * *n* diluvium, dregs, lees, precipitate, precipitation, sediment, settlement, settlings, silt; money, pawn, pledge, security, stake.

depositary *n* fiduciary, guardian, trustee.

deposition *n* affidavit, evidence, testimony; deposit, precipitation, settlement; dethroning, displacement, removal.

depository *n* deposit, depot, storehouse, warehouse.

depot *n* depository, magazine, storehouse, warehouse.

depravation *n* abasement, corruption, deterioration, impairing, injury, vitiation; debasement, degeneracy, degeneration, depravity, impairment.

depraved *adj* abandoned, corrupt, corrupted, debased, debauched, degenerate, dissolute, evil, graceless, hardened, immoral, lascivious, lewd, licentious, lost, perverted, profligate, reprobate, shameless, sinful, vicious, wicked.

depravity *n* corruption, degeneracy, depravedness; baseness, contamination, corruption, corruptness, criminality, demoralization, immorality, iniquity, license, perversion, vice, viciousness, wickedness.

depreciate *vb* underestimate, undervalue, underrate; belittle, censure, decry, degrade, disparage, malign, traduce.

depreciation *n* belittling, censure, derogation, detraction, disparagement, maligning, traducing.

depredation *n* despoiling, devastation, pilfering, pillage, plunder, rapine, robbery, spoliation, theft.

depress *vb* bow, detrude, drop, lower, reduce, sink; abase, abash, degrade, debase, disgrace, humble, humiliate; chill, damp, dampen, deject, discourage, dishearten, dispirit, sadden; deaden, lower.

depression *n* cavity, concavity, dent, dimple, dint, excavation, hollow, hollowness, indentation, pit; blues, cheerlessness, dejection, dejectedness, despondency, disconsolateness, disheartenment, dispiritedness, dole, dolefulness, downheartedness, dumps, gloom, gloominess, hypochondria, melancholy, sadness, vapours; inactivity, lowness, stagnation; abasement, debasement, degradation, humiliation.

deprivation *n* bereavement, dispossession, loss, privation, spoliation, stripping.

deprive *vb* bereave, denude, despoil, dispossess, divest, rob, strip.

depth *n* abyss, deepness, drop, profundity; extent, measure; middle, midst, stillness; astuteness, discernment, penetration, perspicacity, profoundness, profundity, sagacity, shrewdness.

deputation *n* commission, delegation; commissioners, deputies, delegates, delegation, embassies, envoys, legation.

depute *vb* accredit, appoint, authorize, charge, commission, delegate, empower, entrust.

deputy *adj* acting, assistant, vice, subordinate. * *n* agent, commissioner, delegate, envoy, factor, legate, lieutenant, proxy, representative, substitute, viceregent.

derange *vb* confound, confuse, disarrange, disconcert, disorder, displace, madden, perturb, unsettle; discompose, disconcert, disturb, perturb, ruffle, upset; craze, madden, unbalance, unhinge.

derangement *n* confusion, disarrangement, disorder, irregularity; discomposure, disturbance, perturbation; aberration, alienation, delirium, dementia, hallucination, insanity, lunacy, madness, mania.

derelict *adj* abandoned, forsaken, left, relinquished; delinquent, faithless, guilty, neglectful, negligent, unfaithful. * *n* castaway, castoff, outcast, tramp, vagrant, wreck, wretch.

dereliction *n* abandonment, desertion, relinquishement, renunciation; delinquency, failure, faithlessness, fault, neglect, negligence.

deride *vb* chaff, flout, gibe, insult, jeer, lampoon, mock, ridicule, satirize, scoff, scorn, sneer, taunt.

derision *n* contempt, disrespect, insult, laughter, mockery, ridicule, scorn.

derisive *adj* contemptuous, contumelious, mocking, ridiculing, scoffing, scornful.

derivation *n* descent, extraction, genealogy; etymology; deducing, deriving, drawing, getting, obtaining; beginning, foundation, origination, source.

derive *vb* draw, get, obtain, receive; deduce, follow, infer, trace.

derogate *vb* compromise, depreciate, detract, diminish, disparage, lessen.

derogatory *adj* belittling, depreciative, deprecatory, detracting, dishonouring, disparaging, injurious.

descant *vb* amplify, animadvert, dilate, discourse, discuss, enlarge, expatiate. * *n* melody, soprano, treble; animadversion, commentary, remarks; discourse, discussion.

descend *vb* drop, fall, pitch, plunge, sink, swoop; alight, dismount; go, pass, proceed, devolve; derive, issue, originate.

descendants *npl* offspring, issue, posterity, progeny.

descent *n* downrush, drop, fall; descending; decline, declivity, dip, pitch, slope; ancestry, derivation, extraction, genealogy, lineage, parentage, pedigree; assault, attack, foray, incursion, invasion, raid.

describe *vb* define, delineate, draw, illustrate, limn, sketch, specify, trace; detail; depict, explain, narrate, portray, recount, relate, represent; characterize.

description *n* delineation, tracing; account, depiction, explanation, narration, narrative, portrayal, recital, relation, report, representation; class, kind, sort, species.

descry *vb* behold, discover, discern, distinguish, espy, observe, perceive, see; detect, recognize.

desecrate *vb* abuse, pervert, defile, pollute, profane, violate.

desert[1] *n* due, excellence, merit, worth; punishment, reward.

desert[2] *vb* abandon, abscond, forsake, leave, quit, relinquish, renounce, resign, quit, vacate.

desert³ *adj* barren, desolate, forsaken, lonely, solitary, uncultivated, uninhabited, unproductive, untilled, waste, wild.

deserted *adj* abandoned, forsaken, relinquished.

deserter *n* abandoner, forsaker, quitter, runaway; apostate, backslider, fugitive, recreant, renegade, revolter, traitor, turncoat.

desertion *n* abandonment, dereliction, recreancy, relinquishment.

deserve *vb* earn, gain, merit, procure, win.

desiderate *vb* desire, lack, miss, need, want.

design *vb* brew, concoct, contrive, devise, intend, invent, mean, plan, project, scheme; intend, mean, purpose; delineate, describe, draw, outline, sketch, trace. * *n* aim, device, drift, intent, intention, mark, meaning, object, plan, proposal, project, purport, purpose, scheme, scope; delineation, draught, drawing, outline, plan, sketch; adaptation, artifice, contrivance, invention, inventiveness.

designate *vb* denote, distinguish, indicate, particularize, select, show, specify, stipulate; characterize, define, describe; call, christen, denominate, dub, entitle, name, style; allot, appoint, christen.

designation *n* indication, particularization, selection, specification; class, description, kind; appellation, denomination, name, style, title.

designing *adj* artful, astute, crafty, crooked, cunning, deceitful, insidious, intriguing, Machiavellian, scheming, sly, subtle, treacherous, trickish, tricky, unscrupulous, wily.

desirable *adj* agreeable, beneficial, covetable, eligible, enviable, good, pleasing, preferable.

desire *vb* covet, crave, desiderate, fancy, hanker after, long for, lust after, want, wish, yearn for; ask, entreat, request, solicit. * *n* eroticism, lasciviousness, libidinousness, libido, lust, lustfulness, passion; eagerness, fancy, hope, inclination, mind, partiality, penchant, pleasure, volition, want, wish.

desirous *adj* avid, eager, desiring, longing, solicitous, wishful.

desist *vb* cease, discontinue, forbear, pause, stay, stop.

desolate *vb* depopulate, despoil, destroy, devastate, pillage, plunder, ravage, ruin, sack. * *adj* bare, barren, bleak, desert, forsaken, lonely, solitary, unfrequented, uninhabited, waste, wild; companionable, lonely, lonesome, solitary; desolated, destroyed, devastated, ravaged, ruined; cheerless, comfortless, companionless, disconsolate, dreary, forlorn, forsaken, miserable, wretched.

desolation *n* destruction, devastation, havoc, ravage, ruin; barrenness, bleakness, desolateness, dreariness, loneliness, solitariness, solitude, wildness; gloom, gloominess, misery, sadness, unhappiness, wretchedness.

despair *vb* despond, give up, lose hope. * *n* dejection, desperation, despondency, disheartenment, hopelessness.

despatch *see* **dispatch**.

desperado *n* daredevil, gangster, marauder, ruffian, thug, tough.

desperate *adj* despairing, despondent, desponding, hopeless; forlorn, irretrievable; extreme; audacious, daring, foolhardy, frantic, furious, headstrong, precipitate, rash, reckless, violent, wild, wretched; extreme, great, monstrous, prodigious, supreme.

desperation *n* despair, hopelessness; fury, rage.

despicable *adj* abject, base, contemptible, degrading, low, mean, paltry, pitiful, shameful, sordid, vile, worthless.

despise *vb* contemn, disdain, disregard, neglect, scorn, slight, spurn, undervalue.

despite *n* malevolence, malice, malignity, spite; contempt, contumacy, defiance. * *prep* notwithstanding.

despoil *vb* bereave, denude, deprive, dispossess, divest, strip; devastate, fleece, pillage, plunder, ravage, rifle, rob.

despond *vb* despair, give up, lose hope, mourn, sorrow.

despondency *n* blues, dejection, depression, discouragement, gloom, hopelessness, melancholy, sadness.

despondent *adj* dejected, depressed, discouraged, disheartened, dispirited, low-spirited, melancholy.

despot *n* autocrat, dictator; oppressor, tyrant.

despotic *adj* absolute, arrogant, autocratic, dictatorial, imperious; arbitrary, oppressive, tyrannical, tyrannous.

despotism *n* absolutism, autocracy, dictatorship; oppression, tyranny.

destination *n* appointment, decree, destiny, doom, fate, foreordainment, foreordination, fortune, lot, ordination, star; aim, design, drift, end, intention, object, purpose, scope; bourne, goal, harbour, haven, journey's end, resting-place, terminus.

destine *vb* allot, appoint, assign, consecrate, devote, ordain; design, intend, predetermine; decree, doom, foreordain, predestine.

destitute *adj* distressed, indigent, moneyless, necessitous, needy, penniless, penurious, pinched, poor, reduced, wanting.

destitution *n* indigence, need, penury, poverty, privation, want.

destroy *vb* demolish, overthrow, overturn, subvert, raze, ruin; annihilate, dissolve, efface, quench; desolate, devastate, devour, ravage, waste; eradicate, extinguish, extirpate, kill, uproot, slay.

destruction *n* demolition, havoc, overthrow, ruin, subversion; desolation, devastation, holocaust, ravage; annihilation, eradication, extinction, extirpation; death, massacre, murder, slaughter.

destructive *adj* baleful, baneful, deadly, deleterious, detrimental, fatal, hurtful, injurious, lethal, mischievous, noxious, pernicious, ruinous; annihilatory, eradicative, exterminative, extirpative.

desultory *adj* capricious, cursory, discursive, erratic, fitful, inconstant, inexact, irregular, loose, rambling, roving, slight, spasmodic, unconnected, unmethodical, unsettled, unsystematic, vague, wandering.

detach *vb* disengage, disconnect, disjoin, dissever, disunite, divide, part, separate, sever, unfix; appoint, detail, send.

detail *vb* delineate, depict, describe, enumerate, narrate, particularize, portray, recount, rehearse, relate, specify; appoint, detach, send. * *n* account, narration, narrative, recital, relation; appointment, detachment; item, part.

details *npl* facts, minutiae, particulars, parts.

detain *vb* arrest, check, delay, hinder, hold, keep, restrain, retain, stay, stop; confine.

detect *vb* ascertain, catch, descry, disclose, discover, expose, reveal, unmask.

detention *n* confinement, delay, hindrance, restraint, withholding.

deter *vb* debar, discourage, frighten, hinder, prevent, restrain, stop, withhold.

deteriorate *vb* corrupt, debase, degrade, deprave, disgrace, impair, spoil, vitiate; decline, degenerate, depreciate, worsen.

deterioration *n* corruption, debasement, degradation, depravation, vitiation, perversion; caducity, decadence, decay, decline, degeneracy, degeneration, impairment.

determinate *adj* absolute, certain, definite, determined, established, explicit, express, fixed, limited, positive, settled; conclusive, decided, decisive, definitive.

determination *n* ascertainment, decision, deciding, determining, fixing, settlement, settling; conclusion, judgment, purpose, resolution, resolve, result; direction, leaning, tendency; firmness, constancy, effort, endeavour, exertion, grit, persistence, stamina, resoluteness; definition, limitation, qualification.

determine *vb* adjust, conclude, decide, end, establish, fix, resolve, settle; ascertain, certify, check, verify; impel, incline, induce, influence, lead, turn; decide, resolve; condition, define, limit; compel, necessitate.

detest *vb* abhor, abominate, despise, execrate, hate, loathe, nauseate, recoil from.

detestable *adj* abhorred, abominable, accursed, cursed, damnable, execrable, hateful, odious; disgusting, loathsome, nauseating, offensive, repulsive, sickening, vile.

dethrone *vb* depose, uncrown.

detract *vb* abuse, asperse, belittle, calumniate, debase, decry, defame, depreciate, derogate, disparage, slander, traduce, vilify; deprecate, deteriorate, diminish, lessen.

detraction *n* abuse, aspersion, calumny, censure, defamation, depreciation, derogation, disparagement, slander.

detriment *n* cost, damage, disadvantage, evil, harm, hurt, injury, loss, mischief, prejudice.

detrimental *adj* baleful, deleterious, destructive, harmful, hurtful, injurious, mischievous, pernicious, prejudicial.

devastate *vb* desolate, despoil, destroy, lay waste, harry, pillage, plunder, ravage, sack, spoil, strip, waste.

devastation *n* despoiling, destroying, harrying, pillaging, plundering, ravaging, sacking, spoiling, stripping, wasting; desolation, destruction, havoc, pillage, rapine, ravage, ruin, waste.

develop *vb* disentangle, disclose, evolve, exhibit, explicate, uncover, unfold, unravel; cultivate, grow, mature, open, progress.

development *n* disclosure, disentanglement, exhibition, unfolding, unravelling; growth, increase, maturation, maturing; evolution, growth, progression; elaboration, expansion, explication.

deviate *vb* alter, deflect, digress, diverge, sheer off, slew, tack, turn aside, wheel, wheel about; err, go astray, stray, swerve, wander; differ, vary.

deviation *n* aberration, departure, depression, divarication, divergence, turning; alteration, change, difference, variance, variation.

device *n* contraption, contrivance, gadget, invention; design, expedient, plan, project, resort, resource, scheme, shift; artifice, evasion, fraud, manoeuvre, ruse, stratagem, trick, wile; blazon, emblazonment, emblem, sign, symbol, type.

devil *n* archfiend, demon, fiend, goblin; Apollyon, Belial, Deuce, Evil One, Lucifer, Old Harry, Old Nick, Old Serpent, Prince of Darkness, Satan.

devilish *adj* demon, demonic, demonical, demoniac, demoniacal, diabolic, diabolical, fiendish, hellish, infernal, Mephistophelean, Mephistophelian, satanic; atrocious, barbarous, cruel, malevolent, malicious, malign, malignant, wicked.

devilry *n* devilment, diablerie, mischief; devilishness, fiendishness, wickedness.

devious *adj* deviating, erratic, roundabout, wandering; circuitous, confusing, crooked, labyrinthine, mazy, obscure; crooked, disingenuous, misleading, treacherous.

devise *vb* brew, compass, concert, concoct, contrive, dream up, excogitate, imagine, invent, plan, project, scheme; bequeath, demise, leave, will.

devoid *adj* bare, destitute, empty, vacant, void.

devolve *vb* alienate, consign, convey, deliver over, demise, fall, hand over, make over, pass, transfer.

devote *vb* appropriate, consecrate, dedicate, destine; set apart; addict, apply, give up, resign; consign, doom, give over.

devoted *adj* affectionate, attached, loving; ardent, assiduous, earnest, zealous.

devotee *n* bigot, enthusiast, fan, fanatic, zealot.

devotion *n* consecration, dedication, duty; devotedness, devoutness, fidelity, godliness, holiness, piety, religion, religiousness, saintliness, sanctity; adoration, prayer, worship; affection, attachment, love; ardour, devotedness, eagerness, earnestness, fervour, passion, spirit, zeal.

devotional *adj* devout, godly, pious, religious, saintly.

devour *vb* engorge, gorge, gulp down, raven, swallow eagerly, wolf; annihilate, consume, destroy, expend, spend, swallow up, waste.

devout *adj* devotional, godly, holy, pious, religious, saint-like, saintly; earnest, grave, serious, sincere, solemn.

dexterity *n* ability, address, adroitness, aptitude, aptness, art, cleverness, expertness, facility, knack, quickness, readiness, skilfulness, skill, tact.

dexterous, dextrous *adj* able, adept, adroit, apt, deft, clever, expert, facile, handy, nimble-fingered, quick, ready, skilful.

diabolic, diabolical *adj* atrocious, barbarous, cruel, devilish, fiendish, hellish, impious, infernal, malevolent, malign, malignant, satanic, wicked.

diagram *n* chart, delineation, figure, graph, map, outline, plan, sketch.

dialect *n* idiom, localism, provincialism; jargon, lingo, patois, patter; language, parlance, phraseology, speech, tongue.

dialectal *adj* idiomatic, local, provincial.

dialectic, dialectical *adj* analytical, critical, logical, rational, rationalistic.

dialogue *n* colloquy, communication, conference, conversation, converse, intercourse, interlocution; playbook, script, speech, text, words.

diaphanous *adj* clear, filmy, gossamer, pellucid, sheer, translucent, transparent.

diarrhoea *n* (*med*) flux, looseness, purging, relaxation.

diary *n* chronicle, daybook, journal, register.

diatribe *n* disputation, disquisition, dissertation; abuse, harangue, invective, philippic, reviling, tirade.

dictate *vb* bid, direct, command, decree, enjoin, ordain, order, prescribe, require. * *n* bidding, command, decree, injunction, order; maxim, precept, rule.

dictation *n* direction, order, prescription.

dictator *n* autocrat, despot, tyrant.

dictatorial *adj* absolute, unlimited, unrestricted; authoritative, despotic, dictatory, domineering, imperious, overbearing, peremptory, tyrannical.

dictatorship *n* absolutism, authoritarianism, autocracy, despotism, iron rule, totalitarianism, tyranny.

diction *n* expression, language, phraseology, style, vocabulary, wording.

dictionary *n* glossary, lexicon, thesaurus, vocabulary, wordbook; cyclopedia, encyclopedia.

dictum *n* affirmation, assertion, saying; (*law*) award, arbitrament, decision, opinion.

didactic, didactical *adj* educational, instructive, pedagogic, preceptive.

die *vb* decease, demise, depart, expire, pass on; decay, decline, fade, fade out, perish, wither; cease, disappear, vanish; faint, fall, sink.

diet[1] *vb* eat, feed, nourish; abstain, fast, regulate, slim. * *n* aliment, fare, food, nourishment, nutriment, provision, rations, regimen, subsistence, viands, victuals.

diet[2] *n* assembly, congress, convention, convocation, council, parliament.

differ *vb* deviate, diverge, vary; disagree, dissent; bicker, contend, dispute, quarrel, wrangle.

difference *n* contrariety, contrast, departure, deviation, disagreement, disparity, dissimilarity, dissimilitude, divergence, diversity, heterogeneity, inconformity, nuance, opposition, unlikeness, variation; alienation, altercation, bickering, breach, contention, contest, controversy, debate, disaccord, disagreement, disharmony, dispute, dissension, embroilment, falling out, irreconcilability, jarring, misunderstanding, quarrel, rupture, schism, strife, variance, wrangle; discrimination, distinction.

different *adj* distinct, nonidentical, separate, unlike; contradistinct, contrary, contrasted, deviating, disagreeing, discrepant, dissimilar, divergent, diverse, incompatible, incongruous, unlike, variant, various; divers, heterogeneous, manifold, many, sundry.

difficult *adj* arduous, exacting, hard, Herculean, stiff, tough, uphill; abstruse, complex, intricate, knotty, obscure, perplexing; austere, rigid, unaccommodating, uncompliant, unyielding; dainty, fastidious, squeamish.

difficulty *n* arduousness, laboriousness; bar, barrier, crux, deadlock, dilemma, embarrassment, emergency, exigency, fix, hindrance, impediment, knot, obstacle, obstruction, perplexity, pickle, pinch, predicament, stand, standstill, thwart, trial, trouble; cavil, objection; complication, controversy, difference, embarrassment, embroilment, imbroglio, misunderstanding.

diffidence *n* distrust, doubt, hesitance, hesitancy, hesitation, reluctance; bashfulness, modesty, sheepishness, shyness, timidity.

diffident *adj* distrustful, doubtful, hesitant, hesitating, reluctant; bashful, modest, over-modest, sheepish, shy, timid.

diffuse[1] *vb* circulate, disperse, disseminate, distribute, intermingle, propagate, scatter, spread, strew.

diffuse[2] *adj* broadcast, dispersed, scattered, sparse, sporadic, widespread; broad, extensive, liberal, profuse, wide; copious, loose, prolix, rambling, verbose, wordy.

diffusion *n* circulation, dispersion, dissemination, distribution, extension, propagation, spread, strewing.

diffusive *adj* expansive, permeating, wide-reaching; spreading, dispersive, disseminative, distributive, distributory.

dig *vb* channel, delve, excavate, grub, hollow out, quarry, scoop, tunnel. * *n* poke, punch, thrust.

digest[1] *vb* arrange, classify, codify, dispose, methodize, systemize, tabulate; concoct; assimilate, consider, contemplate, meditate, ponder, reflect upon, study; master; macerate, soak, steep.

digest² *n* code, system; abridgement, abstract, brief, breviary, compend, compendium, conspectus, epitome, summary, synopsis.

dignified *adj* august, courtly, decorous, grave, imposing, majestic, noble, stately.

dignify *vb* advance, aggrandize, elevate, ennoble, exalt, promote; adorn, grace, honour.

dignity *n* elevation, eminence, exaltation, excellence, glory, greatness, honour, place, rank, respectability, standing, station; decorum, grandeur, majesty, nobleness, stateliness; preferment; dignitary, magistrate; elevation, height.

digress *vb* depart, deviate, diverge, expatiate, wander.

digression *n* departure, deviation, divergence; episode, excursus.

dilapidate *vb* demolish, destroy, disintegrate, ruin, waste.

dilapidated *adj* decayed, ruined, run down, wasted.

dilapidation *n* decay, demolition, destruction, disintegration, disrepair, dissolution, downfall, ruin, waste.

dilate *vb* distend, enlarge, expand, extend, inflate, swell, tend, widen; amplify, descant, dwell, enlarge, expatiate.

dilation *n* amplification, bloating, distension, enlargement, expanding, expansion, spreading, swelling.

dilatory *adj* backward, behind-hand, delaying, laggard, lagging, lingering, loitering, off-putting, procrastinating, slack, slow, sluggish, tardy.

dilemma *n* difficulty, fix, plight, predicament, problem, quandary, strait.

diligence *n* activity, application, assiduity, assiduousness, attention, care, constancy, earnestness, heedfulness, industry, laboriousness, perseverance, sedulousness.

diligent *adj* active, assiduous, attentive, busy, careful, constant, earnest, hard-working, indefatigable, industrious, laborious, notable, painstaking, persevering, persistent, sedulous, tireless.

dilly-dally *vb* dally, dawdle. delay, lag, linger, loiter, saunter, trifle.

dilute *vb* attenuate, reduce, thin, weaken. * *adj* attenuated, diluted, thin, weak, wishy-washy.

dim *vb* blur, cloud, darken, dull, obscure, sully, tarnish. * *adj* cloudy, dark, dusky, faint, ill-defined, indefinite, indistinct, mysterious, obscure, shadowy; dull, obtuse; clouded, confused, darkened, faint, obscured; blurred, dulled, sullied, tarnished.

dimension *n* extension, extent, measure.

dimensions *npl* amplitude, bigness, bulk, capacity, greatness, largeness, magnitude, mass, massiveness, size, volume; measurements.

diminish *vb* abate, belittle, contract, decrease, lessen, reduce; curtail, cut, dwindle, melt, narrow, shrink, shrivel, subside, taper off, weaken.

diminution *n* abatement, abridgement, attenuation, contraction, curtailment, decrescendo, cut, decay, decrease, deduction, lessening, reduction, retrenchment, weakening.

diminutive *adj* contracted, dwarfish, little, minute, puny, pygmy, small, tiny.

din *vb* beat, boom, clamour, drum, hammer, pound, repeat, ring, thunder. * *n* bruit, clamour, clash, clatter, crash, crashing, hubbub, hullabaloo, hurlyburly, noise, outcry, racket, row, shout, uproar.

dingle *n* dale, dell, glen, vale, valley.

dingy *adj* brown, dun, dusky; bedimmed, colourless, dimmed, dulled, faded, obscure, smirched, soiled, sullied.

dint *n* blow, stroke; dent, indentation, nick, notch; force, power.

diocese *n* bishopric, charge, episcopate, jurisdiction, see.

dip *vb* douse, duck, immerse, plunge, souse; bail, ladle; dive, pitch; bend, incline, slope. * *n* decline, declivity, descent, drop, fall; concavity, depression, hole, hollow, pit, sink; bathe, dipping, ducking, sousing, swim.

diplomat *n* diplomatist, envoy, legate, minister, negotiator.

dire *adj* alarming, awful, calamitous, cruel, destructive, disastrous, dismal, dreadful, fearful, gloomy, horrible, horrid, implacable, inexorable, portentous, shocking, terrible, terrific, tremendous, woeful.

direct *vb* aim. cast, level, point, turn; advise, conduct, control, dispose, guide, govern, manage, regulate, rule; command, bid, enjoin, instruct, order; lead, show; address, superscribe. * *adj* immediate, straight, undeviating; absolute, categorical, express, plain, unambiguous; downright, earnest, frank, ingenuous, open, outspoken, sincere, straightforward, unequivocal.

direction *n* aim; tendency; bearing, course; administration, conduct, control, government, management, oversight, superintendence; guidance, lead; command, order, prescription; address, superscription.

directly *adv* absolutely, expressly, openly, unambiguously; forthwith, immediately, instantly, quickly, presently, promptly, soon, speedily.

director *n* boss, manager, superintendent; adviser, counsellor, guide, instructor, mentor, monitor.

direful *adj* awful, calamitous, dire, dreadful, fearful, gloomy, horrible, shocking, terrible, terrific, tremendous.

dirge *n* coronach, elegy, lament, monody, requiem, threnody.

dirty *vb* befoul, defile, draggle, foul, pollute, soil, sully. * *adj* begrimed. defiled, filthy, foul, mucky, nasty, soiled, unclean; clouded, cloudy, dark, dull, muddy, sullied; base, beggarly, contemptible, despicable, grovelling, low, mean, paltry, pitiful, scurvy, shabby, sneaking, squalid; disagreeable, rainy, sloppy, uncomfortable.

disability *n* disablement, disqualification, impotence, impotency, inability, incapacity, incompetence, incompetency, unfitness, weakness.

disable *vb* cripple, enfeeble, hamstring, impair, paralyse, unman, weaken; disenable, disqualify, incapacitate, unfit.

disabuse *vb* correct, undeceive.

disadvantage *n* disadvantageousness, inconvenience, unfavourableness; damage, detriment, disservice, drawback, harm, hindrance, hurt, injury, loss, prejudice.

disadvantageous *adj* inconvenient, inexpedient, unfavourable; deleterious, detrimental, harmful, hurtful, injurious, prejudicial.

disaffect *vb* alienate, disdain, dislike, disorder, estrange.

disaffected *adj* alienated, disloyal, dissatisfied, estranged.

disaffection *n* alienation, breach, disagreement, dislike, disloyalty, dissatisfaction, estrangement, repugnance, ill will, unfriendliness.

disagree *vb* deviate, differ, diverge, vary; dissent; argue, bicker, clash, debate, dispute, quarrel, wrangle.

disagreeable *adj* contrary, displeasing, distasteful, nasty, offensive, unpleasant, unpleasing, unsuitable.

disagreement *n* deviation, difference, discrepancy, dissimilarity, dissimilitude, divergence, diversity, incongruity, unlikeness; disaccord, dissent; argument, bickering, clashing, conflict, contention, dispute, dissension, disunion, disunity, jarring, misunderstanding, quarrel, strife, variance, wrangle.

disallow *vb* forbid, prohibit; disapprove, reject; deny, disavow, disclaim, dismiss, disown, repudiate.

disappear *vb* depart, fade, vanish; cease, dissolve.

disappoint *vb* baffle, balk, deceive, defeat, delude, disconcert, foil, frustrate, mortify, tantalize, thwart, vex.

disappointment *n* baffling, balk, failure, foiling, frustration, miscarriage, mortification, unfulfilment.

disapprobation *n* blame, censure, condemnation, disapproval, dislike, displeasure, reproof.

disapprove *vb* blame, censure, condemn, deprecate, dislike; disallow, reject.

disarrange *vb* agitate, confuse, derange, disallow, dishevel, dislike, dislocate, disorder, disorganize, disturb, jumble, reject, rumple, tumble, unsettle.

disarray *n* confusion, disorder; dishabille.

disaster *n* accident, adversity, blow, calamity, casualty, catastrophe, misadventure, mischance, misfortune, mishap, reverse, ruin, stroke.

disastrous *adj* adverse, calamitous, catastrophic, destructive, hapless, ill-fated, ill-starred, ruinous, unfortunate, unlucky, unpropitious, unprosperous, untoward.

disavow *vb* deny, disallow, disclaim, disown.

disband *vb* break up, disperse, scatter, separate.

disbelief *n* agnosticism, doubt, nonconviction, rejection, unbelief.

disburden *vb* alleviate, diminish, disburden, discharge, disencumber, ease, free, relieve, rid.

disbursement *n* expenditure, spending.

discard *vb* abandon, cast off, lay aside, reject; banish, break, cashier, discharge, dismiss, remove, repudiate.

discern *vb* differentiate, discriminate, distinguish, judge; behold, descry, discover, espy, notice, observe, perceive, recognize, see.

discernible *adj* detectable, discoverable, perceptible.

discerning *adj* acute, astute, clear-sighted, discriminating, discriminative, eagle-eyed, ingenious, intelligent, judicious, knowing, perspicacious, piercing, sagacious, sharp, shrewd.

discernment *n* acumen, acuteness, astuteness, brightness, cleverness, discrimination, ingenuity, insight, intelligence, judgement, penetration, perspicacity, sagacity, sharpness, shrewdness; beholding, descrying, discerning, discovery, espial, notice, perception.

discharge *vb* disburden, unburden, unload; eject, emit, excrete, expel, void; cash, liquidate, pay; absolve, acquit, clear, exonerate, free, release, relieve; cashier, discard, dismiss, sack; destroy, remove; execute, perform, fulfil, observe; annul, cancel, invalidate, nullify, rescind. * *n* disburdening, unloading; acquittal, dismissal, displacement, ejection, emission, evacuation, excretion, expulsion, vent, voiding; blast, burst, detonation, explosion, firing; execution, fulfilment, observance; annulment, clearance, liquidation, payment, satisfaction, settlement; exemption, liberation, release; flow, flux, execration.

disciple *n* catechumen, learner, pupil, scholar, student; adherent, follower, partisan, supporter.

discipline *vb* breed, drill, educate, exercise, form, instruct, teach, train; control, govern, regulate, school; chasten, chastise, punish. * *n* culture, drill, drilling, education, exercise, instruction, training; control, government, regulation, subjection; chastisement, correction, punishment.

disclaim *vb* abandon, disallow, disown, disavow; reject, renounce, repudiate.

disclose *vb* discover, exhibit, expose, manifest, uncover; bare, betray, blab, communicate, divulge, impart, publish, reveal, show, tell, unfold, unveil, utter.

disclosure *n* betrayal, discovery, exposé, exposure, revelation, uncovering. discolour *vb* stain, tarnish, tinge.

discomfit *vb* beat, checkmate, conquer, defeat, overcome, overpower, overthrow, rout, subdue, vanquish, worst; abash, baffle, balk, confound, disconcert, foil, frustrate, perplex, upset.

discomfiture *n* confusion, defeat, frustration, overthrow, rout, vexation.

discomfort *n* annoyance, disquiet, distress, inquietude, malaise, trouble, uneasiness, unpleasantness, vexation.

discommode *vb* annoy, disquiet, disturb, harass, incommode, inconvenience, molest, trouble.

discompose *vb* confuse, derange, disarrange, disorder, disturb, embroil, jumble, unsettle; agitate, annoy, chafe, displease, disquiet, fret, harass, irritate, nettle, plague, provoke, ruffle, trouble, upset, vex, worry; abash, bewilder, disconcert, embarrass, fluster, perplex.

disconcert *vb* baffle, balk, contravene, defeat, disarrange, frustrate, interrupt, thwart, undo, upset; abash, agitate, bewilder, confuse, demoralize, discompose, disturb, embarrass, faze, perplex, perturb, unbalance, worry.

disconnect *vb* detach, disengage, disjoin, dissociate, disunite, separate, sever, uncouple, unlink.

disconsolate *adj* broken-hearted, cheerless, comfortless, dejected, desolate, forlorn, gloomy, heartbroken, inconsolable, melancholy, miserable, sad, sorrowful, unhappy, woeful, wretched.

discontent *n* discontentment, displeasure, dissatisfaction, inquietude, restlessness, uneasiness.

discontinuance *n* cessation, discontinuation, disjunction, disruption, intermission, interruption, separation, stop, stoppage, stopping, suspension.

discontinue *vb* cease, intermit, interrupt, quit, stop.

discord *n* contention, difference, disagreement, dissension, opposition, quarrelling, rupture, strife, variance, wrangling; cacophony, discordance, dissonance, harshness, jangle, jarring.

discordance *n* conflict, disagreement, incongruity, inconsistency, opposition, repugnance; discord, dissonance.

discordant *adj* contradictory, contrary, disagreeing, incongruous, inconsistent, opposite, repugnant; cacophonous, dissonant, harsh, inharmonious, jangling, jarring.

discount *vb* allow for, deduct, lower, rebate, reduce, subtract; disregard, ignore, overlook. * *n* abatement, drawback; allowance, deduction, rebate, reduction.

discourage *vb* abase, awe, damp, daunt, deject, depress, deject, dismay, dishearten, dispirit, frighten, intimidate; deter, dissuade, hinder; disfavour, discountenance.

discouragement *n* disheartening; dissuasion; damper, deterrent, embarrassment, hindrance, impediment, obstacle, wet blanket.

discourse *vb* expiate, hold forth, lucubrate, sermonize, speak; advise, confer, converse, parley, talk; emit, utter. * *n* address, disquisition, dissertation, homily, lecture, preachment, sermon, speech, treatise; colloquy, conversation, converse, talk.

discourteous *adj* abrupt, brusque, curt, disrespectful, ill-bred, ill-mannered, impolite, inurbane, rude, uncivil, uncourtly, ungentlemanly, unmannerly.

discourtesy *n* abruptness, brusqueness, ill-breeding, impoliteness, incivility, rudeness.

discover *vb* communicate, disclose, exhibit, impart, manifest, show, reveal, tell; ascertain, behold, discern, espy, see; descry, detect, determine, discern; contrive, invent, originate.

discredit *vb* disbelieve, doubt, question; depreciate, disgrace, dishonour, disparage, reproach. * *n* disbelief, distrust; disgrace, dishonour, disrepute, ignominy, notoriety, obloquy, odium, opprobrium, reproach, scandal.

discreditable *adj* derogatory, disgraceful, disreputable, dishonourable, ignominious, infamous, inglorious, scandalous, unworthy.

discreet *adj* careful, cautious, circumspect, considerate, discerning, heedful, judicious, prudent, sagacious, wary, wise.

discrepancy *n* contrariety, difference, disagreement, discordance, dissonance, divergence, incongruity, inconsistency, variance, variation.

discrete *adj* discontinuous, disjunct, distinct, separate; disjunctive.

discretion *n* care, carefulness, caution, circumspection, considerateness, consideration, heedfulness, judgement, judicious, prudence, wariness; discrimination, maturity, responsibility; choice, option, pleasure, will.

discrimination *n* difference, distinction; acumen, acuteness, discernment, in-sight, judgement, penetration, sagacity.

discriminatory *adj* characteristic, characterizing, discriminating, discriminative, distinctive, distinguishing.

discursive *adj* argumentative, reasoning; casual, cursory, desultory, digressive, erratic, excursive, loose, rambling, roving, wandering, wave.

discus *n* disk, quoit.

discuss *vb* agitate, argue, canvass, consider, debate, deliberate, examine, sift, ventilate.

disdain *vb* contemn, deride, despise, disregard, reject, scorn, slight, scout, spurn. * *n* arrogance, contempt, contumely, haughtiness, hauteur, scorn, sneer, superciliousness.

disdainful *adj* cavalier, contemptuous, contumelious, haughty, scornful, supercilious.

disease *n* affection, affliction, ail, ailment, complaint, disorder, distemper, illness, indisposition, infirmity, malady, sickness.

disembarrass *vb* clear, disburden, disencumber, disengage, disentangle, extricate, ease, free, release, rid.

disembodied *adj* bodiless, disincarnate, immaterial, incorporeal, spiritual, unbodied.

disembowel *vb* degut, embowel, eviscerate.

disengage *vb* clear, deliver, discharge, disembarrass, disembroil, disencumber, disentangle, extricate, liberate, release; detach, disjoin, dissociate, disunite, divide, separate; wean, withdraw.

disentangle *vb* loosen, separate, unfold, unravel, untwist; clear, detach, disconnect, disembroil, disengage, extricate, liberate, loose, unloose.

disfavour *n* disapproval, disesteem, dislike, disrespect; discredit, disregard, disrepute, unacceptableness;

disservice, unkindness. * *vb* disapprove, dislike, object, oppose.

disfigure *vb* blemish, deface, deform, injure, mar, spoil.

disfigurement *n* blemishing, defacement, deforming, disfiguration, injury, marring, spoiling; blemish, defect, deformity, scar, spot, stain.

disgorge *vb* belch, cast up, spew, throw up, vomit; discharge, eject; give up, relinquish, surrender, yield.

disgrace *vb* degrade, humble, humiliate; abase, debase, defame, discredit, disfavour, dishonour, disparage, reproach, stain, sully, taint, tarnish. * *n* abomination, disrepute, humiliation, ignominy, infamy, mortification, shame, scandal.

disgraceful *adj* discreditable, dishonourable, disreputable, ignominious, infamous, opprobrious, scandalous, shameful.

disguise *vb* cloak, conceal, cover, dissemble, hide, mask, muffle, screen, secrete, shroud, veil. * *n* concealment, cover, mask, veil; blind, cloak, masquerade, pretence, pretext, veneer.

disguised *adj* cloaked, masked, veiled.

disgust *vb* nauseate, sicken; abominate, detest, displease, offend, repel, repulse, revolt. * *n* disrelish, distaste, loathing, nausea; abhorrence, abomination, antipathy, aversion, detestation, dislike, repugnance, revulsion.

dish *vb* deal out, give, ladle, serve; blight, dash, frustrate, mar, ruin, spoil. * *n* bowl, plate, saucer, vessel.

dishearten *vb* cast down, damp, dampen, daunt, deject, depress, deter, discourage, dispirit.

dished *adj* baffled, balked, disappointed, disconcerted, foiled, frustrated, upset.

dishevelled *adj* disarranged, disordered, messed, tousled, tumbled, unkempt, untidy, untrimmed.

dishonest *adj* cheating, corrupt, crafty, crooked, deceitful, deceiving, deceptive, designing, faithless, false, falsehearted, fraudulent, guileful, knavish, perfidious, slippery, treacherous, unfair, unscrupulous.

dishonesty *n* deceitfulness, faithlessness, falsehood, fraud, fraudulence, fraudulency, improbity, knavery, perfidious, treachery, trickery.

dishonour *vb* abase, defame, degrade, discredit, disfavour, dishonour, disgrace, disparage, reproach, shame, taint. * *n* abasement, basement, contempt, degradation, discredit, disesteem, disfavour, disgrace, dishonour, disparagement, disrepute, ignominy, infamy, obloquy, odium, opprobrium, reproach, scandal, shame.

dishonourable *adj* discreditable, disgraceful, disreputable, ignominious, infamous, scandalous, shameful; base, false, falsehearted, shameless.

disinclination *n* alienation, antipathy, aversion, dislike, indisposition, reluctance, repugnance, unwillingness.

disinfect *vb* cleanse, deodorize, fumigate, purify, sterilize.

disingenuous *adj* artful, deceitful, dishonest, hollow, insidious, insincere, uncandid, unfair, wily.

disintegrate *vb* crumble, decompose, dissolve, disunite, pulverize, separate.

disinter *vb* dig up, disentomb, disinhume, exhume, unbury.

disinterested *adj* candid, fair, high-minded, impartial, indifferent, unbiased, unselfish, unprejudiced; generous, liberal, magnanimous.

disjoin *vb* detach, disconnect, dissever, dissociate, disunite, divide, part, separate, sever, sunder.

disjointed *adj* desultory, disconnected, incoherent, loose.

disjunction *n* disassociation, disconnection, disunion, isolation, parting, separation, severance.

dislike *vb* abominate, detest, disapprove, disrelish, hate, loathe. * *n* antagonism, antipathy, aversion, disapproval, disfavour, disgust, disinclination, displeasure, disrelish, distaste, loathing, repugnance.

dislocate *vb* disarrange, displace, disturb; disarticulate, disjoint, luxate, slip.

dislodge *vb* dismount, dispel, displace, eject, expel, oust, remove.

disloyal *adj* disaffected, faithless, false, perfidious, traitorous, treacherous, treasonable, undutiful, unfaithful, unpatriotic, untrue.

disloyalty *n* faithlessness, perfidy, treachery, treason, undutifulness, unfaithfulness.

dismal *adj* cheerless, dark, dreary, dull, gloomy, lonesome; blue, calamitous, doleful, dolorous, funereal, lugubrious, melancholy, mournful, sad, sombre, sorrowful.

dismantle *vb* divest, strip, unrig.

dismay *vb* affright, alarm, appal, daunt, discourage, dishearten, frighten, horrify, intimidate, paralyse, scare, terrify. * *n* affright, alarm, consternation, fear, fright, horror, terror.

dismember *vb* disjoint, dislimb, dislocate, mutilate; divide, separate, rend, sever.

dismiss *vb* banish, cashier, discard, discharge, disperse, reject, release, remove.

dismount *vb* alight, descend, dismantle, unhorse; dislodge, displace.

disobedient *adj* froward, noncompliant, noncomplying, obstinate, rebellious, refractory, uncomplying, undutiful, unruly, unsubmissive.

disobey *vb* infringe, transgress, violate.

disobliging *adj* ill-natured, unaccommodating, unamiable, unfriendly, unkind.

disorder *vb* confound, confuse, derange, disarrange, discompose, disorganize, disturb, unsettle, upset. * *n* confusion, derangement, disarrangement, disarray, disorganization, irregularity, jumble, litter, mess, topsy-turvy; brawl, commotion, disturbance, fight, quarrel, riot, tumult; riotousness, tumultuousness, turbulence; ail, ailment, complaint, distemper, illness, indisposition, malady, sickness.

disorderly *adj* chaotic, confused, intemperate, irregular, unmethodical, unsystematic, untidy; lawless, rebellious, riotous, tumultuous, turbulent, ungovernable, unmanageable, unruly.

disorganization *n* chaos, confusion, demoralization, derangement, disorder.

disorganize *vb* confuse, demoralize, derange, disarrange, discompose, disorder, disturb, unsettle, upset.

disown *vb* disavow, disclaim, reject, renounce, repudiate; abnegate, deny, disallow.

disparage *vb* belittle, decry, depreciate, derogate from, detract from, doubt, question, run down, underestimate, underpraise, underrate, undervalue; asperse, defame, inveigh against, reflect on, reproach, slur, speak ill of, traduce, vilify.

disparagement *n* belittlement, depreciation, derogation, detraction, underrating, undervaluing; derogation, detraction, diminution, harm, impairment, injury, lessening, prejudice, worsening; aspersion, calumny, defamation, reflection, reproach, traduction, vilification; blackening, disgrace, dispraise, indignity, reproach.

disparity *n* difference, disproportion, inequality; dissimilarity, dissimilitude, unlikeness.

dispassionate *adj* calm, collected, composed, cool, imperturbable, inexcitable, moderate, quiet, serene, sober, staid, temperate, undisturbed, unexcitable, unexcited, unimpassioned, unruffled; candid, disinterested, fair, impartial, neutral, unbiased.

dispatch, despatch *vb* assassinate, kill, murder, slaughter, slay; accelerate, conclude, dismiss, expedite, finish, forward, hasten, hurry, quicken, speed. * *n* dispatching, sending; diligence, expedition, haste, rapidity, speed; completion, conduct, doing, transaction; communication, document, instruction, letter, message, missive, report.

dispel *vb* banish, disperse, dissipate, scatter.

dispensation *n* allotment, apportioning, apportionment, dispensing, distributing, distribution; administration, stewardship; economy, plan, scheme, system; exemption, immunity, indulgence, licence, privilege.

dispense *vb* allot, apportion, assign, distribute; administer, apply, execute; absolve, excuse, exempt, exonerate, release, relieve.

disperse *vb* dispel, dissipate, dissolve, scatter, separate; diffuse, disseminate, spread; disappear, vanish.

dispirit *vb* damp, dampen, depress, deject, discourage, dishearten.

dispirited *adj* chapfallen, dejected, depressed, discouraged, disheartened, down-cast, downhearted.

displace *vb* dislocate, mislay, misplace, move; dislodge, remove; cashier, depose, discard, discharge, dismiss, oust, replace, unseat.

display *vb* expand, extend, open, spread, unfold; exhibit, show; flaunt, parade. * *n* exhibition, manifestation, show; flourish, ostentation, pageant, parade, pomp.

displease *vb* disgruntle, disgust, disoblige, dissatisfy, offend; affront, aggravate, anger, annoy, chafe, chagrin, fret, irritate, nettle, pique, provoke, vex.

displeasure *n* disaffection, disapprobation, disapproval, dislike, dissatisfaction, distaste; anger, annoyance, indignation, irritation, pique, resentment, vexation, wrath; injury, offence.

disport *vb* caper, frisk, frolic, gambol, play, sport, wanton; amuse, beguile, cheer, divert, entertain, relax, solace.

disposal *n* arrangement, disposition; conduct, control, direction, disposure, government, management, ordering, regulation; bestowment, dispensation, distribution.

dispose *vb* arrange, distribute, marshal, group, place, range, rank, set; adjust, determine, regulate, settle; bias, incline, induce, lead, move, predispose; control, decide, regulate, rule, settle; arrange, bargain, compound; alienate, convey, demise, sell, transfer.

disposed *adj* apt, inclined, prone, ready, tending.

disposition *n* arrangement, arranging, classification, disposing, grouping, location, placing; adjustment, control, direction, disposure, disposal, management, ordering, regulation; aptitude, bent, bias, inclination, nature, predisposition, proclivity, proneness, propensity, tendency; character, constitution, humour, native, nature, temper, temperament, turn; inclination, willingness; bestowal, bestowment, dispensation, distribution.

dispossess *vb* deprive, divest, expropriate, strip; dislodge, eject, oust; disseise, disseize, evict, oust.

dispraise *n* blame, censure; discredit, disgrace, dishonour, disparagement, opprobrium, reproach, shame.

disproof *n* confutation, rebuttal, refutation.

disproportion *n* disparity, inadequacy, inequality, insufficiency, unsuitableness; incommensurateness.

disprove *vb* confute, rebel, rebut.

disputable *adj* controvertible, debatable, doubtful, questionable.

disputation *n* argumentation, controversy, debate, dispute.

disputatious *adj* argumentative, bickering, captious, caviling, contentious, dissentious, litigious, polemical, pugnacious, quarrelsome.

dispute *vb* altercate, argue, debate, litigate, question; bicker, brawl, jangle, quarrel, spar, spat, squabble, tiff, wrangle; agitate, argue, debate, ventilate; challenge, contradict, controvert, deny, impugn; contest, struggle for. * *n* controversy, debate, discussion, disputation; altercation, argument, bickering, brawl, disagreement, dissension, spat, squabble, tiff, wrangle.

disqualification *n* disability, incapitation.

disqualify *vb* disable, incapacitate, unfit; disenable, preclude, prohibit.

disquiet *vb* agitate, annoy, bother, discompose, disturb, excite, fret, harass, incommode, molest, plague, pester, trouble, vex, worry. * *n* anxiety, discomposure, disquietude, disturbance, restlessness, solicitude, trouble, uneasiness, unrest, vexation, worry.

disquisition *n* dissertation, discourse, essay, paper, thesis, treatise.

disregard *vb* contemn, despise, disdain, disobey, disparage, ignore, neglect, overlook, slight. * *n* contempt, ignoring, inattention, neglect, pretermit, oversight, slight; disesteem, disfavour, indifference.

disrelish *vb* dislike, loathe. * *n* dislike, distaste; flatness, insipidity, insipidness, nauseousness; antipathy, aversion, repugnance.

disreputable *adj* derogatory, discreditable, dishonourable, disgraceful, infamous, opprobrious, scandalous, shameful; base, contemptible, low, mean, vicious, vile, vulgar.

disrepute *n* abasement, degradation, derogation, discredit, disgrace, dishonour, ill-repute, odium.

disrespect *n* disesteem, disregard, irreverence, neglect, slight.

disrespectful *adj* discourteous, impertinent, impolite, rude, uncivil, uncourteous.

dissatisfaction *n* discontent, disquiet, inquietude, uneasiness; disapprobation, disapproval, dislike, displeasure.

dissect *vb* analyze, examine, explore, investigate, scrutinize, sift; cut apart.

dissemble *vb* cloak, conceal, cover, disguise, hide; counterfeit, dissimulate, feign, pretend.

dissembler *n* dissimulator, feigner, hypocrite, pretender, sham.

disseminate *vb* circulate, diffuse, disperse, proclaim, promulgate, propagate, publish, scatter, spread.

dissension *n* contention, difference, disagreement, discord, quarrel, strife, variance.

dissent *vb* decline, differ, disagree, refuse. * *n* difference, disagreement, nonconformity, opposition, recusancy, refusal.

dissentient *adj* disagreeing, dissenting, dissident, factious.

dissertation *n* discourse, disquisition, essay, thesis, treatise.

disservice *n* disadvantage, disfavour, harm, hurt, ill-turn, injury, mischief.

dissidence *n* disagreement, dissent, nonconformity, sectarianism.

dissimilar *adj* different, divergent, diverse, heterogeneous, unlike, various.

dissimilarity *n* dissimilitude, disparity, divergent, diversity, unlikeness, variation.

dissimulation *n* concealment, deceit, dissembling, double-dealing, duplicity, feigning, hypocrisy, pretence.

dissipate *vb* dispel, disperse, scatter; consume, expend, lavish, spend, squander, waste; disappear, vanish.

dissipation *n* dispersion, dissemination, scattering, vanishing; squandering, waste; crapulence, debauchery, dissoluteness, drunkenness, excess, profligacy.

dissociate *vb* disjoin, dissever, disunite, divide, separate, sever, sunder.

dissolute *adj* abandoned, corrupt, debauched, depraved, disorderly, dissipated, graceless, lax, lewd, licentious, loose, profligate, rakish, reprobate, shameless, vicious, wanton, wild.

dissolution *n* liquefaction, melting, solution; decomposition, putrefaction; death, disease; destruction, overthrow, ruin; termination.

dissolve *vb* liquefy, melt; disorganize, disunite, divide, loose, separate, sever; destroy, ruin; disappear, fade, scatter, vanish; crumble, decompose, disintegrate, perish.

dissonance *n* cacophony, discord, discordance, harshness, jarring; disagreement, discrepancy, incongruity, inconsistency.

dissonant *adj* discordant, grating, harsh, jangling, jarring, unharmonious; contradictory, disagreeing, discrepant, incongruous, inconsistent.

distance *vb* excel, outdo, outstrip, surpass. * *n* farness, remoteness; aloofness, coldness, frigidity, reserve, stiffness, offishness; absence, separation, space.

distant *adj* far, far-away, remote; aloof, ceremonious, cold, cool, frigid, haughty, reserved, stiff, uncordial; faint, indirect, obscure, slight.

distaste *n* disgust, disrelish; antipathy, aversion, disinclination, dislike, displeasure, dissatisfaction, repugnance.

distasteful *adj* disgusting, loathsome, nauseating, nauseous, unpalatable, unsavoury; disagreeable, displeasing, offensive, repugnant, repulsive, unpleasant.

distemper *n* ail, ailment, complaint, disease, disorder, illness, indisposition, malady, sickness.

distempered *adj* diseased, disordered; immoderate, inordinate, intemperate, unregulated.

distend *vb* bloat, dilate, enlarge, expand, increase, inflate, puff, stretch, swell, widen.

distil *vb* dribble, drip, drop; extract, separate.

distinct *adj* definite, different, discrete, disjunct, individual, separate, unconnected; clear, defined, manifest, obvious, plain, unconfused, unmistakable, well-defined.

distinction *n* discernment, discrimination, distinguishing; difference; account, celebrity, credit, eminence, fame, name, note, rank, renown, reputation, repute, respectability, superiority.

distinctive *adj* characteristic, differentiating, discriminating, distinguishing.

distinctness *n* difference, separateness; clearness, explicitness, lucidity, lucidness, perspicuity, precision.

distinguish *vb* characterize, mark; differentiate, discern, discriminate, perceive, recognize, see, single out, tell; demarcate, divide, separate; celebrate, honour, signalize.

distinguished *adj* celebrated, eminent, famous, illustrious, noted; conspicuous, extraordinary, laureate, marked, shining, superior, transcendent.

distort *vb* contort, deform, gnarl, screw, twist, warp, wrest; falsify, misrepresent, pervert.

distortion *n* contortion, deformation, deformity, twist, wryness; falsification, misrepresentation, perversion, wresting.

distract *vb* divert, draw away; bewilder, confound, confuse, derange, discompose, disconcert, disturb, embarrass, harass, madden, mystify, perplex, puzzle.

distracted *adj* crazed, crazy, deranged, frantic, furious, insane, mad, raving, wild.

distraction *n* abstraction, bewilderment, confusion, mystification, embarrassment, perplexity; agitation, commotion, discord, disorder, disturbance, division, perturbation, tumult, turmoil; aberration, alienation, delirium, derangement, frenzy, hallucination, incoherence, insanity, lunacy, madness, mania, raving, wandering.

distress *vb* afflict, annoy, grieve, harry, pain, perplex, rack, trouble; distrain, seize, take. * *n* affliction, calamity, disaster, misery, misfortune, adversity, hardship, perplexity, trial, tribulation; agony, anguish, dolour, grief, sorrow, suffering; gnawing, gripe, griping, pain, torment, torture; destitution, indigence, poverty, privation, straits, want.

distribute *vb* allocate, allot, apportion, assign, deal, dispense, divide, dole out, give, mete, partition, prorate, share; administer, arrange, assort, class, classify, dispose.

distribution *n* allocation, allotment, apportionment, assignment, assortment, dispensation, dispensing; arrangement, disposal, disposition, classification, division, dole, grouping, partition, sharing.

district *n* circuit, department, neighbourhood, province, quarter, region, section, territory, tract, ward.

distrust *vb* disbelieve, discredit, doubt, misbelieve, mistrust, question, suspect. * *n* doubt, misgiving, mistrust, question, suspicion.

distrustful *adj* doubting, dubious, suspicious.

disturb *vb* agitate, shake, stir; confuse, derange, disarrange, disorder, unsettle, upset; annoy, discompose, disconcert, disquiet, distract, fuss, incommode, molest, perturb, plague, trouble, ruffle, vex, worry; impede, interrupt, hinder.

disturbance *n* agitation, commotion, confusion, convulsion, derangement, disorder, perturbation, unsettlement; annoyance, discomposure, distraction, excitement, fuss; hindrance, interruption, molestation; brawl, commotion, disorder, excitement, fracas, hubbub, riot, rising, tumult, turmoil, uproar.

disunion *n* disconnection, disjunction, division, separation, severance; breach, feud, rupture, schism.

disunite *vb* detach, disconnect, disjoin, dissever, dissociate, divide, part, rend, separate, segregate, sever, sunder; alienate, estrange.

disuse *n* desuetude, discontinuance, disusage, neglect, nonobservance.

ditch *vb* canalize, dig, excavate, furrow, gouge, trench; abandon, discard, dump, jettison, scrap. * *n* channel, drain, fosse, moat, trench.

divagation *n* deviation, digression, rambling, roaming, straying, wandering.

divan *n* bed, chesterfield, couch, settee, sofa.

divaricate *vb* diverge, fork, part.

dive *vb* explore, fathom, penetrate, plunge, sound. * *n* drop, fall, header, plunge; bar, den, dump, joint, saloon.

diverge *vb* divide, radiate, separate; divaricate, separate; deviate, differ, disagree, vary.

divers *adj* different, manifold, many, numerous, several, sundry, various.

diverse *adj* different, differing, disagreeing, dissimilar, divergent, heterogeneous, multifarious, multiform, separate, unlike, variant, various, varying.

diversion *n* deflection, diverting; amusement, delight, distraction, enjoyment, entertainment, game, gratification, pastime, play, pleasure, recreation, sport; detour, digression.

diversity *n* difference, dissimilarity, dissimilitude, divergence, unlikeness, variation; heterogeneity, manifoldness, multifariousness, multiformity, variety.

divert *vb* deflect, distract, disturb; amuse, beguile, delight, entertain, exhilarate, give pleasure, gratify, recreate, refresh, solace.

divest *vb* denude, disrobe, strip, unclothe, undress; deprive, dispossess, strip.

divide *vb* bisect, cleave, cut, dismember, dissever, disunite, open, part, rend, segregate, separate, sever, shear, split, sunder; allocate, allot, apportion, assign, dispense, distribute, dole, mete, portion, share; compartmentalize, demarcate, partition; alienate, disunite, estrange.

divination *n* augury, divining, foretelling, incantation, magic, sooth-saying, sorcery; prediction, presage, prophecy.

divine *vb* foretell, predict, presage, prognosticate, vaticinate, prophesy; believe, conjecture, fancy, guess, suppose, surmise, suspect, think. * *adj* deiform, godlike, superhuman, supernatural; angelic, celestial, heavenly, holy, sacred, seraphic, spiritual; exalted, exalting, rapturous, supreme, transcendent. * *n* churchman, clergyman, ecclesiastic, minister, parson, pastor, priest.

division *n* compartmentalization, disconnection, disjunction, dismemberment, segmentation, separation, severance; category, class, compartment, head, parcel, portion, section, segment; demarcation, partition; alienation, allotment, apportionment, distribution; breach, difference, disagreement, discord, disunion, estrangement, feud, rupture, variance.

divorce *vb* disconnect, dissolve, disunite, part, put away, separate, sever, split up, sunder, unmarry. * *n* disjunction, dissolution, disunion, division, divorcement, parting, separation, severance.

divulge *vb* communicate, declare, disclose, discover, exhibit, expose, impart, proclaim, promulgate, publish, reveal, tell, uncover.

dizzy *adj* giddy, vertiginous; careless, heedless, thoughtless.

do *vb* accomplish, achieve, act, commit, effect, execute, perform; complete, conclude, end, finish, settle, terminate; conduct, transact; observe, perform, practice; translate, render; cook, prepare; cheat, chouse, cozen, hoax, swindle; serve, suffice. * *n* act, action, adventure, deed, doing, exploit, feat, thing; banquet, event, feast, function, party.

docile *adj* amenable, obedient, pliant, teachable, tractable, yielding.

dock[1] *vb* clip, curtail, cut, deduct, truncate; lessen, shorten.

dock[2] *vb* anchor, moor; join, meet. * *n* anchorage, basin, berth, dockage, dockyard, dry dock, harbour, haven, marina, pier, shipyard, wharf.

doctor *vb* adulterate, alter, cook, falsify, manipulate, tamper with; attend, minister to, cure, heal, remedy, treat; fix, mend, overhaul, repair, service. * *n* general practitioner, GP, healer, leech, medic, physician; adept, savant.

doctrinaire *adj* impractical, theoretical. * *n* ideologist, theorist, thinker.

doctrine *n* article, belief, creed, dogma, opinion, precept, principle, teaching, tenet.

dodge *vb* equivocate, evade, prevaricate, quibble, shuffle. * *n* artifice, cavil, evasion, quibble, subterfuge, trick.

dogged *adj* cantankerous, headstrong, inflexible, intractable, mulish, obstinate, pertinacious, perverse, resolute, stubborn, tenacious, unyielding, wilful; churlish, morose, sour, sullen, surly.

dogma *n* article, belief, creed, doctrine, opinion, precept, principle, tenet.

dogmatic *adj* authoritative, categorical, formal, settled; arrogant, confident, dictatorial, imperious, magisterial, opinionated, oracular, overbearing, peremptory, positive; doctrinal.

dole *vb* allocate, allot, apportion, assign, deal, distribute, divide, share. * *n* allocation, allotment, apportionment, distribution; part, portion, share; alms, donation, gift, gratuity, pittance; affliction, distress, grief, sorrow, woe.

doleful *adj* lugubrious, melancholy, piteous, rueful, sad, sombre, sorrowful, woebegone, woeful; cheerless, dark, dismal, dolorous, dreary, gloomy.

dolorous *adj* cheerless, dark, dismal, gloomy; doleful, lugubrious, mournful, piteous, rueful, sad, sorrowful, woeful.

dolt *n* blockhead, booby, dullard, dunce, fool, ignoramus, simpleton.

domain *n* authority, dominion, jurisdiction, province, sway; empire, realm, territory; lands, estate; branch, department, region.

domestic *n* charwoman, help, home help, maid, servant. * *adj* domiciliary, family, home, household, private; domesticated; internal, intestine.

domesticate *vb* tame; adopt, assimilate, familiarize, naturalize.

domicile *vb* domiciliate, dwell, inhabit, live, remain, reside. * *n* abode, dwelling, habitation, harbour, home, house, residence.

dominant *adj* ascendant, ascending, chief, controlling, governing, influential, outstanding, paramount, predominant, pre-eminent, preponderant, presiding, prevailing, ruling.

dominate *vb* control, rule, sway; command, overlook, overtop, surmount.

domineer *vb* rule, tyrannize; bluster, bully, hector, menace, swagger, swell, threaten.

dominion *n* ascendancy, authority, command, control, domain, domination, government, jurisdiction, mastery, rule, sovereign, sovereignty, supremacy, sway; country, kingdom, realm, region, territory.

donation *n* alms, benefaction, boon, contribution, dole, donative, gift, grant, gratuity, largesse, offering, present, subscription.

done *adj* accomplished, achieved, effected, executed, performed; completed, concluded, ended, finished, terminated; carried on, transacted; rendered, translated; cooked, prepared; cheated, cozened, hoaxed, swindled; (*with* **for**) damned, dished, *hors de combat*, ruined, shelved, spoiled, wound up.

donkey *n* ass, mule; dunce, fool, simpleton.

donor *n* benefactor, bestower, giver; donator.

double *vb* fold, plait; duplicate, geminate, increase, multiply, repeat; return. * *adj* binary, coupled, geminate, paired; dual, twice, twofold; deceitful, dishonest, double-dealing, false, hollow, insincere, knavish, perfidious, treacherous, twofaced. * *adv* doubly, twice, twofold. * *n* doubling, fold, plait; artifice, manoeuvre, ruse, shift, stratagem, trick, wile; copy, counterpart, twin.

doublet *n* jacket, jerkin.

doubt *vb* demur, fluctuate, hesitate, vacillate, waver; distrust, mistrust, query, question, suspect. * *n* dubiety, dubiousness, dubitation, hesitance, hesitancy, hesitation, incertitude, indecision, irresolution, question, suspense, uncertainty, vacillation; distrust, misgiving, mistrust, scepticism, suspicion.

doubtful *adj* dubious, hesitating, sceptical, undecided, undetermined, wavering; ambiguous, dubious, enigmatical, equivocal, hazardous, obscure, problematical, unsure; indeterminate, questionable, undecided, unquestioned.

doubtless *adv* certainly, unquestionably; clearly, indisputably, precisely.

doughty *adj* adventurous, bold, brave, chivalrous, courageous, daring, dauntless, fearless, gallant, heroic, intrepid, redoubtable, valiant, valorous.

douse *see* **dowse.**

dowdy *adj* awkward, dingy, ill-dressed, shabby, slatternly, slovenly; old-fashioned, unfashionable.

dowel *n* peg, pin, pinion, tenon.

dower *n* endowment, gift; dowry; portion, share.

downcast *adj* chapfallen, crestfallen, dejected, depressed, despondent, discouraged, disheartened, dispirited, downhearted, low-spirited, sad, unhappy.

downfall *n* descent, destruction, fall, ruin.

downhearted *adj* chapfallen, crestfallen, dejected, depressed, despondent, discouraged, disheartened, dispirited, downcast, low-spirited, sad, unhappy.

downright *adj* absolute, categorical, clear, explicit, plain, positive, sheer, simple, undisguised, unequivocal, utter; above-board, artless, blunt, direct, frank, honest, ingenuous, open, sincere, straightforward, unceremonious.

downy *adj* lanate, lanated, lanose.

dowse, douse *vb* dip, immerse, plunge, souse, submerge.

doxy *n* mistress, paramour; courtesan, drab, harlot, prostitute, strumpet, streetwalker, whore.

doze *vb* drowse, nap, sleep, slumber. * *n* drowse, forty-winks, nap.

dozy *adj* drowsy, heavy, sleepy, sluggish.

draft *vb* detach, select; commandeer, conscript, impress; delineate, draw, outline, sketch. * *n* conscription, drawing, selection; delineation, outline, sketch; bill, cheque, order.

drag *vb* draw, haul, pull, tow, tug; trail; linger, loiter. * *n* favour, influence, pull; brake, check, curb, lag, resistance, retardation, scotch, skid, slackening, slack-off, slowing.

draggle *vb* befoul, bemire, besmirch, dangle, drabble, trail.

dragoon *vb* compel, drive, force, harass, harry, persecute. * *n* cavalier, equestrian, horse-soldier.

drain *vb* milk, sluice, tap; empty, evacuate, exhaust; dry. * *n* channel, culvert, ditch, sewer, sluice, trench, watercourse; exhaustion, withdrawal.

draught *n* current, drawing, pulling, traction; cup, dose, drench, drink, potion; delineation, design, draft, outline, sketch.

draw *vb* drag, haul, tow, tug, pull; attract; drain, suck, syphon; extract, extort; breathe in, inhale, inspire; allure, engage, entice, induce, influence, lead, move, persuade; extend, protract, stretch; delineate, depict, sketch; deduce, derive, infer; compose, draft, formulate, frame, prepare; blister, vesicate, write.

drawback *n* defect, deficiency, detriment, disadvantage, fault, flaw, imperfection, injury; abatement, allowance, deduction, discount, rebate, reduction.

drawing *n* attracting, draining, inhaling, pulling, traction; delineation, draught, outline, picture, plan, sketch.

dread *vb* apprehend, fear. * *adj* dreadful, frightful, horrible, terrible; awful, venerable. * *n* affright, alarm, apprehension, fear, terror; awe, veneration.

dreadful *adj* alarming, appalling, awesome, dire,

direful, fearful, formidable, frightful, horrible, horrid, terrible, terrific, tremendous; awful, venerable.

dream *vb* fancy, imagine, think. * *n* conceit, daydream, delusion, fancy, fantasy, hallucination, illusion, imagination, reverie, vagary, vision.

dreamer *n* enthusiast, visionary.

dreamy *adj* absent, abstracted, fanciful, ideal, misty, shadowy, speculative, unreal, visionary.

dreary *adj* cheerless, chilling, comfortless, dark, depressing, dismal, drear, gloomy, lonely, lonesome, sad, solitary, sorrowful; boring, dull, monotonous, tedious, tiresome, uninteresting, wearisome.

dregs *npl* feculence, grounds, lees, off-scourings, residuum, scourings, sediment, waste; draff, dross, refuse, scum, trash.

drench *vb* dowse, drown, imbrue, saturate, soak, souse, steep, wet; physic, purge.

dress *vb* align, straighten; adjust, arrange, dispose, fit, prepare; accoutre, apparel, array, attire, clothe, robe, rig; adorn, bedeck, deck, decorate, drape, embellish, trim. * *n* apparel, attire, clothes, clothing, costume, garb, guise, garments, habiliment, habit, raiment, suit, toilet, vesture; bedizenment, bravery; frock, gown, rob.

dressing *n* compost, fertilizer, manure; forcemeat, stuffing.

dressy *adj* flashy, gaudy, showy.

driblet *n* bit, drop, fragment, morsel, piece, scrap.

drift *vb* accumulate, drive, float, wander. * *n* bearing, course, direction; aim, design, intent, intention, mark, object, proposal, purpose, scope, tendency; detritus, deposit, diluvium; gallery, passage, tunnel; current, rush, sweep; heap, pile.

drill[1] *vb* bore, perforate, pierce; discipline, exercise, instruct, teach, train. * *n* borer; discipline, exercise, training.

drill[2] *n* channel, furrow, trench.

drink *vb* imbibe, sip, swill; carouse, indulge, revel, tipple, tope; swallow, quaff; absorb. * *n* beverage, draught, liquid, potation, potion; dram, nip, sip, snifter, refreshment.

drip *vb* dribble, drop, leak, trickle; distil, filter, percolate; ooze, reek, seep, weep. * *n* dribble, drippings, drop, leak, leakage, leaking, trickle, tricklet; bore, nuisance, wet blanket.

drive *vb* hurl, impel, propel, send, shoot, thrust; actuate, incite, press, urge; coerce, compel, constrain, force, harass, oblige, overburden, press, rush; go, guide, ride, travel; aim, intend. * *n* effort, energy, pressure; airing, ride; road.

drivel *vb* babble, blether, dote, drool, slaver, slobber. * *n* balderdash, drivelling, fatuity, nonsense, prating, rubbish, slaver, stuff, twaddle.

drizzle *vb* mizzle, rain, shower, sprinkle. * *n* haar, mist, mizzle, rain, sprinkling.

droll *adj* comic, comical, farcical, funny, jocular, ludicrous, laughable, ridiculous; amusing, diverting, facetious, odd, quaint, queer, waggish. * *n* buffoon, clown, comedian, fool, harlequin, jester, punch, Punchinello, scaramouch, wag, zany.

drollery n archness, buffoonery, fun, humour, jocularity, pleasantry, waggishness, whimsicality.

drone vb dawdle, drawl, idle, loaf, lounge; hum. * n idler, loafer, lounger, sluggard.

drool vb drivel, slaver.

droop vb fade, wilt, wither; decline, fail, faint, flag, languish, sink, weaken; bend, hang.

drop vb distil, drip, shed; decline, depress, descend, dump, lower, sink; abandon, desert, forsake, forswear, leave, omit, relinquish, quit; cease, discontinue, intermit, remit; fall, precipitate. * n bead, droplet, globule; earring, pendant.

dross n cinder, lees, recrement, scoria, scum, slag; refuse, waste.

drought n aridity, drouth, dryness, thirstiness.

drove n flock, herd; collection, company, crowd.

drown vb deluge, engulf, flood, immerse, inundate, overflow, sink, submerge, swamp; overcome, overpower, overwhelm.

drowse vb doze, nap, sleep, slumber, snooze. * n doze, forty winks, nap, siesta, sleep, snooze.

drowsy adj dozy, sleepy; comatose, lethargic, stupid; lulling, soporific.

drub vb bang, beat, cane, cudgel, flog, hit, knock, pommel, pound, strike, thrash, thump, whack.

drubbing n beating, caning, cudgelling, flagellation, flogging, pommelling, pounding, thrashing, thumping, whacking.

drudge vb grub, grind, plod, slave, toil, work. * n grind, hack, hard worker, menial, plodder, scullion, servant, slave, toiler, worker.

drug vb dose, medicate; disgust, surfeit. * n medicine, physic, remedy; poison.

drunk adj boozed, drunken, inebriated, intoxicated, maudlin, soaked, tipsy; ablaze, aflame, delirious, fervent, suffused. * n alcoholic, boozer, dipsomaniac, drunkard, inebriate, lush, soak; bacchanal, bender, binge.

drunkard n alcoholic, boozer, carouser, dipsomaniac, drinker, drunk, inebriate, reveller, sot, tippler, toper.

dry vb dehydrate, desiccate, drain, exsiccate, parch. * adj desiccated, dried, juiceless, sapless, unmoistened; arid, droughty, parched; drouthy, thirsty; barren, dull, insipid, jejune, plain, pointless, tame, tedious, tiresome, unembellished, uninteresting, vapid; cutting, keen, sarcastic, severe, sharp, sly.

dub vb call, christen, denominate, designate, entitle, name, style, term.

dubious adj doubtful, fluctuating, hesitant, irresolute, skeptical, uncertain, undecided, unsettled, wavering; ambiguous, doubtful, equivocal, improbable, questionable, uncertain.

duck vb dip, dive, immerse, plunge, submerge, souse; bend, bow, dodge, stoop.

duct n canal, channel, conduit, pipe, tube; blood-vessel.

ductile adj compliant, docile, facile, tractable, yielding; flexible, malleable, pliant; extensible, tensile.

dudgeon n anger, indignation, ill will, ire, malice, resentment, umbrage, wrath.

due adj owed, owing; appropriate, becoming, befitting, bounden, fit, proper, suitable, right. * adv dead, direct, directly, exactly, just, right, squarely, straight. * n claim, debt, desert, right.

dulcet adj delicious, honeyed, luscious, sweet; harmonious, melodious; agreeable, charming, delightful, pleasant, pleasing.

dull vb blunt; benumb, besot, deaden, hebetate, obtund, paralyse, stupefy; dampen, deject, depress, discourage, dishearten, dispirit; allay, alleviate, assuage, mitigate, moderate, quiet, soften; deaden, dim, sully, tarnish. * adj blockish, brutish, doltish, obtuse, stolid, stupid, unintelligent; apathetic, callous, dead, insensible, passionless, phlegmatic, unfeeling, unimpassioned, unresponsive; heavy, inactive, inanimate, inert, languish, lifeless, slow, sluggish, torpid; blunt, dulled, hebetate, obtuse; cheerless, dismal, dreary, gloomy, sad, sombre; dim, lack-lustre, lustreless, matt, obscure, opaque, tarnished; dry, flat, insipid, irksome, jejune, prosy, tedious, tiresome, uninteresting, wearisome.

duly adv befittingly, decorously, fitly, properly, rightly; regularly.

dumb adj inarticulate, mute, silent, soundless, speechless, voiceless.

dumbfound, dumfound vb amaze, astonish, astound, bewilder, confound, confuse, nonplus, pose.

dumps npl blues, dejection, depression, despondency, gloom, gloominess, melancholy, sadness.

dun[1] adj greyish-brown, brown, drab.

dun[2] vb beset, importune, press, urge.

dunce n ass, block, blockhead, clodpole, dolt, donkey, dullard, dunderhead, fool, goose, halfwit, ignoramus, jackass, lackwit, loon, nincompoop, numskull, oaf, simpleton, thickhead, witling.

dupe vb beguile, cheat, chouse, circumvent, cozen, deceive, delude, gull, hoodwink, outwit, overreach, swindle, trick. * n gull, simpleton.

duplicate vb copy, double, repeat, replicate, reproduce. * adj doubled, twofold. * n copy, counterpart, facsimile, replica, transcript.

duplicity n artifice, chicanery, circumvention, deceit, deception, dishonesty, dissimulation, double-dealing, falseness, fraud, guile, hypocrisy, perfidy.

durable adj abiding, constant, continuing, enduring, firm, lasting, permanent, persistent, stable.

duration n continuance, continuation, permanency, perpetuation, prolongation; period, time.

duress n captivity, confinement, constraint, durance, hardship, imprisonment, restraint; compulsion.

dusky adj cloudy, darkish, dim, murky, obscure, overcast, shady, shadowy; dark, swarthy, tawny.

dutiful adj duteous, obedient, submissive; deferential, respectful, reverential.

duty n allegiance, devoirs, obligation, responsibility, reverence; business, engagement, function, office, service; custom, excise, impost, tariff, tax, toll.

dwarf *vb* lower, stunt. * *n* bantam, homunculus, manikin, midget, pygmy.

dwarfish *adj* diminutive, dwarfed, little, low, pygmy, small, stunted, tiny, undersized.

dwell *vb* abide, inhabit, live, lodge, remain, reside, rest, sojourn, stay, stop, tarry, tenant.

dwelling *n* abode, cot, domicile, dugout, establishment, habitation, home, house, hutch, lodging, mansion, quarters, residence.

dwindle *vb* decrease, diminish, lessen, shrink; decay, decline, deteriorate, pine, sink, waste away.

dye *vb* colour, stain, tinge. * *n* cast, colour, hue, shade, stain, tinge, tint.

dying *adj* expiring; mortal, perishable. * *n* death, decease, demise, departure, dissolution, exit.

dynasty *n* dominion, empire, government, rule, sovereignty.

dyspepsia *n* indigestion.

E

eager *adj* agog, avid, anxious, desirous, fain, greedy, impatient, keen, longing, yearning; animated, ardent, earnest, enthusiastic, fervent, fervid, forward, glowing, hot, impetuous, sanguine, vehement, zealous.

eagerness *n* ardour, avidity, earnestness, enthusiasm, fervour, greediness, heartiness, hunger, impatience, impetuosity, intentness, keenness, longing, thirst, vehemence, yearning, zeal.

eagle-eyed *adj* discerning, hawk-eyed, sharp-sighted.

ear[1] *n* attention, hearing, heed, regard.

ear[2] *n* head, spike.

early *adj* opportune, seasonable, timely; forward, premature; dawning, matutinal. * *adv* anon, beforehand, betimes, ere, seasonably, shortly, soon.

earn *vb* acquire, gain, get, obtain, procure, realize, reap, win; deserve, merit.

earnest *adj* animated, ardent, eager, cordial, fervent, fervid, glowing, hearty, impassioned, importune, warm, zealous; fixed, intent, steady; sincere, true, truthful; important, momentous, serious, weighty. * *n* reality, seriousness, truth; foretaste, pledge, promise; handsel, payment.

earnings *npl* allowance, emoluments, gains, income, pay, proceeds, profits, remuneration, reward, salary, stipend.

earth *n* globe, orb, planet, world; clay, clod, dirt, glebe, ground, humus, land, loam, sod, soil, turf; mankind, world.

earthborn *adj* abject, base, earthly, grovelling, low, mean, unspiritual.

earthly *adj* terrestrial; base, carnal, earthborn, low, gross, grovelling, sensual, sordid, unspiritual, worldly; bodily, material, mundane, natural, secular, temporal.

earthy *adj* clayey, earth-like, terrene; earthly, terrestrial; coarse, gross, material, unrefined.

ease *vb* disburden, disencumber, pacify, quiet, relieve, still; abate, allay, alleviate, appease, assuage, diminish, mitigate, soothe; loosen, release; facilitate, favour. * *n* leisure, quiescence, repose, rest; calmness, content, contentment, enjoyment, happiness, peace, quiet, quietness, quietude, relief, repose, satisfaction, serenity, tranquillity; easiness, facility, readiness; flexibility, freedom, liberty, lightness, naturalness, unconcern, unconstraint; comfort, elbowroom.

easy *adj* light; careless, comfortable, contented, effortless, painless, quiet, satisfied, tranquil, untroubled; accommodating, complaisant, compliant, complying, facile, indolent, manageable, pliant, submissive, tractable, yielding; graceful, informal, natural, unconstrained; flowing, ready, smooth, unaffected; gentle, lenient, mild, moderate; affluent, loose, unconcerned, unembarrassed.

eat *vb* chew, consume, devour, engorge, ingest, ravage, swallow; corrode, demolish, erode; breakfast, dine, feed, lunch, sup.

eatable *adj* edible, esculent, harmless, wholesome.

ebb *vb* abate, recede, retire, subside; decay, decline, decrease, degenerate, deteriorate, sink, wane. * *n* refluence, reflux, regress, regression, retrocedence, retrocession, retrogression, return; caducity, decay, decline, degeneration, deterioration, wane, waning; abatement, decrease, decrement, diminution.

ebullience *n* ebullition, effervescence; burst, bursting, overenthusiasm, overflow, rush, vigour.

ebullition *n* boiling, bubbling; effervescence, fermentation; burst, fit, outbreak, outburst, paroxysm.

eccentric *adj* decentred, parabolic; aberrant, abnormal, anomalous, cranky, erratic, fantastic, irregular, odd, outlandish, peculiar, singular, strange, uncommon, unnatural, wayward, whimsical. * *n* crank, curiosity, original.

eccentricity *n* ellipticity, flattening, flatness, oblateness; aberration, irregularity, oddity, oddness, peculiarity, singularity, strangeness, waywardness.

ecclesiastic[1], **ecclesiastical** *adj* churchish, churchly, clerical, ministerial, nonsecular, pastoral, priestly, religious, sacerdotal.

ecclesiastic[2] *n* chaplain, churchman, clergyman, cleric, clerk, divine, minister, parson, pastor, priest, reverend, shepherd.

echo *vb* reply, resound, reverberate, ring; re-echo, repeat. * *n* answer, repetition, reverberation; imitation.

éclat *n* acclamation, applause, brilliancy, effect, glory, lustre, pomp, renown, show, splendour.

eclipse *vb* cloud, darken, dim, obscure, overshadow, veil; annihilate, annul, blot out, extinguish. * *n* clouding, concealment, darkening, dimming, disappearance, hiding, obscuration, occultation, shrouding, vanishing, veiling; annihilation, blotting out, destruction, extinction, extinguishment, obliteration.

eclogue n bucolic, idyl, pastoral.

economize vb husband, manage, save; retrench.

economy n frugality, husbandry, parsimony, providence, retrenchment, saving, skimping, stinginess, thrift, thriftiness; administration, arrangement, management, method, order, plan, regulation, system; dispensation.

ecstasy n frenzy, madness, paroxysm, trance; delight, gladness, joy, rhapsody, rapture, ravishment, transport.

eddy vb gurgle, surge, spin, swirl, whirl. * n countercurrent; swirl, vortex, whirlpool.

edge vb sharpen; border, fringe, rim. * n border, brim, brink, bound, crest, fringe, hem, lip, margin, rim, verge; animation, intensity, interest, keenness, sharpness, zest; acrimony, bitterness, gall, sharpness, sting.

edging n border, frill, fringe, trimming.

edible adj eatable, esculent, harmless, wholesome.

edict n act, command, constitution, decision, decree, law, mandate, manifesto, notice, order, ordinance, proclamation, regulation, rescript, statute.

edifice n building, fabric, habitation, house, structure.

edify vb educate, elevate, enlightenment, improve, inform, instruct, nurture, teach, upbuild.

edition n impression, issue, number.

educate vb breed, cultivate, develop, discipline, drill, edify, exercise, indoctrinate, inform, instruct, mature, nurture, rear, school, teach, train.

educated adj cultured, lettered, literate.

education n breeding, cultivation, culture, development, discipline, drilling, indoctrination, instruction, nurture, pedagogics, schooling, teaching, training, tuition.

educe vb bring out, draw out, elicit, evolve, extract.

eerie adj awesome, fearful, frightening, strange, uncanny, weird.

efface vb blot, blot out, cancel, delete, destroy, erase, expunge, obliterate, remove, sponge.

effect vb cause, create, effectuate, produce; accomplish, achieve, carry, compass, complete, conclude, consummate, contrive, do, execute, force, negotiate, perform, realize, work. * n consequence, event, fruit, issue, outcome, result; efficiency, fact, force, power, reality; validity, weight; drift, import, intent, meaning, purport, significance, tenor.

effective adj able, active, adequate, competent, convincing, effectual, sufficient; cogent, efficacious, energetic, forcible, potent, powerful.

effects npl chattels, furniture, goods, movables, property.

effectual adj operative, successful; active, effective, efficacious, efficient.

effectuate vb accomplish, achieve, complete, do, effect, execute, fulfil, perform, secure.

effeminate adj delicate, feminine, soft, tender, timorous, unmanly, womanish, womanlike, womanly; camp.

effervesce vb bubble, ferment, foam, froth.

effete adj addle, barren, fruitless, sterile, unfruitful, unproductive, unprolific; decayed, exhausted, spent, wasted.

efficacious adj active, adequate, competent, effective, effectual, efficient, energetic, operative, powerful.

efficacy n ability, competency, effectiveness, efficiency, energy, force, potency, power, strength, vigour, virtue.

efficient adj active, capable, competent, effective, effectual, efficacious, operative, potent; able, energetic, ready, skilful.

effigy n figure, image, likeness, portrait, representation, statue.

effloresce vb bloom, flower.

efflorescence n blooming, blossoming, flowering.

effluence n discharge, efflux, effluvium, emanation, emission, flow, outflow, outpouring.

effort n application, attempt, endeavour, essay, exertion, pains, spurt, strain, strife, stretch, struggle, trial, trouble.

effrontery n assurance, audacity, boldness, brass, disrespect, hardihood, impudence, incivility, insolence, presumption, rudeness, sauciness, shamelessness.

effulgent adj burning, beaming, blazing, bright, brilliant, dazzling, flaming, glowing, lustrous, radiant, refulgent, resplendent, shining, splendid.

effusion n discharge, efflux, emission, gush, outpouring; shedding, spilling, waste; address, speech, talk, utterance.

egg vb (with on) encourage, incite, instigate, push, stimulate, urge; harass, harry, provoke.

ego n id, self, me, subject, superego.

egotism n self-admiration, self-assertion, self-commendation, self-conceit, self-esteem, self-importance, self-praise; egoism, selfishness.

egotistic, egotistical adj bumptious, conceited, egoistical, opinionated, self-asserting, self-admiring, self-centred, self-conceited, self-important, self-loving, vain.

egregious adj conspicuous, enormous, extraordinary, flagrant, great, gross, huge, monstrous, outrageous, prodigious, remarkable, tremendous.

egress n departure, emergence, exit, outlet, way out.

eject vb belch, discharge, disgorge, emit, evacuate, puke, spew, spit, spout, spurt, void, vomit; bounce, cashier, discharge, dismiss, disposes, eliminate, evict, expel, fire, oust; banish, reject, throw out.

elaborate vb develop, improve, mature, produce, refine, ripen. * adj complicated, decorated, detailed, dressy, laboured, laborious, ornate, perfected, studied.

elapse vb go, lapse, pass.

elastic adj rebounding, recoiling, resilient, springy; buoyant, recuperative.

elated *adj* animated, cheered, elate, elevated, excited, exhilarated, exultant, flushed, puffed up, roused.

elbow *vb* crowd, force, hustle, jostle, nudge, push, shoulder. * *n* angle, bend, corner, flexure, joining, turn.

elder *adj* older, senior; ranking; ancient, earlier, older. * *n* ancestor, senior; presbyter, prior, senator.

elect *vb* appoint, choose, cull, designate, pick, prefer, select. * *adj* choice, chosen, picked, selected; appointed, elected; predestinated, redeemed.

election *n* appointment, choice, preference, selection; alternative, freedom, freewill, liberty; predestination.

elector *n* chooser, constituent, selector, voter.

electrify *vb* charge, galvanize; astonish, enchant, excite, rouse, startle, stir, thrill.

elegance, elegancy *n* beauty, grace, propriety, symmetry; courtliness, daintiness, gentility, nicety, polish, politeness, refinement, taste.

elegant *adj* beautiful, chaste, classical, dainty, graceful, fine, handsome, neat, symmetrical, tasteful, trim, well-made, well-proportioned; accomplished, courtly, cultivated, fashionable, genteel, polished, polite, refined.

elegiac *adj* dirgeful, mournful, plaintive, sorrowful.

elegy *n* dirge, epicedium, lament, ode, threnody.

element *n* basis, component, constituent, factor, germ, ingredient, part, principle, rudiment, unit; environment, milieu, sphere.

elementary *adj* primordial, simple, uncombined, uncomplicated, uncompounded; basic, component, fundamental, initial, primary, rudimental, rudimentary.

elevate *vb* erect, hoist, lift, raise; advance, aggrandize, exalt, promote; dignify, ennoble, exalt, greaten, improve, refine; animate, cheer, elate, excite, exhilarate, rouse.

elfin *adj* elflike, elvish, mischievous, weird.

elicit *vb* draw out, educe, evoke, extort, fetch, obtain, pump, wrest, wring; deduce, educe.

eligible *adj* desirable, preferable; qualified, suitable, worthy.

eliminate *vb* disengage, eradicate, exclude, expel, remove, separate; ignore, omit, reject.

ellipsis *n* gap, hiatus, lacuna, omission.

elliptical *adj* oval; defective, incomplete.

elocution *n* declamation, delivery, oratory, rhetoric, speech, utterance.

elongate *vb* draw, draw out, extend, lengthen, protract, stretch.

elope *vb* abscond, bolt, decamp, disappear, leave.

eloquence *n* fluency, oratory, rhetoric.

else *adv* besides, differently, otherwise.

elucidate *vb* clarify, demonstrate, explain, expound, illuminate, illustrate, interpret, unfold.

elucidation *n* annotation, clarification, comment, commentary, elucidating, explaining, explanation, exposition, gloss, scholium.

elude *vb* avoid, escape, evade, shun, slip; baffle, balk, disappoint, disconcert, escape, foil, frustrate, thwart.

elusive *adj* deceptive, deceitful, delusive, evasive, fallacious, fraudulent, illusory; equivocatory, equivocating, shuffling.

Elysian *adj* blissful, celestial, delightful, enchanting, heavenly, ravishing, seraphic.

emaciation *n* attenuation, lankness, leanness, meagreness, tabes, tabescence, thinness.

emanate *vb* arise, come, emerge, flow, issue, originate, proceed, spring.

emancipate *vb* deliver, discharge, disenthral, enfranchise, free, liberate, manumit, release, unchain, unfetter, unshackle.

emancipation *n* deliverance, enfranchisement, deliverance, freedom, liberation, manumission, release.

emasculate *vb* castrate, geld; debilitate, effeminize, enervate, unman, weaken.

embalm *vb* cherish, consecrate, conserve, enshrine, preserve, store, treasure; perfume, scent.

embargo *vb* ban, bar, blockade, debar, exclude, prohibit, proscribe, restrict, stop, withhold. * *n* ban, bar, blockade, exclusion, hindrance, impediment, prohibition, prohibitory, proscription, restraint, restriction, stoppage.

embark *vb* engage, enlist.

embarrass *vb* beset, entangle, perplex; annoy, clog, bother, distress, hamper, harass, involve, plague, trouble, vex; abash, confound, confuse, discomfit, disconcert, dumbfound, mortify, nonplus, pose, shame.

embellish *vb* adorn, beautify, bedeck, deck, decorate, emblazon, enhance, enrich, garnish, grace, ornament.

embellishment *n* adornment, decoration, enrichment, ornament, ornamentation.

embezzle *vb* appropriate, defalcate, filch, misappropriate, peculate, pilfer, purloin, steal.

embitter *vb* aggravate, envenom, exacerbate; anger, enrage, exasperate, madden.

emblem *n* badge, cognizance, device, mark, representation, sign, symbol, token, type.

embody *vb* combine, compact, concentrate, incorporate; comprehend, comprise, contain, embrace, include; codify, methodize, systematize.

embolden *vb* animate, cheer, elate, encourage, gladden, hearten, inspirit, nerve, reassure.

embosom *vb* bury, cherish, clasp, conceal, enfold, envelop, enwrap, foster, hide, nurse, surround.

embrace *vb* clasp; accept, seize, welcome; comprehend, comprise, contain, cover, embody, encircle, enclose, encompass, enfold, hold, include. * *n* clasp, fold, hug.

embroil *vb* commingle, encumber, ensnarl, entangle, implicate, involve; confuse, discompose, disorder, distract, disturb, perplex, trouble.

embryo *n* beginning, germ, nucleus, root, rudiment.

embryonic *adj* incipient, rudimentary, undeveloped.

emendation *n* amendment, correction, improvement, rectification.

emerge *vb* rise; emanate, escape, issue; appear, arise, outcrop.

emergency *n* crisis, difficulty, dilemma, exigency, extremity, necessity, pass, pinch, push, strait, urgency; conjuncture, crisis, juncture, pass.

emigration *n* departure, exodus, migration, removal.

eminence *n* elevation, hill, projection, prominence, protuberance; celebrity, conspicuousness, distinction, exaltation, fame, loftiness, note, preferment, reputation, repute, renown.

eminent *adj* elevated, high, lofty; celebrated, conspicuous, distinguished, exalted, famous, illustrious, notable, prominent, remarkable, renowned.

emissary *n* messenger, scout, secret agent, spy.

emit *vb* breathe out, dart, discharge, eject, emanate, exhale, gust, hurl, jet, outpour, shed, shoot, spurt, squirt.

emollient *adj* relaxing, softening. soothing. * *n* softener.

emolument *n* compensation, gain, hire, income, lucre, pay, pecuniary, profits, salary, stipend, wages; advantage, benefit, profit, perquisites.

emotion *n* agitation, excitement, feeling, passion, perturbation, sentiment, sympathy, trepidation.

emphasis *n* accent, stress; force, importance, impressiveness, moment, significance, weight.

emphatic *adj* decided, distinct, earnest, energetic, expressive, forcible, impressive, intensive, positive, significant, strong, unequivocal.

empire *n* domain, dominion, sovereignty, supremacy; authority, command, control, government, rule, sway.

empirical, empiric *adj* experimental, experiential; hypothetical, provisional, tentative; charlatanic, quackish.

employ *vb* busy, devote, engage, engross, enlist, exercise, occupy, retain; apply, commission, use. * *n* employment, service.

employee *n* agent, clerk, employee, hand, servant, workman.

employment *n* avocation, business, calling, craft, employ, engagement, occupation, profession, pursuit, trade, vocation, work.

emporium *n* market, mart, shop, store.

empower *vb* authorize, commission, permit, qualify, sanction, warrant; enable.

empty *vb* deplete, drain, evacuate, exhaust; discharge, disembogue; flow, embogue. * *adj* blank, hollow, unoccupied, vacant, vacuous, void; deplete, destitute, devoid, hungry; unfilled, unfurnished, unsupplied; unsatisfactory, unsatisfying, unsubstantial, useless, vain; clear, deserted, desolate, exhausted, free, unburdened, unloaded, waste; foolish, frivolous, inane, senseless, silly, stupid, trivial, weak.

empyrean, empyreal *adj* aerial, airy, ethereal, heavenly, refined, sublimated, sublimed.

emulation *n* competition, rivalry, strife, vying; contention, envy, jealousy.

enable *vb* authorize, capacitate, commission, empower, fit, permit, prepare, qualify, sanction, warrant.

enact *vb* authorize, command, decree, establish, legislate, ordain, order, sanction; act, perform, personate, play, represent.

enactment *n* act, decree, law, edict, ordinance.

enamour *vb* bewitch, captivate, charm, enchant, endear, fascinate.

enchain *vb* bind, confine, enslave, fetter, hold, manacle, restrain, shackle.

enchant *vb* beguile, bewitch, charm, delude, fascinate; captivate, catch, enamour, win; beatify, delight, enrapture, rapture, ravish, transport.

enchanting *adj* bewitching, blissful, captivating, charming, delightful, enrapturing, fascinating, rapturous, ravishing.

enchantment *n* charm, conjuration, incantation, magic, necromancy, sorcery, spell, witchery; bliss, delight, fascination, rapture, ravishment, transport.

encase *vb* encircle, enclose, incase, infix, set; chase, emboss, engrave, inlay, ornament.

encage *vb* confine, coop up, impound, imprison, shut up.

encircle *vb* belt, circumscribe, encompass, enclose, engird, enring, environ, gird, ring, span, surround, twine; clasp, embrace, enfold, fold.

enclose, inclose *vb* circumscribe, corral, coop, embosom, encircle, encompass, environ, fence in, hedge, include, pen, shut in, surround; box, cover, encase, envelop, wrap.

encomium *n* applause, commendation, eulogy, laudation, panegyric, praise.

encompass *vb* belt, compass, encircle, enclose, engird, environ, gird, surround; beset, besiege, hem in, include, invest, surround.

encounter *vb* confront, face, meet; attack, combat, contend, engage, strive, struggle. * *n* assault, attack, clash, collision, meeting, onset; action, affair, battle, brush, combat, conflict, contest, dispute, engagement, skirmish.

encourage *vb* animate, assure, cheer, comfort, console, embolden, enhearten, fortify, hearten, incite, inspirit, instigate, reassure, stimulate, strengthen; abet, aid, advance, approve, countenance, favour, foster, further, help, patronize, promote, support.

encroach *vb* infringe, invade, intrude, tench, trespass, usurp.

encumber *vb* burden, clog, hamper, hinder, impede, load, obstruct, overload, oppress, retard; complicate, embarrass, entangle, involve, perplex.

encumbrance *n* burden, clog, deadweight, drag, embarrassment, hampering, hindrance, impediment, incubus, load; claim, debt, liability, lien.

end *vb* abolish, close, conclude, discontinue, dissolve, drop, finish, stop, terminate; annihilate, destroy, kill; cease, terminate. * *n* extremity, tip; cessation, close, denouement, ending, expiration, finale, finis, finish, last, period, stoppage, wind-up; completion, conclusion, consummation; annihilation, catastrophe, destruction, dissolution; bound, limit, termination, terminus; consequence, event, issue, result, settlement, sequel, upshot; fragment, remnant, scrap, stub, tag, tail; aim, design, goal, intent, intention, object, objective, purpose.

endanger *vb* compromise, hazard, imperil, jeopardize, peril, risk.

endear *vb* attach, bind, captivate, charm, win.

endearment *n* attachment, fondness, love, tenderness; caress, blandishment, fondling.

endeavour *vb* aim, attempt, essay, labour, seek, strive, struggle, study, try. * *n* aim, attempt, conatus, effort, essay, exertion, trial, struggle, trial.

endless *adj* boundless, illimitable, immeasurable, indeterminable, infinite, interminable, limitless, unlimited; dateless, eternal, everlasting, never-ending, perpetual, unending; deathless, ever-enduring, ever-living, immortal, imperishable, undying.

endorse, indorse *vb* approve, back, confirm, guarantee, ratify, sanction, superscribe, support, visé, vouch for, warrant; superscribe.

endow *vb* bequeath, clothe, confer, dower, endue, enrich, gift, indue, invest, supply.

endowment *n* bequest, boon, bounty, gift, grant, largesse, present; foundation, fund, property, revenue; ability, aptitude, capability, capacity, faculty, genius, gift, parts, power, qualification, quality, talent.

endurance *n* abiding, bearing, sufferance, suffering, tolerance, toleration; backbone, bottom, forbearance, fortitude, guts, patience, resignation.

endure *vb* bear, support, sustain; experience, suffer, undergo, weather; abide, brook, permit, pocket, swallow, tolerate, stomach, submit, withstand; continue, last, persist, remain, wear.

enemy *n* adversary, foe; antagonist, foeman, opponent, rival.

energetic *adj* active, effective, efficacious, emphatic, enterprising, forceful, forcible, hearty, mettlesome, potent, powerful, strenuous, strong, vigorous.

energy *n* activity, dash, drive, efficacy, efficiency, force, go, impetus, intensity, mettle, might, potency, power, strength, verve, vim; animation, life, manliness, spirit, spiritedness, stamina, vigour, zeal.

enervate *vb* break, debilitate, devitalize, emasculate, enfeeble, exhaust, paralyse, relax, soften, unhinge, unnerve, weaken.

enfeeble *vb* debilitate, devitalize, enervate, exhaust, relax, unhinge, unnerve, weaken.

enfold, infold *vb* enclose, envelop, fold, enwrap, wrap; clasp, embrace.

enforce *vb* compel, constrain, exact, force, oblige, require, urge.

enfranchise *vb* emancipate, free, liberate, manumit, release.

engage *vb* bind, commit, obligate, pledge, promise; affiance, betroth, plight; book, brief, employ, enlist, hire, retain; arrest, allure, attach, draw, entertain, fix, gain, win; busy, commission, contract, engross, occupy; attack, encounter; combat, contend, contest, fight, interlock, struggle; embark, enlist; agree, promise, stipulate, undertake, warrant.

engagement *n* appointment, assurance, contract, obligation, pledge, promise, stipulation; affiancing, betrothment, betrothal, plighting; avocation, business, calling, employment, enterprise, occupation; action, battle, combat, encounter, fight.

engender *vb* bear, beget, breed, create, generate, procreate, propagate; cause, excite, incite, occasion, produce.

engine *n* invention, machine; agency, agent, device, implement, instrument, means, method, tool, weapon.

engorge *vb* bolt, devour, eat, gobble, gorge, gulp, swallow; glut, obstruct, stuff.

engrave *vb* carve, chisel, cut, etch, grave, hatch, incise, sculpt; grave, impress, imprint, infix.

engross *vb* absorb, engage, occupy, take up; buy up, forestall, monopolize.

engrossment *n* absorption, forestalling, monopoly.

engulf, ingulf *vb* absorb, overwhelm, plunge, swallow up.

enhance *vb* advance, aggravate, augment, elevate, heighten, increase, intensify, raise, swell.

enhearten *vb* animate, assure, cheer, comfort, console, embolden, encourage, hearten, incite, inspirit, reassure, stimulate.

enigma *n* conundrum, mystery, problem, puzzle, riddle.

enigmatic, enigmatical *adj* ambiguous, dark, doubtful, equivocal, hidden, incomprehensible, mysterious, mystic, obscure, occult, perplexing, puzzling, recondite, uncertain, unintelligible.

enjoin *vb* admonish, advise, urge; bid, command, direct, order, prescribe, require; prohibit, restrain.

enjoy *vb* like, possess, relish.

enjoyment *n* delight, delectation, gratification, happiness, indulgence, pleasure, satisfaction; possession.

enkindle *vb* inflame, ignite, kindle; excite, incite, instigate, provoke, rouse, stimulate.

enlarge *vb* amplify, augment, broaden, develop, dilate, distend, expand, extend, grow, increase, magnify, widen; aggrandize, engreaten, ennoble, expand, exaggerate, greaten; swell.

enlighten *vb* illume, illuminate, illumine; counsel, educate, civilize, inform, instruct, teach.

enlist *vb* enrol, levy, recruit, register; enrol, list; embark, engage.

enliven *vb* animate, invigorate, quicken, reanimate, rouse, wake; exhilarate, cheer, brighten, delight, elate, gladden, inspire, inspirit, rouse.

enmity *n* animosity, aversion, bitterness, hate, hatred, hostility, ill-will, malevolence, malignity, rancour.

ennoble *vb* aggrandize, dignify, elevate, engreaten, enlarge, exalt, glorify, greaten, raise.

ennui *n* boredom, irksomeness, languor, lassitude, listlessness, tedium, tiresomeness, weariness.

enormity *n* atrociousness, atrocity, depravity, flagitiousness, heinousness, nefariousness, outrageousness, villainy, wickedness.

enormous *adj* abnormal. exceptional, inordinate, irregular; colossal, Cyclopean, elephantine, Herculean, huge, immense, monstrous, vast, gigantic, prodigious, titanic, tremendous.

enough *adj* abundant, adequate, ample, plenty, sufficient. * *adv* satisfactorily, sufficiently. * *n* abundance, plenty, sufficiency.

enquire *see* **inquire.**

enrage *vb* anger, chafe, exasperate, incense, inflame, infuriate, irritate, madden, provoke.

enrapture *vb* beatify, bewitch, delight, enchant, enravish, entrance, surpassingly, transport.

enrich *vb* endow; adorn, deck, decorate, embellish, grace, ornament.

enrobe *vb* clothe, dress, apparel, array, attire, invest, robe.

enrol *vb* catalogue, engage, engross, enlist, list, register; chronicle, record.

ensconce *vb* conceal, cover, harbour, hide, protect, screen, secure, settle, shelter, shield, snugly.

enshrine *vb* embalm, enclose, entomb; cherish, treasure.

ensign *n* banner, colours, eagle, flag, gonfalcon, pennon, standard, streamer; sign, signal, symbol; badge, hatchment.

enslave *vb* captivate, dominate, master, overmaster, overpower, subjugate.

ensnare *vb* catch, entrap; allure, inveigle, seduce; bewilder, confound, embarrass, encumber, entangle, perplex.

ensue *vb* follow, succeed; arise, come, flow, issue, proceed, result, spring.

entangle *vb* catch, ensnare, entrap; confuse, enmesh, intertwine, intertwist, interweave, knot, mat, ravel, tangle; bewilder, embarrass, encumber, ensnare, involve, nonplus, perplex, puzzle.

enterprise *n* adventure, attempt, cause, effort, endeavour, essay, project, undertaking, scheme, venture; activity, adventurousness, daring, dash, energy, initiative, readiness, push.

enterprising *adj* adventurous, audacious, bold, daring, dashing, venturesome, venturous; active, adventurous, alert, efficient, energetic, prompt, resourceful, smart, spirited, stirring, strenuous, zealous.

entertain *vb* fete, receive, regale, treat; cherish, foster, harbour, hold, lodge, shelter; admit, consider; amuse, cheer, divert, please, recreate.

entertainment *n* hospitality; banquet, collation, feast, festival, reception, treat; amusement, diversion, pastime, recreation, sport.

enthusiasm *n* ecstasy, exaltation, fanaticism; ardour, earnestness, devotion, eagerness, fervour, passion, warmth, zeal.

enthusiast *n* bigot, devotee, fan, fanatic, freak, zealot; castle-builder, dreamer, visionary.

entice *vb* allure, attract, bait, cajole, coax, decoy, inveigle, lure, persuade, prevail on, seduce, tempt, wheedle, wile.

enticement *n* allurement, attraction, bait, blandishment, inducement, inveiglement, lure, persuasion, seduction.

entire *adj* complete, integrated, perfect, unbroken, undiminished, undivided, unimpaired, whole; complete, full, plenary, thorough; mere, pure, sheer, unalloyed, unmingled, unmitigated, unmixed.

entitle *vb* call, characterize, christen, denominate, designate, dub, name, style; empower, enable, fit for, qualify for.

entomb *vb* bury, inhume, inter.

entrails *npl* bowels, guts, intestines, inwards, offal, viscera.

entrance[1] *n* access, approach, avenue, incoming, ingress; adit, avenue, aperture, door, doorway, entry, gate, hallway, inlet, lobby, mouth, passage, portal, stile, vestibule; beginning, commencement, debut, initiation, introduction; admission, entrée.

entrance[2] *vb* bewitch, captivate, charm, delight, enchant, enrapture, fascinate, ravish, transport.

entrap *vb* catch, ensnare; allure, entice, inveigle, seduce; embarrass, entangle, involve, nonplus, perplex, pose, stagger.

entreat *vb* adjure, beg, beseech, crave, enjoin, implore, importune, petition, pray, solicit, supplicate.

entreaty *n* adjuration, appeal, importunity, petition, prayer, request, solicitation, suit, supplication.

entrée *n* access, admission, admittance.

entrench, intrench *vb* furrow; circumvallate, fortify; encroach, infringe, invade, trench, trespass.

entrenchment, intrenchment *n* entrenching; earthwork, fortification; defence, protection, shelter; encroachment, inroad, invasion.

entrust *vb* commit, confide, consign.

entwine *vb* entwist, interlace, intertwine, interweave, inweave, twine, twist, weave; embrace, encircle, encumber, interlace, surround.

enumerate *vb* calculate, cite, compute, count, detail, mention, number, numerate, reckon, recount, specify, tell.

enunciate *vb* articulate, declare, proclaim, promulgate, pronounce, propound, publish, say, speak, utter.

envelop *vb* encase, enfold, enwrap, fold, pack, wrap; cover, encircle, encompass, enshroud, hide, involve, surround.

envelope *n* capsule, case, covering, integument,

shroud, skin, wrapper, veil, vesture, wrap.

envenom *vb* poison, taint; embitter, malign; aggravate, enrage, exasperate, incense, inflame, irritate, madden, provoke.

environ *n* begird, belt, embrace, encircle, encompass, enclose, engrid, envelop, gird, hedge, hem, surround; beset, besiege, encompass, invest.

environs *npl* neighbourhood, vicinage, vicinity.

envoy *n* ambassador, legate, minister, plenipotentiary; courier, messenger.

envy *vb* hate; begrudge, grudge; covet, emulate, desire. * *n* enviousness, hate, hatred, ill-will, jealousy, malice, spite; grudge, grudging.

enwrap *vb* absorb, cover, encase, engross, envelop, infold, involve, wrap, wrap up.

ephemeral *adj* brief, diurnal, evanescent, fleeting, flitting, fugacious, fugitive, momentary, occasional, short-lived, transient, transitory.

epic *adj* Homeric, heroic, narrative.

epicure *n* gastronome, glutton, gourmand, gourmet; epicurean, sensualist, Sybarite, voluptuary.

epidemic *adj* general, pandemic, prevailing, prevalent. * *n* outbreak, pandemia, pestilence, plague, spread, wave.

epidermis *n* cuticle, scarf-skin.

epigrammatic *adj* antithetic, concise, laconic, piquant, poignant, pointed, pungent, sharp, terse.

episcopal *adj* Episcopalian, pontifical, prelatic.

epistle *n* communication, letter, missive, note.

epithet *n* appellation, description, designation, name, predicate, title.

epitome *n* abbreviation, abridgement, abstract, breviary, brief, comment, compendium, condensation, conspectus, digest, summary, syllabus, synopsis.

epitomize *vb* abbreviate, abridge, abstract, condense, contract, curtail, cut, reduce, shorten, summarize.

epoch *n* age, date, era, period, time.

equable *adj* calm, equal, even, even-tempered, regular, steady, uniform, serene, tranquil, unruffled.

equal *vb* equalize, even, match. * *adj* alike, coordinate, equivalent, like, tantamount; even, level, equable, regular, uniform; equitable, even-handed, fair, impartial, just, unbiased; co-extensive, commensurate, corresponding, parallel, proportionate; adequate, competent, fit, sufficient. * *n* compeer, fellow, match, peer; rival.

equanimity *n* calmness, composure, coolness, peace, regularity, self-possession, serenity, steadiness.

equestrian *adj* equine, horse-like, horsy. * *n* horseman, rider; cavalier, cavalryman, chevalier, horse soldier, knight.

equilibrist *n* acrobat, balancer, funambulist, rope-walker.

equip *vb* appoint, arm, furnish, provide, rig, supply; accoutre, array, dress.

equipage *n* accoutrements, apparatus, baggage, effects, equipment, furniture; carriage, turnout,

vehicle; attendance, procession, retinue, suite, train.

equipment *n* accoutrement, apparatus, baggage, equipage, furniture, gear, outfit, rigging.

equipoise *n* balance, equilibrium.

equitable *adj* even-handed, candid, honest, impartial, just, unbiased, unprejudiced, upright; adequate, fair, proper, reasonable, right.

equity *n* just, right; fair play, fairness, impartiality, justice, rectitude, reasonableness, righteousness, uprightness.

equivalent *adj* commensurate, equal, equipollent, tantamount; interchangeable, synonymous. * *n* complement, coordinate, counterpart, double, equal, fellow, like, match, parallel, pendant, quid pro quo.

equivocal *adj* ambiguous; doubtful, dubious, enigmatic, indeterminate, problematical, puzzling, uncertain.

equivocate *vb* dodge, evade, fence, palter, prevaricate, shuffle, quibble.

equivocation *n* evasion, paltering, prevarication, quibbling, shuffling; double entendre, double meaning, quibble.

era *n* age, date, epoch, period, time.

eradicate *vb* extirpate, root, uproot; abolish, annihilate, destroy, obliterate.

erase *vb* blot, cancel, delete, efface, expunge, obliterate, scrape out.

erasure *n* cancellation, cancelling, effacing, expunging, obliteration.

erect *vb* build, construct, raise, rear; create, establish, form, found, institute, plant. * *adj* standing, unrecumbent, uplifted, upright; elevated, vertical, perpendicular, straight; bold, firm, undaunted, undismayed, unshaken, unterrified.

erelong *adv* early, quickly, shortly, soon, speedily.

eremite *n* anchoret, anchorite, hermit, recluse, solitary.

ergo *adv* consequently, hence, therefore.

erode *vb* canker, consume, corrode, destroy, eat away, fret, rub.

erosive *adj* acrid, cathartic, caustic, corroding, corrosive, eating, virulent.

erotic *adj* amorous, amatory, arousing, seductive, stimulating, titillating.

err *vb* deviate, ramble, rove, stray, wander; blunder, misjudge, mistake; fall, lapse, nod, offend, sin, stumble, trespass, trip.

errand *n* charge, commission, mandate, message, mission, purpose.

errant *adj* adventurous, rambling, roving, stray, wandering.

erratic *adj* nomadic, rambling, roving, wandering; moving, planetary; abnormal, capricious, deviating, eccentric, irregular, odd, queer, strange.

erratum *n* correction, corrigendum, error, misprint, mistake.

erroneous *adj* false, incorrect, inaccurate, inexact, mistaken untrue, wrong.

error *n* blunder, fallacy, inaccuracy, misapprehension, mistake, oversight; delinquency, fault, iniquity, misdeed, misdoing, misstep, obliquity, offence, shortcoming, sin, transgression, trespass, wrongdoing.

erudition *n* knowledge, learning, lore, scholarship.

eruption *n* explosion, outbreak, outburst; sally; rash.

escape *vb* avoid, elude, evade, flee from, shun; abscond, bolt, decamp, flee, fly; slip. * *n* flight; release; passage, passing; leakage.

eschew *vb* abstain, avoid, elude, flee from, shun.

escort *vb* convey, guard, protect; accompany, attend, conduct. * *n* attendant, bodyguard, cavalier, companion, convoy, gallant, guard, squire; protection, safe conduct, safeguard; attendance, company.

esculent *adj* eatable, edible, wholesome.

esoteric *adj* hidden, inmost, inner, mysterious, private, recondite, secret.

especial *adj* absolute, chief, distinct, distinguished, marked, particular, peculiar, principal, singular, special, specific, uncommon, unusual; detailed, minute, noteworthy.

espousal *n* affiancing, betrothing, espousing, plighting; adoption, defence, maintenance, support.

espouse *vb* betroth, plight, promise; marry, wed; adopt, champion, defend, embrace, maintain, support.

espy *vb* descry, detect, discern, discover, observe, perceive, spy, watch.

esquire *n* armiger, attendant, escort, gentleman, squire.

essay[1] *vb* attempt, endeavour, try. * *n* aim, attempt, effort, endeavour, exertion, struggle, trial.

essay[2] *n* article, composition, disquisition, dissertation, paper, thesis.

essence *n* nature, quintessence, substance; extract, part; odour, perfume, scent; being, entity, existence, nature.

essential *adj* fundamental, indispensable, important, inward, intrinsic, necessary, requisite, vital; diffusible, pure, rectified, volatile.

establish *vb* fix, secure, set, settle; decree, enact, ordain; build, constitute, erect, form, found, institute, organize, originate, pitch, plant, raise; ensconce, ground, install, place, plant, root, secure; approve, confirm, ratify, sanction; prove, substantiate, verify.

estate *n* condition, state; position, rank, standing; division, order; effects, fortune, possessions, property; interest.

esteem *vb* appreciate, estimate, rate, reckon, value; admire, honour, like, prize, respect, revere, reverence, value, venerate, worship; account, believe, consider, deem, fancy, hold, imagine, suppose, regard, think. * *n* account, appreciation, consideration, estimate, estimation, judgement, opinion, reckoning, valuation; credit, honour, regard, respect, reverence.

estimable *adj* appreciable, calculable, computable;

admirable, credible, deserving, excellent, good, meritorious, precious, respectful, valuable, worthy.

estimate *vb* appraise, appreciate, esteem, prise, rate, value; assess, calculate, compute, count, gauge, judge, reckon. * *n* estimation, judgement, valuation; calculation, computation.

estimation *n* appreciation, estimate, valuation; esteem, estimate, judgement, opinion; honour, reckoning, regard, respect, reverence.

estop *vb* bar, impede, preclude, stop.

estrange *vb* withdraw, withhold; alienate, divert; disaffect, destroy.

estuary *n* creek, inlet, fiord, firth, frith, mouth.

etch *vb* corrode, engrave.

eternal *adj* absolute, inevitable, necessary, self-active, self-existent, self-originated; abiding, ceaseless, endless, ever-enduring, everlasting, incessant, interminable, never-ending, perennial, permanent, perpetual, sempiternal, unceasing, unending; deathless, immortal, imperishable, incorruptible, indestructible, never-dying, undying; immutable, unchangeable; constant, continual, continuous, incessant, persistent, unbroken, uninterrupted.

ethereal *adj* aerial, airy, celestial, empyreal, heavenly, unworldly; attenuated, light, subtle, tenuous, volatile; delicate, fairy, flimsy, fragile, rare, refined, subtle.

eulogize *vb* applaud, commend, extol, laud, magnify, praise.

eulogy *n* discourse, eulogium, panegyric, speech; applause, encomium, commendation, laudation, praise.

euphonious *adj* clear, euphonic, harmonious, mellifluous, mellow, melodious, musical, silvery, smooth, sweet-toned.

evacuant *adj* abstergent, cathartic, cleansing, emetic, purgative. * *n* cathartic, purgative.

evacuate *vb* empty; discharge, clean out, clear out, eject, excrete, expel, purge, void; abandon, desert, forsake, leave, quit, relinquish, withdraw.

evade *vb* elude, escape; avoid, decline, dodge, funk, shun; baffle, elude, foil; dodge, equivocate, fence, palter, prevaricate, quibble, shuffle.

evanescence *n* disappearance, evanishing, evanishment, vanishing; transience, transientness, transitoriness.

evanescent *adj* ephemeral, fleeting, flitting, fugitive, passing, short-lived, transient, transitory, vanishing.

evaporate *vb* distil, volatilize; dehydrate, dry, vaporize; disperse, dissolve, fade, vanish.

evaporation *n* distillation, volatilization; dehydration, drying, vaporization; disappearance, dispersal, dissolution.

evasion *n* artifice, avoidance, bluffing, deceit, dodge, equivocation, escape, excuse, funking, prevarication, quibble, shift, subterfuge, shuffling, sophistical, tergiversation.

evasive *adj* elusive, elusory, equivocating, prevaricating, shuffling, slippery, sophistical.

even *vb* balance, equalize, harmonize, symmetrize; align, flatten, flush, level, smooth, square. * *adj* flat, horizontal, level, plane, smooth; calm, composed, equable, equal, peaceful, placid, regular, steady, uniform, unruffled; direct, equitable, fair, impartial, just, straightforward. * *adv* exactly, just, verily; likewise. * *n* eve, evening, eventide, vesper.

evening *n* dusk, eve, even, eventide, nightfall, sunset, twilight.

event *n* circumstance, episode, fact, happening, incident, occurrence; conclusion, consequence, end, issue, outcome, result, sequel, termination; adventure, affair.

eventful *adj* critical, important, memorable, momentous, remarkable, signal, stirring.

eventual *adj* final, last, ultimate; conditional, contingent, possible. * *adv* always, aye, constantly, continually, eternally, ever evermore, forever, incessantly, perpetually, unceasingly.

everlasting *adj* ceaseless, constant, continual, endless, eternal, ever-during, incessant, interminable, never-ceasing, never-ending, perpetual, unceasing, unending, unintermitting, uninterrupted; deathless, ever-living, immortal, imperishable, never-dying, undying.

evermore *adv* always, constantly, continually, eternally, ever, forever, perpetually.

everyday *adj* accustomed, common, commonplace, customary, habitual, routine, usual, wonted.

evict *vb* dispossess, eject, thrust out.

evidence *vb* evince, make clear, manifest, prove, show, testify, vouch. * *n* affirmation, attestation, averment, confirmation, corroboration, deposition, grounds, indication, proof, testimony, token, trace, voucher, witness.

evident *adj* apparent, bald, clear, conspicuous, distinct, downright, incontestable, indisputable, manifest, obvious, open, overt, palpable, patent, plain, unmistakable.

evil *adj* bad, ill; base, corrupt, malicious, malevolent, malign, nefarious, perverse, sinful, vicious, vile, wicked, wrong; bad, deleterious, baleful, baneful, destructive, harmful, hurtful, injurious, mischievous, noxious, pernicious, profane; adverse, calamitous, diabolic, disastrous, unfortunate, unhappy, unpropitious, woeful. * *n* calamity, disaster, ill, misery, misfortune, pain, reverse, sorrow, suffering, woe; badness, baseness, corruption, depravity, malignity, sin, viciousness, wickedness; bale, bane, blast, canker, curse, harm, injury, mischief, wrong.

evince *vb* establish, evidence, manifest, prove, show; disclose, display, exhibit, indicate, reveal.

eviscerate *vb* disembowel, embowel, gut.

evoke *vb* arouse, elicit, excite, provoke, rouse.

evolve *vb* develop, educe, exhibit, expand, open, unfold, unroll.

exacerbate *vb* aggravate, embitter, enrage, exasperate, excite, inflame, infuriate, irritate, provoke, vex.

exact *vb* elicit, extort, mulch, require, squeeze; ask, claim, compel, demand, enforce, requisition, take. * *adj* rigid, rigorous, scrupulous, severe, strict; diametric, express, faultless, precise, true; accurate, close, correct, definite, faithful, literal, undeviating; accurate, critical, delicate, fine, nice, sensitive; careful, methodical, punctilious, orderly, punctual, regular.

exacting *adj* critical, difficult, exactive, rigid, extortionary.

exaction *n* contribution, extortion, oppression, rapacity, tribute.

exactness *n* accuracy, correctness, exactitude, faithfulness, faultlessness, fidelity, nicety, precision, rigour; carefulness, method, precision, regularity, rigidness, scrupulousity, scrupulousness, strictness.

exaggerate *vb* enlarge, magnify, overcharge, overcolour, overstate, romance, strain, stretch.

exalt *vb* elevate, erect, heighten, lift up, raise; aggrandize, dignify, elevate, ennoble; bless, extol, glorify, magnify, praise.

exalted *adj* elated, elevated, high, highflown, lofty, lordly, magnificent.

examination *n* inspection, observation; exploration, inquiry, inquisition, investigation, perusal, research, search, scrutiny, survey; catechism, probation, review, test, trial.

examine *vb* inspect, observe; canvass, consider, explore, inquire, investigate, scrutinize, study, test; catechize, interrogate.

example *n* archetype, copy, model, pattern, piece, prototype, representative, sample, sampler, specimen, standard; exemplification, illustration, instance, precedent, warning.

exanimate *adj* dead, defunct, inanimate, lifeless; inanimate, inert, sluggish, spiritless, torpid.

exasperate *vb* affront, anger, chafe, enrage, incense, irritate, nettle, offend, provoke, vex; aggravate, exacerbate, inflame, rouse.

exasperation *n* annoyance, exacerbation, irritation, pro- vocation; anger, fury, ire, passion, rage, wrath; aggravation, heightening, increase, worsening.

excavate *vb* burrow, cut, delve, dig, hollow, hollow out, scoop, trench.

exceed *vb* cap, overstep, surpass, transcend; excel, outdo, outstrip, outvie, pass.

excel *vb* beat, eclipse, outdo, outrival, outstrip, outvie, surpass; cap, exceed, transcend.

excellence *n* distinction, eminence, pre-eminence, superiority, transcendence; fineness, fitness, goodness, perfection, purity, quality, superiority; advantage; goodness, probity, uprightness, virtue, worth.

excellent *adj* admirable, choice, crack, eminent, first-rate, prime, sterling, superior, tiptop, transcendent; deserving, estimable, praiseworthy, virtuous, worthy.

except *vb* exclude, leave out, omit, reject. * *conj* unless. * *prep* bar, but, excepting, excluding, save.

exceptional *adj* aberrant, abnormal, anomalous, exceptive, irregular, peculiar, rare, special, strange, superior, uncommon, unnatural, unusual.

excerpt *vb* cite, cull, extract, quote, select, take. * *n* citation, extract, quotation, selection.

excess *adj* excessive, unnecessary, redundant, spare, superfluous, surplus. * *n* disproportion, fulsomeness, glut, oversupply, plethora, redundance, redundancy, surfeit, superabundance, superfluity; overplus, remainder, surplus; debauchery, dissipation, dissoluteness, intemperance, immoderation, overindulgence, unrestraint; extravagance, immoderation, overdoing.

excessive *adj* disproportionate, exuberant, superabundant, superfluous, undue; extravagant, enormous, inordinate, outrageous, unreasonable; extreme, immoderate, intemperate; vehement, violent.

exchange *vb* barter, change, commute, shuffle, substitute, swap, trade, truck; bandy, interchange. * *n* barter, change, commutation, dealing, shuffle, substitution, trade, traffic; interchange, reciprocity; bazaar, bourse, fair, market.

excise[1] *n* capitation, customs, dues, duty, tariff, tax, taxes, toll.

excise[2] *vb* cancel, cut, delete, edit, efface, eradicate, erase, expunge, extirpate, remove, strike out.

excision *n* destruction, eradication, extermination, extirpation.

excitable *adj* impressible, nervous, sensitive, susceptible; choleric, hasty, hot-headed, hot-tempered, irascible, irritable, passionate, quick-tempered.

excite *vb* animate, arouse, awaken, brew, evoke, impel, incite, inflame, instigate, kindle, move, prompt, provoke, rouse, spur, stimulate; create, elicit, evoke, raise; agitate, discompose, disturb, irritate.

excitement *n* excitation, exciting; incitement, motive, stimulus; activity, agitation, bustle, commotion, disturbance, ferment, flutter, perturbation, sensation, stir, tension; choler, heat, irritation, passion, violence, warmth.

exclaim *vb* call, cry, declare, ejaculate, shout, utter, vociferate.

exclude *vb* ban, bar, blackball, debar, ostracize, preclude, reject; hinder, prevent, prohibit, restrain, withhold; except, omit; eject, eliminate, expel, extrude.

exclusive *adj* debarring, excluding; illiberal, narrow, narrow-minded, selfish, uncharitable; aristocratic, choice, clannish, cliquish, fastidious, fashionable, select, snobbish; only, sole, special.

excommunicate *vb* anathematize, ban, curse, denounce, dismiss, eject, exclude, expel, exscind, proscribe, unchurch.

excoriate *vb* abrade, flay, gall, scar, scarify, score, skin, strip.

excrement *n* dejections, dung, faeces, excreta, excretion, ordure, stool.

excrescence *n* fungus, growth, knob, lump, outgrowth, protuberance, tumour, wart.

excrete *vb* discharge, eject, eliminate, separate.

excruciate *vb* agonize, rack, torment, torture.

exculpate *vb* absolve, acquit, clear, discharge, exonerate, free, justify, release, set right, vindicate.

excursion *n* drive, expedition, jaunt, journey, ramble, ride, sally, tour, trip, voyage, walk; digression, episode.

excursive *adj* devious, diffuse, digressive, discursive, erratic, rambling, roaming, roving, wandering.

excusable *adj* allowable, defensible, forgivable, justifiable, pardonable, venial, warrantable.

excursus *n* discussion, disquisition, dissertation.

excuse *vb* absolve, acquit, exculpate, exonerate, forgive, pardon, remit; extenuate, justify; exempt, free, release; overlook. * *n* absolution, apology, defence, extenuation, justification, plea; colour, disguise, evasion, guise, pretence, pretext, makeshift, semblance, subterfuge.

execrable *adj* abhorrent, abominable, accursed, cursed, damnable, detestable, hateful, odious; disgusting, loathsome, nauseating, nauseous, obnoxious, offensive, repulsive, revolting, sickening, vile.

execrate *vb* curse, damn, imprecate; abhor, abominate, detest, hate, loathe.

execute *vb* accomplish, achieve, carry out, complete. consummate, do, effect, effectuate, finish, perform, perpetrate; administer, enforce, seal, sign; behead, electrocute, guillotine, hang.

execution *n* accomplishment, achievement, completion, consummation, operation, performance; warrant, writ; beheading, electrocution, hanging.

executive *adj* administrative, commanding, controlling, directing, managing, ministerial, officiating, presiding, ruling. * *n* administrator, director, manager.

exegetic, exegetical *adj* explanatory, explicative, explicatory, expository, hermeneutic, interpretative.

exemplary *adj* assiduous, close, exact, faithful, punctual, punctilious, rigid, rigorous, scrupulous; commendable, correct, good, estimable, excellent, praiseworthy, virtuous; admonitory, condign, monitory, warning.

exemplify *vb* evidence, exhibit, illustrate, manifest, show.

exempt *vb* absolve, except, excuse, exonerate, free, release, relieve. * *adj* absolved, excepted, excused, exempted, free, immune, liberated, privileged, released.

exemption *n* absolution, dispensation, exception, immunity, privilege, release.

exercise *vb* apply, busy, employ, exert, praxis, use; effect, exert, produce, wield; break in, discipline, drill, habituate, school, train; practise, prosecute, pursue; task, test, try; afflict, agitate, annoy, burden, pain, trouble. * *n* appliance, application, custom, employment, operation, performance, play, plying, practice, usage, use, working; action, activity, effort, exertion, labour, toil, work; discipline, drill, drilling, schooling, training; lesson, praxis, study, task, test, theme.

exert *vb* employ, endeavour, exercise, labour, strain, strive, struggle, toil, use, work.

exertion *n* action, exercise, exerting, use; attempt, effort, endeavour, labour, strain, stretch, struggle, toil, trial.

exhalation *n* emission, evaporation; damp, effluvium, fog, fume, mist, reek, smoke, steam, vapour.

exhale *vb* breathe, discharge, elect, emanate, emit, evaporate, reek; blow, expire, puff.

exhaust *vb* drain, draw, empty; consume, destroy, dissipate, expend, impoverish, lavish, spend, squander, waste; cripple, debilitate, deplete, disable, enfeeble, enervate, overtire, prostrate, weaken.

exhaustion *n* debilitation, enervation, fatigue, lassitude, weariness.

exhibit *vb* demonstrate, disclose, display, evince, expose, express, indicate, manifest, offer, present, reveal, show; offer, present, propose.

exhibition *n* demonstration, display, exposition, manifestation, representation, spectacle, show; allowance, benefaction, grant, pension, scholarship.

exhilarate *vb* animate, cheer, elate, enliven, gladden, inspire, inspirit, rejoice, stimulate.

exhilaration *n* animating, cheering, elating, enlivening, gladdening, rejoicing, stimulating; animation, cheer, cheerfulness, gaiety, gladness, glee, good spirits, hilarity, joyousness.

exhort *vb* advise, caution, encourage, incite, persuade, stimulate, urge, warm; preach.

exhume *vb* disentomb, disinhume, disinter, unbury, unearth.

exigency, exigence *n* demand, necessity, need, requirement, urgency, want; conjuncture, crisis, difficulty, distress, emergency, extremity, juncture, nonplus, quandary, pass, pinch, pressure, strait.

exiguous *adj* attenuated, diminutive, fine, small, scanty, slender, tiny.

exile *vb* banish, expatriate, expel, ostracize, proscribe. * *n* banishment, expatriation, expulsion, ostracism, proscription, separation; outcast, refugee.

exist *vb* be, breathe, live; abide, continue, endure, last, remain.

existence *n* being, subsisting, subsistence; being, creature, entity, essence, thing; animation, continuation, life, living, vitality, vivacity.

exit *vb* depart, egress, go, leave. * *n* departure, withdrawal; death, decrease, demise, end; egress, outlet.

exonerate *vb* absolve, acquit, clear, exculpate, justify, vindicate; absolve, discharge, except, exempt, free, release.

exorbitant *adj* enormous, excessive, extravagant, inordinate, unreasonable.

exorcise *vb* cast out, drive away, expel; deliver, purify; address, conjure.

exordium *n* introduction, opening, preamble, preface, prelude, proem, prologue.

exotic *adj* extraneous, foreign; extravagant.

expand *vb* develop, open, spread, unfold, unfurl; diffuse, enlarge, extend, increase, stretch; dilate, distend, enlarge.

expanse *n* area, expansion, extent, field, stretch.

expansion *n* expansion, opening, spreading; diastole, dilation, distension, swelling; development, diffusion, enlargement, increase; expanse, extent, stretch.

ex parte *adj* biased, one-sided, partisan.

expatiate *vb* amplify, decant, dilate, enlarge, range, rove.

expatriate *vb* banish, exile, expel, ostracize, proscribe. * *adj* banished, exiled, refugee. * *n* displaced person, emigrant, exile.

expect *vb* anticipate, await, calculate, contemplate, forecast, foresee, hope, reckon, rely.

expectancy *n* expectance, expectation; abeyance, prospect.

expectation *n* anticipation, expectance, expectancy, hope, prospect; assurance, confidence, presumption, reliance, trust.

expedient *adj* advisable, appropriate, convenient, desirable, fit, proper, politic, suitable; advantageous, profitable, useful. * *n* contrivance, device, means, method, resort, resource, scheme, shift, stopgap, substitute.

expedite *vb* accelerate, advance, dispatch, facilitate, forward, hasten, hurry, precipitate, press, quicken, urge.

expedition *n* alacrity, alertness, celerity, dispatch, haste, promptness, quickness, speed; enterprise, undertaking; campaign, excursion, journey, march, quest, voyage.

expeditious *adj* quick, speedy, swift, rapid; active, alert, diligent, nimble, prompt, punctual, swift.

expel *vb* dislodge, egest, eject, eliminate, excrete; discharge, eject, evacuate, void; bounce, discharge, exclude, exscind, fire, oust, relegate, remove; banish, disown, excommunicate, exile, expatriate, ostracize, proscribe, unchurch.

expend *vb* disburse, spend; consume, employ, exert, use; dissipate, exhaust, scatter, waste.

expenditure *n* disbursement, outlay, outlaying, spending; charge, cost, expenditure, outlay.

expensive *adj* costly, dear, high-priced; extravagant, lavish, wasteful.

experience *vb* endure, suffer; feel, know; encounter, suffer, undergo. * *n* endurance, practice, trial; evidence, knowledge, proof, test, testimony.

experienced *adj* able, accomplished, expert, instructed, knowing, old, practised, qualified, skilful, trained, thoroughbred, versed, veteran, wise.

experiment *vb* examine, investigate, test, try. * *n* assay, examination, investigation, ordeal, practice, proof, test, testimony, touchstone, trial.

expert *adj* able, adroit, apt, clever, dextrous, proficient, prompt, quick, ready, skilful. * *n* adept, authority, connoisseur, crack, master, specialist.

expertise *n* adroitness, aptness, dexterity, facility, promptness, skilfulness, skill.

expiate *vb* atone, redeem, satisfy.

expiration n death, decease, demise, departure, exit; cessation, close, conclusion, end, termination.

expire *vb* cease, close, conclude, end, stop, terminate; emit, exhale; decease, depart, die, perish.

explain *vb* demonstrate, elucidate, expound, illustrate, interpret, resolve, solve, unfold, unravel; account for, justify, warrant.

explanation *n* clarification, description, elucidation, exegesis, explication, exposition, illustration, interpretation; account, answer, deduction, justification, key, meaning, secret, solution, warrant.

explicit *adj* absolute, categorical, clear, definite, determinate, exact, express, plain, positive, precise, unambiguous, unequivocal, unreserved.

explode *vb* burst, detonate, discharge, displode, shatter, shiver; contemn, discard, repudiate, scorn, scout.

exploit *vb* befool, milk, use, utilize. * *n* achievement, act, deed, feat.

explore *vb* examine, fathom, inquire, inspect, investigate, prospect, scrutinize, seek.

explosion *n* blast, burst, bursting, clap, crack, detonation, discharge, displosion, fulmination, pop.

exponent *n* example, illustration, index, indication, specimen, symbol, type; commentator, demonstrator, elucidator, expounder, illustrator, interpreter.

expose *vb* bare, display, uncover; descry, detect, disclose, unearth; denounce, mask; subject; endanger, jeopardize, risk, venture.

exposé *n* exhibit, exposition, manifesto; denouncement, divulgement, exposure, revelation.

exposition *n* disclosure, interpretation; commentary, critique, elucidation, exegesis, explanation, explication, interpretation; display, show.

expound *vb* develop, present, rehearse, reproduce, unfold; clear, elucidate, explain, interpret.

express *vb* air, assert, asseverate, declare, emit, enunciate, manifest, utter, vent, signify, speak, state, voice; betoken, denote, equal, exhibit, indicate, intimate, present, represent, show, symbolize. * *adj* categorical, clear, definite, determinate, explicit, outspoken, plain, positive, unambiguous; accurate, close, exact, faithful, precise, true; particular, special; fast, nonstop, quick, rapid, speedy, swift. * *n* dispatch, message.

expression *n* assertion, asseveration, communication, declaration, emission, statement, utterance, voicing; language, locution, phrase, remark, saying, term, word; air, aspect, look, mien.

expressive *adj* indicative, meaningful, significant; demonstrative, eloquent, emphatic, energetic, forcible, lively, strong, vivid; appropriate, sympathetic, well-modulated.

expulsion *n* discharge, eviction, expelling, ousting; elimination, evacuation, excretion; ejection, excision, excommunication, extrusion, ostracism, separation.

expunge *vb* annihilate, annul, cancel, delete, destroy, efface, erase, obliterate, wipe out.

expurgate *vb* clean, cleanse, purge, purify; bowdlerize, emasculate.

exquisite *adj* accurate, delicate, discriminating, exact, fastidious, nice, refined; choice, elect, excellent, precious, rare, valuable; complete, consummate, matchless, perfect; acute, keen, intense, poignant. * *n* beau, coxcomb, dandy, fop, popinjay.

extant *adj* existent, existing, present, surviving, undestroyed, visible.

extempore *adj* extemporaneous, extemporary, impromptu, improvised. * *adv* offhand, suddenly, unpremeditatedly, unpreparedly.

extend *vb* reach, stretch; continue, elongate, lengthen, prolong, protract, widen; augment, broaden, dilate, distend, enlarge, expand, increase; diffuse, spread; give, impart, offer, yield; lie, range.

extensible *adj* ductile, elastic, extendible, extensile, protractible, protractile.

extension *n* augmentation, continuation, delay, dilatation, dilation, distension, enlargement, expansion, increase, prolongation, protraction.

extensive *adj* broad, capacious, comprehensive, expanded, extended, far-reaching, large, wide, widespread.

extent *n* amplitude, expanse, expansion; amount, bulk, content, degree, magnitude, size, volume; compass, measure, length, proportions, reach, stretch; area, field, latitude, range, scope; breadth, depth, height, width.

extenuate *vb* diminish, lessen, reduce, soften, weaken; excuse, mitigate, palliate, qualify.

exterior *adj* external, outer, outlying, outside, outward, superficial, surface; extrinsic, foreign. * *n* outside, surface; appearance.

exterminate *vb* abolish, annihilate, destroy, eliminate, eradicate, extirpate, uproot.

external *adj* exterior, outer, outside, outward, superficial; extrinsic, foreign; apparent, visible.

extinct *adj* extinguished, quenched; closed, dead, ended, lapsed, terminated, vanished.

extinction *n* death, extinguishment; abolishment, abolition, annihilation, destruction, excision, extermination, extirpation.

extinguish *vb* choke, douse, put out, quell, smother, stifle, suffocate, suppress; destroy, nullify, subdue; eclipse, obscure.

extirpate *vb* abolish, annihilate, deracinate, destroy, eradicate, exterminate, uproot, weed.

extol *vb* celebrate, exalt, glorify, laud, magnify,

praise; applaud, commend, eulogize, panegyrize.

extort *vb* elicit, exact, extract, force, squeeze, wrench, wrest, wring.

extortion *n* blackmail, compulsion, demand, exaction, oppression, overcharge, rapacity, tribute; exorbitance.

extortionate *adj* bloodsucking, exacting, hard, harsh, oppressive, rapacious, rigorous, severe; exorbitant, unreasonable.

extra *adj* accessory, additional, auxiliary, collateral; another, farther, fresh, further, more, new, other, plus, ulterior; side, spare, supernumerary, supplemental, supplementary, surplus; extraordinary, extreme, unusual. * *adv* additionally, also, beyond, farthermore, furthermore, more, moreover, plus. * *n* accessory, appendage, collateral, nonessential, special, supernumerary, supplement; bonus, premium; balance, leftover, remainder, spare, surplus.

extract *vb* extort, pull out, remove, withdraw; derive, distil, draw, express, squeeze; cite, determine, derive, quote, select. * *n* citation, excerpt, passage, quotation, selection; decoction, distillation, essence, infusion, juice.

extraction *n* drawing out, derivation, distillation, elicitation, essence, pulling out; birth, descent, genealogy, lineage, origin, parentage.

extraneous *adj* external, extrinsic, foreign; additional, adventitious, external, superfluous, supplementary, unessential.

extraordinary *adj* abnormal, amazing, distinguished, egregious, exceptional, marvellous, monstrous, particular, peculiar, phenomenal, prodigious, rare, remarkable, signal, singular, special, strange, uncommon, unprecedented, unusual, unwonted, wonderful.

extravagance *n* excess, enormity, exorbitance, preposterousness, unreasonableness; absurdity, excess, folly, irregularity, wildness; lavishness, prodigality, profuseness, profusion, superabundance; waste.

extravagant *adj* excessive, exorbitant, inordinate, preposterous, unreasonable; absurd, foolish, irregular, wild; lavish, prodigal, profuse, spendthrift.

extreme *adj* farthest, outermost, remotest, utmost, uttermost; greatest, highest; final, last, ultimate; drastic, egregious, excessive, extravagant, immoderate, intense, outrageous, radical, unreasonable. * *n* end, extremity, limit; acme, climax, degree, height, pink; danger, distress.

extremity *n* border, edge, end, extreme, limb, termination, verge.

extricate *vb* clear, deliver, disembarrass, disengage, disentangle, liberate, release, relieve.

extrinsic *adj* external, extraneous, foreign, outside, outward, superabundance, superfluity.

exuberance *n* abundance, copiousness, flood, luxuriance, plenitude; excess, lavishness, overabundance, overflow, overgrowth, over-luxuriance, profusion, rankness, redundancy, superabundance, superfluity.

exuberant *adj* abounding, abundant, copious, fertile, flowing, luxuriant, prolific, rich; excessive, lavish, overabundant, overflowing, over-luxuriant, profuse, rank, redundant, superabounding, superabundant, wanton.

exude *vb* discharge, excrete, secrete, sweat; infiltrate, ooze, percolate.

exult *vb* gloat, glory, jubilate, rejoice, transport, triumph, taunt, vault.

exultation *n* delight, elation, joy, jubilation, transport, triumph.

eye *vb* contemplate, inspect, ogle, scrutinize, survey, view, watch. * *n* estimate, judgement, look, sight, vision, view; inspection, notice, observation, scrutiny, sight, vigilance, watch; aperture, eyelet, peephole, perforation; bud, sho0t.

F

fable *n* allegory, legend, myth, parable, story, tale; fabrication, falsehood, fiction, figment, forgery, untruth.

fabric *n* building, edifice, pile, structure; conformation, make, texture, workmanship; cloth, material, stuff, textile, tissue, web.

fabricate *vb* build, construct, erect, frame; compose, devise, fashion, make, manufacture; coin, fake, feign, forge, invent.

fabrication *n* building, construction, erection; manufacture; fable, fake, falsehood, fiction, figment, forgery, invention, lie.

fabulous *adj* amazing, apocryphal, coined, fabricated, feigned, fictitious, forged, imaginary, invented, legendary, marvellous, mythical, romancing, unbelievable, unreal.

façade *n* elevation, face, front.

face *vb* confront; beard, buck, brave, dare, defy, front, oppose; dress, level, polish, smooth; cover, incrust, veneer. * *n* cover, facet, surface; breast, escarpment, front; countenance, features, grimace, physiognomy, visage; appearance, expression, look, semblance; assurance, audacity, boldness, brass, confidence, effrontery, impudence.

facet *n* cut, face, lozenge, surface.

facetious *adj* amusing, comical, droll, funny, humorous, jocose, jocular, pleasant, waggish, witty; entertaining, gay, lively, merry, sportive, sprightly.

facile *adj* easy; affable, approachable, complaisant, conversable, courteous, mild; compliant, ductile, flexible, fluent, manageable, pliable, pliant, tractable, yielding; dextrous, ready, skilful.

facilitate *vb* expedite, help.

facility *n* ease, easiness; ability, dexterity, expertness, knack, quickness, readiness; ductility, flexibility, pliancy; advantage, appliance, convenience, means, resource; affability, civility, complaisance, politeness.

facsimile *n* copy, duplicate, fax, reproduction.

fact *n* act, circumstance, deed, event, incident, occurrence, performance; actuality, certainty, existence, reality, truth.

faction *n* cabal, clique, combination, division, junta, party, side; disagreement, discord, disorder, dissension, recalcitrance, recalcitrancy, refractoriness, sedition, seditiousness, tumult, turbulence, turbulency.

factious *adj* litigious, malcontent, rebellious, recalcitrant, refractory, seditious. turbulent.

factitious *adj* artful, artificial, conventional, false, unnatural, unreal.

factor *n* agent, bailiff, broker, consignee, go-between, steward, component, element, ingredient; influence, reason.

factory *n* manufactory, mill, work, workshop.

faculty *n* ability, capability, capacity, endowment, power, property, quality; ableness, address, adroitness, aptitude, aptness, clearness, competency, dexterity, efficiency, expertness, facility, forte, ingenuity, knack, qualification, quickness, readiness, skill, skilfulness, talent, turn; body, department, profession; authority, prerogative, license, privilege, right.

fade *vb* disappear, die, evanesce, fall, faint, perish, vanish; decay, decline, droop, fall, languish, wither; bleach, blanch, pale; disperse, dissolve.

faeces *npl* dregs, lees, sediment, settlings; dung, excrement, ordure, settlings.

fag *vb* droop, flag, sink; drudge, toil; fatigue, jade, tire, weary. * *n* drudgery, fatigue, work; drudge, grub, hack; cigarette, smoke.

fail *vb* break, collapse, decay, decline, fade, sicken, sink, wane; cease, disappear; fall, miscarry, miss; neglect, omit; bankrupt, break.

failing *adj* deficient, lacking, needing, wanting; declining, deteriorating, fading, flagging, languishing, sinking, waning, wilting; unsuccessful. * *prep* lacking, needing, wanting. * *n* decay, decline; failure, miscarriage; defect, deficiency, fault, foible, frailty, imperfection, infirmity, shortcoming, vice, weakness; error, lapse, slip; bankruptcy, insolvency.

failure *n* defectiveness, deficiency, delinquency, shortcoming; fail, miscarriage, negligence, neglect, nonobservance, nonperformance, omission, slip; abortion, botch, breakdown, collapse, fiasco, fizzle; bankruptcy, crash, downfall, insolvency, ruin; decay, declension, decline, loss.

fain *adj* anxious, glad, inclined, pleased, rejoiced, well-pleased. * *adv* cheerfully, eagerly, gladly, joyfully, willingly.

faint *vb* swoon; decline, fade, fail, languish, weaken. * *adj* swooning; drooping, exhausted, feeble, languid, listless, sickly, weak; gentle, inconsiderable, little, slight, small, soft, thin; dim, dull, indistinct, perceptible, scarce, slight; cowardly, dastardly, faint-hearted, fearful, timid, timorous; dejected, depressed, discouraged, disheartened, dispirited. * *n* blackout, swoon.

faint-hearted *adj* cowardly, dastardly, faint, fearful, timid, timorous.

fair[1] *adj* spotless, unblemished, unspotted, unstained, untarnished; blond, light, white; beautiful, comely, handsome, shapely; clear, cloudless, pleasant, unclouded; favourable, prosperous; hopeful, promising, propitious; clear, distinct, open, plain, unencumbered, unobstructed; candid, frank, honest, honourable, impartial, ingenuous, just, unbiased, upright; equitable, proper; average, decent, indifferent, mediocre, moderate, ordinary, passable, reasonable, respectful, tolerable.

fair[2] *n* bazaar, carnival, exposition, festival, fete, funfair, gala, kermess.

fairy *n* brownie, elf, demon, fay, sprite.

faith *n* assurance, belief, confidence, credence, credit, dependence, reliance, trust; creed, doctrine, dogma, persuasion, religion, tenet; constancy, faithfulness, fidelity, loyalty, truth, truthfulness.

faithful *adj* constant, devoted, loyal, staunch, steadfast, true; honest, upright, reliable, trustworthy, trusty; reliable, truthful; accurate, close, conscientiousness, exact, nice, strict.

faithless *adj* unbelieving; dishonest, disloyal, false, fickle, fluctuating, inconstant, mercurial, mutable, perfidious, shifting, treacherous, truthless, unsteady, untruthful, vacillating, variable, wavering.

fall *vb* collapse, depend, descend, drop, sink, topple, tumble; abate, decline, decrease, depreciate, ebb, subside; err, lapse, sin, stumble, transgress, trespass, trip; die, perish; befall, chance, come, happen, occur, pass; become, get; come, pass. * *n* collapse, comedown, descent, downcome, dropping, falling, flop, plop, tumble; cascade, cataract, waterfall; death, destruction, downfall, overthrow, ruin, surrender; comeuppance, degradation; apostasy, declension, failure, lapse, slip; decline, decrease, depreciation, diminution, ebb, sinking, subsidence; cadence, close; declivity, inclination, slope.

fallacious *adj* absurd, deceptive, deceiving, delusive, disappointing, erroneous, false, illusive, illusory, misleading; paralogistic, sophistical, worthless.

fallacy *n* aberration, deceit, deception, delusion, error, falsehood, illusion, misapprehension, misconception, mistake, untruth; non sequitur, paralogism, sophism, sophistry.

fallibility *n* frailty, imperfection, uncertainty.

fallible *adj* erring, frail, ignorant, imperfect, uncertain, weak.

fallow *adj* left, neglected, uncultivated, unsowed, untilled; dormant, inactive, inert.

false *adj* lying, mendacious, truthless, untrue, unveracious; dishonest, dishonourable, disingenuous, disloyal, double-faced, double-tongued, faithless, false-hearted, perfidious, treacherous, unfaithful; fictitious, forged, made-up, unreliable, untrustworthy; artificial, bastard, bogus, counterfeit, factitious, feigned, forged, hollow, hypocritical, make-believe, pretended, pseudo, sham, spurious, supposititious; erroneous, improper, incorrect, unfounded, wrong; deceitful, deceiving, deceptive, disappointing, fallacious, misleading.

false-hearted *adj* dishonourable, disloyal, double, double-tongued, faithless, false, perfidious, treacherous.

falsehood *n* falsity; fabrication, fib, fiction, lie, untruth; cheat, counterfeit, imposture, mendacity, treachery.

falsify *vb* alter, adulterate, belie, cook, counterfeit, doctor, fake, falsely, garble, misrepresent, misstate, represent; disprove; violate.

falsity *n* falsehood, untruth, untruthfulness.

falter *vb* halt, hesitate, lisp, quaver, stammer, stutter; fail, stagger, stumble, totter, tremble, waver; dodder.

fame *n* bruit, hearsay, report, rumour; celebrity, credit, eminence, glory, greatness, honour, illustriousness, kudos, lustre, notoriety, renown, reputation, repute.

familiar *adj* acquainted, aware, conversant, well-versed; amicable, close, cordial, domestic, fraternal, friendly, homely, intimate, near; affable, accessible, companionable, conversable, courteous, civil, friendly, kindly, sociable, social; easy, free and easy, unceremonious, unconstrained; common, frequent, well-known. * *n* acquaintance, associate, companion, friend, intimate.

familiarity *n* acquaintance, knowledge, understanding; fellowship, friendship, intimacy; closeness, friendliness, sociability; freedom, informality, liberty; disrespect, overfreedom, presumption; intercourse.

familiarize *vb* accustom, habituate, inure, train, use.

family *n* brood, household, people; ancestors, blood, breed, clan, dynasty, kindred, house, lineage, race, stock, strain, tribe; class, genus, group, kind, subdivision.

famine *n* dearth, destitution, hunger, scarcity, starvation.

famish *vb* distress, exhaust, pinch, starve.

famous *adj* celebrated, conspicuous, distinguished, eminent, excellent, fabled, famed, far-famed, great, glorious, heroic, honoured, illustrious, immortal, notable, noted, notorious, remarkable, renowned, signal.

fan[1] *vb* agitate, beat, move, winnow; blow, cool, refresh, ventilate; excite, fire, increase, rouse, stimulate. * *n* blower, cooler, punkah, ventilator.

fan[2] *n* admirer, buff, devotee, enthusiast, fancier, follower, pursuer, supporter.

fanatic *n* bigot, devotee, enthusiast, visionary, zealot.

fanatical *adj* bigoted, enthusiastic, frenzied, mad, rabid, visionary, wild, zealous.

fanciful *adj* capricious, crotchety, imaginary,

visionary, whimsical; chimerical, fantastical, ideal, imaginary, wild.

fancy *vb* apprehend, believe, conjecture, imagine, suppose, think; conceive, imagine. * *adj* elegant, fine, nice, ornamented; extravagant, fanciful, whimsical. * *n* imagination; apprehension, conceit, conception, impression, idea, image, notion, thought; approval, fondness, inclination, judgement, liking, penchant, taste; caprice, crotchet, fantasy, freak, humour, maggot, quirk, vagary, whim, whimsy; apparition, chimera, daydream, delusion, hallucination, megrim, phantasm, reverie, vision.

fanfaron *n* blatherskite, blusterer, braggadocio, bully, hector, swaggerer, vapourer.

fang *n* claw, nail, talon, tooth; tusk.

fantastic *adj* chimerical, fanciful, imaginary, romantic, unreal, visionary; bizarre, capricious, grotesque, odd, quaint, queer, strange, whimsical, wild.

far *adj* distant, long, protracted, remote; farther, remoter; alienated, estranged, hostile. * *adv* considerably, extremely, greatly, very much; afar, distantly, far away, remotely.

farce *n* burlesque, caricature, parody, travesty; forcemeat, stuffing.

farcical *adj* absurd, comic, droll, funny, laughable, ludicrous, ridiculous.

fardel *n* bundle, burden, load, pack; annoyance, burden, ill, trouble.

fare *vb* go, journey, pass, travel; happen, prosper, prove; feed, live, manage, subsist. * *n* charge, price, ticket money; passenger, traveller; board, commons, food, table, victuals, provisions; condition, experience, fortune, luck, outcome.

farewell *n* adieu, leave-taking, valediction; departure, leave, parting, valedictory.

far-fetched *adj* abstruse, catachrestic, forced, recondite, strained.

farrago *n* gallimaufry, hodgepodge, hotchpotch, jumble, medley, miscellany, mixture, potpourri, salmagundi.

farther *adj* additional; further, remoter, ulterior. * *adv* beyond, further; besides, furthermore, moreover.

farthingale *n* crinoline, hoop, hoop skirt.

fascinate *vb* affect, bewitch, overpower, spellbind, stupefy, transfix; absorb, captivate, catch, charm, delight, enamour, enchant, enrapture, entrance.

fascination *n* absorption, charm, enchantment, magic, sorcery, spell, witchcraft, witchery.

fash *vb* harass, perplex, plague, torment, trouble, vex, worry. * *n* anxiety, care, trouble, vexation.

fashion *vb* contrive, create, design, forge, form, make, mould, pattern, shape; accommodate, adapt, adjust, fit, suit. * *n* appearance, cast, configuration, conformation, cut, figure, form, make, model, mould, pattern, shape, stamp; manner, method, sort, wake; conventionalism, conventionality, custom, fad, mode, style, usage, vogue; breeding, gentility; quality.

fashionable *adj* modish, stylish; current, modern, prevailing, up-to-date; customary, usual; genteel, well-bred.

fast[1] *adj* close, fastened, firm, fixed, immovable, tenacious, tight; constant, faithful, permanent, resolute, staunch, steadfast, unswerving, unwavering; fortified, impregnable, strong; deep, profound, sound; fleet, quick, rapid, swift; dissipated, dissolute, extravagant, giddy, reckless, thoughtless, thriftless, wild. * *adv* firmly, immovably, tightly; quickly, rapidly, swiftly; extravagantly, prodigally, reckless, wildly.

fast[2] *vb* abstain, go hungry, starve. * *n* abstention, abstinence, diet, fasting, starvation.

fasten *vb* attach, bind, bolt, catch, chain, cleat, fix, gird, lace, lock, pin, secure, strap, tether, tie; belay, bend; connect, hold, join, unite.

fastidious *adj* critical, dainty, delicate, difficult, exquisite, finical, hypercritical, meticulous, overdelicate, overnice, particular, precise, precious, punctilious, queasy, squeamish.

fat *adj* adipose, fatty, greasy, oily, oleaginous, unctuous; corpulent, fleshy, gross, obese, paunchy, portly, plump, pudgy, pursy; coarse, dull, heavy, sluggish, stupid; lucrative, profitable, rich; fertile, fruitful, productive, rich. * *n* adipose tissue, ester, grease, oil; best part, cream, flower; corpulence, fatness, fleshiness, obesity, plumpness, stoutness.

fatal *adj* deadly, lethal, mortal; baleful, baneful, calamitous, catastrophic, destructive, mischievous, pernicious, ruinous; destined, doomed, foreordained, inevitable, predestined.

fatality *n* destiny, fate; mortality; calamity, disaster.

fate *n* destination, destiny, fate; cup, die, doom, experience, lot, fortune, portion, weird; death, destruction, ruin.

fated *adj* appointed, destined, doomed, foredoomed, predetermined, predestinated, predestined, preordained.

fatherly *adj* benign, kind, paternal, protecting, tender.

fathom *vb* comprehend, divine, penetrate, reach, understand; estimate, gauge, measure, plumb, probe, sound.

fathomless *adj* abysmal, bottomless, deep, immeasurable, profound; impenetrable, incomprehensible, obscure.

fatigue *vb* exhaust, fag, jade, tire, weaken, weary. * *n* exhaustion, lassitude, tiredness, weariness; hardship, labour, toil.

fatuity *n* foolishness, idiocy, imbecility, stupidity; absurdity, folly, inanity, infatuation, madness.

fatuous *adj* dense, drivelling, dull, foolish, idiotic, stupid, witless; infatuated, mad, senseless, silly, weak.

fault *n* blemish, defect, flaw, foible, frailty, imperfection, infirmity, negligence, obliquity, offence, shortcoming, spot, weakness; delinquency, error, indiscretion, lapse, misdeed, misdemeanour, offence, peccadillo, slip, transgression, trespass, vice, wrong; blame, culpability.

faultless *adj* blameless, guiltless, immaculate, innocent, sinless, spotless, stainless; accurate, correct, perfect, unblemished.

faulty *adj* bad, defective, imperfect, incorrect; blameable, blameworthy, censurable, culpable, reprehensible.

faux pas *n* blunder, indiscretion, mistake.

favour *vb* befriend, countenance, encourage, patronize; approve; ease, facilitate; aid, assist, help, oblige, support; extenuate, humour, indulge, palliate, spare. * *n* approval, benignity, countenance, esteem, friendless, goodwill, grace, kindness; benefaction, benefit, boon, dispensation, kindness; championship, patronage, popularity, support; gift, present, token; badge, decoration, knot, rosette; leave, pardon, permission; advantage, cover, indulgence, protection; bias, partiality, prejudice.

favourable *adj* auspicious, friendly, kind, propitious, well-disposed, willing; conductive, contributing, propitious; adapted, advantage, beneficial, benign, convenient, fair, fit, good, helpful, suitable.

favourite *adj* beloved, darling, dear; choice, fancied, esteemed, pet, preferred.

fawn *vb* bootlick, bow, creep, cringe, crouch, dangle, kneel, stoop, toady, truckle.

fealty *n* allegiance, homage, loyalty, obeisance, submission; devotion, faithfulness, fidelity, honour, loyalty.

fear *vb* apprehend, dread; revere, reverence, venerate. * *n* affright, alarm, apprehension, consternation, dismay, dread, fright, horror, panic, phobia, scare, terror; disquietude, flutter, perturbation, palpitation, quaking, quivering, trembling, tremor, trepidation; anxiety, apprehension, concern, misdoubt, misgiving, qualm, solicitude; awe, dread, reverence, veneration.

fearful *adj* afraid, apprehensive, haunted; chicken-hearted, chicken-livered, cowardly, faint-hearted, lily-livered, nervous, pusillanimous, timid, timorous; dire, direful, dreadful, frightful, ghastly, horrible, shocking, terrible.

fearless *adj* bold, brave, courageous, daring, dauntless, doughty, gallant, heroic, intrepid, unterrified, valiant, valorous.

feasible *adj* achievable, attainable, possible, practicable, suitable.

feast *vb* delight, gladden, gratify, rejoice. * *n* banquet, carousal, entertainment, regale, repast, revels, symposium, treat; celebration, festival, fete, holiday; delight, enjoyment, pleasure.

feat *n* accomplishment, achievement, act, deed, exploit, performance, stunt, trick.

feather *n* plume; kind, nature, species.

featly *adv* adroitly, dextrously, nimbly, skilfully.

feature *vb* envisage, envision, picture, visualize; imagine; specialize; appear in, headline, star. * *n* appearance, aspect, component; conformation,

fashion, make; characteristic, item, mark, particularity, peculiarity, property, point, trait; leader, lead item, special; favour, expression, lineament; article, film, motion picture, movie, story; highlight, high spot.

fecund *adj* fruitful, impregnated, productive, prolific, rich.

fecundity *n* fertility, fruitfulness, productiveness.

federation *n* alliance, allying, confederation, federating, federation, leaguing, union, uniting; affiliation, coalition, combination, compact, confederacy, entente, federacy, league, copartnership.

fee *vb* pay, recompense, reward. * *n* account, bill, charge, compensation, honorarium, remuneration, reward, tip; benefice, fief, feud.

feeble *adj* anaemic, debilitated, declining, drooping, enervated, exhausted, frail, infirm, languid, languishing, sickly; dim, faint, imperfect, indistinct.

feed *vb* contribute, provide, supply; cherish, eat, nourish, subsist, sustain. * *n* fodder, food, foodstuff, forage, provender.

feel *vb* apprehend, intuit, perceive, sense; examine, handle, probe, touch; enjoy, experience, suffer; prove, sound, test, try; appear, look, seem; believe, conceive, deem, fancy, infer, opine, suppose, think. * *n* atmosphere, feeling, quality; finish, surface, texture.

feeling *n* consciousness, impression, notion, perception, sensation; atmosphere, sense, sentience; touch; affecting, emotion, heartstrings, impression, passion, soul, sympathy; sensibility, sentiment, susceptibility, tenderness; attitude, impression, opinion.

feign *vb* devise, fabricate, forge, imagine, invent; affect, assume, counterfeit, imitate, pretend, sham, simulate.

feint *n* artifice, blind, expedient, make-believe, pretence, stratagem, trick.

felicitate *vb* complicate, congratulate; beatify, bless, delight.

felicitous *adj* appropriate, apt, fit, happy, ingenious, inspired, opportune, pertinent, seasonable, skilful, well-timed; auspicious, fortunate, prosperous, propitious, successful.

felicity *n* blessedness, bliss, blissfulness, gladness, happiness, joy; appropriateness, aptitude, aptness, felicitousness, fitness, grace, propriety, readiness, suitableness; fortune, luck, success.

fell[1] *vb* beat, knock down, level, prostrate; cut, demolish, hew.

fell[2] *adj* barbarous, bloodthirsty, bloody, cruel, ferocious, fierce, implacable, inhuman, malicious, malign, malignant, pitiless, relentless, ruthless, sanguinary, savage, unrelenting, vandalistic; deadly, destructive.

fellow *adj* affiliated, associated, joint, like, mutual, similar, twin. * *n* associate, companion, comrade; compeer, equal, peer; counterpart, mate, match; partner; member; boy, character, individual, man, person.

fellowship *n* brotherhood, companionship, comradeship, familiarity, intimacy; participation; partnership; communion, converse, intercourse; affability, kindliness, sociability, sociableness.

felon *n* convict, criminal, culprit, delinquent, malefactor, outlaw; inflammation, whitlow.

felonious *adj* atrocious, cruel, felon, heinous, infamous, malicious, malign, malignant, nefarious, perfidious, vicious, villainous.

female *adj* delicate, gentle, ladylike, soft; fertile, pistil-bearing, pistillate.

feminine *adj* affectionate, delicate, gentle, graceful, modest, soft, tender; female, ladylike, maidenly, womanish, womanly; effeminateness, effeminacy, softness, unmanliness, weakness, womanliness.

fen *n* bog, marsh, moor, morass, quagmire, slough, swamp.

fence *vb* defend, enclose, fortify, guard, protect, surround; circumscribe, evade, equivocate, hedge, prevaricate; guard, parry. * *n* barrier, hedge, hoarding, palings, palisade, stockade, wall; defence, protection, guard, security, shield; fencing, swordplay, swordsmanship; receiver.

fenny *adj* boggy, fennish, swampy, marshy.

feral, ferine *adj* ferocious, fierce, rapacious, ravenous, savage, untamed, wild.

ferment *vb* agitate, excite, heat; boil, brew, bubble, concoct, heat, seethe. * *n* barm, leaven, yeast; agitation, commotion, fever, glow, heat, tumult.

ferocious *adj* feral, fierce, rapacious, ravenous, savage, untamed, wild; barbarous, bloody, bloodthirsty, brutal, cruel, fell, inhuman, merciless, murderous, pitiless, remorseless, ruthless, sanguinary, truculent, vandalistic, violent.

ferocity *n* ferociousness, ferocity, fierceness, rapacity, savageness, wildness; barbarity, cruelty, inhumanity.

fertile *adj* bearing, breeding, fecund, prolific; exuberant, fruitful, luxuriant, plenteous, productive, rich, teeming; female, fruit-bearing, pistillate.

fertility *n* fertileness, fertility; abundance, exuberant, fruitfulness, luxuriance, plenteousness, productiveness, richness.

fervent *adj* burning, hot, glowing, melting, seething; animated, ardent, earnest, enthusiastic, fervid, fierce, fiery, glowing, impassioned, intense, passionate, vehement, warm, zealous.

fervour *n* heat, warmth; animation, ardour, eagerness, earnestness, excitement, fervency, intensity, vehemence, zeal.

fester *vb* corrupt, rankle, suppurate, ulcerate; putrefy, rot. * *n* abscess, canker, gathering, pustule, sore, suppination; festering, rankling.

festival *n* anniversary, carnival, feast, fete, gala, holiday, jubilee; banquet, carousal, celebration, entertainment, treat.

festive *adj* carnival, convivial, festal, festival, gay, jolly, jovial, joyful, merry, mirthful, uproarious.

festivity *n* conviviality, festival, gaiety, jollity, joviality, joyfulness, joyousness, merrymaking, mirth.

festoon *vb* adorn, decorate, embellish, garland, hoop, ornament. * *n* decoration, embellishment, garland, hoop, ornament, ornamentation.

fetch *vb* bring, elicit, get; accomplish, achieve, effect, perform; attain, reach. * *n* artifice, dodge, ruse, stratagem, trick.

fetid *adj* foul, malodorous, mephitic, noisome, offensive, rancid, rank, rank-smelling, stinking, strong-smelling.

fetish *n* charm, medicine, talisman.

fetter *vb* clog, hamper, shackle, trammel; bind, chain, confine, encumber, hamper, restrain, tie, trammel. * *n* bond, chain, clog, hamper, shackle.

feud *vb* argue, bicker, clash, contend, dispute, quarrel. * *n* affray, argument, bickering, broil, clashing, contention, contest, discord, dissension, enmity, fray, grudge, hostility, jarring, quarrel, rupture, strife, vendetta.

fever *n* agitation, excitement, ferment, fire, flush, heat, passion.

fey *adj* clairvoyant, ethereal, strange, unusual, whimsical; death-smitten, doomed.

fiasco *n* failure, fizzle.

fiat *n* command, decree, order, ordinance.

fibre *n* filament, pile, staple, strand, texture, thread; stamina, strength, toughness.

fickle *adj* capricious, changeable, faithless, fitful, inconstant, irresolute, mercurial, mutable, shifting, unsettled, unstable, unsteady, vacillating, variable, veering, violate, volatile, wavering.

fiction *n* fancy, fantasy, imagination, invention; novel, romance; fable, fabrication, falsehood, figment, forgery, invention, lie.

fictitious *adj* assumed, fabulous, fanciful, feigned, imaginary, invented, mythical, unreal; artificial, counterfeit, dummy, false, spurious, supposititious.

fiddle *vb* dawdle, fidget, interfere, tinker, trifle; cheat, swindle, tamper. * *n* fraud, swindle; fiddler, violin, violinist.

fiddle-de-dee *interj* fudge, moonshine, nonsense, stuff.

fiddle-faddle *n* frivolity, gabble, gibberish, nonsense, prate, stuff, trifling, trivia, twaddle.

fidelity *n* constancy, devotedness, devotion, dutifulness, faithfulness, fealty, loyalty, trueheartedness, truth; accuracy, closeness, exactness, faithfulness, precision.

fidget *vb* chafe, fret, hitch, twitch, worry. * *n* fidgetiness, impatience, restlessness, uneasiness.

fiduciary *adj* confident, fiducial, firm, steadfast, trustful, undoubting, unwavering; reliable, trustworthy. * *n* depositary, trustee.

field *n* clearing, glebe, meadow; expanse, extent, opportunity, range, room, scope, surface; department, domain, province, realm, region.

fiendish *adj* atrocious, cruel, demoniac, devilish, diabolical, hellish, implacable, infernal, malevolent, malicious, malign, malignant.

fierce *adj* barbarous, brutal, cruel, fell, ferocious,

furious, infuriate, ravenous, savage; fiery, impetuous, murderous, passionate, tearing, tigerish, truculent, turbulent, uncurbed, untamed, vehement, violent.

fiery *adj* fervent, fervid, flaming, heated, hot, glowing, lurid; ardent, fierce, impassioned, impetuous, inflamed, passionate, vehement.

fight *vb* battle, combat, war; contend, contest, dispute, feud, oppose, strive, struggle, wrestle; encounter, engage; handle, manage, manoeuvre. * *n* affair, affray, action, battle, brush, combat, conflict, confrontation, contest, duel, encounter, engagement, melée, quarrel, struggle, war; brawl, broil, riot, row, skirmish; fighting, pluck, pugnacity, resistance, spirit, temper.

figment *n* fable, fabrication, falsehood, fiction, invention.

figurative *adj* emblematical, representative, symbolic, representative, typical; metaphorical, tropical; florid, flowery, ornate, poetical.

figure *vb* adorn, diversify, ornament, variegate; delineate, depict, represent, signify, symbolize, typify; conceive, image, imagine, picture; calculate, cipher, compute; act, appear, perform. * *n* configuration, conformation, form, outline, shape; effigy, image, likeness, representative; design, diagram, drawing, pattern; image, metaphor, trope; emblem, symbol, type; character, digit, number, numeral.

filament *n* cirrus, fibre, fibril, gossamer, hair, strand, tendril, thread.

filch *vb* crib, nick, pilfer, purloin, rob, snitch, seal, thieve.

file[1] *vb* order, pigeonhole, record, tidy. * *n* data, dossier, folder, portfolio; column, line, list, range, rank, row, series, tier.

file[2] *vb* burnish, furbish, polish, rasp, refine, smooth.

filibuster *vb* delay, frustrate, obstruct, play for time, stall, temporize. * *n* frustrater, obstructionist, thwarter; adventurer, buccaneer, corsair, freebooter, pirate.

fill *vb* occupy, pervade; dilate, distend, expand, stretch, trim; furnish, replenish, stock, store, supply; cloy, congest, content, cram, glut, gorge, line, pack, pall, sate, satiate, satisfy, saturate, stuff, suffuse, swell; engage, fulfil, hold, occupy, officiate, perform.

film *vb* becloud, cloud, coat, cover, darken, fog, mist, obfuscate, obscure, veil; photograph, shoot, take. * *n* cloud, coating, gauze, membrane, nebula, pellicle, scum, skin, veil; thread.

filter *vb* filtrate, strain; exude, ooze, percolate, transude. * *n* diffuser, colander, riddle, sieve, sifter, strainer.

filth *n* dirt, nastiness, ordure; corruption, defilement, foulness, grossness, impurity, obscenity, pollution, squalor, uncleanness, vileness.

filthy *adj* defiled, dirty, foul, licentious, nasty, obscene, pornographic, squalid, unclean; corrupt, gross, impure, unclean; miry, mucky, muddy.

final *adj* eventual, extreme, last, latest, terminal, ultimate; conclusive, decisive, definitive, irrevocable.

finale *n* conclusion, end, termination.

finances *npl* funds, resources, revenues, treasury; income, property.

find *vb* discover, fall upon; gain, get, obtain, procure; ascertain, notice, observe, perceive, remark; catch, detect; contribute, furnish, provide, supply. * *n* acquisition, catch, discovery, finding, plum, prize, strike.

fine[1] *vb* filter, purify, refine. * *adj* comminuted, little, minute, small; capillary, delicate, small; choice, light; exact, keen, sharp; attenuated, subtle, tenuous, thin; exquisite, fastidious, nice, refined, sensitive, subtle; dandy, excellent, superb, superior; beautiful, elegant, handsome, magnificent, splendid; clean, pure, unadulterated.

fine[2] *vb* amerce, mulct, penalize, punish. * *n* amercement, forfeit, forfeiture, mulct, penalty, punishment.

finery *n* decorations, frippery, gewgaws, ornaments, splendour, showiness, trappings, trimmings, trinkets.

finesse *vb* manipulate, manoeuvre. * *n* artifice, contrivance, cunning, craft, manipulation, manoeuvre, manoeuvring, ruses, stratagems, strategy, wiles.

finger *vb* handle, manipulate, play, purloin.

finical *adj* critical, dainty, dapper, fastidious, foppish, jaunty, overnice, overparticular, scrupulous, spruce, squeamish, trim.

finish *vb* accomplish, achieve, complete, consummate, execute, fulfil, perform; elaborate, perfect, polish; close, conclude, end, terminate. * *n* elaboration, elegance, perfection, polish; close, end, death, termination, wind-up.

finite *adj* bounded, circumscribed, conditioned, contracted, definable, limited, restricted, terminable.

fire *vb* ignite, kindle, light; animate, enliven, excite, inflame, inspirit, invigorate, rouse, stir up; discharge, eject, expel, hurl. * *n* combustion; blaze, conflagration; discharge, firing; animation, ardour, enthusiasm, fervour, fervency, fever, force, heat, impetuosity, inflammation, intensity, passion, spirit, vigour, violence; light, lustre, radiance, splendour; imagination, imaginativeness, inspiration, vivacity; affliction, persecution, torture, trouble.

firm[1] *adj* established, coherent, confirmed, consistent, fast, fixed, immovable, inflexible, rooted, secure, settled, stable; compact, compressed, dense, hard, solid; constant, determined, resolute, staunch, steadfast, steady, unshaken; loyal, robust, sinewy, stanch, stout, sturdy, strong.

firm[2] *n* association, business, company, concern, corporation, house, partnership.

firmament *n* heavens, sky, vault, welkin.

firmness *n* compactness, fixedness, hardness, solidity; stability, strength; constancy, soundness, steadfastness, steadiness.

first *adj* capital, chief, foremost, highest, leading, prime, principal; earliest, eldest, original; maiden; elementary, primary, rudimentary; aboriginal, primal, primeval, primitive, pristine. * *adv* chiefly, firstly, initially, mainly, primarily, principally; before, foremost, headmost; before, rather, rather than, sooner, sooner than. * *n* alpha, initial, prime.

first-rate *adj* excellent, prime, superior.

fissure *n* breach, break, chasm, chink, cleft, crack, cranny, crevice, fracture, gap, hole, interstice, opening, rent, rift.

fit[1] *vb* adapt, adjust, suit; become, conform; accommodate, equip, prepare, provide, qualify. * *adj* capacitated, competent, fitted; adequate, appropriate, apt, becoming, befitting, consonant, convenient, fitting, good, meet, pertinent, proper, seemly, suitable.

fit[2] *n* convulsion, fit, paroxysm, qualm, seizure, spasm, spell; fancy, humour, whim; mood, pet, tantrum; interval, period, spell, turn.

fitful *adj* capricious, changeable, convulsive, fanciful, fantastic, fickle, humoursome, impulsive, intermittent, irregular, odd, spasmodic, unstable, variable, whimsical; checkered, eventful.

fitness *n* adaptation, appropriateness, aptitude, aptness, pertinence, propriety, suitableness; preparation, qualification.

fix *vb* establish, fasten, place, plant, set; adjust, correct, mend, repair; attach, bind, clinch, connect, fasten, lock, rivet, stay, tie; appoint, decide, define, determine, limit, seal, settle; consolidate, harden, solidify; abide, remain, rest; congeal, stiffen. * *n* difficulty, dilemma, quandary, pickle, plight, predicament.

flabbergast *vb* abash, amaze, astonish, astound, confound, confuse, disconcert, dumbfound, nonplus.

flabby *adj* feeble, flaccid, inelastic, limp, soft, week, yielding.

flaccid *adj* baggy, drooping, flabby, inelastic, lax, limber, limp, loose, pendulous, relaxed, soft, weak, yielding.

flag[1] *vb* droop, hang, loose; decline, droop, fail, faint, lag, languish, pine, sink, succumb, weaken, weary; stale, pall.

flag[2] *vb* indicate, mark, semaphore, sign, signal. * *n* banner, colours, ensign, gonfalon, pennant, pennon, standard, streamer.

flagellate *vb* beat, castigate, chastise, cudgel, drub, flog, scourge, thrash, whip.

flagitious *adj* abandoned, atrocious, corrupt, flagrant, heinous, infamous, monstrous, nefarious, profligate, scandalous, villainous, wicked.

flagrant *adj* burning, flaming, glowing, raging; crying, enormous, flagitious, glaring, monstrous, nefarious, notorious, outrageous, shameful, wanton, wicked.

flake *vb* desquamate, scale. * *n* lamina, layer, scale.

flamboyant *adj* bright, gorgeous, ornate, rococo.

flame *vb* blaze, shine; burn, flash, glow, warm. * *n* blaze, brightness, fire, flare, vapour; affection, ardour, enthusiasm, fervency, fervour, keenness, warmth.

flaming *adj* blazing; burning, bursting, exciting, glowing, intense, lambent, vehement, violent.

flap *vb* beat, flutter, shake, vibrate, wave. * *n* apron, fly, lap, lappet, tab; beating, flapping, flop, flutter, slap, shaking, swinging, waving.

flare *vb* blaze, flicker, flutter, waver; dazzle, flame, glare; splay, spread, widen. * *n* blaze, dazzle, flame, glare.

flash *vb* blaze, glance, glare, glisten, light, shimmer, scintillate, sparkle, twinkle. * *n* instant, moment, twinkling.

flashy *adj* flaunting, gaudy, gay, loud, ostentatious, pretentious, showy, tawdry, tinsel.

flat *adj* champaign, horizontal, level; even, plane, smooth, unbroken; low, prostrate, overthrow; dull, frigid, jejune, lifeless, monotonous, pointless, prosaic, spiritless, tame, unanimated, uniform, uninteresting; dead, flashy, insipid, mawkish, stale, tasteless, vapid; absolute, clear, direct, downright, peremptory, positive. * *adv* flatly, flush, horizontally, level. * *n* bar, sandbank, shallow, shoal, strand; champaign, lowland, plain; apartment, floor, lodging, storey.

flatter *vb* compliment, gratify, praise; blandish, blarney, butter up, cajole, coax, coddle, court, entice, fawn, humour, inveigle, wheedle.

flattery *n* adulation, blandishment, blarney, cajolery, fawning, obsequiousness, servility, sycophancy, toadyism.

flaunt *vb* boast, display, disport, flourish, parade, sport, vaunt; brandish.

flaunting *adj* flashy, garish, gaudy, ostentatious, showy, tawdry.

flavour *n* gust, gusto, relish, savour, seasoning, smack, taste, zest; admixture, lacing, seasoning; aroma, essence, soul, spirit.

flaw *n* break, breach, cleft, crack, fissure, fracture, gap, rent, rift; blemish, defect, fault, fleck, imperfection, speck, spot.

flay *vb* excoriate, flay; criticize.

fleck *vb* dapple, mottle, speckle, spot, streak, variegate. * *n* speckle, spot, streak.

flecked *adj* dappled, mottled, piebald, spotted, straked, striped, variegated.

flee *vb* abscond, avoid, decamp, depart, escape, fly, leave, run, skedaddle.

fleece *vb* clip, shear; cheat, despoil, pluck, plunder, rifle, rob, steal, strip.

fleer *vb* mock, jeer, gibe, scoff, sneer.

fleet[1] *n* armada, escadrille, flotilla, navy, squadron; company, group.

fleet[2] *adj* fast, nimble, quick, rapid, speedy, swift.

fleeting *adj* brief, caducous, ephemeral, evanescent, flitting, flying, fugitive, passing, short-lived, temporary, transient, transitory.

fleetness *n* celerity, nimbleness, quickness, rapidity, speed, swiftness, velocity.

flesh *n* food, meat; carnality, desires; kindred, race, stock; man, mankind, world.

fleshly *adj* animal, bodily, carnal, lascivious, lustful, lecherous, sensual.

fleshy *adj* corpulent, fat, obese, plump, stout.

flexibility *n* flexibleness, limbersome, lithesome, pliability, pliancy, suppleness; affability, complaisance, compliance, disposition, ductility, pliancy, tractableness, tractability, yielding.

flexible *adj* flexible, limber, lithe, pliable, pliant, supple, willowy; affable, complaisant, ductile, docile, gentle, tractable, tractile, yielding.

flexose, flexuous *adj* bending, crooked, serpentine, sinuate, sinuous, tortuous, waxy, winding.

flibbertigibbet *n* demon, imp, sprite.

flight[1] *n* flying, mounting, soaring, volition; shower, flight; steps, stairs.

flight[2] *n* departure, fleeing, flying, retreat, rout, stampede; exodus, hegira.

flighty *adj* capricious, deranged, fickle, frivolous, giddy, light-headed, mercurial, unbalanced, volatile, wild, whimsical.

flimsy *adj* slight, thin, unsubstantial; feeble, foolish, frivolous, light, puerile, shallow, superficial, trashy, trifling, trivial, weak; insubstantial, sleazy.

flinch *vb* blench, flee, recoil, retreat, shirk, shrink, swerve, wince, withdraw.

fling *vb* cast, chuck, dart, emit, heave, hurl, pitch, shy, throw, toss; flounce, wince. * *n* cast, throw, toss.

flippancy *n* volubility; assuredness, glibness, pertness.

flippant *adj* fluent, glib, talkative, voluble; bold, forward, frivolous, glib, impertinent, inconsiderate, irreverent, malapert, pert, saucy, trifling.

flirt *vb* chuck, fling, hurl, pitch, shy, throw, toss; flutter, twirl, whirl, whisk; coquet, dally, philander. * *n* coquette, jilt, philanderer; jerk.

flirtation *n* coquetry, dalliance, philandering.

flit *vb* flicker, flutter, hover; depart, hasten, pass.

flitting *adj* brief, ephemeral, evanescent, fleeting, fugitive, passing, short, transient, transitory.

float *vb* drift, glide, hang, ride, sail, soar, swim, waft; launch, support.

flock *vb* collect, congregate, gather, group, herd, swarm, throng. * *n* collection, group, multitude; bevy, company, convoy, drove, flight, gaggle, herd, pack, swarm, team, troupe; congregation.

flog *vb* beat, castigate, chastise, drub, flagellate, lash, scourge, thrash, whip.

flood *vb* deluge, inundate, overflow, submerge, swamp. * *n* deluge, freshet, inundation, overflow, tide; bore, downpour, eagre, flow, outburst, spate, rush; abundance, excess.

floor *vb* deck, pave; beat, confound, conquer, overthrow, prevail, prostrate, puzzle; disconcert, nonplus. * *n* storey; bottom, deck, flooring, pavement, stage.

florid *adj* bright-coloured, flushed, red-faced, rubicund; embellished, figurative, luxuriant, ornate, rhetorical, rococo.

flounce[1] *vb* fling, jerk, spring, throw, toss, wince. * *n* jerk, spring.

flounce[2] *n* frill, furbelow, ruffle.

flounder *vb* blunder, flop, flounce, plunge, struggle, toss, tumble, wallow.

flourish *vb* grow, thrive; **boast**, bluster, brag, gasconade, show off, **vaunt, vapour;** brandish, flaunt, swing, wave. * *n* **dash**, display, ostentation, parade, show; bombast, fustian, grandiloquence; brandishing, shake, waving; blast, fanfare, tantivy.

flout *vb* chaff, deride, fleer, gibe, insult, jeer, mock, ridicule, scoff, sneer, taunt. * *n* gibe, fling, insult, jeer, mock, mockery, mocking, scoff, scoffing, taunt.

flow *vb* pour, run, stream; deliquesce, liquefy, melt; arise, come, emanate, follow, grow, issue, proceed, result, spring; glide; float, undulate, wave, waver; abound, run. * *n* current, discharge, flood, flux, gush, rush, stream, trickle; abundance, copiousness.

flower *vb* bloom, blossom, effloresce; develop. * *n* bloom, blossom; best, cream, elite, essence, pick; freshness, prime, vigour.

flowery *adj* bloomy, florid; embellished, figurative, florid, ornate, overwrought.

flowing *adj* abundant, copious, fluent, smooth.

fluctuate *vb* oscillate, swing, undulate, vibrate, wave; change, vary; vacillate, waver.

flue *n* chimney, duct; flew, fluff, nap, floss, fur.

fluency *n* liquidness, smoothness; affluence, copiousness; ease, facility, readiness.

fluent *adj* current, flowing, gliding, liquid; smooth; affluent, copious, easy, facile, glib, ready, talkative, voluble.

fluff *vb* blunder, bungle, forget, fumble, mess up, miscue, misremember, muddle, muff. * *n* down, flew, floss, flue, fur, lint, nap; cobweb, feather, gossamer, thistledown; blunder, bungle, fumble, muff.

flume *n* channel, chute, mill race, race.

flummery *n* chaff, frivolity, froth, moonshine, nonsense, trash, trifling; adulation, blandishment, blarney, flattery; brose, porridge, sowens.

flunky, flunkey *n* footman, lackey, livery servant, manservant, valet; snob, toady.

flurry *vb* agitate, confuse, disconcert, disturb, excite, fluster, hurry, perturb. * *n* gust, flaw, squall; agitation, bustle, commotion, confusion, disturbance, excitement, flutter, haste, hurry, hurry-scurry, perturbation, ruffle, scurry.

flush[1] *vb* flow, rush, start; glow, mantle, redden; animate, elate, elevate, erect, excite; cleanse, drench. * *adj* bright, fresh, glowing, vigorous; abundant, affluent, exuberant, fecund, fertile, generous, lavish, liberal, prodigal, prolific, rich, wealthy, well-supplied; even, flat, level, plane. * *adv* evenly, flat, level; full, point-blank, right, square, squarely, straight. * *n* bloom, blush, glow, redness, rosiness, ruddiness; impulse, shock, thrill.

flush² *vb* disturb, rouse, start, uncover.

fluster *vb* excite, flush, heat; agitate, disturb, flurry, hurry, perturb, ruffle; confound, confuse, discompose, disconcert. * *n* glow, heat; agitation, flurry, flutter, hurry, hurry-scurry, perturbation, ruffle.

fluted *adj* channelled, corrugated, grooved.

flutter *vb* flap, hover; flirt, flit; beat, palpitate, quiver, tremble; fluctuate, oscillate, vacillate, waver. * *n* agitation, tremor; hurry, commotion, confusion, excitement, flurry, fluster, hurry-scurry, perturbation, quivering, tremble, tumult, twitter.

flux *n* flow, flowing; change, mutation, shifting, transition; diarrhoea, dysentery, looseness; fusing, melting, menstruum, solvent.

fly¹ *vb* aviate, hover, mount, soar; flap, float, flutter, play, sail, soar, undulate, vibrate, wave; burst, explode; abscond, decamp, depart, flee, vanish; elapse, flit, glide, pass, slip.

fly² *adj* alert, bright, sharp, smart, wide-awake; astute, cunning, knowing, sly; agile, fleet, nimble, quick, spry.

foal *n* colt, filly.

foam *vb* cream, froth, lather, spume; boil, churn, ferment, fume, seethe, simmer, stew. * *n* bubbles, cream, froth, scum, spray, spume, suds.

fodder *n* feed, food, forage, provender, rations.

foe *n* adversary, antagonist, enemy, foeman, opponent.

fog *vb* bedim, bemist, blear, blur, cloud, dim, enmist, mist; addle, befuddle, confuse, fuddle, muddle. * *n* blear, blur, dimness, film, fogginess, haze, haziness, mist, smog, vapour; befuddlement, confusion, fuddle, maze, muddle.

foggy *adj* blurred, cloudy, dim, dimmed, hazy, indistinct, misty, obscure; befuddled, bewildered, confused, dazed, muddled, muddy, stupid.

foible *n* defect, failing, fault, frailty, imperfection, infirmity, penchant, weakness.

foil¹ *vb* baffle, balk, check, checkmate, circumvent, defeat, disappoint, frustrate, thwart.

foil² *n* film, flake, lamina; background, contrast.

foist *vb* impose, insert, interpolate, introduce, palm off, thrust.

fold¹ *vb* bend, cover, double, envelop, wrap; clasp, embrace, enfold, enwrap, gather, infold, interlace; collapse, fail. * *n* double, doubling, gather, plait, plicature.

fold² *n* cot, enclosure, pen.

foliaceous *adj* foliate, leafy; flaky, foliated, lamellar, lamellate, lamellated, laminated, scaly, schistose.

folk *n* kindred, nation, people.

follow *vb* ensue, succeed; chase, dog, hound, pursue, run after, trail; accompany, attend; conform, heed, obey, observe; cherish, cultivate, seek; practise, pursue; adopt, copy, imitate; arise, come, flow, issue, proceed, result, spring.

follower *n* acolyte, attendant, associate, companion, dependant, retainer, supporter; adherent, admirer, disciple, partisan, pupil; copier, imitator.

folly *n* doltishness, dullness, imbecility, levity, shallowness; absurdity, extravagance, fatuity, foolishness, imprudence, inanity, indiscretion, ineptitude, nonsense, senselessness; blunder, faux pas, indiscretion, unwisdom.

foment *vb* bathe, embrocate, stupe; abet, brew, encourage, excite, foster, instigate, promote, stimulate.

fond *adj* absurd, baseless, empty, foolish, senseless, silly, vain, weak; affectionate, amorous, doting, loving, overaffectionate, tender.

fondle *vb* blandish, caress, coddle, cosset, dandle, pet.

fondness *n* absurdity, delusion, folly, silliness, weakness; liking, partiality, predilection, preference, propensity; appetite, relish, taste.

food *n* aliment, board, bread, cheer, commons, diet, fare, meat, nourishment, nutriment, nutrition, pabulum, provisions, rations, regimen, subsistence, sustenance, viands, victuals; feed, fodder, forage, provender.

fool *vb* jest, play, toy, trifle; beguile, cheat, circumvent, cozen, deceive, delude, dupe, gull, hoodwink, overreach, trick. * *n* blockhead, dolt, driveller, idiot, imbecile, nincompoop, ninny, nitwit, simpleton; antic, buffoon, clown, droll, harlequin, jester, merry-andrew, punch, scaramouch, zany; butt, dupe.

foolery *n* absurdity, folly, foolishness, nonsense; buffoonery, mummery, tomfoolery.

foolhardy *adj* adventurous, bold, desperate, harebrained, headlong, hot-headed, incautious, precipitate, rash, reckless, venturesome, venturous.

foolish *adj* brainless, daft, fatuous, idiotic, inane, inept, insensate, irrational, senseless, shallow, silly, simple, thick-skulled, vain, weak, witless; absurd, ill-judged, imprudent, indiscreet, nonsensical, preposterous, ridiculous, unreasonable, unwise; childish, contemptible, idle, puerile, trifling, trivial, vain.

foolishness *n* doltishness, dullness, fatuity, folly, imbecility, shallowness, silliness, stupidity; absurdity, extravagance, imprudence, indiscretion, nonsense; childishness, puerility, triviality.

footing *n* foothold, purchase; basis, foundation, groundwork, installation; condition, grade, rank, standing, state, status; settlement, establishment.

footman *n* footboy, menial, lackey, runner, servant.

footpad *n* bandit, brigand, freebooter, highwayman, robber.

footpath *n* footway, path, trail.

footprint *n* footfall, footmark, footstep, trace, track.

footstep *n* footmark, footprint, trace, track; footfall, step, tread; mark, sign, token, trace, vestige.

fop *n* beau, coxcomb, dandy, dude, exquisite, macaroni, popinjay, prig, swell.

foppish *adj* coxcombical, dandified, dandyish, dressy, finical, spruce, vain.

forage *vb* feed, graze, provender, provision, victual; hunt for, range, rummage, search, seek; maraud, plunder, raid. * *n* feed, fodder, food, pasturage, provender; hunt, rummage, search.

foray *n* descent, incursion, invasion, inroad, irruption, raid.

forbear *vb* cease, desist, hold, pause, stop, stay; abstain, refrain; endure, tolerate; avoid, decline, shun; abstain, omit, withhold.

forbearance *n* abstinence, avoidance, forbearing, self-restraint, shunning, refraining; indulgence, leniency, long-suffering, mildness, moderation, patience.

forbid *vb* ban, debar, disallow, embargo, enjoin, hinder, inhibit, interdict, prohibit, proscribe, taboo, veto.

forbidding *adj* abhorrent, disagreeable, displeasing, odious, offensive, repellant, repulsive, threatening, unpleasant.

force *vb* coerce, compel, constrain, necessitate, oblige; drive, impel, overcome, press, urge; ravish, violate. * *n* emphasis, energy, head, might, pith, power, strength, stress, vigour, vim; agency, efficacy, efficiency, cogency, potency, validity, virtue; coercion, compulsion, constraint, enforcement, vehemence, violence; army, array, battalion, host, legion, phalanx, posse, soldiery, squadron, troop.

forcible *adj* all-powerful, cogent, impressive, irresistible, mighty, potent, powerful, strong, weighty; impetuous, vehement, violent, unrestrained; coerced, coercive, compulsory; convincing, energetic, effective, efficacious, telling, vigorous.

forcibly *adv* mightily, powerfully; coercively, compulsorily, perforce, violently; effectively, energetically, vigorously.

ford *n* current, flood, stream; crossing, wading place.

fore *adj* anterior, antecedent, first, foregoing, former, forward, preceding, previous, prior; advanced, foremost, head, leading.

forebode *vb* augur, betoken, foreshow, foretell, indicate, portend, predict, prefigure, presage, prognosticate, promise, signify.

foreboding *n* augury, omen, prediction, premonition, presage, presentiment, prognostication.

forecast *vb* anticipate, foresee, predict; calculate, contrive, devise, plan, project, scheme. * *n* anticipation, foresight, forethought, planning, prevision, prophecy, provident.

foreclose *vb* debar, hinder, preclude, prevent, stop.

foredoom *vb* foreordain, predestine, preordain.

forego *see* **forgo**.

foregoing *adj* antecedent, anterior, fore, former, preceding, previous, prior.

foregone *adj* bygone, former, past, previous.

foreign *adj* alien, distant, exotic, exterior, external, outward, outlandish, remote, strange, unnative; adventitious, exterior, extraneous, extrinsic, inappropriate, irrelevant, outside, unnatural, unrelated.

foreknowledge *n* foresight, prescience, prognostication.

foremost *adj* first, front, highest, leading, main, principal.

foreordain *vb* appoint, foredoom, predestinate, predetermine, preordain.

forerunner *n* avant-courier, foregoer, harbinger, herald, precursor, predecessor; omen, precursor, prelude, premonition, prognosticate, sign.

foresee *vb* anticipate, forebode, forecast, foreknow, foretell, prognosticate, prophesy.

foreshadow *vb* forebode, predict, prefigure, presage, presignify, prognosticate, prophesy.

foresight *n* foreknowledge, prescience, prevision; anticipation, care, caution, forecast, forethought, precaution, providence, prudence.

forest *n* wood, woods, woodland.

forestall *vb* hinder, frustrate, intercept, preclude, prevent, thwart; antedate, anticipate, foretaste; engross, monopolize, regrate.

foretaste *n* anticipation, forestalling, prelibation.

foretell *vb* predict, prophesy; augur, betoken, forebode, forecast, foreshadow, foreshow, portend, presage, presignify, prognosticate, prophesy.

forethought *n* anticipation, forecast, foresight, precaution, providence, prudence.

forever *adv* always, constantly, continually, endlessly, eternally, ever, evermore, everlastingly, perpetually, unceasingly.

forewarn *vb* admonish, advise, caution, dissuade.

forfeit *vb* alienate, lose. * *n* amercement, damages, fine, forfeiture, mulct, penalty.

forfend *vb* avert, forbid, hinder, prevent, protect.

forge *vb* beat, fabricate, form, frame, hammer; coin, devise, frame, invent; counterfeit, falsify, feign. * *n* furnace, ironworks, smithy.

forgery *n* counterfeit, fake, falsification, imitation.

forgetful *adj* careless, heedless, inattentive, mindless, neglectful, negligent, oblivious, unmindful.

forgive *vb* absolve, acquit, condone, excuse, exonerate, pardon, remit.

forgiveness *n* absolution, acquittal, amnesty, condoning. exoneration, pardon, remission, reprieve.

forgiving *adj* absolutory, absolvatory, acquitting, clearing, excusing, pardoning, placable, releasing.

forgo *vb* abandon, cede, relinquish, renounce, resign, surrender, yield.

fork *vb* bifurcate, branch, divaricate, divide. * *n* bifurcation, branch, branching, crotch, divarication, division.

forked *adj* bifurcated, branching, divaricated, furcate, furcated.

forlorn *adj* abandoned, deserted, forsaken, friendless, helpless, lost, solitary; abject, comfortless, dejected, desolate, destitute, disconsolate, helpless, hopeless, lamentable, pitiable, miserable, woebegone, wretched.

form *vb* fashion model, mould, shape; build, conceive, construct, create, fabricate, make, produce; contrive, devise, frame, invent; compose, constitute, develop, organize; discipline, educate, teach, train. * *n* body, build, cast, configuration, conformation, contour, cut, fashion, figure, format, mould, outline, pattern, shape; formula, formulary, method, mode, practice, ritual; class, kind, manner, model, order, sort, system, type; arrangement, order, regularity, shapeliness; ceremonial, ceremony, conventionality, etiquette, formality, observance, ordinance, punctilio, rite, ritual; bench, seat; class, rank; arrangement, combination, organization.

formal *adj* explicit, express, official, positive, strict; fixed, methodical, regular, rigid, set, stiff; affected, ceremonious, exact, precise, prim, punctilious, starchy. starched; constitutive, essential; external, outward, perfunctory; formative, innate, organic, primordial.

formality *n* ceremonial, ceremony, conventionality, etiquette, punctilio, rite, ritual.

formation *n* creation, genesis, production; composition, constitution; arrangement, combination, disposal, disposition.

formative *adj* creative, determinative, plastic, shaping; derivative, inflectional, nonradical.

former *adj* antecedent, anterior, earlier, foregoing, preceding, previous, prior; late, old-time, quondam; by, bygone, foregone, gone, past.

formidable *adj* appalling, dangerous, difficult, dreadful, fearful, frightful, horrible, menacing, redoubtable, shocking, terrible, terrific, threatening, tremendous.

forsake *vb* abandon, desert, leave, quit; drop, forgo, forswear, relinquish, renounce, surrender, yield.

forsooth *adv* certainly, indeed, really, surely, truly.

forswear *vb* abandon, desert, drop, forsake, leave, quit, reject, renounce; abjure, deny, eschew, perjure, recant, repudiate, retract.

fort *n* bulwark, castle, citadel, defence, fastness, fortification, fortress, stronghold.

forthwith *adv* directly, immediately, instantly, quickly, straightaway.

fortification *n* breastwork, bulwark, castle, citadel, defence, earthwork, fastness, fort, keep, rampart, redoubt, stronghold, tower.

fortify *vb* brace, encourage, entrench, garrison, protect, reinforce, stiffen, strengthen; confirm, corroborate.

fortitude *n* braveness, bravery, courage, determination, endurance, firmness, hardiness, patience, pluck, resolution, strength, valour.

fortuitous *adj* accidental, casual, chance, contingent, incidental.

fortunate *adj* favoured, happy, lucky, prosperous, providential, successful; advantageous, auspicious, favourable, happy, lucky, propitious, timely.

fortune *n* accident, casualty, chance, contingency, fortuity, hap, luck; estate, possessions, property, substance; affluence, felicity, opulence, prosperity, riches, wealth; destination, destiny, doom, fate, lot, star; event, issue, result; favour, success.

forward *vb* advance; aid, encourage, favour, foster, further, help, promote, support; accelerate, dispatch, expedite, hasten, hurry, quicken, speed; dispatch, post, send, ship, transmit. * *adj* ahead, advanced, onward; anterior, front, fore, head; prompt, eager, earnest, hasty, impulsive, quick, ready, willing, zealous; assuming, bold, brazen, brazen-faced, confident, flippant, impertinent, pert, presumptuous, presuming; advanced, early, premature. * *adv* ahead, onward.

foster *vb* cosset, feed, nurse, nourish, support, sustain; advance, aid, breed, cherish, cultivate, encourage, favour, foment, forward, further, harbour, patronize, promote, rear, stimulate.

foul *vb* besmirch, defile, dirty, pollute, soil, stain, sully; clog, collide, entangle, jam. * *adj* dirty, fetid, filthy, impure, nasty, polluted, putrid, soiled, stained, squalid, sullied, rank, tarnished, unclean; disgusting, hateful, loathsome, noisome, odious, offensive; dishonourable, underhand, unfair, sinister; abominable, base, dark, detestable, disgraceful, infamous, scandalous, scurvy, shameful, wile, wicked; coarse, low, obscene, vulgar; abusive, foul-mouthed, foul-spoken, insulting, scurrilous; cloudy, rainy, rough, stormy, wet; feculent, muddy, thick, turbid; entangled, tangled.

foul-mouthed *adj* abusive, blackguardy, blasphemous, filthy, foul, indecent, insolent, insulting, obscene, scurrilous.

found *vb* base, fix, ground, place, rest, set; build, construct, erect, raise; colonize, establish, institute, originate, plant; cast, mould.

foundation *n* base, basis, bed, bottom, footing, ground, groundwork, substructure, support; endowment, establishment, settlement.

founder[1] *n* author, builder, establisher, father, institutor, originator, organizer, planter.

founder[2] *n* caster, moulder.

founder[3] *vb* sink, swamp, welter; collapse, fail, miscarry; fall, stumble, trip.

fountain *n* fount, reservoir, spring, well; jet, upswelling; cause, fountainhead, origin, original, source.

foxy *adj* artful, crafty, cunning, sly, subtle, wily.

fracas *n* affray, brawl, disturbance, outbreak, quarrel, riot, row, uproar, tumult,

fractious *adj* captious, cross, fretful, irritable, peevish, pettish, perverse, petulant, querulous, snappish, splenetic, touchy, testy, waspish.

fracture *vb* break, crack, split. * *n* breaking, rupture; breach, break, cleft, crack, fissure, flaw, opening, rift, rent.

fragile *adj* breakable, brittle, delicate, frangible; feeble, frail, infirm, weak.

fragility *n* breakability, breakableness, brittleness,

frangibility, frangibleness; feebleness, frailty, infirmity, weakness.

fragment *vb* atomize, break, fracture, pulverize, splinter. * *n* bit, chip, fraction, fracture, morsel, part, piece, remnant, scrap.

fragrance *n* aroma, balminess, bouquet, odour, perfume, redolence, scent, smell.

fragrant *adj* ambrosial, aromatic, balmy, odoriferous, odorous, perfumed, redolent, spicy, sweet, sweet-scented, sweet-smelling.

frail *adj* breakable, brittle, delicate, fragile, frangible, slight; feeble, infirm, weak.

frailty *n* feebleness, frailness, infirmity, weakness; blemish, defect, failing, fault, foible, imperfection, peccability, shortcoming.

frame *vb* build, compose, constitute, construct, erect, form, make, mould, plan, shape; contrive, devise, fabricate, fashion, forge, invest, plan. * *n* body, carcass, framework, framing, shell, skeleton; constitution, fabric, form, structure, scheme, system; condition, humour, mood, state, temper.

franchise *n* privilege, right; suffrage, vote; exemption, immunity.

frangible *adj* breakable, brittle, fragile.

frank *adj* artless, candid, direct, downright, frank-hearted, free, genuine, guileless, ingenuous, naive, open, outspoken, outright, plain, plain-spoken, point-blank, sincere, straightforward, truthful, unequivocal, unreserved, unrestricted.

frankness *n* candour, ingenuousness, openness, outspokenness, plain speaking, truth, straightforwardness.

frantic *adj* crazy, distracted, distraught, frenzied, furious, infuriate, mad. outrageous, phrenetic, rabid, raging, raving, transported, wild.

fraternity *n* association, brotherhood, circle, clan, club, company, fellowship, league, set, society, sodality; brotherliness.

fraternize *vb* associate, coalesce, concur, consort, cooperate, harmonize, sympathize, unite.

fraud *n* artifice, cheat, craft, deception, deceit, duplicity, guile, hoax, humbug, imposition, imposture, sham, stratagem, treachery, trick, trickery, wile.

fraudulent *adj* crafty, deceitful, deceptive, dishonest, false, knavish, treacherous, trickish, tricky, wily.

fraught *adj* abounding, big, burdened, charged, filled, freighted, laden, pregnant, stored, weighted.

fray[1] *n* affray, battle, brawl, broil, combat, fight, quarrel, riot.

fray[2] *vb* chafe, fret, rub, wear; ravel, shred.

freak *adj* bizarre, freakish, grotesque, monstrous, odd, unexpected, unforeseen. * *n* caprice, crotchet, fancy, humour, maggot, quirk, vagary, whim, whimsey; antic, caper, gambol; abnormality, abortion, monstrosity.

freakish *adj* capricious, changeable, eccentric, erratic, fanciful, humoursome, odd, queer, whimsical.

free *vb* deliver, discharge, disenthral, emancipate, enfranchise, enlarge, liberate, manumit, ransom, release, redeem, rescue, save; clear, disencumber, disengage, extricate, rid, unbind, unchain, unfetter, unlock; exempt, immunize, privilege. * *adj* bondless, independent, loose, unattached, unconfined, unentangled, unimpeded, unrestrained, untrammelled; autonomous, delivered, emancipated, freeborn, liberated, manumitted, ransomed, released, self-governing; clear, exempt, immune, privileged; allowed, permitted; devoid, empty, open, unimpeded, unobstructed, unrestricted; affable, artless, candid, frank, ingenuous, sincere, unreserved; bountiful, charitable, free-hearted, generous, hospitable, liberal, munificent, openhanded; immoderate, lavish, prodigal; eager, prompt, ready, willing; available, gratuitous, spontaneous; careless, lax, loose; bold, easy, familiar, informal, overfamiliar, unconstrained. * *adv* openly, outright, unreservedly, unrestrainedly, unstintingly; freely, gratis, gratuitously.

freebooter *n* bandit, brigand, despoiler, footpad, gangster, highwayman, marauder, pillager, plunderer, robber; buccaneer, pirate, rover.

freedom *n* emancipation, independence, liberation, liberty, release; elbowroom, margin, play, range, scope, swing; franchise, immunity, privilege; familiarity, laxity, license, looseness.

freethinker *n* agnostic, deist, doubter, infidel, sceptic, unbeliever.

freeze *vb* congeal, glaciate, harden, stiffen; benumb, chill.

freight *vb* burden, charge, lade, load. * *n* burden, cargo, lading, load.

frenzy *n* aberration, delirium, derangement, distraction, fury, insanity, lunacy, madness, mania, paroxysm, rage, raving, transport.

frequent *vb* attend, haunt, resort, visit. * *adj* iterating, oft-repeated; common, customary, everyday, familiar, habitual, persistent, usual; constant, continual, incessant.

fresh *adj* new, novel, recent; renewed, revived; blooming, flourishing, green, undecayed, unimpaired, unfaded, unobliterated, unwilted, unwithered, well-preserved; sweet; delicate, fair, fresh-coloured, ruddy, rosy; florid, hardy, healthy, vigorous, strong; active, energetic, unexhausted, unfatigued, unwearied, vigorous; keen, lively, unabated, undecayed, unimpaired, vivid; additional, further; uncured, undried, unsalted, unsmoked; bracing, health-giving, invigorating, refreshing, sweet; brink, stiff, strong; inexperienced, raw, uncultivated, unpracticed, unskilled, untrained, unused.

freshen *vb* quicken, receive, refresh, revive.

fret[1] *vb* abrade, chafe, fray, gall, rub, wear; affront, agitate, annoy, gall, harass, irritate, nettle, provoke, ruffle, tease, vex, wear, worry; ripple, roughen; corrode; fume, peeve, rage, stew. * *n* agitation, fretfulness, fretting, irritation, peevishness, vexation.

fret² *vb* diversify, interlace, ornament, variegate. * *n* fretwork, interlacing, ornament; ridge, wale, whelk.

fretful *adj* captious, cross, fractious, ill-humoured, ill-tempered, irritable, peevish, pettish, petulant, querulous, short-tempered, snappish, spleeny, splenetic, testy, touchy, uneasy, waspish.

friable *adj* brittle, crisp, crumbling, powdery, pulverable.

friction *n* abrasion, attrition, grating, rubbing; bickering, disagreement, dissension, wrangling.

friend *adj* benefactor, chum, companion, comrade, crony, confidant, intimate; adherent, ally, associate, confrere, partisan; advocate, defender, encourager, favourer, patron, supporter, well-wisher.

friendly *adj* affectionate, amiable, benevolent, favourable, kind, kind-hearted, kindly, well-disposed; amicable, cordial, fraternal, neighbourly; conciliatory, peaceable, unhostile.

friendship *n* affection, attachment, benevolence, fondness, goodness, love, regard; fellowship, intimacy; amicability, amicableness, amity, cordiality, familiarity, fraternization, friendliness, harmony.

fright *n* affright, alarm, consternation, dismay, funk, horror, panic, scare, terror.

frighten *vb* affright, alarm, appal, daunt, dismay, intimidate, scare, stampede, terrify.

frightful *adj* alarming, awful, dire, direful, dread, dreadful, fearful, horrible, horrid, shocking, terrible, terrific; ghastly, grim, grisly, gruesome, hideous.

frigid *adj* cold, cool, gelid, dull, lifeless, spiritless, tame, unanimated, uninterested, uninteresting; chilling, distant, forbidding, formal, freezing, prim, repellent, repelling, repulsive, rigid, stiff.

frill *n* edging, frilling, furbelow, gathering, ruche, ruching, ruffle; affectation, mannerism.

fringe *vb* border, bound, edge, hem, march, rim, skirt, verge. * *n* border, edge, edging, tassel, trimming. * *adj* edging, extra, unofficial.

frisk *vb* caper, dance, frolic, gambol, hop, jump, play, leap, romp, skip, sport, wanton.

frisky *adj* frolicsome, coltish, gay, lively, playful, sportive.

frivolity *n* flummery, folly, fribbling, frippery, frivolousness, levity, puerility, trifling, triviality.

frivolous *adj* childish, empty, flighty, flimsy, flippant, foolish, giddy, idle, light, paltry. petty, puerile, silly, trashy, trifling, trivial, unimportant, vain, worthless.

frolic *vb* caper, frisk, gambol, lark, play, romp, sport. * *n* escapade, gambol, lark, romp, skylark, spree, trick; drollery, fun, play, pleasantry, sport.

frolicsome *adj* coltish, fresh, frolic, gamesome, gay, lively, playful, sportive.

front *vb* confront, encounter, face, oppose. * *adj* anterior, forward; foremost, frontal, headmost. * *n*

brow, face, forehead; assurance, boldness, brass, effrontery, impudence; breast, head, van, vanguard; anterior, face, forepart, obverse; facade, frontage.

frontier *n* border, boundary, coast, confine, limits, marches.

frosty *adj* chill, chilly, cold, icy, stinging, wintry; cold, cold-hearted, frigid, indifferent, unaffectionate, uncordial, unimpassioned, unloving; dull-hearted, lifeless, spiritless, unanimated; frosted, grey-hearted, hoary, white.

froth *vb* bubble, cream, foam, lather, spume. * *n* bubbles, foam, lather, spume; balderdash, flummery, nonsense, trash, triviality.

frothy *adj* foamy, spumy; empty, frivolous, light, trifling, trivial, unsubstantial, vain.

froward *adj* captious, contrary, contumacious, cross, defiant, disobedient, fractious, impudent, intractable, obstinate, peevish, perverse, petulant, refractory, stubborn, ungovernable, untoward, unyielding, wayward, wilful.

frown *vb* glower, lower, scowl.

frowzy, frowsy *adj* fetid, musty, noisome, rancid, rank, stale; disordered, disorderly, dowdy, slatternly, slovenly.

frugal *adj* abstemious, careful, chary, choice, economical, provident, saving, sparing, temperate, thrifty, unwasteful.

fruit *n* crop, harvest, produce, production; advantage, consequence, effect, good, outcome, product, profit, result; issue, offspring, young.

fruitful *adj* abounding, productive; fecund, fertile, prolific; abundant, exuberant, plenteous, plentiful, rich, teeming.

fruition *n* completion, fulfilment, perfection; enjoyment.

fruitless *adj* acarpous, barren, sterile, infecund, unfertile, unfruitful, unproductive, unprolific; abortive, bootless, futile, idle, ineffectual, profitless, unavailing, unprofitable, useless, vain.

frumpish, frumpy *adj* cross, cross-grained, cross-tempered, dowdy, grumpy, irritable, shabby, slatternly, snappish.

frustrate *vb* baffle, balk, check, circumvent, defeat, disappoint, disconcert, foil, thwart; cross, hinder, outwit.

frustrated *adj* balked, blighted, dashed, defeated, foiled, thwarted; ineffectual, null, useless, vain.

fuddled *adj* befuddled, boozy, corned, crapulous, drunk, groggy, high, inebriated, intoxicated, muddled, slewed, tight, tipsy.

fugacious *adj* evanescent, fleeting, fugitive, transient, transitory.

fugitive *adj* escaping, fleeing, flying; brief, ephemeral, evanescent, fleeting, flitting, fugacious, momentary, short, short-lived, temporal, temporary, transient, transitory, uncertain, unstable, volatile. * *n* émigré, escapee, evacuee, fleer, outlaw, refugee, runaway.

fulfil *vb* accomplish, complete, consummate, effect, effectuate, execute, realize; adhere, discharge, do, keep, obey, observe, perform; answer, fill, meet, satisfy.

full *adj* brimful, filled, flush, replete; abounding, replete, well-stocked; bagging, flowing, loose, voluminous; chock-full, cloyed, crammed, glutted, gorged, overflowing, packed, sated, satiated, saturated, soaked, stuffed, swollen; adequate, complete, entire, mature, perfect; abundant, ample, copious, plenteous, plentiful, sufficient; clear, deep, distinct, loud, rounded, strong; broad, large, capacious, comprehensive, extensive, plump; circumstantial, detailed, exhaustive. * *adv* completely, fully; directly, exactly, precisely.

fullness *n* abundance, affluence, copiousness, plenitude, plenty, profusion; glut, satiety, sating, repletion; completeness, completion, entireness, perfection; clearness, loudness, resonance, strength; dilation, distension, enlargement, plumpness, rotundity, roundness, swelling.

fully *adv* abundantly, amply, completely, copiously, entirely, largely, plentifully, sufficiently.

fulminate *vb* detonate, explode; curse, denounce, hurl, menace, threaten, thunder.

fulsome *adj* excessive, extravagant, fawning; disgusting, nauseous, nauseating, offensive, repulsive; coarse, gross, lustful, questionable.

fumble *vb* bungle, grope, mismanage, stumble; mumble, stammer, stutter.

fume *vb* reek, smoke, vaporize. * *n* effluvium exhalation, reek, smell, smoke, steam, vapour; agitation, fret, fry, fury, passion, pet, rage, storm.

fun *adj* amusing, diverting, droll, entertaining. * *n* amusement, diversion, drollery, frolic, gaiety, humour, jesting, jocularity, jollity, joy, merriment, mirth, play, pranks, sport, pleasantry, waggishness.

function *vb* act, discharge, go, operate, officiate, perform, run, serve, work. * *n* discharge, execution, exercise, operation, performance, purpose, use; activity, business, capacity, duty, employment, occupation, office, part, province, role; ceremony, rite; dependant, derivative.

fund *vb* afford, endow, finance, invest, provide, subsidise, support; garner, hoard, stock, store. * *n* accumulation, capital, endowment, reserve, stock; store, supply; foundation.

fundament *n* bottom, buttocks, seat.

fundamental *adj* basal, basic, bottom, cardinal, constitutional, elementary, essential, indispensable, organic, principal, primary, radical. * *n* essential, principal, rule.

funeral *n* burial, cremation, exequies, internment, obsequies.

funereal *adj* dark, dismal, gloomy, lugubrious, melancholy, mournful, sad, sepulchral, sombre, woeful.

funk *vb* blanch, shrink, quail. * *n* stench, stink; fear, fright, panic.

funny *adj* amusing, comic, comical, diverting, droll, facetious, farcical, humorous, jocose, jocular, laughable, ludicrous, sportive, witty; curious, odd, queer, strange. * *n* jest, joke; cartoon, comic.

furbish *vb* burnish, brighten, polish, renew, renovate, rub, shine.

furious *adj* angry, fierce, frantic, frenzied, fuming, infuriated, mad, raging, violent, wild; boisterous, fierce, impetuous, stormy, tempestuous, tumultuous, turbulent, vehement.

furnish *vb* appoint, endow, provide, supply; decorate, equip, fit; afford, bestow, contribute, give, offer, present, produce, yield.

furniture *n* chattels, effects, household goods, movables; apparatus, appendages, appliances, equipment, fittings, furnishings; decorations, embellishments, ornaments.

furore *n* commotion, craze, enthusiasm, excitement, fad, fury, madness, mania, rage, vogue.

furrow *vb* chamfer, channel, cleave, corrugate, cut, flute, groove, hollow; pucker, seam, wrinkle. * *n* chamfer, channel, cut, depression, fluting, groove, hollow, line, seam, track, trench, rot, wrinkle.

further *vb* advance, aid, assist, encourage, help, forward, promote, succour, strengthen. * *adj* additional. * *adv* also, besides, farther, furthermore, moreover.

furtive *adj* clandestine, hidden, secret, sly, skulking, sneaking, sneaky, stealthy, stolen, surreptitious.

fury *n* anger, frenzy, fit, furore, ire, madness, passion, rage; fierceness, impetuosity, turbulence, turbulency, vehemence; bacchant, bacchante, bedlam, hag, shrew, termagant, virago, vixen.

fuse *vb* dissolve, melt, liquefy, smelt; amalgamate, blend, coalesce, combine, commingle, intermingle, intermix, merge, unite. * *n* match.

fusion *n* liquefaction, melting; amalgamation, blending, commingling, commixture, intermingling, intermixture, union; coalition, merging.

fuss *vb* bustle, fidget; fret, fume, worry. * *n* ado, agitation, bother, bustle, commotion, disturbance, excitement, fidget, flurry, fluster, fret, hurry, pother, stir, worry.

fustian *n* bombast, claptrap, rant, rodomontade; balderdash, inanity, nonsense, stuff, trash, twaddle.

fusty *adj* ill-smelling, malodorous, mildewed, mouldy, musty, rank.

futile *adj* frivolous, trifling, trivial; bootless, fruitless, idle, ineffectual, profitless, unavailing, unprofitable, useless, vain, valueless, worthless.

futility *n* frivolousness, triviality; bootlessness, fruitlessness, uselessness, vanity, worthlessness.

future *adj* coming, eventual, forthcoming, hereafter, prospective, subsequent. * *n* hereafter, outlook, prospect.

G

gabble *vb* babble, chatter, clack, gibber, gossip, prate, prattle. * *n* babble, chatter, clack, gap, gossip, jabber, palaver, prate, prattle, twaddle.

gadabout *n* idler, loafer, rambler, rover, vagrant; gossip, talebearer, vagrant.

gaffer *n* boss, foreman, overseer, supervisor.

gag[1] *n* jape, jest, joke, stunt, wisecrack.

gag[2] *vb* muffle, muzzle, shackle, silence, stifle, throttle; regurgitate, retch, throw up, vomit; choke, gasp, pant. * *n* muzzle.

gage *n* pawn, pledge, security, surety; challenge, defiance, gauntlet, glove.

gaiety *n* animation, blithesomeness, cheerfulness, glee, hilarity, jollity, joviality, merriment, mirth, vivacity.

gain *vb* achieve, acquire, earn, get, obtain, procure, reap, secure; conciliate, enlist, persuade, prevail, win; arrive, attain, reach; clear, net, profit. * *n* accretion, addition, gainings, profits, winnings; acquisition, earnings, emolument, lucre; advantage, benefit, blessing, good, profit.

gainful *adj* advantageous, beneficial, profitable; lucrative, paying, productive, remunerative.

gainsay *vb* contradict, controvert, deny, dispute, forbid.

gait *n* carriage, pace, step, stride, walk.

galaxy *n* assemblage, assembly, cluster, collection, constellation, group.

gale *n* blast, hurricane, squall, storm, tempest, tornado, typhoon.

gall[1] *n* effrontery, impudence; bile; acerbity, bitterness, malice, maliciousness, malignity, rancour, spite.

gall[2] *vb* chafe, excoriate, fret, hurt; affront, annoy, exasperate, harass, incense, irritate, plague, provoke, sting, tease, vex.

gallant *adj* fine, magnificent, showy, splendid, well-dressed; bold, brave, chivalrous, courageous, daring, fearless, heroic, high-spirited, intrepid, valiant, valorous; chivalrous, fine, honourable, high-minded, lofty, magnanimous, noble. * *n* beau, blade, spark; lover, suitor, wooer.

gallantry *n* boldness, bravery, chivalry, courage, courageousness, fearlessness, heroism, intrepidity, prowess, valour; courtesy, courteousness, elegance, politeness.

galling *adj* chafing, irritating, vexing.

gallop *vb* fly, hurry, run, rush, scamper, speed.

gamble *vb* bet, dice, game, hazard, plunge, speculate, wager. * *n* chance, risk, speculation; bet,

punt, wager.

gambol *vb* caper, cut, frisk, frolic, hop, jump, leap, romp, skip. * *n* frolic, hop, jump, skip.

game[1] *vb* gamble, sport, stake. * *n* amusement, contest, diversion, pastime, play, sport; adventure, enterprise, measure, plan, project, scheme, stratagem, undertaking; prey, quarry, victim.

game[2] *adj* brave, courageous, dauntless, fearless, gallant, heroic, intrepid, plucky, unflinching, valorous; enduring, persevering, resolute, undaunted; ready, eager, willing.

game[3] *adj* crippled, disabled, halt, injured, lame.

gameness *n* bravery, courage, grit, heart, mettle, nerve, pith, pluck, pluckiness, spirit, stamina.

gamesome *adj* frisky, frolicsome, lively, merry, playful, sportive, sprightly, vivacious.

gammon *vb* bamboozle, beguile, cheat, circumvent, deceive, delude, dupe, gull, hoax, humbug, inveigle, mislead, overreach, outwit. * *n* bosh, hoax, humbug, imposition, nonsense.

gang *n* band, cabal, clique, company, coterie, crew, horde, party, set, troop.

gaol *see* **jail**.

gap *n* breach, break, cavity, chasm, chink, cleft, crack, cranny, crevice, hiatus, hollow, interval, interstice, lacuna, opening, pass, ravine, rift, space, vacancy.

gape *vb* burst open, dehisce, open, stare, yawn.

garb *vb* attire, clothe, dress. * *n* apparel, attire, clothes, costume, dress, garments, habiliment, habit, raiment, robes, uniform, vestment.

garbage *n* filth, offal, refuse, remains, rubbish, trash, waste.

garble *vb* corrupt, distort, falsify, misquote, misrepresent, mutilate, pervert.

gargantuan *adj* big, Brobdingnagian, colossal, enormous, gigantic, huge, prodigious, tremendous.

garish *adj* bright, dazzling, flashy, flaunting, gaudy, glaring, loud, showy, staring, tawdry.

garland *vb* adorn, festoon, wreathe. * *n* chaplet, coronal, crown, festoon, wreath.

garment *n* clothes, clothing, dress, habit, vestment.

garner *vb* accumulate, collect, deposit, gather, hoard, husband, reserve, save, store, treasure.

garnish *vb* adorn, beautify, bedeck, decorate, deck, embellish, grace, ornament, prank, trim. * *n* decoration, enhancement, ornament, trimming.

garrulous *adj* babbling, loquacious, prating, prattling, talkative.

gasconade *n* bluster, boast, brag, bravado, swagger, vaunt, vapouring.

gasp *vb* blow, choke, pant, puff. * *n* blow, exclamation, gulp, puff.

gather *vb* assemble, cluster, collect, convene, group, muster, rally; accumulate, amass, garner, hoard, huddle, lump; bunch, crop, cull, glean, pick, pluck, rake, reap, shock, stack; acquire, gain, get, win; conclude, deduce, derive, infer; fold, plait, pucker, shirr, tuck; condense, grow, increase, thicken.

gathering *n* acquisition, collecting, earning, gain, heap, pile, procuring; assemblage, assembly, collection, company, concourse, congregation, meeting, muster; abscess, boil, fester, pimple, pustule, sore, suppuration, tumour, ulcer.

gauche *adj* awkward, blundering, bungling, clumsy, inept, tactless, uncouth.

gaudy *adj* bespangled, brilliant, brummagem, cheap, flashy, flaunting, garish, gimcrack, glittering, loud, ostentatious, overdecorated, sham, showy, spurious, tawdry, tinsel.

gauge *vb* calculate, check, determine, weigh; assess, estimate, guess, reckon. * *n* criterion, example, indicator, measure, meter, touchstone, yardstick; bore, depth, height, magnitude, size, thickness, width.

gaunt *adj* angular, attenuated, emaciated, haggard, lank, lean, meagre, scraggy, skinny, slender, spare, thin.

gawky *adj* awkward, boorish, clownish, clumsy, green, loutish, raw, rustic, uncouth, ungainly.

gay *adj* bright, brilliant, dashing, fine, showy; flashy, flaunting, garish, gaudy, glittering, loud, tawdry, tinsel; airy, blithe, blithesome, cheerful, festive, frivolous, frolicsome, gladsome, gleeful, hilarious, jaunty, jolly, jovial, light-hearted, lively, merry, mirthful, sportive, sprightly, vivacious.

gear *vb* adapt, equip, fit, suit, tailor. * *n* apparel, array, clothes, clothing, dress, garb; accoutrements, appliances, appointments, appurtenances, array, harness, goods, movables, subsidiaries; harness, rigging, tackle, trappings; apparatus, machinery, mechanics.

gelid *adj* chill, chilly, cold, freezing, frigid, icy.

gem *n* jewel, stone, treasure.

genealogy *n* ancestry, descent, lineage, pedigree, stock.

general *adj* broad, collective, generic, popular, universal, widespread; catholic, ecumenical; common, current, ordinary, usual; inaccurate, indefinite, inexact, vague.

generally *adv* commonly, extensively, universally, usually.

generate *vb* beget, breed, engender, procreate, propagate, reproduce, spawn; cause, form, make, produce.

generation *n* creation, engendering, formation, procreation, production; age, epoch, era, period, time; breed, children, family, kind, offspring, progeny, race, stock.

generosity *n* disinterestedness, high-mindedness, magnanimity, nobleness; bounteousness, bountifulness, bounty, charity, liberality, openhandedness.

generous *adj* high-minded, honourable, magnanimous, noble; beneficent, bountiful, charitable, free, hospitable, liberal, munificent, openhanded; abundant, ample, copious, plentiful, rich.

genial *adj* cheering, encouraging, enlivening, fostering, inspiring, mild, warm; agreeable, cheerful, cordial, friendly, hearty, jovial, kindly, merry, mirthful, pleasant.

genius *n* aptitude, aptness, bent, capacity, endowment, faculty, flair, gift, talent, turn; brains, creative power, ingenuity, inspiration, intellect, invention, parts, sagacity, wit; adeptness, master, master hand, proficiency; character, disposition, naturalness, nature; deity, demon, spirit.

genteel *adj* aristocratic, courteous, gentlemanly, lady-like, polished, polite, refined, well-bred; elegant, fashionable, graceful, stylish.

gentility *n* civility, courtesy, good breeding, politeness, refinement, urbanity.

gentle *adj* amiable, bland, clement, compassionate, humane, indulgent, kind, kindly, lenient, meek, merciful, mild, moderate, soft, tender, tenderhearted; docile, pacific, peaceable, placid, quiet, tame, temperate, tractable; bland, easy, gradual, light, slight; soft; high-born, noble, well-born; chivalrous, courteous, cultivated, knightly, polished, refined, well-bred.

gentlemanly *adj* civil, complaisant, courteous, cultivated, delicate, genteel, honourable, polite, refined, urbane, well-bred.

genuine *adj* authentic, honest, proper, pure, real, right, true, unadulterated, unalloyed, uncorrupted, veritable; frank, native, sincere, unaffected.

genus *n* class, group, kind, order, race, sort, type.

germ *n* embryo, nucleus, ovule, ovum, seed, seed-bud; bacterium, microbe, microorganism; beginning, cause, origin, rudiment, source.

germane *adj* akin, allied, cognate, related; apposite, appropriate, fitting, pertinent, relevant, suitable.

germinate *vb* bud, burgeon, develop, generate, grow, pollinate, push, shoot, sprout, vegetate.

gesture *vb* indicate, motion, signal, wave. * *n* action, attitude, gesticulation, gesturing, posture, sign, signal.

get *vb* achieve, acquire, attain, earn, gain, obtain, procure, receive, relieve, secure, win; finish, master, prepare; beget, breed, engender, generate, procreate.

gewgaw *n* bauble, gimcrack, gaud, kickshaw, knick-knack, plaything, trifle, toy, trinket.

ghastly *adj* cadaverous, corpse-like, death-like, deathly, ghostly, lurid, pale, pallid, wan; dismal, dreadful, fearful, frightful, grim, grisly, gruesome, hideous, horrible, shocking, terrible.

ghost *n* soul, spirit; apparition, phantom, revenant, shade, spectre, spook, sprite, wraith.

giant *adj* colossal, enormous, Herculean, huge, large, monstrous, prodigious, vast. * *n* colossus, cyclops, Hercules, monster.

gibberish *n* babble, balderdash, drivel, gabble, gobbledygook, jabber, nonsense, prate, prating.

gibe, jibe *vb* deride, fleer, flout, jeer, mock, ridicule, scoff, sneer, taunt. * *n* ridicule, sneer, taunt.

giddiness *n* dizziness, head-spinning, vertigo.

giddy *adj* dizzy, head-spinning, vertiginous; careless, changeable, fickle, flighty, frivolous, harebrained, headlong, heedless, inconstant, irresolute, light-headed, thoughtless, unsteady, vacillating, wild.

gift *n* alms, allowance, benefaction, bequest, bonus, boon, bounty, contribution, donation, dowry, endowment, favour, grant, gratuity, honorarium, largesse, legacy, offering, premium, present, prize, subscription, subsidy, tip; faculty, talent.

gifted *adj* able, capable, clever, ingenious, intelligent, inventive, sagacious, talented.

gigantic *adj* colossal, Cyclopean, enormous, giant, herculean, huge, immense, prodigious, titanic, tremendous, vast.

giggle *vb, n* cackle, grin, laugh, snigger, snicker, titter.

gild *vb* adorn, beautify, bedeck, brighten, decorate, embellish, grace, illuminate.

gimcrack *adj* flimsy, frail, puny; base, cheap, paltry, poor. * *n* bauble, knick-knack, toy, trifle.

gird *vb* belt, girdle; begird, encircle, enclose, encompass, engird, environ, surround; brace, support. * *n* band, belt, cincture, girdle, girth, sash, waistband.

gist *n* basis, core, essence, force, ground, marrow, meaning, pith, point, substance.

give *vb* accord, bequeath, bestow, confer, devise, entrust, present; afford, contribute, donate, furnish, grant, proffer, spare, supply; communicate, impart; deliver, exchange, pay, requite; allow, permit, vouchsafe; emit, pronounce, render, utter; produce, yield; cause, occasion; apply, devote, surrender; bend, sink, recede, retire, retreat, yield.

glad *adj* delighted, gratified, happy, pleased, rejoicing, well-contented; animated, blithe, cheerful, cheery, elated, gladsome, jocund, joyful, joyous, light, light-hearted, merry, playful, radiant; animating, bright, cheering, exhilarating, gladdening, gratifying, pleasing.

gladden *vb* bless, cheer, delight, elate, enliven, exhilarate, gratify, please, rejoice.

gladiator *n* prize-fighter, sword-player, swordsman.

gladness *n* animation, cheerfulness, delight, gratification, happiness, joy, joyfulness, joyousness, pleasure.

gladsome *adj* airy, blithe, blithesome, cheerful,

delighted, frolicsome, glad, gleeful, jocund, jolly, jovial, joyful, joyous, light-hearted, lively, merry, pleased, sportive, sprightly, vivacious.

glamour *n* bewitchment, charm, enchantment, fascination, spell, witchery.

glance *vb* coruscate, gleam, glisten, glister, glitter, scintillate, shine; dart, flit; gaze, glimpse, look, view. * *n* gleam, glitter; gleam, look, view.

glare *vb* dazzle, flame, flare, gleam, glisten, glitter, sparkle; frown, gaze, glower. * *n* flare, glitter.

glaring *adj* dazzling, gleaming, glistening, glittering; barefaced, conspicuous, extreme, manifest, notorious, open.

glassy *adj* brilliant, crystal, crystalline, gleaming, lucent, shining, transparent.

glaze *vb* burnish, calender, furbish, gloss, polish. * *n* coat, enamel, finish, glazing, polish, varnish.

gleam *vb* beam, coruscate, flash, glance, glimmer, glitter, shine, sparkle. * *n* beam, flash, glance, glimmer, glimmering, glow, ray; brightness, coruscation, flashing, gleaming, glitter, glittering, lustre, splendour.

glean *vb* collect, cull, gather, get, harvest, pick, select.

glee *n* exhilaration, fun, gaiety, hilarity, jocularity, jollity, joviality, joy, liveliness, merriment, mirth, sportiveness, verve.

glib *adj* slippery, smooth; artful, facile, flippant, fluent, ready, talkative, voluble.

glide *vb* float, glissade, roll on, skate, skim, slide, slip; flow, lapse, run, roll. * *n* gliding, lapse, sliding, slip.

glimmer *vb* flash, flicker, gleam, glitter, shine, twinkle. * *n* beam, gleam, glimmering, ray; glance, glimpse.

glimpse *vb* espy, look, spot, view. * *n* flash, glance, glimmering, glint, look, sight.

glitter *vb* coruscate, flare, flash, glance, glare, gleam, glisten, glister, scintillate, shine, sparkle. * *n* beam, beaming, brightness, brilliancy, coruscation, gleam, glister, lustre, radiance, scintillation, shine, sparkle, splendour.

gloaming *n* dusk, eventide, nightfall, twilight.

gloat *vb* exult, gaze, rejoice, stare, triumph.

globe *n* ball, earth, orb, sphere.

globular *adj* globate, globated, globe-shaped, globose, globous, round, spheral, spheric, spherical.

globule *n* bead, drop, particle, spherule.

gloom *n* cloud, darkness, dimness, gloominess, obscurity, shade, shadow; cheerlessness, dejection, depression, despondency, downheartedness, dullness, melancholy, sadness.

gloomy *adj* dark, dim, dusky, obscure; cheerless, dismal, lowering, lurid; crestfallen, dejected, depressed, despondent, disheartened, dispirited, downcast, downhearted, glum, melancholy, morose, sad, sullen; depressing, disheartening, dispiriting, heavy, saddening.

glorify *vb* adore, bless, celebrate, exalt, extol, honour, laud, magnify, worship; adorn, brighten, elevate, ennoble, make bright.

glorious *adj* celebrated, conspicuous, distinguished, eminent, excellent, famed, famous, illustrious, pre-eminent, renowned; brilliant, bright, grand, magnificent, radiant, resplendent, splendid; consummate, exalted, high, lofty, noble, supreme.

glory *vb* boast, exult, vaunt. * *n* celebrity, distinction, eminence, fame, honour, illustriousness, praise, renown; brightness, brilliancy, effulgence, lustre, pride, resplendence, splendour; exaltation, exceeding, gloriousness, greatness, grandeur, nobleness; bliss, happiness.

gloss[1] *vb* coat, colour, disguise, extenuate, glaze, palliate, varnish, veneer, veil. * *n* coating, lustre, polish, sheen, varnish, veneer; pretence, pretext.

gloss[2] *vb* annotate, comment, elucidate, explain, interpret. * *n* annotation, comment, commentary, elucidation, explanation, interpretation, note.

glove *n* gantlet, gauntlet, handwear, mitt, mitten; challenge.

glow *vb* incandesce, radiate, shine; blush, burn, flush, redden. * *n* blaze, brightness, brilliance, burning, incandescence, luminosity, reddening; ardour, bloom, enthusiasm, fervency, fervour, flush, impetuosity, vehemence, warmth.

glower *vb* frown, glare, lower, scowl, stare. * *n* frown, glare, scowl.

glum *adj* churlish, crabbed, crestfallen, cross-grained, crusty, depressed, frowning, gloomy, glowering, moody, morose, sour, spleenish, spleeny, sulky, sullen, surly.

glut *vb* block up, cloy, cram, gorge, satiate, stuff. * *n* excess, saturation, surfeit, surplus.

glutinous *adj* adhesive, clammy, cohesive, gluey, gummy, sticky, tenacious, viscid, viscous.

glutton *n* gobbler, gorger, gourmand, gormandizer, greedy-guts, lurcher, pig.

gnarled *adj* contorted, cross-grained, gnarly, knotted, knotty, snaggy, twisted.

go *vb* advance, move, pass, proceed, progress repair; act, operate; be about, extravagate, fare, journey, roam, rove, travel, walk, wend; depart, disappear, cease; elapse, extend, lead, reach, run; avail, concur, contribute, tend, serve; eventuate, fare, turn out; afford, bet, risk, wager. * *n* action, business, case, chance, circumstance, doings, turn; custom, fad, fashion, mode, vogue; energy, endurance, power, stamina, verve, vivacity.

goad *vb* annoy, badger, harass, irritate, sting, worry; arouse, impel, incite, instigate, prod, spur, stimulate, urge. * *n* incentive, incitement, pressure, stimulation.

goal *n* bound, home, limit, mark, mete, post; end, object; aim, design, destination.

gobble *vb* bolt, devour, gorge, gulp, swallow.

goblin *n* apparition, elf, bogey, demon, gnome, hobgoblin, phantom, spectre, sprite.

god *n* almighty, creator, deity, divinity, idol, Jehovah, omnipotence, providence.

godless *adj* atheistic, impious, irreligious, profane, ungodly, wicked.

godlike *adj* celestial, divine, heavenly, supernal.

godly *adj* devout, holy, pious, religious, righteous, saint-like, saintly.

godsend *n* fortune, gift, luck, present, windfall.

golden *adj* aureate, brilliant, bright, gilded, resplendent, shining, splendid; excellent, precious; auspicious, favourable, opportune, propitious; blessed, delightful, glorious, halcyon, happy.

good *adj* advantageous, beneficial, favourable, profitable, serviceable, useful; adequate, appropriate, becoming, convenient, fit, proper, satisfactory, suitable, well-adapted; decorous, dutiful, honest, just, pious, reliable, religious, righteous, true, upright, virtuous, well-behaved, worthy; admirable, capable, excellent, genuine, healthy, precious, sincere, sound, sterling, valid, valuable; benevolent, favourable, friendly, gracious, humane, kind, merciful, obliging, well-disposed; fair, honourable, immaculate, unblemished, unimpeachable, unimpeached, unsullied, untarnished; cheerful, companionable, lively, genial, social; able, competent, dextrous, expert, qualified, ready, skilful, thorough, well-qualified; credit-worthy; agreeable, cheering, gratifying, pleasant. * *n* advantage, benefit, boon, favour, gain, profit, utility; interest, prosperity, welfare, weal; excellence, righteousness, virtue, worth.

good breeding *n* affability, civility, courtesy, good manners, polish, politeness, urbanity.

goodbye *n* adieu, farewell, parting.

goodly *adj* beautiful, comely, good-looking, graceful; agreeable, considerate, desirable, happy, pleasant.

good-natured *adj* amiable, benevolent, friendly, kind, kind-hearted, kindly.

goodness *n* excellence, quality, value, worth; honesty, integrity, morality, principle, probity, righteousness, uprightness, virtue; benevolence, beneficence, benignity, good-will, humaneness, humanity, kindness.

goods *npl* belongings, chattels, effects, furniture, movables; commodities, merchandise, stock, wares.

goodwill *n* benevolence, kindness, good nature; ardour, earnestness, heartiness, willingness, zeal; custom, patronage.

gore *vb* horn, pierce, stab, wound.

gorge[1] *vb* bolt, devour, eat, feed, swallow; cram, fill, glut, gormandize, sate, satiate, stuff, surfeit. * *n* craw, crop, gullet, throat.

gorge[2] *n* canyon, defile, fissure, notch, ravine.

gorgeous *adj* bright, brilliant, dazzling, fine, glittering, grand, magnificent, resplendent, rich, shining, showy, splendid, superb.

Gorgon *n* bugaboo, fright, hobgoblin, hydra, ogre, spectre.

gory *adj* bloody, ensanguined, sanguinary.

gospel *n* creed, doctrine, message, news, revelation, tidings.

gossip *vb* chat, cackle, clack, gabble, prate, prattle, tattle. * *n* babbler, busybody, chatterer, gossipmonger, newsmonger, quidnunc, tale-bearer, tattler, tell-tale; cackle, chat, chit-chat, prate, prattle, tattle.

gourmet *n* connoisseur, epicure, epicurean.

govern *vb* administer, conduct, direct, manage, regulate, reign, rule, superintend, supervise; guide, pilot, steer; bridle, check, command, control, curb, restrain, rule, sway.

government *n* autonomy, command, conduct, control, direction, discipline, dominion, guidance, management, regulation, restraint, rule, rulership, sway; administration, cabinet, commonwealth, polity, sovereignty, state.

governor *n* commander, comptroller, director, head, headmaster, manager, overseer, ruler, superintendent, supervisor; chief magistrate, executive; guardian, instructor, tutor.

grab *vb* capture, clutch, seize, snatch.

grace *vb* adorn, beautify, deck, decorate, embellish; dignify, honour. * *n* benignity, condescension, favour, good-will, kindness, love; devotion, efficacy, holiness, love, piety, religion, sanctity, virtue; forgiveness, mercy, pardon, reprieve; accomplishment, attractiveness, charm, elegance, polish, propriety, refinement; beauty, comeliness, ease, gracefulness, symmetry; blessing, petition, thanks.

graceful *adj* beautiful, becoming, comely, easy, elegant; flowing, natural, rounded, unlaboured; appropriate; felicitous, happy, tactful.

graceless *adj* abandoned, corrupt, depraved, dissolute, hardened, incorrigible, irreclaimable, lost, obdurate, profligate, reprobate, repugnant, shameless,

gracious *adj* beneficent, benevolent, benign, benignant, compassionate, condescending, favourable, friendly, gentle, good-natured, kind, kindly, lenient, merciful, mild, tender; affable, civil, courteous, easy, familiar, polite.

grade *vb* arrange, classify, group, order, rank, sort. * *n* brand, degree, intensity, stage, step, rank; gradient, incline, slope.

gradual *adj* approximate, continuous, gentle, progressive, regular, slow, successive.

graduate *vb* adapt, adjust, proportion, regulate. * *n* alumna, alumnus, laureate, postgraduate.

graft *vb* ingraft, inoculate, insert, transplant. * *n* bud, scion, shoot, slip, sprout; corruption, favouritism, influence, nepotism.

grain *n* kernel, ovule, seed; cereals, corn, grist; atom, bit, glimmer, jot, particle, scintilla, scrap, shadow, spark, tittle, trace, whit; disposition, fibre, humour, temper, texture; colour, dye, hue, shade, stain, texture, tincture, tinge.

granary *n* corn-house, garner, grange, store-house.

grand *adj* august, dignified, elevated, eminent, exalted, great, illustrious, lordly, majestic, princely, stately, sublime; fine, glorious, gorgeous, magnificent, pompous, lofty, noble, splendid, superb; chief, leading, main, pre-eminent, principal, superior.

grandee *n* lord, noble, nobleman.

grandeur *n* elevation, greatness, immensity, impressiveness, loftiness, vastness; augustness, dignity, eminence, glory, magnificence, majesty, nobility, pomp, splendour, state, stateliness.

grandiloquent *adj* bombastic, declamatory, high-minded, high-sounding, inflated, pompous, rhetorical, stilted, swelling, tumid, turgid.

grant *vb* accord, admit, allow, sanction; cede, concede, give, impart, indulge; bestow, confer, deign, invest, vouchsafe; convey, transfer, yield. * *n* admission, allowance, benefaction, bestowal, boon, bounty, concession, donation, endowment, gift, indulgence, largesse, present; conveyance, cession.

graphic *adj* descriptive, diagrammatic, figural, figurative, forcible, lively, pictorial, picturesque, striking, telling, vivid, well-delineated, well-drawn.

grapple *vb* catch, clutch, grasp, grip, hold, hug, seize, tackle, wrestle.

grasp *vb* catch, clasp, clinch, clutch, grapple, grip, seize; comprehend, understand. * *n* clasp, grip, hold; comprehension, power, reach, scope, understanding.

grasping *adj* acquisitive, avaricious, covetous, exacting, greedy, rapacious, sordid, tight-fisted.

grate *vb* abrade, rub, scrape, triturate; comminute, rasp; creak, fret, grind, jar, vex. * *n* bars, grating, latticework, screen; basket, fire bed.

grateful *adj* appreciative, beholden, indebted, obliged, sensible, thankful; pleasant, welcome.

gratification *n* gratifying, indulgence, indulging, pleasing, satisfaction, satisfying; delight, enjoyment, fruition, pleasure, reward.

gratify *vb* delight, gladden, please; humour, fulfil, grant, indulge, requite, satisfy.

gratifying *adj* agreeable, delightful, grateful, pleasing, welcome.

grating *adj* disagreeable, displeasing, harsh, irritating, offensive. * *n* grate, partition.

gratis *adv* freely, gratuitously.

gratitude *n* goodwill, gratitude, indebtedness, thankfulness.

gratuitous *adj* free, spontaneous, unrewarded, voluntary; assumed, baseless, groundless, unfounded, unwarranted, wanton.

gratuity *n* benefaction, bounty, charity, donation, endowment, gift, grant, largesse, present.

grave[1] *n* crypt, mausoleum, ossuary, pit, sepulchre, sepulture, tomb, vault.

grave[2] *adj* cogent, heavy, important, momentous, ponderous, pressing, serious, weighty; dignified, sage, sedate, serious, slow, solemn, staid, thoughtful; dull, grim, plain, quiet, sober, sombre, subdued; cruel, hard, harsh, severe; despicable, dire, dismal, gross, heinous, infamous, outrageous, scandalous, shameful, shocking; heavy, hollow, low, low-pitched, sepulchral.

grave³ *vb* engrave, impress, imprint, infix; carve, chisel, cut, sculpt.

gravel *vb* bewilder, embarrass, nonplus, perplex, pose, puzzle, stagger. * *n* ballast, grit, sand, shingle.

graveyard *n* burial ground, cemetery, churchyard, god's acre, mortuary, necropolis.

gravity *n* heaviness, weight; demureness, sedateness, seriousness, sobriety, thoughtfulness; importance, moment, momentousness, weightiness.

graze *vb* brush, glance, scrape, scratch; abrade, shave, skim; browse, crop, feed, pasture. * *n* abrasion, bruise, scrape, scratch.

great *adj* ample, big, bulky, Cyclopean, enormous, gigantic, Herculean, huge, immense, large, pregnant, vast; decided, excessive, high, much, pronounced; countless, numerous; chief, considerable, grand, important, leading, main, pre-eminent, principal, superior, weighty; celebrated, distinguished, eminent, exalted, excellent, famed, famous, far-famed, illustrious, noted, prominent, renowned; august, dignified, elevated, grand, lofty, majestic, noble, sublime; chivalrous, generous, high-minded, magnanimous; fine, magnificent, rich, sumptuous.

greatness *n* bulk, dimensions, largeness, magnitude, size; distinction, elevation, eminence, fame, importance, renown; augustness, dignity, grandeur, majesty, loftiness, nobility, nobleness, sublimity; chivalry, generosity, magnanimity, spirit.

greed, greediness *n* gluttony, hunger, omnivorousness, ravenousness, voracity; avidity, covetousness, desire, eagerness, longing; avarice, cupidity, graspingness, grasping, rapacity, selfishness.

greedy *adj* devouring, edacious, gluttonous, insatiable, insatiate, rapacious, ravenous, voracious; desirous, eager; avaricious, grasping, selfish.

green *adj* aquamarine, emerald, olive, verdant, verdure, viridescent, viridian; blooming, flourishing, fresh, undecayed; fresh, new, recent; immature, unfledged, unripe; callow, crude, inexpert, ignorant, inexperienced, raw, unskilful, untrained, verdant, young; unseasoned; conservationist, ecological, environmentalist. * *n* common, grass plot, lawn, sward, turf, verdure.

greenhorn *n* beginner, novice, tyro.

greet *vb* accost, address, complement, hail, receive, salute, welcome.

greeting *n* compliment, salutation, salute, welcome.

grief *n* affliction, agony, anguish, bitterness, distress, dole, heartbreak, misery, regret, sadness, sorrow, suffering, tribulation, mourning, woe; grievance, trial; disaster, failure, mishap.

grievance *n* burden, complaint, hardship, injury, oppression, wrong; affliction, distress, grief, sorrow, trial, woe.

grieve *vb* afflict, aggrieve, agonize, discomfort, distress, hurt, oppress, pain, sadden, wound; bewail, deplore, mourn, lament, regret, sorrow, suffer.

grievous *adj* afflicting, afflictive, burdensome, deplorable, distressing, heavy, lamentable, oppressive, painful, sad, sorrowful; baleful, baneful, calamitous, destructive, detrimental, hurtful, injurious, mischievous, noxious, troublesome; aggravated, atrocious, dreadful, flagitious, flagrant, gross, heinous, iniquitous, intense, intolerable, severe, outrageous, wicked.

grill *vb* broil, griddle, roast, toast; sweat; cross-examine, interrogate, question; torment, torture. * *n* grating, gridiron; cross-examination, cross-questioning.

grim *adj* cruel, ferocious, fierce, harsh, relentless, ruthless, savage, stern, unyielding; appalling, dire, dreadful, fearful, frightful, grisly, hideous, horrid, horrible, terrific.

grimace *vb, n* frown, scowl, smirk, sneer.

grime *n* dirt, filth, foulness, smut.

grimy *adj* begrimed, defiled, dirty, filthy, foul, soiled, sullied, unclean.

grind *vb* bruise, crunch, crush, grate, grit, pulverize, rub, triturate; sharpen, whet; afflict, harass, oppress, persecute, plague, trouble. * *n* chore, drudgery, labour, toil.

grip *vb* clasp, clutch, grasp, hold, seize. * *n* clasp, clutch, control, domination, grasp, hold.

grisly *adj* appalling, frightful, dreadful, ghastly, grim, grey, hideous, horrible, horrid, terrible, terrific.

grit *vb* clench, grate, grind. * *n* bran, gravel, pebbles, sand; courage, decision, determination, firmness, perseverance, pluck, resolution, spirit.

groan *vb* complain, lament, moan, whine; creak. * *n* cry, moan, whine; complaint; grouse, grumble.

groom *vb* clean, dress, tidy; brush, tend; coach, educate, nurture, train. * *n* equerry, hostler, manservant, ostler, servant, stable-hand, valet, waiter.

groove *n* channel, cut, furrow, rabbet, rebate, recess, rut, scoring; routine.

gross *vb* accumulate, earn, make. * *adj* big, bulky, burly, fat, great, large; dense, dull, stupid, thick; beastly, broad, carnal, coarse, crass, earthy, impure, indelicate, licentious, low, obscene, unbecoming, unrefined, unseemly, vulgar, rough, sensual; aggravated, brutal, enormous, flagrant, glaring, grievous, manifest, obvious, palpable, plain, outrageous, shameful; aggregate, entire, total, whole. * *n* aggregate, bulk, total, whole.

grossness *n* bigness, bulkiness, greatness; density, thickness; coarseness, ill-breeding, rudeness, vulgarity; bestiality, brutality, carnality, coarseness, impurity, indelicacy, licentiousness, sensuality.

grotesque *adj* bizarre, extravagant, fanciful, fantastic, incongruous, odd, strange, unnatural, whimsical, wild; absurd, antic, burlesque, ludicrous, ridiculous.

ground *vb* fell, place; base, establish, fix, found, set; instruct, train. * *n* area, clod, distance, earth, loam, mould, sod, soil, turf; country, domain, land, region, territory; acres, estate, field, property; base, basis, foundation, groundwork, support; account, consideration, excuse, gist, motive, opinion, reason.

groundless *adj* baseless, causeless, false, gratuitous, idle, unauthorized, unfounded, unjustifiable, unsolicited, unsought, unwarranted.

grounds *npl* deposit, dregs, grouts, lees, precipitate, sediment, settlings; accounts, arguments, considerations, reasons, support; campus, gardens, lawns, premises, yard.

group *vb* arrange, assemble, dispose, order. * *n* aggregation, assemblage, assembly, body, combination, class, clump, cluster, collection, order.

grove *n* copse, glade, spinney, thicket, wood, woodland.

grovel *vb* cower, crawl, creep, cringe, fawn, flatter, sneak.

grovelling *adj* creeping, crouching, squat; abject, base, beggarly, cringing, fawning, low, mean, servile, slavish, sneaking, undignified, unworthy, vile.

grow *vb* enlarge, expand, extend, increase, swell; arise, burgeon, develop, germinate, shoot, sprout, vegetate; advance, extend, improve, progress, thrive, wax; cultivate, produce, raise.

growl *vb* complain, croak, find fault, gnarl, groan, grumble, lament, murmur, snarl. * *n* croak, grown, snarl; complaint.

growth *n* augmentation, development, expansion, extension, growing, increase; burgeoning, excrescence, formation, germination, pollution, shooting, sprouting, vegetation; cultivation, produce, product, production; advance, advancement, development, improvement, progress; adulthood, maturity.

grub *vb* clear, dig, eradicate, root. * *n* caterpillar, larvae, maggot; drudge, plodder.

grudge *vb* begrudge, envy, repine; complain, grieve, murmur. * *n* aversion, dislike, enmity, grievance, hate, hatred, ill-will, malevolence, malice, pique, rancour, resentment, spite, venom.

gruff *adj* bluff, blunt, brusque, churlish, discourteous, grumpy, harsh, impolite, rough, rude, rugged, surly, uncivil, ungracious.

grumble *vb* croak, complain, murmur, repine; gnarl, growl, snarl; roar, rumble. * *n* growl, murmur, complaint, roar, rumble.

grumpy *adj* crabbed, cross, glum, moody, morose, sour, sullen, surly.

guarantee *vb* assure, insure, pledge, secure, warrant. * *n* assurance, pledge, security, surety, warrant, warranty.

guard *vb* defend, keep, patrol, protect, safeguard, save, secure, shelter, shield, watch. * *n* aegis, bulwark, custody, defence, palladium, protection, rampart, safeguard, security, shield; keeper,

guardian, patrol, sentinel, sentry, warden, watch, watchman; conduct, convoy, escort; attention, care, caution, circumspection, heed, watchfulness.

guarded *adj* careful, cautious, circumspect, reserved, reticent, wary, watchful.

guardian *n* custodian, defender, guard, keeper, preserver, protector, trustee, warden.

guerdon *n* recompense, remuneration, requital, reward.

guess *vb* conjecture, divine, mistrust, surmise, suspect; fathom, find out, penetrate, solve; believe, fancy, hazard, imagine, reckon, suppose, think. * *n* conjecture, divination, notion, supposition, surmise.

guest *n* caller, company, visitant.

guidance *n* conduct, control, direction, escort, government, lead, leadership, pilotage, steering.

guide *vb* conduct, escort, lead, pilot; control, direct, govern, manage, preside, regulate, rule, steer, superintend, supervise. * *n* cicerone, conductor, director, monitor, pilot; adviser, counsellor, instructor, mentor; clew, directory, index, key, thread; guidebook, itinerary, landmark.

guild *n* association, brotherhood, company, corporation, fellowship, fraternity, society, union.

guile *n* art, artfulness, artifice, craft, cunning, deceit, deception, duplicity, fraud, knavery, ruse, subtlety, treachery, trickery, wiles, wiliness.

guileless *adj* artless, candid, frank, honest, ingenuous, innocent, open, pure, simple-minded, sincere, straightforward, truthful, undesigning, unsophisticated.

guilt *n* blame, criminality, culpability, guiltless; ill-desert, iniquity, offensiveness, wickedness, wrong; crime, offence, sin.

guiltless *adj* blameless, immaculate, innocent, pure, sinless, spotless, unpolluted, unspotted, unsullied, untarnished.

guilty *adj* criminal, culpable, evil, sinful, wicked, wrong.

guise *n* appearance, aspect, costume, dress, fashion, figure, form, garb, manner, mode, shape; air, behaviour, demeanour, mien; cover, custom, disguise, habit, pretence, pretext, practice.

gulf *n* abyss, chasm, opening; bay, inlet; whirlpool.

gull *vb* beguile, cheat, circumvent, cozen, deceive, dupe, hoax, overreach, swindle, trick. * *n* cheat, deception, hoax, imposition, fraud, trick; cat's paw, dupe.

gullibility *n* credulity, naiveness, naivety, overtrustfulness, simplicity, unsophistication.

gullible *adj* confiding, credulous, naive, overtrustful, simple, unsophisticated, unsuspicious.

gumption *n* ability, astuteness, cleverness, capacity, common sense, discernment, penetration, power, sagacity, shrewdness, skill; courage, guts, spirit.

gun *n* blunderbuss, cannon, carbine, firearm, musket, pistol, revolver, rifle, shotgun.

gurgle *vb* babble, bubble, murmur, purl, ripple. * *n*

babbling, murmur, ripple.

gush *vb* burst, flood, flow, pour, rush, spout, stream; emotionalize, sentimentalize. * *n* flow, jet, onrush, rush, spurt, surge; effusion, effusiveness, loquacity, loquaciousness, talkativeness.

gushing *adj* flowing, issuing, rushing; demonstrative, effusive, sentimental.

gust *vb* blast, blow, puff. * *n* blast, blow, squall; burst, fit, outburst, paroxysm.

gusto *n* enjoyment, gust, liking, pleasure, relish, zest.

gusty *adj* blustering, blustery, puffy, squally, stormy, tempestuous, unsteady, windy.

gut *vb* destroy, disembowel, embowel, eviscerate, paunch. * *n* bowels, entrails, intestines, inwards, viscera.

gutter *n* channel, conduit, kennel, pipe, tube.

guttural *adj* deep, gruff, hoarse, thick, throaty.

guy *vb* caricature, mimic, ridicule. * *n* boy, man, person; dowdy, eccentric, fright, scarecrow.

guzzle *vb* carouse, drink, gorge, gormandize, quaff, swill, tipple, tope.

gyrate *vb* revolve, rotate, spin, whirl.

H

habiliment *n* apparel, attire, clothes, costume, dress, garb, garment, habit, raiment, robes, uniform, vesture, vestment.

habit *vb* accoutre, array, attire, clothe, dress, equip, robe. * *n* condition, constitution, temperament; addiction, custom, habitude, manner, practice, rule, usage, way, wont; apparel, costume, dress, garb, habiliment.

habitation *n* abode, domicile, dwelling, headquarters, home, house, lodging, quarters, residence.

habitual *adj* accustomed, common, confirmed, customary, everyday, familiar, inveterate, ordinary, regular, routine, settled, usual, wonted.

habituate *vb* accustom, familiarize, harden, inure, train, use.

habitude *n* custom, practice, usage, wont.

hack[1] *vb* chop, cut, hew, mangle, mutilate, notch; cough, rasp. * *n* cut, cleft, incision, notch; cough, rasp.

hack[2] *vb* ride. * *adj* hired, mercenary; banal, hackneyed, pedestrian, uninspired, unoriginal. * *n* horse, nag, pony; hireling, mercenary; journalist, scribbler, writer.

hackneyed *adj* banal, common, commonplace, overworked, pedestrian, stale, threadbare, trite.

hag *n* beldame, crone, fury, harridan, jezebel, shemonster, shrew, termagant, virago, vixen, witch.

haggard *adj* intractable, refractory, unruly, untamed, wild, wayward; careworn, emaciated, gaunt, ghastly, lank, lean, meagre, raw, spare, thin, wasted, worn.

haggle *vb* argue, bargain, cavil, chaffer, dispute, higgle, stickle; annoy, badger, bait, fret, harass, tease, worry.

hail[1] *vb* acclaim, greet, salute, welcome; accost, address, call, hallo, signal. * *n* greeting, salute.

hail[2] *vb* assail, bombard, rain, shower, storm, volley. * *n* bombardment, rain, shower, storm, volley.

halcyon *adj* calm, golden, happy, palmy, placid, peaceful, quiet, serene, still, tranquil, unruffled, undisturbed.

hale *adj* hardy, healthy, hearty, robust, sound, strong, vigorous, well.

halfwit *n* blockhead, dunce, moron, simpleton.

halfwitted *adj* doltish, dull, dull-witted, feebleminded, foolish, sappy, shallow, silly, simple, soft, stolid, stupid, thick.

hall *n* chamber, corridor, entrance, entry, hallway, lobby, passage, vestibule; manor, manor-house; auditorium, lecture-room.

halloo *vb* call, cry, shout. * *n* call, cry, hallo, holla, hollo, shout.

hallow *vb* consecrate, dedicate, devote, revere, sanctify, solemnize; enshrine, honour, respect, reverence, venerate.

hallowed *adj* blessed, holy, honoured, revered, sacred.

hallucination *n* blunder, error, fallacy, mistake; aberration, delusion, illusion, phantasm, phantasy, self-deception, vision.

halo *n* aura, aureole, glory, nimbus.

halt[1] *vb* cease, desist, hold, rest, stand, stop. * *n* end, impasse, pause, standstill, stop.

halt[2] *vb* hesitate, pause, stammer, waver; falter, hobble, limp. * *adj* crippled, disabled, lame. * *n* hobble, limp.

hammer *vb* beat, forge, form, shape; excogitate, contrive, invent.

hammer and tongs *adv* earnestly, energetically, resolutely, strenuously, vigorously, zealously.

hamper *vb* bind, clog, confine, curb, embarrass, encumber, entangle, fetter, hinder, impede, obstruct, prevent, restrain, restrict, shackle, trammel. * *n* basket, box, crate, picnic basket; embarrassment, encumbrance, fetter, handicap, impediment, obstruction, restraint, trammel.

hand *vb* deliver, give, present, transmit; conduct, guide, lead. * *n* direction, part, side; ability, dexterity, faculty, skill, talent; course, inning, management, turn; agency, intervention, participation, share; control, possession, power; artificer, artisan, craftsman, employee, labourer, operative, workman; index, indicator, pointer; chirography, handwriting.

handbook *n* guidebook, manual.

handcuff *vb* bind, fetter, manacle, shackle. * *n* fetter, manacle, shackle.

handful *n* fistful, maniple, smattering.

handicap *vb* encumber, hamper, hinder, restrict. * *n* disadvantage, encumbrance, hampering, hindrance, restriction.

handicraft *n* hand manufacture, handwork, workmanship.

handle *vb* feel, finger, manhandle, paw, touch; direct, manage, manipulate, use, wield; discourse, discuss, treat. * *n* haft, helve, hilt, stock.

handsome *adj* admirable, comely, fine-looking, stately, well-formed, well-proportioned; appropriate, suitable, becoming, easy, graceful; generous, gracious, liberal, magnanimous, noble; ample, large, plentiful, sufficient.

handy *adj* adroit, clever, dextrous, expert, ready, skilful, skilled; close, convenient, near.

hang *vb* attach, swing; execute, truss; decline, drop, droop, incline; adorn, drape; dangle, depend, impend, suspend; rely; cling, loiter, rest, stick; float, hover, pay.

hangdog *adj* ashamed, base, blackguard, low, villainous, scurvy, sneaking.

hanger-on *n* dependant, minion, parasite, vassal.

hanker *vb* covet, crave, desire, hunger, long, lust, want, yearn.

hap *n* accident, chance, fate, fortune, lot.

haphazard *adj* aimless, chance, random.

hapless *adj* ill-fated, ill-starred, luckless, miserable, unfortunate, unhappy, unlucky, wretched.

happen *vb* befall, betide, chance, come, occur.

happily *adv* fortunately, luckily; agreeably, delightfully, prosperously, successfully.

happiness *n* brightness, cheerfulness, delight, gaiety, joy, light-heartedness, merriment, pleasure; beatitude, blessedness, bliss, felicity, enjoyment, welfare, well-being.

happy *adj* blessed, blest, blissful, cheerful, contented, joyful, joyous, light-hearted, merry; charmed, delighted, glad, gladdened, gratified, pleased; fortunate, lucky, prosperous, successful; able, adroit, apt, dextrous, expert, ready, skilful; befitting, felicitous, opportune, pertinent, seasonable, well-timed; auspicious, bright, favourable, propitious.

harangue *vb* address, declaim, spout. * *n* address, bombast, declamation, oration, rant, screed, speech, tirade.

harass *vb* exhaust, fag, fatigue, jade, tire, weary; annoy, badger, distress, gall, heckle, disturb, harry, molest, pester, plague, tantalize, tease, torment, trouble, vex, worry.

harbour *vb* protect, lodge, shelter; cherish, entertain, foster, indulge. * *n* asylum, cover, refuge, resting place, retreat, sanctuary, shelter; anchorage, destination, haven, port.

hard *adj* adamantine, compact, firm, flinty, impenetrable, marble, rigid, solid, resistant, stony, stubborn, unyielding; difficult, intricate, knotty, perplexing, puzzling; arduous, exacting, fatiguing, laborious, toilsome, wearying; austere, callous, cruel, exacting, hard-hearted, incorrigible, inflexible, insensible, insensitive, obdurate, oppressive, reprobate, rigorous, severe, unfeeling, unkind, unsusceptible, unsympathetic, unyielding, untender; calamitous, disagreeable, distressing, grievous, painful, unpleasant; acid, alcoholic, harsh, rough, sour; excessive, intemperate. * *adv* close, near; diligently, earnestly, energetically, incessantly, laboriously; distressfully, painfully, rigorously, severely; forcibly, vehemently, violently.

harden *vb* accustom, discipline, form, habituate, inure, season, train; brace, fortify, indurate,

nerve, steel, stiffen, strengthen.

hardened *adj* annealed, case-hardened, tempered, indurated; abandoned, accustomed, benumbed, callous, confirmed, deadened, depraved, habituated, impenitent, incorrigible, inured, insensible, irreclaimable, lost, obdurate, reprobate, seared, seasoned, steeled, trained, unfeeling.

hard-headed *adj* astute, collected, cool, intelligent, sagacious, shrewd, well-balanced, wise.

hardhearted *adj* cruel, fell, implacable, inexorable, merciless, pitiless, relentless, ruthless, unfeeling, uncompassionate, unmerciful, unpitying, unrelenting.

hardihood *n* audacity, boldness, bravery, courage, decision, firmness, fortitude, intrepidity, manhood, mettle, pluck, resolution, stoutness; assurance, audacity, brass, effrontery, impudence.

hardly *adv* barely, scarcely; cruelly, harshly, rigorously, roughly, severely, unkindly.

hardship *n* fatigue, toil, weariness; affliction, burden, calamity, grievance, hardness, injury, misfortune, privation, suffering, trial, trouble.

hardy *adj* enduring, firm, hale, healthy, hearty, inured, lusty, rigorous, robust, rugged, sound, stout, strong, sturdy, tough; bold, brave, courageous, daring, heroic, intrepid, manly, resolute, stout-hearted, valiant.

harebrained *adj* careless, changeable, flighty, giddy, harum-scarum, headlong, heedless, rash, reckless, unsteady, volatile, wild.

hark *interj* attend, hear, hearken, listen.

harlequin *n* antic, buffoon, clown, droll, fool, jester, punch, fool.

harm *vb* damage, hurt, injure, scathe; abuse, desecrate, ill-use, ill-treat, maltreat, molest. * *n* damage, detriment, disadvantage, hurt, injury, mischief, misfortune, prejudice, wrong.

harmful *adj* baneful, detrimental, disadvantageous, hurtful, injurious, mischievous, noxious, pernicious, prejudicial.

harmless *adj* innocent, innocuous, innoxious; inoffensive, safe, unoffending.

harmonious *adj* concordant, consonant, harmonic; dulcet, euphonious, mellifluous, melodious, musical, smooth, tuneful; comfortable, congruent, consistent, correspondent, orderly, symmetrical; agreeable, amicable, brotherly, cordial, fraternal, friendly, neighbourly.

harmonize *vb* adapt, attune, reconcile, unite; accord, agree, blend, chime, comport, conform, correspond, square, sympathize, tally, tune.

harmony *n* euphony, melodiousness, melody; accord, accordance, agreement, chime, concord, concordance, consonance, order, unison; adaptation, congruence, congruity, consistency, correspondence, fairness, smoothness, suitableness; amity, friendship, peace.

harness *vb* hitch, tackle. * *n* equipment, gear, tackle, tackling; accoutrements, armour, array, mail, mounting.

harp *vb* dwell, iterate, reiterate, renew, repeat.

harping n dwelling, iteration, reiteration, repetition.

harrow vb harass, lacerate, rend, tear, torment, torture, wound.

harry vb devastate, pillage, plunder, raid, ravage, rob; annoy, chafe, disturb, fret, gall, harass, harrow, incommode, pester, plague, molest, tease, torment, trouble, vex, worry.

harsh adj acid, acrid, astringent, biting, caustic, corrosive, crabbed, rough, sharp, sour, tart; cacophonous, discordant, grating, jarring, metallic, raucous, strident, unmelodious; abusive, austere, crabbed, crabby, cruel, disagreeable, hard, ill-natured, ill-tempered, morose, rigorous, severe, stern, unfeeling; bearish, bluff, blunt, brutal, gruff, rude, uncivil, ungracious.

harshness n roughness; acerbity, asperity, austerity, churlishness, crabbedness, hardness, ill-nature, ill-temper, moroseness, rigour, severity, sternness, unkindness; bluffness, bluntness, churlishness, gruffness, incivility, ungraciousness, rudeness.

harum-scarum adj hare-brained, precipitate, rash, reckless, volatile, wild.

harvest vb gather, glean, reap. * n crops, produce, yield; consequence, effect, issue, outcome, produce, result.

haste n alacrity, celerity, dispatch, expedition, nimbleness, promptitude, quickness, rapidity, speed, urgency, velocity; flurry, hurry, hustle, impetuosity, precipitateness, precipitation, press, rashness, rush, vehemence.

hasten vb haste, hurry; accelerate, dispatch, expedite, precipitate, press, push, quicken, speed, urge.

hasty adj brisk, fast, fleet, quick, rapid, speedy, swift; cursory, hurried, passing, slight, superficial; ill-advised, rash, reckless; headlong, helter-skelter, pell-mell, precipitate; abrupt, choleric, excitable, fiery, fretful, hot-headed, irascible, irritable, passionate, peevish, peppery, pettish, petulant, testy, touchy, waspish.

hatch vb brew, concoct, contrive, excogitate, design, devise, plan, plot, project, scheme; breed, incubate.

hate vb abhor, abominate, detest, dislike, execrate, loathe, nauseate. * n abomination, animosity, antipathy, detestation, dislike, enmity, execration, hatred, hostility, loathing.

hateful adj malevolent, malicious, malign, malignant, rancorous, spiteful; abhorrent, abominable, accursed, damnable, detestable, execrable, horrid, odious, shocking; disgusting, foul, loathsome, nauseous, obnoxious, offensive, repellent, repugnant, repulsive, revolting, vile.

hatred n animosity, enmity, hate, hostility, ill-will, malevolence, malice, malignity, odium, rancour; abhorrence, abomination, antipathy, aversion, detestation, disgust, execration, horror, loathing, repugnance, revulsion.

haughtiness n arrogance, contempt, contemptu-

ousness, disdain, hauteur, insolence, loftiness, pride, self-importance, snobbishness, stateliness, superciliousness.

haughty adj arrogant, assuming, contemptuous, disdainful, imperious, insolent, lofty, lordly, overbearing, overweening, proud, scornful, snobbish, supercilious.

haul vb drag, draw, lug, pull, tow, trail, tug. * n heaving, pull, tug; booty, harvest, takings, yield.

haunt vb frequent, resort; follow, importune; hover, inhabit, obsess. * n den, resort, retreat.

hauteur n arrogance, contempt, contemptuousness, disdain, haughtiness, insolence, loftiness, pride, self-importance, stateliness, superciliousness.

have vb cherish, exercise, experience, keep, hold, occupy, own, possess; acquire, gain, get, obtain, receive; accept, take.

haven n asylum, refuge, retreat, shelter; anchorage, harbour, port.

havoc n carnage, damage, desolation, destruction, devastation, ravage, ruin, slaughter, waste, wreck.

hawk-eyed adj eagle-eyed, sharp-sighted.

hazard vb adventure, risk, venture; endanger, imperil, jeopardize. * n accident, casualty, chance, contingency, event, fortuity, stake; danger, jeopardy, peril, risk, venture.

hazardous adj dangerous, insecure, perilous, precarious, risky, uncertain, unsafe.

haze n fog, har, mist, smog; cloud, dimness, fume, miasma, obscurity, pall.

hazy adj foggy, misty; cloudy, dim, nebulous, obscure; confused, indefinite, indistinct, uncertain, vague.

head vb command, control, direct, govern, guide, lead, rule; aim, point, tend; beat, excel, outdo, precede, surpass. * adj chief, first, grand, highest, leading, main, principal; adverse, contrary. * n acme, summit, top; beginning, commencement, origin, rise, source; chief, chieftain, commander, director, leader, master, principal, superintendent, superior; intellect, mind, thought, understanding; branch, category, class, department, division, section, subject, topic; brain, crown, headpiece, intellect, mind, thought, understanding; cape, headland, point, promontory.

headiness n hurry, precipitation, rashness; obstinacy, stubbornness.

headless adj acephalous, beheaded; leaderless, undirected; headstrong, heady, imprudent, obstinate, rash, senseless, stubborn.

headlong adj dangerous, hasty, heady, impulsive, inconsiderate, perilous, precipitate, rash, reckless, ruinous, thoughtless; perpendicular, precipitous, sheer, steep. * adv hastily, headfirst, helter-skelter, hurriedly, precipitately, rashly, thoughtlessly.

headstone n cornerstone, gravestone.

headstrong adj cantankerous, cross-grained, dogged, forward, headless, heady, intractable, obstinate, self-willed, stubborn, ungovernable, unruly, violent, wayward.

heady *adj* hasty, headlong, impetuous, impulsive, inconsiderate, precipitate, rash, reckless, rushing, stubborn, thoughtless; exciting, inebriating, inflaming, intoxicating, spirituous, strong.

heal *vb* amend, cure, remedy, repair, restore; compose, harmonize, reconcile, settle, soothe.

healing *adj* curative, palliative, remedial, restoring, restorative; assuaging, assuasive, comforting, composing, gentle, lenitive, mild, soothing.

health *n* healthfulness, robustness, salubrity, sanity, soundness, strength, tone, vigour.

healthy *adj* active, hale, hearty, lusty, sound, vigorous, well; bracing, healthful, health-giving, hygienic, invigorating, nourishing, salubrious, salutary, wholesome.

heap *vb* accumulate, augment, amass, collect, overfill, pile up, store. * *n* accumulation, collection, cumulus, huddle, lot, mass, mound, pile, stack.

hear *vb* eavesdrop, hearken, heed, listen, overhear; ascertain, discover, gather, learn, understand; examine, judge.

heart *n* bosom, breast; centre, core, essence, interior, kernel, marrow, meaning, pith; affection, benevolence, character, disposition, feeling, inclination, love, mind, passion, purpose, will; affections, ardour, emotion, feeling, love; boldness, courage, fortitude, resolution, spirit.

heartache *n* affliction, anguish, bitterness, distress, dole, grief, heartbreak, sorrow, woe.

heartbroken *adj* broken-hearted, cheerless, comfortless, desolate, disconsolate, forlorn, inconsolable, miserable, woebegone, wretched.

hearten *vb* animate, assure, cheer, comfort, console, embolden, encourage, enhearten, incite, inspire, inspirit, reassure, stimulate.

heartfelt *adj* cordial, deep, deep-felt, hearty, profound, sincere, warm.

hearth *n* fireplace, fireside, forge, hearthstone.

heartily *adv* abundantly, completely, cordially, earnestly, freely, largely, sincerely, vigorously.

heartless *adj* brutal, cold, cruel, hard, harsh, merciless, pitiless, unfeeling, unsympathetic; spiritless, timid, timorous, uncourageous.

heart-rending *adj* affecting, afflicting, anguishing, crushing, distressing.

hearty *adj* cordial, deep, earnest, fervent, heartfelt, profound, sincere, true, unfeigned, warm; active, animated, energetic, fit, vigorous, zealous; convivial, hale, healthy, robust, sound, strong, warm; abundant, full, heavy; nourishing, nutritious, rich.

heat *vb* excite, flush, inflame; animate, rouse, stimulate, stir. * *n* calorie, caloricity, torridity, warmth; excitement, fever, flush, impetuosity, passion, vehemence, violence; ardour, earnestness, fervency, fervour, glow, intensity, zeal; exasperation, fierceness, frenzy, rage.

heath *n* field, moor, wasteland, plain.

heathen *adj* animist, animistic; pagan, paganical, paganish, paganistic, unconverted; agnostic, atheist, atheistic, gentile, idolatrous, infidel, irreligious; barbarous, cruel, inhuman, savage. * *n* atheist, gentile, idolater, idolatress, infidel, pagan, unbeliever; barbarian, philistine, savage.

heave *vb* elevate, hoist, lift, raise; breathe, exhale; cast, fling, hurl, send, throw, toss; dilate, expand, pant, rise, swell; retch, throw up; strive, struggle.

heaven *n* empyrean, firmament, sky, welkin; bliss, ecstasy, elysium, felicity, happiness, paradise, rapture, transport.

heavenly *adj* celestial, empyreal, ethereal; angelic, beatific, beatified, cherubic, divine, elysian, glorious, god-like, sainted, saintly, seraphic; blissful, delightful, divine, ecstatic, enrapturing, enravishing, exquisite, golden, rapturous, ravishing, exquisite, transporting.

heaviness *n* gravity, heft, ponderousness, weight; grievousness, oppressiveness, severity; dullness, languor, lassitude, sluggishness, stupidity; dejection, depression, despondency, gloom, melancholy, sadness, seriousness.

heavy *adj* grave, hard, onerous, ponderous, weighty; afflictive, burdensome, crushing, cumbersome, grievous, oppressive, severe, serious; dilatory, dull, inactive, inanimate, indolent, inert, lifeless, listless, sleepy, slow, sluggish, stupid, torpid; chapfallen, crestfallen, crushed, depressed, dejected, despondent, disconsolate, downhearted, gloomy, low-spirited, melancholy, sad, sobered, sorrowful; difficult, laborious; tedious, tiresome, wearisome, weary; burdened, encumbered, loaded; clammy, clayey, cloggy, illraised, miry, muddy, soggy; boisterous, deep, energetic, loud, roaring, severe, stormy, strong, tempestuous, violent; cloudy, dark, dense, gloomy, lowering, overcast.

hebetate *adj* blunt; dull, obtuse, sluggish, stupid, stupefied.

hectic *adj* animated, excited, fevered, feverish, flushed, heated, hot.

hector *vb* bluster, boast, bully, menace, threaten; annoy, fret, harass, harry, irritate, provoke, tease, vex, worry. * *n* blusterer, bully, swaggerer.

hedge *vb* block, encumber, hinder, obstruct, surround; enclose, fence, fortify, guard, protect; disappear, dodge, evade, hide, skulk, temporize. * *n* barrier, hedgerow, fence, limit.

heed *vb* attend, consider, mark, mind, note, notice, observe, regard. * *n* attention, care, carefulness, caution, circumspection, consideration, heedfulness, mindfulness, notice, observation, regard, wariness, vigilance, watchfulness.

heedful *adj* attentive, careful, cautious, circumspect, mindful, observant, observing, provident, regardful, watchful, wary.

heedless *adj* careless, inattentive, neglectful, negligent, precipitate, rash, reckless, thoughtless, unmindful, unminding, unobserving, unobservant.

heft *n* handle, haft, helve; bulk, weight.

hegemony *n* ascendancy, authority, headship, leadership, predominance, preponderance, rule.

height *n* altitude, elevation, tallness; acme, apex, climax, eminence, head, meridian, pinnacle, summit, top, vertex, zenith; eminence, hill, mountain; dignity, exaltation, grandeur, loftiness, perfection.

heighten *vb* elevate, raise; ennoble, exalt, magnify, make greater; augment, enhance, improve, increase, strengthen; aggravate, intensify.

heinous *adj* aggravated, atrocious, crying, enormous, excessive, flagitious, flagrant, hateful, infamous, monstrous, nefarious, odious, villainous.

heir *n* child, inheritor, offspring, product.

helical *adj* screw-shaped, spiral, winding.

hellish *adj* abominable, accursed, atrocious, curst, damnable, damned, demoniacal, detestable, devilish, diabolical, execrable, fiendish, infernal, monstrous, nefarious, satanic.

helm *n* rudder, steering-gear, tiller, wheel; command, control, direction, rein, rule.

help *vb* relieve, save, succour; abet, aid, assist, back, cooperate, second, serve, support, sustain, wait; alleviate, ameliorate, better, cure, heal, improve, remedy, restore; control, hinder, prevent, repress, resist, withstand; avoid, forbear, control. * *n* aid, assistance, succour, support; relief, remedy; assistant, helper, servant.

helper *adj* aider, abettor, ally, assistant, auxiliary, coadjutor, colleague, helpmate, partner, supporter.

helpful *adj* advantageous, assistant, auxiliary, beneficial, contributory, convenient, favourable, kind, profitable, serviceable, useful.

helpless *adj* disabled, feeble, imbecile, impotent, infirm, powerless, prostrate, resourceless, weak; abandoned, defenceless, exposed, unprotected; desperate, irremediable, remediless.

helpmate *n* companion, consort, husband, partner, wife; aider, assistant, associate, helper.

helter-skelter *adj* disorderly, headlong, irregular, pell-mell, precipitate. * *adv* confusedly, hastily, headlong, higgledy-piggledy, pell-mell, precipitately, wildly.

hem *vb* border, edge, skirt; beset, confine, enclose, environ, surround, sew; hesitate. * *n* border, edge, trim.

henchman *n* attendant, follower, retainer, servant, supporter.

herald *vb* announce, proclaim, publish. * *n* announcer, crier, publisher; harbinger, precursor, proclaimer.

heraldry *n* blazonry, emblazonry.

herbage *n* greenery, herb, pasture, plants, vegetation.

herculean *adj* able-bodied, athletic, brawny, mighty, muscular, powerful, puissant, sinewy, stalwart, strong, sturdy, vigorous; dangerous, difficult, hard, laborious, perilous, toilsome, troublesome; colossal, Cyclopean, gigantic, great, large, strapping.

herd *vb* drive, gather, lead, tend; assemble, associate, flock. * *n* drover, herder, herdsman, shepherd; crowd, multitude, populace, rabble; assemblage, assembly, collection, drove, flock, pack.

hereditary *adj* ancestral, inheritable, inherited, patrimonial, transmitted.

heresy *n* dissent, error, heterodoxy, impiety, recusancy, unorthodoxy.

heretic *n* dissenter, dissident, nonconformist, recusant, schismatic, sectarian, sectary, separatist, unbeliever.

heretical *adj* heterodox, impious, schismatic, schismatical, sectarian, unorthodox.

heritage *n* estate, inheritance, legacy, patrimony, portion.

hermetic *adj* airtight, impervious; cabbalistic, emblematic, emblematical, magical, mysterious, mystic, mystical, occult, secret, symbolic, symbolical.

hermit *n* anchoress, anchoret, anchorite, ascetic, eremite, monk, recluse, solitaire, solitary.

heroic *adj* bold, brave, courageous, daring, dauntless, fearless, gallant, illustrious, intrepid, magnanimous, noble, valiant; desperate, extravagant, extreme, violent.

heroism *n* boldness, bravery, courage, daring, endurance, fearlessness, fortitude, gallantry, intrepidity, prowess, valour.

hesitate *vb* boggle, delay, demur, doubt, pause, scruple, shilly-shally, stickle, vacillate, waver; falter, stammer, stutter.

hesitation *n* halting, misgiving, reluctance; delay, doubt, indecision, suspense, uncertainty, vacillation; faltering, stammering, stuttering.

heterodox *adj* heretical, recusant, schismatic, unorthodox, unsound; apocryphal, uncanonical.

heterogeneous *adj* contrasted, contrary, different, dissimilar, diverse, incongruous, indiscriminate, miscellaneous, mixed, opposed, unhomogeneous, unlike.

hew *vb* chop, cut, fell, hack; fashion, form, shape, smooth.

hiatus *n* blank, break, chasm, gap, interval, lacuna, opening, rift.

hidden *adj* blind, clandestine, cloaked, close, concealed, covered, covert, enshrouded, latent, masked, occult, private, secluded, secret, suppressed, undiscovered, veiled; abstruse, cabbalistic, cryptic, dark, esoteric, hermetic, inward, mysterious, mystic, mystical, obscure, oracular, recondite.

hide *vb* bury, conceal, cover, secrete, suppress, withhold; cloak, disguise, eclipse, hoard, mask, screen, shelter, veil.

hideous *adj* abominable, appalling, awful, dreadful, frightful, ghastly, ghoulish, grim, grisly, horrible, horrid, repulsive, revolting, shocking, terrible, terrifying.

hie *vb* hasten, speed.

hieratic *adj* consecrated, devoted, priestly, sacred, sacerdotal.

hieroglyph *n* picture-writing, rebus, sign, symbol.

hieroglyphic *adj* emblematic, emblematical, figurative, obscure, symbolic, symbolical.

higgle *vb* hawk, peddle; bargain, chaffer, haggle, negotiate.

higgledy-piggledy *adj* chaotic, confused, disorderly, jumbled. * *adv* confusedly, in disorder, helter-skelter, pell-mell.

high *adj* elevated, high-reaching, lofty, soaring, tall, towering; distinguished, eminent, pre-eminent, prominent, superior; admirable, dignified, exalted, great, noble; arrogant, haughty, lordly, proud, supercilious; boisterous, strong, tumultuous, turbulent, violent; costly, dear, pricey; acute, high-pitched, high-toned, piercing, sharp, shrill; tainted, malodorous. * *adv* powerfully, profoundly; eminently, loftily; luxuriously, richly.

high-flown *adj* elevated, presumptuous, proud, lofty, swollen; extravagant, high-coloured, lofty, overdrawn, overstrained; bombastic, inflated, pompous, pretentious, strained, swollen, turgid.

high-handed *adj* arbitrary, despotic, dictatorial, domineering, oppressive, overbearing, self-willed, violent, wilful.

highly strung *adj* ardent, excitable, irascible, nervous, quick, tense; high-spirited, sensitive.

high-minded *adj* arrogant, haughty, lofty, proud; elevated, high-toned; generous honourable, magnanimous, noble, spiritual.

highwayman *n* bandit, brigand, footpad, freebooter, marauder, outlaw, robber.

hilarious *adj* boisterous, cheerful, comical, convivial, riotous, uproarious, jovial, joyful, merry, mirthful, noisy.

hilarity *n* cheerfulness, conviviality, exhilarated, gaiety, glee, jollity, joviality, joyousness, merriment, mirth.

hill *n* ascent, ben, elevation, eminence, hillock, knoll, mount, mountain, rise, tor.

hind *adj* back, hinder, hindmost, posterior, rear, rearward.

hinder *vb* bar, check, clog, delay, embarrass, encumber, impede, interrupt, obstruct, oppose, prevent, restrain, retard, stop, thwart.

hindrance *n* check, deterrent, encumbrance, hitch, impediment, interruption, obstacle, obstruction, restraint, stop, stoppage.

hinge *vb* depend, hang, rest, turn.

hint *vb* allude, glance, imply, insinuate, intimate, mention, refer, suggest. * *n* allusion, clue, implication, indication, innuendo, insinuation, intimation, mention, reminder, suggestion, taste, trace.

hire *vb* buy, rent, secure; charter, employ, engage, lease, let. * *n* allowance, bribe, compensation, pay, remuneration, rent, reward, salary, stipend, wages.

hireling *n* employee, mercenary, myrmidon.

hirsute *adj* bristled, bristly, hairy, shaggy; boorish, course, ill-bred, loutish, rough, rude, rustic, uncouth, unmannerly.

hiss *vb* shrill, sibilate, whistle, whir, whiz; condemn, damn, ridicule. * *n* fizzle, hissing, sibilant, sibilation, sizzle.

historian *n* annalist, autobiographer, biographer, chronicler, narrator, recorder.

history *n* account, autobiography, annals, biography, chronicle, genealogy, memoirs, narration, narrative, recital, record, relation, story.

hit *vb* discomfit, hurt, knock, strike; accomplish, achieve, attain, gain, reach, secure, succeed, win; accord, fit, suit; beat, clash, collide, contact, smite. * *n* blow, collision, strike, stroke; chance, fortune, hazard, success, venture.

hitch *vb* catch, impede, stick, stop; attach, connect, fasten, harness, join, tether, tie, unite, yoke. * *n* catch, check, hindrance, impediment, interruption, obstacle; knot, noose.

hoar *adj* ancient, grey, hoary, old, white.

hoard *vb* accumulate, amass, collect, deposit, garner, hive, husband, save, store, treasure. * *n* accumulation, collection, deposit, fund, mass, reserve, savings, stockpile, store.

hoarse *adj* discordant, grating, gruff, guttural, harsh, husky, low, raucous, rough.

hoary *adj* grey, hoar, silvery, white; ancient, old, venerable.

hoax *vb* deceive, dupe, fool, gammon, gull, hoodwink, swindle, trick. * *n* canard, cheat, deception, fraud, humbug, imposition, imposture, joke, trick, swindle.

hobble *vb* falter, halt, hop, limp; fasten, fetter, hopple, shackle, tie. * *n* halt, limp; clog, fetter, shackle; embarrassment, difficulty, perplexity, pickle, strait.

hobgoblin *n* apparition, bogey, bugbear, goblin, imp, spectre, spirit, sprite.

hobnail *n* bumpkin, churl, clodhopper, clown, lout, rustic.

hocus-pocus *n* cheater, impostor, juggler, sharper, swindler, trickster; artifice, cheat, deceit, deception, delusion, hoax, imposition, juggle, trick.

hodgepodge *n* farrago, hash, hotchpotch, jumble, medley, miscellany, mixture, ragout, stew.

hog *n* beast, glutton, pig; grunter, porker, swine.

hoggish *adj* brutish, filthy, gluttonish, piggish, swinish; grasping, greedy, mean, selfish, sordid.

hoist *vb* elevate, heave, lift, raise, rear. * *n* elevator, lift.

hold *vb* clasp, clinch, clutch, grasp, grip, seize; have, keep, occupy, possess, retain; bind, confine, control, detain, imprison, restrain, restrict; connect, fasten, fix, lock; arrest, check, stay, stop, suspend, withhold; continue, keep up, maintain, manage, prosecute, support, sustain; cherish, embrace, entertain; account, believe, consider, count, deem, entertain, esteem, judge, reckon, regard, think; accommodate, admit, carry, contain, receive, stow; assemble, conduct, convene; endure, last, persist, remain; adhere, cleave, cling, cohere, stick. * *n* anchor, bite, clasp, control, embrace, foothold, grasp, grip, possession, retention, seizure; prop, stay, support; claim, footing, vantage point; castle, fort, fortification, fortress, stronghold, tower; locker, storage, storehouse.

hole *n* aperture, opening, perforation; abyss, bore, cave, cavern, cavity, chasm, depression, excavation, eye, hollow, pit, pore, void; burrow, cover, lair, retreat; den, hovel, kennel.

holiday *n* anniversary, celebration, feast, festival, festivity, fete, gala, recess, vacation.

holiness *n* blessedness, consecration, devotion, devoutness, godliness, piety, purity, religiousness, righteousness, sacredness, saintliness, sanctity, sinlessness.

hollow *vb* dig, excavate, groove, scoop. * *adj* cavernous, concave, depressed, empty, sunken, vacant, void; deceitful, faithless, false, false-hearted, hollow-hearted, hypocritical, insincere, pharisaical, treacherous, unfeeling; deep, low, muffled, reverberating, rumbling, sepulchral. * *n* basin, bowl, depression; cave, cavern, cavity, concavity, dent, dimple, dint, depression, excavation, hole, pit; canal, channel, cup, dimple, dig, groove, pocket, sag.

holocaust *n* carnage, destruction, devastation, genocide, massacre.

holy *adj* blessed, consecrated, dedicated, devoted, hallowed, sacred, sanctified; devout, godly, pious, pure, religious, righteous, saintlike, saintly, sinless, spiritual.

homage *n* allegiance, devotion, fealty, fidelity, loyalty; court, deference, duty, honour, obeisance, respect, reverence, service; adoration, devotion, worship.

home *adj* domestic, family; close, direct, effective, penetrating, pointed. * *n* abode, dwelling, seat, quarters, residence.

homely *adj* domestic, familiar, house-like; coarse, commonplace, homespun, inelegant, plain, simple, unattractive, uncomely, unpolished, unpretentious.

homespun *adj* coarse, homely, inelegant, plain, rude, rustic, unpolished.

homicide *n* manslaughter, murder.

homily *n* address, discourse, lecture, sermon.

homogeneous *adj* akin, alike, cognate, kindred, similar, uniform.

honest *adj* equitable, fair, faithful, honourable, open, straight, straightforward; conscientious, equitable, reliable, sound, square, true, trustworthy, trusty, uncorrupted, upright, virtuous; above-board, faithful, genuine, thorough, unadulterated; creditable, decent, proper, reputable, respectable, suitable; chaste, decent; candid, direct, frank, ingenuous, sincere, unreserved.

honesty *n* equity, fairness, faithfulness, fidelity, honour, integrity, justice, probity, trustiness, trustworthiness, uprightness; truth, truthfulness, veracity; genuineness, thoroughness; candour, frankness, ingenuousness, openness, sincerity, straightforwardness, unreserve.

honorary *adj* formal, nominal, titular, unofficial, unpaid.

honour *vb* dignify, exalt, glorify, grace; respect, revere, reverence, venerate; adore, hallow, worship; celebrate, commemorate, keep, observe. * *n* civility, deference, esteem, homage, respect, reverence, veneration; dignity, distinction, elevation, nobleness; consideration, credit, fame, glory, reputation; high-mindedness, honesty, integrity, magnanimity, probity, uprightness; chastity, purity, virtue; boast, credit, ornament, pride.

honourable *adj* elevated, famous, great, illustrious, noble; admirable, conscientious, fair, honest, just, magnanimous, true, trustworthy, upright, virtuous, worshipful; creditable, esteemed, estimable, equitable, proper, respected, reputable, right.

honours *npl* dignities, distinctions, privilege, titles; adornments, beauties, decorations, glories; civilities.

hood *n* capuche, coif, cover, cowl, head.

hoodwink *vb* blind, blindfold; cloak, conceal, cover, hide; cheat, circumvent, cozen, deceive, delete, dupe, fool, gull, impose, overreach, trick.

hook *vb* catch, ensnare, entrap, hasp, snare; bend, curve. * *n* catch, clasp, fastener, hasp; snare, trap; cutter, grass-hook, reaper, reaping-hook, sickle.

hooked *adj* aquiline, bent, crooked, curved, hamate, unciform.

hoop *vb* clasp, encircle, enclose, surround. * *n* band, circlet, girdle, ring; crinoline, farthingale.

hoot *vb* boo, cry, jeer, shout, yell; condemn, decry, denounce, execrate, hiss. * *n* boo, cry, jeer, shout, yell.

hop *vb* bound, caper, frisk, jump, leap, skip, spring; dance, trip; halt, hobble, limp. * *n* bound, caper, dance, jump, leap, skip, spring.

hope *vb* anticipate, await, desire, expect, long; believe, rely, trust. * *n* confidence, belief, faith, reliance, sanguineness, sanguinity, trust; anticipation, desire, expectancy, expectation.

hopeful *adj* anticipatory, confident, expectant, fond, optimistic, sanguine; cheerful, encouraging, promising.

hopeless *adj* abject, crushed, depressed, despondent, despairing, desperate, disconsolate, downcast, forlorn, pessimistic, woebegone; abandoned, helpless, incurable, irremediable, remediless; impossible, impracticable, unachievable, unattainable.

horde *n* clan, crew, gang, troop; crowd, multitude, pack, throng.

horn *vb* gore, pierce. * *n* trumpet, wind instrument; beaker, drinking cup, cornucopia; spike, spur; cusp, prong, wing.

horrid *adj* alarming, awful, bristling, dire, dreadful, fearful, frightful, harrowing, hideous, horrible, horrific, horrifying, rough, terrible, terrific; abominable, disagreeable, disgusting, odious, offensive, repulsive, revolting, shocking, unpleasant, vile.

horrify *vb* affright, alarm, frighten, shock, terrify, terrorise.

horror *n* alarm, awe, consternation, dismay, dread, fear, fright, panic; abhorrence, abomination, antipathy, aversion, detestation, disgust, hatred, loathing, repugnance, revulsion; shuddering.

horse *n* charger, cob, colt, courser, filly, gelding, mare, nag, pad, palfrey, pony, stallion, steed; cavalry, horseman; buck, clotheshorse, frame, sawhorse, stand, support.

horseman *n* cavalier, equestrian, rider; cavalryman, chasseur, dragoon, horse-soldier.

hospitable *adj* attentive, bountiful, kind; bountiful, cordial, generous, liberal, open, receptive, sociable, unconstrained, unreserved.

host[1] *n* entertainer, innkeeper, landlord, master of ceremonies, presenter, proprietor, owner, receptionist.

host[2] *n* array, army, legion; assemblage, assembly, horde, multitude, throng.

host[3] *n* altar bread, bread, consecrated bread, loaf, wafer.

hostile *adj* inimical, unfriendly, warlike; adverse, antagonistic, contrary, opposed, opposite, repugnant.

hostilities *npl* conflict, fighting, war, warfare.

hostility *n* animosity, antagonism, enmity, hatred, ill-will, unfriendliness; contrariness, opposition, repugnance, variance.

hot *adj* burning, fiery, scalding; boiling, flaming, heated, incandescent, parching, roasting, torrid; heated, oppressive, sweltering, warm; angry, choleric, excitable, furious, hasty, impatient, impetuous, irascible, lustful, passionate, touchy, urgent, violent; animated, ardent, eager, fervent, fervid, glowing, passionate, vehement; acrid, biting, highly flavoured, highly seasoned, peppery, piquant, pungent, sharp, stinging.

hotchpotch *n* farrago, jumble, hodgepodge, medley, miscellany, stew.

hotel *n* inn, public house, tavern.

hot-headed *adj* furious, headlong, headstrong, hot-brained, impetuous, inconsiderate, passionate, precipitate, rash, reckless, vehement, violent.

hound *vb* drive, incite, spur, urge; bate, chase, goad, harass, harry, hunt, pursue.

house *vb* harbour, lodge, protect, shelter. * *n* abode, domicile, dwelling, habitation, home, mansion, residence; building, edifice; family, household; kindred, race, lineage, tribe; company, concern, firm, partnership; hotel, inn, public house, tavern.

housing *n* accommodation, dwellings, houses; casing, container, covering, protection, shelter.

hovel *n* cabin, cot, den, hole, hut, shed.

hover *vb* flutter; hang; vacillate, waver.

however *adv* but, however, nevertheless, notwithstanding, still, though, yet.

howl *vb* bawl, cry, lament, ululate, weep, yell, yowl. * *n* cry, yell, ululation.

hoyden *n* romp, tomboy.

hoydenish *adj* bad-mannered, boisterous, bold, ill-behaved, ill-taught, inelegant, romping, rough, rude, rustic, tomboyish, uncouth, ungenteel, unladylike, unruly.

hubbub *n* clamour, confusion, din, disorder, disturbance, hullabaloo, racket, riot, outcry, tumult, uproar.

huckster *n* hawker, peddler, retailer.

huddle *vb* cluster, crowd, gather; crouch, curl up, nestle, snuggle. * *n* confusion, crowd, disorder, disturbance, jumble, tumult.

hue *n* cast, colour, complexion, dye, shade, tinge, tint, tone.

huff *vb* blow, breathe, exhale, pant, puff. * *n* anger, fume, miff, passion, pet, quarrel, rage, temper, tiff.

hug *vb* clasp, cling, cuddle, embrace, grasp, grip, squeeze; cherish, nurse, retain. * *n* clasp, cuddle, embrace, grasp, squeeze.

huge *adj* bulky, colossal, Cyclopean, elephantine, enormous, gigantic, herculean, immense, stupendous, vast,

huggermugger *adj* clandestine, secret, sly; base, contemptible, mean, unfair; confused, disorderly, slovenly.

hull *vb* husk, peel, shell. * *n* covering, husk, rind, shell.

hullabaloo *n* clamour, confusion, din, disturbance, hubbub, outcry, racket, vociferation, uproar.

hum *vb* buzz, drone, murmur; croon, sing.

humane *adj* accommodating, benevolent, benign, charitable, clement, compassionate, gentle, good-hearted, kind, kind-hearted, lenient, merciful, obliging, tender, sympathetic; cultivating, elevating, humanizing, refining, rational, spiritual.

humanity *n* benevolence, benignity, charity, fellow-feeling, humaneness, kind-heartedness, kindness, philanthropy, sympathy, tenderness; humankind, mankind, mortality.

humanize *vb* civilize, cultivate, educate, enlighten, improve, polish, reclaim, refine, soften.

humble *vb* abase, abash, break, crush, debase, degrade, disgrace, humiliate, lower, mortify, reduce, sink, subdue. * *adj* meek, modest, lowly, simple, submissive, unambitious, unassuming, unobtrusive, unostentatious, unpretending; low, obscure, mean, plain, poor, small, undistinguished, unpretentious.

humbug *vb* cheat, cozen, deceive, hoax, swindle, trick. * *n* cheat, dodge, gammon, hoax, imposition, imposture, deception, fraud, trick; cant, charlatanism, charlatanry, hypocrisy, mummery, quackery; charlatan, impostor, fake, quack.

humdrum *adj* boring, dronish, dreary, dry, dull, monotonous, prosy, stupid, tedious, tiresome, wearisome.

humid *adj* damp, dank, moist, wet.

humiliate *vb* abase, abash, debase, degrade, depress, humble, mortify, shame.

humiliation *n* abasement, affront, condescension,

crushing, degradation, disgrace, dishonouring, humbling, indignity, mortification, self-abasement, submissiveness, resignation.

humility *n* diffidence, humbleness, lowliness, meekness, modesty, self-abasement, submissiveness.

humorist *n* comic, comedian, droll, jester, joker, wag, wit.

humorous *adj* comic, comical, droll, facetious, funny, humorous, jocose, jocular, laughable, ludicrous, merry, playful, pleasant, sportive, whimsical, witty.

humour *vb* favour, gratify, indulge. * *n* bent, bias, disposition, predilection, prosperity, temper, vein; mood, state; caprice, crotchet, fancy, freak, vagary, whim, whimsy, wrinkle; drollery, facetiousness, fun, jocoseness, jocularity, pleasantry, wit; fluid, moisture, vapour.

hunch *vb* arch, jostle, nudge, punch, push, shove. * *n* bunch, hump, knob, protuberance; nudge, punch, push, shove; feeling, idea, intuition, premonition.

hungry *adj* covetous, craving, desirous, greedy; famished, starved, starving; barren, poor, unfertile, unproductive.

hunk *n* chunk, hunch, lump, slice.

hunt *vb* chase, drive, follow, hound, pursue, stalk, trap, trail; poach, shoot; search, seek. * *n* chase, field-sport, hunting, pursuit.

hurl *vb* cast, dart, fling, pitch, project, send, sling, throw, toss.

hurly-burly *n* bustle, commotion, confusion, disturbance, hurl, hurly, uproar, tumult, turmoil.

hurricane *n* cyclone, gale, storm, tempest, tornado, typhoon.

hurried *adj* cursory, hasty, slight, superficial.

hurry *vb* drive, precipitate; dispatch, expedite, hasten, quicken, speed; haste, scurry. * *n* agitation, bustle, confusion, flurry, flutter, perturbation, precipitation; celerity, haste, dispatch, expedition, promptitude, promptness, quickness.

hurt *vb* damage, disable, disadvantage, harm, impair, injure, mar; bruise, pain, wound; afflict, grieve, offend; ache, smart, throb. * *n* damage, detriment, disadvantage, harm, injury, mischief; ache, bruise, pain, suffering, wound.

hurtful *adj* baleful, baneful, deleterious, destructive, detrimental, disadvantageous, harmful, injurious, mischievous, noxious, pernicious, prejudicial, unwholesome.

husband *vb* economize, hoard, save, store.

husbandry *n* agriculture, cultivation, farming, geoponics, tillage; economy, frugality, thrift.

hush *vb* quiet, repress, silence, still, suppress; appease, assuage, calm, console, quiet, still. * *n* quiet, quietness, silence, stillness.

hypocrite *n* deceiver, dissembler, impostor, pretender.

hypocritical *adj* deceiving, dissembling, false, insincere, spurious, two-faced.

hypothesis *n* assumption, proposition, supposition, theory.

hypothetical *adj* assumed, imaginary, supposed, theoretical.

hysterical *adj* frantic, frenzied, overwrought, uncontrollable; comical, uproarious.

I

ice *vb* chill, congeal, freeze. * *n* crystal; frosting, sugar.

icy *adj* glacial; chilling, cold, frosty; cold-hearted, distant, frigid, indifferent, unemotional.

idea *n* archetype, essence, exemplar, ideal, model, pattern, plan, model; fantasy, fiction, image, imagination; apprehension, conceit, conception, fancy, illusion, impression, thought; belief, judgement, notion, opinion, sentiment, supposition.

ideal *adj* intellectual, mental; chimerical, fancied, fanciful, fantastic, illusory, imaginary, unreal, visionary, shadowy; complete, consummate, excellent, perfect; impractical, unattainable, utopian. * *n* criterion, example, model, standard.

identical *adj* equivalent, same, selfsame, tantamount.

identity *n* existence, individuality, personality, sameness.

ideology *n* belief, creed, dogma, philosophy, principle.

idiocy *n* fatuity, feebleness, foolishness, imbecility, insanity.

idiosyncrasy *n* caprice, eccentricity, fad, peculiarity, singularity.

idiot *n* blockhead, booby, dunce, fool, ignoramus, imbecile, simpleton.

idiotic *adj* fatuous, foolish, imbecile, irrational, senseless, sottish, stupid.

idle *adj* inactive, unemployed, unoccupied, vacant; indolent, inert, lazy, slothful, sluggish; abortive, bootless, fruitless, futile, groundless, ineffectual, unavailing, useless, vain; foolish, frivolous, trashy, trifling, trivial, unimportant, unprofitable. * *vb* dally, dawdle, laze, loiter, potter, waste; drift, shirk, slack.

idler *n* dawdler, doodle, drone, laggard, lazybones, loafer, lounger, slacker, slowcoach, sluggard, trifler.

idol *n* deity, god, icon, image, pagan, simulacrum, symbol; delusion, falsity, pretender, sham; beloved, darling, favourite, pet.

idolater *n* heathen, pagan; admirer, adorer, worshipper.

idolize *vb* canonize, deify; adore, honour, love, reverence, venerate.

idyll *n* eclogue, pastoral.

if *conj* admitting, allowing, granting, provided, supposing, though, whether. * *n* condition, hesitation, uncertainty.

igneous *adj* combustible, combustive, conflagrative, fiery, molten.

ignite *vb* burn, inflame, kindle, light, torch.

ignoble *adj* base-born, low, low-born, mean, peasant, plebeian, rustic, vulgar; contemptible, degraded, insignificant, mean, worthless; disgraceful, dishonourable, infamous, low, unworthy.

ignominious *adj* discreditable, disgraceful, dishonourable, disreputable, infamous, opprobrious, scandalous, shameful; base, contemptible, despicable.

ignominy *n* abasement, contempt, discredit, disgrace, dishonour disrepute, infamy, obloquy, odium, opprobrium, scandal, shame.

ignoramus *n* blockhead, duffer, dunce, fool, greenhorn, novice, numskull, simpleton.

ignorance *n* benightedness, darkness, illiteracy, nescience, rusticity; blindness, unawareness.

ignorant *adj* blind, illiterate, nescient, unaware, unconversant, uneducated, unenlightened, uninformed, uninstructed, unlearned, unread, untaught, untutored, unwitting.

ignore *vb* disregard, neglect, overlook, reject, skip.

ill *adj* bad, evil, faulty, harmful, iniquitous, naughty, unfavourable, unfortunate, unjust, wicked; ailing, diseased, disordered, indisposed, sick, unwell, wrong; crabbed, cross, hateful, malicious, malevolent, peevish, surly, unkind, ill-bred; ill-favoured, ugly, unprepossessing. * *adv* badly, poorly, unfortunately. * *n* badness, depravity, evil, mischief, misfortune, wickedness; affliction, ailment, calamity, harm, misery, pain, trouble.

ill-advised *adj* foolish, ill-judged, imprudent, injudicious, unwise.

ill-bred *adj* discourteous, ill-behaved, ill-mannered, impolite, rude, uncivil, uncourteous, uncourtly, uncouth.

illegal *adj* contraband, forbidden, illegitimate, illicit, prohibited, unauthorized, unlawful, unlicensed.

illegible *adj* indecipherable, obscure, undecipherable, unreadable.

illegitimate *adj* bastard, misbegotten, natural.

ill-fated *adj* ill-starred, luckless, unfortunate, unlucky.

ill-favoured *adj* homely, ugly, offensive, plain, unpleasant.

ill humour *n* fretfulness, ill-temper, peevishness, petulance, testiness.

illiberal *adj* close, close-fisted, covetous, mean, miserly, narrow, niggardly, parsimonious, penurious, selfish, sordid, stingy, ungenerous; bigoted, narrow-minded, uncharitable, ungentlemanly, vulgar.

illicit *adj* illegal, illegitimate, unauthorized, unlawful, unlegalized, unlicensed; criminal, guilty, forbidden, improper, wrong.

illimitable *adj* boundless, endless, immeasurable, immense, infinite, unbounded, unlimited, vast.

illiterate *adj* ignorant, uneducated, uninstructed, unlearned, unlettered, untaught, untutored.

ill-judged *adj* foolish, ill-advised, imprudent, injudicious, unwise.

ill-mannered *adj* discourteous, ill-behaved, ill-bred, impolite, rude, uncivil, uncourteous, uncourtly, uncouth, unpolished.

ill-natured *adj* disobliging, hateful, malevolent, unamiable, unfriendly, unkind; acrimonious, bitter, churlish, crabbed, cross, cross-grained, crusty, ill-tempered, morose, perverse, petulant, sour, spiteful, sulky, sullen, wayward.

illness *n* ailing, ailment, complaint, disease, disorder, distemper, indisposition, malady, sickness.

illogical *adj* absurd, fallacious, inconsistent, inconclusive, inconsequent, incorrect, invalid, unreasonable, unsound.

ill-proportioned *adj* awkward, ill-made, ill-shaped, misshapen, misproportioned, shapeless.

ill-starred *adj* ill-fated, luckless, unfortunate, unhappy, unlucky.

ill temper *n* bad temper, crabbedness, crossness, grouchiness, ill nature, moroseness, sulkiness, sullenness.

ill-tempered *adj* acrimonious, bad-tempered, crabbed, cross, grouchy, ill-natured, morose, sour, sulky, surly.

ill-timed *adj* inapposite, inopportune, irrelevant, unseasonable, untimely.

ill-treat *vb* abuse, ill-use, injure, maltreat, mishandle, misuse.

illude *vb* cheat, deceive, delude, disappoint, mock, swindle, trick.

illuminate *vb* illume, illumine, light; adorn, brighten, decorate, depict, edify, enlighten, inform, inspire, instruct, make wise.

illusion *n* chimera, deception, delusion, error, fallacy, false appearance, fantasy, hallucination, mockery, phantasm.

illusive, illusory *adj* barmecide, deceitful, deceptive, delusive, fallacious, imaginary, make-believe, mock, sham, unsatisfying, unreal, unsubstantial, visionary, tantalizing.

illustrate *vb* clarify, demonstrate, elucidate, enlighten, exemplify, explain; adorn, depict, draw.

illustration *n* demonstration, elucidation, enlightenment, exemplification, explanation, interpretation; adornment, decoration, picture.

illustrative *adj* elucidative, elucidatory, exemplifying.

illustrious *adj* bright, brilliant, glorious, radiant, splendid; celebrated, conspicuous, distinguished, eminent, famed, famous, noble, noted, remarkable, renowned, signal.

ill will *n* animosity, dislike, enmity, envy, grudge, hate, hatred, hostility, ill nature, malevolence, malice, malignity, rancour, spleen, spite, uncharitableness, unkindness, venom.

image *n* idol, statue; copy, effigy, figure, form, imago, likeness, picture, resemblance, representation, shape, similitude, simulacrum, statue, symbol; conception, counterpart, embodiment, idea, reflection.

imagery *n* dream, phantasm, phantom, vision.

imaginable *adj* assumable, cogitable, conceivable, conjecturable, plausible, possible, supposable, thinkable.

imaginary *adj* chimerical, dreamy, fancied, fanciful, fantastic, fictitious, ideal, illusive, illusory, invented, quixotic, shadowy, unreal, utopian, visionary, wild; assumed, conceivable, hypothetical, supposed.

imagination *n* chimera, conception, fancy, fantasy, invention, unreality; position; contrivance, device, plot, scheme.

imaginative *adj* creative, dreamy, fanciful, inventive, poetical, plastic, visionary.

imagine *vb* conceive, dream, fancy, imagine, picture, pretend; contrive, create, devise, frame, invent, mould, project; assume, suppose, hypothesize; apprehend, assume, believe, deem, guess, opine, suppose, think.

imbecile *adj* cretinous, drivelling, fatuous, feeble, feeble-minded, foolish, helpless, idiotic, imbecilic, inane, infirm, witless. * *n* dotard, driveller.

imbecility *n* debility, feebleness, helplessness, infirmity, weakness; foolishness, idiocy, silliness, stupidity, weak-mindedness.

imbibe *vb* absorb, assimilate, drink, suck, swallow; acquire, gain, gather, get, receive.

imbroglio *n* complexity, complication, embarrassment, entanglement, misunderstanding.

imbrue *vb* drench, embrue, gain, moisten, soak, stain, steep, wet.

imbue *vb* colour, dye, stain, tincture, tinge, tint; bathe, impregnate, infuse, inoculate, permeate, pervade, provide, saturate, steep.

imitate *vb* copy, counterfeit, duplicate, echo, emulate, follow, forge, mirror, reproduce, simulate; ape, impersonate, mimic, mock, personate; burlesque, parody, travesty.

imitation *adj* artificial, fake, man-made, mock, reproduction, synthetic. * *n* aping, copying, imitation, mimicking, parroting; copy, duplicate, likeness, resemblance; mimicry, mocking; burlesque, parody, travesty.

imitative *adj* copying, emulative, imitating, mimetic, simulative; apeish, aping, mimicking.

imitator *n* copier, copycat, copyist, echo, impersonator, mimic, mimicker, parrot.

immaculate *adj* clean, pure, spotless, stainless, unblemished, uncontaminated, undefiled, unpolluted, unspotted, unsullied, untainted, untarnished; faultless, guiltless, holy, innocent, pure, saintly, sinless, stainless.

immanent *adj* congenital, inborn, indwelling, inherent, innate, internal, intrinsic, subjective.

immaterial *adj* bodiless, ethereal, extramundane, impalpable, incorporeal, mental, metaphysical, spiritual, unbodied, unfleshly, unsubstantial; inconsequential, insignificant, nonessential, unessential, unimportant.

immature *adj* crude, green, imperfect, raw, rudimental, rudimentary, unfinished, unformed, unprepared, unripe, unripened, youthful; hasty, premature, unseasonable, untimely.

immaturity *n* crudeness, crudity, greenness, imperfection, rawness, unpreparedness, unripeness.

immeasurable *adj* bottomless, boundless, illimitable, immense, infinite, limitless, measureless, unbounded, vast.

immediate *adj* close, contiguous, near, next, proximate; intuitive, primary, unmeditated; direct, instant, instantaneous, present, pressing, prompt.

immediately *adv* closely, proximately; directly, forthwith, instantly, presently, presto, pronto.

immemorial *adj* ancient, hoary, olden.

immense *adj* boundless, illimitable, infinite, interminable, measureless, unbounded, unlimited; colossal, elephantine, enormous, gigantic, huge, large, monstrous, mountainous, prodigious, stupendous, titanic, tremendous, vast.

immensity *n* boundlessness, endlessness, limitlessness, infiniteness, infinitude, infinity; amplitude, enormity, greatness, hugeness, magnitude, vastness.

immerse *vb* baptize, bathe, dip, douse, duck, overwhelm, plunge, sink, souse, submerge; absorb, engage, engross, involve.

immersion *n* dipping, immersing, plunging; absorption, engagement; disappearance; baptism.

imminent *adj* close, impending, near, overhanging, threatening; alarming, dangerous, perilous.

immobile *adj* fixed, immovable, inflexible, motionless, quiescent, stable, static, stationary, steadfast; dull, expressionless, impassive, rigid, stiff, stolid.

immobility *n* fixedness, fixity, immovability, immovableness, motionlessness, stability, steadfastness, unmovableness; dullness, expressionlessness, inflexibility, rigidity, stiffness, stolidity.

immoderate *adj* excessive, exorbitant, extravagant, extreme, inordinate, intemperate, unreasonable.

immodest *adj* coarse, gross, indecorous, indelicate, lewd, shameless; bold, brazen, forward, impudent, indecent; broad, filthy, impure, indecent, obscene, smutty, unchaste.

immodesty *n* coarseness, grossness, indecorum, indelicacy, shamelessness; impurity, lewdness, obscenity, smuttiness, unchastity; boldness, brass, forwardness, impatience.

immolate *vb* kill, sacrifice.

immoral *adj* antisocial, corrupt, loose, sinful, unethical, vicious, wicked, wrong; bad, depraved, dissolute, profligate, unprincipled; abandoned, indecent, licentious.

immorality *n* corruption, corruptness, criminality, demoralization, depravity, impurity, profligacy, sin, sinfulness, vice, wickedness; wrong.

immortal *adj* deathless, ever-living, imperishable, incorruptible, indestructible, indissoluble, never-dying, undying, unfading; ceaseless, continuing, eternal, endless, everlasting, never-ending, perpetual, sempiternal; abiding, enduring, lasting, permanent. * *n* god, goddess; genius, hero.

immortality *n* deathlessness, incorruptibility, incorruptibleness, indestructibility; perpetuity.

immortalize *vb* apotheosize, enshrine, glorify, perpetuate.

immovable *adj* firm, fixed, immobile, stable, stationary; impassive, steadfast, unalterable, unchangeable, unshaken, unyielding.

immunity *n* exemption, exoneration, freedom, release; charter, franchise, liberty, license, prerogative, privilege, right.

immure *vb* confine, entomb, imprison, incarcerate.

immutability *n* constancy, inflexibility, invariability, invariableness, permanence, stability, unalterableness, unchangeableness.

immutable *adj* constant, fixed, inflexible, invariable, permanent, stable, unalterable, unchangeable, undeviating.

imp *n* demon, devil, elf, flibbertigibbet, hobgoblin, scamp, sprite; graft, scion, shoot.

impact *vb* collide, crash, strike. * *n* brunt, impression, impulse, shock, stroke, touch; collision, contact, impinging, striking.

impair *vb* blemish, damage, deface, deteriorate, injure, mar, ruin, spoil, vitiate; decrease, diminish, lessen, reduce; enervate, enfeeble, weaken.

impale *vb* hole, pierce, puncture, spear, spike, stab, transfix.

impalpable *adj* attenuated, delicate, fine, intangible; imperceptible, inapprehensible, incorporeal, indistinct, shadowy, unsubstantial.

impart *vb* bestow, confer, give, grant; communicate, disclose, discover, divulge, relate, reveal, share, tell.

impartial *adj* candid, disinterested, dispassionate, equal, equitable, even-handed, fair, honourable, just, unbiased, unprejudiced, unwarped.

impassable *adj* blocked, closed, impenetrable, impermeable, impervious, inaccessible, pathless, unattainable, unnavigable, unreachable.

impassioned *adj* animated, ardent, burning, excited, fervent, fervid, fiery, glowing, impetuous, intense, passionate, vehement, warm, zealous.

impassive *adj* calm, passionless; apathetic, callous, indifferent, insensible, insusceptible, unfeeling, unimpressible, unsusceptible.

impassivity *n* calmness, composure, indifference,

insensibility, insusceptibility, passionlessness, stolidity.

impatience *n* disquietude, restlessness, uneasiness; eagerness, haste, impetuosity, precipitation, vehemence; heat, irritableness, irritability, violence.

impatient *adj* restless, uneasy, unquiet; eager, hasty, impetuous, precipitate, vehement; abrupt, brusque, choleric, fretful, hot, intolerant, irritable, peevish, sudden, testy, violent.

impeach *vb* accuse, arraign, charge, indict; asperse, censure, denounce, disparage, discredit, impair, impute, incriminate, lessen.

impeachment *n* accusation, arraignment, indictment; aspersion, censure, disparagement, imputation, incrimination, reproach.

impeccable *adj* faultless, immaculate, incorrupt, innocent, perfect, pure, sinless, stainless, uncorrupt.

impede *vb* bar, block, check, clog, curb, delay, encumber, hinder, interrupt, obstruct, restrain, retard, stop, thwart.

impediment *n* bar, barrier, block, check, curb, difficulty, encumbrance, hindrance, obstacle, obstruction, stumbling block.

impel *vb* drive, push, send, urge; actuate, animate, compel, constrain, embolden, incite, induce, influence, instigate, move, persuade, stimulate.

impend *vb* approach, menace, near, threaten.

impending *adj* approaching, imminent, menacing, near, threatening.

impenetrable *adj* impermeable, impervious, inaccessible; cold, dull, impassive, indifferent, obtuse, senseless, stolid, unsympathetic; dense, proof.

impenitence *n* hardheartedness, impenitency, impenitentness, obduracy, stubbornness.

impenitent *adj* hardened, hard-hearted, incorrigible, irreclaimable, obdurate, recusant, relentless, seared, stubborn, uncontrite, unconverted, unrepentant.

imperative *adj* authoritative, commanding, despotic, domineering, imperious, overbearing, peremptory, urgent; binding, obligatory.

imperceptible *adj* inaudible, indiscernible, indistinguishable, invisible; fine, impalpable, inappreciable, gradual, minute.

imperfect *adj* abortive, crude, deficient, garbled, incomplete, poor; defective, faulty, impaired.

imperfection *n* defectiveness, deficiency, faultiness, incompleteness; blemish, defect, fault, flaw, lack, stain, taint; failing, foible, frailty, limitation, vice, weakness.

imperial *adj* kingly, regal, royal, sovereign; august, consummate, exalted, grand, great, kingly, magnificent, majestic, noble, regal, royal, queenly, supreme, sovereign, supreme, consummate.

imperil *vb* endanger, expose, hazard, jeopardize, risk.

imperious *adj* arrogant, authoritative, commanding, compelling, despotic, dictatorial, domineering, haughty, imperative, lordly, magisterial, overbearing, tyrannical, urgent, compelling.

imperishable *adj* eternal, everlasting, immortal, incorruptible, indestructible, never-ending, perennial, unfading.

impermeable *adj* impenetrable, impervious.

impermissible *adj* deniable, insufferable, objectionable, unallowable, unallowed, unlawful.

impersonate *vb* act, ape, enact, imitate, mimic, mock, personate; embody, incarnate, personify, typify.

impersonation *n* incarnation, manifestation, personification; enacting, imitation, impersonating, mimicking, personating, representation.

impertinence *n* irrelevance, irrelevancy, unfitness, impropriety; assurance, boldness, brass, brazenness, effrontery, face, forwardness, impudence, incivility, insolence, intrusiveness, presumption, rudeness, sauciness, pertness.

impertinent *adj* inapplicable, inapposite, irrelevant; bold, forward, impudent, insolent, intrusive, malapert, meddling, officious, pert, rude, saucy, unmannerly.

imperturbability *n* calmness, collectedness, composure, dispassion, placidity, placidness, sedateness, serenity, steadiness, tranquility.

imperturbable *adj* calm, collected, composed, cool, placid, sedate, serene, tranquil, unmoved, undisturbed, unexcitable, unmoved, unruffled.

impervious *adj* impassable, impenetrable, impermeable.

impetuosity *n* force, fury, haste, precipitancy, vehemence, violence.

impetuous *adj* ardent, boisterous, brash, breakneck, fierce, fiery, furious, hasty, headlong, hot, hot-headed, impulsive, overzealous, passionate, precipitate, vehement, violent.

impetus *n* energy, force, momentum, propulsion.

impiety *n* irreverence, profanity, ungodliness; iniquity, sacreligiousness, sin, sinfulness, ungodliness, unholiness, unrighteousness, wickedness.

impinge *vb* clash, dash, encroach, hit, infringe, strike, touch.

impious *adj* blasphemous, godless, iniquitous, irreligious, irreverent, profane, sinful, ungodly, unholy, unrighteous, wicked.

implacable *adj* deadly, inexorable, merciless, pitiless, rancorous, relentless, unappeasable, unforgiving, unpropitiating, unrelenting.

implant *vb* ingraft, infix, insert, introduce, place.

implement *vb* effect, execute, fulfil. * *n* appliance, instrument, tool, utensil.

implicate *vb* entangle, enfold; compromise, concern, entangle, include, involve.

implication *n* entanglement, involvement, involution; connotation, hint, inference, innuendo, intimation; conclusion, meaning, significance.

implicit *adj* implied, inferred, understood; absolute, constant, firm, steadfast, unhesitating, unquestioning, unreserved, unshaken.

implicitly *adv* by implication, silently, tacitly,

unspokenly, virtually, wordlessly.

implore *vb* adjure, ask, beg, beseech, entreat, petition, pray, solicit, supplicate.

imply *vb* betoken, connote, denote, import, include, infer, insinuate, involve, mean, presuppose, signify.

impolicy *n* folly, imprudence, ill-judgement, indiscretion, inexpediency.

impolite *adj* bearish, boorish, discourteous, disrespectful, ill-bred, insolent, rough, rude, uncivil, uncourteous, ungentle, ungentlemanly, ungracious, unmannerly, unpolished, unrefined.

impoliteness *n* boorishness, discourteousness, discourtesy, disrespect, ill-breeding, incivility, insolence, rudeness, unmannerliness.

impolitic *adj* ill-advised, imprudent, indiscreet, inexpedient, injudicious, unwise.

import *vb* bring in, introduce, transport; betoken, denote, imply, mean, purport, signify. * *n* goods, importation, merchandise; bearing, drift, gist, intention, interpretation, matter, meaning, purpose, sense, signification, spirit, tenor; consequence, importance, significance, weight.

importance *n* concern, consequence, gravity, import, moment, momentousness, significance, weight, weightiness; consequence, pomposity, self-importance.

important *adj* considerable, grave, material, momentous, notable, pompous, ponderous, serious, significant, urgent, valuable, weighty; esteemed, influential, prominent, substantial; consequential, pompous, self-important.

importunate *adj* busy, earnest, persistent, pertinacious, pressing, teasing, troublesome, urgent.

importune *vb* ask, beset, dun, ply, press, solicit, urge.

importunity *n* appeal, beseechment, entreaty, petition, plying, prayer, pressing, suit, supplication, urging; contention, insistence; urgency.

impose *vb* lay, place, put, set; appoint, charge, dictate, enjoin, force, inflict, obtrude, prescribe, tax; (*with* **on, upon**) abuse, cheat, circumvent, deceive, delude, dupe, exploit, hoax, trick, victimize.

imposing *adj* august, commanding, dignified, exalted, grand, grandiose, impressive, lofty, magnificent, majestic, noble, stately, striking.

imposition *n* imposing, laying, placing, putting; burden, charge, constraint, injunction, levy, oppression, tax; artifice, cheating, deception, dupery, fraud, imposture, trickery.

impossibility *n* hopelessness, impracticability, inability, infeasibility, unattainability; inconceivability.

impossible *adj* hopeless, impracticable, infeasible, unachievable, unattainable; inconceivable, self-contradictory, unthinkable.

impost *n* custom, duty, excise, rate, tax, toil, tribute.

impostor *n* charlatan, cheat, counterfeiter, deceiver, double-dealer, humbug, hypocrite, knave,

mountebank, pretender, quack, rogue, trickster.

imposture *n* artifice, cheat, deceit, deception, delusion, dodge, fraud, hoax, imposition, ruse, stratagem, trick, wile.

impotence *n* disability, feebleness, frailty, helplessness, inability, incapability, incapacity, incompetence, inefficaciousness, inefficacy, inefficiency, infirmity, powerlessness, weakness.

impotent *adj* disabled, enfeebled, feeble, frail, helpless, incapable, incapacitated, incompetent, inefficient, infirm, nerveless, powerless, unable, weak; barren, sterile.

impound *vb* confine, coop, engage, imprison.

impoverish *vb* beggar, pauperize; deplete, exhaust, ruin.

impracticability *n* impossibility, impracticableness, impracticality, infeasibility, unpracticability.

impracticable *adj* impossible, infeasible; intractable, obstinate, recalcitrant, stubborn, thorny, unmanageable; impassable, insurmountable.

impracticality *n* impossibility, impracticableness, impractibility, infeasibility, unpracticability; irrationality, unpracticalness, unrealism, unreality, unreasonableness.

imprecate *vb* anathematize, curse, execrate, invoke, maledict.

imprecation *n* anathema, curse, denunciation, execration, invocation, malediction.

imprecatory *adj* appealing, beseeching, entreating, imploratory, imploring, imprecatory, pleading; cursing, damnatory, execrating, maledictory.

impregnable *adj* immovable, impenetrable, indestructible, invincible, inviolable, invulnerable, irrefrangible, secure, unconquerable, unassailable, unyielding.

impregnate *vb* fecundate, fertilize, fructify; dye, fill, imbrue, imbue, infuse, permeate, pervade, saturate, soak, tincture, tinge.

impress *vb* engrave, imprint, print, stamp; affect, move, strike; fix, inculcate; draft, enlist, levy, press, requisition. * *n* impression, imprint, mark, print, seal, stamp; cognizance, device, emblem, motto, symbol.

impressibility *n* affectibility, impressionability, pliancy, receptiveness, responsiveness, sensibility, sensitiveness, susceptibility.

impressible *adj* affectible, excitable, impressionable, pliant, receptive, responsive, sensitive, soft, susceptible, tender.

impression *n* edition, imprinting, printing, stamping; brand, dent, impress, mark, stamp; effect, influence, sensation; fancy, idea, instinct, notion, opinion, recollection.

impressive *adj* affecting, effective, emphatic, exciting, forcible, moving, overpowering, powerful, solemn, speaking, splendid, stirring, striking, telling, touching.

imprint *vb* engrave, mark, print, stamp; impress, inculcate. * *n* impression, mark, print, sign, stamp.

imprison *vb* confine, jail, immure, incarcerate, shut up.

imprisonment *n* captivity, commitment, confinement, constraint, durance, duress, incarceration, restraint.

improbability *n* doubt, uncertainty, unlikelihood.

improbable *adj* doubtful, uncertain, unlikely, unplausible.

improbity *n* dishonesty, faithlessness, fraud, fraudulence, knavery, unfairness.

impromptu *adj* extempore, improvised, offhand, spontaneous, unpremeditated, unprepared, unrehearsed. * *adv* extemporaneously, extemporarily, extempore, offhand, ad-lib.

improper *adj* immodest, inapposite, inappropriate, irregular, unadapted, unapt, unfit, unsuitable, unsuited; indecent, indecorous, indelicate, unbecoming, unseemly; erroneous, inaccurate, incorrect, wrong.

impropriety *n* inappropriateness, unfitness, unsuitability, unsuitableness; indecorousness, indecorum, unseemliness.

improve *vb* ameliorate, amend, better, correct, edify, meliorate, mend, rectify, reform; cultivate; gain, mend, progress; enhance, increase, rise.

improvement *n* ameliorating, amelioration, amendment, bettering, improving, meliorating, melioration; advancement, proficiency, progress.

improvidence *n* imprudence, thriftlessness, unthriftiness.

improvident *adj* careless, heedless, imprudent, incautious, inconsiderate, negligent, prodigal, rash, reckless, shiftless, thoughtless, thriftless, unthrifty, wasteful.

improvisation *n* ad-libbing, contrivance, extemporaneousness, extemporariness, extemporization, fabrication, invention; (*mus*) extempore, impromptu.

improvise *vb* ad-lib, contrive, extemporize, fabricate, imagine, invent.

imprudence *n* carelessness, heedlessness, improvidence, incautiousness, inconsideration, indiscretion, rashness.

imprudent *adj* careless, heedless, ill-advised, ill-judged, improvident, incautious, inconsiderate, indiscreet, rash, unadvised, unwise.

impudence *n* assurance, audacity, boldness, brashness, brass, bumptiousness, cheek, cheekiness, effrontery, face, flippancy, forwardness, front, gall, impertinence, insolence, jaw, lip, nerve, pertness, presumption, rudeness, sauciness, shamelessness.

impudent *adj* bold, bold-faced, brazen, brazen-faced, cool, flippant, forward, immodest, impertinent, insolent, insulting, pert, presumptuous, rude, saucy, shameless.

impugn *vb* assail, attack, challenge, contradict, dispute, gainsay, oppose, question, resist.

impulse *n* force, impetus, impelling, momentum, push, thrust; appetite, inclination, instinct, passion, proclivity; incentive, incitement, influence, instigation, motive, instigation.

impulsive *adj* impelling, moving, propulsive; emotional, hasty, heedless, hot, impetuous, mad-cap, passionate, quick, rash, vehement, violent.

impunity *n* exemption, immunity, liberty, licence, permission, security.

impure *adj* defiled, dirty, feculent, filthy, foul, polluted, unclean; bawdy, coarse, immodest, gross, immoral, indelicate, indecent, lewd, licentious, loose, obscene, ribald, smutty, unchaste; adulterated, corrupt, mixed.

impurity *n* defilement, feculence, filth, foulness, pollution, uncleanness; admixture, coarseness, grossness, immodesty, indecency, indelicacy, lewdness, licentiousness, looseness, obscenity, ribaldry, smut, smuttiness, unchastity, vulgarity.

imputable *adj* ascribable, attributable, chargeable, owing, referable, traceable, owing.

imputation *n* attributing, charging, imputing; accusation, blame, censure, charge, reproach.

impute *vb* ascribe, attribute, charge, consider, imply, insinuate, refer.

inability *n* impotence, incapacity, incapability, incompetence, incompetency, inefficiency; disability, disqualification.

inaccessible *adj* unapproachable, unattainable.

inaccuracy *n* erroneousness, impropriety, incorrectness, inexactness; blunder, defect, error, fault, mistake.

inaccurate *adj* defective, erroneous, faulty, incorrect, inexact, mistaken, wrong.

inaccurately *adv* carelessly, cursorily, imprecisely, incorrectly, inexactly, mistakenly, unprecisely, wrongly.

inactive *adj* inactive; dormant, inert, inoperative, peaceful, quiet, quiescent; dilatory, drowsy, dull, idle, inanimate, indolent, inert, lazy, lifeless, lumpish, passive, slothful, sleepy, stagnant, supine.

inactivity *n* dilatoriness, idleness, inaction, indolence, inertness, laziness, sloth, sluggishness, supineness, torpidity, torpor.

inadequacy *n* inadequateness, insufficiency; defectiveness, imperfection, incompetence, incompetency, incompleteness, insufficiency, unfitness, unsuitableness.

inadequate *adj* disproportionate, incapable, insufficient, unequal; defective, imperfect, inapt, incompetent, incomplete.

inadmissible *adj* improper, incompetent, unacceptable, unallowable, unqualified, unreasonable.

inadvertence, inadvertency *n* carelessness, heedlessness, inattention, inconsiderateness, negligence, thoughtlessness; blunder, error, oversight, slip.

inadvertent *adj* careless, heedless, inattentive, inconsiderate, negligent, thoughtless, unobservant.

inadvertently *adv* accidently, carelessly, heedlessly, inconsiderately, negligently, thoughtlessly, unintentionally.

inalienable *adj* undeprivable, unforfeitable, untransferable.

inane *adj* empty, fatuous, vacuous, void; foolish, frivolous, idiotic, puerile, senseless, silly, stupid, trifling, vain, worthless.

inanimate *adj* breathless, dead, extinct; dead, dull, inert, lifeless, soulless, spiritless.

inanition *n* emptiness, inanity, vacuity; exhaustion, hunger, malnutrition, starvation, want.

inanity *n* emptiness, foolishness, inanition, vacuity; folly, frivolousness, puerility, vanity, worthlessness.

inapplicable *adj* inapposite, inappropriate, inapt, irrelevant, unfit, unsuitable, unsuited.

inapposite *adj* impertinent, inapplicable, irrelevant, nonpertinent; inappropriate, unfit, unsuitable.

inappreciable *adj* impalpable, imperceptible, inconsiderable, inconspicuous, indiscernible, infinitesimal, insignificant, negligible, undiscernible, unnoticed.

inappropriate *adj* inapposite, unadapted, unbecoming, unfit, unsuitable, unsullied.

inapt *adj* inapposite, unapt, unfit, unsuitable; awkward, clumsy, dull, slow, stolid, stupid.

inaptitude *n* awkwardness, inapplicability, inappropriateness, inaptness, unfitness, unsuitableness.

inarticulate *adj* blurred, indistinct, thick; dumb, mute.

inartificial *adj* artless, direct, guileless, ingenuous, naive, simple, simple-minded, sincere, single-minded.

inasmuch as *conj* considering that, seeing that, since.

inattention *n* absent-mindedness, carelessness, disregard, heedlessness, inadvertence, inapplication, inconsiderateness, neglect, remissness, slip, thoughtlessness, unmindfulness, unobservance

inattentive *adj* absent-minded, careless, disregarding, heedless, inadvertent, inconsiderate, neglectful, remiss, thoughtless, unmindful, unobservant.

inaudible *adj* faint, indistinct, muffled; mute, noiseless, silent, still.

inaugurate *vb* induct, install, introduce, invest; begin, commence, initiate, institute, originate.

inauguration *n* beginning, commencement, initiation, institution, investiture, installation, opening, origination.

inauspicious *adj* bad, discouraging, ill-omened, ill-starred, ominous, unfavourable, unfortunate, unlucky, unpromising, unpropitious, untoward.

inborn *adj* congenital, inbred, ingrained, inherent, innate, instinctive, native, natural.

incalculable *adj* countless, enormous, immense, incalculable, inestimable, innumerable, sumless, unknown, untold.

incandescence *n* candescence, glow, gleam, luminousness, luminosity.

incandescent *adj* aglow, candent, candescent, gleaming, glowing, luminous, luminant, radiant.

incantation *n* charm, conjuration, enchantment, magic, necromancy, sorcery, spell, witchcraft, witchery.

incapability *n* disability, inability, incapacity, incompetence.

incapable *adj* feeble, impotent, incompetent, insufficient, unable, unfit, unfitted, unqualified, weak.

incapacious *adj* cramped, deficient, incommodious, narrow, scant.

incapacitate *vb* cripple, disable; disqualify, make unfit.

incapacity *n* disability, inability, incapability, incompetence; disqualification, unfitness.

incarcerate *vb* commit, confine, immure, imprison, jail, restrain, restrict.

incarnate *vb* body, embody, incorporate, personify. * *adj* bodied, embodied, incorporated, personified.

incarnation *n* embodiment, exemplification, impersonation, manifestation, personification.

incautious *adj* impolitic, imprudent, indiscreet, uncircumspect, unwary; careless, headlong, heedless, inconsiderate, negligent, rash, reckless, thoughtless.

incendiary *adj* dissentious, factious, inflammatory, seditious. * *n* agitator, firebrand, fire-raiser.

incense[1] *vb* anger, chafe, enkindle, enrage, exasperate, excite, heat, inflame, irritate, madden, provoke.

incense[2] *n* aroma, fragrance, perfume, scent; admiration, adulation, applause, laudation.

incentive *n* cause, encouragement, goad, impulse, incitement, inducement, instigation, mainspring, motive, provocation, spur, stimulus.

inception *n* beginning, commencement, inauguration, initiation, origin, rise, start.

incertitude *n* ambiguity, doubt, doubtfulness, indecision, uncertainty.

incessant *adj* ceaseless, constant, continual, continuous, eternal, everlasting, never-ending, perpetual, unceasing, unending, uninterrupted, unremitting.

inchoate *adj* beginning, commencing, inceptive, incipient, initial.

incident *n* circumstance, episode, event, fact, happening, occurrence. * *adj* happening; belonging, pertaining, appertaining, accessory, relating, natural; falling, impinging.

incidental *adj* accidental, casual, chance, concomitant, contingent, fortuitous, subordinate; adventitious, extraneous, nonessential, occasional.

incinerate *vb* burn, char, conflagrate, cremate, incremate.

incipient *adj* beginning, commencing, inchoate, inceptive, originating, starting.

incised *adj* carved, cut, engraved, gashed, graved, graven.

incision *n* cut, gash, notch, opening, penetration.

incisive *adj* cutting; acute, biting, sarcastic, satirical, sharp; acute, clear, distinct, penetrating, sharp-cut, trenchant.

incite *vb* actuate, animate, arouse, drive, encourage, excite, foment, goad, hound, impel, instigate, prod, prompt, provoke, push, rouse, spur, stimulate, urge.

incitement *n* encouragement, goad, impulse, incentive, inducement, motive, provocative, spur, stimulus.

incivility *n* discourteousness, discourtesy, disrespect, ill-breeding, ill-manners, impoliteness, impudence, inurbanity, rudeness, uncourtliness, unmannerliness.

inclemency *n* boisterousness, cruelty, harshness, rigour, roughness, severity, storminess, tempestuousness, tyranny.

inclement *adj* boisterous, harsh, rigorous, rough, severe, stormy; cruel, unmerciful.

inclination *n* inclining, leaning, slant, slope; trending, verging; aptitude, bent, bias, disposition, penchant, predilection, predisposition, proclivity, proneness, propensity, tendency, turn, twist; desire, fondness, liking, taste, partiality, predilection, wish; bow, nod, obeisance.

incline *vb* lean, slant, slope; bend, nod, verge; tend; bias, dispose, predispose, turn; bow. * *n* ascent, descent, grade, gradient, rise, slope.

inclose *see* **enclose**.

include *vb* contain, hold; comprehend, comprise, contain, cover, embody, embrace, incorporate, involve, take in.

inclusive *adj* comprehending, embracing, encircling, enclosing, including, taking in.

incognito, incognita *adj* camouflaged, concealed, disguised, unknown. * *n* camouflage, concealment, disguise.

incoherent *adj* detached, loose, nonadhesive, noncohesive; disconnected, incongruous, inconsequential, inconsistent, uncoordinated; confused, illogical, irrational, rambling, unintelligible, wild.

income *n* earnings, emolument, gains, interest, pay, perquisite, proceeds, profits, receipts, rents, return, revenue, salary, wages.

incommensurate *adj* disproportionate, inadequate, insufficient, unequal.

incommode *vb* annoy, discommode, disquiet, disturb, embarrass, hinder, inconvenience, molest, plague, trouble, upset, vex.

incommodious *adj* awkward, cumbersome, cumbrous, inconvenient, unhandy, unmanageable, unsuitable, unwieldy; annoying, disadvantageous, harassing, irritating, vexatious.

incommunicative *adj* exclusive, unsociable, unsocial, reserved.

incomparable *adj* matchless, inimitable, peerless, surpassing, transcendent, unequalled, unparalleled, unrivalled.

incompatibility *n* contrariety, contradictoriness, discrepancy, incongruity, inconsistency, irreconcilability, unsuitability, unsuitableness

incompatible *adj* contradictory, incongruous, inconsistent, inharmonious, irreconcilable, unadapted, unsuitable.

incompetence *n* inability, incapability, incapacity, incompetency; inadequacy, insufficiency; disqualification, unfitness.

incompetent *adj* incapable, unable; inadequate, insufficient; disqualified, incapacitated, unconstitutional, unfit, unfitted.

incomplete *adj* defective, deficient, imperfect, partial; inexhaustive, unaccompanied, uncompleted, unexecuted, unfinished.

incomprehensible *adj* inconceivable, inexhaustible, unfathomable, unimaginable; inconceivable, unintelligible, unthinkable.

incomputable *adj* enormous, immense, incalculable, innumerable, prodigious.

inconceivable *adj* incomprehensible, incredible, unbelievable, unimaginable, unthinkable.

inconclusive *adj* inconsequent, inconsequential, indecisive, unconvincing. illogical, unproved, unproven.

incongruity *n* absurdity, contradiction, contradictoriness, contrariety, discordance, discordancy, discrepancy, impropriety, inappropriateness, incoherence, incompatibility, inconsistency, unfitness, unsuitableness.

incongruous *adj* absurd, contradictory, contrary, disagreeing, discrepant, inappropriate, incoherent, incompatible, inconsistent, inharmonious, unfit, unsuitable.

inconsequent *adj* desultory, disconnected, fragmentary, illogical, inconclusive, inconsistent, irrelevant, loose.

inconsiderable *adj* immaterial, insignificant, petty, slight, small, trifling, trivial, unimportant.

inconsiderate *adj* intolerant, uncharitable, unthoughtful; careless, heedless, giddy, harebrained, hasty, headlong, imprudent, inadvertent, inattentive, indifferent, indiscreet, lightheaded, negligent, rash, thoughtless.

inconsistency *n* incoherence, incompatibility, incongruity, unsuitableness; contradiction, contrariety; changeableness, inconstancy, instability, vacillation, unsteadiness.

inconsistent *adj* different, discrepant, illogical, incoherent, incompatible, incongruous, inconsequent, inconsonant, irreconcilable, unsuitable; contradictory, contrary; changeable, fickle, inconstant, unstable, unsteady, vacillating, variable.

inconsolable *adj* comfortless, crushed, disconsolate, forlorn, heartbroken, hopeless, woebegone.

inconstancy *n* changeableness, mutability, variability, variation, fluctuation, faithlessness, fickleness, capriciousness, vacillation, uncertainty, unsteadiness, volatility.

inconstant *adj* capricious, changeable, faithless, fickle, fluctuating, mercurial, mutable, unsettled, unsteady, vacillating, variable, varying, volatile, wavering; mutable, uncertain, unstable.

incontestable *adj* certain, incontrovertible, indisputable, indubitable, irrefrangible, sure, undeniable, unquestionable.

incontinence *n* excess, extravagance, indulgence, intemperance, irrepressibility, lasciviousness, lewdness, licentiousness, prodigality, profligacy, riotousness, unrestraint, wantonness, wildness.

incontinent *adj* debauched, lascivious, lewd, licentious, lustful, prodigal, unchaste, uncontrolled, unrestrained.

incontrovertible *adj* certain, incontestable, indisputable, indubitable, irrefutable, sure, undeniable, unquestionable.

inconvenience *vb* discommode; annoy, disturb, molest, trouble, vex. * *n* annoyance, disadvantage, disturbance, molestation, trouble, vexation; awkwardness, cumbersomeness, incommodiousness, unwieldiness; unfitness, unseasonableness, unsuitableness.

inconvenient *adj* annoying, awkward, cumbersome, cumbrous, disadvantageous, incommodious, inopportune, troublesome, uncomfortable, unfit, unhandy, unmanageable, unseasonable, unsuitable, untimely, unwieldy, vexatious.

incorporate *vb* affiliate, amalgamate, associate, blend, combine, consolidate, include, merge, mix, unite; embody, incarnate. * *adj* incorporeal, immaterial, spiritual, supernatural; blended, consolidated, merged, united.

incorporation *n* affiliation, alignment, amalgamation, association, blend, blending, combination, consolidation, fusion, inclusion, merger, mixture, unification, union, embodiment, incarnation, personification.

incorporeal *adj* bodiless, immaterial, impalpable, incorporate, spiritual, supernatural, unsubstantial.

incorrect *adj* erroneous, false, inaccurate, inexact, untrue, wrong; faulty, improper, mistaken, ungrammatical, unbecoming, unsound.

incorrectness *n* error, inaccuracy, inexactness, mistake.

incorrigible *adj* abandoned, graceless, hardened, irreclaimable, lost, obdurate, recreant, reprobate, shameless; helpless, hopeless, irremediable, irrecoverable, irreparable, irretrievable, irreversible, remediless.

incorruptibility *n* unpurchasableness; deathlessness, immortality, imperishableness, incorruptibleness, incorruption, indestructibility.

incorruptible *adj* honest, unbribable; imperishable, indestructible, immortal, undying, deathless, everlasting.

increase *vb* accrue, advance, augment, enlarge, extend, grow, intensify, mount, wax; multiply; enhance, greaten, heighten, raise, reinforce; aggravate, prolong. * *n* accession, accretion, accumulation, addition, augmentation, crescendo, development, enlargement, expansion, extension, growth, heightening, increment, intensification,

multiplication, swelling; gain, produce, product, profit; descendants, issue, offspring, progeny.

incredible *adj* absurd, inadmissible, nonsensical, unbelievable.

incredulity *n* distrust, doubt, incredulousness, scepticism, unbelief.

incredulous *adj* distrustful, doubtful, dubious, sceptical, unbelieving.

increment *n* addition, augmentation, enlargement, increase.

incriminate *vb* accuse, blame, charge, criminate, impeach.

incubate *vb* brood, develop, hatch, sit.

inculcate *vb* enforce, implant, impress, infix, infuse, ingraft, inspire, instil.

inculpable *adj* blameless, faultless, innocent, irreprehensible, irreproachable, irreprovable, sinless, unblamable, unblameable.

inculpate *vb* accuse, blame, censure, charge, incriminate, impeach, incriminate.

inculpatory *adj* criminatory, incriminating.

incumbent *adj* binding, devolved, devolving, laid, obligatory; leaning, prone, reclining, resting. * *n* holder, occupant.

incur *vb* acquire, bring, contract.

incurable *adj* cureless, hopeless, irrecoverable, remediless; helpless, incorrigible, irremediable, irreparable, irretrievable, remediless.

incurious *adj* careless, heedless, inattentive, indifferent, uninquisitive, unobservant, uninterested.

incursion *n* descent, foray, raid, inroad, irruption.

incursive *adj* aggressive, hostile, invasive, predatory, raiding.

incurvate *vb* bend, bow, crook, curve. * *adj* (*bot*) aduncous, arcuate, bowed, crooked, curved, hooked.

indebted *adj* beholden, obliged, owing.

indecency *n* impropriety, indecorum, offensiveness, outrageousness, unseemliness; coarseness, filthiness, foulness, grossness, immodesty, impurity, obscenity, vileness.

indecent *adj* bold, improper, indecorous, offensive, outrageous, unbecoming, unseemly; coarse, dirty, filthy, gross, immodest, impure, indelicate, lewd, nasty, obscene, pornographic, salacious, shameless, smutty, unchaste.

indecipherable *adj* illegible, undecipherable, undiscoverable, inexplicable, obscure, unintelligible, unreadable.

indecision *n* changeableness, fickleness, hesitation, inconstancy, irresolution, unsteadiness, vacillation.

indecisive *adj* dubious, hesitating, inconclusive, irresolute, undecided, unsettled, vacillating, wavering.

indecorous *adj* coarse, gross, ill-bred, impolite, improper, indecent, rude, unbecoming, uncivil, unseemly.

indecorum *n* grossness, ill-breeding, ill manners, impoliteness, impropriety, incivility, indecency, indecorousness.

indeed *adv* absolutely, actually, certainly, in fact, in truth, in reality, positively, really, strictly, truly, verily, veritably. * *interj* really! you don't say so! is it possible!

indefatigable *adj* assiduous, never-tiring, persevering, persistent, sedulous, tireless, unflagging, unremitting, untiring, unwearied.

indefeasible *adj* immutable, inalienable, irreversible, irrevocable, unalterable.

indefensible *adj* censurable, defenceless, faulty, unpardonable, untenable; inexcusable, insupportable, unjustifiable, unwarrantable, wrong.

indefinite *adj* confused, doubtful, equivocal, general, imprecise, indefinable, indecisive, indeterminate, indistinct, inexact, inexplicit, lax, loose, nondescript, obscure, uncertain, undefined, undetermined, unfixed, unsettled, vague.

indelible *adj* fast, fixed, ineffaceable, ingrained, permanent.

indelicacy *n* coarseness, grossness, indecorousness, indecorum, impropriety, offensiveness, unseemliness, vulgarity; immodesty, indecency, lewdness, unchastity; foulness, obscenity.

indelicate *adj* broad, coarse, gross, indecorous, intrusive, rude, unbecoming, unseemly; foul, immodest, indecent, lewd, obscene, unchaste, vulgar.

indemnification *n* compensation, reimbursement, remuneration, security.

indemnify *vb* compensate, reimburse, remunerate, requite, secure.

indent *vb* bruise, jag, notch, pink, scallop, serrate; bind, indenture.

indentation *n* bruise, dent, depression, jag, notch.

indenture *vb* bind, indent. * *n* contract, instrument; indentation.

independence *n* freedom, liberty, self-direction; distinctness, nondependence, separation; competence, ease.

independent *adj* absolute, autonomous, free, self-directing, uncoerced, unrestrained, unrestricted, voluntary; (*person*) self-reliant, unconstrained, unconventional.

indescribable *adj* ineffable, inexpressible, nameless, unutterable.

indestructible *adj* abiding, endless, enduring, everlasting, fadeless, imperishable, incorruptible, undecaying.

indeterminate *adj* indefinite, uncertain, undetermined, unfixed.

index *vb* alphabetize, catalogue, codify, earmark, file, list, mark, tabulate. * *n* catalogue, list, register, tally; indicator, lead, mark, pointer, sign, signal, token; contents, table of contents; forefinger; exponent.

indicate *vb* betoken, denote, designate, evince, exhibit, foreshadow, manifest, mark, point out, prefigure, presage, register, show, signify, specify, tell; hint, imply, intimate, sketch, suggest.

indication *n* hint, index, manifestation, mark, note, sign, suggestion, symptom, token.

indicative *adj* significant, suggestive, symptomatic; (*gram*) affirmative, declarative.

indict *vb* (*law*) accuse, charge, present.

indictment *n* (*law*) indicting, presentment; accusation, arraignment, charge, crimination, impeachment.

indifference *n* apathy, carelessness, coldness, coolness, heedlessness, inattention, insignificance, negligence, unconcern, unconcernedness, uninterestedness; disinterestedness, impartiality, neutrality.

indifferent *adj* apathetic, cold, cool, dead, distant, dull, easy-going, frigid, heedless, inattentive, incurious, insensible, insouciant, listless, lukewarm, nonchalant, perfunctory, regardless, stoical, unconcerned, uninterested, unmindful, unmoved; equal; fair, medium, middling, moderate, ordinary, passable, tolerable; mediocre, so-so; immaterial, unimportant; disinterested, impartial, neutral, unbiased.

indigence *n* destitution, distress, necessity, need, neediness, pauperism, penury, poverty, privation, want.

indigenous *adj* aboriginal, home-grown, inborn, inherent, native.

indigent *adj* destitute, distressed, insolvent, moneyless, necessitous, needy, penniless, pinched, poor, reduced.

indigested *adj* unconcocted, undigested; crude, ill-advised, ill-considered, ill-judged; confused, disorderly, ill-arranged, unmethodical.

indigestion *n* dyspepsia, dyspepsy.

indignant *adj* angry, exasperated, incensed, irate, ireful, provoked, roused, wrathful, wroth.

indignation *n* anger, choler, displeasure, exasperation, fury, ire, rage, resentment, wrath.

indignity *n* abuse, affront, contumely, dishonour, disrespect, ignominy, insult, obloquy, opprobrium, outrage, reproach, slight.

indirect *adj* circuitous, circumlocutory, collateral, devious, oblique, roundabout, sidelong, tortuous; deceitful, dishonest, dishonorable, unfair; mediate, remote, secondary, subordinate.

indiscernible *adj* imperceptible, indistinguishable, invisible, undiscernible, undiscoverable.

indiscipline *n* laxity, insubordination.

indiscreet *adj* foolish, hasty, headlong, heedless, imprudent, incautious, inconsiderate, injudicious, rash, reckless, unwise.

indiscretion *n* folly, imprudence, inconsiderateness, rashness; blunder, faux pas, lapse, mistake, misstep.

indiscriminate *adj* confused, heterogeneous, indistinct, mingled, miscellaneous, mixed, promiscuous, undiscriminating, undistinguishable, undistinguishing.

indispensable *adj* essential, expedient, necessary, needed, needful, requisite.

indisputable *adj* certain, incontestable, indubitable, infallible, sure, undeniable, undoubted, unmistakable, unquestionable.

indisposed *adj* ailing, ill, sick, unwell; averse, backward, disinclined, loath, reluctant, unfriendly, unwilling.

indisposition *n* ailment, illness, sickness; aversion, backwardness, dislike, disinclination, reluctance, unwillingness.

indisputable *adj* certain, incontestable, indutitable, infallible, sure, undeniable, undoubted, unmistakable, unquestionable.

indissoluble *adj* abiding, enduring, firm, imperishable, incorruptible, indestructible, lasting, stable, unbreakable.

indistinct *adj* ambiguous, doubtful, uncertain; blurred, dim, dull, faint, hazy, misty, nebulous, obscure, shadowy, vague; confused, inarticulate, indefinite, indistinguishable, undefined, undistinguishable.

indistinguishable *adj* imperceptible, indiscernible, unnoticeable, unobservable; chaotic, confused, dim, indistinct, obscure, vague.

indite *vb* compose, pen, write.

individual *adj* characteristic, distinct, identical, idiosyncratic, marked, one, particular, personal, respective, separate, single, singular, special, unique; peculiar, proper; decided, definite, independent, positive, self-guided, unconventional. * *n* being, character, party, person, personage, somebody, someone; type, unit.

individuality *n* definiteness, indentity, personality; originality, self-direction, self-determination, singularity, uniqueness.

individualize *vb* individuate, particularize, singularize, specify.

indivisible *adj* incommensurable, indissoluble, inseparable, unbreakable, unpartiable.

indocile *adj* cantankerous, contumacious, dogged, froward, inapt, headstrong, intractable, mulish, obstinate, perverse, refractory, stubborn, ungovernable, unmanageable, unruly, unteachable.

indoctrinate *vb* brainwash, imbue, initiate, instruct, rehabilitate, teach.

indoctrination *n* grounding, initiation, instruction, rehabilitation.

indolence *n* idleness, inactivity, inertia, inertness, laziness, listlessness, sloth, slothfulness, sluggishness.

indolent *adj* easy, easy-going, inactive, inert, lazy, listless, lumpish, otiose, slothful, sluggish, supine.

indomitable *adj* invincible, unconquerable, unyielding.

indorse *see* **endorse**.

indubitable *adj* certain, evident, incontestable, incontrovertible, indisputable, sure, undeniable, unquestionable.

induce *vb* actuate, allure, bring, draw, drive, entice, impel, incite, influence, instigate, move, persuade, prevail, prompt, spur, urge; bring on, cause, effect, motivate, lead, occasion, produce.

inducement *n* allurement, draw, enticement, instigation, persuasion; cause, consideration, impulse, incentive, incitement, influence, motive, reason, spur, stimulus.

induct *vb* inaugurate, initiate, install, institute, introduce, invest.

induction *n* inauguration, initiation, institution, installation, introduction; conclusion, generalization, inference.

indue *vb* assume, endow, clothe, endue, invest, supply.

indulge *vb* gratify, license, revel, satisfy, wallow, yield to; coddle, cosset, favour, humour, pamper, pet, spoil; allow, cherish, foster, harbour, permit, suffer.

indulgence *n* gratification, humouring, pampering; favour, kindness, lenience, lenity, liberality, tenderness; (*theol*) absolution, remission.

indulgent *adj* clement, easy, favouring, forbearing, gentle, humouring, kind, lenient, mild, pampering, tender, tolerant.

indurate *vb* harden, inure, sear, strengthen.

induration *n* hardening, obduracy.

industrious *adj* assiduous, diligent, hard-working, laborious, notable, operose, sedulous; brisk, busy, persevering, persistent.

industry *n* activity, application, assiduousness, assiduity, diligence; perseverance, persistence, sedulousness, vigour; effort, labour, toil.

inebriated *adj* drunk, intoxicated, stupefied.

ineffable *adj* indescribable, inexpressible, unspeakable, unutterable.

ineffaceable *adj* indelible, indestructible, inerasable, inexpungeable, ingrained.

ineffectual *adj* abortive, bootless, fruitless, futile, inadequate, inefficacious, ineffective, inoperative, useless, unavailing, vain; feeble, inefficient, powerless, impotent, weak.

inefficacy *n* ineffectualness, inefficiency.

inefficient *adj* feeble, incapable, ineffectual, ineffective, inefficacious, weak.

inelastic *adj* flabby, flaccid, inductile, inflexible, irresilient.

inelegant *adj* abrupt, awkward, clumsy, coarse, constrained, cramped, crude, graceless, harsh, homely, homespun, rough, rude, stiff, tasteless, uncourtly, uncouth, ungainly, ungraceful, unpolished, unrefined.

ineligible *adj* disqualified, unqualified; inexpedient, objectionable, unadvisable, undesirable.

inept *adj* awkward, improper, inapposite, inappropriate, unapt, unfit, unsuitable; null, useless, void, worthless; foolish, nonsensical, pointless, senseless, silly, stupid.

ineptitude *n* inappositeness, inappropriateness, inaptitude, unfitness, unsuitability, unsuitableness; emptiness, nullity, uselessness, worthlessness; folly, foolishness, nonsense, pointlessness, senselessness, silliness, stupidity.

inequality *n* disproportion, inequitableness, injustice, unfairness; difference, disparity, dissimilarity, diversity, imparity, irregularity, roughness, unevenness; inadequacy, incompetency, insufficiency.

inequitable *adj* unfair, unjust.

inert *adj* comatose, dead, inactive, lifeless, motionless, quiescent, passive; apathetic, dronish, dull, idle, indolent, lazy, lethargic, lumpish, phlegmatic, slothful, sluggish, supine, torpid.

inertia *n* apathy, inertness, lethargy, passiveness, passivity, slothfulness, sluggishness.

inestimable *adj* incalculable, invaluable, precious, priceless, valuable.

inevitable *adj* certain, necessary, unavoidable, undoubted.

inexact *adj* imprecise, inaccurate, incorrect; careless, crude, loose.

inexcusable *adj* indefensible, irremissible, unallowable, unjustifiable, unpardonable.

inexhaustible *adj* boundless, exhaustless, indefatigable, unfailing, unlimited.

inexorable *adj* cruel, firm, hard, immovable, implacable, inflexible, merciless, pitiless, relentless, severe, steadfast, unbending, uncompassionate, unmerciful, unrelenting, unyielding.

inexpedient *adj* disadvantageous, ill-judged, impolitic, imprudent, indiscreet, injudicious, inopportune, unadvisable, unprofitable, unwise.

inexperience *n* greenness, ignorance, rawness.

inexperienced *adj* callow, green, raw, strange, unacquainted, unconversant, undisciplined, uninitiated, unpractised, unschooled, unskilled, untrained, untried, unversed, young.

inexpert *adj* awkward, bungling, clumsy, inapt, maladroit, unhandy, unskilful, unskilled.

inexpiable *adj* implacable, inexorable, irreconcilable, unappeasable; irremissible, unatonable, unpardonable.

inexplicable *adj* enigmatic, enigmatical, incomprehensible, inscrutable, mysterious, strange, unaccountable, unintelligible.

inexpressible *adj* indescribable, ineffable, unspeakable, unutterable; boundless, infinite, surpassing.

inexpressive *adj* blank, characterless, dull, unexpressive.

inextinguishable *adj* unquenchable.

in extremis *adv* moribund.

inextricable *adj* entangled, intricate, perplexed, unsolvable.

infallibility *n* certainty, infallibleness, perfection.

infallible *adj* certain, indubitable, oracular, sure, unerring, unfailing.

infamous *adj* abominable, atrocious, base, damnable, dark, detestable, discreditable, disgraceful, dishonorable, disreputable, heinous, ignominious, nefarious, odious, opprobrious, outrageous, scandalous, shameful, shameless, vile, villainous, wicked.

infamy *n* abasement, discredit, disgrace, dishonour, disrepute, ignominy, obloquy, odium, opprobrium, scandal, shame; atrocity, detestableness, disgracefulness, dishonorableness, odiousness, scandalousness, shamefulness, villainy, wickedness.

infancy *n* beginning, commencement; babyhood, childhood, minority, nonage, pupillage.

infant *n* babe, baby, bairn, bantling, brat, chit, minor, nursling, papoose, suckling, tot.

infantile *adj* childish, infantine, newborn, tender, young; babyish, childish, weak; babylike, childlike.

infatuate *vb* befool, besot, captivate, delude, prepossess, stultify.

infatuation *n* absorption, besottedness, folly, foolishness, prepossession, stupefaction.

infeasible *adj* impractical, unfeasible.

infect *vb* affect, contaminate, corrupt, defile, poison, pollute, taint, vitiate.

infection *n* affection, bane, contagion, contamination, corruption, defilement, pest, poison, pollution, taint, virus, vitiation.

infectious *adj* catching, communicable, contagious, contaminating, corrupting, defiling, demoralizing, pestiferous, pestilential, poisoning, polluting, sympathetic, vitiating.

infecund *adj* barren, infertile, sterile, unfruitful, unproductive, unprolific.

infecundity *n* unfruitfulness.

infelicitous *adj* calamitous, miserable, unfortunate, unhappy, wretched; inauspicious, unfavourable, unpropitious; ill-chosen, inappropriate, unfitting.

infer *vb* collect, conclude, deduce, derive, draw, gather, glean, guess, presume, reason.

inference *n* conclusion, consequence, corollary, deduction, generalization, guess, illation, implication, induction, presumption.

inferior *adj* lower, nether; junior, minor, secondary, subordinate; bad, base, deficient, humble, imperfect, indifferent, mean, mediocre, paltry, poor, second-rate, shabby.

inferiority *n* juniority, subjection, subordination, mediocrity; deficiency, imperfection, inadequacy, shortcoming.

infernal *adj* abominable, accursed, atrocious, damnable, dark, demoniacal, devilish, diabolical, fiendish, fiendlike, hellish, malicious, nefarious, satanic, Stygian.

infertility *n* barrenness, infecundity, sterility, unfruitfulness, unproductivity.

infest *vb* annoy, disturb, harass, haunt, molest, plague, tease, torment, trouble, vex, worry; beset, overrun, possess, swarm, throng.

infidel *n* agnostic, atheist, disbeliever, heathen, heretic, sceptic, unbeliever.

infidelity *n* adultery, disloyalty, faithlessness, treachery, unfaithfulness; disbelief, scepticism, unbelief.

infiltrate *vb* absorb, pervade, soak.

infinite *adj* boundless, endless, illimitable, immeasurable, inexhaustible, interminable, limitless, measureless, perfect, unbounded, unlimited; enormous, immense, stupendous, vast;

absolue, eternal, self-determined, self-existent, unconditioned.

infinitesimal *adj* infinitely small; microscopic, miniscule.

infinity *n* absoluteness, boundlessness, endlessness, eternity, immensity, infiniteness, infinitude, interminateness, self-determination, self-existence, vastness.

infirm *adj* ailing, debilitated, enfeebled, feeble, frail, weak, weakened; faltering, irresolute, vacillating, wavering; insecure, precarious, unsound, unstable.

infirmity *n* ailment, debility, feebleness, frailness, frailty, weakness; defect, failing, fault, foible, weakness.

infix *vb* fasten, fix, plant, set; implant, inculcate, infuse, ingraft, instil.

inflame *vb* animate, arouse, excite, enkindle, fire, heat, incite, inspirit, intensify, rouse, stimulate; aggravate, anger, chafe, embitter, enrage, exasperate, incense, infuriate, irritate, madden, nettle, provoke.

inflammability *n* combustibility, combustibleness, inflammableness.

inflammable *adj* combustible, ignitible; excitable.

inflammation *n* burning, conflagration; anger, animosity, excitement, heat, rage, turbulence, violence.

inflammatory *adj* fiery, inflaming; dissentious, incendiary, seditious.

inflate *vb* bloat, blow up, distend, expand, swell, sufflate; elate, puff up; enlarge, increase.

inflated *adj* bloated, distended, puffed-up, swollen; bombastic, declamatory, grandiloquent, high-flown, magniloquent, overblown, pompous, rhetorical, stilted, tumid, turgid.

inflation *n* enlargement, increase, overenlargement, overissue; bloatedness, distension, expansion, sufflation; bombast, conceit, conceitedness, self-conceit, self-complacency, self-importance, self-sufficiency, vaingloriousness, vainglory.

inflect *vb* bend, bow, curve, turn; (*gram*) conjugate, decline, vary.

inflection *n* bend, bending, crook, curvature, curvity, flexure; (*gram*) accidence, conjugation, declension, variation; (*mus*) modulation.

inflexibility *n* inflexibleness, rigidity, stiffness; doggedness, obstinacy, perinacity, stubbornness; firmness, perseverance, resolution, tenacity.

inflexible *adj* rigid, rigorous, stiff, unbending; cantankerous, cross-grained, dogged, headstrong, heady, inexorable, intractable, obdurate, obstinate, pertinacious, refractory, stubborn, unyielding, wilful; firm, immovable, persevering, resolute, steadfast, unbending.

inflict *vb* bring, impose, lay on.

infliction *n* imposition, inflicting; judgment, punishment.

inflorescence *n* blooming, blossoming, flowering.

influence *vb* affect, bias, control, direct, lead, modify, prejudice, prepossess, sway; actuate, arouse, impel, incite, induce, instigate, move, persuade, prevail upon, rouse. * *n* ascendancy, authority, control, mastery, potency, predominance, pull, rule, sway; credit, reputation, weight; inflow, inflowing, influx; magnetism, power, spell.

influential *adj* controlling, effective, effectual, potent, powerful, strong; authoritative, momentous, substantial, weighty.

influx *n* flowing in, introduction.

infold *see* **enfold**.

inform *vb* animate, inspire, quicken; acquaint, advise, apprise, enlighten, instruct, notify, teach, tell, tip, warn.

informal *adj* unceremonious, unconventional, unofficial; easy, familiar, natural, simple; irregular, nonconformist, unusual.

informality *n* unceremoniousness; unconventionality; ease, familiarity, naturalness, simplicity; noncomformity, irregularity, unusualness.

informant *n* advertiser, adviser, informer, intelligencer, newsmonger, notifier, relator; accuser, complainant, informer.

information *n* advice, data, intelligence, knowledge, notice; advertisement, enlightenment, instruction, message, tip, word, warning; accusation, complaint, denunciation.

informer *n* accuser, complainant, informant, snitch.

infraction *n* breach, breaking, disobedience, encroachment, infringement, nonobservance, transgression, violation.

infrangible *adj* inseparable, inviolable, unbreakable.

infrequency *n* rareness, rarity, uncommonness, unusualness.

infrequent *adj* rare, uncommon, unfrequent, unusual; occasional, scant, scarce, sporadic.

infringe *vb* break, contravene, disobey, intrude, invade, transgress, violate.

infringement *n* breach, breaking, disobedience, infraction, nonobservance, transgression, violation.

infuriated *adj* angry, enraged, furious, incensed, maddened, raging, wild.

infuse *vb* breathe into, implant, inculcate, ingraft, insinuate, inspire, instil, introduce; macerate, steep.

infusion *n* inculcation, instillation, introduction; infusing, macerating, steeping.

ingathering *n* harvest.

ingenious *adj* able, adroit, artful, bright, clever, fertile, gifted, inventive, ready, sagacious, shrewd, witty.

ingenuity *n* ability, acuteness, aptitude, aptness, capacity, capableness, cleverness, faculty, genius, gift, ingeniousness, inventiveness, knack, readiness, skill, turn.

ingenuous *adj* artless, candid, childlike, downright, frank, generous, guileless, honest, innocent, naive, open, open-hearted, plain, simple-minded, sincere, single-minded, straightforward, transparent, truthful, unreserved.

ingenuousness *n* artlessness, candour, childlikeness, frankness, guilelessness, honesty, naivety, open-heartedness, openness, sincerity, single-mindedness, truthfulness.

inglorious *adj* humble, lowly, mean, nameless, obscure, undistinguished, unhonoured, unknown, unmarked, unnoted; discreditable, disgraceful, humiliating, ignominous, scandalous, shameful.

ingloriousness *n* humbleness, lowliness, meanness, namelessness, obscurity; abasement, discredit, disgrace, dishonour, disrepute, humiliation, infamy, ignominiousness, ignominy, obloquy, odium, opprobrium, shame.

ingraft *vb* graft, implant, inculcate, infix, infuse, instil.

ingrain *vb* dye, imbue, impregnate.

ingratiate *vb* insinuate.

ingratitude *n* thanklessness, ungratefulness, unthankfulness.

ingredient *n* component, constituent, element.

ingress *n* entrance, entré, entry, introgression.

ingulf *see* **engulf**.

inhabit *vb* abide, dwell, live, occupy, people, reside, sojourn.

inhabitable *adj* habitable, livable.

inhabitant *n* citizen, denizen, dweller, inhabiter, resident.

inhalation *n* breath, inhaling, inspiration; sniff, snuff.

inhale *vb* breathe in, draw in, inbreathe, inspire.

inharmonious *adj* discordant, inharmonic, out of tune, unharmonious, unmusical.

inhere *vb* cleave to, stick, stick fast; abide, belong, exist, lie, pertain, reside.

inherent *adj* essential, immanent, inborn, inbred, indwelling, ingrained, innate, inseparable, intrinsic, native, natural, proper; adhering, sticking.

inherit *vb* get, receive.

inheritance *n* heritage, legacy, patrimony; inheriting.

inheritor *n* heir, (*law*) parcener.

inhibit *vb* bar, check, debar, hinder, obstruct, prevent, repress, restrain, stop; forbid, interdict, prohibit.

inhibition *n* check, hindrance, impediment, obstacle, obstruction, restraint; disallowance, embargo, interdict, interdiction, prevention, prohibition.

inhospitable *adj* cool, forbidding, unfriendly, unkind; bigoted, illiberal, intolerant, narrow, prejudiced, ungenerous, unreceptive; barren, wild.

inhospitality *n* inhospitableness, unkindness; illiberality, narrowness.

inhuman *adj* barbarous, brutal, cruel, fell, ferocious, merciless, pitiless, remorseless, ruthless, savage, unfeeling; nonhuman.

inhumanity *n* barbarity, brutality, cruelty, ferocity,

savageness; hard-heartedness, unkindness.

inhume *vb* bury, entomb, inter.

inimical *adj* antagonistic, hostile, unfriendly; adverse, contrary, harmful, hurtful, noxious, opposed, pernicious, repugnant, unfavourable.

inimitable *adj* incomparable, matchless, peerless, unequalled, unexampled, unmatched, unparagoned, unparalleled, unrivalled, unsurpassed.

iniquitous *adj* atrocious, criminal, flagitious, heinous, inequitable, nefarious, sinful, wicked, wrong, unfair, unjust, unrighteous.

iniquity *n* injustice, sin, sinfulness, unrighteousness, wickedness, wrong; crime, misdeed, offence.

initial *adj* first; beginning, commencing, incipient, initiatory, introductory, opening, original; elementary, inchoate, rudimentary.

initiate *vb* begin, commence, enter upon, inaugurate, introduce, open; ground, indoctrinate, instruct, prime, teach.

initiation *n* beginning, commencement, inauguration, opening; admission, entrance, introduction; indoctrinate, instruction.

initiative *n* beginning; energy, enterprise.

initiatory *adj* inceptive, initiative.

inject *vb* force in, interject, insert, introduce, intromit.

injudicious *adj* foolish, hasty, ill-advised, ill-judged, imprudent, incautious, inconsiderate, indiscreet, rash, unwise.

injunction *n* admonition, bidding, command, mandate, order, precept.

injure *vb* damage, disfigure, harm, hurt, impair, mar, spoil, sully, wound; abuse, aggrieve, wrong; affront, dishonour, insult.

injurious *adj* baneful, damaging, deadly, deleterious, destructive, detrimental, disadvantageous, evil, fatal, hurtful, mischievous, noxious, pernicious, prejudicial, ruinous; inequitable, iniquitous, unjust, wrongful; contumelious, detractory, libellous, slanderous.

injury *n* evil, ill, injustice, wrong; damage, detriment, harm, hurt, impairment, loss, mischief, prejudice.

injustice *n* inequity, unfairness; grievance, iniquity, injury, wrong.

inkhorn *n* inkbottle, inkstand.

inkling *n* hint, intimation, suggestion, whisper.

inky *adj* atramentous, black, murky.

inland *adj* domestic, hinterland, home, upcountry; interior, internal.

inlet *n* arm, bay, bight, cove, creek; entrance, ingress, passage.

inmate *n* denizen, dweller, guest, intern, occupant.

inmost *adj* deepest, innermost.

inn *n* hostel, hostelry, hotel, pub, public house, tavern.

innate *adj* congenital, constitutional, inborn, inbred, indigenous, inherent, inherited, instinctive, native, natural, organic.

inner adj interior, internal.

innermost adj deepest, inmost.

innkeeper n host, innholder, landlady, landlord, tavernkeeper.

innocence n blamelessness, chastity, guilelessness, guiltlessness, purity, simplicity, sinlessness, stainlessness; harmlessness, innocuousness, innoxiousness, inoffensiveness.

innocent adj blameless, clean, clear, faultless, guiltless, immaculate, pure, sinless, spotless, unfallen, upright; harmless, innocuous, innoxious, inoffensive; lawful, legitimate, permitted; artless, guileless, ignorant, ingenuous, simple. * n babe, child, ingénue, naif, naive, unsophisticate.

innocuous adj harmless, innocent, inoffensive, safe.

innovate vb change, introduce.

innovation n change, introduction; departure, novelty.

innuendo n allusion, hint, insinuation, intimation, suggestion.

innumerable adj countless, numberless.

inoculate vb infect, vaccinate.

inoffensive adj harmless, innocent, innocuous, innoxious, unobjectionable, unoffending.

inoperative adj inactive, ineffectual, inefficacious, not in force.

inopportune adj ill-timed, inexpedient, infelicitous, mistimed, unfortunate, unhappy, unseasonable, untimely.

inordinate adj excessive, extravagant, immoderate, intemperate, irregular.

inorganic adj inanimate, unorganized; mineral.

inquest n inquiry, inquisition, investigation, quest, search.

inquietude n anxiety, disquiet, disquietude, disturbance, restlessness, uneasiness.

inquire, enquire vb ask, catechize, interpellate, interrogate, investigate, query, question, quiz.

inquiry, enquiry n examination, exploration, investigation, research, scrutiny, study; interrogation, query, question, quiz.

inquisition n examination, inquest, inquiry, investigation, search.

inquisitive adj curious, inquiring, scrutinizing; curious, meddlesome, peeping, peering, prying.

inroad n encroachment, foray, incursion, invasion, irruption, raid.

insalubrious adj noxious, unhealthful, unhealthy, unwholesome.

insane adj abnormal, crazed, crazy, delirious, demented, deranged, distracted, lunatic, mad, maniacal, unhealthy, unsound.

insanity n craziness, delirium, dementia, derangement, lunacy, madness, mania, mental aberration, mental alienation.

insatiable adj greedy, rapacious, voracious; insatiate, unappeasable.

inscribe vb emblaze, endorse, engrave, enroll, impress, imprint, letter, mark, write; address, dedicate.

inscrutable adj hidden, impenetrable, incomprehensible, inexplicable, mysterious, undiscoverable, unfathomable, unsearchable.

inscrutableness n impenetrability, incomprehensibility, incomprehensibleness, inexplicability, inscrutability, mysteriousness, mystery, unfathomableness, unsearchableness.

insecure adj risky, uncertain, unconfident, unsure; exposed, ill-protected, unprotected, unsafe; dangerous, hazardous, perilous; infirm, shaking, shaky, tottering, unstable, weak, wobbly.

insecurity n riskiness, uncertainty; danger, hazardousness, peril; instability, shakiness, weakness, wobbliness.

insensate adj dull, indifferent, insensible, torpid; brutal, foolish, senseless, unwise; inanimate, insensible, insentient, nonpercipient, unconscious, unperceiving.

insensibility n dullness, insentience, lethargy, torpor; apathy, indifference, insusceptibility, unfeelingness, dullness, stupidity; anaesthesia, coma, stupor, unconsciousness.

insensible adj imperceivable, imperceptible, undiscoverable; blunted, brutish, deaf, dull, insensate, numb, obtuse, senseless, sluggish, stolid, stupid, torpid, unconscious; apathetic, callous, phlegmatic, impassive, indifferent, insensitive, insentient, unfeeling, unimpressible, unsusceptible.

insensibly adv imperceptibly.

insentient adj inert, nonsentient, senseless; inanimate, insensible, insensate, nonpercipient, unconscious, unperceiving.

inseparable adj close, friendly, intimate, together; indissoluble, indivisible, inseverable.

insert vb infix, inject, intercalate, interpolate, introduce, inweave, parenthesize, place, put, set.

inside adj inner, interior, internal; confidential, exclusive, internal, private, secret. * adv indoors, within. * n inner part, interior; nature.

insidious adj creeping, deceptive, gradual, secretive; arch, artful, crafty, crooked, cunning, deceitful, designing, diplomatic, foxy, guileful, intriguing, Machiavellian, sly, sneaky, subtle, treacherous, trickish, tricky, wily.

insight n discernment, intuition, penetration, perception, perspicuity, understanding.

insignia npl badges, marks.

insignificance n emptiness, nothingenss, paltriness, triviality, unimportance.

insignificant adj contemptible, empty, immaterial, inconsequential, inconsiderable, inferior, meaningless, paltry, petty, small, sorry, trifling, trivial, unessential, unimportant.

insincere adj deceitful, dishonest, disingenuous, dissembling, dissimulating, double-faced, double-tongued, duplicitous, empty, faithless, false, hollow, hypocritical, pharisaical, truthless, uncandid, untrue.

insincerity n bad faith, deceitfulness, dishonesty, disingenuousness, dissimulation, duplicity, falseness, faithlessness, hypocrisy.

insinuate *vb* hint, inculcate, infuse, ingratiate, instil, intimate, introduce, suggest.

insipid *adj* dead, dull, flat, heavy, inanimate, jejune, lifeless, monotonous, pointless, prosaic, prosy, spiritless, stupid, tame, unentertaining, uninteresting; mawkish, savourless, stale, tasteless, vapid, zestless.

insipidity, insipidness *n* dullness, heaviness, lifelessness, prosiness, stupidity, tameness; flatness, mawkishness, staleness, tastlessness, unsavouriness, vapidness, zestlessness.

insist *vb* demand, maintain, urge.

insistence *n* importunity, solicitousness, urging, urgency.

insnare *see* **ensnare**.

insolence *n* impertinence, impudence, malapertness, pertness, rudeness, sauciness; contempt, contumacy, contumely, disrespect, frowardness, insubordination.

insolent *adj* abusive, contemptuous, contumelious, disrespectful, domineering, insulting, offensive, overbearing, rude, supercilious; cheeky, impertinent, impudent, malapert, pert, saucy; contumacious, disobedient, froward, insubordinate.

insoluble *adj* indissoluble, indissolvable, irreducible; inexplicable, insolvable.

insolvable *adj* inexplicable.

insolvent *adj* bankrupt, broken, failed, ruined.

insomnia *n* sleeplessness, wakefulness.

inspect *vb* examine, investigate, look into, pry into, scrutinize; oversee, superintend, supervise.

inspection *n* examination, investigation, scrutiny; oversight, superintendence, supervision.

inspector *n* censor, critic, examiner, visitor; boss, overseer, superintendent, supervisor.

inspiration *n* breathing, inhalation; afflatus, fire, inflatus; elevation, exaltation; enthusiasm.

inspire *vb* breathe, inhale; infuse, instil; animate, cheer, enliven, inspirit; elevate, exalt, stimulate; fill, imbue, impart, inform, quicken.

inspirit *vb* animate, arouse, cheer, comfort, embolden, encourage, enhearten, enliven, fire, hearten, incite, invigorate, quicken, rouse, stimulate.

instable *see* **unstable**.

instability *n* changeableness, fickleness, inconstancy, insecurity, mutability.

install, instal *vb* inaugurate, induct, introduce; establish, place, set up.

installation *n* inauguration, induction, instalment, investiture.

instalment *n* earnest, payment, portion.

instance *vb* adduce, cite, mention, specify. * *n* case, example, exemplification, illustration, occasion; impulse, incitement, instigation, motive, prompting, request, solicitation.

instant *adj* direct, immediate, instantaneous, prompt, quick; current, present; earnest, fast, imperative, importunate, pressing, urgent; ready cooked. * n flash, jiffy, moment, second, trice, twinkling; hour, time.

instantaneous *adj* abrupt, immediate, instant, quick, sudden.

instantaneously *adv* forthwith, immediately, presto, quickly, right away.

instauration *n* reconstitution, reconstruction, redintegration, re-establishment, rehabilitation, reinstatement, renewal, renovation, restoration.

instead *adv* in lieu, in place, rather.

instigate *vb* actuate, agitate, encourage, impel, incite, influence, initiate, move, persuade, prevail upon, prompt, provoke, rouse, set on, spur on, stimulate, stir up, tempt, urge.

instigation *n* encouragement, incitement, influence, instance, prompting, solicitation, urgency.

instil, instill *vb* enforce, implant, impress, inculcate, ingraft; impart, infuse, insinuate.

instillation *n* infusion, insinuation, introduction.

instinct *n* natural impulse.

instinctive *adj* automatic, inherent, innate, intuitive, involuntary, natural, spontaneous; impulsive, unreflecting.

institute[1] *n* academy, college, foundation, guild, institution, school; custom, doctrine, dogma, law, maxim, precedent, principle, rule, tenet.

institute[2] *vb* begin, commence, constitute, establish, found, initial, install, introduce, organize, originate, start.

institution *n* enactment, establishment, foundation, institute, society; investiture; custom, law, practice.

instruct *vb* discipline, educate, enlighten, exercise, guide, indoctrinate, inform, initiate, school, teach, train; apprise, bid, command, direct, enjoin, order, prescribe to.

instruction *n* breeding, discipline, education, indoctrination, information, nurture, schooling, teaching, training, tuition; advice, counsel, precept; command, direction, mandate, order.

instructor *n* educator, master, preceptor, schoolteacher, teacher, tutor.

instrument *n* appliance, apparatus, contrivance, device, implement, musical instrument, tool, utensil; agent, means, medium; charter, deed, document, indenture, writing.

instrumental *adj* ancillary, assisting, auxiliary, conducive, contributory, helpful, helping, ministerial, ministrant, serviceable, subservient, subsidiary.

instrumentality *n* agency, intermediary; intervention, means, mediation.

insubordinate *adj* disobedient, disorderly, mutinous, refractory, riotous, seditious, turbulent, ungovernable, unruly.

insubordination *n* disobedience, insurrection, mutiny, revolt, riotousness, sedition; indiscipline, laxity.

insufferable *adj* intolerable, unbearable, unendurable, insupportable; abominable, detestable, disgusting, execrable, outrageous.

insufficiency *n* dearth, defectiveness, deficiency, lack, inadequacy, inadequateness, incapability, incompetence, paucity, shortage.

insufficient *adj* deficient, inadequate, incommensurate, incompetent, scanty; incapable, incompetent, unfitted, unqualified, unsuited, unsatisfactory.

insular *adj* contracted, illiberal, limited, narrow, petty, prejudiced, restricted; isolated, remote.

insulate *vb* detach, disconnect, disengage, disunite, isolate, separate.

insulation *n* disconnection, disengagement, isolation, separation.

insult *vb* abuse, affront, injure, offend, outrage, slander, slight. * *n* abuse, affront, cheek, contumely, indignity, insolence, offence, outrage, sauce, slight.

insulting *adj* abusive, arrogant, contumelious, impertinent, impolite, insolent, rude, vituperative.

insuperable *adj* impassable, insurmountable.

insupportable *adj* insufferable, intolerable, unbearable, unendurable.

insuppressible *adj* irrepressible, uncontrollable.

insurance *n* assurance, security.

insure *vb* assure, guarantee, indemnify, secure, underwrite.

insurgent *adj* disobedient, insubordinate, mutinous, rebellious, revolting, revolutionary, seditious. * *n* mutineer, rebel, revolter, revolutionary.

insurmountable *adj* impassable, insuperable.

insurrection *n* insurgence, mutiny, rebellion, revolt, revolution, rising, sedition, uprising.

intact *adj* scathless, unharmed, unhurt, unimpaired, uninjured, untouched; complete, entire, integral, sound, unbroken, undiminished, whole.

intangible *adj* dim, impalpable, imperceptible, indefinite, insubstantial, intactile, shadowy, vague; aerial, phantom, spiritous.

intangibility *n* imperceptibility, insubstantiality, intangibleness, shadowiness, vagueness.

integral *adj* complete, component, entire, integrant, total, whole.

integrity *n* goodness, honesty, principle, probity, purity, rectitude, soundness, uprightness, virtue; completeness, entireness, entirety, wholeness.

integument *n* coat, covering, envelope, skin, tegument.

intellect *n* brains, cognitive faculty, intelligence, mind, rational faculty, reason, reasoning, faculty, sense, thought, understanding, wit.

intellectual *adj* cerebral, intelligent, mental, scholarly, thoughtful. * *n* academic, highbrow, pundit, savant, scholar.

intelligence *n* acumen, apprehension, brightness, discernment, imagination, insight, penetration, quickness, sagacity, shrewdness, understanding, wits; information, knowledge; advice, instruction, news, notice, notification, tidings; brains, intellect, mentality, sense, spirit.

intelligent *adj* acute, alert, apt, astute, brainy, bright, clear-headed, clear-sighted, clever, discerning, keen-eyed, keen-sighted, knowing,

long-headed, quick, quick-sighted, sagacious, sensible, sharp-sighted, sharp-witted, shrewd, understanding.

intelligibility *n* clarity, comprehensibility, intelligibleness, perspicuity.

intelligible *adj* clear, comprehensible, distinct, evident, lucid, manifest, obvious, patent, perspicuous, plain, transparent, understandable.

intemperate *adj* drunken; excessive, extravagant, extreme, immoderate, inordinate, unbridled, uncontrolled, unrestrained; self-indulgent.

intend *vb* aim at, contemplate, design, determine, drive at, mean, meditate, propose, purpose, think of.

intendant *n* inspector, overseer, superintendent, supervisor.

intense *adj* ardent, earnest, fervid, passionate, vehement; close, intent, severe, strained, stretched, strict; energetic, forcible, keen, potent, powerful, sharp, strong, vigorous, violent; acute, deep, extreme, exquisite, grievous, poignant.

intensify *vb* aggravate, concentrate, deepen, enhance, heighten, quicken, strengthen, whet.

intensity *n* closeness, intenseness, severity, strictness; excess, extremity, violence; activity, energy, force, power, strength, vigour; ardour, earnestness, vehemence.

intensive *adj* emphatic, intensifying.

intent *adj* absorbed, attentive, close, eager, earnest, engrossed, occupied, pre-occupied, zealous; bent, determined, decided, resolved, set. * *n* aim, design, drift, end, import, intention, mark, meaning, object, plan, purport, purpose, purview, scope, view.

intention *n* aim, design, drift, end, import, intent, mark, meaning, object, plan, purport, purpose, purview, scope, view.

intentional *adj* contemplated, deliberate, designed, intended, preconcerted, predetermined, premeditated, purposed, studied, voluntary, wilful.

inter *vb* bury, commit to the earth, entomb, inhume, inurn.

intercalate *vb* insert, interpolate.

intercede *vb* arbitrate, interpose, mediate; entreat, plead, supplicate.

intercept *vb* cut off, interrupt, obstruct, seize.

intercession *n* interposition, intervention, mediation; entreaty, pleading, prayer, supplication.

intercessor *n* interceder, mediator.

interchange *vb* alternate, change, exchange, vary. * *n* alternation.

interchangeableness *n* interchangeability.

interchangeably *adv* alternately.

intercourse *n* commerce, communication, communion, connection, converse, correspondence, dealings, fellowship, truck; acquaintance, intimacy.

interdict *vb* debar, forbid, inhibit, prohibit, proscribe, proscribe, restrain from. * *n* ban, decree, interdiction, prohibition.

interest *vb* affect, concern, touch; absorb, attract, engage, enlist, excite, grip, hold, occupy. * *n* advantage, benefit, good, profit, weal; attention, concern, regard, sympathy; part, participation, portion, share, stake; discount, premium, profit.

interested *adj* attentive, concerned, involved, occupied; biassed, patial, prejudiced; selfish, self-seeking.

interesting *adj* attractive, engaging, entertaining, pleasing.

interfere *vb* intermeddle, interpose, meddle; clash, collide, conflict.

interference *n* intermeddling, interposition; clashing, collision, interfering, opposition.

interim *n* intermediate time, interval, meantime.

interior *adj* inmost, inner, internal, inward; inland, remote; domestic, home. * *n* inner part, inland, inside.

interjacent *adj* intermediate, interposed, intervening, parenthetical.

interject *vb* comment, inject, insert, interpose.

interjection *n* exclamation.

interlace *vb* bind, complicate, entwine, intersperse, intertwine, interweave, inweave, knit, mix, plait, twine, twist, unite.

interlard *vb* difersify, interminate, intersperse, intertwine, mix, vary.

interline *vb* insert, write between.

interlineal *adj* interlinear, interlined.

interlink, interlock *vb* connect, interchain, interrelate, join.

interlocution *n* colloquy, conference, dialogue, interchange.

interlocutor *n* respondent, speaker.

interloper *n* intruder, meddler.

intermeddle *vb* interfere, interpose, meddle.

intermediary *n* go-between, mediator.

intermediate *adj* interjacent, interposed, intervening, mean, median, middle, transitional.

interment *n* burial, entombment, inhumation, sepulture.

interminable *adj* boundless, endless, illimitable, immeasurable, infinite, limitless, unbounded, unlimited; long-drawn-out, tedious, wearisome.

intermingle *vb* blend, commingle, commix, intermix, mingle, mix.

intermission *n* cessation, interruption, interval, lull, pause, remission, respite, rest, stop, stoppage, suspension.

intermit *vb* interrupt, intervene, stop, suspend; discontinue, give over, leave off; abate, subside.

intermittent *adj* broken, capricious, discontinuous, fitful, flickering, intermitting, periodic, recurrent, remittent, spasmodic.

intermix *vb* blend, commingle, commix, intermingle, mingle, mix.

internal *adj* inner, inside, interior, inward; incorporeal, mental, spiritual; deeper, emblematic, hidden, higher, metaphorical, secret, symbolical, under; genuine, inherent, intrinsic, real, true; domestic, home, inland, inside.

international *adj* cosmopolitan, universal.

internecine *adj* deadly, destructive, exterminating, exterminatory, interneciary, internecinal, internecive, mortal.

interpellate *vb* interrogate, question.

interpellation *n* interruption; intercession, interposition; interrogation, questioning.

interplay *n* interaction.

interpolate *vb* add, foist, insert, interpose; (*math*) intercalate, introduce.

interpose *vb* arbitrate, intercede, intervene, mediate; interfere, intermeddle, interrupt, meddle, tamper; insert, interject, put in, remark, sandwich, set between; intrude, thurst in.

interposition *n* intercession, interpellation, intervention, mediation.

interpret *vb* decipher, decode, define, elucidate, explain, expound, solve, unfold, unravel; construe, render, translate.

interpretation *n* meaning, sense, signification; elucidation, explanation, explication, exposition; construction, rendering, rendition, translation, version.

interpreter *n* expositor, expounder, translator.

interrogate *vb* ask, catechize, examine, inquire of, interpellate, question.

interrogation *n* catechizing, examination, examining, interpellation, interrogating, questioning; inquiry, query, question.

interrogative *adj* interrogatory, questioning.

interrupt *vb* break, check, disturb, hinder, intercept, interfere with, obstruct, pretermit, stop; break, cut, disconnect, disjoin, dissever, dissolve, disunite, divide, separate, sever, sunder; break off, cease, discontinue, intermit, leave off, suspend.

interruption *n* hindrance, impediment, obstacle, obstruction, stop, stoppage; cessation, discontinuance, intermission, pause, suspension; break, breaking, disconnecting, disconnection, disjunction, dissolution, disunion, disuniting, division, separation, severing, sundering.

intersect *vb* cross, cut, decussate, divide, interrupt.

intersection *n* crossing.

interspace *n* interlude, interstice, interval.

intersperse *vb* intermingle, scatter, sprinkle; diversify, interlard, mix.

interstice *n* interspace, interval, space; chink, crevice.

interstitial *adj* intermediate, intervening.

intertwine *vb* interlace, intertwine, interweave, inweave, twine.

interval *n* interim, interlude, interregnum, pause, period, recess, season, space, spell, term; interstice, skip.

intervene *vb* come between, interfere, mediate; befall, happen, occur.

intervening *adj* interjacent, intermediate; interstitial.

intervention *n* interference, interposition; agency, mediation.

interview *n* conference, consultation, parley; meeting.

interweave *vb* interlace, intertwine, inweave, weave; intermingle, intermix, mingle, mix.

intestinal *adj* domestic, interior, internal.

intestines *npl* bowels, entrails, guts, insides, inwards, viscera.

intimacy *n* close acquaintance, familiarity, fellowship, friendship; closeness, nearness.

intimate¹ *adj* close, near; familiar, friendly; bosom, chummy, close, dear, homelike, special; confidential, personal, private, secret; detailed, exhaustive, first-hand, immediate, penetrating, profound; cosy, warm. * *n* chum, confidant, companion, crony, friend.

intimate² *vb* allude to, express, hint, impart, indicate, insinuate, signify, suggest, tell.

intimately *adv* closely, confidentially, familiarly, nearly, thoroughly.

intimation *n* allusion, hint, innuendo, insinuation, suggestion.

intimidate *vb* abash, affright, alarm, appal, browbeat, bully, cow, daunt, dishearten, dismay, frighten, overawe, scare, subdue, terrify, terrorize.

intimidation *n* fear, intimidating, terror, terrorism.

intolerable *adj* insufferable, insupportable, unbearable, unendurable.

intolerance *n* bigotry, narrowness; impatience, rejection.

intolerant *adj* bigoted, narrow, proscriptive; dictatorial, impatient, imperious, overbearing, supercilious.

intonation *n* cadence, modulation, tone; musical recitation.

in toto *adv* entirely, wholly.

intoxicate *vb* fuddle, inebriate, muddle.

intoxicated *adj* boozy, drunk, drunken, fuddled, inebriated, maudlin, mellow, muddled, stewed, tight, tipsy.

intoxication *n* drunkenness, ebriety, inebriation, inebriety; excitement, exhilaration, infatuation.

intractability *n* cantankerousness, contrariety, inflexibility, intractableness, obduracy, obstinacy, perverseness, perversity, pig-headedness, stubbornness, wilfulness.

intractable *adj* cantankerous, contrary, contumacious, cross-grained, dogged, froward, headstrong, indocile, inflexible, mulish, obdurate, obstinate, perverse, pig-headed, refractory, restive, stubborn, tough, uncontrollable, ungovernable, unmanageable, unruly, unyielding, wilful.

intrench *see* **entrench**.

intrenchment *see* **entrenchment**.

intrepid *adj* bold, brave, chivalrous, courageous, daring, dauntless, doughty, fearless, gallant, heroic, unappalled, unawed, undaunted, undismayed, unterrified, valiant, valorous.

intrepidity *n* boldness, bravery, courage, daring, dauntlessness, fearlessness, gallantry, heroism, intrepidness, prowess, spirit, valour.

intricacy *n* complexity, complication, difficulty, en-

tanglement, intricateness, involution, obscurity, perplexity.

intricate *adj* complicated, difficult, entangled, involved, mazy, obscure, perplexed.

intrigue *vb* connive, conspire, machinate, plot, scheme; beguile, bewitch, captivate, charm, fascinate. * *n* artifice, cabal, conspiracy, deception, finesse, Machiavelianism, machination, manoeuvre, plot, ruse, scheme, stratagem, wile; amour, liaison, love affair.

intriguing *adj* arch, artful, crafty, crooked, cunning, deceitful, designing, diplomatic, foxy, Machiavelian, insidious, politic, sly, sneaky, subtle, tortuous, trickish, tricky, wily.

intrinsic *adj* essential, genuine, real, sterling, true; inborn, inbred, ingrained, inherent, internal, inward, native, natural.

intrinsically *adv* essentially, really, truly; inherently, naturally.

introduce *vb* bring in, conduct, import, induct, inject, insert, lead in, usher in; present; begin, broach, commence, inaugurate, initiate, institute, start.

introduction *n* exordium, preface, prelude, proem; introducing, ushering in; presentation.

introductory *adj* precursory, prefatory, preliminary, proemial.

introspection *n* introversion, self-contemplation.

intrude *vb* encroach, impose, infringe, interfere, interlope, obtrude, trespass.

intruder *n* interloper, intermeddler, meddler, stranger.

intrusion *n* encroachment, infringement, intruding, obtrusion.

intrusive *adj* obtrusive, trespassing.

intuition *n* apprehension, cognition, insight, instinct; clairvoyance, divination, presentiment.

intuitive *adj* instinctive, intuitional, natural; clear, distinct, full, immediate.

intumesce *vb* bubble up, dilate, expand, swell.

intumescence *n* inturgescence, swelling, tumefaction, turgescence.

inundate *vb* deluge, drown, flood, glut, overflow, overwhelm, submerge.

inundation *n* cataclysm, deluge, flood, glut, overflow, superfluity.

inure *vb* accustom, discipline, familiarize, habituate, harden, toughen, train, use.

inutile *adj* bootless, ineffectual, inoperative, unavailing, unprofitable, useless.

invade *vb* encroach upon, infringe, violate; attack, enter in, march into.

invalid¹ *adj* baseless, fallacious, false, inoperative, nugatory, unfounded, unsound, untrue, worthless; (*law*) null, void.

invalid² *adj* ailing, bedridden, feeble, frail, ill, infirm, sick, sickly, valetudinary, weak, weakly. * *n* convalescent, patient, valetudinarian.

invalidate *vb* abrogate, annul, cancel, nullify, overthrow, quash, repeal, reverse, undo, unmake, vitiate.

invalidity *n* baselessness, fallaciousness, fallacy, falsity, unsoundness.

invaluable *adj* inestimable, priceless.

invariable *adj* changeless, constant, unchanging, uniform, unvarying; changeless, immutable, unalterable, unchangeable.

invariableness *n* changelessness, constancy, uniformity, unvaryingness; changelessness, immutability, unchangeableness, invariability.

invasion *n* encroachment, incursion, infringement, inroad; aggression, assault, attack, foray, raid.

invective *n* abuse, censure, contumely, denunciation, diatribe, railing, reproach, sarcasm, satire, vituperation.

inveigh *vb* blame, censure, condemn, declaim against, denounce, exclaim against, rail at, reproach, vituperate.

inveigle *vb* contrive, devise; concoct, conceive, create, design, excogitate, frame, imagine, originate; coin, fabricate, forge, spin.

invent *vb* concoct, contrive, design, devise, discover, fabricate, find out, frame, originate.

invention *n* creation, discovery, ingenuity, inventing, origination; contrivance, design, device; coinage, fabrication, fiction, forgery.

inventive *adj* creative, fertile, ingenious.

inventor *n* author, contriver, creator, originator.

inventory *n* account, catalogue, list, record, roll, register, schedule.

inverse *adj* indirect, inverted, opposite, reversed.

inversion *n* inverting, reversing, transposal, transposition.

invert *vb* capsize, overturn; reverse, transpose.

invertebrate *adj* invertebral; spineless.

invest *vb* put money into; confer, endow, endue; (*mil*) beset, besiege, enclose, surround; array, clothe, dress.

investigate *vb* canvass, consider, dissect, examine, explore, follow up, inquire into, look into, overhaul, probe, question, research, scrutinize, search into, search out, sift, study.

investigation *n* examination, exploration, inquiry, inquisition, overhauling, research, scrutiny, search, sifting, study.

investiture *n* habilitation, induction, installation, ordination.

investment *n* money invested; endowment; (*mil*) beleaguerment, siege; clothes, dress, garments, habiliments, robe, vestment.

inveteracy *n* inveterateness, obstinacy.

inveterate *adj* accustomed, besetting, chronic, confirmed, deep-seated, habitual, habituated, hardened, ingrained, long-established, obstinate.

invidious *adj* disagreeable, envious, hateful, odious, offensive, unfair.

invigorate *vb* animate, brace, energize, fortify, harden, nerve, quicken, refresh, stimulate, strengthen, vivify.

invincible *adj* impregnable, indomitable, ineradicable, insuperable, insurmountable, irrepressible, unconquerable, unsubduable, unyielding.

inviolable *adj* hallowed, holy, inviolate, sacramental, sacred, sacrosanct, stainless.

inviolate *adj* unbroken, unviolated; pure, stainless, unblemished, undefiled, unhurt, uninjured, unpolluted, unprofaned, unstained; inviolable, sacred.

invisibility *n* imperceptibility, indistinctness, invisibleness, obscurity.

invisible *adj* impalpable, imperceptible, indistinguishable, intangible, unapparent, undiscernable, unperceivable, unseen.

invitation *n* bidding, call, challenge, solicitation, summons.

invite *vb* ask, bid, call, challenge, request, solicit, summon; allure, attract, draw on, entice, lead, persuade, prevail upon.

inviting *adj* alluring, attractive, bewitching, captivating, engaging, fascinating, pleasing, winning; prepossessing, promising.

invocation *n* conjuration, orison, petition, prayer, summoning, supplication.

invoice *vb* bill, list. * *n* bill, inventory, list, schedule.

invoke *vb* adjure, appeal to, beseech, beg, call upon, conjure, entreat, implore, importune, pray, pray to, solicit, summon, supplicate.

involuntary *adj* automatic, blind, instinctive, mechanical, reflex, spontaneous, unintentional; compulsory, reluctant, unwilling.

involve *vb* comprise, contain, embrace, imply, include, lead to; complicate, compromise, embarrass, entangle, implicate, incriminate, inculpate; cover, envelop, enwrap, surround, wrap; blend, conjoin, connect, join, mingle; entwine, interlace, intertwine, interweave, inweave.

invulnerability *n* invincibility, invulnerableness.

invulnerable *adj* incontrovertible, invincible, unassailable, irrefragable.

inward[1] *adj* incoming, inner, interior, internal; essential, hidden, mental, spiritual; private, secret.

inward[2], **inwards** *adv* inwardly, towards the inside, within.

inweave *vb* entwine, interlace, intertwine, interweave, weave together.

iota *n* atom, bit, glimmer, grain, jot, mite, particle, scintilla, scrap, shadow, spark, tittle, trace, whit.

irascibility *n* hastiness, hot-headedness, impatience, irascibleness, irritability, peevishness, petulance, quickness, spleen, testiness, touchiness.

irascible *adj* choleric, cranky, hasty, hot, hotheaded, impatient, irritable, nettlesome, peevish, peppery, pettish, petulant, quick, splenetic, snappish, testy, touchy, waspish.

irate *adj* angry, incensed, ireful, irritated, piqued.

ire *n* anger, choler, exasperation, fury, indignation, passion, rage, resentment, wrath.

ireful *adj* angry, furious, incensed, irate, raging, passionate.

iridescent *adj* irisated, nacreous, opalescent, pavonine, prismatic, rainbow-like.

iris *n* rainbow; (*bot*) fleur-de-lis, flower-de-luce; diaphragm of the eye.

irksome *adj* annoying, burdensome, humdrum, monotonous, tedious, tiresome, wearisome, weary, wearying.

iron *adj* ferric, ferrous.

ironic, ironical *adj* mocking, sarcastic.

irons *npl* chains, fetters, gyves, hampers, manacles, shackles.

irony *n* mockery, raillery, ridicule, sarcasm, satire.

irradiate *vb* brighten, illume, illuminate, illumine, light up, shine upon.

irrational *adj* absurd, extravagant, foolish, injudicious, preposterous, ridiculous, silly, unwise; unreasonable, unreasoning, unthinking; brute, brutish; aberrant, alienated, brainless, crazy, demented, fantastic, idiotic, imbecilic, insane, lunatic.

irrationality *n* absurdity, folly, foolishness, unreasonableness; brutishness.

irreclaimable *adj* hopeless, incurable, irrecoverable, irreparable, irretrievable, irreversible, remediless; abandoned, graceless, hardened, impenitent, incorrigible, lost, obdurate, profligate, recreant, reprobate, shameless, unrepentant.

irreconcilable *adj* implacable, inexorable, inexpiable, unappeasable; incompatible, incongruous, inconsistent.

irrecoverable *adj* hopeless, incurable, irremediable, irreparable, irretrievable, remediless.

irrefragable *adj* impregnable, incontestable, incontrovertible, indisputable, invincible, irrefutable, irresistible, unanswerable, unassailable, undeniable.

irrefutable *adj* impregnable, incontestable, incontrovertible, indisputable, invincible, irrefragable, irresistible, unanswerable, unassailable, undeniable.

irregular *adj* aberrant, abnormal, anomalistic, anomalous, crooked, devious, eccentric, erratic, exceptional, heteromorphous, raged, tortuous, unconformable, unusual; capricious, changeable, desultory, fitful, spasmodic, uncertain, unpunctual, unsettled, variable; disordered, disorderly, improper, uncanonical, unparliamentary, unsystematic; asymmetric, uneven, unsymmetrical; disorderly, dissolute, immoral, loose, wild. * *n* casual, freelance, hireling, mercenary.

irregularity *n* aberration, abnormality, anomaly, anomalousness, singularity; capriciousness, changeableness, uncertainty, variableness; asymmetry; disorderliness, dissoluteness, immorality, laxity, looseness, wildness.

irrelevance, irrelevancy *n* impertinency, inapplicability, nonpertinency.

irrelevant *adj* extraneous, foreign, illogical, impertinent, inapplicable, inapposite, inappropriate, inconsequent, unessential, unrelated.

irreligion *n* atheism, godlessness, impiety, ungodliness.

irreligious *adj* godless, ungodly, undevout; blasphemous, disrespectful, impious, irreverent, profane, ribald, wicked.

irremediable *adj* hopeless, incurable, immedicable, irrecoverable, irreparable, remediless.

irremissible *adj* binding, inexpiable, obligatory, unatonable, unpardonable.

irreparable *adj* irrecoverable, irremediable, irretrievable, remediless.

irreprehensible *adj* blameless, faultless, inculpable, innocent, irreproachable, irreprovable, unblamable.

irrepressible *adj* insuppressible, uncontrollable, unquenchable, unsmotherable.

irreproachable *adj* blameless, faultless, inculpable, innocent, irreprehensible, irreprovable, unblamable.

irresistible *adj* irrefragable, irrepressible, overpowering, overwhelming, resistless.

irresolute *adj* changeable, faltering, fickle, hesitant, hesitating, inconstant, mutable, spineless, uncertain, undecided, undetermined, unsettled, unstable, unsteady, vacillating, wavering.

irrespective *adj* independent, regardless.

irresponsible *adj* unaccountable; untrustworthy.

irretrievable *adj* incurable, irrecoverable, irremediable, irreparable, remediless.

irreverence *n* blasphemy, impiety, profaneness, profanity; disesteem, disrespect.

irreverent *adj* blasphemous, impious, irreligious, profane; disrespectful, slighting.

irreversible *adj* irrepealable, irrevocable, unalterable, unchangeable; changeless, immutable, invariable.

irrevocable *adj* irrepealable, irreversible, unalterable, unchangeable.

irrigate *vb* moisten, wash, water, wet.

irrigation *n* watering.

irritability *n* excitability, fretfulness, irascibility, peevishness, petulance, snappishness, susceptibility, testiness.

irritable *adj* captious, choleric, excitable, fiery, fretful, hasty, hot, irascible, passionate, peppery, peevish, pettish, petulant, snappish, splenetic, susceptible, testy, touchy, waspish.

irritate *vb* anger, annoy, chafe, enrage, exacerbate, exasperate, fret, incense, jar, nag, nettle, offend, provoke, rasp, rile, ruffle, vex; gall, tease; (*med*) excite, inflame, stimulate.

irritation *n* irritating; anger, exacerbation, exasperation, excitement, indignation, ire, passion, provocation, resentment, wrath; (*med*) excitation, inflammation, stimulation; burn, itch.

irruption *n* breaking in, bursting in; foray, incursion, inroad, invasion, raid.

island *n* atoll, isle, islet, reef.

isochronal *adj* isochronous, uniform.

isolate *vb* detach, dissociate, insulate, quarantine, segregate, separate, set apart.

isolated *adj* detached, separate, single, solitary.

isolation *n* detachment, disconnection, insulation, quarantine, segregation, separation; loneliness, solitariness, solitude.

issue *vb* come out, flow out, flow forth, gush, run, rush out, spout, spring, spurt, well; arise, come, emanate, ensue, flow, follow, originate, proceed, spring; end, eventuate, result, terminate; appear, come out, deliver, depart, debouch, discharge, emerge, emit, put forth, send out; distribute, give out; publish, utter. * *n* conclusion, consequence, consummation, denouement, end, effect, event, finale, outcome, result, termination, upshot; antagonism, contest, controversy; debouchment, delivering, delivery, discharge, emergence, emigration, emission, issuance; flux,

outflow, outpouring, stream; copy, edition, number; egress, exit, outlet, passage out, vent, way out; escape, sally, sortie; children, offspring, posterity, progeny.

itch *vb* tingle. * *n* itching; burning, coveting, importunate craving, teasing desire, uneasy hankering.

itching *n* itch; craving, longing, importunate craving, desire, appetite, hankering.

item *adv* also, in like manner. * *n* article, detail, entry, particular, point.

iterate *vb* reiterate, repeat.

itinerant *adj* nomadic, peripatetic, roaming, roving, travelling, unsettled, wandering.

itinerary *n* guide, guidebook; circuit, route.

J

jabber *vb* chatter, gabble, prate, prattle.

jacket *n* casing, cover, sheath; anorak, blazer coat, doublet, jerkin.

jaded *adj* dull, exhausted, fatigued, satiated, tired, weary.

jagged *adj* cleft, divided, indented, notched, serrated, ragged, uneven.

jail, gaol *n* bridewell, (*sl*) clink, dungeon, lockup, (*sl*) nick, penitentiary, prison.

jam *vb* block, crowd, crush, press. * *n* block, crowd, crush, mass, pack, press.

jangle *vb* bicker, chatter, dispute, gossip, jar, quarrel, spar, spat, squabble, tiff, wrangle. * *n* clang, clangour, clash, din, dissonance.

jar[1] *vb* clash, grate, interfere, shake; bicker, contend, jangle, quarrel, spar, spat, squabble, tiff, wrangle; agitate, jolt, jounce, shake. * *n* clash, conflict, disaccord, discord, jangle, dissonance; agitation, jolt, jostle, shake, shaking, shock, start.

jar[2] *n* can, crock, cruse, ewer, flagon.

jarring *adj* conflicting, discordant, inconsistent, inconsonant, wrangling.

jargon *n* gabble, gibberish, nonsense, rigmarole: argot, cant, lingo, slang; chaos, confusion, disarray, disorder, jumble.

jaundiced *adj* biased, envious, prejudiced.

jaunt *n* excursion, ramble, tour, trip.

jaunty *adj* airy, cheery, garish, gay, fine, fluttering, showy, sprightly, unconcerned.

jealous *adj* distrustful, envious, suspicious; anxious, apprehensive, intolerant, solicitous, zealous.

jealousy *n* envy, suspicion, watchfulness.

jeer *vb* deride, despise, flout, gibe, jape, jest, mock, scoff, sneer, spurn, rail, ridicule, taunt. * *n* abuse, derision, mockery, sneer, ridicule, taunt.

jeopardize *vb* endanger, hazard, imperil, risk, venture.

jeopardy *n* danger, hazard, peril, risk, venture.

jerk *vb*, *n* flip, hitch, pluck, tweak, twitch, yank.

jest *vb* banter, joke, quiz. * *n* fun, joke, pleasantry, raillery, sport.

jester *n* humorist, joker, wag; buffoon, clown, droll, fool, harlequin, punch.

jibe *see* **gibe**.

jiffy *n* instant, moment, second, twinkling, trice.

jilt *vb* break with, deceive, disappoint, discard. * *n* coquette, flirt, light-o'-love.

jingle *vb* chink, clink, jangle, rattle, tinkle. * *n* chink, clink, jangle, rattle, tinkle; chorus, ditty, melody, song.

jocose *adj* comical, droll, facetious, funny, humorous, jesting, jocular, merry, sportive, waggish, witty.

jocund *adj* airy, blithe, cheerful, debonair, frolicsome, jolly, joyful, joyous, lively, merry, playful.

jog *vb* jostle, notify, nudge, push, remind, warn; canter, run, trot. * *n* push, reminder.

join *vb* add, annex, append, attach; cement, combine, conjoin, connect, couple, dovetail, link, unite, yoke; amalgamate, assemble, associate, confederate, consolidate.

joint *vb* fit, join, unite. * *adj* combined, concerted, concurrent, conjoint. * *n* connection, junction, juncture, hinge, splice.

joke *vb* banter, jest, frolic, rally. * *n* crank, jest, quip, quirk, witticism.

jolly *adj* airy, blithe, cheerful, frolicsome, gamesome, facetious, funny, gay, jovial, joyous, merry, mirthful, jocular, jocund, playful, sportive, sprightly, waggish; bouncing, chubby, lusty, plump, portly, stout.

jolt *vb* jar, shake, shock. * *n* jar, jolting, jounce, shaking.

jostle *vb* collide, elbow, hustle, joggle, shake, shoulder, shove.

jot *n* ace, atom, bit, corpuscle, iota, grain, mite, particle, scrap, whit.

journal *n* daybook, diary, log; gazette, magazine, newspapers, periodical.

journey *vb* ramble, roam, rove, travel: fare, go, proceed. * *n* excursion, expedition, jaunt, passage, pilgrimage, tour, travel, trip, voyage.

jovial *adj* airy, convivial, festive, jolly, joyous, merry, mirthful.

joy *n* beatification, beatitude, delight, ecstasy, exultation, gladness, glee, mirth, pleasure, rapture, ravishment, transport; bliss, felicity, happiness.

joyful *adj* blithe, blithesome, buoyant, delighted, elate, elated, exultant, glad, happy, jocund, jolly, joyous, merry, rejoicing.

jubilant *adj* exultant, exulting, rejoicing, triumphant.

judge *vb* conclude, decide, decree, determine, pronounce; adjudicate, arbitrate, condemn, doom, sentence, try, umpire; account, apprehend, believe, consider, deem, esteem, guess, hold, imagine, measure, reckon, regard, suppose, think; appreciate, estimate. * *n* adjudicator, arbiter, arbitrator, bencher, justice, magistrate, moderator, referee, umpire, connoisseur, critic.

judgment, judgement *n* brains, ballast, circumspection, depth, discernment, discretion, discrimination, intelligence, judiciousness, penetration, prudence, sagacity, sense, sensibility, taste, understanding, wisdom, wit; conclusion, consideration, decision, determination, estimation, notion, opinion, thought; adjudication, arbitration, award, censure, condemnation, decree, doom, sentence.

judicious *adj* cautious, considerate, cool, critical, discriminating, discreet, enlightened, provident, politic, prudent, rational, reasonable, sagacious, sensible, sober, solid, sound, staid, wise.

jug *n* cruse, ewer, flagon, pitcher, vessel.

juicy *adj* lush, moist, sappy, succulent, watery; entertaining, exciting, interesting, lively, racy, spicy.

jumble *vb* confound, confuse, disarrange, disorder, mix, muddle. * *n* confusion, disarrangement, disorder, medley, mess, mixture, muddle.

jump *vb* bound, caper, clear, hop, leap, skip, spring, vault. * *n* bound, caper, hop, leak, skip, spring, vault; fence, hurdle, obstacle; break, gap, interruption, space; advance, boost, increase, rise; jar, jolt, shock, start, twitch.

junction *n* combination, connection, coupling, hook-up, joining, linking, seam, union; conjunction, joint, juncture.

junta *n* cabal, clique, combination, confederacy, coterie, faction, gang, league, party, set.

just *adj* equitable, lawful, legitimate, reasonable, right, rightful; candid, even-handed, fair, fairminded, impartial; blameless, conscientious, good, honest, honourable, pure, square, straightforward, virtuous; accurate, correct, exact, normal, proper, regular, true; condign, deserved, due, merited, suitable.

justice *n* accuracy, equitableness, equity, fairness, honesty, impartiality, justness, right; judge, justiciary.

justifiable *adj* defensible, fit, proper, right, vindicable, warrantable.

justification *n* defence, exculpation, excuse, exoneration, reason, vindication, warrant.

justify *vb* approve, defend, exculpate, excuse, exonerate, maintain, vindicate, support, warrant.

justness *n* accuracy, correctness, fitness, justice, precision, propriety.

juvenile *adj* childish, immature, puerile, young, youthful. * *n* boy, child, girl, youth.

juxtaposition *n* adjacency, contiguity, contact, proximity.

K

keen[1] *adj* ardent, eager, earnest, fervid, intense, vehement, vivid; acute, sharp; cutting; acrimonious, biting, bitter, caustic, poignant, pungent, sarcastic, severe; astute, discerning, intelligent, quick, sagacious, sharp-sighted, shrewd.

keen[2] *vb* bemoan, bewail, deplore, grieve, lament, mourn, sorrow, weep. * *n* coronach, dirge, elegy, lament, lamentation, monody, plaint, requiem, threnody.

keenness *n* ardour, eagerness, fervour, vehemence, zest; acuteness, sharpness; rigour, severity, sternness; acrimony, asperity, bitterness, causticity, causticness, pungency; astuteness, sagacity, shrewdness.

keep *vb* detain, hold, retain; continue, preserve; confine, detain, reserve, restrain, withhold; attend, guard, preserve, protect; adhere to, fulfil; celebrate, commemorate, honour, observe, perform, solemnize; maintain, support, sustain; husband, save, store; abide, dwell, lodge, stay, remain; endure, last. * *n* board, maintenance, subsistence, support; donjon, dungeon, stronghold, tower.

keeper *n* caretaker, conservator, curator, custodian, defender, gaoler, governor, guardian, jailer, superintendent, warden, warder, watchman.

keeping *n* care, charge, custody, guard, possession; feed, maintenance, support; agreement, conformity, congruity, consistency, harmony.

keepsake *n* memento, souvenir, token.

ken *n* cognizance, sight, view.

key *adj* basic, crucial, essential, important, major, principal. * *n* lock-opener, opener; clue, elucidation, explanation, guide, solution, translation; (*mus*) keynote, tonic; clamp, lever, wedge.

kick *vb* boot, punt; oppose, rebel, resist, spurn. * *n* force, intensity, power, punch, vitality; excitement, pleasure, thrill.

kidnap *vb* abduct, capture, carry off, remove, steal away.

kill *vb* assassinate, butcher, dispatch, destroy, massacre, murder, slaughter, slay.

kin *adj* akin, allied, cognate, kindred, related. * *n* affinity, consanguinity, relationship; connections, family, kindred, kinsfolk, relations, relatives, siblings.

kind[1] *adj* accommodating, amiable, beneficent, benevolent, benign, bland, bounteous, brotherly, charitable, clement, compassionate, complaisant, gentle, good, good-natured, forbearing, friendly, generous, gracious, humane, indulgent, lenient, mild, obliging, sympathetic, tender, tender-hearted.

kind[2] *n* breed, class, family, genus, race, set, species, type; brand, character, colour, denomination, description, form, make, manner, nature, persuasion, sort, stamp, strain, style,

kindle *vb* fire, ignite, inflame, light; animate, awaken, bestir, exasperate, excite, foment, incite, provoke, rouse, stimulate, stir, thrill, warm.

kindliness *n* amiability, benevolence, benignity, charity, compassion, friendliness, humanity, kindness, sympathy; gentleness, mildness, softness.

kindly *adj* appropriate, congenial, kindred, natural, proper; benevolent, considerate, friendly, gracious, humane, sympathetic, well-disposed. * *adv* agreeably, graciously, humanely, politely, thoughtfully.

kindness *n* benefaction, charity, favour; amiability, beneficence, benevolence, benignity, clemency, generosity, goodness, grace, humanity, kindliness, mildness, philanthropy, sympathy, tenderness.

kindred *adj* akin, allied, congenial, connected, related, sympathetic. * *n* affinity, consanguinity, flesh, relationship; folks, kin, kinsfolk, kinsmen, relations, relatives.

king *n* majesty, monarch, sovereign.

kingdom *n* dominion, empire, monarchy, rule, sovereignty, supremacy; region, tract; division, department, domain, province, realm.

kingly *adj* imperial, kinglike, monarchical, regal, royal, sovereign; august, glorious, grand, imperial, imposing, magnificent, majestic, noble, splendid.

kink *n* cramp, crick, curl, entanglement, knot, loop, twist; crochet, whim, wrinkle.

kinsfolk *n* kin, kindred, kinsmen, relations, relatives.

kit *n* equipment, implements, outfit, set, working.

knack *n* ability, address, adroitness, aptitude, aptness, dexterity, dextrousness, expertness, facility, quickness, readiness, skill.

knave *n* caitiff, cheat, miscreant, rascal, rogue, scamp, scapegrace, scoundrel, sharper, swindler, trickster, villain.

knavery *n* criminality, dishonesty, fraud, knavishness, rascality, scoundrelism, trickery, villainy.

knavish *adj* dishonest, fraudulent, rascally, scoundrelly, unprincipled, roguish, trickish, tricky, villainous.

knell *vb* announce, peal, ring, toll. * *n* chime, peal, ring, toll.

knife *vb* cut, slash, stab. * *n* blade, jackknife, lance.

knit *vb* connect, interlace, join, unite, weave.

knob *n* boss, bunch, hunch, lump, protuberance, stud.

knock *vb* clap, cuff, hit, rap, rattle, slap, strike, thump; beat, blow, box. * *n* blow, slap, smack, thump; blame, criticism, rejection, setback.

knoll *n* hill, hillock, mound.

knot *vb* complicate, entangle, gnarl, kink, tie, weave. * *n* complication, entanglement; connection, tie; joint, node, knag; bunch, rosette, tuft; band, cluster, clique, crew, gang, group, pack, set, squad.

knotty *adj* gnarled, hard, knaggy, knurled, knotted, rough, rugged; complex, difficult, harassing, intricate, involved, perplexing, troublesome.

know *vb* apprehend, comprehend, cognize, discern, perceive, recognize, see, understand; discriminate, distinguish.

knowing *adj* accomplished, competent, experienced, intelligent, proficient, qualified, skilful, well-informed; aware, conscious, percipient, sensible, thinking; cunning, expressive, significant.

knowingly *adv* consciously, intentionally, purposely, wittingly.

knowledge *n* apprehension, command, comprehension, discernment, judgment, perception, understanding, wit; acquaintance, acquirement, attainments, enlightenment, erudition, information, learning, lore, mastery, scholarship, science; cognition, cognizance, consciousness, ken, notice, prescience, recognition.

knowledgeable *adj* aware, conscious, experienced, well-informed; educated, intelligent, learned, scholarly.

knuckle *vb* cringe, crouch, stoop, submit, yield.

L

laborious *adj* assiduous, diligent, hardworking, indefatigable, industrious, painstaking, sedulous, toiling; arduous, difficult, fatiguing, hard, Herculean, irksome, onerous, tiresome, toilsome, wearisome.

labour *vb* drudge, endeavour, exert, strive, toil, travail, work. * *n* drudgery, effort, exertion, industry, pains, toil, work; childbirth, delivery, parturition.

labyrinth *n* entanglement, intricacy, maze, perplexity, windings.

labyrinthine *adj* confused, convoluted, intricate, involved, labyrinthian, labyrinthic, perplexing, winding.

lace *vb* attach, bind, fasten, intertwine, tie, twine. * *n* filigree, lattice, mesh, net, netting, network, openwork, web.

lacerate *vb* claw, cut, lancinate, mangle, rend, rip, sever, slash, tear, wound; afflict, harrow, rend, torture, wound.

lack *vb* need, want. * *n* dearth, default, defectiveness, deficiency, deficit, destitution, insufficiency, need, scantiness, scarcity, shortcoming, shortness, want.

lackadaisical *adj* languishing, sentimental, pensive.

laconic *adj* brief, compact, concise, pithy, sententious, short, succinct, terse.

lad *n* boy, schoolboy, stripling, youngster, youth.

lading *n* burden, cargo, freight, load.

ladylike *adj* courtly, genteel, refined, well-bred.

lag *vb* dawdle, delay, idle, linger, loiter, saunter, tarry.

laggard *n* idler, lingerer, loiterer, lounger, saunterer, sluggard.

lair *n* burrow, couch, den, form, resting place.

lambent *adj* flickering, gliding, gleaming, licking, touching, twinkling.

lame *vb* cripple, disable, hobble. * *adj* crippled, defective, disabled, halt, hobbling, limping; feeble, insufficient, poor, unsatisfactory, weak.

lament *vb* complain, grieve, keen, moan, mourn, sorrow, wail, weep; bemoan, bewail, deplore, regret. * *n* complaint, lamentation, moan, moaning, plaint, wailing; coronach, dirge, elegy, keen, monody, requiem, threnody.

lamentable *adj* deplorable, doleful, grievous, lamented, melancholy, woeful; contemptible, miserable, pitiful, poor, wretched.

lamentation *n* dirge, grief, lament, moan, moaning, mourning, plaint, ululation, sorrow, wailing.

lampoon *vb* calumniate, defame, lash, libel, parody, ridicule, satirize, slander. * *n* calumny, defamation, libel, parody, pasquinade, parody, satire, slander.

land *vb* arrive, debark, disembark. * *n* earth, ground, soil; country, district, province, region, reservation, territory, tract, weald.

landlord *n* owner, proprietor; host, hotelier, innkeeper.

landscape *n* prospect, scene, view.

language *n* dialect, speech, tongue, vernacular; conversation; expression, idiom, jargon, parlance, phraseology, slang, style, terminology; utterance, voice.

languid *adj* drooping, exhausted, faint, feeble, flagging, languishing, pining, weak; dull, heartless, heavy, inactive, listless, lukewarm, slow, sluggish, spiritless, torpid.

languish *vb* decline, droop, fade, fail, faint, pine, sicken, sink, wither.

languor *n* debility, faintness, feebleness, languidness, languishment, weakness; apathy, ennui, heartlessness, heaviness, lethargy, listlessness, torpidness, torpor, weariness.

lank *adj* attenuated, emaciated, gaunt, lean, meagre, scraggy, slender, skinny, slim, starveling, thin.

lap[1] *vb* drink, lick, mouth, tongue; plash, ripple, splash, wash; quaff, sip, sup, swizzle, tipple. * *n* draught, dram, drench, drink, gulp, lick, swig, swill, quaff, sip, sup, suck; plash, splash, wash.

lap[2] *vb* cover, enfold, fold, turn, twist, swaddle, wrap; distance, pass, outdistance, overlap. * *n* fold, flap, lappet, lapel, ply, plait; ambit, beat, circle, circuit, cycle, loop, orbit, revolution, round, tour, turn, walk.

lapse *vb* glide, sink, slide, slip; err, fail, fall. * *n* course, flow, gliding; declension, decline, fall; error, fault, indiscretion, misstep, shortcoming, slip.

larceny *n* pilfering, robbery, stealing, theft, thievery.

large *adj* big, broad, bulky, colossal, elephantine, enormous, heroic, great, huge, immense, vast; broad, expanded, extensive, spacious, wide; abundant, ample, copious, full, liberal, plentiful; capacious, comprehensive.

lascivious *adj* concupiscent, immodest, incontinent,

goatish, lecherous, lewd, libidinous, loose, lubricious, lustful, prurient, salacious, sensual, unchaste, voluptuous, wanton.

lash¹ *vb* belay, bind, strap, tie; fasten, join, moor, pinion, secure.

lash² *vb* beat, castigate, chastise, flagellate, flail, flay, flog, goad, scourge, swinge, thrash, whip; assail, censure, excoriate, lampoon, satirize, trounce. * *n* scourge, strap, thong, whip; cut, slap, smack, stroke, stripe.

lass *n* damsel, girl, lassie, maiden, miss.

lassitude *n* dullness, exhaustion, fatigue, languor, languidness, prostration, tiredness, weariness.

last¹ *vb* abide, carry on, continue, dwell, endure, extend, maintain, persist, prevail, remain, stand, stay, survive.

last² *adj* hindermost, hindmost, latest; conclusive, final, terminal, ultimate; eventual, endmost, extreme, farthest, ultimate; greatest, highest, maximal, maximum, most, supreme, superlative, utmost; latest, newest; aforegoing, foregoing, latter, preceding; departing, farewell, final, leaving, parting, valedictory. * *n* conclusion, consummation, culmination, end, ending, finale, finis, finish, termination.

last³ *n* cast, form, matrix, mould, shape, template.

lasting *adj* abiding, durable, enduring, fixed, perennial, permanent, perpetual, stable.

lastly *adv* conclusively, eventually, finally, ultimately.

late *adj* behindhand, delayed, overdue, slow, tardy; deceased, former; recent. * *adv* lately, recently, sometime; tardily.

latent *adj* abeyant, concealed, hidden, invisible, occult, secret, unseen, veiled.

latitude *n* amplitude, breadth, compass, extent, range, room, scope; freedom, indulgence, liberty; laxity.

latter *adj* last, latest, modern, recent.

lattice *n* espalier, grating, latticework, trellis.

laud *vb* approve, celebrate, extol, glorify, magnify, praise.

laudable *adj* commendable, meritorious, praiseworthy.

laugh *vb* cackle, chortle, chuckle, giggle, guffaw, snicker, snigger, titter. * *n* chortle, chuckle, giggle, guffaw, laughter, titter.

laughable *adj* amusing, comical, diverting, droll, farcical, funny, ludicrous, mirthful, ridiculous.

laughter *n* cackle, chortle, chuckle, glee, giggle, guffaw, laugh, laughing.

launch *vb* cast, dart, dispatch, hurl, lance, project, throw; descant, dilate, enlarge, expiate; begin, commence, inaugurate, open, start.

lavish *vb* dissipate, expend, spend, squander, waste. * *adj* excessive, extravagant, generous, immoderate, overliberal, prodigal, profuse, thriftless, unrestrained, unstinted, unthrifty, wasteful.

law *n* act, code, canon, command, commandment, covenant, decree, edict, enactment, order, precept, principle, statute, regulation, rule; jurisprudence; litigation, process, suit.

lawful *adj* constitutional, constituted, legal, legalized, legitimate; allowable, authorized, permissible, warrantable; equitable, rightful, just, proper, valid.

lawless *adj* anarchic, anarchical, chaotic, disorderly, insubordinate, rebellious, reckless, riotous, seditious, wild.

lawyer *n* advocate, attorney, barrister, counsel, counsellor, pettifogger, solicitor.

lax *adj* loose, relaxed, slow; drooping, flabby, soft; neglectful, negligent, remiss; dissolute, immoral, licentious, seditious, wild.

lay¹ *vb* deposit, establish, leave, place, plant, posit, put, set, settle, spread; arrange, dispose, locate, organize, position; bear, produce; advance, lodge, offer, submit; allocate, allot, ascribe, assign, attribute, charge, impute; concoct, contrive, design, plan, plot, prepare; apply, burden, encumber, impose, saddle, tax; bet, gamble, hazard, risk, stake, wager; allay, alleviate, appease, assuage, calm, relieve, soothe, still, suppress; disclose, divulge, explain, reveal, show, unveil; acquire, grab, grasp, seize; assault, attack, beat up; discover, find, unearth; bless, confirm, consecrate, ordain. * *n* arrangement, array, form, formation; attitude, aspect, bearing, demeanour, direction, lie, pose, position, posture, set.

lay² *adj* amateur, inexpert, nonprofessional; civil, laic, laical, nonclerical, nonecclesiastical, nonreligious, secular, temporal, unclerical.

lay³ *n* ballad, carol, ditty, lied, lyric, ode, poem, rhyme, round, song, verse.

layer *n* bed, course, lay, seam, stratum.

laziness *n* idleness, inactivity, indolence, slackness, sloth, fulness, sluggishness, tardiness.

lazy *adj* idle, inactive, indolent, inert, slack, slothful, slow, sluggish, supine, torpid.

lead *vb* conduct, deliver, direct, draw, escort, guide; front, head, precede; advance, excel, outstrip, pass; allure, entice, induce, persuade, prevail; conduce, contribute, serve, tend. * *adj* chief, first, foremost, main, primary, prime, principal. * *n* direction, guidance, leadership; advance; precedence, priority.

leader *n* conductor, director, guide; captain, chief, chieftain, commander, head; superior, dominator, victor.

leading *adj* governing, ruling; capital, chief, first, foremost, highest, principal, superior.

league *vb* ally, associate, band, combine, confederate, unite. * *n* alliance, association, coalition, combination, combine, confederacy, confederation, consortium, union.

leak *vb* drip, escape, exude, ooze, pass, percolate, spill. * *n* chink, crack, crevice, hole, fissure, oozing, opening; drip, leakage, leaking, percolation.

lean¹ *adj* bony, emaciated, gaunt, lank, meagre, poor, skinny, thin; dull, barren, jejune, meagre, tame; inadequate, pitiful, scanty, slender; bare, barren, infertile, unproductive.

lean² *vb* incline, slope; bear, recline, repose, rest; confide, depend, rely, trust.

leaning *n* aptitude, bent, bias, disposition, inclination, liking, predilection, proneness, propensity, tendency.

leap *vb* bound, clear, jump, spring, vault; caper, frisk, gambol, hop, skip. * *n* bound, jump, spring, vault; caper, frisk, gambol, hop, skip.

learn *vb* acquire, ascertain, attain, collect, gain, gather, hear, memorize.

learned *adj* erudite, lettered, literate, scholarly, well-read; expert, experienced, knowing, skilled, versed, well-informed.

learner *n* beginner, novice, pupil, student, tyro.

learning *n* acquirements, attainments, culture, education, information, knowledge, lore, scholarship, tuition.

least *adj* meanest, minutest, smallest, tiniest.

leave¹ *vb* abandon, decamp, go, quit, vacate, withdraw; desert, forsake, relinquish, renounce; commit, consign, refer; cease, desist from, discontinue, refrain, stop; allow, let, let alone, permit; bequeath, demise, desist, will.

leave² *n* allowance, liberty, permission, licence, sufferance; departure, retirement, withdrawal; adieu, farewell, goodbye.

leaven *vb* ferment, lighten, raise; colour, elevate, imbue, inspire, lift, permeate, tinge; infect, vitiate. * *n* barm, ferment, yeast; influence, inspiration.

leavings *npl* bits, dregs, fragments, leftovers, pieces, relics, remains, remnants, scraps.

lecherous *adj* carnal, concupiscent, incontinent, lascivious, lewd, libidinous, lubricious, lustful, wanton, salacious, unchaste.

lechery *n* concupiscence, lasciviousness, lewdness, lubriciousness, lubricity, lust, salaciousness, salacity.

lecture *vb* censure, chide, reprimand, reprove, scold, sermonize; address, harangue, teach. * *n* censure, lecturing, lesson, reprimand, reproof, scolding; address, discourse, prelection.

ledge *n* projection, ridge, shelf.

lees *npl* dregs, precipitate, refuse, sediment, settlings.

leg *n* limb, prop.

legacy *n* bequest, gift, heirloom; heritage, inheritance, tradition.

legal *adj* allowable, authorized, constitutional, lawful, legalized, legitimate, proper, sanctioned.

legalize *vb* authorize, legitimate, legitimatize, legitimize, permit, sanction.

legend *n* fable, fiction, myth, narrative, romance, story, tale.

legendary *adj* fabulous, fictitious, mythical, romantic.

legible *adj* clear, decipherable, fair, distinct, plain, readable; apparent, discoverable, recognizable, manifest.

legion *n* army, body, cohort, column, corps, detachment, detail, division, force, maniple,

phalanx, platoon; squad; army, horde, host, multitude, number, swarm, throng. * *adj* many, multitudinous, myriad, numerous.

legislate *vb* enact, ordain.

legitimacy *n* lawfulness, legality; genuineness.

legitimate *adj* authorized, lawful, legal, sanctioned; genuine, valid; correct, justifiable, logical, reasonable, warrantable, warranted.

leisure *n* convenience, ease, freedom, liberty, opportunity, recreation, retirement, vacation.

lend *vb* advance, afford, bestow, confer, furnish, give, grant, impart, loan, supply.

lengthen *vb* elongate, extend, produce, prolong, stretch; continue, protract.

lengthy *adj* diffuse, lengthened, long, long-drawn-out, prolix, prolonged, protracted.

lenience, leniency *n* clemency, compassion, forbearance, gentleness, lenity, mercy, mildness, tenderness.

lenient *adj* assuasive, lenitive, mitigating, mitigative, softening, soothing; clement, easy, forbearing, gentle, humouring, indulgent, long-suffering, merciful, mild, tender, tolerant.

lesion *n* derangement, disorder, hurt, injury.

less *adj* baser, inferior, lower, smaller; decreased, fewer, lesser, reduced, smaller, shorter; * *adv* barely, below, least, under; decreasingly. * *prep* excepting, lacking, minus, sans, short of, without.

lessen *vb* abate, abridge, contract, curtail, decrease, diminish, narrow, reduce, shrink; degrade, lower; dwindle, weaken.

lesson *n* exercise, task; instruction, precept; censure, chiding, lecture, lecturing, rebuke, reproof, scolding.

let¹ *vb* admit, allow, authorize, permit, suffer; charter, hire, lease, rent.

let² *vb* hinder, impede, instruct, prevent. * *n* hindrance, impediment, interference, obstacle, obstruction, restriction.

lethal *adj* deadly, destructive, fatal, mortal, murderous.

lethargic *adj* apathetic, comatose, drowsy, dull, heavy, inactive, inert, sleepy, stupid, stupefied, torpid.

lethargy *n* apathy, coma, drowsiness, dullness, hypnotism, inactiveness, inactivity, inertia, sleepiness, sluggishness, stupefaction, stupidity, stupor, torpor.

letter *n* epistle, missive, note.

lettered *adj* bookish, educated, erudite, learned, literary, versed, well-read.

levee *n* ceremony, entertainment, reception, party, soiree; embankment.

level *vb* equalize, flatten, horizontalize, smooth; demolish, destroy, raze; aim, direct, point. * *adj* equal, even, flat, flush, horizontal, plain, plane, smooth. * *n* altitude, degree, equality, evenness, plain, plane, smoothness; deck, floor, layer, stage, storey, tier.

levity *n* buoyancy, facetiousness, fickleness,

flightiness, flippancy, frivolity, giddiness, inconstancy, levity, volatility.

levy *vb* collect, exact, gather, tax; call, muster, raise, summon. * *n* duty, tax.

lewd *adj* despicable, impure, lascivious, libidinous, licentious, loose, lustful, profligate, unchaste, vile, wanton, wicked.

liability *n* accountableness, accountability, duty, obligation, responsibility, tendency; exposedness; debt, indebtedness, obligation.

liable *adj* accountable, amenable, answerable, bound, responsible; exposed, likely, obnoxious, subject.

liaison *n* amour, intimacy, intrigue; connection, relation, union.

libel *vb* calumniate, defame, lampoon, satirize, slander, vilify. * *n* calumny, defamation, lampoon, satire, slander, vilification, vituperation.

liberal *adj* beneficent, bountiful, charitable, disinterested, free, generous, munificent, openhearted, princely, unselfish; broad-minded, catholic, chivalrous, enlarged, high-minded, honourable, magnanimous, tolerant, unbiased, unbigoted; abundant, ample, bounteous, full, large, plentiful, unstinted; humanizing, liberalizing, refined, refining.

liberality *n* beneficence, bountifulness, bounty, charity, disinterestedness, generosity, kindness, munificence; benefaction, donation, gift, gratuity, present; broad-mindedness, catholicity, candour, impartiality, large-mindedness, magnanimity, toleration.

liberate *vb* deliver, discharge, disenthral, emancipate, free, manumit, ransom, release.

libertine *adj* corrupt, depraved, dissolute, licentious, profligate, rakish. * *n* debauchee, lecher, profligate, rake, roue, voluptuary.

liberty *n* emancipation, freedom, independence, liberation, self-direction, self-government; franchise, immunity, privilege; leave, licence, permission.

libidinous *adj* carnal, concupiscent, debauched, impure, incontinent, lascivious, lecherous, lewd, loose, lubricious, lustful, salacious, sensual, unchaste, wanton, wicked.

licence *n* authorization, leave, permission, privilege, right; certificate, charter, dispensation, imprimatur, permit, warrant; anarchy, disorder, freedom, lawlessness, laxity, liberty.

license *vb* allow, authorize, grant, permit, warrant; suffer, tolerate.

licentious *adj* disorderly, riotous, uncontrolled, uncurbed, ungovernable, unrestrained, unruly, wanton; debauched, dissolute, lax, libertine, loose, profligate, rakish; immoral, impure, lascivious, lecherous, lewd, libertine, libidinous, lustful, sensual, unchaste, wicked.

lick *vb* beat, flog, spank, thrash; lap, taste. * *n* blow, slap, stroke; salt-spring.

lie¹ *vb* couch, recline, remain, repose, rest; consist, pertain.

lie² *vb* equivocate, falsify, fib, prevaricate, romance. * *n* equivocation, falsehood, falsification, fib, misrepresentation, prevarication, untruth; delusion, illusion.

lief *adv* freely, gladly, willingly.

life *n* activity, alertness, animation, briskness, energy, sparkle, spirit, sprightliness, verve, vigour, vivacity; behaviour, conduct, deportment; being, duration, existence, lifetime; autobiography, biography, curriculum vitae, memoirs, story.

lifeless *adj* dead, deceased, defunct, extinct, inanimate; cold, dull, flat, frigid, inert, lethargic, passive, pulseless, slow, sluggish, tame, torpid.

lift *vb* elevate, exalt, hoist, raise, uplift. * *n* aid, assistance, help; elevator.

light¹ *vb* alight, land, perch, settle. * *adj* porous, sandy, spongy, well-leavened; loose, sandy; free, portable, unburdened, unencumbered; inconsiderable, moderate, negligible, slight, small, trifling, trivial, unimportant; ethereal, feathery, flimsy, gossamer, insubstantial, weightless; easy, effortless, facile; fickle, frivolous, unsettled, unsteady, volatile; airy, buoyant, carefree, lighthearted, lightsome; unaccented, unstressed, weak.

light² *vb* conflagrate, fire, ignite, inflame, kindle; brighten, illume, illuminate, illumine, luminate, irradiate, lighten. * *adj* bright, clear, fair, lightsome, luminous, pale, pearly, whitish. * *n* dawn, day, daybreak, sunrise; blaze, brightness, effulgence, gleam, illumination, luminosity, phosphorescence, radiance, ray; candle, lamp, lantern, lighthouse, taper, torch; comprehension, enlightenment, information, insight, instruction, knowledge; elucidation, explanation, illustration; attitude, construction, interpretation, observation, reference, regard, respect, view.

lighten¹ *vb* allay, alleviate, ease, mitigate, palliate; disburden, disencumber, relieve, unburden, unload.

lighten² *vb* brighten, gleam, shine; light, illume, illuminate, illumine, irradiate; enlighten, inform; emit, flash.

light-headed *adj* dizzy, giddy, vertiginous; confused, delirious, wandering; addle-pated, frivolous, giddy, heedless, indiscreet, light, rattlebrained, thoughtless, volatile.

light-hearted *adj* blithe, blithesome, carefree, cheerful, frolicsome, gay, glad, gladsome, gleeful, happy, jocund, jovial, joyful, lightsome, merry.

lightness *n* flightiness, frivolity, giddiness, levity, volatility; agility, buoyancy, facility.

like¹ *vb* approve, please; cherish, enjoy, love, relish; esteem, fancy, regard; choose, desire, elect, list, prefer, select, wish. * *n* liking, partiality, preference.

like² *adj* alike, allied, analogous, cognate, corresponding, parallel, resembling, similar; equal, same; likely, probable. * *adv* likely, probably. * *n* counterpart, equal, match, peer, twin.

likelihood *n* probability, verisimilitude.

likely *adj* credible, liable, possible, probable; agreeable, appropriate, convenient, likable, pleasing, suitable, well-adapted, well-suited. * *adv* doubtlessly, presumably, probably.

likeness *n* appearance, form, parallel, resemblance, semblance, similarity, similitude; copy, counterpart, effigy, facsimile, image, picture, portrait, representation.

liking *n* desire, fondness, partiality, wish; appearance, bent, bias, disposition, inclination, leaning, penchant, predisposition, proneness, propensity, tendency, turn.

limb *n* arm, extremity, leg, member; bough, branch, offshoot.

limit *vb* bound, circumscribe, define; check, condition, hinder, restrain, restrict. * *n* bound, boundary, bourn, confine, frontier, march, precinct, term, termination, terminus; check, hindrance, obstruction, restraint, restriction.

limitation *n* check, constraint, restraint, restriction.

limitless *adj* boundless, endless, eternal, illimitable, immeasurable, infinite, never-ending, unbounded, undefined, unending, unlimited.

limp[1] *vb* halt, hitch, hobble, totter. * *n* hitch, hobble, shamble, shuffle, totter.

limp[2] *adj* drooping, droopy, floppy, sagging, weak; flabby, flaccid, flexible, limber, pliable, relaxed, slack, soft.

limpid *adj* bright, clear, crystal, crystalline, lucid, pellucid, pure, translucent, transparent.

line *vb* align, line up, range, rank, regiment; border, bound, edge, fringe, hem, interline, march, rim, verge; seam, stripe, streak, striate, trace; carve, chisel, crease, cut, crosshatch; define, delineate, describe. * n mark, streak, stripe; cable, cord, rope, string, thread; rank, row; ancestry, family, lineage, race, succession; course, method; business, calling, employment, job, occupation, post, pursuit.

lineage *n* ancestry, birth, breed, descendants, descent, extraction, family, forebears, forefathers, genealogy, house, line, offspring, progeny, race.

lineament *n* feature, line, outline, trait.

linen *n* cloth, fabric, flax, lingerie.

linger *vb* dally, dawdle, delay, idle, lag, loiter, remain, saunter, stay, tarry, wait.

link *vb* bind, conjoin, connect, fasten, join, tie, unite. * *n* bond, connection, connective, copula, coupler, joint, juncture; division, member, part, piece.

liquefy *vb* dissolve, fuse, melt, thaw.

liquid *adj* fluid; clear, dulcet, flowing, mellifluous, mellifluent, melting, soft. * *n* fluid, liquor.

list[1] *vb* alphabetize, catalogue, chronicle, codify, docket, enumerate, file, index, inventory, record, register, tabulate, tally; enlist, enroll; choose, desire, elect, like, please, prefer, wish. * *n* catalogue, enumeration, index, inventory, invoice, register, roll, schedule, scroll, series, table, tally; border, bound, limit; border, edge, selvedge, strip, stripe; fillet, listel.

list[2] *vb* cant, heel, incline, keel, lean, pitch, tilt, tip. * *n* cant, inclination, incline, leaning, pitch, slope, tilt, tip.

listen *vb* attend, eavesdrop, hark, hear, hearken, heed, obey, observe.

listless *adj* apathetic, careless, heedless, impassive, inattentive, indifferent, indolent, languid, torpid, vacant, supine, thoughtless, vacant.

listlessness *n* apathy, carelessness, heedlessness, impassivity, inattention, indifference, indolence, languidness, languor, supineness, thoughtlessness, torpor, torpidity, vacancy.

literally *adv* actually, really; exactly, precisely, rigorously, strictly.

literary *adj* bookish, book-learned, erudite, instructed, learned, lettered, literate, scholarly, well-read.

literature *n* erudition, learning, letters, lore, writings.

lithe *adj* flexible, flexile, limber, pliable, pliant, supple.

litigation *n* contending, contest, disputing, lawsuit.

litigious *adj* contentious, disputatious, quarrelsome; controvertible, disputable.

litter *vb* derange, disarrange, disorder, scatter, strew; bear. * *n* bedding, couch, palanquin, sedan, stretcher; confusion, disarray, disorder, mess, untidiness; fragments, rubbish, shreds, trash.

little *adj* diminutive, infinitesimal, minute, small, tiny, wee; brief, short, small; feeble, inconsiderable, insignificant, moderate, petty, scanty, slender, slight, trivial, unimportant, weak; contemptible, illiberal, mean, narrow, niggardly, paltry, selfish, stingy. * *n* handful, jot, modicum, pinch, pittance, trifle, whit.

live[1] *vb* be, exist; continue, endure, last, remain, survive; abide, dwell, reside; fare, feed, nourish, subsist, support; continue, lead, pass.

live[2] *adj* alive, animate, living, quick; burning, hot, ignited; bright, brilliant, glowing, lively, vivid; active, animated, earnest, glowing, wide-awake.

livelihood *n* living, maintenance, subsistence, support, sustenance.

liveliness *n* activity, animation, briskness, gaiety, spirit, sprightliness, vivacity.

lively *adj* active, agile, alert, brisk, energetic, nimble, quick, smart, stirring, supple, vigorous, vivacious; airy, animated, blithe, blithesome, buoyant, frolicsome, gleeful, jocund, jolly, merry, spirited, sportive, sprightly, spry; bright, brilliant, clear, fresh, glowing, strong, vivid; dynamic, forcible, glowing, impassioned, intense, keen, nervous, piquant, racy, sparkling, strenuous, vigorous.

living *adj* alive, breathing, existing, live, organic, quick; active, lively, quickening. * *n* livelihood, maintenance, subsistence, support; estate, keeping; benefice.

load *vb* freight, lade; burden, cumber, encumber, oppress, weigh. * *n* burden, freightage, pack, weight; cargo, freight, lading; clog, deadweight, encumbrance, incubus, oppression, pressure.

loafer *n* (*sl*) bum, idler, lounger, vagabond, vagrant.

loath *adj* averse, backward, disinclined, indisposed, reluctant, unwilling.

loathe *vb* abhor, abominate, detest, dislike, hate, recoil.

loathing *n* abhorrence, abomination, antipathy, aversion, detestation, disgust, hatred, horror, repugnance, revulsion.

loathsome *adj* disgusting, nauseating, nauseous, offensive, palling, repulsive, revolting, sickening; abominable, abhorrent, detestable, execrable, hateful, odious, shocking.

local *adj* limited, neighbouring, provincial, regional, restricted, sectional, territorial, topical.

locality *n* location, neighbourhood, place, position, site, situation, spot.

locate *vb* determine, establish, fix, place, set, settle.

lock[1] *vb* bolt, fasten, padlock, seal; confine; clog, impede, restrain, stop; clasp, embrace, encircle, enclose, grapple, hug, join, press. * *n* bolt, fastening, padlock; embrace, grapple, hug.

lock[2] *n* curl, ringlet, tress, tuft.

lodge *vb* deposit, fix, settle; fix, place, plant; accommodate, cover, entertain, harbour, quarter, shelter; abide, dwell, inhabit, live, reside, rest; remain, rest, sojourn, stay, stop. * *n* cabin, cot, cottage, hovel, hut, shed; cave, den, haunt, lair; assemblage, assembly, association club, group, society.

lodging *n* abode, apartment, dwelling, habitation, quarters, residence; cover, harbour, protection, refuge, shelter.

loftiness *n* altitude, elevation, height; arrogance, haughtiness, pride, vanity; dignity, grandeur, sublimity.

lofty *adj* elevated, high, tall, towering; arrogant, haughty, proud; eminent, exalted, sublime; dignified, imposing, majestic, stately.

logical *adj* close, coherent, consistent, dialectical, sound, valid; discriminating, rational, reasoned.

loiter *vb* dally, dawdle, delay, dilly-dally, idle, lag, linger, saunter, stroll, tarry.

loneliness *n* isolation, retirement, seclusion, solitariness, solitude; desolation, dreariness, forlornness.

lonely *adj* apart, dreary, isolated, lonesome, remote, retired, secluded, separate, sequestrated, solitary; alone, lone, companionless, friendless, unaccompanied; deserted, desolate, forlorn, forsaken, withdrawn.

lonesome *adj* cheerless, deserted, desolate, dreary, gloomy, lone, lonely.

long[1] *vb* anticipate, await, expect; aspire, covet, crave, desire, hanker, lust, pine, wish, yearn.

long[2] *adj* drawn-out, extended, extensive, far-reaching, lengthy, prolonged, protracted, stretched; diffuse, long-winded, prolix, tedious, wearisome; backward, behindhand, dilatory, lingering, slack, slow, tardy.

longing *n* aspiration, coveting, craving, desire, hankering, hunger, pining, yearning.

long-suffering *adj* enduring, forbearing, patient. * *n* clemency, endurance, forbearing.

look *vb* behold, examine, notice, see, search; consider, inspect, investigate, observe, study, contemplate, gaze, regard, scan, survey, view; anticipate, await, expect; heed, mind, watch; face, front; appear, seem. * *n* examination, gaze, glance, peep, peer, search; appearance, aspect, complexion; air, aspect, manner, mien.

loophole *n* aperture, crenellation, loop, opening; excuse, plea, pretence, pretext, subterfuge.

loose *vb* free, liberate, release, unbind, undo, unfasten, unlash, unlock, untie; ease, loosen, relax, slacken; detach, disconnect, disengage. * *adj* unbound, unconfined, unfastened, unsewn, untied; disengaged, free, unattached; relaxed; diffuse, diffusive, prolix, rambling, unconnected; ill-defined, indefinite, indeterminate, indistinct, vague; careless, heedless, negligent, lax, slack; debauched, dissolute, immoral, licentious, unchaste, wanton.

loosen *vb* liberate, relax, release, separate, slacken, unbind, unloose, untie.

looseness *n* easiness, slackness; laxity, levity; lewdness, unchastity, wantonness, wickedness; diarrhoea, flux.

loot *vb* pillage, plunder, ransack, rifle, rob, sack. * *n* booty, plunder, spoil.

lop *vb* cut, truncate; crop, curtail, dock, prune; detach, dissever, sever.

loquacious *adj* garrulous, talkative, voluble, wordy; noisy, speaking, talking; babbling, blabbing, tattling, tell-tale.

loquacity *n* babbling, chattering, gabbling, garrulity, loquaciousness, talkativeness, volubility.

lord *n* earl, noble, nobleman, peer, viscount; governor, king, liege, master, monarch, prince, ruler, seigneur, seignior, sovereign, superior; husband, spouse.

lordly *adj* aristocratic, dignified, exalted, grand, lofty, majestic, noble; arrogant, despotic, domineering, haughty, imperious, insolent, masterful, overbearing, proud, tyrannical; large, liberal.

lordship *n* authority, command, control, direction, domination, dominion, empire, government, rule, sovereignty, sway; manor, domain, seigneury, seigniory.

lore *n* erudition, knowledge, learning, letters, scholarship; admonition, advice, counsel, doctrine, instruction, lesson, teaching, wisdom.

lose *vb* deprive, dispossess, forfeit, miss; dislodge, displace, mislay, misspend, squander, waste; decline, fall, succumb, yield.

loss *n* deprivation, failure, forfeiture, privation; casualty, damage, defeat, destruction, detriment, disadvantage, injury, overthrow, ruin; squandering, waste.

lost *adj* astray, missing; forfeited, missed, unredeemed; dissipated, misspent, squandered, wasted; bewildered, confused, distracted, perplexed, puzzled; absent, absent-minded, abstracted, dreamy, napping, preoccupied; abandoned, corrupt, debauched, depraved, dissolute, graceless, hardened, incorrigible, irreclaimable, licentious, profligate, reprobate, shameless, unchaste, wanton; destroyed, ruined.

lot *n* allotment, apportionment, destiny, doom, fate; accident, chance, fate, fortune, hap, haphazard, hazard; division, parcel, part, portion.

loth *adj* averse, disinclined, disliking, reluctant, unwilling

loud *adj* high-sounding, noisy, resounding, sonorous; deafening, stentorian, strong, stunning; boisterous, clamorous, noisy, obstreperous, tumultuous, turbulent, uproarious, vociferous; emphatic, impressive, positive, vehement; flashy, gaudy, glaring, loud, ostentatious, showy, vulgar.

lounge *vb* loll, recline, sprawl; dawdle, idle, loaf, loiter.

love *vb* adore, like, worship. * *n* accord, affection, amity, courtship, delight, fondness, friendship, kindness, regard, tenderness, warmth; adoration, amour, ardour, attachment, passion; devotion, inclination, liking; benevolence, charity, goodwill.

lovely *adj* beautiful, charming, delectable, delightful, enchanting, exquisite, graceful, pleasing, sweet, winning; admirable, adorable, amiable.

loving *adj* affectionate, dear, fond, kind, tender.

low[1] *vb* bellow, moo.

low[2] *adj* basal, depressed, profound; gentle, grave, soft, subdued; cheap, humble, mean, plebeian, vulgar; abject, base, base-minded, degraded, dirty, grovelling, ignoble, low-minded, menial, scurvy, servile, shabby, slavish, vile; derogatory, disgraceful, dishonourable, disreputable, unbecoming, undignified, ungentlemanly, unhandsome, unmanly; exhausted, feeble, reduced, weak; frugal, plain, poor, simple, spare; lowly, reverent, submissive; dejected, depressed, dispirited.

lower[1] *vb* depress, drop, sink, subside; debase, degrade, disgrace, humble, humiliate, reduce; abate, decrease, diminish, lessen. * *adj* baser, inferior, less, lesser, shorter, smaller; subjacent, under.

lower[2] *vb* blacken, darken, frown, glower, threaten.

lowering *adj* dark, clouded, cloudy, lurid, murky, overcast, threatening.

lowliness *n* humbleness, humility, meekness, self-abasement, submissiveness.

lowly *adj* gentle, humble, meek, mild, modest, plain, poor, simple, unassuming, unpretending, unpretentious; low-born, mean, servile.

loyal *adj* constant, devoted, faithful, patriotic, true.

loyalty *n* allegiance, constancy, devotion, faithfulness, fealty, fidelity, patriotism.

lubricious *adj* slippery, smooth; uncertain, unstable, wavering; impure, incontinent, lascivious, lecherous, lewd, libidinous, licentious, lustful, salacious, unchaste, wanton.

lucid *adj* beaming, bright, brilliant, luminous, radiant, resplendent, shining, clear, crystalline, diaphanous, limpid, lucent, pellucid, pure, transparent; clear, distinct, evident, intelligible, obvious, perspicuous, plain; reasonable, sane, sober, sound.

luck *n* accident, casualty, chance, fate, fortune, hap, haphazard, hazard, serendipity, success.

luckless *adj* ill-fated, ill-starred, unfortunate, unhappy, unlucky, unpropitious, unprosperous, unsuccessful.

lucky *adj* blessed, favoured, fortunate, happy, successful; auspicious, favourable, propitious, prosperous.

lucrative *adj* advantageous, gainful, paying, profitable, remunerative.

ludicrous *adj* absurd, burlesque, comic, comical, droll, farcical, funny, laughable, odd, ridiculous, sportive.

lugubrious *adj* complaining, doleful, gloomy, melancholy, mournful, sad, serious, sombre, sorrowful.

lukewarm *adj* blood-warm, tepid, thermal; apathetic, cold, dull, indifferent, listless, unconcerned, torpid.

lull *vb* calm, compose, hush, quiet, still, tranquillize; abate, cease, decrease, diminish, subside. * *n* calm, calmness, cessation.

lumber[1] *vb* rumble, shamble, trudge.

lumber[2] *n* refuse, rubbish, trash, trumpery; wood.

luminous *adj* effulgent, incandescent, radiant, refulgent, resplendent, shining; bright, brilliant, clear; clear, lucid, lucent, perspicuous, plain.

lunacy *n* aberration, craziness, dementia, derangement, insanity, madness, mania.

lunatic *adj* crazy, demented, deranged, insane, mad, psychopathic. * *n* madman, maniac, psychopath.

lurch *vb* appropriate, filch, pilfer, purloin, steal; deceive, defeat, disappoint, evade; ambush, lurk, skulk; contrive, dodge, shift, trick; pitch, sway.

lure *vb* allure, attract, decoy, entice, inveigle, seduce, tempt. * *n* allurement, attraction, bait, decoy, enticement, temptation.

lurid *adj* dismal, ghastly, gloomy, lowering, murky, pale, wan; glaring, sensational, startling, unrestrained.

lurk *vb* hide, prowl, skulk, slink, sneak, snoop.

luscious *adj* delicious, delightful, grateful, palatable, pleasing, savoury, sweet.

lush *adj* fresh, juicy, luxuriant, moist, sappy, succulent, watery.

lust *vb* covet, crave, desire, hanker, need, want, yearn. * *n* cupidity, desire, longing; carnality, concupiscence, lasciviousness, lechery, lewdness, lubricity, salaciousness, salacity, wantonness.

lustful *adj* carnal, concupiscent, hankering, lascivious, lecherous, licentious, libidinous, lubricious, salacious.

lustily *adv* strongly, vigorously.

lustiness *n* hardihood, power, robustness, stoutness, strength, sturdiness, vigour.

lustre *n* brightness, brilliance, brilliancy, splendour.

lusty *adj* healthful, lively, robust, stout, strong, sturdy, vigorous; bulky, burly, corpulent, fat, large, stout.

luxuriance *n* exuberance, profusion, superabundance.

luxuriant *adj* exuberant, plenteous, plentiful, profuse, superabundant.

luxuriate *vb* abound, delight, enjoy, flourish, indulge, revel.

luxurious *adj* epicurean, opulent, pampered, self-indulgent, sensual, sybaritic, voluptuous.

luxury *n* epicureanism, epicurism, luxuriousness, opulence, sensuality, voluptuousness; delight, enjoyment, gratification, indulgence, pleasure; dainty, delicacy, treat.

lying *adj* equivocating, false, mendacious, untruthful, untrue.

lyric *adj* dulcet, euphonious, lyrical, mellifluous, mellifluent, melodic, melodious, musical, poetic, silvery, tuneful.

lyrical *adj* ecstatic, enthusiastic, expressive, impassion; dulcet, lyric, mellifluous, mellifluent, melodic, melodious, musical, poetic.

M

macabre *adj* cadaverous, deathlike, deathly, dreadful, eerie, frightening, frightful, ghoulish, grim, grisly, gruesome, hideous, horrid, morbid, unearthly, weird.

mace *n* baton, staff, truncheon.

macerate *vb* harass, mortify, torture; digest, soak, soften, steep.

Machiavellian *adj* arch, artful, astute, crafty, crooked, cunning, deceitful, designing, diplomatic, insidious, intriguing, shrewd, sly, subtle, tricky, wily.

machination *n* artifice, cabal, conspiracy, contrivance, design, intrigue, plot, scheme, stratagem, trick.

machine *n* instrument, puppet, tool; machinery, organization, system; engine.

mad *adj* crazed, crazy, delirious, demented, deranged, distracted, insane, irrational, lunatic, maniac, maniacal; enraged, furious, rabid, raging, violent; angry, enraged, exasperated, furious, incensed, provoked, wrathful; distracted, infatuated, wild; frantic, frenzied, raving.

madden *vb* annoy, craze, enrage, exasperate, inflame, infuriate, irritate, provoke.

madness *n* aberration, craziness, dementia, derangement, insanity, lunacy, mania; delirium, frenzy, fury, rage.

magazine *n* depository, depot, entrepot, receptacle, repository, storehouse, warehouse; pamphlet, paper, periodical.

magic *adj* bewitching, charming, enchanting, fascinating, magical, miraculous, spellbinding. * *n* conjuring, enchantment, necromancy, sorcery, thaumaturgy, voodoo, witchcraft; char, fascination, witchery.

magician *n* conjurer, enchanter, juggler, magus, necromancer, shaman, sorcerer, wizard.

magisterial *adj* august, dignified, majestic, pompous; authoritative, despotic, domineering, imperious, dictatorial.

magnanimity *n* chivalry, disinterestedness, forbearance, high-mindedness, generosity, nobility.

magnificence *n* brilliance, éclat, grandeur, luxuriousness, luxury, majesty, pomp, splendour.

magnificent *adj* elegant, grand, majestic, noble, splendid, superb; brilliant, gorgeous, imposing, lavish, luxurious, pompous, showy, stately.

magnify *vb* amplify, augment, enlarge; bless, celebrate, elevate, exalt, extol, glorify, laud, praise; exaggerate.

magnitude *n* bulk, dimension, extent, mass, size, volume; consequence, greatness, importance; grandeur, loftiness, sublimity.

maid *n* damsel, girl, lass, lassie, maiden, virgin; maidservant, servant.

maiden *adj* chaste, pure, undefiled, virgin; fresh, new, unused. * *n* girl, maid, virgin.

maidenly *adj* demure, gentle, modest, maidenlike, reserved.

maim *vb* cripple, disable, disfigure, mangle, mar, mutilate. * *n* crippling, disfigurement, mutilation; harm, hurt, injury, mischief.

main[1] *adj* capital, cardinal, chief, leading, principal; essential, important, indispensable, necessary, requisite, vital; enormous, huge, mighty, vast; pure, sheer; absolute, direct, entire, mere. * *n* channel, pipe; force, might, power, strength, violence.

main[2] *n* high seas, ocean; continent, mainland.

maintain *vb* keep, preserve, support, sustain, uphold; hold, possess; defend, vindicate, justify; carry on, continue, keep up; feed, provide, supply; allege, assert, declare; affirm, aver, contend, hold, say.

maintenance *n* defence, justification, preservation, support, sustenance, vindication; bread, food, livelihood, provisions, subsistence, sustenance, victuals.

majestic *adj* august, dignified, imperial, imposing, lofty, noble, pompous, princely, stately, regal, royal; grand, magnificent, splendid, sublime.

majesty *n* augustness, dignity, elevation, grandeur, loftiness, stateliness.

majority *n* bulk, greater, mass, more, most, plurality, preponderance, superiority; adulthood, manhood.

make *vb* create; fashion, figure, form, frame, mould, shape; cause, construct, effect, establish, fabricate, produce; do, execute, perform, practice; acquire, gain, get, raise, secure; cause, compel, constrain, force, occasion; compose, constitute; go, journey, move, proceed, tend, travel; conduce, contribute, effect, favour, operate; estimate, judge, reckon, suppose, think. * *n* brand, build, constitution, construction, form, shape, structure.

maker *n* creator, god; builder, constructor, fabricator, framer, manufacturer; author, composer, poet, writer.

maladministration *n* malversation, misgovernment, misrule.

maladroit *adj* awkward, bungling, clumsy, inept, inexpert, unhandy, unskilful, unskilled.

malady *n* affliction, ailment, complaint, disease, disorder, illness, indisposition, sickness.

malcontent *adj* discontented, dissatisfied, insurgent, rebellious, resentful, uneasy, unsatisfied. * *n* agitator, complainer, fault-finder, grumbler, spoilsport.

malediction *n* anathema, ban, curse, cursing, denunciation, execration, imprecation, malison.

malefactor *n* convict, criminal, culprit, delinquent, evildoer, felon, offender, outlaw.

malevolence *n* hate, hatred, ill-will, malice, malignity, rancour, spite, spitefulness, vindictiveness.

malevolent *adj* evil-minded, hateful, hostile, ill-natured, malicious, malignant, mischievous, rancorous, spiteful, venomous. vindictive.

malice *n* animosity, bitterness, enmity, grudge, hate, ill-will, malevolence, maliciousness, malignity, pique, rancour, spite, spitefulness, venom, vindictiveness.

malicious *adj* bitter, envious, evil-minded, ill-disposed, ill-natured, invidious, malevolent, malignant, mischievous, rancorous, resentful, spiteful, vicious.

malign *vb* abuse, asperse, blacken, calumniate, defame, disparage, revile, scandalize, slander, traduce, vilify. * *adj* malevolent, malicious, malignant, ill-disposed; baneful, injurious, pernicious, unfavourable, unpropitious.

malignant *adj* bitter, envious, hostile, inimical, malevolent, malicious, malign, spiteful, rancorous, resentful, virulent; heinous, pernicious; ill-boding, unfavourable, unpropitious; dangerous, fatal.

malignity *n* animosity, hatred, ill-will, malice, malevolence, maliciousness, rancour, spite; deadliness, destructiveness, fatality, harmfulness, malignancy, perniciousness, virulence; enormity, evilness, heinousness.

malpractice *n* dereliction, malversation, misbehaviour, misconduct, misdeed, misdoing, sin, transgression.

maltreat *vb* abuse, harm, hurt, ill-treat, ill-use, injure.

mammoth *adj* colossal, enormous, gigantic, huge, immense, vast.

man *vb* crew, garrison, furnish; fortify, reinforce, strengthen. * *n* adult, being, body, human, individual, one, person, personage, somebody, soul; humanity, humankind, mankind; attendant, butler, dependant, liege, servant, subject, valet, vassal; employee, workman.

manacle *vb* bind, chain, fetter, handcuff, restrain, shackle, tie. * *n* bond, chain, handcuff, gyve, hand-fetter, shackle.

manage *vb* administer, conduct, direct, guide, handle, operate, order, regulate, superintend, supervise, transact, treat; control, govern, rule; handle, manipulate, train, wield; contrive, economize, husband, save.

manageable *adj* controllable, docile, easy, governable, tamable, tractable.

management *n* administration, care, charge, conduct, control, direction, disposal, economy, government, guidance, superintendence, supervision, surveillance, treatment.

manager *n* comptroller, conductor, director, executive, governor, impresario, overseer, superintendent, supervisor.

mandate *n* charge, command, commission, edict, injunction, order, precept, requirement.

manful *adj* bold, brave, courageous, daring, heroic, honourable, intrepid, noble, stout, strong, undaunted, vigorous.

mangily *adv* basely, foully, meanly, scabbily, scurvily, vilely.

mangle[1] *vb* hack, lacerate, mutilate, rend, tear; cripple, crush, destroy, maim, mar, spoil.

mangle[2] *vb* calender, polish, press, smooth.

manhood *n* virility; bravery, courage, firmness, fortitude, hardihood, manfulness, manliness, resolution; human nature, humanity; adulthood, maturity.

mania *n* aberration, craziness, delirium, dementia, derangement, frenzy, insanity, lunacy, madness; craze, desire, enthusiasm, fad, fanaticism.

manifest *vb* declare, demonstrate, disclose, discover, display, evidence, evince, exhibit, express, reveal, show. * *adj* apparent, clear, conspicuous, distinct, evident, glaring, indubitable, obvious, open, palpable, patent, plain, unmistakable, visible.

manifestation *n* disclosure, display, exhibition, exposure, expression, revelation.

manifold *adj* complex, diverse, many, multifarious, multiplied, multitudinous, numerous, several, sundry, varied, various.

manipulate *vb* handle, operate, work.

manliness *n* boldness, bravery, courage, dignity, fearlessness, firmness, heroism, intrepidity, nobleness, resolution, valour.

manly *adj* bold, brave, courageous, daring, dignified, firm, heroic, intrepid, manful, noble, stout, strong, undaunted, vigorous; male, masculine, virile.

manner *n* fashion, form, method, mode, style, way; custom, habit, practice; degree, extent, measure; kind, kinds, sort, sorts; air, appearance, aspect, behaviour, carriage, demeanour, deportment, look, mien; mannerism, peculiarity; behaviour, conduct, habits, morals; civility, deportment.

mannerly *adj* ceremonious, civil, complaisant, courteous, polite, refined, respectful, urbane, well-behaved, well-bred.

manners *npl* conduct, habits, morals; air, bearing, behaviour, breeding, carriage, comportment, deportment, etiquette.

manoeuvre *vb* contrive, finesse, intrigue, manage, plan, plot, scheme. * *n* evolution, exercise, movement, operation; artifice, finesse, intrigue, plan, plot, ruse, scheme, stratagem, trick.

mansion *n* abode, dwelling, dwelling house, habitation, hall, residence, seat.

mantle *vb* cloak, cover, discover, obscure; expand, spread; bubble, cream, effervesce, foam, froth, sparkle. * *n* chasuble, cloak, toga; cover, covering, hood.

manufacture *vb* build, compose, construct, create, fabricate, forge, form, make, mould, produce, shape. * *n* constructing, fabrication, making, production.

manumission *n* deliverance, emancipation, enfranchisement, freedom, liberation, release.

manumit *vb* deliver, emancipate, enfranchise, free, liberate, release.

manure *vb* enrich, fertilize. * *n* compost, dressing, fertilizer, guano, muck.

many *adj* abundant, diverse, frequent, innumerable, manifold, multifarious, multifold, multiplied, multitudinous, numerous, sundry, varied, various. * *n* crowd, multitude, people.

map *vb* chart, draw up, plan, plot, set out, sketch. * *n* chart, diagram, outline, plot, sketch.

mar *vb* blot, damage, harm, hurt, impair, injure, ruin, spoil, stain; deface, deform, disfigure, maim, mutilate.

marauder *n* bandit, brigand, desperado, filibuster, freebooter, outlaw, pillager, plunderer, ravager, robber, rover.

march *vb* go, pace, parade, step, tramp, walk. * *n* hike, tramp, walk; parade, procession; gait, step, stride; advance, evolution, progress.

marches *npl* borders, boundaries, confines, frontiers, limits, precincts.

margin *n* border, brim, brink, confine, edge, limit, rim, skirt, verge; latitude, room, space, surplus.

marine *adj* oceanic, pelagic, saltwater, sea; maritime, naval, nautical. * *n* navy, shipping; sea-dog, sea soldier, soldier; sea piece, seascape.

mariner *n* navigator, sailor, salt, seafarer, seaman, tar.

marital *adj* connubial, conjugal, matrimonial.

maritime *adj* marine, naval, nautical, oceanic, sea, seafaring, seagoing; coastal, seaside.

mark *vb* distinguish, earmark, label; betoken, brand, characterize, denote, designate, engrave, impress, imprint, indicate, print, stamp; evince, heed, note, notice, observe, regard, remark, show, spot. * *n* brand, character, characteristic, impression, impress, line, note, print, sign, stamp, symbol, token, race; evidence, indication, proof, symptom, trace, track, vestige; badge; footprint; bull's-eye, butt, object, target; consequence, distinction, eminence, fame, importance, notability, position, preeminence, reputation, significance.

marked *adj* conspicuous, distinguished, eminent, notable, noted, outstanding, prominent, remarkable.

marriage *n* espousals, nuptials, spousals, wedding; matrimony, wedlock; union; alliance, association, confederation.

marrow *n* medulla, pith; cream, essence, quintessence, substance.

marsh *n* bog, fen, mire, morass, quagmire, slough, swamp.

marshal *vb* arrange, array, dispose, gather, muster, range, order, rank; guide, herald, lead. * *n* conductor, director, master of ceremonies, regulator; harbinger, herald, pursuivant.

marshy *adj* boggy, miry, mossy, swampy, wet.

martial *adj* brave, heroic, military, soldier-like, warlike.

marvel *vb* gape, gaze, goggle, wonder. * *n* miracle, prodigy, wonder; admiration, amazement, astonishment, surprise.

marvellous *adj* amazing, astonishing, extraordinary, miraculous, prodigious, strange, stupendous, wonderful, wondrous; improbable, incredible, surprising, unbelievable.

masculine *adj* bold, hardy, manful, manlike, manly, mannish, virile; potent, powerful, robust, strong, vigorous; bold, coarse, forward.

mask *vb* cloak, conceal, cover, disguise, hide, screen, shroud, veil. * *n* blind, cloak, disguise, screen, veil; evasion, pretence, plea, pretext, ruse, shift, subterfuge, trick; masquerade; bustle, mummery.

masquerade *vb* cover, disguise, hide, mask, revel, veil. * *n* mask, mummery, revel, revelry.

Mass *n* communion, Eucharist.

mass *vb* accumulate, amass, assemble, collect, gather, rally, throng. * *adj* extensive, general, large-scale, widespread. * *n* cake, clot, lump; assemblage, collection, combination, congeries, heap; bulk, dimension, magnitude, size; accumulation, aggregate, body, sum, total, totality, whole.

massacre *vb* annihilate, butcher, exterminate, kill, murder, slaughter, slay. * *n* annihilation, butchery, carnage, extermination, killing, murder, pogrom, slaughter.

massive *adj* big, bulky, colossal, enormous, heavy, huge, immense, ponderous, solid, substantial, vast, weighty.

master *vb* conquer, defeat, direct, govern, overcome, overpower, rule, subdue, subjugate, vanquish; acquire, learn. * *adj* cardinal, chief, especial, grand, great, main, leading, prime, principal; adept, expert, proficient. * *n* director, governor, lord, manager, overseer, superintendent, ruler; captain, commander; instructor, pedagogue, preceptor, schoolteacher, teacher, tutor; holder, owner, possessor, proprietor; chief, head, leader, principal.

masterly *adj* adroit, clever, dextrous, excellent, expert, finished, skilful, skilled; arbitrary, despotic, despotical, domineering, imperious.

mastery *n* command, dominion, mastership, power, rule, supremacy, sway; ascendancy, conquest, leadership, preeminence, superiority, upper-hand, victory; acquisition, acquirement, attainment; ability, cleverness, dexterity, proficiency, skill.

masticate *vb* chew, eat, munch.

match *vb* equal, rival; adapt, fit, harmonize, proportion, suit; marry, mate; combine, couple, join, sort; oppose, pit; correspond, suit, tally. * *n* companion, equal, mate, tally; competition, contest, game, trial; marriage, union.

matchless *adj* consummate, excellent, exquisite, incomparable, inimitable, peerless, perfect, surpassing, unequalled, unmatched, unparalleled, unrivalled.

mate *vb* marry, match, wed; compete, equal, vie; appal, confound, crush, enervate, subdue, stupefy. * *n* associate, companion, compeer, consort, crony, friend, fellow, intimate; companion, equal, match; assistant, subordinate; husband, spouse, wife.

material *adj* bodily, corporeal, nonspiritual, physical, temporal; essential, important, momentous, relevant, vital, weighty. * *n* body, element, stuff, substance.

maternal *adj* motherlike, motherly.

matrimonial *adj* conjugal, connubial, espousal, hymeneal, marital, nuptial, spousal.

matrimony *n* marriage, wedlock.

matter *vb* import, signify, weigh. * *n* body, content, sense, substance; difficulty, distress, trouble; material, stuff; question, subject, subject matter, topic; affair, business, concern, event; consequence, import, importance, moment, significance; discharge, purulence, pus.

mature *vb* develop, perfect, ripen. * *adj* complete, fit, full-grown, perfect, ripe; completed, prepared, ready, well-considered, well-digested.

maturity *n* completeness, completion, matureness, perfection, ripeness.

mawkish *adj* disgusting, flat, insipid, nauseous, sickly, stale, tasteless, vapid; emotional, feeble, maudlin, sentimental.

maxim *n* adage, aphorism, apothegm, axiom, byword, dictum, proverb, saw, saying, truism.

maze *vb* amaze, bewilder, confound, confuse, perplex. * *n* intricacy, labyrinth, meander; bewilderment, embarrassment, intricacy, perplexity, puzzle, uncertainty.

mazy *adj* confused, confusing, intricate, labyrinthian, labyrinthic, labyrinthine, perplexing, winding.

meagre *adj* emaciated, gaunt, lank, lean, poor, skinny, starved, spare, thin; barren, poor, sterile, unproductive; bald, barren, dry, dull, mean, poor, prosy, feeble, insignificant, jejune, scanty, small, tame, uninteresting, vapid.

mean[1] *vb* contemplate, design, intend, purpose; connote, denote, express, imply, import, indicate, purport, signify, symbolize.

mean[2] *adj* average, medium, middle; intermediate, intervening. * *n* measure, mediocrity, medium, moderation; average; agency, instrument, instrumentality, means, measure, method, mode, way.

mean[3] *adj* coarse, common, humble, ignoble, low, ordinary, plebeian, vulgar; abject, base, base-minded, beggarly, contemptible, degraded, dirty, dishonourable, disingenuous, grovelling, low-minded, pitiful, rascally, scurvy, servile, shabby, sneaking, sorry, spiritless, unfair, vile; illiberal, mercenary, miserly, narrow, narrow-minded, niggardly, parsimonious, penurious, selfish, sordid, stingy, ungenerous, unhandsome; contemptible, despicable, diminutive, insignificant, paltry, petty, poor, small, wretched.

meaning *n* acceptation, drift, import, intention, purport, purpose, sense, signification.

means *npl* instrument, method, mode, way; appliance, expedient, measure, resource, shift, step; estate, income, property, resources, revenue, substance, wealth, wherewithal.

measure *vb* mete; adjust, gauge, proportion; appraise, appreciate, estimate, gauge, value. * *n* gauge, meter, rule, standard; degree, extent, length, limit; allotment, share, proportion; means, step; foot, metre, rhythm, tune, verse.

measureless *adj* boundless, endless, immeasurable, immense, limitless, unbounded, unlimited, vast.

meat *n* aliment, cheer, diet, fare, feed, flesh, food, nourishment, nutriment, provision, rations, regimen, subsistence, sustenance, viands, victuals.

mechanic *n* artificer, artisan, craftsman, hand, handicraftsman, machinist, operative, workman.

meddle *vb* interfere, intermeddle, interpose, intrude.

meddlesome *adj* interfering, intermeddling, intrusive, officious, prying.

mediate *vb* arbitrate, intercede, interpose, intervene, settle. * *adj* interposed, intervening, middle.

mediation *n* arbitration, intercession, interposition, intervention.

mediator *n* advocate, arbitrator, interceder, intercessor, propitiator, umpire.

medicine *n* drug, medicament, medication, physic; therapy.

mediocre *adj* average, commonplace, indifferent, mean, medium, middling, ordinary.

meditate *vb* concoct, contrive, design, devise, intend, plan, purpose, scheme; chew, contemplate, ruminate, study; cogitate, muse, ponder, think.

meditation *n* cogitation, contemplation, musing, pondering, reflection, ruminating, study, thought.

meditative *adj* contemplative, pensive, reflective, studious, thoughtful.

medium *adj* average, mean, mediocre, middle. * *n* agency, channel, intermediary, instrument, instrumentality, means, organ; conditions, environment, influences; average, means.

medley *n* confusion, farrago, hodgepodge, hotchpotch, jumble, mass, melange, miscellany, mishmash, mixture.

meed *n* award, guerdon, premium, prize, recompense, remuneration, reward.

meek *adj* gentle, humble, lowly, mild, modest, pacific, soft, submissive, unassuming, yielding.

meekness *n* gentleness, humbleness, humility, lowliness, mildness, modesty, submission, submissiveness.

meet *vb* cross, intersect, transact; confront, encounter, engage; answer, comply, fulfil, gratify, satisfy; converge, join, unite; assemble, collect, convene, congregate, forgather, muster, rally. * *adj* adapted, appropriate, befitting, convenient, fit, fitting, proper, qualified, suitable, suited.

meeting *n* encounter, interview; assemblage, assembly, audience, company, concourse, conference, congregation, convention, gathering; assignation, encounter, introduction, rendezvous; confluence, conflux, intersection, joining, junction, union; collision.

melancholy *adj* blue, dejected, depressed, despondent, desponding, disconsolate, dismal, dispirited, doleful, down, downcast, downhearted, gloomy, glum, hypochondriac, low-spirited, lugubrious, moody, mopish, sad, sombre, sorrowful, unhappy; afflictive, calamitous, unfortunate, unlucky; dark, gloomy, grave, quiet. * *n* blues, dejection, depression, despondency, dismals, dumps, gloom, gloominess, hypochondria, sadness, vapours.

melee *n* affray, brawl, broil, contest, fight, fray, scuffle.

mellifluous, mellifluent *adj* dulcet, euphonic, euphonical, euphonious, mellow, silver-toned, silvery, smooth, soft, sweet.

mellow *vb* mature, ripen; improve, smooth, soften, tone; pulverize; perfect. * *adj* mature, ripe; dulcet, mellifluous, mellifluent, rich, silver-toned, silvery, smooth, soft; delicate; genial, good-humoured, jolly, jovial, matured, softened; mellowy, loamy, unctuous; perfected, well-prepared; disguised, fuddled, intoxicated, tipsy.

melodious *adj* arioso, concordant, dulcet, euphonious, harmonious, mellifluous, mellifluent, musical, silvery, sweet, tuneful.

melody *n* air, descant, music, plainsong, song, theme, tune.

melt *vb* dissolve, fuse, liquefy, thaw; mollify, relax, soften, subdue; dissipate, waste; blend, pass, shade.

member *n* arm, leg, limb, organ; component, constituent, element, part, portion; branch, clause, division, head.

memento *n* memorial, remembrance, reminder, souvenir.

memoir *n* account, autobiography, biography, journal, narrative, record, register.

memorable *adj* celebrated, distinguished, extraordinary, famous, great, illustrious, important, notable, noteworthy, remarkable, signal, significant.

memorandum *n* minute, note, record.

memorial *adj* commemorative, monumental. * *n* cairn, commemoration, memento, monument, plaque, record, souvenir; memorandum, remembrance.

memory *n* recollection, remembrance, reminiscence; celebrity, fame, renown, reputation; commemoration, memorial.

menace *vb* alarm, frighten, intimidate, threaten. * *n* danger, hazard, peril, threat, warning; nuisance, pest, troublemaker.

menage *n* household, housekeeping, management.

mend *vb* darn, patch, rectify, refit, repair, restore, retouch; ameliorate, amend, better, correct, emend, improve, meliorate, reconcile, rectify, reform; advance, help; augment, increase.

mendacious *adj* deceitful, deceptive, fallacious, false, lying, untrue, untruthful.

mendacity *n* deceit, deceitfulness, deception, duplicity, falsehood, lie, untruth.

mendicant *n* beggar, pauper, tramp.

menial *adj* base, low, mean, servile, vile. * *n* attendant, bondsman, domestic, flunkey, footman, lackey, serf, servant, slave, underling, valet, waiter.

mensuration *n* measurement, measuring; survey, surveying.

mental *adj* ideal, immaterial, intellectual, psychiatric, subjective.

mention *vb* acquaint, allude, cite, communicate, declare, disclose, divulge, impart, inform, name, report, reveal, state, tell. * *n* allusion, citation, designation, notice, noting, reference.

mentor *n* adviser, counsellor, guide, instructor, monitor.

mephitic *adj* baleful, baneful, fetid, foul, mephitical, noisome, noxious, poisonous, pestilential.

mercantile *adj* commercial, marketable, trading.

mercenary *adj* hired, paid, purchased, venal; avaricious, covetous, grasping, mean, niggardly, parsimonious, penurious, sordid, stingy. * *n* hireling, soldier.

merchandise *n* commodities, goods, wares.

merchant *n* dealer, retailer, shopkeeper, trader, tradesman.

merciful *adj* clement, compassionate, forgiving, gracious, lenient, pitiful; benignant, forbearing, gentle, humane, kind, mild, tender, tenderhearted.

merciless *adj* barbarous, callous, cruel, fell, hardhearted, inexorable, pitiless, relentless, remorseless, ruthless, savage, severe, uncompassionate, unfeeling, unmerciful, unrelenting, unrepenting, unsparing.

mercurial *adj* active, lively, nimble, prompt, quick, sprightly; cheerful, light-hearted; changeable, fickle, flighty, inconstant, mobile, volatile.

mercy *n* benevolence, clemency, compassion, gentleness, kindness, lenience, leniency, lenity, mildness, pity, tenderness; blessing, favour, grace; discretion, disposal; forgiveness, pardon.

mere *adj* bald, bare, naked, plain, sole, simple; absolute, entire, pure, sheer, unmixed. * *n* lake, pond, pool.

meretricious *adj* deceitful, brummagem, false,

gaudy, make-believe, sham, showy, spurious, tawdry.

merge *vb* bury, dip, immerse, involve, lose, plunge, sink, submerge.

meridian *n* acme, apex, climax, culmination, summit, zenith; midday, noon, noontide.

merit *vb* deserve, earn, incur; acquire, gain, profit, value. * *n* claim, right; credit, desert, excellence, goodness, worth, worthiness.

meritorious *adj* commendable, deserving, excellent, good, worthy.

merriment *n* amusement, frolic, gaiety, hilarity, jocularity, jollity, joviality, laughter, liveliness, mirth, sport, sportiveness.

merry *adj* agreeable, brisk, delightful, exhilarating, lively, pleasant, stirring; airy, blithe, blithesome, buxom, cheerful, comical, droll, facetious, frolicsome, gladsome, gleeful, hilarious, jocund, jolly, jovial, joyous, light-hearted, lively, mirthful, sportive, sprightly, vivacious.

mess *n* company, set; farrago, hodgepodge, hotchpotch, jumble, medley, mass, melange, miscellany, mishmash, mixture; confusion, muddle, perplexity, pickle, plight, predicament.

message *n* communication, dispatch, intimation, letter, missive, notice, telegram, wire, word.

messenger *n* carrier, courier, emissary, envoy, express, mercury, nuncio; forerunner, harbinger, herald, precursor.

metamorphic *adj* changeable, mutable, variable.

metamorphose *vb* change, mutate, transfigure, transform, transmute.

metamorphosis *n* change, mutation, transfiguration, transformation, transmutation.

metaphorical *adj* allegorical, figurative, symbolic, symbolical.

metaphysical *adj* abstract, allegorical, figurative, general, intellectual, parabolic, subjective, unreal.

mete *vb* dispense, distribute, divide, measure, ration, share. * *n* bound, boundary, butt, limit, measure, term, terminus.

meteor *n* aerolite, falling star, shooting star.

method *n* course, manner, means, mode, procedure, process, rule, way; arrangement, classification, disposition, order, plan, regularity, scheme, system.

methodical *adj* exact, orderly, regular, systematic, systematical.

metropolis *n* capital, city, conurbation.

mettle *n* constitution, element, material, stuff; character, disposition, spirit, temper; ardour, courage, fire, hardihood, life, nerve, pluck, sprightliness, vigour.

mettlesome *adj* ardent, brisk, courageous, fiery, frisky, high-spirited, lively, spirited, sprightly.

mew *vb* confine, coop, encase, enclose, imprison; cast, change, mould, shed.

microscopic *adj* infinitesimal, minute, tiny.

middle *adj* central, halfway, mean, medial, mid; intermediate, intervening. * *n* centre, halfway, mean, midst.

middleman *n* agent, broker, factor, go-between, intermediary.

mien *n* air, appearance, aspect, bearing, behaviour, carriage, countenance, demeanour, deportment, look, manner.

might *n* ability, capacity, efficacy, efficiency, force, main, power, prowess, puissance, strength.

mighty *adj* able, bold, courageous, potent, powerful, puissant, robust, strong, sturdy, valiant, valorous, vigorous; bulky, enormous, huge, immense, monstrous, stupendous, vast.

migratory *adj* nomadic, roving, shifting, strolling, unsettled, wandering, vagrant.

mild *adj* amiable, clement, compassionate, gentle, good-natured, indulgent, kind, lenient, meek, merciful, pacific, tender; bland, pleasant, soft, suave; calm, kind, placid, temperate, tranquil; assuasive, compliant, demulcent, emollient, lenitive, mollifying, soothing.

mildness *n* amiability, clemency, gentleness, indulgence, kindness, meekness, moderation, softness, tenderness, warmth.

mildew *n* blight, blast, mould, must, mustiness, smut, rust.

milieu *n* background, environment, sphere, surroundings.

militant *adj* belligerent, combative, contending, fighting.

military *adj* martial, soldier, soldierly, warlike. * *n* army, militia, soldiers.

mill *vb* comminute, crush, grate, grind, levigate, powder, pulverize. * *n* factory, manufactory; grinder; crowd, throng.

mimic *vb* ape, counterfeit, imitate, impersonate, mime, mock, parody. * *adj* imitative, mock, simulated. * *n* imitator, impersonator, mime, mocker, parodist, parrot.

mince¹ *vb* chop, cut, hash, shatter. * *n* forcemeat, hash, mash, mincemeat.

mince² *vb* attenuate, diminish, extenuate, mitigate, palliate, soften; pose, sashay, simper, smirk.

mind¹ *vb* attend, heed, mark, note, notice, regard, tend, watch; obey, observe, submit; design, incline, intend, mean; recall, recollect, remember, remind; beware, look out, watch out. * *n* soul, spirit; brains, common sense, intellect, reason, sense, understanding; belief, consideration, contemplation, judgement, opinion, reflection, sentiment, thought; memory, recollection, remembrance; bent, desire, disposition, inclination, intention, leaning, purpose, tendency, will.

mind² *vb* balk, begrudge, grudge, object, resent.

mindful *adj* attentive, careful, heedful, observant, regardful, thoughtful.

mindless *adj* dull, heavy, insensible, senseless, sluggish, stupid, unthinking; careless, forgetful, heedless, neglectful, negligent, regardless.

mine *vb* dig, excavate, quarry, unearth; sap, undermine, weaken; destroy, ruin. * *n* colliery, deposit, lode, pit, shaft.

mingle *vb* blend, combine, commingle, compound, intermingle, intermix, join, mix, unite.

miniature *adj* bantam, diminutive, little, small, tiny.

minion *n* creature, dependant, favourite, hanger-on, parasite, sycophant; darling, favourite, flatterer, pet.

minister *vb* administer, afford, furnish, give, supply; aid, assist, contribute, help, succour. * *n* agent, assistant, servant, subordinate, underling; administrator, executive; ambassador, delegate, envoy, plenipotentiary; chaplain, churchman, clergyman, cleric, curate, divine, ecclesiastic, parson, pastor, preacher, priest, rector, vicar.

ministry *n* agency, aid, help, instrumentality, interposition, intervention, ministration, service, support; administration, cabinet, council, government.

minor *adj* less, smaller; inferior, junior, secondary, subordinate, younger; inconsiderable, petty, unimportant, small.

minstrel *n* bard, musician, singer, troubadour.

mint *vb* coin, stamp; fabricate, fashion, forge, invent, make, produce. * *adj* fresh, new, perfect, undamaged. * *n* die, punch, seal, stamp; fortune, (*inf*) heap, million, pile, wad.

minute[1] *adj* diminutive, fine, little, microscopic, miniature, slender, slight, small, tiny; circumstantial, critical, detailed, exact, fussy, meticulous, nice, particular, precise.

minute[2] *n* account, entry, item, memorandum, note, proceedings, record; instant, moment, second, trice, twinkling.

miracle *n* marvel, prodigy, wonder.

miraculous *adj* supernatural, thaumaturgic, thaumaturgical; amazing, extraordinary, incredible, marvellous, unaccountable, unbelievable, wondrous.

mirror *vb* copy, echo, emulate, reflect, show. * *n* looking-glass, reflector, speculum; archetype, exemplar, example, model, paragon, pattern, prototype.

mirth *n* cheerfulness, festivity, frolic, fun, gaiety, gladness, glee, hilarity, festivity, jollity, joviality, joyousness, laughter, merriment, merry-making, rejoicing, sport.

mirthful *adj* cheery, cheery, festive, frolicsome, hilarious, jocund, jolly, merry, jovial, joyous, lively, playful, sportive, vivacious; comic, droll, humorous, facetious, funny, jocose, jocular, ludicrous, merry, waggish, witty.

misadventure *n* accident, calamity, catastrophe, cross, disaster, failure, ill-luck, infelicity, mischance, misfortune, mishap, reverse.

misanthrope *n* cynic, egoist, egotist, man-hater, misanthropist.

misapply *vb* abuse, misuse, pervert.

misapprehend *vb* misconceive, mistake, misunderstand.

misbehaviour *n* ill-behaviour, ill-conduct, incivility, miscarriage, misconduct, misdemeanour, naughtiness, rudeness.

miscarriage *n* calamity, defeat, disaster, failure, mischance, mishap; misbehaviour, misconduct, ill-behaviour.

miscellaneous *adj* confused, diverse, diversified, heterogeneous, indiscriminate, jumbled, many, mingled, mixed, promiscuous, stromatic, stromatous, various.

miscellany *n* collection, diversity, farrago, gallimaufry, hodgepodge, hotchpotch, jumble, medley, mishmash, melange, miscellaneous, mixture, variety.

mischance *n* accident, calamity, disaster, ill-fortune, ill-luck, infelicity, misadventure, misfortune, mishap.

mischief *n* damage, detriment, disadvantage, evil, harm, hurt, ill, injury, prejudice; ill-consequence, misfortune, trouble; devilry, wrong-doing.

mischievous *adj* destructive, detrimental, harmful, hurtful, injurious, noxious, pernicious; malicious, sinful, vicious, wicked; annoying, impish, naughty, troublesome, vexatious.

misconceive *vb* misapprehend, misjudge, mistake, misunderstand.

misconduct *vb* botch, bungle, misdirect, mismanage. * *n* bad conduct, ill-conduct, misbehaviour, misdemeanour, rudeness, transgression; ill-management, mismanagement.

misconstrue *vb* misread, mistranslate; misapprehend, misinterpret, mistake, misunderstand.

miscreant *adj* corrupt, criminal, evil, rascally, unprincipled, vicious, villainous, wicked. * *n* caitiff, knave, ragamuffin, rascal, rogue, ruffian, scamp, scoundrel, vagabond, villain.

misdemeanour *n* fault, ill-behaviour, misbehaviour, misconduct, misdeed, offence, transgression, trespass.

miser *n* churl, curmudgeon, lickpenny, money-grabber, niggard, penny-pincher, pinch-fist, screw, scrimp, skinflint.

miserable *adj* afflicted, broken-hearted, comfortless, disconsolate, distressed, forlorn, heartbroken, unhappy, wretched; calamitous, hapless, ill-starred, pitiable, unfortunate, unlucky; poor, valueless, worthless; abject, contemptible, despicable, low, mean, worthless.

miserly *adj* avaricious, beggarly, close, close-fisted, covetous, grasping, mean, niggardly, parsimonious, penurious, sordid, stingy, tight-fisted.

misery *n* affliction, agony, anguish, calamity, desolation, distress, grief, heartache, heavy-heartedness, misfortune, sorrow, suffering, torment, torture, tribulation, unhappiness, woe, wretchedness.

misfortune *n* adversity, affliction, bad luck, blow, calamity, casualty, catastrophe, disaster, distress, hardship, harm, ill, infliction, misadventure, mischance, mishap, reverse, scourge, stroke, trial, trouble, visitation.

misgiving *n* apprehension, distrust, doubt, hesitation, suspicion, uncertainty.

mishap *n* accident, calamity, disaster, ill luck, misadventure, mischance, misfortune.

misinterpret *vb* distort, falsify, misapprehend, misconceive, misconstrue, misjudge.

mislead *vb* beguile, deceive, delude, misdirect, misguide.

mismanage *vb* botch, fumble, misconduct, mishandle, misrule.

misprize *vb* slight, underestimate, underrate, undervalue.

misrepresent *vb* belie, caricature, distort, falsify, misinterpret, misstate, pervert.

misrule *n* anarchy, confusion, disorder, maladministration, misgovernment, mismanagement.

miss[1] *vb* blunder, err, fail, fall short, forgo, lack, lose, miscarry, mistake, omit, overlook, trip; avoid, escape, evade, skip, slip; feel the loss of, need, want, wish. * *n* blunder, error, failure, fault, mistake, omission, oversight, slip, trip; loss, want.

miss[2] *n* damsel, girl, lass, maid, maiden.

misshapen *adj* deformed, ill-formed, ill-shaped, ill-proportioned, misformed, ugly, ungainly.

missile *n* projectile, weapon.

mission *n* commission, legation; business, charge, duty, errand, office, trust; delegation, deputation, embassy.

missive *n* communication, epistle, letter, message, note.

mist *vb* cloud, drizzle, mizzle, smog. * *n* cloud, fog, haze; bewilderment, obscurity, perplexity.

mistake *vb* misapprehend, miscalculate, misconceive, misjudge, misunderstand; confound, take; blunder, err. * *n* misapprehension, miscalculation, misconception, mistaking, misunderstanding; blunder, error, fault, inaccuracy, oversight, slip, trip.

mistaken *adj* erroneous, inaccurate, incorrect, misinformed, wrong.

mistrust *vb* distrust, doubt, suspect; apprehend, fear, surmise, suspect. * *n* doubt, distrust, misgiving, suspicion.

misty *adj* cloudy, clouded, dark, dim, foggy, obscure, overcast.

misunderstand *vb* misapprehend, misconceive, misconstrue, mistake.

misunderstanding *n* error, misapprehension, misconception, mistake; difference, difficulty, disagreement, discord, dissension, quarrel.

misuse *vb* desecrate, misapply, misemploy, pervert, profane; abuse, ill-treat, maltreat, ill-use; fritter, squander, waste. * *n* abuse, perversion, profanation, prostitution; ill-treatment, ill-use, ill-usage, misusage; misapplication, solecism.

mitigate *vb* abate, alleviate, assuage, diminish, extenuate, lessen, moderate, palliate, relieve; allay, appease, calm, mollify, pacify, quell, quiet, reduce, soften, soothe; moderate, temper.

mitigation *n* abatement, allaying, alleviation, assuagement, diminution, moderation, palliation, relief.

mix *vb* alloy, amalgamate, blend, commingle, combine, compound, incorporate, interfuse, interlard, mingle, unite; associate, join. * *n* alloy, amalgam, blend, combination, compound, mixture.

mixture *n* admixture, association, intermixture, union; compound, farrago, hash, hodgepodge, hotchpotch, jumble, medley, melange, mishmash; diversity, miscellany, variety.

moan *vb* bemoan, bewail, deplore, grieve, groan, lament, mourn, sigh, weep. * *n* groan, lament, lamentation, sigh, wail.

mob *vb* crowd, jostle, surround, swarm, pack, throng. * *n* assemblage, crowd, rabble, multitude, throng, tumult; dregs, canaille, populace, rabble, riffraff, scum.

mobile *adj* changeable, fickle, expressive, inconstant, sensitive, variable, volatile.

mock *vb* ape, counterfeit, imitate, mimic, take off; deride, flout, gibe, insult, jeer, ridicule, taunt; balk, cheat, deceive, defeat, disappoint, dupe, elude, illude, mislead. * *adj* assumed, clap-trap, counterfeit, fake, false, feigned, make-believe, pretended, spurious. * *n* fake, imitation, phoney, sham; gibe, insult, jeer, scoff, taunt.

mockery *n* contumely, counterfeit, deception, derision, imitation, jeering, mimicry, ridicule, scoffing, scorn, sham, travesty.

mode *n* fashion, manner, method, style, way; accident, affection, degree, graduation, modification, quality, variety.

model *vb* design, fashion, form, mould, plan, shape. * *adj* admirable, archetypal, estimable, exemplary, ideal, meritorious, paradigmatic, perfect, praiseworthy, worthy. * *n* archetype, design, mould, original, pattern, protoplast, prototype, type; dummy, example, form; copy, facsimile, image, imitation, representation.

moderate *vb* abate, allay, appease, assuage, blunt, dull, lessen, soothe, mitigate, mollify, pacify, quell, quiet, reduce, repress, soften, still, subdue; diminish, qualify, slacken, temper; control, govern, regulate. * *adj* abstinent, frugal, sparing, temperate; limited, mediocre; abstemious, sober; calm, cool, judicious, reasonable, steady; gentle, mild, temperate, tolerable.

moderation *n* abstemiousness, forbearance, frugality, restraint, sobriety, temperance; calmness, composure, coolness, deliberateness, equanimity, mildness, sedateness.

modern *adj* fresh, late, latest, new, novel, present, recent, up-to-date.

modest *adj* bashful, coy, diffident, humble, meek, reserved, retiring, shy, unassuming, unobtrusive, unostentatious, unpretending, unpretentious; chaste, proper, pure, virtuous; becoming, decent, moderate.

modesty *n* bashfulness, coyness, diffidence, humility, meekness, propriety, prudishness, reserve, shyness, unobtrusiveness; chastity, purity, virtue; decency, moderation.

modification *n* alteration, change, qualification,

reformation, variation; form, manner, mode, state.

modify *vb* alter, change, qualify, reform, shape, vary; lower, moderate, qualify, soften.

modish *adj* fashionable, stylish; ceremonious, conventional, courtly, genteel.

modulate *vb* attune, harmonize, tune; inflict, vary; adapt, adjust, proportion.

moiety *n* half; part, portion, share.

moil *vb* drudge, labour, toil; bespatter, daub, defile, soil, splash, spot, stain; fatigue, weary, tire.

moist *adj* damp, dank, humid, marshy, muggy, swampy, wet.

moisture *n* dampness, dankness, humidity, wetness.

mole *n* breakwater, dike, dyke, jetty, mound, pier, quay.

molecule *n* atom, monad, particle.

molest *vb* annoy, badger, bore, bother, chafe, discommode, disquiet, disturb, harass, harry, fret, gull, hector, incommode, inconvenience, irritate, oppress, pester, plague, tease, torment, trouble, vex, worry.

mollify *vb* soften; appease, calm, compose, pacify, quiet, soothe, tranquillize; abate, allay, assuage, blunt, dull, ease, lessen, mitigate, moderate, relieve, temper; qualify, tone down.

moment *n* flash, instant, jiffy, second, trice, twinkling, wink; avail, consequence, consideration, force, gravity, importance, significance, signification, value, weight; drive, force, impetus, momentum.

momentous *adj* grave, important, serious, significant, vital, weighty.

momentum *n* impetus, moment.

monarch *n* autocrat, despot; chief, dictator, emperor, king, potentate, prince, queen, ruler, sovereign.

monastery *n* abbey, cloister, convent, lamasery, nunnery, priory.

monastic *adj* coenobitic, coenobitical, conventual, monkish, secluded.

money *n* banknotes, cash, coin, currency, riches, specie, wealth.

moneyed, monied *adj* affluent, opulent, rich, well-off, well-to-do.

monitor *vb* check, observe, oversee, supervise, watch. * *n* admonisher, admonitor, adviser, counsellor, instructor, mentor, overseer.

monomania *n* delusion, hallucination, illusion, insanity, self-deception.

monopolize *vb* control, dominate, engross, forestall.

monotonous *adj* boring, dull, tedious, tiresome, undiversified, uniform, unvaried, unvarying, wearisome.

monotony *n* boredom, dullness, sameness, tedium, tiresomeness, uniformity, wearisomeness.

monster *adj* enormous, gigantic, huge, immense, mammoth, monstrous. * *n* enormity, marvel, prodigy, wonder; brute, demon, fiend, miscreant, ruffian, villain, wretch.

monstrous *adj* abnormal, preternatural, prodigious, unnatural; colossal, enormous, extraordinary, huge, immense, stupendous, vast; marvellous, strange, wonderful; bad, base, dreadful, flagrant, frightful, hateful, hideous, horrible, shocking, terrible.

monument *n* memorial, record, remembrance, testimonial; cairn, cenotaph, gravestone, mausoleum, memorial, pillar, tomb, tombstone.

mood *n* disposition, humour, temper, vein.

moody *adj* capricious, humoursome, variable; angry, crabbed, crusty, fretful, ill-tempered, irascible, irritable, passionate, pettish, peevish, petulant, snappish, snarling, sour, testy; crossgrained, dogged, frowning, glowering, glum, intractable, morose, perverse, spleeny, stubborn, sulky, sullen, wayward; abstracted, gloomy, melancholy, pensive, sad, saturnine.

moonshine *n* balderdash, fiction, flummery, fudge, fustian, nonsense, pretence, stuff, trash, twaddle, vanity.

moor[1] *vb* anchor, berth, fasten, fix, secure, tie.

moor[2] *n* bog, common, heath, moorland, morass, moss, wasteland.

moot *vb* agitate, argue, debate, discuss, dispute. * *adj* arguable, debatable, doubtful, unsettled.

mopish *adj* dejected, depressed, desponding, downcast, down-hearted, gloomy, glum, sad.

moral *adj* ethical, good, honest, honourable, just, upright, virtuous; abstract, ideal, intellectual, mental. * *n* intent, meaning, significance.

morals *npl* ethics, morality; behaviour, conduct, habits, manners.

morass *n* bog, fen, marsh, quagmire, slough, swamp.

morbid *adj* ailing, corrupted, diseased, sick, sickly, tainted, unhealthy, unsound, vitiated; depressed, downcast, gloomy, pessimistic, sensitive.

mordacious *adj* acrid, biting, cutting, mordant, pungent, sharp, stinging; caustic, poignant, satirical, sarcastic, scathing, severe.

mordant *adj* biting, caustic, keen, mordacious, nipping, sarcastic.

moreover *adv, conj* also, besides, further, furthermore, likewise, too.

morning *n* aurora, daybreak, dawn, morn, morningtide, sunrise.

morose *adj* austere, churlish, crabbed, crusty, dejected, desponding, downcast, downhearted, gloomy, glum, melancholy, moody, sad, severe, sour, sullen, surly.

morsel *n* bite, mouthful, titbit; bit, fragment, part, piece, scrap.

mortal *adj* deadly, destructive, fatal, final, human, lethal, perishable, vital. * *n* being, earthling, human, man, person, woman.

mortality *n* corruption, death, destruction, fatality.

mortification *n* chagrin, disappointment, discontent, dissatisfaction, displeasure, humiliation, trouble, shame, vexation; humility, penance, self-abasement, self-denial; gangrene, necrosis.

mortify *vb* annoy, chagrin, depress, disappoint, displease, disquiet, dissatisfy, harass, humble, plague, vex, worry; abase, abash, confound, humiliate, restrain, shame, subdue; corrupt, fester, gangrene, putrefy.

mortuary *n* burial place, cemetery, churchyard, graveyard, necropolis; charnel house, morgue.

mostly *adv* chiefly, customarily, especially, generally, mainly, particularly, principally.

mote *n* atom, corpuscle, flaw, mite, particle, speck, spot.

motherly *adj* affectionate, kind, maternal, paternal, tender.

motion *vb* beckon, direct, gesture, signal. * *n* action, change, drift, flux, movement, passage, stir, transit; air, gait, port; gesture, impulse, prompting, suggestion; proposal, proposition.

motionless *adj* fixed, immobile, quiescent, stable, stagnant, standing, stationary, still, torpid, unmoved.

motive *adj* activating, driving, moving, operative. * *n* cause, consideration, ground, impulse, incentive, incitement, inducement, influence, occasion, prompting, purpose, reason, spur, stimulus.

motley *adj* coloured, dappled, mottled, speckled, spotted, variegated; composite, diversified, heterogeneous, mingled, mixed.

mottled *adj* dappled, motley, piebald, speckled, spotted, variegated.

mould[1] *vb* carve, cast, fashion, form, make, model, shape. * *n* cast, character, fashion, form, matrix, pattern, shape; material, matter, substance.

mould[2] *n* blight, mildew, mouldiness, must, mustiness, rot; fungus, lichen, mushroom, puffball, rust, smut, toadstool; earth, loam, soil.

moulder *vb* crumble, decay, perish, waste.

mouldy *adj* decaying, fusty, mildewed, musty.

mound *n* bank, barrow, hill, hillock, knoll, tumulus; bulwark, defence, rampart.

mount[1] *n* hill, mountain, peak.

mount[2] *vb* arise, ascend, climb, rise, soar, tower; escalate, scale; embellish, ornament; bestride, get upon. * *n* charger, horse, ride, steed.

mountain *n* alp, height, hill, mount, peak; abundance, heap, mound, stack.

mountebank *n* charlatan, cheat, impostor, pretender, quack.

mourn *vb* bemoan, bewail, deplore, grieve, lament, sorrow, wail.

mournful *adj* afflicting, afflictive, calamitous, deplorable, distressed, grievous, lamentable, sad, woeful; doleful, heavy, heavy-hearted, lugubrious, melancholy, sorrowful, tearful.

mouth *vb* clamour, declaim, rant, roar, vociferate. * *n* chaps, jaws; aperture, opening, orifice; entrance, inlet; oracle, mouthpiece, speaker, spokesman.

movables *npl* chattels, effects, furniture, goods, property, wares.

move *vb* dislodge, drive, impel, propel, push, shift,

start, stir; actuate, incite, instigate, rouse; determine, incline, induce, influence, persuade, prompt; affect, impress, touch, trouble; agitate, awaken, excite, incense, irritate; propose, recommend, suggest; go, march, proceed, walk; act, live; flit, remove. * *n* action, motion, movement.

movement *n* change, move, motion, passage; emotion; crusade, drive.

moving *adj* impelling, influencing, instigating, persuading, persuasive; affecting, impressive, pathetic, touching.

mucous *adj* glutinous, gummy, mucilaginous, ropy, slimy, viscid.

mud *n* dirt, mire, muck, slime.

muddle *vb* confuse, disarrange, disorder; fuddle, inebriate, stupefy; muff, mull, spoil. * *n* confusion, disorder, mess, plight, predicament.

muddy *vb* dirty, foul, smear, soil; confuse, obscure. * *adj* dirty, foul, impure, slimy, soiled, turbid; bothered, confused, dull, heavy, stupid; incoherent, obscure, vague.

muffle *vb* cover, envelop, shroud, wrap; conceal, disguise, involve; deaden, soften, stifle, suppress.

mulish *adj* cross-grained, headstrong, intractable, obstinate, stubborn.

multifarious *adj* different, divers, diverse, diversified, manifold, multiform, multitudinous, various.

multiloquence *n* garrulity, loquacity, loquaciousness, talkativeness.

multiply *vb* augment, extend, increase, spread.

multitude *n* numerousness; host, legion; army, assemblage, assembly, collection, concourse, congregation, crowd, horde, mob, swarm, throng; commonality, herd, mass, mob, pack, populace, rabble.

mundane *adj* earthly, secular, sublunary, temporal, terrene, terrestrial, worldly.

munificence *n* benefice, bounteousness, bountifulness, bounty, generosity, liberality.

munificent *adj* beneficent, bounteous, bountiful, free, generous, liberal, princely.

murder *vb* assassinate, butcher, destroy, dispatch, kill, massacre, slaughter, slay; abuse, mar, spoil. * *n* assassination, butchery, destruction, homicide, killing, manslaughter, massacre.

murderer *n* assassin, butcher, cut-throat, killer, manslaughterer, slaughterer, slayer.

murderous *adj* barbarous, bloodthirsty, bloody, cruel, fell, sanguinary, savage.

murky *adj* cheerless, cloudy, dark, dim, dusky, gloomy, hazy, lowering, lurid, obscure, overcast.

murmur *vb* croak, grumble, mumble, mutter; hum, whisper. * *n* complaint, grumble, mutter, plaint, whimper; hum, undertone, whisper.

muscular *adj* sinewy; athletic, brawny, powerful, lusty, stalwart, stout, strong, sturdy, vigorous.

muse *vb* brood, cogitate, consider, contemplate, deliberate, dream, meditate, ponder, reflect, ruminate, speculate, think. * *n* abstraction, musing, reverie.

music *n* harmony, melody, symphony.

musical *adj* dulcet, harmonious, melodious, sweet, sweet-sounding, symphonious, tuneful.

musing *adj* absent-minded, meditative, preoccupied. * *n* absent-mindedness, abstraction, contemplation, daydreaming, meditation, muse, reflection, reverie, rumination.

muster *vb* assemble, collect, congregate, convene, convoke, gather, marshal, meet, rally, summon. * *n* assemblage, assembly, collection, congregation, convention, convocation, gathering, meeting, rally.

musty *adj* fetid, foul, fusty, mouldy, rank, sour, spoiled; hackneyed, old, stale, threadbare, trite; ill-favoured, insipid, vapid; dull, heavy, rusty, spiritless.

mutable *adj* alterable, changeable; changeful, fickle, inconstant, irresolute, mutational, unsettled, unstable, unsteady, vacillating, variable, wavering.

mutation *n* alteration, change, variation.

mute *vb* dampen, lower, moderate, muffle, soften. * *adj* dumb, voiceless; silent, speechless, still, taciturn.

mutilate *vb* cripple, damage, disable, disfigure, hamstring, injure, maim, mangle, mar.

mutinous *adj* contumacious, insubordinate, rebellious, refractory, riotous, tumultuous, turbulent, unruly; insurgent, seditious.

mutiny *vb* rebel, revolt, rise, resist. * *n* insubordination, insurrection, rebellion, revolt, revolution, riot, rising, sedition, uprising.

mutter *vb* grumble, muffle, mumble, murmur.

mutual *adj* alternate, common, correlative, interchangeable, interchanged, reciprocal, requited.

myopic *adj* near-sighted, purblind, short-sighted.

myriad *adj* innumerable, manifold, multitudinous, uncounted. * *n* host, million(s), multitude, score(s), sea, swarm, thousand(s).

mysterious *adj* abstruse, cabbalistic, concealed, cryptic, dark, dim, enigmatic, enigmatical, hidden, incomprehensible, inexplicable, inscrutable, mystic, mystical, obscure, occult, puzzling, recondite, secret, sphinx-like, unaccountable, unfathomable, unintelligible, unknown.

mystery *n* enigma, puzzle, riddle, secret; art, business, calling, trade.

mystical *adj* abstruse, cabbalistic, dark, enigmatical, esoteric, hidden, inscrutable, mysterious, obscure, occult, recondite, transcendental; allegorical, emblematic, emblematical, symbolic, symbolical.

mystify *vb* befog, bewilder, confound, confuse, dumbfound, embarrass, obfuscate, perplex, pose, puzzle.

myth *n* fable, legend, tradition; allegory, fiction, invention, parable, story; falsehood, fancy, figment, lie, untruth.

mythical *adj* allegorical, fabled, fabulous, fanciful, fictitious, imaginary, legendary, mythological.

N

nab *vb* catch, clutch, grasp, seize.

nag[1] *vb* carp, fuss, hector, henpeck, pester, torment, worry. * *n* nagger, scold, shrew, tartar.

nag[2] *n* bronco, crock, hack, horse, pony, scrag.

naive *adj* artless, candid, ingenuous, natural, plain, simple, unaffected, unsophisticated.

naked *adj* bare, nude, uncovered; denuded, unclad, unclothed, undressed; defenceless, exposed, open, unarmed, unguarded, unprotected; evident, manifest, plain, stark, unconcealed, undisguised; mere, sheer, simple; bare, destitute, rough, rude, unfurnished, unprovided; uncoloured, unexaggerated, unvarnished.

name *vb* call, christen, denounce, dub, entitle, phrase, style, term; mention; denominate, designate, indicate, nominate, specify. * *n* appellation, cognomen, denomination, designation, epithet, nickname, surname, sobriquet, title; character, credit, reputation, repute; celebrity, distinction, eminence, fame, honour, note, praise, renown.

narcotic *adj* stupefacient, stupefactive, stupefying. * *n* anaesthetic, anodyne, dope, opiate, sedative, stupefacient, tranquillizer.

narrate *vb* chronicle, describe, detail, enumerate, recite, recount, rehearse, relate, tell.

narration *n* account, description, chronicle, history, narrative, recital, rehearsal, relation, story, tale.

narrow *vb* confine, contract, cramp, limit, restrict, straiten. * *adj* circumscribed, confined, contracted, cramped, incapacious, limited, pinched, scanty, straitened; bigoted, hidebound, illiberal, ungenerous; close, near.

nastiness *n* defilement, dirtiness, filth, filthiness, foulness, impurity, pollution, squalor, uncleanness; indecency, grossness, obscenity, pornography, ribaldry, smut, smuttiness.

nasty *adj* defiled, dirty, filthy, foul, impure, loathsome, polluted, squalid, unclean; gross, indecent, indelicate, lewd, loose, obscene, smutty, vile; disagreeable, disgusting, nauseous, odious, offensive, repulsive, sickening; aggravating, annoying, pesky, pestering, troublesome.

nation *n* commonwealth, realm, state; community, people, population, race, stock, tribe.

native *adj* aboriginal, autochthonal, autochthonous, domestic, home, indigenous, vernacular; genuine, intrinsic, natural, original, real; congenital, inborn, inbred, inherent, innate, natal. * *n* aborigine, autochthon, inhabitant, national, resident.

natty *adj* dandyish, fine, foppish, jaunty, neat, nice, spruce, tidy.

natural *adj* indigenous, innate, native, original; characteristic, essential; legitimate, normal, regular; artless, authentic, genuine, ingenious, unreal, simple, spontaneous, unaffected; bastard, illegitimate.

nature *n* universe, world; character, constitution, essence; kind, quality, species, sort; disposition, grain, humour, mood, temper; being, intellect, intelligence, mind.

naughty *adj* bad, corrupt, mischievous, perverse, worthless.

nausea *n* queasiness, seasickness; loathing, qualm; aversion, disgust, repugnance.

nauseous *adj* abhorrent, disgusting, distasteful, loathsome, offensive, repulsive, revolting, sickening.

naval *adj* marine, maritime, nautical.

navigate *vb* cruise, direct, guide, pilot, plan, sail, steer.

navy *n* fleet, shipping, vessels.

near *vb* approach, draw close. * *adj* adjacent, approximate, close, contiguous, neighbouring, nigh; approaching, forthcoming, imminent, impending; dear, familiar, friendly, intimate; direct, immediate, short, straight; accurate, literal; narrow, parsimonious.

nearly *adv* almost, approximately, well-nigh; closely, intimately, pressingly; meanly, parsimoniously, penuriously, stingily.

neat *adj* clean, cleanly, orderly, tidy, trim, unsoiled; nice, smart, spruce; chaste, pure, simple; excellent, pure, unadulterated; adroit, clever, exact, finished; dainty, nice.

nebulous *adj* cloudy, hazy, misty.

necessary *adj* inevitable, unavoidable; essential, expedient, indispensable, needful, requisite; compelling, compulsory, involuntary. * *n* essential, necessity, requirement, requisite.

necessitate *vb* compel, constrain, demand, force, impel, oblige.

necessitous *adj* destitute, distressed, indigent, moneyless, needy, penniless, pinched, poor, poverty-stricken; narrow, pinching.

necessity *n* inevitability, inevitableness, unavoidability, unavoidableness; compulsion, destiny, fatality, fate; emergency, urgency; exigency, indigence, indispensability, indispensableness, need, needfulness, poverty, want; essentiality, essentialness, requirement, requisite.

necromancy n conjuration, divination, enchantment, magic, sorcery, witchcraft, wizardry.

necropolis n burial ground, cemetery, churchyard, crematorium, graveyard, mortuary.

need vb demand, lack, require, want. * n emergency, exigency, extremity, necessity, strait, urgency, want; destitution, distress, indigence, neediness, penury, poverty, privation.

needful adj distressful, necessitous, necessary; essential, indispensable, requisite.

needless adj superfluous, unnecessary, useless.

needy adj destitute, indigent, necessitous, poor.

nefarious adj abominable, atrocious, detestable, dreadful, execrable, flagitious, heinous, horrible, infamous, iniquitous, scandalous, vile, wicked.

negation n denial, disavowal, disclaimer, rejection, renunciation.

neglect vb condemn, despise, disregard, forget, ignore, omit, overlook, slight. * n carelessness, default, failure, heedlessness, inattention, omission, remissness; disregard, disrespect, slight; indifference, negligence.

negligence n carelessness, disregard, heedlessness, inadvertency, inattention, indifference, neglect, remissness, slackness, thoughtlessness; defect, fault, inadvertence, omission, shortcoming.

negligent adj careless, heedless, inattentive, indifferent, neglectful, regardless, thoughtless.

negotiate vb arrange, bargain, deal, debate, sell, settle, transact, treat.

neighbourhood n district, environs, locality, vicinage, vicinity; adjacency, nearness, propinquity, proximity.

neighbourly adj attentive, civil, friendly, kind, obliging, social.

neophyte n beginner, catechumen, convert, novice, pupil, tyro.

nerve vb brace, energize, fortify, invigorate, strengthen. * n force, might, power, strength, vigour; coolness, courage, endurance, firmness, fortitude, hardihood, manhood, pluck, resolution, self-command, steadiness.

nervous adj forcible, powerful, robust, strong, vigorous; irritable, fearful, shaky, timid, timorous, weak, weakly.

nestle vb cuddle, harbour, lodge, nuzzle, snug, snuggle.

nettle vb chafe, exasperate, fret, harass, incense, irritate, provoke, ruffle, sting, tease, vex.

neutral adj impartial, indifferent; colourless, mediocre.

neutralize vb cancel, counterbalance, counterpoise, invalidate, offset.

nevertheless adv however, nonetheless, notwithstanding, yet.

new adj fresh, latest, modern, novel, recent, unused; additional, another, further; reinvigorated, renovated, repaired.

news n advice, information, intelligence, report, tidings, word.

nice adj accurate, correct, critical, definite, delicate, exact, exquisite, precise, rigorous, strict; dainty, difficult, exacting, fastidious, finical, punctilious, squeamish; discerning, discriminating, particular, precise, scrupulous; neat, tidy, trim; fine, minute, refined, subtle; delicate, delicious, luscious, palatable, savoury, soft, tender; agreeable, delightful, good, pleasant.

nicety n accuracy, exactness, niceness, precision, truth, daintiness, fastidiousness, squeamishness; discrimination, subtlety.

niggard n churl, curmudgeon, miser, screw, scrimp, skinflint.

niggardly adj avaricious, close, close-fisted, illiberal, mean, mercenary, miserly, parsimonious, penurious, skinflint, sordid, stingy.

nigh adj adjacent, adjoining, contiguous, near; present, proximate. * adv almost, near, nearly.

nimble adj active, agile, alert, brisk, lively, prompt, quick, speedy, sprightly, spry, swift, tripping.

nobility n aristocracy, dignity, elevation, eminence, grandeur, greatness, loftiness, magnanimity, nobleness, peerage, superiority, worthiness.

noble adj dignified, elevated, eminent, exalted, generous, great, honourable, illustrious, magnanimous, superior, worthy; choice, excellent; aristocratic, gentle, high-born, patrician; grand, lofty, lordly, magnificent, splendid, stately. * n aristocrat, grandee, lord, nobleman, peer.

noctambulist n sleepwalker, somnambulist.

noise vb bruit, gossip, repeat, report, rumour. * n ado, blare, clamour, clatter, cry, din, fuss, hubbub, hullabaloo, outcry, pandemonium, racket, row, sound, tumult, uproar, vociferation.

noiseless adj inaudible, quiet, silent, soundless.

noisome adj bad, baneful, deleterious, disgusting, fetid, foul, hurtful, injurious, mischievous, nocuous, noxious, offensive, pernicious, pestiferous, pestilential, poisonous, unhealthy, unwholesome.

noisy adj blatant, blustering, boisterous, brawling, clamorous, loud, uproarious, riotous, tumultuous, vociferous.

nomadic adj migratory, pastoral, vagrant, wandering.

nominal adj formal, inconsiderable, minimal, ostensible, pretended, professed, so-called, titular.

nominate vb appoint, choose, designate, name, present, propose.

nonchalant adj apathetic, careless, cool, indifferent, unconcerned.

nondescript adj amorphous, characterless, commonplace, dull, indescribable, odd, ordinary, unclassifiable, uninteresting, unremarkable.

nonentity n cipher, futility, inexistence, inexistency, insignificance, nobody, nonexistence, nothingness.

nonplus vb astonish, bewilder, confound, confuse, discomfit, disconcert, embarrass, floor, gravel, perplex, pose, puzzle.

nonsensical adj absurd, foolish, irrational, senseless, silly, stupid.

norm *n* model, pattern, rule, standard.

normal *adj* analogical, legitimate, natural, ordinary, regular, usual; erect, perpendicular, vertical.

notable *adj* distinguished, extraordinary, memorable, noted, remarkable, signal; conspicuous, evident, noticeable, observable, plain, prominent, striking; notorious, rare, well-known. * *n* celebrity, dignitary, notability, worthy.

note *vb* heed, mark, notice, observe, regard, remark; record, register; denote, designate. * *n* memorandum, minute, record; annotation, comment, remark, scholium; indication, mark, sign, symbol, token; account, bill, catalogue, reckoning; billet, epistle, letter; consideration, heed, notice, observation; celebrity, consequence, credit, distinction, eminence, fame, notability, notedness, renown, reputation, respectability; banknote, bill, promissory note; song, strain, tune, voice.

noted *adj* celebrated, conspicuous, distinguished, eminent, famed, famous, illustrious, notable, notorious, remarkable, renowned, well-known.

nothing *n* inexistence, nonentity, nonexistence, nothingness, nullity; bagatelle, trifle.

notice *vb* mark, note, observe, perceive, regard, see; comment on, mention, remark; attend to, heed. * *n* cognizance, heed, note, observation, regard; advice, announcement, information, intelligence, mention, news, notification; communication, intimation, premonition, warning; attention, civility, consideration, respect; comments, remarks.

notify *vb* advertise, announce, declare, publish, promulgate; acquaint, apprise, inform.

notion *n* concept, conception, idea; apprehension, belief, conceit, conviction, expectation, estimation, impression, judgement, opinion, sentiment, view.

notoriety *n* celebrity, fame, figure, name, note, publicity, reputation, repute, vogue.

notorious *adj* apparent, egregious, evident, notable, obvious, open, overt, manifest, patent, well-known; celebrated, conspicuous, distinguished, famed, famous, flagrant, infamous, noted, remarkable, renowned.

notwithstanding *conj* despite, however, nevertheless, yet. * *prep* despite.

nourish *vb* feed, nurse, nurture; maintain, supply, support; breed, educate, instruct, train; cherish, encourage, foment, foster, promote, succour.

nourishment *n* aliment, diet, food, nutriment, nutrition, sustenance.

novel *adj* fresh, modern, new, rare, recent, strange, uncommon, unusual. * *n* fiction, romance, story, tale.

novice *n* convert, proselyte; initiate, neophyte, novitiate, probationer; apprentice, beginner, learner, tyro.

noxious *adj* baneful, deadly, deleterious, destructive, detrimental, hurtful, injurious, insalubrious, mischievous, noisome, pernicious, pestilent, poisonous, unfavourable, unwholesome.

nude *adj* bare, denuded, exposed, naked, uncovered, unclothed, undressed.

nugatory *adj* frivolous, insignificant, trifling, trivial, vain, worthless; bootless, ineffectual, inefficacious, inoperative, null, unavailing, useless.

nuisance *n* annoyance, bore, bother, infliction, offence, pest, plague, trouble.

null *adj* ineffectual, invalid, nugatory, useless, void; characterless, colourless.

nullify *vb* abolish, abrogate, annul, cancel, invalidate, negate, quash, repeal, revoke.

numb *vb* benumb, deaden, stupefy. * *adj* benumbed, deadened, dulled, insensible, paralysed.

number *vb* calculate, compute, count, enumerate, numerate, reckon, tell; account, reckon. * *n* digit, figure, numeral; horde, multitude, numerousness, throng; aggregate, collection, sum, total.

numerous *adj* abundant, many, numberless.

nuncio *n* ambassador, legate, messenger.

nunnery *n* abbey, cloister, convent, monastery.

nuptial *adj* bridal, conjugal, connubial, hymeneal, matrimonial.

nuptials *npl* espousal, marriage, wedding.

nurse *vb* nourish, nurture; rear, suckle; cherish, encourage, feed, foment, foster, pamper, promote, succour; economize, manage; caress, dandle, fondle. * *n* auxiliary, orderly, sister; amah, *au pair*, babysitter, nanny, nursemaid, nurserymaid,

nurture *vb* feed, nourish, nurse, tend; breed, discipline, educate, instruct, rear, school, train. * *n* diet, food, nourishment; breeding, discipline, education, instruction, schooling, training, tuition; attention, nourishing, nursing.

nutriment *n* aliment, food, nourishment, nutrition, pabulum, subsistence, sustenance.

nutrition *n* diet, food, nourishment, nutriment.

nutritious *adj* invigorating, nourishing, strengthening, supporting, sustaining.

nymph *n* damsel, dryad, lass, girl, maid, maiden, naiad.

O

oaf *n* blockhead, dolt, dunce, fool, idiot, simpleton.

oath *n* blasphemy, curse, expletive, imprecation, malediction; affirmation, pledge, promise, vow.

obduracy *n* contumacy, doggedness, obstinacy, stubbornness, tenacity; depravity, impenitence.

obdurate *adj* hard, harsh, rough, rugged; callous, cantankerous, dogged, firm, hardened, inflexible, insensible, obstinate, pigheaded, unfeeling, stubborn, unbending, unyielding; depraved, graceless, lost, reprobate, shameless, impenitent, incorrigible, irreclaimable.

obedience *n* acquiescence, agreement, compliance, duty, respect, reverence, submission, submissiveness, subservience.

obedient *adj* acquiescent, compliant, deferential, duteous, dutiful, observant, regardful, respectful, submissive, subservient, yielding.

obeisance *n* bow, courtesy, curtsy, homage, reverence, salutation.

obelisk *n* column, pillar.

obese *adj* corpulent, fat, fleshy, gross, plump, podgy, portly, stout.

obesity *n* corpulence, corpulency, embonpoint, fatness, fleshiness, obeseness, plumpness.

obey *vb* comply, conform, heed, keep, mind, observe, submit, yield.

obfuscate *vb* cloud, darken, obscure; bewilder, confuse, muddle.

object[1] *vb* cavil, contravene, demur, deprecate, disapprove of, except to, impeach, oppose, protest, refuse.

object[2] *n* particular, phenomenon, precept, reality, thing; aim, butt, destination, end, mark, recipient, target; design, drift, goal, intention, motive, purpose, use, view.

objection *n* censure, difficulty, doubt, exception, protest, remonstrance, scruple.

objurgate *vb* chide, reprehend, reprove.

oblation *n* gift, offering, sacrifice.

obligation *n* accountability, accountableness, responsibility; agreement, bond, contract, covenant, engagement, stipulation; debt, indebtedness, liability.

obligatory *adj* binding, coercive, compulsory, enforced, necessary, unavoidable.

oblige *vb* bind, coerce, compel, constrain, force, necessitate, require; accommodate, benefit, convenience, favour, gratify, please; obligate, bind.

obliging *adj* accommodating, civil, complaisant, considerate, kind, friendly, polite.

oblique *adj* aslant, inclined, sidelong, slanting; indirect, obscure.

obliterate *vb* cancel, delete, destroy, efface, eradicate, erase, expunge.

oblivious *adj* careless, forgetful, heedless, inattentive, mindless, negligent, neglectful.

obloquy *n* aspersion, backbiting, blame, calumny, censure, contumely, defamation, detraction, disgrace, odium, reproach, reviling, slander, traducing.

obnoxious *adj* blameworthy, censurable, faulty, reprehensible; hateful, objectionable, obscene, odious, offensive, repellent, repugnant, repulsive, unpleasant, unpleasing.

obscene *adj* broad, coarse, filthy, gross, immodest, impure, indecent, indelicate, ribald, unchaste, lewd, licentious, loose, offensive, pornographic, shameless, smutty; disgusting, dirty, foul.

obscure *vb* becloud, befog, blur, cloud, darken, eclipse, dim, obfuscate, obnubilate, shade; conceal, cover, equivocate, hide. *adj* dark, darksome, dim, dusky, gloomy, lurid, murky, rayless, shadowy, sombre, unenlightened, unilluminated; abstruse, blind, cabbalistic, difficult, doubtful, enigmatic, high, incomprehensible, indefinite, indistinct, intricate, involved, mysterious, mystic, recondite, undefined, unintelligible, vague; remote, secluded; humble, inglorious, nameless, renownless, undistinguished, unhonoured, unknown, unnoted, unnoticed.

obsequious *adj* cringing, deferential, fawning, flattering, servile, slavish, supple, subservient, sycophantic, truckling.

observant *adj* attentive, heedful, mindful, perceptive, quick, regardful, vigilant, watchful.

observation *n* attention, cognition, notice, observance; annotation, note, remark; experience, knowledge.

observe *vb* eye, mark, note, notice, remark, watch; behold, detect, discover, perceive, see; express, mention, remark, say, utter; comply, conform, follow, fulfil, obey; celebrate, keep, regard, solemnize.

obsolete *adj* ancient, antiquated, antique, archaic, disused, neglected, old, old-fashioned, obsolescent, out-of-date, past, passé, unfashionable.

obstacle *n* barrier, check, difficulty, hindrance, impediment, interference, interruption, obstruction, snag, stumbling block.

obstinacy *n* contumacy, doggedness, headiness, firmness, inflexibility, intractability, obduracy, persistence, perseverance, perversity, resoluteness, stubbornness, tenacity, wilfulness.

obstinate *adj* cross-grained, contumacious, dogged, firm, headstrong, inflexible, immovable, intractable, mulish, obdurate, opinionated, persistent, pertinacious, perverse, resolute, self-willed, stubborn, tenacious, unyielding, wilful.

obstreperous *adj* boisterous, clamorous, loud, noisy, riotous, tumultuous, turbulent, unruly, uproarious, vociferous.

obstruct *vb* bar, barricade, block, blockade, block up, choke, clog, close, glut, jam, obturate, stop; hinder, impede, oppose, prevent; arrest, check, curb, delay, embrace, interrupt, retard, slow.

obstruction *n* bar, barrier, block, blocking, check, difficulty, hindrance, impediment, obstacle, stoppage; check, clog, embarrassment, interruption, obturation.

obtain *vb* achieve, acquire, attain, bring, contrive, earn, elicit, gain, get, induce, procure, secure; hold, prevail, stand, subsist.

obtrude *vb* encroach, infringe, interfere, intrude, trespass.

obtrusive *adj* forward, interfering, intrusive, meddling, officious.

obtuse *adj* blunt; blockish, doltish, dull, dull-witted, heavy, stockish, stolid, stupid, slow, unintellectual, unintelligent.

obviate *vb* anticipate, avert, counteract, preclude, prevent, remove.

obvious *adj* exposed, liable, open, subject; apparent, clear, distinct, evident, manifest, palatable, patent, perceptible, plain, self-evident, unmistakable, visible.

occasion *vb* breed, cause, create, originate, produce; induce, influence, move, persuade. * *n* casualty, event, incident, occurrence; conjuncture, convenience, juncture, opening, opportunity; condition, necessity, need, exigency, requirement, want; cause, ground, reason; inducement, influence; circumstance, exigency.

occasional *adj* accidental, casual, incidental, infrequent, irregular, uncommon; causative, causing.

occasionally *adv* casually, sometimes.

occult *adj* abstruse, cabbalistic, hidden, latent, secret, invisible, mysterious, mystic, mystical, recondite, shrouded, undetected, undiscovered, unknown, unrevealed, veiled. * *n* magic, sorcery, witchcraft.

occupation *n* holding, occupancy, possession, tenure, use; avocation, business, calling, craft, employment, engagement, job, post, profession, trade, vocation.

occupy *vb* capture, hold, keep, possess; cover, fill, garrison, inhabit, take up, tenant; engage, employ, use.

occur *vb* appear, arise, offer; befall, chance, eventuate, happen, result, supervene.

occurrence *n* accident, adventure, affair, casualty, event, happening, incident, proceeding, transaction.

odd *adj* additional, redundant, remaining; casual, incidental; inappropriate, queer, unsuitable; comical, droll, erratic, extravagant, extraordinary, fantastic, grotesque, irregular, peculiar, quaint, singular, strange, uncommon, uncouth, unique, unusual, whimsical.

odds *npl* difference, disparity, inequality; advantage, superiority, supremacy.

odious *adj* abominable, detestable, execrable, hateful, shocking; hated, obnoxious, unpopular; disagreeable, forbidding, loathsome, offensive.

odium *n* abhorrence, detestation, dislike, enmity, hate, hatred; odiousness, repulsiveness; obloquy, opprobrium, reproach, shame.

odorous *adj* aromatic, balmy, fragrant, perfumed, redolent, scented, sweet-scented, sweet-smelling.

odour *n* aroma, fragrance, perfume, redolence, scent, smell.

offal *n* carrion, dregs, garbage, refuse, rubbish, waste.

offence *n* aggression, attack, assault; anger, displeasure, indignation, pique, resentment, umbrage, wrath; affront, harm, injury, injustice, insult, outrage, wrong; crime, delinquency, fault, misdeed, misdemeanour, sin, transgression, trespass.

offend *vb* affront, annoy, chafe, displease, fret, gall, irritate, mortify, nettle, provoke, vex; molest, pain, shock, wound; fall, sin, stumble, transgress.

offender *n* convict, criminal, culprit, delinquent, felon, malefactor, sinner, transgressor, trespasser.

offensive *adj* aggressive, attacking, invading; disgusting, loathsome, nauseating, nauseous, repulsive, sickening; abominable, detestable, disagreeable, displeasing, execrable, hateful, obnoxious, repugnant, revolting, shocking, unpalatable, unpleasant; abusive, disagreeable, impertinent, insolent, insulting, irritating, opprobrious, rude, saucy, unpleasant. * *n* attack, onslaught.

offer *vb* present, proffer, tender; exhibit; furnish, propose, propound, show; volunteer; dare, essay, endeavour, venture. * *n* overture, proffering, proposal, proposition, tender, overture; attempt, bid, endeavour, essay.

offhand *adj* abrupt, brusque, casual, curt, extempore, impromptu, informal, unpremeditated, unstudied. * *adv* carelessly, casually, clumsily, haphazardly, informally, slapdash; ad-lib, extemporaneously, extemporarily, extempore, impromptu.

office *n* duty, function, service, work; berth, place, position, post, situation; business, capacity, charge, employment, trust; bureau, room.

officiate *vb* act, perform, preside, serve.

officious *adj* busy, dictatorial, forward, impertinent, interfering, intermeddling, meddlesome, meddling, obtrusive, pushing, pushy.

offset *vb* balance, counteract, counterbalance, counterpoise. * *n* branch, offshoot, scion, shoot, slip, sprout, twig; counterbalance, counterpoise, set-off, equivalent.

offspring *n* brood, children, descendants, issue, litter, posterity, progeny; cadet, child, scion.

often *adv* frequently, generally, oftentimes, repeatedly.

ogre *n* bugbear, demon, devil, goblin, hobgoblin, monster, spectre.

old *adj* aged, ancient, antiquated, antique, archaic, elderly, obsolete, olden, old-fashioned, superannuated; decayed, done, senile, worn-out; original, primitive, pristine; former, preceding, pre-existing.

oleaginous *adj* adipose, fat, fatty, greasy, oily, sebaceous, unctuous.

omen *n* augury, auspice, foreboding, portent, presage, prognosis, sign, warning.

ominous *adj* inauspicious, monitory, portentous, premonitory, threatening, unpropitious.

omission *n* default, failure, forgetfulness, neglect, oversight.

omit *vb* disregard, drop, eliminate, exclude, miss, neglect, overlook, skip.

omnipotent *adj* almighty, all-powerful.

omniscient *adj* all-knowing, all-seeing, all-wise.

oneness *n* individuality, singleness, unity.

onerous *adj* burdensome, difficult, hard, heavy, laborious, oppressive, responsible, weighty.

one-sided *adj* partial, prejudiced, unfair, unilateral, unjust.

only *adj* alone, single, sole, solitary. * *adv* barely, merely, simply.

onset *n* assault, attack, charge, onslaught, storm, storming.

onus *n* burden, liability, load, responsibility.

ooze *vb* distil, drip, drop, shed; drain, exude, filter, leak, percolate, stain, transude. * *n* mire, mud, slime.

opaque *adj* dark, dim, hazy, muddy; abstruse, cryptic, enigmatic, enigmatical, obscure, unclear.

open *vb* expand, spread; begin, commence, initiate; disclose, exhibit, reveal, show; unbar, unclose, uncover, unlock, unseal, untie. * *adj* expanded, extended, unclosed, spread wide; aboveboard, artless, candid, cordial, fair, frank, guileless, hearty, honest, sincere, openhearted, single-minded, undesigning, undisguised, undissembling, unreserved; bounteous, bountiful, free, generous, liberal, munificent; ajar, uncovered; exposed, undefended, unprotected; clear, unobstructed; accessible, public, unenclosed, unrestricted; mild, moderate; apparent, debatable, evident, obvious, patent, plain, undetermined.

opening *adj* commencing, first, inaugural, initiatory, introductory. * *n* aperture, breach, chasm, cleft, fissure, flaw, gap, gulf, hole, interspace, loophole, orifice, perforation, rent, rift; beginning, commencement, dawn; chance, opportunity, vacancy.

openly *adv* candidly, frankly, honestly, plainly, publicly.

openness *n* candour, frankness, honesty, ingenuousness, plainness, unreservedness.

operate *vb* act, function, work; cause, effect, occasion, produce; manipulate, use, run.

operation *n* manipulation, performance, procedure, proceeding, process; action, affair, manoeuvre, motion, movement.

operative *adj* active, effective, effectual, efficient, serviceable, vigorous; important, indicative, influential, significant. * *n* artisan, employee, labourer, mechanic, worker, workman.

opiate *adj* narcotic, sedative, soporiferous, soporific. * *n* anodyne, drug, narcotic, sedative, tranquillizer.

opine *vb* apprehend, believe, conceive, fancy, judge, suppose, presume, surmise, think.

opinion *n* conception, idea, impression, judgment, notion, sentiment, view; belief, persuasion, tenet; esteem, estimation, judgment.

opinionated *adj* biased, bigoted, cocksure, conceited, dictatorial, dogmatic, opinionative, prejudiced, stubborn.

opponent *adj* adverse, antagonistic, contrary, opposing, opposite, repugnant. * *n* adversary, antagonist, competitor, contestant, counteragent, enemy, foe, opposite, opposer, party, rival.

opportune *adj* appropriate, auspicious, convenient, favourable, felicitous, fit, fitting, fortunate, lucky, propitious, seasonable, suitable, timely, well-timed.

opportunity *n* chance, convenience, moment, occasion.

oppose *vb* combat, contravene, counteract, dispute, obstruct, oppugn, resist, thwart, withstand; check, prevent; confront, counterpoise.

opposite *adj* facing, fronting; conflicting, contradictory, contrary, different, diverse, incompatible, inconsistent, irreconcilable; adverse, antagonistic, hostile, inimical, opposed, opposing, repugnant. * *n* contradiction, contrary, converse, reverse.

opposition *n* antagonism, antinomy, contrariety, inconsistency, repugnance; counteraction, counter-influence, hostility, resistance; hindrance, obstacle, obstruction, oppression, prevention.

oppress *vb* burden, crush, depress, harass, load, maltreat, overburden, overpower, overwhelm, persecute, subdue, suppress, tyrannize, wrong.

oppression *n* abuse, calamity, cruelty, hardship, injury, injustice, misery, persecution, severity, suffering, tyranny; depression, dullness, heaviness, lassitude.

oppressive *adj* close, muggy, stifling, suffocating, sultry.

opprobrious *adj* abusive, condemnatory, contemptuous, damnatory, insolent, insulting, offensive, reproachable, scandalous, scurrilous, vituperative; despised, dishonourable, disreputable, hateful, infamous, shameful.

opprobrium *n* contumely, scurrility; calumny, disgrace, ignominy, infamy, obloquy, odium, reproach.

oppugn *vb* assail, argue, attack, combat, contravene, oppose, resist, thwart, withstand.

option *n* choice, discretion, election, preference, selection.

optional *adj* discretionary, elective, nonobligatory, voluntary.

opulence *n* affluence, fortune, independence, luxury, riches, wealth.

opulent *adj* affluent, flush, luxurious, moneyed, plentiful, rich, sumptuous, wealthy.

oracular *adj* ominous, portentous, prophetic; authoritative, dogmatic, magisterial, positive; aged, grave, wise; ambiguous, blind, dark, equivocal, obscure.

oral *adj* nuncupative, spoken, verbal, vocal.

oration *n* address, declamation, discourse, harangue, speech.

orb *n* ball, globe, sphere; circle, circuit, orbit, ring; disk, wheel.

orbit *vb* circle, encircle, revolve around. * *n* course, path, revolution, track.

ordain *vb* appoint, call, consecrate, elect, experiment, constitute, establish, institute, regulate; decree, enjoin, enact, order, prescribe.

order *vb* adjust, arrange, methodize, regulate, systematize; carry on, conduct, manage; bid, command, direct, instruct, require. * *n* arrangement, disposition, method, regularity, symmetry, system; law, regulation, rule; discipline, peace, quiet; command, commission, direction, injunction, instruction, mandate, prescription; class, degree, grade, kind, rank; family, tribe; brotherhood, community, fraternity, society; sequence, succession.

orderly *adj* methodical, regular, systematic; peaceable, quiet, well-behaved; neat, shipshape, tidy.

ordinance *n* appointment, command, decree, edict, enactment, law, order, prescript, regulation, rule, statute; ceremony, observance, sacrament, rite, ritual.

ordinary *adj* accustomed, customary, established, everyday, normal, regular, settled, wonted, everyday, regular; common, frequent, habitual, usual; average, commonplace, indifferent, inferior, mean, mediocre, second-rate, undistinguished; homely, plain.

organization *n* business, construction, constitution, organism, structure, system.

organize *vb* adjust, constitute, construct, form, make, shape; arrange, coordinate, correlate, establish, systematize.

orgy *n* carousal, debauch, debauchery, revel, saturnalia.

orifice *n* aperture, hole, mouth, perforation, pore, vent.

origin *n* beginning, birth, commencement, cradle, derivation, foundation, fountain, fountainhead, original, rise, root, source, spring, starting point; cause, occasion; heritage, lineage, parentage.

original *adj* aboriginal, first, primary, primeval, primitive, primordial, pristine; fresh, inventive, novel; eccentric, odd, peculiar. * *n* cause, commencement, origin, source, spring; archetype, exemplar, model, pattern, prototype, protoplast, type.

originate *vb* arise, begin, emanate, flow, proceed, rise, spring; create, discover, form, invent, produce.

originator *n* author, creator, former, inventor, maker, parent.

orison *n* petition, prayer, solicitation, supplication.

ornament *vb* adorn, beautify, bedeck, bedizen, decorate, deck, emblazon, garnish, grace. * *n* adornment, bedizenment, decoration, design, embellishment, garnish, ornamentation.

ornate *adj* beautiful, bedecked, decorated, elaborate, elegant, embellished, florid, flowery, ornamental, ornamented.

orthodox *adj* conventional, correct, sound, true.

oscillate *vb* fluctuate, sway, swing, vacillate, vary, vibrate.

ostensible *adj* apparent, assigned, avowed, declared, exhibited, manifest, presented, visible; plausible, professed, specious.

ostentation *n* dash, display, flourish, pageantry, parade, pomp, pomposity, pompousness, show, vaunting; appearance, semblance, showiness.

ostentatious *adj* boastful, dashing, flaunting, pompous, pretentious, showy, vain, vainglorious; gaudy.

ostracize *vb* banish, boycott, exclude, excommunicate, exile, expatriate, expel, evict.

oust *vb* dislodge, dispossess, eject, evict, expel.

outbreak *n* ebullition, eruption, explosion, outburst; affray, broil, conflict, commotion, fray, riot, row; flare-up, manifestation.

outcast *n* exile, expatriate; castaway, pariah, reprobate, vagabond.

outcome *n* conclusion, consequence, event, issue, result, upshot.

outcry *n* cry, scream, screech, yell; bruit, clamour, noise, tumult, vociferation.

outdo *vb* beat, exceed, excel, outgo, outstrip, outvie, surpass.

outlandish *adj* alien, exotic, foreign, strange; barbarous, bizarre, uncouth.

outlaw *vb* ban, banish, condemn, exclude, forbid, make illegal, prohibit. * *n* bandit, brigand, crook, freebooter, highwayman, lawbreaker, marauder, robber, thief.

outlay *n* disbursement, expenditure, outgoings.

outline *vb* delineate, draft, draw, plan, silhouette, sketch. * *n* contour, profile; delineation, draft, drawing, plan, rough draft, silhouette, sketch.

outlive *vb* last, live longer, survive.

outlook *n* future, prospect, sight, view; lookout, watch-tower.

outrage *vb* abuse, injure, insult, maltreat, offend, shock, injure. * *n* abuse, affront, indignity, insult, offence.

outrageous *adj* abusive, frantic, furious, frenzied, mad, raging, turbulent, violent, wild; atrocious, enormous, flagrant, heinous, monstrous, nefarious, villainous; enormous, excessive, extravagant, unwarrantable.

outré *adj* excessive, exorbitant, extravagant, immoderate, inordinate, overstrained, unconventional.

outrun *vb* beat, exceed, outdistance, outgo, outstrip, outspeed, surpass.

outset *n* beginning, commencement, entrance, opening, start, starting point.

outshine *vb* eclipse, outstrip, overshadow, surpass.

outspoken *adj* abrupt, blunt, candid, frank, plain, plainspoken, unceremonious, unreserved.

outstanding *adj* due, owing, uncollected, ungathered, unpaid, unsettled; conspicuous, eminent, prominent, striking.

outward *adj* exterior, external, outer, outside.

outwit *vb* cheat, circumvent, deceive, defraud, diddle, dupe, gull, outmanoeuvre, overreach, swindle, victimize.

overawe *vb* affright, awe, browbeat, cow, daunt, frighten, intimidate, scare, terrify.

overbalance *vb* capsize, overset, overturn, tumble, upset; outweigh, preponderate.

overbearing *adj* oppressive, overpowering; arrogant, dictatorial, dogmatic, domineering, haughty, imperious, overweening, proud, supercilious.

overcast *vb* cloud, darken, overcloud, overshadow, shade, shadow. * *adj* cloudy, darkened, hazy, murky, obscure.

overcharge *vb* burden, oppress, overburden, overload, surcharge; crowd, overfill; exaggerate, overstate, overstrain.

overcome *vb* beat, choke, conquer, crush, defeat, discomfit, overbear, overmaster, overpower, overthrow, overturn, overwhelm, prevail, rout, subdue, subjugate, surmount, vanquish.

overflow *vb* brim over, fall over, pour over, pour out, shower, spill; deluge, inundate, submerge. * *n* deluge, inundation, profusion, superabundance.

overhaul *vb* overtake; check, examine, inspect, repair, survey. * *n* check, examination, inspection.

overlay *vb* cover, spread over; overlie, overpress, smother; crush, overpower, overwhelm; cloud, hide, obscure, overcast. * *n* appliqué, covering, decoration, veneer.

overlook *vb* inspect, oversee, superintend, supervise; disregard, miss, neglect, slight; condone, excuse, forgive, pardon, pass over.

overpower *vb* beat, conquer, crush, defeat, discomfit, overbear, overcome, overmaster, overturn, overwhelm, subdue, subjugate, vanquish.

overreach *vb* exceed, outstrip, overshoot, pass, surpass; cheat, circumvent, deceive, defraud.

override *vb* outride, outweigh, pass, quash, supersede, surpass.

overrule *vb* control, govern, sway; annul, cancel, nullify, recall, reject, repeal, repudiate, rescind, revoke, reject, set aside, supersede, suppress.

oversight *n* care, charge, control, direction, inspection, management, superintendence, supervision, surveillance; blunder, error, fault, inadvertence, inattention, lapse, miss, mistake, neglect, omission, slip, trip.

overt *adj* apparent, glaring, open, manifest, notorious, patent, public, unconcealed.

overthrow *vb* overturn, upset, subvert; demolish, destroy, level; beat, conquer, crush, defeat, discomfit, foil, master, overcome, overpower, overwhelm, rout, subjugate, vanquish, worst. * *n* downfall, fall, prostration, subversion; destruction, demolition, ruin; defeat, discomfiture, dispersion, rout.

overturn *vb* invert, overthrow, reverse, subvert, upset.

overture *n* invitation, offer, proposal, proposition.

overweening *adj* arrogant, conceited, consequential, egotistical, haughty, opinionated, proud, supercilious, vain, vainglorious.

overwhelm *vb* drown, engulf, inundate, overflow, submerge, swallow up, swamp; conquer, crush, defeat, overbear, overcome, overpower, subdue, vanquish.

overwrought *adj* overdone, overelaborate; agitated, excited, overexcited, overworked, stirred.

own[1] *vb* have, hold, possess; avow, confess; acknowledge, admit, allow, concede.

own[2] *adj* particular, personal, private.

owner *n* freeholder, holder, landlord, possessor, proprietor.

P

pace *vb* go, hasten, hurry, move, step, walk. * *n* amble, gait, step, walk.

pacific *adj* appeasing, conciliatory, ironic, mollifying, placating, peacemaking, propitiatory; calm, gentle, peaceable, peaceful, quiet, smooth, tranquil, unruffled.

pacify *vb* appease, conciliate, harmonize, tranquillize; allay, appease, assuage, calm, compose, hush, lay, lull, moderate, mollify, placate, propitiate, quell, quiet, smooth, soften, soothe, still.

pack *vb* compact, compress, crowd, fill; bundle, burden, load, stow. * *n* bale, budget, bundle, package, packet, parcel; burden, load; assemblage, assembly, assortment, collection, set; band, bevy, clan, company, crew, gang, knot, lot, party, squad.

pact *n* agreement, alliance, bargain, bond, compact, concordat, contract, convention, covenant, league, stipulation.

pagan *adj* heathen, heathenish, idolatrous, irreligious, paganist, paganistic. * *n* gentile, heathen, idolater.

pageantry *n* display, flourish, magnificence, parade, pomp, show, splendour, state.

pain *vb* agonize, bite, distress, hurt, rack, sting, torment, torture; afflict, aggrieve, annoy, bore, chafe, displease, disquiet, fret, grieve, harass, incommode, plague, tease, trouble, vex, worry; rankle, smart, shoot, sting, twinge. * *n* ache, agony, anguish, discomfort, distress, gripe, hurt, pang, smart, soreness, sting, suffering, throe, torment, torture, twinge; affliction, anguish, anxiety, bitterness, care, chagrin, disquiet, dolour, grief, heartache, misery, punishment, solicitude, sorrow, trouble, uneasiness, unhappiness, vexation, woe, wretchedness.

painful *adj* agonizing, distressful, excruciating, racking, sharp, tormenting, torturing; afflicting, afflictive, annoying, baleful, disagreeable, displeasing, disquieting, distressing, dolorous, grievous, provoking, troublesome, unpleasant, vexatious; arduous, careful, difficult, hard, severe, sore, toilsome.

pains *npl* care, effort, labour, task, toilsomeness, trouble; childbirth, labour, travail.

painstaking *adj* assiduous, careful, conscientious, diligent, hardworking, industrious, laborious, persevering, plodding, sedulous, strenuous.

paint *vb* delineate, depict, describe, draw, figure, pencil, portray, represent, sketch; adorn, beautify, deck, embellish, ornament. * *n* colouring, dye, pigment, stain; cosmetics, greasepaint, make-up.

pair *vb* couple, marry, mate, match. * *n* brace, couple, double, duo, match, twosome.

pal *n* buddy, chum, companion, comrade, crony, friend, mate, mucker.

palatable *adj* acceptable, agreeable, appetizing, delicate, delicious, enjoyable, flavourful, flavoursome, gustative, gustatory, luscious, nice, pleasant, pleasing, savoury, relishable, tasteful, tasty, toothsome.

palaver *vb* chat, chatter, converse, patter, prattle, say, speak, talk; confer, parley; blandish, cajole, flatter, wheedle. * *n* chat, chatter, conversation, discussion, language, prattle, speech, talk; confab, confabulation, conference, conclave, parley, powwow; balderdash, cajolery, flummery, gibberish.

pale *vb* blanch, lose colour, whiten. * *adj* ashen, ashy, blanched, bloodless, pallid, sickly, wan, white; blank, dim, obscure, spectral. * *n* picket, stake; circuit, enclosure; district, region, territory; boundary, confine, fence, limit.

pall[1] *n* cloak, cover, curtain, mantle, pallium, shield, shroud, veil.

pall[2] *vb* cloy, glut, gorge, satiate, surfeit; deject, depress, discourage, dishearten, dispirit; cloak, cover, drape, invest, overspread, shroud.

palliate *vb* cloak, conceal, cover, excuse, extenuate, hide, gloss, lessen; abate, allay, alleviate, assuage, blunt, diminish, dull, ease, mitigate, moderate, mollify, quell, quiet, relieve, soften, soothe, still.

pallid *adj* ashen, ashy, cadaverous, colourless, pale, sallow, wan, whitish.

palm[1] *vb* foist, impose, obtrude, pass off; handle, touch.

palm[2] *n* bays, crown, laurels, prize, trophy, victory.

palmy *adj* flourishing, fortunate, glorious, golden, halcyon, happy, joyous, prosperous, thriving, victorious.

palpable *adj* corporeal, material, tactile, tangible; evident, glaring, gross, intelligible, manifest, obvious, patent, plain, unmistakable.

palpitate *vb* flutter, pulsate, throb; quiver, shiver, tremble.

palter *vb* dodge, equivocate, evade, haggle, prevaricate, quibble, shift, shuffle, trifle.

paltry *adj* diminutive, feeble, inconsiderable, insignificant, little, miserable, petty, slender, slight, small, sorry, trifling, trivial, unimportant, wretched.

pamper *vb* baby, coddle, fondle, gratify, humour, spoil.

panacea *n* catholicon, cure-all, medicine, remedy.

panegyric *adj* commendatory, encomiastic, encomiastical, eulogistic, eulogistical, laudatory, panegyrical. * *n* eulogy, laudation, praise, paean, tribute.

pang *n* agony, anguish, distress, gripe, pain, throe, twinge.

panic *vb* affright, alarm, scare, startle, terrify; become terrified, overreact. * *n* alarm, consternation, fear, fright, jitters, terror.

pant *vb* blow, gasp, puff; heave, palpitate, pulsate, throb; languish; desire, hunger, long, sigh, thirst, yearn. * *n* blow, gasp, puff.

parable *n* allegory, fable, story.

paraclete *n* advocate, comforter, consoler, intercessor, mediator.

parade *vb* display, flaunt, show, vaunt. * *n* ceremony, display, flaunting, ostentation, pomp, show; array, pageant, review, spectacle; mall, promenade.

paradox *n* absurdity, contradiction, mystery.

paragon *n* flower, ideal, masterpiece, model, nonpareil, pattern, standard.

paragraph *n* clause, item, notice, passage, section, sentence, subdivision.

parallel *vb* be alike, compare, conform, correlate, match. * *adj* abreast, concurrent; allied, analogous, correspondent, equal, like, resembling, similar. * *n* conformity, likeness, resemblance, similarity; analogue, correlative, counterpart.

paramount *adj* chief, dominant, eminent, pre-eminent, principal, superior, supreme.

paraphernalia *n* accoutrements, appendages, appurtenances, baggage, belongings, effects, equipage, equipment, ornaments, trappings.

parasite *n* bloodsucker, fawner, flatterer, flunky, hanger-on, leech, spaniel, sycophant, toady, wheedler.

parcel *vb* allot, apportion, dispense, distribute, divide. * *n* budget, bundle, package; batch, collection, group, lot, set; division, part, patch, pierce, plot, portion, tract.

parched *adj* arid, dry, scorched, shrivelled, thirsty.

pardon *vb* condone, forgive, overlook, remit; absolve, acquit, clear, discharge, excuse, release. * *n* absolution, amnesty, condonation, discharge, excuse, forgiveness, grace, mercy, overlook, release.

parentage *n* ancestry, birth, descent, extraction, family, lineage, origin, parenthood, pedigree, stock.

pariah *n* outcast, wretch.

parish *n* community, congregation, parishioners; district, subdivision.

parity *n* analogy, correspondence, equality, equivalence, likeness, sameness, similarity.

parody *vb* burlesque, caricature, imitate, lampoon, mock, ridicule, satirize, travesty. * *n* burlesque, caricature, imitation, ridicule, satire, travesty.

paroxysm *n* attack, convulsion, exacerbation, fit, outburst, seizure, spasm, throe.

parsimonious *adj* avaricious, close, close-fisted, covetous, frugal, grasping, grudging, illiberal, mean, mercenary, miserly, near, niggardly, penurious, shabby, sordid, sparing, stingy, tightfisted.

parson *n* churchman, clergyman, divine, ecclesiastic, incumbent, minister, pastor, priest, rector.

part *vb* break, dismember, dissever, divide, sever, subdivide, sunder; detach, disconnect, disjoin, dissociate, disunite, separate; allot, apportion, distribute, divide, mete, share; secrete. * *n* crumb, division, fraction, fragment, moiety, parcel, piece, portion, remnant, scrap, section, segment, subdivision; component, constituent, element, ingredient, member, organ; lot, share; concern, interest, participation; allotment, apportionment, dividend; business, charge, duty, function, office, work; faction, party, side; character, cue, lines, role; clause, paragraph, passage.

partake *vb* engage, participate, share; consume, eat, take;evince, evoke, show, suggest.

partial *adj* component, fractional, imperfect, incomplete, limited; biased, influential, interested, one-sided, prejudiced, prepossessed, unfair, unjust, warped; fond, indulgent.

participate *vb* engage in, partake, perform, share.

particle *n* atom, bit, corpuscle, crumb, drop, glimmer, grain, granule, iota, jot, mite, molecule, morsel, mote, scrap, shred, snip, spark, speck, whit.

particular *adj* especial, special, specific; distinct, individual, respective, separate, single; characteristic, distinctive, peculiar; individual, intimate, own, personal, private; notable, noteworthy; circumstantial, definite, detailed, exact, minute, narrow, precise; careful, close, conscientious, critical, fastidious, nice, scrupulous, strict; marked, odd, singular, strange, uncommon. * *n* case, circumstance, count, detail, feature, instance, item, particularity, point, regard, respect.

parting *adj* breaking, dividing, separating; final, last, valedictory; declining, departing. * *n* breaking, disruption, rupture, severing; detachment, division, separation; death, departure, farewell, leave-taking.

partisan *adj* biased, factional, interested, partial, prejudiced. * *n* adherent, backer, champion, disciple, follower, supporter, votary; baton, halberd, pike, quarterstaff, truncheon, staff.

partition *vb* apportion, distribute, divide, portion, separate, share. * *n* division, separation; barrier, division, screen, wall; allotment, apportionment, distribution.

partner *n* associate, colleague, copartner, partaker, participant, participator; accomplice, ally, coadjutor, confederate; companion, consort, spouse.

partnership *n* association, company, copartnership, firm, house, society; connection, interest, participation, union.

parts *npl* abilities, accomplishments, endowments, faculties, genius, gifts, intellect, intelligence, mind, qualities, powers, talents; districts, regions.

party *n* alliance, association, cabal, circle, clique, combination, confederacy, coterie, faction, group, junta, league, ring, set; body, company, detachment, squad, troop; assembly, gathering; partaker, participant, participator, sharer; defendant, litigant, plaintiff; individual, one, person, somebody; cause, division, interest, side.

pass[1] *vb* devolve, fall, go, move, proceed; change, elapse, flit, glide, lapse, slip; cease, die, fade, expire, vanish; happen, occur; convey, deliver, send, transmit, transfer; disregard, ignore, neglect; exceed, excel, surpass; approve, ratify, sanction; answer, do, succeed, suffice, suit; express, pronounce, utter; beguile, wile.

pass[2] *n* avenue, ford, road, route, way; defile, gorge, passage, ravine; authorization, licence, passport, permission, ticket; condition, conjecture, plight, situation, state; lunge, push, thrust, tilt; transfer, trick.

passable *adj* admissible, allowable, mediocre, middling, moderate, ordinary, so-so, tolerable; acceptable, current, receivable; navigable, traversable.

passage *n* going, passing, progress, transit; evacuation, journey, migration, transit, voyage; avenue, channel, course, pass, path, road, route, thoroughfare, vennel, way; access, currency, entry, reception; act, deed, event, feat, incidence, occurrence, passion; corridor, gallery, gate, hall; clause, paragraph, sentence, text; course, death, decease, departure, expiration, lapse; affair, brush, change, collision, combat, conflict, contest, encounter, exchange, joust, skirmish, tilt.

passenger *n* fare, itinerant, tourist, traveller, voyager, wayfarer.

passionate *adj* animated, ardent, burning, earnest, enthusiastic, excited, fervent, fiery, furious, glowing, hot-blooded, impassioned, impetuous, impulsive, intense, vehement, warm, zealous; hot-headed, irascible, quick-tempered, tempestuous, violent.

passive *adj* inactive, inert, quiescent, receptive; apathetic, enduring, long-suffering, nonresistant, patient, stoical, submissive, suffering, unresisting.

past *adj* accomplished, elapsed, ended, gone, spent; ancient, bygone, former, obsolete, outworn. * *adv* above, extra, beyond, over. * *prep* above, after, beyond, exceeding. * *n* antiquity, heretofore, history, olden times, yesterday.

pastime *n* amusement, diversion, entertainment, hobby, play, recreation, sport.

pastor *n* clergyman, churchman, divine, ecclesiastic, minister, parson, priest, vicar.

pat[1] *vb* dab, hit, rap, tap; caress, chuck, fondle, pet. * *n* dab, hit, pad, rap, tap; caress.

pat[2] *adj* appropriate, apt, fit, pertinent, suitable. * *adv* aptly, conveniently, fitly, opportunely, seasonably.

patch *vb* mend, repair. * *n* repair; parcel, plot, tract.

patent *adj* expanded, open, spreading; apparent, clear, conspicuous, evident, glaring, indisputable, manifest, notorious, obvious, public, open, palpable, plain, unconcealed, unmistakable. * *n* copyright, privilege, right.

paternity *n* derivation, descent, fatherhood, origin.

path *n* access, avenue, course, footway, passage, pathway, road, route, track, trail, way.

pathetic *adj* affecting, melting, moving, pitiable, plaintive, sad, tender, touching.

patience *n* endurance, fortitude, long-sufferance, resignation, submission, sufferance; calmness, composure, quietness; forbearance, indulgence, leniency; assiduity, constancy, diligence, indefatigability, indefatigableness, perseverance, persistence.

patient *adj* meek, passive, resigned, submissive, uncomplaining, unrepining; calm, composed, contented, quiet; indulgent, lenient, long-suffering; assiduous, constant, diligent, indefatigable, persevering, persistent. * *n* case, invalid, subject, sufferer.

patrician *adj* aristocratic, blue-blooded, highborn, noble, senatorial, well-born. * *n* aristocrat, blue blood, nobleman.

patron *n* advocate, defender, favourer, guardian, helper, protector, supporter.

patronize *vb* aid, assist, befriend, countenance, defend, favour, maintain, support; condescend, disparage, scorn.

pattern *vb* copy, follow, imitate. * *n* archetype, exemplar, last, model, original, paradigm, plan, prototype; example, guide, sample, specimen; mirror, paragon; design, figure, shape, style, type.

paucity *n* deficiency, exiguity, insufficiency, lack, poverty, rarity, shortage.

paunch *n* abdomen, belly, gut, stomach.

pauperism *n* beggary, destitution, indigence, mendicancy, mendicity, need, poverty, penury, want.

pause *vb* breathe, cease, delay, desist, rest, stay, stop, wait; delay, forbear, intermit, stay, stop, tarry, wait; deliberate, demur, hesitate, waver. * *n* break, caesura, cessation, halt, intermission, interruption, interval, remission, rest, stop, stoppage, stopping, suspension; hesitation, suspense, uncertainty; paragraph.

pawn[1] *n* cat's-paw, dupe, plaything, puppet, stooge, tool, toy.

pawn[2] *vb* bet, gage, hazard, lay, pledge, risk, stake, wager. * *n* assurance, bond, guarantee, pledge, security.

pay *vb* defray, discharge, discount, foot, honour, liquidate, meet, quit, settle; compensate, recompense, reimburse, requite, reward; punish, revenge; give, offer, render. * *n* allowance, commission, compensation, emolument, hire, recompense, reimbursement, remuneration, requital, reward, salary, wages.

peace *n* calm, calmness, quiet, quietness, repose, stillness; accord, amity, friendliness, harmony; composure, equanimity, imperturbability, placidity, quietude, tranquillity; agreement, armistice.

peaceable *adj* pacific, peaceful; amiable, amicable, friendly, gentle, inoffensive, mild; placid, quiet, serene, still, tranquil, undisturbed, unmoved.

peaceful *adj* quiet, undisturbed; amicable, concordant, friendly, gentle, harmonious, mild, pacific, peaceable; calm, composed, placid, serene, still.

peak *vb* climax, culminate, top; dwindle, thin. * *n* acme, apex, crest, crown, pinnacle, summit, top, zenith.

peaked *adj* piked, pointed, thin.

peasant *n* boor, countryman, clown, hind, labourer, rustic, swain.

peculate *vb* appropriate, defraud, embezzle, misappropriate, pilfer, purloin, rob, steal.

peculiar *adj* appropriate, idiosyncratic, individual, proper; characteristic, eccentric, exceptional, extraordinary, odd, queer, rare, singular, strange, striking, uncommon, unusual; individual, especial, particular, select, special, specific.

peculiarity *n* appropriateness, distinctiveness, individuality, speciality; characteristic, idiosyncrasy, oddity, peculiarity, singularity.

pedantic *adj* conceited, fussy, officious, ostentatious, over-learned, particular, pedagogical, pompous, pragmatical, precise, pretentious, priggish, stilted.

pedlar *n* chapman, costermonger, hawker, packman, vendor.

pedigree *adj* purebred, thoroughbred. * *n* ancestry, breed, descent, extraction, family, genealogy, house, line, lineage, race, stock, strain.

peer[1] *vb* gaze, look, peek, peep, pry, squinny, squint; appear, emerge.

peer[2] *n* associate, co-equal, companion, compeer, equal, equivalent, fellow, like, mate, match; aristocrat, baron, count, duke, earl, grandee, lord, marquis, noble, nobleman, viscount.

peerless *adj* excellent, incomparable, matchless, outstanding, superlative, unequalled, unique, unmatched, unsurpassed.

peevish *adj* acrimonious, captious, churlish, complaining, crabbed, cross, crusty, discontented, fretful, ill-natured, ill-tempered, irascible, irritable, pettish, petulant, querulous, snappish, snarling, splenetic, spleeny, testy, waspish; forward, headstrong, obstinate, self-willed, stubborn; childish, silly, thoughtless, trifling.

pellucid *adj* bright, clear, crystalline, diaphanous, limpid, lucid, transparent.

pelt[1] *vb* assail, batter, beat, belabour, bombard, pepper, stone, strike; cast, hurl, throw; hurry, rush, speed, tear.

pelt[2] *n* coat, hide, skin.

pen[1] *vb* compose, draft, indite, inscribe, write.

pen[2] *vb* confine, coop, encage, enclose, impound, imprison, incarcerate. * *n* cage, coop, corral, crib, hutch, enclosure, paddock, pound, stall, sty.

penalty *n* chastisement, fine, forfeiture, mulct, punishment, retribution.

penance *n* humiliation, maceration, mortification, penalty, punishment.

penchant *n* bent, bias, disposition, fondness, inclination, leaning, liking, predilection, predisposition, proclivity, proneness, propensity, taste, tendency, turn.

penetrate *vb* bore, burrow, cut, enter, invade, penctrate, percolate, perforate, pervade, pierce, soak, stab; affect, sensitize, touch; comprehend, discern, perceive, understand.

penetrating *adj* penetrative, permeating, piercing, sharp, subtle; acute, clear-sighted, discerning, intelligent, keen, quick, sagacious, sharp-witted, shrewd.

penetration *n* acuteness, discernment, insight, sagacity.

penitence *n* compunction, contrition, qualms, regret, remorse, repentance, sorrow.

penitent *adj* compunctious, conscience-stricken, contrite, regretful, remorseful, repentant, sorrowing, sorrowful. * *n* penance-doer, penitentiary, repentant.

penniless *adj* destitute, distressed, impecunious, indigent, moneyless, pinched, poor, necessitous, needy, pensive, poverty-stricken, reduced.

pensive *adj* contemplative, dreamy, meditative, reflective, sober, thoughtful; grave, melancholic, melancholy, mournful, sad, serious, solemn.

penurious *adj* inadequate, ill-provided, insufficient, meagre, niggardly, poor, scanty, stinted; avaricious, close, close-fisted, covetous, illiberal, grasping, grudging, mean, mercenary, miserly, near, niggardly, parsimonious, sordid, stingy, tightfisted.

penury *n* beggary, destitution, indigence, need, poverty, privation, want.

people *vb* colonize, inhabit, populate. * *n* clan, country, family, nation, race, state, tribe; folk, humankind, persons, population, public; commons, community, democracy, populace, proletariat; mob, multitude, rabble.

perceive *vb* behold, descry, detect, discern, discover, discriminate, distinguish, note, notice, observe, recognize, remark, see, spot; appreciate, comprehend, know, understand.

perceptible *adj* apparent, appreciable, cognizable, discernible, noticeable, perceivable, understandable, visible.

perception *n* apprehension, cognition, discernment, perceiving, recognition, seeing; comprehension, conception, consciousness, perceptiveness, perceptivity, understanding, feeling.

perchance *adv* haply, maybe, mayhap, peradventure, perhaps, possibly, probably.

percolate *vb* drain, drip, exude, filter, filtrate, ooze, penetrate, stain, transude.

percussion *n* collision, clash, concussion, crash, encounter, shock.

perdition *n* damnation, demolition, destruction, downfall, hell, overthrow, ruin, wreck.

peremptory *adj* absolute, authoritative, categorical, commanding, decisive, express, imperative, imperious, positive; determined, resolute, resolved; arbitrary, dogmatic, incontrovertible.

perennial *adj* ceaseless, constant, continual, deathless, enduring, immortal, imperishable, lasting, never-failing, permanent, perpetual, unceasing, undying, unfailing, uninterrupted.

perfect *vb* accomplish, complete, consummate, elaborate, finish. * *adj* completed, finished; complete, entire, full, unqualified, utter, whole; capital, consummate, excellent, exquisite, faultless, ideal; accomplished, disciplined, expert, skilled; blameless, faultless, holy, immaculate, pure, spotless, unblemished.

perfection *n* completeness, completion, consummation, correctness, excellence, faultlessness, finish, maturity, perfection, perfectness, wholeness; beauty, quality.

perfidious *adj* deceitful, dishonest, disloyal, double-faced, faithless, false, false-hearted, traitorous, treacherous, unfaithful, untrustworthy, venal.

perfidy *n* defection, disloyalty, faithlessness, infidelity, perfidiousness, traitorousness, treachery, treason.

perforate *vb* bore, drill, penetrate, pierce, pink, prick, punch, riddle, trepan.

perform *vb* accomplish, achieve, compass, consummate, do, effect, transact; complete, discharge, execute, fulfil, meet, observe, satisfy; act, play, represent.

performance *n* accomplishment, achievement, completion, consummation, discharge, doing, execution, fulfilment; act, action, deed, exploit, feat, work; composition, production; acting, entertainment, exhibition, play, representation, hold; execution, playing.

perfume *n* aroma, balminess, bouquet, fragrance, incense, odour, redolence, scent, smell, sweetness.

perfunctory *adj* careless, formal, heedless, indifferent, mechanical, negligent, reckless, slight, slovenly, thoughtless, unmindful.

perhaps *adv* haply, peradventure, perchance, possibly.

peril *vb* endanger, imperil, jeopardize, risk. * *n* danger, hazard, insecurity, jeopardy, pitfall, risk, snare, uncertainty.

perilous *adj* dangerous, hazardous, risky, unsafe.

period *n* aeon, age, cycle, date, eon, epoch, season, span, spell, stage, term, time; continuance, duration; bound, conclusion, determination, end, limit, term, termination; clause, phrase, proposition, sentence.

periodical *adj* cyclical, incidental, intermittent, recurrent, recurring, regular, seasonal, systematic. * *n* magazine, paper, review, serial, weekly.

periphery *n* boundary, circumference, outside, perimeter, superficies, surface.

perish *vb* decay, moulder, shrivel, waste, wither; decease, die, expire, vanish.

perishable *adj* decaying, decomposable, destructible; dying, frail, mortal, temporary.

perjured *adj* false, forsworn, perfidious, traitorous, treacherous, untrue.

permanent *adj* abiding, constant, continuing, durable, enduring, fixed, immutable, invariable, lasting, perpetual, persistent, stable, standing, steadfast, unchangeable, unchanging, unfading, unmovable.

permissible *adj* admissible, allowable, free, lawful, legal, legitimate, proper, sufferable, unprohibited.

permission *n* allowance, authorization, consent, dispensation, leave, liberty, licence, permit, sufferance, toleration, warrant.

permit *vb* agree, allow, endure, let, suffer, tolerate; admit, authorize, consent, empower, license, warrant. * *n* leave, liberty, licence, passport, permission, sanction, warrant.

pernicious *adj* baleful, baneful, damaging, deadly, deleterious, destructive, detrimental, disadvantageous, fatal, harmful, hurtful, injurious, malign, mischievous, noisome, noxious, prejudicial, ruinous; evil-hearted, malevolent, malicious, malignant, mischief-making, wicked.

perpetrate *vb* commit, do, execute, perform.

perpetual *adj* ceaseless, continual, constant, endless, enduring, eternal, ever-enduring, everlasting, incessant, interminable, never-ceasing, never-ending, perennial, permanent, sempiternal, unceasing, unending, unfailing, uninterrupted.

perplex *vb* complicate, encumber, entangle, involve, snarl, tangle; beset, bewilder, confound, confuse, corner, distract, embarrass, fog, mystify, nonplus, pother, puzzle, set; annoy, bother, disturb, harass, molest, pester, plague, tease, trouble, vex, worry.

persecute *vb* afflict, distress, harass, molest, oppress, worry; annoy, beset, importune, pester, solicit, tease.

perseverance *n* constancy, continuance, doggedness, indefatigableness, persistence, persistency, pertinacity, resolution, steadfastness, steadiness, tenacity.

persevere *vb* continue, determine, endure, maintain, persist, remain, resolve, stick.

persist *vb* continue, endure, last, remain; insist, persevere.

persistent *adj* constant, continuing, enduring, fixed, immovable, persevering, persisting, steady, tenacious; contumacious, dogged, indefatigable, obdurate, obstinate, pertinacious, perverse, pigheaded, stubborn.

personable *adj* comely, good-looking, graceful, seemly, well-turned-out.

personal *adj* individual, peculiar, private, special; bodily, corporal, corporeal, exterior, material, physical.

personate *vb* act, impersonate, personify, play, represent; disguise, mast; counterfeit, feign, simulate.

perspective *n* panorama, prospect, view, vista; proportion, relation.

perspicacious *adj* keen-sighted, quick-sighted, sharp-sighted; acute, clever, discerning, keen, penetrating, sagacious, sharp-witted, shrewd.

perspicacity *n* acumen, acuteness, astuteness, discernment, insight, penetration, perspicaciousness, sagacity, sharpness, shrewdness.

perspicuity *n* clearness, distinctness, explicitness, intelligibility, lucidity, lucidness, perspicuousness, plainness, transparency.

perspicuous *adj* clear, distinct, explicit, intelligible, lucid, obvious, plain, transparent, unequivocal.

perspire *vb* exhale, glow, sweat, swelter.

persuade *vb* allure, actuate, entice, impel, incite, induce, influence, lead, move, prevail upon, urge; advise, counsel; convince, satisfy; inculcate, teach.

persuasion *n* exhortation, incitement, inducement, influence; belief, conviction, opinion; creed, doctrine, dogma, tenet; kind, sort, variety.

persuasive *adj* cogent, convincing, inducing, inducible, logical, persuading, plausible, sound, valid, weighty.

pert *adj* brisk, dapper, lively, nimble, smart, sprightly, perky; bold, flippant, forward, free, impertinent, impudent, malapert, presuming, smart, saucy.

pertain *vb* appertain, befit, behove, belong, concern, refer, regard, relate.

pertinacious *adj* constant, determined, firm, obdurate, persevering, resolute, staunch, steadfast, steady; dogged, headstrong, inflexible, mulish, intractable, obstinate, perverse, stubborn, unyielding, wayward, wilful.

pertinent *adj* adapted, applicable, apposite, appropriate, apropos, apt, fit, germane, pat, proper, relevant, suitable; appurtenant, belonging, concerning, pertaining, regarding.

perturb *vb* agitate, disquiet, distress, disturb, excite, trouble, unsettle, upset, vex, worry; confuse.

pervade *vb* affect, animate, diffuse, extend, fill, imbue, impregnate, infiltrate, penetrate, permeate.

perverse *adj* bad, disturbed, oblique, perverted; contrary, dogged, headstrong, mulish, obstinate, pertinacious, perversive, stubborn, ungovernable, intractable, unyielding, wayward, wilful; cantankerous, churlish, crabbed, cross, cross-grained, crusty, cussed, morose, peevish, petulant, snappish, snarling, spiteful, spleeny, surly, testy, touchy, wicked, wrong-headed; inconvenient, troublesome, untoward, vexatious.

perversion *n* abasement, corruption, debasement, impairment, injury, prostitution, vitiation.

perverted *adj* corrupt, debased, distorted, evil, impaired, misguiding, vitiated, wicked.

pessimistic *adj* cynical, dark, dejected, depressed, despondent, downhearted, gloomy, glum, melancholy, melancholic, morose, sad.

pest *n* disease, epidemic, infection, pestilence, plague; annoyance, bane, curse, infliction, nuisance, scourge, trouble.

pestilent *adj* contagious, infectious, malignant, pestilential; deadly, evil, injurious, malign, mischievous, noxious, poisonous; annoying, corrupt, pernicious, troublesome, vexatious.

petition *vb* ask, beg, crave, entreat, pray, solicit, sue, supplicate. * *n* address, appeal, application, entreaty, prayer, request, solicitation, supplication, suit.

petrify *vb* calcify, fossilize, lapidify; benumb, deaden; amaze, appal, astonish, astound, confound, dumbfound, paralyse, stun, stupefy.

petty *adj* diminutive, frivolous, inconsiderable, inferior, insignificant, little, mean, slight, small, trifling, trivial, unimportant.

petulant *adj* acrimonious, captious, cavilling, censorious, choleric, crabbed, cross, crusty, forward, fretful, hasty, ill-humoured, ill-tempered, irascible, irritable, peevish, perverse, pettish, querulous, snappish, snarling, testy, touchy, waspish.

phantom *n* apparition, ghost, illusion, phantasm, spectre, vision, wraith.

pharisaism *n* cant, formalism, hypocrisy, phariseeism, piety, sanctimoniousness, self-righteousness.

phenomenal *adj* marvellous, miraculous, prodigious, wondrous.

philanthropy *n* alms-giving, altruism, benevolence, charity, grace, humanitarianism, humanity, kindness.

philosophical, philosophic *adj* rational, reasonable, sound, wise; calm, collected, composed, cool, imperturbable, sedate, serene, stoical, tranquil, unruffled.

phlegmatic *adj* apathetic, calm, cold, cold-blooded, dull, frigid, heavy, impassive, indifferent, inert, sluggish, stoical, tame, unfeeling.

phobia *n* aversion, detestation, dislike, distaste, dread, fear, hatred.

phrase *vb* call, christen, denominate, designate, describe, dub, entitle, name, style. * *n* diction, expression, phraseology, style.

phraseology *n* diction, expression, language, phrasing, style.

physical *adj* material, natural; bodily, corporeal, external, substantial, tangible, sensible.

physiognomy *n* configuration, countenance, face, look, visage.

picaroon *n* adventurer, cheat, rogue; buccaneer, corsair, freebooter, marauder, pirate, plunderer, sea-rover.

pick *vb* peck, pierce, strike; cut, detach, gather, pluck; choose, cull, select; acquire, collect, get; pilfer, steal. * *n* pickaxe, pike, spike, toothpick.

picture *vb* delineate, draw, imagine, paint, represent. * *n* drawing, engraving, painting, print; copy, counterpart, delineation, embodiment, illustration, image, likeness, portraiture, portrayal, semblance, representation, resemblance, similitude; description.

picturesque *adj* beautiful, charming, colourful, graphic, scenic, striking, vivid.

piece *vb* mend, patch, repair; augment, complete, enlarge, increase; cement, join, unite. * *n* amount, bit, chunk, cut, fragment, hunk, part, quantity, scrap, shred, slice; portion; article, item, object; composition, lucubration, work, writing.

pied *adj* irregular, motley, mottled, particoloured, piebald, spotted, variegated.

pierce *vb* gore, impale, pink, prick, stab, transfix; bore, drill, excite, penetrate, perforate, puncture; affect, move, rouse, strike, thrill, touch.

piety *n* devotion, devoutness, holiness, godliness, grace, religion, sanctity.

pile[1] *vb* accumulate, amass; collect, gather, heap, load. * *n* accumulation, collection, heap, mass, stack; fortune, wad; building, edifice, erection, fabric, pyramid, skyscraper, structure, tower; reactor, nuclear reactor.

pile[2] *n* beam, column, pier, pillar, pole, post.

pile[3] *n* down, feel, finish, fur, fluff, fuzz, grain, nap, pappus, shag, surface, texture.

pilfer *vb* filch, purloin, rob, steal, thieve.

pilgrim *n* journeyer, sojourner, traveller, wanderer, wayfarer; crusader, devotee, palmer.

pilgrimage *n* crusade, excursion, expedition, journey, tour, trip.

pillage *vb* despoil, loot, plunder, rifle, sack, spoil, strip. * *n* depredation, destruction, devastation, plundering, rapine, spoliation; despoliation, plunder, rifling, sack, spoils.

pillar *n* column, pier, pilaster, post, shaft, stanchion; maintainer, prop, support, supporter, upholder.

pilot *vb* conduct, control, direct, guide, navigate, steer. * *adj* experimental, model, trial. * *n* helmsman, navigator, steersman; airman, aviator, conductor, director, flier, guide.

pinch *vb* compress, contract, cramp, gripe, nip, squeeze; afflict, distress, famish, oppress, straiten, stint; frost, nip; apprehend, arrest; economize, spare, stint. * *n* gripe, nip; pang, throe; crisis, difficulty, emergency, exigency, oppression, pressure, push, strait, stress.

pine *vb* decay, decline, droop, fade, flag, languish, waste, wilt, wither; desire, long, yearn.

pinion *vb* bind, chain, fasten, fetter, maim, restrain, shackle. * *n* pennon, wing; feather, quill, pen, plume, wing; fetter.

pinnacle *n* minaret, turret; acme, apex, height, peak, summit, top, zenith.

pious *adj* filial; devout, godly, holy, religious, reverential, righteous, saintly.

piquant *adj* biting, highly flavoured, piercing, prickling, pungent, sharp, stinging; interesting, lively, racy, sparkling, stimulating; cutting, keen, pointed, severe, strong, tart.

pique *vb* goad, incite, instigate, spur, stimulate, urge; affront, chafe, displease, fret, incense, irritate, nettle, offend, provoke, sting, vex, wound. * *n* annoyance, displeasure, irritation, offence, resentment, vexation.

pirate *vb* copy, crib, plagiarize, reproduce, steal. * *n* buccaneer, corsair, freebooter, marauder, picaroon, privateer, seadog, sea-robber, sea-rover, sea wolf.

pit *vb* match, oppose; dent, gouge, hole, mark, nick, notch, scar. * *n* cavity, hole, hollow; crater, dent, depression, dint, excavation, well; abyss, chasm, gulf; pitfall, snare, trap: auditorium, orchestra.

pitch *vb* fall, lurch, plunge, reel; light, settle, rest; cast, dart, fling, heave, hurl, lance, launch, send, toss, throw; erect, establish, fix, locate, place, plant, set, settle, station. * *n* degree, extent, height, intensity, measure, modulation, rage, rate; declivity, descent, inclination, slope; cast, jerk, plunge, throw, toss; place, position, spot; field, ground; line, patter.

piteous *adj* affecting, distressing, doleful, grievous, mournful, pathetic, rueful, sorrowful, woeful; deplorable, lamentable, miserable, pitiable, wretched; compassionate, tender.

pith *n* chief, core, essence, heart, gist, kernel, marrow, part, quintessence, soul, substance; importance, moment, weight; cogency, force, energy, strength, vigour.

pithy *adj* cogent, energetic, forcible, powerful; compact, concise, brief, laconic, meaty, pointed, short, sententious, substantial, terse; corky, porous.

pitiable *adj* deplorable, lamentable, miserable, pathetic, piteous, pitiable, woeful, wretched; abject, base, contemptible, despicable, disreputable, insignificant, low, paltry, mean, rascally, sorry, vile, worthless.

pitiably *adv* deplorably, distressingly, grievously, lamentably, miserably, pathetically, piteously, woefully, wretchedly.

pitiful *adj* compassionate, kind, lenient, merciful, mild, sympathetic, tender, tenderhearted; deplorable, lamentable, miserable, pathetic, piteous, pitiable, wretched; abject, base, contemptible, despicable, disreputable, insignificant, mean, paltry, rascally, sorry, vile, worthless.

pitiless *adj* cruel, hardhearted, implacable, inexorable, merciless, unmerciful, relentless, remorseless, unfeeling, unpitying, unrelenting, unsympathetic.

pittance *n* allowance, allotment, alms, charity, dole, gift; driblet, drop, insufficiency, mite, modicum, trifle.

pity *vb* commiserate, condole, sympathize. * *n* clemency, commiseration, compassion, condolence, fellow-feeling, grace, humanity, leniency, mercy, quarter, sympathy, tenderheartedness.

pivot *vb* depend, hinge, turn. * *n* axis, axle, centre, focus, hinge, joint.

place *vb* arrange, bestow, commit, deposit, dispose, fix, install, lay, locate, lodge, orient, orientate, pitch, plant, pose, put, seat, set, settle, situate, stand, station, rest; allocate, arrange, class, classify, identify, order, organize, recognize; appoint, assign, commission, establish, induct, nominate. * n area, courtyard, square; bounds, district, division, locale, locality, location, part, position, premises, quarter, region, scene, site, situation, spot, station, tract, whereabouts; calling, charge, employment, function, occupation, office, pitch, post; calling, condition, grade, precedence, rank, sphere, stakes, standing; abode, building, dwelling, habitation, mansion, residence, seat; city, town, village; fort, fortress, stronghold; paragraph, part, passage, portion; ground, occasion, opportunity, reason, room; lieu, stead.

placid *adj* calm, collected, composed, cool, equable, gentle, peaceful, quiet, serene, tranquil, undisturbed, unexcitable, unmoved, unruffled; halcyon, mild, serene.

plague *vb* afflict, annoy, badger, bore, bother, pester, chafe, disquiet, distress, disturb, embarrass, harass, fret, gall, harry, hector, incommode, irritate, molest, perplex, tantalize, tease, torment, trouble, vex, worry. * n disease, pestilence, pest; affliction, annoyance, curse, molestation, nuisance, thorn, torment, trouble, vexation, worry.

plain *adj* dull, even, flat, level, plane, smooth, uniform; clear, open, unencumbered, uninterrupted; apparent, certain, conspicuous, evident, distinct, glaring, manifest, notable, notorious, obvious, overt, palpable, patent, prominent, pronounced, staring, transparent, unmistakable, visible; explicit, intelligible, perspicuous, unambiguous, unequivocal; homely, ugly; aboveboard, blunt, crude, candid, direct, downright, frank, honest, ingenuous, open, openhearted, sincere, single-minded, straightforward, undesigning, unreserved, unsophisticated; artless, common, natural, simple, unaffected, unlearned; absolute, mere, unmistakable; clear, direct, easy; audible, articulate, definite; frugal, homely; unadorned, unfigured, unornamented, unvariegated. * n expanse, flats, grassland, pampas, plateau, prairie, steppe, stretch.

plaint *n* complaint, cry, lament, lamentation, moan, wail.

plaintiff *n* accuser, prosecutor.

plaintive *adj* dirge-like, doleful, grievous, melancholy, mournful, piteous, rueful, sad, sorrowful, woeful.

plan *vb* arrange, calculate, concert, delineate, devise, diagram, figure, premeditate, project, represent, study; concoct, conspire, contrive, design, digest, hatch, invent, manoeuvre, machinate, plot, prepare, scheme. * n chart, delineation, diagram, draught, drawing, layout, map, plot, sketch; arrangement, conception, contrivance, design, device, idea, method, programme, project, proposal, proposition, scheme, system; cabal, conspiracy, intrigue, machination; custom, process, way.

plane *vb* even, flatten, level, smooth; float, fly, glide, skate, skim, soar. * adj even, flat, horizon-tal, level, smooth. * n degree, evenness, level, levelness, smoothness; aeroplane, aircraft; groover, jointer, rabbet, rebate, scraper.

plant *vb* bed, sow; breed, engender; direct, point, set; colonize, furnish, inhabit, settle; establish, introduce; deposit, establish, fix, found, hide. * n herb, organism, vegetable; establishment, equipment, factory, works.

plaster *vb* bedaub, coat, cover, smear, spread. * n cement, gypsum, mortar, stucco.

plastic *adj* ductile, flexible, formative, mouldable, pliable, pliant, soft.

platitude *n* dullness, flatness, insipidity, mawkishness; banality, commonplace, truism; balderdash, chatter, flummery, fudge, jargon, moonshine, nonsense, palaver, stuff, trash, twaddle, verbiage.

plaudit *n* acclaim, acclamation, applause, approbation, clapping, commendation, encomium, praise.

plausible *adj* believable, credible, probable, reasonable; bland, fair-spoken, glib, smooth, suave.

play *vb* caper, disport, frisk, frolic, gambol, revel, romp, skip, sport; dally, flirt, idle, toy, trifle, wanton; flutter, hover, wave; act, impersonate, perform, personate, represent; bet, gamble, stake, wager. * n amusement, exercise, frolic, gambols, game, jest, pastime, prank, romp, sport; gambling, gaming; act, comedy, drama, farce, performance, tragedy; action, motion, movement; elbowroom, freedom, latitude, movement, opportunity, range, scope, sweep, swing, use.

playful *adj* frisky, frolicsome, gamesome, jolly, kittenish, merry, mirthful, rollicking, sportive; amusing, arch, humorous, lively, mischievous, roguish, skittish, sprightly, vivacious.

plead *vb* answer, appeal, argue, reason; argue, defend, discuss, reason, rejoin; beg, beseech, entreat, implore, petition, sue, supplicate.

pleasant *adj* acceptable, agreeable, delectable, delightful, enjoyable, grateful, gratifying, nice, pleasing, pleasurable, prepossessing, seemly, welcome; cheerful, enlivening, good-humoured, gracious, likable, lively, merry, sportive, sprightly, vivacious; amusing, facetious, humorous, jocose, jocular, sportive, witty.

please *vb* charm, delight, elate, gladden, gratify, pleasure, rejoice; content, oblige, satisfy; choose, like, prefer.

pleasure *n* cheer, comfort, delight, delectation, elation, enjoyment, exhilaration, joy, gladness, gratifying, gusto, relish, satisfaction, solace; amusement, diversion, entertainment, indulgence, refreshment, treat; gratification, luxury, sensuality, voluptuousness; choice, desire, preference, purpose, will, wish; favour, kindness.

plebeian *adj* base, common, ignoble, low, lowborn, mean, obscure, popular, vulgar. * n commoner, peasant, proletarian.

pledge *vb* hypothecate, mortgage, pawn, plight;

affiance, bind, contract, engage, plight, promise. * *n* collateral, deposit, gage, pawn; earnest, guarantee, security; hostage, security.

plenipotentiary *n* ambassador, envoy, legate, minister.

plenitude *n* abundance, completeness, fullness, plenteousness, plentifulness, plenty, plethora, profusion, repletion.

plentiful *adj* abundant, ample, copious, full, enough, exuberant, fruitful, luxuriant, plenteous, productive, sufficient.

plenty *n* abundance, adequacy, affluence, amplitude, copiousness, enough, exuberance, fertility, fruitfulness, fullness, overflow, plenteousness, plentifulness, plethora, profusion, sufficiency, supply.

pleonastic *adj* circumlocutory, diffuse, redundant, superfluous, tautological, verbose, wordy.

plethora *n* fullness, plenitude, repletion; excess, redundance, redundancy, superabundance, superfluity, surfeit.

pliable *adj* flexible, limber, lithe, lithesome, pliable, pliant, supple; adaptable, compliant, docile, ductile, facile, manageable, obsequious, tractable, yielding.

plight[1] *n* case, category, complication, condition, dilemma, imbroglio, mess, muddle, pass, predicament, scrape, situation, state, strait.

plight[2] *vb* avow, contract, covenant, engage, honour, pledge, promise, propose, swear, vow. * *n* avowal, contract, covenant, oath, pledge, promise, troth, vow, word; affiancing, betrothal, engagement.

plod *vb* drudge, lumber, moil, persevere, persist, toil, trudge.

plot[1] *vb* connive, conspire, intrigue, machinate, scheme; brew, concoct, contrive, devise, frame, hatch, compass, plan, project; chart, map. * *n* blueprint, chart, diagram, draft, outline, plan, scenario, skeleton; cabal, combination, complicity, connivance, conspiracy, intrigue, plan, project, scheme, stratagem; script, story, subject, theme, thread, topic.

plot[2] *n* field, lot, parcel, patch, piece, plat, section, tract.

pluck[1] *vb* cull, gather, pick; jerk, pull, snatch, tear, tug, twitch.

pluck[2] *n* backbone, bravery, courage, daring, determination, energy, force, grit, hardihood, heroism, indomitability, indomitableness, manhood, mettle, nerve, resolution, spirit, valour.

plump[1] *adj* bonny, bouncing, buxom, chubby, corpulent, fat, fleshy, full-figured, obese, portly, rotund, round, sleek, stout, well-rounded; distended, full, swollen, tumid.

plump[2] *vb* dive, drop, plank, plop, plunge, plunk, put; choose, favour, support * *adj* blunt, complete, direct, downright, full, unqualified, unreserved.

plunder *vb* desolate, despoil, devastate, fleece, forage, harry, loot, maraud, pillage, raid, ransack, ravage, rifle, rob, sack, spoil, spoliate, plunge. * *n* freebooting, devastation, harrying, marauding, rapine, robbery, sack; booty, pillage, prey, spoil.

ply[1] *vb* apply, employ, exert, manipulate, wield; exercise, practise; assail, belabour, beset, press; importune, solicit, urge; offer, present.

ply[2] *n* fold, layer, plait, twist; bent, bias, direction, turn.

pocket *vb* appropriate, steal; bear, endure, suffer, tolerate. * *n* cavity, cul-de-sac, hollow, pouch, receptacle.

poignant *adj* bitter, intense, penetrating, pierce, severe, sharp; acrid, biting, mordacious, piquant, prickling, pungent, sharp, stinging; caustic, irritating, keen, mordant, pointed, satirical, severe.

point *vb* acuminate, sharpen; aim, direct, level; designate indicate, show; punctuate. * *n* apex, needle, nib, pin, prong, spike, stylus, tip; cape, headland, projection, promontory; eve, instant, moment, period, verge; place, site, spot, stage, station; condition, degree, grade, state; aim, design, end, intent, limit, object, purpose; nicety, pique, punctilio, trifle; position, proposition, question, text, theme, thesis; aspect, matter, respect; characteristic, peculiarity, trait; character, mark, stop; dot, jot, speck; epigram, quip, quirk, sally, witticism; poignancy, sting.

point-blank *adj* categorical, direct, downright, explicit, express, plain, straight. * *adv* categorically, directly, flush, full, plainly, right, straight.

pointless *adj* blunt, obtuse; aimless, dull, flat, fruitless, futile, meaningless, vague, vapid, stupid.

poise *vb* balance, float, hang, hover, support, suspend. * *n* aplomb, balance, composure, dignity, equanimity, equilibrium, equipoise, serenity.

poison *vb* adulterate, contaminate, corrupt, defile, embitter, envenom, impair, infect, intoxicate, pollute, taint, vitiate. * *adj* deadly, lethal, poisonous, toxic. * *n* bane, canker, contagion, pest, taint, toxin, venom, virulence, virus.

poisonous *adj* baneful, corruptive, deadly, fatal, noxious, pestiferous, pestilential, toxic, venomous.

poke *vb* jab, jog, punch, push, shove, thrust; interfere, meddle, pry, snoop. * *n* jab, jog, punch, push, shove, thrust; bag, pocket, pouch, sack.

pole[1] *n* caber, mast, post, rod, spar, staff, stick; bar, beam, pile, shaft; oar, paddle, scull.

pole[2] *n* axis, axle, hub, pivot, spindle.

poles *npl* antipodes, antipoles, counterpoles, opposites.

policy *n* administration, government, management, rule; plan, plank, platform, role; art, address, cunning, discretion, prudence, shrewdness, skill, stratagem, strategy, tactics; acumen, astuteness, wisdom, wit.

polish *vb* brighten, buff, burnish, furbish, glaze, gloss, scour, shine, smooth; civilize, refine. * *n* brightness, brilliance, brilliancy, lustre, splendour; accomplishment, elegance, finish, grace, refinement.

polished *adj* bright, burnished, glossed, glossy, lustrous, shining, smooth; accomplished, cultivated, elegant, finished, graceful, polite, refined.

polite *adj* attentive, accomplished, affable, chivalrous, civil, complaisant, courtly, courteous, cultivated, elegant, gallant, genteel, gentle, gentlemanly, gracious, mannerly, obliging, polished, refined, suave, urbane, well, well-bred, well-mannered.

politic *adj* civic, civil, political; astute, discreet, judicious, long-headed, noncommittal, provident, prudent, prudential, sagacious, wary, wise; artful, crafty, cunning, diplomatic, expedient, foxy, ingenious, intriguing, Machiavellian, shrewd, skilful, sly, subtle, strategic, timeserving, unscrupulous, wily; well-adapted, well-devised.

political *adj* civic, civil, national, politic, public.

pollute *vb* defile, foul, soil, taint; contaminate, corrupt, debase, demoralize, deprave, impair, infect, pervert, poison, stain, tarnish, vitiate; desecrate, profane; abuse, debauch, defile, deflower, dishonour, ravish, violate.

pollution *n* abomination, contamination, corruption, defilement, foulness, impurity, pollutedness, taint, uncleanness, vitiation.

poltroon *n* coward, crave, dastard, milksop, recreant, skulk, sneak.

pomp *n* display, flourish, grandeur, magnificence, ostentation, pageant, pageantry, parade, pompousness, pride, show, splendour, state, style.

pompous *adj* august, boastful, bombastic, dignified, gorgeous, grand, inflated, lofty, magisterial, ostentatious, pretentious, showy, splendid, stately, sumptuous, superb, vainglorious.

ponder *vb* cogitate, consider, contemplate, deliberate, examine, meditate, muse, reflect, study, weigh.

ponderous *adj* bulky, heavy, massive, weighty; dull, laboured, slow-moving; important, momentous; forcible, mighty.

poniard *n* dagger, dirk, stiletto.

poor *adj* indigent, necessitous, needy, pinched, straitened; destitute, distressed, embarrassed, impecunious, impoverished, insolvent, moneyless, penniless, poverty-stricken, reduced, seedy, unprosperous; emaciated, gaunt, spare, lank, lean, shrunk, skinny, spare, thin; barren, fruitless, sterile, unfertile, unfruitful, unproductive, unprolific; flimsy, inadequate, insignificant, insufficient, paltry, slender, slight, small, trifling, trivial, unimportant, valueless, worthless; decrepit, delicate, feeble, frail, infirm, unsound, weak; inferior, shabby, valueless, worthless; bad, beggarly, contemptible, despicable, humble, inferior, low, mean, pitiful, sorry; bald, cold, dry, dull, feeble, frigid, jejune, languid, meagre, prosaic, prosing, spiritless, tame, vapid, weak; ill-fated, ill-starred, inauspicious, indifferent, luckless, miserable, pitiable, unfavourable, unfortunate, unhappy, unlucky, wretched; deficient, imperfect, inadequate, insufficient, mediocre, scant, scanty; faulty, unsatisfactory; feeble.

populace *n* citizens, crowd, inhabitants, masses, people, public, throng.

popular *adj* lay, plebeian, public; comprehensible, easy, familiar, plain; acceptable, accepted, accredited, admired, approved, favoured, liked, pleasing, praised, received; common, current, prevailing, prevalent; cheap, inexpensive.

pore[1] *n* hole, opening, orifice, spiracle.

pore[2] *vb* brood, consider, dwell, examine, gaze, read, study.

porous *adj* honeycombed, light, loose, open, penetrable, perforated, permeable, pervious, sandy.

porridge *n* broth, gruel, mush, pap, pottage, soup.

port[1] *n* anchorage, harbour, haven, shelter; door, entrance, gate, passageway; embrasure, porthole.

port[2] *n* air, appearance, bearing, behaviour, carriage, demeanour, deportment, mien, presence.

portable *adj* convenient, handy, light, manageable, movable, portative, transmissible.

portend *vb* augur, betoken, bode, forebode, foreshadow, foretoken, indicate, presage, procrastinate, signify, threaten.

portent *n* augury, omen, presage, prognosis, sign, warning; marvel, phenomenon, wonder.

portion *vb* allot, distribute, divide, parcel; endow, supply. * *n* bit, fragment, morsel, part, piece, scrap, section; allotment, contingent, dividend, division, lot, measure, quantity, quota, ration, share; inheritance.

portly *adj* dignified, grand, imposing, magisterial, majestic, stately; bulky, burly, corpulent, fleshy, large, plump, round, stout.

portray *vb* act, draw, depict, delineate, describe, paint, picture, represent, pose, position, sketch.

pose *vb* arrange, place, set; bewilder, confound, dumbfound, embarrass, mystify, nonplus, perplex, place, puzzle, set, stagger; affect, attitudinize. * *n* attitude, posture; affectation, air, facade, mannerism, pretence, role.

position *vb* arrange, array, fix, locate, place, put, set, site, stand. * *n* locality, place, post, site, situation, spot, station; relation; attitude, bearing, posture; affirmation, assertion, doctrine, predication, principle, proposition, thesis; caste, dignity, honour, rank, standing, status; circumstance, condition, phase, place, state; berth, billet, incumbency, place, post, situation.

positive *adj* categorical, clear, defined, definite, direct, determinate, explicit, express, expressed, precise, unequivocal, unmistakable, unqualified; absolute, actual, real, substantial, true, veritable; assured, certain, confident, convinced, sure; decisive, incontrovertible, indisputable, indubitable, inescapable; imperative, unconditional, undeniable; decided, dogmatic, emphatic, obstinate, overbearing, overconfident, peremptory, stubborn, tenacious.

possess *vb* control, have, hold, keep, obsess, obtain, occupy, own, seize.

possession *n* monopoly, ownership, proprietorship; control, occupation, occupancy, retention, tenancy, tenure; bedevilment, lunacy, madness, obsession; (pl) assets, effects, estate, property, wealth.

possessor n owner, proprietor.

possible adj conceivable, contingent, imaginable, potential; accessible, feasible, likely, practical, practicable, workable.

possibly adv haply, maybe, mayhap, peradventure, perchance, perhaps.

post[1] vb advertise, announce, inform, placard, publish; brand, defame, disgrace, vilify; enter, slate, record, register. * n column, picket, pier, pillar, stake, support.

post[2] vb establish, fix, place, put, set, station. * n billet, employment, office, place, position, quarter, seat, situation, station.

post[3] vb drop, dispatch, mail. * n carrier, courier, express, mercury, messenger, postman; dispatch, haste, hurry, speed.

posterior adj after, ensuing, following, later, latter, postprandial, subsequent. * n back, buttocks, hind, hinder, rump.

posterity n descendants, offspring, progeny, seed; breed, brood, children, family, heirs, issue.

postpone vb adjourn, defer, delay, procrastinate, prorogue, retard.

postscript n addition, afterthought, appendix, supplement.

postulate vb assume, presuppose; beseech, entreat, solicit, supplicate. * n assumption, axiom, conjecture, hypothesis, proposition, speculation, supposition, theory.

posture vb attitudinize, pose. * n attitude, pose, position; condition, disposition, mood, phase, state.

pot n kettle, pan, saucepan, skillet; can, cup, mug, tankard; crock, jar, jug.

potency n efficacy, energy, force, intensity, might, power, strength, vigour; authority, control, influence, sway.

potent adj efficacious, forceful, forcible, intense, powerful, strong, virile; able, authoritative, capable, efficient, mighty, puissant, strong; cogent, influential.

potentate n emperor, king, monarch, prince, sovereign, ruler.

potential adj able, capable, inherent, latent, possible. * n ability, capability, dynamic, possibility, potentiality, power.

pother vb beset, bewilder, confound, confuse, embarrass, harass, perplex, pose, puzzle, tease. * n bustle, commotion, confusion, disturbance, flutter, fuss, huddle, hurly-burly, rumpus, tumult, turbulence, turmoil.

pound[1] vb beat, strike, thump; bray, bruise, comminute, crush, levigate, pulverize, triturate; confound, coop, enclose, impound.

pound[2] n enclosure, fold, pen.

pour vb cascade, emerge, flood, flow, gush, issue, rain, shower, stream.

pouting adj bad-tempered, cross, ill-humoured, moody, morose, sulky, sullen.

poverty n destitution, difficulties, distress, impecuniosity, impecuniousness, indigence, necessity, need, neediness, penury, privation, straits, want; beggary, mendicancy, pauperism, pennilessness; dearth, jejuneness, lack, scantiness, sparingness, meagreness; exiguity, paucity, poorness, smallness; humbleness, inferiority, lowliness; barrenness, sterility, unfruitfulness, unproductiveness.

power n ability, ableness, capability, cogency, competency, efficacy, faculty, might, potency, validity, talent; energy, force, strength, virtue; capacity, susceptibility; endowment, faculty, gift, talent; ascendancy, authoritativeness, authority, carte blanche, command, control, domination, dominion, government, influence, omnipotence, predominance, prerogative, pressure, proxy, puissance, rule, sovereignty, sway, warrant; governor, monarch, potentate, ruler, sovereign; army, host, troop.

powerful adj mighty, potent, puissant; able-bodied, herculean, muscular, nervous, robust, sinewy, strong, sturdy, vigorous, vivid; able, commanding, dominating, forceful, forcible, overpowering; cogent, effective, effectual, efficacious, efficient, energetic, influential, operative, valid.

practicable adj achievable, attainable, bearable, feasible, performable, possible, workable; operative, passable, penetrable.

practical adj hardheaded, matter-of-fact, pragmatic, pragmatical; able, experienced, practised, proficient, qualified, trained, skilled, thoroughbred, versed; effective, useful, virtual, workable.

practice n custom, habit, manner, method, repetition; procedure, usage, use; application, drill, exercise, pursuit; action, acts, behaviour, conduct, dealing, proceeding.

practise vb apply, do, exercise, follow, observe, perform, perpetrate, pursue.

practised adj able, accomplished, experienced, instructed, practical, proficient, qualified, skilled, thoroughbred, trained, versed.

pragmatic adj impertinent, intermeddling, interfering, intrusive, meddlesome, meddling, obtrusive, officious, over-busy; earthy, hard-headed, matter-of-fact, practical, pragmatical, realistic, sensible, stolid.

praise vb approbate, acclaim, applaud, approve, commend; celebrate, compliment, eulogize, extol, flatter, laud; adore, bless, exalt, glorify, magnify, worship. * n acclaim, approbation, approval, commendation; encomium, eulogy, glorification, laud, laudation, panegyric; exaltation, extolling, glorification, homage, tribute, worship; celebrity, distinction, fame, glory, honour, renown; desert, merit, praiseworthiness.

praiseworthy adj commendable, creditable, good, laudable, meritorious.

prank n antic, caper, escapade, frolic, gambol, trick.

prate vb babble, chatter, gabble, jabber, palaver, prattle, tattle. * n chatter, gabble, nonsense, palaver, prattle, twaddle.

pray vb ask, beg, beseech, conjure, entreat, implore, importune, invoke, petition, request, solicit, supplicate.

prayer n beseeching, entreaty, imploration, petition, request, solicitation, suit, supplication; adoration, devotion(s), litany, invocation, orison, praise, suffrage.

preach vb declare, deliver, proclaim, pronounce, publish; inculcate, press, teach, urge; exhort, lecture, moralize, sermonize.

preamble n foreword, introduction, preface, prelude, prologue.

precarious adj critical, doubtful, dubious, equivocal, hazardous, insecure, perilous, unassured, riskful, risky, uncertain, unsettled, unstable, unsteady.

precaution n care, caution, circumspection, foresight, forethought, providence, prudence, safeguard, wariness; anticipation, premonition, provision.

precautionary adj preservative, preventative, provident.

precede vb antedate, forerun, head, herald, introduce, lead, utter.

precedence n advantage, antecedence, lead, preeminence, preference, priority, superiority, supremacy.

precedent n antecedent, authority, custom, example, instance, model, pattern, procedure, standard, usage.

precept n behest, bidding, canon, charge, command, commandment, decree, dictate, edict, injunction, instruction, law, mandate, ordinance, ordination, order, regulation; direction, doctrine, maxim, principle, teaching, rubric, rule.

preceptor n instructor, lecturer, master, pedagogue, professor, schoolteacher, teacher, tutor.

precinct n border, bound, boundary, confine, environs, frontier, enclosure, limit, list, march, neighbourhood, purlieus, term, terminus; area, district.

precious adj costly, inestimable, invaluable, priceless, prized, valuable; adored, beloved, cherished, darling, dear, idolized, treasured; fastidious, overnice, over-refined, precise.

precipice n bluff, cliff, crag, steep.

precipitate vb advance, accelerate, dispatch, expedite, forward, further, hasten, hurry, plunge, press, quicken, speed. * adj hasty, hurried, headlong, impetuous, indiscreet, overhasty, rash, reckless; abrupt, sudden, violent.

precipitous adj abrupt, cliffy, craggy, perpendicular, uphill, sheer, steep.

precise adj accurate, correct, definite, distinct, exact, explicit, express, nice, pointed, severe, strict, unequivocal, well-defined; careful, scrupulous; ceremonious, finical, formal, prim, punctilious, rigid, starched, stiff.

precision n accuracy, correctness, definiteness, distinctness, exactitude, exactness, nicety, preciseness.

preclude vb bar, check, debar, hinder, inhibit, obviate, prevent, prohibit, restrain, stop.

precocious adj advanced, forward, overforward, premature.

preconcert vb concoct, prearrange, predetermine, premeditate, prepare.

precursor n antecedent, cause, forerunner, predecessor; harbinger, herald, messenger, pioneer; omen, presage, sign.

precursory adj antecedent, anterior, forerunning, precedent, preceding, previous, prior; initiatory, introductory, precursive, prefatory, preliminary, prelusive, prelusory, premonitory, preparatory, prognosticative.

predatory adj greedy, pillaging, plundering, predacious, rapacious, ravaging, ravenous, voracious.

predestination n doom, fate, foredoom, foreordainment, foreordination, necessity, predetermination, preordination.

predicament n attitude, case, condition, plight, position, posture, situation, state; corner, dilemma, emergency, exigency, fix, hole, impasse, mess, pass, pinch, push, quandary, scrape.

predict vb augur, betoken, bode, divine, forebode, forecast, foredoom, foresee, forespeak, foretell, foretoken, forewarn, portend, prognosticate, prophesy, read, signify, soothsay.

predilection n bent, bias, desire, fondness, inclination, leaning, liking, love, partiality, predisposition, preference, prejudice, prepossession.

predisposition n aptitude, bent, bias, disposition, inclination, leaning, proclivity, proneness, propensity, willingness.

predominant adj ascendant, controlling, dominant, overruling, prevailing, prevalent, reigning, ruling, sovereign, supreme.

predominate vb dominate, preponderate, prevail, rule.

pre-eminent adj chief, conspicuous, consummate, controlling, distinguished, excellent, excelling, paramount, peerless, predominant, renowned, superior, supreme, surpassing, transcendent, unequalled.

preface vb begin, introduce, induct, launch, open, precede. * n exordium, foreword, induction, introduction, preamble, preliminary, prelude, prelusion, premise, proem, prologue, prolusion.

prefatory adj antecedent, initiative, introductory, precursive, precursory, preliminary, prelusive, prelusory, preparatory, proemial.

prefer vb address, offer, present, proffer, tender; advance, elevate, promote, raise; adopt, choose, elect, fancy, pick, select, wish.

preference n advancement, choice, election, estimation, precedence, priority, selection.

preferment n advancement, benefice, dignity, elevation, exaltation, promotion.

pregnant *adj* big, enceinte, parturient; fraught, full, important, replete, significant, weighty; fecund, fertile, fruitful, generative, potential, procreant, procreative, productive, prolific.

prejudice *vb* bias, incline, influence, turn, warp; damage, diminish, hurt, impair, injure. * *n* bias, intolerance, partiality, preconception, predilection, prejudgement, prepossession, unfairness; damage, detriment, disadvantage, harm, hurt, impairment, injury, loss, mischief.

prejudiced *adj* biased, bigoted, influenced, one-sided, partial, partisan, unfair.

preliminary *adj* antecedent, initiatory, introductory, precedent, precursive, precursory, prefatory, prelusive, prelusory, preparatory, previous, prior, proemial. * *n* beginning, initiation, introduction, opening, preamble, preface, prelude, start.

prelude *n* introduction, opening, overture, prelusion, preparation, voluntary; exordium, preamble, preface, preliminary, proem.

premature *adj* hasty, ill-considered, precipitate, unmatured, unprepared, unripe, unseasonable, untimely.

premeditation *n* deliberation, design, forethought, intention, prearrangement, predetermination, purpose.

premise *vb* introduce, preamble, preface, prefix. * *n* affirmation, antecedent, argument, assertion, assumption, basis, foundation, ground, hypothesis, position, premiss, presupposition, proposition, support, thesis, theorem.

premium *n* bonus, bounty, encouragement, fee, gift, guerdon, meed, payment, prize, recompense, remuneration, reward; appreciation, enhancement.

premonition *n* caution, foreboding, foreshadowing, forewarning, indication, omen, portent, presage, presentiment, sign, warning.

preoccupied *adj* absent, absentminded, abstracted, dreaming, engrossed, inadvertent, inattentive, lost, musing, unobservant.

prepare *vb* adapt, adjust, fit, qualify; arrange, concoct, fabricate, make, order, plan, procure, provide.

preponderant *adj* outweighing, overbalancing, preponderating.

prepossessing *adj* alluring, amiable, attractive, bewitching, captivating, charming, engaging, fascinating, inviting, taking, winning.

preposterous *adj* absurd, excessive, exorbitant, extravagant, foolish, improper, irrational, monstrous, nonsensical, perverted, ridiculous, unfit, unreasonable, wrong.

prerogative *n* advantage, birthright, claim, franchise, immunity, liberty, privilege, right.

presage *vb* divine, forebode; augur, betoken, bode, foreshadow, foretell, foretoken, indicate, portend, predict, prognosticate, prophesy, signify, soothsay. * *n* augury, auspice, boding, foreboding, foreshowing, indication, omen, portent,

prognostication, sign, token; foreknowledge, precognition, prediction, premonition, presentiment, prophecy.

prescribe *vb* advocate, appoint, command, decree, dictate, direct, enjoin, establish, institute, ordain, order.

presence *n* attendance, company, inhabitance, inhabitancy, nearness, neighbourhood, occupancy, propinquity, proximity, residence, ubiquity, vicinity; air, appearance, carriage, demeanour, mien, personality.

present[1] *adj* near; actual, current, existing, happening, immediate, instant, living; available, quick, ready; attentive, favourable. * *n* now, time being, today.

present[2] *n* benefaction, boon, donation, favour, gift, grant, gratuity, largesse, offering.

present[3] *vb* introduce, nominate; exhibit, offer; bestow, confer, give, grant; deliver, hand; advance, express, prefer, proffer, tender.

presentiment *n* anticipation, apprehension, foreboding, forecast, foretaste, forethought, prescience.

presently *adv* anon, directly, forthwith, immediately, shortly, soon.

preservation *n* cherishing, conservation, curing, maintenance, protection, support; safety, salvation, security; integrity, keeping, soundness.

preserve *vb* defend, guard, keep, protect, rescue, save, secure, shield; maintain, uphold, sustain, support; conserve, economize, husband, retain. * *n* comfit, compote, confection, confiture, conserve, jam, jelly, marmalade, sweetmeat; enclosure, warren.

preside *vb* control, direct, govern, manage, officiate.

press *vb* compress, crowd, crush, squeeze; flatten, iron, smooth; clasp, embrace, hug; force, compel, constrain; emphasize, enforce, enjoin, inculcate, stress, urge; hasten, hurry, push, rush; crowd, throng; entreat, importune, solicit. * *n* crowd, crush, multitude, throng; hurry, pressure, urgency; case, closet, cupboard, repository.

pressing *adj* constraining, critical, distressing, imperative, importunate, persistent, serious, urgent, vital.

pressure *n* compressing, crushing, squeezing; influence, force; compulsion, exigency, hurry, persuasion, press, stress, urgency; affliction, calamity, difficulty, distress, embarrassment, grievance, oppression, straits; impression, stamp.

prestidigitation *n* conjuring, juggling, legerdemain, sleight-of-hand.

prestige *n* credit, distinction, importance, influence, reputation, weight.

presume *vb* anticipate, apprehend, assume, believe, conjecture, deduce, expect, infer, surmise, suppose, think; consider, presuppose; dare, undertake, venture.

presumption *n* anticipation, assumption, belief, concession, conclusion, condition, conjecture, deduction, guess, hypothesis, inference, opinion, supposition, understanding; arrogance, assurance, audacity, boldness, brass, effrontery, forwardness, haughtiness, presumptuousness; probability.

presumptuous *adj* arrogant, assuming, audacious, bold, brash, forward, irreverent, insolent, intrusive, presuming; foolhardy, overconfident, rash.

pretence *n* affectation, cloak, colour, disguise, mask, semblance, show, simulation, veil, window-dressing; excuse, evasion, fabrication, feigning, makeshift, pretext, sham, subterfuge; claim, pretension.

pretend *vb* affect, counterfeit, deem, dissemble, fake, falsify, feign, sham, simulate; act, imagine, lie, profess; aspire, claim.

pretension *n* assertion, assumption, claim, demand, pretence; affectation, airs, conceit, ostentation, pertness, pretentiousness, priggishness, vanity.

pretentious *adj* affected, assuming, conceited, conspicuous, ostentatious, presuming, priggish, showy, tawdry, unnatural, vain.

preternatural *adj* abnormal, anomalous, extraordinary, inexplicable, irregular, miraculous, mysterious, odd, peculiar, strange, unnatural.

pretext *n* affectation, appearance, blind, cloak, colour, guise, mask, pretence, semblance, show, simulation, veil; excuse, justification, plea, vindication.

pretty *adj* attractive, beautiful, bonny, comely, elegant, fair, handsome, neat, pleasing, trim; affected, foppish. * *adv* fairly, moderately, quite, rather, somewhat.

prevail *vb* overcome, succeed, triumph, win; obtain, predominate, preponderate, reign, rule.

prevailing *adj* controlling, dominant, effectual, efficacious, general, influential, operative, overruling, persuading, predominant, preponderant, prevalent, ruling, successful.

prevalent *adj* ascendant, compelling, efficacious, governing, predominant, prevailing, successful, superior; extensive, general, rife, widespread.

prevaricate *vb* cavil, deviate, dodge, equivocate, evade, palter, pettifog, quibble, shift, shuffle, tergiversate.

prevent *vb* bar, check, debar, deter, forestall, help, hinder, impede, inhibit, intercept, interrupt, obstruct, obviate, preclude, prohibit, restrain, save, stop, thwart.

prevention *n* anticipation, determent, deterrence, deterrent, frustration, hindrance, interception, interruption, obstruction, preclusion, prohibition, restriction, stoppage.

previous *adj* antecedent, anterior, earlier, foregoing, foregone, former, precedent, preceding, prior.

prey *vb* devour, eat, feed on, live off; exploit, intimidate, terrorize; burden, distress, haunt, oppress, trouble, worry. * *n* booty, loot, pillage, plunder, prize, rapine, spoil; food, game, kill, quarry, victim; depredation, ravage.

price *vb* assess, estimate, evaluate, rate, value. * *n* amount, cost, expense, outlay, value; appraisal, charge, estimation, excellence, figure, rate, quotation, valuation, value, worth; compensation, guerdon, recompense, return, reward.

priceless *adj* dear, expensive, precious, inestimable, invaluable, valuable; amusing, comic, droll, funny, humorous, killing, rich.

prick *vb* perforate, pierce, puncture, stick; drive, goad, impel, incite, spur, urge; cut, hurt, mark, pain, sting, wound; hasten, post, ride. * *n* mark, perforation, point, puncture; prickle, sting, wound.

pride *vb* boast, brag, crow, preen, revel in. * *n* conceit, egotism, self-complacency, self-esteem, self-exaltation, self-importance, self-sufficiency, vanity; arrogance, assumption, disdain, haughtiness, hauteur, insolence, loftiness, lordliness, pomposity, presumption, superciliousness, vainglory; decorum, dignity, elevation, self-respect; decoration, glory, ornament, show, splendour.

priest *n* churchman, clergyman, divine, ecclesiastic, minister, pastor, presbyter.

prim *adj* demure, formal, nice, precise, prudish, starch, starched, stiff, strait-laced.

primary *adj* aboriginal, earliest, first, initial, original, prime, primitive, primeval, primordial, pristine; chief, main, principal; basic, elementary, fundamental, preparatory: radical.

prime[1] *adj* aboriginal, basic, first, initial, original, primal, primary, primeval, primitive, primordial, pristine; chief, foremost, highest, leading, main, paramount, principal; blooming, early; capital, cardinal, dominant, predominant; excellent, first-class, first-rate, optimal, optimum, quintessential, superlative; beginning, opening. * *n* beginning, dawn, morning, opening; spring, springtime, youth; bloom, cream, flower, height, heyday, optimum, perfection, quintessence, zenith.

prime[2] *vb* charge, load, prepare, undercoat; coach, groom, train, tutor.

primeval *adj* original, primitive, primordial, pristine.

primitive *adj* aboriginal, first, fundamental, original, primal, primary, prime, primitive, primordial, pristine; ancient, antiquated, crude, old-fashioned, quaint, simple, uncivilized, unsophisticated.

prince *n* monarch, potentate, ruler, sovereign; dauphin, heir apparent, infant; chief, leader, potentate.

princely *adj* imperial, regal, royal; august, generous, grand, liberal, magnanimous, magnificent, majestic, munificent, noble, pompous, splendid, superb, titled; dignified, elevated, high-minded, lofty, noble, stately.

principal *adj* capital, cardinal, chief, essential, first, foremost, highest, leading, main, pre-eminent, prime. * *n* chief, head, leader; head teacher, master.

principally *adv* chiefly, essentially, especially, mainly, particularly.

principle *n* cause, fountain, fountainhead, groundwork, mainspring, nature, origin, source, spring; basis, constituent, element, essence, substratum; assumption, axiom, law, maxim, postulation; doctrine, dogma, impulse, maxim, opinion, precept, rule; tenet, theory; conviction, ground, motive, reason; equity, goodness, honesty, honour, incorruptibility, integrity, justice, probity, rectitude, righteousness, trustiness, truth, uprightness, virtue, worth; faculty, power.

prink *vb* adorn, deck, decorate; preen, primp, spruce.

print *vb* engrave, impress, imprint, mark, stamp; issue, publish. * *n* book, periodical, publication; copy, engraving, photograph, picture; characters, font, fount, lettering, type, typeface.

prior *adj* antecedent, anterior, earlier, foregoing, precedent, preceding, precursory, previous, superior.

priority *n* antecedence, anteriority, precedence, pre-eminence, pre-existence, superiority.

priory *n* abbey, cloister, convent, monastery, nunnery.

prison *n* confinement, dungeon, gaol, jail, keep, lockup, penitentiary, reformatory; can, clink, cooler, jug.

pristine *adj* ancient, earliest, first, former, old, original, primary, primeval, primitive, primordial.

privacy *n* concealment, secrecy; retirement, retreat, seclusion, solitude.

private *adj* retired, secluded, sequestrated, solitary; individual, own, particular, peculiar, personal, special, unofficial; confidential, privy; clandestine, concealed, hidden, secret. * *n* GI, soldier, tommy.

privation *n* bereavement, deprivation, dispossession, loss; destitution, distress, indigence, necessity, need, want; absence, negation; degradation.

privilege *n* advantage, charter, claim, exemption, favour, franchise, immunity, leave, liberty, licence, permission, prerogative, right.

privy *adj* individual, particular, peculiar, personal, private, special; clandestine, secret; retired, sequestrated.

prize[1] *vb* appreciate, cherish, esteem, treasure, value.

prize[2] *adj* best, champion, first-rate, outstanding, winning. * *n* guerdon, honours, meed, premium, reward; cup, decoration, medal, laurels, palm, trophy; booty, capture, lot, plunder, spoil; advantage, gain, privilege.

probability *n* chance, prospect, likelihood, presumption; appearance, credibility, credibleness, likeliness, verisimilitude.

probable *adj* apparent, credible, likely, presumable, reasonable.

probably *adv* apparently, likely, maybe, perchance, perhaps, presumably, possibly, seemingly.

probation *n* essay, examination, ordeal, proof, test, trial; novitiate.

probe *vb* examine, explore, fathom, investigate, measure, prove, scrutinize, search, sift, sound, test, verify. * *n* examination, exploration, inquiry, investigation, scrutiny, study.

probity *n* candour, conscientiousness, equity, fairness, faith, goodness, honesty, honour, incorruptibility, integrity, justice, loyalty, morality, principle, rectitude, righteousness, sincerity, soundness, trustworthiness, truth, truthfulness, uprightness, veracity, virtue, worth.

problem *adj* difficult, intractable, uncontrollable, unruly. * *n* dilemma, dispute, doubt, enigma, exercise, proposition, puzzle, riddle, theorem.

problematic *adj* debatable, disputable, doubtful, dubious, enigmatic, problematical, puzzling, questionable, suspicious, uncertain, unsettled.

procedure *n* conduct, course, custom, management, method, operation, policy, practice, process; act, action, deed, measure, performance, proceeding, step, transaction.

proceed *vb* advance, continue, go, pass, progress; accrue, arise, come, emanate, ensue, flow, follow, issue, originate, result, spring.

proceeds *npl* balance, earnings, effects, gain, income, net, produce, products, profits, receipts, returns, yield.

process *vb* advance, deal with, fulfil, handle, progress; alter, convert, refine, transform. * *n* advance, course, progress, train; action, conduct, management, measure, mode, operation, performance, practice, procedure, proceeding, step, transaction, way; action, case, suit, trial; outgrowth, projection, protuberance.

procession *n* cavalcade, cortege, file, march, parade, retinue, train.

proclaim *vb* advertise, announce, blazon, broach, broadcast, circulate, cry, declare, herald, promulgate, publish, trumpet; ban, outlaw, proscribe.

proclamation *n* advertisement, announcement, blazon, declaration, promulgation, publication; ban, decree, edict, manifesto, ordinance.

proclivity *n* bearing, bent, bias, determination, direction, disposition, drift, inclination, leaning, predisposition, proneness, propensity, tendency, turn; aptitude, facility, readiness.

procrastinate *vb* adjourn, defer, delay, postpone, prolong, protract, retard; neglect, omit; lag, loiter.

procrastination *n* delay, dilatoriness, postponement, protraction, slowness, tardiness.

procreate *vb* beget, breed, engender, generate, produce, propagate.

procurable *adj* acquirable, compassable, obtainable.

procurator *n* agent, attorney, deputy, proctor, proxy, representative, solicitor.

procure *vb* acquire, gain, get, obtain; cause, compass, contrive, effect.

procurer *n* bawd, pander, pimp.

prodigal *adj* abundant, dissipated, excessive, extravagant, generous, improvident, lavish, profuse, reckless, squandering, thriftless, unthrifty, wasteful. * *n* spendthrift, squanderer, waster, wastrel.

prodigality *n* excess, extravagance, lavishness, profusion, squandering, unthriftiness, waste, wastefulness.

prodigious *adj* amazing, astonishing, astounding, extraordinary, marvellous, miraculous, portentous, remarkable, startling, strange, surprising, uncommon, wonderful, wondrous; enormous, huge, immense, monstrous, vast.

prodigy *n* marvel, miracle, phenomenon, portent, sign, wonder; curiosity, monster, monstrosity.

produce *vb* exhibit, show; bear, beget, breed, conceive, engender, furnish, generate, hatch, procreate, yield; accomplish, achieve, cause, create, effect, make, occasion, originate; accrue, afford, give, impart, make, render; extend, lengthen, prolong, protract; fabricate, fashion, manufacture. * *n* crop, fruit, greengrocery, harvest, product, vegetables, yield.

producer *n* creator, inventor, maker, originator; agriculturalist, farmer, greengrocer, husbandman, raiser.

product *n* crops, fruits, harvest, outcome, proceeds, produce, production, returns, yield; consequence, effect, fruit, issue, performance, production, result, work.

production *n* fruit, produce, product; construction, creation, erection, fabrication, making, performance; completion, fruition; birth, breeding, development, growth, propagation; opus, publication, work; continuation, extension, lengthening, prolongation.

productive *adj* copious, fertile, fruitful, luxuriant, plenteous, prolific, teeming; causative, constructive, creative, efficient, life-giving, producing.

proem *n* exordium, foreword, introduction, preface, prelims, prelude, prolegomena.

profane *vb* defile, desecrate, pollute, violate; abuse, debase. * *adj* blasphemous, godless, heathen, idolatrous, impious, impure, pagan, secular, temporal, unconsecrated, unhallowed, unholy, unsanctified, worldly, unspiritual; impure, polluted, unholy.

profanity *n* blasphemy, impiety, irreverence, profaneness, sacrilege.

profess *vb* acknowledge, affirm, allege, aver, avouch, avow, confess, declare, own, proclaim, state; affect, feign, pretend.

profession *n* acknowledgement, assertion, avowal, claim, declaration; avocation, evasion, pretence, pretension, protestation, representation; business, calling, employment, engagement, occupation, office, trade, vocation.

proffer *vb* offer, propose, propound, suggest, tender, volunteer. * *n* offer, proposal, suggestion, tender.

proficiency *n* advancement, forwardness, improvement; accomplishment, aptitude, competency, dexterity, mastery, skill.

proficient *adj* able, accomplished, adept, competent, conversant, dextrous, expert, finished, masterly, practised, skilled, skilful, thoroughbred, trained, qualified, well-versed. * *n* adept, expert, master, master-hand.

profit *vb* advance, benefit, gain, improve. * *n* aid, clearance, earnings, emolument, fruit, gain, lucre, produce, return; advancement, advantage, benefit, interest, perquisite, service, use, utility, weal.

profitable *adj* advantageous, beneficial, desirable, gainful, productive, useful; lucrative, remunerative.

profitless *adj* bootless, fruitless, unprofitable, useless, valueless, worthless.

profligate *adj* abandoned, corrupt, corrupted, degenerate, depraved, dissipated, dissolute, graceless, immoral, shameless, vicious, vitiated, wicked. * *n* debauchee, libertine, rake, reprobate, roué.

profound *adj* abysmal, deep, fathomless; heavy, undisturbed; erudite, learned, penetrating, sagacious, skilled; deeply felt, far-reaching, heartfelt, intense, lively, strong, touching, vivid; low, submissive; abstruse, mysterious, obscure, occult, subtle, recondite; complete, thorough.

profundity *n* deepness, depth, profoundness.

profuse *adj* abundant, bountiful, copious, excessive, extravagant, exuberant, generous, improvident, lavish, overabundant, plentiful, prodigal, wasteful.

profusion *n* abundance, bounty, copiousness, excess, exuberance, extravagance, lavishness, prodigality, profuseness, superabundance, waste.

progenitor *n* ancestor, forebear, forefather.

progeny *n* breed, children, descendants, family, issue, lineage, offshoot, offspring, posterity, race, scion, stock, young.

prognostic *adj* foreshadowing, foreshowing, foretokening. * *n* augury, foreboding, indication, omen, presage, prognostication, sign, symptom, token; foretelling, prediction, prophecy.

prognosticate *vb* foretell, predict, prophesy; augur, betoken, forebode, foreshadow, foreshow, foretoken, indicate, portend, presage.

prognostication *n* foreknowledge, foreshowing, foretelling, prediction, presage; augury, foreboding, foretoken, indication, portent, prophecy.

progress *vb* advance, continue, proceed; better, gain, improve, increase. * *n* advance, advancement, progression; course, headway, ongoing, passage; betterment, development, growth, improvement, increase, reform; circuit, procession.

prohibit *vb* debar, hamper, hinder, preclude, prevent; ban, disallow, forbid, inhibit, interdict.

prohibition *n* ban, bar, disallowance, embargo, forbiddance, inhibition, interdict, interdiction, obstruction, prevention, proscription, taboo, veto.

prohibitive *adj* forbidding, prohibiting, refraining, restrictive.

project *vb* cast, eject, fling, hurl, propel, shoot, throw; brew, concoct, contrive, design, devise, intend, plan, plot, purpose, scheme; delineate, draw, exhibit; bulge, extend, jut, protrude. * *n* contrivance, design, device, intention, plan, proposal, purpose, scheme.

projectile *n* bullet, missile, shell.

projection *n* delivery, ejection, emission, propulsion, throwing; contriving, designing, planning, scheming; bulge, extension, outshoot, process, prominence, protuberance, salience, saliency, salient, spur; delineation, map, plan.

proletarian *adj* mean, plebeian, vile, vulgar. * *n* commoner, plebeian.

proletariat *n* commonality, hoi polloi, masses, mob, plebs, working class.

prolific *adj* abundant, fertile, fruitful, generative, productive, teeming.

prolix *adj* boring, circumlocutory, discursive, diffuse, lengthy, long, long-winded, loose, prolonged, protracted, prosaic, rambling, tedious, tiresome, verbose, wordy.

prologue *n* foreword, introduction, preamble, preface, preliminary, prelude, proem.

prolong *vb* continue, extend, lengthen, protract, sustain; defer, postpone.

promenade *vb* saunter, walk. * *n* dance, stroll, walk; boulevard, esplanade, parade, walkway.

prominent *adj* convex, embossed, jutting, projecting, protuberant, raised, relieved; celebrated, conspicuous, distinguished, eminent, famous, foremost, influential, leading, main, noticeable, outstanding; conspicuous, distinctive, important, manifest, marked, principal, salient.

promiscuous *adj* confused, heterogeneous, indiscriminate, intermingled, mingled, miscellaneous, mixed; abandoned, dissipated, dissolute, immoral, licentious, loose, unchaste, wanton.

promise *vb* covenant, engage, pledge, subscribe, swear, underwrite, vow; assure, attest, guarantee, warrant; agree, bargain, engage, stipulate, undertake. * *n* agreement, assurance, contract, engagement, oath, parole, pledge, profession, undertaking, vow, word.

promising *adj* auspicious, encouraging, hopeful, likely, propitious.

promote *vb* advance, aid, assist, cultivate, encourage, further, help, promote; dignify, elevate, exalt, graduate, honour, pass, prefer, raise.

promotion *n* advancement, encouragement, furtherance; elevation, exaltation, preferment.

prompt *vb* actuate, dispose, impel, incite, incline, induce, instigate, stimulate, urge; remind; dictate, hint, influence, suggest. * *adj* active, alert, apt, quick, ready; forward, hasty; disposed, inclined, prone; early, exact, immediate, instant, precise, punctual, seasonable, timely. * *adv* apace, directly, forthwith, immediately, promptly. * *n* cue, hint, prompter, reminder, stimulus.

promptly *adv* apace, directly, expeditiously, forthwith, immediately, instantly, pronto, punctually, quickly, speedily, straightway, straightaway, summarily, swiftly.

promptness *n* activity, alertness, alacrity, promptitude, readiness, quickness.

promulgate *vb* advertise, announce, broadcast, bruit, circulate, declare, notify, proclaim, publish, spread, trumpet.

prone *adj* flat, horizontal, prostrate, recumbent; declivitous, inclined, inclining, sloping; apt, bent, disposed, inclined, predisposed, tending; eager, prompt, ready.

pronounce *vb* articulate, enunciate, frame, say, speak, utter; affirm, announce, assert, declare, deliver, state.

proof *adj* firm, fixed, impenetrable, stable, steadfast. * *n* essay, examination, ordeal, test, trial; attestation, certification, conclusion, conclusiveness, confirmation, corroboration, demonstration, evidence, ratification, substantiation, testimony, verification.

prop *vb* bolster, brace, buttress, maintain, shore, stay, support, sustain, truss, uphold. * *n* support, stay; buttress, fulcrum, pin, shore, strut.

propaganda *n* inculcation, indoctrination, promotion.

propagate *vb* continue, increase, multiply; circulate, diffuse, disseminate, extend, promote, promulgate, publish, spread, transmit; beget, breed, engender, generate, originate, procreate.

propel *vb* drive, force, impel, push, urge; cast, fling, hurl, project, throw.

propensity *n* aptitude, bent, bias, disposition, inclination, ply, proclivity, proneness, tendency.

proper *adj* individual, inherent, natural, original, particular, peculiar, special, specific; adapted, appropriate, becoming, befitting, convenient, decent, decorous, demure, fit, fitting, legitimate, meet, pertinent, respectable, right, seemly, suitable; accurate, correct, exact, fair, fastidious, formal, just, precise; actual, real.

property *n* attribute, characteristic, disposition, mark, peculiarity, quality, trait, virtue; appurtenance, assets, belongings, chattels, circumstances, effects, estate, goods, possessions, resources, wealth; ownership, possession, proprietorship, tenure; claim, copyright, interest, participation, right, title.

prophecy *n* augury, divination, forecast, foretelling, portent, prediction, premonition, presage, prognostication; exhortation, instruction, preaching.

prophesy *vb* augur, divine, foretell, predict, prognosticate.

propinquity *n* adjacency, contiguity, nearness, neighbourhood, proximity, vicinity; affinity, connection, consanguinity, kindred, relationship.

propitiate *vb* appease, atone, conciliate, intercede, mediate, pacify, reconcile, satisfy.

propitious *adj* benevolent, benign, friendly, gracious, kind, merciful; auspicious, encouraging, favourable, fortunate, happy, lucky, opportune, promising, prosperous, thriving, timely, well-disposed.

proportion *vb* adjust, graduate, regulate; form, shape. * *n* arrangement, relation; adjustment, commensuration, dimension, distribution, symmetry; extent, lot, part, portion, quota, ratio, share.

proposal *n* design, motion, offer, overture, proffer, proposition, recommendation, scheme, statement, suggestion, tender.

propose *vb* move, offer, pose, present, propound, proffer, put, recommend, state, submit, suggest, tender; design, intend, mean, purpose.

proposition *vb* accost, proffer, solicit. * *n* offer, overture, project, proposal, suggestion, tender, undertaking; affirmation, assertion, axiom, declaration, dictum, doctrine, position, postulation, predication, statement, theorem, thesis.

proprietor *n* lord, master, owner, possessor, proprietary.

propriety *n* accuracy, adaptation, appropriation, aptness, becomingness, consonance, correctness, fitness, justness, reasonableness, rightness, seemliness, suitableness; conventionality, decency, decorum, demureness, fastidiousness, formality, modesty, properness, respectability.

prorogation *n* adjournment, continuance, postponement.

prosaic *adj* commonplace, dull, flat, humdrum, matter-of-fact, pedestrian, plain, prolix, prosing, sober, stupid, tame, tedious, tiresome, unentertaining, unimaginative, uninspired, uninteresting, unromantic, vapid.

proscribe *vb* banish, doom, exile, expel, ostracize, outlaw; exclude, forbid, interdict, prohibit; censure, condemn, curse, denounce, reject.

prosecute *vb* conduct, continue, exercise, follow, persist, pursue; arraign, indict, sue, summon.

prospect *vb* explore, search, seek, survey. * *n* display, field, landscape, outlook, perspective, scene, show, sight, spectacle, survey, view, vision, vista; picture, scenery; anticipation, calculation, contemplation, expectance, expectancy, expectation, foreseeing, foresight, hope, presumption, promise, trust; likelihood, probability.

prospectus *n* announcement, conspectus, description, design, outline, plan, programme, sketch, syllabus.

prosper *vb* aid, favour, forward, help; advance, flourish, grow rich, thrive, succeed; batten, increase.

prosperity *n* affluence, blessings, happiness, felicity, good luck, success, thrift, weal, welfare, well-being; boom, heyday.

prosperous *adj* blooming, flourishing, fortunate, golden, halcyon, rich, successful, thriving; auspicious, booming, bright, favourable, good, golden, lucky, promising, propitious, providential, rosy.

prostrate *vb* demolish, destroy, fell, level, over-

throw, overturn, ruin; depress, exhaust, overcome, reduce. * *adj* fallen, prostrated, prone, recumbent, supine; helpless, powerless.

prostration *n* demolition, destruction, overthrow; dejection, depression, exhaustion.

prosy *adj* prosaic, unpoetic, unpoetical; dull, flat, jejune, stupid, tedious, tiresome, unentertaining, unimaginative, uninteresting.

protect *vb* cover, defend, guard, shield; fortify, harbour, house, preserve, save, screen, secure, shelter; champion, countenance, foster, patronize.

protector *n* champion, custodian, defender, guardian, patron, warden.

protest *vb* affirm, assert, asseverate, attest, aver, avow, declare, profess, testify; demur, expostulate, object, remonstrate, repudiate. * *n* complaint, declaration, disapproval, objection, protestation.

prototype *n* archetype, copy, exemplar, example, ideal, model, original, paradigm, precedent, protoplast, type.

protract *vb* continue, extend, lengthen, prolong; defer, delay, postpone.

protrude *vb* beetle, bulge, extend, jut, project.

protuberance *n* bulge, bump, elevation, excrescence, hump, lump, process, projection, prominence, roundness, swelling, tumour.

proud *adj* assuming, conceited, contended, egotistical, overweening, self-conscious, self-satisfied, vain; arrogant, boastful, haughty, high-spirited, highly strung, imperious, lofty, lordly, presumptuous, supercilious, uppish, vainglorious.

prove *vb* ascertain, conform, demonstrate, establish, evidence, evince, justify, manifest, show, substantiate, sustain, verify; assay, check, examine, experiment, test, try.

proverb *n* adage, aphorism, apothegm, byword, dictum, maxim, precept, saw, saying.

proverbial *adj* acknowledged, current, notorious, unquestioned.

provide *vb* arrange, collect, plan, prepare, procure; gather, keep, store; afford, contribute, feed, furnish, produce, stock, supply, yield; cater, purvey; agree, bargain, condition, contract, covenant, engage, stipulate.

provided, providing *conj* granted, if, supposing.

provident *adj* careful, cautious, considerate, discreet, farseeing, forecasting, forehanded, foreseeing, prudent; economical, frugal, thrifty.

province *n* district, domain, region, section, territory, tract; colony, dependency; business, calling, capacity, charge, department, duty, employment, function, office, part, post, sphere; department, division, jurisdiction.

provincial *adj* annexed, appendant, outlying; bucolic, countrified, rude, rural, rustic, unpolished, unrefined; insular, local, narrow. * *n* peasant, rustic, yokel.

provision *n* anticipation, providing; arrangement, care, preparation, readiness; equipment, fund, grist, hoard, reserve, resources, stock, store, supplies, supply; clause, condition, prerequisite, proviso, reservation, stipulation.

provisions *npl* eatables, fare, food, provender, supplies, viands, victuals.

proviso *n* clause, condition, provision, stipulation.

provocation *n* incentive, incitement, provocativeness, stimulant, stimulus; affront, indignity, insult, offence; angering, vexation.

provoke *vb* animate, arouse, awaken, excite, impel, incite, induce, inflame, instigate, kindle, move, rouse, stimulate; affront, aggravate, anger, annoy, chafe, enrage, exacerbate, exasperate, incense, infuriate, irritate, nettle, offend, pique, vex; cause, elicit, evoke, instigate, occasion, produce, promote.

provoking *adj* aggravating, annoying, exasperating, irritating, offensive, tormenting, vexatious, vexing.

prowess *n* bravery, courage, daring, fearlessness, gallantry, heroism, intrepidity, valour; aptitude, dexterity, expertness, facility.

proximity *n* adjacency, contiguity, nearness, neighbourhood, propinquity, vicinage, vicinity.

proxy *n* agent, attorney, commissioner, delegate, deputy, lieutenant, representative, substitute.

prudence *n* carefulness, caution, circumspection, common sense, considerateness, discretion, forecast, foresight, judgment, judiciousness, policy, providence, sense, tact, wariness, wisdom.

prudent *adj* cautious, careful, circumspect, considerate, discreet, foreseeing, heedful, judicious, politic, provident, prudential, wary, wise.

prudish *adj* coy, demure, modest, precise, prim, reserved, strait-laced.

prune *vb* abbreviate, clip, cut, dock, lop, thin, trim; dress, preen.

prurient *adj* covetous, craving, desiring, hankering, itching, lascivious, libidinous, longing, lustful.

pry *vb* examine, ferret, inspect, investigate, peep, peer, question, scrutinize, search; force, lever, prise.

public *adj* civil, common, countrywide, general, national, political, state; known, notorious, open, popular, published, well-known. * *n* citizens, community, country, everyone, general public, masses, nation, people, population; audience, buyers, following, supporters.

publication *n* advertisement, announcement, disclosure, divulgement, divulgence, proclamation, promulgation, report; edition, issue, issuance, printing.

publicity *n* daylight, currency, limelight, notoriety, spotlight; outlet, vent.

publish *vb* advertise, air, bruit, announce, blaze, blazon, broach, communicate, declare, diffuse, disclose, disseminate, impart, placard, post, proclaim, promulgate, reveal, tell, utter, vent, ventilate.

pucker *vb* cockle, contract, corrugate, crease, crinkle, furrow, gather, pinch, purse, shirr, wrinkle. * *n* crease, crinkle, fold, furrow, wrinkle.

puerile *adj* boyish, childish, infantile, juvenile, youthful; foolish, frivolous, idle, nonsensical, petty, senseless, silly, simple, trifling, trivial, weak.

puffy *adj* distended, swelled, swollen, tumid, turgid; bombastic, extravagant, inflated, pompous.

pugnacious *adj* belligerent, bellicose, contentious, fighting, irascible, irritable, petulant, quarrelsome.

puissant *adj* forcible, mighty, potent, powerful, strong.

pull *vb* drag, draw, haul, row, tow, tug; cull, extract, gather, pick, pluck; detach, rend, tear, wrest. * *n* pluck, shake, tug, twitch, wrench; contest, struggle; attraction, gravity, magnetism; graft, influence, power.

pulsate *vb* beat, palpitate, pant, throb, thump, vibrate.

pulverize *vb* bruise, comminute, grind, levigate, triturate.

pun *vb* assonate, alliterate, play on words. * *n* assonance, alliteration, clinch, conceit, double-meaning, paranomasia, play on words, quip, rhyme, witticism, wordplay.

punctilious *adj* careful, ceremonious, conscientious, exact, formal, nice, particular, precise, punctual, scrupulous, strict.

punctual *adj* exact, nice, precise, punctilious; early, prompt, ready, regular, seasonable, timely.

puncture *vb* bore, penetrate, perforate, pierce, prick. * *n* bite, hole, sting, wound.

pungent *adj* acid, acrid, biting, burning, caustic, hot, mordant, penetrating, peppery, piercing, piquant, prickling, racy, salty, seasoned, sharp, smart, sour, spicy, stimulating, stinging; acute, acrimonious, cutting, distressing, irritating, keen, painful, peevish, poignant, pointed, satirical, severe, tart, trenchant, waspish.

punish *vb* beat, castigate, chasten, chastise, correct, discipline, flog, lash, scourge, torture, whip.

punishment *n* castigation, chastening, chastisement, correction, discipline, infliction, retribution, scourging, trial; judgment, nemesis, penalty.

puny *adj* feeble, inferior, weak; dwarf, dwarfish, insignificant, diminutive, little, petty, pygmy, small, stunted, tiny, underdeveloped, undersized.

pupil *n* beginner, catechumen, disciple, learner, neophyte, novice, scholar, student, tyro.

pupillage *n* minority, nonage, tutelage, wardship.

puppet *n* doll, image, manikin, marionette; cat's-paw, pawn, tool.

purchase *vb* buy, gain, get, obtain, pay for, procure; achieve, attain, earn, win. * *n* acquisition, buy, gain, possession, property; advantage, foothold, grasp, hold, influence, support.

pure *adj* clean, clear, fair, immaculate, spotless, stainless, unadulterated, unalloyed, unblemished, uncorrupted, undefiled, unpolluted, unspotted, unstained, unsullied, untainted, untarnished; chaste, continent, guileless, guiltless, holy, honest, incorrupt, innocent, modest, sincere, true, uncorrupt, upright, virgin, virtuous; genuine, perfect, real, simple, true, unadorned; absolute, essential, mere, sheer, thorough; classic, classical.

purge *vb* cleanse, clear, purify; clarify, defecate, evacuate; deterge, scour; absolve, pardon, shrive. * *n* elimination, eradication, expulsion, removal, suppression; cathartic, emetic, enema, laxative, physic.

purify *vb* clean, cleanse, clear, depurate, expurgate, purge, refine, wash; clarify, fine.

puritanical *adj* ascetic, narrow-minded, overscrupulous, prim, prudish, rigid, severe, strait-laced, strict.

purity *n* clearness, fineness; cleanness, correctness, faultlessness, immaculacy, immaculateness; guilelessness, guiltlessness, holiness, honesty, innocence, integrity, piety, simplicity, truth, uprightness, virtue; excellence, genuineness; homogeneity, simpleness; chasteness, chastity, continence, modesty, pudency, virginity.

purlieus *npl* borders, bounds, confines, environs, limits, neighbourhood, outskirts, precincts, suburbs, vicinage, vicinity.

purloin *vb* abstract, crib, filch, pilfer, rob, steal, thieve.

purport *vb* allege, assert, claim, maintain, pretend, profess; denote, express, imply, indicate, mean, signify, suggest. * *n* bearing, current, design, drift, gist, import, intent, meaning, scope, sense, significance, signification, spirit, tendency, tenor.

purpose *vb* contemplate, design, intend, mean, meditate; determine, resolve. * *n* aim, design, drift, end, intent, intention, object, resolution, resolve, view; plan, project; meaning, purport, sense; consequence, effect.

pursue *vb* chase, dog, follow, hound, hunt, shadow, track; conduct, continue, cultivate, maintain, practise, prosecute; seek, strive; accompany, attend.

pursuit *n* chase, hunt, race; conduct, cultivation, practice, prosecution, pursuance; avocation, calling, business, employment, fad, hobby, occupation, vocation.

pursy *adj* corpulent, fat, fleshy, plump, podgy, pudgy, short, thick; short-breathed, short-winded; opulent, rich.

purview *n* body, compass, extent, limit, reach, scope, sphere, view.

push *vb* elbow, crowd, hustle, impel, jostle, shoulder, shove, thrust; advance, drive, hurry, propel, urge; importune, persuade, tease. * *n* pressure, thrust; determination, perseverance; emergency, exigency, extremity, pinch, strait, test, trial; assault, attack, charge, endeavour, onset.

pusillanimous *adj* chicken, chicken-hearted, cowardly, dastardly, faint-hearted, feeble, lily-livered, mean-spirited, spiritless, timid, recreant, timorous, weak.

pustule *n* abscess, blain, blister, blotch, boil, fester, gathering, pimple, sore, ulcer.

put *vb* bring, collocate, deposit, impose, lay, locate, place, set; enjoin, impose, inflict, levy; offer, present, propose, state; compel, constrain, force, oblige; entice, incite, induce, urge; express, utter.

putative *adj* deemed, reckoned, reported, reputed, supposed.

putrefy *vb* corrupt, decay, decompose, fester, rot, stink.

putrid *adj* corrupt, decayed, decomposed, fetid, rank, rotten, stinking.

puzzle *vb* bewilder, confound, confuse, embarrass, gravel, mystify, nonplus, perplex, pose, stagger; complicate, entangle.* *n* conundrum, enigma, labyrinth, maze, paradox, poser, problem, riddle; bewilderment, complication, confusion, difficulty, dilemma, embarrassment, mystification, perplexity, point, quandary, question.

pygmy *adj* diminutive, dwarf, dwarfish, Lilliputian, little, midget, stunted, tiny. * *n* dwarf, Lilliputian, midget.

Q

quack[1] *vb, n* cackle, cry, squeak.

quack[2] *adj* fake, false, sham. * *n* charlatan, empiric, humbug, impostor, mountebank, pretender.

quadruple *adj* fourfold, quadruplicate.

quagmire *n* bog, fen, marsh, morass, slough, swamp; difficulty, impasse, muddle, predicament.

quail *vb* blench, cower, droop, faint, flinch, shrink, tremble.

quaint *adj* antiquated, antique, archaic, curious, droll, extraordinary, fanciful, odd, old-fashioned, queer, singular, uncommon, unique, unusual; affected, fantastic, far-fetched, whimsical; artful, ingenious.

quake *vb* quiver, shake, shiver, shudder; move, vibrate. * *n* earthquake, shake, shudder.

qualification *n* ability, accomplishment, capability, competency, eligibility, fitness, suitability; condition, exception, limitation, modification, proviso, restriction, stipulation; abatement, allowance, diminution, mitigation.

qualified *adj* accomplished, certificated, certified, competent, fitted, equipped, licensed, trained; adapted, circumscribed, conditional, limited, modified, restricted.

qualify *vb* adapt, capacitate, empower, entitle, equip, fit; limit, modify, narrow, restrain, restrict; abate, assuage, ease, mitigate, moderate, reduce, soften; diminish, modulate, temper, regulate, vary.

quality *n* affection, attribute, characteristic, colour, distinction, feature, flavour, mark, nature, peculiarity, property, singularity, timbre, tinge, trait, character, condition, disposition, humour, mood, temper; brand, calibre, capacity, class, description, excellence, grade, kind, rank, sort, stamp, standing, station, status, virtue; aristocracy, gentility, gentry, noblesse, nobility.

qualm *n* agony, pang, throe; nausea, queasiness, sickness; compunction, remorse, uneasiness, twinge.

quandary *n* bewilderment, difficulty, dilemma, doubt, embarrassment, perplexity, pickle, plight, predicament, problem, puzzle, strait, uncertainty.

quantity *n* content, extent, greatness, measure, number, portion, share, size; aggregate, batch, amount, bulk, lot, mass, quantum, store, sum, volume; duration, length.

quarrel *vb* altercate, bicker, brawl, carp, cavil, clash, contend, differ, dispute, fight, jangle, jar, scold, scuffle, spar, spat, squabble, strive, wrangle. * *n* altercation, affray, bickering, brawl, breach, breeze, broil, clash, contention, contest, controversy, difference, disagreement, discord, dispute, dissension, disturbance, feud, fight, fray, imbroglio, jar, miff, misunderstanding, quarrelling, row, rupture, spat, squabble, strife, tiff, tumult, variance, wrangle.

quarrelsome *adj* argumentative, choleric, combative, contentious, cross, discordant, disputatious, dissentious, fiery, irascible, irritable, petulant, pugnacious, ugly, wranglesome.

quarter *vb* billet, lodge, post, station; allot, furnish, share. * *n* abode, billet, dwelling, habitation, lodgings, posts, quarters, stations; direction, district, locality, location, lodge, position, region, territory; clemency, mercy, mildness.

quash *vb* abate, abolish, annul, cancel, invalidate, nullify, overthrow; crush, extinguish, repress, stop, subdue, suppress.

queasy *adj* nauseated, pukish, seasick, sick, squeamish.

queer *vb* botch, harm, impair, mar, spoil. * *adj* curious, droll, extraordinary, fantastic, odd, peculiar, quaint, singular, strange, uncommon, unusual, whimsical; gay, homosexual.

quell *vb* conquer, crush, overcome, overpower, subdue; bridle, check, curb, extinguish, lay, quench, rein in, repress, restrain, stifle; allay, calm, compose, hush, lull, pacify, quiet, quieten, still, tranquillize; alleviate, appease, blunt, deaden, dull, mitigate, mollify, soften, soothe.

quench *vb* extinguish, put out; check, destroy, repress, satiate, stifle, still, suppress; allay, cool, dampen, extinguish, slake.

querulous *adj* bewailing, complaining, cross, discontented, dissatisfied, fretful, fretting, irritable, mourning, murmuring, peevish, petulant, plaintive, touchy, whining.

query *vb* ask, enquire, inquire, question; dispute, doubt. * *n* enquiry, inquiry, interrogatory, issue, problem, question.

quest *n* expedition, journey, search, voyage; pursuit, suit; examination, enquiry, inquiry; demand, desire, invitation, prayer, request, solicitation.

question *vb* ask, catechize, enquire, examine, inquire, interrogate, quiz, sound out; doubt, query; challenge, dispute. * *n* examination, enquiry,

191

inquiry, interpellation, interrogation; enquiry, inquiry, interrogatory, query; debate, discussion, disquisition, examination, investigation, issue, trial; controversy, dispute, doubt; motion, mystery, point, poser, problem, proposition, puzzle, topic.

questionable *adj* ambiguous, controversial, controvertible, debatable, doubtful, disputable, equivocal, problematic, problematical, suspicious, uncertain, undecided.

quibble *vb* cavil, equivocate, evade, prevaricate, shuffle. * *n* equivocation, evasion, pretence, prevarication, quirk, shift, shuffle, sophism, subtlety, subterfuge.

quick *adj* active, agile, alert, animated, brisk, lively, nimble, prompt, ready, smart, sprightly; expeditious, fast, fleet, flying, hurried, rapid, speedy, swift; adroit, apt, clever, dextrous, expert, skilful; choleric, hasty, impetuous, irascible, irritable, passionate, peppery, petulant, precipitate, sharp, unceremonious, testy, touchy, waspish; alive, animate, live, living.

quicken *vb* animate, energize, resuscitate, revivify, vivify; cheer, enliven, invigorate, reinvigorate, revive, whet; accelerate, dispatch, expedite, hasten, hurry, speed; actuate, excite, incite, kindle, refresh, sharpen, stimulate; accelerate, live, take effect.

quickly *adv* apace, fast, immediately, nimbly, quick, rapidly, readily, soon, speedily, swiftly.

quickness *n* celerity, dispatch, expedition, haste, rapidity, speed, swiftness, velocity; agility, alertness, activity, briskness, liveliness, nimbleness, promptness, readiness, smartness; adroitness, aptitude, aptness, dexterity, facility, knack; acumen, acuteness, keenness, penetration, perspicacity, sagacity, sharpness, shrewdness.

quiescent *adj* at rest, hushed, motionless, quiet, resting, still; calm, mute, placid, quiet, serene, still, tranquil, unagitated, undisturbed, unruffled.

quiet *adj* hushed, motionless, quiescent, still, unmoved; calm, contented, gentle, mild, meek, modest, peaceable, peaceful, placid, silent, smooth, tranquil, undemonstrative, unobtrusive, unruffled; patient; retired, secluded. * *n* calmness, peace, repose, rest, silence, stillness.

quieten *vb* arrest, discontinue, intermit, interrupt, still, stop, suspend; allay, appease, calm, compose, lull, pacify, sober, soothe, tranquillize; hush, silence; alleviate, assuage, blunt, dull, mitigate, moderate, mollify, soften.

quip *n* crank, flout, gibe, jeer, mock, quirk, repartee, retort, sarcasm, sally, scoff, sneer, taunt, witticism.

quit *vb* absolve, acquit, deliver, free, release; clear, deliver, discharge from, free, liberate, relieve; acquit, behave, conduct; carry through, perform; discharge, pay, repay, requite; relinquish, renounce, resign, stop, surrender; depart from, leave, withdraw from; abandon, desert, forsake, forswear. * *adj* absolved, acquitted, clear, discharged, free, released.

quite *adv* completely, entirely, exactly, perfectly, positively, precisely, totally, wholly.

quiver *vb* flicker, flutter, oscillate, palpitate, quake, play, shake, shiver, shudder, tremble, twitch, vibrate. * *n* shake, shiver, shudder, trembling.

quixotic *adj* absurd, chimerical, fanciful, fantastic, fantastical, freakish, imaginary, mad, romantic, utopian, visionary, wild.

quiz *vb* examine, question, test; peer at; banter, hoax, puzzle, ridicule. * *n* enigma, hoax, jest, joke, puzzle; jester, joker, hoax.

quota *n* allocation, allotment, apportionment, contingent, portion, proportion, quantity, share.

quotation *n* citation, clipping, cutting, extract, excerpt, reference, selection; estimate, rate, tender.

quote *vb* adduce, cite, excerpt, extract, illustrate, instance, name, repeat, take; estimate, tender.

R

rabble *n* commonality, horde, mob, populace, riff-raff, rout, scum, trash.

rabid *adj* frantic, furious, mad, raging, wild; bigoted, fanatical, intolerant, irrational, narrow-minded, rampant.

race[1] *n* ancestry, breed, family, generation, house, kindred, line, lineage, pedigree, stock, strain; clan, folk, nation, people, tribe; breed, children, descendants, issue, offspring, progeny, stock.

race[2] *vb* career, compete, contest, course, hasten, hurry, run, speed. * *n* career, chase, competition, contest, course, dash, heat, match, pursuit, run, sprint; flavour, quality, smack, strength, taste.

rack *vb* agonize, distress, excruciate, rend, torment, torture, wring; exhaust, force, harass, oppress, strain, stretch, wrest. * *n* agony, anguish, pang, torment, torture; crib, manger; neck, crag; dampness, mist, moisture, vapour.

racket *n* clamour, clatter, din, dissipation, disturbance, fracas, frolic, hubbub, noise, outcry, tumult, uproar; game, graft, scheme, understanding.

racy *adj* flavoursome, palatable, piquant, pungent, rich, spicy, strong; forcible, lively, pungent, smart, spirited, stimulating, vigorous, vivacious.

radiance *n* brightness, brilliance, brilliancy, effluence, efflux, emission, glare, glitter, light, lustre, refulgence, resplendence, shine, splendour.

radiant *adj* beaming, brilliant, effulgent, glittering, glorious, luminous, lustrous, resplendent, shining, sparkling, splendid; ecstatic, happy, pleased.

radiate *vb* beam, gleam, glitter, shine; emanate, emit; diffuse, spread.

radical *adj* constitutional, deep-seated, essential, fundamental, ingrained, inherent, innate, native, natural, organic, original, uncompromising; original, primitive, simple, uncompounded, underived; complete, entire, extreme, fanatic, insurgent, perfect, rebellious, thorough, total. * *n* etymon, radix, root; fanatic, revolutionary.

rage *vb* bluster, boil, chafe, foam, fret, fume, ravage, rave. * *n* excitement, frenzy, fury, madness, passion, rampage, raving, vehemence, wrath; craze, fashion, mania, mode, style, vogue.

ragged *adj* rent, tattered, torn; contemptible, mean, poor, shabby; jagged, rough, rugged, shaggy, uneven; discordant, dissonant, inharmonious, unmusical.

raid *vb* assault, forage, invade, pillage, plunder. * *n* attack, foray, invasion, inroad, plunder.

rail *vb* abuse, censure, inveigh, scoff, scold, sneer, upbraid.

raillery *n* banter, chaff, irony, joke, pleasantry, ridicule, satire.

raiment *n* array, apparel, attire, clothes, clothing, costume, dress, garb, garments, habiliment, habit, vestments, vesture.

rain *vb* drizzle, drop, fall, pour, shower, sprinkle, teem; bestow, lavish. * *n* cloudburst, downpour, drizzle, mist, shower, sprinkling.

raise *vb* boost, construct, erect, heave, hoist, lift, uplift, upraise, rear; advance, elevate, ennoble, exalt, promote; aggravate, amplify, augment, enhance, heighten, increase, invigorate; arouse, awake, cause, effect, excite, originate, produce, rouse, stir up, occasion, start; assemble, collect, get, levy, obtain; breed, cultivate, grow, propagate, rear; ferment, leaven, work.

rake[1] *vb* collect, comb, gather, scratch; ransack, scour.

rake[2] *n* debauchee, libertine, profligate, roué.

rakish *adj* debauched, dissipated, dissolute, lewd, licentious; cavalier, jaunty.

ramble *vb* digress, maunder, range, roam, rove, saunter, straggle, stray, stroll, wander. * *n* excursion, rambling, roving, tour, trip, stroll, wandering.

rambling *adj* discursive, irregular; straggling, strolling, wandering.

ramification *n* arborescence, branching, divarication, forking, radiation; branch, division, offshoot, subdivision; consequence, upshot.

ramify *vb* branch, divaricate, extend, separate.

rampant *adj* excessive, exuberant, luxuriant, rank, wanton; boisterous, dominant, headstrong, impetuous, predominant, raging, uncontrollable, unbridled, ungovernable, vehement, violent.

rampart *n* bulwark, circumvallation, defence, fence, fortification, guard, security, wall.

rancid *adj* bad, fetid, foul, fusty, musty, offensive, rank, sour, stinking, tainted.

rancorous *adj* bitter, implacable, malevolent, malicious, malign, malignant, resentful, spiteful, vindictive, virulent.

rancour *n* animosity, antipathy, bitterness, enmity, gall, grudge, hate, hatred, ill-will, malevolence, malice, malignity, spite, venom, vindictiveness.

random *adj* accidental, casual, chance, fortuitous,

haphazard, irregular, stray, wandering.

range *vb* course, cruise, extend, ramble, roam, rove, straggle, stray, stroll, wander; bend, lie, run; arrange, class, dispose, rank. * *n* file, line, row, rank, tier; class, kind, order, sort; excursion, expedition, ramble, roving, wandering; amplitude, bound, command, compass, distance, extent, latitude, reach, scope, sweep, view; register.

rank[1] *vb* arrange, class, classify, range. * *n* file, line, order, range, row, tier; class, division, group, order, series; birth, blood, caste, degree, estate, grade, position, quality, sphere, stakes, standing; dignity, distinction, eminence, nobility.

rank[2] *adj* dense, exuberant, luxuriant, overabundant, overgrown, vigorous, wild; excessive, extreme, extravagant, flagrant, gross, rampant, sheer, unmitigated, utter, violent; fetid, foul, fusty, musty, offensive, rancid; fertile, productive, rich; coarse, disgusting.

ransack *vb* pillage, plunder, ravage, rifle, sack, strip; explore, overhaul, rummage, search thoroughly.

ransom *vb* deliver, emancipate, free, liberate, redeem, rescue, unfetter. * *n* money, payment payoff, price; deliverance, liberation, redemption, release.

rant *vb* declaim, mouth, spout, vociferate. * *n* bombast, cant, exaggeration, fustian.

rapacious *adj* predacious, preying, raptorial; avaricious, grasping, greedy, ravenous, voracious.

rapid *adj* fast, fleet, quick, swift; brisk, expeditious, hasty, hurried, quick, speedy.

rapine *n* depredation, pillage, plunder, robbery, spoliation.

rapt *adj* absorbed, charmed, delighted, ecstatic, engrossed, enraptured, entranced, fascinated, inspired, spellbound.

rapture *vb* enrapture, ravish, transport. * *n* delight, exultation, enthusiasm, rhapsody; beatification, beatitude, bliss, ecstasy, felicity, happiness, joy, spell, transport.

rare[1] *adj* sparse, subtle, thin; extraordinary, infrequent, scarce, singular, strange, uncommon, unique, unusual; choice, excellent, exquisite, fine, incomparable, inimitable.

rare[2] *adj* bloody, underdone.

rarity *n* attenuation, ethereality, etherealness, rarefaction, rareness, tenuity, tenuousness, thinness; infrequency, scarcity, singularity, sparseness, uncommonness, unwontedness.

rascal *n* blackguard, caitiff, knave, miscreant, rogue, reprobate, scallywag, scapegrace, scamp, scoundrel, vagabond, villain.

rash[1] *adj* adventurous, audacious, careless, foolhardy, hasty, headlong, headstrong, heedless, incautious, inconsiderate, indiscreet, injudicious, impetuous, impulsive, incautious, precipitate, quick, rapid, reckless, temerarious, thoughtless, unguarded, unwary, venturesome.

rash[2] *n* breaking-out, efflorescence, eruption; epidemic, flood, outbreak, plague, spate.

rashness *n* carelessness, foolhardiness, hastiness, heedlessness, inconsideration, indiscretion, precipitation, recklessness, temerity, venturesomeness.

rate[1] *vb* appraise, compute, estimate, value. * *n* cost, price; class, degree, estimate, rank, value, valuation, worth; proportion, ration; assessment, charge, impost, tax.

rate[2] *vb* abuse, berate, censure, chide, criticize, find fault, reprimand, reprove, scold.

ratify *vb* confirm, corroborate, endorse, establish, seal, settle, substantiate; approve, bind, consent, sanction.

ration *vb* apportion, deal, distribute, dole, restrict. * *n* allowance, portion, quota, share.

rational *adj* intellectual, reasoning; equitable, fair, fit, just, moderate, natural, normal, proper, reasonable, right; discreet, enlightened, intelligent, judicious, sagacious, sensible, sound, wise.

raucous *adj* harsh, hoarse, husky, rough.

ravage *vb* consume, desolate, despoil, destroy, devastate, harry, overrun, pillage, plunder, ransack, ruin, sack, spoil, strip, waste. * *n* desolation, despoilment, destruction, devastation, havoc, pillage, plunder, rapine, ruin, spoil, waste.

ravenous *adj* devouring, ferocious, gluttonous, greedy, insatiable, omnivorous, ravening, rapacious, voracious.

ravine *n* canyon, cleft, defile, gap, gorge, gulch, gully, pass.

raving *adj* delirious, deranged, distracted, frantic, frenzied, furious, infuriated, mad, phrenetic, raging. * *n* delirium, frenzy, fury, madness, rage.

ravish *vb* abuse, debauch, defile, deflower, force, outrage, violate; captivate, charm, delight, enchant, enrapture, entrance, overjoy, transport; abduct, kidnap, seize, snatch, strip.

raw *adj* fresh, inexperienced, unpractised, unprepared, unseasoned, untried, unskilled; crude, green, immature, unfinished, unripe; bare, chafed, excoriated, galled, sensitive, sore; bleak, chilly, cold, cutting, damp, piercing, windswept; uncooked.

ray *n* beam, emanation, gleam, moonbeam, radiance, shaft, streak, sunbeam.

raze *vb* demolish, destroy, dismantle, extirpate, fell, level, overthrow, ruin, subvert; efface, erase, obliterate.

reach *vb* extend, stretch; grasp, hit, strike, touch; arrive at, attain, gain, get, obtain, win. * *n* capability, capacity, grasp.

readily *adv* easily, promptly, quickly; cheerfully, willingly.

readiness *n* alacrity, alertness, expedition, quickness, promptitude, promptness; aptitude, aptness, dexterity, easiness, expertness, facility, quickness, skill; preparation, preparedness, ripeness; cheerfulness, disposition, eagerness, ease, willingness.

ready *vb* arrange, equip, organize, prepare. * *adj* alert, expeditious, prompt, quick, punctual, speedy; adroit, apt, clever, dextrous, expert, facile, handy, keen, nimble, prepared, prompt, ripe, quick, sharp, skilful, smart; cheerful, disposed, eager, free, inclined, willing; accommodating, available, convenient, near, handy; easy, facile, fluent, offhand, opportune, short, spontaneous.

real *adj* absolute, actual, certain, literal, positive, practical, substantial, substantive, veritable; authentic, genuine, true; essential, internal, intrinsic.

realize *vb* accomplish, achieve, discharge, effect, effectuate, perfect, perform; apprehend, comprehend, experience, recognize, understand; externalize, substantiate; acquire, earn, gain, get, net, obtain, produce, sell.

reality *n* actuality, certainty, fact, truth, verity.

really *adv* absolutely, actually, certainly, indeed, positively, truly, verily, veritably.

reap *vb* acquire, crop, gain, gather, get, harvest, obtain, receive.

rear[1] *adj* aft, back, following, hind, last. * *n* background, reverse, setting; heel, posterior, rear end, rump, stern, tail; path, trail, train, wake.

rear[2] *vb* construct, elevate, erect, hoist, lift, raise; cherish, educate, foster, instruct, nourish, nurse, nurture, train; breed, grow; rouse, stir up.

reason *vb* argue, conclude, debate, deduce, draw from, infer, intellectualize, syllogize, think, trace. * *n* faculty, intellect, intelligence, judgement, mind, principle, sanity, sense, thinking, understanding; account, argument, basis, cause, consideration, excuse, explanation, gist, ground, motive, occasion, pretence, proof; aim, design, end, object, purpose; argument, reasoning; common sense, reasonableness, wisdom; equity, fairness, justice, right; exposition, rationale, theory.

reasonable *adj* equitable, fair, fit, honest, just, proper, rational, right, suitable; enlightened, intelligent, judicious, sagacious, sensible, wise; considerable, fair, moderate, tolerable; credible, intellectual, plausible, well-founded; sane, sober, sound; cheap, inexpensive, low-priced.

rebate *vb* abate, bate, blunt, deduct, diminish, lessen, reduce; cut, pare, rabbet. * *n* decrease, decrement, diminution, lessening; allowance, deduction, discount, reduction.

rebel *vb* mutiny, resist, revolt, strike. * *adj* insubordinate, insurgent, mutinous, rebellious. * *n* insurgent, mutineer, traitor.

rebellion *n* anarchy, insubordination, insurrection, mutiny, resistance, revolt, revolution, uprising.

rebellious *adj* contumacious, defiant, disloyal, disobedient, insubordinate, intractable, obstinate, mutinous, rebel, refractory, seditious.

rebuff *vb* check, chide, oppose, refuse, reject, repel, reprimand, resist, snub. * *n* check, defeat, discouragement, opposition, rejection, resistance, snub.

rebuke *vb* blame, censure, chide, lecture, upbraid; reprehend, reprimand, reprove, scold, silence. * *n* blame, censure, chiding, expostulation, remonstrance, reprimand, reprehension, reproach, reproof, reproval; affliction, chastisement, punishment.

recall *vb* abjure, abnegate, annul, cancel, countermand, deny, nullify, overrule, recant, repeal, repudiate, rescind, retract, revoke, swallow, withdraw; commemorate, recollect, remember, retrace, review, revive. * *n* abjuration, abnegation, annulment, cancellation, nullification, recantation, repeal, repudiation, rescindment, retraction, revocation, withdrawal; memory, recollection, remembrance, reminiscence.

recant *vb* abjure, annul, disavow, disown, recall, renounce, repudiate, retract, revoke, unsay.

recapitulate *vb* epitomize, recite, rehearse, reiterate, repeat, restate, review, summarize.

recede *vb* desist, ebb, retire, regress, retreat, retrograde, return, withdraw.

receive *vb* accept, acquire, derive, gain, get, obtain, take; admit, shelter, take in; entertain, greet, welcome; allow, permit, tolerate; adopt, approve, believe, credit, embrace, follow, learn, understand; accommodate, carry, contain, hold, include, retain; bear, encounter, endure, experience, meet, suffer, sustain.

recent *adj* fresh, new, novel; latter, modern, young; deceased, foregoing, late, preceding, retiring.

reception *n* acceptance, receipt, receiving; entertainment, greeting, welcome; levee, soiree, party; admission, credence; belief, credence, recognition.

recess *n* alcove, corner, depth, hollow, niche, nook, privacy, retreat, seclusion; break, holiday, intermission, interval, respite, vacation; recession, retirement, retreat, withdrawal.

reciprocal *adj* alternate, commutable, complementary, correlative, correspondent, mutual.

recital *n* rehearsal, repetition, recitation; account, description, detail, explanation, narration, relation, statement, telling.

recite *vb* declaim, deliver, rehearse, repeat; describe, mention, narrate, recount, relate, tell; count, detail, enumerate, number, recapitulate.

reckless *adj* breakneck, careless, desperate, devil-may-care, flighty, foolhardy, giddy, harebrained, headlong, heedless, inattentive, improvident, imprudent, inconsiderate, indifferent, indiscreet, mindless, negligent, rash, regardless, remiss, thoughtless, temerarious, uncircumspect, unconcerned, unsteady, volatile, wild.

reckon *vb* calculate, cast, compute, consider, count, enumerate, guess, number; account, class, esteem, estimate, regard, repute, value.

reckoning *n* calculation, computation, consideration, counting; account, bill, charge, estimate, register, score; arrangement, settlement.

reclaim *vb* amend, correct, reform; recover, redeem, regenerate, regain, reinstate, restore; civilize, tame.

recline *vb* couch, lean, lie, lounge, repose, rest.

recluse *adj* anchoritic, anchoritical, cloistered,

eremitic, eremitical, hermitic, hermitical, reclusive, solitary. * *n* anchorite, ascetic, eremite, hermit, monk, solitary.

reclusive *adj* recluse, retired, secluded, sequestered, sequestrated, solitary.

recognition *n* identification, memory, recollection, remembrance; acknowledgement, appreciation, avowal, comprehension, confession, notice; allowance, concession.

recognize *vb* apprehend, identify, perceive, remember; acknowledge, admit, avow, confess, own; allow, concede, grant; greet, salute.

recoil *vb* react, rebound, reverberate; retire, retreat, withdraw; blench, fail, falter, quail, shrink. * *n* backstroke, boomerang, elasticity, kick, reaction, rebound, repercussion, resilience, revulsion, ricochet, shrinking.

recollect *vb* recall, remember, reminisce.

recollection *n* memory, remembrance, reminiscence.

recommend *vb* approve, commend, endorse, praise, sanction; commit; advise, counsel, prescribe, suggest.

recommendation *n* advocacy, approbation, approval, commendation, counsel, credential, praise, testimonial.

recompense *vb* compensate, remunerate, repay, requite, reward, satisfy; indemnify, redress, reimburse. * *n* amends, compensation, indemnification, indemnity, remuneration, repayment, reward, satisfaction; requital, retribution.

reconcilable *adj* appeasable, forgiving, placable; companionable, congruous, consistent.

reconcile *vb* appease, conciliate, pacify, placate, propitiate, reunite; content, harmonize, regulate; adjust, compose, heal, settle.

recondite *adj* concealed, dark, hidden, mystic, mystical, obscure, occult, secret, transcendental.

record *vb* chronicle, enter, note, register. * *n* account, annals, archive, chronicle, diary, docket, enrolment, entry, file, list, minute, memoir, memorandum, memorial, note, proceedings, register, registry, report, roll, score; mark, memorial, relic, trace, track, trail, vestige; memory, remembrance; achievement, career, history.

recount *vb* describe, detail, enumerate, mention, narrate, particularize, portray, recite, relate, rehearse, report, tell.

recover *vb* recapture, reclaim, regain; rally, recruit, repair, retrieve; cure, heal, restore, revive; redeem, rescue, salvage, save; convalesce, recuperate.

recreant *adj* base, cowardly, craven, dastardly, faint-hearted, mean-spirited, pusillanimous, yielding; apostate, backsliding, faithless, false, perfidious, treacherous, unfaithful, untrue. * *n* coward, dastard; apostate, backslider, renegade.

recreation *n* amusement, cheer, diversion, entertainment, fun, game, leisure, pastime, play, relaxation, sport.

recreational *adj* amusing, diverting, entertaining, refreshing, relaxing, relieving.

recruit *vb* repair, replenish; recover, refresh, regain, reinvigorate, renew, renovate, restore, retrieve, revive, strengthen, supply. * *n* auxiliary, beginner, helper, learner, novice, tyro.

rectify *vb* adjust, amend, better, correct, emend, improve, mend, redress, reform, regulate, straighten.

rectitude *n* conscientiousness, equity, goodness, honesty, integrity, justice, principle, probity, right, righteousness, straightforwardness, uprightness, virtue.

recumbent *adj* leaning, lying, prone, prostrate, reclining; idle, inactive, listless, reposing.

recur *vb* reappear, resort, return, revert.

recusancy *n* dissent, heresy, heterodoxy, nonconformity.

redeem *vb* reform, regain, repurchase, retrieve; free, liberate, ransom, rescue, save; deliver, reclaim, recover, reinstate; atone, compensate for, recompense; discharge, fulfil, keep, perform, satisfy.

redemption *n* buying, compensation, recovery, repurchase, retrieval; deliverance, liberation, ransom, release, rescue, salvation; discharge, fulfilment, performance.

redolent *adj* aromatic, balmy, fragrant, odoriferous, odorous, scented, sweet, sweet-smelling.

redoubtable *adj* awful, doughty, dreadful, formidable, terrible, valiant.

redound *vb* accrue, conduce, contribute, result, tend.

redress *vb* amend, correct, order, rectify, remedy, repair; compensate, ease, relieve. * *n* abatement, amends, atonement, compensation, correction, cure, indemnification, rectification, repair, righting, remedy, relief, reparation, satisfaction.

reduce *vb* bring; form, make, model, mould, remodel, render, resolve, shape; abate, abbreviate, abridge, attenuate, contract, curtail, decimate, decrease, diminish, lessen, minimize, shorten, thin; abase, debase, degrade, depress, dwarf, impair, lower, weaken; capture, conquer, master, overpower, overthrow, subject, subdue, subjugate, vanquish; impoverish, ruin; resolve, solve.

redundant *adj* copious, excessive, exuberant, fulsome, inordinate, lavish, needless, overflowing, overmuch, plentiful, prodigal, superabundant, replete, superfluous, unnecessary, useless; diffuse, periphrastic, pleonastic, tautological, verbose, wordy.

reel[1] *n* capstan, winch, windlass; bobbin, spool.

reel[2] *vb* falter, flounder, heave, lurch, pitch, plunge, rear, rock, roll, stagger, sway, toss, totter, tumble, wallow, welter, vacillate; spin, swing, turn, twirl, wheel, whirl. * *n* gyre, pirouette, spin, turn, twirl, wheel, whirl.

re-establish *vb* re-found, rehabilitate, reinstall, reinstate, renew, renovate, replace, restore.

refer *vb* commit, consign, direct, leave, relegate, send, submit; ascribe, assign, attribute, impute;

appertain, belong, concern, pertain, point, relate, respect, touch; appeal, apply, consult; advert, allude, cite, quote.

referee *vb* arbitrate, judge, umpire. * *n* arbiter, arbitrator, judge, umpire.

reference *n* concern, connection, regard, respect; allusion, ascription, citation, hint, intimation, mark, reference, relegation.

refine *vb* clarify, cleanse, defecate, fine, purify; cultivate, humanize, improve, polish, rarefy, spiritualize.

refined *adj* courtly, cultured, genteel, polished, polite; discerning, discriminating, fastidious, sensitive; filtered, processed, purified.

refinement *n* clarification, filtration, purification, sublimation; betterment, improvement; delicacy, cultivation, culture, elegance, elevation, finish, gentility, good breeding, polish, politeness, purity, spirituality, style.

reflect *vb* copy, imitate, mirror, reproduce; cogitate, consider, contemplate, deliberate, meditate, muse, ponder, ruminate, study, think.

reflection *n* echo, shadow; cogitation, consideration, contemplation, deliberation, idea, meditation, musing, opinion, remark, rumination, thinking, thought; aspersion, blame, censure, criticism, disparagement, reproach, slur.

reflective *adj* reflecting, reflexive; cogitating, deliberating, musing, pondering, reasoning, thoughtful.

reform *vb* amend, ameliorate, better, correct, improve, mend, meliorate, rectify, reclaim, redeem, regenerate, repair, restore; reconstruct, remodel, reshape. * *n* amendment, correction, progress, reconstruction, rectification, reformation.

reformation *n* amendment, emendation, improvement, reform; adoption, conversion, redemption; refashioning, regeneration, reproduction, reconstruction.

refractory *adj* cantankerous, contumacious, cross-grained, disobedient, dogged, headstrong, heady, incoercible, intractable, mulish, obstinate, perverse, recalcitrant, self-willed, stiff, stubborn, sullen, ungovernable, unmanageable, unruly, unyielding.

refrain[1] *vb* abstain, cease, desist, forbear, stop, withhold.

refrain[2] *n* chorus, song, undersong.

refresh *vb* air, brace, cheer, cool, enliven, exhilarate, freshen, invigorate, reanimate, recreate, recruit, reinvigorate, revive, regale, slake.

refreshing *adj* comfortable, cooling, grateful, invigorating, pleasant, reanimating, restful, reviving.

refuge *n* asylum, covert, harbour, haven, protection, retreat, safety, sanction, security, shelter.

refulgent *adj* bright, brilliant, effulgent, lustrous, radiant, resplendent, shining.

refund *vb* reimburse, repay, restore, return. * *n* reimbursement, repayment.

refuse[1] *n* chaff, discard, draff, dross, dregs, garbage, junk, leavings, lees, litter, lumber, offal, recrement, remains, rubbish, scoria, scum, sediment, slag, sweepings, trash, waste.

refuse[2] *vb* decline, deny, withhold; disallow, disavow, exclude, rebuff, reject, renege, renounce, repel, repudiate, repulse, revoke, veto.

refute *vb* confute, defeat, disprove, overcome, overthrow, rebut, repel, silence.

regain *vb* recapture, recover, re-obtain, repossess, retrieve.

regal *adj* imposing, imperial, kingly, noble, royal, sovereign.

regale *vb* delight, entertain, gratify, refresh; banquet, feast.

regard *vb* behold, gaze, look, notice, mark, observe, remark, see, view, watch; attend to, consider, heed, mind, respect; esteem, honour, revere, reverence, value; account, believe, estimate, deem, hold, imagine, reckon, suppose, think, treat, use. * *n* aspect, gaze, look, view; attention, attentiveness, care, concern, consideration, heed, notice, observance; account, reference, relation, respect; admiration, affection, attachment, deference, esteem, estimation, favour, honour, interest, liking, love, respect, reverence, sympathy, value; account, eminence, note, reputation, repute; condition, matter, point.

regardful *adj* attentive, careful, considerate, deferential, heedful, mindful, observing, thoughtful, watchful.

regarding *prep* concerning, respecting, touching.

regardless *adj* careless, disregarding, heedless, inattentive, indifferent, mindless, neglectful, negligent, unconcerned, unmindful, unobservant. * *adv* however, irrespectively, nevertheless, nonetheless, notwithstanding.

regenerate *vb* reproduce; renovate, revive; change, convert, renew, sanctify. * *adj* born-again, converted, reformed, regenerated.

regime *n* administration, government, rule.

region *n* climate, clime, country, district, division, latitude, locale, locality, province, quarter, scene, territory, tract; area, neighbourhood, part, place, portion, spot, space, sphere, terrain, vicinity.

register *vb* delineate, portray, record, show. * *n* annals, archive, catalogue, chronicle, list, record, roll, schedule; clerk, registrar, registry; compass, range.

regret *vb* bewail, deplore, grieve, lament, repine, sorrow; bemoan, repent, mourn, rue. * *n* concern, disappointment, grief, lamentation, rue, sorrow, trouble; compunction, contrition, penitence, remorse, repentance, repining, self-condemnation, self-reproach.

regular *adj* conventional, natural, normal, ordinary, typical; correct, customary, cyclic, established, fixed, habitual, periodic, periodical, recurring, reasonable, rhythmic, seasonal, stated, usual; steady, constant, uniform, even; just, methodical, orderly, punctual, systematic, unvarying; complete, genuine, indubitable, out-and-out, perfect, thorough; balanced, consistent, symmetrical.

regulate *vb* adjust, arrange, dispose, methodize, order, organize, settle, standardize, time, systematize; conduct, control, direct, govern, guide, manage, rule.

regulation *adj* customary, mandatory, official, required, standard. * *n* adjustment, arrangement, control, disposal, disposition, law, management, order, ordering, precept, rule, settlement.

rehabilitate *vb* reinstate, re-establish, restore; reconstruct, reconstitute, reintegrate, reinvigorate, renew, renovate.

rehearsal *n* drill, practice, recital, recitation, repetition; account, history, mention, narration, narrative, recounting, relation, statement, story, telling.

rehearse *vb* recite, repeat; delineate, depict, describe, detail, enumerate, narrate, portray, recapitulate, recount, relate, tell.

reign *vb* administer, command, govern, influence, predominate, prevail, rule. * *n* control, dominion, empire, influence, power, royalty, sovereignty, power, rule, sway.

reimburse *vb* refund, repay, restore; compensate, indemnify, requite, satisfy.

rein *vb* bridle, check, control, curb, guide, harness, hold, restrain, restrict. * *n* bridle, check, curb, harness, restraint, restriction.

reinforce *vb* augment, fortify, strengthen.

reinstate *vb* re-establish, rehabilitate, reinstall, replace, restore.

reject *vb* cashier, discard, dismiss, eject, exclude, pluck; decline, deny, disallow, despise, disapprove, disbelieve, rebuff, refuse, renounce, repel, repudiate, scout, slight, spurn, veto. * *n* cast-off, discard, failure, refusal, repudiation.

rejoice *vb* cheer, delight, enliven, enrapture, exhilarate, gladden, gratify, please, transport; crow, exult, delight, gloat, glory, jubilate, triumph, vaunt.

rejoin *vb* answer, rebut, respond, retort.

relate *vb* describe, detail, mention, narrate, recite, recount, rehearse, report, tell; apply, connect, correlate.

relation *n* account, chronicle, description, detail, explanation, history, mention, narration, narrative, recital, rehearsal, report, statement, story, tale; affinity, application, bearing, connection, correlation, dependency, pertinence, relationship; concern, reference, regard, respect; alliance, nearness, propinquity, rapport; blood, consanguinity, cousinship, kin, kindred, kinship, relationship; kinsman, kinswoman, relative.

relax *vb* loose, loosen, slacken, unbrace, unstrain; debilitate, enervate, enfeeble, prostrate, unbrace, unstring, weaken; abate, diminish, lessen, mitigate, reduce, remit; amuse, divert, ease, entertain, recreate, unbend.

release *vb* deliver, discharge, disengage, exempt, extricate, free, liberate, loose, unloose; acquit,

discharge, quit, relinquish, remit. * *n* deliverance, discharge, freedom, liberation; absolution, dispensation, excuse, exemption, exoneration; acquaintance, clearance.

relentless *adj* cruel, hard, impenitent, implacable, inexorable, merciless, obdurate, pitiless, rancorous, remorseless, ruthless, unappeasable, uncompassionate, unfeeling, unforgiving, unmerciful, unpitying, unrelenting, unyielding, vindictive.

relevant *adj* applicable, appropriate, apposite, apt, apropos, fit, germane, pertinent, proper, relative, suitable.

reliable *adj* authentic, certain, constant, dependable, sure, trustworthy, trusty, unfailing.

reliance *n* assurance, confidence, credence, dependence, hope, trust.

relic *n* keepsake, memento, memorial, remembrance, souvenir, token, trophy; trace, vestige.

relics *npl* fragments, leavings, remainder, remains, remnants, ruins, scraps; body, cadaver, corpse, remains.

relict *n* dowager, widow.

relief *n* aid, alleviation, amelioration, assistance, assuagement, comfort, deliverance, ease, easement, help, mitigation, reinforcement, respite, rest, succour, softening, support; indemnification, redress, remedy; embossment, projection, prominence, protrusion; clearness, distinction, perspective, vividness.

relieve *vb* aid, comfort, help, spell, succour, support, sustain; abate, allay, alleviate, assuage, cure, diminish, ease, lessen, lighten, mitigate, remedy, remove, soothe; indemnify, redress, right, repair; disengage, free, release, remedy, rescue.

religious *adj* devotional, devout, god-fearing, godly, holy, pious, prayerful, spiritual; conscientious, exact, rigid, scrupulous, strict; canonical, divine, theological.

relinquish *vb* abandon, desert, forsake, forswear, leave, quit, renounce, resign, vacate; abdicate, cede, forbear, forgo, give up, surrender, yield.

relish *vb* appreciate, enjoy, like, prefer; season, flavour, taste. * *n* appetite, appreciation, enjoyment, fondness, gratification, gusto, inclination, liking, partiality, predilection, taste, zest; cast, flavour, manner, quality, savour, seasoning, sort, tang, tinge, touch; appetizer, condiment.

reluctance *n* aversion, backwardness, disinclination, dislike, loathing, repugnance, unwillingness.

reluctant *adj* averse, backward, disinclined, hesitant, indisposed, loath, unwilling.

rely *vb* confide, count, depend, hope, lean, reckon, repose, trust.

remain *vb* abide, continue, endure, last; exceed, persist, survive; abide, continue, dwell, halt, inhabit, rest, sojourn, stay, stop, tarry, wait.

remainder *n* balance, excess, leavings, remains, remnant, residue, rest, surplus.

remark *vb* heed, notice, observe, regard; comment, express, mention, observe, say, state, utter. * *n* consideration, heed, notice, observation, regard; annotation, comment, gloss, note, stricture; assertion, averment, comment, declaration, saying, statement, utterance.

remarkable *adj* conspicuous, distinguished, eminent, extraordinary, famous, notable, noteworthy, noticeable, pre-eminent, rare, singular, strange, striking, uncommon, unusual, wonderful.

remedy *vb* cure, heal, help, palliate, relieve; amend, correct, rectify, redress, repair, restore, retrieve. * *n* antidote, antitoxin, corrective, counteractive, cure, help, medicine, nostrum, panacea, restorative, specific; redress, reparation, restitution, restoration; aid, assistance, relief.

remembrance *n* recollection, reminiscence, retrospection; keepsake, memento, memorial, memory, reminder, souvenir, token; consideration, regard, thought.

reminiscence *n* memory, recollection, remembrance, retrospective.

remiss *adj* backward, behindhand, dilatory, indolent, languid, lax, lazy, slack, slow, tardy; careless, dilatory, heedless, idle, inattentive, neglectful, negligent, shiftless, slothful, thoughtless.

remission *n* abatement, decrease, diminution, lessening, mitigation, moderation, reduction, relaxation; cancellation, discharge, release, relinquishment; intermission, interruption, pause, rest, stop, stoppage, suspense, suspension; absolution, acquittal, excuse, exoneration, forgiveness, indulgence, pardon.

remit *vb* replace, restore, return; abate, bate, diminish, relax; release; absolve, condone, excuse, forgive, overlook, pardon; relinquish, resign, surrender; consign, forward, refer, send, transmit. * *n* authorization, brief, instructions, orders.

remnant *n* remainder, remains, residue, rest, trace; fragment, piece, scrap.

remorse *n* compunction, contrition, penitence, qualm, regret, repentance, reproach, self-reproach, sorrow.

remorseless *adj* cruel, barbarous, hard, harsh, implacable, inexorable, merciless, pitiless, relentless, ruthless, savage, uncompassionate, unmerciful, unrelenting.

remote *adj* distant, far, out-of-the-way; alien, far-fetched, foreign, inappropriate, unconnected, unrelated; abstracted, separated; inconsiderable, slight; isolated, removed, secluded, sequestrated.

removal *n* abstraction, departure, dislodgement; displacement, relegation, remove, shift, transference; elimination, extraction, withdrawal; abatement, destruction; discharge, dismissal, ejection, expulsion.

remove *vb* carry, dislodge, displace, shift, transfer, transport; abstract, extract, withdraw; abate, banish, destroy, suppress; cashier, depose, dis-

charge, dismiss, eject, expel, oust, retire; depart, move.

remunerate *vb* compensate, indemnify, pay, recompense, reimburse, repay, requite, reward, satisfy.

remuneration *n* compensation, earnings, indemnity, pay, payment, recompense, reimbursement, reparation, repayment, reward, salary, wages.

remunerative *adj* gainful, lucrative, paying, profitable; compensatory, recompensing, remuneratory, reparative, requiting, rewarding.

rend *vb* break, burst, cleave, crack, destroy, dismember, dissever, disrupt, divide, fracture, lacerate, rive, rupture, sever, shiver, snap, split, sunder, tear.

render *vb* restore, return, surrender; assign, deliver, give, present; afford, contribute, furnish, supply, yield; construe, interpret, translate.

rendition *n* restitution, return, surrender; delineation, exhibition, interpretation, rendering, representation, reproduction; translation, version.

renegade *adj* apostate, backsliding, disloyal, false, outlawed, rebellious, recreant, unfaithful. * *n* apostate, backslider, recreant, turncoat; deserter, outlaw, rebel, revolter, traitor; vagabond, wretch.

renew *vb* rebuild, recreate, re-establish, refit, refresh, rejuvenate, renovate, repair, replenish, restore, resuscitate, revive; continue, recommence, repeat; iterate, reiterate; regenerate, transform.

renounce *vb* abjure, abnegate, decline, deny, disclaim, disown, forswear, neglect, recant, repudiate, reject, slight; abandon, abdicate, drop, forgo, forsake, desert, leave, quit, relinquish, resign.

renovate *vb* reconstitute, re-establish, refresh, refurbish, renew, restore, revamp; reanimate, recreate, regenerate, reproduce, resuscitate, revive, revivify.

renown *n* celebrity, distinction, eminence, fame, figure, glory, honour, greatness, name, note, notability, notoriety, reputation, repute.

renowned *adj* celebrated, distinguished, eminent, famed, famous, honoured, illustrious, remarkable, wonderful.

rent[1] *n* breach, break, crack, cleft, crevice, fissure, flaw, fracture, gap, laceration, opening, rift, rupture, separation, split, tear; schism.

rent[2] *vb* hire, lease, let. * *n* income, rental, revenue.

repair[1] *vb* mend, patch, piece, refit, retouch, tinker, vamp; correct, recruit, restore, retrieve. * *n* mending, refitting, renewal, reparation, restoration.

repair[2] *vb* betake oneself, go, move, resort, turn.

repairable *adj* curable, recoverable, reparable, restorable, retrievable.

reparable *adj* curable, recoverable, repairable, restorable, retrievable.

reparation *n* renewal, repair, restoration; amends, atonement, compensation, correction, indemnification, recompense, redress, requital, restitution, satisfaction.

repay *vb* refund, reimburse, restore, return; compensate, recompense, remunerate, reward, satisfy; avenge, retaliate, revenge.

repeal *vb* abolish, annul, cancel, recall, rescind, reverse, revoke. * *n* abolition, abrogation, annulment, cancellation, rescission, reversal, revocation.

repeat *vb* double, duplicate, iterate; cite, narrate, quote, recapitulate, recite, rehearse; echo, renew, reproduce. * *n* duplicate, duplication, echo, iteration, recapitulation, reiteration, repetition.

repel *vb* beat, disperse, repulse, scatter; check, confront, oppose, parry, rebuff, resist, withstand; decline, refuse, reject; disgust, revolt, sicken.

repellent *adj* abhorrent, disgusting, forbidding, repelling, repugnant, repulsive, revolting, uninviting.

repent *vb* atone, regret, relent, rue, sorrow.

repentance *n* compunction, contriteness, contrition, penitence, regret, remorse, self-accusation, self-condemnation, self-reproach.

repentant *adj* contrite, penitent, regretful, remorseful, rueful, sorrowful, sorry.

repercussion *n* rebound, recoil, reverberation; backlash, consequence, result.

repetition *n* harping, iteration, recapitulation, reiteration; diffuseness, redundancy, tautology, verbosity; narration, recital, rehearsal, relation, retailing; recurrence, renewal.

repine *vb* croak, complain, fret, grumble, long, mope, murmur.

replace *vb* re-establish, reinstate, reset; refund, repay, restore; succeed, supersede, supplant.

replenish *vb* fill, refill, renew, re-supply; enrich, furnish, provide, store, supply.

replete *adj* abounding, charged, exuberant, fraught, full, glutted, gorged, satiated, well-stocked.

repletion *n* abundance, exuberance, fullness, glut, profusion, satiation, satiety, surfeit.

replica *n* autograph, copy, duplicate, facsimile, reproduction.

reply *vb* answer, echo, rejoin, respond. * *n* acknowledgement, answer, rejoinder, repartee, replication, response, retort.

report *vb* announce, annunciate, communicate, declare; advertise, broadcast, bruit, describe, detail, herald, mention, narrate, noise, promulgate, publish, recite, relate, rumour, state, tell; minute, record. * *n* account, announcement, communication, declaration, statement; advice, description, detail, narration, narrative, news, recital, story, tale, talk, tidings; gossip, hearsay, rumour; clap, detonation, discharge, explosion, noise, repercussion, sound; fame, reputation, repute; account, bulletin, minute, note, record, statement.

repose[1] *vb* compose, recline, rest, settle; couch, lie, recline, sleep, slumber; confide, lean. * *n* quiet, recumbence, recumbency, rest, sleep, slumber; breathing time, inactivity, leisure, respite, relaxation; calm, ease, peace, peacefulness, quietness, quietude, stillness, tranquillity.

repose[2] *vb* place, put, stake; deposit, lodge, reposit, store.

repository *n* conservatory, depository, depot, magazine, museum, receptacle, repertory, storehouse, storeroom, thesaurus, treasury, vault.

reprehend *vb* accuse, blame, censure, chide, rebuke, reprimand, reproach, reprove, upbraid.

reprehensible *adj* blameable, blameworthy, censurable, condemnable, culpable, reprovable.

reprehension *n* admonition, blame, censure, condemnation, rebuke, reprimand, reproof.

represent *vb* exhibit, express, show; delineate, depict, describe, draw, portray, sketch; act, impersonate, mimic, personate, personify; exemplify, illustrate, image, reproduce, symbolize, typify.

representation *n* delineation, exhibition, show; impersonation, personation, simulation; account, description, narration, narrative, relation, statement; image, likeness, model, portraiture, resemblance, semblance; sight, spectacle; expostulation, remonstrance.

representative *adj* figurative, illustrative, symbolic, typical; delegated, deputed, representing. * *n* agent, commissioner, delegate, deputy, emissary, envoy, legate, lieutenant, messenger, proxy, substitute.

repress *vb* choke, crush, dull, overcome, overpower, silence, smother, subdue, suppress, quell; bridle, chasten, chastise, check, control, curb, restrain; appease, calm, quiet.

reprimand *vb* admonish, blame, censure, chide, rebuke, reprehend, reproach, reprove, upbraid. * *n* admonition, blame, censure, rebuke, reprehension, reproach, reprobation, reproof, reproval.

reprint *vb* republish. * *n* reimpression, republication; copy.

reproach *vb* blame, censure, rebuke, reprehend, reprimand, reprove, upbraid; abuse, accuse, asperse, condemn, defame, discredit, disparage, revile, traduce, vilify. * *n* abuse, blame, censure, condemnation, contempt, contumely, disapprobation, disapproval, expostulation, insolence, invective, railing, rebuke, remonstrance, reprobation, reproof, reviling, scorn, scurrility, upbraiding, vilification; abasement, discredit, disgrace, dishonour, disrepute, indignity, ignominy, infamy, insult, obloquy, odium, offence, opprobrium, scandal, shame, slur, stigma.

reproachful *adj* abusive, censorious, condemnatory, contemptuous, contumelious, damnatory, insolent, insulting, offensive, opprobrious, railing, reproving, sacrifice, scolding, scornful, scurrilous, upbraiding, vituperative; base, discreditable, disgraceful, dishonourable, disreputable, infamous, scandalous, shameful, vile.

reprobate *vb* censure, condemn, disapprove, discard, reject, reprehend; disallow; abandon, disown. * *adj* abandoned, base, castaway, corrupt, depraved, graceless, hardened, irredeemable, lost, profligate, shameless, vile, vitiated, wicked.

* *n* caitiff, castaway, miscreant, outcast, rascal, scamp, scoundrel, sinner, villain.

reproduce *vb* copy, duplicate, emulate, imitate, print, repeat, represent; breed, generate, procreate, propagate.

reproof *n* admonition, animadversion, blame, castigation, censure, chiding, condemnation, correction, criticism, lecture, monition, objurgation, rating, rebuke, reprehension, reprimand, reproach, reproval, upbraiding.

reprove *vb* admonish, blame, castigate, censure, chide, condemn, correct, criticize, inculpate, lecture, objurgate, rate, rebuke, reprimand, reproach, scold, upbraid.

reptilian *adj* abject, crawling, creeping, grovelling, low, mean, treacherous, vile, vulgar.

repudiate *vb* abjure, deny, disavow, discard, disclaim, disown, nullify, reject, renounce.

repugnance *n* contrariety, contrariness, incompatibility, inconsistency, irreconcilability, irreconcilableness, unsuitability, unsuitableness; contest, opposition, resistance, struggle; antipathy, aversion, detestation, dislike, hatred, hostility, reluctance, repulsion, unwillingness.

repugnant *adj* incompatible, inconsistent, irreconcilable; adverse, antagonistic, contrary, hostile, inimical, opposed, opposing, unfavourable; detestable, distasteful, offensive, repellent, repulsive.

repulse *vb* check, defeat, refuse, reject, repel. * *n* repelling, repulsion; denial, refusal; disappointment, failure.

repulsion *n* abhorrence, antagonism, anticipation, aversion, discard, disgust, dislike, hatred, hostility, loathing, rebuff, rejection, repugnance, repulse, spurning.

repulsive *adj* abhorrent, cold, disagreeable, disgusting, forbidding, frigid, harsh, hateful, loathsome, nauseating, nauseous, odious, offensive, repellent, repugnant, reserved, revolting, sickening, ugly, unpleasant.

reputable *adj* creditable, estimable, excellent, good, honourable, respectable, worthy.

reputation *n* account, character, fame, mark, name, repute; celebrity, credit, distinction, eclat, esteem, estimation, glory, honour, prestige, regard, renown, report, respect; notoriety.

repute *vb* account, consider, deem, esteem, estimate, hold, judge, reckon, regard, think.

request *vb* ask, beg, beseech, call, claim, demand, desire, entreat, pray, solicit, supplicate. * *n* asking, entreaty, importunity, invitation, petition, prayer, requisition, solicitation, suit, supplication.

require *vb* beg, beseech, bid, claim, crave, demand, dun, importune, invite, pray, requisition, request, sue, summon; need, want; direct, enjoin, exact, order, prescribe.

requirement *n* claim, demand, exigency, market, need, needfulness, requisite, requisition, request, urgency, want; behest, bidding, charge,

command, decree, exaction, injunction, mandate, order, precept.

requisite *adj* essential, imperative, indispensable, necessary, needful, needed, required. * *n* essential, necessity, need, requirement.

requite *vb* compensate, pay, remunerate, reciprocate, recompense, repay, reward, satisfy; avenge, punish, retaliate, satisfy.

rescind *vb* abolish, abrogate, annul, cancel, countermand, quash, recall, repeal, reverse, revoke, vacate, void.

rescue *vb* deliver, extricate, free, liberate, preserve, ransom, recapture, recover, redeem, release, retake, save. * *n* deliverance, extrication, liberation, redemption, release, salvation.

research *vb* analyse, examine, explore, inquire, investigate, probe, study. * *n* analysis, examination, exploration, inquiry, investigation, scrutiny, study.

resemblance *n* affinity, agreement, analogy, likeness, semblance, similarity, similitude; counterpart, facsimile, image, representation.

resemble *vb* compare, liken; copy, counterfeit, imitate.

resentful *adj* angry, bitter, choleric, huffy, hurt, irascible, irritable, malignant, revengeful, sore, touchy.

resentment *n* acrimony, anger, annoyance, bitterness, choler, displeasure, dudgeon, fury, gall, grudge, heartburning, huff, indignation, ire, irritation, pique, rage, soreness, spleen, sulks, umbrage, vexation, wrath.

reservation *n* reserve, suppression; appropriation, booking, exception, restriction, saving; proviso, salvo; custody, park, reserve, sanctuary.

reserve *vb* hold, husband, keep, retain, store. * *adj* alternate, auxiliary, spare, substitute. * *n* reservation; aloofness, backwardness, closeness, coldness, concealment, constraint, suppression, reservedness, retention, restraint, reticence, uncommunicativeness, unresponsiveness; coyness, demureness, modesty, shyness, taciturnity; park, reservation, sanctuary.

reserved *adj* coy, demure, modest, shy, taciturn; aloof, backward, cautious, cold, distant, incommunicative, restrained, reticent, self-controlled, unsociable, unsocial; bespoken, booked, excepted, held, kept, retained, set apart, taken, withheld.

reside *vb* abide, domicile, domiciliate, dwell, inhabit, live, lodge, remain, room, sojourn, stay.

residence *n* inhabitance, inhabitancy, sojourn, stay, stop, tarrying; abode, domicile, dwelling, habitation, home, house, lodging, mansion.

residue *n* leavings, remainder, remains, remnant, residuum, rest; excess, overplus, surplus.

resign *vb* abandon, abdicate, abjure, cede, commit, disclaim, forego, forsake, leave, quit, relinquish, renounce, surrender, yield.

resignation *n* abandonment, abdication, relinquishment, renunciation, retirement, surrender;

acquiescence, compliance, endurance, forbearance, fortitude, long-sufferance, patience, submission, sufferance.

resist *vb* assail, attack, baffle, block, check, confront, counteract, disappoint, frustrate, hinder, impede, impugn, neutralize, obstruct, oppose, rebel, rebuff, stand against, stem, stop, strive, thwart, withstand.

resolute *adj* bold, constant, decided, determined, earnest, firm, fixed, game, hardy, inflexible, persevering, pertinacious, relentless, resolved, staunch, steadfast, steady, stout, stouthearted, sturdy, tenacious, unalterable, unbending, undaunted, unflinching, unshaken, unwavering, unyielding.

resolution *n* boldness, disentanglement, explication, unravelling; backbone, constancy, courage, decision, determination, earnestness, energy, firmness, fortitude, grit, hardihood, inflexibility, intention, manliness, pluck, perseverance, purpose, relentlessness, resolve, resoluteness, stamina, steadfastness, steadiness, tenacity.

resolve *vb* analyse, disperse, scatter, separate, reduce; change, dissolve, liquefy, melt, reduce, transform; decipher, disentangle, elucidate, explain, interpret, unfold, solve, unravel; conclude, decide, determine, fix, intend, purpose, will. * *n* conclusion, decision, determination, intention, will; declaration, resolution.

resonant *adj* booming, clangorous, resounding, reverberating, ringing, roaring, sonorous, thundering, vibrant.

resort *vb* frequent, haunt; assemble, congregate, convene, go, repair. * *n* application, expedient, recourse; haunt, refuge, rendezvous, retreat, spa; assembling, confluence, concourse, meeting; recourse, reference.

resound *vb* echo, re-echo, reverberate, ring; celebrate, extol, praise, sound.

resource *n* dependence, resort; appliance, contrivance, device, expedient, instrumentality, means, resort.

resources *npl* capital, funds, income, money, property, reserve, supplies, wealth.

respect *vb* admire, esteem, honour, prize, regard, revere, reverence, spare, value, venerate; consider, heed, notice, observe. * *n* attention, civility, courtesy, consideration, deference, estimation, homage, honour, notice, politeness, recognition, regard, reverence, veneration; consideration, favour, goodwill, kind; aspect, bearing, connection, feature, matter, particular, point, reference, regard, relation.

respects *npl* compliments, greetings, regards.

respectable *adj* considerable, estimable, honourable, presentable, proper, upright, worthy; adequate, moderate; tolerable.

respectful *adj* ceremonious, civil, complaisant, courteous, decorous, deferential, dutiful, formal, polite.

respire *vb* breathe, exhale, live.

respite *vb* delay, relieve, reprieve. * *n* break, cessation, delay, intermission, interval, pause, recess, rest, stay, stop; forbearance, postponement, reprieve.

resplendent *adj* beaming, bright, brilliant, effulgent, lucid, glittering, glorious, gorgeous, luminous, lustrous, radiant, shining, splendid.

respond *vb* answer, reply, rejoin; accord, correspond, suit.

response *n* answer, replication, rejoinder, reply, retort.

responsible *adj* accountable, amenable, answerable, liable, trustworthy.

rest[1] *vb* cease, desist, halt, hold, pause, repose, stop; breathe, relax, unbend; repose, sleep, slumber; lean, lie, lounge, perch, recline, ride; acquiesce, confide, trust; confide, rely, trust; calm, comfort, ease. * *n* fixity, immobility, inactivity, motionlessness, quiescence, quiet, repose; hush, peace, peacefulness, quietness, relief, security, stillness, tranquillity; cessation, intermission, interval, lull, pause, relaxation, respite, stop, stay; siesta, sleep, slumber; death; brace, stay, support; axis, fulcrum, pivot.

rest[2] *vb* be left, remain. * *n* balance, remainder, remnant, residuum; overplus, surplus.

restaurant *n* bistro, café, cafeteria, chophouse, eatery, eating house, pizzeria, trattoria.

restitution *n* restoration, return; amends, compensation, indemnification, recompense, rehabilitation, remuneration, reparation, repayment, requital, satisfaction.

restive *adj* mulish, obstinate, stopping, stubborn, unwilling; impatient, recalcitrant, restless, uneasy, unquiet.

restless *adj* disquieted, disturbed, restive, sleepless, uneasy, unquiet, unresting; changeable, inconstant, irresolute, unsteady, vacillating; active, astatic, roving, transient, unsettled, unstable, wandering; agitated, fidgety, fretful, turbulent.

restoration *n* recall, recovery, re-establishment, reinstatement, reparation, replacement, restitution, return; reconsideration, redemption, reintegration, renewal, renovation, repair, resuscitation, revival; convalescence, cure, recruitment, recuperation.

restorative *adj* curative, invigorating, recuperative, remedial, restoring, stimulating. * *n* corrective, curative, cure, healing, medicine, remedy, reparative, stimulant.

restore *vb* refund, repay, return; caulk, cobble, emend, heal, mend, patch, reintegrate, re-establish, rehabilitate, reinstate, renew, repair, replace, retrieve; cure, heal, recover, revive; resuscitate.

restrain *vb* bridle, check, coerce, confine, constrain, curb, debar, govern, hamper, hinder, hold, keep, muzzle, picket, prevent, repress, restrict, rule, subdue, tie, withhold; abridge, circumscribe, narrow.

restraint *n* bridle, check, coercion, control, compulsion, constraint, curb, discipline, repression, suppression; arrest, deterrence, hindrance, inhibition, limitation, prevention, prohibition, restriction, stay, stop; confinement, detention, imprisonment, shackles; constraint, stiffness, reserve, unnaturalness.

restrict *vb* bound, circumscribe, confine, limit, qualify, restrain, straiten.

restriction *n* confinement, limitation; constraint, restraint; reservation, reserve.

result *vb* accrue, arise, come, ensue, flow, follow, issue, originate, proceed, spring, rise; end, eventuate, terminate. * *n* conclusion, consequence, deduction, inference, outcome; corollary, effect, end, event, eventuality, fruit, harvest, issue, product, sequel, termination; decision, determination, finding, resolution, resolve, solution, verdict.

resume *vb* continue, recommence, renew, restart, summarize.

résumé *n* abstract, curriculum vitae, epitome, recapitulation, summary, synopsis.

resuscitate *vb* quicken, reanimate, renew, resurrect, restore, revive, revivify.

retain *vb* detain, hold, husband, keep, preserve, recall, recollect, remember, reserve, save, withhold; engage, maintain.

retainer *n* adherent, attendant, dependant, follower, hanger-on, servant.

retaliate *vb* avenge, match, repay, requite, retort, return, turn.

retaliation *n* boomerang, counterstroke, punishment, repayment, requital, retribution, revenge.

retard *vb* check, clog, hinder, impede, obstruct, slacken; adjourn, defer, delay, postpone, procrastinate.

reticent *adj* close, reserved, secretive, silent, taciturn, uncommunicative.

retinue *n* bodyguard, cortege, entourage, escort, followers, household, ménage, suite, tail, train.

retire *vb* discharge, shelve, superannuate, withdraw; depart, leave, resign, retreat.

retired *adj* abstracted, removed, withdrawn; apart, private, secret, sequestrated, solitary.

retirement *n* isolation, loneliness, privacy, retreat, seclusion, solitude, withdrawal.

retiring *adj* coy, demure, diffident, modest, reserved, retreating, shy, withdrawing.

retort *vb* answer, rejoin, reply, respond. * *n* answer, rejoinder, repartee, reply, response; crucible, jar, vessel, vial.

retract *vb* reverse, withdraw; abjure, cancel, disavow, recall, recant, revoke, unsay.

retreat *vb* recoil, retire, withdraw; recede. * *n* departure, recession, recoil, retirement, withdrawal; privacy, seclusion, solitude; asylum, cove, den, habitat, haunt, niche, recess, refuge, resort, shelter.

retrench *vb* clip, curtail, cut, delete, dock, lop, mutilate, pare, prune; abridge, decrease, diminish, lessen; confine, limit; economize, encroach.

retribution *n* compensation, desert, judgement,

nemesis, penalty, recompense, repayment, requital, retaliation, return, revenge, reward, vengeance.

retrieve *vb* recall, recover, recoup, recruit, re-establish, regain, repair, restore.

retrograde *vb* decline, degenerate, recede, retire, retrocede. * *adj* backward, inverse, retrogressive, unprogressive.

retrospect *n* recollection, re-examination, reminiscence, re-survey, review, survey.

return *vb* reappear, recoil, recur, revert; answer, reply, respond; recriminate, retort; convey, give, communicate, reciprocate, recompense, refund, remit, repay, report, requite, send, tell, transmit; elect. * *n* payment, reimbursement, remittance, repayment; recompense, recovery, recurrence, renewal, repayment, requital, restitution, restoration, reward; advantage, benefit, interest, profit, rent, yield.

reunion *n* assemblage, assembly, gathering, meeting, re-assembly; rapprochement, reconciliation.

reveal *vb* announce, communicate, confess, declare, disclose, discover, display, divulge, expose, impart, open, publish, tell, uncover, unmask, unseal, unveil.

revel *vb* carouse, disport, riot, roister, tipple; delight, indulge, luxuriate, wanton. * *n* carousal, feast, festival, saturnalia, spree.

revelry *n* bacchanal, carousal, carouse, debauch, festivity, jollification, jollity, orgy, revel, riot, rout, saturnalia, wassail.

revenge *vb* avenge, repay, requite, retaliate, vindicate. * *n* malevolence, rancour, reprisal, requital, retaliation, retribution, vengeance, vindictiveness.

revengeful *adj* implacable, malevolent, malicious, malignant, resentful, rancorous, spiteful, vengeful, vindictive.

revenue *n* fruits, income, produce, proceeds, receipts, return, reward, wealth.

reverberate *vb* echo, re-echo, resound, return.

revere *vb* adore, esteem, hallow, honour, reverence, venerate, worship.

reverence *vb* adore, esteem, hallow, honour, revere, venerate, worship. * *n* adoration, awe, deference, homage, honour, respect, veneration, worship.

reverential *adj* deferential, humble, respectful, reverent, submissive.

reverse *vb* invert, transpose; overset, overthrow, overturn, quash, subvert, undo, unmake; annul, countermand, repeal, rescind, retract, revoke; back, back up, retreat. * *adj* back, converse, contrary, opposite, verso. * *n* back, calamity, check, comedown, contrary, counterpart, defeat, opposite, tail; change, vicissitude; adversity, affliction, hardship, misadventure, mischance, misfortune, mishap, trial.

revert *vb* repel, reverse; backslide, lapse, recur, relapse, return.

review *vb* inspect, overlook, reconsider, re-examine, retrace, revise, survey; analyse, criticize, discuss, edit, judge, scrutinize, study. * n reconsideration, re-examination, re-survey, retrospect, survey; analysis, digest, synopsis; commentary, critique, criticism, notice, review, scrutiny, study.

revile vb abuse, asperse, backbite, calumniate, defame, execrate, malign, reproach, slander, traduce, upbraid, vilify.

revise vb reconsider, re-examine, review; alter, amend, correct, edit, overhaul, polish.

revive vb reanimate, reinspire, reinspirit, reinvigorate, resuscitate, revitalize, revivify; animate, cheer, comfort, invigorate, quicken, reawaken, recover, refresh, renew, renovate, rouse, strengthen; reawake, recall.

revocation n abjuration, recall, recantation, repeal, retraction, reversal.

revoke vb abolish, abrogate, annul, cancel, countermand, invalidate, quash, recall, recant, repeal, repudiate, rescind, retract.

revolt vb desert, mutiny, rebel, rise; disgust, nauseate, repel, sicken. * n defection, desertion, faithlessness, inconstancy; disobedience, insurrection, mutiny, outbreak, rebellion, sedition, strike, uprising.

revolting adj abhorrent, abominable, disgusting, hateful, monstrous, nauseating, nauseous, objectionable, obnoxious, offensive, repulsive, shocking, sickening; insurgent, mutinous, rebellious.

revolution n coup, disobedience, insurrection, mutiny, outbreak, rebellion, sedition, strike, uprising; change, innovation, reformation, transformation, upheaval; circle, circuit, cycle, lap, orbit, rotation, spin, turn..

revolve vb circle, circulate, rotate, swing, turn, wheel; devolve, return; consider, mediate, ponder, ruminate, study.

revulsion n abstraction, shrinking, withdrawal; change, reaction, reversal, transition; abhorrence, disgust, loathing, repugnance.

reward vb compensate, gratify, indemnify, pay, punish, recompense, remember, remunerate, requite. * n compensation, gratification, guerdon, indemnification, pay, recompense, remuneration, requital; bounty, bonus, fee, gratuity, honorarium, meed, perquisite, premium, remembrance, tip; punishment, retribution.

rhythm n cadence, lilt, pulsation, swing; measure, metre, number.

ribald adj base, blue, coarse, filthy, gross, indecent, lewd, loose, low, mean, obscene, vile.

rich adj affluent, flush, moneyed, opulent, prosperous, wealthy; costly, estimable, gorgeous, luxurious, precious, splendid, sumptuous, superb, valuable; delicious, luscious, savoury; abundant, ample, copious, enough, full, plentiful, plenteous, sufficient; fertile, fruitful, luxuriant, productive, prolific; bright, dark, deep, exuberant, vivid; harmonious, mellow, melodious, soft, sweet; comical, funny, humorous, laughable.

riches npl abundance, affluence, fortune, money, opulence, plenty, richness, wealth, wealthiness.

rickety adj broken, imperfect, shaky, shattered, tottering, tumbledown, unsteady, weak.

rid vb deliver, free, release; clear, disburden, disencumber, scour, sweep; disinherit, dispatch, dissolve, divorce, finish, sever.

riddance n deliverance, disencumberment, extrication, escape, freedom, release, relief.

riddle[1] vb explain, solve, unriddle. * n conundrum, enigma, mystery, puzzle, rebus.

riddle[2] vb sieve, sift, perforate, permeate, spread. * n colander, sieve, strainer.

ridge n chine, hogback, ledge, saddle, spine, rib, watershed, weal, wrinkle.

ridicule vb banter, burlesque, chaff, deride, disparage, jeer, mock, lampoon, rally, satirize, scout, taunt. * n badinage, banter, burlesque, chaff, derision, game, gibe, irony, jeer, mockery, persiflage, quip, raillery, sarcasm, satire, sneer, squib, wit.

ridiculous adj absurd, amusing, comical, droll, eccentric, fantastic, farcical, funny, laughable, ludicrous, nonsensical, odd, outlandish, preposterous, queer, risible, waggish.

rife adj abundant, common, current, general, numerous, plentiful, prevailing, prevalent, replete.

riffraff n horde, mob, populace, rabble, scum, trash.

rifle vb despoil, fleece, pillage, plunder, ransack, rob, strip.

rift vb cleave, rive, split. * n breach, break, chink, cleft, crack, cranny, crevice, fissure, fracture, gap, opening, reft, rent.

rig vb accoutre, clothe, dress. * n costume, dress, garb; equipment, team.

right vb adjust, correct, regulate, settle, straighten, vindicate. * adj direct, rectilinear, straight; erect, perpendicular, plumb, upright; equitable, evenhanded, fair, just, justifiable, honest, lawful, legal, legitimate, rightful, square, unswerving; appropriate, becoming, correct, conventional, fit, fitting, meet, orderly, proper, reasonable, seemly, suitable, well-done; actual, genuine, real, true, unquestionable; dexter, dextral, right-handed. * adv equitably, fairly, justly, lawfully, rightfully, rightly; correctly, fitly, properly, suitably, truly; actually, exactly, just, really, truly, well. * n authority, claim, liberty, permission, power, privilege, title; equity, good, honour, justice, lawfulness, legality, propriety, reason, righteousness, truth.

righteous adj devout, godly, good, holy, honest, incorrupt, just, pious, religious, saintly, uncorrupt, upright, virtuous; equitable, fair, right, rightful.

righteousness n equity, faithfulness, godliness, goodness, holiness, honesty, integrity, justice, piety, purity, right, rightfulness, sanctity, uprightness, virtue.

rightful adj lawful, legitimate, true; appropriate, correct, deserved, due, equitable, fair, fitting, honest, just, legal, merited, proper, reasonable, suitable.

rigid *adj* firm, hard, inflexible, permanent, stiff, stiffened, unbending, unpliant, unyielding; bristling, erect, precipitous, steep; austere, conventional, correct, exact, formal, harsh, meticulous, precise, rigorous, severe, sharp, stern, strict, unmitigated; cruel.

rigmarole *n* balderdash, flummery, gibberish, gobbledegook, jargon, nonsense, palaver, trash, twaddle, verbiage.

rigour *n* hardness, inflexibility, rigidity, rigidness, stiffness; asperity, austerity, harshness, severity, sternness; evenness, strictness; inclemency.

rile *vb* anger, annoy, irritate, upset, vex.

rim *n* brim, brink, border, confine, curb, edge, flange, girdle, margin, ring, skirt.

ring[1] *vb* circle, encircle, enclose, girdle, surround. * *n* circle, circlet, girdle, hoop, round, whorl; cabal, clique, combination, confederacy, coterie, gang, junta, league, set.

ring[2] *vb* chime, clang, jingle, knell, peal, resound, reverberate, sound, tingle, toll; call, phone, telephone. * *n* chime, knell, peal, tinkle, toll; call, phone call, telephone call.

riot *vb* carouse, luxuriate, revel. * *n* affray, altercation, brawl, broil, commotion, disturbance, fray, outbreak, pandemonium, quarrel, squabble, tumult, uproar; dissipation, excess, luxury, merrymaking, revelry.

riotous *adj* boisterous, luxurious, merry, revelling, unrestrained, wanton; disorderly, insubordinate, lawless, mutinous, rebellious, refractory, seditious, tumultuous, turbulent, ungovernable, unruly, violent.

ripe *adj* advanced, grown, mature, mellow, seasoned, soft; fit, prepared, ready; accomplished, complete, consummate, finished, perfect, perfected.

ripen *vb* burgeon, develop, mature, prepare.

rise *vb* arise, ascend, clamber, climb, levitate, mount; excel, succeed; enlarge, heighten, increase, swell, thrive; revive; grow, kindle, wax; begin, flow, head, originate, proceed, spring, start; mutiny, rebel, revolt; happen, occur. * *n* ascension, ascent, rising; elevation, grade, hill, slope; beginning, emergence, flow, origin, source, spring; advance, augmentation, expansion, increase.

risible *adj* amusing, comical, droll, farcical, funny, laughable, ludicrous, ridiculous.

risk *vb* bet, endanger, hazard, jeopardize, peril, speculate, stake, venture, wager. * *n* chance, danger, hazard, jeopardy, peril, venture.

rite *n* ceremonial, ceremony, form, formulary, ministration, observance, ordinance, ritual, rubric, sacrament, solemnity.

ritual *adj* ceremonial, conventional, formal, habitual, routine, stereotyped. * *n* ceremonial, ceremony, liturgy, observance, rite, sacrament, service; convention, form, formality, habit, practice, protocol.

rival *vb* emulate, match, oppose. * *adj* competing, contending, emulating, emulous, opposing. * *n* antagonist, competitor, emulator, opponent.

rive *vb* cleave, rend, split.

river *n* affluent, current, reach, stream, tributary.

road *n* course, highway, lane, passage, path, pathway, roadway, route, street, thoroughfare, track, trail, turnpike, way.

roam *vb* jaunt, prowl, ramble, range, rove, straggle, stray, stroll, wander.

roar *vb* bawl, bellow, cry, howl, vociferate, yell; boom, peal, rattle, resound, thunder. * *n* bellow, roaring; rage, resonance, storm, thunder; cry, outcry, shout; laugh, laughter, shout.

rob *vb* despoil, fleece, pilfer, pillage, plunder, rook, strip; appropriate, deprive, embezzle, plagiarize.

robber *n* bandit, brigand, desperado, depredator, despoiler, footpad, freebooter, highwayman, marauder, pillager, pirate, plunderer, rifler, thief.

robbery *n* depredation, despoliation, embezzlement, freebooting, larceny, peculation, piracy, plagiarism, plundering, spoliation, theft.

robe *vb* array, clothe, dress, invest. * *n* attire, costume, dress, garment, gown, habit, vestment; bathrobe, dressing gown, housecoat.

robust *adj* able-bodied, athletic, brawny, energetic, firm, forceful, hale, hardy, hearty, iron, lusty, muscular, powerful, seasoned, self-assertive, sinewy, sound, stalwart, stout, strong, sturdy, vigorous.

rock[1] *n* boulder, cliff, crag, reef, stone; asylum, defence, foundation, protection, refuge, strength, support; gneiss, granite, marble, slate, etc.

rock[2] *vb* calm, cradle, lull, quiet, soothe, still, tranquillize; reel, shake, sway, teeter, totter, wobble.

rogue *n* beggar, vagabond, vagrant; caitiff, cheat, knave, rascal, scamp, scapegrace, scoundrel, sharper, swindler, trickster, villain.

roguish *adj* dishonest, fraudulent, knavish, rascally, scoundrelly, trickish, tricky; arch, sportive, mischievous, puckish, waggish, wanton.

role *n* character, function, impersonation, part, task.

roll *vb* gyrate, revolve, rotate, turn, wheel; curl, muffle, swathe, wind; bind, involve, enfold, envelop; flatten, level, smooth, spread; bowl, drive; trundle, wheel; gybe, lean, lurch, stagger, sway, yaw; billow, swell, undulate; wallow, welter; flow, glide, run. * *n* document, scroll, volume; annals, chronicle, history, record, rota; catalogue, inventory, list, register, schedule; booming, resonance, reverberation, thunder; cylinder, roller.

rollicking *adj* frisky, frolicking, frolicsome, jolly, jovial, lively, swaggering.

romance *vb* exaggerate, fantasize. * *n* fantasy, fiction, legend, novel, story, tale; exaggeration, falsehood, lie; ballad, idyll, song.

romantic *adj* extravagant, fanciful, fantastic, ideal, imaginative, sentimental, wild; chimerical, fabulous, fantastic, fictitious, imaginary, improbable, legendary, picturesque, quixotic, sentimental. * *n* dreamer, idealist, sentimentalist, visionary.

romp *vb* caper, gambol, frisk, sport. * *n* caper, frolic, gambol.

room *n* accommodation, capacity, compass, elbow-room, expanse, extent, field, latitude, leeway, play, scope, space, swing; place, stead; apartment, chamber, lodging; chance, occasion, opportunity.

roomy *adj* ample, broad, capacious, comfortable, commodious, expansive, extensive, large, spacious, wide.

root[1] *vb* anchor, embed, fasten, implant, place, settle; confirm, establish. * *n* base, bottom, foundation; cause, occasion, motive, origin, reason, source; etymon, radical, radix, stem.

root[2] *vb* destroy, eradicate, extirpate, exterminate, remove, unearth, uproot; burrow, dig, forage, grub, rummage; applaud, cheer, encourage.

rooted *adj* chronic, confirmed, deep, established, fixed, radical.

roseate *adj* blooming, blushing, rose-coloured, rosy, rubicund; hopeful.

rostrum *n* platform, stage, stand, tribune.

rosy *adj* auspicious, blooming, blushing, favourable, flushed, hopeful, roseate, ruddy, sanguine.

rot *vb* corrupt, decay, decompose, degenerate, putrefy, spoil, taint. * *n* corruption, decay, decomposition, putrefaction.

rotary *adj* circular, rotating, revolving, rotatory, turning, whirling.

rotten *adj* carious, corrupt, decomposed, fetid, putrefied, putrescent, putrid, rank, stinking; defective, unsound; corrupt, deceitful, immoral, treacherous, unsound, untrustworthy.

rotund *adj* buxom, chubby, full, globular, obese, plump, round, stout; fluent, grandiloquent.

roué *n* debauchee, libertine, profligate, rake.

rough *vb* coarsen, roughen; manhandle, mishandle, molest. * *adj* bumpy, craggy, irregular, jagged, rugged, scabrous, scraggy, scratchy, stubby, uneven; approximate, cross-grained, crude, formless, incomplete, knotty, rough-hewn, shapeless, sketchy, uncut, unfashioned, unfinished, unhewn, unpolished, unwrought, vague; bristly, bushy, coarse, disordered, hairy, hirsute, ragged, shaggy, unkempt; austere, bearish, bluff, blunt, brusque, burly, churlish, discourteous, gruff, harsh, impolite, indelicate, rude, surly, uncivil, uncourteous, ungracious, unpolished, unrefined; harsh, severe, sharp, violent; astringent, crabbed, hard, sour, tart; discordant, grating, inharmonious, jarring, raucous, scabrous, unmusical; boisterous, foul, inclement, severe, stormy, tempestuous, tumultuous, turbulent, untamed, violent, wild; acrimonious, brutal, cruel, disorderly, riotous, rowdy, severe, uncivil, unfeeling, ungentle. * *n* bully, rowdy, roughneck, ruffian; draft, outline, sketch, suggestion; unevenness.

round *vb* curve; circuit, encircle, encompass, surround. * *adj* bulbous, circular, cylindrical, globular, orbed, orbicular, rotund, spherical; complete, considerable, entire, full, great, large, unbroken, whole; chubby, corpulent, plump, stout, swelling; continuous, flowing, harmonious, smooth; brisk, quick; blunt, candid, fair, frank, honest, open, plain, upright. * *adv* around, circularly, circuitously. * *prep* about, around. * *n* bout, cycle, game, lap, revolution, rotation, succession, turn; canon, catch, dance; ball, circle, circumference, cylinder, globe, sphere; circuit, compass, perambulation, routine, tour, watch.

roundabout *adj* circuitous, circumlocutory, indirect, tortuous; ample, broad, extensive; encircling, encompassing.

rouse *vb* arouse, awaken, raise, shake, wake, waken; animate, bestir, brace, enkindle, excite, inspire, kindle, rally, stimulate, stir, whet; startle, surprise.

rout *vb* beat, conquer, defeat, discomfit, overcome, overpower, overthrow, vanquish; chase away, dispel, disperse, scatter. * *n* defeat, discomfiture, flight, ruin; concourse, multitude, rabble; brawl, disturbance, noise, roar, uproar.

route *vb* direct, forward, send, steer. * *n* course, circuit, direction, itinerary, journey, march, road, passage, path, way.

routine *adj* conventional, familiar, habitual, ordinary, standard, typical, usual; boring, dull, humdrum, predictable, tiresome. * *n* beat, custom, groove, method, order, path, practice, procedure, round, rut.

rove *vb* prowl, ramble, range, roam, stray, struggle, stroll, wander.

row[1] *n* file, line, queue, range, rank, series, string, tier; alley, street, terrace.

row[2] *vb* argue, dispute, fight, quarrel, squabble. * *n* affray, altercation, brawl, broil, commotion, dispute, disturbance, noise, outbreak, quarrel, riot, squabble, tumult, uproar.

royal *adj* august, courtly, dignified, generous, grand, imperial, kingly, kinglike, magnanimous, magnificent, majestic, monarchical, noble, princely, regal, sovereign, splendid, superb.

rub *vb* abrade, chafe, grate, graze, scrape; burnish, clean, massage, polish, scour, wipe; apply, put, smear, spread. * *n* caress, massage, polish, scouring, shine, wipe; catch, difficulty, drawback, impediment, obstacle, problem.

rubbish *n* debris, detritus, fragments, refuse, ruins, waste; dregs, dross, garbage, litter, lumber, scoria, scum, sweepings, trash, trumpery.

rubicund *adj* blushing, erubescent, florid, flushed, red, reddish, ruddy.

rude *adj* coarse, crude, ill-formed, rough, rugged, shapeless, uneven, unfashioned, unformed, unwrought; artless, barbarous, boorish, clownish, ignorant, illiterate, loutish, raw, savage, uncivilized, uncouth, uncultivated, undisciplined, unpolished, ungraceful, unskilful, unskilled, untaught, untrained, untutored, vulgar; awkward, barbarous, bluff, blunt, boorish, brusque, brutal, churlish, gruff, ill-bred, impertinent, impolite, impudent, insolent, insulting, ribald, saucy, uncivil, uncourteous, unrefined; boisterous, fierce, harsh, severe, tumultuous, turbulent, violent; artless, inelegant, rustic, unpolished; hearty, robust.

rudimentary *adj* elementary, embryonic, fundamental, initial, primary, rudimental, undeveloped.

rue *vb* deplore, grieve, lament, regret, repent.

rueful *adj* dismal, doleful, lamentable, lugubrious, melancholic, melancholy, mournful, penitent, regretful, sad, sorrowful, woeful.

ruffian *n* bully, caitiff, cutthroat, hoodlum, miscreant, monster, murderer, rascal, robber, roisterer, rowdy, scoundrel, villain, wretch.

ruffle *vb* damage, derange, disarrange, dishevel, disorder, ripple, roughen, rumple; agitate, confuse, discompose, disquiet, disturb, excite, harass, irritate, molest, plague, perturb, torment, trouble, vex, worry; cockle, flounce, pucker, wrinkle. * *n* edging, frill, ruff; agitation, bustle, commotion, confusion, contention, disturbance, excitement, fight, fluster, flutter, flurry, perturbation, tumult.

rugged *adj* austere, bristly, coarse, crabbed, cragged, craggy, hard, hardy, irregular, ragged, robust, rough, rude, scraggy, severe, seamed, shaggy, uneven, unkempt, wrinkled; boisterous, inclement, stormy, tempestuous, tumultuous, turbulent, violent; grating, harsh, inharmonious, unmusical, scabrous.

ruin *vb* crush, damn, defeat, demolish, desolate, destroy, devastate, overthrow, overturn, overwhelm, seduce, shatter, smash, subvert, wreck; beggar, impoverish. * *n* damnation, decay, defeat, demolition, desolation, destruction, devastation, discomfiture, downfall, fall, loss, perdition, prostration, rack, ruination, shipwreck, subversion, undoing, wrack, wreck; bane, mischief, pest.

ruination *n* demolition, destruction, overthrow, ruin, subversion.

ruinous *adj* decayed, demolished, dilapidated; baneful, calamitous, damnatory, destructive, disastrous, mischievous, noisome, noxious, pernicious, subversive, wasteful.

rule *vb* bridle, command, conduct, control, direct, domineer, govern, judge, lead, manage, reign, restrain; advise, guide, persuade; adjudicate, decide, determine, establish, settle; obtain, prevail, predominate. * *n* authority, command, control, direction, domination, dominion, empire, government, jurisdiction, lordship, mastery, mastership, regency, reign, sway; behaviour, conduct; habit, method, order, regularity, routine, system; aphorism, canon, convention, criterion, formula, guide, law, maxim, model, precedent, precept, standard, system, test, touchstone; decision, order, prescription, regulation, ruling.

ruler *n* chief, governor, king, lord, master, monarch, potentate, regent, sovereign; director, head, manager, president; controller, guide, rule; straight-edge.

ruminate *vb* brood, chew, cogitate, consider, contemplate, meditate, muse, ponder, reflect, think.

rumour *vb* bruit, circulate, report, tell. * *n* bruit, gossip, hearsay, report, talk; news, report, story, tidings; celebrity, fame, reputation, repute.

rumple *vb* crease, crush, corrugate, crumple, disarrange, dishevel, pucker, ruffle, wrinkle. * *n* crease, corrugation, crumple, fold, pucker, wrinkle.

run *vb* bolt, career, course, gallop, haste, hasten, hie, hurry, lope, post, race, scamper, scour, scud, scuttle, speed, trip; flow, glide, go, move, proceed, stream; fuse, liquefy, melt; advance, pass, proceed, vanish; extend, lie, spread, stretch; circulate, pass, press; average, incline, tend; flee; pierce, stab; drive, force, propel, push, thrust, turn; cast, form, mould, shape; follow, perform, pursue, take; discharge, emit; direct, maintain, manage. * *n* race, running; course, current, flow, motion, passage, progress, way, wont; continuance, currency, popularity; excursion, gallop, journey, trip, trot; demand, pressure; brook, burn, flow, rill, rivulet, runlet, runnel, streamlet.

rupture *vb* break, burst, fracture, sever, split. * *n* breach, break, burst, disruption, fracture, split; contention, faction, feud, hostility, quarrel, schism.

rural *adj* agrarian, bucolic, country, pastoral, rustic, sylvan.

ruse *n* artifice, deception, deceit, fraud, hoax, imposture, manoeuvre, sham, stratagem, trick, wile.

rush *vb* attack, career, charge, dash, drive, gush, hurtle, precipitate, surge, sweep, tear. * *n* dash, onrush, onset, plunge, precipitance, precipitancy, rout, stampede, tear.

rust *vb* corrode, decay, degenerate. * *n* blight, corrosion, crust, mildew, must, mould, mustiness.

rustic *adj* country, rural; awkward, boorish, clownish, countrified, loutish, outlandish, rough, rude, uncouth, unpolished, untaught; coarse, countrified, homely, plain, simple, unadorned; artless, honest, unsophisticated. * *n* boor, bumpkin, clown, countryman, peasant, swain, yokel.

ruthless *adj* barbarous, cruel, fell, ferocious, hardhearted, inexorable, inhuman, merciless, pitiless, relentless, remorseless, savage, truculent, uncompassionate, unmerciful, unpitying, unrelenting, unsparing.

S

sable *adj* black, dark, dusky, ebony, sombre.

sabulous *adj* gritty, sabulose, sandy.

sack[1] *n* bag, pouch.

sack[2] *vb* despoil, devastate, pillage, plunder, ravage, spoil. * *n* desolation, despoliation, destruction, devastation, havoc, ravage, sacking, spoliation, waste; booty, plunder, spoil.

sacred *adj* consecrated, dedicated, devoted, divine, hallowed, holy; inviolable, inviolate; sainted, venerable.

sacrifice *vb* forgo, immolate, surrender. * *n* immolation, oblation, offering; destruction, devotion, loss, surrender.

sacrilege *n* desecration, profanation, violation.

sacrilegious *adj* desecrating, impious, irreverent, profane.

sad *adj* grave, pensive, sedate, serious, sober, sombre, staid.

saddle *vb* burden, charge, clog, encumber, load.

sadly *adv* grievously, miserable, mournfully, sorrowfully; afflictively, badly, calamitously; darkly; gravely, seriously, soberly.

sadness *n* dejection, depression, despondency, melancholy, mournful, sorrow, sorrowfulness; dolefulness, gloominess, grief, mournfulness, sorrow; gravity, sedateness, seriousness.

safe *adj* undamaged, unharmed, unhurt, unscathed; guarded, protected, secure, snug, unexposed; certain, dependable, reliable, sure, trustworthy; good, harmless, sound, whole. * *n* chest, coffer, strongbox.

safeguard *vb* guard, protect. * *n* defence, protection, security; convoy, escort, guard, safe-conduct; pass, passport.

sagacious *adj* acute, apt, astute, clear-sighted, discerning, intelligent, judicious, keen, penetrating, perspicacious, rational, sage, sharp-witted, wise, shrewd.

sagacity *n* acuteness, astuteness, discernment, ingenuity, insight, penetration, perspicacity, quickness, readiness, sense, sharpness, shrewdness, wisdom.

sage *adj* acute, discerning, intelligent, prudent, sagacious, sapient, sensible, shrewd, wise; judicious, well-judged; grave, serious, solemn. * *n* philosopher, pundit, savant.

sailor *n* mariner, navigator, salt, seafarer, seaman, tar.

saintly *adj* devout, godly, holy, pious, religious.

sake *n* end, cause, purpose, reason; account, consideration, interest, regard, respect, score.

saleable *adj* marketable, merchantable, vendible.

salacious *adj* carnal, concupiscent, incontinent, lascivious, lecherous, lewd, libidinous, loose, lustful, prurient, unchaste, wanton.

salary *n* allowance, hire, pay, stipend, wages.

salient *adj* bounding, jumping, leaping; beating, springing, throbbing; jutting, projecting, prominent; conspicuous, remarkable, striking.

saline *adj* briny, salty.

sally *vb* issue, rush. * *n* digression, excursion, sortie, run, trip; escapade, frolic; crank, fancy, jest, joke, quip, quirk, sprightly, witticism.

salt *adj* saline, salted, salty; bitter, pungent, sharp. * *n* flavour, savour, seasoning, smack, relish, taste; humour, piquancy, poignancy, sarcasm, smartness, wit, zest; mariner, sailor, seaman, tar.

salubrious *adj* beneficial, benign, healthful, healthy, salutary, sanitary, wholesome.

salutary *adj* healthy, healthful, helpful, safe, salubrious, wholesome; advantageous, beneficial, good, profitable, serviceable, useful.

salute *vb* accost, address, congratulate, greet, hail, welcome. * *n* address, greeting, salutation.

salvation *n* deliverance, escape, preservation, redemption, rescue, saving.

same *adj* ditto, identical, selfsame; corresponding, like, similar.

sample *vb* savour, sip, smack, sup, taste; test, try; demonstrate, exemplify, illustrate, instance. * *adj* exemplary, illustrative, representative. * *n* demonstration, exemplification, illustration, instance, piece, specimen; example, model, pattern.

sanctify *vb* consecrate, hallow, purify; justify, ratify, sanction.

sanctimonious *adj* affected, devout, holy, hypocritical, pharisaical, pious, self-righteous.

sanction *vb* authorize, countenance, encourage, support; confirm, ratify. * *n* approval, authority, authorization, confirmation, countenance, endorsement, ratification, support, warranty; ban, boycott, embargo, penalty.

sanctity *n* devotion, godliness, goodness, grace, holiness, piety, purity, religiousness, saintliness.

sanctuary *n* altar, church, shrine, temple; asylum, protection, refuge, retreat, shelter.

sane *adj* healthy, lucid, rational, reasonable, sober, sound.

sang-froid *n* calmness, composure, coolness,

imperturbability, indifference, nonchalance, phlegm, unconcern.

sanguinary *adj* bloody, gory, murderous; barbarous, bloodthirsty, cruel, fell, pitiless, savage, ruthless.

sanguine *adj* crimson, florid, red; animated, ardent, cheerful, lively, warm; buoyant, confident, enthusiastic, hopeful, optimistic; full-blooded.

sanitary *adj* clean, curative, healing, healthy, hygienic, remedial, therapeutic, wholesome.

sanity *n* normality, rationality, reason, saneness, soundness.

sapient *adj* acute, discerning, intelligent, knowing, sagacious, sage, sensible, shrewd, wise.

sarcastic *adj* acrimonious, biting, cutting, mordacious, mordant, sardonic, satirical, sharp, severe, sneering, taunting.

sardonic *adj* bitter, derisive, ironical, malevolent, malicious, malignant, sarcastic.

satanic *adj* devilish, diabolical, evil, false, fiendish, hellish, infernal, malicious.

satellite *adj* dependent, subordinate, tributary, vassal. * *n* attendant, dependant, follower, hanger-on, retainer, vassal.

satiate *vb* fill, sate, satisfy, suffice; cloy, glut, gorge, overfeed, overfill, pall, surfeit.

satire *n* burlesque, diatribe, invective, fling, irony, lampoon, pasquinade, philippic, ridicule, sarcasm, skit, squib.

satirical *adj* abusive, biting, bitter, censorious, cutting, invective, ironical, keen, mordacious, poignant, reproachful, sarcastic, severe, sharp, taunting.

satirize *vb* abuse, censure, lampoon, ridicule.

satisfaction *n* comfort, complacency, contentment, ease, enjoyment, gratification, pleasure, satiety; amends, appeasement, atonement, compensation, indemnification, recompense, redress, remuneration, reparation, requital, reward.

satisfactory *adj* adequate, conclusive, convincing, decisive, sufficient; gratifying, pleasing.

satisfy *vb* appease, content, fill, gratify, please, sate, satiate, suffice; indemnify, compensate, liquidate, pay, recompense, remunerate, requite; discharge, settle; assure, convince, persuade; answer, fulfil, meet.

saturate *vb* drench, fill, fit, imbue, soak, steep, wet.

saturnine *adj* dark, dull, gloomy, grave, heavy, leaden, morose, phlegmatic, sad, sedate, sombre; melancholic, mournful, serious, unhappy; mischievous, naughty, troublesome, vexatious, wicked.

sauce *n* cheekiness, impudence, insolence; appetizer, compound, condiment, relish, seasoning.

saucy *adj* bold, cavalier, disrespectful, flippant, forward, immodest, impertinent, impudent, insolent, pert, rude.

saunter *vb* amble, dawdle, delay, dilly-dally, lag, linger, loiter, lounge, stroll, tarry. * *n* amble, stroll, walk.

savage *vb* attack, lacerate, mangle, maul. * *adj* rough, uncultivated, wild; rude, uncivilized, unpolished, untaught; bloodthirsty, feral, ferine, ferocious, fierce, rapacious, untamed, vicious; beastly, bestial, brutal, brutish, inhuman; atrocious, barbarous, barbaric, bloody, brutal, cruel, fell, fiendish, hardhearted, heathenish, merciless, murderous, pitiless, relentless, ruthless, sanguinary, truculent; native, rough, rugged. * *n* barbarian, brute, heathen, vandal.

save *vb* keep, liberate, preserve, rescue; salvage, recover, redeem; economize, gather, hoard, husband, reserve, store; hinder, obviate, prevent, spare. * *prep* but, deducting, except.

saviour *n* defender, deliverer, guardian, protector, preserver, rescuer, saver.

savour *vb* affect, appreciate, enjoy, like, partake, relish; flavour, season. * *n* flavour, gusto, relish, smack, taste; fragrance, odour, smell, scent.

savoury *adj* agreeable, delicious, flavourful, luscious, nice, palatable, piquant, relishing.

saw *n* adage, aphorism, apothegm, axiom, byword, dictum, maxim, precept, proverb, sententious saying.

say *vb* declare, express, pronounce, speak, tell, utter; affirm, allege, argue; recite, rehearse, repeat; assume, presume, suppose. * *n* affirmation, declaration, speech, statement; decision, voice, vote.

saying *n* declaration, expression, observation, remark, speech, statement; adage, aphorism, byword, dictum, maxim, proverb, saw.

scale[1] *n* basin, dish, pan; balance.

scale[2] *n* flake, lamina, lamella, layer, plate.

scale[3] *vb* ascend, climb, escalate, mount. * *n* graduation.

scamp *n* cheat, knave, rascal, rogue, scapegrace, scoundrel, swindler, trickster, villain.

scamper *vb* haste, hasten, hie, run, scud, speed, trip.

scan *vb* examine, investigate, scrutinize, search, sift.

scandal *vb* asperse, defame, libel, traduce. * *n* aspersion, calumny, defamation, obloquy, reproach; discredit, disgrace, dishonour, disrepute, ignominy, infamy, odium, opprobrium, offence, shame.

scandalize *vb* offend; asperse, backbite, calumniate, decry, defame, disgust, lampoon, libel, reproach, revile, satirize, slander, traduce, vilify.

scandalous *adj* defamatory, libellous, opprobrious, slanderous; atrocious, disgraceful, disreputable, infamous, inglorious, ignominious, odious, shameful.

scanty *adj* insufficient, meagre, narrow, scant, small; hardly, scarce, short, slender; niggardly, parsimonious, penurious, scrimpy, skimpy, sparing.

scar[1] *vb* hurt, mark, wound. * *n* cicatrice, cicatrix, seam; blemish, defect, disfigurement, flaw, injury, mark.

scar[2] *n* bluff, cliff, crag, precipice.

scarce *adj* deficient, wanting; infrequent, rare,

uncommon. * *adv* barely, hardly, scantily.

scarcely *adv* barely, hardly, scantily.

scarcity *n* dearth, deficiency, insufficiency, lack, want; infrequency, rareness, rarity, uncommonness.

scare *vb* affright, alarm, appal, daunt, fright, frighten, intimidate, shock, startle, terrify. * *n* alarm, fright, panic, shock, terror.

scathe *vb* blast, damage, destroy, injure, harm, haste. * *n* damage, harm, injury, mischief, waste.

scatter *vb* broadcast, sprinkle, strew; diffuse, disperse, disseminate, dissipate, distribute, separate, spread; disappoint, dispel, frustrate, overthrow.

scene *n* display, exhibition, pageant, representation, show, sight, spectacle, view; place, situation, spot; arena, stage.

scent *vb* breathe in, inhale, nose, smell, sniff; detect, smell out, sniff out; aromatize, perfume. * *n* aroma, balminess, fragrance, odour, perfume, smell, redolence.

sceptic *n* doubter, freethinker, questioner, unbeliever.

sceptical *adj* doubtful, doubting, dubious, hesitating, incredulous, questioning, unbelieving.

scepticism *n* doubt, dubiety, freethinking, incredulity, unbelief.

schedule *vb* line up, list, plan, programme, tabulate. * *n* document, scroll; catalogue, inventory, list, plan, record, register, roll, table, timetable.

scheme *vb* contrive, design, frame, imagine, plan, plot, project. * *n* plan, system, theory; cabal, conspiracy, contrivance, design, device, intrigue, machination, plan, plot, project, stratagem; arrangement, draught, diagram, outline.

schism *n* division, separation, split; discord, disunion, division, faction, separation.

scholar *n* disciple, learner, pupil, student; don, fellow, intellectual, pedant, savant.

scholarship *n* accomplishments, acquirements, attainments, erudition, knowledge, learning; bursary, exhibition, foundation, grant, maintenance.

scholastic *adj* academic, bookish, lettered, literary; formal, pedantic.

school *vb* drill, educate, exercise, indoctrinate, instruct, teach, train; admonish, control, chide, discipline, govern, reprove, tutor. * *adj* academic, collegiate, institutional, scholastic, schoolish. * *n* academy, college, gymnasium, institute, institution, kindergarten, lyceum, manège, polytechnic, seminary, university; adherents, camarilla, circle, clique, coterie, disciples, followers; body, order, organization, party, sect.

schooling *n* discipline, education, instruction, nurture, teaching, training, tuition.

scintillate *vb* coruscate, flash, gleam, glisten, glitter, sparkle, twinkle.

scoff *vb* deride, flout, jeer, mock, ridicule, taunt; gibe, sneer. * *n* flout, gibe, jeer, sneer, mockery, taunt; derision, ridicule.

scold *vb* berate, blame, censure, chide, rate, reprimand, reprove; brawl, rail, rate, reprimand, upbraid, vituperate. * *n* shrew, termagant, virago, vixen.

scope *n* aim, design, drift, end, intent, intention, mark, object, purpose, tendency, view; amplitude, field, latitude, liberty, margin, opportunity, purview, range, room, space, sphere, vent; extent, length, span, stretch, sweep.

scorch *vb* blister, burn, char, parch, roast, sear, shrivel, singe.

score *vb* cut, furrow, mark, notch, scratch; charge, note, record; impute, note; enter, register. * *n* incision, mark, notch; account, bill, charge, debt, reckoning; consideration, ground, motive, reason.

scorn *vb* condemn, despise, disregard, disdain, scout, slight, spurn. * *n* contempt, derision, disdain, mockery, slight, sneer; scoff.

scornful *adj* contemptuous, defiant, disdainful, contemptuous, regardless.

scot-free *adj* untaxed; clear, unhurt, uninjured, safe.

scoundrel *n* cheat, knave, miscreant, rascal, reprobate, rogue, scamp, swindler, trickster, villain.

scour[1] *vb* brighten, buff, burnish, clean, cleanse, polish, purge, scrape, scrub, rub, wash, whiten; rake; efface, obliterate, overrun.

scour[2] *vb* career, course, range, scamper, scud, scuttle; comb, hunt, rake, ransack, rifle, rummage, search.

scourge *vb* lash, whip; afflict, chasten, chastise, correct, punish; harass, torment. * *n* cord, cowhide, lash, strap, thong, whip; affliction, bane, curse, infliction, nuisance, pest, plague, punishment.

scout *vb* contemn, deride, disdain, despise, ridicule, scoff, scorn, sneer, spurn; investigate, probe, search. * *n* escort, lookout, precursor, vanguard.

scowl *vb* frown, glower, lower. * *n* frown, glower, lower.

scraggy *adj* broken, craggy, rough, rugged, scabrous, scragged, uneven; attenuated, bony, emaciated, gaunt, lank, lean, meagre, scrawny, skinny, thin.

scrap[1] *vb* discard, junk, trash. * *n* bit, fragment, modicum, particle, piece, snippet; bite, crumb, morsel, mouthful; debris, junk, litter, rubbish, rubble, trash, waste.

scrap[2] *vb* altercate, bicker, dispute, clash, fight, hassle, quarrel, row, spat, squabble, tiff, tussle, wrangle. * *n* affray, altercation, bickering, clash, dispute, fight, fray, hassle, melee, quarrel, row, run-in, set-to, spat, squabble, tiff, tussle, wrangle.

scrape *vb* bark, grind, rasp, scuff; accumulate, acquire, collect, gather, save; erase, remove. * *n* difficulty, distress, embarrassment, perplexity, predicament.

scream *vb* screech, shriek, squall, ululate. * *n* cry, outcry, screech, shriek, shrill, ululation.

screen *vb* cloak, conceal, cover, defend, fence, hide,

mask, protect, shelter, shroud. * *n* blind, curtain, lattice, partition; defence, guard, protection, shield; cloak, cover, veil, disguise; riddle, sieve.

screw *vb* force, press, pressurize, squeeze, tighten, twist, wrench; oppress, rack; distort. * *n* extortioner, extortionist, miser, scrimp, skinflint; prison guard; sexual intercourse.

scrimmage *n* brawl, melee, riot, scuffle, skirmish.

scrimp *vb* contract, curtail, limit, pinch, reduce, scant, shorten, straiten.

scrimpy *adj* contracted, deficient, narrow, scanty.

scroll *n* inventory, list, parchment, roll, schedule.

scrub[1] *adj* contemptible, inferior, mean, niggardly, scrubby, shabby, small, stunted. * *n* brushwood, underbrush, underwood.

scrub[2] *vb* clean, cleanse, rub, scour, scrape, wash.

scruple *vb* boggle, demur, falter, hesitate, object, pause, stickle, waver. * *n* delicacy, hesitancy, hesitation, nicety, perplexity, qualm.

scrupulous *adj* conscientious, fastidious, nice, precise, punctilious, rigorous, strict; careful, cautious, circumspect, exact, vigilant.

scrutinize *vb* canvass, dissect, examine, explore, investigate, overhaul, probe, search, sift, study.

scrutiny *n* examination, exploration, inquisition, inspection, investigation, search, searching, sifting.

scud *vb* flee, fly, haste, hasten, hie, post, run, scamper, speed, trip.

scuffle *vb* contend, fight, strive, struggle. * *n* altercation, brawl, broil, contest, encounter, fight, fray, quarrel, squabble, struggle, wrangle.

sculpt *vb* carve, chisel, cut, sculpture; engrave, grave.

scurrilous *adj* abusive, blackguardly, contumelious, foul, foul-mouthed, indecent, infamous, insolent, insulting, offensive, opprobrious, reproachful, ribald, vituperative; coarse, gross, low, mean, obscene, vile, vulgar.

scurry *vb* bustle, dash, hasten, hurry, scamper, scud, scutter. * *n* burst, bustle, dash, flurry, haste, hurry, scamper, scud, spurt.

scurvy *adj* scabbed, scabby, scurfy; abject, bad, base, contemptible, despicable, low, mean, pitiful, sorry, vile, vulgar, worthless; malicious, mischievous, offensive.

scuttle[1] *vb* hurry, hustle, run, rush, scamper, scramble, scud, scurry. * *n* dash, drive, flurry, haste, hurry, hustle, race, rush, scamper, scramble, scud, scurry.

scuttle[2] *vb* capsize, founder, go down, sink, overturn, upset. * *n* hatch, hatchway.

seal *vb* close, fasten, secure; attest, authenticate, confirm, establish, ratify, sanction; confine, enclose, imprison. * *n* fastening, stamp, wafer, wax; assurance, attestation, authentication, confirmation, pledge, ratification.

seamy *adj* disreputable, nasty, seedy, sordid, unpleasant.

sear *vb* blight, brand, cauterize, dry, scorch, wither. * *adj* dried up, dry, sere, withered.

search *vb* examine, explore, ferret, inspect, investigate, overhaul, probe, ransack, scrutinize, sift; delve, hunt, forage, inquire, look, rummage. * *n* examination, exploration, hunt, inquiry, inspection, investigation, pursuit, quest, research, seeking, scrutiny.

searching *adj* close, keen, penetrating, trying; examining, exploring, inquiring, investigating, probing, seeking.

seared *adj* callous, graceless, hardened, impenitent, incorrigible, obdurate, shameless, unrepentant.

season *vb* acclimatize, accustom, form, habituate, harden, inure, mature, qualify, temper, train; flavour, spice. * *n* interval, period, spell, term, time, while.

seasonable *adj* appropriate, convenient, fit, opportune, suitable, timely.

seasoning *n* condiment, flavouring, relish, salt, sauce.

seat *vb* establish, fix, locate, place, set, station. * *n* place, site, situation, station; abode, capital, dwelling, house, mansion, residence; bottom, fundament; bench, chair, pew, settle, stall, stool.

secede *vb* apostatize, resign, retire, withdraw.

secluded *adj* close, covert, embowered, isolated, private, removed, retired, screened, sequestrated, withdrawn.

seclusion *n* obscurity, privacy, retirement, secrecy, separation, solitude, withdrawal.

second[1] *n* instant, jiffy, minute, moment, trice.

second[2] *vb* abet, advance, aid, assist, back, encourage, forward, further, help, promote, support, sustain; approve, favour. * *adj* inferior, secondrate, secondary; following, next, subsequent; additional, extra, other; double, duplicate. * *n* another, other; assistant, backer, supporter.

secondary *adj* collateral, inferior, minor, subsidiary, subordinate. * *n* delegate, deputy, proxy.

secrecy *n* clandestineness, concealment, furtiveness, stealth, surreptitiousness.

secret *adj* close, concealed, covered, covert, cryptic, hid, hidden, mysterious, privy, shrouded, veiled, unknown, unrevealed, unseen; cabbalistic, clandestine, furtive, privy, sly, stealthy, surreptitious, underhand; confidential, private, retired, secluded, unseen; abstruse, latent, mysterious, obscure, occult, recondite, unknown. * *n* confidence, enigma, key, mystery.

secretary *n* clerk, scribe, writer; escritoire, writing-desk.

secrete[1] *vb* bury, cache, conceal, disguise, hide, shroud, stash; screen, separate.

secrete[2] *vb* discharge, emit, excrete, exude, release, secern.

secretive *adj* cautious, close, reserved, reticent, taciturn, uncommunicative, wary.

sect *n* denomination, faction, schism, school.

section *n* cutting, division, fraction, part, piece, portion, segment, slice.

secular *adj* civil, laic, laical, lay, profane, temporal, worldly.

secure vb guard, protect, safeguard; assure, ensure, guarantee, insure; fasten; acquire, gain, get, obtain, procure. * adj assured, certain, confident, sure; insured, protected, safe; fast, firm, fixed, immovable, stable; careless, easy, undisturbed, unsuspecting; heedless, inattentive, incautious, negligent, overconfident.

security n bulwark, defence, guard, palladium, protection, safeguard, safety, shelter; bond, collateral, deposit, guarantee, pawn, pledge, stake, surety, warranty; carelessness, heedlessness, overconfidence, negligence; assurance, assuredness, certainty, confidence, ease.

sedate adj calm, collected, composed, contemplative, cool, demure, grave, placid, philosophical, quiet, serene, serious, sober, still, thoughtful, tranquil, undisturbed, unemotional, unruffled.

sedative adj allaying, anodyne, assuasive, balmy, calming, composing, demulcent, lenient, lenitive, soothing, tranquillizing. * n anaesthetic, anodyne, hypnotic, narcotic, opiate.

sedentary adj inactive, motionless, sluggish, torpid.

sediment n dregs, grounds, lees, precipitate, residue, residuum, settlings.

sedition n insurgence, insurrection, mutiny, rebellion, revolt, riot, rising, treason, tumult, uprising, uproar.

seditious adj factious, incendiary, insurgent, mutinous, rebellious, refractory, riotous, tumultuous, turbulent.

seduce vb allure, attract, betray, corrupt, debauch, deceive, decoy, deprave, ensnare, entice, inveigle, lead, mislead.

seductive adj alluring, attractive, enticing, tempting.

sedulous adj active, assiduous, busy, diligent, industrious, laborious, notable, painstaking, persevering, unremitting, untiring.

see vb behold, contemplate, descry, glimpse, sight, spot, survey; comprehend, conceive, distinguish, espy, know, notice, observe, perceive, recognize, remark, understand; beware, consider, envisage, regard, visualize; experience, feel, suffer; examine, inspire, notice, observe; discern, look; call on, visit.

seed n semen, sperm; embryo, grain, kernel, matured ovule; germ, original; children, descendants, offspring, progeny; birth, generation, race.

seedy adj faded, old, shabby, worn; destitute, distressed, indigent, needy, penniless, pinched, poor.

seek vb hunt, look, search; court, follow, prosecute, pursue, solicit; attempt, endeavour, strive, try.

seem vb appear, assume, look, pretend.

seeming adj apparent, appearing, ostensible, specious. * n appearance, colour, guise, look, semblance.

seemly adj appropriate, becoming, befitting, congruous, convenient, decent, decorous, expedient, fit, fitting, meet, proper, right, suitable; beautiful, comely, fair, good-looking, graceful, handsome, pretty, well-favoured.

seer n augur, diviner, foreteller, predictor, prophet, soothsayer.

segment n bit, division, part, piece, portion, section, sector.

segregate vb detach, disconnect, disperse, insulate, part, separate.

segregation n apartheid, discrimination, insulation, separation.

seize vb capture, catch, clutch, grab, grapple, grasp, grip, snatch; confiscate, impress, impound; apprehend, comprehend; arrest, take.

seldom adv infrequently, occasionally, rarely.

select vb choose, cull, pick, prefer. * adj choice, chosen, excellent, exquisite, good, picked, rare, selected.

selection n choice, election, pick, preference.

self-conscious adj awkward, diffident, embarrassed, insecure, nervous.

self-control n restraint, willpower.

self-important adj assuming, consequential, proud, haughty, lordly, overbearing, overweening.

selfish adj egoistic, egotistical, greedy, illiberal, mean, narrow, self-seeking, ungenerous.

self-possessed adj calm, collected, composed, cool, placid, sedate, undisturbed, unexcited, unruffled.

self-willed adj contumacious, dogged, headstrong, obstinate, pig-headed, stubborn, uncompliant, wilful.

sell vb barter, exchange, hawk, market, peddle, trade, vend.

semblance n likeness, resemblance, similarity; air, appearance, aspect, bearing, exterior, figure, form, mien, seeming, show; image, representation, similitude.

seminal adj important, original; germinal, radical, rudimental, rudimentary, unformed.

seminary n academy, college, gymnasium, high school, institute, school, university.

send vb cast, drive, emit, fling, hurl, impel, lance, launch, project, propel, throw, toss; delegate, depute, dispatch; forward, transmit; bestow, confer, give, grant.

senile adj aged, doddering, superannuated; doting, imbecile.

senior adj elder, older; higher.

seniority n eldership, precedence, priority, superiority.

sensation n feeling, sense, perception; excitement, impression, thrill.

sensational adj exciting, melodramatic, startling, thrilling.

sense vb appraise, appreciate, estimate, notice, observe, perceive, suspect, understand. * n brains, intellect, intelligence, mind, reason, understanding; appreciation, apprehension, discernment, feeling, perception, recognition, tact; connotation, idea, implication, judgment, notion, opinion, sentiment, view; import, interpretation, meaning, purport, significance; sagacity, soundness, substance, wisdom.

senseless *adj* apathetic, inert, insensate, unfeeling; absurd, foolish, ill-judged, nonsensical, silly, unmeaning, unreasonable, unwise; doltish, foolish, simple, stupid, witless, weak-minded.

sensible *adj* apprehensible, perceptible; aware, cognizant, conscious, convinced, persuaded, satisfied; discreet, intelligent, judicious, rational, reasonable, sagacious, sage, sober, sound, wise; observant, understanding; impressionable, sensitive.

sensitive *adj* perceptive, sentient; affected, impressible, impressionable, responsive, susceptible; delicate, tender, touchy.

sensual *adj* animal, bodily, carnal, voluptuous; gross, lascivious, lewd, licentious, unchaste.

sentence *vb* condemn, doom, judge. * *n* decision, determination, judgment, opinion, verdict; doctrine, dogma, opinion, tenet; condemnation, conviction, doom; period, proposition.

sententious *adj* compendious, compact, concise, didactic, laconic, pithy, pointed, succinct, terse.

sentiment *n* judgment, notion, opinion; maxim, saying; emotion, tenderness; disposition, feeling, thought.

sentimental *adj* impressible, impressionable, overemotional, romantic, tender.

sentinel *n* guard, guardsman, patrol, picket, sentry, watchman.

separate *vb* detach, disconnect, disjoin, disunite, dissever, divide, divorce, part, sever, sunder; eliminate, remove, withdraw; cleave, open. * *adj* detached, disconnected, disjoined, disjointed, dissociated, disunited, divided, parted, severed; discrete, distinct, divorced, unconnected; alone, segregated, withdrawn.

separation *n* disjunction, disjuncture, dissociation; disconnection, disseverance, disseveration, disunion, division, divorce; analysis, decomposition.

sepulchral *adj* deep, dismal, funereal, gloomy, grave, hollow, lugubrious, melancholy, mournful, sad, sombre, woeful.

sepulchre *n* burial place, charnel house, grave, ossuary, sepulture, tomb.

sequel *n* close, conclusion, denouement, end, termination; consequence, event, issue, result, upshot.

sequence *n* following, graduation, progression, succession; arrangement, series, train.

sequestrated *adj* hidden, private, retired, secluded, unfrequented, withdrawn; seized.

seraphic *adj* angelic, celestial, heavenly, sublime; holy, pure, refined.

serene *adj* calm, collected, placid, peaceful, quiet, tranquil, sedate, undisturbed, unperturbed, unruffled; bright, calm, clear, fair, unclouded.

serenity *n* calm, calmness, collectedness, composure, coolness, imperturbability, peace, peaceful-

ness, quiescence, sedateness, tranquillity; brightness, calmness, clearness, fairness, peace, quietness, stillness.

serf *n* bondman, servant, slave, thrall, villein.

serfdom *n* bondage, enslavement, enthralment, servitude, slavery, subjection, thraldom.

series *n* chain, concatenation, course, line, order, progression, sequence, succession, train.

serious *adj* earnest, grave, demure, pious, resolute, sedate, sober, solemn, staid, thoughtful; dangerous, great, important, momentous, weighty.

sermon *n* discourse, exhortation, homily, lecture.

serpentine *adj* anfractuous, convoluted, crooked, meandering, sinuous, spiral, tortuous, twisted, undulating, winding.

servant *n* attendant, dependant, factotum, helper, henchman, retainer, servitor, subaltern, subordinate, underling; domestic, drudge, flunky, lackey, menial, scullion, slave.

serve *vb* aid, assist, attend, help, minister, oblige, succour; advance, benefit, forward, promote; content, satisfy, supply; handle, officiate, manage, manipulate, work.

service *vb* check, maintain, overhaul, repair. * *n* labour, ministration, work; attendance, business, duty, employ, employment, office; advantage, benefit, good, gain, profit; avail, purpose, use, utility; ceremony, function, observance, rite, worship.

serviceable *adj* advantageous, available, beneficial, convenient, functional, handy, helpful, operative, profitable, useful.

servile *adj* dependent, menial; abject, base, beggarly, cringing, fawning, grovelling, low, mean, obsequious, slavish, sneaking, sycophantic, truckling.

servility *n* bondage, dependence, slavery; abjection, abjectness, baseness, fawning, meanness, obsequiousness, slavishness, sycophancy.

servitor *n* attendant, dependant, footman, lackey, retainer, servant, squire, valet, waiter.

servitude *n* bondage, enslavement, enthralment, serfdom, service, slavery, thraldom.

set[1] *vb* lay, locate, mount, place, put, stand, station; appoint, determine, establish, fix, settle; risk, stake, wager; adapt, adjust, regulate; adorn, stud, variegate; arrange, dispose, pose, post; appoint, assign, predetermine, prescribe; estimate, prize, rate, value; embarrass, perplex, pose; contrive, produce; decline, sink; congeal, concern, consolidate, harden, solidify; flow, incline, run, tend; (*with* **about**) begin, commence; (*with* **apart**) appropriate, consecrate, dedicate, devote, reserve, set aside; (*with* **aside**) abrogate, annul, omit, reject; reserve, set apart; (*with* **before**) display, exhibit; (*with* **down**) chronicle, jot down, record, register, state, write down; (*with* **forth**) display, exhibit, explain, expound, manifest, promulgate, publish, put forward, represent, show; (*with* **forward**) advance, further, promote; (*with* **free**) acquit, clear, emancipate, liberate, release; (*with* **off**) adorn, decorate, embellish; define, portion off; (*with* **on**) actuate, encourage, impel, influence, incite, instigate, prompt, spur, urge; attack, assault, set upon; (*with* **out**) display, issue, publish, proclaim, prove, recommend, show; (*with* **right**) correct, put in order; (*with* **to rights**) adjust, regulate; (*with* **up**) elevate, erect, exalt, raise; establish, found, institute; (*with* **upon**) assail, assault, attack, fly at, rush upon. * *adj* appointed, established, formal, ordained, prescribed, regular, settled; determined, fixed, firm, obstinate, positive, stiff, unyielding; immovable, predetermined; located, placed, put. * *n* attitude, position, posture; scene, scenery, setting.

set² *n* assortment, collection, suit; class, circle, clique, cluster, company, coterie, division, gang, group, knot, party, school, sect.

setback *n* blow, hitch, hold-up, rebuff; defeat, disappointment, reverse.

set-off *n* adornment, decoration, embellishment, ornament; counterbalance, counterclaim, equivalent.

settle *vb* adjust, arrange, compose, regulate; account, balance, close up, conclude, discharge, liquidate, pay, pay up, reckon, satisfy, square; allay, calm, compose, pacify, quiet, repose, rest, still, tranquillize; confirm, decide, determine, make clear; establish, fix, set; fall, gravitate, sink, subside; abide, colonize, domicile, dwell, establish, inhabit, people, place, plant, reside; (*with* **on**) determine on, fix on, fix upon; establish. * *n* bench, seat, stool.

settled *adj* established, fixed, stable; decided, deep-rooted, steady, unchanging; adjusted, arranged; methodical, orderly, quiet; common, customary, everyday, ordinary, usual, wonted.

set-to *n* combat, conflict, contest, fight.

sever *vb* divide, part, rend, separate, sunder; detach, disconnect, disjoin, disunite.

several *adj* individual, single, particular; distinct, exclusive, independent, separate; different, divers, diverse, manifold, many, sundry, various.

severance *n* partition, separation.

severe *adj* austere, bitter, dour, hard, harsh, inexorable, morose, painful, relentless, rigid, rigorous, rough, sharp, stern, stiff, strait-laced, unmitigated, unrelenting, unsparing; accurate, exact, methodical, strict; chaste, plain, restrained, simple, unadorned; biting, caustic, cruel, cutting, harsh, keen, sarcastic, satirical, trenchant; acute, afflictive, distressing, excruciating, extreme, intense, stringent, violent; critical, exact.

severity *n* austerity, gravity, harshness, rigour, seriousness, sternness, strictness; accuracy, exactness, niceness; chasteness, plainness, simplicity; acrimony, causticity, keenness, sharpness; afflictiveness, extremity, keenness, stringency, violence; cruelty.

sew *vb* baste, bind, hem, stitch, tack.

sex *n* gender, femininity, masculinity, sexuality;

coitus, copulation, fornication, love-making.

shabby *adj* faded, mean, poor, ragged, seedy, threadbare, worn, worn-out; beggarly, mean, paltry, penurious, stingy, ungentlemanly, unhandsome.

shackle *vb* chain, fetter, gyve, hamper, manacle; bind, clog, confine, cumber, embarrass, encumber, impede, obstruct, restrict, trammel. * *n* chain, fetter, gyve, hamper, manacle.

shade *vb* cloud, darken, dim, eclipse, obfuscate, obscure; cover, ensconce, hide, protect, screen, shelter. * *n* darkness, dusk, duskiness, gloom, obscurity, shadow; cover, protection, shelter; awning, blind, curtain, screen, shutter, veil; degree, difference, kind, variety; cast, colour, complexion, dye, hue, tinge, tint, tone; apparition, ghost, manes, phantom, shadow, spectre, spirit.

shadow *vb* becloud, cloud, darken, obscure, shade; adumbrate, foreshadow, symbolize, typify; conceal, cover, hide, protect, screen, shroud. * *n* penumbra, shade, umbra, umbrage; darkness, gloom, obscurity; cover, protection, security, shelter; adumbration, foreshadowing, image, prefiguration, representation; apparition, ghost, phantom, shade, spirit; image, portrait, reflection, silhouette.

shadowy *adj* shady, umbrageous; dark, dim, gloomy, murky, obscure; ghostly, imaginary, impalpable, insubstantial, intangible, spectral, unreal, unsubstantial, visionary.

shady *adj* shadowy, umbrageous; crooked.

shaft *n* arrow, missile, weapon; handle, helve; pole, tongue; axis, spindle; pinnacle, spire; stalk, stem, trunk.

shaggy *adj* rough, rugged.

shake *vb* quake, quaver, quiver, shiver, shudder, totter, tremble; agitate, convulse, jar, jolt, stagger; daunt, frighten, intimidate; endanger, move, weaken; oscillate, vibrate, wave; move, put away, remove, throw off. * *n* agitation, concussion, flutter, jar, jolt, quaking, shaking, shivering, shock, trembling, tremor.

shaky *adj* jiggly, quaky, shaking, tottering, trembling.

shallow *adj* flimsy, foolish, frivolous, puerile, trashy, trifling, trivial; empty, ignorant, silly, slight, simple, superficial, unintelligent.

sham *vb* ape, feign, imitate, pretend; cheat, deceive, delude, dupe, impose, trick. * *adj* assumed, counterfeit, false, feigned, mock, make-believe, pretended, spurious. * *n* delusion, feint, fraud, humbug, imposition, imposture, pretence, trick.

shamble *vb* hobble, shuffle.

shambles *npl* abattoir, slaughterhouse; confusion, disorder, mess.

shame *vb* debase, degrade, discredit, disgrace, dishonour, stain, sully, taint, tarnish; abash, confound, confuse, discompose, disconcert, humble, humiliate; deride, flout, jeer, mock, ridicule, sneer. * *n* contempt, degradation, derision, discredit, disgrace, dishonour, disrepute, ignominy, infamy, obloquy, odium, opprobrium; abashment, chagrin, confusion, embarrassment, humiliation, mortification; reproach, scandal; decency, decorousness, decorum, modesty, propriety, seemliness.

shamefaced *adj* bashful, diffident, overmodest.

shameful *adj* atrocious, base, disgraceful, dishonourable, disreputable, heinous, ignominous, infamous, nefarious, opprobrious, outrageous, scandalous, vile, villainous, wicked; degrading, indecent, unbecoming.

shameless *adj* assuming, audacious, bold-faced, brazen, brazen-faced, cool, immodest, impudent, indecent, indelicate, insolent, unabashed, unblushing; abandoned, corrupt, depraved, dissolute, graceless, hardened, incorrigible, irreclaimable, lost, obdurate, profligate, reprobate, sinful, unprincipled, vicious.

shape *vb* create, form, make, produce; fashion, model, mould; adjust, direct, frame, regulate; conceive, conjure up, figure, image, imagine. * *n* appearance, aspect, fashion, figure, form, guise, make; build, cast, cut, model, mould, pattern; apparition, image.

shapeless *adj* amorphous, formless; grotesque, irregular, rude, uncouth, unsymmetrical.

shapely *adj* comely, symmetrical, trim, well-formed.

share *vb* apportion, distribute, divide, parcel out, portion, split; partake, participate; experience, receive. * *n* part, portion, quantum; allotment, allowance, contingent, deal, dividend, division, interest, lot, proportion, quantity, quota.

sharer *n* communicant, partaker, participator.

sharp *adj* acute, cutting, keen, keen-edged, knife-edged, razor-edged, trenchant; acuminate, needle-shaped, peaked, pointed, ridged; apt, astute, canny, clear-sighted, clever, cunning, discerning, discriminating, ingenious, inventive, keen-witted, penetrating, perspicacious, quick, ready, sagacious, sharp-witted, shrewd, smart, subtle, witty; acid, acrid, biting, bitter, burning, high-flavoured, high-seasoned, hot, mordacious, piquant, poignant, pungent, sour, stinging; acrimonious, biting, caustic, cutting, harsh, mordant, sarcastic, severe, tart, trenchant; cruel, hard, rigid; afflicting, distressing, excruciating, intense, painful, piercing, shooting, sore, violent; nipping, pinching; ardent, eager, fervid, fierce, fiery, impetuous, strong; high, screeching, shrill; attentive, vigilant; severe; close, exacting, shrewd, cold, crisp, freezing, icy wintry. * *adv* abruptly, sharply, suddenly; exactly, precisely, punctually.

sharp-cut *adj* clear, distinct, well-defined.

sharpen *vb* edge, intensify, point.

sharper *n* cheat, deceiver, defrauder, knave, rogue, shark, swindler, trickster.

sharply *adv* rigorously, roughly, severely; acutely, keenly; vehemently, violently; accurately, exactly, minutely, trenchantly, wittily; abruptly, steeply.

sharpness *n* acuteness, keenness, trenchancy; acuity, spinosity; acumen, cleverness, discernment, ingenuity, quickness, sagacity, shrewdness, smartness, wit; acidity, acridity, piquancy, pungency, sting, tartness; causticness, incisiveness, pungency, sarcasm, satire, severity; afflictiveness, intensity, painfulness, poignancy; ardour, fierceness, violence; discordance, dissonance, highness, screechiness, squeakiness, shrillness.

sharp-sighted *adj* clear-sighted, keen, keen-eyed, keen-sighted.

sharp-witted *adj* acute, clear-sighted, cunning, discerning, ingenious, intelligent, keen, keen-sighted, long-headed, quick, sagacious, sharp, shrewd.

shatter *vb* break, burst, crack, rend, shiver, smash, splinter, split; break up, derange, disorder, overthrow.

shave *vb* crop, cut off, mow, pare; slice; graze, skim, touch.

shaver *n* boy, child, youngster; bargainer, extortioner, sharper.

shear *vb* clip, cut, fleece, strip; divest; break off.

sheath *n* case, casing, covering, envelope, scabbard, sheathing.

sheathe *vb* case, cover, encase, enclose.

shed[1] *n* cabin, cot, hovel, hut, outhouse, shack, shelter.

shed[2] *vb* effuse, let fall, pour out, spill; diffuse, emit, give out, scatter, spread; cast, let fall, put off, slough, throw off.

sheen *n* brightness, gloss, glossiness, shine, spendour.

sheep *n* ewe, lamb, ram.

sheepish *adj* bashful, diffident, overmodest, shamefaced, timid, timorous.

sheer[1] *adj* perpendicular, precipitous, steep, vertical; clear, downright, mere, pure, simple, unadulterated, unmingled, unmixed, unqualified, utter; clear; fine, transparent. * *adv* outright; perpendicularly, steeply.

sheer[2] *vb* decline, deviate, move aside, swerve. * *n* bow, curve.

shelf *n* bracket, console, ledge, mantelpiece.

shell *vb* exfoliate, fall off, peel off; bombard. * *n* carapace, case, covering, shard; bomb, grenade, sharpnel; framework.

shelter *vb* cover, defend, ensconce, harbour, hide, house, protect, screen, shield, shroud. * *n* asylum, cover, covert, harbour, haven, hideaway, refuge, retreat, sanctuary; defence, protection, safety, screen, security, shield; guardian, protector.

shelve *vb* dismiss, put aside; incline, slope.

shepherd *vb* escort, guide, marshal, usher; direct, drive, drove, herd, lead; guard, tend, watch over. * *n* drover, grazier, herder, herdsman; chaplain, churchman, clergyman, cleric, divine, ecclesiastic, minister, padre, parson, pastor; chaperon, duenna, escort, guide, squire, usher.

shield *vb* cover, defend, guard, protect, shelter; repel, ward off; avert, forbid, forfend. * *n* aegis, buckler, escutcheon, scutcheon, targe; bulwark, cover, defence, guard, palladium, protection, rampart, safeguard, security, shelter.

shift *vb* alter, change, fluctuate, move, vary; chop, dodge, swerve, veer; contrive, devise, manage, plan, scheme, shuffle. * *n* change, substitution, turn; contrivance, expedient, means, resort, resource; artifice, craft, device, dodge, evasion, fraud, mask, ruse, stratagem, subterfuge, trick, wile; chemise, smock.

shiftless *adj* improvident, imprudent, negligent, slack, thriftless, unresourceful.

shifty *adj* tricky, undependable, wily.

shillyshally *vb* hesitate, waver. * *n* hesitation, irresolute, wavering.

shimmer *vb* flash, glimmer, glisten, shine. * *n* blink, glimmer, glitter, twinkle.

shin *vb* climb, swarm. * *n* shinbone, tibia.

shindy *n* disturbance, riot, roughhouse, row, spree, uproar.

shine *vb* beam, blaze, coruscate, flare, give light, glare, gleam, glimmer, glisten, glitter, glow, lighten, radiate, sparkle; excel. * *n* brightness, brilliancy, glaze, gloss, polish, sheen.

shining *adj* beaming, bright, brilliant, effulgent, gleaming, glowing, glistening, glittering, luminous, lustrous, radiant, resplendent, splendid; conspicuous, distinguished, illustrious.

shiny *adj* bright, clear, luminous, sunshiny, unclouded; brilliant, burnished, glassy, glossy, polished.

ship *n* boat, craft, steamer, vessel.

shipshape *adj* neat, orderly, tidy, trim, well-arranged.

shipwreck *vb* cast away, maroon, strand, wreck. * *n* demolition, destruction, miscarriage, overthrow, perdition, ruin, subversion, wreck.

shirk *vb* avoid, dodge, evade, malinger, quit, slack; cheat, shark, trick.

shiver[1] *vb* break, shatter, splinter. * *n* bit, fragment, piece, slice, sliver, splinter.

shiver[2] *vb* quake, quiver, shake, shudder, tremble. * *n* shaking, shivering, shuddering, tremor.

shivery[1] *adj* brittle, crumbly, frangible, friable, shatterable, splintery.

shivery[2] *adj* quaking, quavering, quivering, shaky, trembly, tremulous, chilly, shivering.

shoal[1] *vb* crowd, throng. * *n* crowd, horde, multitude, swarm, throng.

shoal[2] *n* sandbank, shallows; danger.

shock *vb* appall, horrify; disgust, disquiet, disturb, nauseate, offend, outrage, revolt, scandalize, sicken; astound, stagger, stun; collide with, jar, jolt, shake, strike against; encounter, meet. * *n* agitation, blow, offence, stroke, trauma; assault, brunt, conflict; clash, collision, concussion, impact, percussion.

shocking *adj* abominable, detestable, disgraceful, disgusting, execrable, foul, hateful, loathsome, obnoxious, odious, offensive, repugnant, repulsive, revolting; appalling, awful, dire, dreadful, fearful, frightful, ghastly, hideous, horrible, horrid, horrific, monstrous, terrible.

shoot *vb* catapult, expel, hurl, let fly, propel; discharge, fire, let off; dart, fly, pass, pelt; extend, jut, project, protrude, protuberate, push, put forth, send forth, stretch; bud, germinate, sprout; (*with* **up**) grow increase, spring up, run up, start up. * *n* branch, offshoot, scion, sprout, twig.

shop *n* emporium, market, mart, store; workshop.

shore[1] *n* beach, brim, coast, seabord, seaside, strand, waterside.

shore[2] *vb* brace, buttress, prop, stay, support. * *n* beam, brace, buttress, prop, stay, support.

shorn *adj* cut-off; deprived.

short *adj* brief, curtailed; direct, near, straight; compendious, concise, condensed, laconic, pithy, terse, sententious, succinct, summary; abrupt, curt, petulant, pointed, sharp, snappish, uncivil; defective, deficient, inadequate, insufficient, niggardly, scanty, scrimpy; contracted, desitute, lacking, limited, minus, wanting, dwarfish, squat, undersized; brittle, crisp, crumbling, friable. * *adv* abruptly, at once, forthwith, suddenly.

shortcoming *n* defect, deficiency, delinquency, error, failing, failure, fault, imperfection, inadequacy, remissness, slip, weakness.

shorten *vb* abbreviate, abridge, curtail, cut short; abridge, contract, diminish, lessen, retrench, reduce; cut off, dock, lop, trim; confine, hinder, restrain, restrict.

shortening *n* abbreviation, abridgment, contraction, curtailment, diminution, retrenchment, reduction.

shorthand *n* brachygraphy, stenography, tachygraphy.

short-lived *adj* emphemeral, transient, transitory.

shortly *adv* quickly, soon; briefly, concisely, succinctly, tersely.

short-sighted *adj* myopic, nearsighted, purblind; imprudent, indiscreet.

shot[1] *n* discharge; ball, bullet, missile, projectile; marksman, shooter.

shot[2] *adj* chatoyant, iridescent, irisated, moiré, watered; intermingled, interspersed, interwoven.

shoulder *vb* bear, bolster, carry, hump, maintain, pack, support, sustain, tote; crowd, elbow, jostle, press forward, push, thrust. * *n* projection, protuberance.

shoulder blade *n* blade bone, omoplate, scapula, shoulder bone.

shout *vb* bawl, cheer, clamour, exclaim, halloo, roar, vociferate, whoop, yell. * *n* cheer, clamour, exclamation, halloo, hoot, huzza, outcry, roar, vociferation, whoop, yell.

shove *vb* jostle, press against, propel, push, push aside; (*with* **off**) push away, thrust away.

show *vb* blazon, display, exhibit, flaunt, parade, present; indicate, mark, point out; disclose, discover, divulge, explain, make clear, make known, proclaim, publish, reveal, unfold; demonstrate, evidence, manifest, prove, verify; conduct, guide, usher; direct, inform, instruct, teach; expound, elucidate, interpret; (*with* **off**) display, exhibit, make a show, set off; (*with* **up**) expose. * *n* array, exhibition, representation, sight, spectacle; blazonry, bravery, ceremony, dash, demonstration, display, flourish, ostentation, pageant, pageantry, parade, pomp, splendour, splurge; likeness, resemblance, semblance; affectation, appearance, colour, illusion, mask, plausibility, pose, pretence, pretext, simulation, speciousness; entertainment, production.

showy *adj* bedizened, dressy, fine, flashy, flaunting, garish, gaudy, glaring, gorgeous, loud, ornate, smart, swanky, splendid; grand, magnificent, ostentatious, pompous, pretentious, stately, sumptuous.

shred *vb* tear. * *n* bit, fragment, piece, rag, scrap, strip, tatter.

shrew *n* brawler, fury, scold, spitfire, termagant, virago, vixen.

shrewd *adj* arch, artful, astute, crafty, cunning, Machiavellian, sly, subtle, wily; acute, astute, canny, discerning, discriminating, ingenious, keen, knowing, penetrating, sagacious, sharp, sharp-sighted.

shrewdness *n* address, archness, art, artfulness, astuteness, craft, cunning, policy, skill, slyness, subtlety; acumen, acuteness, discernment, ingenuity, keenness, penetration, perspicacity, sagacity, sharpness, wit.

shrewish *adj* brawling, clamorous, froward, peevish, petulant, scolding, vixenish.

shriek *vb* scream, screech, squeal, yell, yelp. * *n* cry, scream, screech, yell.

shrill *adj* acute, high, high-toned, high-pitched, piercing, piping, sharp.

shrine *n* reliquary, sacred tomb; altar, hallowed place, sacred place.

shrink *vb* contract, decrease, dwindle, shrivel, wither; balk, blench, draw back, flinch, give way, quail, recoil, retire, swerve, wince, withdraw.

shrivel *vb* dry, dry up, parch; contract, decrease, dwindle, shrink, wither, wrinkle.

shroud *vb* bury, cloak, conceal, cover, hide, mask, muffle, protect, screen, shelter, veil. * *n* covering, garment; grave clothes, winding sheet.

shrub *n* bush, dwarf tree, low tree.

shrubby *adj* bushy.

shudder *vb* quake, quiver, shake, shiver, tremble. * *n* shaking, shuddering, trembling, tremor.

shuffle *vb* confuse, disorder, intermix, jumble, mix, shift; cavil, dodge, equivocate, evade, prevaricate, quibble, vacillate; struggle. * *n* artifice, cavil, evasion, fraud, pretence, pretext, prevarication, quibble, ruse, shuffling, sophism, subterfuge, trick.

shun *vb* avoid, elude, eschew, escape, evade, get clear of.

shut *vb* close, close up, stop; confine, coop up, enclose, imprison, lock up, shut up; (*with* **in**) confine, enclose; (*with* **off**) bar, exclude, intercept; (*with* **up**) close up, shut; confine, enclose, fasten in, imprison, lock in, lock up.

shy *vb* cast, chuck, fling, hurl, jerk, pitch, sling, throw, toss; boggle, sheer, start aside. * *adj* bashful, coy, diffident, reserved, retiring, sheepish, shrinking, timid; cautious, chary, distrustful, heedful, wary. * *n* start; fling, throw.

sibilant *adj* buzzing, hissing, sibilous.

sick *adj* ailing, ill, indisposed, laid-up, unwell, weak; nauseated, queasy; disgusted, revolted, tired, weary; diseased, distempered, disordered, feeble, morbid, unhealthy, unsound, weak; languishing, longing, pining.

sicken *vb* ail, disease, fall sick, make sick; nauseate; disgust, weary; decay, droop, languish, pine.

sickening *adj* nauseating, nauseous, palling, sickish; disgusting, distasteful, loathsome, offensive, repulsive, revolting.

sickly *adj* ailing, diseased, faint, feeble, infirm, languid, languishing, morbid, unhealthy, valetudinary, weak, weakly.

sickness *n* ail, ailment, complaint, disease, disorder, distemper, illness, indisposition, invalidism, malady, morbidity; nausea, qualmishness, queasiness.

side *vb* border, bound, edge, flank, frontier, march, rim, skirt, verge; avert, turn aside; (*with* **with**) befriend, favour, flock to, join with, second, support. * *adj* flanking, later, skirting; indirect, oblique; extra, odd, off, spare. * *n* border, edge, flank, margin, verge; cause, faction, interest, party, sect.

sideboard *n* buffet, dresser.

side by side abreast, alongside, by the side.

sidelong *adj* lateral, oblique. * *adv* laterally, obliquely; on the side.

sidewalk *n* footpath, footway, pavement.

sideways, sidewise *adv* laterally. * *adv* athwart, crossways, crosswise, laterally, obliquely, sidelong, sidewards.

siesta *n* doze, nap.

sift *vb* part, separate; bolt, screen, winnow; analyse, canvass, discuss, examine, fathom, follow up, inquire into, investigate, probe, scrutinze, sound, try.

sigh *vb* complain, grieve, lament, mourn. * *n* long breath, sough, suspiration.

sight *vb* get sight of, perceive, see. * *n* cognizance, ken, perception, view; beholding, eyesight, seeing, vision; exhibition, prospect, representation, scene, show, spectacle, wonder; consideration, estimation, knowledge; examination, inspection.

sightless *adj* blind, eyeless, unseeing.

sightly *adj* beautiful, comely, handsome.

sign *vb* indicate, signal, signify; countersign, endorse, subscribe. * *n* emblem, index, indication, manifestation, mark, note, proof, signal, signification, symbol, symptom, token; beacon; augury, auspice, foreboding, miracle, omen, portent, presage, prodigy, prognostic, wonder; type; countersign, password.

signal *vb* flag, glance, hail, nod, nudge, salute, sign, signalize, sound, speak, touch, wave, wink. * *adj* conspicuous, eminent, extraordinary, memorable, notable, noteworthy, remarkable. * *n* cue, indication, mark, sign, token.

signalize *vb* celebrate, distinguish, make memorable.

signature *n* mark, sign, stamp; autograph, hand.

significance *n* implication, import, meaning, purport, sense; consequence, importance, moment, portent, weight; emphasis, energy, expressiveness, force, impressiveness.

significant *adj* betokening, expressive, indicative, significative, signifying; important, material, momentous, portentous, weighty; forcible, emphatic, expressive, telling.

signification *n* expression; acceptation, import, meaning, purport, sense.

signify *vb* betoken, communication, express, indicate, intimate; denote, imply, import, mean, purport, suggest; announce, declare, give notice of, impart, make known, manifest, proclaim, utter; augur, foreshadow, indicate, portend, represent; matter, weigh.

silence *vb* hush, muzzle, still; allay, calm, quiet. * *interj* be silent, be still, hush, soft, tush, tut, whist. * *n* calm, hush, lull, noiselessness, peace, quiet, quietude, soundlessness, stillness; dumbness, mumness, muteness, reticence, speechlessness, taciturnity.

silent *adj* calm, hushed, noiseless, quiet, soundless, still; dumb, inarticulate, mum, mute, nonvocal, speechless, tacit; reticent, taciturn, uncommunicative.

silken *adj* flossy, silky, soft.

silkiness *n* smoothness, softness.

silly *adj* brainless, childish, foolish, inept, senseless, shallow, simple, stupid, weak-minded, witless; absurd, extravagant, frivolous, imprudent, indiscreet, nonsensical, preposterous, trifling, unwise. * *n* ass, duffer, goose, idiot, simpleton.

silt *n* alluvium, deposit, deposition, residue, settlement, settlings, sediment.

silver *adj* argent, silvery; bright, silvery, white; clear, mellifluous, soft.

similar *adj* analogous, duplicate, like, resembling, twin; homogeneous, uniform.

similarity *n* agreement, analogy, correspondence, likeness, parallelism, parity, resemblance, sameness, semblance, similitude.

simile *n* comparison, metaphor, similitude.

similitude *n* image, likeness, resemblance; comparison, metaphor, simile.

simmer *vb* boil, bubble, seethe, stew.

simper *vb* smile, smirk.

simple *adj* bare, elementary, homogeneous, incomplex, mere, single, unalloyed, unblended, uncombined, uncompounded, unmingled, unmixed; chaste, plain, homespun, inornate, natural, neat, unadorned, unaffected, unembellished, unpretentious, unstudied, unvarnished; artless, downright, frank, guileless, inartificial, ingenuous, naive, open, simple-hearted, simple-minded, sincere, single-minded, straightforward, true, unconstrained, undesigning, unsophisticated; credulous, fatuous, foolish, shallow, silly, unwise, weak; clear, intelligible, understandable, uninvolved, unmistakable.

simple-hearted *adj* artless, frank, ingenuous, open, simple, single-hearted.

simpleton *n* fool, greenhorn, nincompoop, ninny.

simplicity *n* chasteness, homeliness, naturalness, neatness, plainness; artlessness, frankness, naivety, openness, simplesse, sincerity; clearness; gullibility, folly, silliness, weakness.

simply *adv* artlessly, plainly, sincerely, unaffectedly; barely, merely, of itself, solely; absolutely, alone.

simulate *vb* act, affect, ape, assume, counterfeit, dissemble, feign, mimic, pretend, sham.

simulation *n* counterfeiting, feigning, personation, pretence.

simultaneous *adj* coeval, coincident, concomitant, concurrent, contemporaneous, synchronous.

sin *vb* do wrong, err, transgress, trespass. * *n* delinquency, depravity, guilt, iniquity, misdeed, offence, transgression, unrighteousness, wickedness, wrong.

since *conj* as, because, considering, seeing that. * *adv* ago, before this; from that time. * *prep* after, from the time of, subsequently to.

sincere *adj* pure, unmixed; genuine, honest, inartificial, real, true, unaffected, unfeigned, unvarnished; artless, candid, direct, frank, guileless, hearty, honest, ingenuous, open, plain, single, straightforward, truthful, undissembling, upright, whole-hearted.

sincerity *n* artlessness, candour, earnestness, frankness, genuineness, guilelessness, honesty, ingenuousness, probity, truth, truthfulness, unaffectedness, veracity.

sinew *n* ligament, tendon; brawn, muscle, nerve, strength.

sinewy *adj* able-bodied, brawny, firm, Herculean, muscular, nervous, powerful, robust, stalwart, strapping, strong, sturdy, vigorous, wiry.

sinful *adj* bad, criminal, depraved, immoral, iniquitous, mischievous, peccant, transgressive, unholy, unrighteous, wicked, wrong.

sinfulness *n* corruption, criminality, depravity, iniquity, irreligion, ungodliness, unholiness, unrighteousness, wickedness.

sing *vb* cantillate, carol, chant, hum, hymn, intone, lilt, troll, warble, yodel.

singe *vb* burn, scorch, sear.

singer *n* cantor, caroler, chanter, gleeman, prima donna, minstrel, psalmodist, songster, vocalist.

single *vb* (*with* out) choose, pick, select, single. * *adj* alone, isolated, one only, sole, solitary; individual, particular, separate; celibate, unmarried, unwedded; pure, simple, uncompounded, unmixed; honest, ingenuous, sincere, unbiased, uncorrupt, upright.

single-handed *adj* alone, by one's self, unaided, unassisted.

single-minded *adj* artless, candid, guileless, ingenuous, sincere.

singleness *n* individuality, unity; purity, simplicity; ingenuousness, integrity, sincerity, uprightness.

singular *adj* eminent, exceptional, extraordinary, rare, remarkable, strange, uncommon, unusual, unwonted; particular, unexampled, unparalleled, unprecedented; unaccountable; bizarre, curious, eccentric, fantastic, odd, peculiar, queer; individual, single; not complex, single, uncompounded, unique.

singularity *n* aberration, abnormality, irregularity, oddness, rareness, rarity, strangeness, uncommonness; characteristic, idiosyncrasy, individuality, particularity, peculiarity; eccentricity, oddity.

sinister *adj* baleful, injurious, untoward; boding ill, inauspicious, ominous, unlucky; left, on the left hand.

sink *vb* droop, drop, fall, founder, go down, submerge, subside; enter, penetrate; collapse, fail; decay, decline, decrease, dwindle, give way, languish, lose strength; engulf, immerse, merge, submerge, submerse; dig, excavate, scoop out; abase, bring down, crush, debase, degrade, depress, diminish, lessen, lower, overbear; destroy, overthrow, overwhelm, reduce, ruin, swamp, waste. * *n* basin, cloaca, drain.

sinless *adj* faultless, guiltless, immaculate, impeccable, innocent, spotless, unblemished, undefiled, unspotted, unsullied, untarnished.

sinner *n* criminal, delinquent, evildoer, offender, reprobate, wrongdoer.

sinuosity *n* crook, curvature, flexure, sinus, tortuosity, winding.

sinuous *adj* bending, crooked, curved, curvilinear, flexuous, serpentine, sinuate, sinuated, tortuous, undulating, wavy, winding.

sip *vb* drink, suck up, sup; absorb, drink in. * *n* small draught, taste.

sire *vb* father, reproduce; author, breed, conceive, create, generate, originate, produce, propagate. * *n* father, male parent, progenitor; man, male person; sir, sirrah; author, begetter, creator, father, generator, originator.

siren *adj* alluring, bewitching, fascinating, seducing, tempting. * *n* mermaid; charmer, Circe, seducer, seductress, tempter, temptress.

sit *vb* be, remain, repose, rest, stay; bear on, lie, rest; abide, dwell, settle; perch; brood, incubate; become, be suited, fit.

site *vb* locate, place, position, situate, station. * *n* ground, locality, location, place, position, seat, situation, spot, station, whereabouts.

sitting *n* meeting, session.

situation *n* ground, locality, location, place, position, seat, site, spot, whereabouts; case, category, circumstances, condition, juncture, plight, predicament, state; employment, office, place, post, station.

size *n* amplitude, bigness, bulk, dimensions, expanse, greatness, largeness, magnitude, mass, volume.

skeleton *n* framework; draft, outline, sketch.

sketch *vb* design, draft, draw out; delineate, depict, paint, portray, represent. * *n* delineation, design, draft, drawing, outline, plan, skeleton.

sketchy *adj* crude, incomplete, unfinished.

skilful *adj* able, accomplished, adept, adroit, apt, clever, competent, conversant, cunning, deft, dexterous, dextrous, expert, handy, ingenious, masterly, practised, proficient, qualified, quick, ready, skilled, trained, versed, well-versed.

skill *n* ability, address, adroitness, aptitude, aptness, art, cleverness, deftness, dexterity, expertise, expertness, facility, ingenuity, knack, quickness, readiness, skilfulness; discernment, discrimination, knowledge, understanding, wit.

skim *vb* brush, glance, graze, kiss, scrape, scratch, sweep, touch lightly; coast, flow, fly, glide, sail, scud, whisk; dip into, glance at, scan, skip, thumb over, touch upon.

skin *vb* pare, peel; decorticate, excoriate, flay. * *n* cuticle, cutis, derm, epidermis, hide, integument, pellicle, pelt; hull, husk, peel, rind.

skinflint *n* churl, curmudgeon, lickpenny, miser, niggard, scrimp.

skinny *adj* emaciated, lank, lean, poor, shrivelled, shrunk, thin.

skip *vb* bound, caper, frisk, gambol, hop, jump, leap, spring; disregard, intermit, miss, neglect, omit, pass over, skim. * *n* bound, caper, frisk, gambol, hop, jump, leap, spring.

skirmish *vb* battle, brush, collide, combat, contest, fight, scuffle, tussle. * *n* affair, affray, battle, brush, collision, combat, conflict, contest, encounter, fight, scuffle, tussle.

skirt *vb* border, bound, edge, fringe, hem, march, rim; circumnavigate, circumvent, flank, go along. * *n* border, boundary, edge, margin, rim, verge; flap, kilt, overskirt, petticoat.

skittish *adj* changeable, fickle, inconstant; hasty, volatile, wanton; shy, timid, timorous.

skulk *vb* hide, lurk, slink, sneak.

skulker *n* lurker, sneak; shirk, slacker, malingerer.

skull *n* brain pan, cranium.

sky *n* empyrean, firmament, heaven, heavens, welkin.

sky-blue *adj* azure, cerulean, sapphire, sky-coloured.

skylarking *n* carousing, frolicking, sporting.

slab *adj* slimy, thick, viscous. * *n* beam, board, layer, panel, plank, slat, table, tablet; mire, mud, puddle, slime.

slabber *vb* drivel, slaver, slobber; drop, let fall, shed, spill.

slack *vb* ease off, let up; abate, ease up, relax,

slacken; malinger, shirk; choke, damp, extinguish, smother, stifle. * adj backward, careless, inattentive, lax, negligent, remiss; abated, dilatory, diminished, lingering, slow, tardy; loose, relaxed; dull, idle, inactive, quiet, sluggish. * n excess, leeway, looseness, play; coal dust, culm, residue.

slacken vb abate, diminish, lessen, lower, mitigate, moderate, neglect, remit, relieve, retard, slack; loosen, relax; flag, slow down; bridle, check, control, curb, repress, restrain.

slackness n looseness; inattention, negligence, remissness; slowness, tardiness.

slander vb asperse, backbite, belie, brand, calumniate, decry, defame, libel, malign, reproach, scandalize, traduce, vilify; detract from, disparage. * n aspersion, backbiting, calumny, defamation, detraction, libel, obloquy, scandal, vilification.

slanderous adj calumnious, defamatory, false, libellous, malicious, maligning.

slang n argo, cant, jargon, lingo.

slant vb incline, lean, lie obliquely, list, slope. * n inclination, slope, steep, tilt.

slap vb dab, clap, pat, smack, spank, strike. * adv instantly, quickly, plumply. * n blow, clap.

slapdash adv haphazardly, hurriedly, precipitately.

slash vb cut, gash, slit. * n cut, gash, slit.

slashed adj cut, slit; (bot) jagged, laciniate, multifid.

slattern adj slatternly, slovenly, sluttish. * n drab, slut, sloven, trollop.

slatternly adj dirty, slattern, slovenly, sluttish, unclean, untidy. * adv carelessly, negligently, sluttishly.

slaughter vb butcher, kill, massacre, murder, slay. * n bloodshed, butchery, carnage, havoc, killing, massacre, murder, slaying.

slaughterer n assassin, butcher, cutthroat, destroyer, killer, murderer, slayer.

slave vb drudge, moil, toil. * n bondmaid, bondservant, bondslave, bondman, captive, dependant, henchman, helot, peon, serf, thrall, vassal, villein; drudge, menial.

slavery n bondage, bond-service, captivity, enslavement, enthralment, serfdom, servitude, thraldom, vassalage, villeinage; drudgery, mean labour.

slavish adj abject, beggarly, base, cringing, fawning, grovelling, low, mean, obsequious, servile, sycophantic; drudging, laborious, menial, servile.

slay vb assassinate, butcher, dispatch, kill, massacre, murder, slaughter; destroy, ruin.

slayer n assassin, destroyer, killer, murderer, slaughterer.

sledge n drag, sled; cutter, pung, sleigh.

sleek adj glossy, satin, silken, silky, smooth.

sleekly adv evenly, glossily, nicely, smoothly.

sleep vb catnap, doze, drowse, nap, slumber. * n dormancy, hypnosis, lethargy, repose, rest, slumber.

sleeping adj dormant, inactive, quiescent.

sleepwalker n night-walker, noctambulist, somnambulist.

sleepwalking n somnambulism.

sleepy adj comatose, dozy, drowsy, heavy, lethargic, nodding, somnolent; narcotic, opiate, slumberous, somniferous, somnific, soporiferous, soporific; dull, heavy, inactive, lazy, slow, sluggish, torpid.

sleight n adroitness, dexterity, manoeuvring.

sleight of hand n conjuring, hocus-pocus, jugglery, legerdemain, prestdigitation.

slender adj lank, lithe, narrow, skinny, slim, spindly, thin; feeble, fine, flimsy, fragile, slight, tenuous, weak; inconsiderable, moderate, small, trivial; exiguous, inadequate, insufficient, lean, meagre, pitiful, scanty; abstemious, light, simple, spare, sparing.

slice vb cut, divide, part, section; cut off, sever. * n chop, collop, piece.

slick adj glassy, glossy, polished, sleek, smooth; alert, clever, cunning, shrewd, slippery, unctuous. vb burnish, gloss, lacquer, polish, shine, sleek, varnish; grease, lubricate, oil.

slide vb glide, move smoothly, slip. * n glide, glissade, skid, slip.

sliding adj gliding, slippery, uncertain. * n backsliding, falling, fault, lapse, transgression.

slight vb cold-shoulder, disdain, disregard, neglect, snub; overlook; scamp, skimp, slur. * adj inconsiderable, insignificant, little, paltry, petty, small, trifling, trivial, unimportant, unsubstantial; delicate, feeble, frail, gentle, weak; careless, cursory, desultory, hasty, hurried, negligent, scanty, superficial; flimsy, perishable, slender, slim. * n discourtesy, disregard, disrespect, inattention, indignity, neglect.

slightingly adv contemptuously, disrespectfully, scornfully, slightly.

slightly adv inconsiderably, little, somewhat; feebly, slenderly, weakly; cursorily, hastily, negligently, superficially.

slim vb bant, diet, lose weight, reduce, slenderize. * adj gaunt, lank, lithe, narrow, skinny, slender, spare; inconsiderable, paltry, poor, slight, trifling, trivial, unsubstantial, weak; insufficient, meagre.

slime n mire, mud, ooze, sludge.

slimy adj miry, muddy, oozy; clammy, gelatinous, glutinous, gummy, lubricious, mucilaginous, mucous, ropy, slabby, viscid, viscous.

sling vb cast, fling, hurl, throw; hang up, suspend.

slink vb skulk, slip away, sneak, steal away.

slip vb glide, slide; err, mistake, trip; lose, omit; disengage, throw off; escape, let go, loose, loosen, release, . * n glide, slide, slipping; blunder, lapse, misstep, mistake, oversight, peccadillo, trip; backsliding, error, fault, impropriety, indiscretion, transgression; desertion, escape; cord, leash, strap, string; case, covering, wrapper.

slippery adj glib, slithery, smooth; changeable,

insecure, mutable, perilous, shaky, uncertain, unsafe, unstable, unsteady; cunning, dishonest, elusive, faithless, false, knavish, perfidious, shifty, treacherous.

slipshod *adj* careless, shuffling, slovenly, untidy.

slit *vb* cut; divide, rend, slash, split, sunder. * *n* cut, gash.

slobber *vb* drivel, drool, slabber, slaver; daub, obscure, smear, stain.

slobbery *adj* dank, floody, moist, muddy, sloppy, wet.

slope *vb* incline, slant, tilt. * *n* acclivity, cant, declivity, glacis, grade, gradient, incline, inclination, obliquity, pitch, ramp.

sloping *adj* aslant, bevelled, declivitous, inclining, oblique, shelving, slanting.

sloppy *adj* muddy, plashy, slabby, slobbery, splashy, wet.

sloth *n* dilatoriness, slowness, tardiness; idleness, inaction, inactivity, indolence, inertness, laziness, lumpishness, slothfulness, sluggishness, supineness, torpor.

slothful *adj* dronish, idle, inactive, indolent, inert, lazy, lumpish, slack, sluggish, supine, torpid.

slouch *vb* droop, loll, slump; shamble, shuffle. * *n* malingerer, shirker, slacker; shamble, shuffle, stoop.

slouching *adj* awkward, clownish, loutish, lubberly, uncouth, ungainly.

slough[1] *n* bog, fen, marsh, morass, quagmire; dejection, depression, despondence, despondency.

slough[2] *vb* cast, desquamate, excuviate, moult, shed, throw off; cast off, discard, divest, jettison, reject. * *n* cast, desquamation.

sloven *n* slattern, slob, slouch, slut.

slovenly *adj* unclean, untidy; blowsy, disorderly, dowdy, frowsy, loose, slatternly, tacky, unkempt, untidy; careless, heedless, lazy, negligent, perfunctory.

slow *vb* abate, brake, check, decelerate, diminish, lessen, mitigate, moderate, modulate, reduce, weaken; delay, detain, retard; ease, ease up, relax, slack, slacken, slack off. * *adj* deliberate, gradual; dead, dull, heavy, inactive, inert, sluggish, stupid; behindhand, late, tardy, unready; delaying, dilatory, lingering, slack.

sludge *n* mire, mud; slosh, slush.

sluggard *n* dawdler, drone, idler, laggard, lounger, slug.

sluggish *adj* dronish, drowsy, idle, inactive, indolent, inert, languid, lazy, listless, lumpish, phlegmatic, slothful, torpid; slow; dull, stupid, supine, tame.

sluice *vb* drain, drench, flood, flush, irrigate. * *n* floodgate, opening, vent.

slumber *vb* catnap, doze, nap, repose, rest, sleep. * *n* catnap, doze, nap, repose, rest, siesta, sleep.

slumberous *adj* drowsy, sleepy, somniferous, somnific, soporific.

slump *vb* droop, drop, fall, flop, founder, sag, sink, sink down; decline, depreciate, deteriorate, ebb,

fail, fall away, lose ground, recede, slide, slip, subside, wane. * *n* droop, drop, fall, flop, lowering, sag, sinkage; decline, depreciation, deterioration, downturn, downtrend, subsidence, ebb, falling off, wane; crash, recession, smash.

slur *vb* asperse, calumniate, disparage, depreciate, reproach, traduce; conceal, disregard, gloss over, obscure, pass over, slight. * *n* mark, stain; brand, disgrace, reproach, stain, stigma; innuendo.

slush *n* slosh, sludge.

slushy *vb* plashy, sloppy, sloshy, sludgy.

slut *n* drab, slattern, sloven, trollop.

sluttish *adj* careless, dirty, disorderly, unclean, untidy.

sly *adj* artful, crafty, cunning, insidious, subtle, wily; astute, cautious, shrewd; arch, knowing, clandestine, secret, stealthy, underhand.

smack[1] *vb* smell, taste. * *n* flavour, savour, tang, taste, tincture; dash, infusion, little, space, soupçon, sprinkling, tinge, touch; smattering.

smack[2] *vb* slap, strike; crack, slash, snap; buss, kiss. * *n* crack, slap, slash, snap; buss, kiss.

small *adj* diminutive, Lilliputian, little, miniature, petite, pygmy, tiny, wee; infinitesimal, microscopic, minute; inappreciable, inconsiderable, insignificant, petty, trifling, trivial, unimportant; moderate, paltry, scanty, slender; faint, feeble, puny, slight, weak; illiberal, mean, narrow, narrow-minded, paltry, selfish, sorded, ungenerous, unworthy.

small talk *n* chat, conversation, gossip.

smart[1] *vb* hurt, pain, sting; suffer. * *adj* keen, painful, poignant, pricking, pungent, severe, sharp, stinging.

smart[2] *adj* active, agile, brisk, fresh, lively, nimble, quick, spirited, sprightly, spry; effective, efficient, energetic, forcible, vigorous; adroit, alert, clever, dexterous, dextrous, expert, intelligent, stirring; acute, apt, pertinent, ready, witty; chic, dapper, fine, natty, showy, spruce, trim.

smartness *n* acuteness, keenness, poignancy, pungency, severity, sharpness; efficiency, energy, force, vigour; activity, agility, briskness, liveliness, nimbleness, sprightliness, spryness, vivacity; alertness, cleverness, dexterity, expertise, expertness, intelligence, quickness; acuteness, aptness, pertinency, wit, wittiness; chic, nattiness, spruceness, trimness.

smash *vb* break, crush, dash, mash, shatter. * *n* crash, debacle, destruction, ruin; bankruptcy, failure.

smattering *n* dabbling, smatter, sprinkling.

smear *vb* bedaub, begrime, besmear, daub, plaster, smudge; contaminate, pollute, smirch, smut, soil, stain, sully, tarnish. * *n* blot, blotch, daub, patch, smirch, smudge, spot, stain; calumny, defamation, libel, slander.

smell *vb* scent, sniff, stench, stink. * *n* aroma, bouquet, fragrance, fume, odour, perfume, redolence, scent, stench, stink; sniff, snuff.

smelt *vb* fuse, melt.

smile vb grin, laugh, simper, smirk. * n grin, simper, smirk.

smite vb beat, box, collide, cuff, knock, strike, wallop, whack; destroy, kill, slay; afflict, chasten, punish; blast, destroy.

smitten adj attracted, captivated, charmed, enamoured, fascinated, taken; destroyed, killed, slain; smit, struck; afflicted, chastened, punished.

smock n chemise, shift, slip; blouse, gaberdine.

smoke vb emit, exhale, reek, steam; fumigate, smudge; discover, find out, smell out. * n effluvium, exhalation, fume, mist, reek, smother, steam, vapour; fumigation, smudge.

smoky adj fuliginous, fumid, fumy, smudgy; begrimed, blackened, dark, reeky, sooty, tanned.

smooth vb flatten, level, plane; ease, lubricate; extenuate, palliate, soften; allay, alleviate, assuage, calm, mitigate, mollify. * adj even, flat, level, plane, polished, unruffled, unwrinkled; glabrous, glossy, satiny, silky, sleek, soft, velvet; euphonious, flowing, liquid, mellifluent; fluent, glib, voluble; bland, flattering, ingratiating, insinuating, mild, oily, smooth-tongued, soothing, suave, unctuous.

smoothly adv evenly; easily, readily, unobstructedly; blandly, flatteringly, gently, mildly, pleasantly, softly, soothingly.

smooth-tongued adj adulatory, cozening, flattering, plausible, smooth, smooth-spoken.

smother vb choke, stifle, suffocate; conceal, deaden, extinguish, hide, keep down, repress, suppress; smoke, smoulder.

smudge vb besmear, blacken, blur, smear, smut, smutch, soil, spot, stain. * n blur, blot, smear, smut, spot, stain.

smug adj complacent, self-satisfied; neat, nice, spruce, trim.

smuggler n contrabandist, runner.

smut vb blacken, smouch, smudge, soil, stain, sully, taint, tarnish. * n dirt, smudge, smutch, soot; nastiness, obscenity, ribaldry, smuttiness; pornography.

smutty adj coarse, gross, immodest, impure, indecent, indelicate, loose, nasty; dirty, foul, nasty, soiled, stained.

snack n bite, light meal, nibble.

snag vb catch, enmesh, entangle, hook, snare, sniggle, tangle. * n knarl, knob, knot, projection, protuberance, snub; catch, difficulty, drawback, hitch, rub, shortcoming, weakness; obstacle.

snaky adj serpentine, snaking, winding; artful, cunning, deceitful, insinuating, sly, subtle.

snap vb break, fracture; bite, catch at, seize, snatch at, snip; crack; crackle, crepitate, decrepitate, pop. * adj casual, cursory, hasty, offhand, sudden, superficial. * n bite, catch, nip, seizure; catch, clasp, fastening, lock; crack, fillip, flick, flip, smack; briskness, energy, verve, vim.

snappish adj acrimonious, captious, churlish, crabbed, cross, crusty, froward, irascible, ill-tempered, peevish, perverse, pettish, petulant, snarl-

ing, splenetic, surly, tart, testy, touchy, waspish.

snare vb catch, ensnare, entangle, entrap. * n catch, gin, net, noose, springe, toil, trap, wile.

snarl¹ vb girn, gnarl, growl, grumble, murmur. * n growl, grumble.

snarl² vb complicate, disorder, entangle, knot; confuse, embarrass, ensnare. * n complication, disorder, entanglement, tangle; difficulty, embarrassment, intricacy.

snatch vb catch, clutch, grasp, grip, pluck, pull, seize, snip, twich, wrest, wring. * n bit, fragment, part, portion; catch, effort.

sneak vb lurk, skulk, slink, steal; crouch, truckle. * adj clandestine, concealed, covert, hidden, secret, sly, underhand. * n informer, telltale; lurker, shirk.

sneaky adj furtive, skulking, slinking; abject, crouching, grovelling, mean; clandestine, concealed, covert, hidden, secret, sly, underhand.

sneer vb flout, gibe, jeer, mock, rail, scoff; (with at) deride, despise, disdain, laugh at, mock, rail at, scoff, spurn. * n flouting, gibe, jeer, scoff.

snicker vb giggle, laugh, snigger, titter.

sniff vb breathe, inhale, snuff; scent, smell.

snip vb clip, cut, nip; snap, snatch. * n bit, fragment, particle, piece, shred; share, snack.

snivel vb blubber, cry, fret, sniffle, snuffle, weep, whimper, whine.

snively adj snotty; pitiful, whining.

snob n climber, toady.

snooze vb catnap, doze, drowse, nap, sleep, slumber. * n catnap, nap, sleep, slumber.

snout n muzzle, nose; nozzle.

snowy adj immaculate, pure, spotless, unblemished, unstained, unsullied, white.

snub¹ vb abash, cold-shoulder, cut, discomfit, humble, humiliate, mortify, slight, take down. * n check, rebuke, slight.

snub² vb check, clip, cut short, dock, nip, prune, stunt. * adj pug, retroussé, snubbed, squashed, squat, stubby, turned-up.

snuff¹ vb breathe, inhale, sniff; scent, smell; snort.

snuff² vb (with out) annihilate, destroy, efface, extinguish, obliterate.

snuffle vb sniffle; snort, snuff.

snug adj close, concealed; comfortable, compact, convenient, neat, trim.

snuggle vb cuddle, nestle, nuzzle.

so adv thus, with equal reason; in such a manner; in this way, likewise; as it is, as it was, such; for this reason, therefore; be it so, thus be it. * conj in case that, on condition that, provided that.

soak vb drench, moisten, permeate, saturate, wet; absorb, imbibe; imbue, macerate, steep.

soar vb ascend, fly aloft, glide, mount, rise, tower.

sob vb cry, sigh convulsively, weep.

sober vb (with up) calm down, collect oneself, compose oneself, control oneself, cool off, master, moderate, simmer down. * adj abstemious, abstinent, temperate, unintoxicated; rational, reasonable, sane, sound; calm, collected, composed, cool, dispassionate, moderate, rational, reasonabler, regular, restrained, steady, temperate, unimpassioned, unruffled, well-regulated; demure, grave, quiet, sedate, serious, solemn, sombre, staid; dark, drab, dull-looking, quiet, sad, subdued.

sobriety *n* abstemiousness, abstinence, soberness, temperance; calmness, coolness, gravity, sedateness, sober-mindedness, staidness, thoughtfulness; gravity, seriousness, solemnity.

sobriquet *n* appellation, nickname, nom de plume, pseudonym.

sociability *n* companionableness, comradeship, good fellowship, sociality.

sociable *adj* accessible, affable, communicative, companionable, conversable, friendly, genial, neighbourly, social.

social *adj* civic, civil; accessible, affable, communicative, companionable, familiar, friendly, hospitable, neighbourly, sociable; convivial, festive, gregarious. * *n* conversazione, gathering, get-together, party, reception, soiree.

society *n* association, companionship, company, converse, fellowship; the community, populace, the public, the world; élite, *monde*; body, brotherhood, copartnership, corporation, club, fraternity, partnersnip, sodality, union.

sodden *adj* drenched, saturated, soaked, steeped, wet; boiled, decocted, seethed, stewed.

sofa *n* couch, davenport, divan, ottoman, settee.

soft *adj* impressible, malleable, plastic, pliable, yielding; downy, fleecy, velvety, mushy, pulpy, squashy; compliant, facile, irresolute, submissive, undecided, weak; bland, mild, gentle, kind, lenient, soft-hearted, tender; delicate; easy, even, quiet, smooth-going, steady; effeminate, luxurious, unmanly; dulcet, fluty, mellifluous, melodious, smooth. * *interj* hold, stop.

soften *vb* intenerate, mellow, melt, tenderize; abate, allay, alleviate, appease, assuage, attemper, balm, blunt, calm, dull, ease, lessen, make easy, mitigate, moderate, mollify, milden, qualify, quell, quiet, relent, relieve, soothe, still, temper; extenuate, modify, palliate, qualify; enervate, weaken.

soil[1] *n* earth, ground loam, mould; country, land.

soil[2] *vb* bedaub, begrime, bemire, besmear, bespatter, contaminate, daub, defile, dirty, foul, pollute, smirch, stain, sully, taint, tarnish. * *n* blemish, defilement, dirt, filth, foulness; blot, spot, stain, taint, tarnish.

sojourn *vb* abide, dwell, live, lodge, remain, reside, rest, stay, stop, tarry, visit. * *n* residence, stay.

solace *vb* cheer, comfort, console, soothe; allay, assuage, mitigate, relieve, soften. * *n* alleviation, cheer, comfort, consolation, relief.

soldier *n* fighting man, man-at-arms, warrior; GI, private.

soldierly *adj* martial, military, warlike; brave, courageous, gallant, heroic, honourable, intrepid, valiant.

sole *adj* alone, individual, one, only, single, solitary, unique.

solecism *n* barbarism, blunder, error, faux pas, impropriety, incongruity, mistake, slip.

solemn *adj* ceremonial, formal, ritual; devotional, devout, religious, reverential, sacred; earnest, grave, serious, sober; august, awe-inspiring, awful, grand, imposing, impressive, majestic, stately, venerable.

solemnity *n* celebration, ceremony, observance, office, rite; awfulness, sacredness, sanctity; gravity, impressiveness, seriousness.

solemnize *vb* celebrate, commemorate, honour, keep, observe.

solicit *vb* appeal to, ask, beg, beseech, conjure, crave, entreat, implore, importune, petition, pray, press, request, supplicate, urge; arouse, awaken, entice, excite, invite, summon; canvass, seek.

solicitation *n* address, appeal, asking, entreaty, imploration, importunity, insistence, petition, request, suit, supplication, urgency; bidding, call, invitation, summons.

solicitor *n* attorney, law agent, lawyer; asker, canvasser, drummer, petitioner, solicitant.

solicitous *adj* anxious, apprehensive, careful, concerned, disturbed, eager, troubled, uneasy.

solicitude *n* anxiety, care, carefulness, concern, perplexity, trouble.

solid *adj* congealed, firm, hard, impenetrable, rock-like; compact, dense, impermeable, massed; cubic; sound, stable, stout, strong, substantial; just, real, true, valid, weighty; dependable, faithful, reliable, safe, staunch, steadfast, trustworthy, well established.

solidarity *n* communion of interests, community, consolidation, fellowship, joint interest, mutual responsibility.

solidify *vb* compact, congeal, consolidate, harden, petrify.

solidity *n* compactness, consistency, density, firmness, hardness, solidness; fullness; massiveness, stability, strength; dependability, gravity, justice, reliability, soundness, steadiness, validity, weight; cubic content, volume.

soliloquy *n* monologue.

solitariness *n* isolation, privacy, reclusion, retirement, seclusion; loneliness, solitude.

solitary *adj* alone, companionless, lone, lonely, only, separate, unaccompanied; individual, single, sole; desert, deserted, desolate, isolated, lonely, remote, retired, secluded, unfrequented.

solitude *n* isolation, loneliness, privacy, recluseness, retiredness, retirement, seclusion, solitariness; desert, waste, wilderness.

solution *n* answer, clue, disentanglement, elucidation, explication, explanation, key, resolution, unravelling, unriddling; disintegration, dissolution, liquefaction, melting, resolution, separation; breach, disconnection, discontinuance, disjunction, disruption.

solve *vb* clear, clear up, disentangle, elucidate, explain, expound, interpret, make plain, resolve, unfold.

solvent *n* diluent, dissolvent, menstruum.

somatic *adj* bodily, corporeal.

sombre *adj* cloudy, dark, dismal, dull, dusky, gloomy, murky, overcast, rayless, shady, sombrous, sunless; doleful, funereal, grave, lugubrious, melancholy, mournful, sad, sober.

some *adj* a, an, any, one; about, near; certain, little, moderate, part, several.

somebody *n* one, someone, something; celebrity, VIP.

somehow *adv* in some way.

something *n* part, portion, thing; somebody; affair, event, matter.

sometime *adj* former, late. * *adv* formerly, once; now and then, at one time or other, sometimes.

sometimes *adv* at intervals, at times, now and then, occasionally; at a past period, formerly, once.

somewhat *adv* in some degree, more or less, rather, something. * *n* something, a little, more or less, part.

somewhere *adv* here and there, in one place or another, in some place.

somnambulism *n* sleepwalking, somnambulation.

somnambulist *n* night-walker, noctambulist, sleepwalker, somnambulator, somnambule.

somniferous *adj* narcotic, opiate, slumberous, somnific, soporific, soporiferous.

somnolence *n* doziness, drowsiness, sleepiness, somnolency.

somnolent *adj* dozy, drowsy, sleepy.

son *n* cadet, heir, junior, scion.

song *n* aria, ballad, canticle, canzonet, carol, ditty, glee, lay, lullaby, snatch; descant, melody; anthem, hymn, poem, psalm, strain; poesy, poetry, verse.

sonorous *adj* full-toned, resonant, resounding, ringing, sounding; high-sounding, loud.

soon *adv* anon, before long, by and by, in a short time, presently, shortly; betimes, early, forthwith, promptly, quick; gladly, lief, readily, willingly.

soot *n* carbon, crock, dust.

soothe *vb* cajole, flatter, humour; appease, assuage, balm, calm, compose, lull, mollify, pacify, quiet, soften, still, tranquillize; allay, alleviate, blunt, check, deaden, dull, ease, lessen, mitigate, moderate, palliate, qualify, relieve, repress, soften, subdue, temper.

soothsayer *n* augur, diviner, foreteller, necromancer, predictor, prophet, seer, sorcerer, vaticinator.

sooty *adj* black, dark, dusky, fuliginous, murky, sable.

sophism *n* casuistry, fallacy, paralogism, paralogy, quibble, specious argument.

sophist *n* quibbler.

sophistical *adj* casuistical, fallacious, illogical, quibbling, subtle, unsound.

soporific *adj* dormitive, hypnotic, narcotic, opiate,

sleepy, slumberous, somnific, somniferous, soporiferous, soporous.

soppy *adj* drenched, saturated, soaked, sopped; emotional, mawkish, sentimental.

soprano *n* (*mus*) descant, discant, treble.

sorcerer *n* charmer, conjurer, diviner, enchanter, juggler, magician, necromancers, seer, shaman, soothsayer, thaumaturgist, wizard.

sorcery *n* black art, charm, divination, enchantment, necromancy, occultism, shamanism, spell, thaumaturgy, voodoo, witchcraft.

sordid *adj* base, degraded, low, mean, vile; avaricious, close-fisted, covetous, illiberal, miserly, niggardly, penurious, stingy, ungenerous.

sore *adj* irritated, painful, raw, tender, ulcerated; aggrieved, galled, grieved, hurt, irritable, vexed; afflictive, distressing, severe, sharp, violent. * *n* abscess, boil, fester, gathering, imposthume, pustule, ulcer; affliction, grief, pain, sorrow, trouble.

sorely *adv* greatly, grievously, severely, violently.

sorrily *adv* despicably, meanly, pitiably, poorly, wretchedly.

sorrow *vb* bemoan, bewail, grieve, lament, mourn, weep. * *n* affliction, dolour, grief, heartache, mourning, sadness, trouble, woe.

sorrowful *adj* afflicted, dejected, depressed, grieved, grieving, heartsore, sad; baleful, distressing, grievous, lamentable, melancholy, mournful, painful; disconsolate, dismal, doleful, dolorous, drear, dreary, lugubrious, melancholy, piteous, rueful, woebegone, woeful.

sorry *adj* afflicted, dejected, grieved, pained, poor, sorrowful; distressing, pitiful; chagrined, mortified, pained, regretful, remorseful, sad, vexed; abject, base, beggarly, contemptible, despicable, low, mean, paltry, insignificant, miserable, shabby, worthless, wretched.

sort *vb* arrange, assort, class, classify, distribute, order; conjoin, join, put together; choose, elect, pick out, select; associate, consort, fraternize; accord, agree with, fit, suit. * *n* character, class, denomination, description, kind, nature, order, race, rank, species, type; manner, way.

sortie *n* attack, foray, raid, sally.

so-so *adj* indifferent, mediocre, middling, ordinary, passable, tolerable.

sot *n* blockhead, dolt, dullard, dunce, fool, simpleton; drunkard, tippler, toper.

sottish *adj* doltish, dull, foolish, senseless, simple, stupid; befuddled, besotted, drunken, insensate, senseless, tipsy.

sotto voce *adv* in a low voice, in an undertone, softly.

sough *n* murmur, sigh; breath, breeze, waft.

soul *n* mind, psyche, spirit; being, person; embodiment, essence, personification, spirit, vital principle; ardour, energy, fervour, inspiration, vitality.

soulless *adj* dead, expressionless, lifeless, unfeeling.

sound[1] *adj* entire, intact, unbroken, unhurt,

unimpaired, uninjured, unmutilated, whole; hale, hardy, healthy, hearty, vigorous; good, perfect, undecayed; sane, well-balanced; correct, orthodox, right, solid, valid, well-founded; legal; deep, fast, profound, unbroken, undisturbed; forcible, lusty, severe, stout.

sound² *n* channel, narrows, strait.

sound³ *vb* resound; appear, seem; play on; express, pronounce, utter; announce, celebrate, proclaim, publish, spread. * *n* noise, note, tone, voice, whisper.

sound⁴ *vb* fathom, gauge, measure, test; examine, probe, search, test, try.

sounding *adj* audible, resonant, resounding, ringing, sonorous; imposing, significant.

soundless *adj* dumb, noiseless, silent; abysmal, bottomless, deep, profound, unfathomable, unsounded.

soundly *adv* satisfactorily, thoroughly, well; healthily, heartily; forcibly, lustily, severely, smartly, stoutly; correctly, rightly, truly; firmly, strongly; deeply, fast, profoundly.

soundness *n* entireness, entirety, integrity, wholeness; healthiness, vigour, saneness, sanity; correctness, orthodoxy, rectitude, reliability, truth, validity; firmness, solidity, strength, validity.

soup *n* broth, consommé, purée.

sour *vb* acidulate; embitter, envenom. * *adj* acetose, acetous, acid, astringent, pricked, sharp, tart, vinegary; acrimonious, crabbed, cross, crusty, fretful, glum, ill-humoured, ill-natured, ill-tempered, peevish, pettish, petulant, snarling, surly; bitter, disagreeable, unpleasant; austere, dismal, gloomy, morose, sad, sullen; bad, coagulated, curdled, musty, rancid, turned.

source *n* beginning, fountain, fountainhead, head, origin, rise, root, spring, well; cause, original.

sourness *n* acidity, sharpness, tartness; acrimony, asperity, churlishness, crabbedness, crossness, discontent, harshness, moroseness, peevishness.

souse *vb* pickle; dip, douse, immerse, plunge, submerge.

souvenir *n* keepsake, memento, remembrance, reminder.

sovereign *adj* imperial, monarchical, princely, regal, royal, supreme; chief, commanding, excellent, highest, paramount, predominant, principal, supreme, utmost; efficacious, effectual. * *n* autocrat, monarch, suzerain; emperor, empress, king, lord, potentate, prince, princess, queen, ruler.

sovereignty *n* authority, dominion, empire, power, rule, supremacy, sway.

sow *vb* scatter, spread, strew; disperse, disseminate, propagate, spread abroad; plant; besprinkle, scatter.

space *n* expanse, expansion, extension, extent, proportions, spread; accommodation, capacity, room, place; distance, interspace, interval.

spacious *adj* extended, extensive, vast, wide; ample, broad, capacious, commodious, large, roomy, wide.

span *vb* compass, cross, encompass, measure, overlay. * *n* brief period, spell; pair, team, yoke.

spank *vb* slap, strike.

spar¹ *n* beam, boom, pole, sprit, yard.

spar² *vb* box, fight; argue, bicker, contend, dispute, quarrel, spat, squabble, wrangle.

spare *vb* lay aside, lay by, reserve, save, set apart, set aside; dispense with, do without, part with; forbear, omit, refrain, withhold; exempt, forgive, keep from; afford, allow, give, grant; save; economize, pinch. * *adj* frugal, scanty, sparing, stinted; chary, parsimonious; emaciated, gaunt, lank, lean, meagre, poor, thin, scraggy, skinny, raw-boned; additional, extra, supernumerary.

sparing *adj* little, scanty, scarce; abstemious, meagre, spare; chary, economical, frugal, parsimonious, saving; compassionate, forgiving, lenient, merciful.

spark *vb* scintillate, sparkle; begin, fire, incite, instigate, kindle, light, set off, start, touch off, trigger. * *n* scintilla, scintillation, sparkle; beginning, element, germ, seed.

sparkle *vb* coruscate, flash, gleam, glisten, glister, glitter, radiate, scintillate, shine, twinkle; bubble, effervesce, foam, froth. * *n* glint, scintillation, spark; luminosity, lustre.

sparkling *adj* brilliant, flashing, glistening, glittering, glittery, twinkling; bubbling, effervescing, eloquent, foaming, frothing, mantling; brilliant, glowing, lively, nervous, piquant, racy, spirited, sprightly, witty.

sparse *adj* dispersed, infrequent, scanty, scattered, sporadic, thin.

spartan *adj* bold, brave, chivalric, courageous, daring, dauntless, doughty, fearless, hardy, heroic, intrepid, lion-hearted, undaunted, valiant, valorous; austere, exacting, hard, severe, tough, unsparing; enduring, long-suffering, self-controlled, stoic.

spasm *n* contraction, cramp, crick, twitch; fit, paroxysm, seizure, throe.

spasmodic *adj* erratic, fitful, intermittent, irregular, sporadic; convulsive, paroxysmal, spasmodical, violent.

spat *vb* argue, bicker, dispute, jangle, quarrel, spar, squabble, wrangle.

spatter *vb* bespatter, besprinkle, plash, splash, sprinkle; spit, sputter.

spawn *vb* bring forth, generate, produce. * *n* eggs, roe; fruit, offspring, product.

speak *vb* articulate, deliver, enunciate, express, pronounce, utter; announce, confer, declare, disclose, mention, say, tell; celebrate, make known, proclaim, speak abroad; accost, address, greet, hail; exhibit; argue, converse, dispute, talk; declaim, discourse, hold forth, harangue, orate, plead, spout, treat.

speaker *n* discourse, elocutionist, orator, prolocutor, spokesman; chairman, presiding officer.

speaking *adj* rhetorical, talking; eloquent, expressive; lifelike. * *n* discourse, talk, utterance; declamation, elocution, oratory.

spear *n* dart, gaff, harpoon, javelin, lance, pike; shoot, spire.

special *adj* specific, specifical; especial, individual, particular, peculiar, unique; exceptional, extraordinary, marked, particular, uncommon; appropriate, express.

speciality, specialty *n* particularity; feature, forte, pet subject.

species *n* assemblage, class, collection, group; description, kind, sort, variety; (*law*) fashion, figure, form, shape.

specific *adj* characteristic, especial, particular, peculiar; definite, limited, precise, specified.

specification *n* characterization, designation; details, particularization.

specify *vb* define, designate, detail, indicate, individualize, name, show, particularize.

specimen *n* copy, example, model, pattern, sample.

specious *adj* manifest, obvious, open, showy; flimsy, illusory, ostensible, plausible, sophistical.

speck *n* blemish, blot, flaw, speckle, spot, stain; atom, bit, corpuscle, mite, mote, particle, scintilla.

spectacle *n* display, exhibition, pageant, parade, representation, review, scene, show, sight; curiosity, marvel, phenomenon, wonder.

spectacles *npl* glasses, goggles, shades.

spectator *n* beholder, bystander, observer, onlooker, witness.

spectral *adj* eerie, ghostlike, ghostly, phantomlike, shadowy, spooky, weird, wraithlike.

spectre, specter *n* apparition, banshee, ghost, goblin, hobgoblin, phantom, shade, shadow, spirit, sprite, wraith.

spectrum *n* appearance, image, representation.

speculate *vb* cogitate, conjecture, contemplate, imagine, meditate, muse, ponder, reflect, ruminate, theorize, think; bet, gamble, hazard, risk, trade, venture.

speculation *n* contemplation, intellectualization; conjecture, hypothesis, scheme, supposition, reasoning, reflection, theory, view.

speculative *adj* contemplative, philosophical, speculatory, unpractical; ideal, imaginary, theoretical; hazardous, risky, unsecured.

speculator *n* speculatist, theorist, theorizer; adventurer, dealer, gambler, trader.

speech *n* articulation, language, words; dialect, idiom, locution, tongue; conversation, oral communication, parlance, talk, verbal intercourse; mention, observation, remark, saying; address, declaration, discourse, harangue, oration, palaver.

speechless *adj* dumb, gagged, inarticulate, mute, silent; dazed, dumbfounded, flabbergasted, shocked.

speed *vb* hasten, hurry, rush, scurry; flourish, prosper, succeed, thrive; accelerate, expedite, hasten, hurry, quicken, press forward, urge on; carry through, dispatch, execute; advance, aid, assist, help; favour. * *n* acceleration, celerity, dispatch, expedition, fleetness, haste, hurry, quickness, rapidity, swiftness, velocity; good fortune, good luck, prosperity, success; impetuosity.

speedy *adj* fast, fleet, flying, hasty, hurried, hurrying, nimble, quick, rapid, swift; expeditious, prompt, quick; approaching, early, near.

spell[1] *n* charm, exorcism, hoodoo, incantation, jinx, witchery; allure, bewitchment, captivation, enchantment, entrancement, fascination.

spell[2] *vb* decipher, interpret, read, unfold, unravel, unriddle.

spell[3] *n* fit, interval, period, round, season, stint, term, turn.

spellbound *adj* bewitched, charmed, enchanted, entranced, enthralled, fascinated.

spend *vb* disburse, dispose of, expend, lay out, part with; consume, dissipate, exhaust, lavish, squander, use up, wear, waste; apply, bestow, devote, employ, pass.

spendthrift *n* prodigal, spender, squanderer, waster.

spent *adj* exhausted, fatigued, played out, used up, wearied, worn out.

spew *vb* cast up, puke, throw up, vomit; cast forth, eject.

spheral *adj* complete, perfect, symmetrical.

sphere *n* ball, globe, orb, spheroid; ambit, beat, bound, circle, circuit, compass, department, function, office, orbit, province, range, walk; order, rank, standing; country, domain, quarter, realm, region.

spherical *adj* bulbous, globated, globous, globular, orbicular, rotund, round, spheroid; planetary.

spice *n* flavour, flavouring, relish, savour, taste; admixture, dash, grain, infusion, particle, smack, soupçon, sprinkling, tincture.

spicily *adv* pungently, wittily.

spicy *adj* aromatic, balmy, fragrant; keen, piquant, pointed, pungent, sharp; indelicate, off-colour, racy, risqué, sensational, suggestive.

spill *vb* effuse, pour out, shed. * *n* accident, fall, tumble.

spin *vb* twist; draw out, extend; lengthen, prolong, protract, spend; pirouette, turn, twirl, whirl. * *n* drive, joyride, ride; autorotation, gyration, loop, revolution, rotation, turning, wheeling; pirouette, reel, turn, wheel, whirl.

spindle *n* axis, shaft.

spine *n* barb, prickle, thorn; backbone; ridge.

spinose *adj* briery, spinous, spiny, thorny.

spiny *adj* briery, prickly, spinose, spinous, thorny; difficult, perplexed, troublesome.

spiracle *n* aperture, blowhole, orifice, pore, vent.

spiral *adj* cochlear, cochleated, curled, helical, screw-shaped, spiry, winding. * *n* helix, winding, worm.

spire *n* curl, spiral, twist, wreath; steeple; blade, shoot, spear, stalk; apex, summit.

spirit *vb* animate, encourage, excite, inspirit; carry

off, kidnap. * *n* immaterial substance, life, vital essence; person, soul; angel, apparition, demon, elf, fairy, genius, ghost, phantom, shade, spectre, sprite; disposition, frame of mind, humour, mood, temper; spirits; ardour, cheerfulness, courage, earnestness, energy, enterprise, enthusiasm, fire, force, mettle, resolution, vigour, vim, vivacity, zeal; animation, cheerfulness, enterprise, esprit, glow, liveliness, piquancy, spice, spunk, vivacity, warmth; drift, gist, intent, meaning, purport, sense, significance, tenor; character, characteristic, complexion, essence, nature, quality, quintessence; alcohol, liquor; (*with* **the**) Comforter, Holy Ghost, Paraclete.

spirited *adj* active, alert, animated, ardent, bold, brisk, courageous, earnest, frisky, high-mettled, high-spirited, high-strung, lively, mettlesome, sprightly, vivacious.

spiritless *adj* breathless, dead, extinct, lifeless; dejected, depressed, discouraged, dispirited, low-spirited; apathetic, cold, dull, feeble, languid, phlegmatic, sluggish, soulless, torpid, unenterprising; dull, frigid, heavy, insipid, prosaic, prosy, stupid, tame, uninteresting.

spiritual *adj* ethereal, ghostly, immaterial incorporeal, psychical, supersensible; ideal, moral, unwordly; divine, holy, pure, sacred; ecclesiastical.

spiritualize *vb* elevate, etherealize, purify, refine.

spirituous *adj* alcoholic, ardent, spiritous.

spit[1] *vb* impale, thrust through, transfix.

spit[2] *vb* eject, throw out; drivel, drool, expectorate, salivate, slobber, spawl, splutter. * *n* saliva, spawl, spittle, sputum.

spite *vb* injure, mortify, thwart; annoy, offend, vex. * *n* grudge, hate, hatred, ill-nature, ill-will, malevolence, malice, maliciousness, malignity, pique, rancour, spleen, venom, vindictiveness.

spiteful *adj* evil-minded, hateful, ill-disposed, ill-natured, malevolent, malicious, malign, malignant, rancorous.

spittoon *n* cuspidor.

splash *vb* dabble, dash, plash, spatter, splurge, swash, swish. * *n* blot, daub, spot.

splay *adj* broad, spreading out, turned out, wide.

spleen *n* anger, animosity, chagrin, gall, grudge, hatred, ill-humour, irascibility, malevolence, malice, malignity, peevishness, pique, rancour, spite.

spleeny *adj* angry, fretful, ill-tempered, irritable, peevish, spleenish, splenetic.

splendid *adj* beaming, bright, brilliant, effulgent, glowing, lustrous, radiant, refulgent, resplendent, shining; dazzling, gorgeous, imposing, kingly, magnificent, pompous, showy, sumptuous, superb; celebrated, conspicuous, distinguished, eminent, excellent, famous, glorious, illustrious, noble, pre-eminent, remarkable, signal; grand, heroic, lofty, noble, sublime.

splendour *n* brightness, brilliance, brilliancy, lustre, radiance, refulgence; display, éclat, gorgeousness, grandeur, magnificence, parade, pomp, show, showiness, stateliness; celebrity, eminence, fame, glory, grandeur, renown; grandeur, loftiness, nobleness, sublimity.

splenetic *adj* choleric, cross, fretful, irascible, irritable, peevish, pettish, petulant, snappish, testy, touchy, waspish; churlish, crabbed, morose, sour, sulky, sullen; gloomy, jaundiced.

splice *vb* braid, connect, join, knit, mortise.

splinter *vb* rend, shiver, sliver, split. * *n* fragment, piece.

split *vb* cleave, rive; break, burst, rend, splinter; divide, part, separate, sunder. * *n* crack, fissure, rent; breach, division, separation.

splotch *n* blot, daub, smear, spot, stain.

splutter *vb* sputter, stammer, stutter.

spoil *vb* despoil, fleece, loot, pilfer, plunder, ravage, rob, steal, strip, waste; corrupt, damage, destroy, disfigure, harm, impair, injure, mar, ruin, vitiate; decay, decompose. * *n* booty, loot, pillage, plunder, prey; rapine, robbery, spoliation, waste.

spoiler *n* pillager, plunderer, robber; corrupter, destroyer.

spokesman *n* mouthpiece, prolocutor, speaker.

spoliate *vb* despoil, destroy, loot, pillage, plunder, rob, spoil.

spoliation *n* depradation, deprivation, despoliation, destruction, robbery; destruction, devastation, pillage, plundering, rapine, ravagement.

sponge *vb* cleanse, wipe; efface, expunge, obliterate, rub out, wipe out.

sponger *n* hanger-on, parasite.

spongy *adj* absorbent, porous, spongeous; rainy, showery, wet; drenched, marshy, saturated, soaked, wet.

sponsor *vb* back, capitalize, endorse, finance, guarantee, patronize, promote, support, stake, subsidize, take up, underwrite. * *n* angel, backer, guarantor, patron, promoter, supporter, surety, underwriter; godfather, godmother, godparent.

spontaneity *n* improvisation, impulsiveness, spontaneousness.

spontaneous *adj* free, gratuitous, impulsive, improvised, instinctive, self-acting, self-moving, unbidden, uncompelled, unconstrained, voluntary, willing.

sporadic *adj* dispersed, infrequent, isolated, rare, scattered, separate, spasmodic.

sport *vb* caper, disport, frolic, gambol, have fun, make merry, play, romp, skip; trifle; display, exhibit. * *n* amusement, diversion, entertainment, frolic, fun, gambol, game, jollity, joviality, merriment, merry-making, mirth, pastime, pleasantry, prank, recreation; jest, joke; derision, jeer, mockery, ridicule; monstrosity.

sportive *adj* frisky, frolicsome, gamesome, hilarious, lively, merry, playful, prankish, rollicking, sprightly, tricksy; comic, facetious, funny, humorous, jocose, jocular, lively, ludicrous, mirthful, vivacious, waggish.

spot *vb* besprinkle, dapple, dot, speck, stud,

variegate; blemish, disgrace, soil, splotch, stain, sully, tarnish; detect, discern, espy, make out, observe, see, sight. * n blot, dapple, fleck, freckle, maculation, mark, mottle, patch, pip, speck, speckle; blemish, blotch, flaw, pock, splotch, stain, taint; locality, place, site.

spotless adj perfect, undefaced, unspotted; blameless, immaculate, innocent, irreproachable, pure, stainless, unblemished, unstained, untainted, untarnished.

spotted adj bespeckled, bespotted, dotted, flecked, freckled, maculated, ocellated, speckled, spotty.

spousal adj bridal, conjugal, connubial, hymeneal, marital, matrimonial, nuptial, wedded.

spouse n companion, consort, husband, mate, partner, wife.

spout vb gush, jet, pour out, spirit, spurt, squirt; declaim, mouth, speak, utter. * n conduit, tube; beak, nose, nozzle, waterspout.

sprain vb overstrain, rick, strain, twist, wrench, wrick.

spray[1] vb atomize, besprinkle, douche, gush, jet, shower, splash, splatter, spout, sprinkle, squirt. * n aerosol, atomizer, douche, foam, froth, shower, sprinkler, spume.

spray[2] n bough, branch, shoot, sprig, twig.

spread vb dilate, expand, extend, mantle, stretch; diffuse, disperse, distribute, radiate, scatter, sprinkle, strew; broadcast, circulate, disseminate, divulge, make known, make public, promulgate, propagate, publish; open, unfold, unfurl; cover, extend over, overspread. * n compass, extent, range, reach, scope, stretch; expansion, extension; circulation, dissemination, propagation; cloth, cover; banquet, feast, meal.

spree n bacchanal, carousal, debauch, frolic, jollification, orgy, revel, revelry, saturnalia.

sprig n shoot, spray, twig; lad, youth.

sprightliness n animation, activity, briskness, cheerfulness, frolicsomeness, gaiety, life, liveliness, nimbleness, vigour, vivacity.

sprightly adj airy, animated, blithe, blithesome, brisk, buoyant, cheerful, debonair, frolicsome, joyous, lively, mercurial, vigorous, vivacious.

spring vb bound, hop, jump, leap, prance, vault; arise, emerge, grow, issue, proceed, put forth, shoot forth, stem; derive, descend, emanate, flow, originate, rise, start; fly back, rebound, recoil; bend, warp; grow, thrive, wax. * adj hopping, jumping, resilient, springy. * n bound, hop, jump, leap, vault; elasticity, flexibility, resilience, resiliency, springiness; fount, fountain, fountainhead, geyser, springhead, well; cause, origin, original, principle, source; seed time, springtime.

springe n gin, net, noose, snare, trap.

springiness n elasticity, resilience, spring; sponginess, wetness.

springy adj bouncing, bounding, elastic, rebounding, recoiling, resilient.

sprinkle vb scatter, strew; bedew, besprinkle, dust,

powder, sand, spatter; wash, cleanse, purify, shower.

sprinkling n affusion, baptism, bedewing, spattering, splattering, spraying, wetting; dash, scattering, seasoning, smack, soupçon, suggestion, tinge, touch, trace, vestige.

sprite n apparition, elf, fairy, ghost, goblin, hobgoblin, phantom, pixie, shade, spectre, spirit.

sprout vb burgeon, burst forth, germinate, grow, pullulate, push, put forth, ramify, shoot, shoot forth. * n shoot, sprig.

spruce vb preen, prink; adorn, deck, dress, smarten, trim. * adj dandyish, dapper, fine, foppish, jaunty, natty, neat, nice, smart, tidy, trig, trim.

spry adj active, agile, alert, brisk, lively, nimble, prompt, quick, ready, smart, sprightly, stirring, supple.

spume n foam, froth, scum, spray.

spumy adj foamy, frothy, spumous.

spur vb gallop, hasten, press on, prick; animate, arouse, drive, goad, impel, incite, induce, instigate, rouse, stimulate, urge forward. * n goad, point, prick, rowel; fillip, impulse, incentive, incitement, inducement, instigation, motive, provocation, stimulus, whip; gnarl, knob, knot, point, projection, snag.

spurious adj bogus, counterfeit, deceitful, false, feigned, fictitious, make-believe, meretricious, mock, pretended, sham, supposititious, unauthentic.

spurn vb drive away, kick; contemn, despise, disregard, flout, scorn, slight; disdain, reject, repudiate.

spurt vb gush, jet, spirt, spout, spring out, stream out, well. * n gush, jet, spout, squirt; burst, dash, rush.

sputter vb spawl, spit, splutter, stammer.

spy vb behold, discern, espy, see; detect, discover, search out; explore, inspect, scrutinize, search; shadow, trail, watch. * n agent, detective, double agent, mole, scout, undercover agent.

squabble vb brawl, fight, quarrel, scuffle, struggle, wrangle; altercate, bicker, contend, dispute, jangle. * n brawl, dispute, fight, quarrel, rumpus, scrimmage.

squad n band, bevy, crew, gang, knot, lot, relay, set.

squalid adj dirty, filthy, foul, mucky, slovenly, unclean, unkempt.

squalidness n filthiness, foulness, squalidity, squalor.

squall vb bawl, cry, cry out, scream, yell. * n bawl, cry, outcry, scream, yell; blast, flurry, gale, gust, hurricane, storm, tempest.

squally adj blustering, blustery, gusty, stormy, tempestuous, windy.

squander vb dissipate, expend, lavish, lose, misuse, scatter, spend, throw away, waste.

squanderer n lavisher, prodigal, spendthrift, waster.

square vb make square, quadrate; accommodate,

adapt, fit, mould, regulate, shape, suit; adjust, balance, close, make even, settle; accord, chime in, cohere, comport, fall in, fit, harmonize, quadrate, suit. * *adj* four-square, quadrilateral, quadrate; equal, equitable, exact, fair, honest, just, upright; adjusted, balanced, even, settled; true, suitable. * *n* four-sided figure, quadrate, rectangle, tetragon; open area, parade, piazza, plaza.

squash *vb* crush, mash.

squashy *adj* pulpy, soft.

squat *vb* cower, crouch; occupy, plant, settle. * *adj* cowering, crouching; dumpy, pudgy, short, stocky, stubby, thickset.

squeal *vb* creak, cry, howl, scream, screech, shriek, squawk, yell; betray, inform on. * *n* creak, cry, howl, scream, screech, shriek, squawk, yell.

squeamish *adj* nauseated, qualmish, queasy, sickish; dainty, delicate, fastidious, finical, hypercritical, nice, over-nice, particular, priggish.

squeeze *vb* clutch, compress, constrict, grip, nip, pinch, press; drive, force; crush, harass, oppress; crowd, force through; press; (*with* **out**) extract. * *n* congestion, crowd, crush, throng; compression.

squelch *vb* crush, quash, quell, silence, squash, suppress.

squib *n* firework, fuse; lampoon, pasquinade, satire.

squint *vb* look askance, look obliquely, peer. * *adj* askew, aslant, crooked, oblique, skew, skewed, twisted.

squire *vb* accompany, attend, escort, wait on.

squirm *vb* twist, wriggle, writhe.

squirt *vb* eject, jet, splash, spurt.

stab *vb* broach, gore, jab, pierce, pink, spear, stick, transfix, transpierce; wound. * *n* cut, jab, prick, thrust; blow, dagger-stroke, injury, wound.

stability *n* durability, firmness, fixedness, immovability, permanence, stableness, steadiness; constancy, firmness, reliability.

stable *adj* established, fixed, immovable, immutable, invariable, permanent, unalterable, unchangeable; constant, firm, staunch, steadfast, steady, unwavering; abiding, durable, enduring, fast, lasting, permanent, perpetual, secure, sure.

staff *n* baton, cane, pole, rod, stick, wand; bat, bludgeon, club, cudgel, mace; prop, stay, support; employees, personnel, team, workers, work force.

stage *vb* dramatize, perform, present, produce, put on. * *n* dais, platform, rostrum, scaffold, staging, stand; arena, field; boards, playhouse, theatre; degree, point, step; diligence, omnibus, stagecoach.

stagey *adj* bombastic, declamatory, dramatic, melodramatic, ranting, theatrical.

stagger *vb* reel, sway, totter; alternate, fluctuate, overlap, vacillate, vary; falter, hesitate, waver; amaze, astonish, astound, confound, dumbfound, nonplus, pose, shock, surprise.

stagnant *adj* close, motionless, quiet, standing; dormant, dull, heavy, inactive, inert, sluggish, torpid.

stagnate *vb* decay, deteriorate, languish, rot, stand still, vegetate.

staid *adj* calm, composed, demure, grave, sedate, serious, settled, sober, solemn, steady, unadventurous.

stain *vb* blemish, blot, blotch, discolour, maculate, smirch, soil, splotch, spot, sully, tarnish; colour, dye, tinge; contaminate, corrupt, debase, defile, deprave, disgrace, dishonour, pollute, taint. * *n* blemish, blot, defect, discoloration, flaw, imperfection, spot, tarnish; contamination, disgrace, dishonour, infamy, pollution, reproach, shame, taint, tarnish.

stainless *adj* spotless, unspotted, untarnished; blameless, faultless, innocent, guiltless, pure, spotless, uncorrupted, unsullied.

stairs *npl* flight of steps, staircase, stairway.

stake[1] *vb* brace, mark, prop, secure, support. * *n* pale, palisade, peg, picket, post, stick.

stake[2] *vb* finance, pledge, wager; hazard, imperil, jeopardize, peril, risk, venture. * *n* bet, pledge, wager; adventure, hazard, risk, venture.

stale *adj* flat, fusty, insipid, mawkish, mouldy, musty, sour, tasteless, vapid; decayed, effete, faded, old, time-worn, worn-out; common, commonplace, hackneyed, stereotyped, threadbare, trite.

stalk[1] *n* culm, pedicel, peduncle, petiole, shaft, spire, stem, stock.

stalk[2] *vb* march, pace, stride, strut, swagger; follow, hunt, shadow, track, walk stealthily.

stall[1] *n* stable; cell, compartment, recess; booth, kiosk, shop, stand.

stall[2] *vb* block, delay, equivocate, filibuster, hinder, postpone, procrastinate, temporize; arrest, check, conk out, die, fail, halt, stick, stop.

stalwart *adj* able-bodied, athletic, brawny, lusty, muscular, powerful, robust, sinewy, stout, strapping, strong, sturdy, vigorous; bold, brave, daring, gallant, indomitable, intrepid, redoubtable, resolute, valiant, valorous. * *n* backer, member, partisan, supporter.

stamina *n* energy, force, lustiness, power, stoutness, strength, sturdiness, vigour.

stammer *vb* falter, hesitate, stutter. * *n* faltering, hesitation, stutter.

stamp *vb* brand, impress, imprint, mark, print. * *n* brand, impress, impression, print; cast, character, complexion, cut, description, fashion, form, kind, make, mould, sort, type.

stampede *vb* charge, flee, panic. * *n* charge, flight, rout, running away, rush.

stanch *see* **staunch**[1].

stanchion *n* prop, shore, stay, support.

stand *vb* be erect, remain upright; abide, be fixed, continue, endure, hold good, remain; halt, pause, stop; be firm, be resolute, stand ground, stay; be valid, have force; depend, have support, rest; bear, brook, endure, suffer, sustain, weather; abide, admit, await, submit, tolerate, yield; fix, place, put, set upright; (*with* **against**) oppose, resist, withstand; (*with* **by**) be near, be present; aid, assist, defend, help, side with, support; defend, make good, justify, maintain, support, vindicate; (*naut*) attend, be ready; (*with* **fast**) be fixed, be immovable; (*with* **for**) mean, represent, signify; aid, defend, help, maintain, side with, support; (*with* **off**) keep aloof, keep off; not to comply; (*with* **out**) be prominent, jut, project, protrude; not comply, not yield, persist; (*with* **up for**) defend, justify, support, sustain, uphold; (*with* **with**) agree. * *n* place, position, post, standing place, station; halt, stay, stop; dais, platform, rostrum; booth, stall; opposition, resistance.

standard¹ *n* banner, colours, ensign, flag, gonfalon, pennon, streamer.

standard² *adj* average, conventional, customary, normal, ordinary, regular, usual; accepted, approved, authoritative, orthodox, received; formulary, prescriptive, regulation. * *n* canon, criterion, model, norm, rule, test, type; gauge, measure, model, scale; support, upright.

standing *adj* established, fixed, immovable, settled; durable, lasting, permanent, settled; motionless, stagnant. * *n* position, stand, station; continuance, duration, existence; footing, ground, hold; condition, estimation, rank, reputation, status.

standpoint *n* point of view, viewpoint.

standstill *n* cessation, interruption, stand, stop; deadlock.

stanza *n* measure, staff, stave, strophe, verse.

staple *adj* basic, chief, essential, fundamental, main, primary, principal. * *n* fibre, filament, pile, thread; body, bulk, mass, substance.

star *vb* act, appear, feature, headline, lead, perform, play; emphasize, highlight, stress, underline. * *adj* leading, main, paramount, principal; celebrated, illustrious, well-known. * *n* heavenly body, luminary; asterisk, pentacle, pentagram; destiny, doom, fate, fortune, lot; diva, headliner, hero, heroine, lead, leading lady, leading man, prima ballerina, prima donna, principal, protagonist.

starchy *adj* ceremonious, exact, formal, precise, prim, punctilious, rigid, starched, stiff.

stare *vb* gape, gaze, look intently, watch.

stark *adj* rigid, stiff; absolute, bare, downright, entire, gross, mere, pure, sheer, simple. * *adv* absolutely, completely, entirely, fully, wholly.

starry *adj* astral, sidereal, star-spangled, stellar; bright, brilliant, lustrous, shining, sparkling, twinkling.

start *vb* begin, commence, inaugurate, initiate, institute; discover, invent; flinch, jump, shrink, startle, wince; alarm, disturb, fright, rouse, scare; depart, set off, take off; arise, call forth, evoke, raise; dislocate, move suddenly, spring. * *n* beginning, commencement, inauguration, outset; fit, jump, spasm, twitch; impulse, sally.

startle *vb* flinch, shrink, start, wince; affright, alarm, fright, frighten, scare, shock; amaze, astonish, astound.

startling *adj* abrupt, alarming, astonishing, shocking, sudden, surprising, unexpected, unforeseen, unheard of.

starvation *n* famine, famishment.

starve *vb* famish, perish; be in need, lack, want; kill, subdue.

starveling *adj* attenuated, emaciated, gaunt, hungry, lank, lean, meagre, scraggy, skinny, thin. * *n* beggar, mendicant, pauper.

state *vb* affirm, assert, aver, declare, explain, expound, express, narrate, propound, recite, say, set forth, specify, voice. * *adj* civic, national, public. * *n* case, circumstances, condition, pass, phase, plight, position, posture, predicament, situation, status; condition, guise, mode, quality, rank; dignity, glory, grandeur, magnificence, pageantry, parade, pomp, spendour; body politic, civil community, commonwealth, nation, realm.

statecraft *n* diplomacy, political subtlety, state management, statesmanship.

stated *adj* established, fixed, regular, settled; detailed, set forth, specified.

stately *adj* august, dignified, elevated, grand, imperial, imposing, lofty, magnificent, majestic, noble, princely, royal; ceremonious, formal, magisterial, pompous, solemn.

statement *n* account, allegation, announcement, communiqué, declaration, description, exposition, mention, narration, narrative, recital, relation, report, specification; assertion, predication, proposition, pronouncement, thesis.

statesman *n* politician.

station *vb* establish, fix, locate, place, post, set. * *n* location, place, position, lost, seat, situation; business, employment, function, occupation, office; character, condition, degree, dignity, footing, rank, standing, state, status; depot, stop, terminal.

stationary *adj* fixed, motionless, permanent, quiescent, stable, standing, still.

statuary *n* carving, sculpture, statues.

statue *n* figurine, image, statuette.

stature *n* height, physique, size, tallness; altitude, consequence, elevation, eminence, prominence.

status *n* caste, condition, footing, position, rank, standing, station.

statute *n* act, decree, edict, enactment, law, ordinance, regulation.

staunch¹, **stanch** *vb* arrest, block, check, dam, plug, stem, stop.

staunch² *adj* firm, sound, stout, strong; constant, faithful, firm, hearty, loyal, resolute, stable, steadfast, steady, strong, trustworthy, trusty, unwavering, zealous.

stave *vb* break, burst; (*with* **off**) adjourn, defer, delay, postpone, procrastinate, put off, waive.

stay *vb* abide, dwell, lodge, rest, sojourn, tarry;

continue, halt, remain, stand still, stop; attend, delay, linger, wait; arrest, check, curb, hold, keep in, prevent, rein in, restrain, withhold; delay, detain, hinder, obstruct; hold up, prop, shore up, support, sustain, uphold. * *n* delay, repose, rest, sojourn; halt, stand, stop; bar, check, curb, hindrance, impediment, interruption, obstacle, obstruction, restraint, stumbling block; buttress, dependence, prop, staff, support, supporter.

stead *n* place, room.

steadfast *adj* established, fast, firm, fixed, stable; constant, faithful, implicit, persevering, pertinacious, resolute, resolved, staunch, steady, unhesitating, unreserved, unshaken, unwavering, wholehearted.

steadiness *n* constancy, firmness, perseverance, persistence, resolution, steadfastness; fixedness, stability.

steady *vb* balance, counterbalance, secure, stabilize, support. * *adj* firm, fixed, stable; constant, equable, regular, undeviating, uniform, unremitting; persevering, resolute, staunch, steadfast, unchangeable, unwavering.

steal *vb* burglarize, burgle, crib, embezzle, filch, peculate, pilfer, plagiarize, poach, purloin, shoplift, thieve; creep, sneak, pass stealthily.

stealing *n* burglary, larceny, peculation, shoplifting, robbery, theft, thievery.

stealth *n* secrecy, slyness, stealthiness.

stealthy *adj* clandestine, furtive, private, secret, skulking, sly, sneaking, surreptitious, underhand.

steam *vb* emit vapour, fume; evaporate, vaporize; coddle, cook, poach; navigate, sail; be hot, sweat. * *n* vapour; effluvium, exhalation, fume, mist, reek, smoke.

steamboat *n* steamer, steamship.

steamy *adj* misty, moist, vaporous; erotic, voluptuous.

steed *n* charger, horse, mount.

steel *vb* case-harden, edge; brace, fortify, harden, make firm, nerve, strengthen.

steep[1] *adj* abrupt, declivitous, precipitous, sheer, sloping, sudden. * *n* declivity, precipice.

steep[2] *vb* digest, drench, imbrue, imbue, macerate, saturate, soak.

steeple *n* belfry, spire, tower, turret.

steer *vb* direct, conduct, govern, guide, pilot, point.

steersman *n* conductor, guide, helmsman, pilot.

stellar *adj* astral, starry, star-spangled, stellary.

stem[1] *vb* (*with* **from**) bud, descend, generate, originate, spring, sprout. * *n* axis, stipe, trunk; pedicel, peduncle, petiole, stalk; branch, descendant, offspring, progeny, scion, shoot; ancestry, descent, family, generation, line, lineage, pedigree, race, stock; (*naut*) beak, bow, cutwater, forepart, prow; helm, lookout; etymon, radical, radix, origin, root.

stem[2] *vb* breast, oppose, resist, withstand; check, dam, oppose, staunch, stay, stop.

stench *n* bad smell, fetor, offensive odour, stink.

stenography *n* brachygraphy, shorthand, tachygraphy.

stentorian *adj* loud-voiced, powerful, sonorous, thundering, trumpet-like.

step *vb* pace, stride, tramp, tread, walk. * *n* footstep, pace, stride; stair, tread; degree, gradation, grade, interval; advance, advancement, progression; act, action, deed, procedure, proceeding; footprint, trace, track, vestige; footfall, gait, pace, walk; expedient, means, measure, method; round, rundle, rung.

steppe *n* pampa, prairie, savannah.

sterile *adj* barren, infecund, unfruitful, unproductive, unprolific; bare, dry, empty, poor; (*bot*) acarpous, male, staminate.

sterility *n* barrenness, fruitlessness, infecundity, unfruitfulness, unproductiveness.

sterling *adj* genuine, positive, pure, real, sound, standard, substantial, true.

stern[1] *adj* austere, dour, forbidding, grim, severe; bitter, cruel, hard, harsh, inflexible, relentless, rigid, rigorous, severe, strict, unrelenting; immovable, incorruptible, steadfast, uncompromising.

stern[2] *n* behind, breach, hind part, posterior, rear, tail; (*naut*) counter, poop, rudderpost, tailpost; butt, buttocks, fundament, rump.

sternness *n* austerity, rigidity, severity; asperity, cruelty, harshness, inflexibility, relentlessness, rigour.

sternum *n* (*anat*) breastbone, sternon.

stertorous *adj* hoarsely breathing, snoring.

stew *vb* boil, seethe, simmer, stive. * *n* ragout; confusion, difficulty, mess, scrape.

steward *n* chamberlain, majordomo, seneschal; manciple, purveyor.

stick[1] *vb* gore, penetrate, pierce, puncture, spear, stab, transfix; infix, insert, thrust; attach, cement, glue, paste; fix in, set; adhere, cleave, cling, hold; abide, persist, remain, stay, stop; doubt, hesitate, scruple, stickle, waver; (*with* **by**) adhere to, be faithful, support. * *n* prick, stab, thrust.

stick[2] *n* birch, rod, switch; bat, bludgeon, club, cudgel, shillelah; cane, staff, walking stick; cue, pole, spar, stake.

stickiness *n* adhesiveness, glutinousness, tenacity, viscosity, viscousness.

stickle *vb* altercate, contend, contest, struggle; doubt, hesitate, scruple, stick, waver.

sticky *adj* adhesive, clinging, gluey, glutinous, gummy, mucilaginous, tenacious, viscid, viscous.

stiff *adj* inflexible, rigid, stark, unbending, unyielding; firm, tenacious, thick; obstinate, pertinacious, strong, stubborn; absolute, austere, dogmatic, inexorable, peremptory, positive, rigorous, severe, straitlaced, strict, stringent, uncompromising; ceremonious, chilling, constrained, formal, frigid, prim, punctilious, stately, starchy, stilted; abrupt, cramped, crude, graceless, harsh, inelegant.

stiff-necked *adj* contumacious, cross-grained, dogged, headstrong, intractable, mulish, obdurate, obstinate, stubborn, unruly.

stiffness *n* hardness, inflexibility, rigidity, rigidness, rigour, starkness; compactness, consistence, denseness, density, thickness; contumaciousness, inflexibility, obstinacy, pertinacity, stubbornness; austerity, harshness, rigorousness, severity, sternness, strictness; constraint, formality, frigidity, precision, primness, tenseness.

stifle *vb* choke, smother, suffocate; check, deaden, destroy, extinguish, quench, repress, stop, suppress; conceal, gag, hush, muffle, muzzle, silence, smother, still.

stigma *n* blot, blur, brand, disgrace, dishonour, reproach, shame, spot, stain, taint, tarnish.

stigmatize *vb* brand, defame, discredit, disgrace, dishonour, post, reproach, slur, villify.

stiletto *n* dagger, dirk, poniard, stylet; bodkin, piercer.

still[1] *vb* hush, muffle, silence, stifle; allay, appease, calm, compose, lull, pacify, quiet, smooth, tranquillize; calm, check, immobilize, restrain, stop, subdue, suppress. * *adj* hushed, mum, mute, noiseless, silent; calm, placid, quiet, serene, stilly, tranquil, unruffled; inert, motionless, quiescent, stagnant, stationary. * *n* hush, lull, peace, quiet, quietness, quietude, silence, stillness, tranquillity; picture, photograph, shot.

still[2] *n* distillery, still-house; distillatory, retort, stillatory.

still[3] *adv, conj* till now, to this time, yet; however, nevertheless, notwithstanding; always, continually, ever, habitually, uniformly; after that, again, in continuance.

stilted *adj* bombastic, fustian, grandiloquent, grandiose, high-flown, high-sounding, inflated, magniloquent, pompous, pretentious, stilty, swelling, tumid, turgid.

stimulant *adj* exciting, stimulating, stimulative. * *n* bracer, cordial, pick-me-up, tonic; fillip, incentive, provocative, spur, stimulus.

stimulate *vb* animate, arouse, awaken, brace, encourage, energize, excite, fire, foment, goad, impel, incite, inflame, inspirit, instigate, kindle, prick, prompt, provoke, rally, rouse, set on, spur, stir up, urge, whet, work up.

stimulus *n* encouragement, fillip, goad, incentive, incitement, motivation, motive, provocation, spur, stimulant.

sting *vb* hurt, nettle, prick, wound; afflict, cut, pain.

stinging *adj* acute, painful, piercing; biting, nipping, pungent, tingling.

stingy *adj* avaricious, close, close-fisted, covetous, grudging, mean, miserly, narrow-hearted, niggardly, parsimonious, penurious.

stink *vb* emit a stench, reek, smell bad. * *n* bad smell, fetor, offensive odour, stench.

stint *vb* bound, confine, limit, restrain; begrudge, pinch, scrimp, skimp, straiten; cease, desist,

stop. * *n* bound, limit, restraint; lot, period, project, quota, share, shift, stretch, task, time, turn.

stipend *n* allowance, compensation, emolument, fee, hire, honorarium, pay, remuneration, salary, wages.

stipulate *vb* agree, bargain, condition, contract, covenant, engage, provide, settle terms.

stipulation *n* agreement, bargain, concordat, condition, contract, convention, covenant, engagement, indenture, obligation, pact.

stir *vb* budge, change place, go, move; agitate, bestir, disturb, prod; argue, discuss, moot, raise, start; animate, arouse, awaken, excite, goad, incite, instigate, prompt, provoke, quicken, rouse, spur, stimulate; appear, happen, turn up; get up, rise; (*with* **up**) animate, awaken, incite, instigate, move, provoke, quicken, rouse, stimulate. * *n* activity, ado, agitation, bustle, confusion, excitement, fidget, flurry, fuss, hurry, movement; commotion, disorder, disturbance, tumult, uproar.

stirring *adj* active, brisk, diligent, industrious, lively, smart; animating, arousing, awakening, exciting, quickening, stimulating.

stitch *vb* backstitch, baste, bind, embroider, fell, hem, seam, sew, tack, whip.

stive *vb* stow, stuff; boil, seethe, stew; make close, hot or sultry.

stock *vb* fill, furnish, store, supply; accumulate, garner, hoard, lay in, reposit, reserve, save, treasure up. * *adj* permanent, standard, standing. * *n* assets, capital, commodities, fund, principal, shares; accumulation, hoard, inventory, merchandise, provision, range, reserve, store, supply; ancestry, breed, descent, family, house, line, lineage, parentage, pedigree, race; cravat, neckcloth; butt, haft, hand; block, log, pillar, post, stake; stalk, stem, trunk.

stockholder *n* shareholder.

stocking *n* hose, sock.

stock market *n* stock exchange; cattle market.

stocks *npl* funds, public funds, public securities; shares.

stockstill *adj* dead-still, immobile, motionless, stationary, still, unmoving.

stocky *adj* chubby, chunky, dumpy, plump, short, stout, stubby, thickset.

stoic, stoical *adj* apathetic, cold-blooded, impassive, imperturbable, passionless, patient, philosophic, philosophical, phlegmatic, unimpassioned.

stoicism *n* apathy, coldness, coolness, impassivity, indifference, insensibility, nonchalance, phlegm.

stolen *adj* filched, pilfered, purloined; clandestine, furtive, secret, sly, stealthy, surreptitious.

stolid *adj* blockish, doltish, dull, foolish, heavy, obtuse, slow, stockish, stupid.

stolidity *n* doltishness, dullness, foolishness, obtuseness, stolidness, stupidity.

stomach *vb* abide, bear, brook, endure, put up with, stand, submit to, suffer, swallow, tolerate.

* *n* abdomen, belly, gut, paunch, pot, tummy; appetite, desire, inclination, keenness, liking, relish, taste.

stone *vb* cover, face, slate, tile; lapidate, pelt. * *n* boulder, cobble, gravel, pebble, rock; gem, jewel, precious stone; cenotaph, gravestone, monument, tombstone; nut, pit; adamant, agate, flint, gneiss, granite, marble, slate, etc.

stony *adj* gritty, hard, lapidose, lithic, petrous, rocky; adamantine, flinty, hard, inflexible, obdurate; cruel, hard-hearted, inexorable, pitiless, stony-hearted, unfeeling, unrelenting.

stoop *vb* bend forward, bend down, bow, lean, sag, slouch, slump; abase, cower, cringe, give in, submit, succumb, surrender; condescend, deign, descend, vouchsafe; fall, sink. * *n* bend, inclination, sag, slouch, slump; descent, swoop.

stop *vb* block, blockade, close, close up, obstruct, occlude; arrest, check, halt, hold, pause, stall, stay; bar, delay, embargo, hinder, impede, intercept, interrupt, obstruct, preclude, prevent, repress, restrain, staunch, suppress, thwart; break off, cease, desist, discontinue, forbear, give over, leave off, refrain from; intermit, quiet, quieten, terminate; lodge, tarry. * *n* halt, intermission, pause, respite, rest, stoppage, suspension, truce; block, cessation, check, hindrance, interruption, obstruction, repression; bar, impediment, obstacle; full stop, point.

stopcock *n* cock, faucet, tap.

stoppage *n* arrest, block, check, closure, hindrance, interruption, obstruction, prevention.

stopper *n* cork, plug, stopple.

store *vb* accumulate, amass, cache, deposit, garner, hoard, husband, lay by, lay in, lay up, put by, reserve, save, store up, stow away, treasure up; furnish, provide, replenish, stock, supply. * *n* accumulation, cache, deposit, fund, hoard, provision, reserve, stock, supply, treasure, treasury; abundance, plenty; storehouse; emporium, market, shop.

storehouse *n* depository, depot, godown, magazine, repository, store, warehouse.

storm *vb* assail, assault, attack; blow violently; fume, rage, rampage, rant, rave, tear. * *n* blizzard, gale, hurricane, squall, tempest, tornado, typhoon, whirlwind; agitation, clamour, commotion, disturbance, insurrection, outbreak, sedition, tumult, turmoil; adversity, affliction, calamity, distress; assault, attack, brunt, onset, onslaught; violence.

storminess *n* inclemency, roughness, tempestuousness.

stormy *adj* blustering, boisterous, gusty, squally, tempestuous, windy; passionate, riotous, rough, turbulent, violent, wild; agitated, furious.

story *n* annals, chronicle, history, record; account, narration, narrative, recital, record, rehearsal, relation, report, statement, tale; fable, fiction, novel, romance; anecdote, incident, legend, tale; canard, fabrication, falsehood, fib, figure, invention, lie, untruth.

storyteller *n* bard, chronicler, narrator, raconteur.

stout *adj* able-bodied, athletic, brawny, lusty, robust, sinewy, stalwart, strong, sturdy, vigorous; courageous, hardy, indomitable, stouthearted; contumacious, obstinate, proud, resolute, stubborn; compact, firm, solid, staunch; bouncing, bulky, burly, chubby, corpulent, fat, heavy, jolly, large, obese, plump, portly, stocky, strapping, thickset.

stouthearted *adj* fearless, heroic, redoubtable; bold, brave, courageous, dauntless, doughty, firm, gallant, hardy, indomitable, intrepid, resolute, valiant, valorous.

stow *vb* load, pack, put away, store, stuff.

straddle *vb* bestride.

straggle *vb* rove, wander; deviate, digress, ramble, range, roam, stray, stroll.

straggling *adj* rambling, roving, straying, strolling, wandering; scattered.

straight *adj* direct, near, rectilinear, right, short, undeviating, unswerving; erect, perpendicular, plumb, right, upright, vertical; equitable, fair, honest, honourable, just, square, straightforward. * *adv* at once, directly, forthwith, immediately, straightaway, straightway, without delay.

straightaway, straightway *adv* at once, directly, forthwith, immediately, speedily, straight, suddenly, without delay.

straighten *vb* arrange, make straight, neaten, order, tidy.

straight-laced *see* strait-laced.

strain[1] *vb* draw tightly, make tense, stretch, tighten; injure, sprain, wrench; exert, overexert, overtax, rack; embrace, fold, hug, press, squeeze; compel, constrain, force; dilute, distill, drain, filter, filtrate, ooze, percolate, purify, separate; fatigue, overtask, overwork, task, tax, tire. * *n* stress, tenseness, tension, tensity; effort, exertion, force, overexertion; burden, task, tax; sprain, wrech; lay, melody, movement, snatch, song, stave, tune.

strain[2] *n* manner, style, tone, vein; disposition, tendency, trait, turn; descent, extraction, family, lineage, pedigree, race, stock.

strait *adj* close, confined, constrained, constricted, contracted, narrow; rigid, rigorous, severe, strict; difficult, distressful, grievous, straitened. * *n* channel, narrows, pass, sound.

straits *npl* crisis, difficulty, dilemma, distress, embarrassment, emergency, exigency, extremity, hardship, pass, perplexity, pinch, plight, predicament.

straiten *vb* confine, constrain, constrict, contract, limit; narrow; intensify, stretch; distress, embarrass, perplex, pinch, press.

straitened *adj* distressed, embarrassed limited, perplexed, pinched.

strait-laced, straight-laced *adj* austere, formal, prim, rigid, rigorous, stern, stiff, strict, uncompromising.

straitness *n* narrowness, rigour, severity, strictness;

difficulty, distress, trouble; insufficiency, narrowness, scarcity, want.

strand[1] *vb* abandon, beach, be wrecked, cast away, go aground, ground, maroon, run aground, wreck. * *n* beach, coast, shore.

strand[2] *n* braid, cord, fibre, filament, line, rope, string, tress.

stranded *adj* aground, ashore, cast away, lost, shipwrecked, wrecked.

strange *adj* alien, exotic, far-fetched, foreign, outlandish, remote; new, novel; curious, exceptional, extraordinary, irregular, odd, particular, peculiar, rare, singular, surprising, uncommon, unusual; abnormal, anomalous, extraordinary, inconceivable, incredible, inexplicable, marvellous, mysterious, preternatural, unaccountable, unbelievable, unheard of, unique, unnatural, wonderful; bizarre, droll, grotesque, quaint, queer; inexperienced, unacquainted, unfamiliar, unknown; bashful, distant, distrustful, reserved, shy, uncommunicative.

strangeness *n* foreignness; bashfulness, coldness, distance, reserve, shyness, uncommunicativeness; eccentricity, grotesqueness, oddness, singularity, uncommonness, uncouthness.

stranger *n* alien, foreigner, newcomer, immigrant, outsider; guest, visitor.

strangle *vb* choke, contract, smother, squeeze, stifle, suffocate, throttle, tighten; keep back, quiet, repress, still, suppress.

strap *vb* beat, thrash, whip; bind, fasten, sharpen, strop. * *n* thong; band, ligature, strip, tie; razorstrap, strop.

strapping *adj* big, burly, large, lusty, stalwart, stout, strong, tall.

stratagem *n* artifice, cunning, device, dodge, finesse, intrigue, machination, manoeuvre, plan, plot, ruse, scheme, trick, wile.

strategic, strategical *adj* calculated, deliberate, diplomatic, manoeuvering, planned, politic, tactical; critical, decisive, key, vital.

strategy *n* generalship, manoeuvering, plan, policy, stratagem, strategetics, tactics.

stratum *n* band, bed, layer.

straw *n* culm, stalk, stem; button, farthing, fig, penny, pin, rush, snap.

stray *vb* deviate, digress, err, meander, ramble, range, roam, rove, straggle, stroll, swerve, transgress, wander. * *adj* abandoned, lost, strayed, wandering; accidental, erratic, random, scattered.

streak *vb* band, bar, striate, stripe, vein; dart, dash, flash, hurtle, run, speed, sprint, stream, tear. * *n* band, bar, belt, layer, line, strip, stripe, thread, trace, vein; cast, grain, tone, touch, vein; beam, bolt, dart, dash, flare, flash, ray, stream.

streaky *adj* streaked, striped, veined.

stream *vb* course, flow, glide, pour, run, spout; emit, pour out, shed; emanate, go forth, issue, radiate; extend, float, stretch out, wave. * *n*

brook, burn, race, rill, rivulet, run, runlet, runnel, trickle; course, current, flow, flux, race, rush, tide, torrent, wake, wash; beam, gleam, patch, radiation, ray, streak.

streamer *n* banner, colours, ensign, flag, pennon, standard.

street *n* avenue, highway, road, way.

strength *n* force, might, main, nerve, potency, power, vigour; hardness, solidity, toughness; impregnability, proof; brawn, grit, healthy, lustiness, muscle, robustness, sinew, stamina, thews, vigorousness; animation, courage, determination, firmness, fortitude, resolution, spirit; cogency, efficacy, soundness, validity; emphasis, energy; security, stay, support; brightness, brilliance, clearness, intensity, vitality, vividness; body, excellence, virtue; impetuosity, vehemence, violence; boldness.

strengthen *vb* buttress, recruit, reinforce; fortify; brace, energize, harden, nerve, steel, stimulate; freshen, invigorate, vitalize; animate, encourage; clench, clinch, confirm, corroborate, establish, fix, justify, sustain, support.

strenuous *adj* active, ardent, eager, earnest, energetic, resolute, vigorous, zealous; bold, determined, doughty, intrepid, resolute, spirited, strong, valiant.

stress *vb* accent, accentuate, emphasize, highlight, point up, underline, underscore; bear, bear upon, press, pressurize; pull, rack, strain, stretch, tense, tug. * *n* accent, accentuation, emphasis; effort, force, pull, strain, tension, tug; boisterousness, severity, violence; pressure, urgency.

stretch *vb* brace, screw, strain, tense, tighten; elongate, extend, lengthen, protract, pull; display, distend, expand, spread, unfold, widen; sprain, strain; distort, exaggerate, misrepresent. * *n* compass, extension, extent, range, reach, scope; effort, exertion, strain, struggle; course, direction.

strict *adj* close, strained, tense, tight; accurate, careful, close, exact, literal, particular, precise, scrupulous; austere, inflexible, harsh, orthodox, puritanical, rigid, rigorous, severe, stern, straitlaced, stringent, uncompromising, unyielding.

stricture *n* animadversion, censure, denunciation, criticism, compression, constriction, contraction.

strife *n* battle, combat, conflict, contention, contest, discord, quarrel, struggle, warfare.

strike *vb* bang, beat, belabour, box, buffet, cudgel, cuff, hit, knock, lash, pound, punch, rap, slap, slug, smite, thump, whip; impress, imprint, stamp; afflict, chastise, deal, give, inflict, punish; affect, astonish, electrify, stun; clash, collide, dash, touch; surrender, yield; mutiny, rebel, rise.

stringent *adj* binding, contracting, rigid, rigorous, severe, strict.

strip[1] *n* piece, ribbon, shred, slip.

strip[2] *vb* denude, hull, skin, uncover; bereave, deprive, deforest, desolate, despoil, devastate, disarm, dismantle, disrobe, divest, expose, fleece, loot, shave; plunder, pillage, ransack, rob, sack, spoil; disrobe, uncover, undress.

strive *vb* aim, attempt, endeavour, exert, labour, strain, struggle, toil; contend, contest, fight, tussle, wrestle; compete, cope.

stroke[1] *n* blow, glance, hit, impact, knock, lash, pat, percussion, rap, shot, switch, thump; attack, paralysis, stroke; affliction, damage, hardship, hurt, injury, misfortune, reverse, visitation; dash, feat, masterstroke, touch.

stroke[2] *vb* caress, feel, palpate, pet, knead, massage, nuzzle, rub, touch.

stroll *vb* loiter, lounge, ramble, range, rove, saunter, straggle, stray, wander. * *n* excursion, promenade, ramble, rambling, roving, tour, trip, walk, wandering.

strong *adj* energetic, forcible, powerful, robust, sturdy; able, enduring; cogent, firm, valid.

structure *vb* arrange, constitute, construct, make, organize. * *n* arrangement, conformation, configuration, constitution, construction, form, formation, make, organization; anatomy, composition, texture; building, edifice, fabric, framework, pile.

struggle *vb* aim, endeavour, exert, labour, strive, toil, try; battle, contend, contest, fight, wrestle; agonize, flounder, writhe. * n effort, endeavour, exertion, labour, pains; battle, conflict, contention, contest, fight, strife; agony, contortions, distress.

stubborn *adj* contumacious, dogged, headstrong, heady, inflexible, intractable, mulish, obdurate, obstinate, perverse, positive, refractory, ungovernable, unmanageable, unruly, unyielding, willful; constant, enduring, firm, hardy, persevering, persistent, steady, stoical, uncomplaining, unremitting; firm, hard, inflexible, stiff, strong, tough, unpliant, studied.

studious *adj* contemplative, meditative, reflective, thoughtful; assiduous, attentive, desirous, diligent, eager, lettered, scholarly, zealous.

study *vb* cogitate, lucubrate, meditate, muse, ponder, reflect, think; analyze, contemplate, examine, investigate, ponder, probe, scrutinize, search, sift, weigh. * *n* exercise, inquiry, investigation, reading, research, stumble; cogitation, consideration, contemplation, examination, meditation, reflection, thought; stun; model, object, representation, sketch; den, library, office, studio.

stunning *adj* deafening, stentorian; dumbfounding, stupefying.

stunted *adj* checked, diminutive, dwarfed, dwarfish, lilliputian, little, nipped, small, undersized.

stupendous *adj* amazing, astonishing, astounding, marvellous, overwhelming, surprising, wonderful; enormous, huge, immense, monstrous, prodigious, towering, tremendous, vast.

stupid *adj* brainless, crass, doltish, dull, foolish, idiotic, inane, inept, obtuse, pointless, prosaic, senseless, simple, slow, sluggish, stolid, tedious,

tiresome, witless.

stupor *n* coma, confusion, daze, lethargy, narcosis, numbness, stupefaction, torpor.

sturdy *adj* bold, determined, dogged, firm, hardy, obstinate, persevering, pertinacious, resolute, stiff, stubborn, sturdy; athletic, brawny, forcible, lusty, muscular, powerful, robust, stalwart, stout, strong, thickset, vigorous, well-set.

style *vb* address, call, characterize, denominate, designate, dub, entitle, name, term. * *n* dedication, expression, phraseology, turn; cast, character, fashion, form, genre, make, manner, method, mode, model, shape, vogue, way; appellation, denomination, designation, name, title; chic, elegance, smartness; pen, pin, point, stylus.

stylish *adj* chic, courtly, elegant, fashionable, genteel, modish, polished, smart.

suave *adj* affable, agreeable, amiable, bland, courteous, debonair, delightful, glib, gracious, mild, pleasant, smooth, sweet, oily, unctuous, urbane.

subdue *vb* beat, bend, break, bow, conquer, control, crush, defeat, discomfit, foil, master, overbear, overcome, overpower, overwhelm, quell, rout, subject, subjugate, surmount, vanquish, worst; allay, choke, curb, mellow, moderate, mollify, reduce, repress, restrain, soften, suppress, temper.

subject *vb* control, master, overcome, reduce, subdue, subjugate, tame; enslave, enthral; abandon, refer, submit, surrender. * *adj* beneath, subjacent, underneath; dependent, enslaved, inferior, servile, subjected, subordinate, subservient; conditional, obedient, submissive; disposed, exposed to, liable, obnoxious, prone. * *n* dependent, henchman, liegeman, slave, subordinate; matter, point, subject matter, theme, thesis, topic; nominative, premise; case, object, patient, recipient; ego, mind, self, thinking.

subjoin *vb* add, affix, annex, append, join, suffix.

subjugate *vb* conquer, enslave, enthral, master, overcome, overpower, overthrow, subdue, subject, vanquish.

sublimate *vb* alter, change, repress.

sublime *adj aloft, elevated, high,* sacred; eminent, exalted, grand, great, lofty, mighty; august, glorious, magnificent, majestic, noble, stately, solemn, sublunary; elated, elevated, eloquent, exhilarated, raised.

submission *n* capitulation, cession, relinquishment, surrender, yielding; acquiescence, compliance, obedience, resignation; deference, homage, humility, lowliness, obeisance, passiveness, prostration, self-abasement, submissiveness.

submissive *adj* amenable, compliant, docile, pliant, tame, tractable, yielding; acquiescent, long-suffering, obedient, passive, patient, resigned, unassertive, uncomplaining, unrepining; deferential, humble, lowly, meek, obsequious, prostrate, self-abasing.

submit *vb* cede, defer, endure, resign, subject, surrender, yield; commit, propose, refer; offer;

acquiesce, bend, capitulate, comply, stoop, succumb.

subordinate *adj* ancillary, dependent, inferior, junior, minor, secondary, subject, subservient, subsidiary. * *n* assistant, dependant, inferior, subject, underling.

subscribe *vb* accede, approve, agree, assent, consent, yield; contribute, donate, give, offer, promise.

subscription *n* aid, assistance, contribution, donation, gift, offering.

subsequent *adj* after, attendant, ensuing, later, latter, following, posterior, sequent, succeeding.

subservient *adj* inferior, obsequious, servile, subject, subordinate; accessory, aiding, auxiliary, conducive, contributory, helpful, instrumental, serviceable, useful.

subside *vb* settle, sink; abate, decline, decrease, diminish, drop, ebb, fall, intermit, lapse, lessen, lower, lull, wane.

subsidence *n* settling, sinking; abatement, decline, decrease, descent, ebb, diminution, lessening.

subsidiary *adj* adjutant, aiding, assistant, auxiliary, cooperative, corroborative, helping, subordinate, subservient.

subsidize *vb* aid, finance, fund, sponsor, support, underwrite.

subsidy *n* aid, bounty, grant, subvention, support, underwriting.

subsist *vb* be, breathe, consist, exist, inhere, live, prevail; abide, continue, endure, persist, remain; feed, maintain, ration, support.

subsistence *n* aliment, food, livelihood, living, maintenance, meat, nourishment, nutriment, provision, rations, support, sustenance, victuals.

substance *n* actuality, element, groundwork, hypostasis, reality, substratum; burden, content, core, drift, essence, gist, heart, import, meaning, pith, sense, significance, solidity, soul, sum, weight; estate, income, means, property, resources, wealth.

substantial *adj* actual, considerable, essential, existent, hypostatic, pithy, potential, real, subsistent, virtual; concrete, durable, positive, solid, tangible, true; corporeal, bodily, material; bulky, firm, goodly, heavy, large, massive, notable, significant, sizable, solid, sound, stable, stout, strong, well-made; cogent, just, efficient, influential, valid, weighty.

substantially *adv* adequately, essentially, firmly, materially, positively, really, truly.

substantiate *vb* actualize, confirm, corroborate, establish, prove, ratify, verify.

subterfuge *n* artifice, evasion, excuse, expedient, mask, pretence, pretext, quirk, shift, shuffle, sophistry, trick.

subtle *adj* arch, artful, astute, crafty, crooked, cunning, designing, diplomatic, intriguing, insinuating, sly, tricky, wily; clever, ingenious; acute, deep, discerning, discriminating, keen, profound, sagacious, shrewd; airy, delicate, ethereal,

light, nice, rare, refined, slender, subtle, thin, volatile.

subtlety *n* artfulness, artifice, astuteness, craft, craftiness, cunning, guile, subtleness; acumen, acuteness, cleverness, discernment, intelligence, keenness, sagacity, sharpness, shrewdness; attenuation, delicacy, fitness, nicety, rareness, refinement.

subtract *vb* deduct, detract, diminish, remove, take, withdraw.

suburbs *npl* environs, confines, neighbourhood, outskirts, precincts, purlieus, vicinage.

subversive *adj* destructive, overthrowing, pervasive, ruining, upsetting. * *n* collaborator, dissident, insurrectionist, saboteur, terrorist, traitor.

subvert *vb* invert, overset, overthrow, overturn, reverse, upset; demolish, destroy, extinguish, raze, ruin; confound, corrupt, injure, pervert.

succeed *vb* ensue, follow, inherit, replace; flourish, gain, hit, prevail, prosper, thrive, win.

success *n* attainment, issue, result; fortune, happiness, hit, luck, prosperity, triumph.

successful *adj* auspicious, booming, felicitous, fortunate, happy, lucky, prosperous, victorious, winning.

succession *n* chain, concatenation, cycle, consecution, following, procession, progression, rotation, round, sequence, series, suite; descent, entail, inheritance, lineage, race, reversion.

succinct *adj* brief, compact, compendious, concise, condensed, curt, laconic, pithy, short, summary, terse.

succour *vb* aid, assist, help, relieve; cherish, comfort, encourage, foster, nurse. * *n* aid, assistance, help, relief, support.

succulent *adj* juicy, luscious, lush, nutritive, sappy.

succumb *vb* capitulate, die, submit, surrender, yield.

sudden *adj* abrupt, hasty, hurried, immediate, instantaneous, rash, unanticipated, unexpected, unforeseen, unusual; brief, momentary, quick, rapid.

sue *vb* charge, court, indict, prosecute, solicit, summon, woo; appeal, beg, demand, entreat, implore, petition, plead, pray, supplicate.

suffer *vb* feel, undergo; bear, endure, sustain, tolerate; admit, allow, indulge, let, permit.

sufferable *adj* allowable, bearable, endurable, permissible, tolerable.

sufferance *n* endurance, inconvenience, misery, pain, suffering; long-suffering, moderation, patience, submission; allowance, permission, toleration.

suffice *vb* avail, content, satisfy, serve.

sufficient *adj* adequate, ample, commensurate, competent, enough, full, plenteous, satisfactory; able, equal, fit, qualified, responsible.

suffocate *vb* asphyxiate, choke, smother, stifle, strangle.

suffrage *n* ballot, franchise, voice, vote; approval, attestation, consent, testimonial, witness.

suggest *vb* advise, allude, hint, indicate, insinuate, intimate, move, present, prompt, propose, propound, recommend.

suggestion *n* allusion, hint, indication, insinuation, intimation, presentation, prompting, proposal, recommendation, reminder.

suit *vb* accommodate, adapt, adjust, fashion, fit, level, match; accord, become, befit, gratify, harmonize, please, satisfy, tally. * *n* appeal, entreaty, invocation, petition, prayer, request, solicitation, supplication; courtship, wooing; action, case, cause, process, prosecution, trial; clothing, costume, habit.

suitable *adj* adapted, accordant, agreeable, answerable, apposite, applicable, appropriate, apt, becoming, befitting, conformable, congruous, convenient, consonant, correspondent, decent, due, eligible, expedient, fit, fitting, just, meet, pertinent, proper, relevant, seemly, worthy.

suite *n* attendants, bodyguard, convoy, cortege, court, escort, followers, staff, retainers, retinue, train; collection, series, set, suit; apartment, rooms.

sulky *adj* aloof, churlish, cross, cross-grained, dogged, grouchy, ill-humoured, ill-tempered, moody, morose, perverse, sour, spleenish, spleeny, splenetic, sullen, surly, vexatious, wayward.

sullen *adj* cross, crusty, glum, grumpy, ill-tempered, moody, morose, sore, sour, sulky; cheerless, cloudy, dark, depressing, dismal, foreboding, funereal, gloomy, lowering, melancholy, mournful, sombre; dull, heavy, slow, sluggish; intractable, obstinate, perverse, refractory, stubborn, vexatious; baleful, evil, inauspicious, malign, malignant, sinister, unlucky, unpropitious.

sully *vb* blemish, blot, contaminate, deface, defame, dirty, disgrace, dishonour, foul, smirch, soil, slur, spot, stain, tarnish.

sultry *adj* close, damp, hot, humid, muggy, oppressive, stifling, stuffy, sweltering.

sum *vb* add, calculate, compute, reckon; collect, comprehend, condense, epitomize, summarize. * *n* aggregate, amount, total, totality, whole; compendium, substance, summary; acme, completion, height, summit.

summary *adj* brief, compendious, concise, curt, laconic, pithy, short, succinct, terse; brief, quick, rapid. * *n* abridgement, abstract, brief, compendium, digest, epitome, precis, résumé, syllabus, synopsis.

summit *n* acme, apex, cap, climax, crest, crown, pinnacle, top, vertex, zenith.

summon *vb* arouse, bid, call, cite, invite, invoke, rouse; convene, convoke; charge, indict, prosecute, subpoena, sue.

sumptuous *adj* costly, dear, expensive, gorgeous, grand, lavish, luxurious, magnificent, munificent, pompous, prodigal, rich, showy, splendid, stately, superb.

sunburnt *adj* bronzed, brown, ruddy, tanned.

sunder *vb* break, disconnect, disjoin, dissociate, dissever, disunited, divide, part, separate, sever.

sundry *adj* different, divers, several, some, various.

sunny *adj* bright, brilliant, clear, fine, luminous, radiant, shining, unclouded, warm; cheerful, genial, happy, joyful, mild, optimistic, pleasant, smiling.

superannuated *adj* aged, anile, antiquated, decrepit, disqualified, doting, effete, imbecile, passé, retired, rusty, time-worn, unfit.

superb *adj* august, beautiful, elegant, exquisite, grand, gorgeous, imposing, magnificent, majestic, noble, pompous, rich, showy, splendid, stately, sumptuous.

supercilious *adj* arrogant, condescending, contemptuous, dictatorial, domineering, haughty, high, imperious, insolent, intolerant, lofty, lordly, magisterial, overbearing, overweening, proud, scornful, vainglorious.

superficial *adj* external, flimsy, shallow, untrustworthy.

superfluity *n* excess, exuberance, redundancy, superabundance, surfeit.

superfluous *adj* excessive, redundant, unnecessary.

superintend *vb* administer, conduct, control, direct, inspect, manage, overlook, oversee, supervise.

superintendence *n* care, charge, control, direction, guidance, government, inspection, management, oversight, supervision, surveillance.

superior *adj* better, greater, high, higher, finer, paramount, supreme, ultra, upper; chief, foremost, principal; distinguished, matchless, noble, pre-eminent, preferable, sovereign, surpassing, unrivalled, unsurpassed; predominant, prevalent. * *n* boss, chief, director, head, higher-up, leader, manager, principal, senior, supervisor.

superiority *n* advantage, ascendency, lead, odds, predominance, pre-eminence, prevalence, transcendence; excellence, nobility, worthiness.

superlative *adj* consummate, greatest, incomparable, peerless, pre-eminent, supreme, surpassing, transcendent.

supernatural *adj* abnormal, marvellous, metaphysical, miraculous, otherworldly, preternatural, unearthly.

supernumerary *adj* excessive, odd, redundant, superfluous.

supersede *vb* annul, neutralize, obviate, overrule, suspend; displace, remove, replace, succeed, supplant.

supervise *vb* administer, conduct, control, direct, inspect, manage, overlook, oversee, superintend.

supine *adj* apathetic, careless, drowsy, dull, idle, indifferent, indolent, inert, languid, lethargic, listless, lumpish, lazy, negligent, otiose, prostrate, recumbent, sleepy, slothful, sluggish, spineless, torpid.

supplant *vb* overpower, overthrow, undermine;

displace, remove, replace, supersede.

supple *adj* elastic, flexible, limber, lithe, pliable, pliant; compliant, humble, submissive, yielding; adulatory, cringing, fawning, flattering, grovelling, obsequious, oily, parasitical, servile, slavish, sycophantic.

supplement *vb* add, augment, extend, reinforce, supply. * *n* addendum, addition, appendix, codicil, complement, continuation, postscript.

suppliant *adj* begging, beseeching, entreating, imploring, precative, precatory, praying, suing, supplicating. * *n* applicant, petitioner, solicitor, suitor, supplicant.

supplicate *vb* beg, beseech, crave, entreat, implore, importune, petition, pray, solicit.

supplication *n* invocation, orison, petition, prayer; entreaty, petition, prayer, request, solicitation.

supply *vb* endue, equip, furnish, minister, outfit, provide, replenish, stock, store; afford, accommodate, contribute, furnish, give, grant, yield. * *n* hoard, provision, reserve, stock, store.

support *vb* brace, cradle, pillow, prop, sustain, uphold; bear, endure, undergo, suffer, tolerate; cherish, keep, maintain, nourish, nurture; act, assume, carry, perform, play, represent; accredit, confirm, corroborate, substantiate, verify; abet, advocate, aid, approve, assist, back, befriend, champion, countenance, encourage, favour, float, hold, patronize, relieve, reinforce, succour, vindicate. * *n* bolster, brace, buttress, foothold, guy, hold, prop, purchase, shore, stay, substructure, supporter, underpinning; groundwork, mainstay, staff; base, basis, bed, foundation; keeping, living, livelihood, maintenance, subsistence, sustenance; confirmation, evidence; aid, assistance, backing, behalf, championship, comfort, countenance, encouragement, favour, help, patronage, succour.

suppose *vb* apprehend, believe, conceive, conclude, consider, conjecture, deem, imagine, judge, presume, presuppose, think; assume, hypothesize; imply, posit, predicate, think; fancy, opine, speculate, surmise, suspect, theorize, wean.

supposition *n* conjecture, guess, guesswork, presumption, surmise; assumption, hypothesis, postulation, theory, thesis; doubt, uncertainty.

suppress *vb* choke, crush, destroy, overwhelm, overpower, overthrow, quash, quell, quench, smother, stifle, subdue, withhold; arrest, inhibit, obstruct, repress, restrain, stop; conceal, extinguish, keep, retain, secret, silence, stifle, strangle.

supremacy *n* ascendancy, domination, headship, lordship, mastery, predominance, pre-eminence, primacy, sovereignty.

supreme *adj* chief, dominant, first, greatest, highest, leading, paramount, predominant, pre-eminent, principal, sovereign.

sure *adj* assured, certain, confident, positive; accurate, dependable, effective, honest, infallible, precise, reliable, trustworthy, undeniable, undoubted, unmistakable, well-proven; guaranteed, inevitable, irrevocable; fast, firm, safe, secure, stable, steady.

surely *adv* assuredly, certainly, infallibly, sure, undoubtedly; firmly, safely, securely, steadily.

surety *n* bail, bond, certainty, guarantee, pledge, safety, security.

surfeit *vb* cram, gorge, overfeed, sate, satiate; cloy, nauseate, pall. * *n* excess, fullness, glut, oppression, plethora, satiation, satiety, superabundance, superfluity.

surge *vb* billow, rise, rush, sweep, swell, swirl, tower. * *n* billow, breaker, roller, wave, white horse.

surly *adj* churlish, crabbed, cross, crusty, discourteous, fretful, gruff, grumpy, harsh, ill-natured, ill-tempered, morose, peevish, perverse, pettish, petulant, rough, rude, snappish, snarling, sour, sullen, testy, touchy, uncivil, ungracious, waspish; dark, tempestuous.

surmise *vb* believe, conclude, conjecture, consider, divine, fancy, guess, imagine, presume, suppose, think, suspect. * *n* conclusion, conjecture, doubt, guess, notion, possibility, supposition, suspicion, thought.

surmount *vb* clear, climb, crown, overtop, scale, top, vault; conquer, master, overcome, overpower, subdue, vanquish; exceed, overpass, pass, surpass, transcend.

surpass *vb* beat, cap, eclipse, exceed, excel, outdo, outmatch, outnumber, outrun, outstrip, override, overshadow, overtop, outshine, surmount, transcend.

surplus *adj* additional, leftover, remaining, spare, superfluous, supernumerary, supplementary. * *n* balance, excess, overplus, remainder, residue, superabundance, surfeit.

surprise *vb* amaze, astonish, astound, bewilder, confuse, disconcert, dumbfound, startle, stun. * *n* amazement, astonishment, blow, shock, wonder.

surprising *adj* amazing, astonishing, astounding, extraordinary, marvellous, unexpected, remarkable, startling, strange, unexpected, wonderful.

surrender *vb* cede, sacrifice, yield; abdicate, abandon, forgo, relinquish, renounce, resign, waive; capitulate, comply, succumb. * *n* abandonment, capitulation, cession, delivery, relinquishment, renunciation, resignation, yielding.

surreptitious *adj* clandestine, fraudulent, furtive, secret, sly, stealthy, unauthorized, underhand.

surround *vb* beset, circumscribe, compass, embrace, encircle, encompass, environ, girdle, hem, invest, loop.

surveillance *n* care, charge, control, direction, inspection, management, oversight, superintendence, supervision, surveyorship, vigilance, watch.

survey *vb* contemplate, observe, overlook, reconnoitre, review, scan, scout, view; examine, inspect, scrutinize; oversee, supervise; estimate, measure, plan, plot, prospect. * n prospect, retrospect, sight, view; examination, inspection, reconnaissance, review; estimating, measuring, planning, plotting, prospecting, work-study.

survive vb endure, last, outlast, outlive.

susceptible adj capable, excitable, impressible, impressionable, inclined, predisposed, receptive, sensitive.

suspect vb believe, conclude, conjecture, fancy, guess, imagine, judge, suppose, surmise, think; distrust, doubt, mistrust. * adj doubtful, dubious, suspicious.

suspend vb append, hang, sling, swing; adjourn, arrest, defer, delay, discontinue, hinder, intermit, interrupt, postpone, stay, withhold; debar, dismiss, rusticate.

suspicion n assumption, conjecture, dash, guess, hint, inkling, suggestion, supposition, surmise, trace; apprehension, distrust, doubt, fear, jealousy, misgiving, mistrust.

suspicious adj distrustful, jealous, mistrustful, suspect, suspecting; doubtful, questionable.

sustain vb bear, bolster, fortify, prop, strengthen, support, uphold; maintain, nourish, perpetuate, preserve; aid, assist, comfort, relieve; brave, endure, suffer, undergo; approve, confirm, ratify, sanction, validate; confirm, establish, justify, prove.

sustenance n maintenance, subsistence, support; aliment, bread, food, nourishment, nutriment, nutrition, provisions, supplies, victuals.

swagger vb bluster, boast, brag, bully, flourish, hector, ruffle, strut, swell, vapour. * n airs, arrogance, bluster, boastfulness, braggadocio, ruffling, strut.

swain n clown, countryman, hind, peasant, rustic; adorer, gallant, inamorata, lover, suitor, wooer.

swallow vb bolt, devour, drink, eat, englut, engorge, gobble, gorge, gulp, imbibe, ingurgitate, swamp; absorb, appropriate, arrogate, devour, engulf, submerge; consume, employ, occupy; brook, digest, endure, pocket, stomach; recant, renounce, retract. * n gullet, oesophagus, throat; inclination, liking, palate, relish, taste; deglutition, draught, gulp, ingurgitation, mouthful, taste.

swamp vb engulf, overwhelm, sink; capsize, embarrass, overset, ruin, upset, wreck. * n bog, fen, marsh, morass, quagmire, slough.

sward n grass, lawn, sod, turf.

swarm vb abound, crowd, teem, throng. * n cloud, concourse, crowd, drove, flock, hive, horde, host, mass, multitude, press, shoal, throng.

swarthy adj black, brown, dark, dark-skinned, dusky, tawny.

sway vb balance, brandish, move, poise, rock, roll, swing, wave, wield; bend, bias, influence, persuade, turn, urge; control, dominate, direct, govern, guide, manage, rule; hoist, raise; incline, lean, lurch, yaw. * n ascendency, authority, command, control, domination, dominion, empire, government, mastership, mastery, omnipotence, predominance, power, rule, sovereignty; bias, direction, influence, weight; preponderance, preponderation; oscillation, sweep, swing, wag, wave.

swear vb affirm, attest, avow, declare, depose, promise, say, state, testify, vow; blaspheme, curse.

sweep vb clean, brush; graze, touch; rake, scour, traverse. * n amplitude, compass, drive, movement, range, reach, scope; destruction, devastation, havoc, ravage; curvature, curve.

sweeping adj broad, comprehensive, exaggerated, extensive, extravagant, general, unqualified, wholesale.

sweet adj candied, cloying, honeyed, luscious, nectareous, nectarous, sugary, saccharine; balmy, fragrant, odorous, redolent, spicy; harmonious, dulcet, mellifluous, mellow, melodious, musical, pleasant, soft, tuneful, silver-toned, silvery; beautiful, fair, lovely; agreeable, charming, delightful, grateful, gratifying; affectionate, amiable, attractive, engaging, gentle, mild, lovable, winning; benignant, serene; clean, fresh, pure, sound. * n fragrance, perfume, redolence; blessing, delight, enjoyment, gratification, joy, pleasure; candy, treat.

swell vb belly, bloat, bulge, dilate, distend, expand, inflate, intumesce, puff, swell, tumefy; augment, enlarge, increase; heave, rise, surge; strut, swagger. * n swelling; augmentation, excrescence, protuberance; ascent, elevation, hill, rise; force, intensity, power; billows, surge, undulation, waves; beau, blade, buck, coxcomb, dandy, exquisite, fop, popinjay.

swerve vb deflect, depart, deviate, stray, turn, wander; bend, incline, yield; climb, swarm, wind.

swift adj expeditious, fast, fleet, flying, quick, rapid, speedy; alert, eager, forward, prompt, ready, zealous; instant, sudden.

swiftness n celerity, expedition, fleetness, quickness, rapidity, speed, velocity.

swindle vb cheat, con, cozen, deceive, defraud, diddle, dupe, embezzle, forge, gull, hoax, overreach, steal, trick, victimize. * n cheat, con, deceit, deception, fraud, hoax, imposition, knavery, roguery, trickery.

swindler n blackleg, cheat, defaulter, embezzler, faker, fraud, impostor, jockey, knave, peculator, rogue, sharper, trickster.

swing vb oscillate, sway, vibrate, wave; dangle, depend, hang; brandish, flourish, whirl; administer, manage. * n fluctuation, oscillation, sway, undulation, vibration; elbow-room, freedom, margin, play, range, scope, sweep; bias, tendency.

swoop vb descend, pounce, rush, seize, stoop, sweep. * n clutch, pounce, seizure; stoop, descent.

sword n brand, broadsword, claymore, cutlass, epee, falchion, foil, hanger, rapier, sabre, scimitar.

sybarite *n* epicure, voluptuary.

sycophancy *n* adulation, cringing, fawning, flattery, grovelling, obsequiousness, servility.

sycophant *n* cringer, fawner, flunky, hanger-on, lickspittle, parasite, spaniel, toady, wheedler.

syllabus *n* abridgement, abstract, breviary, brief, compendium, digest, epitome, outline, summary, synopsis.

symbol *n* badge, emblem, exponent, figure, mark, picture, representation, representative, sign, token, type.

symbolic, symbolical *adj* emblematic, figurative, hieroglyphic, representative, significant, typical.

symmetry *n* balance, congruity, evenness, harmony, order, parallelism, proportion, regularity, shapeliness.

sympathetic *adj* affectionate, commiserating, compassionate, condoling, kind, pitiful, tender.

sympathy *n* accord, affinity, agreement, communion, concert, concord, congeniality, correlation, correspondence, harmony, reciprocity, union; commiseration, compassion, condolence, fellow-feeling, kindliness, pity, tenderness, thoughtfulness.

symptom *n* diagnostic, indication, mark, note, prognostic, sign, token.

symptomatic *adj* characteristic, indicative, symbolic, suggestive.

synonymous *adj* equipollent, equivalent, identical, interchangeable, similar, tantamount.

synopsis *n* abridgement, abstract, compendium, digest, epitome, outline, precis, résumé, summary, syllabus.

system *n* method, order, plan.

systematic *adj* methodic, methodical, orderly, regular.

T

tabernacle *n* pavilion, tent; cathedral, chapel, church, minster, synagogue, temple.

table *vb* enter, move, propose, submit, suggest. * *n* plate, slab, tablet; board, counter, desk, stand; catalogue, chart, compendium, index, list, schedule, syllabus, synopsis, tabulation; diet, fare, food, victuals.

tableau *n* picture, scene, representation.

taboo *vb* forbid, interdict, prohibit, proscribe. * *adj* banned, forbidden, inviolable, outlawed, prohibited, proscribed. * *n* ban, interdict, prohibition, proscription.

tacit *adj* implicit, implied, inferred, silent, understood, unexpressed, unspoken.

taciturn *adj* close, dumb, laconic, mum, reserved, reticent, silent, tight-lipped, uncommunicative.

tack *vb* add, affix, append, attach, fasten, tag; gybe, yaw, zigzag. * *n* nail, pin, staple; bearing, course, direction, heading, path, plan, procedure.

tackle *vb* attach, grapple, seize; attempt, try, undertake. * *n* apparatus, cordage, equipment, furniture, gear, harness, implements, rigging, tackling, tools, weapons.

tact *n* address, adroitness, cleverness, dexterity, diplomacy, discernment, finesse, insight, knack, perception, skill, understanding.

tail *vb* dog, follow, shadow, stalk, track. * *adj* abridged, curtailed, limited, reduced. * *n* appendage, conclusion, end, extremity, stub; flap, skirt; queue, retinue, train.

taint *vb* imbue, impregnate; contaminate, corrupt, defile, inflect, mildew, pollute, poison, spoil, touch; blot, stain, sully, tarnish. * *n* stain, tincture, tinge, touch; contamination, corruption, defilement, depravation, infection, pollution; blemish, defect, fault, flaw, spot.

take *vb* accept, obtain, procure, receive; clasp, clutch, grasp, grip, gripe, seize, snatch; filch, misappropriate, pilfer, purloin, steal; abstract, apprehend, appropriate, arrest, bag, capture, ensnare, entrap; attack, befall, smite; capture, carry off, conquer, gain, win; allure, attract, bewitch, captivate, charm, delight, enchant, engage, fascinate, interest, please; consider, hold, interrupt, suppose, regard, understand; choose, elect, espouse, select; employ, expend, use; claim, demand, necessitate, require; bear, endure, experience, feel, perceive, tolerate; deduce, derive, detect, discover, draw; carry, conduct, convey, lead, transfer; clear, surmount; drink, eat, imbibe,

inhale, swallow. * *n* proceeds, profits, return, revenue, takings, yield.

tale *n* account, fable, legend, narration, novel, parable, recital, rehearsal, relation, romance, story, yarn; catalogue, count, enumeration, numbering, reckoning, tally.

talent *n* ableness, ability, aptitude, capacity, cleverness, endowment, faculty, forte, genius, gift, knack, parts, power, turn.

talk *vb* chatter, communicate, confer, confess, converse, declaim, discuss, gossip, pontificate, speak. * *n* chatter, communication, conversation, diction, gossip, jargon, language, rumour, speech, utterance.

talkative *adj* chatty, communicative, garrulous, loquacious, voluble.

tally *vb* accord, agree, conform, coincide, correspond, harmonize, match, square, suit. * *n* match, mate; check, counterpart, muster, roll call; account, reckoning.

tame *vb* domesticate, reclaim, train; conquer, master, overcome, repress, subdue, subjugate. * *adj* docile, domestic, domesticated, gentle, mild, reclaimed; broken, crushed, meek, subdued, unresisting, submissive; barren, commonplace, dull, feeble, flat, insipid, jejune, languid, lean, poor, prosaic, prosy, spiritless, tedious, uninteresting, vapid.

tamper *vb* alter, conquer, dabble, damage, interfere, meddle; intrigue, seduce, suborn.

tang *n* aftertaste, flavour, relish, savour, smack, taste; keenness, nip, sting.

tangible *adj* corporeal, material, palpable, tactile, touchable; actual, certain, embodied, evident, obvious, open, perceptible, plain, positive, real, sensible, solid, stable, substantial.

tangle *vb* complicate, entangle, intertwine, interweave, mat, perplex, snarl; catch, ensnare, entrap, involve, catch; embarrass, embroil, perplex. * *n* complication, disorder, intricacy, jumble, perplexity, snarl; dilemma, embarrassment, quandary, perplexity.

tantalize *vb* balk, disappoint, frustrate, irritate, provoke, tease, torment, vex.

tantamount *adj* equal, equivalent, synonymous.

tantrum *n* fit, ill-humour, outburst, paroxysm, temper, whim.

tap[1] *vb* knock, pat, rap, strike, tip, touch. * *n* pat, tip, rap, touch.

tap[2] *vb* broach, draw off, extract, pierce; draw on,

exploit, mine, use, utilize; bug, eavesdrop, listen in. *n faucet, plug, spigot, spout, stopcock, valve; bug, listening device, transmitter.

tardiness n delay, dilatoriness, lateness, procrastination, slackness, slowness.

tardy adj slow, sluggish, snail-like; backward, behindhand, dilatory, late, loitering, overdue, slack.

tarn n bog, fen, marsh, morass, swamp.

tarnish vb blemish, deface, defame, dim, discolour, dull, slur, smear, soil, stain, sully. * n blemish, blot, soiling, spot, stain.

tarry vb delay, dally, linger, loiter, remain, stay, stop, wait; defer; abide, lodge, rest, sojourn.

tart adj acid, acidulous, acrid, astringent, piquant, pungent, sharp, sour; acrimonious, caustic, crabbed, curt, harsh, ill-humoured, ill-tempered, keen, petulant, sarcastic, severe, snappish, testy.

task vb burden, overwork, strain, tax. * n drudgery, labour, toil, work; business, charge, chore, duty, employment, enterprise, job, mission, stint, undertaking; assignment, exercise, lesson.

taste vb experience, feel, perceive, undergo; relish, savour, sip. * n flavour, gusto, relish, savour, smack, piquancy; admixture, bit, dash, fragment, hint, infusion, morsel, mouthful, sample, shade, sprinkling, suggestion, tincture; appetite, desire, fondness, liking, partiality, predilection; acumen, cultivation, culture, delicacy, discernment, discrimination, elegance, fine-feeling, grace, judgement, polish, refinement; manner, style.

tasteful adj appetizing, delicious, flavoursome, palatable, savoury, tasty, toothsome; aesthetic, artistic, attractive, elegant.

tasteless adj flat, insipid, savourless, stale, watery; dull, mawkish, uninteresting, vapid.

tattle vb babble, chat, chatter, jabber, prate, prattle; blab, gossip, inform. * n gabble, gossip, prate, prattle, tittle-tattle, twaddle.

taunt vb censure, chaff, deride, flout, jeer, mock, scoff, sneer, revile, reproach, ridicule, twit, upbraid. * n censure, derision, gibe, insult, jeer, quip, quirk, reproach, ridicule, scoff.

taut adj strained, stretched, tense, tight.

tautology n iteration, pleonasm, redundancy, reiteration, repetition, verbosity, wordiness.

tavern n bar, chophouse, hostelry, inn, pub, public house.

tawdry adj flashy, gaudy, garish, glittering, loud, meretricious, ostentatious, showy.

tax vb burden, demand, exact, load, overtax, require, strain, task; accuse, charge. * n assessment, custom, duty, excise, impost, levy, rate, taxation, toll, tribute; burden, charge, demand, requisition, strain; accusation, censure.

teach vb catechize, coach, discipline, drill, edify, educate, enlighten, inform, indoctrinate, initiate, instruct, ground, prime, school, train, tutor; communicate, disseminate, explain, expound, impart, implant, inculcate, infuse, instil, interpret,

preach, propagate; admonish, advise, counsel, direct, guide, signify, show.

teacher n coach, educator, inculcator, informant, instructor, master, pedagogue, preceptor, schoolteacher, trainer, tutor; adviser, counsellor, guide, mentor; pastor, preacher.

tear vb burst, slit, rive, rend, rip; claw, lacerate, mangle, shatter, rend, wound; sever, sunder; fume, rage, rant, rave. * n fissure, laceration, rent, rip, wrench.

tease vb annoy, badger, beg, bother, chafe, chagrin, disturb, harass, harry, hector, importune, irritate, molest, pester, plague, provoke, tantalize, torment, trouble, vex, worry.

tedious adj dull, fatiguing, irksome, monotonous, tiresome, trying, uninteresting, wearisome; dilatory, slow, sluggish, tardy.

teem vb abound, bear, produce, swarm; discharge, empty, overflow.

teeming adj abounding, fraught, full, overflowing, pregnant, prolific, replete, swarming.

tell vb compute, count, enumerate, number, reckon; describe, narrate, recount, rehearse, relate, report; acknowledge, announce, betray, confess, declare, disclose, divulge, inform, own, reveal; acquaint, communicate, instruct, teach; discern, discover, distinguish; express, mention, publish, speak, state, utter.

temper vb modify, qualify; appease, assuage, calm, mitigate, mollify, moderate, pacify, restrain, soften, soothe; accommodate, adapt, adjust, fit, suit. * n character, constitution, nature, organization, quality, structure, temperament, type; disposition, frame, grain, humour, mood, spirits, tone, vein; calmness, composure, equanimity, moderation, tranquillity; anger, ill-temper, irritation, spleen, passion.

temperament n character, constitution, disposition, habit, idiosyncrasy, nature, organization, temper.

temperate adj abstemious, ascetic, austere, chaste, continent, frugal, moderate, self-controlled, self-denying, sparing; calm, cool, dispassionate, mild, sober, sedate.

tempest n cyclone, gale, hurricane, squall, storm, tornado; commotion, disturbance, excitement, perturbation, tumult, turmoil.

temporal adj civil, lay, mundane, political, profane, secular, terrestrial, worldly; brief, ephemeral, evanescent, fleeting, momentary, short-lived, temporal, transient, transitory.

temporary adj brief, ephemeral, evanescent, fleeting, impermanent, momentary, short-lived, transient, transitory.

tempt vb prove, test, try; allure, decoy, entice, induce, inveigle, persuade, seduce; dispose, incite, incline, instigate, lead, prompt, provoke.

tempting adj alluring, attractive, enticing, inviting, seductive.

tenable adj defensible, maintainable, rational, reasonable, sound.

tenacious *adj* retentive, unforgetful; adhesive, clinging, cohesive, firm, glutinous, gummy, resisting, retentive, sticky, strong, tough, unyielding, viscous; dogged, fast, obstinate, opinionated, opinionative, pertinacious, persistent, resolute, stubborn, unwavering.

tenacity *n* retentiveness, tenaciousness; adhesiveness, cohesiveness, glutinosity, glutinousness, gumminess, toughness, stickiness, strength, viscidity; doggedness, firmness, obstinacy, perseverance, persistency, pertinacity, resolution, stubbornness.

tend[1] *vb* accompany, attend, graze, guard, keep, protect, shepherd, watch.

tend[2] *vb* aim, exert, gravitate, head, incline, influence, lead, lean, point, trend, verge; conduce, contribute.

tendency *n* aim, aptitude, bearing, bent, bias, course, determination, disposition, direction, drift, gravitation, inclination, leaning, liability, predisposition, proclivity, proneness, propensity, scope, set, susceptibility, turn, twist, warp.

tender[1] *vb* bid, offer, present, proffer, propose, suggest, volunteer. * *n* bid, offer, proffer, proposal; currency, money.

tender[2] *adj* callow, delicate, effeminate, feeble, feminine, fragile, immature, infantile, soft, weak, young; affectionate, compassionate, gentle, humane, kind, lenient, loving, merciful, mild, pitiful, sensitive, sympathetic, tender-hearted; affecting, disagreeable, painful, pathetic, touching, unpleasant.

tenebrous *adj* cloudy, dark, darksome, dusky, gloomy, murky, obscure, shadowy, shady, sombre, tenebrious.

tenement *n* abode, apartment, domicile, dwelling, flat, house.

tenet *n* belief, creed, position, dogma, doctrine, notion, opinion, position, principle, view.

tenor *n* cast, character, cut, fashion, form, manner, mood, nature, stamp, tendency, trend, tone; drift, gist, import, intent, meaning, purport, sense, significance, spirit.

tense *vb* flex, strain, tauten, tighten. * *adj* rigid, stiff, strained, stretched, taut, tight; excited, highly strung, intent, nervous, rapt.

tentative *adj* essaying, experimental, provisional, testing, toying.

tenure *n* holding, occupancy, occupation, possession, tenancy, tenement, use.

term *vb* call, christen, denominate, designate, dub, entitle, name, phrase, style. * *n* bound, boundary, bourn, confine, limit, mete, terminus; duration, period, season, semester, span, spell, termination, time; denomination, expression, locution, name, phrase, word.

termagant *n* beldam, hag, scold, shrew, spitfire, virago, vixen.

terminal *adj* bounding, limiting; final, terminating, ultimate. * *n* end, extremity, termination; bound, limit; airport, depot, station, terminus.

terminate *vb* bound, limit; end, finish, close, complete, conclude; eventuate, issue, prove.

termination *n* ending, suffix; bound, extend, limit; end, completion, conclusion, consequence, effect, issue, outcome, result.

terms *npl* conditions, provisions, stipulations.

terrestrial *adj* earthly, mundane, subastral, subcelestial, sublunar, sublunary, tellurian, worldly. * *n* earthling, human.

terrible *adj* appalling, dire, dreadful, fearful, formidable, frightful, gruesome, hideous, horrible, horrid, shocking, terrific, tremendous; alarming, awe-inspiring, awful, dread; great, excessive, extreme, severe.

terrific *adj* marvellous, sensational, superb; immense, intense; alarming, dreadful, formidable, frightful, terrible, tremendous.

terrify *vb* affright, alarm, appal, daunt, dismay, fright, frighten, horrify, scare, shock, startle, terrorize.

territory *n* country, district, domain, dominion, division, land, place, province, quarter, region, section, tract.

terror *n* affright, alarm, anxiety, awe, consternation, dismay, dread, fear, fright, horror, intimidation, panic, terrorism.

terse *adj* brief, compact, concise, laconic, neat, pithy, polished, sententious, short, smooth, succinct.

test *vb* assay; examine, prove, try. * *n* attempt, essay, examination, experiment, ordeal, proof, trial; criterion, standard, touchstone; example, exhibition; discrimination, distinction, judgment.

testify *vb* affirm, assert, asseverate, attest, avow, certify, corroborate, declare, depose, evidence, state, swear.

testimonial *n* certificate, credential, recommendation, voucher; monument, record.

testimony *n* affirmation, attestation, confession, confirmation, corroboration, declaration, deposition, profession; evidence, proof, witness.

testy *adj* captious, choleric, cross, fretful, hasty, irascible, irritable, quick, peevish, peppery, pettish, petulant, snappish, splenetic, touchy, waspish.

tetchy *adj* crabbed, cross, fretful, irritable, peevish, sullen, touchy.

tether *vb* chain, fasten, picket, stake, tie. * *n* chain, fastening, rope.

text *n* copy, subject, theme, thesis, topic, treatise.

texture *n* fabric, web, weft; character, coarseness, composition, constitution, fibre, fineness, grain, make-up, nap, organization, structure, tissue.

thankful *adj* appreciative, beholden, grateful, indebted, obliged.

thankfulness *n* appreciation, gratefulness, gratitude.

thankless *adj* profitless, ungracious, ungrateful, unthankful.

thaw *vb* dissolve, liquefy, melt, soften, unbend.

theatre *n* opera house, playhouse; arena, scene, seat, stage.

theatrical *adj* dramatic, dramaturgic, dramaturgical, histrionic, scenic, spectacular; affected, ceremonious, meretricious, ostentatious, pompous, showy, stagy, stilted, unnatural.

theft *n* depredation, embezzlement, fraud, larceny, peculation, pilfering, purloining, robbery, spoliation, stealing, swindling, thieving.

theme *n* composition, essay, motif, subject, text, thesis, topic, treatise.

theoretical *adj* abstract, conjectural, doctrinaire, ideal, hypothetical, pure, speculative, unapplied.

theory *n* assumption, conjecture, hypothesis, idea, plan, postulation, principle, scheme, speculation, surmise, system; doctrine, philosophy, science; explanation, exposition, philosophy, rationale.

therefore *adv* accordingly, afterward, consequently, hence, so, subsequently, then, thence, whence.

thesaurus *n* dictionary, encyclopedia, repository, storehouse, treasure.

thick *adj* bulky, chunky, dumpy, plump, solid, squab, squat, stubby, thickset; clotted, coagulated, crass, dense, dull, gross, heavy, viscous; blurred, cloudy, dirty, foggy, hazy, indistinguishable, misty, obscure, vaporous; muddy, roiled, turbid; abundant, frequent, multitudinous, numerous; close, compact, crowded, set, thickset; confused, guttural, hoarse, inarticulate, indistinct; dim, dull, weak; familiar, friendly, intimate, neighbourly, well-acquainted. * *adv* fast, frequently, quick; closely, densely, thickly. * *n* centre, middle, midst.

thicket *n* clump, coppice, copse, covert, forest, grove, jungle, shrubbery, underbrush, undergrowth, wood, woodland.

thief *n* depredator, filcher, pilferer, lifter, marauder, purloiner, robber, shark, stealer; burglar, corsair, defaulter, defrauder, embezzler, footpad, highwayman, housebreaker, kidnapper, pickpocket, pirate, poacher, privateer, sharper, swindler, peculator.

thieve *vb* cheat, embezzle, peculate, pilfer, plunder, purloin, rob, steal, swindle.

thin *vb* attenuate, dilute, diminish, prune, reduce, refine, weaken. * *adj* attenuated, bony, emaciated, fine, fleshless, flimsy, gaunt, haggard, lank, lanky, lean, meagre, peaked, pinched, poor, scanty, scraggy, scrawny, slender, slight, slim, small, sparse, spindly.

thing *n* being, body, contrivance, creature, entity, object, something, substance; act, action, affair, arrangement, circumstance, concern, deed, event, matter, occurrence, transaction.

think *vb* cogitate, contemplate, dream, meditate, muse, ponder, reflect, ruminate, speculate; consider, deliberate, reason, undertake; apprehend, believe, conceive, conclude, deem, determine, fancy, hold, imagine, judge, opine, presume, reckon, suppose, surmise; design, intend, mean, purpose; account, count, deem, esteem, hold, regard; compass, design, plan, plot. * *n* assessment, contemplation, deliberation, meditation, opinion, reasoning, reflection.

thirst *n* appetite, craving, desire, hunger, longing, yearning; aridity, drought, dryness.

thirsty *adj* arid, dry, parched; eager, greedy, hungry, longing, yearning.

thorn *n* prickle, spine; annoyance, bane, care, evil, infliction, nettle, nuisance, plague, torment, trouble, scourge.

thorny *adj* briary, briery, prickly, spinose, spinous, spiny; acuminate, barbed, pointed, prickling, sharp, spiky; annoying, difficult, harassing, perplexing, rugged, troublesome, trying, vexatious.

thorough, thoroughgoing *adj* absolute, arrant, complete, downright, entire, exhaustive, finished, perfect, radical, sweeping, total unmitigated, utter; accurate, correct, reliable, trustworthy.

though *conj* admitting, allowing, although, granted, granting, if, notwithstanding, still. * *adv* however, nevertheless, still, yet.

thought *n* absorption, cogitation, engrossment, meditation, musing, reflection, reverie, rumination; contemplation, intellect, ratiocination, thinking, thoughtfulness; application, conception, consideration, deliberation, idea, pondering, speculation, study; consciousness, imagination, intellect, perception, understanding; conceit, fancy, notion; conclusion, judgment, motion, opinion, sentiment, supposition, view; anxiety, attention, care, concern, provision, regard, solicitude, thoughtfulness; design, expectation, intention, purpose.

thoughtful *adj* absorbed, contemplative, deliberative, dreamy, engrossed, introspective, pensive, philosophic, reflecting, reflective, sedate, speculative; attentive, careful, cautious, circumspect, considerate, discreet, heedful, friendly, kindhearted, kindly, mindful, neighbourly, provident, prudent, regardful, watchful, wary; quiet, serious, sober, studious.

thoughtless *adj* careless, casual, flighty, heedless, improvident, inattentive, inconsiderate, neglectful, negligent, precipitate, rash, reckless, regardless, remiss, trifling, unmindful, unthinking; blank, blockish, dull, insensate, stupid, vacant, vacuous.

thraldom *n* bondage, enslavement, enthralment, serfdom, servitude, slavery, subjection, thrall, vassalage.

thrash *vb* beat, bruise, conquer, defeat, drub, flog, lash, maul, pommel, punish, thwack, trounce, wallop, whip.

thread *vb* course, direction, drift, tenor; reeve, trace. * *n* cord, fibre, filament, hair, line, twist; pile, staple.

threadbare *adj* napless, old, seedy, worn; common,

commonplace, hackneyed, stale, trite, worn-out.

threat *n* commination, defiance, denunciation, fulmination, intimidation, menace, thunder, thunderbolt.

threaten *vb* denounce, endanger, fulminate, intimidate, menace, thunder; augur, forebode, foreshadow, indicate, portend, presage, prognosticate, warn.

threshold *n* doorsill, sill; door, entrance, gate; beginning, commencement, opening, outset, start.

thrift *n* economy, frugality, parsimony, saving, thriftiness; gain, luck, profit, prosperity, success.

thriftless *adj* extravagant, improvident, lavish, profuse, prodigal, shiftless, unthrifty, wasteful.

thrifty *adj* careful, economical, frugal, provident, saving, sparing; flourishing, prosperous, thriving, vigorous.

thrill *vb* affect, agitate, electrify, inspire, move, penetrate, pierce, rouse, stir, touch. * *n* excitement, sensation, shock, tingling, tremor.

thrilling *adj* affecting, exciting, gripping, moving, sensational, touching.

thrive *vb* advance, batten, bloom, boom, flourish, prosper, succeed.

throng *vb* congregate, crowd, fill, flock, pack, press, swarm. * *n* assemblage, concourse, congregation, crowd, horde, host, mob, multitude, swarm.

throttle *vb* choke, silence, strangle, suffocate.

throw *vb* cast, chuck, dart, fling, hurl, lance, launch, overturn, pitch, pitchfork, send, sling, toss, whirl. * *n* cast, fling, hurl, launch, pitch, sling, toss, whirl; chance, gamble, try, venture.

thrust *vb* clap, dig, drive, force, impel, jam, plunge, poke, propel, push, ram, run, shove, stick. * *n* dig, jab, lunge, pass, plunge, poke, propulsion, push, shove, stab, tilt.

thump *vb* bang, batter, beat, belabour, knock, punch, strike, thrash, thwack, whack. * *n* blow, knock, punch, strike, stroke.

thwart *vb* baffle, balk, contravene, counteract, cross, defeat, disconcert, frustrate, hinder, impede, oppose, obstruct, oppugn; cross, intersect, traverse.

tickle *vb* amuse, delight, divert, enliven, gladden, gratify, please, rejoice, titillate.

ticklish *adj* dangerous, precarious, risky, tottering, uncertain, unstable, unsteady; critical, delicate, difficult, nice.

tide *n* course, current, ebb, flow, stream.

tidings *npl* advice, greetings, information, intelligence, news, report, word.

tidy *vb* clean, neaten, order, straighten. * *adj* clean, neat, orderly, shipshape, spruce, trig, trim.

tie *vb* bind, confine, fasten, knot, lock, manacle, secure, shackle, fetter, yoke; complicate, entangle, interlace, knit; connect, hold, join, link, unite; constrain, oblige, restrain, restrict. * *n* band, fastening, knot, ligament, ligature; allegiance, bond, obligation; bow, cravat, necktie.

tier *n* line, rank, row, series.

tiff *n* fit, fume, passion, pet, miff, rage.

tight *adj* close, compact, fast, firm; taut, tense, stretched; impassable, narrow, strait.

till *vb* cultivate, plough, harrow.

tillage *n* agriculture, cultivation, culture, farming, geoponics, husbandry.

tilt *vb* cant, incline, slant, slope, tip; forge, hammer; point, thrust; joust, rush. * *n* awning, canopy, tent; lunge, pass, thrust; cant, inclination, slant, slope, tip.

time *vb* clock, control, count, measure, regulate, schedule. * *n* duration, interim, interval, season, span, spell, tenure, term, while; aeon, age, date, epoch, eon, era; term; cycle, dynasty, reign; confinement, delivery, parturition; measure, rhythm.

timely *adj* acceptable, appropriate, apropos, early, opportune, prompt, punctual, seasonable, well-timed.

timid *adj* afraid, cowardly, faint-hearted, fearful, irresolute, meticulous, nervous, pusillanimous, skittish, timorous, unadventurous; bashful, coy, diffident, modest, shame-faced, shrinking.

tincture *vb* colour, dye, shade, stain, tinge, tint; flavour, season; imbue, impregnate, impress, infuse. * *n* grain, hue, shade, stain, tinge, tint, tone; flavour, smack, spice, taste; admixture, dash, infusion, seasoning, sprinkling, touch.

tinge *vb* colour, dye, stain, tincture, tint; imbue, impregnate, impress, infuse. * *n* cast, colour, dye, hue, shade, stain, tincture, tint; flavour, smack, spice, quality, taste.

tint *n* cast, colour, complexion, dye, hue, shade, tinge, tone.

tiny *adj* diminutive, dwarfish, Lilliputian, little, microscopic, miniature, minute, puny, pygmy, small, wee.

tip[1] *n* apex, cap, end, extremity, peak, pinnacle, point, top, vertex.

tip[2] *vb* incline, overturn, tilt; dispose of, dump. * *n* donation, fee, gift, gratuity, perquisite, reward; inclination, slant; hint, pointer, suggestion; strike, tap.

tirade *n* abuse, denunciation, diatribe, harangue, outburst.

tire *vb* exhaust, fag, fatigue, harass, jade, weary; bore, bother, irk.

tiresome *adj* annoying, arduous, boring, dull, exhausting, fatiguing, fagging, humdrum, irksome, laborious, monotonous, tedious, wearisome, vexatious.

tissue *n* cloth, fabric; membrane, network, structure, texture, web; accumulation, chain, collection, combination, conglomeration, mass, series, set.

titanic *adj* colossal, Cyclopean, enormous, gigantic, herculean, huge, immense, mighty, monstrous, prodigious, stupendous, vast.

title *vb* call, designate, name, style, term. * *n* caption, legend, head, heading; appellation, application, cognomen, completion, denomination, designation, epithet, name; claim, due, ownership, part, possession, prerogative, privilege, right.

tittle *n* atom, bit, grain, iota, jot, mite, particle, scrap, speck, whit.

tittle-tattle *vb, n* babble, cackle, chatter, discourse, gabble, gossip, prattle.

toast *vb* brown, dry, heat; honour, pledge, propose, salute. * *n* compliment, drink, pledge, salutation, salute; favourite, pet.

toil *vb* drudge, labour, strive, work. * *n* drudgery, effort, exertion, exhaustion, grinding, labour, pains, travail, work; gin, net, noose, snare, spring, trap.

toilsome *adj* arduous, difficult, fatiguing, hard, laborious, onerous, painful, severe, tedious, wearisome.

token *adj* nominal, superficial, symbolic. * *n* badge, evidence, index, indication, manifestation, mark, note, sign, symbol, trace, trait; keepsake, memento, memorial, reminder, souvenir.

tolerable *adj* bearable, endurable, sufferable, supportable; fair, indifferent, middling, ordinary, passable, so-so.

tolerance *n* endurance, receptivity, sufferance, toleration.

tolerate *vb* admit, allow, indulge, let, permit, receive; abide, brook, endure, suffer.

toll[1] *n* assessment, charge, customs, demand, dues, duty, fee, impost, levy, rate, tax, tribute; cost, damage, loss.

toll[2] *vb* chime, knell, peal, ring, sound. * *n* chime, knell, peal, ring, ringing, tolling.

tomb *n* catacomb, charnel house, crypt, grave, mausoleum, sepulchre, vault.

tone *vb* blend, harmonize, match, suit. * *n* note, sound; accent, cadence, emphasis, inflection, intonation, modulation; key, mood, strain, temper; elasticity, energy, force, health, strength, tension, vigour; cast, colour, manner, hue, shade, style, tint; drift, tenor.

tongue *n* accent, dialect, language, utterance, vernacular; discourse, parlance, speech, talk; nation, race.

too *adv* additionally, also, further, likewise, moreover, overmuch.

toothsome *adj* agreeable, dainty, delicious, luscious, nice, palatable, savoury.

top *vb* cap, head, tip; ride, surmount; outgo, surpass. * *adj* apical, best, chief, culminating, finest, first, foremost, highest, leading, prime, principal, topmost, uppermost. * *n* acme, apex, crest, crown, head, meridian, pinnacle, summit, surface, vertex, zenith.

topic *n* business, question, subject, text, theme, thesis; division, head, subdivision; commonplace, dictum, maxim, precept, proposition, principle, rule; arrangement, scheme.

topple *vb* fall, overturn, tumble, upset.

torment *vb* annoy, agonize, distress, excruciate, pain, rack, torture; badger, fret, harass, harry, irritate, nettle, plague, provoke, tantalize, tease,

trouble, vex, worry. * *n* agony, anguish, pang, rack, torture.

tornado *n* blizzard, cyclone, gale, hurricane, storm, tempest, typhoon, whirlwind.

torpid *adj* benumbed, lethargic, motionless, numb; apathetic, dormant, dull, inactive, indolent, inert, listless, sleepy, slothful, sluggish, stupid.

torpor *n* coma, insensibility, lethargy, numbness, torpidity; inaction, inactivity, inertness, sluggishness, stupidity.

torrid *adj* arid, burnt, dried, parched; burning, fiery, hot, parching, scorching, sultry, tropical, violent.

tortuous *adj* crooked, curved, curvilineal, curvilinear, serpentine, sinuate, sinuated, sinuous, twisted, winding; ambiguous, circuitous, crooked, deceitful, indirect, perverse, roundabout.

torture *vb* agonize, distress, excruciate, pain, rack, torment. * *n* agony, anguish, distress, pain, pang, rack, torment.

toss *vb* cast, fling, hurl, pitch, throw; agitate, rock, shake; disquiet, harass, try; roll, writhe. * *n* cast, fling, pitch, throw.

total *vb* add, amount to, reach, reckon. * *adj* complete, entire, full, whole; integral, undivided. * *n* aggregate, all, gross, lump, mass, sum, totality, whole.

totter *vb* falter, reel, stagger, vacillate; lean, oscillate, reel, rock, shake, sway, tremble, waver; fail, fall, flag.

touch *vb* feel, graze, handle, hit, pat, strike, tap; concern, interest, regard; affect, impress, move, stir; grasp, reach, stretch; melt, mollify, soften; afflict, distress, hurt, injure, molest, sting, wound. * *n* hint, smack, suggestion, suspicion, taste, trace; blow, contract, hit, pat, tap.

touchiness *n* fretfulness, irritability, irascibility, peevishness, pettishness, petulance, snappishness, spleen, testiness.

touching *adj* affecting, heart-rending, impressive, melting, moving, pathetic, pitiable, tender; abutting, adjacent, bordering, tangent.

touchy *adj* choleric, cross, fretful, hot-tempered, irascible, irritable, peevish, petulant, quick-tempered, snappish, splenetic, tetchy, testy, waspish.

tough *adj* adhesive, cohesive, flexible, tenacious; coriaceous, leathery; clammy, ropy, sticky, viscous; inflexible, intractable, rigid, stiff; callous, hard, obdurate, stubborn; difficult, formidable, hard, troublesome. * *n* brute, bully, hooligan, ruffian, thug.

tour *vb* journey, perambulate, travel, visit. * *n* circuit, course, excursion, expedition, journey, perambulation, pilgrimage, round.

tow *vb* drag, draw, haul, pull, tug. * *n* drag, lift, pull.

tower *vb* mount, rise, soar, transcend. * *n* belfry, bell tower, column, minaret, spire, steeple, turret; castle, citadel, fortress, stronghold; pillar, refuge, rock, support.

towering *adj* elevated, lofty; excessive, extreme, prodigious, violent.

toy *vb* dally, play, sport, trifle, wanton. * *n* bauble, doll, gewgaw, gimmick, knick-knack, plaything, puppet, trinket; bagatelle, bubble, trifle; play, sport.

trace *vb* follow, track, train; copy, deduce, delineate, derive, describe, draw, sketch. * *n* evidence, footmark, footprint, footstep, impression, mark, remains, sign, token, track, trail, vestige, wake; memorial, record; bit, dash, flavour, hint, suspicion, streak, tinge.

track *vb* chase, draw, follow, pursue, scent, track, trail. * *n* footmark, footprint, footstep, spoor, trace, vestige; course, pathway, rails, road, runway, trace, trail, wake, way.

trackless *adj* pathless, solitary, unfrequented, unused.

tract[1] *n* area, district, quarter, region, territory; parcel, patch, part, piece, plot, portion.

tract[2] *n* disquisition, dissertation, essay, homily, pamphlet, sermon, thesis, tractate, treatise.

tractable *adj* amenable, docile, governable, manageable, submissive, willing, yielding; adaptable, ductile, malleable, plastic, tractile.

trade *vb* bargain, barter, chaffer, deal, exchange, interchange, sell, traffic. * *n* bargaining, barter, business, commerce, dealing, traffic; avocation, calling, craft, employment, occupation, office, profession, pursuit, vocation.

traditional *adj* accustomed, apocryphal, customary, established, historic, legendary, old, oral, transmitted, uncertain, unverified, unwritten.

traduce *vb* abuse, asperse, blemish, brand, calumniate, decry, defame, depreciate, disparage, revile, malign, slander, vilify.

traducer *n* calumniator, defamer, detractor, slanderer, vilifier.

traffic *vb* bargain, barter, chaffer, deal, exchange, trade. * *n* barter, business, chaffer, commerce, exchange, intercourse, trade, transportation, truck.

tragedy *n* drama, play; adversity, calamity, catastrophe, disaster, misfortune.

tragic *adj* dramatic; calamitous, catastrophic, disastrous, dreadful, fatal, grievous, heart-breaking, mournful, sad, shocking, sorrowful.

trail *vb* follow, hunt, trace, track; drag, draw, float, flow, haul, pull. * *n* footmark, footprint, footstep, mark, trace, track.

train *vb* drag, draw, haul, trail, tug; allure, entice; discipline, drill, educate, exercise, instruct, school, teach; accustom, break in, familiarize, habituate, inure, prepare, rehearse, use. * *n* trail, wake; entourage, cortege, followers, retinue, staff, suite; chain, consecution, sequel, series, set, succession; course, method, order, process; allure, artifice, device, enticement, lure, persuasion, stratagem, trap.

trait *n* line, mark, stroke, touch; characteristic, feature, lineage, particularity, peculiarity, quality.

traitor *n* apostate, betrayer, deceiver, Judas, miscreant, quisling, renegade, turncoat; conspirator, deserter, insurgent, mutineer, rebel, revolutionary.

traitorous *adj* faithless, false, perfidious, recreant, treacherous; insidious, treasonable.

trammel *vb* clog, confine, cramp, cumber, hamper, hinder, fetter, restrain, restrict, shackle, tie. * *n* bond, chain, fetter, hindrance, impediment, net, restraint, shackle.

tramp *vb* hike, march, plod, trudge, walk. * *n* excursion, journey, march, walk; landloper, loafer, stroller, tramper, vagabond, vagrant.

trample *vb* crush, tread; scorn, spurn.

trance *n* dream, ecstasy, hypnosis, rapture; catalepsy, coma.

tranquil *adj* calm, hushed, peaceful, placid, quiet, serene, still, undisturbed, unmoved, unperturbed, unruffled, untroubled.

tranquillity *n* calmness, peace, peacefulness, placidity, placidness, quiet, quietness, serenity, stillness, tranquilness.

tranquillize *vb* allay, appease, assuage, calm, compose, hush, lay, lull, moderate, pacify, quell, quiet, silence, soothe, still.

transact *vb* conduct, dispatch, enact, execute, do, manage, negotiate, perform, treat.

transaction *n* act, action, conduct, doing, management, negotiation, performance; affair, business, deal, dealing, incident, event, job, matter, occurrence, procedure, proceeding.

transcend *vb* exceed, overlap, overstep, pass, transgress; excel, outstrip, outrival, outvie, overtop, surmount, surpass.

transcendent *adj* consummate, inimitable, peerless, pre-eminent, supereminent, surpassing, unequalled, unparalleled, unrivalled, unsurpassed; metempiric, metempirical, noumenal, supersensible.

transcript *n* duplicate, engrossment, rescript.

transfer *vb* convey, dispatch, move, remove, send, translate, transmit, transplant, transport; abalienate, alienate, assign, cede, confer, convey, consign, deed, devise, displace, forward, grant, pass, relegate. * *n* abalienation, alienation, assignment, bequest, carriage, cession, change, conveyance, copy, demise, devisal, gift, grant, move, relegation, removal, shift, shipment, transference, transferring, transit, transmission, transportation.

transfigure *vb* change, convert, dignify, idealize, metamorphose, transform.

transform *vb* alter, change, metamorphose, transfigure; convert, resolve, translate, transmogrify, transmute.

transgress *vb* exceed, transcend, overpass, overstep; break, contravene, disobey, infringe, violate; err, intrude, offend, sin, slip, trespass.

transgression *n* breach, disobedience, encroachment, infraction, infringement, transgression, violation; crime, delinquency, error, fault, iniquity, misdeed, misdemeanour, misdoing, offence, sin, slip, trespass, wrongdoing.

transient *adj* diurnal, ephemeral, evanescent, fleeting, fugitive, impertinent, meteoric, mortal, passing, perishable, short-lived, temporary, transitory, volatile; hasty, imperfect, momentary, short.

transitory *adj* brief, ephemeral, evanescent, fleeting, flitting, fugacious, momentary, passing, short, temporary, transient.

translate *vb* remove, transfer, transport; construe, decipher, decode, interpret, render, turn.

translucent *adj* diaphanous, hyaline, pellucid, semi-opaque, semi-transparent.

transmit *vb* forward, remit, send; communicate, conduct, radiate; bear, carry, convey.

transparent *adj* bright, clear, diaphanous, limpid, lucid; crystalline, hyaline, pellucid, serene, translucent, transpicuous, unclouded; open, porous, transpicuous; evident, obvious, manifest, patent.

transpire *vb* befall, chance, happen, occur; evaporate, exhale.

transport *vb* bear, carry, cart, conduct, convey, fetch, remove, ship, take, transfer, truck; banish, expel; beatify, delight, enrapture, enravish, entrance, ravish. * *n* carriage, conveyance, movement, transportation, transporting; beatification, beatitude, bliss, ecstasy, felicity, happiness, rapture, ravishment; frenzy, passion, vehemence, warmth.

transude *vb* exude, filter, ooze, percolate, strain.

trap *vb* catch, ensnare, entrap, noose, snare, springe; ambush, deceive, dupe, trick; enmesh, tangle, trepan. * *n* gin, snare, springe, toil; ambush, artifice, pitfall, stratagem, trepan.

trappings *npl* adornments, decorations, dress, embellishments, frippery, gear, livery, ornaments, paraphernalia, rigging; accoutrements, caparisons, equipment, gear.

trash *n* dregs, dross, garbage, refuse, rubbish, trumpery, waste; balderdash, nonsense, twaddle.

travel *vb* journey, peregrinate, ramble, roam, rove, tour, voyage, walk, wander; go, move, pass. * *n* excursion, expedition, journey, peregrination, ramble, tour, trip, voyage, walk.

traveller *n* excursionist, explorer, globe-trotter, itinerant, passenger, pilgrim, rover, sightseer, tourist, trekker, tripper, voyager, wanderer, wayfarer.

traverse *vb* contravene, counteract, defeat, frustrate, obstruct, oppose, thwart; ford, pass, play, range.

travesty *vb* imitate, parody, take off. * *n* burlesque, caricature, imitation, parody, take-off.

treacherous *adj* deceitful, disloyal, faithless, false, false-hearted, insidious, perfidious, recreant, sly, traitorous, treasonable, unfaithful, unreliable, unsafe, untrustworthy.

treachery *n* betrayal, deceitfulness, disloyalty, double-dealing, faithlessness, foul play, infidelity, insidiousness, perfidiousness, treason, perfidy.

treason *n* betrayal, disloyalty, lèse-majesté, lese-majesty, perfidy, sedition, traitorousness, treachery.

treasonable *adj* disloyal, traitorous, treacherous.

treasure *vb* accumulate, collect, garner, hoard, husband, save, store; cherish, idolize, prize, value, worship. * *n* cash, funds, jewels, money, riches, savings, valuables, wealth; abundance, reserve, stock, store.

treasurer *n* banker, bursar, purser, receiver, trustee.

treat *vb* entertain, feast, gratify, refresh; attend, doctor, dose, handle, manage, serve; bargain, covenant, negotiate, parley. * *n* banquet, entertainment, feast; delight, enjoyment, entertainment, gratification, luxury, pleasure, refreshment.

treatise *n* commentary, discourse, dissertation, disquisition, monograph, tractate.

treatment *n* usage, use; dealing, handling, management, manipulation; doctoring, therapy.

treaty *n* agreement, alliance, bargain, compact, concordat, convention, covenant, entente, league, pact.

tremble *vb* quake, quaver, quiver, shake, shiver, shudder, vibrate, wobble. * *n* quake, quiver, shake, shiver, shudder, tremor, vibration, wobble.

tremendous *adj* colossal, enormous, huge, immense; excellent, marvellous, wonderful; alarming, appalling, awful, dreadful, fearful, frightful, horrid, horrible, terrible.

tremor *n* agitation, quaking, quivering, shaking, trembling, trepidation, tremulousness, vibration.

tremulous *adj* afraid, fearful, quavering, quivering, shaking, shaky, shivering, timid, trembling, vibrating.

trench *vb* carve, cut; ditch, channel, entrench, furrow. * *n* channel, ditch, drain, furrow, gutter, moat, pit, sewer, trough; dugout, entrenchment, fortification.

trenchant *adj* cutting, keen, sharp; acute, biting, caustic, crisp, incisive, pointed, piquant, pungent, sarcastic, sententious, severe, unsparing, vigorous.

trend *vb* drift, gravitate, incline, lean, run, stretch, sweep, tend, turn. * *n* bent, course, direction, drift, inclination, set, leaning, tendency, trending.

trepidation *n* agitation, quaking, quivering, shaking, trembling, tremor; dismay, excitement, fear, perturbation, tremulousness.

trespass *vb* encroach, infringe, intrude, trench; offend, sin, transgress. * *n* encroachment, infringement, injury, intrusion, invasion; crime, delinquency, error, fault, sin, misdeed, misdemeanour, offence, transgression; trespasser.

trial *adj* experimental, exploratory, testing. * *n* examination, experiment, test; experience, knowledge; aim, attempt, effort, endeavour, essay, exertion, struggle; assay, criterion, ordeal, prohibition, proof, test, touchstone; affliction, burden, chagrin, dolour, distress, grief, hardship, heartache, inclination, misery, mortification, pain, sorrow, suffering, tribulation, trouble, unhappiness, vexation, woe, wretchedness; action, case, cause, hearing, suit.

tribe *n* clan, family, lineage, race, sept, stock; class, distinction, division, order.

tribulation *n* adversity, affliction, distress, grief, misery, pain, sorrow, suffering, trial, trouble, unhappiness, woe, wretchedness.

tribunal *n* bench, judgement seat; assizes, bar, court, judicature, session.

tribute *n* subsidy, tax; custom, duty, excise, impost, tax, toll; contribution, grant, offering.

trice *n* flash, instant, jiffy, moment, second, twinkling.

trick *vb* cheat, circumvent, cozen, deceive, defraud, delude, diddle, dupe, fob, gull, hoax, overreach. * *n* artifice, blind, deceit, deception, dodge, fake, feint, fraud, game, hoax, imposture, manoeuvre, shift, ruse, swindle, stratagem, wile; antic, caper, craft, deftness, gambol, sleight; habit, mannerism, peculiarity, practice.

trickle *vb* distil, dribble, drip, drop, ooze, percolate, seep. * *n* dribble, drip, percolation, seepage.

tricky *adj* artful, cunning, deceitful, deceptive, subtle, trickish.

trifle *vb* dally, dawdle, fool, fribble, palter, play, potter, toy. * *n* bagatelle, bauble, bean, fig, nothing, triviality; iota, jot, modicum, particle, trace.

trifling *adj* empty, frippery, frivolous, inconsiderable, insignificant, nugatory, petty, piddling, shallow, slight, small, trivial, unimportant, worthless.

trill *vb* shake, quaver, warble. * *n* quaver, shake, tremolo, warbling.

trim *vb* adjust, arrange, prepare; balance, equalize, fill; adorn, array, bedeck, decorate, dress, embellish, garnish, ornament; clip, curtail, cut, lop, mow, poll, prune, shave, shear; berate, chastise, chide, rebuke, reprimand, reprove, trounce; fluctuate, hedge, shift, shuffle, vacillate. * *adj* compact, neat, nice, shapely, snug, tidy, well-adjusted, well-ordered; chic, elegant, finical, smart, spruce. * *n* dress, embellishment, gear, ornaments, trappings, trimmings; case, condition, order, plight, state.

trinket *n* bagatelle, bauble, bijoux, gewgaw, gimcrack, knick-knack, toy, trifle.

trinkets *npl* bijouterie, jewellery, jewels, ornaments.

trip *vb* caper, dance, frisk, hop, skip; misstep, stumble; bungle, blunder, err, fail, mistake; overthrow, supplant, upset; catch, convict, detect. * *n* hop, skip; lurch, misstep, stumble; blunder, bungle, error, failure, fault, lapse, miss, mistake, oversight, slip; circuit, excursion, expedition, jaunt, journey, ramble, route, stroll, tour.

trite *adj* banal, beaten, common, commonplace, hackneyed, old, ordinary, stale, stereotyped, threadbare, usual, worn.

triturate *vb* beat, bray, bruise, grind, pound, rub, thrash; comminute, levigate, pulverize.

triumph *vb* exult, rejoice; prevail, succeed, win; flourish, prosper, thrive; boast, brag, crow, gloat, swagger, vaunt. * *n* celebration, exultation, joy, jubilation, jubilee, ovation; accomplishment, achievement, conquest, success, victory.

triumphant *adj* boastful, conquering, elated, exultant, exulting, jubilant, rejoicing, successful, victorious.

trivial *adj* frivolous, gimcrack, immaterial, inconsiderable, insignificant, light, little, nugatory, paltry, petty, small, slight, slim, trifling, trumpery, unimportant.

trollop *n* prostitute, slattern, slut, whore.

troop *vb* crowd, flock, muster, throng. * *n* company, crowd, flock, herd, multitude, number, throng; band, body, party, squad, troupe.

trophy *n* laurels, medal, palm, prize.

troth *n* candour, sincerity, truth, veracity, verity; allegiance, belief, faith, fidelity, word; betrothal.

trouble *vb* agitate, confuse, derange, disarrange, disorder, disturb; afflict, ail, annoy, badger, concern, disquiet, distress, fret, grieve, harass, molest, perplex, perturb, pester, plague, torment, vex, worry. * *n* adversity, affliction, calamity, distress, dolour, grief, hardship, misfortune, misery, pain, sorrow, suffering, tribulation, woe; ado, annoyance, anxiety, bother, care, discomfort, embarrassment, fuss, inconvenience, irritation, pains, perplexity, plague, torment, vexation, worry; commotion, disturbance, row; bewilderment, disquietude, embarrassment, perplexity, uneasiness.

troublesome *adj* annoying, distressing, disturbing, galling, grievous, harassing, painful, perplexing, vexatious, worrisome; burdensome, irksome, tiresome, wearisome; importunate, intrusive, teasing; arduous, difficult, hard, inconvenient, trying, unwieldy.

troublous *adj* agitated, disquieted, disturbed, perturbed, tumultuous, turbulent.

trough *n* hutch, manger; channel, depression, hollow, furrow.

truant *vb* be absent, desert, dodge, malinger, shirk, skive. * *n* absentee, deserter, idler, laggard, loiterer, lounger, malingerer, quitter, runaway, shirker, vagabond.

truce *n* armistice, breathing space, cessation, delay, intermission, lull, pause, recess, reprieve, respite, rest.

truck *vb* barter, deal, exchange, trade, traffic. * *n* lorry, van, wagon.

truckle *vb* roll, trundle; cringe, crouch, fawn, knuckle, stoop, submit, yield.

truculent *adj* barbarous, bloodthirsty, ferocious, fierce, savage; cruel, malevolent, relentless; destructive, deadly, fatal, ruthless.

true *adj* actual, unaffected, authentic, genuine, legitimate, pure, real, rightful, sincere, sound, truthful, veritable; substantial, veracious; constant, faithful, loyal, staunch, steady; equitable, honest, honourable, just, upright, trusty, trustworthy, virtuous; accurate, correct, even, exact, right, straight, undeviating. * *adv* good, well.

truism *n* axiom, commonplace, platitude.

trumpery *adj* pinchbeck, rubbishy, trashy, trifling, worthless. * *n* deceit, deception, falsehood, humbug, imposture; frippery, rubbish, stuff, trash, trifles.

truncheon *n* club, cudgel, nightstick, partisan, staff; baton, wand.

trunk *n* body, bole, butt, shaft, stalk, stem, stock, torso; box, chest, coffer.

trundle *vb* bowl, revolve, roll, spin, truckle, wheel.

truss *vb* bind, bundle, close, cram, hang, pack. * *n* bundle, package, packet; apparatus, bandage, support.

trust *vb* confide, depend, expect, hope, rely; believe, credit; commit, entrust. * *n* belief, confidence, credence, faith; credit, tick; charge, deposit; commission, duty, errand; assurance, conviction, expectation, hope, reliance, secutrity.

trustful *adj* confiding, trusting, unquestioning, unsuspecting; faithful, trustworthy, trusty.

trustworthy *adj* confidential, constant, credible, dependable, faithful, firm, honest, incorrupt, upright, reliable, responsible, straightforward, staunch, true, trusty, uncorrupt, upright.

truth *n* fact, reality, veracity; actuality, authenticity, realism; canon, law, oracle, principle; right, truthfulness, veracity; candour, fidelity, frankness, honesty, honour, ingenuousness, integrity, probity, sincerity, virtue; constancy, devotion, faith, fealty, loyalty, steadfastness; accuracy, correctness, exactitude, exactness, nicety, precision, regularity, trueness.

truthful *adj* correct, reliable, true, trustworthy, veracious; artless, candid, frank, guileless, honest, ingenuous, open, sincere, straightforward, trusty.

truthless *adj* canting, disingenuous, dishonest, false, faithless, hollow, hypocritical, insincere, pharisaical, treacherous, unfair, untrustworthy.

try *vb* examine, prove, test; attempt, essay; adjudicate, adjudge, examine, hear; purify, refine; sample, sift, smell, taste; aim, attempt, endeavour, seek, strain, strive. * *n* attempt, effort, endeavour, experiment, trial.

trying *adj* difficult, fatiguing, hard, irksome, tiresome, wearisome; afflicting, afflictive, calamitous, deplorable, dire, distressing, grievous, hard, painful, sad, severe.

tryst *n* appointment, assignation, rendezvous.

tube *n* bore, bronchus, cylinder, duct, hollow, hose, pipe, pipette, worm.

tuft *n* brush, bunch, crest, feather, knot, plume, topknot, tussock; clump, cluster, group.

tug *vb* drag, draw, haul, pull, tow, wrench; labour, strive, struggle. * *n* drag, haul, pull, tow, wrench.

tuition *n* education, instruction, schooling, teaching, training.

tumble *vb* heave, pitch, roll, toss, wallow; fall, sprawl, stumble, topple, trip; derange, disarrange, dishevel, disorder, disturb, rumple, tousle. * *n* collapse, drop, fall, plunge, spill, stumble, trip.

tumbler *n* acrobat, juggler; glass.

tumid *adj* bloated, distended, enlarged, puffed-up, swelled, swollen, turgid; bombastic, declamatory, fustian, grandiloquent, grandiose, high-flown, inflated, pompous, puffy, rhetorical, stilted, swelling.

tumour *n* boil, carbuncle, swelling, tumefaction.

tumult *n* ado, affray, agitation, altercation, bluster, brawl, disturbance, ferment, flurry, feud, fracas, fray, fuss, hubbub, huddle, hurly-burly, melee, noise, perturbation, pother, quarrel, racket, riot, row, squabble, stir, turbulence, turmoil, uproar.

tumultuous *adj* blustery, breezy, bustling, confused, disorderly, disturbed, riotous, turbulent, unruly.

tune *vb* accord, attune, harmonize, modulate; adapt, adjust, attune. * *n* air, aria, melody, strain, tone; agreement, concord, harmony; accord, order.

tuneful *adj* dulcet, harmonious, melodious, musical.

turbid *adj* foul, impure, muddy, thick, unsettled.

turbulence *n* agitation, commotion, confusion, disorder, disturbance, excitement, tumult, tumultuousness, turmoil, unruliness, uproar; insubordination, insurrection, mutiny, rebellion, riot, sedition.

turbulent *adj* agitated, disturbed, restless, tumultuous, wild; blatant, blustering, boisterous, brawling, disorderly, obstreperous, tumultuous, uproarious, vociferous; factious, insubordinate, insurgent, mutinous, raging, rebellious, refractory, revolutionary, riotous, seditious, stormy, violent.

turf *n* grass, greensward, sod, sward; horse racing, racecourse, race-ground.

turgid *adj* bloated, distended, protuberant, puffed-up, swelled, swollen, tumid; bombastic, declamatory, diffuse, digressive, fustian, high-flown, inflated, grandiloquent, grandiose, ostentatious, pompous, puffy, rhetorical, stilted.

turmoil *n* activity, agitation, bustle, commotion, confusion, disorder, disturbance, ferment, flurry, huddle, hubbub, hurly-burly, noise, trouble, tumult, turbulence, uproar.

turn *vb* revolve, rotate; bend, cast, defect, inflict, round, spin, sway, swivel, twirl, twist, wheel; crank, grind, wind; deflect, divert, transfer, warp; form, mould, shape; adapt, fit, manoeuvre, suit; alter, change, conform, metamorphose, transform, transmute, vary; convert, persuade, prejudice; construe, render, translate; depend, hang, hinge, pivot; eventuate, issue, result, terminate; acidify, curdle, ferment. * n cycle, gyration, revolution, rotation, round; bending, deflection, deviation, diversion, doubling, flection, flexion, flexure, reel, retroversion, slew, spin, sweep, swing, swirl, swivel, turning, twist, twirl, whirl, winding; alteration, change, variation, vicissitude; bend, circuit, drive, ramble, run, round, stroll; bout, hand, innings, opportunity, shift, spell; act, action, deed, office; convenience, occasion, purpose; cast, fashion, form, guise, manner, mould, phase, shape; aptitude, bent, bias, disposition, faculty, genius, gift, inclination, leaning, proclivity, proneness, propensity, talent, tendency.

turncoat n apostate, backslider, deserter, recreant, renegade, traitor, wretch.

turpitude n baseness, degradation, depravity, vileness, wickedness.

turret n cupola, minaret, pinnacle.

tussle vb conflict, contend, contest, scuffle, struggle, wrestle. * n conflict, contest, fight, scuffle, struggle.

tutelage n care, charge, dependence, guardianship, protection, teaching, tutorage, tutorship, wardship.

tutor vb coach, educate, instruct, teach; discipline, train. * n coach, governess, governor, instructor, master, preceptor, schoolteacher, teacher.

twaddle vb chatter, gabble, maunder, prate, prattle. * n balderdash, chatter, flummery, gabble, gibberish, gobbledegook, gossip, jargon, moonshine, nonsense, platitude, prate, prattle, rigmarole, stuff, tattle.

tweak vb, n jerk, pinch, pull, twinge, twitch.

twig[1] n bough, branch, offshoot, shoot, slip, spray, sprig, stick, switch.

twig[2] vb catch on, comprehend, discover, grasp, realize, recognize, see, understand.

twin vb couple, link, match, pair. * adj double, doubled, duplicate, geminate, identical, matched, matching, second, twain. * n corollary, double, duplicate, fellow, likeness, match.

twine vb embrace, encircle, entwine, interlace, surround, wreathe; bend, meander, wind; coil, twist. * n convolution, coil, twist; embrace, twining, winding; cord, string.

twinge vb pinch, tweak, twitch. * n pinch, tweak, twitch; gripe, pang, spasm.

twinkle vb blink, twink, wink; flash, glimmer, scintillate, sparkle. * n blink, flash, gleam, glimmer, scintillation, sparkle; flash, instant, jiffy, moment, second, tick, trice, twinkling.

twinkling n flashing, sparkling, twinkle; flash, instant, jiffy, moment, second, tick, trice.

twirl vb revolve, rotate, spin, turn, twist, twirl. * n convolution, revolution, turn, twist, whirling.

twist vb purl, rotate, spin, twine; complicate, contort, convolute, distort, pervert, screw, wring; coil, writhe; encircle, wind, wreathe. * n coil, curl, spin, twine; braid, roll; change, complication, development, variation; bend, convolution, turn; defect, distortion, flaw, imperfection; jerk, pull, sprain, wrench; aberration, characteristic, eccentricity, oddity, peculiarity, quirk.

twit[1] vb banter, blame, censure, reproach, taunt, tease, upbraid.

twit[2] n blockhead, fool, idiot, nincompoop, nitwit.

twitch vb jerk, pluck, pull, snatch. * n jerk, pull; contraction, pull, quiver, spasm, twitching.

type n emblem, mark, stamp; adumbration, image, representation, representative, shadow, sign, symbol, token; archetype, exemplar, model, original, pattern, prototype, protoplast, standard; character, form, kind, nature, sort; figure, letter, text, typography.

typical adj emblematic, exemplary, figurative, ideal, indicative, model, representative, symbolic, true.

typify vb betoken, denote, embody, exemplify, figure, image, indicate, represent, signify.

tyrannical adj absolute, arbitrary, autocratic, cruel, despotic, dictatorial, domineering, high, imperious, irresponsible, severe, tyrannical, unjust; galling, grinding, inhuman, oppressive, overbearing, severe.

tyranny n absolutism, autocracy, despotism, dictatorship, harshness, oppression.

tyrant n autocrat, despot, dictator, oppressor.

tyro n beginner, learner, neophyte, novice; dabbler, smatterer.

U

ubiquitous *adj* omnipresent, present, universal.

udder *n* nipple, pap, teat.

ugly *adj* crooked, homely, ill-favoured, plain, ordinary, unlovely, unprepossessing, unshapely, unsightly; forbidding, frightful, gruesome, hideous, horrible, horrid, loathsome, monstrous, shocking, terrible, repellent, repulsive; bad-tempered, cantankerous, churlish, cross, quarrelsome, spiteful, surly, spiteful, vicious.

ulcer *n* boil, fester, gathering, pustule, sore.

ulterior *adj* beyond, distant, farther; hidden, personal, secret, selfish, undisclosed.

ultimate *adj* conclusive, decisive, eventual, extreme, farthest, final, last. * *n* acme, consummation, culmination, height, peak, pink, quintessence, summit.

ultra *adj* advanced, beyond, extreme, radical.

umbrage *n* shadow, shade; anger, displeasure, dissatisfaction, dudgeon, injury, offence, pique, resentment.

umpire *vb* adjudicate, arbitrate, judge, referee. * *n* adjudicator, arbiter, arbitrator, judge, referee.

unabashed *adj* bold, brazen, confident, unblushing, undaunted, undismayed.

unable *adj* impotent, incapable, incompetent, powerless, weak.

unacceptable *adj* disagreeable, distasteful, offensive, unpleasant, unsatisfactory, unwelcome.

unaccommodating *adj* disobliging, noncompliant, uncivil, ungracious.

unaccomplished *adj* incomplete, unachieved, undone, unperformed, unexecuted, unfinished; illeducated, uncultivated, unpolished.

unaccountable *adj* inexplicable, incomprehensible, inscrutable, mysterious, unintelligible; irresponsible, unanswerable.

unaccustomed *adj* uninitiated, unskilled, unused; foreign, new, strange, unfamiliar, unusual.

unaffected *adj* artless, honest, naive, natural, plain, simple, sincere, real, unfeigned; chaste, pure, unadorned; insensible, unchanged, unimpressed, unmoved, unstirred, untouched.

unanimity *n* accord, agreement, concert, concord, harmony, union, unity.

unanimous *adj* agreeing, concordant, harmonious, like-minded, solid, united.

unassuming *adj* humble, modest, reserved, unobtrusive, unpretending, unpretentious.

unattainable *adj* inaccessible, unobtainable.

unavailing *adj* abortive, fruitless, futile, ineffectual, ineffective, inept, nugatory, unsuccessful, useless, vain.

unbalanced *adj* unsound, unsteady; unadjusted, unsettled.

unbearable *adj* insufferable, insupportable, unendurable.

unbecoming *adj* inappropriate, indecent, indecorous, improper, unbefitting, unbeseeming, unseemly, unsuitable.

unbelief *n* disbelief, dissent, distrust, incredulity, incredulousness, miscreance, miscreancy, nonconformity; doubt, freethinking, infidelity, scepticism.

unbeliever *n* agnostic, deist, disbeliever, doubter, heathen, infidel, sceptic.

unbending *adj* inflexible, rigid, stiff, unpliant, unyielding; firm, obstinate, resolute, stubborn.

unbiased *adj* disinterested, impartial, indifferent, neutral, uninfluenced, unprejudiced, unwarped.

unbind *vb* loose, undo, unfasten, unloose, untie; free, unchain, unfetter.

unblemished *adj* faultless, guiltless, immaculate, impeccable, innocent, intact, perfect, pure, sinless, spotless, stainless, undefiled, unspotted, unsullied, untarnished.

unblushing *adj* boldfaced, impudent, shameless.

unbounded *adj* absolute, boundless, endless, immeasurable, immense, infinite, interminable, measureless, unlimited, vast; immoderate, uncontrolled, unrestrained, unrestricted.

unbridled *adj* dissolute, intractable, lax, licensed, licentious, loose, uncontrolled, ungovernable, unrestrained, violent, wanton.

unbroken *adj* complete, entire, even, full, intact, unimpaired; constant, continuous, fast, profound, sound, successive, undisturbed; inviolate, unbetrayed, unviolated.

unbuckle *vb* loose, unfasten, unloose.

uncanny *adj* inopportune, unsafe; eerie, eery, ghostly, unearthly, unnatural, weird.

unceremonious *adj* abrupt, bluff, blunt, brusque, course, curt, gruff, plain, rough, rude, ungracious; casual, familiar, informal, offhand, unconstrained.

uncertain *adj* ambiguous, doubtful, dubious, equivocal, indefinite, indeterminate, indistinct, questionable, unsettled; insecure, precarious, problematical; capricious, changeable, desultory, fitful, fluctuating, irregular, mutable, shaky, slippery, unreliable, variable.

unchaste *adj* dissolute, incontinent, indecent, immoral, lascivious, lecherous, libidinous, lewd, loose, obscene, wanton.

unchecked *adj* uncurbed, unhampered, unhindered, unobstructed, unrestrained, untrammelled.

uncivil *adj* bearish, blunt, boorish, brusque, discourteous, disobliging, disrespectful, gruff, ill-bred, ill-mannered, impolite, irreverent, rough, rude, uncomplaisant, uncourteous, uncouth, ungentle, ungracious, unmannered, unseemly.

unclean *adj* abominable, beastly, dirty, filthy, foul, grimy, grubby, miry, muddy, nasty, offensive, purulent, repulsive, soiled, sullied; improper, indecent, indecorous, obscene, polluted, risqué, sinful, smutty, unholy, uncleanly.

uncomfortable *adj* disagreeable, displeasing, disquieted, distressing, disturbed, uneasy, unpleasant, restless; cheerless, close, oppressive; dismal, miserable, unhappy.

uncommon *adj* choice, exceptional, extraordinary, infrequent, noteworthy, odd, original, queer, rare, remarkable, scarce, singular, strange, unexampled, unfamiliar, unusual, unwonted.

uncommunicative *adj* close, inconversable, reserved, reticent, taciturn, unsociable, unsocial.

uncomplaining *adj* long-suffering, meek, patient, resigned, tolerant.

uncompromising *adj* inflexible, narrow, obstinate, orthodox, rigid, stiff, strict, unyielding.

unconcerned *adj* apathetic, careless, indifferent.

unconditional *adj* absolute, categorical, complete, entire, free, full, positive, unlimited, unqualified, unreserved, unrestricted.

uncongenial *adj* antagonistic, discordant, displeasing, ill-assorted, incompatible, inharmonious, mismatched, unsuited, unsympathetic.

uncouth *adj* awkward, boorish, clownish, clumsy, gawky, inelegant, loutish, lubberly, rough, rude, rustic, uncourtly, ungainly, unpolished, unrefined, unseemly; odd, outlandish, strange, unfamiliar, unusual.

uncover *vb* denude, divest, lay bare, strip; disclose, discover, expose, reveal, unmask, unveil; bare, doff; open, unclose, unseal.

unctuous *adj* adipose, greasy, oily, fat, fatty, oleaginous, pinguid, sebaceous; bland, lubricious, smooth, slippery; bland, fawning, glib, obsequious, plausible, servile, suave, sycophantic; fervid, gushing.

uncultivated *adj* fallow, uncultured, unreclaimed, untilled; homely, ignorant, illiterate, rude, uncivilized, uncultured, uneducated, unfit, unlettered, unpolished, unread, unready, unrefined, untaught; rough, savage, sylvan, uncouth, wild.

undaunted *adj* bold, brave, courageous, dauntless, fearless, intrepid, plucky, resolute, undismayed.

undefiled *adj* clean, immaculate, pure, spotless, stainless, unblemished, unspotted, unsullied, untarnished; honest, innocent, inviolate, pure, uncorrupted, unpolluted, unstained.

undemonstrative *adj* calm, composed, demure, impassive, modest, placid, quiet, reserved, sedate, sober, staid, tranquil.

undeniable *adj* certain, conclusive, evident, incontestable, incontrovertible, indisputable, indubitable, obvious, unquestionable.

under *prep* below, beneath, inferior to, lower than, subordinate to, underneath. *adv* below, beneath, down, lower.

underestimate *vb* belittle, underrate, undervalue.

undergo *vb* bear, endure, experience, suffer, sustain.

underhand *adj* clandestine, deceitful, disingenuous, fraudulent, hidden, secret, sly, stealthy, underhanded, unfair. * *adv* clandestinely, privately, secretly, slyly, stealthily, surreptitiously; fraudulently, unfairly.

underling *n* agent, inferior, servant, subordinate.

undermine *vb* excavate, mine, sap; demoralize, foil, frustrate, thwart, weaken.

understand *vb* apprehend, catch, comprehend, conceive, discern, grasp, know, penetrate, perceive, see, seize, twig; assume, interpret, take; imply, mean.

understanding *adj* compassionate, considerate, forgiving, kind, kindly, patient, sympathetic, tolerant. * *n* brains, comprehension, discernment, faculty, intellect, intelligence, judgement, knowledge, mind, reason, sense.

undertake *vb* assume, attempt, begin, embark on, engage in, enter upon, take in hand; agree, bargain, contract, covenant, engage, guarantee, promise, stipulate.

undertaking *n* adventure, affair, attempt, business, effort, endeavour, engagement, enterprise, essay, move, project, task, venture.

undesigned *adj* spontaneous, unintended, unintentional, unplanned, unpremeditated.

undigested *adj* crude, ill-advised, ill-considered, ill-judged; confused, disorderly, ill-arranged, unmethodical.

undivided *adj* complete, entire, whole; one, united.

undo *vb* annul, cancel, frustrate, invalidate, neutralize, nullify, offset, reverse; disengage, loose, unfasten, unmake, unravel, untie; crush, destroy, overturn, ruin.

undoubted *adj* incontrovertible, indisputable, indubitable, undisputed, unquestionable, unquestioned.

undress *vb* denude, dismantle, disrobe, unclothe, unrobe, peel, strip. * *n* disarray, nakedness, nudity; mufti, negligee.

undue *adj* illegal, illegitimate, improper, unlawful, excessive, disproportionate, disproportioned, immoderate, unsuitable; unfit.

undulation *n* billowing, fluctuation, pulsation, ripple, wave.

undying *adj* deathless, endless, immortal, imperishable.

unearthly *adj* preternatural, supernatural, uncanny, weird.

uneasy *adj* disquieted, disturbed, fidgety, impatient, perturbed, restless, restive, unquiet, worried; awkward, stiff, ungainly, ungraceful; constraining, cramping, disagreeable, uncomfortable.

unending *adj* endless, eternal, everlasting, interminable, never-ending, perpetual, unceasing.

unequal *adj* disproportionate, disproportioned, ill-matched, inferior, irregular, insufficient, not alike, uneven.

unequalled *adj* exceeding, incomparable, inimitable, matchless, new, nonpareil, novel, paramount, peerless, pre-eminent, superlative, surpassing, transcendent, unheard of, unique, unparalleled, unrivalled.

unequivocal *adj* absolute, certain, clear, evident, incontestable, indubitable, positive; explicit, unambiguous, unmistakable.

uneven *adj* hilly, jagged, lumpy, ragged, rough, rugged, stony; motley, unequal, variable, variegated.

uneventful *adj* commonplace, dull, eventless, humdrum, quiet, monotonous, smooth, uninteresting.

unexceptionable *adj* excellent, faultless, good, irreproachable.

unexpected *adj* abrupt, sudden, unforeseen.

unfair *adj* dishonest, dishonourable, faithless, false, hypocritical, inequitable, insincere, oblique, one-sided, partial, unequal, unjust, wrongful.

unfaithful *adj* adulterous, derelict, deceitful, dishonest, disloyal, false, faithless, fickle, perfidious, treacherous, unreliable; negligent; changeable, inconstant, untrue.

unfamiliar *adj* bizarre, foreign, new, novel, outlandish, queer, singular, strange, uncommon, unusual.

unfashionable *adj* antiquated, destitute, disused, obsolete, old-fashioned, unconventional.

unfavourable *adj* adverse, contrary, disadvantageous, discouraging, ill, inauspicious, inimical, inopportune, indisposed, malign, sinister, unfriendly, unlucky, unpropitious, untimely; foul, inclement.

unfeeling *adj* apathetic, callous, heartless, insensible, numb, obdurate, torpid, unconscious, unimpressionable; adamantine, cold-blooded, cruel, hard, merciless, pitiless, stony, unkind, unsympathetic.

unfit *vb* disable, disqualify, incapacitate. * *adj* improper, inappropriate, incompetent, inconsistent, unsuitable; ill-equipped, inadequate, incapable, unqualified, useless; debilitated, feeble, flabby, unhealthy, unsound.

unflagging *adj* constant, indefatigable, never-ending, persevering, steady, unfaltering, unremitting, untiring, unwearied.

unflinching *adj* firm, resolute, steady, unshrinking.

unfold *vb* display, expand, open, separate, unfurl, unroll; declare, disclose, reveal, tell; decipher, develop, disentangle, evolve, explain, illustrate, interpret, resolve, unravel.

unfortunate *adj* hapless, ill-fated, ill-starred, infelicitous, luckless, unhappy, unlucky, unprosperous, unsuccessful, wretched; calamitous, deplorable, disastrous; inappropriate, inexpedient.

unfrequented *adj* abandoned, deserted, forsaken, lone, solitary, uninhabited, unoccupied.

unfruitful *adj* barren, fruitless, sterile; infecund, unprolific; unprofitable, unproductive.

ungainly *adj* awkward, boorish, clownish, clumsy, gawky, inelegant, loutish, lubberly, lumbering, slouching, stiff, uncourtly, uncouth, ungraceful.

ungentlemanly *adj* ill-bred, impolite, rude, uncivil, ungentle, ungracious, unmannerly.

unhappy *adj* afflicted, disastrous, dismal, distressed, drear, evil, inauspicious, miserable, painful, unfortunate, wretched.

unhealthy *adj* ailing, diseased, feeble, indisposed, infirm, poorly, sickly, toxic, unsanitary, unsound, toxic, venomous.

uniform *adj* alike, constant, even, equable, equal, smooth, steady, regular, unbroken, unchanged, undeviating, unvaried, unvarying. * *n* costume, dress, livery, outfit, regalia, suit.

uniformity *n* constancy, continuity, permanence, regularity, sameness, stability; accordance, agreement, conformity, consistency, unanimity.

unimportant *adj* immaterial, inappreciable, inconsequent, inconsequential, inconsiderable, indifferent, insignificant, mediocre, minor, paltry, petty, small, slight, trifling, trivial.

unintentional *adj* accidental, casual, fortuitous, inadvertent, involuntary, spontaneous, undesigned, unmeant, unplanned, unpremeditated, unthinking.

uninterrupted *adj* continuous, endless, incessant, perpetual, unceasing.

union *n* coalescence, coalition, combination, conjunction, coupling, fusion, incorporation, joining, junction, unification, uniting; agreement, concert, concord, concurrence, harmony, unanimity, unity; alliance, association, club, confederacy, federation, guild, league.

unique *adj* choice, exceptional, matchless, only, peculiar, rare, single, sole, singular, uncommon, unexampled, unmatched.

unison *n* accord, accordance, agreement, concord, harmony.

unite *vb* amalgamate, attach, blend, centralize, coalesce, confederate, consolidate, embody, fuse, incorporate, merge, weld; associate, conjoin, connect, couple, link, marry; combine, join; harmonize, reconcile; agree, concert, concur, cooperate, fraternize.

universal *adj* all-reaching, catholic, cosmic, encyclopedic, general, ubiquitous, unlimited; all, complete, entire, total, whole.

unjust *adj* inequitable, injurious, partial, unequal,

unfair, unwarranted, wrong, wrongful; flagitious, heinous, influenced, iniquitous, nefarious, unrighteous, wicked; biased, prejudiced, uncandid.

unjustifiable *adj* indefensible, unjust, unreasonable, unwarrantable; inexcusable, unpardonable.

unknown *adj* unappreciated, unascertained; undiscovered, unexplored, uninvestigated; concealed, dark, enigmatic, hidden, mysterious, mystic; anonymous, incognito, inglorious, nameless, obscure, renownless, undistinguished, unheralded, unnoted.

unladylike *adj* ill-bred, impolite, rude, uncivil, ungentle, ungracious, unmannerly.

unlamented *adj* unmourned, unregretted.

unlimited *adj* boundless, infinite, interminable, limitless, measureless, unbounded; absolute, full, unconfined, unconstrained, unrestricted; indefinite, undefined.

unlucky *adj* baleful, disastrous, ill-fated, ill-starred, luckless, unfortunate, unprosperous, unsuccessful; ill-omened, inauspicious; miserable, unhappy.

unmanageable *adj* awkward, cumbersome, inconvenient, unwieldy; intractable, unruly, unworkable, vicious; difficult, impractical.

unmatched *adj* matchless, unequalled, unparalleled, unrivalled.

unmitigated *adj* absolute, complete, consummate, perfect, sheer, stark, thorough, unqualified, utter.

unnatural *adj* aberrant, abnormal, anomalous, foreign, irregular, prodigious, uncommon; brutal, cold, heartless, inhuman, unfeeling, unusual; affected, artificial, constrained, forced, insincere, self-conscious, stilted, strained; factitious.

unpleasant *adj* disagreeable, displeasing, distasteful, obnoxious, offensive, repulsive, unlovely, ungrateful, unacceptable, unpalatable, unwelcome.

unpremeditated *adj* extempore, impromptu, off-hand, spontaneous, undesigned, unintentional, unstudied.

unprincipled *adj* bad, crooked, dishonest, fraudulent, immoral, iniquitous, knavish, lawless, profligate, rascally, roguish, thievish, trickish, tricky, unscrupulous, vicious, villainous, wicked.

unqualified *adj* disqualified, incompetent, ineligible, unadapted, unfit; absolute, certain, consummate, decided, direct, downright, full, outright, unconditional, unmeasured, unrestricted, unmitigated; exaggerated, sweeping.

unreal *adj* chimerical, dreamlike, fanciful, flimsy, ghostly, illusory, insubstantial, nebulous, shadowy, spectral, visionary, unsubstantial.

unreasonable *adj* absurd, excessive, exorbitant, foolish, ill-judged, illogical, immoderate, impractical, injudicious, irrational, nonsensical, preposterous, senseless, silly, stupid, unfair, unreasoning, unwarrantable, unwise.

unreliable *adj* fallible, fickle, irresponsible, treacherous, uncertain, undependable, unstable, unsure, untrustworthy.

unremitting *adj* assiduous, constant, continual, diligent, incessant, indefatigable, persevering, sedulous, unabating, unceasing.

unrepentant *adj* abandoned, callous, graceless, hardened, impenitent, incorrigible, irreclaimable, lost, obdurate, profligate, recreant, seared, shameless.

unrequited *adj* unanswered, unreturned, unrewarded.

unreserved *adj* absolute, entire, full, unlimited; above-board, artless, candid, communicative, fair, frank, guileless, honest, ingenuous, open, sincere, single-minded, undesigning, undissembling; demonstrative, emotional, open-hearted.

unresisting *adj* compliant, long-suffering, non-resistant, obedient, passive, patient, submissive, yielding.

unresponsive *adj* irresponsive, unsympathetic.

unrestrained *adj* unbridled, unchecked, uncurbed, unfettered, unhindered, unobstructed, unreserved; broad, dissolute, incontinent, inordinate, lax, lewd, licentious, loose, wanton; lawless, wild.

unrestricted *adj* free, unbridled, unconditional, unconfined, uncurbed, unfettered, unlimited, unqualified, unrestrained; clear, open, public, unobstructed.

unrevealed *adj* hidden, occult, secret, undiscovered, unknown.

unrewarded *adj* unpaid, unrecompensed.

unriddle *vb* explain, expound, solve, unfold, unravel.

unrighteous *adj* evil, sinful, ungodly, unholy, vicious, wicked, wrong; heinous, inequitable, iniquitous, nefarious, unfair, unjust.

unripe *adj* crude, green, hard, immature, premature, sour; incomplete, unfinished.

unrivalled *adj* incomparable, inimitable, matchless, peerless, unequalled, unexampled, unique, unparalleled.

unrobe *vb* disrobe, undress.

unroll *vb* develop, discover, evolve, open, unfold; display, lay open.

unromantic *adj* literal, matter-of-fact, prosaic.

unroot *vb* eradicate, extirpate, root out, uproot.

unruffled *adj* calm, peaceful, placid, quiet, serene, smooth, still, tranquil; collected, composed, cool, imperturbable, peaceful, philosophical, placid, tranquil, undisturbed, unexcited, unmoved.

unruly *adj* disobedient, disorderly, fractious, headstrong, insubordinate, intractable, mutinous, obstreperous, rebellious, refractory, riotous, seditious, turbulent, ungovernable, unmanageable, wanton, wild; lawless, obstinate, rebellious, stubborn, vicious.

unsafe *adj* dangerous, hazardous, insecure, perilous, precarious, risky, treacherous, uncertain, unprotected.

unsaid *adj* tacit, unmentioned, unspoken, unuttered.

unsanctified *adj* profane, unhallowed, unholy.

unsatisfactory *adj* insufficient; disappointing; faulty, feeble, imperfect, poor, weak.

unsatisfied *adj* insatiate, unsated, unsatiated, unstaunched; discontented, displeased, dissatisfied, malcontent; undischarged, unpaid, unperformed, unrendered.

unsavoury *adj* flat, insipid, mawkish, savourless, tasteless, unflavoured, unpalatable, vapid; disagreeable, disgusting, distasteful, nasty, nauseating, nauseous, offensive, rank, revolting, sickening, uninviting, unpleasing.

unsay *vb* recall, recant, retract, take back.

unscathed *adj* unharmed, uninjured.

unschooled *adj* ignorant, uneducated, uninstructed; undisciplined, untrained.

unscrupulous *adj* dishonest, reckless, ruthless, unconscientious, unprincipled, unrestrained.

unsealed *adj* open, unclosed.

unsearchable *adj* hidden, incomprehensible, inscrutable, mysterious.

unseasonable *adj* ill-timed, inappropriate, infelicitous, inopportune, untimely; late, too late; inexpedient, undesireable, unfit, ungrateful, unsuitable, unwelcome; premature, too early.

unseasonably *adv* malapropos, unsuitably, untimely.

unseasoned *adj* inexperienced, unaccustomed, unqualified, untrained; immoderate, inordinate, irregular; green; fresh, unsalted.

unseeing *adj* blind, sightless.

unseemly *adj* improper, indecent, inappropriate, indecorous, unbecoming, uncomely, unfit, unmeet, unsuitable.

unseen *adj* undiscerned, undiscovered, unobserved, unperceived; imperceptible, indiscoverable, invisible, latent.

unselfish *adj* altruistic, devoted, disinterested, generous, high-minded, impersonal, liberal, magnanimous, self-denying, self-forgetful, selfless, self-sacrificing.

unserviceable *adj* ill-conditioned, unsound, useless; profitless, unprofitable.

unsettle *vb* confuse, derange, disarrange, disconcert, disorder, disturb, trouble, unbalance, unfix, unhinge, upset.

unsettled *adj* changeable, fickle, inconstant, restless, transient, unstable, unsteady, vacillating, wavering; inequable, unequal; feculent, muddy, roiled, roily, turbid; adrift, afloat, homeless, unestablished, uninhabited; open, tentative, unadjusted, undecided, undetermined; due, outstanding, owing, unpaid; perturbed, troubled, unnerved.

unshackle *vb* emancipate, liberate, loose, release, set free, unbind, unchain, unfetter.

unshaken *adj* constant, firm, resolute, steadfast, steady, unmoved.

unshapen *adj* deformed, grotesque, ill-formed, ill-made, ill-shaped, misshapen, shapeless, ugly, uncouth.

unsheltered *adj* exposed, unprotected.

unshrinking *adj* firm, determined, persisting, resolute, unblenching, unflinching.

unshroud *vb* discover, expose, reveal, uncover.

unsightly *adj* deformed, disagreeable, hideous, repellent, repulsive, ugly.

unskilful, unskillful *adj* awkward, bungling, clumsy, inapt, inexpert, maladroit, rough, rude, unhandy, unskilled, unversed.

unskilled *adj* inexperienced, raw, undisciplined, undrilled, uneducated, unexercised, unpractised, unprepared, unschooled; unskilful.

unslaked *adj* unquenched, unslacked.

unsleeping *adj* unslumbering, vigilant, wakeful, watchful.

unsmirched *adj* undefiled, unpolluted, unspotted.

unsociable *adj* distant, reserved, retiring, segregative, shy, solitary, standoffish, taciturn, uncommunicative, uncompanionable, ungenial, unsocial; inhospitable, misanthropic, morose.

unsoiled *adj* clean, spotless, unspotted, unstained, unsullied, untarnished.

unsophisticated *adj* genuine, pure, unadulterated; good, guileless, innocent, undepraved, unpolluted, invitiated; artless, honest, ingenuous, naive, natural, simple, sincere, straightforward, unaffected, undesigning, unstudied.

unsound *adj* decayed, defective, impaired, imperfect, rotten, thin, wasted, weak; broken, disturbed, light, restless; diseased, feeble, infirm, morbid, poorly, sickly, unhealthy, weak; deceitful, erroneous, fallacious, false, faulty, hollow, illogical, incorrect, invalid, ill-advised, irrational, questionable, sophistical, unreasonable, unsubstantial, untenable, wrong; dishonest, false, insincere, unfaithful, untrustworthy, untrue; insubstantial, unreal; heretical, heterodox, unorthodox.

unsparing *adj* bountiful, generous, lavish, liberal, profuse, ungrudging; harsh, inexorable, relentless, rigorous, ruthless, severe, uncompromising, unforgiving.

unspeakable *adj* indescribable, ineffable, inexpressible, unutterable.

unspiritual *adj* bodily, carnal, fleshly, sensual.

unspotted *adj* clean, spotless, unsoiled, unstained, unsullied, untarnished; faultless, immaculate, innocent, pure, stainless, unblemished, uncorrupted, undefiled, untainted.

unstable *adj* infirm, insecure, precarious, topheavy, tottering, unbalanced, unballasted, unreliable, unsafe, unsettled, unsteady; changeable, erratic, fickle, inconstant, irresolute, mercurial, mutable, vacillating, variable, wavering, weak, volatile.—*also* **instable**.

unstained *adj* colourless, uncoloured, undyed, untinged; clean, spotless, unspotted.

unsteady *adj* fluctuating, oscillating, unsettled; insecure, precarious, unstable; changeable, desultory, ever-changing, fickle, inconstant, irresolute, mutable, unreliable, variable, wavering; drunken, jumpy, tottering, vacillating, wobbly, tipsy.

unstinted *adj* abundant, ample, bountiful, full, large, lavish, plentiful, prodigal, profuse.

unstrung *adj* overcome, shaken, unnerved, weak.

unstudied *adj* extempore, extemporaneous, impromptu, offhand, spontaneous, unpremeditated; inexpert, unskilled, unversed.

unsubdued *adj* unbowed, unbroken, unconquered, untamed.

unsubmissive *adj* disobedient, contumacious, indocile, insubordinate, obstinate, perverse, refractory, uncomplying, ungovernable, unmanageable, unruly, unyielding.

unsubstantial *adj* airy, flimsy, gaseous, gossamery, light, slight, tenuous, thin, vaporous; apparitional, bodiless, chimerical, cloudbuilt, dreamlike, empty, fantastical, ideal, illusory, imaginary, imponderable, moonshiny, spectral, unreal, vague, visionary; erroneous, fallacious, flimsy, groundless, illogical, unfounded, ungrounded, unsolid, unsound, untenable, weak.

unsuccessful *adj* abortive, bootless, fruitless, futile, ineffectual, profitless, unavailing, vain; ill-fated, ill-starred, luckless, unfortunate, unhappy, unlucky, unprosperous.

unsuitable *adj* ill-adapted, inappropriate, malapropos, unfit, unsatisfactory, unsuited; improper, inapplicable, inapt, incongruous, inexpedient, infelicitous, unbecoming, unbeseeming, unfitting.

unsuited *adj* unadapted, unfitted, unqualified.

unsullied *adj* chaste, clean, spotless, unsoiled, unspotted, unstained, untarnished; immaculate, pure, stainless, unblemished, uncorrupted, undefiled, untainted, untouched, virginal.

unsupplied *adj* destitute, unfurnished, unprovided.

unsupported *adj* unaided, unassisted; unbacked, unseconded, unsustained, unupheld.

unsurpassed *adj* matchless, peerless, unequalled, unexampled, unexcelled, unmatched, unparagoned, unparalleled, unrivalled.

unsusceptible *adj* apathetic, cold, impassive, insusceptible, phlegmatic, stoical, unimpressible, unimpressionable.

unsuspecting *adj* confiding, credulous, trusting, unsuspicious.

unsuspicious *adj* confiding, credulous, gullible, simple, trustful, unsuspecting.

unsustainable *adj* insupportable, intolerable; controvertible, erroneous, unmaintainable, untenable.

unswerving *adj* direct, straight, undeviating; constant, determined, firm, resolute, staunch, steadfast, steady, stable, unwavering.

unsymmetrical *adj* amorphous, asymmetric, disproportionate, formless, irregular, unbalanced.

unsystematic, unsystematical *adj* casual, disorderly, haphazard, irregular, planless, unmethodical.

untainted *adj* chaste, clean, faultless, fresh, healthy, pure, sweet, wholesome; spotless, unsoiled, unstained, unsullied, untarnished; immaculate, stainless, unblemished, uncorrupted, undefiled, unspotted.

untamable *adj* unconquerable.

untamed *adj* fierce, unbroken, wild.

untangle *vb* disentangle, explain, explicate.

untarnished *adj* chaste, clean, spotless, unsoiled, unspotted, unstained, unsullied; immaculate, pure, spotless, stainless, unblemished, uncorrupted, undefiled, unspotted, unsullied, untainted, virginal, virtuous.

untaught *adj* illiterate, unenlightened, uninformed, unlettered; ignorant, inexperienced, undisciplined, undrilled, uneducated, uninitiated, uninstructed, untutored.

untenable *adj* indefensible, unmaintainable, unsound; fallacious, hollow, illogical, indefensible, insupportable, unjustifiable, weak.

untenanted *adj* deserted, empty, tenantless, uninhabited, unoccupied.

unterrified *adj* fearless, unappalled, unawed, undismayed, undaunted, unscared.

unthankful *adj* thankless, ungrateful.

unthinking *adj* careless, heedless, inconsiderate, thoughtless, unreasoning, unreflecting; automatic, mechanical.

unthoughtful *adj* careless, heedless, inconsiderable, thoughtless.

unthrifty *adj* extravagant, improvident, lavish, prodigal, profuse, thriftless, wasteful.

untidy *adj* careless, disorderly, dowdy, frumpy, mussy, slatternly, slovenly, unkempt, unneat.

untie *vb* free, loose, loosen, unbind, unfasten, unknot, unloose; clear, resolve, solve, unfold.

until *adv, conj* till, to the time when; to the place, point, state or degree that; * *prep* till, to.

untimely *adj* ill-timed, immature, inconvenient, inopportune, mistimed, premature, unseasonable, unsuitable; ill-considered, inauspicious, uncalled for, unfortunate. * *adv* unseasonably, unsuitably.

untinged *adj* achromatic, colourless, hueless, uncoloured, undyed, unstained.

untiring *adj* persevering, incessant, indefatigable, patient, tireless, unceasing, unfatiguable, unflagging, unremitting, unwearied, unwearying.

untold *adj* countless, incalculable, innumerable, uncounted, unnumbered; unrelated, unrevealed.

untouched *adj* intact, scatheless, unharmed, unhurt, uninjured, unscathed; insensible, unaffected, unmoved, unstirred.

untoward *adj* adverse, froward, intractable, perverse, refractory, stubborn, unfortunate; annoying, ill-timed, inconvenient, unmanageable, vexatious; awkward, uncouth, ungainly, ungraceful.

untrained *adj* green, ignorant, inexperienced, raw, unbroken, undisciplined, undrilled, uneducated, uninstructed, unpractised, unskilled, untaught, untutored.

untrammelled *adj* free, unhampered.

untried *adj* fresh, inexperienced, maiden, new, unassayed, unattempted, unattested, virgin; undecided.

untrodden *adj* pathless, trackless, unbeaten.

untroubled *adj* calm, careless, composed, peaceful, serene, smooth, tranquil, undisturbed, unvexed.

untrue *adj* contrary, false, inaccurate, wrong; disloyal, faithless, perfidious, recreant, treacherous, unfaithful.

untrustworthy *adj* deceitful, dishonest, inaccurate, rotten, slippery, treacherous, undependable, unreliable; disloyal, false; deceptive, fallible, illusive, questionable.

untruth *n* error, faithlessness, falsehood, falsity, incorrectness, inveracity, treachery; deceit, deception, fabrication, fib, fiction, forgery, imposture, invention, lie, misrepresentation, misstatement, story.

untutored *adj* ignorant, inexperienced, undisciplined, undrilled, uneducated, uninitiated, uninstructed, untaught; artless, natural, simple, unsophisticated.

untwist *vb* disentangle, disentwine, ravel, unravel, unwreathe.

unused *adj* idle, unemployed, untried; new, unaccustomed, unfamiliar.

unusual *adj* abnormal, curious, exceptional, extraordinary, odd, peculiar, queer, rare, recherché, remarkable, singular, strange, unaccustomed, uncommon, unwonted.

unutterable *adj* incommunicable, indescribable, ineffable, inexpressible, unspeakable.

unvarnished *adj* unpolished; candid, plain, simple, true, unadorned, unembellished.

unvarying *adj* constant, invariable, unchanging.

unveil *vb* disclose, expose, reveal, show, uncover, unmask.

unveracious *adj* false, lying, mendacious, untruthful.

unversed *adj* inexperienced, raw, undisciplined, undrilled, uneducated, unexercised, unpractised, unprepared, unschooled; unskilful.

unviolated *adj* inviolate, unbetrayed, unbroken.

unwarlike *adj* pacific, peaceful.

unwarped *adj* impartial, unbiased, undistorted, unprejudiced.

unwarrantable *adj* improper, indefensible, unjustifiable.

unwary *adj* careless, hasty, heedless, imprudent, incautious, indiscreet, precipitate, rash, reckless, remiss, uncircumspect, unguarded.

unwavering *adj* constant, determined, firm, fixed, resolute, settled, staunch, steadfast, steady, unhesitating.

unwearied *adj* unfatigued; constant, continual, incessant, indefatigable, persevering, persistent,

unceasing, unremitting, untiring.

unwelcome *adj* disagreeable, unacceptable, ungrateful, unpleasant, unpleasing.

unwell *adj* ailing, delicate, diseased, ill, indisposed, sick.

unwept *adj* unlamented, unmourned, unregretted.

unwholesome *adj* baneful, deleterious, injurious, insalubrious, noisome, noxious, poisonous, unhealthful, unhealthy; injudicious, pernicious, unsound; corrupt, tainted.

unwieldy *adj* bulky, clumsy, cumbersome, cumbrous, elephantine, heavy, hulking, large, massy, ponderous, unmanageable, weighty.

unwilling *adj* averse, backward, disinclined, indisposed, laggard, loath, opposed, recalcitrant, reluctant; forced, grudging.

unwind *vb* unravel, unreel, untwine, wind off; disentangle.

unwise *adj* brainless, foolish, ill-advised, ill-judged, impolitic, imprudent, indiscreet, injudicious, inexpedient, senseless, silly, stupid, unwary, weak.

unwitnessed *adj* unknown, unseen, unspied.

unwittingly *adv* ignorantly, inadvertently, unconsciously, undesignedly, unintentionally, unknowingly.

unwonted *adj* infrequent, rare, uncommon, unusual; unaccustomed, unused.

unworthy *adj* undeserving; bad, base, blameworthy, worthless; shameful, unbecoming, vile; contemptible, derogatory, despicable, discreditable, mean, paltry, reprehensible, shabby.

unwrap *vb* open, unfold.

unwrinkled *adj* smooth, unforrowed.

unwritten *adj* oral, traditional, unrecorded; conventional, customary.

unwrought *adj* crude, rough, rude, unfashioned, unformed.

unyielding *adj* constant, determined, indomitable, inflexible, pertinacious, resolute, staunch, steadfast, steady, tenacious, uncompromising, unwavering; headstrong, intractable, obstinate, perverse, self-willed, stiff, stubborn, wayward, wilful; adamantine, firm, grim, hard, immovable, implastic, inexorable, relentless, rigid, unbending.

unyoke *vb* disconnect, disjoin, part, separate.

unyoked *adj* disconnected, separated; licentious, loose, unrestrained.

upbraid *vb* accuse, blame, chide, condemn, criticize, denounce, fault, reproach, reprove, revile, scold, taunt, twit.

upheaval *n* elevation, upthrow; cataclysm, convulsion, disorder, eruption, explosion, outburst, overthrow.

uphill *adj* ascending, upward; arduous, difficult, hard, laborious, strenuous, toilsome, wearisome.

uphold *vb* elevate, raise; bear up, hold up, support, sustain; advocate, aid, champion, countenance, defend, justify, maintain, vindicate.

upland *n* down, fell, ridge, plateau.

uplift *vb* raise, upraise; animate, elevate, inspire, lift, refine. * *n* ascent, climb, elevation, lift, rise, upthrust; exaltation, inspiration, uplifting; improvement, refinement.

upon *prep* on, on top of, over; about, concerning, on the subject of, relating to; immediately after, with.

upper hand *n* advantage, ascendancy, control, dominion, mastership, mastery, pre-eminence, rule, superiority, supremacy, whip hand.

uppermost *adj* foremost, highest, loftiest, supreme, topmost, upmost.

uppish *adj* arrogant, assuming, haughty, perky, proud, smart.

upright *adj* erect, perpendicular, vertical; conscientious, equitable, fair, faithful, good, honest, honourable, incorruptible, just, pure, righteous, straightforward, true, trustworthy, upstanding, virtuous.

uprightness *n* erectness, perpendicularity, verticality; equity, fairness, goodness, honesty, honour, incorruptibility, integrity, justice, probity, rectitude, righteousness, straightforwardness, trustiness, trustworthiness, virtue, worth.

uproar *n* clamour, commotion, confusion, din, disturbance, fracas, hubbub, hurly-burly, noise, pandemonium, racket, riot, tumult, turmoil, vociferation.

uproarious *adj* boisterous, clamorous, loud, noisy, obstreperous, riotous, tumultuous.

uproot *vb* eradicate, extirpate, root out.

upset *vb* capsize, invert, overthrow, overtumble, overturn, spill, tip over, topple, turn turtle; agitate, confound, confuse, discompose, disconcert, distress, disturb, embarrass, excite, fluster, muddle, overwhelm, perturb, shock, startle, trouble, unnerve, unsettle; checkmate, defeat, overthrow, revolutionize, subvert; foil, frustrate, nonplus, thwart. * *adj* disproved, exposed, overthrown; bothered, confused, disconcerted, flustered, mixed-up, perturbed; shocked, startled, unsettled; beaten, defeated, overcome, overpowered, overthrown; discomfited, distressed, discomposed, overexcited, overwrought, shaken, troubled, unnerved. * *n* confutation, refutation; foiling, frustration, overthrow, revolution, revulsion, ruin, subversdion, thwarting.

upshot *n* conclusion, consummation, effect, end, event, issue, outcome, result, termination.

upside down *adj* bottom side up, bottom up, confused, head over heels, inverted, topsy-turvy.

upstart *n* adventurer, arriviste, parvenu, snob, social cimber, yuppie.

upturned *adj* raised, uplifted; retroussé.

upward *adj* ascending, climbing, mounting, rising, uphill. * *adv* above, aloft, overhead, up; heavenwards, skywards.

urbane *adj* civil, complaisant, courteous, courtly, elegant, mannerly, polished, polite, refined, smooth, suave, well-mannered.

urbanity *n* amenity, civility, complaisance, cour-

tesy, politeness, smoothness, suavity.

urchin *n* brat, child, kid, ragamuffin, rascal, scrap, squirt, tad.

urge *vb* crowd, drive, force on, impel, press, press on, push, push on; beg, beseech, conjure, entreat, exhort, implore, importune, ply, solicit, tease; animate, egg on, encourage, goad, hurry, incite, instigate, quicken, spur, stimulate. * *n* compulsion, desire, drive, impulse, longing, pressure, wish, yearning.

urgency *n* drive, emergency, exigency, haste, necessity, press, pressure, push, stress; clamorousness, entreaty, insistence, importunity, instance, solicitation; goad, incitement, spur, stimulus.

urgent *adj* cogent, critical, crucial, crying, exigent, immediate, imperative, important, importunate, insistent, instant, pertinacious, pressing, serious.

urinal *n* chamber, chamber pot, lavatory, pot, potty, jordan, toilet.

urinate *vb* make water, pee, pee-pee, piddle, piss, stale, wee.

usage *n* treatment; consuetude, custom, fashion, habit, method, mode, practice, prescription, tradition, use.

use *vb* administer, apply, avail oneself of, drive, employ, handle, improve, make use of, manipulate, occupy, operate, ply, put into action, take advantage of, turn to account, wield, work; exercise, exert, exploit, practice, profit by, utilize; absorb, consume, exhaust, expend, swallow up, waste, wear out; accustom, familiarize, habituate, harden, inure, train; act toward, behave toward, deal with, manage, treat; be accustomed, be wont. * *n* appliance, application, consumption, conversion, disposal, exercise, employ, employment, practice, utilization; adaptability, advantage, avail, benefit, convenience, profit, service, usefulness, utility, wear; exigency, necessity, indispensability, need, occasion, requisiteness; custom, habit, handling, method, treatment, usage, way.

useful *adj* active, advantageous, available, availing, beneficial, commodious, conducive, contributory, convenient, effective, good, helpful, instrumental, operative, practical, profitable, remunerative, salutary, suitable, serviceable, utilitarian; available, helpful, serviceable, valuable.

usefulness *n* advantage, profit, serviceableness, utility, value.

useless *adj* abortive, bootless, fruitless, futile, helpless, idle, incapable, incompetent, ineffective, ineffectual, inutile, nugatory, null, profitless, unavailing, unprofitable, unproductive, unserviceable, valueless, worthless; good for nothing, waste.

usher *vb* announce, forerun, herald, induct, introduce, precede; conduct, direct, escort, shepherd, show. * *n* attendant, conductor, escort, shepherd, squire.

usual *adj* accustomed, common, customary, everyday, familiar, frequent, general, habitual, normal, ordinary, prevailing, prevalent, regular, wonted.

usurp *vb* appropriate, arrogate, assume, seize.

usurpation *n* assumption, dispossession, infringement, seizure.

usury *n* interest; exploitation, extortion, profiteering.

utensil *n* device, implement, instrument, tool.

utility *n* advantageousness, avail, benefit, profit, service, use, usefulness; happiness, welfare.

utilize *vb* employ, exploit, make use of, put to use, turn to account, use.

utmost *adj* extreme, farthest, highest, last, main, most distant, remotest; greatest, uttermost. * *n* best, extreme, maximum, most.

Utopian *adj* air-built, air-drawn, chimerical, fanciful, ideal, imaginary, visionary, unreal.

utricle *n* bladder, cyst, sac, vesicle.

utter[1] *adj* complete, entire, perfect, total; absolute, blank, diametric, downright, final, peremptory, sheer, stark, thorough, thoroughgoing, unconditional, unqualified, total.

utter[2] *vb* articulate, breathe, deliver, disclose, divulge, emit, enunciate, express, give forth, pronounce, reveal, speak, talk, tell, voice; announce, circulate, declare, issue, publish.

utterance *n* articulation, delivery, disclosure, emission, expression, pronouncement, pronunciation, publication, speech.

utterly *adv* absolutely, altogether, completely, downright, entirely, quite, totally, unconditionally, wholly.

uttermost *adj* extreme, farthest; greatest, utmost.

V

vacant *adj* blank, empty, unfilled, void; disengaged, free, unemployed, unoccupied, unencumbered; thoughtless, unmeaning, unthinking, unreflective; uninhabited, untenanted.

vacate *vb* abandon, evacuate, relinquish, surrender; abolish, abrogate, annul, cancel, disannul, invalidate, nullify, overrule, quash, rescind.

vacillate *vb* dither, fluctuate, hesitate, oscillate, rock, sway, waver.

vacillation *n* faltering, fluctuation, hesitation, inconstancy, indecision, irresolution, reeling, rocking, staggering, swaying, unsteadiness, wavering.

vacuity *n* emptiness, inanition, vacancy; emptiness, vacancy, vacuum, void; expressionlessness, inanity, nihility.

vacuous *adj* empty, empty-headed, unfilled, vacant, void; inane, unintelligent.

vacuum *n* emptiness, vacuity, void.

vagabond *adj* footloose, idle, meandering, rambling, roving, roaming, strolling, vagrant, wandering. * *n* beggar, castaway, landloper, loafer, lounger, nomad, outcast, tramp, vagrant, wanderer.

vagary *n* caprice, crotchet, fancy, freak, humour, whim.

vagrant *adj* erratic, itinerant, roaming, roving, nomadic, strolling, unsettled, wandering. * *n* beggar, castaway, landloper, loafer, lounger, nomad, outcast, tramp, vagabond, wanderer.

vague *adj* ambiguous, confused, dim, doubtful, indefinite, ill-defined, indistinct, lax, loose, obscure, uncertain, undetermined, unfixed, unsettled.

vain *adj* baseless, delusive, dreamy, empty, false, imaginary, shadowy, suppositional, unsubstantial, unreal, void; abortive, bootless, fruitless, futile, ineffectual, nugatory, profitless, unavailing, unprofitable; trivial, unessential, unimportant, unsatisfactory, unsatisfying, useless, vapid, worthless; arrogant, conceited, egotistical, flushed, high, inflated, opinionated, ostentatious, overweening, proud, self-confident, self-opinionated, vainglorious; gaudy, glittering, gorgeous, showy.

valediction *n* adieu, farewell, goodbye, leave-taking.

valet *n* attendant, flunky, groom, lackey, servant.

valetudinarian *adj* delicate, feeble, frail, infirm, sickly.

valiant *adj* bold, brave, chivalrous, courageous, daring, dauntless, doughty, fearless, gallant, heroic, intrepid, lion-hearted, redoubtable, Spartan, valorous, undaunted.

valid *adj* binding, cogent, conclusive, efficacious, efficient, good, grave, important, just, logical, powerful, solid, sound, strong, substantial, sufficient, weighty.

valley *n* basin, bottom, canyon, dale, dell, dingle, glen, hollow, ravine, strath, vale.

valorous *adj* bold, brave, courageous, dauntless, doughty, intrepid, stout.

valour *n* boldness, bravery, courage, daring, gallantry, heroism, prowess, spirit.

valuable *adj* advantageous, precious, profitable, useful; costly, expensive, rich; admirable, estimable, worthy. * *n* heirloom, treasure.

value *vb* account, appraise, assess, estimate, price, rate, reckon; appreciate, esteem, prize, regard, treasure. * *n* avail, importance, usefulness, utility, worth; cost, equivalent, price, rate; estimation, excellence, importance, merit, valuation.

valueless *adj* miserable, useless, worthless.

vandal *n* barbarian, destroyer, savage.

vandalism *n* barbarism, barbarity, savagery.

vanish *vb* disappear, dissolve, fade, melt.

vanity *n* emptiness, falsity, foolishness, futility, hollowness, insanity, triviality, unreality, worthlessness; arrogance, conceit, egotism, ostentation, self-conceit.

vanquish *vb* conquer, defeat, outwit, overcome, overpower, overthrow, subdue, subjugate; crush, discomfit, foil, master, quell, rout, worst.

vapid *adj* dead, flat, insipid, lifeless, savourless, spiritless, stale, tasteless; dull, feeble, jejune, languid, meagre, prosaic, prosy, tame.

vapour *n* cloud, exhalation, fog, fume, mist, rack, reek, smoke, steam; daydream, dream, fantasy, phantom, vagary, vision, whim, whimsy.

variable *adj* changeable, mutable, shifting; aberrant, alterable, capricious, fickle, fitful, floating, fluctuating, inconstant, mobile, mutable, protean, restless, shifting, unsteady, vacillating, wavering.

variance *n* disagreement, difference, discord, dissension, incompatibility, jarring, strife.

variation *n* alteration, change, modification; departure, deviation, difference, discrepancy, innovation; contrariety, discordance.

variegated *adj* chequered, dappled, diversified,

flecked, kaleidoscopic, mottled, multicoloured, pied, spotted, striped.

variety *n* difference, dissimilarity, diversity, diversification, medley, miscellany, mixture, multiplicity, variation; kind, sort.

various *adj* different, diverse, manifold, many, numerous, several, sundry.

varnish *vb* enamel, glaze, japan, lacquer; adorn, decorate, embellish, garnish, gild, polish; disguise, excuse, extenuate, gloss over, palliate. * *n* enamel, lacquer, stain; cover, extenuation, gloss.

vary *vb* alter, metamorphose, transform; alternate, exchange, rotate; diversify, modify, variegate; depart, deviate, swerve.

vassal *n* bondman, liegeman, retainer, serf, slave, subject, thrall.

vassalage *n* bondage, dependence, serfdom, servitude, slavery, subjection.

vast *adj* boundless, infinite, measureless, spacious, wide; colossal, enormous, gigantic, huge, immense, mighty, monstrous, prodigious, tremendous; extraordinary, remarkable.

vaticination *n* augury, divination, prediction, prognostication, prophecy.

vault[1] *vb* arch, bend, curve, span. * *n* cupola, curve, dome; catacomb, cell, cellar, crypt, dungeon, tomb; depository, strongroom.

vault[2] *vb* bound, jump, leap, spring; tumble, turn. * *n* bound, leap, jump, spring.

vaunt *vb* advertise, boast, brag, display, exult, flaunt, flourish, parade.

veer *vb* change, shift, turn.

vegetate *vb* blossom, develop, flourish, flower, germinate, grow, shoot, sprout, swell; bask, hibernate, idle, stagnate.

vehemence *n* impetuosity, violence; ardour, eagerness, earnestness, enthusiasm, fervency, fervour, heat, keenness, passion, warmth, zeal; force, intensity.

vehement *adj* furious, high, hot, impetuous, passionate, rampant, violent; ardent, burning, eager, earnest, enthusiastic, fervid, fiery, keen, passionate, sanguine, zealous; forcible, mighty, powerful, strong.

veil *vb* cloak, conceal, cover, curtain, envelop, hide, invest, mask, screen, shroud. * *n* cover, curtain, film, shade, screen; blind, cloak, disguise, mask, muffler, visor.

vein *n* course, current, lode, seam, streak, stripe, thread, wave; bent, character, faculty, humour, mood, talent, turn.

velocity *n* acceleration, celerity, expedition, fleetness, haste, quickness, rapidity, speed, swiftness.

velvety *adj* delicate, downy, smooth, soft.

venal *adj* corrupt, mean, purchasable, sordid.

vend *vb* dispose, flog, hawk, retail, sell.

venerable *adj* grave, respected, revered, sage, wise; awful, dread, dreadful; aged, old, patriarchal.

venerate *vb* adore, esteem, honour, respect, revere.

veneration *n* adoration, devotion, esteem, respect, reverence, worship.

vengeance *n* retaliation, retribution, revenge.

venial *adj* allowed, excusable, pardonable, permitted, trivial.

venom *n* poison, virus; acerbity, acrimony, bitterness, gall, hate, ill-will, malevolence, malice, maliciousness, malignity, rancour, spite, virulence.

venomous *adj* deadly, poisonous, septic, toxic, virulent; caustic, malicious, malignant, mischievous, noxious, spiteful.

vent *vb* emit, express, release, utter. * *n* air hole, hole, mouth, opening, orifice; air pipe, air tube, aperture, blowhole, bunghole, hydrant, plug, spiracle, spout, tap, orifice; effusion, emission, escape, outlet, passage; discharge, expression, utterance.

ventilate *vb* aerate, air, freshen, oxygenate, purify; fan, winnow; canvass, comment, discuss, examine, publish, review, scrutinize.

venture *vb* adventure, dare, hazard, imperil, jeopardize, presume, risk, speculate, test, try, undertake. * *n* adventure, chance, hazard, jeopardy, peril, risk, speculation, stake.

venturesome *adj* adventurous, bold, courageous, daring, doughty, enterprising, fearless, foolhardy, intrepid, presumptuous, rash, venturous.

veracious *adj* reliable, straightforward, true, trustworthy, truthful; credible, genuine, honest, unfeigned.

veracity *n* accuracy, candour, correctness, credibility, exactness, fidelity, frankness, honesty, ingenuousness, probity, sincerity, trueness, truth, truthfulness.

verbal *adj* nuncupative, oral, spoken, unwritten.

verbose *adj* diffusive, long-winded, loquacious, talkative, wordy.

verdant *adj* fresh, green, verdure, verdurous; green, inexperienced, raw, unsophisticated.

verdict *n* answer, decision, finding, judgement, opinion, sentence.

verge *vb* bear, incline, lean, slope, tend; approach, border, skirt. * *n* mace, rod, staff; border, boundary, brink, confine, edge, extreme, limit, margin; edge, eve, point.

verification *n* authentication, attestation, confirmation, corroboration.

verify *vb* attest, authenticate, confirm, corroborate, prove, substantiate.

verily *adv* absolutely, actually, confidently, indeed, positively, really, truly.

verity *n* certainty, reality, truth, truthfulness.

vermicular *adj* convoluted, flexuose, flexuous, meandering, serpentine, sinuous, tortuous, twisting, undulating, waving, winding, wormish, wormlike.

vernacular *adj* common, indigenous, local, mother, native, vulgar. * *n* cant, dialect, jargon, patois, speech.

versatile *adj* capricious, changeable, erratic, mobile, variable; fickle, inconstant, mercurial, unsteady; adaptable, protean, plastic, varied.

versed *adj* able, accomplished, acquainted, clever,

conversant, practised, proficient, qualified, skilful, skilled, trained.

version *n* interpretation, reading, rendering, translation.

vertex *n* apex, crown, height, summit, top, zenith.

vertical *adj* erect, perpendicular, plumb, steep, upright.

vertiginous *adj* rotatory, rotary, whirling; dizzy, giddy.

vertigo *n* dizziness, giddiness.

verve *n* animation, ardour, energy, enthusiasm, force, rapture, spirit.

very *adv* absolutely, enormously, excessively, hugely, remarkably, surpassingly. * *adj* actual, exact, identical, precise, same; bare, mere, plain, pure, simple.

vesicle *n* bladder, blister, cell, cyst, follicle.

vest *vb* clothe, cover, dress, envelop; endow, furnish, invest. * *n* dress, garment, robe, vestment, vesture, waistcoat.

vestibule *n* anteroom, entrance hall, lobby, porch.

vestige *n* evidence, footprint, footstep, mark, record, relic, sign, token.

veteran *adj* adept, aged, experienced, disciplined, seasoned, old. * *n* campaigner, old soldier; master, past master, old-timer, old-stager.

veto *vb* ban, embargo, forbid, interdict, negate, prohibit. * *n* ban, embargo, interdict, prohibition, refusal.

vex *vb* annoy, badger, bother, chafe, cross, distress, gall, harass, harry, hector, molest, perplex, pester, plague, tease, torment, trouble, roil, spite, worry; affront, displease, fret, irk, irritate, nettle, offend, provoke; agitate, disquiet, disturb.

vexation *n* affliction, agitation, chagrin, discomfort, displeasure, disquiet, distress, grief, irritation, pique, sorrow, trouble; annoyance, curse, nuisance, plague, torment; damage, troubling, vexing.

vexed *adj* afflicted, agitated, annoyed, bothered, disquieted, harassed, irritated, perplexed, plagued, provoked, troubled, worried.

vibrate *vb* oscillate, sway, swing, undulate, wave; impinge, quiver, sound, thrill; fluctuate, hesitate, vacillate, waver.

vibration *n* nutation, oscillation, vibration.

vicarious *adj* commissioned, delegated, indirect, second-hand, substituted.

vice *n* blemish, defect, failing, fault, imperfection, infirmity; badness, corruption, depravation, depravity, error, evil, immorality, iniquity, laxity, obliquity, sin, viciousness, vileness, wickedness.

vicinity *n* nearness, proximity; locality, neighbourhood, vicinage.

vicious *adj* abandoned, atrocious, bad, corrupt, degenerate, demoralized, depraved, devilish, diabolical, evil, flagrant, hellish, immoral, iniquitous, mischievous, profligate, shameless, sinful, unprincipled, wicked; malicious, spiteful, venomous; foul, impure; debased, faulty; contrary, refractory.

viciousness *n* badness, corruption, depravity, immorality, profligacy.

vicissitude *n* alteration, interchange; change, fluctuation, mutation, revolution, variation.

victim *n* martyr, sacrifice, sufferer; prey; cat's-paw, cull, cully, dupe, gull, gudgeon, puppet.

victimize *vb* bamboozle, befool, beguile, cheat, circumvent, cozen, deceive, defraud, diddle, dupe, fool, gull, hoax, hoodwink, overreach, swindle, trick.

victor *n* champion, conqueror, vanquisher, winner.

victorious *adj* conquering, successful, triumphant, winning.

victory *n* achievement, conquest, mastery, triumph.

victuals *npl* comestibles, eatables, fare, food, meat, provisions, repast, sustenance, viands.

vie *vb* compete, contend, emulate, rival, strive.

view *vb* behold, contemplate, eye, inspect, scan, survey; consider, inspect, regard, study. * *n* inspection, observation, regard, sight; outlook, panorama, perspective, prospect, range, scene, survey, vista; aim, intent, intention, design, drift, object, purpose, scope; belief, conception, impression, idea, judgement, notion, opinion, sentiment, theory; appearance, aspect, show.

vigilance *n* alertness, attentiveness, carefulness, caution, circumspection, observance, watchfulness.

vigilant *adj* alert, attentive, careless, cautious, circumspect, unsleeping, wakeful, watchful.

vigorous *adj* lusty, powerful, strong; active, alert, cordial, energetic, forcible, strenuous, vehement, vivid, virile; brisk, hale, hardy, robust, sound, sturdy, healthy; fresh, flourishing; bold, emphatic, impassioned, lively, nervous, piquant, pointed, severe, sparkling, spirited, trenchant.

vigour *n* activity, efficacy, energy, force, might, potency, power, spirit, strength; bloom, elasticity, haleness, health, heartiness, pep, punch, robustness, soundness, thriftiness, tone, vim, vitality; enthusiasm, freshness, fire, intensity, liveliness, piquancy, strenuousness, vehemence, verve, raciness.

vile *adj* abject, base, beastly, beggarly, brutish, contemptible, despicable, disgusting, grovelling, ignoble, low, odious, paltry, pitiful, repulsive, scurvy, shabby, slavish, sorry, ugly; bad, evil, foul, gross, impure, iniquitous, lewd, obscene, sinful, vicious, wicked; cheap, mean, miserable, valueless, worthless.

vilify *vb* abuse, asperse, backbite, berate, blacken, blemish, brand, calumniate, decry, defame, disparage, lampoon, libel, malign, revile, scandalize, slander, slur, traduce, vituperate.

villain *n* blackguard, knave, miscreant, rascal, reprobate, rogue, ruffian, scamp, scapegrace, scoundrel.

villainous *adj* base, mean, vile; corrupt, depraved, knavish, unprincipled, wicked; atrocious, heinous, outrageous, sinful; mischievous, sorry.

vindicate *vb* defend, justify, uphold; advocate, avenge, assert, maintain, right, support.

vindication *n* apology, excuse, defence, justification.

vindictive *adj* avenging, grudgeful, implacable, malevolent, malicious, malignant, retaliative, revengeful, spiteful, unforgiving, unrelenting, vengeful.

violate *vb* hurt, injure; break, disobey, infringe, invade; desecrate, pollute, profane; abuse, debauch, defile, deflower, outrage, ravish, transgress.

violent *adj* boisterous, demented, forceful, forcible, frenzied, furious, high, hot, impetuous, insane, intense, stormy, tumultuous, turbulent, vehement, wild; fierce, fiery, fuming, heady, heavy, infuriate, passionate, obstreperous, strong, raging, rampant, rank, rapid, raving, refractory, roaring, rough, tearing, towering, ungovernable; accidental, unnatural; desperate, extreme, outrageous, unjust; acute, exquisite, poignant, sharp.

virago *n* amazon, brawler, fury, shrew, tartar, vixen.

virgin *adj* chaste, maidenly, modest, pure, undefiled, stainless, unpolluted, vestal, virginal; fresh, maiden, untouched, unused. * *n* celibate, damsel, girl, lass, maid, maiden.

virile *adj* forceful, manly, masculine, robust, vigorous.

virtual *adj* constructive, equivalent, essential, implicit, implied, indirect, practical, substantial.

virtue *n* chastity, goodness, grace, morality, purity; efficacy, excellence, honesty, integrity, justice, probity, quality, rectitude, worth.

virtuous *adj* blameless, equitable, exemplary, excellent, good, honest, moral, noble, righteous, upright, worthy; chaste, continent, immaculate, innocent, modest, pure, undefiled; efficacious, powerful.

virulent *adj* deadly, malignant, poisonous, toxic, venomous; acrid, acrimonious, bitter, caustic.

visage *n* aspect, countenance, face, guise, physiognomy, semblance.

viscera *n* bowels, entrails, guts, intestines.

viscous *adj* adhesive, clammy, glutinous, ropy, slimy, sticky, tenacious.

visible *adj* observable, perceivable, perceptible, seeable, visual; apparent, clear, conspicuous, discoverable, distinct, evident, manifest, noticeable, obvious, open, palpable, patent, plain, revealed, unhidden, unmistakable.

vision *n* eyesight, seeing, sight; eyeshot, ken; apparition, chimera, dream, ghost, hallucination, illusion, phantom, spectre.

visionary *adj* imaginative, impractical, quixotic, romantic; chimerical, dreamy, fancied, fanciful, fantastic, ideal, illusory, imaginary, romantic, shadowy, unsubstantial, utopian, wild. * *n* dreamer, enthusiast, fanatic, idealist, optimist, theorist, zealot.

vital *adj* basic, cardinal, essential, indispensable, necessary, needful; animate, alive, existing, lifegiving, living; paramount.

vitality *n* animation, life, strength, vigour, virility.

vitiate *vb* adulterate, contaminate, corrupt, debase, defile, degrade, deprave, deteriorate, impair, infect, injure, invalidate, poison, pollute, spoil.

vitiation *n* adulteration, corruption, degeneracy, degeneration, degradation, depravation, deterioration, impairment, injury, invalidation, perversion, pollution, prostitution.

vituperate *vb* abuse, berate, blame, censure, denounce, overwhelm, rate, revile, scold, upbraid, vilify.

vituperation *n* abuse, blame, censure, invective, reproach, railing, reviling, scolding, upbraiding.

vivacious *adj* active, animated, breezy, brisk, buxom, cheerful, frolicsome, gay, jocund, lighthearted, lively, merry, mirthful, spirited, sportive, sprightly.

vivacity *n* animation, cheer, cheerfulness, gaiety, liveliness, sprightliness.

vivid *adj* active, animated, bright, brilliant, clear, intense, fresh, lively, living, lucid, quick, sprightly, strong; expressive, graphic, striking, telling.

vivify *vb* animate, arouse, awake, quicken, vitalize.

vixen *n* brawler, scold, shrew, spitfire, tartar, virago.

vocabulary *n* dictionary, glossary, lexicon, wordbook; language, terms, words.

vocation *n* call, citation, injunction, summons; business, calling, employment, occupation, profession, pursuit, trade.

vociferate *vb* bawl, bellow, clamour, cry, exclaim, rant, shout, yell.

vociferous *adj* blatant, clamorous, loud, noisy, obstreperous, ranting, stunning, uproarious.

vogue *adj* fashionable, modish, stylish, trendy. * *n* custom, fashion, favour, mode, practice, repute, style, usage, way.

voice *vb* declare, express, say, utter. * *n* speech, tongue, utterance; noise, notes, sound; opinion, option, preference, suffrage, vote; accent, articulation, enunciation, inflection, intonation, modulation, pronunciation, tone; expression, language, words.

void *vb* clear, eject, emit, empty, evacuate. * *adj* blank, empty, hollow, vacant; clear, destitute, devoid, free, lacking, wanting, without; inept, ineffectual, invalid, nugatory, null; imaginary, unreal, vain. * *n* abyss, blank, chasm, emptiness, hole, vacuum.

volatile *adj* gaseous, incoercible; airy, buoyant, frivolous, gay, jolly, lively, sprightly, vivacious; capricious, changeable, fickle, flighty, flyaway, giddy, harebrained, inconstant, light-headed, mercurial, reckless, unsteady, whimsical, wild.

volition *n* choice, determination, discretion, option, preference, will.

volley *n* fusillade, round, salvo; blast, burst, discharge, emission, explosion, outbreak, report, shower, storm.

voluble *adj* fluent, garrulous, glib, loquacious, talkative.

volume *n* book, tome; amplitude, body, bulk, compass, dimension, size, substance, vastness; fullness, power, quantity.

voluminous *adj* ample, big, bulky, full, great, large; copious, diffuse, discursive, flowing.

voluntary *adj* free, spontaneous, unasked, unbidden, unforced; deliberate, designed, intended, purposed; discretionary, optional, willing.

volunteer *vb* offer, present, proffer, propose, tender.

voluptuary *n* epicure, hedonist, sensualist.

voluptuous *adj* carnal, effeminate, epicurean, fleshy, licentious, luxurious, sensual, sybaritic.

vomit *vb* discharge, eject, emit, puke, regurgitate, spew, throw up.

voracious *adj* devouring, edacious, greedy, hungry, rapacious, ravenous.

vortex *n* eddy, maelstrom, whirl, whirlpool.

votary *adj* devoted, promised. * *n* adherent, devotee, enthusiast, follower, supporter, votarist, zealot.

vote *vb* ballot, elect, opt, return; judge, pronounce, propose, suggest. * *n* ballot, franchise, poll, referendum, suffrage, voice.

vouch *vb* affirm, asseverate, attest, aver, declare, guarantee, support, uphold, verify, warrant.

vouchsafe *vb* accord, cede, deign, grant, stoop, yield.

vow *vb* consecrate, dedicate, devote; asseverate. * *n* oath, pledge, promise.

voyage *vb* cruise, journey, navigate, ply, sail. * *n* crossing, cruise, excursion, journey, passage, sail, trip.

vulgar *adj* base-born, common, ignoble, lowly, plebeian; boorish, cheap, coarse, discourteous, flashy, homespun, garish, gaudy, ill-bred, inelegant, loud, rustic, showy, tawdry, uncultivated, unrefined; general, ordinary, popular, public; base, broad, loose, low, gross, mean, ribald, vile; inelegant, unauthorized.

vulgarity *n* baseness, coarseness, grossness, meanness, rudeness.

vulnerable *adj* accessible, assailable, defenceless, exposed, weak.

W

waddle *vb* toddle, toggle, waggle, wiggle, wobble.

waft *vb* bear, carry, convey, float, transmit, transport. * *n* breath, breeze, draught, puff.

wag[1] *vb* shake, sway, waggle; oscillate, vibrate, waver; advance, move, progress, stir. * *n* flutter, nod, oscillation, vibration.

wag[2] *n* humorist, jester, joker, wit.

wage *vb* bet, hazard, lay, stake, wager; conduct, undertake.

wager *vb* back, bet, gamble, lay, pledge, risk, stake. * *n* bet, gamble, pledge, risk, stake.

wages *npl* allowance, compensation, earnings, emolument, hire, pay, payment, remuneration, salary, stipend.

waggish *adj* frolicsome, gamesome, mischievous, roguish, tricksy; comical, droll, facetious, funny, humorous, jocular, jocose, merry, sportive.

wagon *n* cart, lorry, truck, van, waggon, wain.

wail *vb* bemoan, deplore, lament, mourn; cry, howl, weep. * *n* complaint, cry, lamentation, moan, wailing.

waist *n* bodice, corsage, waistline.

wait *vb* delay, linger, pause, remain, rest, stay, tarry; attend, minister, serve; abide, await, expect, look for. * *n* delay, halt, holdup, pause, respite, rest, stay, stop.

waiter, waitress *n* attendant, lackey, servant, servitor, steward, valet.

waive *vb* defer, forgo, surrender, relinquish, remit, renounce; desert, reject.

wake[1] *vb* arise, awake, awaken; activate, animate, arouse, awaken, excite, kindle, provoke, stimulate. * *n* vigil, watch, watching.

wake[2] *n* course, path, rear, track, trail, wash.

wakeful *adj* awake, sleepless, restless; alert, observant, vigilant, wary, watchful.

wale *n* ridge, streak, stripe, welt, whelk.

walk *vb* advance, depart, go, march, move, pace, saunter, step, stride, stroll, tramp. * *n* amble, carriage, gait, step; beat, career, course, department, field, province; conduct, procedure; alley, avenue, cloister, esplanade, footpath, path, pathway, pavement, promenade, range, sidewalk, way; constitutional, excursion, hike, ramble, saunter, stroll, tramp, turn.

wall *n* escarp, parapet, plane, upright.

wallet *n* bag, knapsack, pocketbook, purse, sack.

wan *adj* ashen, bloodless, cadaverous, colourless, haggard, pale, pallid.

wand *n* baton, mace, truncheon, sceptre.

wander *vb* forage, prowl, ramble, range, roam, rove, stroll; deviate, digress, straggle, stray; moon, rave. * *n* amble, cruise, excursion, ramble, stroll.

wane *vb* abate, decrease, ebb, subside; decline, fail, sink. * *n* decrease, diminution, lessening; decay, declension, decline, failure.

want *vb* crave, desire, need, require, wish; fail, lack, neglect, omit. * *n* absence, defect, default, deficiency, lack; defectiveness, failure, inadequacy, insufficiency, meagreness, paucity, poverty, scantiness, scarcity, shortness; requirement; craving, desire, longing, wish; destitution, distress, indigence, necessity, need, penury, poverty, privation, straits.

wanton *vb* caper, disport, frisk, frolic, play, revel, romp, sport; dally, flirt, toy, trifle. * *adj* free, loose, unchecked, unrestrained, wandering; abounding, exuberant, luxuriant, overgrown, rampant; airy, capricious, coltish, frisky, playful, skittish, sportive; dissolute, irregular, licentious, loose; carnal, immoral, incontinent, lascivious, lecherous, lewd, libidinous, light, lustful, prurient, salacious, unchaste; careless, gratuitous, groundless, heedless, inconsiderate, needless, perverse, reckless, wayward, wilful. * *n* baggage, flirt, harlot, light-o'-love, prostitute, rake, roué, slut, whore.

war *vb* battle, campaign, combat, contend, crusade, engage, fight, strive. * *n* contention, enmity, hostility, strife, warfare.

warble *vb* sing, trill, yodel. * *n* carol, chant, hymn, hum.

ward *vb* guard, watch; defend, fend, parry, protect, repel. * *n* care, charge, guard, guardianship, watch; defender, guardian, keeper, protector, warden; custody; defence, garrison, protection; minor, pupil; district, division, precinct, quarter; apartment, cubicle.

warehouse *n* depot, magazine, repository, store, storehouse.

wares *npl* commodities, goods, merchandise, movables.

warfare *n* battle, conflict, contest, discord, engagement, fray, hostilities, strife, struggle, war.

warily *adv* carefully, cautiously, charily, circumspectly, heedfully, watchfully, vigilantly.

wariness *n* care, caution, circumspection, foresight, thought, vigilance.

warlike *adj* bellicose, belligerent, combative,

hostile, inimical, martial, military, soldierly, watchful.

warm *vb* heat, roast, toast; animate, chafe, excite, rouse. * *adj* lukewarm, tepid; genial, mild, pleasant, sunny; close, muggy, oppressive; affectionate, ardent, cordial, eager, earnest, enthusiastic, fervent, fervid, glowing, hearty, hot, zealous; excited, fiery, flushed, furious, hasty, keen, lively, passionate, quick, vehement, violent.

warmth *n* glow, tepidity; ardour, fervency, fervour, zeal; animation, cordiality, eagerness, earnestness, enthusiasm, excitement, fervency, fever, fire, flush, heat, intensity, passion, spirit, vehemence.

warn *vb* caution, forewarn; admonish, advise; apprise, inform, notify; bid, call, summon.

warning *adj* admonitory, cautionary, cautioning, monitory. * *n* admonition, advice, caveat, caution, monition; information, notice; augury, indication, intimation, omen, portent, presage, prognostic, sign, symptom; call, summons; example, lesson, sample.

warp *vb* bend, bias, contort, deviate, distort, pervert, swerve, turn, twist. * *n* bent, bias, cast, crook, distortion, inclination, leaning, quirk, sheer, skew, slant, slew, swerve, twist, turn.

warrant *vb* answer for, certify, guarantee, secure; affirm, assure, attest, avouch, declare, justify, state; authorize, justify, license, maintain, sanction, support, sustain, uphold. * *n* guarantee, pledge, security, surety, warranty; authentication, authority, commission, verification; order, pass, permit, summons, subpoena, voucher, writ.

warrantable *adj* admissible, allowable, defensible, justifiable, lawful, permissible, proper, right, vindicable.

warrior *n* champion, captain, fighter, hero, soldier.

wary *adj* careful, cautious, chary, circumspect, discreet, guarded, heedful, prudent, scrupulous, vigilant, watchful.

wash *vb* purify, purge; moisten, wet; bathe, clean, flush, irrigate, lap, lave, rinse, sluice; colour, stain, tint. * *n* ablution, bathing, cleansing, lavation, washing; bog, fen, marsh, swamp, quagmire; bath, embrocation, lotion; laundry, washing.

washy *adj* damp, diluted, moist, oozy, sloppy, thin, watery, weak; feeble, jejune, pointless, poor, spiritless, trashy, trumpery, unmeaning, vapid, worthless.

waspish *adj* choleric, fretful, irascible, irritable, peevish, petulant, snappish, testy, touchy; slender, slim, small-waisted.

waste *vb* consume, corrode, decrease, diminish, emaciate, wear; absorb, deplete, devour, dissipate, drain, empty, exhaust, expend, lavish, lose, misspend, misuse, scatter, spend, squander; demolish, desolate, destroy, devastate, devour, dilapidate, harry, pillage, plunder, ravage, ruin, scour, strip; damage, impair, injure; decay,

dwindle, perish, wither. * *adj* bare, desolated, destroyed, devastated, empty, ravaged, ruined, spoiled, stripped, void; dismal, dreary, forlorn; abandoned, bare, barren, uncultivated, unimproved, uninhabited, untilled, wild; useless, valueless, worthless; exuberant, superfluous. * *n* consumption, decrement, diminution, dissipation, exhaustion, expenditure, loss, wasting; destruction, dispersion, extravagance, loss, squandering, wanton; decay, desolation, destruction, devastation, havoc, pillage, ravage, ruin; chaff, debris, detritus, dross, excrement, husks, junk, matter, offal, refuse, rubbish, trash, wastrel, worthlessness; barrenness, desert, expanse, solitude, wild, wilderness.

wasteful *adj* destructive, ruinous; extravagant, improvident, lavish, prodigal, profuse, squandering, thriftless, unthrifty.

watch *vb* attend, guard, keep, oversee, protect, superintend, tend; eye, mark, observe. * *n* espial, guard, outlook, wakefulness, watchfulness, watching, vigil, ward; alertness, attention, inspection, observation, surveillance; guard, picket, sentinel, sentry, watchman; pocket watch, ticker, timepiece, wristwatch.

watchful *adj* alert, attentive, awake, careful, circumspect, guarded, heedful, observant, vigilant, wakeful, wary.

watchword *n* catchword, cry, motto, password, shibboleth, word.

waterfall *n* cascade, cataract, fall, linn.

watery *adj* diluted, thin, waterish, weak; insipid, spiritless, tasteful, vapid; moist, wet.

wave *vb* float, flutter, heave, shake, sway, undulate, wallow; brandish, flaunt, flourish, swing; beckon, signal. * *n* billow, bore, breaker, flood, flush, ripple, roll, surge, swell, tide, undulation; flourish, gesture, sway; convolution, curl, roll, unevenness.

waver *vb* flicker, float, undulate, wave; reel, totter; falter, fluctuate, flutter, hesitate, oscillate, quiver, vacillate.

wax *vb* become, grow, increase, mount, rise.

way *n* advance, journey, march, progression, transit, trend; access, alley, artery, avenue, beat, channel, course, highroad, highway, passage, path, road, route, street, track, trail; fashion, manner, means, method, mode, system; distance, interval, space, stretch; behaviour, custom, form, guise, habit, habitude, practice, process, style, usage; device, plan, scheme.

wayfarer *n* itinerant, nomad, passenger, pilgrim, rambler, traveller, walker, wanderer.

wayward *adj* capricious, captious, contrary, forward, headstrong, intractable, obstinate, perverse, refractory, stubborn, unruly, wilful.

weak *adj* debilitated, delicate, enfeebled, enervated, exhausted, faint, feeble, fragile, frail, infirm, invalid, languid, languishing, shaky, sickly, spent, strengthless, tender, unhealthy, unsound, wasted, weakly; accessible, defenceless, unprotected, vulnerable; light, soft, unstressed; boneless, cowardly, infirm; compliant, irresolute, pliable, pliant, undecided, undetermined, unsettled, unstable, unsteady, vacillating, wavering, yielding; childish, foolish, imbecile, senseless, shallow, silly, simple, stupid, weak-minded, witless; erring, foolish, indiscreet, injudicious, unwise; gentle, indistinct, low, small; adulterated, attenuated, diluted, insipid, tasteless, thin, watery; flimsy, frivolous, poor, sleazy, slight, trifling; futile, illogical, inconclusive, ineffective, ineffectual, inefficient, lame, unconvincing, unsatisfactory, unsupported, unsustained, vague, vain; unsafe, unsound, unsubstantial, untrustworthy; helpless, impotent, powerless; breakable, brittle, delicate, frangible; inconsiderable, puny, slender, slight, small.

weaken vb cramp, cripple, debilitate, devitalize, enervate, enfeeble, invalidate, relax, sap, shake, stagger, undermine, unman, unnerve, unstring; adulterate, attenuate, debase, depress, dilute, exhaust, impair, impoverish, lessen, lower, reduce.

weakness n debility, feebleness, fragility, frailty, infirmity, languor, softness; defect, failing, fault, flaw; fondness, inclination, liking.

weal n advantage, good, happiness, interest, profit, utility, prosperity, welfare; ridge, streak, stripe.

wealth n assets, capital, cash, fortune, funds, goods, money, possessions, property, riches, treasure; abundance, affluence, opulence, plenty, profusion.

wean vb alienate, detach, disengage, withdraw.

wear vb bear, carry, don; endure, last; consume, impair, rub, use, waste. * n corrosion, deterioration, disintegration, erosion, wear and tear; consumption, use; apparel, array, attire, clothes, clothing, dress, garb, gear.

wearied adj apathetic, bored, exhausted, fagged, fatigued, jaded, tired, weary, worn.

weariness n apathy, boredom, ennui, exhaustion, fatigue, languor, lassitude, monotony, prostration, sameness, tedium.

wearisome adj annoying, boring, dull, exhausting, fatiguing, humdrum, irksome, monotonous, prolix, prosaic, slow, tedious, tiresome, troublesome, trying, uninteresting, vexatious.

weary vb debilitate, exhaust, fag, fatigue, harass, jade, tire. * adj apathetic, bored, drowsy, exhausted, jaded, spent, tired, worn; irksome, tiresome, wearisome.

weave vb braid, entwine, interlace, lace, mat, plait, pleat, twine; compose, construct, fabricate, make.

wed vb contract, couple, espouse, marry, unite.

wedding n bridal, espousal, marriage, nuptials.

wedlock n marriage, matrimony.

ween vb fancy, imagine, suppose, think.

weep vb bemoan, bewail, complain, cry, lament, sob.

weigh vb balance, counterbalance, lift, raise; consider, deliberate, esteem, examine, study.

weight vb ballast, burden, fill, freight, load; weigh. * n gravity, heaviness, heft, tonnage; burden, load, pressure; consequence, efficacy, emphasis, importance, impressiveness, influence, moment, pith, power, significance, value.

weighty adj heavy, massive, onerous, ponderous, unwieldy; considerable, efficacious, forcible, grave, important, influential, serious, significant.

weird adj eerie, ghostly, strange, supernatural, uncanny, unearthly, witching.

welcome vb embrace, greet, hail, receive. * adj acceptable, agreeable, grateful, gratifying, pleasant, pleasing, satisfying. * n greeting, reception, salutation.

welfare n advantage, affluence, benefit, happiness, profit, prosperity, success, thrift, weal, wellbeing.

well[1] vb flow, gush, issue, jet, pour, spring. * n fount, fountain, reservoir, spring, wellhead, wellspring; origin, source; hole, pit, shaft.

well[2] adj hale, healthy, hearty, sound; fortunate, good, happy, profitable, satisfactory, useful. * adv accurately, adequately, correctly, efficiently, properly, suitably; abundantly, considerably, fully, thoroughly; agreeably, commendably, favourably, worthily.

wellbeing n comfort, good, happiness, health, prosperity, welfare.

welter vb flounder, roll, toss, wallow. * n confusion, jumble, mess.

wet vb dabble, damp, dampen, dip, drench, moisten, saturate, soak, sprinkle, water. * adj clammy, damp, dank, dewy, dripping, humid, moist; rainy, showery, sprinkly. * n dampness, humidity, moisture, wetness.

whack vb, n bang, beat, rap, strike, thrash, thump, thwack.

wharf n dock, pier, quay.

wheedle vb cajole, coax, flatter, inveigle, lure.

wheel vb gyrate, revolve, roll, rotate, spin, swing, turn, twist, whirl, wind. * n circle, revolution, roll, rotation, spin, turn, twirl.

whet vb grind, sharpen; arouse, awaken, excite, provoke, rouse, stimulate; animate, inspire, kindle, quicken, warm.

whiff vb, n blast, gust, puff.

whim n caprice, crotchet, fancy, freak, frolic, humour, notion, quirk, sport, vagary, whimsy, wish.

whimsical adj capricious, crotchety, eccentric, erratic, fanciful, frolicsome, odd, peculiar, quaint, singular.

whine vb cry, grumble, mewl, moan, snivel, wail, whimper. * n complaint, cry, grumble, moan, sob, wail, whimper.

whip vb beat, lash, strike; flagellate, flog, goad, horsewhip, scourge, slash; hurt, sting; jerk, snap, snatch, whisk. * n bullwhip, cane, crop, horsewhip, knout, lash, scourge, switch, thong.

whipping n beating, castigation, dusting, flagellation, flogging, thrashing.

whirl vb gyrate, pirouette, roll, revolve, rotate, turn, twirl, twist, wheel. * n eddy, flurry, flutter, gyration, rotation, spin, swirl, twirl, vortex.

whit n atom, bit, grain, iota, jot, mite, particle, scrap, speck, tittle.

white adj argent, canescent, chalky, frosty, hoary, ivory, milky, silver, snowy; grey, pale, pallid, wan; candid, clean, chaste, immaculate, innocent, pure, spotless, unblemished.

whole adj all, complete, entire, intact, integral, total, undivided; faultless, firm, good, perfect, strong, unbroken, undivided, uninjured; healthy, sound, well. * adv entire, in one. * n aggregate, all, amount, ensemble, entirety, gross, sum, total, totality.

wholesome adj healthy, healthful, invigorating, nourishing, nutritious, salubrious, salutary; beneficial, good, helpful, improving, salutary; fresh, sound, sweet.

wholly adv altogether, completely, entirely, fully, totally, utterly.

whoop vb halloo, hoot, roar, shout, yell. * n bellow, hoot, roar, shout, yell.

whore n bawd, courtesan, drab, harlot, prostitute, streetwalker, strumpet.

wicked adj abandoned, abominable, depraved, devilish, godless, graceless, immoral, impious, infamous, irreligious, irreverent, profane, sinful, ungodly, unholy, unprincipled, unrighteous, vicious, vile, worthless; atrocious, bad, black, criminal, dark, evil, heinous, ill, iniquitous, monstrous, nefarious, unjust, villainous.

wide adj ample, broad, capacious, comprehensive, distended, expanded, large, spacious, vast; distant, remote; prevalent, rife, widespread. * adv completely, farthest, fully.

wield vb brandish, flourish, handle, manipulate, ply, work; control, manage, sway, use.

wild adj feral, undomesticated, untamed; desert, desolate, native, rough, rude, uncultivated; barbarous, ferocious, fierce, savage, uncivilized; dense, luxuriant, rank; disorderly, distracted, frantic, frenzied, furious, impetuous, irregular, mad, outrageous, raving, turbulent, ungoverned, uncontrolled, violent; dissipated, fast, flighty, foolish, giddy, harebrained, heedless, ill-advised, inconsiderate, reckless, thoughtless, unwise; boisterous, rough, stormy; crazy, extravagant, fanciful, grotesque, imaginary, strange. * n desert, waste, wilderness.

wilderness n desert, waste, wild.

wilful adj cantankerous, contumacious, dogged, headstrong, heady, inflexible, intractable, mulish, obdurate, obstinate, perverse, pig-headed, refractory, self-willed, stubborn, unruly, unyielding; arbitrary, capricious; deliberate, intended, intentional, planned, premeditated.

will vb bid, command, decree, direct, enjoin, ordain; choose, desire, elect, wish; bequeath, convey, demise, devise, leave. * n decision, determination, resoluteness, resolution, self-reliance; desire, disposition, inclination, intent, pleasure, purpose, volition, wish; behest, command, decree, demand, direction, order, request, requirement.

willing adj adaptable, amenable, compliant, desirous, disposed, inclined, minded; deliberate, free, intentional, spontaneous, unasked, unbidden, voluntary; cordial, eager, forward, prompt, ready.

willingly adv cheerfully, gladly, readily, spontaneously, voluntarily.

wily adj arch, artful, crafty, crooked, cunning, deceitful, designing, diplomatic, foxy, insidious, intriguing, politic, sly, subtle, treacherous, tricky.

win vb accomplish, achieve, acquire, catch, earn, effect, gain, gather, get, make, obtain, procure, reach, realize, reclaim, recover; gain, succeed, surpass, triumph; arrive; allure, attract, convince, influence, persuade. * n conquest, success, triumph, victory.

wind[1] n air, blast, breeze, draught, gust, hurricane, whiff, zephyr; breath, breathing, expiration, inspiration, respiration; flatulence, gas, windiness.

wind[2] vb coil, crank, encircle, involve, reel, roll, turn, twine, twist; bend, curve, meander, zigzag. * n bend, curve, meander, twist, zigzag.

winding adj circuitous, devious, flexuose, flexuous, meandering, serpentine, tortuous, turning, twisting. * n bend, curve, meander, turn, twist.

windy adj breezy, blowy, blustering, boisterous, draughty, gusty, squally, stormy, tempestuous; airy, empty, hollow, inflated. **winning** adj alluring, attractive, bewitching, brilliant, captivating, charming, dazzling, delightful, enchanting, engaging, fascinating, lovely, persuasive, pleasing, prepossessing; conquering, triumphant, victorious.

winnow vb cull, glean, divide, fan, part, select, separate, sift.

winsome adj blithe, blithesome, bonny, buoyant, charming, cheerful, debonair, jocund, lighthearted, lively, lovable, merry, pleasant, sportive, winning.

wintry adj arctic, boreal, brumal, cold, frosty, icy, snowy.

wipe vb clean, dry, mop, rub. * n mop, rub, blow, hit, strike; gibe, jeer, sarcasm, sneer, taunt.

wisdom n depth, discernment, far-sightedness, foresight, insight, judgement, judiciousness, prescience, profundity, prudence, sagacity, sapience, sense, solidity, understanding, wiseness; attainment, edification, enlightenment, erudition, information, knowledge, learning, lore, scholarship; reason.

wise adj deep, discerning, enlightened, intelligent, judicious, penetrating, philosophical, profound, rational, seasonable, sensible, sage, sapient, solid, sound; erudite, informed, knowing, learned, scholarly; crafty, cunning, designing, foxy, politic, sly, subtle, wary, wily.

wish *vb* covet, desire, hanker, list, long; bid, command, desire, direct, intend, mean, order, want. * *n* behest, desire, intention, mind, pleasure, want, will; craving, desire, hankering, inclination, liking, longing, want, yearning.

wistful *adj* contemplative, engrossed, meditative, musing, pensive, reflective, thoughtful; desirous, eager, earnest, longing.

wit *n* genius, intellect, intelligence, reason, sense, understanding; brightness, banter, cleverness, drollery, facetiousness, fun, humour, jocularity, piquancy, point, raillery, satire, sparkle, whim; conceit, epigram, jest, joke, pleasantry, quip, quirk, repartee, sally, witticism; humorist, joker, wag.

witch *n* charmer, enchantress, fascinator, sorceress; crone, hag, sibyl.

witchcraft *n* conjuration, enchantment, magic, necromancy, sorcery, spell.

withdraw *vb* abstract, deduct, remove, retire, separate, sequester, sequestrate, subduct, subtract; disengage, wean; abjure, recall, recant, relinquish, resign, retract, revoke; abdicate, decamp, depart, dissociate, retire, shrink, vacate.

wither *vb* contract, droop, dry, sear, shrivel, wilt, wizen; decay, decline, languish, pine, waste.

withhold *vb* check, detain, hinder, repress, restrain, retain, suppress.

withstand *vb* confront, defy, face, oppose, resist.

witless *adj* daft, dull, foolish, halfwitted, obtuse, senseless, shallow, silly, stupid, unintelligent.

witness *vb* corroborate, mark, note, notice, observe, see. * *n* attestation, conformation, corroboration, evidence, proof, testimony; beholder, bystander, corroborator, deponent, eyewitness, onlooker, spectator, testifier.

witty *adj* bright, clever, droll, facetious, funny, humorous, jocose, jocular, pleasant, waggish; alert, penetrating, quick, sparkling, sprightly.

wizard *n* charmer, diviner, conjurer, enchanter, magician, necromancer, seer, soothsayer, sorcerer.

woe *n* affliction, agony, anguish, bitterness, depression, distress, dole, grief, heartache, melancholy, misery, sorrow, torture, tribulation, trouble, unhappiness, wretchedness.

woeful *adj* afflicted, agonized, anguished, burdened, disconsolate, distressed, melancholy, miserable, mournful, piteous, sad, sorrowful, troubled, unhappy, wretched; afflicting, afflictive, calamitous, deplorable, depressing, disastrous, distressing, dreadful, tragic, tragical, grievous, lamentable, pitiable, saddening.

wonder *vb* admire, gape, marvel; conjecture, ponder, query, question, speculate. * *n* amazement, astonishment, awe, bewilderment, curiosity, marvel, miracle, prodigy, surprise, stupefaction, wonderment.

wonderful *adj* amazing, astonishing, astounding, awe-inspiring, awesome, awful, extraordinary, marvellous, miraculous, portentous, prodigious, startling, stupendous, surprising.

wont *adj* accustomed, customary, familiar, habitual, ordinary, usual. * *n* custom, habit, practice, rule, usage.

wonted *adj* accustomed, common, conventional, customary, everyday, familiar, frequent, habitual, ordinary, regular, usual.

wood *n* coppice, copse, covert, forest, greenwood, grove, spinney, thicket, woodland.

word *vb* express, phrase, put, say, state, term, utter. * *n* expression, name, phrase, term, utterance; account, advice, information, intelligence, message, news, report, tidings; affirmation, assertion, averment, avowal, declaration, statement; conversation, speech; agreement, assurance, engagement, parole, pledge, plight, promise; behest, bidding, command, direction, order, precept; countersign, password, signal, watchword.

wordy *adj* circumlocutory, diffuse, garrulous, inflated, lengthened, long-winded, loquacious, periphrastic, rambling, talkative, tedious, verbose, windy.

work *vb* act, operate; drudge, fag, grind, grub, labour, slave, sweat, toil; move, perform, succeed; aim, attempt, strive, try; effervesce, ferment, leaven, rise; accomplish, beget, cause, effect, engender, manage, originate, produce; exert, strain; embroider, stitch. * *n* exertion, drudgery, grind, labour, pain, toil; business, employment, function, occupation, task; action, accomplishment, achievement, composition, deed, feat, fruit, handiwork, opus, performance, product, production; fabric, manufacture; ferment, leaven; management, treatment.

workman *n* journeyman, employee, labourer, operative, worker, wright; artisan, craftsman, mechanic.

world *n* cosmos, creation, earth, globe, nature, planet, sphere, universe.

worldly *adj* common, earthly, human, mundane, sublunary, terrestrial; carnal, fleshly, profane, secular, temporal; ambitious, grovelling, irreligious, selfish, proud, sordid, unsanctified, unspiritual; sophisticated, worldly-wise.

worry *vb* annoy, badger, bait, beset, bore, bother, chafe, disquiet, disturb, fret, gall, harass, harry, hector, infest, irritate, molest, persecute, pester, plague, tease, torment, trouble, vex. * *n* annoyance, anxiety, apprehensiveness, care, concern, disquiet, fear, misgiving, perplexity, solicitude, trouble, uneasiness, vexation.

worship *vb* adore, esteem, honour, revere, venerate; deify, idolize; aspire, pray. * *n* adoration, devotion, esteem, homage, idolatry, idolizing, respect, reverence; aspiration, exultation, invocation, laud, praise, prayer, supplication.

worst *vb* beat, choke, conquer, crush, defeat, discomfit, foil, master, overpower, overthrow, quell, rout, subdue, subjugate, vanquish.

worth *n* account, character, credit, desert, excellence, importance, integrity, merit, nobleness, worthiness, virtue; cost, estimation, price, value.

worthless *adj* futile, meritless, miserable, nugatory, paltry, poor, trifling, unproductive, unsalable, unserviceable, useless, valueless, wretched; abject, base, corrupt, degraded, ignoble, low, mean, vile.

worthy *adj* deserving, fit, suitable; estimable, excellent, exemplary, good, honest, honourable, reputable, righteous, upright, virtuous. * *n* celebrity, dignitary, luminary, notability, personage, somebody, VIP.

wound *vb* damage, harm, hurt, injure; cut, gall, harrow, irritate, lacerate, pain, prick, stab; annoy, mortify, offend. * *n* blow, hurt, injury; damage, detriment; anguish, grief, pain, pang, torture.

wraith *n* apparition, ghost, phantom, spectre, vision.

wrangle *vb* argue, bicker, brawl, cavil, dispute, jangle, jar, quarrel, squabble, spar, spat. * *n* altercation, argument, bickering, brawl, contest, controversy, jar, quarrel, squabble.

wrap *vb* cloak, cover, encase, envelop, muffle, swathe, wind. * *n* blanket, cape, cloak, cover, overcoat, shawl.

wrath *n* anger, choler, exasperation, fury, heat, resentment, indignation, ire, irritation, offence, passion, rage.

wrathful *adj* angry, enraged, exasperated, furious, hot, indignant, infuriated, irate, mad, passionate, provoked, rageful.

wreak *vb* execute, exercise, indulge, inflict, work.

wreath *n* chaplet, curl, festoon, garland, ring, twine.

wreathe *vb* encircle, festoon, garland, intertwine, surround, twine, twist.

wreck *vb* founder, shipwreck, strand; blast, blight, break, devastate, ruin, spoil. * *n* crash, desolation, destruction, perdition, prostration, ruin, shipwreck, smash, undoing.

wrench *vb* distort, pervert, twist, wrest, wring; sprain, strain; extort, extract. * *n* twist, wring; sprain, strain; monkey wrench, spanner.

wrest *vb* force, pull, strain, twist, wrench, wring.

wrestle *vb* contend, contest, grapple, strive, struggle.

wretch *n* outcast, pariah, pilgarlic, troglodyte,

vagabond, victim, sufferer; beggar, criminal, hound, knave, miscreant, rascal, ruffian, rogue, scoundrel, villain.

wretched *adj* afflicted, comfortless, distressed, forlorn, sad, unfortunate, unhappy, woebegone; afflicting, calamitous, deplorable, depressing, pitiable, sad, saddening, shocking, sorrowful; bad, beggarly, contemptible, mean, paltry, pitiful, poor, shabby, sorry, vile, worthless.

wring *vb* contort, twist, wrench; extort, force, wrest; anguish, distress, harass, pain, rack, torture.

wrinkle[1] *vb* cockle, corrugate, crease, gather, pucker, rumple. * *n* cockle, corrugation, crease, crimp, crinkle, crumple, fold, furrow, gather, plait, ridge, rumple.

wrinkle[2] *n* caprice, fancy, notion, quirk, whim; device, tip, trick.

writ *n* decree, order, subpoena, summons.

write *vb* compose, copy, indite, inscribe, pen, scrawl, scribble, transcribe.

writer *n* amanuensis, author, clerk, penman, scribe, secretary.

writhe *vb* contort, distort, squirm, twist, wriggle.

written *adj* composed, indited, inscribed, penned, transcribed.

wrong *vb* abuse, encroach, injure, maltreat, oppress. * *adj* inequitable, unfair, unjust, wrongful; bad, criminal, evil, guilty, immoral, improper, iniquitous, reprehensible, sinful, vicious, wicked; amiss, improper, inappropriate, unfit, unsuitable; erroneous, false, faulty, inaccurate, incorrect, mistaken, untrue. * *adv* amiss, erroneously, falsely, faultily, improperly, inaccurately, incorrectly, wrongly. * *n* foul, grievance, inequity, injury, injustice, trespass, unfairness; blame, crime, dishonesty, evil, guilt, immorality, iniquity, misdeed, misdoing, sin, transgression, unrighteousness, vice, wickedness, wrongdoing; error, falsity.

wroth *adj* angry, enraged, exasperated, furious, incensed, indignant, irate, passionate, provoked, resentful.

wrought *adj* done, effected, performed, worked.

wry *adj* askew, awry, contorted, crooked, distorted, twisted.

XYZ

xanthous *adj* blonde, fair, light-complexioned, xanthic, yellow.

xiphoid *adj* ensiform, gladiate, sword-like, sword-shaped.

Xmas *n* Christmas, Christmastide, Noel, Yule, Yuletide.

X-ray *n* roentgen ray, röntgen ray.

xylograph *n* cut, woodcut, wood engraving.

xylographer *n* wood engraver.

xylophagous *adj* wood-eating, wood-nourished.

yap *vb* bark, cry, yelp. * *n* bark, cry, yelp.

yard *n* close, compound, court, courtyard, enclosure, garden.

yarn *n* anecdote, boasting, fabrication, narrative, story, tale, untruth.

yawn *vb* dehisce, gape, open wide. * *n* gap, gape, gulf.

yearn *vb* crave, desire, hanker after, long for.

yell *vb* bawl, bellow, cry out, howl, roar, scream, screech, shriek, squeal.* *n* cry, howl, roar, scream, screech, shriek.

yellow *adj* aureate, gilded, gilt, gold, golden, lemon, primrose, saffron, xanthic, xanthous.

yelp *vb* bark, howl, yap; complain, bitch, grouse. * *n* bark, sharp cry, howl.

yet *adv* at last, besides, further, however, over and above, so far, still, thus far, ultimately.* *conj* moreover, nevertheless, notwithstanding, now.

yield *vb* afford, bear, bestow, communicate, confer, fetch, furnish, impart, produce, render, supply; accede, accord, acknowledge, acquiesce, allow, assent, comply, concede, give, grant, permit; abandon, abdicate, cede, forgo, give up, let go, quit, relax, relinquish, resign, submit, succumb, surrender, waive. * *n* earnings, income, output, produce, profit, return, revenue.

yielding *adj* accommodating, acquiescent, affable, compliant, complaisant, easy, manageable, obedient, passive, submissive, unresisting; bending, flexible, flexile, plastic, pliant, soft, supple, tractable; fertile, productive.

yoke *vb* associate, bracket, connect, couple, harness, interlink, join, link, unite. * *n* bond, chain, ligature, link, tie, union; bondage, dependence, enslavement, service, servitude, subjection, vassalage; couple, pair.

yokel *n* boor, bumpkin, countryman, peasant, rustic.

yore *adj* ancient, antique, old, olden. * *n* long ago, long since, olden times.

young *adj* green, ignorant, inexperienced, juvenile, new, recent, youthful. * *n* young people, youth; babies, issue, brood, offspring, progeny, spawn.

youngster *n* adolescent, boy, girl, lad, lass, stripling, youth.

youth *n* adolescence, childhood, immaturity, juvenile, juvenility, minority, nonage, pupillage, wardship; boy, girl, lad, lass, schoolboy, schoolgirl, slip, sprig, stripling, youngster.

youthful *adj* boyish, childish, girlish, immature, juvenile, puerile, young.

zany *adj* comic, comical, crazy, droll, eccentric, funny, imaginative, scatterbrained; clownish, foolish, ludicrous, silly. * *n* buffoon, clown, droll, fool, harlequin, jester, punch.

zeal *n* alacrity, ardour, cordiality, devotedness, devotion, earnestness, eagerness, energy, enthusiasm, fervour, glow, heartiness, intensity, jealousness, passion, soul, spirit, warmth.

zealot *n* bigot, devotee, fanatic, freak, partisan.

zealous *adj* ardent, burning, devoted, eager, earnest, enthusiastic, fervent, fiery, forward, glowing, jealous, keen, passionate, prompt, ready, swift, warm.

zenith *n* acme, apex, climax, culmination, heyday, pinnacle, prime, summit, top, utmost, height.

zero *n* cipher, naught, nadir, nil, nothing, nought.

zest *n* appetite, enjoyment, exhilaration, gusto, liking, piquancy, relish, thrill; edge, flavour, salt, savour, tang, taste; appetizer, sauce.

zone *n* band, belt, cincture, girdle, girth; circuit, clime, region.

zymotic *adj* bacterial, fermentative, germinating.

Phrasefinder

A

A

—**A1** first class, of the highest quality: *The produce must be A1. The firm has an A1 staff.* <A1 is the highest rating given to the condition of ships for Lloyd's Register, Lloyds of London being a major insurance company>.

—**ABC** basic knowledge: *The book sets out the ABC of carpentry.*

—**as easy as ABC** very simple: *Getting them to agree was as easy as ABC.*

—**from A to Z** thoroughly, comprehensively: *They have studied the facts from A to Z.*

aback

—**taken aback** surprised, disconcerted: *She was taken aback when she discovered that he was her cousin.* <A sailing ship was said to be taken aback when the sails were blown against the mast causing the ship to stop suddenly>.

above

—**above board** open, honest and without trickery: *His negotiations to get planning permission were all above board.* <Card cheats tend to keep their cards under the table, or board>.

—**above (someone's) head** too difficult to understand: *Computers are away above his head.*

—**above suspicion** too much respected or thought to be too honourable to be suspected of doing wrong: *The police must be above suspicion.*

—**get a bit above oneself** to become very vain or conceited: *Since his promotion he has got a bit above himself.*

accident

—**accidents will happen** things go wrong at some time in everyone's life: *It's a pity the child broke the vase, but accidents will happen*

—**a chapter of accidents** a series of misfortunes: *Their holiday seems to have been a chapter of accidents.*

accord

—**according to one's lights** in keeping with one's beliefs or attitudes: *I disapprove of his actions, but he acted according to his lights.*

—**of one's own accord** of one's own free will, without being forced: *He left his job of his own accord.*

—**with one accord** together, in unison: *With one accord the audience left.*

account

—**by all accounts** in the opinion of most people: *By all accounts he is not very honest.*

—**give a good account of oneself** to do well: *They didn't win the match, but they gave a good account of themselves.*

—**on my** *or* **your** *or* **his** *or* **her, etc, account** because of me, etc, for my, etc, sake: *Don't leave early on my account.*

—**on no account** not for any reason whatsoever: *On no account accept a lift from a stranger.*

ace

—**an ace in the hole** something kept in reserve for emergencies: *The hostages were regarded by the terrorists as their ace in the hole.* <From the game of stud poker>.

—**within an ace of** very close to: *He came within an ace of winning the match.* <From the game of dice, ace being the term for the side of a dice with one spot>.

Achilles

—**Achilles' heel** the one weak spot in a person. *The boy is a good student, but maths is his Achilles' heel.* <Achilles, the legendary Greek hero, is said to have been dipped in the River Styx by his mother at birth to make him invulnerable but his heel, by which she was holding him, remained unprotected and he was killed by an arrow through his heel>.

acid

—**acid test** a test that will prove or disprove something conclusively: *He claims to be a good golfer but playing against the professional will be the acid test.* <From the use of nitric acid to ascertain whether a metal was gold or not. If it was not gold the acid decomposed it>.

acquire

—**acquired taste** something that one comes to like gradually, often after an original dislike: *To some people very dry wine is an acquired taste.*

across

—**across the board** applying to everyone or to all cases: *The pay increase was across the board.*

—**put one across on (someone)** to deceive or

trick (someone): *I really thought he was penni-less. He certainly put one across on me.*

act

—**act of faith** an action that demonstrates one's trust in someone or something: *Lending the young man such a large sum of money was a real act of faith.*

—**act of God** a happening, usually sudden and unexpected, for which no human can be held responsible: *It is difficult to obtain insurance coverage against acts of God such as earthquakes and floods.*

—**act of war** an act of violence or other hostile act for which only war is thought to be a suitable response: *Invading Belgium was an act of war.*

—**act up** to behave badly, to act badly or wrongly: *The child acts up when her father is here. The car is acting up again.*

—**catch (someone) in the act** *see* **catch.**

—**get in on the act** to become involved in some profitable or advantageous activity, especially an activity related to someone else's success: *Now that her fashion business is making a profit her sister wants to get in on the act and become a partner.*

—**get one's act together** to get organized: *If you are hoping to pass the exams you had better get your act together and allow some time for study.*

action

—**action stations** a state of preparedness for some activity: *Action stations! The guests are arriving.* <From positions taken up by soldiers in readiness for battle>.

—**get a piece** *or* **slice of the action** to be involved in something, get a share of something: *He's setting up a new company. If you want a piece of the action you had better go and see him.*

actress

—**as the actress said to the bishop** an expression added to a seemingly ordinary statement to draw attention to its possible sexual double meaning: *You can't have it both ways at once, as the actress said to the bishop.*

ad

—**ad hoc** for a particular (usually exclusive) purpose: *This is an ad hoc bonus. It will not be an annual occurrence.* <Latin, to this>.

—**ad infinitum** without limit or end: *This road seems to go on ad infinitum.* <Latin>.

—**ad-lib** to speak without preparation, to improvise: *I have forgotten my notes. I shall have to*

ad-lib. <Latin *ad libitum*, according to pleasure>.

—**ad nauseam** to an excessive degree, seemingly endlessly: *He talks about his work ad nauseam.* <Latin, literally to sickness>.

Adam <refers to the biblical Adam>

—**Adam's ale** water: *We have no beer or wine. It will have to be Adam's ale.*

—**not to know (someone) from Adam** not to recognize (someone): *He said he was my neighbour's son, but I didn't know him from Adam.*

—**the old Adam in us** the sin or evil that is in everyone: *I was surprised that he had an affair, but I suppose it was just the old Adam in him.*

add

—**add fuel to the fire** to make a difficult situation worse: *Making excuses for being late will just add fuel to the fire.*

—**add insult to injury** to make matters worse: *Having given his first play a bad review, the critic added insult to injury by ignoring his next one.*

—**add up** to seem logical: *No one understands why he left so suddenly. It just doesn't add up.*

Adonis

—**an Adonis** a very attractive young man: *The advert for suntan lotion showed a bronzed Adonis.* <In Greek legend Adonis was a beautiful young man who was loved by Aphrodite, the goddess of love, and who was killed by a boar while hunting>.

advantage

—**have the advantage of (someone)** to recognize (someone) without oneself being recognized by that person: *She looked in puzzlement at the woman who spoke to her and said, "I am afraid that you have the advantage of me."*

—**take advantage of (someone)** to exploit or make use of (someone) for one's own ends: *The young mother takes advantage of her neighbour by asking her to babysit practically every evening.*

—**take advantage of (something)** to make use of (something), to put (something) to good use: *You should take advantage of that holiday offer.*

—**to advantage** favourably, so that the good points are emphasized: *She rarely wears dresses that show her figure to advantage.*

aegis

—**under the aegis of (someone)** with the support or backing of (someone): *The project is under the aegis of the local council.* <In Greek legend *aegis* was the shield of the god Zeus>.

after

—**after a fashion** in a manner that is barely adequate: *She cleaned the silver after a fashion, but it was not very shiny.*

—**aftermath** something that happens after, or as a result of, an important, often a disastrous, event: *Housing was scarce in the aftermath of the flood.* <A 'math' was a crop of grass and an 'aftermath' was a second crop of grass mowed in the same season>.

—**after (someone's) own heart** to one's liking; liked or admired by (someone): *His son-in-law is a man after his own heart. They are both avid football fans.*

—**after the fact** after something, especially a crime, has taken place: *His wife was an accessory after the fact.*

against

—**against the clock** in a hurry to get something done before a certain time: *The staff are working against the clock to finish the order on time.*

—**be up against it** to be in a difficult or dangerous situation: *The family have really been up against it since the father lost his job.*

age

—**a golden age** a time of great achievement: *The reign of Elizabeth Tudor is often regarded as having been a golden age.*

—**a ripe old age** a very old age: *Despite her injury she lived to a ripe old age.*

—**of a certain age** no longer young: *Women of a certain age sometimes feel jealous of younger women.*

—**come of age** to reach the age when one is legally considered an adult (in Britain 18): *The boy will receive his inheritance when he comes of age.*

—**the age of consent** the age someone must be before he or she can legally have sexual intercourse: *She looks quite old but she is below the age of consent. The boy in the homosexual relationship was below the age of consent.*

—**under age** under the legal age for something, too young: *The teenagers won't be served at the bar. They're under age.*

agony

—**agony aunt** *or* **uncle** a woman or man who gives advice on personal problems either in a newspaper or magazine column, or on television or radio: *The battered wife wrote to the agony aunt of her local paper for advice.*

—**agony column** a newspaper or magazine column in which readers write in with their problems, which are answered by the agony aunt or uncle. <Originally a newspaper column containing advertisements for missing relatives and friends>.

ahead

—**ahead of the game** in an advantageous position; in front of one's rivals: *Their firm always seems to be ahead of the game. They keep getting most of the orders.*

—**ahead of time** early, before the appointed time: *It's as well to get to the theatre ahead of time to get a good seat.*

—**streets ahead of (someone** *or* **something)** much better than (someone or something): *The local firm's furniture is streets ahead of the chain store's.*

aid

—**aid and abet (someone)** to help and encourage (someone), especially in something wrong or illegal: *He was the thief but he was aided and abetted by his sister.* <A legal term>.

—**what is (something) in aid of?** what is (something) for? why has (something) been done?: *What are those labels in aid of? What's all this formality in aid of?*

air

—**air** *or* **wash one's dirty linen in public** to discuss private or personal matters in public: *When they were quarrelling they really aired their dirty linen in public by making all those comments about their marriage.*

—**air one's grievances** to make public one's complaints: *After suffering in silence she aired her grievances about her neighbours.*

—**clear the air** to make a situation less tense: *If you discuss your disagreement you will at least clear the air.*

—**hot air** boasting; empty or meaningless words: *He says he's going to climb Everest but it's just hot air.*

—**in the air** current; around; in circulation: *There's hostility in the air.*

—**into thin air** seemingly into nowhere: *One minute she was there, the next she had disappeared into thin air.*

—**on the air** on radio or television.

—**put on airs** to behave as though one were superior to others, to act in a conceited way: *She's really put on airs since she got promotion.*

—**take the air** go for a walk or a drive: *It's such a nice evening. Let's take some air.*

—**up in the air** uncertain, undecided: *Her career plans are still up in the air.*

—**walk on air** to be very happy: *They've been walking on air since they got engaged.*

Aladdin

—**Aladdin's cave** a place full of valuable or desirable objects: *The local toyshop is an Aladdin's cave to the children.* <From the tale of Aladdin in the Arabian Nights who gained access to such a cave with the help of the genie from his magic lamp>.

alarm

—**a false alarm** a warning about some danger or difficulty which does not happen: *Someone told him that he might lose his job but it proved to have been a false alarm.*

—**alarms** or **alarums and excursions** confused and noisy activity: *There were alarums and excursions when we thought we heard a burglar.* <In Shakespeare's history plays, the expression 'alarms and excursions' was used as a stage direction calling for activity typical of the scene at the edge of a battle>.

alive

—**alive and kicking** in a good or healthy condition: *His old mother is still alive and kicking. Some ancient New Year customs are alive and kicking.*

—**alive with** full of, covered in: *The place was alive with tourists.*

all

—**all and sundry** everybody, one and all: *They invited all and sundry from the village to the party.*

—**all chiefs and no Indians** a surplus of people wishing to give orders or to administrate and a deficiency of people willing to carry orders out or to do the work: *The firm failed largely because it was a case of all chiefs and no Indians to do the actual work.*

—**all ears** listening intently: *Tell me all the details. I'm all ears.*

—**all for (someone** or **something)** completely in favour of (someone or something): *We're all for having an extra holiday.*

—**all hours** for long periods of time, from early in the morning until late at night: *The shop is open all hours.*

—**all in** exhausted: *The marathon runners are all in.*

—**all in a day's work** *see* **day**.

—**all in all** taking everything into consideration: *We had some rain but all in all it was a good summer.*

—**all in one piece** safely, undamaged: *I was glad to see the children back all in one piece after their bike ride.*

—**all my eye and Betty Martin** *see* **eye**.

—**all out** with as much effort as possible: *He's going all out to win the race.*

—**all over** at an end: *Their romance is all over.*

—**all over bar the shouting** at an end to all intents and purposes: *The other competitors can't overtake him now. It's all over bar the shouting.*

—**all set** ready to go, prepared: *We're all set for the journey.*

—**all systems go** *see* **system**.

—**all the best** best wishes, good luck: *All the best with the exams.*

—**all the rage** *see* **rage**.

—**all there** having all one's faculties, alert and intelligent: *She is not academically clever, but she's all there when it comes to dealing with money.*

—**all told** altogether, including everything or everyone: *There were 20 cars and 60 people all told.*

—**be all things to all men** to try constantly to agree with or fit in with whomever one is with at the time: *The young man seems to have no opinions of his own but is trying to be all things to all men.*

—**it is all up with (someone)** there is no hope left for (someone): *It is all up with the accused. He has been identified by an eye witness.*

—**on all fours** on one's hands and knees: *He got down on all fours to look for the contact lens.*

alley

—**alley cat** a wild or promiscuous person: *The woman he married is respectable now but she used to be a real alley cat.*

—**blind alley** an action or situation that cannot be advantageous: *His present job is just a blind alley. There's no hope of advancement.*

allowance

—**make allowances for (someone)** to expect a less high standard from (someone) because of particular circumstances: *The teacher should make allowances for the pupil as he has been ill.*

alma mater

—one's old university, college or school: *They are going to a reunion at their alma mater.* <Latin, 'bountiful mother'>.

alpha

—**alpha and omega** the beginning and the end: *We have witnessed the alpha and omega of the relationship.* <The first and last letters of the Greek alphabet>.

also

—**also-ran** an unsuccessful person: *He will never get promotion. He's an also-ran.* <A horse-racing term for a horse that is not one of the first three horses in a race>.

alter ego

—a person who is very close or dear to someone: *The girl next door is our daughter's alter ego. They're never apart.* <Latin, "other self">.

alternative

—**alternative medicine** the treatment of diseases or disorders that uses techniques other than those of conventional medicine, including homoeopathy, osteopathy, acupuncture, aroma-therapy, etc: *She is reluctant to take drugs and so she is turning to alternative medicine for herbal remedies.*

—**have no alternative** to be forced to take a certain course of action because it is the only possible one: *He does not wish to resign, but after his quarrel with management he has no alternative.*

altogether

—**in the altogether** in the nude: *You can't answer the door—you're in the altogether.*

Amazon

—a very strong or well-built woman: *He expected the women's rugby team to be Amazons .*<In Greek legend the Amazons were a race of female warriors who had their right breasts removed in order to draw their bows better>.

amiss

—**take (something) amiss** to take offence or be upset at (something): *They took it amiss that they were not invited to the wedding although they could not have gone to it.*

angel

—**an angel of mercy** a person who gives help and comfort, especially one who appears unexpectedly: *When he collapsed in the street an unknown angel of mercy took him to hospital.*

—**angels' visits** visits that are rare and short but very pleasant: *Her son lives far away but pays his mother a series of angels' visits.*

—**entertain an angel unawares** to meet and talk to someone whose worth or fame one is unaware of: *The winner of the literary prize was at the party but we were entertaining an angel unawares. No one told us who he was.*

—**on the side of the angels** supporting or agreeing with what is regarded as being the good or the right side: *The teacher has to pretend to be on the side of the angels and support his col-leagues although he has some sympathy with the pupils.*

—**fools rush in where angels fear to tread** see **fool**.

—**write like an angel** to write well and movingly: *I cannot wait for her next novel. She writes like an angel.* <Originally the term referred to handwriting rather than to style of writing, being derived from the name of Angelo Vergece, who was a famous 16th-century calligrapher at the court of Francis I of France>.

anger

—**more in sorrow than in anger** see **sorrow**.

angry

—**angry young man** a person who expresses angry dissatisfaction with established social, political and intellectual values. <A term applied to British dramatist, John Osborne, author of the play *Look Back in Anger*>.

answer

—**know all the answers** to have all the information that is required to deal successfully with a situation, especially when one is conceited about this: *She won't listen to any advice. She acts as if she knows all the answers.*

—**not to take no for an answer** to urge very strongly that one's request, invitation or suggestion is accepted: *Of course you must stay and have dinner. I won't take no for an answer.*

—**the answer to a maiden's prayer** exactly what one desires and is looking for: *She's found the perfect job—the answer to a maiden's prayer.* <The answer to a maiden's prayer was thought to be an eligible bachelor>.

ant

—**have ants in one's pants** to be restless or agitated: *She's got ants in her pants waiting to hear the results of the exams.*

ante

—**up** or **raise the ante** to increase the amount of money required or offered for something: *If you want to buy that house you'll have to up the ante.* <Refers to increasing the money one bets in a game of cards, the other player having to match this amount in order to stay in the game>.

any

—**anybody's guess** something which no one can be certain about: *How they make their money is anybody's guess.*

—**any day** whatever the circumstances: *I would rather read a book than watch television any day.*

—**any old how** in an untidy and careless way: *The books in the bookcase were arranged any old how.*

—**anything but** not at all: *He doesn't dislike her—anything but.*

—**anything goes** any kind of behaviour, dress, etc, is acceptable: *It's not a formal party—anything goes.*

—**like anything** very much, hard, fast, energetically, etc: *He tried like anything to get a job.*

apart

—**be poles** or **worlds apart** to be completely different: *Husband and wife are poles apart in their attitudes to bringing up children.*

—**take (someone) apart** to scold or criticize (someone) severely: *Your mother will take you apart if you break the window.*

apology

—**an apology for (something)** a very poor example of (something): *The cafe served us up an apology for a meal.*

appearance

—**from** or **to all appearances** judging only from what can be seen: *Apparently they are going to divorce but to all appearances they made the perfect couple.*

—**keep up appearances** to behave in public in such a way as to hide what is going on in private: *He has lost his job but he keeps up appearances by leaving the house at his usual time every morning.*

—**put in an appearance at (something)** to attend a meeting, function, etc, especially for a short time or because it is one's duty to do so: *All the teachers are expected to put in an appearance at the school's annual concert.*

apple

—**apple of discord** a cause of quarrelling: *The leather coat in the sale was a real apple of discord. Several women were fighting over it.* <From the golden apple in Greek legend inscribed "for the fairest", which Eris, the goddess of discord, threw and which three other goddesses, Aphrodite, Pallas Athene and Hera, quarrelled over>.

—**apple-pie bed** a bed made up, as a practical joke, in such a way that it is impossible to get into: *She was so tired that she didn't notice that the children had made her an apple-pie bed.*

—**in apple-pie order** with everything tidy and correctly arranged: *She always leaves the office files in apple-pie order.* <From the French *nappe pliée*, "folded linen," linen neatly laid out>.

—**rotten apple** a person who is bad or unsatisfactory and will have a bad influence on others: *The class is mostly well-behaved, but there are one or two rotten apples who cause trouble.*

—**the apple of (someone's) eye** a favourite, a person who is greatly loved by (someone): *There are five girls in the family but the only boy is the apple of his father's eye.* <Apple refers to the pupil of the eye>.

—**upset the apple-cart** to spoil plans or arrangements: *The teenagers were going to have a party but their parents upset the apple-cart by coming home early.* <From the practice of selling fruit from carts in street markets>.

apron

—**tied to (someone's) apron-strings** completely dependent on a woman, especially one's mother or wife: *He's so tied to his mother's apron-strings that I cannot see him getting married.*

ark

—**like something out of the ark** very old-fashioned looking: *She wears clothes that are like something out of the ark.* <From Noah's ark in the Bible>.

arm

—**armed to the hilt** or **teeth** provided with all the equipment that one could possibly need: *The enemy soldiers were armed to the hilt. The tourists were armed to the teeth with guide books and cameras.*

—**a shot in the arm** see **shot**.

—**be up in arms** to protest angrily: *The residents are up in arms about the proposed shopping centre.*

—**chance one's arm** to take a risk: *You're really chancing your arm by asking for more time off. We're so understaffed.*

—**cost an arm and a leg** to cost a great deal of money: *His new car must have cost him an arm and a leg.*

—**give one's right arm for (something)** to be willing to go to any lengths to get something: *He'd give his right arm to get a job as a pilot.*

—**keep (someone) at arm's length** to avoid becoming too close to or too friendly with someone: *As the boss he has to keep everyone at arm's length or he gets accused of favouritism.*

—**lay down one's arms** to stop fighting or opposing: *We lost our appeal against the new road. Now we will just have to lay down our arms.* <A military reference to soldiers laying down their arms when they surrender>.

—**the long arm of the law** the power or authority of the police: *The crook thought he had got away with the bank robbery, but the long arm of the law caught up with him as he was leaving the country.*

—**right arm** chief source of help and support: *His secretary is his right arm, and he can't cope without her.*

—**take up arms** to become actively involved in a quarrel or dispute: *The whole village took up arms when the post office was threatened with closure.* <A military reference to soldiers taking up arms to go into battle>.

—**twist (someone's) arm** to force (someone) to do (something), to persuade (someone) to do (something): *If you want to get him to cut the grass you'll have to twist his arm—he hates doing it. I don't really want another drink but you could twist my arm.*

—**with one arm tied behind one's back** very easily: *She could beat him at tennis with one arm tied behind her back.*

—**with open arms** welcomingly: *They will receive your offer of help with open arms.*

armour

—**chink in (someone's) armour** a weak or vulnerable spot in someone who is otherwise very strong and difficult to get through to or attack: *The old man is very stern but his granddaughter has found the chink in his armour. The Opposition are always trying to find a chink in the Government's armour.* <A knight in armour could be injured only through a flaw or opening in his protective armour>.

—**knight in shining armour** a person who it is hoped will save a situation or come to one's aid: *A knight in shining armour helped her to change the wheel of her car.* <From medieval legends in which knights in armour came to the aid of damsels in distress>.

around

—**have been around** (1) to have had a lot of experience of life: *She's not as innocent as she looks. She's been around a bit.* (2) to have been alive. *He said that he had been around so long he could remember Queen Victoria.*

ashes

—**rake over the ashes** to discuss things that are passed, especially things that are best forgotten: *There's no point in raking over the ashes of their relationship. They're divorced, and that's that.*

—**rise from the ashes** to develop and flourish out of ruin and destruction: *The firm had to close last year but a new one has risen from the ashes.* <In Greek legend the phoenix, a mythical bird, who after a certain number of years of life set fire to itself and was then reborn from the ashes>.

—**sackcloth and ashes** *see* **sack**.

—**the Ashes** the trophy, originally mythical, contended for in the cricket test matches between Britain and Australia: *The winner of the Ashes will be decided by the third test match.* <When England was beaten by Australia in 1882 the *Sporting Times* published a humorous epitaph on English cricket saying, "The body will be cremated and the ashes taken back to Australia">.

ask

—**ask for the moon** *see* **moon**.

—**be asking for it** to behave in such a way as to invite something unpleasant, such as a beating: *You shouldn't have hit that young man even if he was asking for it by making nasty comments about you.*

—**be (someone's) for the asking** for something to be available to someone who wishes it without payment: *I don't want any money for the books. They're yours for the asking.*

attendance

—**dance attendance on (someone)** to stay close to (someone) in order to carry out all his or her wishes and so gain favour: *The new girl in the office has all the men dancing attendance on her.*

auld lang syne

—times that are past, especially times remembered with fondness: *The two men who had been at school together had a drink together for auld lang syne.* <A Scots phrase meaning 'old long since'>.

aunt

—**Aunt Sally** a person or thing that is being subjected to general abuse, mockery and criticism: *Whenever people are angry about the high cost of living they treat the government like an Aunt Sally.* <An Aunt Sally at a fair was a wooden model of a woman's head, mounted on a pole, at which people threw sticks or balls in order to win a prize>.

avail

—**of no avail** of no use, without effect: *All our efforts to revive him were of no avail.*

—**to no avail** without success: *We tried to dissuade her from leaving but to no avail.*

away

—**do away with (someone** *or* **something)** to get rid of something, to abolish something: *They've done away with all the old customs.*

—**get away from it all** to escape from the problems of daily life, usually by taking a holiday: *He's going to a small island in Scotland to get away from it all.*

—**get away with you!** I don't believe you!: *Get away with you! You can't have seen a ghost.*

—**the one that got away** a chance of success which one either did not or could not take of advantage at the time but which one always remembers: *He talks frequently of his first girlfriend, the one that got away.* <Refers to a supposedly large fish which an angler fails to catch but about which he tells many stories>.

axe

—**get the axe** to be dismissed: *With so few orders some of the workers are bound to get the axe.*

—**have an axe to grind** to have a personal, often selfish, reason for being involved in something: *She has an axe to grind by being so kind to her old uncle. She hopes he will leave her some money in his will.* <From a story told by Benjamin Franklin, the American politician, about how a man had once asked him in his boyhood to demonstrate the working of his father's grindstone and had sharpened his own axe on it while it was working>.

B

babe

—**babe in arms** an inexperienced or naive person: *He'll never succeed in business. He's just a babe in arms.*

baby

—**be left holding the baby** to be left to cope with a difficult situation that has been abandoned by the person who is really responsible for it: *They were meant to be organizing the birthday party but I was left holding the baby.*

—**throw out the baby with the bathwater** accidentally to get rid of something desirable or essential when trying to get rid of undesirable or unnecessary things: *We must try to salvage some of the best of the old methods when we reorganize. Let's not throw out the baby with the bathwater.*

—**wet the baby's head** to drink the health of a new-born baby: *The father got drunk wetting the baby's head.*

back

—**at the back of (something)** responsible for something, usually something bad: *You should have guessed that he was at the back of the smear campaign.*

—**backhanded compliment** a supposed compliment that sounds more like criticism: *It's a backhanded compliment for him to tell the girl that she is as attractive as her mother. He thoroughly dislikes her mother.*

—**back number** a person or thing that is no longer of importance or of use: *He used to be a famous comedian but he is a back number now.* <Refers to an out-of-date or back copy of a newspaper or magazine>.

—**backscratching** doing favours for someone so that he or she will in turn do favours for one: *There's a lot of backscratching goes on in the financial world.*

—**backseat driver** (1) a passenger in a car who gives unasked-for and unwanted advice: *His mother doesn't drive but she's a real backseat driver who's always shouting out directions when she's in the car.* (2) a person who is not directly involved in some activity but who offers unwanted advice: *It's his wife who's our account-ant but he's a backseat driver who tells us what to do about our tax problems.*

—**back to the drawing board** it will be necessary to start again on a project or activity: *Our holiday tour's been cancelled, so it's back to the drawing board.* <Refers to the board on which plans of buildings, etc, are drawn before being built>.

—**back to the grindstone** back to work: *We've had lunch and so it's back to the grindstone.*

—**backwater** an isolated place unaffected by what is happening in the world outside: *How can he bear to live in such a backwater where nothing ever happens?*

—**behind someone's back** without the knowledge or permission of the person concerned: *She married him behind her father's back.*

—**bend over backwards** to go to great trouble: *We bent over backwards to be nice to the shy new girl.*

—**break one's back** to put in a great deal of effort: *The salesman really broke his back to get that order.*

—**break the back of (something)** to complete the largest or most difficult part: *He hasn't finished the essay but at least he's broken the back of it.*

—**flat on one's back** ill in bed: *He's been flat on his back since the accident.*

—**get off (someone's) back** to stop harassing or bothering (someone): *The teacher should get off Tom's back or he'll leave school.*

—**get one's own back** to take one's revenge: *He is determined to get his own back on the person who damaged his car.*

—**give one's back** or **eye teeth** *see* **teeth**.

—**have (someone** or **something) at one's back** have (someone or something) as a help or support: *She is a single parent but she has her parents at her back.*

—**have one's back to the wall**: to be in a very difficult or desperate situation: *They had their backs to the wall so they had no choice but to accept his offer.* <Someone being pursued has to face his or her pursuers or be captured when a wall prevents retreat>.

—**know (something) backwards** *or* **like the back of one's hand** to know all there is to know about (something): *The professor knows his subject backwards.*

—**know (someone** *or* **something) like the back of one's hand** to know (someone or something) very well indeed: *She can always tell when her husband is lying. She knows him like the back of her hand.*

—**put one's back into (something)** to put the greatest possible effort into (something): *They're really putting their backs into their new business.*

—**put (someone's) back up:** to annoy (someone): *My friend always puts my back up when she's late.* <A cat's back arches up when it is angry>.

—**see the back of (someone** *or* **something)** to get rid of (someone or something), not to see (someone or something) again: *He'll be glad to see the back of his lodger.*

—**take a back seat** to take an unimportant or minor role: *The older children have taken a back seat with the arrival of the new baby.*

—**talk through the back of one's head** to talk nonsense: *If she said that he's married she's talking through the back of her head.*

—**the back of beyond** a very remote place: *We hardly ever visit them because they live in the back of beyond.*

—**when (someone's) back is turned** when (someone) is either not present or is not noticing what is happening: *The children steal money from their mother's purse when her back is turned.*

bacon

—**bring home the bacon** (1) to earn money to support one's family: *She regards her husband just as someone who brings home the bacon.* (2) to succeed in doing (something): *Mending the table's a difficult task but that carpenter will bring home the bacon.* <Perhaps from the winning of a greased pig as a prize at a country fair>.

—**save (someone's) bacon** to save someone from a danger or difficulty: *If you hadn't saved my bacon by giving me a lift I would have been late.*

bad

—**bad egg** a worthless or law-breaking person: *Her husband was a bad egg who ended up in prison.*

—**badly off** without much money: *They're too badly off to go on holiday.*

—**go to the bad** to become immoral or criminal: *Her parents are afraid of her coming to the city in case she goes to the bad.*

—**hit a bad patch** to encounter difficulties or a difficult period: *You've hit a bad patch but things will improve.*

—**in bad odour** in disfavour: *He's been in bad odour with her parents since he brought her home late.*

—**in (someone's) bad** *or* **black books** out of favour with (someone): *They're in the teacher's bad books for being late.* <Refers to an account book where bad debts are noted>.

—**not half bad** quite good, very good: *This cake's not half bad.*

—**too bad** unfortunate: *It's too bad you have to leave early.*

—**with a bad grace** in an unwilling and bad-tempered way: *They eventually came with us but with a bad grace.*

bag

—**bag and baggage** all one's belongings, or equipment: *They had to get out of the house bag and baggage when the new tenant came.*

—**bag lady** a homeless woman who carries all her belongings with her in bags: *During the recession more and more bag ladies appeared on the streets.*

—**bag of bones** a person who is extremely thin: *The student had so little money to spend on food that he was a bag of bones.*

—**bag of nerves** a very nervous or anxious person: *She worries about everything. She's just a bag of nerves.*

—**bag of tricks** the equipment necessary to do something: *The joiner arrived with his bag of tricks to mend the floor.*

—**cannot punch one's way out of a paper bag** to be totally lacking in ability or power: *He won't succeed in business. He couldn't punch his way out of a paper bag.*

—**in the bag** certain to be obtained: *He think's the job's in the bag but I think he's wrong.* <From the bag used in hunting to carry what one has shot or caught>.

—**let the cat out of the bag** *see* **cat.**

—**mixed bag** a very varied mixture: *This new set of pupils is a mixed bag.*

bait

—**rise to the bait** to do what someone has been trying to get one to do: *She knew that he was trying to get her to lose her temper but she refused to rise to the bait.* <Refers to fish rising to the

surface to reach the bait on an angler's line>.

—**swallow the bait** to accept completely an offer, proposal, etc, that has been made purely to tempt one: *They swallowed the bait and took the money from the company without realizing that they had actually sold their houses to them.* <As above>.

baker

—**baker's dozen** thirteen. <From the former custom of bakers adding an extra bun or loaf to a dozen in order to be sure of not giving short weight>.

balance

—**in the balance** undecided, uncertain: *The fate of the old building is in the balance although we have worked hard to preserve it.* <A balance is a pair of hanging scales>.

—**on balance** considering everything: *There are good points on each side but on balance I think the older man is the better candidate.*

—**strike a balance** to reach an acceptable compromise: *Try to strike a balance between going out every night and never going out at all.*

—**throw (someone) off balance** to cause (someone) to be disconcerted or confused: *The lecturer was thrown off balance by some of the questions from the audience.*

—**tip the balance** to exert an influence which, although slight, is enough to alter the outcome of something: *There was very little to choose between the candidates but one of them lived locally, which tipped the balance.*

bald

—**bald as a coot** extremely bald. <A coot is a bird with a spot of white feathers on its head>.

ball[1]

—**have a ball** to have a very enjoyable time: *The children had a ball at the birthday party.*

ball[2]

—**have the ball at one's feet** to be in a position to be successful: *The young graduate thought he had the ball at his feet when he got his degree.* <From football>.

—**on the ball** alert, quick-witted, attentive to what is going on around one: *If he had been on the ball he would have sold his shares earlier.* <Referring to a football player who watches the ball carefully in order to be prepared if it comes to him>.

—**play ball** to act in accordance with someone else's wishes: *We had hoped that he would play ball and leave quietly.*

—**play ball with (someone)** to cooperate with (someone): *He's decided to play ball with the police and tell them all he knows.*

—**set** or **start the ball rolling** to start off an activity of some kind, often a discussion: *Now that we are all present for the staff meeting perhaps someone will set the ball rolling.*

balloon

—**when the balloon goes up** when something serious, usually something that is expected and feared, happens: *The real trouble-makers had run away before the balloon went up and the headmaster discovered the broken windows.* <From balloons sent up to undertake military observation in World War I, signifying that action was about to start>.

banana

—**go bananas** to go mad, to get extremely angry: *Her mother will go bananas if she comes home late.*

—**slip on a banana skin** to do something that causes one humiliation or public embarrassment: *The politician thought that her speech was going very well until she slipped on a banana skin and got the name of the town wrong.* <Cartoons often show people literally slipping on banana skins>.

band

—**jump on the bandwagon** to show an interest in, or become involved in, something simply because it is fashionable or financially advantageous: *When blue denim became popular a lot of manufacturers jumped on the bandwagon.* <Refers to a brightly coloured wagon for carrying the band at the head of a procession>.

—**looking as though one has stepped out of a bandbox** looking very neat and elegant: *Even after the long journey she still looked as though she had stepped out of a bandbox.* <Refers to a lightweight box formerly used for holding small articles of clothing such as hats>.

—**to beat the band** *see* **beat**.

bang

—**bang goes (something)** that puts a sudden end to (something): *I have extra work to do, so bang goes my holiday.*

—**bang one's head against a brick wall** to do (something) in vain: *You're banging your head against a brick wall if you try to get him to change his mind.*

—**bang on** exactly, precisely: *He was bang on time.*

—**go with a bang** to be very successful: *The jum-*

ble sale went with a bang—we made a lot of money.

bank

—**break the bank** to leave (onself or someone) without any money: *If he buys a cup of coffee it won't exactly break the bank.* <In gambling terms, to win all the money that a casino is prepared to pay out in one night>.

baptism

—**baptism of fire** a first, usually difficult or unpleasant, experience of something: *She had a real baptism of fire when she had to represent her new company at an international conference.* <From Christian baptism>.

bar

—**behind bars** in prison: *The victim's family want to see the accused behind bars.*

bare

—**bare one's soul** to tell (someone) one's private feelings or thoughts: *She bared her soul to her best friend after the break-up of the marriage.*

—**the bare bones of (something)** the essential and basic details of (something): *Tell me the bare bones of the project.*

—**with one's bare hands** using one's hands rather than tools or weapons: *He tried to dig the dog's grave with his own hands.*

bargain

—**into the bargain** in addition, as well: *We bought their house and their car into the bargain.*

—**drive a hard bargain** to try to get a deal that is very favourable to oneself: *We're going to refuse his offer to buy the firm because he's trying to drive too hard a bargain.*

—**strike a bargain** to reach a settlement or agreement: *They struck a bargain that one firm would do the production work and the other the marketing.*

barge

—**wouldn't touch (someone** *or* **something) with a bargepole:** to wish to have absolutely no contact with (someone or something): *I'm not considering him for the job—I wouldn't touch him with a bargepole.*

bark

—**bark up the wrong tree** to have the wrong idea or impression about (something), to approach (something) in the wrong way: *You are barking up the wrong tree if you ask him for help because he is incredibly mean.* <From raccoon-hunting, in which dogs were used to locate trees that had raccoons in them>.

—**(someone's) bark is worse than his** *or* **her**

bite a person is not as dangerous or as harmful as he or she appears to be: *His father shouts a lot but his bark is worse than his bite. He never hits his son.* <Refers to a barking dog that is often quite friendly>.

barrel

—**have (someone) over a barrel** to get (someone) into such a position that one can get him or her to do anything that one wants: *Since she owes the landlord a lot of money he has her over a barrel.* <From holding someone over a barrel of boiling oil, etc, where the alternatives for the victim are to agree to demands or be dropped in the barrel>.

—**scrape the (bottom of the) barrel** to have to use someone or something of poor or inferior quality because that is all that is available: *They are really scraping the bottom of the barrel if they have appointed him to the job since he has absolutely no experience.* <Referring to the fact that people will only scrape out the bottom of an empty barrel if they have no more full ones left>.

base

—**get to** *or* **make** *or* **reach first base** to complete the important first stage of a process: *He has some good ideas but none of his projects ever gets to first base.* <From baseball, to complete the first section of a run>.

bat[1]

—**not to bat an eyelid** *see* **eye**.

—**off one's own bat** by oneself, without the help or permission of any one else: *Her mother didn't tell her to write to you. She did it off her own bat.* <From the game of cricket>.

bat[2]

—**blind as a bat** having very poor eyesight: *Her aunt can't look up the number in the telephone directory since she's blind as a bat.* <Referring to the fact that bats live their lives in darkness>.

—**like a bat out of hell** very quickly: *When he saw the police he ran away like a bat out of hell.*

bate

—**with bated breath** anxiously: *They waited with bated breath for the results of the tests.*

bay

—**keep (someone** *or* **something) at bay** to to keep (someone or something) from coming too close: *She tries to keep her inquisitive neighbours at bay.*

be

—**the be-all and end-all** the most important aim or purpose: *Making a lot of money is the be-*

all and end-all of her existence. <From Shakespeare's *Macbeth*, Act 1, scene vii.

beam

—**broad in the beam** wide in the hips or buttocks: *She really is too broad in the beam to wear those trousers.* <Used of a ship to mean wide according to its length>.

—**off beam** (1) on the wrong course: *The police are looking for the criminal in the wrong place—they are away off beam.* (2) inaccurate: *The results of your calculations are completely off beam.* <From the radio beam that is used to bring aircraft to land in poor visibility>.

—**on one's beam ends** very short of money: *Neither of them can get a job and they're now on their beam ends.* <Originally a nautical term used to describe a ship lying on its side and in danger of capsizing completely>.

bean

—**full of beans** very lively, in good spirits: *She was ill and depressed but she's full of beans after her holiday.* <Originally referring to a horse fed on beans, a high energy food>.

—**know how many beans make five** to be experienced in the ways of the world: *The new barmaid will be able to cope with the difficult customers. She knows how many beans make five.*

—**not have a bean** to have no money whatsoever: *The rent is due and they haven't a bean.*

—**not know beans about (something)** to know nothing whatsoever about (something): *He's bought a pub but he does not know beans about running a business.*

—**spill the beans** to reveal a secret or confidential information: *His mother asked him not to tell anyone her age, but he spilled the beans to his friends.*

bear[1]

—**bear down on (someone)** to come towards (someone) in a determined and often threatening way: *The child saw his angry mother bearing down on him waving the letter from the school.*

—**bear fruit** to produce results: *Our fashion ideas are beginning to bear fruit—we've made a profit this year.*

—**bear fruit** a disorderly gathering: *Parliament sometimes resembles a bear garden.*

—**bear in mind** to remember: *Bear in mind that Monday is a public holiday.*

—**bear (something) out** to confirm (something): *The evidence at the scene of the crime bore out the witnesses' account of the attack.*

—**bear up** to keep cheerful or strong under strain or stress: *I know you've a lot to put up with but you must try to bear up.*

—**grin and bear it** see **grin**.

—**have a cross to bear** see **cross**.

bear[2]

—**bear garden** a noisy, rowdy place: *With all those kids around, their house is a bear garden.* <Originally referred to a public place used for bear-baiting, in which dogs were made to attack bears and get them angry, for public amusement>.

—**like a bear with a sore head** extremely bad-tempered: *When the boss has a hangover he's like a bear with a sore head.*

beard

—**beard the lion in its den** to confront or face (someone) openly and boldly: *If you want to get a rise you'll have to go the boss's office and beard the lion in his den.*

beat

—**beat about the bush** to approach (something) in an indirect way: *If you want her to leave, tell her frankly. Don't beat about the bush.* <In game-bird hunting, bushes are beaten to make the birds appear>.

—**beat a (hasty) retreat** to run away: *The boys beat a hasty retreat when they saw the police.* <Military orders used to be conveyed by a series of different drum signals>.

—**beat (someone) hollow** to defeat (someone) soundly: *He beat his father hollow at chess.*

—**beat it** to run away: *When the old man saw the children stealing apples in his garden he told them to beat it.*

—**beat the drum** to try to attract public attention: *They're beating the drum for their new perfume at the exhibition.* <The noise of a drum makes people stop and listen>.

—**beat (someone) to it** to succeed in doing something before someone else can: *He was going to pay the restaurant bill but his partner beat him to it.*

—**if you can't beat them** or **'em, join them** or **'em** if you cannot persuade other people to think and act like you, the most sensible course of action is for you to begin to think and act like them: *Go on, take the money from the gamblers. After all, if you can't beat 'em, join 'em.*

—**off the beaten track** in an isolated position, away from towns or cities: *She likes to live somewhere quiet that is off the beaten track.*

—**take some** *or* **a lot of beating** to be of such high quality that it is difficult to improve on: *His performance will take some beating. The food at that restaurant takes a lot of beating.*

—**to beat the band** with great force or vigour: *The child is yelling to beat the band.* <Refers to a sound that is louder than that produced by a band>.

beauty

—**beauty is in the eye of the beholder** different people have different ideas of what is beautiful: *Beauty is certainly in the eye of the beholder. He said his new wife is wildly attractive, but to me she's plain.*

—**beauty is only skin deep** people have more important qualities than how they look: *Beauty is only skin deep. His sister may be very pretty but she is also very spiteful.*

beaver

—**eager beaver** a very enthusiastic and hard-working person: *The new employee is a real eager beaver who works late every night.*

—**work like a beaver** to work very industriously and enthusiastically: *They're working like beavers to decorate the house.* <Beavers are small animals that build dams, etc, with great speed and skill>.

beck

—**at (someone's) beck and call** having to be always available to carry out (someone's) orders or wishes: *She isn't as much of an invalid as she makes out—she likes having everyone at her beck and call.* <Beck is a form of "beckon">.

bed

—**bed of nails** *or* **thorns** a very unpleasant or difficult situation: *His early life in the slums was an absolute bed of thorns.*

—**bed of roses** an easy, comfortable or happy situation: *He says that being a travel writer is not a bed of roses.*

—**get out of bed on the wrong side** to start the day in a very bad-tempered mood: *The boss is criticizing everybody. He must have got out of bed on the wrong side today.*

bee

—**have a bee in one's bonnet** to have an idea that one cannot stop thinking or talking about, to have an obsession: *The old lady has got a bee in her bonnet about going on a cruise but she is not fit to go.* <A bee trapped under one's hat cannot escape>.

—**busy bee** a person who is very active and industrious: *Her mother's such a busy bee that she*

never seems to rest. <Bees are reputed to be very hard-working creatures>.

—**make a beeline for (someone** *or* **something)** to go directly and quickly to (someone or something): *The children made a beeline for the table where the food was.* <Bees are reputed to fly back to their hives in straight lines>.

—**the birds and the bees** *see* **bird**.

—**think one** *or* **someone is the bee's knees** to consider oneself or someone else to very special and important: *She think she's the bees knees and won't speak to any of the other workers.*

beer

—**not all beer and skittles** not consisting just of pleasant or enjoyable things: *He's discovered that being a travel courier is definitely not all beer and skittles.*

—**small beer** something unimportant: *His present job is very small beer compared with his last one.*

beetroot

—**go beetroot** to blush deeply: *The girl went beetroot when he paid her a compliment.*

before

—**before one can say Jack Robinson** very rapidly, in an instant: *The waiter brought the food before we could say Jack Robinson.*

—**before one knows where one is** very quickly, before one can grasp the situation: *Before we knew where we were he had booked the tickets for the holiday.*

—**before the flood** a very long time ago: *They've known each other since before the flood.* <Referring to the Flood described in the Bible in Genesis 7:9>.

beg

—**beggar description** to be such that words cannot describe it: *The richness of the furnishings beggars description.* <From Shakespeare's *Antony and Cleopatra*, Act 2, scene ii>.

—**beg the question** in an argument, to take for granted the very point that requires to be proved; to fail to deal effectively with the point being discussed: *Politicians are noted for their ability to beg the question.*

—**going a-begging** unclaimed or unsold: *At the end of the sale several articles were going a-begging.*

bell

—**bell the cat** to be the person in a group who undertakes something dangerous for the good of the group: *Someone has to bell the cat and tell the boss that we want more money.* <Re-

ferring to a story about some mice who wanted to put a bell on the neck of the cat so that they would hear it coming and who needed a volunteer to do it>.

—**ring a bell** to bring back vague memories: *His name rings a bell but I can't think where I've heard it.*

—**saved by the bell** rescued from an unpleasant situation by something suddenly bringing that situation to an end: *The teacher asked him for his homewor, which he hadn't done. He was saved by the bell by a parent arriving to see her.* <From the bell that marks the end of a round in boxing>.

belt

—**below the belt** unfair: *To refer in public to his father being in prison was below the belt.* <In boxing, a blow below the belt is against the rules>.

—**tighten one's belt** to reduce one's expenditure: *In the recession most firms had to tighten their belts.* <Belts have to be tightened if one loses weight—in this case from spending less on food>.

—**under one's belt** achieved or accomplished: *We've got 200 miles under our belts.*

bend

—**bend over backwards** *see* **back.**

—**on bended knee** very humbly or earnestly: *On bended knee I ask you not to sack them.*

—**round the bend** mad: *The children are driving their father round the bed with their noise.*

berth

—**give (someone) a wide berth** to keep well away from (someone): *Give that man a wide berth. He looks violent.* <Refers to a ship that keeps a good distance away from others>.

beside

—**be beside oneself** to be in a state of great emotion: *The child was beside himself with joy at receiving the prize.*

—**beside the point** not directly concerned with the issue being discussed: *She has to stay here. Whether she wants to go abroad is beside the point.*

best

—**do one's level best** to try as hard as one can: *We'll do our level best to get there on time.*

—**have the best of both worlds** to benefit from the advantages of two sets of circumstances: *She thinks she has the best of both worlds by working at home. She earns some money but can look after the children herself.*

—**put one's best foot forward** to make the best attempt possible: *If you want to pass the exam you had better put your best foot forward.*

—**the best part of (something)** most of (something), nearly all of (something): *They spent the best part of £3000 on plane fares.*

—**with the best of them** as well as other people who are more experienced, better qualified, etc: *She started to learn to skate only this year but already she can skate with the best of them*

—**with the best will in the world** no matter how much one wants to do something: *With the best will in the world I couldn't get there in time.*

bet

—**hedge one's bets** to try to protect oneself from possible loss, failure, disappointment, etc: *We decided to hedge our bets and book seats for both performances in case we missed the first one.* <From betting the same amount on each side to make sure of not losing>.

better

—**better off** (1) happier: *She says that she's better off without her husband.* (2) richer: *His family is much better off than hers.*

—**go one better than (someone)** to improve on something that someone has done: *She won three prizes but her sister went one better and won five.*

—**get the better of (someone)** to overcome or defeat (someone): *His son always gets the better of him at chess.*

—**have seen better days**: to be no longer new or fresh: *This coat has seen better days. I need a new one.*

—**the better part of (something)** a large part of (something), most of (something): *They stayed for the better part of four hours.*

—**think better of (something)** to reconsider (something), to change one's mind about (something): *They should think better of buying such an expensive house when money is tight.*

beyond

—**beyond compare** unrivalled, without equal: *The queen's beauty was beyond compare.*

—**beyond one's ken** *see* **ken.**

—**beyond the pale** beyond normal or acceptable limits: *When he drinks too much his behaviour is completely beyond the pale.* <The pale was an area of English government in Ireland in the 16th century>.

bide

—**bide one's time** to wait for a suitable opportunity: *They haven't given up the plan to climb the mountain. They're biding their time until the weather improves.*

big

—**a big fish in a small pond** a person who seems better, more important, etc, than he or she is because he or she operates in a small, limited area: *He did well in the village school where he was a big fish in a small pond, but when he went to a large city school he was just average.*

—**be big of (someone)** to be generous of (someone): *It was big of them to give us a day's holiday.*

—**Big Brother** *see* **brother**.

—**big guns** the most important people in an organization: *The big guns are having a board meeting.*

—**the Big Apple** New York: *He's excited about flying to the Big Apple.*

—**the Big Smoke** London: *They would hate to live in the Big Smoke.*

bill

—**a clean bill of health** verification that someone is well and fit: *The footballer has been given a clean bill of health after treatment for his injury.* <Ships were given clean bills of health and allowed to sail when it was certified that no one aboard had an infectious disease>.

—**fill the bill** to be exactly what is required: *They're seeking peace and quiet. At last they've found a cottage that fits the bill.* <Refers originally to a handbill or public notice>.

—**foot the bill** to pay for something, usually something expensive: *He had to foot the bill for the repairs to his own car and the other one.*

—**top the bill** to be the most important performer in a show: *A world-famous pianist topped the bill.* <On theatrical advertising bills or posters the star performer's name is at the top>.

bird

—**a bird in the hand is worth two in the bush** something that one already has is much more valuable than things that one might or might not acquire. *Hang on to that old car. A bird in the hand is worth two in the bush.* <A bird in the bush might fly away>.

—**a little bird told me** I found out by a means which I do not wish to reveal: *A little bird told me that she is having a baby.*

—**birds of a feather flock together** people who share the same interests, ideas, etc, usually form friendships. *The football fans are like birds of a feather, they flock together.*

—**give (someone) the bird** of an audience, to express its disapproval of a performer by hissing or booing so that he or she leaves the stage: *The comic was so bad that the gave him the bird after five minutes.* <From the resemblance of the noise of the audience to the hissing of geese>.

—**go like a bird** to go very well or very easily: *The car goes like a bird with the new engine.*

—**kill two birds with one stone** to fulfil two purposes with one action: *By spending the weekend there we were able to kill two birds with one stone. We did some business and we were able to visit my parents.*

—**strictly for the birds** acceptable only to people who are not very clever, fashionable, etc. *You can't tell me the moon is made of green cheese. That's strictly for the birds.*

—**the birds and the bees** the basic facts of human sexual behaviour and reproduction: *The mother explained to her young daughter about the birds and the bees.*

—**the early bird catches the worm** a person who arrives early or acts promptly is in a position to gain advantage over others.

biscuit

—**take the biscuit** to be much worse than anything that has happened so far: *He is always rude but his latest insults take the biscuit.*

bit

—**champing at the bit** very impatient: *The children are champing at the bit to open their presents.*<A horse chews at its bit when it is impatient>.

—**take the bit between one's teeth** to act on one's own and cease to follow other people's instructions or advice: *He dismissed his advisers, took the bit between his teeth and ruled the country on his own.* <Refers to a horse escaping from the control of its rider>.

bite

—**bite off more than one can chew** to try to do more than one can without too much difficulty: *When she took over the running of both firms she was biting off more than she can chew.*

—**bite the bullet** to do something unpleasant but unavoidable with courage: *He can't afford to take a reduction in salary but he's just going to have to bite the bullet and agree to it.*

—**bite the dust** to die or cease to operate or function: *The society bit the dust for lack of membership.*

—**bite the hand that feeds one** to treat badly

someone who has helped one: *He got the girl her first job but she won't even speak to him now—a real case of biting the hand that feeds you.*

—**have more than one bite at the cherry** to have more than one opportunity to succeed at something: *You can always take the exam again. You have more than one bite at the cherry.*

bitter

—**a bitter pill to swallow** something unpleasant or difficult that one has to accept: *When he got engaged to someone else it was a bitter pill for her to swallow.*

—**to the bitter end** right to the very end, however unpleasant that is: *We had to stay at the boring concert to the bitter end.* <A bitt is a post on a ship's deck for tying cable or rope to and the part of the cable fastened round it is the bitter end. When the cable is let out to the bitter end, no further adjustment is possible>.

black

—**as black as one is painted** as bad as everyone says one is: *She can be very helpful, not nearly as black as she is painted.*

—**black sheep** a member of a family or group who is not up to the standard of the rest of the group. *They never talk about the youngest son. He was the black sheep of the family.*

—**in black and white** in writing or in print: *We must have the details of the agreement in black and white.*

—**in (someone's) black books** same as **in (someone's) bad books**—*see* **bad**.

—**in the black** showing a profit, not in debt: *His bank account is rarely in the black.* <From the use of black ink to make entries on the credit side of a ledger>.

—**the pot calling the kettle black** *see* **pot**.

blank

—**blank cheque** permission to do exactly what one wants: *The manager has been given a blank cheque in the reorganization of the firm.* <Refers to a cheque made out to someone with the amount left blank>.

—**draw a blank** to fail to find out anything after much searching or research.

blanket

—**on the wrong side of the blanket** illegitimate: *The prince fathered many children who were born on the wrong side of the blanket.*

—**wet blanket** a dull person who makes other people feel depressed: *We were all enjoying the party until the host's girlfriend started asking everyone to leave. She's such a wet blanket.*

blessing

—**a blessing in disguise** something that turns out to advantage after at first seeming unfortunate: *Getting the sack was a blessing in disguise. He got a much better job after that.*

—**a mixed blessing** something that has disadvantages as well as advantages: *Having a lodger was a mixed blessing. The extra income was useful but he interfered with their privacy.*

blind

—**blind alley** *see* **alley**.

—**blind as a bat** *see* **bat**.

—**the blind leading the blind** referring to a situation in which the person who is in charge of others knows as little as they do: *He's supposed to be a skiing instructor but he's only a beginner himself. It's an obvious case of the blind leading the blind.*

blood

—**bad blood** hostile feelings: *There has been bad blood between the two sisters.*

—**in cold blood** deliberately and calmly: *She killed her husband in cold blood. She wasn't hysterical at the time.*

—**like getting blood out of a stone** very difficult, almost impossible: *Getting him to say anything is like getting blood out of a stone.*

—**new blood** new members of an organization: *Most of the members of the club are old and it desperately needs some new blood.*

—**sweat blood** to put a very deal of effort into something: *She sweated blood to save the money.*

blow

—**blow hot and cold** to keep changing one's mind or attitude: *Sometimes he's friendly, sometimes he's nasty. He keeps blowing hot and cold.*

—**blow over** to cease and be forgotten: *Their disagreement soon blew over.*

—**blow one's own trumpet** to boast about one's achievements: *We're tired of her blowing her own trumpet since she won the contest.*

—**blow the gaff** to tell something secret, often something illegal, to someone, often the police: *He blew the gaff on his fellow burglar.* <Perhaps from gaff, meaning mouth>.

—**blow the whistle on (someone)** to reveal or report someone's wrongdoing so that it will be stopped: *He blew the whistle on the smugglers.* <From the practice of blowing a whistle to indicate a foul in some ball games>.

—**see which way the wind blows** to wait and find out how a situation is developing before making a decision: *He's going to wait and see* which way the wind blows before asking for promotion. <From sailing>.

blue

—**blue-eyed boy** a person who is someone's favourite: *The young clerk will soon be promoted. He's the manager's blue-eyed boy.*

—**bluestocking** an educated, intellectual woman: *He calls any intelligent woman a bluestocking.* <From a group of women in the 18th century who met in London to discuss intellectual and philosophical issues and some of whom wore blue worsted stockings>.

—**once in a blue moon** hardly ever: *Once in a blue moon he sends her flowers.*

—**out of the blue** without warning: *The news of his death came out of the blue.*

bluff

—**call (someone's) bluff** to make (someone) prove that what he or she says is true is really genuine: *He kept telling his colleagues that he wanted to leave until the boss called his bluff and asked him if it was indeed the case.* <Refers to poker, the card game>.

board

—**above board** *see* **above**.

—**across the board** *see* **across**.

—**go by the board** to be abandoned: *His dreams of going to university have gone by the board with the death of his father.* <The board here is a ship's board or side, and to go by the board literally was to vanish overboard>.

—**sweep the board** to win all the prizes: *The young tennis player has swept the board at all the local contests.* <The board referred to is the surface on which card games are played and on which the bets are placed>.

boat

—**burn one's boats** to do something that makes it impossible to go back to one's previous position: *You've given up your job, you'll have to go now—you've burned your boats.*

—**in the same boat** in the same situation: *Both of them are in the same boat—they're both single mothers.*

—**miss the boat** to fail to take advantage of a opportunity: *The application forms had to be in yesterday—so you've missed the boat.*

—**rock the boat** to do something to endanger or spoil a comfortable or happy situation: *You have a good job here—so don't rock the boat by calling a strike.*

bolt

—**a bolt from the blue** something very sudden and unexpected: *His transfer to another branch was a bolt from the blue.*

—**shoot one's bolt** to make one's final effort, have no other possible course of action: *When he reported the teacher to the headteacher he shot his bolt because the head rejected the complaint.*

bone

—**a bone of contention** a cause of dispute: *The state of her bedroom is a bone of contention between her and her mother.* <Dogs fight over bones>.

—**have a bone to pick with (someone)** to have a matter to disagree about with (someone): *He said to the other man that he had a bone to pick with him for going out with his girlfriend.* <From dogs fighting over a bone>.

—**make no bones about (something)** to have no hesitation or restraint about (saying or doing something openly): *She made no bones about the fact that she disliked him.* <Originally a reference to finding no bones in one's soup, which was therefore easier to eat>.

—**near the bone** (1) referring too closely to something that should not be mentioned; tactless: *Some of the guests remarks about adultery were a bit near the bone. The host's having an affair.* (2) slightly indecent or crude: *Some of the comedian's jokes were a bit near the bone.*

—**the bare bones (of something)** *see* **bare**.

boo

—**would not say boo to a goose** to be extremely timid: *She's very aggressive but her husband wouldn't say boo to a goose.*

book

—**a closed book** something about which one knows nothing, something that one does not understand: *The new technology is a closed book to older members of staff.*

—**an open book** something that is easily understood: *His motives were an open book to all of us.*

—**bring (someone) to book** to make (someone) explain or be punished for his or her actions: *They thought they could cause the damage and walk away but they were soon brought to book.* <Perhaps referring to a book where a police officer keeps a note of crimes>.

—**by the book** strictly according to the rules: *The headteacher won't give us a day off. He does everything by the book.*

—**cook the books** illegally to alter accounts or financial records: *He had been cooking the books, so they did not know money had gone missing.*

—**in someone's black books** *see* **bad**.

—**read (someone) like a book** to understand (someone) completely, not to be deceived by someone: *I know that he's planning something nasty. I can read him like a book.*

—**suit (someone's) book** to be advantageous to (someone): *It doesn't suit her book for him to leave.* <Perhaps referring to a bookmaker who accepts bets only if he thinks he will not lose too much money on them, in other words if the bets suit his book>.

—**take a leaf out of (someone's) book** *see* **leaf.**

—**throw the book at (someone)** to criticize or punish (someone) severely, to charge (someone) with several crimes at once: *The judge threw the book at him. He's got a ten-year sentence.* <Literally, to charge someone with every crime listed in a book>.

boot

—**get the boot** to be dismissed or discharged from one's job: *The woman got the boot for stealing.*

—**give (someone) the boot** to dismiss or discharge (someone): *They're giving all the older workers the boot.*

—**hang up one's boots** to retire from work, to cease doing an activity: *The elderly man has played bowls for years but he is hanging up his boots now.* <From hanging up football boots after a game>.

—**lick (someone's) boots** to flatter (someone) and do everything he or she wants: *The new boy is licking the boss's boots to get promotion.*

—**pull oneself up by one's bootstraps** to become successful through one's own efforts: *He owns several stores but he started as an errand boy and pulled himself up by his bootstraps.*

—**put the boot in (someone)** (1) to kick (someone) when he or she is already lying on the ground injured: *The bullies put the boot in and kicked their victim to death.* (2) to treat (someone) cruelly or harshly after he or she has suffered already: *He lost his job and his wife put the boot in and left him.*

—**the boot is on the other foot** the situation has been completely turned round: *She begged him to stay but now the boot is on the other foot and he is pleading to be allowed back.*

—**too big for one's boots** too conceited: *Since she won the beauty contest she has been too big for her boots.*

bottle

—**crack a bottle** to open a bottle: *Let's crack a bottle of wine to celebrate.*

—**hit the bottle** to drink a great deal of alcohol: *Since his wife died he's been hitting the bottle.*

—**on the bottle** drinking a great deal of alcohol regularly: *He's been on the bottle since he lost his job.*

bottom

—**at the bottom of (something)** the cause of (something): *I might have known that he was at the bottom of the rumours that were going around about his wife.*

—**bottom drawer** a collection of articles for the home, which a young woman gathered together before her marriage: *She's keen to get married so she's already started collecting linen and cutlery for her bottom drawer.*

—**get to the bottom of (something)** to find out the exact cause of (something) or the true nature of (something): *The doctors cannot get to the bottom of her chest complaint.*

—**hit rock bottom** to reach the lowest possible level: *Share prices hit rock bottom last week. Her spirits have hit rock bottom since her friend left.*

—**scrape the (bottom of the) barrel** *see* **barrel.**

bow¹

—**bow and scrape** to behave in a very humble and respectful way: *They expect the staff to bow and scrape to the rich guests.*

—**bow out** to leave or cease to take part in a project, organization, etc: *She's been secretary for three years but she's bowing out now.* <From performers bowing to the audience at the end of a show>.

—**take a bow** to accept acknowledgement of one's achievements: *Everyone thinks you've done a good job, so take a bow.* <As above>.

bow²

—**draw the long bow** to exaggerate: *He said that she was absolutely penniless but he was drawing the long bow.* <An archer carries a spare bow in case one breaks>.

—**have another** *or* **more than one string to one's bow** to have another possibility, plan, etc, available to one: *He's applied for other jobs as well as that one because it's as well to have more than one string to your bow.*

brain

—**cudgel** *or* **rack one's brains** to think very hard: *I racked my brains to remember the first name of her husband.*

—**have (something) on the** *or* **one's brain** to think or worry about (something) continuously: *She's got marriage on the brain.*

—**pick (someone's) brains** to find out (someone's) ideas and knowledge about a subject so that one can put them to one's own use: *Stop picking my brains and use an encyclopedia.*

brass

—**get down to brass tacks** to consider the basic facts or issues of something: *We must get down to brass tacks and discuss how much rent we can afford.*

—**the top brass** the most important people in an organization, especially originally in the army: *The top brass have individual offices but the staff all work in one room.* <From the metal decoration on military uniforms>.

bread

—**bread and butter** one's basic living: *How does he earn his bread and butter?*

—**know which side one's bread is buttered** to know the course of action that is to one's greatest advantage: *He certainly won't leave his wife. He knows which side his bread is buttered.*

—**on the breadline** with scarcely enough money to live on: *Since the father lost his job the family has been on the breadline.*

—**the greatest thing since sliced bread** a person or thing that is greatly admired and appreciated: *He is a careless worker but he thinks he is the greatest thing since sliced bread.*

break

—**break even** to have one's losses balanced by one's gains, to make neither a loss nor a profit: *I didn't make any money on my investment but at least I broke even.*

—**break of day** dawn: *The first train to town leaves at break of day.*

—**break the bank** *see* **bank**.

—**break the ice** *see* **ice**.

—**break the news** *see* **news**.

—**make a break for it** to attempt to escape: *The prisoner made a break for it when he was being led into court.*

breath

—**catch one's breath** (1) to breathe in sharply in fear, surprise or pain: *She caught her breath when she saw the huge dark shape.* (2) to rest for a short time: *I'll have to catch my breath after climbing the hill.*

—**hold one's breath** to wait anxiously for something: *We held our breath as the child walked along the roof edge.*

—**save one's breath** to stop talking since one's words are having no effect: *Save your breath. He'll leave school if he wants to.*

—**take (someone's) breath away** to surprise

(someone) greatly: *They took her parents' breath away when they announced that they were married.*

—**under one's breath** very quietly, in a whisper: *He asked what time it was under his breath.*

—**waste one's breath** to say something that is not taken heed of: *I tried to persuade them to stay but I was wasting my breath.*

breathe

—**be able to breathe again** to be able to relax after a period of anxiety, etc: *You can breathe again! The police have gone.*

—**breathe down (someone's) neck** (1) to be very close behind (someone): *He was in the lead but there were several runners breathing down his neck.* (2) to be waiting impatiently for something from (someone): *The boss is breathing down her neck for those letters.*

—**breathe one's last** to die: *He breathed his last just before midnight.*

brick

—**bang one's head against a brick wall** *see* **bang**.

—**drop a brick** to say something tactless or undiplomatic: *She dropped a brick when she introduced the boss's wife as the cleaner.*

—**like a cat on hot bricks** very nervous or restless: *He is like a cat on hot bricks when he is waiting for a phone call from her.*

—**like a ton of bricks** to treat or punish (someone) severely: *The headmaster came down on the boys like a ton of bricks for playing truant.*

—**try to make bricks without straw** to try to do something without the necessary materials or equipment: *She has so few supplies in her kitchen that trying to make a meal there is like trying to make bricks without straw.* <A biblical reference, from Pharaoh's command concerning the Israelites in Exodus 5:7>.

bridge

—**burn one's bridges** *same as* **burn one's boats** —*see* **boat**.

—**cross a bridge when one comes to it** to worry about or deal with a problem only when it actually arises: *She keeps worrying about what might happen in the future. She must learn to cross a bridge only when she comes to it.*

—**try to build bridges** to try to put right a disagreement or a quarrel: *The feud's still on. I tried to build bridges but without success.*

—**water under the bridge** *see* **water**.

brief

—**hold no brief for (someone *or* something)**

not to support or defend (someone or something): *I hold no brief for these new methods.*

bright

—**bright-eyed and bushy-tailed** very cheerful and lively: *They were both bright-eyed and bushy-tailed when they came back from holiday.*

—**look on the bright side** to be optimistic, to see the advantages of one's situation: *You might not like your present job but look on the bright side—it's well paid.*

bring

—**bring down to earth** *see* **earth**.

—**bring home the bacon** *see* **bacon**.

—**bring home to** *see* **home**.

—**bring (someone) round** (1) to bring (someone) back from unconsciousness: *The doctor brought him round with the kiss of life.* (2) to persuade (someone) to do something: *He was reluctant to participate but we brought him round eventually.*

—**bring to a head** *see* **head**.

broad

—**broad in the beam** *see* **beam**.

—**have broad shoulders** to be able to accept a great deal of responsibility, criticism, etc: *I don't mind them blaming me. I've got broad shoulders.*

—**in broad daylight** during the day: *The child was attacked in broad daylight.*

broken

—**broken reed** *see* **reed**.

brother

—**am I my brother's keeper?** the actions or affairs of other people are not my responsibility: *So my colleague was rude to you. Am I my brother's keeper?* <From the biblical story of Cain and Abel, Genesis 4:9>.

—**Big Brother** a powerful person or organization thought to be constantly monitoring and controlling people's actions: *I prefer to work for a small company. In a big organization I get a feeling that Big Brother is watching me.* <From the dictator in George Orwell's novel *1984*>.

brown

—**in a brown study** deep in thought: *She won't hear you. She's in a brown study.*

brush

—**brush up on (something)** to refresh one's knowledge of (something): *You should brush up on your French before you go on holiday.*

—**get the brush-off** to be rejected or refused abruptly: *He asked her to the cinema but he got the brush-off when she said "no."*

bucket

—**a drop in the bucket** a very small part of what is needed: *Our contribution to the famine fund is only a drop in the bucket.*

—**come down in buckets** to rain heavily: *As usual in August, it's coming down in buckets.*

—**kick the bucket** to die: *They were just waiting for the old man to kick the bucket.* <"Bucket" here is perhaps a beam from which pigs were hung after being killed>.

—**weep buckets** to cry a great deal: *She wept buckets at the sad film.*

Buggins

—**Buggins' turn** one's turn to be promoted, according to some automatic or routine system, not according to merit. *He got the job because it's Buggins' turn, not because he's good.*

bull

—**hit the bull's eye** to do or say something that is very appropriate or relevant: *You hit the bull's eye when you said you thought she was pregnant.* <The exact centre of a dart board>.

—**like a bull in a china shop** in a very clumsy way: *She went charging off like a bull in a china shop and knocked my papers to the floor.*

—**like a red rag to a bull** *see* **red**.

—**take the bull by the horns** to tackle (something) boldly: *If you want them to stop the noise you'll have to take the bull by the horns and complain.*

bullet

—**bite the bullet** *see* **bite**.

—**get the bullet** to be dismissed or discharged: *Half the firm have got the bullet.*

—**give (someone) the bullet** to dismiss or discharge (someone): *The boss will give you the bullet if you don't turn up.*

burden

—**the burden of proof** the responsibility for proving something: *The burden of proof lies with the accuser.* <A legal term>.

burn

—**burn one's boats** *or* **bridges** *see* **boat**.

—**burn one's fingers** *see* **finger**.

—**burn the candle at both ends** *see* **candle**.

—**burn the midnight oil** *see* **midnight**.

—**the burning question** a question of great interest to many people: *The burning question is who is our new owner?*

Burton

—**gone for a Burton** dead, ruined, broken, etc: *The old car's gone for a Burton.* <Originally a military term from Burton, a kind of ale>.

bus

—**busman's holiday** a holiday spent doing much the same as one does when one is at work: *The house-painter's wife expects him to take a busman's holiday and redecorate their house.* <Refers to a bus driver who drives a bus on holiday>.

bush

—**beat about the bush** *see* **beat**.

—**bush telegraph** the fast spreading of information by word of mouth: *I heard on the bush telegraph that he had resigned.* <A reference to the Australian bush>.

bushel

—**hide one's light under a bushel** *see* **light**.

business

—**mean business** to be determined (to do something), to be serious: *He was not joking about the redundancies. He means business.*

—**mind one's own business** to concern oneself with one's own affairs and not interfere in those of other people: *When he tried to give advice to the girl she asked him to mind his own business.*

bust

—**bust a gut** *see* **gut**.

—**go bust** to fail, to be financially ruined: *During the recession many firms went bust.*

butter

—**butterfingers** a person who often drops things: *She's such a butterfingers. She dropped the tray full of dishes.*

—**butter (someone) up** to flatter (someone) a great deal, usually in order to get him or her to do something for one. *He doesn't really like the boss, but he's buttering him up to get a pay rise.*

—**know which side of one's bread is buttered** *see* **bread**.

—**look as though butter would not melt in one's mouth** to appear very innocent, respectable, etc: *The girl looks as though butter wouldn't melt in her mouth but she actually behaves very wildly.*

butterfly

—**have butterflies in one's stomach** to have a fluttering sensation in one's stomach as a sign of nervousness. *Every night she has butterflies in her stomach before she goes on stage.*

button

—**buttonhole (someone)** to catch (someone's) attention and engage him or her in conversation: *The minister buttonholed me as I came out of the church.* <Originally "button hold", to hold by the button>.

C

cabbage

—**not as green as one is cabbage-looking** not as foolish or inexperienced as one appears to be: *He won't accept a reduction in salary. He's not as green as he is cabbage-looking.*

cahoots

—**in cahoots with (someone)** forming a secret partnership with (someone), especially to do something dishonest or illegal: *The police think that the bank clerk was in cahoots with the robbers.* <Cahoot, a partnership, perhaps from *cahute*, French, a cabin>.

Cain

—**raise Cain** to make a great deal of noise or fuss: *He will raise Cain when he sees the damage to his car.* <Refers to Cain in the Bible who killed his brother Abel, Genesis 4>.

cake

—**a piece of cake** something easy to do: *Winning the race was a piece of cake.*

—**a slice** *or* **share of the cake** a share of something desirable or valuable: *You should invest some money in the firm and get a slice of the cake.*

—**cakes and ale** pleasant or enjoyable activity: *A student's life is not all cakes and ale. You have to do some work.* <From Shakespeare's *Twelfth Night*, Act 2, scene iii>.

—**have one's cake and eat it** *or* **eat one's cake and have it** to have the advantages of two things or situations when doing, possessing, etc, one of them would normally make the other one impossible: *He's engaged to one of the sisters but he would like to have his cake and eat it and go out with the other one.*

—**icing on the cake** *see* **ice**.

—**sell** *or* **go like hot cakes** to sell very quickly: *That computer game is selling like hot cakes since it was advertised on TV.*

—**take the cake** *same as* **take the biscuit**—*see* **biscuit**.

calf

—**calf love** love felt by a very young, inexperienced person: *He is unhappy that she has gone away but calf love soon passes.*

—**kill the fatted calf** to provide a lavish meal, especially to mark a celebration of someone's

arrival or return: *Our daughter's coming home from Canada, so we're killing the fatted calf.* <From the parable of the prodigal son in the Bible, Luke 15:23>.

call

—**a close call** *same as* **a close shave**—*see* **close**[2].

—**answer** *or* **obey the call of nature** to go to the toilet: *Where is the nearest public toilet? I need to answer the call of nature.*

—**call a spade** *see* **spade**.

—**call it a day** *see* **day**.

—**call it quits** *see* **quit**.

—**call the shots** *see* **shot**.

—**pay a call** to go to the toilet: *Excuse me, I have to pay a call.*

camel

—**the straw that breaks the camel's back** *see* **straw**.

—**swallow a camel** to regard something as being acceptable, true, fair, etc, when it is quite clearly not so: *How can they swallow the camel of their colleague's unfair dismissal?*

camp

—**have a foot in both camps** to have associations with two groups who have opposing and conflicting views and attitudes: *He is a member of staff but he has shares in the company, so he has a foot in both camps.*

can

—**carry the can** to accept blame or responsibility, usually for something that someone else has done: *Several of the pupils set fire to the school but the one who was caught carried the can.*

—**in the can** certain, agreed or decided upon: *He had a good interview so the job's in the can.* <Refers to a completed cinema film that is stored in large metal containers or cans>.

candle

—**burn the candle at both ends** to work and/or to play during too many hours of the day: *He has a full-time job and studies at night. He is certainly burning the candle at both ends.*

—**cannot hold a candle to (someone)** to be not nearly as good or as talented as (someone): *The rest of the football team cannot hold a candle to the new player.* <Literally, someone who is

not good enough even to hold a light while someone else does the work>.

—**the game is not worth the candle** something that is not worth the effort that has to be spent on it: *She's well paid but she works such long hours that she has decided that the game is not worth the candle.* <From the translation of the French phrase *le jeu n'en vaut la chandelle*, referring to a gambling session in which the amount of money at stake was not enough to pay for the candles required to give light at the game>.

canoe

—**paddle one's own canoe** to control one's own affairs without help from anyone else: *Now her father's dead she'll have to paddle her own canoe.*

cap

—**a feather in one's cap** *see* **feather**.

—**cap in hand** humbly: *He has gone back cap in hand to ask for his job back.* <Removing one's cap in someone's presence is a sign of respect>.

—**if the cap fits, wear it** if what has been said applies to you, then you should take note of it: *I simply said that honesty was not common these days, but if the cap fits, wear it.*

—**put one's thinking cap on** to think very carefully about a problem: *If we put our thinking caps on I am sure we can find our way out of the difficulty.*

—**set one's cap at (someone)** to try to attract (someone of the opposite sex): *She was so anxious to get married that she set her cap at every man in sight.* <Perhaps a mistranslation of French *metter le cap*, to head towards>.

—**to cap it all** on top of everything else, finally: *I was late for work and then to cap it all I missed the bus.*

capital

—**make capital out of (something)** to make use of (something) for one's own advantage: *The counsel for the defence made capital out of the witness's nervousness.*

—**with a capital A, B, C, etc** used to emphasize that the person or thing described is an extreme example of his, her or its kind: *They are certainly villains with a capital V.*

card

—**get one's cards** to be dismissed or discharged: *The clerk got his cards for stealing money.*

—**have a card up one's sleeve** to have an idea, plan of action, etc, in reserve to be used if nec-

essary: *They think that they have won but their opponent has a card up his sleeve.* <From cheating at cards>.

—**on the cards** likely: *Their dismissal is very much on the cards.* <From reading the cards in fortune-telling>.

—**play one's cards close to one's chest** to be secretive or non-communicative about one's plans or intentions: *I think that they are moving overseas but they are playing their cards very close to their chest.* <From holding one's cards close to one in card-playing so that one's opponents will not see them>.

—**play one's cards right** to act in such a way as to take advantage of a situation: *If she plays her cards right he will marry her.*

—**put one's cards on the table** to make known one's plans or intentions: *If you want us to help you'll have to put your cards on the table.* <In card-playing, to show one's opponent one's cards>.

—**stack the cards against (someone)** to make it very difficult for (someone) to succeed: *The cards are stacked against him finding a job because he has no qualifications.*

carpet

—**on the carpet** about to be rebuked or punished by someone in authority: *She will be on the carpet when the boss discovers that she is late.* <Refers to the piece of carpet in front of a desk, where someone might stand to be rebuked>.

—**sweep (something) under the carpet** to try to hide or forget about (something unpleasant): *They try to sweep under the carpet the fact that their son's in prison.*

—**the red carpet** special, respectful treatment: *They're rolling out the red carpet. They've invited the boss and his wife to dinner.* <Refers to the red carpet put down for a royal person to walk on during official visits>.

carrot

—**carrot and stick** reward and punishment as a method of persuasion: *The headmaster uses a policy of carrot and stick with the pupils. He praises them a lot but he punishes them a lot also.* <See below>.

—**hold out a carrot to (someone)** to promise (someone) a reward in order to get him or her to do something: *If you want them to work late you'll have to hold out the carrot of extra money.* <From urging a donkey forward by holding a carrot in front of it>.

carry

—**carry a torch for (someone)** to be in love with someone, especially with someone who does not return it: *She's carried the torch for the boss for years but he doesn't even notice her.* <A torch or a flame was regarded as symbolic of love>.

—**carry coals to Newcastle** *see* **coal**.

—**carry the can** *see* **can**.

—**carry the day** *see* **day**.

cart

—**put the cart before the horse** to do or say things in the wrong order: *He painted the walls before the ceiling. He certainly put the cart before the horse.*

carte

—**be given carte blanche** to be given complete freedom to act as one wishes: *The owner has given him carte blanche to furnish her house.* <Literally, a blank card>.

Casanova

—**Casanova** a man who has relationships with many women: *He's a real Casanova. He's been out with most of the girls in the office.* <From Giacomo Casanova, a famous 18th-century Italian lover and adventurer>.

Cassandra

—**Cassandra** a person who makes predictions about unpleasant future events but who is never believed: *She's a real Cassandra, she's always seeing gloom ahead.* <In Greek legend, Cassandra, who was the daughter of Priam, king of Troy, had the gift of prophecy but was destined never to be believed. She predicted the fall of Troy>.

cast

—**cast pearls before swine** to offer something valuable or desirable to someone who does not appreciate it: *Taking her to the opera was a case of casting pearls before swine.* <A biblical reference to Matthew 7:6>.

—**cast the first stone** to be the first person to blame or criticize someone: *Eventually everyone blamed him but it was his sister who cast the first stone.* <A biblical reference to John 8:7, about a woman who was to be punished by being stoned to death>.

—**the die is cast** *see* **die**².

castle

—**castles in the air** *or* **castles in Spain** dreams or hopes that are unlikely ever to be realized: *She builds castles in the air about being a princess.*

cat

—**a cat may look at a king** there is nothing to prevent an ordinary person from looking at someone important: *She asked me why I was looking at her but I just said, "A cat can look at a king".*

—**bell the cat** *see* **bell**.

—**curiosity killed the cat** said as a warning not to pry into other people's affairs: *One day someone is going to hit him for asking personal questions, and he'll find out that curiosity killed the cat.*

—**has the cat got your tongue?** said to someone who does not say anything out of timidity, etc, to encourage him or her to speak: *What have you got to say in your defence? Has the cat got your tongue?*

—**let the cat out of a bag** to reveal something secret or confidential, especially accidentally or at an inappropriate time. *They didn't want anyone to know that they had been married that day but their friend let the cat out of the bag.* <Supposedly referring to a fairground trick in which a customer was offered a cat in a bag when he or she thought it was a piglet in the bag>.

—**like a cat on hot bricks** *see* **brick**.

—**like a scalded cat** in a rapid, excited way: *She's rushing around like a scalded cat to get the meal ready for the guests.*

—**like something the cat brought** *or* **dragged in** very untidy or bedraggled: *After the football match the boys looked like something the cat brought in.*

—**not to be enough room to swing a cat** for there to be very little space: *She can't stay at her daughter's house. There's not enough room there to swing a cat.*

—**not to have a cat's chance in hell** *or* **a cat's chance in hell** to have no chance at all: *They don't have a cat's chance in hell of winning.*

—**play cat and mouse with (someone)** to treat (someone) in such a way that he or she does not know what is going to happen to them at any time: *The terrorists were playing cat and mouse with the hostages. One minute they thought that they were going to be released, the next they thought that they were going to be killed.* <A cat often plays with its prey, a mouse, before killing it>.

—**put** *or* **set the cat among the pigeons** to cause a disturbance, especially a sudden or unexpected one: *Her neighbour certainly put the cat among the pigeons when he accidentally mentioned her husband's affair.*

—**rain cats and dogs** to rain very heavily: *The picnic's cancelled—it's raining cats and dogs.*

—**see which way the cat jumps** to wait and see what other people are going to do and how the situation is developing before deciding on one's course of action: *I'm not going to rush into putting in an offer for the house. I'm going to wait and see how the cat jumps.*

—**the cat's pyjamas** *or* **whiskers** a person who is very highly regarded: *He thinks he's the cat's pyjamas in his new sports car.*

—**there's more than one way to kill** *or* **skin a cat** there's more than one way method of doing things: *He left, not because he disliked the work, but because his colleagues were so unpleasant to him. There's more than one way to kill a cat*

—**when the cat's away, the mice will play** when the person in charge or in control is not present the people whom he or she is in charge of will work less hard, misbehave, etc. *When the boss is away, they take very long lunch breaks. When the cat's away, the mice will play.*

catch

—**catch (someone) in the act** to catch (someone) actually doing something wrong or bad: *He hoped to steal the money and run but he was caught in the act by the police.*

—**catch it** to be scolded or punished: *He'll catch it when his father sees what he's done to the car.*

—**catch one's breath** *see* **breath**.

—**catch one's death (of cold)** *see* **death**.

—**catch (someone) napping** to surprise (someone) when he or she is unprepared or inattentive: *The early winter caught them napping. They had no fuel for the fire.*

—**catch (someone) on the hop** *see* **hop**.

—**catch (someone) red-handed** *see* **red**.

—**catch the sun** to become sunburnt or suntanned: *The child's caught the sun although she was outside for only a short time.*

—**Catch 22** a situation in which one can never win or from which one can never escape, being constantly hindered by a rule or restriction that itself changes to block any change in one's plans; a difficulty that prevents one from escaping from an unpleasant or dangerous situation. *If you need an emergency loan you can apply to the Social Fund, but it is a loan for credit-worthy people so you won't get it. It's Catch 22.* <From the title of a novel by Joseph Heller>.

—**catch (someone) with his** *or* **her pants** *or* **trousers down** to surprise (someone) when he or she is unprepared or doing something wrong, especially when this causes embarrassment: *The boss found his assistant manager chatting to his secretary instead of writing the monthly report. He certainly regretted being caught with his pants down.* <Refers to walking in on someone partially dressed>.

caviar

—**caviar to the general** something considered to be too sophisticated to be appreciated by ordinary people: *Only intellectuals read his books. They're caviar to the general.* <From Shakespeare's *Hamlet*, Act 2, scene ii>.

ceiling

—**go through the ceiling** to rise very high, to soar: *House prices went through the ceiling.*

—**hit the ceiling** *or* **roof** to lose one's temper completely: *She hit the ceiling when he cancelled the appointment.*

ceremony

—**stand on ceremony** to behave in a formal manner: *You can take your jacket off. You don't have to stand on ceremony.*

certain

—**in a certain condition** pregnant: *She has been sick because she is in a certain condition.*

—**of a certain age** *see* **age**.

chalk

—**as different as chalk and cheese** completely different: *They're sisters but they are as different as chalk and cheese.*

—**chalk it up to experience** accept the inevitability of something: *You won't get your money back from the con-man. You might as well chalk it up to the experience*

—**not by a long chalk** not by a long way, by no means: *They haven't given up yet, not by a long chalk.* <From the vertical chalk lines drawn to mark scores in a game, the longer lines representing the greater number of points>.

champ

—**champing at the bit** *see* **bit**.

chance

—**chance it** to take a risk: *I won't take an umbrella. I think I'll chance it.*

—**chance one's arm** *see* **arm**.

—**fancy one's chances** to think that one is highly likely to succeed: *Even with so many top-class competitors he still fancies his chances.*

—**have a fighting chance** to have a possibility of success if a great effort is made: *The team still have a fighting chance of winning the tournament but they face tough opposition.*

—**have an eye to the main chance** to watch carefully for what will be advantageous or profitable to oneself: *He's learning to play golf because the boss plays it and he always has an eye to the main chance.*

—**have a sporting chance** to have a reasonable chance of success: *Many experienced people have applied for the job but with his qualifications he has at least a sporting chance.*

—**not to have a cat's chance in hell** *see* **cat**.

—**not to have the ghost of a chance** not to have the slightest possibility of success: *He hopes to win the race but he really doesn't have the ghost of a chance.*

—**on the off-chance (of** *or* **that)** in the hope (of or that), assuming there is the possibility (of or that): *We went to the theatre on the off-chance of getting seats. You should go early in the off-chance that you get in.*

—**take one's chance** *or* **chances** to take a risk or take advantage of an opportunity on the understanding that one accepts whatever happens: *You'll just have to take your chance and apply for the job. If your present employer finds out it's too bad.*

change

—**change hands** to pass into different ownership: *Houses in that street change hands extremely quickly.*

—**change horses in mid-stream** to change one's opinions, plans, sides, etc, in the middle of something: *At the beginning of the election campaign he was going to vote Conservative but he changed horses in mid-stream.*

—**change one's mind** to alter one's decision or intention: *They were going to go to Greece but they have changed their mind.*

—**change one's tune** to change one's attitude or opinion: *He disagreed with me yesterday but he changed his tune when he heard the facts.*

—**chop and change** *see* **chop**.

—**have a change of heart** to alter one's opinion or decision, usually to a better or kinder one: *The headmaster was going to expel the girl but he had a change of heart when he saw how sorry she was.*

—**ring the changes** to add variety by doing or arranging things in different ways: *She cannot afford new furniture but she rings the changes by shifting the furniture around from room to room.*

chapter

—**a chapter of accidents** *see* **accident**.

—**chapter and verse** detailed sources for a piece of information: *Don' t just make vague references in your essay to other writers. You must give chapter and verse.* <From the method of referring to biblical texts>.

charity

—**charity begins at home** one must take care of oneself and one's family before concerning oneself with others: *She would like to be able to contribute to the welfare of children overseas but her own children need new clothes and charity begins at home.*

—**cold as charity** extremely cold: *When the central heating went off in the huge house it was as cold as charity.* <Charity is referred to as cold since it tends to be given to the poor and disadvantaged by organizations rather than by individual people and so lacks human feeling or warmth>.

charm

—**lead a charmed life** regularly to have good fortune and avoid misfortune, harm or danger: *The racing driver seems to lead a charmed life. He has never been involved in an accident.*

—**work like a charm** to be very effective, to work very well: *His efforts to persuade her to go out with him worked like a charm.*

chase

—**chase after rainbows** to spend time and effort in thinking about, or in trying to obtain, things that it is impossible for one to achieve: *He should concentrate on doing his job and stop applying for ones he won't get. He spends most of his time chasing rainbows.*

cheek

—**cheek by jowl** side by side, very close together: *Workers and management work cheek by jowl in the same large office.*

—**turn the other cheek** to take no action against someone who has harmed one, thereby giving him or her the opportunity to harm one again: *I know he insulted you but it will cause less trouble for everyone if you turn the other cheek rather than take your revenge on him.* <A biblical reference to Matthew 5:39, "Whosoever shall smite thee on thy right cheek, turn to him the left one also">.

cheese

—**as different as chalk and cheese** *see* **chalk**.

—**cheesed off** bored, weary or dissatisfied: *He's really cheesed off with his present job.*

—**hard cheese** bad luck, a sentiment usually expressed by someone who does not care about another's misfortune: *It's hard cheese for him if* *he has to work late but the rest of us can leave early.*

—**say "cheese"** to smile when one has one's photograph taken: *Don't look so glum, say "cheese".* <When one says "cheese" one's mouth forms a smile>.

cherry
—**have more than one bite at the cherry** *see* bite.

cheque
—**blank cheque** *see* blank.

Cheshire
—**grin like a Cheshire cat** to smile broadly so as to show one's teeth: *She was grinning like a Cheshire cat as they handed her the prize.* <Refers to *Alice's Adventures in Wonderland* by Lewis Carroll, in which the Cheshire cat gradually disappears except for its smile>.

chest
—**get (something) off one's chest** to tell (someone) about something that is upsetting, worrying or annoying one: *If you know something about the accident you had better get it off your chest and tell the police.*

—**play one's cards close to one's chest** *see* card.

chestnut
—**old chestnut** an old joke, usually one no longer funny: *The comedian wasn't amusing. His jokes were old chestnuts I had heard before.*

—**pull (someone's) chestnuts out of the fire** to rescue (someone) from a difficult or dangerous situation, often by putting oneself in difficulty or danger: *He is continually getting himself into financial trouble and he always expects his brother to pull his chestnuts out of the fire and lend him money.* <From a story by the 17th-century French writer La Fontaine, in which a monkey use a cat's paw to get hot nuts from a fire>.

chew
—**bite off more than one can chew** *see* bite.

—**chew the cud** to think deeply about something: *I'll have to chew the cud a lot before deciding whether or not to move house.*

—**chew the fat** to have a discussion or conversation: *Let's not rush out anywhere. I think we should chew the fat first.*

chicken
—**chicken-feed** something of very little value or importance; an insignificant amount of money: *They paid her chicken-feed for that valuable desk.*

—**chickens come home to roost** misdeeds, mistakes, etc, that come back with an unpleasant effect on the person who performed the misdeed, especially after a considerable time: *He told everyone that he had never been married, but his chickens came home to roost when his ex-wife turned up.*

—**count one's chickens before they are hatched** to make plans which depend on something that is still uncertain: *Don't give up this job before you are officially offered the other. It's unwise to count your chickens before they're hatched.*

child
—**child's play** something that is very easy to do: *you will find the work child's play.*

—**second childhood** a time when an adult person, often an old person, behaves like a child: *The little boy's father seems to be in his second childhood and keeps playing with the train set. The old man seems to have entered a second childhood—he won't let anyone touch his belongings.*

—**the child is father of the man** the character of an adult is formed from childhood influences: *He's been in and out of prison but his father and uncle were both burglars. The child is father of the man.*

chin
—**keep one's chin up** not to show feelings of depression, worry or fear: *I know it's difficult to find a job but you should keep your chin up and go on trying.*

—**stick one's chin out** to show determination in opposing someone or something: *Her parents tried to stop her going to university but she stuck her chin out and went ahead against their wishes.*

—**take it on the chin** to accept or to suffer (something) with courage: *He was upset when she broke their engagement but he took it on the chin and went out with other girls.*

chink
—**chink in (someone's) armour** *see* armour.

chip
—**a chip off the old block** a person who is very like one of his or her parents: *That boy's a real chip off the old block. He's already as good a salesman as his father.*

—**cash in one's chips** to die: *I hear that the old man cashed in his chips on the way to the hospital.* <Refers to a gambler cashing in his or her chips or tokens in exchange for money at the end of a session>.

—**have a chip on one's shoulder** to have an aggressive attitude and act as if everyone is going to insult or ill-treat one, often because one feels inferior: *He has a chip on his shoulder about his lack of education and is always belligerent towards academics.* <Refers to a former American custom by which a young man who wished to provoke a fight would place a piece of wood on his shoulder and dare someone to knock it off>.

—**have had one's chips** to have had, and failed at, all the chances of success one is likely to get: *If he fails the exam this time he's had his chips because he's not allowed to resit it.* <Refers to gambling tokens>.

—**when the chips are down** when a situation has reached a critical stage: *He thought he had many friends but when the chips were down and he was unemployed he found he had only one.* <A gambling terms indicating that the bets have been placed>.

choice

—**Hobson's choice** no choice at all; a choice between accepting what is offered or having nothing at all: *We've only got one empty room for tonight. It's Hobson's choice, I'm afraid.* <Refers to the practice of Tobias Hobson, an English stable-owner in the 17th century, of offering customers only the horse nearest the stable door>.

chop

—**chop and change** to keep altering (something), to keep changing (something): *He's furious at them for chopping and changing their holiday arrangements.*

—**get the chop** (1) to be dismissed or discontinued: *Both he and his research project got the chop.* (2) to be killed: *The gang made sure that their enemy got the chop.*

chord

—**strike a chord** to be familiar in some way: *Something about his voice struck a chord.*

—**touch a chord** to arouse emotion or sympathy: *He is usually very hard-hearted but the little girl's tears touched a chord.*

circle

—**come full circle** to return to the position or situation from which one started: *Diet advice has come full circle. Dieters used to be told to avoid bread but now they are told to eat it.*

—**go round in circles** to keep going over the same ideas without reaching a satisfactory decision or answer: *I think we should postpone this discussion until we have more information. We're just going round in circles.*

—**run round in circles** to dash about and appear to be very busy without accomplishing anything: *She's been running round in circles preparing for the guests—none of the rooms is ready yet.*

—**vicious circle** an unfortunate or bad situation, the result of which produces the original cause of the situation or something similar: *They're stuck in a vicious circle—his wife nags him for going out, and he has to go out to get away from her nagging.* <In logic, the term for the fallacy of proving one statement by the evidence of another which is itself only valid if the first statement is valid>.

clanger

—**drop a clanger** same as **drop a brick**—see **brick**.

clapper

—**like the clappers** extremely rapidly: *You'll have to go like the clappers to get there on time.*

class

—**in a class by oneself** *or* **itself,** *or* **in a class of its, etc, own** far better than other people or things of the same type, without equal: *The ice cream in that shop is in a class by itself. As an actress, she's in a class of her own.*

clay

—**have feet of clay** see **feet**.

clean

—**a clean bill of health** see **bill**.

—**a clean slate** a record free of any discredit; an opportunity to make a fresh start: *He has paid the penalty for his wrongdoing and now starts the new job with a clean slate.* <Slates were formerly used for writing on in schools>.

—**clean as a whistle** (1) extremely clean: *The kitchen surfaces were clean as a whistle.* (2) completely without guilt, blameless: *They thought that he was selling drugs but he was found to be clean as a whistle.*

—**cleanliness is next to godliness** it is almost as important to be clean as it is to be religious and virtuous: *The teacher was always trying to get the children to wash their hands by telling them that cleanliness is next to godliness.*

—**come clean** to tell the truth about something, especially after lying about it: *He finally decided to come clean and tell the police about his part in the crime.*

—**(my** *or* **his** *or* **her) hands are clean** I am or he or she is, etc, not guilty or responsible: *The police can question him if they like but his hands are clean.*

—**keep one's nose clean** to keep out of trouble,

to behave well or legally: *If you keep your nose clean for the rest of the term I think the teacher will forget about what you did.*

—**make a clean breast of (something)** to admit to (something), especially after having denied it: *At first they said that they hadn't been involved but then they made a clean breast of it.*

—**make a clean sweep** to get rid of everything which is unnecessary or unwanted: *If you have doubts about most of the existing staff you should make a clean sweep and dismiss them all.*

—**Mr Clean** a person who is highly trusted or respected: *Some of the members of the government are under suspicion but he's Mr Clean.*

—**pick (something) clean** to take or steal everything that can be removed from (something or somewhere): *The burglars picked his house clean.*

—**show a clean pair of heels** to run away very quickly: *When the burglar saw the police he instantly showed a clean pair of heels.*

—**squeaky clean** free of all guilt or blame: *The police investigated him but he's squeaky clean.* <Clean surfaces tend to squeak when wiped>.

—**take (someone) to the cleaners** to cause (someone) to spend or lose a great deal of money: *The firm was really taken to the cleaners by the suppliers who provided the goods in a hurry.*

clear

—**clear as a bell** very easy to hear: *The international telephone call was clear as a bell.* <Bells, such as church bells, are very audible>.

—**clear as crystal** very easy to understand or grasp: *It's clear as crystal that he's in love with her.*

—**clear as mud** not at all easy to understand or grasp: *He tried to explain but his explanation was clear as mud.*

—**clear the air** *see* **air**.

—**clear the decks** to tidy up, especially as a preparation for some activity or project: *I'll have to clear the decks and put all this shopping away before I start cooking lunch.* <Refers to getting a ship ready for battle>.

—**in the clear** free from suspicion: *the police suspected him but he has an alibi so he's in the clear.*

—**steer clear of (someone *or* something)** to keep away from or avoid (someone or something): *You should steer clear of badly lit streets.*

—**the coast is clear** the danger or difficulty is now past: *She doesn't want to go into the house when her father's there, so tell her when he's gone out and the coast is clear.* <Probably a military term indicating that there were no enemy forces near the coast and so an invasion was possible>.

cleft

—**in a cleft stick** unable to decide between two equally important or difficult courses of action: *He's in a cleft stick. He's promised to take his wife out to celebrate their wedding anniversary but his boss is insisting on him working late.*

clip

—**clip (someone's) wings** to limit the freedom, power or influence of (someone): *She used to go out every night but her wings have been clipped since she had a baby.* <From the practice of clipping the wings of a bird to prevent it flying away>.

cloak

—**cloak-and-dagger** involving or relating to a great deal of plotting and scheming: *He's resigned from the board of directors because of all the cloak-and dagger business surrounding the sacking of the chairman.* <The combination of a cloak and a dagger suggests conspiracy>.

clock

—**against the clock** *see* **against**.

—**as regular as clockwork** perfectly regularly: *His visits to his mother were as regular as clockwork.*

—**like clockwork** very smoothly, without problems: *The escape plan worked like clockwork.*

—**put back the clock** *or* **turn the clock back** to return to the conditions or situation of a former time: *Some employers would like to put back the clock sixty years and pay their employers practically nothing. He wishes he could turn the clock back and be at home again with his family.*

—**round the clock** all the time; for twenty-four hours a day: *The rescue services are working round the clock searching for survivors.*

close¹

—**a closed book** *see* **book**.

—**behind closed doors** in secret: *The committee is meeting behind closed doors.*

—**close one's eyes to (something)** *see* **eye**.

—**close ranks** *see* **rank**.

close²

—**a close shave** something that was only just avoided, especially an escape from danger, failure, etc: *He had a close shave when his car skidded out of control and ran into a wall.*

—**at close quarters** very close, from a position

nearby: *I thought she was young but when you see her at close quarters she looks quite old.*

—**close to home** referring to something about which someone is very sensitive or which relates very closely to someone: *Talking about law and order in front of her was a bit close to home since her husband's in prison.*

—**sail close to the wind** *see* **sail.**

—**too close for comfort** so near that one feels uncomfortable, worried, etc: *The meeting is a bit close for comfort as I haven't prepared for it.*

cloud

—**cast a cloud over (something)** to spoil (something), to introduce something unpleasant or sad into a pleasant or happy situation: *Her mother's illness cast a cloud over their holiday.*

—**cloud cuckoo land** an imaginary place, where everything is perfect; an unreal world: *They're living in cloud cuckoo land if they think they can afford that house.*

—**every cloud has a silver lining** something good happens for every bad or unpleasant thing: *He has no job, but every cloud has a silver lining as he is able to spend time with his children.*

—**have one's head in the clouds** to be daydreaming and not paying attention to what is going on around one: *She has her head in the clouds thinking about her wedding.*

—**on cloud nine** extremely happy: *She's been on cloud nine since she met her new boyfriend.*

—**under a cloud** under suspicion, in trouble: *He left his previous job under a cloud.*

clover

—**in clover** in great comfort: *They're living in clover since he won the pools.* <Refers to farm animals which have rich food>.

club

—**in the club** pregnant: *His girlfriend just told him that she's in the club.*

—**join the club** you are in the same unfortunate situation that I am or we are: *If you haven't done any work for the exams join the club. Neither have we.*

clue

—**be clued up on (something)** to be very well-informed about (something): *You'll have to be clued up on computers to get that job.*

—**not to have a clue about (something)** to have no knowledge of (something), to be badly-informed about (something): *She set off without having a clue about how to get to her destination.*

clutch

—**clutch at straws** *see* **straw.**

coach

—**drive a coach and horses through (something)** to destroy (an argument etc) completely by detecting and making use of the weak points in it: *The defence lawyer drove a coach and horses through the prosecution's case against his client.* <Refers to the fact that the defects (or holes) in the argument are so large as to let a coach and horses through them>.

coal

—**carry** *or* **take coals to Newcastle** to do something that is completely unnecessary, especially to take something to a place where there is already a great deal of it: *Taking a cake to her would be like carrying coals to Newcastle. She spends most of her time baking.* <Refers to Newcastle in England, which was a large coal-mining centre>.

—**haul (someone) over the coals** to scold (someone) very severely: *The assistant was hauled over the coals for being rude to a customer.*

—**heap coals of fire on** *or* **upon (someone's) head** to do good or be kind to (someone) who has done one harm so that he or she feels sorry or ashamed: *When the boy tried to steal her purse she heaped coals of fire on his head by offering him money to buy food.* <A biblical reference to Proverbs 25:21-22>.

—**rake over the coals** same as **rake over the ashes**—*see* **ashes.**

coast

—**the coast is clear** *see* **clear.**

coat

—**cut one's coat according to one's cloth** to organize one's ideas and aims, particularly one's financial aims, so that they are within the limits of what one has or possesses: *We'd like to buy a big house but we'll have to cut our coat according to our cloth and buy a smaller one. Our income is not large.*

—**turn one's coat** to change sides: *He supported the king at first but he turned his coat and joined the enemy army.* <Refers to a soldier's coat whose colour and markings showed which army he belonged to. If he turned it inside out the colour was hidden>.

cock

—**a cock-and-bull story** an absurd story that is unlikely to be believed: *She told me some cock-and-bull story about finding the money in a waste-paper basket.*

—**cock a snook at (someone)** to express one's defiance or contempt of (someone): *Now that* he has another job he can cock a snook at his previous employer. <Originally referring to a rude gesture of contempt made by putting the end of one's thumb on the end of one's nose and spreading out and moving one's fingers>.

—**cock of the walk** the person who is the most important or influential member in a group and who is very proud of this fact: *The boy was cock of the walk at school until a new boy beat him in a fight.* <The pen in which fighting cocks were kept and bred was called a walk>.

—**go off at half cock** to be unsuccessful because of lack of preparation or because of a premature start: *The government scheme went off at half cock because of lack of preliminary research.* <Refers to a gun that fires too soon>.

coffin

—**a nail in (someone's) coffin** *see* **nail**.

cog

—**a cog in the wheel** a person who plays a small or unimportant part in a large organization: *He boasts about his job in the international company but he's really just a cog in the wheel.*

coin

—**coin it in** to make a great deal of money: *Local shopkeepers have been coining it in since the oil business came to the area.*

—**pay (someone) back in his** *or* **her own coin** to get one's revenge on someone who has done harm to one by treating him or her in the same way. *Now he's in charge he's paying his former boss back in his own coin by not promoting him.*

—**the other side of the coin** the opposite argument, point of view, etc: *She has a really successful career and a family, but the other side of the coin is that she can spend hardly any time with her children.*

cold

—**as cold as charity** *see* **charity**.

—**cold comfort** no consolation at all: *When one suffers a misfortune it is cold comfort to be told that there are other people who are much worse off.*

—**come in from the cold** to be allowed to take part in some activity that one was excluded from before: *After months of not being selected, he's come in from the cold and been offered a game with the team this week.*

—**get cold feet** to become nervous and change one's mind about being involved in (something): *He was going to row the Atlantic but got cold feet at the last minute.*

—**give (someone) the cold shoulder** to act in an

unfriendly way to (someone) by ignoring him or her: *She has tried to be friendly to her parents-in-law but they keep giving her the cold shoulder.*

—**in a cold sweat** in a state of great fear or anxiety: *He was in a cold sweat when the police were searching his flat.* <From the fact that the skin tends to become cold and damp when one is very frightened>.

—**in cold blood** *see* **blood**.

—**leave (someone) cold** to fail to impress or excite (someone): *The new dance group left the audience cold.*

—**make (someone's) blood run cold** to cause terror or great distress in (someone): *The ghostly figure made my blood run cold.*

—**out in the cold** not taking part, not included: *Only her richer friends were asked to her party—the rest of us were out in the cold.*

—**pour** *or* **throw cold water on (something)** to discourage enthusiasm for (something): *We were all looking forward to the dance but the organizer poured cold water on the idea by saying it would run at a loss.*

—**stone cold** extremely cold: *This soup's supposed to be hot but it's stone cold.*

colour¹

—**a horse of a different colour** someone or something that is completely different from someone or something else: *The previous headmaster was very kind to the pupils but the new one is a horse of a different colour.*

colour²

—**change colour** to become either very pale or else very red in the face through fear, distress, embarrassment, anger, guilt, etc: *She changed colour when she was caught with the money in her hands.*

—**nail one's colours to the mast** to commit oneself to a point of view or course of action in a very obvious and final way: *Most people are undecided about who to vote for in the election but the young people have nailed their colours to the mast by putting up posters for the Green Party candidate.* <Refers to a ship's colours or flag. If this was nailed to the mast it could not be lowered, lowering the flag being a sign of surrender>.

—**off-colour** unwell: *Travelling always makes her feel off-colour.* <People tend to turn pale when they are unwell>.

—**show oneself in one's true colours** to reveal what one is really like after pretending to be otherwise: *She pretended to be his friend but she* showed herself in her true colours by reporting him to the boss. <Refers to a ship raising its colours or flag to indicate which country or side it was supporting>.

—**with flying colours** with great success: *They both passed the exam with flying colours.* <Refers to a ship leaving a battle with its colours or flag still flying as opposed to lowering them in surrender>.

come

—**come a cropper** to suffer misfortune, to fail: *He came a cropper when he bought a hotel without knowing anything about the business.* <Originally a hunting phrase meanint to take a serious fall>.

—**come clean** *see* **clean**.

—**come down on (someone) like a ton of bricks** *see* **brick**.

—**come in for (something)** to be the receiver or target of (something): *The organizers came in for a great deal of criticism when the fete was cancelled.*

—**come in from the cold** *see* **cold**.

—**come into one's own** *see* **own**.

—**come of age** *see* **age**.

—**come off it** don't be ridiculous, don't try to deceive me: *Come off it! You couldn't possibly have been at work and be back so early.*

—**come to grief** *see* **grief**.

—**come to grips with (something)** *see* **grip**.

—**come to light** *see* **light**.

—**come to nothing** *see* **nothing**.

—**come to one's senses** *see* **sense**.

—**come to that** taking into consideration other facts: *She's not qualified for the job, but come to that he's not qualified for it either.*

—**come unstuck** to fail, to suffer a major setback: *Our holiday plans have come unstuck. I have to work that week.*

—**have it coming to one** to deserve the punishment, misfortune, etc, that one is going to get: *I'm not sorry that he's been dismissed. He's had it coming for years.*

common

—**common-or-garden** completely ordinary: *I'm not going to wear anything special: I'll wear a common-or-garden skirt and top.*

—**the common touch** the ability to get on well with ordinary people: *He is a prince but most of his friends are just ordinary students. He has the common touch.*

compare

—**beyond compare** *see* **beyond**.

confidence

—**a vote of confidence** *see* **vote**.

—**confidence trick** the act of a swindler who gains the trust of someone and then persuades him or her to hand over money: *The old lady thought she was giving money to charity but the collector played a confidence trick on her and kept the money for himself.*

conjure

—**a name to conjure with** the name of someone very important, influential or well-known: *Now that's a name to conjure with. He was one of our really great players.* <The suggestion is that such people have magical powers>.

conscience

—**in all conscience** being completely fair and honest: *In all conscience we cannot appoint him if he is not qualified for the job.*

contention

—**a bone of contention** *see* **bone**.

contradiction

—**a contradiction in terms** a statement, idea, etc, that contains a contradiction: *He is a cynic and thinks that a happy husband is a contradiction in terms.*

convert

—**preach to the converted** to speak enthusiatically in favour of something to people who already admire it or are in favour of it: *You are preaching to the converted by praising the candidate to us. We already voted for him.*

cook

—**cook (someone's) goose** *see* **goose**.

—**cook the books** *see* **book**.

—**too many cooks spoil the broth** if there are a great many people involved in a project they are more likely to hinder it than help it: *Let's appoint a very small organizing committee. Too many cooks spoil the broth.*

—**what's cooking?** what is happening?, what is going on?: *What's cooking? Everyone seems very busy.*

cookie

—**that's the way the cookie crumbles** that is the situation and one must just accept it: *He doesn't like working at weekends but that's the way the cookie crumbles.* <Cookie is American English for biscuit>.

cool

—**cool as a cucumber** very calm and unexcited: *She hit the burglar over the head, cool as a cucumber.*

—**cool, calm and collected** completely calm, in

full control of one's emotions: *She was cool, calm and collected when she told him to get out.*

—**cool** or **kick one's heels** to be kept waiting: *My meeting has not finished yet. You'll just have to cool your heels.*

—**keep one's cool** to remain calm: *She always keeps her cool in a crisis.*

—**lose one's cool** to become angry, excited etc: *It's easy to lose one's cool when the children are naughty.*

coot
—**bald as a coot** see **bald**.

cop
—**cop it** (1) to be scolded or punished: *You'll cop it from your father if you go home late.* (2) to die: *Three terrorists copped it in the attack.*

—**not much cop** not very good, desirable, useful, etc: *The new teacher isn't much cop.*

copy
—**blot one's copybook** to spoil a previously good record of behaviour, achievement, etc, by doing something wrong: *He was thought certain to get the manager's job but he blotted his copybook by losing a large export order.*

—**carbon copy** a person or thing that is very like someone or something else: *His new girlfriend's a carbon copy of his previous one.*

corn
—**tread on (someone's) corns** to offend (someone): *You fairly trod on her corns by criticizing the new secretary—that's her daughter.*

corner
—**cut corners** to use less money, materials, effort, time, etc, than is usually required or than is required to give a good result: *The production department is going to have to have a tighter budget and cut a few corners.*

—**drive (someone) into a corner** to force (someone) into a difficult or dangerous situation: *The firm are trying to drive their competitors into a corner by charging low prices.*

—**from all (four) corners of the earth** from every part of the world, from everywhere: *The conference was attended by people from all corners of the earth.*

—**in a tight corner** in an awkward, difficult or dangerous situation: *They were in a tight corner with their escape route cut off by the enemy.*

—**turn the corner** to begin to get better or improve: *The accident victim was very ill but he has turned the corner at last.*

cost
—**at all cost** or **costs** no matter what must be

done, given, suffered etc, whatever happens: *We must stop the enemy advancing at all costs.*

—**cost a bomb** or **a packet** to cost a very great deal of money: *His new car cost him a bomb.*

—**cost an arm and a leg** to cost an excessive amount of money: *Those houses cost an arm and a leg.*

—**cost the earth** to cost a very great deal of money: *That holiday cost them the earth.*

—**count the cost** to consider the risks, difficulties and possible losses involved in doing something: *He didn't stop to count the cost before he had an affair, and his wife left him.*

—**to one's cost** to one's disadvantage or loss: *It will be to your cost if you offend the office manager. She's the chairman's wife.*

count
—**count one's chickens before they are hatched** see **chicken**.

—**count the cost** see **cost**.

—**out for the count** unconscious or deeply asleep: *The children are out for the count after their long walk.* <Refers to boxing where a boxer who has been knocked down by his opponent has to get up again before the referee counts to ten in order to stay in the match>.

—**stand up and be counted** see **stand**.

counter
—**under the counter** secretly or illegally: *When meat was rationed he used to supply his richer customers under the counter.*

country
—**country cousin** a person from the country, considered unsophisticated by a town or city dweller: *His country cousin has never been to a pop concert.*

—**go to the country** to hold a general election: *When the government was defeated on the employment bill the prime minister decided to go to the country.*

courage
—**Dutch courage** see **Dutch**.

—**have the courage of one's convictions** to be brave enough to do what one thinks one should: *If you are sure that your colleague stole the money you should have the courage of your convictions and report him.*

—**pluck up** or **screw up courage** to force oneself to be brave: *Finally he plucked up courage and asked her to marry him.*

course
—**horses for courses** see **horse**.

—**par for the course** see **par**.

—**run its course** *see* **run**.

—**stay the course** *see* **stay**.

court

—**laugh (someone** *or* **something) out of court** not to give serious consideration to (someone or something): *Management laughed our request for a salary increase out of court*. <Refers to a trivial legal case>.

—**pay court to (someone)** to try to gain the love of (someone): *The prince is paying court to a foreign princess*.

—**the ball is in (someone's) court** it is (someone's) turn to take action: *I've done all I can. The ball's in your court now*.

—**rule (something) out of court** to prevent (something) from being considered for (something): *His prospects of marrying her have been ruled out of court by her father because he cannot afford to support a wife*. <Refers to a court of law where evidence, etc, ruled out of court has no effect on the case>.

Coventry

—**send (someone) to Coventry** collectively to refuse to associate with (someone): *His colleagues sent him to Coventry for working during the strike*. <Perhaps from an incident in the English Civil War when Royalists captured in Birmingham were sent to the stronghold of Coventry>.

cow

—**a sacred cow** something that is regarded with too much respect for people to be allowed to criticize it freely: *You musn't say the old town hall is ugly—it's one of the village's sacred cows*. <The cow is considered sacred by Hindus>.

—**till** *or* **until the cows come home** for an extremely long time: *I could listen to her music until the cows come home*. <Cows walk very slowly from the field to the milking sheds unless someone hurries them along>.

crack

—**a fair crack of the whip** a fair share, a fair chance of doing (something): *The children were supposed to take turns at playing on the swing but the little ones did not get a fair crack of the whip*.

—**a hard nut to crack** *see* **nut**.

—**at (the) crack of dawn** very early in the morning: *We must leave for the airport at crack of dawn*.

—**crack a bottle** *see* **bottle**.

—**crack the whip** to treat sternly or severely those under one's control or charge: *If you want the workers to finish the orders on time*

you'll have to start cracking the whip. They take too much time off. <From the use of a whip to punish people>.

—**get cracking** to start moving, working, etc, quickly: *You had better get cracking or you'll miss the train*.

—**have a crack at (something)** to have a try at (something): *Why not have a crack at the competition?*

—**not all it's cracked up to be** not to be as good as it is said to be: *The holiday resort is not all it's cracked up to be*.

—**paper over the cracks** *see* **paper**.

—**take a sledgehammer to crack a nut** to spend a great deal of effort on a small task or problem: *We don't need a whole team of workmen to mend one small hole in the roof. That really is taking a sledgehammer to crack a nut*.

creature

—**creature comforts** things that contribute to one's physical well-being: *Her adult son still lives at home because he likes his creature comforts*.

creek

—**up the creek** in trouble, in serious difficulties: *We'll be up the creek if the car breaks down here. It's miles to the nearest garage*.

creep

—**give (someone) the creeps** to arouse dislike, disgust or fear in (someone): *I don't like the new boss. He gives me the creeps*.

—**make (someone's) flesh creep** to arouse fear or horror in (someone): *The eerie howling made my flesh creep*.

cricket

—**lively as a cricket** very lively: *The old lady's as lively as a cricket*. <A reference to the insect>.

—**not cricket** not fair or honourable, unsportsmanlike: *It's not cricket to ask him to pay the bill for all of us*. <The game of cricket is regarded as being played in a gentlemanly way>.

crocodile

—**crocodile tears** a pretended show of grief or sorrow: *She wept at her uncle's funeral, but they were crocodile tears as she really disliked him*. <Refers to an old belief that crocodiles weep while eating their prey>.

cross

—**cross a bridge when one comes to it** *see* **bridge**.

—**cross one's fingers** *see* **finger**.

—**cross one's heart** *see* **heart**.

—**cross one's mind** *see* **mind**.

—**cross swords with (someone)** *see* **sword**.

—**cross the Rubicon** to do something that commits one completely to a course of action that cannot be undone: *He has crossed the Rubicon. He has sent in his letter of resignation.* <Julius Caesar's crossing of the River Rubicon in 49BC committed him to war with the Senate>.

—**dot the i's and cross the t's** *see* **dot**.

—**have a cross to bear** to have to suffer or tolerate a responsibility, inconvenience or source of distress: *He certainly has a cross to bear. He has to look after both his elderly parents and go to work.* <Refers to the fact that in the days of crucifixions, those being crucified had to carry their own crosses>.

—**talk at cross purposes** to be involved in a misunderstanding because of talking or thinking about different things without realizing it: *We've been talking at cross purposes. I was referring to a different Mr Smith.*

crow

—**as the crow flies** measured in a straight line: *As the crow flies the town is five miles away but by road it is ten.*

—**eat crow** to have to admit or accept that one was wrong: *He had to eat crow when he got the capital of Australia wrong.*

crunch

—**when it comes to the crunch** when a time of testing comes, when a decision has to be made: *When it came to the crunch I decided not to leave.*

cry

—**a crying shame** a great shame, a disgrace: *It's a crying shame that those children are dressed in rags.*

—**a far cry from (something)** a long way from (something), very different from (something): *His present lifestyle is a far cry from that of his parents.*

—**a shoulder to cry on** *see* **shoulder**.

—**cry for the moon** *same as* **ask for the moon**— *see* **moon**.

—**crying out for (something)** to be badly in need of something or something to be done: *The old house is in a bad state. It's crying out for a new coat of paint.*

—**cry one's eyes out** *see* **eye**.

—**cry over spilt milk** to waste time regretting a misfortune or accident that cannot be undone: *I know you're sorry that you didn't get the job but there's no use crying over spilt milk.*

—**cry wolf** *see* **wolf**.

—**for crying out loud** a phrase used to express annoyance, impatience, irritation, etc: *For crying out loud! Their phone's been engaged for hours.*

—**in full cry** enthusiastically and excitedly pursuing something: *The crowd were in full cry after the thief.* <Refers to the cry made by hunting dogs>.

cuckoo

—**cloud cuckoo land** *see* **cloud**.

cucumber

—**cool as a cucumber** *see* **cool**.

cud

—**chew the cud** *see* **chew**.

cudgel

—**cudgel one's brains** *see* **brain**.

—**take up the cudgels on behalf of (someone** *or* **something)** to fight strongly on behalf of (someone or something), to support (someone or something) vigorously: *She's taken up the cudgels on behalf of children's rights.*

cue

—**take one's cue from (someone)** to use the actions or reactions of (someone) as a guide to one's own, to copy (someone's) actions: *The children took their cue from their mother and remained silent.* <A theatrical term, literally meaning to use the words of another actor as a signal for one to speak or move>.

cuff

—**off the cuff** without preparation: *The speaker gave a clever talk, completely off the cuff.* <Refers to the habit of some after-dinner speakers of making brief headings on the celluloid cuffs of their evening shirts as a reminder of what he or she wanted to say rather than preparing a formal speech>.

cup

—**not be one's cup of tea** not to be something which one likes or appreciates: *Seaside holidays are not really our cup of tea.*

—**in one's cups** under the influence of alcohol: *He starts singing when he's in his cups.*

—**there's many a slip 'twixt cup and lip** *see* **slip**.

cupboard

—**cupboard love** pretended affection shown for a person because of the things he or she gives one: *The child always kisses her aunt but that's because she knows she will bring her a present. It's just cupboard love.* <From people and animals liking those who feed them, food being kept in cupboards>.

—**have a skeleton in the cupboard** *see* **skeleton**.

curiosity
—**curiosity killed the cat** see **cat**.

curry
—**curry favour with (someone)** to try to gain the approval or favour of (someone) by insincere flattery or by being extremely nice to him or her all the time: *The girl thinks that she will pass the test if she curries favour with the teacher.* <Originally curry favel, from Old French *estriller fauvel, fauvel* being a chestnut horse>.

curtain
—**be curtains for (someone** or **something)** to be the end of (someone or something): *The change of ownership means curtains for the present manager.* <Refers to curtains falling at the end of a stage performance>.

—**curtain lecture** a private scolding, especially one given by a wife to a husband: *I bet he got a curtain lecture when he got home for flirting at the party.* <From the curtains that formerly were hung round a bed>.

—**curtain raiser** something that begins or acts as an introduction to something: *Her appearance on the school stage was a curtain raiser for a long and successful career as an actress.*

—**ring down the curtain on (something)** to cause (something) to come to an end: *The government are ringing down the curtain on that scheme.* <See above>.

cut
—**a cut above (someone** or **something)** rather better than (someone or something): *The office workers think they are a cut above the factory workers.*

—**cut a long story short** to give a brief account of something quite complicated or lengthy: *I could go into a great deal of detail but, to cut a long story short, they've gone.*

—**cut and dried** settled and definite: *We cannot change our plans. They're cut and dried.* <Refers to wood that has been cut and dried and made ready for use>.

—**cut and thrust** methods and techniques of rivalry, argument or debate: *The politician is skilled in the cut and thrust of parliamentary debate.* <Refers to sword fighting>.

—**cut both ways** to have an equal or the same effect on both parts of a question or on both people involved in something: *We can impose sanctions on the enemy country but sanctions can cut both ways.*

—**cut corners** see **corner**.

—**cut (someone) dead** see **dead**.

—**cut (someone) down to size** see **size**.

—**cut it fine** to allow hardly enough time to do or get something: *You're cutting it a bit fine. You might miss the bus.*

—**cut it out** to stop doing (something): *The children were teasing the cat but I told them to cut it out.*

—**cut no ice** see **ice**.

—**cut off one's nose to spite one's face** see **nose**.

—**cut one's coat according to one's cloth** see **coat**.

—**cut one's teeth on (something)** see **teeth**.

—**cut one's own (own) throat** see **throat**.

—**cut the Gordian knot** see **Gordian**.

—**cut (someone) to the quick** see **quick**.

—**cut up** upset: *She is cut up about the death of her dog.*

—**cut up rough** see **rough**.

—**not cut out for (something)** not naturally suited to: *He wants to be a doctor, but he's not cut out for medicine.*

cylinder
—**firing on all cylinders** working or operating at full strength: *The factory hasn't been firing on all cylinders for some time.* <Literally used of an internal combustion engine>.

D

dab

—**a dab hand at (something)** an expert at (something): *He's a dab hand at carpentry.*

daddy

—**the daddy of them all** the most extreme example of (something), the finest or the worst example, often the worst: *He has made many mistakes so far but his latest one is the daddy of them all.*

dagger

—**at daggers drawn** feeling or showing great hostility towards each other: *They're been at daggers drawn ever since the breakup of their marriage.*

—**cloak-and-dagger** *see* **cloak**.

—**look daggers at (someone)** to look with great dislike or hostility at (someone): *When she won the prize her fellow contestants looked daggers at her.*

daily

—**daily bread** basic living costs: *They have to struggle to earn the daily bread for their family.*

—**daily dozen** a series of physical exercises done every day, usually every morning: *He always does his daily dozen before breakfast.*

—**the daily round** the usual routine of daily life: *He's tired of the daily round and he's given up his job to travel round the world.*

daisy

—**be pushing up the daisies** to be dead: *I saw his obituary today but I thought he'd been pushing up the daisies for years.*

—**fresh as a daisy** not at all tired, lively: *The old lady was fresh as a daisy after her long journey.*

damage

—**what's the damage?** what does it cost?, what's the total cost?: *"What's the damage?" the diners asked the waiter.*

Damocles

—**the sword of Damocles** *see* **sword**.

Damon

—**Damon and Pythias** sworn friends: *His political opinions would have estranged Damon and Pythias.* <Refers to a Classical legend.>

damp

—**a damp squib** something that is expected to be exciting, effective, etc, but fails to live up to its expectations: *Everyone looked forward to the Christmas party but it turned out to be a damp squib.* <Refers to a wet firework that fails to go off>.

—**put a damper on (something)** to reduce the enjoyment, optimism, happiness of (something): *Her parents arrived home early and instantly put a damper on the party.*

dance

—**dance attendance on (someone)** *see* **attendance**.

—**dance to a different tune** to act or think in a completely different way, especially when forced to do so: *At first she refused to leave but she danced to a different tune when the police arrived.*

—**lead (someone) a (merry) dance** to cause (someone) a series of great, usually unnecessary, problems or irritations: *Their daughter led them a merry dance by going to stay with an old school friend without telling them. They spent ages looking for her.*

dander

—**get one's dander up** to become very angry: *The headmaster's really got his dander up about people who play truant.* <Originally Northern English dialect>.

dandy

—**fine and dandy** quite all right: *We had problems with the holiday bookings but everything's fine and dandy now.*

Darby

—**Darby and Joan** a devoted elderly couple: *So many people get divorced nowadays that it is a refreshing change to meet a Darby and Joan.* <From the names of such a couple in an 18th-century English ballad>.

dark

—**a leap in the dark** an action or decision, the result of which is unknown or unpredictable: *Her new job is a bit of a leap in the dark but there are no other possibilities at the moment.*

—**a shot in the dark** an attempt or guess based on very little information: *We don't know his exact address, but it's worth taking a shot in the* *dark and looking up his name in the telephone directory.*

—**dark horse** a person or thing whose abilities, worth, etc, is unknown: *He thinks that he is certain to win but there is at least one dark horse in the race.*

—**in the dark** lacking knowledge or awareness: *Everyone else seems to know all about the plans but I am still in the dark.*

—**keep it** *or* **something dark** to keep it or something secret: *We know all about his prison record but we must keep it dark from other people in the firm.*

—**not darken (someone's) door** not to dare to visit (someone): *When his daughter stole his money he told her not to darken his door again.*

dash

—**cut a dash** to wear very smart or unusual clothes and so impress others: *He cut quite a dash in his scarlet suit.*

daunt

—**nothing daunted** not discouraged in any way: *She had a bad start to the race but nothing daunted she went on to win.*

Davy Jones

—**Davy Jones's locker** the bottom of the sea: *The ship and all the sailors on board went to Davy Jones's locker.* <Davy Jones was a name given in the 18th century to the ruler of the evil spirits of the sea>.

dawn

—**at (the) crack of dawn** *see* **crack**.

day

—**all in a day's work** all part of one's normal routine, not requiring extra or unusual effort: *Of course the hotel receptionist will get the theatre tickets for you. It's all in a day's work.*

—**any day of the week** whatever the circumstances: *His horse can race faster than yours any day of the week.*

—**at the end of the day** when everything has been taken into consideration: *At the end of the day we must find someone to do the job.*

—**call it a day** to put an end to (something); to stop doing (something), especially to stop working: *It's too dark to see to work. Let's call it a day.*

—**carry** *or* **win the day** to be successful, to gain a victory: *The lawyer's argument carried the day.* <Originally a military term meaning to win a battle>.

—**day in, day out** every day without exception: *It's rained day in, day out for a month.*

—**daylight robbery** the charging of prices that are far too high: *Taxi prices in that city are daylight robbery.*

—**(your, etc) days are numbered** you are about to be dismissed, be killed, etc: *When the boss finds out about that mistake your days are numbered.*

—**every dog has his day** everyone will get an opportunity at some time: *Every dog has his day. Your turn will come.*

—**happy as the day is long** very happy: *The children are happy as the day is long playing on the beach.*

—**have a field day** *see* **field**.

—**have had one's** *or* **its day** to be past the most successful part of one's or its life: *I thought the cinema had had its day but it has been revived.*

—**have seen better days** *see* **better**.

—**live from day to day** to think only about the present without making any plans for the future: *With so little money it is difficult to do anything other than live from day to day.*

—**make (someone's) day** to make (someone) very pleased or happy: *He really made his mother's day by sending her flowers.*

—**name the day** to announce the date of one's wedding: *At last the engaged couple have named the day.*

—**not to be one's day** to be a day when nothing seems to go right for one: *I couldn't find a place to park, I got a parking ticket and then I ran out of petrol. It just hasn't been my day.*

—**one of these days** at some time in the future: *One of these days you'll have a home of your own.*

—**one of those days** a day when nothing seems to go right: *I'll be glad to go to bed. It's been one of those days.*

—**save the day** to prevent something from going wrong or from being a failure: *When it rained we had no place to hold the fete but the headmaster saved the day by lending us the school hall.*

—**see daylight** to be coming to the end of a long task: *I've been working for weeks on the research project but at last I'm beginning to see daylight.*

—**that will be the day** that is extremely unlikely to happen: *"Perhaps your boss will offer you a salary increase." "That'll be the day."*

—**the order of the day** *see* **order**.

—**the other day** one day recently: *I saw him just the other day.*

—**those were the days** the times in the past about which we are talking were good times:

Do you remember our schooldays? Those were the days!

dead

—**a dead duck** a person or thing that is very unlikely to survive or continue: *The proposed new traffic scheme is a dead duck. Most of the committee are going to vote against it.*

—**a dead end** a situation from which it is impossible to progress: *That factory job's a dead end. You have no prospects.*

—**a dead loss** a person or thing that is completely useless or unprofitable: *He's a dead loss as a teacher as he can't maintain discipline.*

—**a dead ringer** *see* **ring**.

—**at dead of night** in the middle of the night when people are usually asleep: *The burglars broke in at dead of night.*

—**cut (someone) dead** to ignore (someone) completely: *My neighbour's been cutting me dead since our children quarrelled.*

—**dead and buried** completely dead or extinct with no chance of being revived: *The issue of the proposed new motorway is dead and buried.*

—**dead as a dodo** completely dead or out of fashion: *They're trying to revive village traditions that have been dead as a dodo for years.* <Refers to a flightless bird that has been extinct since 1700>.

—**dead beat** exhausted: *I'm dead beat after walking up that hill.*

—**dead from the neck up** extremely stupid: *Don't take his advice. He's dead from the neck up.*

—**Dead Sea fruit** a thing that appears to be, or is expected to be, of great value but proves to be valueless: *Her job abroad sounded very glamorous but it turned out to be a case of Dead Sea fruit.* <Refers to a fruit, the apple of Sodom, that was thought to grow on trees beside the shores of the Dead Sea. It was beautiful to look at but fell to ashes when touched or tasted>.

—**dead set on (something)** determined to have or to do (something): *His son is dead set on going to university.*

—**dead to the world** in a very deep sleep: *I didn't hear the phone. I was dead to the world.*

—**dead wood** a person or thing that is no longer necessary or useful: *The new management say that they are going to get rid of all the dead wood.*

—**enough to waken the dead** extremely loud: *The children's rowdy game was enough to waken the dead.*

—**flog a dead horse** *see* **horse**.

—**let the dead bury their dead** past problems, quarrels, etc, are best forgotten: *You must stop thinking about your divorce. It was a long time ago and you should let the dead bury their dead.* <A biblical reference to Matthew 8:22, in which Jesus said, "Follow me and let the dead bury their dead">.

—**over my dead body** in the face of my fierce opposition: *The council will pull my house down over my dead body.*

—**step into** *or* **fill dead men's shoes** to take over the position of someone who has died or left under unfortunate circumstances: *If you want promotion in that firm you'll have to step into dead men's shoes. No one ever leaves to go elsewhere.*

—**would not be seen dead in** *or* **with, etc**, extremely unlikely to be seen wearing something, accompanying someone, etc, because of an extreme dislike or aversion: *He wouldn't be seen dead in flared trousers. She wouldn't be seen dead in public with him.*

deaf

—**deaf as a post** completely deaf: *There's no point in shouting. The old man is deaf as a post.*

—**fall on deaf ears** not to be listened to, to go unnoticed or disregarded: *There's no point in giving her advice. It will just fall on deaf ears.*

—**stone deaf** completely deaf: *The old man is stone deaf but he refuses to wear a hearing aid.*

—**turn a deaf ear to (something)** to refuse to listen to (something), to take no notice of (something): *He turned a deaf ear to her appeals for help.*

deal

—**a raw deal** unfair treatment: *The younger son got a raw deal when his father's estate was divided.*

—**a square deal** fair or honest treatment: *I don't feel that I got a square deal when I bought that car.*

—**wheeling and dealing** *see* **wheel**.

death

—**at death's door** extremely ill, dying: *He seemed to be at death's door yesterday but he shows signs of recovery today.*

—**be in at the death** to be present at the end or final stages of something: *The factory closed today. It was sad to be in at the death.* <Refers originally to being present at the death of the prey in a hunt>.

—**catch one's death (of cold)** to become infected with a very bad cold: *You'll catch your death of cold in those wet clothes.*

—**death trap** a building that is in a dangerous state: *That high building with no fire escape is a death trap.*

—**dice with death** to do something extremely risky and dangerous: *She's dicing with death driving a car with faulty brakes.*

—**die the death** to be badly received: *His proposals have died the death. They were rejected by the committee.* <Refers originally to an actor or performer getting a poor reception from the audience>.

—**flog (something) to death** to discuss or deal with (something) to such an extent that it is no longer interesting: *The newspapers have really flogged the story about the politician and the model to death.*

—**hang on** or **hold on like grim death** *see* **grim**.

—**kiss of death** *see* **kiss**.

—**look** or **feel like death warmed up** to look or feel very unwell or very tired: *You've looked like death warmed up ever since you had the flu.*

—**put the fear of death** or **God into (someone)** *see* **fear**.

—**sick** or **tired to death of (someone** or **something)** extremely weary or bored with (someone or something): *I'm sick to death of that piece of music.*

—**sign one's own death warrant** to bring about one's own downfall, ruin, etc: *He signed his own death warrant when he criticized the firm's product to a competitor.*

—**will be the death of (someone)** (1) to cause the death of (someone): *That son of hers worries his mother so much that he'll be the death of her.* (2) to make (someone) laugh a great deal: *"That comedian will be the death of me," gasped my father.*

deck

—**clear the decks** *see* **clear**.

deep

—**beauty is only skin deep** *see* **beauty**.

—**be thrown in at the deep end** to be put suddenly into a difficult situation of which one has no experience: *The trainee journalist was thrown in at the deep end and sent out on a story on his first morning in the office.* <Refers to the deep end of a swimming pool>.

—**go off at the deep end** to lose one's temper: *His father went off at the deep end when he saw his wrecked car.* (See above).

—**in deep water** in great difficulties or trouble: *Financially they've been in deep water since he lost his job.*

—**still waters run deep** *see* **still**.

degree

—**give (someone) the third degree** to subject (someone) to intense questioning, especially by using severe methods: *The officer gave the captured enemy soldiers the third degree.*

—**one degree under** slightly unwell: *She's not at work—she's feeling one degree under.*

—**to the nth degree** to the greatest possible degree, extent or amount: *They will back you to the nth degree.* <Refers to the use of n as a symbol to represent a number, especially a large number>.

delicate

—**in a delicate condition** pregnant: *She announced to the group that her daughter was in a delicate condition.*

dent

—**make a dent in (something)** to reduce (something) by a considerable amount: *My holiday abroad has made a dent in my savings.*

depth

—**in depth** thoroughly: *You must study the problem in depth before making a recommendation.*

—**out of one's depth** in a situation which one cannot cope with: *The child is out of his depth in that class. The work is too hard for him.* <Refers literally to being in water deeper than one can stand up in>.

—**plumb the depths of (something)** to reach the lowest level of unhappiness, misfortune, etc: *He really plumbed the depths of misery when his wife died.*

deserts

—**get one's just deserts** to be treated as one deserves, especially to receive deserved punishment: *The burglar got his just deserts when he was sent to prison.*

design

—**have designs upon (someone** or **something)** to wish to possess (someone or something), usually belonging to someone else: *Look out. I think he has designs on your job.*

device

—**leave (someone) to his** or **her own devices** to leave (someone) to look after himself or herself, often after having tried unsuccessfully to help him or her: *You've done all you can. Now you must leave him to his own devices.*

devil

—**be the very devil** to be very difficult or troublesome: *Getting to that town by public transport is the very devil.*

—**better the devil you know** it is preferable to have someone or something that one knows to be bad than take a chance with someone or something that might turn out even worse: *I think we should keep our present suppliers. At least we can cope with their faults, and it's a case of better the devil you know.*

—**between the devil and the deep blue sea** faced with two possible courses of action each of which is as unacceptable as the other: *He's between the devil and the deep sea. If he takes promotion he has to move to another part of the country. If he stays where he is he will be downgraded.*

—**devil take the hindmost** the person who is last must accept the worst fate or the least acceptable conditions, so everyone should take care to avoid this position: *There are so few jobs and so many young people looking for them nowadays that it is devil take the hindmost.*

—**give the devil his due** to be fair to someone, even although one dislikes him or her: *I cannot stand him but give the devil his due he's an excellent worker.*

—**needs must when the devil drives** if it is absolutely necessary that something must be done then one must do it: *I would like to take some time off, but this work is needed for next week and needs must when the devil drives.*

—**play the devil's advocate** to put forward objections to a plan, idea, etc, simply in order to test the strength of the arguments in its favour: *It's really important that there are no flaws in our proposal for change. That's why I'm playing devil's advocate.*

—**speak of the devil** here is the very person whom we have just been referring to: *Speak of the devil. There's the man we've been discussing.* <Short for "speak of the devil and he will appear", which refers to a superstition by which it was thought that talking about evil gave it the power to appear>.

—**there will be the devil to pay** there will be serious trouble: *There'll be the devil to pay when the boss finds out we all left early.* <From legendary bargains struck with the devil by which one could have immediate worldly success, happiness and riches, if one gave him one's soul at a later date.>

diamond

—**rough diamond** a person who behaves in a rough manner but who has good or valuable qualities: *He's extremely good at his job but he'll hate the formal reception. He's a real rough diamond.*

dice

—**dice with death** *see* **death**.

—**load the dice against (someone)** to arrange things so that (someone) has no chance of success: *Since he has no qualifications the dice are loaded against him in his job hunt.* <Refers to a method of cheating in gambling by putting lead or similar heavy material into a dice so that only certain numbers will come up>.

die[1]

—**be dying for (something)** to be longing for (something): *He's dying for a cigarette.*

—**die hard** to take a long time to disappear or become extinct: *He can't get used to new methods of production—old habits die hard.*

—**die laughing** to be extremely amused: *We nearly died at the clown's antics.*

—**die the death** *see* **death**.

—**die with one's boots on** to die while still working: *He refused to retire but died with his boots on.* <Refers to soldiers dying in active service>.

—**do or die** *see* **do**.

—**never say die** never give up hope: *You may have lost your girlfriend but never say die. You'll find someone else.*

die[2]

—**the die is cast** a step has been taken that makes the course of future events inevitable: *The die is cast—he has asked her to marry him.* <A translation of the Latin *iacta alea est*, supposedly said by Julius Caesar when he crossed the Rubicon in 49 BC and so committed himself to a war with the Senate>.

differ

—**a different kettle of fish** *see* **kettle**.

—**agree to differ** to agree not to argue about something any more since neither party is likely to change his or her opinion: *We are reasonably friendly now since we agreed to differ about politics. We used to quarrel all the time.*

—**as different as chalk and cheese** *see* **chalk**.

—**sink one's differences** to forget about past disagreements: *The two members of the board will never agree about company policy but in the interests of the firm they have agreed to sink their differences.*

—**split the difference** to agree on an amount of money halfway between two amounts, especially between the amount that one person is charging for something and the amount that someone else is willing to pay for it: *He's asking £200 for the bike and you only want to pay £100. Why don't you split the difference and offer him £150?*

dig

—**dig one's heels in** to show great determination, especially in order to get one's own wishes carried out: *You won't persuade him to attend the meeting. He's digging his heels in and refusing to go.*

—**dig one's own grave** to be the cause of one's own misfortune: *I feel sorry for the young man who lost his job but he dug his own grave when he kept taking days off.*

dilemma

—**on the horns of a dilemma** in a position where it is necessary to choose between two courses of action: *The old lady's on the horns of a dilemma. She can't decide which of her grandchildren's invitations to accept.* <In medieval rhetoric a dilemma was likened to a two-horned animal on one of whose horns the person making the decision had to throw himself or herself>.

dim

—**take a dim view of (something)** to look with disapproval on (something) *The boss takes a dim view of his employee's inability to get to work on time.*

dine

—**dine out on (something)** to be given social invitations because of information, gossip, etc, one can pass on: *Ever since he got back to America he's been dining out on having met the queen.*

dinner

—**like a dog's dinner** an untidy mess: *The pupil's written work is like a dog's dinner.*

—**more of (something) than you have had hot dinners** a very great deal of (something): *He's been in jail for burglary more times than I've had hot dinners.*

dirt

—**dirty old man** an elderly man who shows a sexual interest in young girls or young boys: *The police are keeping an eye on the dirty old man in the park.*

—**do (someone's) dirty work** to do something wrong or unpleasant on behalf of (someone else): *The manager has asked his deputy to do his dirty work and sack half the workforce.*

—**do the dirty on (someone)** to treat (someone) in an unfair, dishonest or disloyal way: *He did the dirty on his friend and told the police about her part in the crime.*

—**(someone's) name is dirt** *or* **mud** (someone) is in great disfavour: *When he was company secretary he embezzled money, so now his name is dirt around here.*

—**treat (someone) like dirt** to treat (someone) with contempt: *The new head of the household treats the staff like dirt.*

—**wash one's dirty linen in public** *same as* **air one's dirty linen**—*see* **air.**

discord

—**apple of discord** *see* **apple.**

discretion

—**discretion is the better part of valour** it is wise not to take any unnecessary risks: *I thought of betting all my winnings on the next race but I decided that discretion was the better part of valour.* <Refers to Shakespeare's *Henry IV Part 1*, Act 5,.scene iv.>.

distance

—**go the distance** to complete something successfully, to last until the end of something: *I didn't think that he would go the distance but he finished the marathon race easily.*

—**keep one's distance** not to come too close, not to be too friendly: *It is important for teachers to keep their distance from their pupils.*

—**within striking distance** reasonably close: *He was within striking distance of the town when he collapsed.*

do

—**do (someone) a good turn** *see* **turn.**

—**do away with (someone** *or* **something)** *see* **away.**

—**do one's bit** to do one's share of the work, etc: *If we all do our bit to collect donations we should reach our target amount.*

—**do (someone) down** (1) to do (someone) harm, to cheat (someone): *The businessman made his fortune from doing other people down.* (2) to speak unfavourably of or criticize (someone): *Salesmen usually do down the products of their competitors.*

—**do (someone) in** to kill (someone): *The police are looking for the person who did her in.*

—**do (someone** *or* **something) justice** *see* **justice.**

—**do one's level best** *see* **best.**

—**done for** without any hope of rescue, help or recovery: *We're done for. Our enemies are gaining on us.*

—**done to a turn** *see* **turn.**

—do one's nut *see* **nut**.

—do one's own thing *see* **thing**.

—do or die to make the greatest effort possible at the risk of killing, injuring, ruining, etc, oneself: *The soldiers were told that if the battle was to be won their next attack on the enemy would be a case of do or die.*

—do (someone) out of (something) to prevent (someone) from getting (something), usually by dishonest or deceitful means: *The other brothers did the youngest brother out of his inheritance by telling their father that he was dead.*

—do (someone) proud *see* **proud**.

—do the honours to act as host, to serve food or drink to one's guests: *His wife did the honours and poured the cocktails.*

—do the trick *see* **trick**.

—do time to serve a prison sentence: *I'm sure he'll do time for shooting the policeman.*

—do (something) up to renovate or redecorate (something): *We're doing up an old coach house.*

—fair do's (1) fair treatment: *Everybody in the group is entitled to fair do's.* (2) be fair! *Fair do's! It's my turn to have the car.*

—make do with (something) to make use of (something) as a substitute for something better: *They would really like to buy a house but they will have to make do meanwhile with rented accommodation.*

—not the done thing not acceptable behaviour: *It's not the done thing to smoke at the table.*

—nothing doing certainly not: *"Would you lend me £10?" "Nothing doing!"*

—take some doing to take a great deal of effort: *We might just get there on time but it'll take some doing.*

—the do's and don'ts what one should or should not do in a particular situation: *It's difficult to know the do's and don'ts when you go to a new school.*

doctor

—just what the doctor ordered exactly what is required: *A cool drink is just what the doctor ordered in this heat.*

dodo

—dead as a dodo *see* **dead**.

dog

—a dog in the manger a person who stops someone else from doing or having something which he or she does not want: *The child's a real dog in the manger. He doesn't want to play with his model cars but he won't lend them to his friends.* <From one of Aesop's fables in which a dog prevents the horses from eating the hay in the feeding rack although he himself did not want to eat the hay>.

—a dog's life a miserable life: *He leads a dog's life with his nagging wife.*

—a hair of the dog (that bit one) *see* **hair**.

—dog eat dog a ruthless struggle against one's rivals to survive or be successful: *It's dog eat dog in the business world during a recession.*

—dogsbody someone who is given all the odd jobs, particularly unpleasant ones, to do: *The boss treats her like the office dogsbody and gets her to run errands and make the coffee.*

—every dog has his day *see* **day**.

—go to the dogs to be no longer good, moral, successful, etc: *He used to be such a hard-working young man but since his mother died he's gone to the dogs.*

—give a dog a bad name if bad things are said about a person's character they will stay with him or her for the rest of his or her life: *He's actually a very good worker, but he's got a reputation for laziness, and you know what they say about giving a dog a bad name.*

—in the doghouse in disfavour: *He's in the doghouse for being late for dinner.*

—keep a dog and bark oneself to employ someone to do a job and then do it oneself: *She has a secretary and yet she does all her own typing. Talk about keeping a dog and barking oneself.*

—let sleeping dogs lie do not look for trouble; if there is no trouble, do not cause any: *I think that she's forgotten about my mistake, so don't remind her. Just let sleeping dogs lie.*

—let the dog see the rabbit let me, etc, come near, get a view, etc: *Could you all get away from the television screen and let the dog see the rabbit. I want to watch something.*

—like a dog's dinner *see* **dinner**.

—rain cats and dogs *see* **cat**.

—shaggy dog story a very long joke with a pointless or a ridiculous ending: *His uncle's shaggy dog stories go on for ages.*

—throw (someone) to the dogs deliberately to cause (someone) to suffer an unpleasant fate, especially when this is done for selfish or dishonest reasons: *It was he who made the mistake but he threw his assistant to the dogs and had him sacked for it.*

—top dog the person who is in charge: *Now that the manager has left, several of the workers are fighting to be top dog.*

—**you can't teach an old dog new tricks** the older you get the more difficult it is to learn new skills or accept ideas or new fashions: *The old man resigned from his caretaker's job when they called for new security methods. "You can't teach a dog new tricks," he said.*

doggo
—**lie doggo** to remain in hiding, not to do anything that will draw attention to oneself: *Lie doggo. The police are looking for you.*

done *see* **do**.

donkey
—**donkey's ages** *or* **years** a very long time: *He's been with that firm for donkey's ages.* <Perhaps from a pun on donkey's ears, which are very long>.
—**donkey work** the hard, often tiring or physical, part of any job: *They're doing all the painting of the house themselves but they're hiring someone to the donkey work.*
—**talk the hind legs off a donkey** to talk too much or to talk for a very long time: *I try to avoid my neighbour if I'm in a hurry. She can talk the hind legs off a donkey.*

door
—**at death's door** *see* **death**.
—**darken (someone's) door** to come or go into (someone's) house: *He told his son never to darken his door again.*
—**behind closed doors** in private, secretly: *Something's wrong. The boss is talking to them behind closed doors.*
—**have a** *or* **one foot in the door** to start to gain entrance to somewhere or something when entrance is difficult: *He hasn't been invited to join the golf club but he's been asked to play there. That's one foot in the door.* <Refers to someone putting a foot in a door to wedge it open in order to gain entrance>.
—**keep the wolf from the door** *see* **wolf**.
—**lay (something) at (someone's) door** to blame (someone) for (something): *The police are trying to lay the crime at his door just because he's an ex-convict.*
—**on (someone's) doorstep** very close to where (someone) lives: *Understandably they don't want a motorway on their doorstep.*
—**open doors** to give someone an opportunity to improve his or her position, to improve someone's chances of success: *Having his father in the same profession will open doors for him when he applies for a job.*
—**show (someone) the door** to make (someone)

leave: *If those people are disturbing the other customers show them the door.*

dose
—**a dose** *or* **taste of one's own medicine** something unpleasant done to a person who is in the habit of doing similar things to other people: *He's always bullying the younger boys but he got a dose of his own medicine when one of their brothers beat him up.*
—**like a dose of salts** very quickly or very efficiently: *She got through the typing like a dose of salts.* <Refers to Epsom salts which is used as a purgative>.

dot
—**dot the i's and cross the t's** to attend to details: *She's good at general planning but you'll need someone to dot the i's and cross the t's.*
—**on the dot** (1) exactly on time: *They arrived on the dot for the meeting.* (2) exactly at the time stated: *You must be there at six o'clock on the dot.* <Refers to the dots on the face of a clock>.

double
—**at the double** very quickly: *You had better get your homework handed in—on the double.* <A military term, literally at twice the normal marching speed>.
—**do a double take** to look at or think about (someone or something) a second time because one has not taken it in or understood it the first time: *I did a double take when I saw my old friend. I hadn't seen him for thirty years.*
—**double back** to turn round and go back the way one has come: *The fox doubled back and avoided the hounds.*
—**double Dutch** unintelligible words or language: *I couldn't understand what the lecturer was talking about—it was double Dutch to me.* <Refers to the fact that Dutch sounds a very difficult language to those who are not native speakers of it>.
—**see double** to see two images of everything instead of one: *I thought I was seeing double when the twins walked into the room.*

doubt
—**a doubting Thomas** a person who will not believe something without strong proof: *He won't believe that you're back until he sees you. You know what a doubting Thomas he is.* <Refers to the biblical story Thomas, the disciple who doubted Christ, John 21:24-29>.

down
—**down-and-out** (a person who is) without money or a means of support, homeless: *The*

down-and-outs are sleeping under the bridge.

—**down-at-heel** untidy, uncared-for, poorly dressed: *She's a bit down-at-heel but she can't afford to buy new clothes.*

—**down in the dumps** or **down in the mouth** depressed, in low spirits: *He's always down in the dumps in the winter.*

—**down on one's luck** *see* **luck.**

—**down the drain** completely wasted: *Something went wrong with the computer and I lost all my material when it crashed. That was a day's work down the drain.*

—**down-to-earth** very practical: *He does not wish to be involved with the theory of the project. He is a very down-to earth person.*

—**down under** Australia: *He has many relatives down under.*

—**get down to (something)** to begin to work at (something) in earnest: *The exams are next week. You'll have to get down to some revising.*

—**go down big** to be a great success: *The conjuror went down big with the children.*

—**go downhill** to get worse and worse, to deteriorate: *The old lady's gone downhill mentally since I last saw her.*

—**have a down on (someone** or **something)** to be very hostile or opposed to (someone or something): *The teacher seems to have a down on the new boy for some reason.*

—**let the side down** *see* **side.**

—**play (something) down** *see* **play.**

—**sell (someone) down the river** *see* **river.**

—**suit (someone) down to the ground** *see* **ground.**

—**talk down to (someone)** *see* **talk.**

dozen

—**baker's dozen** *see* **baker.**

—**daily dozen** *see* **daily.**

—**talk nineteen to the dozen** *see* **talk.**

draw

—**back to the drawing board** *see* **back.**

—**draw a blank** *see* **blank.**

—**draw a veil over (something)** *see* **veil.**

—**draw in one's horns** *see* **horn.**

—**draw on** to approach (of time): *And so the time of depature drew on.*

—**draw rein** to stop, to check one's course: *The rider drew rein at the door.*

—**draw the line** *see* **line.**

—**draw the long bow** *see* **bow.**

—**draw the teeth of (someone** or **something)** *see* **teeth.**

—**long drawn out** going on for a long time, es-

pecially unnecessarily: *The reception was a long-drawn-out affair.*

—**bottom drawer** *see* **bottom.**

—**out of the top drawer** from the upper classes or aristocracy: *They are out of the top drawer although they are absolutely penniless.*

dress

—**dressed to kill** or **dressed to the nines** dressed in one's smartest clothes so as to attract attention: *She was dressed to kill for their first date.*

drift

—**get the drift** to understand the general meaning of something: *I got the drift of the lecturer's talk although I didn't understand all the details.*

drink

—**drink like a fish** to drink a great deal of alcoholic drinks. *He has a terrible complexion as he drinks like a fish.*

—**drink to (someone** or **something)** to toast (someone's) health: *Let's drink to the new baby.*

drive

—**be driving at** to be suggesting or trying to say: *I wasn't sure what he was driving at but I thought that he was implying I was lying.*

—**drive a coach and horses through (something)** *see* **coach.**

—**drive a hard bargain** *see* **bargain.**

—**drive (something) home to (someone)** *see* **home.**

drop

—**a drop in the bucket** *see* **bucket.**

—**at the drop of a hat** immediately, requiring only the slightest excuse: *He will start singing at the drop of a hat.*

—**drop a brick** *see* **brick.**

—**drop in** to pay a casual visit: *Do drop in if you are passing.*

—**drop into (someone's) lap** to happen to (someone) without any effort: *The job abroad just dropped into his lap. He didn't even apply for it.*

—**drop off** to fall asleep: *My father dropped off during the sermon.*

—**drop out** to withdraw from school, university, etc, or from society: *After his first year at college he dropped out. He hated his parent's lifestyle so much that he decided to drop out and live rough.*

—**let (something) drop** to let (something) be known accidentally: *She let it drop that he was married.*

—**the penny drops** *see* **penny.**

—**you could have heard a pin drop** *see* **pin.**

drown

—**drown one's sorrows** to take alcoholic drink in order to forget one's unhappiness. *The day he was made redundant he drowned his sorrows in the pub.*

drum

—**beat the drum** *see* **beat**.

—**drum (someone) out** to send (someone) away, to ask (someone) to leave: *They've drummed him out of the club for starting a fight.* <Refers to the use of drums when an officer was being publicly dismissed from his regiment>.

dry

—**a dry run** a practice attempt, a rehearsal: *The headmaster wants a dry run of tomorrow's speech day.*

—**dry as a bone** extremely dry: *The grass is dry as a bone.*

—**dry as dust** extremely dull or boring: *Some of the texts we have to read this year are dry as dust.*

—**dry up** to forget what one was going to say: *It was embarrassing for everyone when the speaker dried up.*

—**home and dry** *see* **home**.

—**keep one's powder dry** to remain calm and prepared for immediate action: *Don't do anything just now. Keep your powder dry and wait to see what the opposition do.* <Refers to the fact that gunpowder must be kept dry to be effective>.

—**leave (someone) high and dry** *see* **high**.

duck

—**a dead duck** *see* **dead**.

—**a lame duck** a weak or inefficient person or organization: *You shouldn't keep helping him. He's just a lame duck who's relying on you too much.*

—**a sitting duck** a person or thing that is very easy to attack: *Their firm was a sitting duck for take-over bids as it was obviously in financial trouble.* <Refers to the fact that a sitting duck is easier to shoot at than one flying in the air>.

—**be water off a duck's back** be totally ineffective: *Don't bother offering him advice—it's water off a duck's back.* <Refers to the fact that water runs straight off the oily feathers on a duck's back>.

—**break one's duck** to have one's first success: *We were worried about the trainee salesman but he's broken his duck. He's made his first sale.* <A cricketing term—no score in cricket is known as a duck>.

—**take to (something) like a duck to water**: to be able to do (something) right from the beginning naturally and without difficulty. *The child took to skiing like a duck to water.*

—**ugly duckling** an unattractive or uninteresting person or thing that develops in time into someone or something very attractive, interesting or successful: *She is now an international model but as a child she was a real ugly duckling.* <Refers to the story by Hans Andersen about a baby swan that is brought up by ducks who consider it ugly by their standards until it grows into a beautiful swan>.

dust

—**bite the dust** *see* **bite**.

—**be like gold dust** *see* **gold**.

—**dry as dust** *see* **dry**.

—**shake the dust from one's feet** to leave somewhere, usually gladly: *I've been in this town long enough. It's time to shake the dust from my feet.*

—**throw dust in (someone's eyes)** to attempt to confuse or deceive (someone): *They threw dust in the policeman's eyes by saying that they had seen an intruder but this was just to give the real burglar time to get away.* <Dust temporarily blinds people if it gets into their eyes>.

—**not see (someone) for dust** not to see (someone) again because he has run away: *When he discovers that he's the father of her child you won't see him for dust.* <Refers to clouds of dust left behind by horses or vehicles when they are moving fast>.

Dutch

—**double Dutch** *see* **double**.

—**Dutch auction** an auction in which the auctioneer starts with a high price and reduces it until someone puts in a bid: *I got the table quite cheaply in a Dutch auction.*

—**Dutch courage** courage that is not real courage but induced by drinking alcohol: *He needed some Dutch courage before asking for a salary increase.* <Perhaps from a Dutch military custom of drinking alcohol before going into battle, perhaps from the fact that gin was introduced into England by the Dutch followers of William III>.

—**Dutch treat** a kind of entertainment or celebration where everyone concerned pays for himself or herself: *He's asked us to help him celebrate his promotion but it's to be a Dutch treat.* <From Dutch lunch, to which all of the guests were expected to contribute some of the food>.

—**go Dutch** to share expenses: *I'll accept your dinner invitation if we go Dutch.*

—**I'm a Dutchman** a phrase used to indicate that one does not at all believe what is being said: *If that politician means what he says then I'm a Dutchman.*

—**talk to (someone) like a Dutch uncle** to scold (someone) or talk to (someone) for what is supposedly his or her own good: *He's her younger brother but he talks to her like a Dutch uncle.* <Perhaps from the reputation that the Dutch have for maintaining strict family discipline>.

dye

—**dyed-in-the-wool** thorough, of firmly fixed opinions: *He's a dyed-in-the-wool Arsenal supporter.* <Refers to the dyeing of material while it is in its raw state before being spun so that the colour is deeper and lasts longer>.

—**dying** *see* **die**.

E

eager

eager beaver *see* **beaver**.

ear

—**a flea in one's ear** *see* **flea**.

—**all ears** *see* **all**.

—**be out on one's ear** to be suddenly dismissed: *He was out on his ear as soon as the manager discovered that he had taken money from the till.*

—**fall on deaf ears** *see* **deaf**.

—**give one's ears for (something)** *same as* **give one's right arm for (something)** *see* **arm**.

—**go in one ear and out the other** not to make any lasting impression: *I gave my assistant detailed instructions but they went in one ear and out the other.*

—**have (someone's) ear** to have the sympathetic attention of (someone, usually someone influential): *He may well get the manager's job—he has the ear of the directors.*

—**have** *or* **keep one's ear to the ground** to keep oneself informed about what is happening around one: *The caretaker will know if there are any vacant rooms. He keeps his ear to the ground.* <Perhaps from a North American Indian method of tracking prey>.

—**(my, etc) ears are burning** someone somewhere is talking about (me, etc): *My ears should have been burning this morning—I believe the board were discussing my promotion.* <The belief that one's ears grow hot when someone is talking about one is mentioned by Pliny, the Roman writer>.

—**pin back one's ears** to listen attentively: *Pin back your ears if you hear his name mentioned.*

—**play it by ear** to deal with matters as they arise without making plans beforehand: *It's difficult to know how they will react to your suggestion. You will have to play it by ear.* <Refers to playing a piece of music from memory rather than from printed music>.

—**prick up one's ears** to begin to listen attentively: *He was bored by the speech but he pricked up his ears when he heard his name mentioned.* <Refers to animals literally pricking up their ears when they are listening attentively>.

—**turn a deaf ear to (something)** *see* **deaf**.

—**up to one's ears in (something)** deeply involved in (something): *I'm up to my ears in work this week.* <A comparison with someone who is almost submerged by very deep water>.

—**walls have ears** *see* **wall**.

—**wet behind the ears** *see* **wet**.

—**you can't make a silk purse out of a pig's ear** *see* **silk**.

early

—**the early bird catches the worm** *see* **bird**.

earth

—**bring (someone) (back) down to earth** to make (someone) aware of the practicalities of life or of a situation: *She was daydreaming about a career on the stage but was brought down to earth by her boss asking her to do some typing.*

—**cost the earth** *see* **cost**.

—**go to earth** to go into hiding: *The criminals went to earth after the robbery.* <Refers to a fox escaping into its earth or hole during a hunt>.

—**move heaven and earth** *see* **heaven**.

—**not have** *or* **stand an earthly** (1) not to have the slightest chance: *The youngest competitor doesn't stand an earthly in the competition against the experienced players.* (2) to have no knowledge or information: *I haven't an earthly where he lives.* <A shortened form of a religious expression, not to have an earthly hope>.

—**run (someone** *or* **something) to earth** to find (someone or something) after a long search: *I finally ran the book to earth in a second-hand book shop.* <Refers to a hunting term for chasing a fox into its earth or hole>.

—**the salt of the earth** *see* **salt**.

easy

—**easy as falling off a log** *or* **easy as pie** extremely easy: *Passing the exam was easy as falling off a log.*

—**easy meat** someone or something that is easily taken advantage of: *She was so naive that she was easy meat for lecherous men.*

—**easy on the eye** very attractive: *He always employs secretaries who are easy on the eye.*

—**go easy on (someone** *or* **something)** (1) not to

treat (someone) too sternly: *Go easy on the child—she didn't mean to spill the coffee.* (2) not to use very much of (something): *Go easy on the milk—we haven't much left.*

—**take it easy** (1) not to hurry or expend much effort: *Take it easy. We've got plenty of time to catch the bus.* (2) not to get upset or angry: *Take it easy. Losing your temper won't help the situation.*

eat

—**eat crow** *see* **crow**.

—**eat one's heart out** *see* **heart**.

—**eat humble pie** *see* **humble**.

—**eat one's words** *see* **word**.

—**have one's cake and eat it** *see* **cake**.

—**have (someone) eating out of one's hand** to have (someone) doing everything that one wishes, because he or she likes or admires one: *The boss is usually a very stern, unfriendly man but the secretary has him eating out of her hand.* <Refers to an animal that is so tame that it will eat out of someone's hand>.

—**I'll eat my hat** *see* **hat**.

—**what's eating you?** what's annoying or troubling you?: *What's eating you? You've been in a bad mood all morning.*

ebb

—**at a low ebb** in a poor or depressed state: *She has been at a low ebb since the death of her husband.* <Refers to the tide when it has flowed away from the land>.

edge

—**get a word in edgeways** *or* **edgewise** *see* **word**.

—**have the edge on (someone** *or* **something)** to have the advantage of (someone or something): *He should win. With his experience he has the edge on the other competitors.*

—**on edge** nervous: *She was on edge until she heard the results of the tests.*

—**set one's teeth on edge** *see* **teeth**.

—**take the edge off (something)** to reduce (something), to make (something) less sharp, etc: *His smile took the edge of his criticism.*

egg

—**a nest-egg** *see* **nest**.

—**bad egg** *see* **bad**.

—**be left with egg on one's face** to be left looking foolish: *He told everyone that his horse would certainly win but he was left with egg on his face when it came in last.*

—**put all one's eggs in one basket** to rely entirely on the success of one project, etc: *The young graduate has put all her eggs in one basket and only applied for one job.*

—**teach one's grandmother to suck eggs** to try to tell someone how to do something when he or she is much more experienced than oneself at it: *We've been playing chess for years, but the young beginner was giving us hints—certainly a case of teaching one's grandmother to suck eggs.*

eight

—**be** *or* **have one over the eight** to be or to have had too much to drink: *He started a fight when he was one over the eight.* <Refers to a former belief that one could have eight drinks before one is drunk>.

elbow

—**elbow grease** hard physical work: *New polishes are all very well but it will take elbow grease to get a shine on that table.*

—**elbow room** space enough to move or to do something: *I'll need elbow room in the kitchen if I am to get the meal ready.*

—**give (someone) the elbow** to get rid of (someone), to end a relationship with (someone): *She's given her fiance the elbow and is going out with someone else.*

—**more power to (someone's) elbow** *see* **power**.

—**out at elbow** ragged, having holes: *That old sweater is out at elbow. Throw it out.*

—**up to one's elbows** *same as* **up to one's ears** *see* **ear**.

element

—**in one's element** in a situation in which one is happy or at one's best: *He's in his element sailing boats.* <Refers to the four elements of medieval science of fire, earth, air and water>.

elephant

—**a white elephant** something which is useless and troublesome to look after: *The vase my aunt gave me is a real white elephant. It's ugly and impossible to dust.* <White elephants were given by the Kings of Siam by followers who had displeased them since the cost of keeping such an elephant was such that it would ruin the follower>.

—**have a memory like an elephant** never to forget things: *Her mother won't forget that I borrowed her dress. She's got a memory like an elephant.*

—**see pink elephants** to have hallucinations, especially when one has drunk too much alcohol: *The drunk man saw pink elephants at the foot of his bed.*

eleventh

—**at the eleventh hour** at the last possible minute: *She handed in her essay at the eleventh hour.* <A biblical reference to the parable of the labourers in the vineyard in Matthew 20>.

empty

—**empty vessels make most noise** the most foolish or least informed people are most likely to voice their opinions: *She complains all the time about the new scheme but she knows nothing about them. Empty vessels make most noise.*

end

—**a dead end** see **dead**.

—**at a loose end** with nothing to do, with no plans: *The young man's been at a loose end since he finished his exams.*

—**at the end of the day** see **day**.

—**at the end of one's tether** at the end of one's patience, tolerance, etc: *She's at the end of her tether looking after three small children.* <Refers to a rope that will only extend a certain distance to let the animal attached to it graze>.

—**at one's wits' ends** see **wit**.

—**come to a sticky end** see **stick**.

—**keep one's end up** to perform as well as other people involved: *I didn't know much about the subject being discussed but I kept my end up.*

—**make ends meet** to live within the limits of one's income: *He earns very little but somehow they make ends meet.* <The ends referred to are the start and finish of one's annual accounts>.

—**the end justifies the means** if the result is good it does not matter how one achieved it: *She cheated in order to pass the exam but she says that the end justifies the means.*

—**the end of the line** or **road** the point beyond which survival is impossible: *Their marriage has reached the end of the line.*

—**get hold of the wrong end of the stick** see **stick**.

—**the thin end of the wedge** see **wedge**.

enfant

—**enfant terrible** a younger person who embarrasses older people with his or her unconventional ideas or behaviour: *The new committee member is an enfant terrible and shocked the older members by suggesting radical changes.*

error

—**trial and error** see **trial**.

essence

—**of the essence** of the greatest importance: *Speed is of the essence in this project.*

establishment

—**the Establishment** the group who hold positions of authority in a country, society, etc: *Young people often rebel against the Establishment.*

eternal

—**eternal rest** death: *The old man has gone to his eternal rest.*

—**eternal triangle** a sexual relationship between two men and one woman or between two women and one man: *He is married but he has a mistress—the eternal triangle.*

even

—**break even** see **even**.

—**get even with (someone)** to be revenged on (someone): *He vowed to get even with his opponent for committing a foul.*

—**get** or **keep on an even keel** to be or keep steady or calm with no sudden changes: *One minute she's up, the next she's down. She must get on an even keel.*

event

—**be wise after the event** to realize how a situation should have been dealt with after it is over: *Her father never knows what to do at the time but he's always wise after the event.*

—**in the event** as it happened: *We thought he would lose but in the event he lost.*

—**in the event of (something)** if (something) happens: *He inherits in the event of his father's death.*

every

—**every inch a** or **the** see **inch**.

—**every man jack** see **jack**.

evidence

—**in evidence** easily seen: *His love for her is much in evidence.*

—**turn Queen's** or **King's evidence** to give evidence against a fellow criminal in order to have one's own sentence reduced: *The accused turned Queen's evidence and spilled the beans about his accomplice.*

evil

—**the evil eye** see **eye**.

—**put off the evil hour** or **day** to keep postponing something unpleasant: *He should go to the dentist but he keeps postponing the evil hour.*

ewe

—**(someone's) ewe lamb** (someone's) favourite: *Her youngest son is her ewe lamb.* <A biblical reference to Samuel 12:3>.

exception

—**the exception that proves the rule** the fact

that an exception has to be made for a particular example of something proves that the general rule is valid: *All the family have black hair. The youngest member who is fair-haired is the exception that proves the rule.*

—**take exception to (something)** to take offence at (something): *I took exception to his overcritical comments about my outfit.*

exhibition

—**make an exhibition of oneself** to behave embarrassingly in public: *She made an exhibition of herself at the office party by getting very drunk.*

expense

—**at the expense of (someone *or* something)** causing loss, harm, embarrassment, etc: *He won the race, but at the expense of his health.*

eye

—**all my eye (and Betty Martin)** completely untrue: *He told me he was wealthy, but I knew that it was all my eye.*

—**an eye for an eye (and a tooth for a tooth)** a punishment to match the offence committed: *He killed the son of the man who murdered his daughter.* <A biblical reference to Exodus 21:23>.

—**a sight for sore eyes** a pleasant or welcome sight: *"Well, you're a sight for sore eyes," said the old man to his son who was just back from a long trip abroad.*

—**a smack in the eye for (someone)** an insult or rebuff for (someone): *When she married someone else it was a real smack in the eye for her ex-boyfriend.*

—**beauty is in the eye of the beholder** *see* **beauty**.

—**be one in the eye for (someone)** to be something unpleasant that happens to someone who deserves it: *He tried to get the boss to sack her, but it was one in the eye for him when she was promoted.*

—**can see with half an eye** to see or understand without difficulty: *You can see with half an eye that he is seriously ill.*

—**close one's eyes to (something)** deliberately to ignore (something blameworthy): *The local policeman closed his eyes to the pub being open after closing time.*

—**cry one's eyes out** to weep bitterly: *The little girl cried her eyes out when her rabbit died.*

—**easy on the eye** *see* **easy**.

—**eye-opener** something which reveals an unexpected fact: *When he stood up to the bully it was a real eye-opener to her. She'd thought he was a coward.*

—**eyesore** something extremely ugly: *That new building is an eyesore.*

—**give one's eye teeth** *see* **teeth**.

—**give (someone) the glad eye** *see* **glad**.

—**have an eye for (someone *or* something)** to be a good judge of (someone or something), to be able to spot (someone or something) as a good example: *She has an eye for a bargain when it comes to antiques.*

—**have an eye to the main chance** *see* **chance**.

—**in the twinkling of an eye** very rapidly, immediately: *The child disappeared in the twinkling of an eye.*

—**keep a weather eye open** *or* **keep one's eyes peeled** *or* **skinned** to keep a close watch, to be alert: *Keep your eyes peeled in case the police come.* <A nautical term for watching for changes in the weather>.

—**make eyes at (someone)** to look at (someone) with sexual interest: *She was making eyes at the man at the bar.*

—**not to bat an eyelid** not to show any surprise, distress, etc: *He didn't bat an eyelid when the police charged him.*

—**open (someone's) eyes to (something)** to make (someone) aware of (something, usually unpleasant) previously unknown: *They finally opened his eyes to his wife's adultery.*

—**pull the wool over (someone's) eyes** *see* **wool**.

—**see eye to eye with (someone)** to be in agreement with (someone): *The couple rarely see eye to eye about how to bring up their children.*

—**the apple of (someone's) eye** *see* **apple**.

—**the evil eye** the supposed power of causing harm by a look: *I think he's put the evil eye on me. I always play chess badly when I'm playing against him.*

—**there's more to (someone *or* something) than meets the eye** the true worth or state of (someone or something) is not immediately obvious: *I think that there's more to his illness than meets the eye.*

—**turn a blind eye to (something)** same as **close one's eyes to (something)** *see above.*

—**up to one's eyes** same as **up to one's ears (in something)** *see* **ear**.

—**with one's eyes open** fully aware of one's actions: *She married him with her eyes open. She knew he was violent.*

F

face

—**a slap in the face** *see* **slap**.

—**cut off one's nose to spite one's face** *see* **nose**.

—**face the music** to face and deal with a situation caused by one's actions: *At first he ran away after the crime but he returned to face the music.* <Perhaps from a performer facing the musicians below the front of the stage as he or she makes an entrance on stage>.

—**fly in the face of (something)** to oppose or defy (something): *She takes pleasure in flying in the face of convention.* <Refers to a dog attacking>.

—**give (something) a face-lift** to make (something) look better, to renovate (something): *They've given the old house a complete face-lift.* <Refers to a cosmetic operation to raise the skin of the lower face to improve the appearance>.

—**have a long face** to look unhappy. *Judging from his long face I assume that he didn't get the job.*

—**have a face like thunder** to be very angry-looking: *She had a face like thunder when he was late for dinner.*

—**in the face of (something)** while having to cope with (something unpleasant): *She succeeded in the face of great hardship.*

—**laugh on the other side of one's face** *see* **laugh**.

—**lose face** to suffer a loss of respect or reputation: *She refused to apologize to her employee because she thought she would lose face by doing so.*

—**make** *or* **pull a face** to twist one's face into a strange or funny expression: *She made a face behind her father's back.*

—**put a brave face on it** to try to appear brave when one is feeling afraid, distressed, etc: *I'm nervous about the interview but I'm putting a brave face on it.*

—**save (someone's) face** to prevent (someone) from appearing stupid or wrong: *It was her mistake but her secretary saved her face by taking responsibility for it.*

—**set one's face against (someone** *or* **something)** to oppose (someone or something)

with great determination: *The chairman has set his face against the proposal and that's the end of it.*

—**show one's face** to put in an appearance, especially when one will not be welcome or when one will be embarrassed: *I'm surprised that she showed her face at the party after she got so drunk at the last one.*

—**take (someone** *or* **something) at face value** to judge (someone or something) on outward appearance: *She takes him at face value, but his sincerity is false.* <Refers to the value of a coin or note printed on it>.

faint

—**faint heart never won fair lady** boldness is necessary to achieve what one desires: *You won't get a job sitting there. Faint heart never won fair lady.*

—**not to have the faintest** not to have the slightest idea: *I haven't the faintest who he is.*

fair

—**a fair crack of the whip** *see* **crack**.

—**by fair means or foul** by any method whatsoever: *He's determined to get that job by fair means or foul.*

—**fair and square** (1) honestly, in a fair way: *He won the contest fair and square, not because he was the umpire's son.* (2) straight, directly: *He hit him fair and square on the nose.*

—**fair do's** *see* **do**.

—**fair game** a person or thing that it is considered quite reasonable to attack, make fun of, etc: *Politicians are fair game to the press.*

—**fair play** fairness and justice: *The children are organizing the sports themselves but there will have to be some teachers there to see fair play.*

—**fairweather friends** people who are friendly towards one only when one is not in trouble: *All his fairweather friends deserted him when he lost his job.*

—**in a fair way to** very likely to: *He's in a fair way to becoming a director.*

faith

—**in (all) good faith** with honest and sincere intentions: *I recommended the job to him in all good faith.*

fall

—**fall about** to be extremely amused: *The children fell about at the clown's antics.*

—**fall back on (someone** or **something)** to rely on (someone or something) if all else fails: *When her husband left her she knew that she could fall back on her parents.*

—**fall between two stools** *see* **stool**.

—**fall by the wayside** *see* **wayside**.

—**fall down on (something)** to do badly at (something): *Since he was ill he has been falling down on his job.*

—**fall flat** to fail, to have no effect: *The comedian's jokes fell completely flat.*

—**fall for (someone** or **something)** (1) to be deceived by (something): *She fell for his charm but he was a rogue.* (2) to be attracted to or fall in love with (someone or something): *He fell for his best friend's girlfriend.*

—**fall foul of (something** or **something)** to do something that arouses someone's anger or hostility: *He fell foul of the law at an early age.*

—**fall from grace** to lose (someone's) favour: *She used to be her father's favourite but she fell from grace when she married without his permission.*

—**fall into place** *see* **place**.

—**fall on deaf ears** *see* **deaf**.

—**fall** or **land on one's feet** *see* **feet**.

—**fall out** to quarrel: *He fell out with his neighbour over the repair of their communal wall.*

—**fall over oneself to** to set about doing something with great willingness and eagerness: *She fell over herself to make her rich guest welcome.*

false

—**a false alarm** *see* **alarm**.

—**a false start** *see* **start**.

—**under false pretences** by using deceit: *They got into the house under false pretences by saying they were workmen.*

familiarity

—**familiarity breeds contempt** people cease to appreciate people or things they know well: *He doesn't realize what a marvellous wife he has because familiarity has bred contempt.*

family

—**in the family way** pregnant: *Her son's scarcely a year old, but she's in the family way again.*

—**run in the family** to be a characteristic found in many members of the same family: *Violence runs in that family. At least three of them are in prison.*

fancy

—**(footloose and) fancy free** not in love with anyone, not romantically attached: *He used to be married but he's fancy free now.*

—**fancy one's chances** *see* **chance**.

—**take** or **tickle one's fancy** to attract one, to arouse a liking in one: *She has seen a dress that took her fancy.*

far

—**a far cry from (something)** *see* **cry**.

—**far and away** by a very great amount: *He's far and away the best salesman.*

—**far be it from (someone) to** (someone) has no right to do something: *Far be it from me to presume to advise you, but are you doing the right thing?*

—**go far** to be very successful: *The boy is not academic but I think he will go far.*

—**go too far** to do or say something that is beyond the limits of what is acceptable: *The young employee went too far when he hit the supervisor.*

—**so far, so good** up until now the project, etc, has been successful: *So far so good, but we don't know what will happen in the future.*

fashion

—**after a fashion** *see* **after**.

fast

—**hard-and-fast** *see* **hard**.

—**play fast and loose with (something)** to act irresponsibly with (something): *He had no intentions of marrying her. He was just playing fast and loose with her affections.*

—**pull a fast one on (someone)** to deceive (someone): *He pulled a fast one on me by selling me a stolen car.* <Refers to bowling a fast ball in cricket>.

fat

—**chew the fat** *see* **chew**.

—**kill the fatted calf** *see* **calf**.

—**live off the fat of the land** to live in a luxurious fashion: *While he was successful they lived off the fat of the land.*

—**the fat is in the fire** trouble has been started and it cannot be stopped: *The fat was in the fire when his parents discovered he had been out all night.* <Fat causes a fire to flare up>.

fate

—**a fate worse than death** something terrible that happens to one, often rape: *The village girls suffered a fate worse than death at the hands of the invaders.*

—**seal (someone's) fate** to ensure that something, usually unpleasant, happens to (someone): *The workers' fate was sealed when the firm was bought over. They lost their jobs.*

—**tempt fate** to act in a way that is likely to bring one ill luck or misfortune: *You're tempting fate by having a party outside. It's bound to rain now.*

father

—**the child is father of the man** *see* **child**.

—**the father and mother of (something)** an extreme example of (something, usually something bad): *The couple had the father and mother of a row last night.*

fault

—**to a fault** to too great an extent: *He embarrasses her by his lavish gifts. He's generous to a fault.*

favour

—**curry favour with (someone)** *see* **curry**.

fear

—**put the fear of death** *or* **God into (someone)** to terrify (someone): *Hearing the eerie shrieks in the graveyard put the fear of God into him.*

—**there is no fear of (something)** it is not likely that (something) will happen: *There's no fear of our getting an extra holiday.*

—**without fear or favour** with complete fairness: *You must conduct the investigation into the frauds without fear or favour.*

feather

—**a feather in one's cap** something of which one can be proud: *Winning the tournament was a real feather in the young player's cap.*

—**birds of a feather flock together** *see* **bird**.

—**feather one's (own) nest** to make a profit for oneself, often at the expense of someone else: *All the years that he was storekeeper with the firm he was feathering his nest.*

—**make the feathers** *or* **fur fly** to cause trouble or a quarrel: *The politician made the feathers fly when he announced the privatization of the industry.* <Refers to birds or animals fighting>.

—**show the white feather** to show signs of cowardice: *His colleagues accused him of showing the white feather when he refused to ask for a salary increase.* <A white feather in the tail of a fighting cock was a sign of inferior breeding>.

feel

—**feel at home** *see* **home**.

—**feel free** to do what you wish: *Feel free to borrow the car.*

—**feel in one's bones** to know (something) by instinct: *I felt in my bones that he was lying.*

—**feel one's feet** to be becoming used to a situation: *He's not very good at the job yet but he's just feeling his feet.*

—**feel the pinch** *see* **pinch**.

feet

—**at (someone's) feet** easily within (someone's) reach or power: (1) *With his qualifications the world is at his feet.* 2 greatly admiring of (someone): *All the young men were at the feet of the beautiful woman.*

—**fall** *or* **land on one's feet** to be fortunate or successful, especially after a period of uncertainty or misfortune: *After being unemployed he landed on his feet with a job in management.*

—**find one's feet** to become capable of coping with a situation: *She felt overwhelmed by motherhood at first but she's finding her feet now.*

—**get cold feet** *see* **cold**.

—**have feet of clay** to have a surprising weakness, despite having been thought to be perfect: *He thought his wife was an angel, but he discovered that she had feet of clay when she was rude to the workman.* <A biblical reference to Daniel 2:31-34>.

—**have both feet on the ground** *or* have one's feet on the ground to be practical and sensible: *Her husband is a dreamer but she has her feet on the ground.*

—**have the ball at one's feet** *see* **ball**.

—**have two left feet** *see* **left**.

—**get under (someone's) feet** to hinder or get in (someone's) way: *The children get under her feet when she's doing the housework.*

—**put one's feet up** to take a rest: *He's been working hard all his life and it's time for him to put his feet up.*

—**shake the dust from one's feet** *see* **dust**.

—**sit at (someone's) feet** receive tuition from (someone) and be influenced by (him or her): *He sat at Picasso's feet as a student.*

—**stand on one's own feet** to be independent: *Your children will have to learn to stand on their own feet some day.*

—**sweep (someone) off his** *or* **her feet** to affect (someone) with great enthusiasm or emotion; to influence (someone) to do as one wishes: *She should never have married her but he swept her off his feet.*

fence

—**mend fences** to put things right after a quarrel, etc: *Your quarrel with your father was a long time ago. You should try to mend fences now.*

—**rush one's fences** to act too hurriedly or

rashly: *I know you're attracted to her, but don't rush your fences by asking her to marry you until you get to know her properly.* <A horse-riding term>.

—**sit on the fence** to refuse to take sides in a dispute, etc: *My mother and my sister have quarrelled but I find it's wiser to sit on the fence.*

fiddle

—**fiddle while Rome burns** *see* **Rome**.

—**fit as a fiddle** extremely fit: *His father has been ill but he's fit as a fiddle now.*

—**play second fiddle to (someone)** to be in a subordinate or inferior position to (someone): *She always plays second fiddle to her glamorous sister at parties.*

field

—**fresh fields and pastures new** new areas of activity, new places: *I'm tired of working here. I'm looking for fresh fields and pastures new.* <From Lycidas, a poem by John Milton>.

—**have a field day** to have a very busy, successful or enjoyable day: *The journalists had a field day when the prime minister resigned.*

—**play the field** to take advantage of many chances offered to one, especially to go out with several members of the opposite sex: *He's played the field for years but she wants to get married now.*

fight

—**fighting fit** extremely healthy and in good condition: *The player was injured but he's fighting fit now.*

—**fight like Kilkenny cats** to fight fiercely: *The two boys fought like Kilkenny cats.* <Refers to a story of two cats in the town of Kilkenny who were tied together by their tails and fought until only the tails were left>.

—**fight shy of (something)** to avoid (something): *He's been fighting shy of telling her he's leaving.*

—**have a fighting chance** *see* **chance**.

fill

—**fill a dead man's shoes** *same as* **step into a dead man's shoes**—*see* **dead**.

—**fill out** to get plumper: *She was very thin but she's beginning to fill out.*

—**fill the bill** *see* **bill**.

—**have had one's fill** to have had enough, to be unable to tolerate any more: *He says he's had his fill of his boring job.*

find

—**find one's feet** *see* **feet**.

—**find one's** *or* **its own level** *see* **level**.

—**find out the hard way** to find out (something) by one's own experience rather than from others: *He found out the hard way that it's difficult to get into acting.*

fine

—**cut it fine** *see* **cut**.

—**get (something) down to a fine art** to have learned to do (something) extremely well: *She's got getting out quickly in the morning down to a fine art.*

—**go through (something) with a fine-tooth comb**: to search (something) very carefully: *You must go through the written contract with a fine-tooth comb.* <A fine-tooth comb is used to remove lice from hair>.

finger

—**be all fingers and thumbs** to be clumsy or awkward when using one's hands: *I'm so nervous. I'm all fingers and thumbs.*

—**burn one's fingers** *or* **get one's fingers burnt** to suffer because of something that one has been involved in: *He hoped to make money by investing in the firm but he got his fingers burnt when it went bankrupt*

—**cross one's fingers** to hope for good fortune: *Cross your fingers that it doesn't rain tomorrow.*

—**get** *or* **pull one's finger out** to stop wasting time and get on with something: *If that job is to be finished on time you'll have to get your finger out.*

—**have a finger in every pie** to be involved in a large number of projects, organizations, etc: *I'm not sure what business he's in—he has a finger in every pie.*

—**have a finger in the pie** to be involved in something: *I wondered who had caused the trouble. I might have known that he would have a finger in the pie.*

—**have (something) at one's fingertips** to know all the information about (something): *She has the history of the village at her fingertips.*

—**have green fingers** *see* **green**.

—**keep one's finger on the pulse** *see* **pulse**.

—**let (something) slip through one's fingers** to lose (an advantage, opportunity, etc), often by one's inaction: *He let the job slip through his fingers by not applying in time.*

—**point the finger at (someone)** to indicate who is to blame: *She would point the finger at anyone to save her son who has been accused.*

—**put one's finger on (something)** to identify (something) exactly: *I could not put my finger on why I disliked him.*

—**twist** or **wrap (someone) round one's little finger** to be able to get (someone) to do exactly as one wishes: *Her father will lend her the money. She can twist him round her little finger.*

fire

—**add fuel to the fire** see **add**.

—**baptism of fire** see **baptism**.

—**firing on all cylinders** see **cylinder**.

—**get on like a house on fire** to get on very well: *I didn't think my two friends would like each other but they get on like a house on fire.*

—**hang fire** to wait or be delayed: *His holiday plans are hanging fire until his health improves.* <Refers to a gun in which there is a delay between the trigger being pulled and the gun being fired>.

—**have many** or **several irons in the fire** see **iron**.

—**out of the frying pan into the fire** see **fry**.

—**play with fire** to take tasks, to do something dangerous: *The child is playing with fire by teasing that dog. It will bite him.*

—**pull (someone's) chestnuts out of the fire** see **chestnut**.

—**set the Thames** or **world on fire** to do something remarkable: *He'll never set the Thames on fire but he'll do quite well at his job.* <Refers to the River Thames, which it would be impossible to set alight>.

—**the fat is in the fire** see **fat**.

—**there's no smoke without fire** see **smoke**.

—**under fire** being attacked: *The new traffic plans have come under fire from several organizations.* <Refers literally to being shot at>.

first

—**at first hand** directly: *I got my information about the council meeting at first hand from my cousin who attended it.*

—**first thing** early in the morning or in the working day: *The boss wants to see you first thing.*

—**get to** or **make** or **reach first base** see **base**.

—**in the first flush of (something)** in the early and vigorous stages of (something): *He offered to work overtime in the first flush of enthusiasm for the job.*

—**in the first place** see **place**.

—**not to know the first thing about (something)** to know nothing about (something): *He doesn't know the first thing about computers.*

—**of the first water** of the highest quality, of the most extreme type: *She is a doctor of the first water.* <Refers to a top-quality diamond, dia-

monds being graded into three "waters" according to clarity>.

fish

—**a big fish in a small pond** see **big**.

—**a pretty kettle of fish** see **kettle**.

—**a queer fish** a person who is considered strange or eccentric: *He's a queer fish who seems to have no friends.*

—**drink like a fish** see **drink**.

—**fish in muddy** or **troubled waters** to concern oneself with matters that are unpleasant or confused: *You'll really be fishing in troubled waters if you investigate the employment practices in that firm.*

—**have other fish to fry** to have something else to do, especially something that is more important or more profitable: *We asked him to join us but he had other fish to fry. He has a new girlfriend.*

—**like a fish out of water** ill at ease and unaccustomed to a situation: *Having come from a small office she felt like a fish out of water in the huge firm.*

—**there's plenty more fish in the sea** many more opportunities will arise; many more members of the opposite sex are around: *I know your girlfriend has left you but there are plenty more fish in the sea.*

fit

—**by fits and starts** irregularly, often stopping and starting: *He tends to work by fits and starts, rather than continuously.*

—**fit as a fiddle** see **fiddle**.

—**fit like a glove** see **glove**.

—**if the cap fits, wear it** see **cap**.

five

—**a bunch of fives** a clenched fist, a blow with one's fist: *The bully said he'd give him a bunch of fives if he didn't give him money.*

—**know how many beans make five** see **bean**.

fix

—**in a fix** in an awkward or difficult situation: *I'm in a fix now that I've lost my wallet.*

flag

—**hang** or **put the flags out** to celebrate something (a rare event): *The day she smiles at a customer I'll hang the flags out.*

—**show the flag** to attend an event only so that one can say that one has been present, or in order to make sure that one's firm, organization, etc, is represented: *I really don't want to go to the bank's party but as no one else from the company is going. I'll have to show the flag.*

flame

—**an old flame** a former boyfriend or girlfriend: *His wife objected to him seeing an old flame who was in town.*

—**fan the flames** to make a difficult situation worse: *She quarrelled with him, and her friend fanned the flames by telling her what he had said about her in anger.*

—**shoot (someone) down in flames** *see* **shoot**.

flash

—**a flash in the pan** a sudden, brief success: *He did well in the first match but it was just a flash in the pan. He lost the rest.* <Refers to a flintlock gun in which the spark from the flint ignited the gunpowder in the priming pan, the flash then travelling to the main barrel. If this failed to go off there was only a flash>.

flat

—**fall flat** *see* **fall**.

—**flat on one's back** *see* **back**.

—**in a flat spin** in a state of confused excitement: *She was in a flat spin when she heard her fiancé was coming home from the war.*

flea

—**a flea in one's ear** a sharp scolding: *He got a flea in his ear from the teacher for being late.*

—**flea-market** a market where second-hand or cheap clothes and goods are sold: *She got a lovely skirt at a stall in the flea-market.* <From the *Marché aux Puces* in Paris>.

flesh

—**a thorn in (someone's) flesh** a permanent source of annoyance or irritation: *Her younger son is a thorn in her flesh. He's always getting into trouble.* <A biblical reference to II Corinthians 12:7>.

—**flesh and blood** (1) family, relations: *Surely they'll take her in. She's their own flesh and blood.* (2) human beings in general: *Resisting the delicious-looking cake was more than flesh and blood could stand.*

—**get** *or* **have one's pound of flesh** to obtain everything that one is entitled to, especially if this causes difficulties or suffering to those who have to give it: *The factory owner gets his pound of flesh from his workers. They work long hours at boring work.* <Refers to Shakespeare's play *The Merchant of Venice*, in which Shylock tries to enforce an agreement by which he can cut a pound of flesh from Antonio>.

—**in the flesh** in real life, not in a photograph: *She never dreamt that she'd see her favourite film-star in the flesh.*

—**make (someone's) flesh creep** *see* **creep**.

—**the flesh-pots** luxurious living: *She's enjoying the flesh-pots of the Bahamas.* <A biblical reference to Exodus 16:3>.

—**the spirit is willing (but the flesh is weak)** *see* **spirit**.

flog

—**flog a dead horse** *see* **horse**.

flood

—**before the flood** a very long time ago: *The clothes she wears were in fashion before the flood.* <Refers to the Great Flood in the Bible in Genesis 7:9>.

floor

—**get in on the ground floor** *see* **ground**.

—**take the floor** (1) to rise to make a public speech: *The chairman took the floor to introduce the speakers.* (2) to begin to dance: *The couple took the floor to do the tango.*

—**wipe the floor with (someone)** to defeat (someone) thoroughly: *The experienced player wiped the floor with the young player.*

flush

—**in the first flush of (something)** *see* **first**.

fly[1]

—**a fly in the ointment** something that spoils something: *The holiday was enjoyable—the only fly in the ointment was that I lost my wallet.*

—**there are no flies on (someone)** there is no possibility of deceiving (someone), there is no lack of sense in (someone): *She won't buy his old car—there are no flies on her.*

—**would like to be a fly on the wall** would like to be present and able to hear what is going on without being seen: *I would like to have been a fly on the wall when she told him what she thought of him.*

fly[2]

—**as the crow flies** *see* **crow**.

—**be flying high** to be very successful, to be in a position of power: *He's flying high nowadays as chairman of the company, but he started off as the errand boy.*

—**fly a kite** *see* **kite**.

—**fly in the face of (something)** *see* **face**.

—**fly off the handle** *see* **handle**.

—**get off to a flying start** to have a very successful beginning: *Our appeal got off to a flying start with a donation of £1000.*

—**pigs might fly** *see* **pig**.

—**with flying colours** *see* **colour**.

foam

—**foam at the mouth** to be very angry: *He was*

foaming at the mouth when he got a parking ticket. <Mad dogs foam at the mouth>.

fog

—**not to have the foggiest** not to have the slightest idea: *I haven't the foggiest where she's gone.*

follow

—**follow in (someone's) footsteps** *see* **foot**.

—**follow one's nose** *see* **nose**.

—**follow suit** to do just as someone else has done: *He got up to leave and everyone followed suit.* <A reference to card-playing when a player plays the same suit as the previous player>.

food

—**food for thought** something to make one think carefully: *The managing director's talk about the state of the firm gave us food for thought.*

fool

—**a fool's paradise** a state of happiness that is based on something that is not true or realistic: *She lived in a fool's paradise thinking that he was going to marry her.*

—**be nobody's fool** to have a good deal of common sense: *She's nobody's fool. She knows the salary they offered her is too low.*

—**fools rush in (where angels fear to tread)** an ignorant person can sometimes achieve what a warier person cannot: *Fools rush in—he went straight to the top person and got our complaint settled.* <From Alexander Pope's *An Essay on Criticism*>.

—**make a fool of oneself** to make oneself appear ridiculous or stupid: *He thought that he would make a fool of himself if he sang in public.*

—**make a fool of (someone)** to make (someone) appear ridiculous or stupid: *She made a fool of him by imitating his accent.*

—**not to suffer fools gladly** not to have any patience with foolish or stupid people: *Clever children get on with that teacher but she doesn't suffer fools gladly.*

foot

—**follow in (someone's) footsteps** to do the same as someone else, particularly a relative, has done before: *He's following in his father's footsteps and studying medicine.*

—**footloose and fancy free** *see* **fancy**.

—**get off on the wrong foot** to get off to a bad or unfortunate start: *He got off on the wrong foot with her parents by arriving late.*

—**have a** *or* **one foot in the door** *see* **door**.

—**have one foot in the grave** to be very old: *Young people tend to think that anyone over 50 has one foot in the grave!*

—**the boot is on the other foot** *see* **boot**.

—**put one's best foot forward** *see* **best**.

—**put one's foot down** to be firm about something, to forbid someone to do something: *She wanted to hitch-hike but her mother put her foot down and she's going by bus.*

—**put one's foot in it** to do or say something tactless: *You put your foot in it when you mentioned her husband. He's just left her.*

fork

—**speak with a forked tongue** to tell lies: *He was speaking with a forked tongue when he said he loved her.* <Supposedly a phrase used by North American Indians>.

form

—**be good** *or* **bad form** be in or not in accordance with social conventions or customs: *It is bad form to smoke between courses at the dinner table.*

—**on form** in good condition, fit and in a good humour: *He's been ill but he's back on form again.* <Form refers to the condition of a horse>.

—**true to form** in accordance with someone's usual pattern of behaviour: *True to form, he arrived about an hour early.*

fort

—**hold the fort** to take temporary charge of something: *The owner of the shop is in hospital and I'm holding the fort.*

forty

—**forty winks** a short nap: *I'll just have forty winks before I go out.*

foul

—**by fair means or foul** *see* **fair**

—**fall foul of (someone** *or* **something)** *see* **fall**.

—**foul play** a criminal act, especially one involving murder: *The police have found a body and they're suspecting foul play.* <A legal term>.

four

—**on all fours** *see* **all**.

free

—**(footloose and) fancy free** *see* **fancy**.

—**feel free** *see* **feel**.

—**free and easy** informal, casual: *He's the boss but he's always very free and easy with his employees.*

—**free-for-all** an argument or fight in which everyone joins in an uncontrolled way: *It started off as a quarrel between husband and wife* but it ended up as a free-for-all with all the neighbours involved.

—**give (someone) a free hand** give (someone) permission to do as he or she wishes: *They gave the interior decorator a free hand with the renovation of their house.*

—**scot-free** unhurt or unpunished: *He was charged with the crime but he got away scot-free for lack of evidence.*

French

—**take French leave** to stay away from work, etc, without permission: *He might well be dismissed for taking French leave.* <Refers to an 18th-century French custom of leaving a party without saying goodbye to one's host>.

fresh

—**fresh as a daisy** *see* **daisy**.

—**fresh fields and pastures new** *see* **field**.

Freudian

—**a Freudian slip** the use of a wrong word while speaking that is supposed to indicate an unconscious thought: *The policeman made a Freudian slip when he said the accused was being persecuted for hitting another policeman. He meant to say prosecuted.* <Refers to the theories of the psychologist Sigmund Freud>.

Friday

—**man** *or* **girl Friday** an invaluable assistant: *The boss cannot find anything in the office when his man Friday is away.* <Refers to Friday, a character in *Robinson Crusoe* by Daniel Defoe.

friend

—**a friend in need is a friend indeed** a friend who helps when one is in trouble is truly a friend: *She visited him regularly in prison. A friend in need is a friend indeed.*

—**fairweather friends** *see* **fair**.

—**have a friend at court** *or* **have a friend in high places** to have a friend in an influential position who will be able to help one: *They say she got a the job because she has a friend at court. Her cousin is on the board.*

frog

—**have a frog in one's throat** to to be hoarse: *We couldn't hear what she was saying as she had a frog in her throat.*

fruit

—**bear fruit** *see* **bear**.

—**Dead Sea fruit** *see* **dead**.

—**forbidden fruit** something desirable that is made even more so because one is forbidden for some reason to obtain it: *He is in love with her but she is forbidden fruit, being his brother's*

wife. <Refers to the biblical tree in the Garden of Eden whose fruit Adam was forbidden by God to eat in Genesis 3>.

fry

—**have other fish to fry** *see* **fish**.

—**out of the frying pan into the fire** free of a difficult or dangerous situation only to get into a worse one: *He was in debt to the bank and now he is in debt to a money-lender—he's definitely out of the frying pan and into the fire.*

fuel

—**add fuel to the fire** *see* **add**.

full

—**be full of oneself** to be very conceited: *She's so full of herself since she married a rich man.*

—**come full circle** *see* **circle**.

—**full of beans** *see* **bean**.

—**in full** completely, with nothing left out: *You must complete the form in full.*

—**in full cry** *see* **cry**.

—**in full swing** *see* **swing**.

—**in the fullness of time** when the proper time has arrived, eventually: *In the fullness of time her baby was born.*

fun

—**fun and games** a lively time, an amusing time: *We had fun and games when the grandchildren came to stay.*

—**make fun of (someone)** *or* **poke fun at (someone)** to laugh at (someone), to make mocking remarks about (someone): *Her classmates made fun of her for wearing old-fashioned clothes.*

funeral

—**that's my, etc, funeral** that's my, etc, problem and I must deal with it: *He's spent all his money but that's his funeral.*

funny

—**funny business** unfair activities, deception: *There's some funny business going on in that firm because they keep losing staff.*

fur

—**make the fur fly** *same as* **make the feathers fly** *see* **feather**.

furrow

—**plough a lonely furrow** to work or make one's way alone without help: *Single parents often have to plough a lonely furrow.*

fuss

—**make a fuss** to complain vigorously: *She got her money back from the shop when she made a fuss.*

—**make a fuss of (someone)** to pay a lot of attention to (someone), to show (someone) a lot of affection: *She always makes a fuss of her niece.*

G

gab

—**the gift of the gab** the ability to talk readily and easily: *He loves public speaking. He has the gift of the gab.*

gaff

—**blow the gaff** *see* **blow**.

gain

—**gain ground** to make progress, to become more generally acceptable or popular: *The campaign against the nuclear base is gaining ground.*

—**gain time** to arrange things so that one has more time to do something: *The student should have handed in his essay yesterday but he pretended to be ill to gain time.*

—**nothing ventured, nothing gained** *see* **nothing**.

gallery

—**play to the gallery** to act in an amusing or showy way to the ordinary people in an organization, etc, in order to gain popularity or their support: *The politician was playing to the gallery at the party conference.*

game

—**beat (someone) at his** *or* **her own game** to do better than (someone) at his or her activity, especially a cunning or dishonest one: *In previous years he won the cross-country race by taking a short cut but this year another competitor beat him at his own game.*

—**fair game** *see* **fair**.

—**give the game away** to reveal a secret plan, trick, etc, usually accidentally: *We planned a surprise party for her birthday but her mother gave the game away.*

—**play the game** to behave fairly and honourably: *Play the game. You shouldn't accuse him in his absence.*

—**the game is not worth the candle** *see* **candle**.

—**the game is up** the plan, trick, crime, etc, has been discovered and so has failed: *The game is up. Our parents have found out about our plan to hold a party when they are away.*

—**the name of the game** *see* **name**.

garden

—**bear garden** *see* **bear**.

—**everything in the garden is lovely** everything is fine: *She was unhappy in that job but she says everything in the garden's lovely now that she's used to it.*

—**lead (someone) up the garden path** to mislead or deceive (someone): *She thought he was going to marry her but he was just leading her up the garden path.*

gasp

—**at one's last gasp** just about to collapse, be ruined, die, etc: *We were at our last gasp when we reached the top of the mountain.*

gauntlet

—**run the gauntlet** to be exposed or subjected to blame, criticism or risk: *Before he married her he had to run the gauntlet of her family's disapproving comments.* <"Gauntlet" is a mistaken form of Swedish *gatlopp*. "Running the gatlopp" was a military punishment in which the culprit had to run between two lines of men with whips who struck him as he passed>.

—**throw down the gauntlet** to issue a challenge: *The work force threw down the gauntlet to management by saying they would go on strike unless their pay was increased.* <Throwing down a gauntlet, a protective glove, was the traditional method of challenging someone to a fight in medieval times>.

get

—**be getting on for (something)** to be close to (a particular age, time, etc): *It's getting on for midnight. Despite his young appearance he's getting on for fifty.*

—**get a bit above oneself** *see* **above**.

—**get away from it all** *see* **away**.

—**get even with (someone)** *see* **even**.

—**get nowhere** to make no progress: *We've been looking for the lost dog for hours and we're getting nowhere.*

—**get** *or* **pull one's finger out** *see* **finger**.

—**play hard to get** *see* **play**.

—**tell (someone) where to get off** to tell (someone) that one will not tolerate him or her or his or her behaviour anymore: *He kept borrowing things from me until I finally told him where to get off.*

ghost

—**give up the ghost** to die, stop working, etc: *My old washing machine finally gave up the ghost.* <Ghost refers to a person's spirit—a biblical reference to Job 14:10>.

—**not to have the ghost of a chance** *see* **chance.**

gift

—**Greek gift** *see* **Greek.**

—**look a gift horse in the mouth** to criticize something that has been given to one: *Don't look for flaws in that table. It was a gift and you mustn't look a gift horse in the mouth.* <Looking at a horse's teeth is a way of telling its age and so estimating its value>.

—**the gift of the gab** *see* **gab.**

—**think one is God's gift (to someone)** *see* **God.**

gild

—**gild the lily** to add unnecessary decoration or detail: *She looks at her best without make-up but she gilds the lily by wearing a lot of cosmetics.* <An adaptation of a speech from Shakespeare's *King John*, Act 4, scene ii>.

gilt

—**take the gilt off the gingerbread** to take away what makes something attractive: *She loved the job when she travelled a lot but the gilt was taken off the gingerbread when her boss asked her to stay in the office all day.* <Gingerbread used to be sold in fancy shapes and decorated with gold leaf>.

gird

—**gird up one's loins** to prepare oneself for action: *I'll be late for work. I had better gird up my loins.* <A biblical phrase from the fact that robes had to be tied up with a girdle before men began work, Acts 12:8>.

give

—**give a dog a bad name** *see* **dog.**

—**give a good account of oneself** *see* **account.**

—**give and take** willingness to compromise: *There has to be some give and take in marriage. You can't get your own way all the time.*

—**give as good as one gets** *see* **good.**

—**give (something) away** to let (some information, etc) be revealed accidentally: *I meant to keep our destination a secret but my father gave it away.*

—**give (someone) his** *or* **her head** *see* **head.**

—**give (someone) the glad eye** *see* **glad.**

—**give the game away** *see* **game.**

—**give up the ghost** *see* **ghost.**

glad

—**glad rags** best clothes worn for special occa-sions: *They got into their glad rags and went out for dinner.*

—**give (someone) the glad eye** to look at (someone) in a way that shows that one is romantically or sexually interested in him or her: *He was giving the glad eye to all the girls at the party.*

glass

—**people who live in glass houses should not throw stones** people with faults themselves should not criticize faults in others: *He criticized his wife for arriving late, but he himself is hardly ever on time. Someone should tell him that people in glass houses shouldn't throw stones.*

glove

—**be hand in glove (with someone)** *see* **hand.**

—**fit like a glove** to fit perfectly: *That new dress fits her like a glove.*

—**handle (someone** *or* **something) with kid gloves** *see* **kid.**

—**take the gloves off** to begin to fight, argue, etc, in earnest: *So far our discussions about the disputed will have been gentlemanly but now the gloves are off.* <Refers to boxers who wear protective gloves to soften their blows>.

gnat

—**strain at a gnat (and swallow a camel)** to trouble oneself over a matter of no importance, something only slightly wrong, etc, (but be unconcerned about a matter of great importance, something very wrong, etc): *The headmaster was really straining at a gnat when he expelled four boys for smoking.* <A biblical reference to Matthew 23:23-24>.

go

—**from the word go** right from the very start: *Their marriage went wrong right from the word go.*

—**give (someone** *or* **something) the go-by** to ignore or disregard (someone or something): *He asked her out but she gave him the go-by.*

—**go against the grain** *see* **grain.**

—**go bust** *see* **bust.**

—**go downhill** *see* **downhill.**

—**go far** *see* **far.**

—**go for (someone** *or* **something)** (1) to attack (someone or something) either physically or verbally: *The press really went for the government about the unemployment figures.* (2) be attracted by: *He always goes for older women.*

—**go great guns** *see* **gun.**

—**go halves with (someone)** *see* **half.**

—**go places** *see* **place.**

—**go steady** *see* **steady.**

—**go the whole hog** *see* **hog**.

—**go to (someone's) head** *see* **head**.

—**go to town** *see* **town**.

—**go to the wall** *see* **wall**.

—**go with a bang** *see* **bang**.

—**go with a swing** *see* **swing**.

—**have a go** (1) to make an attempt: *I'm no cook, but I'll have a go at baking a cake.* (2) to try to stop a criminal escaping from the scene of a crime: *The old man got badly injured when he had a go at the armed bank-robber.*

—**it's touch and go** *see* **go**.

—**make a go of it** *or* **something** to make a success of something: *I hope he makes a go of it in his new job. Perhaps they will make a go of their new project.*

—**no go** impossible, not given approval: *We asked if we could leave early but it was no go.*

—**on the go** continually active, busy: *She's quite elderly but she's always on the go.*

goat

—**act the goat** to behave in an intentionally silly way: *He was acting the goat to amuse the children.*

—**get (someone's) goat** to irritate (someone): *Her high-pitched laugh really gets my goat.*

—**separate the sheep from the goats** *see* **sheep**.

God, god

—**act of God** *see* **act**.

—**a little tin god** a person who thinks that he or she is more important than he or she is and tries to order others around: *The workers are tired of the little tin god that is the deputy manager.*

—**in the lap of the gods** uncertain, left to chance or fate: *It's in the lap of the gods whether we get there on time or not.*

—**put the fear of God into (someone)** *see* **fear**.

—**there but for the grace of God go I** if I had not been fortunate that could easily have happened to me: *My colleague is now unemployed, and there but for the grace of God go I. There were many redundancies in the firm.*

—**think one is God's gift to (someone)** to have a very conceited opinion of oneself: *He thinks he's God's gift to women.*

gold

—**a golden age** *see* **age**.

—**a gold mine** a source of wealth or profit: *The health food shop turned out to be a real gold mine.*

—**be like gold dust** be very scarce: *Food is like gold dust in some areas of the world.*

—**golden boy** a young man who is popular or successful: *He was the golden boy in our year at school winning all the academic and all the sports prizes.*

—**golden handshake** a large amount of money given to someone who is leaving a job, usually because he or she has been declared redundant: *He has started his own business with his golden handshake.*

—**good as gold** very well-behaved: *The children were good as gold when their grandmother was looking after them.*

—**kill the goose that lays the golden egg** *see* **goose**.

—**the crock** *or* **pot of gold at the end of the rainbow** wealth or good fortune that one will never achieve: *He's always looking for a well-paid job, but with his lack of qualifications it's as much use as looking for the crock of gold at the end of the rainbow.*

—**silence is golden** *see* **silence**.

—**the golden rule** a principle or practice that it is vital to remember: *The golden rule when making a sponge cake is never to open the oven door while it is cooking.* <Originally the golden rule was that one should do to others as one would wish them to do to oneself>.

—**worth its** *or* **one's weight in gold** extremely valuable or useful: *Their baby-sitter is worth her weight in gold.*

gone

—**gone on (someone)** very much attracted to (someone): *He's gone on my sister.*

good

—**a good job** a satisfactory or fortunate state of affairs: *It was a good job that I took an umbrella. It was pouring.*

—**all to the good** to one's benefit or advantage: *He arrived late but that was all to the good as we were not quite ready.*

—**be as good as one's word** to do what one has promised do: *He said he would lend her the money and he was as good as his word.*

—**be on to a good thing** *or* **have a good thing going** to be in a desirable or profitable situation: *He lives there rent free. He's certainly on to a good thing.*

—**be up to no good** to be planning something wrong or illegal: *His wife knew before the robbery that he was up to no good.*

—**for good (and all)** for ever, permanently: *They're leaving town for good and all.*

—**for good measure** *see* **measure**.

—**give as good as one gets** to be as successful as

one's opponent in an argument, contest, fight, etc: *He was shouting at his wife but she gave as good as she got by yelling back.*

—**good as gold** *see* **gold**.

—**good for nothing** worthless: *She's a hard worker but she married a man who's good for nothing.*

—**have a good mind to (do something)** *see* **mind**.

—**in (someone's) good books** in favour with (someone): *She's in her mother's good books for cleaning the house.*

—**in good hands** *see* **hand**.

—**in good time** *see* **time**.

—**in (someone's) own good time** *see* **time**.

—**make good** to be successful in one's career or business: *He was penniless when he arrived, but he soon made good.*

—**make good time** *see* **time**.

—**put in a good word for (someone)** *see* **word**.

—**take (something) in good part** to accept (something) without being offended or angry: *We thought she would be furious at the practical joke but she took it in good part.*

—**to good purpose** with useful or successful results: *She used her qualifications to good purpose.*

—**to the good** richer: *After the fete the charity was £500 to the good.*

—**with a bad** *or* **good grace** *see* **grace**.

goods

—**deliver the goods** to do what one is required or expected to do: *Don't promise to help if you can't deliver the goods.*

—**goods and chattels** movable property: *He was asked to leave taking all his goods and chattels.* <An old legal term>.

goose

—**a wild-goose chase** *see* **wild**.

—**cook (someone's) goose** to ruin (someone's) chances of success: *She had a good job but she cooked her goose by arriving late every morning and so she was sacked.*

—**kill the goose that lays the golden egg** to destroy something that is a source of profit or advantage to oneself: *Her mother used to babysit for them regularly but she stopped after they left the children with her for three weeks. They certainly killed the goose that laid the golden egg.* <Refers to one of Aesop's fables in which the owner of a goose that laid golden eggs killed it and opened it up, thinking to get all the golden eggs at once, only to discover that there were none>.

—**what's sauce for the goose is sauce for the gander** what applies to one person should apply to another, usually to a member of the opposite sex: *If women have to work and look after the house so should men. After all, what's sauce for the goose is sauce for the gander.*

—**would not say boo to a goose** *see* **boo**.

gooseberry

—**play gooseberry** to be the third person present with a couple who wish to be alone: *When they go to the cinema her young sister always plays gooseberry.*

Gordian

—**cut the Gordian knot** to solve a problem or end a great difficulty by a vigorous or drastic method: *He was going to give the lazy worker a warning, but he decided to cut the Gordian knot and sack her right away.* <Refers to a legend in which whoever could untie a knot in a rope belonging to King Gordius, king of Phrygia, would be made ruler of all Asia. Alexander the Great severed the knot by cutting through it with a sword>.

gospel

—**take (something) as gospel** to accept (something) as absolutely true: *She takes everything her husband says as gospel, although everyone else knows that he is a liar.* <The gospel refers to the books of the Bible dealing with the life and teachings of Christ>.

grab

—**how does that grap you?** what do you think of that?: *I thought we might go out for a meal. How does that grab you?*

—**up for grabs** ready to be taken, bought, etc: *There's a job up for grabs at the factory.*

grace

—**fall from grace** *see* **fall**.

—**(someone's** *or* **something's) saving grace** a good quality that prevents someone or something from being completely bad, worthless, etc: *She is rather a horrible person. Her saving grace is that she is a good mother.*

—**there but for the grace of God go I** *see* **God**.

—**with a bad** *or* **good grace** in an unpleasant or pleasant and unwilling or willing way: *He acknowledged his opponent the winner with a good grace.*

grain

—**go against the grain** to be against someone's inclinations, feelings or wishes: *It goes against the grain for her to be pleasant to him. She loathes him.* <Refers to the direction of the grain in

wood, it being easier to cut or smooth wood with the grain rather than across or against it>.

—**take (something) with a grain** *or* **pinch of salt** *see* **salt**.

grape

—**sour grapes** saying that something that one cannot have is not worth having: *He said that it was a very boring job but that was just sour grapes because he wasn't offered it.* <Refers to one of Aesop's fables in which a fox that failed to reach a bunch of grapes growing above his head said that they were sour anyhow>.

—**the grapevine** an informal and unofficial way of passing news and information from person to person, gossip: *I heard on the grapevine that they had got married.*

grasp

—**grasp the nettle** *see* **nettle**.

grass

—**a snake in the grass** *see* **snake**.

—**grass widow** a woman whose husband is away from home for a short time for reasons of business or sport: *She's a grass widow while her husband is abroad on business.* <Originally the term referred to an unmarried woman who had sexual relations with a man or men, the origin being that such relations usually took place out of doors>.

—**let the grass grow under one's feet** to delay or waste time: *If you want that contract you had better apply for it now. Don't let the grass grow under your feet.*

—**put** *or* **turn (someone) out to grass** to cause (someone) to retire: *The company have decided to put the caretaker out to grass although he's not retirement age yet.* <Refers to turning out a horse into a field after its working life>.

—**the grass is always greener on the other side of the fence** another set of circumstances or lifestyle always seems preferable to one's own: *She has just started a new job but she's already envying her sister's. The grass is always greener on the other side of the fence.* <Refers to the habit of grazing animals of grazing through the fence separating them from the next field>.

—**the grass roots** the ordinary people in an organization, etc: *The politician ignored the grass roots opinion in his constituency.*

grasshopper

—**knee-high to a grasshopper** extremely small: *Our family have known her since she was knee-high to a grasshopper.*

grave

—**dig one's own grave** *see* **dig**.

—**have one foot in the grave** *see* **foot**.

—**(someone) would turn in his** *or* **her grave** (someone) would be very annoyed or upset: *Her father would turn in his grave if he could see her in prison.*

gravy

—**the gravy train** an easy method of getting a great deal of money or other advantages: *His present job allows him such a generous expenses budget that he is on a real gravy train.* <Gravy is a slang term for a gain or profit made easily>.

great

—**go great guns** *see* **gun**.

—**great minds think alike** *see* **mind**.

Greek

—**be all Greek to me, etc,** I, etc, don't understand any of it: *They demonstrated the machine, but it was all Greek to me.* <Refers to the fact that ancient Greek was considered a difficult language to learn>.

—**Greek gift** a gift that is dangerous or disadvantageous to the person given it: *The loan of his cottage turned out to be a Greek gift. The roof fell in and injured us.* <Refers to the gift of a wooden horse to the Trojans from the Greeks which contained Greek soldiers who attacked the Trojans and led to the fall of Troy>.

—**the Greek calends** never: *They will get married on the Greek calends.* <It was the Roman calendar, not the Greek, that had calends, the first day of the month>.

green

—**give the green light to (something)** give one's permission for (something): *The new road has been given the green light by the council.*

—**green about the gills** looking as though one were going to be sick: *They were decidedly green about the gills during the sea crossing.*

—**have green fingers** to be good at growing plants: *He grows a whole range of vegetables. He really has green fingers.*

—**not as green one is cabbage-looking** *see* **cabbage**.

—**the green-eyed monster** jealousy: *She is suffering from the green-eyed monster over her sister's new car.*

grey

—**a grey area** a part of a subject, etc, where it is difficult to distinguish between one category and another, an area of confusion: *The question of school security is a grey area. The teachers are responsible for some aspects and the caretaker for others.*

—**grey matter** brain, powers of reasoning: *You'll just have to use your grey matter to work out how to get there.*

grief

—**come to grief** to suffer misfortune or failure: *Our plans have come to grief. The council have turned them down.*

grim

—**hang on** or **hold on like grim death** to take a firm, determined hold of something in difficult or dangerous circumstances: *The boy held on like grim death to the high branch of the tree until help arrived.*

grin

—**grin like a Cheshire cat** see **Cheshire**.

—**grin and bear it** to tolerate something without complaining: *It's a boring job but you'll just have to grin and bear it. Jobs are so scarce.*

grind

—**grind to a halt** slowly begin to stop or cease working: *Without more money the work of the charity will grind to a halt.*

—**back to the grindstone** see **back**.

—**keep (one's** or **someone's) nose to the grindstone** see **nose**.

—**have an axe to grind** see **axe**.

grip

—**get a grip (of** or **on something** or **oneself)** to take firm control (of something or oneself): *He must get a grip on his drinking or he will lose his job.*

—**get** or **come to grips with (something)** to begin to deal with (something): *You cannot ignore the naughtiness of the children. You must come to grips with the problem.*

—**in the grip of (someone** or **something)** in the control or power of (someone or something): *The country is in the grip of a cruel tyrant.*

grist

—**it's all grist to the** or **someone's mill** all this experience, information will prove useful in some way: *His job as a paper boy pays very little but all is grist to the mill. He's saving to go on holiday.* <Grist means corn for grinding>.

grit

—**grit one's teeth** to make every effort not to show one's feelings of pain, disappointment, etc: *He gritted his teeth as the nurse cleaned his wound.*

ground

—**break new** or **fresh ground** to deal with a subject, etc, for the first time: *She's breaking new ground by writing fiction. She usually writes biographies.*

—**cut the ground from under (someone's) feet** to cause (someone's) actions, arguments, etc, to be ineffective, often by acting before he or she does: *When the boss sacked him he cut the ground from under his feet by telling him he had already posted his letter of resignation.*

—**gain ground** see **gain**.

—**get in on the ground floor** to be in at the very start of a project, business, etc: *You might get in on the ground floor of the company. They're looking for investors.*

—**get (something) off the ground** to get (a project) started: *I don't think his research scheme will ever get off the ground.* <Refers literally to a plane>.

—**have both feet on the ground** or **have one's feet on the ground** see **feet**.

—**have** or **keep one's ear to the ground** see **ear**.

—**ground rules** basic rules which must be obeyed or applied: *If we're going to share a house we must have a few ground rules.*

—**lose ground** see **lose**.

—**on one's own ground** dealing with a subject, situation, etc, with which one is familiar: *He's usually shy but he's on his own ground when it comes to discussing golf.*

—**run (someone** or **something) to ground** same as **run (someone** or **something) to earth** see **earth**.

—**shift one's ground** to change one's opinions, attitude, etc: *He was wildly opposed to the scheme but he's shifted his ground.*

—**stand one's ground** to remain firm, not to yield: *Everyone tried to get him to change his mind but he stood his ground.*

—**suit (someone) down to the ground** to suit someone perfectly: *The cottage suits them down to the ground. It's in the country but near town.*

—**thin** or **thick on the ground** scarce or plentiful: *Tourists are thick on the ground in summer but thin on the ground in winter.*

Grundy

—**Mrs Grundy** a narrow-minded person who is censorious of other people's behaviour: *The old woman's a Mrs Grundy who objected to the young couple kissing in the park.* <Refers to a character in *Speed the Plough* by Thomas Morton>.

guard

—**on** *or* **off one's guard** prepared or unprepared for any situation, especially a dangerous or difficult one: *The examiner caught him off guard by asking him about a subject which he hadn't revised.* <Refers to fencing>.

—**the old guard** *see* **old**.

guess

—**anybody's guess** *see* **anybody**.

—**your guess is as good as mine** I have no idea: *Your guess is as good as mine as to how we'll get home.*

guinea

—**guinea pig** a person who is the subject of an experiment: *The patient felt that the doctor had used him as a guinea pig with the new treatment.* <Refers to the use of guinea pigs in medical experiments>.

gullet

—**stick in one's gullet** *same as* **stick in one's throat**—*see* **throat**.

gum

—**gum up the works** to cause a machine, system, etc, to break down: *When the computer broke down it gummed up the entire works.*

—**up a gum tree** in a very difficult or hopeless situation: *He's up a gum tree if he can't get his car to start.* <Refers to an opossum climbing such a tree when being hunted>.

gun

—**be gunning for (someone)** to plan to harm (someone): *Her head of department is gunning for her, and she's scared of losing her job.*

—**big guns** *see* **big**.

—**go great guns** to be going or performing very well: *The firm's going great guns with a full order book.*

—**jump the gun** to start before the proper time: *You jumped the gun by applying for the job. It's not been advertised yet.* <Refers to athletes starting a race before the starting gun goes>.

—**spike (someone's) guns** to cause (someone's) plans or actions to be ineffective: *He was planning to come to our party uninvited but we spiked his guns by changing the date.* <Refers historically to driving a metal spike into the touchhole of a captured enemy gun in order to render it useless>.

—**stick to one's guns** to remain firm in one's opinions, etc: *They tried to get him to say he was mistaken about the time of the offence was committed but he stuck to his guns.* <Refers to a soldier who keeps shooting at the enemy and does not run away>.

gut

—**bust a gut** to make a tremendous effort to do something: *We'll have to bust a gut to finish this project in time.*

H

hackles

—**make (someone's) hackles rise** to make (someone) angry: *The shop assistant's rudeness made my mother's hackles rise.* <Hackles are the feathers on the necks of male birds which rise when the bird is angry>.

hair

—**a hair of the dog (that bit one)** an alcoholic drink taken as a supposed cure for having consumed too much alcohol the night before: *He took a hair of the dog the morning after the party.* <From an old belief that if you were bitten by a mad dog and got rabies you could be cured by having hairs of the dog laid on the wound>.

—**get in (someone's) hair** to irritate (someone): *She's not in a good mood—the children are getting in her hair.*

—**keep one's hair on** to remain calm and not get angry: *Keep your hair on. He didn't mean to bump your car.*

—**let one's hair down** to behave in an informal, relaxed manner: *She fairly let her hair down at the party and danced on the table.*

—**make (someone's) hair stand on end** to terrify or horrify (someone): *Some of the policeman's accounts of murders he had investigated made her hair stand on end.*

—**not to turn a hair** not to show any sign of fear, distress, etc: *He didn't turn a hair when the bully threatened him.*

—**split hairs** to argue about small unimportant details, to quibble: *He's a crook. There's no point in splitting hairs over whether he's a burglar or a robber.*

—**tear one's hair (out)** to show frustration or irritation: *The shop assistant was tearing her hair out over the indecision of her customer.*

half

—**(someone's) better half** (someone's) wife or husband: *Where's your better half this evening?*

—**can see with half an eye** see **eye**.

—**do things by half**: to do things in an incomplete, careless way: *He will have attended to every detail. He never does things by halves.*

—**go halves with (someone)** to share costs with (someone): *The rent won't be all that expensive if we go halves.*

—**go off at half cock** see **cock**.

—**half a loaf is better than no bread** a little of something desirable is better than nothing: *We would have liked a bigger garden but half a loaf is better than no bread.*

—**meet (someone) halfway** to reach a compromise agreement with (someone): *Neither of us got all our demands. We met each other halfway.*

—**not half** very much so: *"Is he a good player?" "Not half, he's brilliant".*

—**the half of it** only part of the problem, situation, etc: *I had heard he was violent towards her but I didn't know the half of it.*

hammer

—**come under the hammer** to be for sale at an auction: *The paintings came under the hammer as one lot.* <Refers to the hammer that an auctioneer bangs on the table to indicate that a sale has been made>.

—**go at it hammer and tongs** to fight or quarrel loudly and fiercely: *The two neighbours were going at it hammer and tongs over repairs to the garden fence.* <Refers to a blacksmith holding a piece of heated iron in his tongs and striking it loudly with his hammer>.

hand

—**a dab hand at (something)** see **dab**.

—**an old hand** see **old**.

—**at first hand** see **first**.

—**at** or **on hand** available, ready for use, ready to help: *The invalid needs to keep his painkillers at hand. The nurse is on hand if you need her.*

—**be hand in glove with (someone)** to be closely associated with (someone) for a bad or illegal purpose: *One of the assistants in the jewellery shop was hand in glove with the jewel thieves.*

—**bite the hand that feeds one** see **bite**.

—**cap in hand** see **cap**.

—**change hands** see **change**.

—**close at hand** very near: *Her mother lives close at hand.*

—**force (someone's) hand** to force (someone) to do something that he or she may not want to do or be ready to do: *He didn't want to move to a new house yet but his wife forced his hand.*

—**give (someone) a free hand** *see* **free**.

—**give** *or* **lend (someone) a (helping) hand** to help (someone): *She gave her mother a hand with the housework.*

—**go hand in hand** to be closely connected: *Poverty and crime often go hand in hand.*

—**hand (something) down** to pass (something) from one generation to another: *Some of the village traditions have been handed down from Tudor times.*

—**hand over fist** in large amounts, very rapidly: *The owners of the new restaurant are making money hand over fist.* <Originally a nautical term meaning rapid progress such as can be made by hauling on a rope putting one hand after the other>.

—**have a hand in (something)** to be involved in (something), to have contributed to the cause of (something): *The police are sure that he had a hand in the robbery.*

—**have (someone) eating out of one's hand** *see* **eat**.

—**have (something) handed to one on a plate** *see* **plate**.

—**have one's hands full** to be very busy: *She has her hands full.*

—**have** *or* **get the upper hand (of** *or* **over someone)** *see* **upper**.

—**have the whip hand over (someone)** *see* **whip**.

—**in good hands** well looked after: *The patient is in good hands. He's an excellent doctor.*

—**in hand** (1) remaining, not used, etc: *After we have paid all the bills we will have £30 in hand.* (2) being dealt with: *The matter of your complaint is in hand.*

—**keep one's hand in** to retain one's skill at something by doing it occasionally: *The ex-champion doesn't play tennis very often but he plays enough to keep his hand in.*

—**know (someone** *or* **something) backwards** *or* **like the back of one's hand** *see* **back**.

—**lend (someone) a hand** to help (someone): *Could you lend me a hand to change the wheel? I have a flat tyre.*

—**live from hand to mouth** to have enough money only to pay for one's present needs without having any to save: *They earn so little that all they can do is to live from hand to mouth.* <Whatever money comes into one's hand is used to put food in one's mouth>.

—**many hands make light work** a job is easier to do if there are several people doing it: *If we all help we'll soon get the house painted. Many hands make light work.*

—**my, etc, hands are tied** something prevents me from acting as I, etc, might wish to: *I would like to refund your money but my hands are tied. There is a shop rule against this.*

—**not to do a hand's turn** to do nothing: *I've been cleaning the house all morning but she's not done a hand's turn.*

—**off hand** (1) without further consideration or research: *I can't say off hand what the population of the town is.* (2) abrupt, curt: *The customers complained about her being so off hand.*

—**out of hand** (1) out of control: *The protest march was getting out of hand.* (2) without consideration of the matter: *She dismissed my suggestion out of hand.*

—**play into (someone's) hands** to do exactly what someone wants one to do because it is to his or her advantage: *You shouldn't have got angry. You played right into his hands because he had just told the boss that you are bad-tempered with the staff.* <Refers to playing one's hand at cards so as to benefit another player>.

—**put one's hand in one's pocket** to spend or give money: *All of you will have to put your hands in your pockets to pay for the damage.*

—**show one's hand** to reveal to others one's plans or intentions, previously kept secret: *She really showed her hand when she told his wife about their affair. She wanted to marry him.* <Refers to showing one's hand to other players in a card game>.

—**take (someone) in hand** to train or discipline (someone): *It's time (someone) took that boy in hand. He's out of control.*

—**take one's life in one's hands** *see* **life**.

—**take the law into one's hands** *see* **law**.

—**throw in one's hand** to give up, to abandon a course of action, etc: *He tried to persuade her to marry him but finally threw in his hand.* <Refers to a card player throwing his cards on the table to indicate that he is out of the game>.

—**turn one's hand to (something)** to do, to be able to do: *He is a philosopher but he can turn his hand to carpentry and plumbing.*

—**wait on (someone) hand and foot** to look after (someone) to such an extent that he or she does not have to do anything for himself or herself: *The mother waits on her sons hand and foot.*

—**wash one's hands of (someone** or **something)** to refuse to be involved any longer in (something) or to be responsible for (someone or something): *His father said he would wash his hands of him if he got into trouble with the police again.* <A biblical reference to the action of Pontius Plate after the crucifixion of Jesus in Matthew 27:24>.

—**with one hand tied behind one's back** very easily: *He could have won the fight with one hand tied behind his back.*

handle
—**fly off the handle** to lose one's temper: *She flies off the handle whenever anyone disagrees with her.* <Refers to an axehead which flies off the handle when it is being used>.

hang
—**a hanging matter** a very serious subject or deed: *I was surprised that he was dismissed. I wouldn't have thought what he did was a hanging matter.* <Literally, a crime punishable by death or by hanging>.

—**get the hang of (something)** to learn how to do (something) or begin to understand (something): *I think she's finally got the hang of changing gears.*

—**hang by a thread** see **thread**.

—**hang fire** see **fire**.

—**hang one's head** to look ashamed or embarrassed: *The little girl hung her head when her mother scolded her.*

—**hang on** or **hold on like grim death** see **grim**.

—**hang on (someone's) words** see **word**.

—**hang the flags out** see **flag**.

—**hang up one's hat** see **hat**.

—**hung up on (someone** or **something)** obsessed with (someone or something): *He's completely hung up on horror movies.*

—**(someone) might as well be hanged for a sheep as a lamb** see **sheep**.

—**thereby hangs a tale** see **tale**.

happy
—**go to the happy hunting ground** to die: *I didn't realize the old man had gone to the happy hunting ground.* <Originally an American Indian phrase>.

—**happy as a lark** or **sand-boy** extremely happy: *The child was happy as a sand-boy playing with her new doll.*

—**happy event** the birth of a baby: *When is the happy event?*

—**happy hunting ground** a place where someone finds what he or she desires or where he or she is successful: *That shop is a happy hunting ground for her. She buys most of her clothes there.*

—**the** or **a happy medium** a sensible middle course between two extremes: *She's spends her time either over-eating or fasting. She should find a happy medium.*

hard
—**a hard nut to crack** see **nut**.

—**be hard put to it (to do something)** to have great difficulty (in doing something): *You would be hard put to it to find a better teacher.*

—**give (someone) a hard time** to act in an unpleasant, unsympathetic or tough way towards (someone): *They wanted him to leave and gave him a hard time until he did.*

—**hard-and-fast** not to be changed or ignored: *There is a hard-and-fast office rule that no one takes time off without prior permission.* <Refers to a ship that is stuck fast from having run aground>.

—**hard as nails** lacking in pity, sympathy, softer feelings, etc: *She wasn't moved by that child's tears but then she's hard as nails.*

—**hard-bitten** tough, toughened by experience of life: *She was very gentle when she was young but years in business have made her hard-bitten.*

—**hard-boiled** not influenced by emotion: *Even the hard-boiled politician shed a tear at the sight of the starving children.* <Refers to hard-boiled eggs>.

—**hard cash** coins and bank-notes as opposed to cheques, etc: *The workman wanted to be paid in hard cash and refused a cheque.*

—**hard done by** unfairly treated: *She felt hard done by because her father gave her less money than he gave her brother.*

—**hard facts** facts that cannot be disputed: *The hard facts are that we are losing money.*

—**hard-headed** practical and not influenced by emotion: *She's too hard-headed a business woman to give you a job because she's sorry for you.*

—**hard lines** bad luck: *It was hard lines that the champion didn't win.* <Perhaps a reference to a ship's ropes being made hard by ice>.

—**hard-luck story** a story of misfortune told to gain sympathy: *He got money from all of us by telling us all the same hard-luck story.*

—**hard of hearing** rather deaf: *The old lady's hard of hearing but she won't wear a hearing-aid.*

—**hard-pressed** in difficulties, in trouble: *They will be hard-pressed this month to pay the rent.*

—**hard up** not having much money: *They're too hard up to go on holiday.*

—**take a hard line** to take strong, stern or unyielding action or have strong opinions about something: *The headmaster took a hard line with pupils who played truant.*

—**the hard stuff** strong alcoholic drink, spirits: *He drinks wine but not the hard stuff.*

hare

—**mad as a March hare** *see* **mad**.

—**run with the hare and hunt with the hounds** to try to give one's support to two opposing sides at once: *You're going to have to vote for one of the candidates. You can't go on running with the hare and hunting with the hounds.*

—**start a hare** to raise a subject in the course of a discussion, often to divert attention from what was the main subject of it: *During the discussion about increasing salaries the manager started a hare about people smoking in the office.* <Refers to causing a hare to leave its hiding place to distract the hounds taking part in a fox hunt>.

hark

—**hark back to (something)** to refer to (something that has been said or has happened early): *She kept harking back to how things used to be done.* <Refers to a hunting term which is a command to the hounds and their handlers to double back and try to pick up a lost scent>.

harp

—**harp on (something)** to keep on talking about (something): *She kept harping on about how badly paid she was.* <Refers to playing the harp with one string only>.

hash

—**make a hash of (something)** to ruin or spoil (something), to do (something) badly: *He made a real hash of putting up those shelves.* <Refers to a dish made from chopped up pieces of meat mixed together, which looks rather messy>.

—**settle (someone's) hash** to deal with (someone) in such a way that he or she causes no more trouble or is prevented from doing what was intended: *He refused to give up the key to her flat but sh settled his hash by changing the locks.*

haste

—**more haste less speed** if one attempts to do something in too much of a hurry one makes careless mistakes and ends up taking longer to do it: *If you try to hurry the typist she makes mistakes. You know what they say about more haste less speed.*

hat

—**at the drop of a hat** *see* **drop**.

—**hang up one's hat** to move into a house, job, etc, with the intention of staying a long time: *She thought her father-in-law was just staying for the weekend but he's really hung up his hat.* <Refers to hanging up one's hat in someone's hat stand>.

—**hats off to (someone)** (someone) should be praised and congratulated: *Hats off to the new girl for slapping the office womanizer on the face.*

—**hat trick** any action done three times in a row: *We sold three houses this morning—a hat trick.* <Refers originally to a cricketer receiving a hat from his club for putting out three batsmen with three balls in a row>.

—**I'll eat my hat** an expression used to express total disbelief in a fact, statement, etc: *I'll eat my hat if he isn't guilty.*

—**keep (something) under one's hat** to keep (something) secret: *He was told to keep his salary increase under his hat.*

—**knock (someone *or* something) into a cocked hat** to defeat or surpass (someone or something) completely: *Her dress knocked all the others into a cocked hat.* <A cocked hat was a three-cornered hat in the 18th-century made by folding the edges of a round hat into corners>.

—**old hat** *see* **old**.

—**pass the hat round** to ask for contributions of money: *We passed the hat round the office for her leaving present.*

—**take one's hat off to (someone)** to express or show one's admiration for someone): *You must take your hat off to her for supporting the family all these years.*

—**talk through one's hat** to talk about something without any knowledge about it, to talk nonsense: *Pay no attention to his advice on investments. He knows nothing whatsoever about finance and is talking through his hat.*

—**throw one's hat in the ring** to declare oneself a contender or candidate for something: *He's decided to throw his hat in the ring and apply for the post of managing director.* <Refers to a method of making a challenge in prize boxing matches at fairgrounds, etc>.

—**wear a different *or* another hat** to speak as the holder of a different position: *She was* *speaking as a teacher but now she's wearing a different hat and speaking as a parent.*

hatch

—**batten down the hatches** to prepare for trouble: *In the recession a lot of firms had to batten down the hatches and think of ways of saving money.* <Refers to preparations for a storm on a ship at sea>.

—**hatches, matches and despatches** the announcement of births, marriages and deaths in a newspaper.

hatchet

—**bury the hatchet** to agree to be friends again after a quarrel: *The two families have been hostile to each other for years but they've finally decided to bury the hatchet.* <Refers to an American Indian custom of burying tomahawks when peace was made>.

hatter

—**mad as a hatter** *see* **mad**.

haul

—**haul (someone) over the coals** *see* **coal**.

have

—**have had it** to have no hope of survival, success, etc: *The little corner shop will have had it when the supermarket opens.*

—**have it coming to one** *see* **come**.

—**have it in for (someone)** to try to cause trouble for (someone): *The manager has had it in for her since she refused to go out with him.*

—**have it in one** to have the ability, courage, etc, to do something: *I didn't think he had it in him to argue with the boss.*

—**have it out with (someone)** to discuss areas of disagreement or discontent with someone in order to settle it: *Don't go around complaining about her treatment of you. Have it out with her.*

—**have (someone) on** to try to deceive (someone), often for a joke: *The police aren't looking for you. Your friends are having you on.*

—**let (someone) have it** suddenly to attack (someone) either physically or verbally: *She was tired of never arriving on time and finally let him have it.*

havoc

—**play havoc with (something)** to cause serious damage to (something): *His stressful job played havoc with his health.*

hawk

—**watch (someone) like a hawk** to watch (someone) very carefully: *They are watching her like a hawk because they suspect her of stealing money.*

hay

—**go haywire** to go completely wrong, to go out of control: *The organization of the office went haywire when she was away.* <Refers to wire that was used to bind hay. It very easily became twisted and therefore came to symbolize confusion>.

—**hit the hay** or **sack** to go to bed: *He was so tired that he hit the hay immediately after dinner.* <Beds were formerly filled with hay or made from the same material as sacks>.

—**like looking for a needle in a haystack** *see* **needle**.

—**make hay (while the sun shines)** to profit or take advantage of an opportunity while one has the chance: *He's been offered a lot of overtime and he needs the money. He might as well make hay while the sun shines.* <Haymaking is only possible in fine weather>.

head

—**above (someone's) head** *see* **above**.

—**bang one's head against a brick wall** *see* **bang**.

—**bite** or **eat** or **snap (someone's) head off** to speak very sharply and angrily to (someone): *What's wrong with her? She's been biting everyone's head off all morning.*

—**bring (something) to a head** to bring something to a state where something must be done about it: *There has been hostility between them for some time but his public criticism of her brought matters to a head.* <Refers to bringing a boil, etc, to a head>.

—**bury one's head in the sand** to deliberately ignore a situation so that one does not have to deal with it: *He says his job is safe but he is burying his head in the sand. The factory is closing down.* <Refers to the old belief that ostriches hide their heads in the sand when they are in danger because they think that then they cannot be seen>.

—**cannot make head nor tail of (something)** cannot understand (something) at all: *I can't make head nor tail of these instructions.*

—**get one's head down** (1) to start working hard: *The exams are next week. I had better get my head down.* (2) to have a sleep or a nap: *If I just get my head down for an hour I'll be all right.*

—**give (someone) his** or **her head** to allow (someone) to do as he or she wishes: *The owner gives the manager his head in the running of the firm.* <Refers literally to slackening one's hold on the reins of a horse>.

—**go to (someone's) head** (l) to make (someone) arrogant or conceited: *Winning the prize went to his head and he goes around boasting.* (2) to make (someone) slightly drunk: *One glass of wine seems to go to her head.*

—**hang one's head** *see* **hang**.

—**have a head for (something)** to have an ability or aptitude for (something): *He can't climb the ladder. He has no head for heights.*

—**have a (good) head on one's shoulders** to be clever or sensible: *The boy should go to college. He has a good head on his shoulders.*

—**have one's head screwed on the right way** to to be sensible: *He won't give up his job. He's got his head screwed on the right way.*

—**head over heels** completely: *They're head over heels in love.*

—**heads will roll** someone is going to get into serious trouble: *Heads will roll when mother sees the mess the house is in.* <Refers to the use of the guillotine to execute criminals>.

—**hit the headlines** to attract a great deal of media attention: *He hit the headlines last year when he married a film-star.*

—**hold a pistol to (someone's) head** *see* **pistol**.

—**hold one's head up (high)** not to feel ashamed or guilty, to remain dignified: *After her crime she'll never hold her head up in the village again.*

—**keep a level head** *or* **keep one's head** to remain calm and sensible, especially in a difficult situation: *When he discovered the fire he kept a level head and phoned for the fire brigade.*

—**keep one's head above water** to have enough money to keep out of debt: *With so many children they have great difficulty in keeping their heads above water.*

—**knock (something) on the head** to put an end to (something): *Our plans for a picnic were knocked on the head by the rain.*

—**laugh one's head off** to laugh very loudly: *They laughed their heads off when he slipped on a banana skin.*

—**like a bear with a sore head** *see* **bear**.

—**lose one's head** to cease to remain calm, to act foolishly: *She lost her head during her driving test and made a lot of mistakes.*

—**make headway** to make progress: *They don't seem to be making much headway with their research project.* <Refers originally to ships>.

—**need one's head examined** to be foolish or insane: *If you believe his story you need your head examined.*

—**not to know whether one is on one's head** *or* **one's feet** *or* **heels** to be totally confused: *I served so many customers that I didn't know whether I was on my head or my feet.*

—**off one's head** insane, not rational: *The old man was off his head to give his daughters his house.*

—**off the top of one's head** *see* **top**.

—**on (someone's) (own) head be it** (someone) must take responsibility or blame: *On your head be it if mother is annoyed. You made us late.*

—**over (someone's) head** (l) too difficult for (someone) to understand: *The explanation of the scientific experiment was right over my head.* (2) when (someone) seems to have a better right: *They promoted him over her head although she was better qualified.* (3) beyond (someone) to a person of higher rank: *He went over the departmental manager's head and reported the matter to the managing director.*

—**put** *or* **lay one's head on the block** to leave oneself open to blame, punishment, danger, etc: *He laid his head on the block by letting his assistants have the afternoon off.* <Refers to laying one's head on the block before being beheaded>.

—**put our, etc, heads together** to discuss something together, to share thoughts on something: *If we put our heads together we'll come up with a plan.*

—**rear its ugly head** to appear or happen: *They were happy at first but jealousy reared its ugly head.*

—**scratch one's head** to be puzzled: *The police are scratching their heads over the motive for the crime.*

—**soft** *or* **weak in the head** not very intelligent, mentally retarded: *He must be soft in the head to trust her again.*

—**talk one's head off** to talk a great deal: *We hadn't seen each other for a long time and so we talked our heads off.*

—**talk through the back of one's head** *see* **back**.

—**turn (someone's) head** to make (someone) conceited: *Her head was turned by his extravagant compliments.*

heart

—**after (someone's) own heart** *see* **after**.

—**a heart-to-heart** a private talk where one tells one's thoughts, troubles, etc, openly: *She had a heart-to-heart with her mother about her health fears.*

—**at heart** basically, really: *He seems unfriendly at*

first but at heart he's very kind and sympathetic.

—**break (someone's) heart** to make (someone) very sad: *He broke her heart when he left town without telling her.*

—**cross one's heart** said to emphasize the truth of what one is saying: *I'll be there on time. Cross my heart.*

—**do (someone's) heart good** to give (someone) pleasure: *It did my heart good to see the children playing.*

—**eat one's heart out** to be distressed because one cannot have someone or something which one is longing for: *She is eating her heart out for her ex-fiancé.*

—**faint heart never won fair lady** *see* **faint.**

—**from the bottom of one's heart** most sincerely, very much: *I apologize from the bottom of my heart for the mistake.*

—**have a change of heart** *see* **change.**

—**have (something) at heart** to be deeply interested or concerned about (something): *Your father may seem discouraging about the job but he has your interests at heart.*

—**have one's heart in one's mouth** to feel afraid or anxious: *She had her heart in her mouth as she watched the young man standing on the edge of the roof.*

—**heart and soul** completely, with all one's energy: *She pledged herself heart and soul to look after the children.*

—**(someone's) heart goes out to (someone)** (someone) feels sympathy or pity for (someone): *Our hearts went out to the orphaned children.*

—**(someone's) heart is in the right place** (someone) is basically kind, sympathetic, etc, although not appearing to be so: *Our neighbour seems very stern, but her heart's in the right place.*

—**(someone's) heart is not in it** (someone) is not enthusiastic about something: *He's given up teaching because his heart wasn't in it.*

—**(someone's) heart sinks** (someone) feels depressed, disappointed, etc: *Her heart sank as she saw the policeman standing on her doorstep.*

—**in good heart** cheerful and confident: *The soldiers were in good heart before the battle.*

—**in (someone's) heart of hearts** in the deepest part of one's mind or feelings: *In her heart of hearts she knew her mother was right.*

—**learn something by heart** to memorize (something) thoroughly: *The teacher told the pupils to learn the poem by heart.*

—**lose heart** to grow discouraged: *She was very*

enthusiastic about her plan but she lost heart when no one seemed interested.

—**not to have the heart (to do something)** not to be unkind, unsympathetic, etc, enough (to do something): *I didn't have the heart to tell her that her husband was a rogue.*

—**put new heart into (someone)** to make (someone) feel encouraged and more hopeful: *Scoring a goal put new heart into the team.*

—**set one's heart on** or **have one's heart set on (something)** to desire (something) very much: *He's set his heart on buying a motor bike.*

—**take heart** to become encouraged: *The travellers took heart when they saw the town ahead.*

—**take (something) to heart** (1) to be upset by (something): *He was only teasing but she took his remarks to heart.* (2) to be influenced by and take notice of (something): *She took the doctor's advice to heart.*

—**warm the cockles of the heart** to make one feel happy and contented: *Watching her with the baby would warm the cockles of the heart.*

—**wear one's heart on one's sleeve** to let one's feelings be obvious: *She was badly hurt by him although she's not one to wear her heart on her sleeve.*

—**with a heavy heart** *see* **heavy.**

—**with all one's heart** most sincerely: *I hope with all my heart that you will be happy.*

heat

—**in the heat of the moment** while influenced by the excitement or emotion of the occasion: *They were having a quarrel and in the heat of the moment she threatened to kill him.*

—**take the heat out of (something)** to make (a situation) less emotional, tense, etc: *They were just about to fight each other when their friend took the heat out of the situation by suggesting they sit down and talk.*

heave

—**give (someone) the (old) heave-ho** to get rid of (someone), to dismiss (someone): *He's been given the old heave-ho from the firm for embezzlement.*

heaven

—**in seventh heaven** extremely happy: *She was in seventh heaven when her son was born.* <In Jewish literature the seventh heaven is the highest of all heavens and the one where God lives>.

—**manna from heaven** something advantageous which happens unexpectedly, especially in a time of trouble: *My parents' offer of a* *loan was manna from heaven. We were practically penniless.* <A biblical reference to Exodus 16:15>.

—**move heaven and earth** to make every effort possible: *The doctor moved heaven and earth to save the patient's life.*

—**pennies from heaven** a sudden and unexpected sum of money: *They were very poor, so the prize money from the competition was pennies from heaven.*

—**smell** *or* **stink to high heaven** to have a strong and nasty smell: *The drains stink to high heaven.*

heavy

—**heavy-going** difficult to make progress with or cope with: *I found the climb heavy going.* <Refers originally to the surface of a horse-race track>.

—**make heavy weather of (something)** to make more effort to do something than should be required: *The pupils made heavy weather of the exam paper although it was quite easy.* <Refers originally to a ship which does not handle well in difficult conditions>.

—**with a heavy heart** with great sadness or despondency: *It was with a heavy heart that she left her family home.*

hedge

—**hedge one's bets** *see* **bet**.

—**look as though one has been dragged through a hedge backwards** to look very untidy: *The little boy always looks as though he has been dragged through a hedge backwards when he comes home from school.*

heel

—**Achilles' heel** *see* **Achilles**.

—**bring (someone) to heel** to bring (someone) under one's control: *The new teacher soon brought the unruly class to heel.* <Refers to making a dog walk to heel>.

—**cool** *or* **kick one's heels** *see* **heel**.

—**dig one's heels in** *see* **dig**.

—**down-at-heel** *see* **down**.

—**head over heels** *see* **head**.

—**show a clean pair of heels** *see* **clean**.

—**take to one's heels** to run away: *She took to her heels when she saw the bull in the field.*

—**turn on one's heel** to turn and walk away in the opposite direction: *When he was rude she turned on her heel and left.*

helm

—**at the helm** in charge: *With a new person at the helm in the company there are bound to be changes.* <Refers to the helm of a ship>.

help

—**give** *or* **lend (someone) a (helping) hand** *see* **hand**.

hen

—**like a hen on a hot girdle** very nervous and restless: *She was like a hen on a hot girdle waiting for the telephone to ring.*

here

—**neither here nor there** of no importance: *It's neither here nor there whether he comes or not.*

—**the hereafter** life after death: *He does not believe in the hereafter.*

herring

—**a red herring** a piece of information which misleads (someone) or draws (someone's) attention away from the truth, often introduced deliberately: *She told the police that she had seen a man at the door of the burgled house but it proved to be a red herring.* <A red herring is a strong-smelling fish whose scent could mislead hunting dogs if it were dragged across the path they were pursuing>.

—**neither fish nor fowl nor good red herring** neither one thing nor the other: *He has lived in so many parts of the country that his accent is neither fish nor fowl, nor good red herring.*

—**packed like herring in a barrel**: very tightly packed: *The audience were packed like herring in a barrel at the pop concert.*

hide

—**hide one's light under a bushel** *see* **light**.

—**neither hide nor hair of (someone** *or* **something)** no trace at all of (someone or something): *The police searched for the missing prisoner but they could find nether hide nor hair of him.*

—**on a hiding to nothing** in a situation where one cannot possibly win: *She wants to be a vet but she's on a hiding to nothing because she hasn't the academic ability.* <Perhaps a reference to boxing>.

—**tan (someone's) hide** to beat or thrash (someone): *The boy's father threatened to tan his hide if he got into trouble at school again.* <Refers to leather-making>.

high

—**a high flier** a person who is bound to be very successful or who has achieved great success: *She was one of the high fliers in our year at university.*

—**be for the high jump** to be about to be punished or scolded: *You're for the high jump when your mother sees that torn jacket.*

—**be high time** to be time something was done without delay: *It is high time you cut the grass.*

—**be** *or* **get on one's high horse** to be or become offended in a haughty manner: *She gets on her high horse if you ask her to do some typing. She says she is a personal assistant.*

—**high and mighty** arrogant: *Since he became rich he's so high and mighty he won't speak to his former neighbours.*

—**high spot** an exceptionally good part of something: *One of the high spots of their holiday was their visit to Rome.*

—**hunt** *or* **search high and low for (someone** *or* **something)** to search absolutely everywhere for (someone or something): *I've hunted high and low for my address book but in vain.*

—**leave (someone) high and dry** to leave (someone) in a difficult or helpless state: *His secretary walked out and left him and dry in middle of the busiest time of year.*

—**riding high** very successful: *The firm was riding high until the recession began.* <Used literally of the moon being high in the sky>.

—**run high** of feelings, tempers, etc, to be extremely angry, agitated, etc: *Feelings ran high among the crowd when the police arrested the young boy.* <Refers to the sea when there is a strong current and high waves>.

hill

—**old as the hills** *see* **old**.

—**over the hill** past one's youth or one's best: *In that firm you're over the hill at 35.*

hilt

—**armed to the hilt** *see* **armed**.

—**back (someone) to the hilt** to support (someone) totally: *Her parents backed her to the hilt when she decided to have the baby.* <Refers to the hilt of a sword>.

hind

—**devil take the hindmost** *see* **devil**.

history

—**be history** to be past, to be no longer relevant or important: *I know he has a police record but that's history. It happened when he was a youth.*

—**make history** to do something remarkable that will be remembered in the future: *He made medical history by performing the first heart transplant.*

hit

—**a smash hit** *see* **smash**.

—**be a hit with (someone)** to be popular with (someone): *The magician was a real hit with the children at the party.*

—**hit a bad patch** *see* **bad**.

—**hit a man when he's down** to attack someone who is already suffering from some misfortune: *His wife left him just after he lost his job. She really knows how to hit a man when he's down.*

—**hit-and-run accident** an accident involving a vehicle where the driver who caused it does not stop or report the accident: *The little girl was killed in a hit-and-run accident.*

—**hit it off** to get on well, to become friendly: *I knew they would hit it off. They have so much in common.*

—**hit the ceiling** *or* **roof** *see* **ceiling**.

—**hit the hay** *or* **sack** *see* **hay**.

—**hit the headlines** *see* **head**.

—**hit the jackpot** *see* **jackpot**.

—**hit the mark** *see* **mark**.

—**hit the nail on the head** *see* **nail**.

—**hit the road** *see* **road**.

Hobson

—**Hobson's choice** *see* **choice**.

hog

—**go the whole hog** to do something completely and thoroughly: *We decorated one room and then decided to go the whole hog and do the whole house.* <Perhaps referring to buying a whole pig for meat rather than just parts of it>.

hoist

—**hoist with one's own petard** *see* **petard**.

hold

—**hang on** *or* **hold on like grim death** *see* **grim**.

—**have a hold over (someone)** to have power or influence over (someone): *I think the old man has some kind of hold over him. He always does what he says.*

—**hold (something) against (someone)** to dislike (someone) because of (something) he or she has done: *He always held it against her that she had her child adopted.*

—**hold a pistol to (someone's) head** *see* **pistol**.

—**hold forth** to talk for a long time forcefully or pompously: *The lecturer held forth on his views on the political situation.*

—**hold good** to be valid or applicable: *The rules that applied last year hold good this year.*

—**hold one's breath** *see* **breath**.

—**hold one's head up (high)** *see* **head**.

—**hold one's horses** *see* **horse**.

—**hold one's own** *see* **own**.

—**hold one's tongue** *see* **tongue**.

—**hold out on (someone)** not to tell (someone):

He's been holding out on us. He's engaged to be married.

—**hold the fort** *see* **fort**.

—**no holds barred** no restrictions on what is permitted: *It was a case of no holds barred in the election campaign. All the candidates criticized their opponents savagely.*

hole

—**hole-and-corner** secret and often dishonourable: *Their romance is a hole-and-corner affair because she is married.*

—**in a hole** in an awkward or difficult situation: *They're in a real hole. They've lost their return plane tickets.*

—**make a hole in (something)** to use a large part of (something): *Holding the party left a huge hole in our supply of wine.*

—**need (something) like (someone) needs a hole in the head** to regard (something) as being completely unwelcome or undesirable: *The firm needs a strike at the moment like they need a hole in the head.*

—**pick holes in (something)** to find faults in (a theory, plan, etc): *He had no suggestions of his own but he picked holes in mine.*

—**talk through a hole in one's head** *same as* **talk through the back of one's head** *see* **back**.

holy

—**holier-than-thou** acting as though one is more moral, more pious, etc, than other people: *She is so holier-than-thou that you wouldn't believe that she once spent a night in the police cells.* <A biblical reference to Isaiah 65.5>.

—**the holy of holies** a private or special place inside a building: *That's her father's study. It's the holy of holies in their house.* <A literal translation of the the Hebrew name of the inner sanctuary in the Jewish Temple where the Ark of the Covenant was kept>.

home

—**a home from home** a place where one feels comfortable and relaxed: *Our holiday accommodation was a home from home.*

—**bring** *or* **drive (something) home to (someone)** to cause someone fully to understand or believe (something): *Their mother's illness really brought home to them how much they relied on her.*

—**do one's homework** to prepare thoroughly for a meeting, etc, by getting all the necessary information: *You will have to do your homework if you are going to win that export order.*

—**feel at home** to feel comfortable and relaxed:

She's from Italy originally but she feels completely at home here now.

—**home and dry** having successfully completed an objective: *I didn't think we'd get the contract but it's just been signed so we're home and dry.*

—**home truth** a plain, direct statement of something that is true but unpleasant or difficult for someone to accept: *I told her a few home truths about how his behaviour was affecting the family.*

—**make oneself at home** to make oneself comfortable and relaxed: *Make yourself at home while I prepare the meal.*

—**nothing to write home about** not very special, not remarkable: *The food in the hotel was all right but nothing to write home about.*

—**romp home** to win easily: *Our candidate romped home to win the election by a huge majority.* <Refers to horse-racing>.

—**till** *or* **until the cows come home** *see* **cow**.

honour

—**do the honours** *see* **do**.

hook

—**by hook or by crook** by any means possible: *She's says she'll get to the party by hook or by crook although she has no transport.*

—**off the hook** free from some difficulty, problem, etc, or something one does not want to do: *I didn't want to go to the party and my friend let me off the hook by asking me to baby-sit.* <A reference to angling>.

—**sling one's hook** to go away: *Why don't you sling your hook and leave us alone?*

—**swallow (something) hook, line and sinker** to believe (something) completely: *His story was obviously untrue but she swallowed it hook, line and sinker.* <Refers to a fish that swallows not only the hook but the whole of the end section of the fishing line>.

hoop

—put (someone) through the hoop to cause (someone) to experience something unpleasant or difficult: *The interviewers certainly put the candidates through the hoop by asking searching questions.* <Refers to circus performers who jump through hoops set on fire>.

hop

—**catch (someone) on the hop** to find (someone) unprepared: *My guests arrived early and caught me on the hop without the meal ready.*

—**hopping mad** extremely angry: *He was hopping mad when his new car broke down.*

—**keep (someone) on the hop** to keep (someone) busy or active: *Her grandchildren keep her on the hop.*

hope

—**great white hope** someone or something that is expected to bring victory, fame, glory, etc, to a group: *We have won nothing so far but the youngest member of the team is our great white hope in the 100 metres race.* <Refers originally to a white boxer attempting to defeat a black boxer, black boxers often being the champions>.

—**have high hopes of (something)** to be extremely hopeful of success in (something): *He has high hopes of getting into university.*

—**hope against hope** to continue to hope although there is little reason to be hopeful: *She is seriously ill but they are hoping against hope that she will recover completely.*

—**hope springs eternal (in the human breast)** it is of the nature of human beings to hope: *So far he doesn't have a job but hope springs eternal (in the human breast).* <Refers to a quotation from Alexander Pope's poem *An Essay on Criticism*>.

—**pin one's hopes on (someone or something)** to rely on (someone or something) helping one in some way: *They have no money and they're pinning their hopes on the horse they backed winning.*

horn

—**draw in one's horns** to restrain one's actions, particularly the spending of money: *Now that they have a child they will have to draw in their horns.* <Refers to a snail drawing in its horns if it is in danger>.

—**horn in on (something)** to join in on (something) uninvited and unwanted: *She's trying to horn in on the organization of the party.*

—**lock horns** to argue or fight: *It wasn't long before the new boss and the union leader locked horns*: <Refers to horned male animals who sometimes get their horns caught together when fighting>.

—**on the horns of a dilemma** *see* **dilemma**.

hornet

—**stir up a hornet's nest** to cause a great deal of trouble: *The headmaster stirred up a hornet's nest when he suggested changing the school uniform.*

horse

—**a horse of a different colour** *see* **colour**[1].
—**back the wrong horse** to show support for the person, side, plan, etc, that turns out to be the loser in some way: *You backed the wrong horse*

when you appointed him treasurer. He's hopeless with money.

—**be** *or* **get on one's high horse** *see* **high**.

—**change horses in mid-stream** *see* **change**.

—**dark horse** *see* **dark**.

—**eat like a horse** to eat a great deal: *Like most teenage boys he eats like a horse.*

—**flog a dead horse** to continue to try to arouse interest, enthusiasm, etc, in something which is obviously not, or no longer, of interest: *He's trying to sell life insurance to his neighbours but he's flogging a dead horse. An agent from another firm has already been round the area.*

—**hold one's horses** not to move so fast: *Hold your horses! I haven't agreed to your plan yet.*

—**horse sense** common sense, practicability: *She has no specialist knowledge of the business but she has horse sense.*

—**horses for courses** certain people are better suited to certain tasks or situations: *He's good at planning things and she is good at putting plans into action. It's a case of horses for courses.* <Some horses run better on certain types of ground>.

—**lock the stable door after the horse has bolted** *see* **stable**.

—**look a gift horse in the mouth** *see* **gift**.

—**put the cart before the horse** *see* **cart**.

—**straight from the horse's mouth** from someone closely connected with a situation and therefore knowledgeable about it: *I got it straight from the horse's mouth. She told me herself she was leaving.* <As though a horse is giving a tip about a race in which it is running>.

—**wild horses would not drag (someone) to something** *or* **somewhere** nothing would persuade (someone) to attend something or go somewhere: *Wild horses wouldn't drag me to his party. I loathe him.*

—**willing horse** someone who is keen to work or help: *She is chairman of the organizing committee but it's the willing horses who do all the work.*

—**you can take a horse to the water but you cannot make it drink** you can encourage someone to do something but you cannot force him or her to do it: *You can get the university prospectuses for your son, but after that it's for him to decide. You can take a horse to water but you can't make it drink.*

hot

—**blow hot and cold** *see* **blow**.
—**hot air** *see* **air**.

—**hot line** a direct telephone line for use in emergencies: *The two leaders have spoken on the hot line.*

—**hot on (someone's) heels** close behind (someone): *She arrived and then hot on her heels he rushed in.*

—**hot potato** something which it is difficult or dangerous to deal with: *The complaint about faulty goods is a hot potato. Pass it to the manager.*

—**hot under the collar** angry or agitated: *He got very hot under the collar when she refused to believe him.*

—**in hot water** in trouble: *The boy will be in hot water when his father sees the damage he caused.*

—**in the hot seat** in a position where one has responsibility for important and difficult issues: *The acting manager director is in the hot seat now.*

—**like a cat on hot bricks** *see* **cat**.

—**make it** *or* **things hot for (someone)** to make a situation unpleasant or impossible for (someone): *You might as well leave. He'll just make things hot for you if you stay.*

—**piping hot** very hot: *I like soup to be piping hot.*

—**sell** *or* **go like hot cakes** *see* **cake**.

hour

—**after hours** during the period when a shop, etc, would be normally be shut for business: *The pub owner has been selling alcohol after hours.*

—**all hours** *see* **all**.

—**at the eleventh hour** *see* **eleven**.

—**put off the evil hour** *see* **evil**.

—**the (wee) small hours** the hours immediately following midnight (1 a.m, 2 a.m, etc): *They danced until the wee small hours.*

—**the witching hour** midnight: *It's time we went home. It's the witching hour.* <Witches traditionally are supposed to be active at midnight>.

house

—**bring the house down** to cause great amusement or applause: *The comedian's jokes brought the house down.*

—**eat (someone) out of house and home**: to eat a great deal and so be expensive to feed: *When all the grandchildren stayed with their grandparents they ate them out of house and home.*

—**get on like a house on fire** *see* **fire**.

—**keep open house** always to be ready and willing to welcome guests: *Why don't you pay them a visit. They keep open house.*

—**on the house** paid by the owner of shop, pub, etc: *The drinks are on the house to celebrate the birth of the baby.*

—**put one's house in order** to make sure that one's affairs are well arranged and organized: *His will is perfectly legal. He put his house in order before his death.*

—**safe as houses** completely safe: *The children will be safe as houses with their grandmother.*

hue

—**a hue and cry** a loud protest: *There was a hue and cry about the council's proposal to close the local school.* <An old legal term meaning a summons for people to join in a hunt for a criminal>.

humble

—**eat humble pie** to have to admit that one has been wrong: *He had to eat humble pie when his wife passed her driving test. He said she wasn't good enough.* <Refers originally to a dish made from the umble or offal of a deer eaten by the lower classes>.

hunt

—**hunt high and low for (someone** *or* **something)** *see* **high**.

—**run with the hare and hunt with the hounds** *see* **hare**.

I

i

—**dot the i's and cross the t's** *see* **dot**.

ice

—**break the ice** to ease the shyness or formality of a social occasion: *The baby's laughter broke the ice at the lunch party*.

—**cut no ice** to have no effect: *His charm cut no ice with her mother*.

—**icing on the cake** a desirable but unnecessary addition: *The garden's the icing on the cake. It's the size of the house that matters*.

—**on ice** put aside for future use or attention: *Our expansion plans will have to be put on ice*.

—**(skate) on thin ice** (to be) in a risky or dangerous position: *You're skating on thin ice by criticizing his sister*.

—**the tip of the iceberg** a small sign of a much larger problem: *Painting the new house will cost about £1000 and that's the tip of the iceberg—we need new carpets and curtains*. <Refers to the fact that the bulk of an iceberg is hidden underwater>.

ill

—**ill-gotten gains** possessions acquired dishonestly: *He got her jewels from her by blackmail and then sold his ill-gotten gains* .

—**it's an ill wind** (that blows nobody any good) in almost every misfortune there is something of benefit to someone: *There was an accident on the road and we might have been involved in it if the car hadn't broken down. It's an ill wind*.

—**take (something) ill out** to be offended or annoyed at (something): *She took it ill out that we hadn't invited her*.

image

—**be the spitting image of** *or* **the spit and image of (someone** *or* **something)** *see* **spit**.

imagination

—**a figment of one's imagination** something which has no reality: *His cottage in the country is a figment of his imagination*.

immemorial

—**from time immemorial** from a time beyond anyone's memory, written records, etc; for an extremely long time: *The family has lived in the village from time immemorial*. <In legal phraseology the expression means "before the beginning of legal memory">.

in

—**be in for (something)** to be likely to experience (something, often something unpleasant): *The sky looks as if we're in for a storm*.

—**be in on (something)** to be involved in (something), to know about (something): *Not many were in on the secret*.

—**be in with (someone)** to be friendly with or in favour with (someone): *She's in with the boss*.

—**have it in for (someone)** *see* **have**.

—**the ins and outs of (something)** the details of (something): *I don't know the ins and outs of their disagreement*.

inch

—**be** *or* **come within an inch of (something)** to be or come very close to: *He came within an inch of being killed by the falling chimney*.

—**every inch a** *or* **the (something)** exactly the type of (something): *The old man is every inch a gentleman*.

—**give (someone) an inch (and he** *or* **she will take a mile** *or* **an ell)** if someone yields in any way to (someone) he or she will make even greater demands: *If you give him an extra day to write his essay he will expect an extra week next time. Give him an inch and he'll take a mile*. <An ell is an old form of measurement>.

Indian

—**an Indian summer** a time of fine, warm weather in autumn: *I've put away all my light clothes but we are having an Indian summer*. <Perhaps from a feature of the climate of North America whose original inhabitants were Indians>.

innings

—**have a good innings** to enjoy a considerable period of life, success etc: *To die at 90 is to have had a good innings*. <Refers to the batting turn of a player or team in cricket>.

insult

—**add insult to injury** *see* **add**.

interest

—**a vested interest in (something)** a personal and biased interest in (something): *She has a* *vested interest in campaigning against the proposed new pub. It would be competition for hers.*

—**in an interesting condition** pregnant: *She's not drinking alcohol because she's in an interesting condition.*

—**with interest** to an even greater extent than something has been done, etc, to someone: *He returned his insults with interest.*

iron

—**have many** or **several irons in the fire** to be involved in several projects, etc, at the same time: *One of his firms has gone bankrupt but he has several irons in the fire.* < Refers to a blacksmith who heats pieces of iron before shaping them>.

—**rule (someone** or **something) with a rod of iron** to rule with the sternness or ruthlessness. *All the children are scared of the head teacher. She rules them with a rod of iron.*

—**strike while the iron is hot** to act at a point at which things are favourable to one: *Your father is in a good mood. Why don't you strike while the iron is hot and ask him for a loan now.* <Refers to a blacksmith's work>.

—**the iron hand in the velvet glove** sternness or ruthlessness hidden under an appearance of gentleness: *Her father looks very kindly but he frequently beats his children. It's a case of the iron hand in the velvet glove.*

—**the iron horse** railway engines or trains: *Travel was much more difficult before the invention of the iron horse.*

itch

—**be itching to (do something)** to want very much to (do something): *He was itching to slap the naughty little boy.*

—**have an itching palm** to be greedy for money: *The shopkeeper always overcharges—she's got an itching palm.*

ivory

—**live in an ivory tower** to have a way of life protected from difficulty or unpleasantness: *The writer lives in an ivory tower. He doesn't realize how badly off his family are.* <*La toure d'ivoire*, French for "ivory tower", was coined by the poet Charles Augustin Saint-Beuve in 1837>.

—**tickle the ivories** to play the piano: *There's a man in the pub who likes to tickle the ivories.* <The keys of a piano are made of ivory>.

J

jack, Jack

—**a jack of all trades (and master of none)** someone who can do several different kinds of job (but does not do any of them very well): *He's their gardener as well as their plumber. He's a jack of all trades.*

—**a jack in office** a pompous, dictatorial official: *That jack in office says that we will have to fill in all the forms again.*

—**all work and no play makes Jack a dull boy** *see* **work**.

—**before you can say Jack Robinson** extremely rapidly: *Your mother will be home before you can say Jack Robinson.*

—**every man jack** absolutely everyone: *Every man jack of you must attend tomorrow.* <Perhaps from the fact that Jack is a very common first name>.

—**I'm all right, Jack** my situation is satisfactory, the implication being that it does not matter about anyone else: *The manager has got a pay increase and it's a case of I'm all right Jack. He's not bothered about the workers' pay.*

jackpot

—**hit the jackpot** to have a great success, often involving a large sum of money: *He hit the jackpot when he married the boss's daughter.* <Refers to the pool of money in poker>.

jam

—**jam tomorrow** the promise of better things in the future: *Governments often promise jam tomorrow but many people would prefer some improvements now.* <From a statement by the Red Queen in *Alice Through the Looking-Glass* by Lewis Carroll>.

—**money for jam** or **old rope** *see* **money**.

—**want jam on it** to want an even better situation, etc, than one has already: *She should be glad that she has a well-paid job but she wants jam on it. She wants longer holidays.* <Refers to asking for jam on bread when bread is quite sufficient>.

Jekyll

—**a Jekyll and Hyde** someone with two completely different sides to his or her personality: *One day he is charming, the next he is very rude. He's a real Jekyll and Hyde.* <Refers to the character in *The Strange Case of Dr Jekyll and Mr Hyde*, a novel by Robert Louis Stevenson>.

Jeremiah

—**a Jeremiah** a pessimist: *My neighbour's a Jeremiah who says that the economic situation is going to get even worse.* <A biblical reference to the Lamentations of Jeremiah>.

jet

—**the jet set** wealthy people who can afford to travel a great deal. <Refers to jet planes>.

job

—**a good job** *see* **good**.

—**a job lot** a mixed collection: *The furniture in the flat is a real job lot.* <Refers to auctioneering>.

—**a put-up job** *see* **put**.

—**give (something) up as a bad job** to stop doing (something) because one has little hope of success: *I tried to persuade her to stay but I eventually gave it up as a bad job.*

—**have a job** to have difficulty: *If you're trying to get a contribution from her you'll have a job. She's incredibly mean.*

—**just the job** exactly what is required: *This cold drink is just the job in this heat.*

—**jobs for the boys** employment given to friends or supporters: *As soon as he got elected he gave appointments to most of his campaign committee—a clear case of jobs for the boys.*

—**make the best of a bad job** to obtain the best results possible from something unsatisfactory: *The house is in a terrible state of disrepair but we'll just have to make the best of a bad job and paint it.*

Job

—**a Job's comforter** someone who brings no comfort at all but makes one feel worse: *She supposedly came to cheer me up but she was a real Job's comforter and told me how ill I looked.* <A biblical reference to the friends of Job>.

—**enough to try the patience of Job** so irritating as to make the most patient of people angry: *Their deliberate lack of cooperation was enough to try the patience of Job.* <A biblical reference to

Job who had to suffer many misfortunes patiently>.

jockey

—**jockey for position** to try to manoeuvre oneself into a favourable or advantageous position: *Very few people will be promoted and ambitious members of staff are jockeying for position.*

Joe

—**Joe Bloggs** *or* **Public** *or* **Soap** the ordinary, average person: *Some politicians only bother about what Joe Bloggs thinks at election times.*

join

—**if you can't beat them** *or* **'em join them** *or* **'em** *see* **beat**.

—**join the club** *see* **club**.

joint

—**case the joint** to inspect premises carefully, especially with a view to later burglary: *They weren't window-cleaners at all. They were burglars casing the joint.*

—**put (someone's) nose out of joint** *see* **nose**.

joke

—be no joke to be a serious matter: *It was no joke when we missed the last bus.*

—**beyond a joke** no longer amusing, rather serious or annoying: *His remarks about women drivers are beyond a joke.*

—**crack a joke** to make a funny remark, to tell a funny story: *The comedian cracked a series of bad jokes.*

Jonah

—a Jonah someone who brings bad luck: *His workmates regard him as a Jonah. Things always go wrong when he's around.* <a biblical reference to the book of Jonah, Jonah 1:4-7>.

Jones

—**keep up with the Joneses** to make an effort to remain on the same social level as one's neighbours by buying what they have, etc: *Their neighbours are going to Florida, so they'll be going next year. They spend their time keeping up with the Joneses.*

jowl

—**cheek by jowl** *see* **cheek**.

joy

—**full of the joys of spring** very happy and

cheerful: *She was full of the joys of spring when she was planning her holiday.*

—**no joy** no success, no luck: *We looked for the missing glove but no joy.*

—**wish (someone) joy of (something)** *see* **wish**.

juice

—**stew in one's juice** to suffer because of one's own foolish actions: *She'll just have to stew in her own juice. She shouldn't have left her husband.*

jump

—**a jumping-off point** a place from which to begin: *We have to start the investigation somewhere. This is as good a jumping-off point as any.*

—**be for the high jump** *see* **high**.

—**be** *or* **stay one jump ahead** to be or keep slightly ahead of someone or something in some way: *Both of them are looking for clues but the policeman is one jump ahead of the private investigator.*

—**jump down (someone's) throat** *see* **throat**.

—**jump on the bandwagon** *see* **band**.

—**jump out of one's skin** *see* **skin**.

—**jump the gun** *see* **gun**.

—**jump the queue** *see* **queue**.

—**jump to it** hurry up: *Jump to it! You're going to be late.*

jungle

—**the law of the jungle** *see* **law**.

just

—**get one's just deserts** *see* **desert**.

—**just so** very neatly arranged: *She likes everything in her kitchen to be just so.*

—**just the job** *see* **job**.

justice

—**do (someone** *or* **something) justice** (1) to show the true value of (someone or something): *The photograph doesn't do justice to her beauty.* (2) to eat (a meal, etc) with a good appetite: *I really couldn't do justice to the dessert. I had eaten too much meat.*

—**do justice to oneself** to behave in a way that is worthy of one's ability: *The pupil didn't do justice to himself in the exam.*

—**poetic justice** *see* **poetic**.

K

keel

—get *or* keep on an even keel *see* even.

keen

—keen as mustard *see* mustard.

keep

—bear *or* keep (something) in mind *see* bear.

—for keeps permanently: *She's gone abroad for keeps.*

—keep a level head *or* keep one's head *see* head.

—keep an open mind *see* open.

—keep (someone) at arm's length *see* arm.

—keep in with (someone) to remain friendly with (someone) or in (someone's) favour: *She keeps in with her aunt because the old lady is wealthy.*

—keep it up to carry on doing something as well as one is doing it: *There's been an improvement in your work—keep it up.* <Perhaps from the game of shuttlecock the aim of which was to keep the shuttlecock in the air>.

—keep on at (someone) to urge (someone) constantly to do something, to nag (someone): *She kept on at him to get a new car.*

—keep one's chin up *see* chin.

—keep one's cool *see* cool.

—keep one's distance *see* distance.

—keep one's end up *see* end.

—keep one's hair on *see* hair.

—keep one's hand in *see* hand.

—keep one's head above water *see* head.

—keep one's nose clean *see* clean.

—keep one's own counsel to keep one's opinions, problems, etc, secret: *I thought of telling him about my health fears but decided to keep my own counsel.*

—keep oneself to oneself not to seek the company of others much, to tell others very little about oneself: *Our new neighbours keep themselves very much to themselves.*

—keep one's shirt on *see* shirt.

—keep one's word *see* word.

—keep pace with (someone *or* something) *see* pace.

—keep (someone) posted *see* post[2].

—keep tabs on (someone *or* something) *see* tab.

—keep the peace *see* peace.

—keep the wolf from the door *see* wolf.

—keep time *see* time.

—keep (something) to oneself to keep (something) secret: *The child kept her worries about school to herself.*

—keep *or* lose track of (something) *see* track.

—keep (something) under one's hat *see* hat.

—keep (something) under wraps *see* wrap.

—keep up appearances *see* appear.

—keep up with the Joneses *see* Jones.

ken

—beyond one's ken outside the range of one's knowledge or understanding: *Why he did it is beyond my ken.* <Literally, ken used to mean range of vision>.

kettle

—a different kettle of fish a completely different set of circumstances: *Your previous suggestion was turned down, but your latest one is a completely different kettle of fish.*

—a pretty kettle of fish an awkward or difficult situation: *We're lost without a map. This is a pretty kettle of fish.*

—the pot calling the kettle black *see* pot.

kibosh

—put the kibosh on (something) to spoil or ruin (something's) chances of success: *My broken arm put the kibosh on my holiday plans last year.*

kick

—alive and kicking *see* alive.

—for kicks for thrills or fun: *The children broke the windows for kicks.*

—kick oneself to be annoyed with oneself: *I could have kicked myself when I realized my mistake.*

—kick one's heels *same as* cool one's heels—*see* cool.

—kick (someone) in the teeth *see* teeth.

—kick over the traces to defy rules that control one's behaviour: *Her parents were very strict but she kicked over the traces and eloped.* <Refers to a horse drawing a cart which gets out of control of the driver>.

—kick the bucket *see* bucket.

kid

—**handle (someone** or **something) with kid gloves** to deal with (someone or something) very tactfully or delicately: *The boss is furious. You'll have to handle him with kid gloves today.*

Kilkenny

—**fight like Kilkenny cats** *see* **fight**.

kill

—**curiosity killed the cat** *see* **cat**.

—**kill the fatted calf** *see* **calf**.

—**kill the goose that lays the golden egg** *see* **goose**.

—**kill time** *see* **time**.

—**kill two birds with one stone** *see* **bird**.

—**kill (someone) with kindness** to spoil (someone) to the extent that it is a disadvantage to him or her: *The old lady is killing her dog with kindness by over-feeding it.*

—**make a killing** to make a large profit: *He made a killing when he sold his shop.*

kind1

—**of a kind** of poor quality: *They provided a meal of a kind.*

—**two of a kind** *see* **two**.

kind2

—**kill (someone) with kindness** *see* **kill**.

—**the milk of human kindness** *see* **milk**.

king

—**a cat may look at a king** *see* **cat**.

—**a king's ransom** a vast sum of money: *They paid a king's ransom for that house.*

kingdom

—**till kingdom come** for a very long time: *Those two will gossip until kingdom come.* <Refers to the Lord's Prayer>.

—**to kingdom come** to death: *That bomb would blow us to kingdom come.* <See above>.

kiss

—**kiss of death** something which causes the end, ruin or death of something: *His appointment as managing director was the kiss of death to the firm.* <A biblical reference to the kiss by which Judas betrayed Jesus>.

kite

—**fly a kite** to start a rumour about a new project to see how people would react if the project were put into operation: *I think the rumour going around about moving to a new building is a kite flown by management.* <Refers to the use of kites to discover the direction and strength of the wind>.

kitten

—**have kittens** to get very agitated or angry: *She'll have kittens when she sees the mess in the kitchen.*

knee

—**bring (someone) to his** or **her knees** to humble or ruin (someone): *The workers went on strike but they were brought to their knees by lack of money.* <Refers to going on one's knees to beg for something>.

—**knee-high to a grasshopper** *see* **grasshopper**.

knickers

—**get one's knickers in a twist** to become agitated: *Don't get your knickers in a twist. They'll be here soon.*

knife

—**have one's knife in (someone)** to wish to harm (someone): *He's got his knife in her because she got the job his sister wanted.*

—**on a knife edge** in a very uncertain or risky state: *The financial state of the company is on a knife edge.*

—**the night of the long knives** a time when an act of great disloyalty is carried out, usually by the sudden removal of several people from power or employment: *She went in one morning to discover that she and her team had been sacked. It had been the night of the long knives.* <Refers to 19 June 1934, when the German leader Adolf Hitler had a number of his Nazi colleagues imprisoned or killed>.

knock

—**beat** or **knock the living daylights out of (someone)** *see* **live**.

—**knock (someone) for six** *see* **six**.

—**knock (something) into a cocked hat** *see* **hat**.

—**knock (someone** or **something) into shape** *see* **shape**.

—**knock (something) on the head** *see* **head**.

—**knock spots off (someone)** *see* **spot**.

—**knock the stuffing out of (someone)** *see* **stuff**.

knot

—**at a rate of knots** extremely rapidly: *She's getting through the work at a rate of knots.* <Refers to a method of measuring the speed of ships>.

—**cut the Gordian knot** *see* **Gordian**.

—**tie (oneself** or **someone) in knots** to get (oneself or someone) in a confused state: *The defence lawyer is tying the witness in knots.*

know

—**in the know** knowing facts, etc, that are known only to a small group of people: *Someone in the know told me that he has won.*

—**know all the answers** *see* **answer**.

—know a thing or two *see* thing.

—know (something) backwards *or* like the back of one's hand *see* back.

—know (someone) by sight *see* sight.

—know one's onions *see* onion.

—know one's place *see* place.

—know the ropes *see* rope.

—know the score *see* score.

—know which side one's bread is buttered *see* bread.

—know what's what *see* what.

—know where one stands *see* stand.

—not to know one is born to lead a trouble-free, protected life: *She doesn't know she's born. She has a well-paid job and works very few hours.*

knuckle

—near the knuckle *or* bone *see* bone.

—rap (someone) over the knuckles to scold or criticize (someone): *They were rapped over the knuckles for being rude to customers.*

L

labour

—**a labour of love** a long or difficult job done for one's own satisfaction or from affection for someone rather than for reward: *Ironing all her husband's shirts is a real labour of love.*

la-di-dah

—**la-di-dah** upper-class: *The children laugh at the teacher's la-di-da accent.* <From the supposed sound of upper-class speech>.

lady

—**ladies' man** a man who likes the company of women and tries to charm them: *He rarely goes out with male friends. He's a real ladies' man.*

—**lady bountiful** a rich, generous, and often patronizing woman: *She likes playing lady bountiful to her badly off relatives.* <Refers to a character in George Farquhar's play, *The Beaux' Stratagem*>.

—**lady-killer** a man who likes going out with women: *He still goes out with other women even now that they are married. He always was a lady-killer.*

lamb

—**(someone's) ewe lamb** *see* **ewe**.

—**in two shakes of a lamb's tail** *see* **shake**.

—**like a lamb to the slaughter** meekly, without arguing or resisting, often because unaware of danger or difficulty: *Young soldiers went to fight in World War I like lambs to the slaughter.* <A biblical reference to Isaiah 53:7>.

—**(someone) might as well be hanged for a sheep as a lamb** *see* **sheep**.

—**mutton dressed as lamb** *see* **mutton**.

lame

—**a lame duck** *see* **duck**.

—**help a lame dog over a stile** to give help to someone in difficulties: *The old lady has very little money but she's always helping lame dogs over stiles.*

lamp

—**smell of the lamp** of a piece of writing, to show signs of research and revision rather than originality: *He doesn't show much creativity in his essays. They smell of the lamp.*

land

—**a land of milk and honey** a place where life is pleasant, with plenty of food and possibilities of success: *The refugees saw their new country as a land of milk and honey.* <A biblical reference to the Promised Land of the Israelites described in Exodus 3:8>.

—**cloud cuckoo land** *see* **cloud**.

—**fall** *or* **land on one's feet** *see* **feet**.

—**live off the fat of the land** *see* **fat**.

—**see how the land lies** to look carefully at a situation before taking any action or decision: *I don't know how long I'll stay with my friends. I'll see how the land lies.* <Refers literally to sailors looking at the shore before landing>.

—**the land of Nod** *see* **nod**.

lane

—**it's a long lane that has no turning** every period of misfortune, unhappiness, etc, comes to an end or changes to happier circumstances eventually: *He'll find happiness one day. It's a long lane that has no turning.*

language

—**speak the same language** to have similar tastes and views: *It's good to meet someone who speaks the same language.*

lap

—**drop into (someone's) lap** *see* **drop**.

—**in the lap of luxury** in luxurious conditions: *Film-stars usually live in the lap of luxury.*

—**in the lap of the gods** *see* **god**.

large

—**large as life** in person, actually present: *We had just been asking where he was when he came in large as life.* <From works of art, particularly sculptural, which are life-size>.

—**larger than life** extraordinary, behaving, etc, in an extravagant way: *He is very quiet and shy but his wife is larger than life.*

lark

—**get up** *or* **rise with the lark** to rise very early in the morning: *We got up with the lark to catch the train.*

—**happy as a lark** *see* **happy**.

last[1]

—**as a** *or* **in the last resort** when all other methods have failed: *In the last resort you can sell your house to pay your debts.*

—**at one's last gasp** *see* **gasp**.

—**breathe one's last** *see* **breathe**.

—**have the last laugh** *see* **laugh**.

—**have the last word** to make the last or decisive statement in an argument, etc: *His wife always has to have the last word*.

—**on one's** *or* **its last legs** near to collapse: *The factory is on its last legs after losing a major order*.

—**the last straw** same as **the straw that breaks the camel's back**—*see* **straw**.

—**the last word** the most fashionable or up-to-date example of something: *He has the last word in recording equipment*.

last²

—**stick to one's last** to continue to do the job that one is experienced in: *He's a computer specialist and he should stick to his last rather than try to become a journalist*. <From the sayin, "The cobbler should stick to his last", literally, a shoemaker should concern himself only with making or mending shoes>.

late

—**better late than never** better for something to arrive, happen, etc, late than never to do so at all: *He arrived at midnight but that was better late than never*.

—**late in the day** when a project, activity, etc, is well advanced: *It's a bit late in the day to propose changes to the scheme*.

laugh

—**have the last laugh** to be victorious or proved right in the end, especially after being scorned, criticized, etc: *His neighbours teased him for entering the garden competition, but he had the last laugh when he won it*. <From the saying that he who laughs last laughs longest>.

—**laugh and the world laughs with you (weep and you weep alone)** when someone is cheerful or happy, other people share in his or her joy (but when he or she is sad or miserable, people tend to avoid him or her): *His friends all went to see him when he won the prize, but the year when he came last in the compeition, no one went near him. Laught and the world laughs with you, weep and you weep alone*.

—**laugh like a drain** *or* **laugh one's head off** to laugh very loudly: *They laughed like a drain when the bully tripped and fell*.

—**laugh on the other side of one's face** to suffer disappointment or misfortune after seeming to be successful or happy: *They were sure his side had won but they laughed on the other side of their faces when the opposing side scored a late goal*.

—**laugh (someone** *or* **something) out of court** *see* **court**.

—**laugh up one's sleeve** to be secretly amused: *She thought she was impressing them but they were laughing up their sleeves at her*.

—**no laughing matter** a very serious matter: *His playing truant is no laughing matter*.

laurel

—**look to one's laurels** to be careful not to lose one's position or reputation because of better performances by one's rivals: *The champion had better look to her laurels. The new young tennis player is very good.* <A reference to to the laurel wreath with which the ancient Greeks crowned their poets and victors>.

—**rest on one's laurels** to be content with past successes without trying for any more: *The firm used to have a good reputation but it has been resting on its laurels for too long*. <Another reference to the Greek laurel wreath>.

law

—**be a law unto oneself** to behave as one wishes rather than obeying the usual rules and conventions: *He was the only one not wearing evening dress but then he's always a law unto himself*.

—**lay down the law** to state one's opinions with great force, to give orders dictatorially: *Her father lays the law down about which friends she should see*.

—**take the law into one's own hands** to take action against a crime or injustice witnout involving the police or courts: *The villagers took the law into their own hands and nearly killed the child's murderer*.

—**the law of the jungle** the unofficial rules for survival or success in a dangerous or difficult situation where civilized laws are not effective: *He's beating him up because he raped his sister. The law of the jungle applies in these parts*.

—**the letter of the law** *see* **letter**.

—**the long arm of the law** *see* **arm**.

lay

—**lay (something) at (someone's) door** *see* **door**.

—**lay down one's arms** *see* **arm**.

—**lay it on the line** *see* **line**.

—**lay it on thick** *or* **lay it on with a trowel** to exaggerate greatly in one's praise, compliments, etc, to someone: *He was laying it on with a trowel when he was telling her how beautiful she was*.

—lay (someone) low to make (someone) ill: *He's been laid low by a stomach bug.*

—lay odds *see* **odd**.

—lay *or* **put (something) on the line** *see* **line**.

—lay waste *see* **waste**.

—lay oneself (wide) open to (something) *see* **open**.

lead¹

—a leading question a question asked in such a way as to suggest the answer the questioner wants to hear: *The defence counsel asked his witness a series of leading questions.*

—lead (someone) by the nose *see* **nose**.

—leading light an important person in a certain group, field, etc: *She's one of the leading lights of the local dramatic society.*

—lead the way *see* **way**.

—lead (someone) up the garden path *see* **garden**.

lead²

—swing the lead to avoid doing one's work, usually by inventing deceitful excuses: *He said the soil was too dry to dig but he knew he was swinging the lead.* <Originally an expression from naval slang>.

leaf

—take a leaf out of (someone's) book to use (someone) as an example: *You should take a leaf out of your sister's book and start doing some work.*

—turn over a new leaf to change one's behaviour, etc, for the better: *He was wild as a teenager but he's turned over a new leaf now.*

league

—be in league with (someone) to have joined together with (someone), usually for a bad purpose: *He was in league with the men who broke into the shop.*

—not be in the same league as (someone) not to be as able as (someone): *The new teacher's not in the same league as our previous one.* <Refers to the grouping of clubs in soccer, etc, according to ability>.

lean

—lean on (someone) to use force on (someone) to persuade him or her to do something: *They must have leant on him to get him to give them an alibi.*

—lean over backwards *same as* **bend over backwards**—*see* **back**.

leap

—a leap in the dark an action or decision the results of which cannot be foreseen: *It's foolish to take a leap in the dark and emigrate to a new country without a job.*

—by leaps and bounds very quickly or successfully: *The children are progressing by leaps and bounds in their new school.*

—look before you leap *see* **look**.

lease

—give (someone *or* **something) a new lease of life** to cause (someone) to have a longer period of active life or usefulness or to have a happier or more interesting life: *Her hip operation has given the old lady a new lease of life.*

leash

—strain at the leash to be impatient or very eager to do something: *The children were straining at the leash to get out to play.* <Refers to a dog on a leash straining to get its freedom>.

least

—least said soonest mended the less one says in a difficult situation the less harm will be done: *I was so angry that I wanted to tell her what I thought of her but least said soonest mended.*

leave

—leave (someone) in the lurch to leave (someone) in a difficult or dangerous situation without any help: *She walked out and left her husband in the lurch with three young children.* <A lurch refers to a position at the end of certain games, such as cribbage, in which the loser has either lost by a huge margin or scored no points at all>.

—leave *or* **let well alone** to make no change to something that is already reasonably satisfactory: *You've just made the television picture worse by trying to fix it. You should have left well alone.*

—take French leave *see* **French**.

—take it or leave it *see* **take**.

—take leave of one's senses *see* **sense**.

leech

—stick to (someone) like a leech to be constantly with (someone) or constantly to follow (someone): *His new girlfriend sticks to him like a leech. His friends never see him alone.* <Formerly leeches were used in medicine and were stuck firmly to patients to suck blood>.

leeway

—make up leeway to take action to recover from a setback or loss of advantage: *After his illness he had a lot of schoolwork to do in order to catch up on his classmates but he soon made up leeway.* <Leeway refers to the distance a sail-

ing ship is blown sideways off its course by the wind>.

left

—**have two left feet** to be clumsy or awkward with one's feet, e.g. when dancing: *I tried to waltz with him but he has two left feet.*

—**left, right and centre** everywhere, to an extreme degree: *He gives a bad impression of the firm left, right and centre.*

—**(someone's) left hand does not know what his** *or* **her right hand is doing** (someone's) affairs are extremely complicated: *He has so many different business interests that his left hand doesn't know what his right hand is doing.*

leg

—**cost an arm and a leg** *see* **arm**.

—**give (someone) a leg up** to give (someone) some assistance to achieve advancement: *The manager would still be working on the factory floor if the previous manager hadn't given him a leg up.*

—**not to have a leg to stand on** to have no defence or justification for one's actions: *He was drunk when he ran over the old man and he does not have a leg to stand on.*

—**on one's** *or* **its last legs** *see* **last**.

—**pull (someone's) leg** to try as a joke to make (someone) believe something that is not true: *There's not really an escaped lion in the street. He's pulling your leg.*

—**stretch one's legs** to go for a walk: *I'm stiff from sitting in the car for so long. I must stretch my legs.*

legion

—**their name is legion** there are a great many of them: *It's difficult to estimate how many people have applied. Their name is legion.* <A biblical reference to Mark 5:9>.

length

—**go to great lengths** to take absolutely any action in order to achieve what one wants: *He'll go to any lengths to get that job, including bribery.*

leopard

—**the leopard never changes its spots** a person's basic character does not change. *I don't believe that he was acting out of kindness. The leopard never changes his spots.*

let

—**let alone (someone** *or* **something)** not taking into consideration (someone or something): *We haven't really enough room for her, let alone the three children.*

—**let oneself go** (1) to enjoy oneself without restraint: *He seems very formal but he really lets himself go at parties.* (2) to stop taking trouble over one's appearance: *She used to be elegantly dressed but since her husband's death she's let herself go.*

—**let (someone) have it** *see* **have**.

—**let (someone) in on something** to share something secret with (someone): *They let him in on their plans to escape.*

—**let off steam** *see* **steam**.

—**let (something) slip** *see* **slip**.

—**let the grass grow under one's feet** *see* **grass**.

—**let well alone** *same as* **leave well alone**—*see* **leave**.

letter

—**a red-letter day** *see* **red**.

—**the letter of the law** the exact wording of a law, rule, agreement clause: *According to the letter of the law, you are responsible for half the costs of the repairs, but in your financial circumstances, it would be unreasonable of him to expect you to pay it.* <A biblical reference to II Corinthians 3:6>.

—**to the letter** in every detail: *You must follow the instructions to the letter.*

level

—**do one's level best** *see* **best**.

—**find one's** *or* **its (own) level** to find out what situation, position, etc, one is naturally suited to: *There's no point in expecting all the pupils to go to university. Each has to find his or her own level.*

—**on the level** honest, trustworthy: *His father's a crook but he's on the level.*

liberty

—**Liberty Hall** a place where one can do as one pleases: *It's Liberty Hall in their house at the moment. Their parents are abroad for a year.*

—**take liberties with (something)** to treat (something) with too much freedom or with not enough respect: *The writer of the book thought that the makers of the film had taken liberties with her text and had changed the plot totally.*

—**take the liberty of (doing something)** to dare to do (something) without prior permission or without being asked to: *I took the liberty of borrowing a pen from your desk. I hope you don't mind.*

licence

—**poetic licence** *see* **poetic**.

lick

—**a lick and a promise** a quick, not thorough,

wash or clean: *She's given the kitchen floor a lick and a promise.*

—**lick (someone** *or* **something) into shape** to improve (someone or something) greatly to bring up to standard: *The report he wrote was inadequate, but I helped him lick it into shape.* <Refers to an old belief that bear cubs are born shapeless and have to be licked into shape by their mothers>.

—**lick one's lips** *see* **lip**.

lid

—**blow** *or* **take the lid off (something)** to reveal the truth about (something): *The sacked worker blew the lid off the company's tax evasion.*

—**put the (tin) lid on (something)** to finish (something) off usually in an unpleasant way: *The recession put the tin lid on his already failing business.*

lie[1]

—**give the lie to (something)** to show that (something) is untrue: *The letters the police found gave the lie to his denial of the crime.*

—**lie in** *or* **through one's teeth** to tell lies obviously and unashamedly: *He was lying through his teeth when he told the police that he hadn't been near the scene of the crime.*

—**live a lie** to live a way of life about which there is something dishonest: *His wife didn't know that he had committed bigamy and was living a lie.*

—**white lie** *see* **white**.

lie[2]

—**lie heavy on (someone)** to be a burden or source of anxiety to (someone): *The guilt of his crime lay heavy on him.*

—**lie in wait for (someone)** *see* **wait**.

—**lie low** *see* **low**.

—**see how the land lies** *see* **land**.

—**take (something) lying down** to accept an unpleasant situation without protesting or taking action against it: *The workers have been dismissed unfairly but they're not taking it lying down. They're taking it to a tribunal.*

—**the lie of the land** the nature and details of a situation: *Find out the lie of the land before applying for a job with that organization.* <Refers to sailors studying the nature of the coastline>.

life

—**a dog's life** *see* **dog**.

—**a matter of life and death** *see* **matter**.

—**breathe new life into (something)** to make (something) more lively, active or successful: *The club needs new members to breathe new life into it.*

—**come to life** to become active or lively: *The restaurants there don't come to life until late in the evening.*

—**large as life** *see* **large**.

—**for dear life** *or* **for dear life's sake** to a very great extent, very rapidly, hard, etc: *We had to run for dear life to catch the bus.*

—**for the life of me** if my life depended on it: *I can't for the life of me remember his name.*

—**give (someone** *or* **something) a new lease of life** *see* **lease**.

—**have the time of one's life** *see* **time**.

—**lead a charmed life** *see* **charm**.

—**lead a double life** to follow two completely different ways of life, one of which is usually secret and deceitful: *The salesman was leading a double life. He had one wife in London and one in Leeds.*

—**lead** *or* **live the life of Riley** to lead a comfortable and trouble-free life: *She married a rich old man and led the life of Riley.*

—**not on your life** certainly not: *"Are you going to accept that?" "Not on your life."*

—**risk life and limb** to risk death or physical injury, to take extreme risks: *Soldiers know they must risk life and limb in the course of their jobs.*

—**see life** to have wide experience, especially of varying conditions of life: *She certainly sees life as a social worker.*

—**take one's life in one's hands** to take the risk of being killed, injured or harmed: *You take your life in your hands when you cross that road.*

—**the facts of life** the facts about sex or reproduction: *The child is too young to understand the facts of life.*

—**the life and soul of the party** someone who is very lively and amusing on social occasions: *Although she is quite an elderly person, she was the life and soul of the party.*

—**(someone) to the life** exactly like (someone): *The old man's Churchill to the life.*

—**while** *or* **where there's life there's hope** one should not despair of a situation while there is still a possibility of improvement: *The firm is in a pretty bad state financially but while there's life there's hope.*

light[1]

—**according to one's lights** *see* **accord**.

—**bring (something) to light** to reveal or uncover (something): *The police investigation has brought new facts to light.*

—**come to light** to be revealed or uncovered: *New evidence has come to light.*

—**give the green light to (something)** *see* **green**.

—**hide one's light under a bushel** to be modest or silent about one's abilities or talents: *We discovered accidentally that she's a marvellous piano player. She's certainly been hiding her light under a bushel.* <A biblical reference to Matthew 5:15, quoting Christ>.

—**in the cold light of day** when one looks at something practically and calmly: *At the party we planned a world trip but in the cold light of day we realized that we couldn't afford it.*

—**leading light** *see* **lead**.

—**light at the end of the tunnel** possibility of success, happiness, etc, after a long period of suffering, misery etc: *He's been depressed about being unemployed. Now he's been promised a job there is light at the end of the tunnel.*

—**see the light** (1) to understand something after not doing so: *She was having trouble with the maths problem but she suddenly saw the light.* (2) to agree with someone's opinions or beliefs after not doing so: *She laughed at vegetarianism but then she suddenly saw the light.* (3) (*also* **see the light of day**) to come into existence: *I don't think the book he's supposed to be writing will ever see the light.*

—**shed** *or* **throw light on (something)** to make (something) clearer, e.g. by providing more information about it: *Can his parents shed any light on why he ran away?*

—**the light of (someone's) life** the most important person or thing in (someone's) life: *Her dogs are the light of her life.*

light²

—**be light-fingered** to be likely to steal: *Lock your money and jewels away. I think she is light-fingered.*

—**make light of (something)** to treat (something) as unimportant: *He made light of his injury and worked on.*

—**many hands make light work** *see* **hand**.

lightning

—**lightning never strikes twice (in the same place)** the same misfortune is unlikely to occur more than once: *Having been burgled once we're hoping lightning doesn't strike twice.*

—**quick as lightning** *or* **like greased lightning** extremely rapidly: *Quick as lightning he snatched my purse from my hand.*

lily

—**be lily-livered** to be cowardly: *He's lily-livered. He won't accept a challenge to fight.* <Refers to an old belief that the liver had no blood in it>.

—**gild the lily** *see* **gild**.

limb

—**out on a limb** in a risky and often lonely position; having ideas, opinions, etc, different from other people: *He went out on a limb and disagreed publicly with the scientific research of his professor.* <Refers to being stuck in an isolated position on the branch of a tree>.

—**risk life and limb** *see* **life**.

limbo

—**in limbo** in a forgotten or neglected position: *He's in limbo in a small department far from the head office.*

limelight

—**in the limelight** in a situation where one attracts a great deal of public attention: *Leading politicians must get used to being in the limelight.*

limit

—**be the limit** to be as much as, or more than, one can tolerate: *That postman's the limit. He gets later and later.*

—**off limits** beyond what is allowed: *They told him not to go out with their sister but he can't resist someone that's off limits.*

—**the sky's the limit** *see* **sky**.

line

—**all along the line** at every point in an action, process, etc: *All along the line it was obvious that their marriage was in difficulties.*

—**along** *or* **on the lines of (something)** similar to (something): *Our pay scale should be along the lines of that of the other parts of the firm.*

—**be in line for (something)** to be likely to get (something): *He's in line for promotion.*

—**bring (something) into line with (something)** to make (something) the same as or comparable with (something else): *The aim is to bring the agricultural policies of all the countries into line.*

—**draw the line** to fix a limit: *We can't invite everyone. We must draw the line somewhere.*

—**hard lines** *see* **hard**.

—**hot line** *see* **hot**.

—**lay it on the line** to make (something) absolutely clear to someone: *If you want him to understand the seriousness of the position you will have to lay it on the line to him.*

—**lay** *or* **put (something) on the line** to risk losing (something): *He laid his job on the line by supporting the strikers.*

—**line one's pocket** *see* **pocket**.

—**read between the lines** to understand or deduce something from a statement, situation, etc, although this has not actually been stated: *Her family says that she is well but, reading between the lines, I think that she is unlikely to recover.* <Refers to a method of writing secret messages by writing in invisible ink between the lines of other messages>.

—**shoot a line** to to exaggerate or boast about one's abilities, achievements, etc: *Beware of candidates who shoot a line at their interviews.*

—**step out of line** to behave differently from what is usually acceptable or expected: *There's no point in deliberately stepping out of line and wearing jeans to the formal party.* <Refers to a line of soldiers on parade>.

—**take a hard line** *see* **hard**.

—**the line of least resistance** the course of action that will cause one least effort or trouble: *She won't disagree with the rest of the committee. She always takes the line of least resistance.*

—**toe the line** to obey the rules or orders: *The new teacher will soon get the children to toe the line.* <Refers to competitors having to stand with their toes to a line when starting a race, etc>.

linen

—**air** *or* **wash one's dirty linen in public** *see* **air**.

lion

—**beard the lion in its den** *see* **beard**.

—**lion-hunter** a person who tries very hard to become friendly with famous people: *When the actor became famous he tried to avoid lion-hunters.* <Refers to people formerly going to see the lions at the Tower of London as part of the sight-seeing tour of London>.

—**put one's head in the lion's mouth** to put oneself in a very dangerous or difficult position: *She put her head in the lion's mouth by asking her boss for a rise when he had just paid all the bills.*

—**the lion's share** a much larger share than anyone else: *His eldest son got the lion's share of the old man's estate.* <Refers to one of Aesop's fables in which the lion, being a very fierce animal, claimed three quarters of the food which he and other animals had hunted for>.

—**throw (someone) to the lions** deliberately to put (someone) in a in a dangerous or difficult position, often to protect oneself: *They were both responsible for the mistakes, but he threw his colleague to the lions by telling the manager it was*

her fault alone. <Refers to a form of entertainment in ancient Rome in which prisoners were thrown to wild animals to be attacked and killed>.

lip

—**keep a stiff upper lip** to show no emotion, such as fear or disappointment when danger, trouble, etc, arises: *The boy was sad not to receive a present but his father had taught him to keep a stiff upper lip.*

—**lick one's lips** to look forward to something with pleasure: *He was licking his lips at the thought of his holiday cruise.* <A reference to licking one's lips at the thought of appetizing food>.

—**(someone's) lips are sealed** (someone) will not reveal something secret: *I know what he has got you for your birthday but my lips are sealed.*

—**pay lip-service to (something)** to say that one believes in or agrees with (something) without really doing so and without acting as if one did: *She pays lip-service to feminism but she pays her female workers a lot less than her male ones.*

—**there's many a skip 'twixt cup and lip** *see* **slip**.

list

—**enter the lists** to join in a contest or argument: *My father and brother are arguing about holidays and my sister has now entered the lists.*

live[1]

—**beat** *or* **knock the living daylights out of (someone)** to give (someone) a severe beating: *He'll knock the living daylights out of you if he finds out you lost him his job.*

—**live and let live** to get on with one's own life and let other people get on with theirs without one interfering: *I wouldn't complain about my neighbours. I believe in live and let live.*

—**live by one's wits** *see* **wit**.

—**live from hand to mouth** *see* **hand**.

—**live in sin** *see* **sin**.

—**live it up** to have an enjoyable and expensive time: *He was living it up on his trips at the firm's expense.*

—**live like a lord** *see* **lord**.

—**live up to one's reputation** *see* **reputation**.

live[2]

—**a live wire** an energetic, enthusiastic person: *She's a live wire who'll introduce new ideas.* <Refers to a live electrical wire>.

load

—**a loaded question** a question intended to lead

someone into admitting to or agreeing with something when he or she does not wish to do so: *The accused was tricked into admitting his presence at the crime by a loaded question from the prosecuting barrister*. <Refers to a dice loaded or weighted so that it tends always to show the same score>.

loaf

—**half a loaf is better than no bread** *see* **half**.

—**use one's loaf** to use one's brains, to think clearly: *He'll have to use his loaf if he is to do the navigating on our car journey*.

lock

—**lock horns** *see* **lock**.

—**lock, stock and barrel** completely, with everything included: *They are moving overseas lock, stock and barrel*. <Refers to the main components of a gun>.

—**lock the stable door after the horse has bolted** *see* **stable**.

—**under lock and key** in a place which is locked for security: *She keeps her jewels under lock and key*.

log

—**easy as falling off a log** *see* **easy**.

—**sleep like a log** to sleep very soundly: *We slept like logs after our long journey*.

loin

—**gird up one's loins** *see* **gird**.

lone

—**a lone wolf** someone who prefers to be alone: *We asked him to join us on holiday but he went off somewhere by himself. He's a real lone wolf*.

long

—**a long shot** *see* **shot**.

—**be** *or* **get long in the tooth** *see* **tooth**.

—**draw the long bow** *see* **bow**[2].

—**have a long face** *see* **face**.

—**in the long run** in the end, after everything has been considered: *In the long run you would be better to buy a house than rent one*.

—**it's a long lane that has no turning** *see* **lane**.

—**the long and the short of it** the only thing that need be said, to sum the story up in a few words: *The long and the short of it is that she left him*.

—**the long arm of the law** *see* **arm**.

look

—**look askance at (someone** *or* **something)** to regard with disapproval or distrust: *He always looked askance at the neighbour's offers of help*.

—**look before you leap** give careful considera-tion before you act: *Don't rush into changing jobs. Look before you leap*.

—**look daggers at (someone)** *see* **dagger**.

—**look down one's nose at (someone** *or* **some-thing)** *see* **nose**.

—**look down on (someone)** to regard and treat (someone) as being inferior: *She looks down on people who work in factories*.

—**look in on (someone)** to pay (someone) a brief visit, usually without prior notice or in-vitation: *I'll look in on the old lady on my way past*.

—**look sharp** *see* **sharp**.

—**look the other way** *see* **other**.

—**look the part** *see* **part**.

—**look to one's laurels** *see* **laurel**.

—**look up** (1) to improve: *Things are looking up. He's found a job*. (2) to pay (someone) a visit: *We decided to look you up as we were passing through your village*.

—**look (someone) up and down** to look at someone carefully and critically: *She looked him up and down and then said he wasn't suitable for the job*.

—**look up to (someone)** to regard (someone) with great respect or admiration: *He always looked up his elder brother*.

—**make (someone) look small** *see* **small**.

—**not to get a look-in** not to have a chance of winning, succeeding, being noticed, etc: *He entered the race but he didn't get a look-in*.

loose

—**at a loose end** *see* **end**.

—**have a screw loose** *see* **screw**.

—**on the loose** enjoying freedom and pleasure: *The girls from the boarding school were on the loose in the town at the weekend*. <Refers origi-nally to prisoners escaped from jail>.

lord

—**drunk as a lord** extremely drunk: *He staggered home drunk as a lord*.

—**live like a lord** to live in rich and luxurious way: *He lives like a lord in big house while his mother lives in a rented room*.

—**lord it over (someone)** to act in a proud and commanding manner to (someone): *He lords it over the poorer children in the class*.

lose

—**lose face** *see* **face**.

—**lose ground** to lose one's advantage or strong position: *The political party is losing ground to its nearest rival*.

—**lose heart** *see* **heart**.

—**lose one's cool** *see* **cool**.

—**lose one's grip** to lose control: *They sacked the manager because he was losing his grip.*

—**lose one's head** *see* **head**.

—**lose one's nerve** *see* **nerve**.

—**lose one's rag** *see* **rag**.

—**lose one's touch** *see* **touch**.

—**lose one's way** *see* **way**.

—**lose out** to suffer loss or disadvantage: *New workers lost out on the bonus payments.*

—**lose sleep over (something)** *see* **sleep**.

—**lose the thread** *see* **thread**.

—**lose track of (someone** *or* **something)** *see* **track**.

—**lost cause** an aim, ideal, etc, that cannot be achieved: *They are hopeful that the campaign to save the whale will not be yet another lost cause.*

—**lost on (someone)** not appreciated by, or having no effect on, (someone): *The humour of the situation was lost on her.*

—**play a losing game** to go on with something that is obviously going to be unsuccessful: *The campaigners are still trying to stop the building of the new airport but they're playing a losing game.*

loss

—**cut one's losses** not to spend any more time, money or effort on something on which one has already spent a lot to little benefit: *You've tried to help her and she's rejected you. It's time to cut your losses.*

love

—**a labour of love** *see* **labour**.

—**not for love nor money** not in any way at all: *We couldn't get a taxi for love nor money on Saturday night.*

—**there's no love lost between them** they are hostile to each other: *They are brothers-in-law but there's no love lost between them.*

low

—**hunt** *or* **search high and low for (someone** *or* **something)** *see* **high**.

—**keep a low profile** not to draw attention to oneself or one's actions or opinions: *She kept a low profile after the boss gave her a warning.*

—**lay (someone) low** *see* **lay**.

—**lie low** to stay quiet or hidden: *The criminals are lying low until the police hunt is called off.*

—**the low-down** information, especially of a secret or damaging nature: *The press have got hold of the low-down on the politician's affair.*

luck

—**down on one's luck** experiencing misfortune: *He's helping a friend who's down on his luck.*

—**hard-luck story** *see* **hard**.

—**push one's luck** to risk failure by trying to gain too much: *He's pushing his luck by asking for yet more time off.*

—**strike it lucky** to have good fortune: *The actor struck it lucky when he met a film director at a party.*

—**take pot-luck** *see* **pot**.

—**thank one's lucky stars** to be grateful for one's good fortune: *You should thank your lucky stars that you have a job.*

—**worse luck** unfortunately: *We have to stay and work, worse luck.*

lull

—**lull (someone) into a false sense of security** to lead (someone) into thinking that all is well in order to attack when he or she is not prepared: *The workers were lulled into a false sense of security by the management's statement and then received their redundancy notices the following week.*

lumber

—**get lumbered with (something)** to be given an unwanted task or responsibility: *She's got lumbered with looking after the children all day.*

lump

—**lump it** to put up with (something) whether one likes it or not: *I don't like the new arrangement but I can't change it and so I'll just have to lump it.*

lurch

—**leave (someone) in the lurch** *see* **leave**.

lute

—**a rift in the lute** *see* **rift**.

luxury

—**in the lap of luxury** *see* **lap**.

M

mackerel

—a sprat to catch a mackerel *see* sprat.

mad

—go *or* run mad after (something) to develop a violent passion for (something): *As Dryden wrote, "The world is running mad after farce".*

—hopping mad *see* hop.

—in *or* for the main for the most part: *New ideas on education have, for the main, been current for about a year.*

—like mad in an excited fashion, hurriedly: *No one would have recognized the head teacher in the figure that came flying across the meadow, his hat dangling and leapng like mad behind him.*

—mad as a hatter utterly insane, extremely foolish or eccentric: *The villagers thought the inventor of strange gadgets was mad as a hatter.* <Hatmaking used to involve the use of nitrate of mercury, exposure to which could cause a nervous illness which people thought was a symptom of insanity>.

—mad as a March hare insane, silly, extremely eccentric: *His neighbours regard him as being mad as a March hare because of the peculiar clothes he wears.* <Hares tend to leap around wildly in the fields during March, which is their breeding season>.

—midsummer madness *see* midsummer.

maiden

—maiden speech the first speech made as a member of the British House of Commons: *The press were heavily critical of the politician's maiden speech.*

—maiden voyage the first voyage undertaken by a ship: *The ship ran aground on its maiden voyage.*

main

—have an eye to the main chance *see* chance.

—splice the mainbrace *see* splice.

—with might and main *see* might.

make

—be the making of (someone) to cause the improvement or successful development of (someone): *People said that being in the army would be the making of him.*

—have the makings of (something) to have the abilities or qualities necessary to become (something): *That young man has the makings of an excellent teacher.*

—in the making being formed or developed: *Some of the members of the school debating society may be politicians in the making.*

—make a day *or* night of it to spend a whole day or night enjoying oneself in some way: *After dinner we decided to make a night of it and go to a nightclub.*

—make *or* pull a face *see* face.

—make a fool of (someone) *see* fool.

—make a go of (something) *see* go.

—make a meal of (something) *see* meal.

—make a name for oneself *see* name.

—make a pass at (someone) *see* pass.

—make a play for (someone *or* something) *see* play.

—make a point of (doing something) *see* point.

—make as if to (do something) to act as if one were about to (do something). *He made as if to hit her.*

—make a stand against (something) *see* stand.

—make believe to pretend or imagine: *The children made believe that they were soldiers.*

—make bricks without straw to work without having the necessary materials supplied: *To expect him to write an autobiography when he is only twenty-five is like making bricks without straw.* <A biblical reference to Exodus 5:7>.

—make do with (something) to use (something) as a poor or temporary substitute for something: *The poor family had no carpet but had to make do with a piece of sacking on the floor.*

—make eyes at (someone) *see* eye.

—make free with (something) to use without permission or ceremony: *In his review the literary critic made free with the greatest names.*

—make good *see* good.

—make hay (while the sun shines) *see* hay.

—make headway against (something) to progress, to overcome some obstacle: *With the new evidence, his defence lawyer hopes to make headway against the prosecution's case.* <Originally a nautical term>.

—**make heavy weather of (something)** *see* **heavy**.

—**make it** (1) to be successful: *He was determined to make it before he was 30.* (2) to arrive somewhere: *I will be at the meeting if I can make it in time.*

—**make it up** to become friendly again after a quarrel: *The feuding families have made it up.*

—**make light of (something)** *see* **light**.

—**make one's mark** *see* **mark**.

—**make merry** *see* **merry**.

—**make much of (someone** *or* **something)** *see* **much**.

—**make off with (something)** to run away: *The burglar made off with his loot.*

—**make-or-break** bringing either success or failure: *This is a make or-break year for the team.*

—**make one's peace with (someone)** *see* **peace**.

—**make one's point** *see* **point**.

—**make the best of a bad job** *see* **job**.

—**make the grade** to do as well as necessary for something, to reach the required standard: *She didn't become an opera singer. She didn't make the grade.* <Originally referred to a train that succeeded in climbing a steep section of track>.

—**make the most of (something)** *see* **most**.

—**make tracks (for)** *see* **track**.

—**make up one's mind** *see* **mind**.

—**make up to (someone)** to flatter or try to please (someone) in order to gain favour.

—**make one's way** *see* **way**.

—**make way (for someone** *or* **something)** *see* **way**.

—**on the make** trying to make a profit for oneself: *Don't buy a car from him. He's always on the make.*

man

—**a man of his word** someone who always does as he promises: *He'll be there if he said he would be. He's a man of his word.*

—**be a marked man** *see* **mark**.

—**be one's own man** to be independent in one's actions, opinions, etc: *He's not his own man since he married. He simply agrees with what his wife says.*

—**every man jack** *see* **jack**.

—**hit a man when he's down** *see* **hit**.

—**man-about-town** a sophisticated, fashionable man: *He likes football and beer but his brother's a man-about-town.*

—**man Friday** *see* **Friday**.

—**man of straw** a man who is considered to be

of not much worth or substance: *He won't oppose the powerful members of the board. He is a man of straw.*

—**man to man** frankly: *They need to talk man to man about their disagreement.*

—**odd man out** *see* **odd**.

—**right-hand man** *or* **woman** *see* **right**.

—**the man in the street** *or* **in the Clapham omnibus** the ordinary, average person: *Politicians should pay more attention to the man in the street.*

—**the man of the moment** the person who is currently dealing with a situation: *The defence secretary is the man of the moment. He is taking part in talks to try to end the war.*

—**to a man** everyone without exception: *The workers voted to a man to return to work.*

manger

—**a dog in the manger** *see* **dog**.

manna

—**manna from heaven** *see* **heaven**.

manner

—**in a manner of speaking** in a way, in a sense: *I suppose you could call him her guardian in a manner of speaking.*

—**to the manner born** as if accustomed since birth to a particular way of behaviour etc: *She comes from a poor family but she acts like an aristocrat to the manner born.* <Refers to a quotation from Shakespeare's *Hamlet*, act 1, scene iv>.

many

—**many hands make light work** *see* **hand**.

map

—**put (somewhere) on the map** to cause (somewhere) to become well-known or important: *Finding gold there certainly put the town on the map.*

marble

—**have marbles in one's mouth** to speak with an upper-class accent: *Since she went to that school she sounds as though she has marbles in her mouth.*

—**lose one's marbles** to become insane or senile: *The poor old man is losing his marbles.*

march

—**get one's marching orders** to be told to leave, to be dismissed: *She was given her marching orders for persistent late arrival.* <Refers to a military term>.

—**steal a march on (someone)** to gain an advantage over (someone) by doing something earlier than expected: *We stole a march on them by* launching our new product before they could launch a similar one. <Refers literally to moving an army unexpectedly while the enemy is resting>.

mare

—**a mare's nest** a supposed discovery of something, which turns out to be imaginary or completely different from what was expected: *The publicized new cure for cancer turned out to be a mare's nest.*

marine

—**tell that to the marines** I do not believe you: *You're working hard when you have time to gossip? Tell that to the marines.* <Refers to the fact that sailors used to consider marines to be ignorant about the sea>.

mark

—**be a marked man** *or* **woman** to be in danger or trouble because people are trying to harm one: *He's marked man. His wife's brother has just found out he's having an affair.* <In this case, "marked" means watched>.

—**beside** *or* **wide of the mark** off the target or subject: *His guess was wide of the mark.* <Refers to hitting the target in archery>.

—**be up to the mark** to reach the required or normal standard: *His work just isn't up to the mark.*

—**get off one's mark** to get started quickly on an undertaking: *If you want to buy his car you better get off your mark. Someone else is interested.* <Refers to track events in athletics>.

—**hit the mark** to be correct or accurate: *You certainly hit the mark when you said the house would be expensive.* <Refers to the target in archery>.

—**make one's mark** to make oneself well-known, to make a lasting impression: *He wants to make his mark in the world of theatre.*

—**mark time** *see* **time**.

—**quick off the mark** quick to act: *You'll have to be quick off the mark if you want to get to the shop before it closes.* <Refers literally to a runner starting quickly in a race>.

marrow

—**chilled** *or* **frozen to the marrow** extremely cold: *We got chilled to the marrow waiting for the bus.*

mass

—**the masses** the ordinary people, taken as a whole: *He wants to provide entertainment for the masses.*

mast

—**sail** *or* **serve before the mast** to be an ordinary sailor: *He had spent his career sailing before the mast.* <In sailing ships, the sailors' quarters, or forecastle, are in the bow of the vessel.

master

—**old master** *see* **old**.

—**past master** *see* **past**.

match

—**meet one's match** to find oneself against someone who has the ability to defeat one in a contest, argument or activity: *She has been winning the annual tennis match for years but she has met her match in that young player.*

matter

—**a matter of life or death** something of great urgency, something that might involve loss of life: *Tell the doctor that it is a matter of life and death.*

—**as a matter of course** as part of a routine: *That garage is very good. They'll clean your car as a matter of course.*

—**be the matter** be the problem, be what is wrong: *There is something the matter with this car.*

meal

—**make a meal of (something)** to treat (something) as it it is more complicated or time-consuming than it is: *He's really making a meal of painting that door.*

—**square meal** *see* **square**.

means

—**ways and means** *see* **way**.

measure

—**for good measure** as something in addition to what is necessary: *He locked the door and for good measure put the chain on.*

—**have (someone's) measure** to have formed an impression or judgement of (someone): *You had his measure when you said he was not to be trusted.*

meat

—**be meat and drink to (someone)** be very important to (someone): *Reading is meat and drink to the old lady.*

—**one man's meat is another man's poison** people have different tastes: *I liked the film but you may not. After all, one man's meat is another man's poison.*

Mecca

—**a Mecca** a place that is important to a certain group of people and is visited by them: *Liverpool was a Mecca for fans of the Beatles.* <Refers to the birthplace of Mohammed to which Muslims make pilgrimages>.

medicine

—a **dose** or **taste of one's own medicine** see **dose**.

medium

—**the** or **a happy medium** see **happy**.

meet

—**meet (someone) halfway** see **half**.

—**meet one's match** see **match**.

—**meet one's Waterloo** to be finally defeated: *The tennis champion met his Waterloo when he played the younger player.* <Napoleon was defeated for the last time at the Battle of Waterloo by Wellington in 1815>.

melt

—**be in the melting-pot** to be in the process of changing: *The government's education policy is in the melting-pot again.* <Refers to melting down and reshaping metal>.

mend

—**be on the mend** to be getting better: *He nearly died, but now he's on the mend.*

—**least said, soonest mended** see **least**.

—**mend one's ways** see **way**.

mercy

—**an angel of mercy** see **angel**.

—**at the mercy of (someone** or **something)** wholly in the power or control of (someone or something): *The villagers are at the mercy of the cruel tyrant.*

—**be thankful for small mercies** to be grateful for minor benefits or advantages in an otherwise difficult situation: *We have no meat or vegetables but we do have some bread. Let's be thankful for small mercies.*

merry

—**make merry** to have an enjoyable, entertaining time, to have a party: *The students are making merry after their exams.*

—**the more the merrier** see **more**.

message

—**get the message** to understand: *When he made cocoa his guests got the message. He wanted them to go.*

method

—**there is method in one's madness** someone has a good, logical reason for acting as he or she does, although his or her actions may appear to be strange or unreasonable: *We thought he was a fool to resign but he got his redundancy money and the firm went bankrupt two months later. There was method in his madness.* <A reference to Shakespeare's *Hamlet* Act 2, scene ii>.

mettle

—**on one's mettle** prepared to make a great effort: *You'd better be on your mettle. The owner of the firm is making a tour of inspection today.*

mickey, micky

—**Mickey Finn** a drink that has been drugged: *They gave him a Mickey Finn and kidnapped him.*

—**take the mickey** or **micky out of (someone)** to make fun of or ridicule (someone): *The other pupils take the mickey out of her because of her accent.*

Midas

—**the Midas touch** the ability to make money or be successful easily: *All his firms are extremely profitable. He has the Midas touch.* <Refers to a Greek legend about a king of Phrygia whose touch turned everything to gold>.

middle

—**middle-of-the-road** moderate, midway between extremes: *His political views are middle-of-the-road.*

midnight

—**burn the midnight oil** to work or study until late at night: *The student had to burn the midnight oil to finish his essay.*

midsummer

—**midsummer madness** utter lunacy: To expect him to win the election is midsummer madness.

might

—**high and mighty** see **high**.

—**with might and main** with maximum strength and power: *He rowed with might and main in the stormy sea.*

mile

—**a miss is as good as a mile** see **miss**.

—**give (someone) an inch** or **ell and he** or **she will take a mile** see **inch**.

—**milestone** a very important event: *The discovery of anaesthetics was a milestone in medical history.* <Refers literally to a stone set at the edge of a road to indicate the number of miles to the next town, etc>.

—**stand** or **stick out a mile** to be extremely obvious: *It stuck out a mile that he was jealous.*

milk

—**a land of milk and honey** see **land**.

—**cry over spilt milk** see **cry**.

—**the milk of human kindness** natural kindness and sympathy towards others: *He won't give anything to charity. He's completely lacking in the milk of human kindness.* <A quotation from Shakespeare's *Macbeth*, Act 1, scene v>.

mill

—**a millstone round one's neck** a heavy burden or responsibility: *Our high mortgage is a millstone round our necks.*

—**calm as a millpond** extremely calm: *The sea was calm as a millpond.*

—**it's all grist to the** or **someone's mill** see **grist**.

—**go through the mill** to experience a series of difficult or troublesome events, periods or tests: *She's really been through the mill recently. She's had one illness after another.* <From the grinding of corn in a mill>.

—**run-of-the-mill** usual, not special: *They're wealthy but they live in a run-of-the mill kind of house.*

—**the mills of God grind slowly (but they grind exceedingly small)** the proper punishment or reward for someone's actions may be slow in coming but it will certainly come: *His second wife has left him in the same way as he left his first wife. The mills of God grind slowly.*

million

—**one in a million** someone or something that is exceptionally good or special in some way: *The teacher is one in a million. She has helped many parents as well as the children.*

mince

—**make mincemeat of (someone** or **something)** to defeat (someone) soundly, to destroy (something): *The defence barrister made mincemeat of the prosecution's allegations against his client.*

—**not to mince matters** to speak completely frankly without trying to be too kind, etc: *Her tutor didn't mince matters when he told the student her essay was very poor.*

mind

—**a gold mine** see **gold**.

—**a mine of information** a rich or productive source of information: *The old man's a mine of information on local history.*

—**be** or **go out of one's mind** to be or become insane: *She must be out of her mind to go to live in that remote place.*

—**bear** or **keep (something) in mind** see **bear**.

—**blow (someone's) mind** to amaze (someone), to excite (someone) greatly: *The singer's excellent performance really blew our minds.*

—**cross one's mind** to enter one's mind briefly: *It crossed my mind that I hadn't seen him for a while.*

—**give (someone) a piece of one's mind** to scold or criticize (someone) angrily: *She gave the bus driver a piece of her mind for not stopping at the bus stop.*

—**great minds think alike** clever people tend to have the same ideas and opinions: *I see we both bought him the same book. Great minds think alike!*

—**have a good mind to (do something)** to feel inclined to (do something): *I have a good mind to take the day off.*

—**have a mind of one's own** to form one's own opinions, to be independent: *She won't vote for the party her husband tells her to. She has a mind of her own.*

—**have a one-track mind** see **one**.

—**have half a mind to (do something)** to feel slightly inclined to (do something): *I have half a mind to go and live in the country.*

—**in one's right mind** sane, rational: *Her family say that she cannot have been in her right mind when she signed the will.*

—**in two minds** undecided: *They're in two minds about moving house.*

—**keep an open mind** see **open**.

—**make up one's mind** to reach a decision: *I can't make up my mind where to go on holiday.*

—**mind one's own business** see **business**.

—**mind one's p's and q's** see **p**.

—**not to know one's own mind** not to know what one really wants to do: *She doesn't know her own mind. She can't decide whether to live in the town or the country.*

—**out of sight, out of mind** see **sight**.

—**presence of mind** see **presence**.

—**put (someone) in mind of (someone** or **something)** to remind (someone) of (someone or something): *She puts me in mind of her mother when she was that age.*

—**put** or **set (someone's) mind at rest** to free (someone) from anxiety and worry: *Telephone and tell your mother that you're all right. It'll put her mind at rest.*

—**slip one's mind** to be temporarily forgotten: *I meant to telephone you but it slipped my mind.*

—**to my mind** in my opinion: *To my mind she would be better staying here.*

mint

—**a mint of money** a large fortune: *She shopped as if she had a mint of money instead of a small bequest.*

—**in mint condition** used but in extremely good condition: *He'll buy your books only if they're in mint condition.* <Literally the unused condition of a newly minted coin>.

minute

—**up to the minute** modern or fashionable: *He's up to the minute on information about computers. She wears up-to-the-minute clothes.*

miscarriage

—**a miscarriage of justice** a mistaken verdict or decision in a court of law, etc: *The accused was released from jail after a year. The appeal court found that there had been a miscarriage of justice.*

mischief

—**do (oneself** or **someone) a mischief** to hurt or harm (oneself or someone): *The child might do herself a mischief if she plays on that fence.*

—**make mischief** to cause trouble: *Her mother tried to make mischief between husband and wife.*

misery

—**put (someone) out of his** or **her misery** to end a time of worry, anxiety or suspense for (someone): *Put the students out of their misery and tell them which of them passed.* <Originally a term for putting to death a wounded and suffering animal>.

miss

—**a miss is as good as a mile** if one fails at something it does not matter how close he or she came to succeeding: *He failed the exam by two marks but a miss is as good as a mile.*

—**a near miss** *see* **near.**

—**give (something) a miss** not to go to or attend (something): *I think I'll give the party a miss.*

—**miss the boat** *see* **boat.**

mistake

—**and no mistake** without any doubt: *I was terrified and no mistake.*

mix

—**a mixed blessing** *see* **bless.**

—**mixed bag** *see* **bag.**

moment

—**have one's moments** to have times of success, happiness: *She may live a boring life now but she's had her moments.*

—**in a weak moment** *see* **weak.**

—**not for a moment** not at all: *I didn't for one moment believe him.*

—**on the spur of the moment** *see* **spur.**

—**the man of the moment** *see* **man.**

—**the moment of truth** a crucial time, a time when one has to make an important decision, face a crisis, etc: *It was the moment of truth for her. She had to decide whether to marry him or not.*

money

—**a run for (someone's) money** *see* **run.**

—**be in the money** to be well off, sometimes temporarily: *Let him pay for dinner. He's in the money for once.*

—**for my money** in my opinion, as my choice: *For my money I'd rather live in the city than the country.* <Literally what one would spend one's money on>.

—**have money to burn** to have enough money to be able to spend it in ways considered foolish: *She must have money to burn if she can afford clothes like that.*

—**money for jam** or **old rope** money obtained in exchange for very little work, effort, etc: *She gets paid very highly for writing two reports a week. It's money for jam.* <Originally army slang>.

—**money** or **distance, etc, is no object** *see* **object.**

—**money talks** rich people have influence simply because they have money: *The local council should not alter their plans because of the local landowners but money talks.*

—**not for love nor money** *see* **love.**

—**put one's money where one's mouth is** to give money for a cause or purpose which one claims to support: *She is in favour of a new library being built but she won't put her money where her mouth is and contribute to the building fund.*

—**ready money** *see* **ready.**

—**spend money like water** to spend money very freely: *When he received his redundancy pay the family spent money like water.*

—**throw good money after bad** to spend money in an unsuccessful attempt to retrieve money which one has already lost: *Borrowing thousands of pounds from the bank to try to make that firm profitable is simply throwing good money after bad.*

monkey

—**monkey business** action likely to cause trouble, illegal or unfair activities: *There seems to have been some monkey business in the accounts department.*

—**not to give a monkey's** not to care at all: *He says he doesn't give a monkey's whether he gets the sack or not.*

month

—**a month of Sundays** an extremely long time: *You'll never finish that piece of work in a month of Sundays.*

moon

—**ask** or **cry for the moon** to ask for something that it is impossible to get: *The young woman is* looking for a well-paid and undemanding job without any qualifications. *She is crying for the moon.*

—**do a moonlight (flit)** to move away suddenly: *They did a moonlight to avoid paying the rent.*

—**over the moon** extremely happy: *They were over the moon to hear that they had passed their exams.*

moral

—**moral support** encouragement but not actual physical, financial, etc, help: *Her parents could not afford to give her money to help with her college studies but they gave her their moral support.*

more

—**the more the merrier** the more people that are involved the better: *Come and join our outing to the cinema. It'll be fun—the more the merrier.*

morning

—**the morning after the night before** a morning when one is suffering from a hangover caused by drinking too much alcohol the night before: *He looked absolutely terrible at this morning's meeting. It was obviously a case of the morning after the night before.*

most

—**make the most of (something)** to take maximum advantage of (an opportunity, occasion, etc): *Make the most of your last university vacation. You probably won't get such a long holiday again.*

mother

—**a mother's** or **mummy's boy** a boy or man who depends too much on his mother; a weak, effeminate boy or man: *He's such a mother's boy that he probably won't marry till his mother dies.*

—**mother's milk** something that one needs or enjoys very much: *Modern novels are mother's milk to him.*

—**the father and mother of** *see* **father.**

motion

—**go through the motions** to make a show of doing something, to pretend to do something: *I'm bored stiff but I'll have to go through the motions of enjoying myself.*

—**set the wheels in motion** *see* **wheel.**

mould

—**cast in the same mould (as someone)** very similar (to someone): *She's cast in the same mould as her cousin. They're both hot-tempered.* <Refers to iron-working>.

mountain

—**make a mountain out of a molehill** greatly to

exaggerate the extent of a problem, etc: *It's not a very complicated journey. She's just making a mountain out of a molehill.*

mouth

—**down in the dumps** or **down in the mouth** *see* **down.**

—**foam at the mouth** *see* **foam.**

—**have a big mouth** to talk a lot, especially about things, such as secrets, that one should not: *She told him where we're going. She's got a big mouth.*

—**put one's money where one's mouth is** *see* **money.**

—**shoot one's mouth off** to talk in a loud and often boastful or threatening manner: *He was shooting his mouth off about what he would do if he didn't get a pay increase.*

move

—**get a move on** to hurry: *We had better get a move on or we'll miss the bus.*

—**move heaven and earth** *see* **heaven.**

much

—**make much of (someone** or **something)** to pay (someone or something) a great deal of attention: *Their grandmother always makes much of the children.*

—**make much of (something)** to treat (something) as being of great importance: *They made much of the fact that I was late although it was only by a few minutes.*

—**much ado about nothing** a great fuss about something very minor: *The boy only broke a very small window but the owner sent for the police. It was a case of much ado about nothing.* <From Shakespeare's play of the same name>.

—**much of a muchness** very similar: *The houses we looked at were much of a muchness. We're still looking.*

—**not much of a (something)** not a very good (something): *She's not much of a cook.*

—**not to think much of (someone** or **something)** *see* **think.**

—**not up to much** not very good: *The holiday hotel was not up to much.*

—**without so much as** without even: *They left suddenly without so much as saying goodbye.*

muck

—**muck in** to join in a task, etc: *If we all muck in we should finish by this evening.* <Originally army slang>.

—**muck-raking** searching for scandalous information, usually with the intention of publishing it: *The Sunday newspaper was accused of muck-raking to discredit the new president.*

—**where there's muck there's brass** where there is dirt and ugliness in a place there is often industry and so wealth: *The son objected to the ugly factory chimneys but his wealthy grandfather said, "Where there's muck there's brass".*

mud

—**clear as mud** *see* **clear**.

—**(someone's) name is mud** (someone) is in disfavour or is being criticized: *Your name will be mud if you don't go to her party.*

—**sling** *or* **throw mud at (someone** *or* **something)** to say bad or insulting things about (someone or something): *The candidates in the election kept slinging mud at each other.*

—**stick-in-the mud** *see* **stick**.

mug

—**a mug's game** something that only foolish people would involve themselves in: *He has decided that marriage is a mug's game.*

mule

—**stubborn as a mule** extremely stubborn: *The old lady is stubborn as a mule and will not accept help with her housework.*

multitude

—**cover a multitude of sins** to be able to apply or refer to a large number of different things: *In an office the term personal assistant can cover a multitude of sins.* <A misquotation from the Bible, I Peter 4:8—"Charity shall cover the multitude of sins">.

mum

—**keep mum** to stay silent: *He was told to keep mum if anyone questioned him about the accident.*

—**mum's the word** do not say anything: *We're planning a surprise party for her and so mum's the word.*

mummy

—**mummy's boy** *same as* **mother's boy** *see* **mother**.

murder

—**get away with murder** to do something bad, irresponsible, etc, without suffering punishment: *When their mother's away their father lets the children away with murder.*

mustard

—**keen as mustard** very eager and enthusiastic: *The trainee chef is keen as mustard.*

mutton

—**mutton dressed as lamb** an older person, usually a woman, dressed in clothes suitable for young people: *She thinks she looks very smart but she's mutton dressed as lamb.*

N

n

—**to the nth degree** see **degree**.

nail

—**a nail in (someone's) coffin** something which helps to bring about (someone's) downfall or destruction: *The customer's complaint about him was yet another nail in his coffin.*

—**hard as nails** see **hard**.

—**hit the nail on the head** to be extremely accurate in one's description, judgement, etc, of someone or something: *She certainly hit the nail on the head when she said he was work-shy.*

—**nail one's colours to the mast** see **colour**.

—**pay (something) on the nail** to pay (something) immediately: *He always pays his account on the nail.*

name

—**a name to conjure with** see **conjure**.

—**call (someone) names** to apply insulting or rude names to (someone): *The other children called him names because he wore second-hand clothes.*

—**clear (someone's) name** to prove that (someone) was not involved in a crime or misdeed of which he or she was accused: *He finally cleared his name by finding out the real culprit.*

—**give (someone or something) a bad name** to damage the reputation of (someone or something): *All these complaints about late deliveries are giving the firm a bad name.*

—**in name only** not in practice: *They're man and wife in name only. They don't live together.*

—**make a name for oneself** to become famous or well-known: *She's already made a name for herself as a dancer.*

—**name-dropping** the habit of mentioning the names of famous or important people as though they were friends: *She was trying to impress us by name-dropping but it was just embarrassing.*

—**(someone's) name is mud** see **mud**.

—**name names** to give the names of people, especially people who are guilty or accused of wrong-doing: *The children are being bullied but they are afraid of naming names.*

—**name the day** see **day**.

—**no names, no pack-drill** no names will be mentioned and so no one will get into trouble: *If you repair the damage you have done, there will be no names, no pack-drill.* <"Pack-drill" refers to a form of army punishment in which the soldiers being punished were forced to march up and down carrying all their equipment>.

—**the name of the game** the important or central thing: *Persistence—that's the name of the game in job-hunting.*

—**take (someone's) name in vain** see **vain**.

—**their name is legion** see **legion**.

—**to one's name** in one's possession or ownership: *He has scarcely a penny to his name.*

—**worthy of the name** deserving to be so called: *Any teacher worthy of the name would punish the pupil.*

nap

—**catch (someone) napping** see **catch**.

narrow

—**a narrow squeak** see **squeak**.

—**the straight and narrow (path)** see **straight**.

nasty

—**a nasty piece of work** someone who is very unpleasant or behaves very unpleasantly: *Try not to argue with him. He's a really nasty piece of work.*

native

—**go native** to live according to the customs, fashions, etc, of the foreign country in which one is living: *Although she has only been in India a short time she's gone native and wears a sari.*

nature

—**answer or obey the call of nature** see **call**.

—**in a state of nature** naked: *The man was found in the cave in a state of nature and raving mad.*

—**second nature** see **second**.

near

—**a near miss** something unpleasant that very nearly happened, often the near collision of two planes in the sky: *The chimney fell to the ground just beside me. It was a near miss.*

—**a near thing** the act of just avoiding an accident, misfortune, etc: *We arrived at the station on time but it was a near thing.*

—**one's nearest and dearest** one's close family: *Even her nearest and dearest criticize her.*

neat

—**neat as a pin** very neat and tidy: Everything was as neat as a pin in the house.

neck

—**a millstone round one's neck** *see* **mill**.

—**a pain in the neck** *see* **pain**.

—**be in (something) up to one's neck** to be very much involved in something bad or illegal: *The police were convinced that he was up to his neck in drug-smuggling.*

—**be neck or nothing** to be a braving of all dangers, the risking of everything: *It's neck or nothing for the party if it wants to win the election.*

—**breathe down (someone's) neck** *see* **breathe**.

—**get it in the neck** to be severely scolded or punished: *You'll get it in the neck if you're not home by midnight.*

—**have the brass neck to (do something)** to have the impertinence or brazenness to (do something): *She had the brass neck to expect us to pay for her cinema ticket.*

—**neck and neck** exactly equal: *The two football teams were neck and neck at the end of the season.*

—**risk one's neck** to put one's life, job, etc, in danger: *Firemen risk their necks to save other people.*

—**stick one's neck out** to take a risk, to or do something that may cause trouble: *I know I'm sticking my neck out but hasn't your husband had too much to drink?*

—**this *or* that, etc, neck of the woods** this or that, etc, part of the country: *Why did you come to this neck of the woods?* <Originally a term for a remote community in the woods of the early 19th-century American frontier>.

need

—**needs must when the devil drives** *see* **devil**.

—**the needful** money: *We don't have the needful to pay the rent.*

needle

—**like looking for a needle in a haystack** an impossible search: *Looking for a contact lens on this carpet is like looking like for a needle in a haystack.*

—**on pins and needles** *see* **pin**.

nerve

—**bag of nerves** *see* **bag**.

—**get on (someone's) nerves** to irritate (someone): *His constant whistling gets on my nerves.*

—**have a nerve** to be impertinent or brazen: *They had the nerve to ask us for another loan when they still owed us money.*

—**lose one's nerve** to become scared, and so be unable to continue with an activity or course of action: *The diver lost his nerve on the high diving-board.*

nest

—**a mare's nest** *see* **mare**.

—**a nest-egg** savings for the future: *She had to spend her nest-egg to pay her son's fine.*

—**feather one's nest** *see* **feather**.

nettle

—**grasp the nettle** to set about an unpleasant or difficult task in a firm and determined manner: *You must grasp the nettle and tell her that her work is not up to standard.*

never

—**never-never land** an imaginary land where conditions are ideal: *They live in a never-never land and don't seem to realize how bad their financial situation is.* <Refers to the idealized land in J. M. Barrie's play *Peter Pan*>.

—**never say die** don't despair, persevere: *You'll pass your exams if you study properly—never say die.*

—**on the never-never** by hire purchase: *They're buying the furniture for their new house on the never-never.*

new

—**new blood** *see* **blood**.

—**new broom** someone who has just been appointed to a post and who is eager to be efficient, make changes, etc: *Our office system works very well but the new manager is a new broom who wants to revolutionize the whole thing.* <From the saying a new broom sweeps clean, a new broom being more effective than the old one>.

—**put new heart into (someone)** *see* **heart**.

—**turn over a new leaf** *see* **leaf**.

news

—**break the news to (someone)** to tell (someone) about something, usually something unpleasant or sad, that has happened: *The policewoman had to break the news of her son's fatal road accident to her.*

—**no news is good news** if one has not received any information about someone or something then all is likely to be well since if something bad, such as an accident, had happened one would have heard: *Our son is very late but no news is good news. He's probably just been delayed on the journey.*

next

—**next door to (something)** very nearly (something): *Her recent actions have been next door to insanity.*

—**next one's heart** very dear to one: *Football is a subject that is next his heart.*

—**next to nothing** almost nothing, very little: *The second-hand furniture cost next to nothing.*

nick

—**in good** or **poor nick** in good or poor condition: *The car is in good nick for its age.*

—**in the nick of time** just in time, at the last possible time: *We arrived in the nick of time to save him from drowning.*

night

—**a one-night stand** *see* **one**.

—**night-owl** someone who is in the habit of staying up very late at night: *She never goes to bed before 2 a.m. She's a real night-owl.*

nine

—**a nine days' wonder** something that arouses surprise and interest for a short time only: *His marriage to a much younger girl was a nine days' wonder.* <Refers to a saying quoted by Chaucer—"where is no wonder so great that it lasts more than nine days">.

—**a stitch in time saves nine** *see* **stitch**.

—**dressed to the nines** *see* **dress**.

nineteen

—**talk nineteen to the dozen** *see* **talk**.

nip

—**nip (something) in the bud** to put a stop or end to (something) as soon as it develops: *Her father tried to nip the romance in the bud by sending her to college in France.*

nit

—**get down to the nitty-gritty** to begin to deal with the basic practical details, problems, etc: *It's time to get down to the nitty-gritty and discuss the funding of the project.*

—**nit-picking** the act of finding very minor faults in something, quibbling: *He ignores all the major issues and spends his time nit-picking.* <Refers to picking nits out of hair>.

no

—**be no joke** *see* **joke**.

—**no end of (something)** a great deal of (something): *There will be no end of trouble if the boss finds out.*

—**no go** unsuccessful, in vain: *We applied for planning permission but it was no go.*

—**no holds barred** *see* **hold**.

—**no time at all** *see* **time**.

—**no way** under no circumstances: *There's no way that we'll get there in time.*

noble

—**noble savage** a primitive person brought up in primitive surroundings, thought of as being less corrupt, more worthy, more innocent, etc, than people brought up in a more civilized environment: *The explorer was a great believer in the concept of the noble savage and eventually went to live in the jungle.* <From a quotation by John Dryden, the English dramatist, and a theory developed by Jean Jacques Rousseau, the French philosopher>.

nobody

—**be nobody's fool** *see* **fool**.

—**like nobody's business** very rapidly, energetically, etc: *We worked liked nobody's business to finish the job in time.*

nod

—**a nod is as good as a wink (to a blind horse)** there is no use repeating a sign to those who cannot or do not choose to see: *Management won't improve conditions unless the workers take action—a nod is as good as a wink.*

—**have a nodding acquaintance with (someone** or **something)** to know (someone or something) slightly: *I have a nodding acquaintance with the history of the period.* <Refers to knowing someone well enough to nod in greeting to him or her>.

—**nod off** to fall asleep, sometimes accidentally: *His lecture was so boring that the students nodded off.*

—**the land of Nod** sleep: *It's time the children were in the land of Nod.* <Refers to a place mentioned in the Bible in Genesis 4:16 and the fact that nodding is associated with falling asleep>.

noise

—**big noise** an important person: *The big noises on the board are looking round the factory today.*

—**empty vessels make most noise** *see* **empty**.

none

—**none the wiser** *see* **wise**.

—**none too** not very: *He looks none too happy.*

nook

—**every nook and cranny** absolutely everywhere: *We searched in every nook and cranny of the house for the last earring.* <Literally, in all the corners and cracks>.

nose

—**cut off one's nose to spite one's face** to do something that harms oneself, usually in order to harm someone else: *Refusing to work overtime because you quarrelled with your boss is cutting off your nose to spite your face. You need the extra money.*

—**follow one's nose** to go straight forward: *You'll reach the village if you follow your nose all the way from here.*

—**keep one's nose clean** *see* **clean**.

—**keep (one's** *or* **someone's) nose to the grindstone** to keep (someone) working hard without stopping: *I'll have to keep my nose to the grindstone to finish this in time.*

—**lead (someone) by the nose** to get (someone) to do whatever one wants: *He leads the other children in the class by the nose.* <Refers to the ring on a bull's nose>.

—**look down one's nose at (someone** *or* **something)** to regard or treat (someone or something) with disdain or contempt: *She looks down her nose at people from the council housing estate.*

—**nosey parker** someone who is too inquisitive about other people's affairs: *I'm tired of that nosey parker asking where I'm going.*

—**no skin off my, etc, nose** *see* **skin**.

—**pay through the nose** to pay a great deal of money for something: *You'll pay through the nose for a house in that area.*

—**poke one's nose into (something)** to pry into or interfere in other people's affairs: *I wish she'd stop poking her nose into my mother's business.* <Refers literally to a dog>.

—**put (someone's) nose out of joint** to make (someone) jealous or offended by taking a place usually held by him or her e.g. in the affections of a person whom he or she loves: *The teenager's nose has been put out of joint by the new baby in the house.* <Refers to a person whose nose has been broken by being hit in the face>.

—**rub (someone's) nose in it** to keep on reminding (someone) about something he or she has done wrong: *I know I shouldn't have lent him money but there's no need to rub my nose in it.* <Refers literally to rubbing a dog's nose in its faeces when house-training it>.

—**see further than the end of one's nose** to be concerned with more than just what is happening in the immediate present and in the immediate vicinity: *He can't see further than the end of his nose, so he doesn't give any thought to what his children will do if he and his wife emigrate.*

—**thumb one's nose at (someone** *or* **something)** *see* **thumb**.

—**turn up one's nose at (something)** to treat (something) with dislike or disgust: *The child was used to sophisticated food and turned up his nose at fish fingers.*

—**under (someone's) (very) nose** (1) right in front of (someone) and so easily seen: *The book which I couldn't find had been right under my nose all the time.* (2) while (someone) is actually present: *She stole my suitcase from under my very nose.*

note

—**of note** famous or important: *They want someone of note to open the new store.*

—**strike the right note** to say or do something suitable for the occasion: *The clothes which the princess wore struck just the right note at the children's sports day.* <Refers to playing a musical instrument>.

nothing

—**come to nothing** to fail: *His plans to start his own business came to nothing.*

—**go for nothing** to be wasted or unsuccessful: *All our efforts to save the old building went for nothing.*

—**have nothing on (someone)** (1) not to be nearly as good, skilful, bad, etc, as (someone else): *She may have a quick temper but I bet she has nothing on my mother.* (2) to have no proof or evidence of (someone's) wrong doing: *The police have nothing on the burglar. They can't arrest him.*

—**have nothing to do with (someone** *or* **something)** to avoid contact with (someone or something): *They have had nothing to do with each other since their divorce.*

—**next to nothing** *see* **next**.

—**nothing to write home about** *see* **home**.

—**nothing ventured, nothing gained** one cannot achieve anything if one does not make an attempt or take a risk: *It's not a good time to open a small business but there again nothing ventured nothing gained.*

—**stop at nothing** *see* **stop**.

—**sweet nothings** *see* **sweet**.

—**there is nothing to choose between (two people** *or* **things)** there is hardly any difference in quality, ability, etc, between (two people or things): *Either of the candidates will do for the job. There's nothing to choose between them in qualifications or experience.*

—**there's nothing to it** it is very easy: *I'm sure*

that you can assemble the furniture yourself. There's nothing to it.

—**think nothing of (something)** not to regard (something) as out of the ordinary, difficult, etc: *She thinks nothing of driving hundreds of miles every weekend to see her boyfriend.*

—**think nothing of it** do not worry about it. It does not matter: *"I'm sorry that I took your coat by mistake." "Think nothing of it."*

nowhere

—**get** *or* **be nowhere** to make no progress, to have no success: *I tried to explain my difficulty to the passport office but I got absolutely nowhere.*

—**nowhere near** not nearly: *They've nowhere near enough money to put a deposit on a house.*

number

—**back number** *see* **back.**

—**(your, etc) days are numbered** *see* **day.**

—**get** *or* **have (someone's) number** to find out or know what kind of person (someone) is and what he or she is likely to do: *I've got his number. He's a con-man who's trying to get money out of my aunt.*

—**in penny numbers** *see* **penny.**

—**(someone's) number is up** (someone) is about to suffer something unpleasant, such as dy-

ing, failing, being punished, being caught, etc: *He has been stealing from the firm for years but his number is up. The manager is conducting an investigation.*

—**number one** oneself: *For once I must think of number one.*

—**(someone's) opposite number** *see* **opposite.**

—**there's safety in numbers** *see* **safe.**

nut

—**a hard nut to crack** a difficult problem or person to deal with: *I don't know how we'll get there by public transport. That's a hard nut to crack.*

—**be nuts about (someone** *or* **something)** to like (someone or something) a very great deal, to be wildly enthusiastic about (someone or something): *He's nuts about jazz.*

—**do one's nut** to get very angry: *The teacher will do her nut if you're late again.*

—**in a nutshell** briefly, to sum up: *The trial went on for days but in a nutshell he was acquitted.*

—**the nuts and bolts of (something)** the basic details or practicalities of (something): *He wants to buy a pub but he knows nothing whatsoever about the nuts and bolts of running a business.*

O

oar

—**put** *or* **stick one's oar in** to interfere in another's affairs, conversation, e.g. by offering unwanted opinions: *They would have settled their argument if she had not stuck her oar in.* <Perhaps refers to someone who is being rowed in a boat by others and who suddenly decides to take part in the rowing unasked>.

—**rest on one's oars** to take a rest after working very hard: *The students are resting on their oars after their exams before looking for holiday jobs.* <Refers literally to rowing>.

oat

—**off one's oats** not feeling well and so not eating much: *I've been off my oats ever since I had flu last week.* <Literally used of horses>.

—**sow one's wild oats** *see* **wild**.

oath

—**take one's oath** to swear that something one has said is true: *I will take my oath that I saw him enter my office.*

object

—**money, distance, etc, is no object** it does not matter how much money, distance, etc, is involved in the particular situation: *The delivery service says that distance is no object in their business.* <Originally "money is no object" meant money or profits were not the main aim but it came to be misapplied>.

occasion

—**rise to the occasion** to be able to carry out whatever action is required in an important or urgent situation: *He had never played the piano in public before but he rose to the occasion.*

ocean

—**a drop in the ocean** *same as* **a drop in the bucket** *see* **bucket**.

odd

—**against all the odds** in spite of major difficulties: *Traffic conditions were terrible but against all the odds we arrived in time.*

—**be at odds with (someone** *or* **something)** to be in disagreement with (someone or something), not to be in accordance with (something): *His work performance is at odds with his brilliant reference.*

—**lay odds** to bet: *I'll lay odds that he won't turn up.* <Refers to betting on horses>.

—**make no odds** to be of no importance, to make no difference: *It makes no odds whether it rains or not. The party is indoors.*

—**odd man out** someone or something that is different from others: *He's the odd man out in the family. He doesn't have black hair.* <Refers literally to someone left out of a game when the teams have been chosen>.

—**odds and ends** small objects of different kinds: *All our holiday packing is done apart from odds and ends such as suntan oil.*

—**odds and sods** a mixed selection of people or things not considered important: *I knew most of the people at the party but there were a few odds and sods that I didn't recognize.*

—**over the odds** more than one would usually expect to pay: *The restaurant charges over the odds in the tourist season.* <Refers originally to a horse-racing term>.

odour

—**an odour of sanctity** an air of excessive piety or virtue: *There's such an odour of sanctity about her that he's afraid to ask her out.*

—**in bad odour** in disfavour: *He's in bad odour with management for supporting the strikers.* <From a French term for the sweet smell reputed to be given off by the corpses of saints>.

off

—**badly** *or* **well off** *see* **bad** *or* **well**.

—**get off (something)** to be given a lesser punishment than expected: *She got off with a fine instead of imprisonment.*

—**go off** to begin to dislike (someone or something previously liked): *She went off cheese when she was pregnant.*

—**know (something) off by heart** to have committed to memory: *He was so fond of the poem he knew it off by heart.*

—**off and on** *or* **on and off** occasionally: *We've met for lunch off and on over the years.*

—**off-colour** *see* **colour**.

—**off one's head** *see* **head**.

—**off the cuff** *see* **cuff**.

—**off the hook** *see* **hook**.

—**off the peg** *see* **peg**.

—**off the rails** *see* **rail**.

—**off the record** *see* **record**.

—**off the top of one's head** *see* **top**.

—**on the off-chance (of** *or* **that)** *see* **chance**.

—**put (someone) off his** *or* **her stroke** *see* **stroke**.

office

—**seek office** to wish or apply for a position: *The minister is retiring shortly and has told his colleagues he will not be seeking office.*

—**the usual offices** a lavatory: *The estate agent assured the client that the building had the usual offices.*

offing

—**in the offing** about to or likely to happen, appear, etc: *He doesn't have a job yet but there are one or two in the offing.* <A nautical term—refers to the whole area of sea that can be seen from a particular point on shore>.

oil

—**burn the midnight oil** *see* **midnight**.

—**oil the wheels** to make something easier to do or obtain: *She got a visa quite quickly. Knowing someone at the embassy oiled the wheels.* <Wheels turn more easily if oil is applied to them>.

—**pour oil on troubled waters** to to attempt to bring a state of calm and peace to a situation of disagreement or dispute: *When the children quarrel their mother always tries to pour oil on troubled waters.* <Since oil floats on water it has the effect of making waves flat>.

—**strike oil** to obtain exactly what one wants, to be successful: *We've never found a comfortable holiday house but this year we struck oil.*

ointment

—**a fly in the ointment** *see* **fly**[1].

old

—**an old hand** someone who is very experienced (at doing something): *She's an old hand at serving in a bar.*

—**any old how** *see* **any**.

—**a ripe old age** *see* **age**.

—**money for old rope** *see* **money**.

—**old as the hills** extremely old: *Some of the village traditions are old as the hills.*

—**old hat** old-fashioned, no longer popular: *His ideas are considered old hat nowadays.*

—**old master** (a work by) any great painter before the 19th century, especially of the 15th and 16th centuries: *The art gallery has had several old masters stolen.*

—**the old-boy network** a system in which jobs and other advantages are obtained on the basis of knowing the right people rather than on ability or worth: *His father got him a job in a bank although he's hopeless with figures. It was obviously a case of the old-boy network.* <The basic connection with such people is often that one was at school with them>.

—**the old country** the country from which an immigrant or his or her parents or grandparents originally came: *The Swedish farmer enjoyed his new life in the USA, but his wife would often think about the old country.*

—**the old guard** the older members of a group who are old-fashioned in their opinions and tastes: *The old guard in the club voted against having women members.* <The translation of the name applied to the most experienced section of Napoleon's army>.

olive

—**olive branch** a sign of a wish for peace: *He had a bitter quarrel with his wife then sent her a huge bouquet of flowers as an olive branch.* <The olive branch was an ancient symbol of peace>.

on

—**be on to (someone)** having discovered some previously secret or unknown information about (someone) or his or her activities: *The police are on to his drug-dealing.*

—**be on for (something)** to be ready to take part in (something): *Are you on for a row on the river?*

—**on and off** *see* **off**.

once

—**give (someone) the once-over** to look at or study (someone or something) quickly: *I know that you're in a hurry but would you give this report the once-over?*

—**once and for all** *or* **once for all** now and for the last time, finally: *Once and for all I am telling you to go.*

—**once and again** repeatedly, often: *I have told you once and again that you must not smoke in this room.*

—**once in a blue moon** *see* **blue**.

—**you're only young once** *see* **young**.

one

—**a one-horse race** a competition, contest, etc, in which one person or side is certain to win: *There was no point in advertising the manager's job. It's a one-horse race because his assistant is bound to get it.*

—**a one-night stand** a relationship, arrangement, etc, that lasts for one evening or night only: *She should be careful. One-night stands can be dangerous.* <Literally a single performance in one place given by a pop group, etc, on tour>.

—**a quick one** *see* **quick**.

—**be at one with (someone)** to be in agreement with (someone): *I am at one with her on the subject of childcare.*

—**be one in the eye for (someone)** *see* **eye**.

—**be one too many for (someone)** to be more powerful or cunning than (someone): *The interviewer and the opposition politician were one too many for the minister.*

—**be one up on (someone)** to have an advantage over (someone): *They've both applied for the post but with his qualifications he's one up on his rival.*

—**have a one-track mind** to think only of one subject all the time: *She has a one-track mind. She can't stop thinking about getting married.*

—**just one of those things** *see* **thing**.

—**not be oneself** to be feeling slightly unwell, to be more depressed, etc, than usual: *She's not been herself since the death of her husband.*

—**number one** *see* **number**.

—**one for the road** *see* **road**.

—**one in a million** *see* **million**.

—**one of these days** soon, shortly: *There will be a general election one of these days.*

—**one way and another** *see* **way**.

—**the one that got away** *see* **away**.

onion

—**know one's onions** to know a subject, one's job, etc: *He'll be able to fix the computer. He really knows his onions.*

open

—**an open book** *see* **book**.

—**an open-and-shut case** free from uncertainty, having an obvious outcome: *The trial will not take long. It's an open-and-shut case.*

—**an open secret** a supposed secret that is known to many people: *It's an open secret that he's having an affair with his friend's wife while the friend is working abroad.*

—**be open as the day** to be utterly without deception or hypocrisy: *Open as the day, he made no secret of the fact that he was alone in the world.*

—**keep an open mind** to be willing to listen to other people's suggestions, ideas, etc, instead of just concentrating on one's own point of view: *The members of the jury should keep an open mind until all the evidence has been heard.*

—**keep open house** *see* **house**.

—**keep one's options open** *see* **option**.

—**lay oneself (wide) open to (something)** to put oneself in a position in which one is liable to be in receipt of (blame, criticism, accusations, attack, etc): *If you go out to dinner with one of the job applicants you'll be laying yourself open to charges of bribery.*

—**with one's eyes open** *see* **eye**.

—**with open arms** *see* **arm**.

opposite

—**(someone's) opposite number** the person in another company, country, etc, whose job or role corresponds to someone's: *The Chancellor of the Exchequer met with his opposite numbers in the EEC countries.*

option

—**keep one's options open** to delay making a definite decision so that all choices are available as long as possible: *Try to avoid replying to the job offer until you hear about the others. It is as well to keep your options open.*

—**soft option** *see* **soft**.

oracle

—**work the oracle** to produce the desired result, to obtain what one wants, especially by using cunning, influence or bribery: *We couldn't get tickets but her uncle's the theatre manager so she phoned him and that worked the oracle.* <Refers to the oracle at Delphi that foretold the future in Greek legend>.

order

—**a tall order** *see* **tall**.

—**call (someone or something) to order**: to restore calm to: *He kept on interrupting the meeting so the chairman had to call him to order.*

—**get one's marching orders** *see* **march**.

—**in apple-pie order** *see* **apple**.

—**just what the doctor ordered** *see* **doctor**.

—**out of order** (1) not working properly: *The coffee machine is out of order.* (2) not according to the conventions or rules of meetings, etc: *The chairman should have ruled his interruption out of order.*

—**take orders** to become a member of the clergy: *Although he never could be persuaded to take orders, theology was his favourite subject.*

—**the order of the day** something that should be done, worn, etc, because conventional, common, fashionable, etc: *Hats will be the order of the day at the royal garden party.*

—**the orders of the day** the list of business to be conducted on a particular day by an organization, especially Parliament: *The Speaker announced the orders of the day.*

other

—**look the other way** to ignore or disregard something wrong, illegal, etc: *The local policeman would look the other way when the village pub was open after hours.*

—**or other** not known or decided: *Someone or other will have to go.*

—**pass by on the other side** *see* **pass**.

out

—**be** *or* **go out of one's mind** *see* **mind**.

—**be well out of (something)** *see* **well**.

—**be out of place** to be unsuitable or improper: *Smoking in church is out of place.*

—**come out** to make public the fact that one is a homosexual: *He came out when they began living together.*

—**have it out with (someone)** *see* **have**.

—**out and about** going around outside, e.g. after an illness: *He was confined to bed for weeks but he's out and about now.*

—**out-and-out** thoroughgoing, complete: *It's an out-and-out scandal—he's left his wife for another woman.*

—**out at elbow** *see* **elbow**.

—**out for (something)** wanting and trying to get (something): *She's only out for a good time.*

—**out of hand** *see* **hand**.

—**out of order** *see* **order**.

—**out of pocket** *see* **pocket**.

—**out of sight, out of mind** *see* **sight**.

—**out of sorts** *see* **sort**.

—**out of turn** *see* **turn**.

—**out on a limb** *see* **limb**.

—**out to (do something)** determined to (do something): *She's out to cause trouble.*

—**take it out on (someone)** *see* **take**.

outside

—**at the outside** at the most: *The drive will take an hour at the outside.*

over

—**be all over (someone)** to be extremely friendly and attentive to (someone): *She was all over him as soon as she discovered he had money.*

—**over and above** in addition, besides, extra: *He earns a commission over and above his salary.*

—**over and done with** completely finished, at an end: *They once went out with each other but that's over and done with.*

—**over my dead body** *see* **dead**.

—**over the hill** *see* **hill**.

—**over the odds** *see* **odd**.

—**over the top** *see* **top**.

overboard

—**go overboard (about** *or* **for someone** *or* **something)** to be extremely enthusiastic about (someone or something): *All the men have gone overboard for the new girl in the office.*

own

—**be one's own man** *see* **man**.

—**come into one's own** to have the opportunity to show one's good qualities, talent, skill, etc: *She is a marvellous hostess and really comes into her own at dinner parties.*

—**do one's (own) thing** *see* **thing**.

—**get one's own back** *see* **back**.

—**hold one's own** (1) to perform as well as one's opponents in a contest, an argument, etc: *The younger team held their own against the much more experienced side.* (2) to be surviving, to be holding on to life: *The accident is very bad but he is holding his own.*

—**in one's own right** *see* **right**.

P

p

—**mind one's p's and q's** to be very careful, to be polite and well-behaved: *You'll have to mind your p's and q's when you meet your girl-friend's mother for the first time.* <Perhaps refers to a warning to a printer to be careful of the letters p and q so as not to confuse them>.

pace

—**keep pace with (someone** *or* **something)** to progress or develop at the same rate as (a person, subject or situation) with regard to social or financial standing, knowledge, etc: *Their salaries have not kept pace with those of workers in comparable industries.* <Literally refers to going as fast as someone else in a race>.

—**put (someone** *or* **something) through its** *or* **his** *or* **her paces** to test the ability of (someone or something) by getting them to demonstrate what it, he or she is capable of: *He wants to see the car put through his paces before he buys it.* <Refers originally to assessing how a horse walks, ambles, trots, canters and gallops>.

—**set the pace for** to establish the rate at which, or the manner in which, an activity is carried out: *Their research team has made such rapid progress with cancer drugs that they have set the pace for the other teams.* <Refers originally to horse-racing>.

—**show one's paces** to demonstrate one's abilities: *The sales manager went round with all the salesmen to watch them show their paces with the customers.*

—**stay the pace** to maintain progress in an activity at the same rate as others: *Small electronic firms find it difficult to stay the pace in these days of rapid technological change.*

pack

—**no names, no pack-drill** *see* **name**.

—**packed like herring in a barrel** *see* **herring**.

—**packed like sardines** *see* **sardine**.

—**pack it in** to stop doing something, e.g. working at something: *I've nearly finished this project so I think I'll pack it in for tonight.*

—**send (someone) packing** to send (someone) away firmly and frankly: *She always sends door-to-door salesmen packing immediately.*

paddle

—**paddle one's own canoe** *see* **canoe**.

pain

—**a pain in the neck** someone or something that constantly irritates one: *I work with a real pain in the neck who's always complaining.*

—**be at** *or* **take pains** to take trouble, to be careful: *He is at at pains to be on good terms with his mother-in-law.*

—**for one's pains** as reward for one's trouble and effort: *She nursed the old man for years and got nothing for her pains when he died.*

—**on pain of (something)** at the risk of (some kind of punishment, etc): *The workers were told on pain of instant dismissal not to talk to the rival company about the new product.*

paint

—**paint the town red** to go out and celebrate in a lively, noisy manner: *As soon as they finished their exams the students went out to paint the town red.*

pair

—**pair** *or* **pair off** (1) of a member of Parliament, to abstain from voting having made an arrangement with a member of the opposite side that he or she will also abstain: *The members for Kensington and Cardiff have paired for the vote.* (2) to take as a partner: *He paired off for the dance with the most attractive girl in the room.*

pale

—**beyond the pale** *see* **beyond**.

palm[1]

—**grease (someone's) palm** to give (someone) money, to bribe (someone): *We had to grease the hotel owner's palm to get our passports back.*

—**have an itching palm** *see* **itch**.

—**have (someone) in the palm of one's hand** to have (someone) in one's power and ready to do as one wishes: *The landowner has the local officials in the palm of his hand.*

palm[2]

—**bear the palm** to be pre-eminent: *The promising young athlete bore the palm at the Olympic Games when he won the 100 metres.* <Like the laurel, the leaves of the palm tree were used

as symbols of victory, and a palm leaf or branch was carried before a conqueror>.

—**give the palm to (someone)** to acknowledge (someone) as superior: *The retiring footballer gave the palm to the young player.*

pan

—**a flash in the pan** *see* **flash.**

—**out of the frying pan into the fire** *see* **fry.**

Pandora

—**Pandora's box** a collection of evils: *Pandora's box was opened for him, and all the pains and griefs his imagination had ever figured were abroad.* <Refers to the Greek legend of Prometheus in which Pandora, the all-gifted goddess, is said to have brought from heaven a box containing all human ills, which, the lid having been opened, escaped and spread over the world>.

pants

—**catch (someone) with his** *or* **her pants** *or* **trousers down** *see* **catch.**

paper

—**paper over the cracks** to try to hide faults, mistakes, difficulties, etc, in a hasty or careless way in order to pretend that there were no faults, mistakes, etc: *The couple tried to paper over the cracks in their marriage and always appeared very loving in public but they divorced soon after.*

—**paper tiger** someone or something that has the outward appearance of being powerful and threatening but is in fact ineffective: *The president of the country used to be feared by everyone but ever since the attempted coup he's been a paper tiger.*

—**paper war** a dispute carried on in writing: *The two columnists carried on a paper war in their respective newspapers.*

par

—**below** *or* **not up to par** (1) not up to the usual or required standard: *Her work has been below par recently.* (2) not completely well: *He's been feeling below par since he had the flu.*

—**on a par with (something)** of the same standard as (something), as good as (something): *His painting is not on a par with that of his contemporaries.*

—**par for the course** what might be expected, what usually happens: *He came late to the party but that's par for the course.* <Originally a golfing term meaning the number of strokes that would be made in a perfect round on the course>.

paradise

—**a fool's paradise** *see* **fool.**

parrot

—**parrot-fashion** repeating words or ideas without understanding what they mean: *The student learns her notes parrot-fashion but can't apply them when writing essays.*

—**sick as a parrot** *see* **sick.**

part

—**for my, etc, part** as far as I, etc, am concerned: *For my part I prefer autumn to spring.*

—**look the part** to have the appropriate appearance of a particular kind of person: *If she wants to be a top executive, she must look the part.*

—**(someone) of parts** an able person: *The position as head of the arts organization requires and man or woman of parts and experience.*

—**part and parcel (of something)** something that is naturally or basically part (of something): *Stress is part and parcel of a senior job.*

—**take (something) in good part** to accept (something) without being angry or offended: *She took the other children's teasing in good part.*

—**take (someone's) part** to support (someone) in an argument, etc: *She always takes her brother's part when he quarrels with their sister.*

—**the parting of the ways** the point at which people must go different ways, take different courses of action, make different decisions, etc: *The sale of their company was the parting of the ways for the two business partners.* <A biblical reference to Ezekiel 21:21>.

party

—**(someone's) party piece** an act, joke, speech that someone frequently performs in public: *The managing director always gives the same welcoming speech to new employees. It's his party piece.*

—**the life and soul of the party** *see* **life.**

—**the party line** the official opinions, ideas, attitudes, etc, as set down by the leaders of a particular group: *The politician refused to follow the party line.*

—**the party's over** a pleasant or happy time has come to an end: *This used to be a pleasant department but the party's over now. The new manager is very strict and gloomy.*

pass

—**come to a pretty pass** *see* **pretty.**

—**let (something) pass** to choose to disregard (something): *He was very rude to me but I let it pass. I could see he was upset.*

—**make a pass at (someone)** to try to start a romantic or sexual relationship with (someone): *He made a pass at the girl at the next table.* <Originally a fencing term, meaning to thrust with a foil>.

—**pass away** to die: *The old lady passed away in the night.*

—**pass by on the other side** to ignore someone in trouble and not help him or her: *When he was made homeless he did not expect his friends to pass by on the other side.* <A biblical reference to the parable of the Samaritan—Luke 10>.

—**pass for (someone** *or* **something)** to be mistaken for (someone or something): *She could easily pass for her sister.*

—**pass out** to faint: *She passed out in the extreme heat.*

—**pass the hat round** *see* **hat**.

—**pass (something) up** not to accept (something): *I'm going to have to pass up her invitation. I have another engagement.*

—**ships that pass in the night** *see* **ship**.

passage

—**passage of arms** a dispute, a quarrel, real or playful: *It seemed as if the two women could not meet without a passage of arms.*

—**rite of passage** *see* **rite**.

passing

—**passing rich** very wealthy: *As Alexander Pope wrote, "A man he was to all the country dear / And passing rich on forty pounds a year."* <Passing is frequently used as an intensifier by Shakespeare>.

past

—**I, etc, would not put it past (someone) to (do something)** I, etc, think (someone) is quite capable of (doing something bad): *I wouldn't put it past him to steal money from an old woman.*

—**past one's** *or* **its best** *or* **past it** less good, etc, than when one or it was not so old: *The runner is still fast but he's past his best.*

—**past master** someone extremely talented or skilful: *He is a past master at the art of charming women.*

pat

—**a pat on the back** an indication of praise or approval: *She got a pat on the back for her handling of the difficult customer.*

patch

—**hit a bad patch** *see* **bad**.

—**not to be a patch on (someone** *or* **something)** not to be nearly as good as (someone or something): *Her cooking isn't a patch on his.*

—**patch it** *or* **things up** to become friends again after a quarrel: *The two sisters haven't spoken to each other for years but we're trying to get them to patch things up.*

path

—**beat a path to (someone's) door** to visit (someone) very frequently or in large numbers: *The world's press beat a path to the door of the new tennis champion.*

patience

—**enough to try the patience of Job** *see* **Job**.

pave

—**pave the way for (something)** to make it possible or easier for (something to happen): *The student's research paved the way for the development of the new drug.*

pay

—**pay (someone) back in his** *or* **her own coin** *see* **coin**.

—**pay court to (someone)** *see* **court**.

—**pay lip-service to (something)** *see* **lip**.

—**pay one's way** to pay one's own expenses without going into debt, to meet one's obligations, to live free of debt: *He did not have a credit card as he wanted to be able to pay his way.*

—**pay the piper** *see* **piper**.

—**pay through the nose** *see* **nose**.

—**put paid to (something)** to prevent (an action, plan, etc) from being carried out: *She was planning to come uninvited to our party but we put paid to that by changing the date.*

—**rob Peter to pay Paul** *see* **rob**.

—**there will be the devil to pay** *see* **devil**.

pea

—**like as two peas in a pod** exactly or extremely alike: *The twins are like as two peas in a pod.*

peace

—**keep the peace** to prevent disturbances, fighting, quarrelling, etc: *The police were on duty at the football match to keep the peace.*

—**make one's peace with (someone)** to become, or try to become, friendly with (someone) again after a period of disagreement: *She made peace with her family before she died.*

peacock

—**proud as a peacock** extremely proud: *He's proud as a peacock of his baby son.*

pearl

—**cast pearls before swine** *see* **cast**.

peck

—**keep one's pecker up** to remain in good spirits: *Keep your pecker up. You'll get a job soon.* <Pecker means beak or nose>.

pedestal
—**put (someone) on a pedestal** to treat (someone) with great respect and admiration: *She put her music teacher on a pedestal.* <Refers to the practice of putting statues of famous people on pedestals>.

peep
—**a peeping Tom** *see* **Tom**.

peg
—**bring (someone) down a peg or two** to make (someone) more humble: *He was boasting about his wealth but she took him down a peg or two by reminding of his poverty-stricken youth.* <Refers to the tuning of musical instruments by adjusting pegs>.

—**off the peg** of clothes, ready to wear, not made for one specially: *He's so tall it is difficult for him to buy clothes off the peg.*

penny
—**a penny for them** *or* **your thoughts** what are you thinking of?: *You were lost in thought. A penny for them.*

—**cost a pretty penny** *see* **pretty**.

—**in for a penny, in for a pound** if one is going to do something one might as well do it boldly and thoroughly: *We've very little money but if we're going on holiday we might as well go somewhere exciting. In for a penny, in for a pound.*

—**in penny numbers** a very few, a very little at a time: *They came to the jumble sale in penny numbers.* <Refers to a method of selling encyclopedias, etc, in parts, originally at a penny per part>.

—**not to have a penny to one's name** to have no money at all: *When he died he didn't have a penny to his name.*

—**penny wise and pound foolish** being careful with small items of expenditure and extravagant with large ones: *She always buys the cheapest food and then goes on world cruises. She really is penny wise and pound foolish.*

—**spend a penny** to urinate: *Their little girl wants to spend a penny.* <From the former price of admission to the cubicle of a public toilet>.

—**the penny drops** I, etc, suddenly understand: *At first she didn't know what he was talking about but then the penny dropped.* <Refers to a coin in a slot machine>.

—**turn up like a bad penny** to reappear or keep reappearing although not wanted or welcome: *Her son turned up like a bad penny to borrow money from her.*

—**two a penny** of little value because very common: *China bowls like that are two a penny. There's no point in selling it.*

perfect
—**the pink of perfection** *see* **pink**.

period
—**period piece** something or someone that is exceptionally typical of the time when he or she was born or it was made: *She has a houseful of Victorian furniture—all period pieces.*

person
—**in person** not through a deputy, with bodily presence: *Her curt reply on the phone brought him in person to her apartment.*

petard
—**hoist with one's own petard** to be the victim of one's own action which was intended to harm someone else: *My neighbour was hoist with his own petard. He put broken glass on the top of his wall to prevent trespassers and then cut his hand on it.* <Refers to Shakespeare's *Hamlet*, Act 3, scene iv. A petard was a kind of bomb used by military engineers>.

petrel
—**a stormy petrel** *see* **storm**.

petticoat
—**in petticoats** still a child, still in the nursery: *I was earning my own living while you were still in petticoats.*

—**petticoat government** the rule of women: *The friendship of Queen Anne and the Duchess of Marlborough constituted a kind of petticoat government.*

philistine
—someone who is not interested in artistic or intellectual pursuits: *Don't ask her to go to the opera. She's a real Philistine.* <The Philistines were a fierce race of people who fought against the Israelites in biblical times. The present meaning was influenced by German>.

phoenix
—**rise like a phoenix from the ashes** *same as* **rise from the ashes**—*see* **ashes**.

pick
—**have a bone to pick with (someone)** *see* **bone**.

—**pick and choose** to choose very carefully from a range of things: *Surely there are enough dresses here for you to pick and choose from.*

—**pick (someone's) brains** *see* **brain**.

—**pick holes in (something)** *see* **hole**.

—**pick up the tab (for something)** *see* **tab**.

picture
—**put (someone) in the picture** to give (some-

one) all the information and detail about a situation: *Could you put me in the picture about what happened while I was on holiday.*

pie

—**have a finger in every pie** *see* **finger**.

—**have a finger in the pie** *see* **finger**.

—**pie in the sky** something good expected or promised in the future which is unlikely to come about: *He is planning a trip round the world but it's pie in the sky. He'll never save that much money.* <Refers to a quotation from a poem by the American poet Joe Hill>.

piece

—**a nasty piece of work** *see* **nasty**.

—**a piece of cake** *see* **cake**.

—**give (someone) a piece of one's mind** *see* **mind**.

—**go to pieces** to be unable to continue coping with a situation, life, etc: *She goes to pieces in an emergency.*

—**nasty piece of work** *see* **nasty**.

pig

—**buy a pig in a poke** to buy (something) without examining it carefully or without knowing its worth: *The second-hand washing machine she bought doesn't work. She bought a pig in a poke.* <Supposedly referring to a fairground trick in which a prospective customer was sold a cat in a bag thinking that it was a piglet>.

—**make a pig of oneself** to eat greedily, to eat a great deal. *The food was so good that we all made pigs of ourselves.*

—**make a pig's ear of (something)** to make a mess of (something) to do (something) very badly or clumsily: *She made a real pig's ear of knitting a sweater.*

—**pigs might fly** it is extremely unlikely that that will happen: *You think he'll marry her? Pigs might fly.*

pigeon

—**put** *or* **set the cat among the pigeons** *see* **cat**.

—**that's not my pigeon** that is not my responsibility or area of interest: *The accounts are not in order but that's not my pigeon. We have an accountant.* <Originally "not my pidgin" with its origins in pidgin English>.

pikestaff

—**plain as a pikestaff** very obvious: *The motive for his crime is plain as pikestaff.* <Pikestaff was originally packstaff, a staff for holding a traveller's pack and lacking any ornamentation. This sense of plain has been confused with

that of plain meaning clear>.

pill

—**sugar the pill** *see* **sugar**.

pillar

—**from pillar to post** from one place to another, often repeatedly: *The authorities sent us from pillar to post in search of a visa.* <Refers originally to the game of real tennis>.

pin

—**for two pins** given the least encouragement or reason: *For two pins I'd take the day off.*

—**on pins and needles** in a state of anxiety or suspense: *We're on pins and needles waiting to find out who's won.*

—**pin back one's ears** *see* **ear**.

—**pin one's hopes on (someone** *or* **something)** *see* **hope**.

—**you could have heard a pin drop** there was silence: *You could have heard a pin drop after she made the accusation.*

pinch

—**at a pinch** if it is absolutely necessary: *At a pinch we could accommodate three of you.*

—**feel the pinch** to have financial problems: *We were all right last year but the firm is feeling the pinch this year.*

—**take (something) with a grain** *or* **pinch of salt** *see* **salt**..

pink

—**be tickled pink** *see* **tickle**.

—**in the pink** in good health: *The family have all been ill but we're in the pink now.* <Refers to the pink complexion of some healthy people>.

—**the pink of perfection** absolute perfection: *If her cakes are not in the pink of perfection she throws them out.* <Refers to a quotation from Oliver Goldsmith's play, *She Stoops to Conquer*>.

pip

—**pipped at the post** beaten at the last minute: *I thought we would get the house for the price we offered but we were pipped at the post by someone who suddenly offered more.* <Refers originally to horse-racing. A horse is pipped at the post if another horse passes it at the end of the race>.

pipe

—**put that in your pipe and smoke it!** listen to that remark and think it over: *Always allow time for traffic delays if you want to arrive in time—put that in your pipe and smoke it!* <Generally accompanies a rebuke>.

—**pipe dream** a wish or idea that can never be

realized: *She talks of buying a cottage in the country but it's a pipe dream. She has very little money.* <Refers to visions experienced by opium smokers>.

pipeline

—**in the pipeline** in preparation, happening soon: *There are some new jobs in the pipeline but appointments will not be made until next year.* <Refers to crude oil being piped from the well to the refineries>.

piper

—**pay the piper** to provide the money for something and therefore be entitled to have a say in the organization of it: *Father should be allowed a say in where we go on holiday. After all he's paying the piper.* <Refers to the saying "He who pays the piper calls the tune">.

—**piping hot** *see* **hot**.

—**put that in your pipe and smoke it!** See how you like that!: *I know you think you're better at French than I am, but I've just heard that I passed the exam and you failed. Put that in your pipe and smoke it!*

pistol

—**hold a pistol to (someone's) head** to use force or threats to get (someone) to do as one wishes: *He had to sell the firm to get some money. The bank was holding a pistol to his head.*

pitch

—**black as pitch** extremely black: *The night was black as pitch.*

—**queer (someone's) pitch** *see* **queer**.

place

—**fall into place** to become understood when seen in terms of its relationship to other things: *The reason for her fear of men fell into place when we realized that she had been abused by her father as a child.*

—**go places** to be successful in one's career: *That young research worker is going places.*

—**in the first place** (1) in the beginning, to start with: *I regret going. I didn't want to go in the first place.* (2) as the first point in an argument, etc: *We can't cope with so many people. In the first place we have not got enough food.*

—**know one's place** to accept the lowliness of one's position and act accordingly: *It was made clear to the trainee teacher that she should know her place in the staff-room.*

—**out of place** *see* **out**.

—**pride of place** *see* **pride**.

—**put oneself in (someone's) place** to imagine what it would be like to be in (someone else's) circumstances: *I know you don't approve of strikes but put yourself in the workers' place. What else could they do?*

—**put (someone) in his** *or* **her place** to remind (someone) angrily of the lowliness of his or her position or of his or her lack of experience, knowledge, etc: *He tried to take over the running of the meeting but the chairman soon put him in his place.*

plain

—**plain as a pikestaff** *see* **pikestaff**.

—**plain sailing** easy progress: *Making alterations to the building will be plain sailing if we get planning permission.* <Perhaps confused with plane sailing, a method of making navigational calculations at sea in which the earth's surface is treated as though it were flat>.

plate

—**have (something) handed to one on a plate** to get (something) without having to put any effort into it: *Her schoolfriend works at weekends to buy clothes but she has a clothes allowance from her father. She has everything handed to her on a plate.*

play

—**all work and no play makes Jack a dull boy** *see* **work**.

—**bring into play** to begin to use or employ: *He had to bring all his powers of persuasion into play to get her to go.*

—**child's play** *see* **child**.

—**fair play** *see* **fair**.

—**make a play for (someone** *or* **something)** to try to obtain (someone or something): *He's making a play for his friend's job.*

—**play a losing game** *see* **lose**.

—**play (something) down** to try to make (something) appear less important, grave, etc: *Management are trying to play down the seriousness of the firm's financial position.*

—**played out** (1) exhausted: *The children are played out after the part.* (2) no longer having any interest, influence, usefulness, etc: *His ideas on education are played out.*

—**play fast and loose with (something)** *see* **fast**.

—**play for time** *see* **time**.

—**play gooseberry** *see* **gooseberry**.

—**play hard to get** to make it difficult for someone to get to know one in order to make him or her more keen to do so: *She regretted playing hard to get when he started going out with another girl.*

—**play havoc with (something)** *see* **havoc**.

—**play it by ear** *see* **ear**.

—**play (someone) off against (someone else)** to use two people for one's own purposes, to make two people act upon each other so as to bring about a desired result: *The spoiled child played his father off against his mother so that he was always getting treats*.

—**play possum** *see* **possum**.

—**play second fiddle (to someone)** *see* **fiddle**.

—**play the devil's advocate** *see* **devil**.

—**play the field** *see* **field**.

—**play the game** *see* **game**.

—**play one's trump card** *see* **trump**.

—**play (someone) up** to cause trouble to or annoy (someone): *The children always play their father up when he's looking after them*.

—**play up to (someone)** to flatter (someone) and pay (someone) a great deal of attention for one's own advantage: *She's playing up to her father because she wants him to buy her a new dress*.

—**play with fire** *see* **fire**.

please

—**pleased as Punch** *see* **Punch**.

plot

—**the plot thickens** the situation is getting more complicated and more interesting: *He is having an affair with his secretary and it turns out that his wife is having an affair with her boss. The plot thickens*. <Refers to a quotation from George Villiers' play *The Rehearsal*>.

plough

—**put one's hand to the plough** to begin serious work, to undertake important duties: *The students must put their hands to the plough and begin studying for the examination*.

pocket

—**in (someone's) pocket** under the control or influence of (someone): *The board will vote with the managing director. He has them all in his pocket*.

—**line one's pocket** to make money for oneself dishonestly: *The boss found out that he had been lining his pocket by taking bribes from suppliers*.

—**out of pocket** having made a loss: *Not only did the dance not make a profit but the organizing committee were all out of pocket*.

poetic

—**poetic justice** deserved but accidental punishment or reward: *The burglar left his bag of stolen jewellery on the train. That was poetic justice*.

—**poetic licence** the disregarding of established rules of form, grammar, fact, etc, by writers to achieve a desired effect: *The poet uses no capital letters or punctuation and includes other forms of poetic licence in his works*.

point

—**a sore point** *see* **sore**.

—**beside the point** *see* **beside**.

—**come** *or* **get to the point** to reach the most important part of a discussion, etc: *I wish the lecturer would stop rambling on and get to the point*.

—**make a point of (doing something)** to be exceptionally careful about (doing something): *She makes a point of visiting her elderly parents at least once a week*.

—**make one's point** to state one's opinion clearly: *Now you've made your point please give others the chance to speak*.

—**point the finger at (someone** *or* **something)** *see* **finger**.

—**stretch a point** *see* **stretch**.

—**the point of no return** the stage in a process, etc. when it becomes impossible either to stop or change one's mind: *The divorce papers have been signed. They've reached the point of no return*. <Originally referred to the point in the flight of an aircraft after which it did not have enough fuel to return to its place of departure>.

—**up to a point** to some extent but not completely: *I agree with your views up to a point but I do have reservations*.

poison

—**poison-pen letter** an anonymous letter saying bad things about someone: *She received a poison-pen letter saying her husband was an adulterer*.

pole

—**be poles apart** *see* **apart**.

pony

—**on shanks's pony** *see* **shanks**.

pop

—**pop the question** *see* **question**.

port

—**any port in a storm** any solution to a problem or difficulty will suffice. *I don't like asking my parents for a loan but my rent is overdue. It's a case of any port in a storm*.

possum

—**play possum** to pretend to be asleep, unconscious or dead: *He played possum when the children crept into his bedroom. He was too tired to play with them*. <The possum pretends to be

dead when it is under threat of attack from another animal>.

post¹

—**deaf as a post** see **deaf**.

—**from pillar to post** from one place to another, often repeatedly: *The authorities chased us from pillar to post trying to get a visa.*

—**pipped at the post** see **pip**.

post²

—**keep (someone) posted** to keep (someone) informed about developments in a situation: *The boss wants to be kept posted about the export deal although he's on holiday.*

pot

—**go to pot** to get into a bad or worse state: *The firm went to pot when the old man died.* <Refers to meat being cut up and stewed in a pot).

—**take pot-luck** to have a meal at someone's house, etc, without having anything specially prepared for one: *You're welcome to stay to dinner but you'll have to take pot-luck.* <Literally to take whatever happens to be in the cooking-pot at the time>.

—**the pot calling the kettle black** someone criticizing (someone) for doing (something) that he or she does himself or herself: *His father scolded him for being untidy although he himself leaves things lying around—a case of the pot calling the kettle black.*

—**the** or **a watched pot never boils** when one is waiting for something to happen, etc, the time taken seems longer if one is constantly thinking about it. *Stop thinking about the letter with the exam results. It won't make the postman arrive any sooner. A watched pot never boils.*

potato

—**hot potato** see **hot**.

pound

—**get** or **have one's pound of flesh** see **flesh**.

pour

—**it never rains but it pours** when something goes wrong it goes wrong very badly or other things go wrong too: *I forgot where I parked the car and then I got a parking ticket. It never rains but it pours.*

—**pour oil on troubled waters** see **oil**.

power

—**more power to (someone's) elbow** may (someone) be successful: *I hear that he's started a charity for handicapped children. More power to his elbow.*

—**the power behind the throne** the person who is really in charge of or in control of an or-

ganization, etc, while giving the impression that it is someone else: *He is the chairman of the company, but his wife is the power behind the throne.*

—**the powers that be** the people in charge, the authorities: *The powers that be have decided that the shop assistants should wear a uniform.*

practice

—**practice makes perfect** if one practises doing something one will eventually be good at it: *They say that practice makes perfect, but I'll never be good at sewing.*

—**sharp practice** see **sharp**.

practise

—**practise what one preaches** to act in the way that one recommends to others: *He tells the children to come home on time but he's always late himself. He should practise what he preaches.*

praise

—**praise (someone** or **something) to the skies** see **sky**.

—**sing (someone's** or **something's) praises** to praise (someone or something) with great enthusiasm: *She keeps singing the praises of her new washing machine.*

preach

—**preach to the converted** see **convert**.

—**practise what he preaches** see **practise**.

premium

—**be at a premium** to be much in demand and, therefore, difficult to obtain: *Tickets for the pop concert are at a premium. The group is very popular.* <A financial term meaning literally "sold at more than the nominal value">.

presence

—**presence of mind** the ability to keep calm and think and act sensibly whatever the situation: *She had the presence of mind to throw a wet cloth over the pan when it caught fire.*

present

—**there's no time like the present** see **time**.

press

—**be pressed for (something)** to be short of (something, such as time or money): *I'm really pressed for time.*

—**press-gang (someone) into (doing something)** to force (someone) or persuade (someone) against his or her will to (do something): *She's pressganged us into being in charge of a stall at the fête.* <The press gang was a group of sailors in the 18th century who seized men and forced them to join the navy>.

—**press (someone** or **something) into service** to

make use of (someone or something), especially in an emergency or on a special occasion: *My vacuum cleaner has broken down and so I'll have to press the old one into service.*

pressure

—**pressure group** a group of people who try to bring the attention of the authorities, etc, to certain issues, usually with a view to influencing them into making some changes: *She's part of a pressure group that is campaigning for more state nursery schools.*

pretence

—**under false pretences** *see* **false**.

pretty

—**a pretty kettle of fish** *see* **kettle**.

—**come to a pretty pass** to get into a bad state: *Things have come to a pretty pass if the firm is making people redundant.*

—**cost a pretty penny** to cost a large amount of money: *His new car must have cost a pretty penny.*

—**sitting pretty** in a very comfortable or advantageous position: *She's the boss's daughter. She's sitting pretty while the rest of us are worried about our jobs.*

prey

—**be a prey to (something)** regularly to suffer from (something): *She has been a prey to headaches all her life.*

—**prey on (someone's) mind** to cause constant worry or anxiety to (someone): *The accident in which he knocked over a child preyed on his mind all his life.*

price

—**at a price** at a very high price: *You can get a drink in the hotel—at a price!*

—**a price on (someone's) head** a reward offered for the capture or killing of (someone): *The escaped convict was never found even though there was a price on his head.*

—**what price (something)?** what do you think of (something)?, what is the value of (something)?: *He's been charged with drink driving. What price his lectures on the dangers of alcohol abuse now?*

prick

—**kick against the pricks** to show opposition to those in control or power: *The ordinary people will start kicking against the pricks if the government raise interest rates again.* <From cattle kicking against being driven forward by a sharp stick>.

—**prick up one's ears** *see* **ear**.

pride

—**pride goes before a fall** being too conceited often leads to misfortune: *The player who was boasting about how good she was got beaten. It just proves that pride goes before a fall.*

—**pride of place** the most important or privileged position: *Her son's photograph has pride of place on her mantelpiece.*

—**swallow one's pride** to behave in a more humble way than one usually does or than one would wish to do: *She had no money for food and so she swallowed her pride and asked her father for some.*

prime

—**be cut off in one's prime** to die or be killed in one's youth or at the most successful period in one's life: *They mourned for the soldiers cut off in their prime.*

—**prime mover** someone or something that gets something started: *She was the prime mover in the campaign against the new motorway.*

print

—**the small print** *see* **small**.

private

—**private eye** a private detective: *He hired a private eye to discover the identity of his wife's lover.*

pro

—**the pros and cons** the arguments for and against: *The council will consider the pros and cons of the new road tomorrow.* <Latin *pro*, for, and *contra*, against>.

profile

—**keep a low profile** *see* **low**.

proof

—**the proof of the pudding is in the eating** the real worth of something is found only when it has been into practice or use: *The government's theories on education are all very well, but the proof of the pudding will be in the eating.*

proportion

—**sense of proportion** the ability to decide what is important, etc, and what is not: *She has no sense of proportion. She went into hysterics just because she got a small stain on her dress.*

proud

—**do (someone) proud** to treat (someone) exceptionally well or lavishly: *I must say they did the old age pensioners proud at their Christmas party.*

public

—**public spirit** a wish to do things for the good of the community as a whole: *He's full of public spirit. He even picks up the litter in the park.*

pull

—**pull a face** *see* **face**.

—**pull a fast one on (someone)** *see* **fast**.

—**pull (something) off** to be successful in (something): *We were all surprised when he pulled off a victory against the golf champion.*

—**pull one's punches** *see* **punch**.

—**pull one's socks up** *see* **sock**.

—**pull one's weight** *see* **weight**.

—**pull out all the stops** *see* **stop**.

—**pull strings** *see* **string**.

—**pull through** to survive, to get better: *We thought that he was going to die after the operation but he pulled through.*

pulse

—**keep one's finger on the pulse** to keep oneself informed about recent developments in a situation, organization, etc, or in the world: *The old man has retired but still keeps his finger on the pulse by reading all the company reports.* <Refers to a doctor checking the rate of someone's pulse for health reasons>.

Punch

—**pleased as Punch** extremely pleased or happy: *The little girl was pleased as Punch with her new dress.* <Refers to the puppet show character who is usually portrayed smiling gleefully>.

punch

—**pull one's punches** to be less forceful or harsh in one's attack or criticism than one is capable of: *The manager rarely pulls his punches when he is criticizing someone's work.* <Refers to striking blows in boxing without using one's full strength>.

pup

—**sell (someone) a pup** to deceive (someone), often to sell or recommend something that turns out not to be as good as he or she thought: *That computer keeps breaking down. I think we've been sold a pup.*

pure

—**pure as the driven snow** exceptionally virtuous or moral: *She was pure as the driven snow but her sister was wild.* <Refers to snow that has been blown into heaps by the wind and has not yet become dirty>.

purpose

—**at cross purposes** involved in a misunderstanding because of talking or thinking about different things without realizing it: *No wonder I couldn't understand what she was talking about. We were talking at cross purposes.*

—**serve a** *or* **the purpose** to be useful in a particular situation, to fulfil a need: *I really need a lever for this but a knife will serve the purpose.*

purse

—**you can't make a silk purse out of a sow's ear** *see* **silk**.

push

—**push one's luck** *see* **luck**.

—**push off** to go away: *It's getting late. I'd better push off.*

put

—**be put upon** to be made use of for someone else's benefit, to be taken advantage of: *Her mother's really put upon by her daughter. She expects her to baby-sit every night.*

—**put a brave face on it** *see* **face**.

—**put (someone) in mind of (someone** *or* **something)** *see* **mind**.

—**put (someone) in his** *or* **her place** *see* **place**.

—**put (someone) in the picture** *see* **picture**.

—**put it on** to feign, to pretend: *She said that she had sprained her ankle but she was putting it on.*

—**put (someone's) nose out of joint** *see* **nose**.

—**put one across (someone)** *see* **across**.

—**put one's finger on (something)** *see* **finger**.

—**put the cat among the pigeons** *see* **cat**.

—**put-up job** something done to deceive or trick (someone): *The police pretended to believe him but it was a put-up job. They were trying to get him to confess.*

pyjamas

—**the cat's pyjamas** *see* **cat**.

putty

—**putty in (someone's) hands** easily influenced or manipulated by (someone): *She'll do whatever he wants. She's putty in his hands.* <Putty is a malleable substance>.

Pyrrhic

—**Pyrrhic victory** a a success of some kind in which what it takes to achieve is not worth it: *She was eventually awarded compensation for unfair dismissal but the money all went in legal costs. It was indeed a Pyrrhic victory.* <From the costly victory of Pyrrhus, king of Epirus, over the Romans at Heraclea in 280 BC>.

Q

q

—**mind one's p's and q's** *see* **p**.

quantity

—**an unknown quantity** someone or something of which very little is known: *One of the players in the tournament is an unknown quantity.* <Refers literally to a mathematical term>.

quarter

—**at close quarters** nearby, at or from a short distance away: *At close quarters she looks older.*

—**give** *or* **show quarter** to act with clemency, to be merciful, to be lenient: *The general ordered that no quarter should be given and that all prisoners should be killed.*

queer

—**a queer fish** *see* **fish**.

—**in Queer Street** in financial difficulties: *If we both lose our jobs we'll be in Queer Street.* <Perhaps changed from Carey Street in London where the bankruptcy courts were>.

—**queer (someone's) pitch** to upset (someone's) plans or arrangements: *He was going to ask her out but his best friend queered his pitch by asking her first.* <Pitch here refers to the site of a market stall. Originally to queer someone's pitch was to set up a stall beside it selling the same kind of goods>.

question

—**a loaded question** *see* **load**.

—**a vexed question** *see* **vex**.

—**beg the question** *see* **beg**.

—**call (something) in question** to express doubts regarding (something), to find fault with (something): *After the bad traffic jam, the police were called in question for their handling of it.*

—**out of the question** not possible: *Further salary increases are out of question.*

—**pop the question** to ask (someone) to marry one: *He popped the question on her birthday.*

—**rhetorical question** *see* **rhetorical**.

—**the burning question** *see* **burn**.

—**the sixty-four (thousand) dollar question** *see* **sixty**.

queue

—**jump the queue** to go ahead of others in a queue without waiting for one's proper turn: *She jumped the queue and went straight up to the shop counter.*

qui

—**on the qui vive** very alert: *The child was on the qui vive and heard her father's car.* <From the challenge of a French sentry *Qui vive?*— "Long live who, whose side are you on?">.

quick

—**a quick one** a quick drink: *The pubs will be closing soon but there's time for a quick one.*

—**cut (someone) to the quick** to hurt (someone's) feelings very badly: *She cut him to the quick when she rejected his present.* <The quick is the sensitive skin under the nail>.

—**quick as lightning** *see* **lightning**.

—**quick on the uptake** *see* **uptake**.

quid

—**quids in** a fortunate position: *If you get a job with that firm you'll be quids in.*

quit

—**call it quits** to agree that neither person owes the other one anything and that neither one has any kind of advantage over the other: *You paid for lunch and I paid for dinner. Let's call it quits.*

quite

—**quite something** something special or remarkable: *Her new hat is quite something.*

R

R

—**the three R's** reading, writing and arithmetic, thought of as the essential basics of education: *The teacher spends much time on the three R's.* <From reading, writing and arithmetic>.

race

—**one-horse race** *see* **one**.

—**the rat race** *see* **rat**.

rack[1]

—**go to rack and ruin** to fall into a state of disrepair or into a worthless condition: *The estate has gone to rack and ruin because the duke has no money.* <"Rack" means destruction>.

rack[2]

—**on the rack** in distress, under strain: *He's on the rack worrying about losing his job.* <The rack was an instrument of torture on which a person's body was stretched in both directions at once>.

—**rack one's brains** *see* **brain**.

racket

—**be on the racket** to spend one's time in idleness and dissipation: *He had been off on the racket for perhaps a week at a time.*

rag

—**like a red rag to a bull** *see* **red**.

—**lose one's rag** to lose one's temper: *The teacher completely lost her rag and shouted at the children.*

—**the ragtag and bobtail** the common people: *The decent citizens did not attend the meeting; only the ragtag and bobtail were present, and their views carry no weight.*

rage

—**all the rage** very fashionable or popular: *Mini skirts were all the rage then.*

rail

—**off the rails** not sensible, disorganized, deranged: *He used to be one of our best workers but he seems to have gone a bit off the rails.* <Refers to a train leaving the track>.

rain

—**it never rains but it pours** a rapid succession of events: *He not only received a legacy from his uncle but also one from his friend—it never rains but it pours.*

—**keep** *or* **put away** *or* **save (something) for a rainy day** to keep (something, especially money) until one really needs it: *The old lady does not have enough food but she insists on keeping a large sum of money for a rainy day.* <Formerly most jobs, such as farm jobs, were dependent on the weather. Since they could not be carried out in rainy weather no money was earned then>.

—**right as rain** perfectly all right, completely well: *She's had flu but she's right as rain now.*

—**rain or shine** whatever the weather: *He plays golf rain or shine.*

—**rain like cats and dogs** *see* **cat**.

raise

—**raise Cain** *see* **Cain**.

—**raise one's back** to grow obstinate, to rebel: *The clergyman raised his back against orders emanating from the bishop's palace.*

—**raise the wind** *see* **wind**.

rake

—**thin as a rake** extremely thin: *She eats huge amounts but stays thin as a rake.*

ram

—**ram (something) down (someone's) throat** *see* **throat**.

rampage

—**be** *or* **go on the rampage** to rush about wildly or violently: *The crowd went on the rampage and some people were trampled to death.*

rank

—**close ranks** to act together and support each other as a defensive measure: *The dead patient's husband tried to enquire into the cause of her death but the doctors closed ranks and would tell him nothing.*

—**the rank and file** the ordinary people or the ordinary members of an organization, etc: *The union leaders should pay attention to the views of the rank and file.* <Literally ranks and files were the horizontal and vertical lines in which battalions of soldiers were drawn up on parade>.

ransom

—**a king's ransom** *see* **king**.

—**hold (someone) to ransom** to demand something (from someone) by threatening to take harmful action if it is not given: *The newspaper said that the firemen were holding the government to ransom by threatening to go on strike.* <Literally to hold someone as a hostage until a sum of money is paid for his or her release>.

rant

—**rant and rave** to shout angrily: *Her father's ranting and raving about how late she came home.*

rap

—**not care a rap** not to care at all about what anybody says: *I shall do as I like—I don't care a rap.*

—**rap over the knuckles** to administer a sharp reproof, to censure sharply: *The children were rapped over the knuckles by the policeman for running out onto the road without looking.*

—**take the rap for (something)** to take the blame or punishment for (something): *He committed the crime but his friend took the rap for it and went to prison.*

rarin'

—**rarin' to go** extremely eager to begin or set off: *I promised to take the children on a picnic and they're rarin' to go.* <Dialect for "rearing">.

rat

—**like a drowned rat** soaking wet: *They came in from the storm like drowned rats.*

—**rat on (someone)** to report or betray (someone): *The head knew that they had played truant because another pupil had ratted on them.*

—**smell a rat** to have a suspicion that something is wrong or that one is being deceived: *I smelt a rat when he did not invite me into the house.* <Refers to a terrier hunting>.

—**the rat race** the fierce competitive struggle for success in business, etc: *He's given up the rat race and gone to live on an island.* <A nautical phrase for a fierce tidal current>.

rate

—**at a rate of knots** see **knot**.

raw

—**a raw deal** see **deal**.

—**in the raw** in the natural state without civilization, comfort, etc: *He chose life in the raw rather than city life and lives in a hut in the country.*

—**touch (someone) on the raw** to hurt or anger (someone): *You touched him on the raw when you mentioned his children. He's lost contact with them.*

razor

—**sharp as a razor** quick-witted and very intelli-

gent: *The child's sharp as a razor. Watch what you say in front of him.*

read

—**take (something) as read** to assume (something): *You can take it as read that all the candidates are suitably qualified.*

ready

—**ready money** money that can be immediately made use of, money in one's hands, cash: *He couldn't pay the window cleaner as he had no ready money.*

real

—**the real McCoy** something genuine and very good as opposed to others like it which are not: *This lasagne is the real McCoy, not something out of a freezer.* <Perhaps from Kid McCoy, an American boxer who was called The Real McCoy to distinguish him from other boxers of the same name>.

reason

—**it stands to reason that** it is logical, or obvious that: *It stands to reason that she would be in pain. Her leg is broken.*

—**ours, etc, not to reason why** it is not for us, etc, to question orders: *If the boss says to come in half-an-hour early tomorrow we had better do it. Ours not to reason why.*

—**see reason** to be persuaded by someone's advice, etc, to act or think sensibly.

—**within reason** within sensible limits: *You can choose your birthday present—within reason.*

—**without rhyme or reason** see **rhyme**.

rebound

—**on the rebound** while suffering from the disappointment of the end of a relationship: *She married him on the rebound from a broken engagement.*

rebuff

—**meet with a rebuff** to encounter opposition: *The poor man met with a rebuff when he asked the millionaire for his daughter's hand. He was refused absolutely.*

reckon

—**reckon on** or **upon** to expect: *You reckon on losing your friends' kindness if you impose too much.*

—**reckon without one's host** to calculate blindly, to enter rashly on any undertaking: *We thought our troubles would end after the election but we reckoned without our host.*

record

—**break the record** to do something better, faster, etc, than it has been done before: *The sprinter has broken the world record.*

—**for the record** so that it will be noted: *For the record I do not agree with the committee's decision.*

—**off the record** not to be made public: *Don't say anything off the record to a journalist. He'll just publish it anyhow.*

—**on record** noted officially: *The politician is on record as saying that he won't resign.*

—**set the record straight** to put right a mistake or misunderstanding: *He thought that I had voted against him but I was able to set the record straight.*

—**(someone's) track record** *see* **track**.

red

—**a red herring** *see* **herring**.

—**a red-letter day** a day remembered because something particularly pleasant or important happened or happens on it: *It will be a red-letter day for her when her husband comes home from the war.* <From the fact that important dates in the year are sometimes shown in red on calendars>.

—**catch (someone) red-handed** to find (someone) in the act of doing something wrong or unlawful: *We caught the thief red-handed with the stolen necklace in his hand.* <Refers to finding a murderer with the blood of a victim on his or her hands>.

—**in the red** in debt, overdrawn: *My bank account is in the red but it's nearly pay-day.* <From the use of red ink to make entries on the debit side of an account>.

—**like a red rag to a bull** certain to make (someone) angry: *Any criticism of the government is like a red rag to a bull to the old man.* <From the widespread belief that bulls are angered by the sight of the colour red although they are in fact colour-blind>.

—**on red alert** ready for an an immediate danger: *The area was put on red alert because of the forest fire.* <Originally a military term for mobilizing civilians during an air-raid>.

—**paint the town red** *see* **paint**.

—**red-hot** very enthusiastic or dedicated: *She's a red-hot fan of the group.*

—**red tape** the rules and regulations official papers, etc, that are thought to characterize government departments: *With all the red tape it could take quite a long time to get a visa.* <From the reddish tape used by government offices to tie bundles of papers>.

—**see red** to get very angry: *She saw red when she witnessed him kick the dog.*

—**the red carpet** *see* **carpet**.

reed

—**a broken reed** someone who is too weak or unreliable to be depended upon: *She has to work to support her five children because her husband is a broken reed.*

region

—**in the region of (something)** about, approximately: *The price will be in the region of £60,000.*

rein

—**give free rein to (something)** to allow complete freedom to (one's imagination, emotions, etc) : *She gave free rein to her creative powers in her recent writings.* <Refers to a horse that is allowed to go as fast as it likes>.

—**keep a tight rein on (someone *or* something)** to keep strict control over (someone or something): *We must keep a tight rein on our expenditure this year.* <Refers to a horse strictly controlled by the rider>.

reputation

—**live up to one's reputation** to behave in the way that one is reputed or expected to behave: *He lived up to his reputation as as womanizer by making a pass at our hostess.*

resort

—**as a *or* in the last resort** *see* **last**.

resistance

—**the line of least resistance** *see* **line**.

resource

—**leave (someone) to his *or* her own resources** to let (someone) find his or her own way of solving a problem, entertaining himself or herself, etc: *You can't be responsible for her all the time. You'll have to leave her to her own resources some time.*

respect

—**be no respecter of persons** not to be influenced by the standing, importance, money, etc, of people: *Illness is no respecter of persons.*

rest

—**come to rest** to stop: *The child's train came to rest just in front of me.*

—**lay (someone) to rest** to bury (someone): *We laid the old man to rest yesterday.*

—**rest assured** you can be quite certain: *Rest assured we will do a good job.*

—**rest on one's laurels** *see* **laurel**.

—**rest on one's oars** *see* **oar**.

retreat

—**beat a (hasty) retreat** *see* **beat**.

return

—**return to the fold** to come or back to one's

family, an organization, a set of principles or beliefs, etc, which one has previously left: *He left the firm to work overseas but he has now returned to the fold.* <Refers to a sheep returning to the sheep-pen>.

—**the point of no return** *see* **point**.

rhetorical

—**rhetorical question** a question which does not require an answer: *What happened to the summers of our youth?*

rhyme

—**without rhyme or reason** without any logical or sensible reason or explanation: *His attitude to his children is without rhyme or reason.*

rich

—**rich as Croesus** extremely rich: *He can well afford to pay for the party. He's rich as Croesus.* <Croesus was a ruler of the kingdom of Lydia who was very wealthy>.

—**strike it rich** to obtain wealth, often suddenly or unexpectedly: *He struck it rich when he went to work for the old lady. She left him all her money.*

Richmond

—**another Richmond in the field** another unexpected adversary: *When a rival suitor appeared, his temper rose when he saw another Richmond in the field.* <From Shakespeare's Richard III, act V, scene iv, when at the Battle of Bosworth King Richard replies to his attendant Catesby, who urges him to flee, "I think there be six Richmonds in the field. Five I have slain today instead of him.">

riddance

—**good riddance to (someone *or* something)** I am glad to have got rid of (someone or something): *Good riddance to him. He was just a troublemaker.*

ride

—**be riding for a fall** to be on a course of action that is likely to lead to unpleasant results or disaster for oneself: *Just because she's a friend of the manager she thinks she can come to work as late as she likes. She's riding for a fall.* <Refers originally to hunting>.

—**have a rough ride** to receive harsh treatment or suffer an unpleasant experience: *I hear he had rather a rough ride at his interview.*

—**ride out (something)** to survive until (something difficult) is over: *Many small companies did not ride out the recession.* <Used literally of a ship keeping afloat during a storm>.

—**ride roughshod over (someone)** *see* **rough**.

—**riding high** *see* **high**.

—**take (someone) for a ride** to deceive or trick (someone): *He was taking her for a ride pretending to be wealthy. He's actually penniless.* <Originally American gangsters' slang for killing someone, from the practice of killing someone in a moving vehicle so as not to attract attention>.

rift

—**a rift in the lute** a slight disagreement or difficulty that might develop into a major one and ruin a project or relationship: *They've only been divorced for a short time but I noticed a rift in the lute right at the beginning of their marriage.* <Refers to a quotation from Tennyson's *Idylls*>.

rig

—**rig the market** to buy shares of a stock in which one is interested in order to force up the price so that a profit is made on reselling: *The financier was not interested in the company—he was rigging the market.*

right

—**by rights** rightly, justly: *By rights he should not be in a senior position.*

—**get *or* keep on the right side of (someone)** to act in such a way that (someone) feels or continues to feel friendly and well disposed towards one: *It is important to keep on the right side of your girlfriend's mother.*

—**give one's right arm for (something)** *see* **arm**.

—**have one's heart in the right place** *see* **heart**.

—**in one's own right** independently, because of one's own social position, ability, work, etc: *She is a princess in her own right, not because her husband is a prince.*

—**in one's right mind** *see* **mind**.

—**(someone's) left hand does not know what his *or* her right one is doing** *see* **left**.

—**left, right and centre** *see* **left**.

—**Mr *or* Miss Right** the perfect man or woman for one to marry: *She's turned down several proposals of marriage. She says she's waiting for Mr Right.*

—**not right in the head** deranged, insane, mentally handicapped: *The young man who attacked her is not right in the head.*

—**on the right track** *see* **track**.

—**put (something) right** to repair, to make all right, to rectify: *The machine has been put right. The misunderstanding between them has been put right.*

—**put (someone) right** to cause (someone) to realize his mistake, incorrect beliefs, etc: *He* thought they were still married but I was able to put him right.

—**right arm** see **arm**.

—**right as a trivet** safe and sound, in a thoroughly satisfactory condition: *Once he had won the lottery his financial affairs were right as a trivet.*

—**right as rain** see **rain**.

—**right-hand man** or **woman** someone's most valuable and helpful assistant: *The chief mechanic is the garage owner's right-hand man.*

—**right off** immediately: *They told me the name of the nearest supplier right off.*

—**serve (someone) right** to be something unpleasant that (someone) deserves: *It serves her right that he has left her. She was having an affair with his best friend.*

—**set (something) to rights** to bring (something) into a correct, organized, desired, etc, state: *The filing system is chaotic but we'll soon set it to rights.*

—**strike the right note** see **note**.

ring

—**a dead ringer** someone who looks extremely like someone else: *He's a dead ringer for my younger brother.* <Perhaps from the use of the phrase to mean a horse, similar to the original, illegally substituted in a race>.

—**have a ringside seat** to be in a position to observe clearly what is happening: *His mother's had a ringside seat at their marital quarrels for years.* <Originally refers to boxing>.

—**ring a bell** see **bell**.

—**ring down the curtain (on something)** see **curtain**.

—**ring the changes** see **change**.

—**ring true** to sound true, to be convincing: *Something about his account of the accident did not hold true.*

riot

—**read the riot act to (someone)** to scold (someone) severely and warn him or her to behave better: *Their mother read the riot act to the children about the state of their rooms.* <The Riot Act of 1715 was read to unlawful gatherings of people to break the gathering up. If the people refused to disperse action could be taken against them>.

—**riotous living** extravagant, energetic living: *After the riotous living of Christmas I'm glad to take things quietly.*

—**run riot** to get out of control: *The children run riot in her class. Wild roses run riot in her garden.*

ripe

—**a ripe old age** see **age**.

rise

—**get up with** or **rise with the lark** see **lark**.

—**rise and shine** to get out of bed and be lively and cheerful: *It's time to rise and shine.*

—**rise from the ashes** see **ashes**.

—**rise to the bait** see **bait**.

—**rise to the occasion** see **occasion**.

—**take a rise out of (someone)** to tease or make fun of (someone) so that he or she gets annoyed: *You should try to ignore it when he takes a rise out of you.*

risk

—**risk life and limb** see **life**.

—**risk one's neck** see **neck**.

—**run the risk of (something** or **doing something)** to do (something) that involves a risk of (something or doing something): *He runs the risk of killing himself when he drives so fast.*

—**rite of passage** a ceremony or event marking the transition from one period or status in life to the next: *The*

river

—**sell (someone) down the river** to betray or be disloyal to (someone): *He sold his friend down the river by telling the police that she had been present at the crime.* <Refers historically to selling slaves from the upper Mississippi states to buyers in Louisiana where working and living conditions were much harsher>.

road

—**all roads lead to Rome** see **Rome**.

—**a royal road** a road without difficulties: *There is no royal road to learning.*

—**get the show on the road** see **show**.

—**hit the road** start out on a journey: *If we're to get there by nightfall we'll have to hit the road now.*

—**one for the road** one last drink before leaving: *Don't go yet. Let's have one for the road.*

roaring

—**do a roaring trade in (something)** to be selling a lot of (something): *We're doing a roaring trade in ice-cream in this hot weather.*

—**roaring drunk** extremely, and often noisily, drunk: *They all got roaring drunk after their team won.*

rob

—**daylight robbery** see **day**.

—**rob Peter to pay Paul** to pay (someone) with the money that should go to pay a debt owed to (someone else): *He paid the gas bill with the* rent money, which was just robbing Peter to pay Paul. <Refers to Saints Peter and Paul who share the same feast day, 29 July>.

rock

—**on the rocks** (1) in difficulties, in danger of being destroyed or ruined: *Their marriage is on the rocks.* (2) of a drink, served with ice cubes: *The customer in the bar asked for a whisky on the rocks.*

—**steady as a rock** extremely steady, motionless: *The surgeon's hand was steady as a rock.*

rod

—**make a rod for one's own back** to do something that is going to cause harm or problems for oneself in the future: *If you charge too little for your work now you will be making a rod for one's own back. Your employers will not want to raise the rate.*

—**rule (someone or something) with a rod of iron** see **iron**.

—**spare the rod and spoil the child** if a child is not punished for being naughty it will have a bad effect on his or her character: *She lets that child do what he likes and she will regret it. It will be a case of spare the rod and spoil the child.*

rogue

—**a rogue's gallery** a police collection of photographs of known criminals: *When she was attacked the police asked her if she recognized anybody in their rogue's gallery.*

roll

—**a rolling stone (gathers no moss)** a person who does not stay very long in one place (does not acquire very much in the way of possessions or responsibilities): *He has no furniture to put in an unfurnished flat. He's a rolling stone.*

—**be rolling in it** or **in money** to have a great deal of money: *He lives in a very small flat although he's rolling in it.*

—**be rolling in the aisles** to be laughing very heartily: *The comedian had the audience rolling in the aisles.*

—**heads will roll** see **head**.

—**roll on** may (a particular time) come soon: *Roll on the return to school! The children are driving me mad.*

Rome

—**all roads lead to Rome** all ways of fulfilling an aim or intention end in the same result and so it does not does not matter which way one uses: *You might not like my method of fund-raising but all roads lead to Rome.*

—**fiddle while Rome burns** to do nothing while something important is being ruined or destroyed: *By doing nothing about the rate of unemployment the government is being accused of fiddling while Rome burns.* <The Emperor Nero was said to have played on a lyre while Rome was burning>.

—**Rome was not built in a day** a difficult task cannot be completed satisfactorily quickly: *The new company has very few orders yet, but Rome was not built in a day.*

—**when in Rome do as the Romans do** one should follow the customs, behaviour, etc, of the people one is visiting or living with: *He should try to eat some Spanish food instead of looking for somewhere that sells English food. When in Rome do as the Romans do.* <A saying of St Ambrose>.

romp

—**romp home** see **home**.

roof

—**have a roof over one's head** to have somewhere to live: *It's just a small room in a flat but at least it's a roof over your head.*

—**hit the roof** same as **hit the ceiling**—see **ceiling**.

room

—**not to be enough room to swing a cat** see **cat**.

roost

—**chickens come home to roost** see **chicken**.

—**rule the roost** to be the person in charge whose wishes or orders are obeyed: *The son rules the roost in that household. The father hardly ever speaks.*

root

—**root and branch** thoroughly and completely: *The government should get rid of that out-dated law root and branch.*

—**rooted to the spot** see **spot**.

—**root (something) out** to destroy or get rid of something completely: *The new regime was determined to root out any opposition.*

—**the grass roots** see **grass**.

rope

—**give (someone) enough rope (and he will hang himself)** let (someone foolish) act as he or she pleases and he or she will bring about his or her own ruin, downfall, misfortune, etc: *I know he's running the department badly but don't interfere. Give him enough rope and he will hang himself.*

—**know the ropes** to know the details and methods associated with a business, procedure, activity, etc: *This is his first day as manager. He'll soon to get to know the ropes.*

—**money for old rope** *see* **money.**

—**rope (someone) in** to include (someone), to ask (someone) to join in, often against his or her will: *I've been roped in to help with the running of the school dance.* <Refers to lassoing cattle in the American West>.

—**show (someone) the ropes** to teach (someone) the details and methods involved (in something): *You'll soon know your way around the school. Your sister will show you the ropes.*

rose

—**bed of roses** *see* **bed.**

—**everything's coming up roses** everything is turning out to be successful or happy: *The business was doing badly last year but now everything's coming up roses.*

—**look at (someone** *or* **something) through rose-coloured** *or* **rose-tinted spectacles** *or* **glasses** to view (someone or something) in an extremely optimistic light: *She doesn't see his faults. She looks at him through rose-coloured spectacles.*

rough

—**cut up rough** to get very nasty: *He always seemed so pleasant but he cut up rough when he didn't get his own way.*

—**give (someone) the rough edge of one's tongue** to scold or criticize (someone) severely: *I'll give that child the rough edge of my tongue for letting the dog out.*

—**live rough** to live without proper housing, often outside all the time, and without the usual amenities: *The escaped prisoner lived rough before he was caught.*

—**ride roughshod over (someone)** to treat (someone) without any respect and without any regard for his or her views or feelings: *He never listens to anything anyone else suggests. He just rides roughshod over them and carries out his own ideas.* <Horses are roughshod to give a better grip on icy, etc, roads>.

—**rough and ready** (1) not polished or carefully done or made, but good enough: *His cooking is a bit rough and ready but the food tastes all right.* (2) not having polished manners: *The villagers made us welcome but they were a bit rough and ready.*

—**rough and tumble** disorderly struggle: *He was too timid for the rough and tumble of the business world.* <Originally boxing slang for a fight in which the usual rules do not apply>.

—**rough diamond** *see* **diamond.**

—**take the rough with the smooth** to accept the disadvantages as well as the advantages and benefits of a situation: *The baby cries all night but she's adorable and you have to take the rough with the smooth.*

round

—**get round to (something)** to find time and opportunity to do (something), to do something when one can: *I never seem to get round to writing letters.*

—**go the rounds** to be passed from person to person : *I believe there's flu going the rounds.*

—**in round figures** *or* **numbers** to the nearest whole number, especially one that can be divided by ten: *He would prefer the quote in round figures, i.e. £500.*

—**round the twist** *see* **twist.**

—**round trip** the journey to somewhere plus the journey back: *The round trip to my parents' home will take about five hours.*

royal

—**royal road** *see* **road.**

rub

—**rub (something) in** to keep reminding someone about (something which he or she would rather forget): *I know I shouldn't have offended her, but there's no need to rub it in.*

—**rub (someone's) nose in it** *see* **nose.**

—**rub off on (to) (someone)** to be passed to (someone), to affect (someone): *Some of his rudeness seems to have rubbed off onto his friends.*

—**rub salt in the wound** *see* **salt.**

—**rub shoulders with (someone)** *see* **shoulder.**

—**rub (someone) up the wrong way** to irritate (someone): *He always seems to rub people up the wrong way.* <Refers to rubbing an animal's coat up the wrong way>.

—**there's the rub** that's the problem: *We need an assistant but we need to find the money to pay one. There's the rub.* <Refers to a quotation from Shakespeare's *Hamlet*, Act 3, scene i, "To sleep, perchance to dream. Ay, there's the rub.">.

Rubicon

—**cross the Rubicon** *see* **cross.**

rug

—**pull the rug (out) from under (someone)** suddenly to stop giving important help or support to (someone), to leave (someone) in a weak position: *The landlord pulled the rug from under her by asking her to leave when the baby was born.*

ruin

—**go to rack and ruin** *see* **rack.**

rule

—**ground rules** *see* **ground.**

—**rule of thumb** a rough or inexact guide used for calculations of some kind: *I just measured the windows by rule of thumb.*

—**rule (someone** *or* **something) with a rod of iron** *see* **iron.**

—**rule the roost** *see* **roost.**

—**the exception proves the rule** *see* **exception.**

—**the golden rule** *see* **gold.**

run

—**a dry run** *see* **dry.**

—**a run for (someone's) money** a creditable or worthy performance or opposition: *They thought they would defeat us easily but we gave them a run for their money and nearly won.* <A racing term indicating that the horse one has backed has actually raced although it has not won>.

—**(someone's) cup runneth over** someone feels very happy: *Her cup runneth over. Her son has returned from the war.* <A biblical reference to Psalm 23:5>.

—**in the long run** *see* **long.**

—**in the running** with a chance of success: *We don't know if he'll get the job but he's certainly in the running for it.*

—**make the running** to be the leader, to set the pace, fashion or standard: *The large firms make the running in the technological industry.*

—**on the run** running away: *There are two prisoners on the run.*

—**run across (someone** *or* **something)** to meet or find (someone or something) by chance: *I ran across an old friend yesterday.*

—**run a tight ship** *see* **tight.**

—**run high** *see* **high.**

—**run in the family** *see* **family.**

—**run its course** to continue to its natural end, to develop naturally: *Your child will be all right. Just let the infection run its course.*

—**runner-up** the person, animal or thing that comes second in a competition, race, etc. : *The runner-up got a silver medal.*

—**run-of-the-mill** *see* **mill.**

—**run out of steam** *see* **steam.**

—**run out on (someone** *or* **something)** to abandon (someone or something): *She ran out on her husband and children.*

—**run riot** *see* **riot.**

—**run the gauntlet** *see* **gauntlet.**

—**run (someone** *or* **something) to earth** *see* **earth.**

—**run wild** *see* **wild.**

—**take a running jump** to go away: *He asked her out but she told him to take a running jump.*

rush

—**be rushed off one's feet** to be very busy: *We were rushed off our feet in the shop today.*

—**rush one's fences** *see* **fence.**

—**the rush hour** a period when there is a lot of traffic on the roads, usually when people are going to, or leaving, work: *I avoid the rush hour by going to work early.*

rut

—**in a rut** in a routine, monotonous way of life: *He's leaving his job because he feels he's in a rut.* <Refers to the rut made by a cartwheel, etc>.

S

sabre
—**rattle one's sabre** to put on a show of anger or fierceness without resorting to physical force in order to frighten someone: *It is unlikely the dictator will invade the neighbouring country. He's only rattling his sabre.*

sack
—**get the sack** to be dismissed from one's job: *If he's late for work once more he'll get the sack.* <From the sack in which workman carried their tools and belongings>.
—**sackcloth and ashes** sorrow or apology for what one has done or failed to do: *He apologized profusely to her for being so late. It was a case of sackcloth and ashes.* <People in mourning used to wear sackcloth and throw ashes over their heads. The phrase has several biblical references, e.g. Matthew 11:21>.

sacred
—**a sacred cow** *see* **cow**.

safe
—**be on the safe side** not to take any risks: *I don't think it will rain but I'll take my umbrella to be on the same side.*
—**safe and sound** totally unharmed: *The missing children were found safe and sound at a friend's house.*
—**safe as houses** *see* **house**.
—**there's safety in numbers** it is safer to undertake a risky venture if there are several people involved: *He wouldn't go on strike on his own but his colleagues are joining him and there's safety in numbers.*

sail
—**plain sailing** *see* **plain**.
—**sail before the mast** *see* **mast**.
—**sail close to the wind** to come close to breaking the law or a rule: *The second-hand car dealer is not a convicted criminal but he sails very close to the wind.*
—**sail under false colours** to pretend to be different in character, beliefs, status, work, etc, than is really the case: *He said that he is a qualified teacher but he is sailing under false colours.* <Refers to a ship flying a flag other than its own, as pirate ships sometimes did>.

—**take the wind out of (someone's) sails** *see* **wind**.

salad
—**(someone's) salad days** (someone's) carefree and inexperienced youth: *In our salad days we didn't mind the discomfort of camping.*

salt
—**below the salt** in a humble, lowly or despised position: *Now that she is in an executive position she regards all her former colleagues as being below the salt.* <Formerly the salt container marked the division at a dinner table between the rich and important people and the more lowly people, the important people being near the top and so above the salt>.
—**like a dose of salts** *see* **dose**.
—**rub salt in the wound** to make someone feel worse: *He left her and rubbed salt in the wound by laughing about it with his friends.* <Salt used to be used as an antiseptic but it was painful on raw wounds>.
—**take (something) with a grain** *or* **pinch of salt** to treat (something) with some disbelief: *He says that he is an experienced sailor but I'd take that with a pinch of salt.*
—**the salt of the earth** someone very worthy or good: *Her mother would help anyone in trouble. She's the salt of the earth.* <A biblical reference to Matthew 5:13>.
—**worth one's salt** worth the money one is paid, of any worth: *If she can't take telephone messages properly she's not worth her salt.* <Salt was once a valuable commodity and the reference is to that given to servants or workers>.

Samaritan
—**a good Samaritan** someone who helps people when they are in need : *A good Samaritan gave me a lift to the garage when I ran out of petrol.* <A biblical reference to the parable in Luke 10>.

same
—**be all the same to (someone)** to be a matter of no importance to (someone): *It's all the same to me if he goes or stays.*
—**not be in the same league as (someone)** *see* **league**.
—**the same old story** *see* **story**.

sand

—**build (something) on sand** to establish (something) without having enough support, money, likelihood of survival, etc, to make it secure or practicable: *The new business is built on sand. The market for its products is too small.* <A biblical reference to Matthew 7:26>.

—**happy as a sandboy** *see* **happy**.

sardine

—**packed like sardines** crowded very close together: *So many people turned up to the protest meeting that we were packed like sardines.* <Sardines are sold tightly packed in tins>.

savage

—**noble savage** *see* **noble**.

save

—**keep** *or* **put away** *or* **save (something) for a rainy day** *see* **rain**.

—**saved by the bell** *see* **bell**.

—**save one's skin** *see* **skin**.

—**save the day** *see* **day**.

sauce

—**what's sauce for the goose is sauce for the gander** *see* **goose**.

say

—**say the word** *see* **word**.

—**say** *or* **have one's say** to tell one's own story in one's own way: *He was an enlightened employer and let his employees say their say.*

—**there's no saying** it is impossible to know or guess, there is no way of knowing or guessing: *There's no saying how long the meeting will last.*

—**you can say that again!** you're absolutely right!: *"I think that shop is very expensive." "You can say that again!"*

scales

—**tip the scales** to be the factor that decides some issue, or causes events to happen in a certain way: *We couldn't decide between a holiday in Greece or one in Italy but the cheaper flight tipped the scales in favour of Italy.*

scarce

—**make oneself scarce** to withdraw, to go off: *When he hears his parents arguing he makes himself scarce.*

scarlet

—**scarlet woman** an immoral or promiscuous woman: *His mother treats her like a scarlet woman because she is divorced.* <A biblical reference to the woman in scarlet in Revelation 17>.

scene

—**behind the scenes** out of sight of the public, etc: *Our hostess took all the credit for the successful dinner party but she had a team of caterers working behind the scenes.* <Refers literally to people in a theatrical production who work behind the scenery offstage>.

—**come on the scene** to arrive or appear: *They were happily married until that young woman came on the scene.*

—**not (someone's) scene** not the kind of thing that (someone) likes: *Opera is not his scene; he prefers pop.*

—**set the scene for (something)** to prepare the way for (something), to be the forerunner of (something): *His disagreement with his assistant on his first day in the job set the scene for their working relationship all the time he was with the firm.* <Refers originally to the preparation of the stage for theatrical action>.

scent

—**throw (someone) off the scent** to distract (someone) from a search for someone or something, e.g. by giving him or her wrong information: *The police were put off the scent of the real killer by someone making a false confession.* <Refers literally to dogs>.

scheme

—**the best-laid schemes of mice and men (gang aft agley)** the most carefully arranged plans (often go wrong): *We had checked our holiday itinerary to the last detail but you know what they say about the best laid plans of mice and men.* <Refers to a quotation from Robert Burns's poem, "To a Mouse">.

school

—**of the old school** believing in or practising customs, codes of behaviour, ideas, etc, no longer popular: *She's of the old school. She always wears a hat and gloves when going out.*

—**the schoolmaster is abroad** good education is spreading everywhere: *The improvement in the area's examination results means the schoolmaster has been abroad.* <Often wrongly used in the opposite sense to imply that the schoolmaster is absent and is much needed>.

score

—**know the score** to know exactly what is involved, to know all the facts of a situation : *They knew the score. They were aware that he had a police record before they employed him.* <Literally to know from the score in a game who is likely to win or lose>.

—**settle old scores** to get revenge for wrongs

committed in the past: *I know he went off with your wife years ago but there's no point in settling old scores.*

scot
—**scot-free** without being punished or hurt: *The police knew he was guilty but he got off scot-free because she gave him a false alibi.* <Originally referred to not having to pay a form of tax>.

scrape
—**scrape the (bottom of the) barrel** see **barrel**.

scratch
—**backscratching** see **back**.

—**scratch the surface (of something)** see **surface**.

—**start from scratch** to start from the very beginning, without any advantages: *There were no furniture and fittings at all in the new house. We had to start from scratch and buy it.* <Refers to the starting line (formerly scratched on the ground), from which runners start unless their handicap allows them to start further down the track>.

—**up to scratch** up to the required standard: *The pupil will have to repeat the year if his work is not up to scratch.* <Refers originally to a scratch in the centre of a boxing ring to which boxers had to make their way unaided after being knocked down to prove that they were fit to continue>.

screw
—**have a screw loose** to be deranged, to be very foolish: *She must have a screw loose to marry such a violent man.* <Refers literally to malfunctioning machinery>.

—**put the screws on (someone)** to exert pressure or force to get (someone) to do something: *He didn't want to give them a room but they really put the screws on him.* <Refers to thumbscrews, an instrument of torture>.

—**screw up one's courage** see **courage**.

Scrooge
—**Scrooge** an extremely mean person: *He didn't give them a wedding present. He's an old Scrooge.* <Refers to a character in Charles Dickens's *A Christmas Carol*>.

sea
—**all at sea** puzzled, bewildered: *She was all at sea trying to cope with the rows of figures.*

seal
—**(someone's) lips are sealed** see **lip**.

—**seal (someone's) fate** see **fate**.

—**set one's** *or* **the seal (of approval) on (something)** to give one's agreement or approval to (something): *The council have set their seal on our proposal for a new nursery school.* <Literally to sign (something) by attaching a wax seal to it>.

seam
—**come** *or* **fall apart at the seams** to be in a state of collapse or ruin: *The educational system there is in danger of falling apart at the seams.* <From clothes coming to pieces>.

—**the seamy side (of life)** the rough, nasty, low aspect (of life): *She saw the seamy side of life when she was homeless.* <Refers to the seamed or wrong side of a garment in Shakespeare's *Othello*, Act 4, scene ii.>.

search
—**search high and low for (someone or something)** same as **hunt high and low**—see **high**.

season
—**the silly season** see **silly**.

seat
—**have a ringside seat** see **ring**.

—**in the hot seat** see **hot**.

second
—**at second hand** not directly, from someone else: *I didn't hear about his injury from him. I heard it at second hand.*

—**come off second best** to be defeated: *In the fight the younger boxer came off second best.*

—**play second fiddle to (someone)** see **fiddle**.

—**second childhood** see **child**.

—**second nature** a firmly established habit: *It is second nature to her to work night shift.*

—**second-rate** not of the highest quality, inferior: *Their team last year was very good but this year's one is second-rate.*

—**second sight** the supposed power of seeing into the future: *She said that she had second sight and knew that she would die young.*

—**second thoughts** a change of opinion, decision, etc: *They've had second thoughts about emigrating.*

secret
—**an open secret** see **open**.

see
—**have seen better days** of people, to have been in a higher social position; of things, to have been in a better condition: *His clothes were threadbare and had obviously seen better days.*

—**see daylight** see **day**.

—**see double** see **double**.

—**see eye to eye with (someone)** see **eye**.

—**see further than the end of one's nose** see **nose**.

—**see how the land lies** *see* **land**.

—**see life** *see* **life**.

—**see red** *see* **red**.

—**see stars** *see* **star**.

—**see things** *see* **thing**.

—**see through (someone *or* something)** not to be deceived by (someone or something): *We saw through his trick to get us out of the house.*

—**see which way the wind blows** *see* **blow**.

seed

—**go to seed** to become shabby and uncared-for: *This area of town has gone to seed.* <Refers literally to plants seeding after flowering and being no longer attractive or useful>.

sell

—**sell (someone) a pup** *see* **pup**.

—**sell (someone) down the river** *see* **river**.

send

—**send (someone) packing** *see* **pack**.

—**send (someone) to Coventry** *see* **Coventry**.

—**send (something) up** to ridicule or make fun of (something), especially through parody or satire: *In the playwright's latest comedy he sends up the medical profession.*

sense

—**a sixth sense** *see* **six**.

—**come to one's senses** to begin to behave or think sensibly: *He was going to leave his job but he came to his senses when he looked around for another.*

—**horse sense** *see* **horse**.

—**sense of proportion** *see* **proportion**.

—**take leave of one's senses** to become deranged or very foolish: *I think she's taken leave of her senses. She's going to marry that womanizer from the office.*

separate

—**separate the sheep from the goats** *see* **sheep**.

sepulchre

—**whited sepulchre** *see* **white**.

serve

—**serve a *or* the purpose** *see* **purpose**.

—**serve (someone) right** *see* **right**.

service

—**at (someone's) service** ready to be of assistance to (someone): *His chauffeur is at our service for the day.*

—**have seen good service** to have been well used and reliable.

—**press (someone *or* something) into service** *see* **press**.

set

—**set about (someone *or* something)** (1) to begin (something or doing something): *How will you set about finding someone for the job?* (2) to attack (someone): *The thug set about the old man with an iron bar.*

—**set one's cap at (someone)** *see* **cap**.

—**set one's face against (someone *or* something)** *see* **face**.

—**set one's heart on (something)** *see* **heart**.

—**set one's *or* the seal (of approval) on (something)** *see* **seal**.

—**set one's sights on (something)** *see* **sight**.

—**set one's teeth on edge** *see* **teeth**.

—**set the cat among the pigeons** *see* **cat**.

—**set the pace for** *see* **pace**.

—**set the Thames *or* world on fire** to be conspicuously able or important: *I don't expect he'll set the Thames on fire, but I hope his mother will be proud of him.*

—**set the wheels in motion** *see* **wheel**.

—**set (something) to rights** *see* **right**.

settle

—**settle old scores** *see* **score**.

—**settle up (with someone)** to pay what one owes (someone): *If you pay the bill now we'll settle up with you later.*

seven

—**at sixes and seven** *see* **six**.

—**in seventh heaven** *see* **heaven**.

sewn

—**(all) sewn up** completely settled or arranged: *If we get the finance, our expansion plans are all sewn up.*

shade

—**put (someone *or* something) in the shade** to be much better, etc, than (someone or something): *Her dancing puts that of her fellow pupils totally in the shade.* <Refers to making someone seem dark by being so much brighter oneself>.

—**shades of (someone *or* something)** that reminds me of (someone or something): *Shades of school! The food served at this conference is exactly like school dinners.* <It is as though the shade or ghost of someone or something were present>.

shadow

—**worn to a shadow** made exhausted and thin by over-working: *She's worn to a shadow because of all the overtime she has had to do.*

shaggy

—**a shaggy dog story** *see* **dog**.

shakes

—**in two shakes of a lamb's tail** in a very short

time: *I'll get it for you in two shakes of a lamb's tail.*

—**no great shakes** not very good or important: *She's no great shakes as tennis player.*

shame
—**a crying shame** *see* cry.

shank
—**on shanks's pony** on foot: *There's no proper road. You'll have to go on shanks's pony.* <Refers to shank meaning leg>.

shape
—**knock (someone** *or* **something) into shape** to get (something) into the desired or good condition: *The office system is chaotic but we'll soon knock it into shape.*

—**lick (someone** *or* **something) into shape** *see* lick.

—**shape up** to be developing into the desired state or form: *The new player wasn't very good to start with but he's shaping up.*

sharp
—**look sharp** be quick: *Look sharp. The bus is coming.*

—**sharp as a razor** *see* razor.

—**sharp practice** dishonest dealing: *Their accounts department has been found guilty of sharp practice.*

sheep
—**a wolf in sheep's clothing** *see* wolf.

—**black sheep** *see* black.

—**(someone) might as well be hanged for a sheep as a lamb** if (someone) is going to do something slightly wrong and have to pay a penalty one might as well do something really wrong and get more benefit: *Your wife is going to be angry at you being late home, anyhow. Have another drink and be hanged for a sheep as a lamb.* <Refers to the fact that stealing a lamb or a sheep used to be punishable by death>.

—**separate the sheep from the goats** to distinguish in some way the good, useful, talented, etc, people from the bad, useless or stupid, etc, ones: *The teacher said that the exam would separate the sheep from the goats.* <A biblical reference to Matthew 25:32>.

sheet
—**white as a sheet** extremely pale: *She went white as a sheet when she heard the news.*

shelf
—**on the shelf** unmarried and unlikely to get married because of being unattractive, old, etc: *She thinks she's on the shelf at 23!* <Refers to goods that are not sold>.

shell
—**come out of one's shell** to become less shy: *The child has come out of her shell since she went to school.* <Refers to a tortoise or crab, etc>.

shine
—**take a shine to (someone)** to become fond of (someone): *He's taken a real shine to the girl in the office.*

ship
—**run a tight ship** *see* tight.

—**shipshape and Bristol fashion** neat, in good order: *She likes everything shipshape and Bristol fashion.* <Originally applied to ships. Bristol was formerly the largest port in Britain>.

—**ships that pass in the night** people who meet by chance and only on one occasion: *I met her at a conference but she was just a ship that passed in the night.* <Refers to a quotation from "Tales of a Wayside Inn" poem by Henry Wadsworth Longfellow>.

—**spoil the ship for a ha'porth of tar** to spoil something of value by not buying or doing something which would improve it but not cost very much: *She spent a fortune on an evening dress but refused to buy an evening bag— she carries her old handbag. Trust her to spoil a ship for a ha'porth of tar.* <Ship is dialect here for sheep—tar used to be used to prevent infections in sheep or to treat wounds>.

—**when (someone's) ship comes in** when (someone) becomes rich or successful: *We'll buy a new car when my ship comes in.* <Refers to merchants waiting for their ships to return with goods to sell>.

shirt
—**a stuffed shirt** *see* stuff.

—**keep one's shirt on** not to become angry: *Keep your shirt on. She didn't mean to bump your car.*

—**put one's shirt on (someone** *or* **something)** to bet everything on (someone or something): *I would have put my shirt on her winning the match.*

shoe
—**in (someone's) shoes** in (someone else's) place: *I wouldn't want to be in your shoes when he sees the damage.*

—**on a shoestring** using very little money: *We organized our holiday on a shoestring.*

—**step into dead men's shoes** *see* dead.

shoot
—**shoot a line** *see* line.

—**shoot (something) down in flames** to destroy: *Recent research will shoot his theory down* *in flames*. <Refers literally to destroying aircraft by shooting at them>.

—**shoot one's mouth off** *see* **mouth**.

—**the whole (bang) shoot** *or* **the whole shooting match** absolutely the whole lot: *He wants to sell the whole bang shoot before he goes abroad.*

shop

—**all over the shop** all over the place: *In her office there are books all over the shop.*

—**shut up shop** to stop working: *It's 5 o'clock—time to shut up shop.*

—**talk shop** to talk about one's work: *I try to avoid my colleagues socially. They keep talking shop.*

short

—**by a short head** by a very small amount: *She got there before me by a short head.* <Refers to horse-racing>.

—**caught** *or* **taken short** having a sudden, urgent need to go to the toilet: *He was caught short and looked for a public toilet.*

—**cut a long story short** *see* **cut**.

—**give (someone** *or* **something) short shrift** to spend very little time or thought on (someone or something): *He gave her short shrift when she asked for her job back.* <Short shrift was the short time given to a criminal for confession before execution>.

—**go short** not to have or take enough of something that one needs: *She goes short of food herself to feed the children.*

—**make short work of (something)** to deal with or get rid of (something) very quickly: *We'll make short work of washing these dishes.*

—**run short of (something)** to begin not to have enough of (something): *We're running short of milk.*

—**sell (someone** *or* **something) short** not to do justice to, to belittle (someone or something): *He always sells his wife short but she's very pleasant and efficient.* <Literally to give a customer less than the correct amount of something>.

—**short and sweet** short and to the point: *His goodbye was short and sweet.*

—**stop short of (something)** *see* **stop**.

shot

—**a long shot** a guess or attempt unlikely to be accurate or successful, but worth trying: *It's a long shot but you might get his name from the local shop.*

—**a shot across the bows** something given as a warning: *The lawyer's letter was just a shot across the bows.* <From naval warfare>.

—**a shot in the arm** something that helps to revive (something): *He should look for more investors. The business needs a shot in the arm.* <Literally, an injection in the arm>.

—**a shot in the dark** *see* **dark**.

—**big shot** an important person: *The big shots on the board are having a meeting.*

—**call the shots** to be in charge of events or a situation: *The old man's retired and it's his son who's calling the shots in the firm now.*

—**like a shot** very quickly or willingly: *If they invite me to visit them I'll go like a shot.*

—**shotgun wedding** a forced wedding, usually because the bride is pregnant: *He was forced into a shotgun wedding by her father.* <From the idea that the groom was forced into the wedding by shotgun>.

shoulder

—**a shoulder to cry on** a sympathetic listener: *She doesn't need someone to scold her. She needs a shoulder to cry on.*

—**give (someone) the cold shoulder** *see* **cold**.

—**have a chip on one's shoulder** *see* **chip**.

—**have a (good) head on one's shoulders** *see* **head**.

—**have broad shoulders** *see* **broad**.

—**put one's shoulder to the wheel** to begin to work hard: *If this project is going to be finished on time, we'll have to put our shoulders to the wheel.* <Refers to putting one's shoulder to the wheel of a cart, etc, to push it out of muddy ground, etc>.

—**rub shoulders with (someone)** to associate closely with (someone): *She rubbed shoulders with all kinds of people in her job.*

—**shoulder to shoulder** side by side: *The two men fought shoulder to shoulder in the last war.*

show

—**a show of hands** a vote expressed by people raising their hands: *The decision to strike was taken by a show of hands.*

—**for show** for appearance, in order to impress people: *The country's annual military procession is just for show.*

—**get the show on the road** to get something started or put into operation: *Get everybody out of bed! It's time we got this show on the road.* <Used originally of a theatre company going on tour>.

—**run the show** to be in charge of an organisation, etc: *I don't know what will happen to our jobs. There's a new man running the show now.* <Refers literally to the theatre>.

—**show one's face** *see* **face**.

—**show one's hand** *see* **hand**.

—**show oneself in one's true colours** *see* **colour**.

—**show off** to behave in such a way as to impress others with one's possessions, ability, etc: *The child has just learnt to dance and is showing off.*

—**show one's paces** *see* **pace**.

—**show one's teeth** *see* **teeth**.

—**show the flag** *see* **flag**.

—**show the white feather** *see* **feather**.

—**show (someone) up** to reveal to the world a person's real character: *His reaction to the beggar showed him up as a miser.*

—**steal the show** to attract the most attention at an event: *The little flower girl stole the show at her sister's wedding.* <Refers to someone getting most of the applause at a theatrical performance>.

shrift

—**give (someone *or* something) short shrift** *see* **short**.

shy

—**fight shy of (something)** *see* **fight**.

sick

—**sick and tired of something** weary of or bored of something: *I'm sick of the sight of this old coat. I wish I had a new one.*

—**sick as a parrot** very disappointed: *He's sick as a parrot he didn't get the job.*

—**sick at heart** very sad: *She is sick at heart because her husband is seriously ill.*

side

—**get *or* keep on the right side of (someone)** *see* **right**.

—**get on the wrong side of (someone)** *see* **wrong**.

—**let the side down** to hinder one's colleagues by not performing, etc, as well as they have: *His team-mates all won their matches but he let the side down by being beaten very badly.*

—**on the side** in a way other than by means of one's ordinary occupation: *He has a full-time job as a teacher but he earns a lot on the side as a barman.*

—**on the side of the angels** *see* **angel**.

—**pass by on the other side** *see* **other**.

—**side by side** beside one another: *They climbed the hill side by side.*

—**take sides** to support a particular person, group, etc, against another: *Two of the women in the office quarrelled and everyone else took sides.*

sieve

—**have a memory like a sieve** to be extremely forgetful: *Don't expect him to remember the date of the party. He's got a memory like a sieve.*

sight

—**a sight for sore eyes** *see* **eye**.

—**have *or* set one's sights on (something)** to try to obtain (something): *She set her sights on the big house at the edge of the village.* <Refers to the sights of a gun>.

—**know (someone) by sight** to be able to recognise (someone) without ever having spoken to them: *I know some of the other parents by sight.*

—**not be able to stand the sight of (someone)** to dislike (someone) very much: *The two women are friendly but their husbands can't stand the sight of each other.*

—**out of sight** beyond comparison, incomparably: *The new automobile is out of sight the best car on the market.*

—**out of sight, out of mind** one ceases to think about someone who has gone away or about something which is no longer in front of one: *He rarely mentions his girlfriend, who is overseas. It seems to be a case of out of sight, out of mind.*

—**second sight** *see* **second**.

silence

—**silence is golden** it is better to say nothing in a particular situation: *In order to keep the children quiet the teacher told them that silence is golden.*

silent

—**silent as the grave** wholly silent, saying nothing, making no noise: *The children promised to be silent as the grave in the theatre.*

—**the silent majority** the people who make up most of the population but who rarely make their views known although these are thought to be moderate and reasonable: *The politician said it was time the silent majority had an influence on the country.*

silk

—**take silk** to be made a Queen's or King's Counsel at the bar and be entitled to wear a silk robe: *The law student eventually became a distinguished barrister and in due course took silk.*

—**you can't make a silk purse out of a sow's ear** one cannot make something good or special out of poor materials: *She is not really a poor teacher. The pupils aren't very bright and you can't make a silk purse out of a sow's ear.*

silly

—**the silly season** a period of the year, usually late summer, when the newspapers have a lot of unimportant stories in the absence of important news: *There's a story in this about a funny-shaped potato. It must be the silly season.*

silver

—**born with a silver spoon in one's mouth** to be born into an aristocratic or wealthy family: *She's never worked in her life. She was born with a silver spoon in her mouth.* <Perhaps from the custom of giving a christening present of a silver teaspoon>.

—**every cloud has a silver lining** *see* **cloud**.

sin

—**cover a multitude of sins** *see* **multitude**.

—**live in sin** to live together without being married: *Her parents regard their living together as living in sin.*

—**ugly as sin** extremely ugly: *He said the girl we invited as his partner was ugly as sin.*

sink

—**leave (someone) to sink or swim** to let (someone) succeed or fail without helping: *When he came out of prison his parents left him to sink or swim.*

sing

—**sing (someone's *or* something's) praises** *see* **praise**.

sit

—**a sitting duck** *see* **duck**.

—**sit at (someone's) feet** *see* **feet**.

—**sit on the fence** *see* **fence**.

—**sit (something) out** to do nothing and simply wait for the end of (something) unpleasant: *Small firms should try to sit out the recession.*

—**sit tight** *see* **tight**.

—**sitting pretty** *see* **pretty**.

six

—**a sixth sense** intuition, an ability to feel or realize something not perceived by the five senses: *A sixth sense told him he was not alone.*

—**at sixes and sevens** in a state of confusion and chaos: *With so many visitors staying the house was at sixes and sevens.*

—**knock (someone) for six** to take (someone) completely by surprise: *The news of his promotion knocked him for six.* <Refers to cricket—literally to score six runs off a bowl>.

—**six of one and half a dozen of another** so similar as to make no difference: *We can either go by train or car. It is six of one and half a dozen of another.* <Half a dozen is six>.

sixty

—**the sixty-four (thousand) dollar question** the most important and/or difficult question: *Only one of us will be promoted. The sixty-four thousand dollar question is who it will be.* <From an American quiz game in which the contestant won one dollar for the first question, two for the second, four for the third, up to the last when he or she won sixty-four dollars or lost it all.>

size

—**cut (someone) down to size** to humble (someone), to reduce (someone's) sense of his or her own importance: *He threatened to cut his assistant down to size for being impertinent.*

—**size up (someone *or* something)** to consider carefully and form an opinion of the worth, nature, etc, of (someone or something): *You should size up the employment situation before leaving your job.*

skate

—**get one's skates on** to hurry up: *Get your skates on. We'll miss the train.*

—**skate on thin ice** *see* **ice**.

skeleton

—**have a skeleton in the cupboard** to have a closely kept secret about some cause of shame: *We didn't know that they had a skeleton in the cupboard until a family friend told us that their grandfather had murdered their grandmother.*

skin

—**by the skin of one's teeth** only just, very narrowly: *He passed the exam by the skin of his teeth.*

—**jump out of one's skin** to get a very great fright or shock: *I jumped out of my skin when the door creaked.*

—**no skin off my, etc, nose** no difference to me, etc, of no concern to me, etc: *It's no skin off my nose whether he comes to the party or not.*

—**save one's skin** to save one's life or one's career: *He didn't bother about his wounded friend. He just wanted to save his own skin.*

—**skin and bone** extremely thin: *That pony is just skin and bone.*

sky

—**go sky-high** to go very high: *The price of petrol has gone sky-high.*

—**pie in the sky** *see* **pie**.

—**praise (someone *or* something) to the skies** to praise (someone) extremely highly: *He praises his new assistant to the skies.*

—**the sky's the limit** there is no upper limit: *He*

doesn't think about money when he buys her presents. The sky's the limit.

slap

—**a slap in the face** a rebuff: *Her refusal to come to dinner was a slap in the face to her mother.*

—**a slap on the wrist** a reprimand: *She'll get a slap on the wrist for forgetting to give the boss that message.*

—**slap and tickle** playful lovemaking: *They were having a bit of slap and tickle on the park bench.*

sleep

—**let sleeping dogs lie** *see* **dog**.

—**lose sleep (over something)** to worry or be anxious about (something): *She's left him but he won't lose any sleep over that.*

—**put (something) to sleep** to kill (an animal) painlessly because it is incurably ill, etc: *The vet put the dog to sleep when it lost the use of its limbs.*

—**sleep around** to be promiscuous: *She seems very respectable now but she slept around in her youth.*

—**sleep like a log** *see* **log**.

—**sleep like a top** *see* **top**.

—**sleep with (someone)** to have sexual intercourse with (someone): *His wife doesn't know that he is sleeping with another woman.*

sleeve

—**have** *or* **keep (something) up one's sleeve** to keep (a plan, etc) in reserve or secret for possible use at a later time: *We're not beaten yet. I have a scheme up my sleeve.* <Refers to cheating at cards by having a card up one's sleeve>.

—**laugh up one's sleeve at (someone** *or* **something)** *see* **laugh**.

—**wear one's heart on one's sleeve** *see* **heart**.

slice

—**a slice of the cake** *see* **cake**.

slip

—**a Freudian slip** *see* **Freudian**.

—**a slip of the tongue** a word or phrase said in mistake for another: *He called her Mary but it was just a slip of the tongue.*

—**give (someone) the slip** to succeed in escaping from or evading (someone): *The escaped prisoner gave the police the slip.*

—**let (something) slip** to say or reveal (something) accidentally: *I'm sorry I let slip that you are leaving.*

—**slip one's mind** *see* **mind**.

—**there's many a slip 'twixt cup and lip** something can easily go wrong with a project, etc, before it is completed: *We hope we'll get the*

house but the contract isn't signed yet and there's many a slip 'twixt cup and lip.

slow

—**go slow** deliberately to work less quickly than usual as a form of protest: *The voters voted not to strike but to go slow.*

—**slow on the uptake** *see* **uptake**.

small

—**it's a small world** an expression used when one meets someone one knows somewhere unexpected: *We went to India on holiday and met our next-door neighbours. It's a small world!*

—**make (someone) look small** to make (someone) seem foolish or insignificant: *He made her look small by criticizing her work in front of all of us.*

—**small talk** light conversation about trivial matters: *He always talks about his work. He has no small talk.*

—**small wonder** it is not at all surprising: *Small wonder she's got no money. She spends it all on clothes.*

—**the small print** the parts of a document where important information is given without being easily noticed: *Read all those legal clauses very carefully. If you ignore the small print you could be signing anything.*

—**the (wee) small hours** *see* **hour**.

smart

—**a smart Alec** someone who thinks he or she is very clever: *He's such a smart Alec that he tries to teach us our jobs.*

—**look smart** to be quick: *If you look smart you'll catch the last bus.*

smash

—**a smash-and-grab** a robbery in which a shop window is smashed and goods grabbed from behind it.

—**a smash hit** a great success: *The magician was a smash hit at the children's party.* <Originally referred to a very successful popular song>.

smear

—**smear campaign** an attempt to blacken or damage someone's reputation by making accusations or spreading rumours about him or her: *He started a smear campaign against the opposing candidate.*

smell

—**smell a rat** *see* **rat**.

—**smell of the lamp** *see* **lamp**.

smoke

—**go up in smoke** to end in nothing: *He had a great many plans but they all went up in smoke.*

—**put that in your pipe and smoke it!** *see* **pipe**.

—**there's no smoke without fire** there is always some kind of basis to a rumour, however untrue it appears to be: *He denies that he ever fathered a son but there's no smoke without fire.*

snail

—**at a snail's pace** extremely slowly: *The children wandered along at a snail's pace.*

snake

—**a snake in the grass** a treacherous person: *Be careful of him. He appears to be very friendly and helpful but he's a real snake in the grass.* <From Virgil's *Aeneid*>.

sneeze

—**not to be sneezed at** not to be ignored or disregarded: *It's not a large salary but on the other hand it's not to be sneezed at.*

snook

—**cock a snook at (someone)** *see* **cock**.

snow

—**pure as the driven snow** *see* **pure**.

—**snowed under** overwhelmed: *We're snowed under with work just now.*

soap

—**soap opera** a radio or television serial broadcast regularly and dealing with the daily lives, problems, etc, of the characters: *Life in their house is like a soap opera. They've had to cope with all kinds of problems.* <Refers to the fact that such series were often sponsored by soap manufacturers in America where they were first made>.

sock

—**pull one's socks up** to make an effort to improve: *You had better pull your socks up or you won't pass your exams.*

—**put a sock in it** to be quiet: *I wish you'd put a sock in it. I want to listen to the music.*

—**sock it to (someone)** to put as much effort and energy as possible into (something): *The singer really socked it to the audience.*

soft[1]

—**have a soft spot for (someone)** to have a weakness, affection or exceptional liking for (someone): *The old man has soft spot for his youngest granddaughter.*

—**soft in the head** *see* **head**.

soft[2]

—**a soft touch** *or* **mark** someone who is easily taken advantage of, deceived etc: *He would lend money to anyone. He's a soft touch.*

—**soft option** a choice or alternative which is easier or more pleasant than the others: *At school camp there was a choice of climbing the mountain or walking along the river bank and most of the children chose the soft option.*

sold

—**be sold on (something)** to be keen on (something): *They're sold on the idea of going to Turkey on holiday.*

song

—**for a song** for very little money: *They bought that house for a song.*

—**make a song and dance about (something)** to cause an unnecessary fuss about (something): *She really made a song and dance about losing her glove.*

—**(someone's) swan song** *see* **swan**.

soon

—**no sooner said than done** a request will be fulfilled as soon as it is made: *You asked for a pizza? No sooner said than done.*

—**speak too soon** to say something that takes for granted something not yet accomplished: *We started to congratulate him on his horse winning but we spoke too soon. It was disqualified.*

sore

—**a sight for sore eyes** *see* **eye**.

—**a sore point** a subject which annoys or offends someone: *Don't mention cars—they're a sore point with him. He's just had his stolen.*

—**stick out like a sore thumb** to be very noticeable: *The fact that they had been quarrelling stuck out like a sore thumb.*

sorrow

—**drown one's sorrows** *see* **drown**.

—**more in sorrow than in anger** more disappointed than angry at someone's behaviour: *The headmaster said that it was more in sorrow than in anger that he was expelling the boys.*

sort

—**it takes all sorts (to make a world)** one should be tolerant of everyone whatever they are like: *Don't be so critical of your fellow workers. It takes all sorts.*

—**not a bad sort** quite a nice person: *He's not a bad sort when you get to know him.*

—**out of sorts** not feeling quite well, rather bad-tempered: *He's been out of sorts ever since he had flu.*

soul

—**not to be able to call one's soul one's own** to be under the constant control of someone else: *Since he married he's not been able to call his soul his own. His wife orders him around.*

—**the soul of (something)** a perfect example of

(something): *She's the soul of tact. She won't say anything indiscreet.*

soup
—**in the soup** in serious trouble: *We'll be in the soup if we're caught in the school after hours.*

sour
—**sour grapes** *see* **grape.**

sow[1]
—**sow one's wild oats** *see* **wild.**

sow[2]
—**you can't make a silk purse out of a sow's ear** *see* **silk.**

spade
—**call a spade a spade** to speak bluntly and forthrightly: *Stop trying to break the news to me gently. I'd rather you called a spade a spade.*
—**do the spadework** to do the hard preparatory work at the beginning of a project: *There's a lot of spadework to be done before we open for business.* <Digging is the first stage of building houses, etc>.

spanner
—**throw a spanner in the works** to hinder or spoil (a project, plan, etc): *We were going on holiday but my boss threw a spanner in the works by asking me to do some urgent work.*

spar
—**sparring partner** someone with whom one often enjoys a lively argument: *I missed my brother when he left home. He was a good sparring partner.* <Literally refers to someone with whom a boxer practises>.

spare
—**go spare** to become very angry or distressed: *You're so late that your wife will be going spare.*
—**spare tyre** a roll of fat round the middle of the body: *She's trying to get rid of her spare tyre before the start of her holiday.* <From its supposed resemblance to a spare car tyre>.

speak
—**be on speaking terms** to be friendly towards someone and communicate with him or her: *He is not on speaking terms with her since she crashed his car.*
—**in a manner of speaking** *see* **manner.**
—**speak for itself** to need no explanation: *The evidence speaks for itself. They're obviously guilty.*
—**speak the same language** *see* **language.**
—**speak too soon** *see* **soon.**
—**speak volumes** *see* **volume.**
—**speak with a forked tongue** *see* **fork.**
—**to speak of** worth mentioning: *He has no money to speak of.*

spectacles
—**look at (someone or something) through rose-coloured** *or* **rose-tinted spectacles** *or* **glasses** *see* **rose.**

spell
—**spell (something) out** to explain (something) plainly and in detail: *Let me spell out what will happen if you get into trouble with the police again.*

spend
—**spend a penny** *see* **penny.**
—**spend money like water** *see* **money.**

spice
—**variety is the spice of life** *see* **variety.**

spick
—**spick and span** clean and tidy: *The old lad's house was spick and span.*

spike
—**spike (someone's) guns** *see* **gun.**

spill
—**cry over spilt milk** *see* **cry.**
—**spill the beans** *see* **bean.**

spin
—**in a flat spin** *see* **flat.**
—**spin a yarn** *see* **yarn.**

spirit
—**public spirit** *see* **public.**
—**spirit (someone or something) away** to carry away (someone or something) secretly and suddenly: *They spirited the princess away before the press could interview her.*
—**the spirit is willing (but the flesh is weak)** one is not always physically able to do the things that one wishes do: *They've asked him to join their climbing expedition but he says he won't—the spirit is willing but the flesh is weak.* <A biblical quotation—Matthew 26:40–41>.

spit
—**be the spitting image** *or* **the spit and image** *or* **the dead spit of (someone or something)** to be extremely like (someone or something): *The child is the spitting image of his grandfather.*
—**spit and polish** cleaning: *The house could be doing with a bit of spit and polish.* <Refers to the habit of using spit as well as polish to clean boots>.

splash
—**splash out on (something)** to spend a great deal of money on (something): *Let's splash out on some champagne.*

spleen
—**vent one's spleen** to express one's anger and frustration: *He had a row with his wife and*

vented his spleen by shouting at the children. <The spleen was thought to be the source of spite and melancholy>.

splice

—**splice the mainbrace** to serve alcoholic drinks. *It's six o'clock. It's time to splice the mainbrace.* <Naval slang>.

splinter

—**splinter group** a group that is formed by breaking away from a larger one: *we formed a splinter group because we didn't agree with all the views of the parent group.*

split

—**a split second** a fraction of a second: *For a split second she thought she was going to be killed.*

—**split hairs** *see* **hair**.

spoil

—**be spoiling for (something)** to be eager for (a fight, etc): *He was drunk and spoiling for a fight.*

—**spoil the ship for a ha'porth of tar** *see* **ship**.

—**too many cooks spoil the broth** *see* **cook**.

spoke

—**put a spoke in (someone's) wheel** to hinder (someone's) activity: *They had a monopoly of the market in electrical goods and charged a lot in the area but a local firm has put a spoke in their wheel.* <Spoke is from Dutch spoak, a bar formerly jammed under a cartwheel to act as a brake when going downhill>.

sponge

—**throw up the sponge** to give up a contest, struggle, argument, etc: *He was getting beaten badly at chess and so he threw up the sponge.* <Refers originally to a method of conceding defeat in boxing>.

spoon

—**born with a silver spoon in one's mouth** *see* **silver**.

sport

—**have a sporting chance** *see* **chance**.

spot

—**have a soft spot for (someone)** *see* **soft**.

—**in a spot** in trouble, in difficulties: *He's in a spot. His car is beyond repair, and he lives in a remote cottage.*

—**knock spots off (someone)** to beat or surpass (someone) thoroughly: *The youngest Scrabble player knocked spots off the rest of the family.*

—**put (someone) on the spot** to place (someone) in a difficult or awkward situation: *Having boasted about his ability at chess for a long time, he was put on the spot when he was challenged to a match.*

—**rooted to the spot** unable to move from fear, horror, etc: *She stood rooted to the spot as the bull charged.*

—**spot on** absolutely accurate: *His answer was spot on.*

sprat

—**a sprat to catch a mackerel** something minor or trivial given or conceded in order to obtain some major gain or advantage: *Our chairman asked the owner of that small local firm to a supposedly informal friendly lunch but it was a sprat to catch a mackerel. He wants to buy his firm.*

spread

—**spread like wildfire** *see* **wild**.

—**spread one's wings** *see* **wing**.

spur

—**on the spur of the moment** suddenly, without previous planning: *They decided to go on holiday on the spur of the moment.*

square

—**a square deal** *see* **deal**.

—**back to square one** back at the beginning: *I thought I'd found a job but it's back to square one. I'm back job hunting again.* <Refers to an instruction in board games>.

—**fair and square** *see* **fair**.

—**square meal** a nourishing and filling meal: *He's been living on snacks. He hasn't had a square meal in ages.*

—**square up with (someone)** to settle a bill with (someone): *You paid my train fare. I had better square up with you.*

—**square up to (someone or something)** to face and tackle (someone or something) boldly: *She is going to have to square up to her financial problems.*

squeak

—**a narrow squeak** a narrow escape: *That was a narrow squeak. That car nearly ran me over.*

squib

—**a damp squib** *see* **damp**.

stab

—**have a stab at (something)** to have a try at (something): *I've never papered a room but I'll have a stab at it.*

—**stab (someone) in the back** to behave treacherously towards (someone), to betray (someone): *He stabbed his best friend in the back by going off with his wife when he was in hospital.*

stable

—**lock the stable door after the horse has bolted** to take precautions against something happening after it has already happened:

Now that they have been burgled they have installed a burglar alarm. It is a case of locking the stable door after the horse has bolted.

stack

—**stack the cards against (someone)** *see* **card**.

stage

—**a stage whisper** a loud whisper that is intended to be heard by people other than the person to whom it is directed: *She said to me in a stage whisper that she would like to meet the man by the bar.* <From the fact that whispers on stage have to be audible to the audience>.

—**stage fright** the nervousness, sometimes leading to him or her forgetting words, felt by an actor when in front of an audience; often extended to that felt by anyone making a public appearance: *She suddenly got stage fright when she saw the size of the gathering that she was to address.*

—**stage-manage (something)** to be in overall charge of (something): *She stage-managed the business conference.* <Literally to be in charge of the scenery and equipment for a play>.

stake

—**be at stake** to be in peril or at risk: *If the publishing company does not get the book out on time, its future is at stake.*

—**go to the stake** to suffer severe punishment or retribution: *The women won't mind going to the stake if they can stop the nuclear waste dump being sited here.* <From people being burned while tied to a stake, often because of their religious beliefs>.

—**have a stake in (something)** to have an interest or investment in (something): *We all have a stake in the family business.*

—**stake a claim in (something)** to assert or establish one's right to or ownership of (something): *The youngest sister got a lawyer to stake her claim to a share in the family home.* <Refers originally to gold-mining>.

stamp

—**(someone's) stamping ground** a place where (someone) goes regularly: *The pub in the village is his stamping ground.* <Refers literally to animals>.

stand

—**a standing joke** *see* **joke**.

—**it stands to reason that** *see* **reason**.

—**know where one stands** to know the exact nature of one's position or situation: *With so much talk of redundancy the workers must know where they stand.*

—**make a stand against (something)** to oppose or resist (something one believes to be wrong etc): *We should all make a stand against racism.*

—**not to stand an earthly** *same as* **not to have an earthly**—*see* **earthly**.

—**stand at ease** to take the position of rest allowed to soldiers in the intervals of drill: *The sergeant major told the company to stand at ease while the orders of the day were read.*

—**stand by** (1) to provide help and support for (someone): *Her parents stood by her when she had the baby.* (2) to be ready to take action: *The emergency services are standing by. There has been an accident at the mine.*

—**stand corrected** to accept that one has been wrong: *I thought they lived in Leeds but he tells me it's Liverpool. I stand corrected.*

—**stand one's ground** *see* **ground**.

—**stand in for (someone)** to act as a substitute for (someone): *She is just standing in for his usual nurse who is on holiday.*

—**stand (someone) in good stead** *see* **stead**.

—**stand on ceremony** to be very formal: *Take your jacket off if you like. There is no need to stand on ceremony.*

—**stand on end** of the hairs on the head of a frightened person, to stand erect: *The thought of a ghost in the house makes my hair stand on end.*

—**stand out for (something)** to go on protesting or resisting until one gets (something): *The unions are standing out for more money.*

—**stand to reason** to be logially certain, to be an undoubted fact: *It stands to reason that I must either be driven along with the crowd or else be left behind.*

—**stand (someone) up** not to keep a promise to meet (someone): *We were supposed to be going to the cinema together but he stood me up.*

—**stand up and be counted** to declare one's opinions publicly: *She says she's in favour of equal rights for women but she won't stand up and be counted by coming with us to ask the boss for fairer wages.*

—**stand up for (someone)** to support or defend (someone): *His brother stood up for him when he was being bullied.*

—**stand up to (someone)** to face (someone) boldly, to show resistance to (someone): *She should stand up to her husband and refuse to be bullied.*

star

—**see stars** to see flashes of light as a result of a

bang on the head: *I saw stars when the branch fell on my head.*

start

—**a false start** an unsuccessful beginning, resulting in one in having to start again: *He's had one false start with his first restaurant and he's now bought another.* <From a start in a race which has to be repeated, e.g. because a runner has left the starting line before the signal has been given>.

—**for starters** to begin with: *For starters we need more money.* <Starter refers literally to the first course of a meal>.

—**start from scratch** *see* **scratch**.

statistics

—**vital statistics** *see* **vital**.

status

—**status quo** the situation as it is, or was, before a change: *The experiment has obviously failed and we should return to the status quo.* <Latin, literally "the state in which">.

—**status symbol** a possession that supposedly demonstrates someone's elevated social position: *He bought his Rolls Royce as a status symbol.*

stay

—**stay the course** to continue to the end or completion of (something): *She's gone on a diet but she'll never stay the course.*

—**stay the pace** *see* **pace**.

stead

—**stand (someone) in good stead** to be useful or advantageous in the future: *The job may not be interesting but the experience of it will stand you in good stead when you look for another.*

steady

—**steady as a rock** *see* **rock**.

—**go steady** to go out together regularly, to have a romantic attachment to each other: *The young people are not engaged but they're going steady.*

steal

—**steal a march on (someone)** *see* **march**.

—**steal the show** *see* **show**.

—**steal (someone's) thunder** *see* **thunder**.

steam

—**get all steamed up** to get angry or agitated: *There's no point in getting all steamed up about the ugly new building . There's nothing you can do about it.*

—**get up steam** to gather energy and impetus to do (something): *I should finish this work today but I can't seem to get up steam.* <Literally used

of increasing the pressure of steam in an engine before it goes into operation>.

—**let off steam** to give free expression to one's feelings or energies: *He wrote the letter to the council to let off steam about his objections to the new road. The children need to let off steam after they've been sitting in school all day.* <Literally to release steam from a steam engine to in order to reduce pressure>.

—**run out of steam** to become exhausted, to lose enthusiasm: *I think our campaign is running out of steam. Hardly anyone turns up to our public meetings.* <Refers literally to the steam engine>.

—**under one's own steam** entirely through one's own efforts: *He got the job under his own steam even although his father's in the same business.*

step

—**step by step** gradually: *You won't get better right away. You must take it step by step.*

—**step in** to intervene: *The two children are quarrelling but the parents shouldn't step in.*

—**step on it** to hurry: *Step on it. We're going to be late.* <Refers to putting one's foot down hard on the accelerator of a car>.

—**step out of line** *see* **line**.

—**step (something) up** to increase (something): *The police are going to step up their investigation.*

—**take steps** to take action of some kind: *The government must take steps to improve the economy.*

stick

—**be on a sticky wicket** to be in a difficult or awkward situation that is difficult to defend: *He's on a sticky wicket if he sold goods that he knew had been stolen.* <Refers to cricket when the state of the ground or the weather makes it difficult for the batsman or woman to hit the ball>.

—**come to a sticky end** to meet some misfortune or an unpleasant death: *He was murdered by a gang. People weren't surprised that he came to a sticky end after the life of violence he had led.*

—**get hold of the wrong end of the stick** to misunderstand a situation or something said or done: *I didn't tell her she could go. She must have got hold of the wrong end of the stick.*

—**give (someone) stick** to scold or criticize (someone): *His father will give him stick when he hears his exam results.* <Refers literally to beating someone with a stick>.

—**in a cleft stick** *see* **cleft**.

—**stick by (someone)** to support and defend (someone), especially when he or she is in trouble: *His wife stuck by him when he was in prison.*

—**stick-in-the-mud** someone who is unwilling to try anything new or exciting: *She certainly won't go trekking in the Himalayas. She's a real stick-in-the-mud.*

—**stick one's neck out** *see* **neck.**

—**stick one's oar in** *see* **oar.**

—**stick out a mile** *see* **mile.**

—**stick out like a sore thumb** *see* **sore.**

—**stick to one's guns** *see* **gun.**

—**stick to one's last** *see* **last[2].**

—**stick up for (someone):** *When all the other children were blaming him she stuck up for him.*

stiff

—**bore (someone) stiff** to bore (someone) a great deal: *The audience were bored stiff by the play.*

—**keep a stiff upper lip** *see* **lip.**

still

—**still waters run deep** quiet people often think very deeply or have strong emotions: *He hardly said a word during the discussion, but that doesn't mean he doesn't feel strongly about it. Still waters run deep.*

stitch

—**a stitch in time saves nine** prompt action at the first sign of trouble saves a lot of time and effort later: *You should repair that broken roof tile or your ceiling may get damaged. A stitch in time saves nine.*

—**have (someone) in stitches** to make (someone) laugh a great deal: *The comedian had the audience in stitches.*

—**without a stitch on** completely naked: *He stood at the window without a stitch on.*

stock

—**on the stocks** in preparation, in the process of being made or arranged: *We have a new product on the stocks but it won't be on the market until next year.* <Refers to the fact that a ship is supported on stocks, a wooden frame, while being built>.

—**take stock (of something)** to assess (a situation): *I took stock of my life and decided I need a change.*

stomach

—**have no stomach for (something)** not to have the inclination, toughness, etc, for (something): *They are a peace-loving people. They have no stomach for a war.* <Refers to a medieval be-

lief that the stomach was the seat of physical courage>.

—**turn (someone's) stomach** to make (someone) feel sick, to disgust (someone): *The sight of blood turns his stomach.*

stone

—**a stone's throw** a very short distance: *Their house is a stone's throw away from here.*

—**leave no stone unturned** to try every means possible: *The police left no stone unturned in their search for clues.*

stool

—**fall between two stools** to try to gain two aims and fail with regard to both of them, usually because of indecision: *The student's essay falls between two stools. In part of it he is trying to be funny and in the other he is trying to be very serious and the two styles don't marry.*

stop

—**pull out all the stops** to put as much effort and energy into something as possible: *If you're going to win that race you'll have to pull out all the stops.* <Refers to pulling out the stops of an organ so that it plays at full volume>.

—**stop at nothing** to be willing to do absolutely anything, however wrong, etc: *He will stop at nothing to get those jewels.*

—**stop dead** to stop suddenly and abruptly: *He stopped dead when saw his ex-wife.*

—**stop over** to stay overnight somewhere while on a journey: *He stopped over at Amsterdam.*

—**stop short of (something** or **doing something)** not to go as far as (something or doing something): *I hope he would stop short of murder.*

store

—**in cold storage** in reserve: *Our plans for expansion are in cold storage until the recession is over.*

—**in store** in the future, coming to one: *There's trouble in store for you if you go home late again.*

—**set great store by (something)** to consider (something) to be of great importance or value: *My neighbour sets great store by a tidy house.*

storm

—**any port in a storm** *see* **port.**

—**a storm in a teacup** a great fuss made over a trivial matter: *She kept going on about her ruined dress but it was a storm in a teacup. You could hardly see the stain.* <Refers to the title of a farce written by William Bernard in 1854>.

—**stormy petrel** someone whose presence indicates that there is likely to be some kind of trouble in the near future: *She's a stormy petrel in a bar. Men always end up fighting over her.* <Refers to a small bird that lives in areas where storms are common>.

—**take (someone** *or* **something) by storm** to make a very great and immediate impression (on someone or something): *The young opera singer took London by storm.* <Literally to capture a fort, etc, by a sudden violent military attack>.

—**weather the storm** to survive a difficult or troublesome situation or period of time: *The company found it difficult to weather the storm during the recession.* <Refers originally to ships>.

story

—**a tall story** *see* **tall.**

—**cut a long story short** *see* **cut.**

—**the same old story** a situation, etc, that occurs frequently: *It was the same old story. As soon as he got out of prison he committed another crime.*

—**the story goes (that)** people say that, rumours suggest (that): *The story goes that they are not married.*

straight

—**go straight** to start leading an honest life: *He has been in prison twice but he's going straight now.*

—**get (something) straight** to get all the facts and details of a situation so as to understand it fully: *Let's get this straight. You say that you have never met the man who claims to be your husband.*

—**set the record straight** *see* **record.**

—**straight as a die** completely honest and fair. *You can trust that estate agent. He's straight as a die.*

—**straight from the horse's mouth** *see* **horse.**

—**straight talking** a frank and honest statement or conversation: *You've tried to tell her tactfully she has to leave. Now it's time for some straight talking.*

—**the straight and narrow (path)** a good, virtuous way of life: *He left the straight and narrow when he left home.* <A variation on a biblical reference—"Straight is the gate and narrow is the way which leadeth unto life", Matthew 7:4>.

stranger

—**be a stranger to (something)** to have no experience of (something): *He is a stranger to poverty.*

straw

—**a straw in the wind** a small or minor incident, etc, that indicates what may happen in the future: *The bye-election result might be interpreted as a straw in the wind for the general election.*

—**clutch at straws** to hope that something may happen to get one out of a difficulty or danger when this is extremely unlikely: *He is hoping that his wife will live but he's clutching at straws. She's terminally ill with cancer.* <From the saying "A drowning man will clutch at a straw">.

—**man of straw** *see* **man.**

—**straw poll** an unofficial poll to get some idea of general opinion: *The union took a straw poll on the possibility of a strike.* <Refers to drawing straws>.

—**the last straw** *or* **the straw that breaks the camel's back** an event, etc, which, added to everything that has already happened, makes a situation impossible: *Her boss's criticism was the last straw and she walked out.* <From the saying that it is the last straw added to its burden that breaks the camel's back>.

—**try to make bricks without straw** *see* **brick.**

street

—**be on the streets** to be homeless: *They'll be on the streets soon if they can't pay the rent.*

—**be right up (someone's) street** to be exactly what what one likes or what is suitable for one: *That job abroad is right up her street.*

—**go on the streets** to become a prostitute: *She went on the streets to support herself and the children.*

—**in Queer Street** *see* **queer.**

—**streets ahead of (someone** *or* **something)** *see* **ahead.**

—**the man in the street** *see* **man.**

strength

—**a tower of strength** *see* **tower.**

—**from strength to strength** to progress successfully from one achievement to another: *The firm's going from strength to strength since it expanded.*

—**on the strength of (something)** relying on (something): *We're going on a cruise on the strength of our pools win.*

stretch

—**at full stretch** using all one's energy, abilities, powers, etc, as much as possible: *We're working at full stretch these days.*

—**stretch a point** to go further than the rules or regulations allow in giving permission, etc, for something: *I shouldn't really let you take this book out but I suppose I could stretch a point.*

—**stretch one's legs** see **leg.**

stride

—**get into one's stride** to become accustomed to doing something and so do it well and effectively: *He was slow at the job at first but he soon got into his stride.* <A reference to the pace one is comfortable with when running>.

—**make great strides** to make very good progress: *Her son is making great strides with his studies in senior school.*

—**take (something) in one's stride** to cope with (something) without worrying about it: *She failed the exam but she took it in her stride.* <Refers to a horse jumping an obstacle without altering its stride>.

strike

—**strike a balance** see **balance.**

—**strike a bargain** see **bargain.**

—**strike a chord** see **chord.**

—**strike it lucky** see **luck.**

—**strike it rich** see **rich.**

—**strike (someone) off (something)** to remove (something—especially a doctor's name) from a professional register, etc, e.g. for misconduct: *I won't go to that doctor. From the rumours I hear he'll soon be struck off.*

—**strike the right note** see **note.**

—**strike while the iron is hot** see **iron.**

string

— **have another** or **more than one string to one's bow** see **bow.**

—**have (someone) on a string** to have (someone) in one's control: *He has her on a string—she owes him money.* <Refers to someone manipulating a puppet>.

—**pull strings** to use influence to gain an advantage or benefit of some kind: *He may have to pull a few strings to get a visa for her.* <As above>.

—**tied to (someone's) apron-strings** see **apron.**

—**with no strings attached** without any conditions or provisos: *Father will lend us the money with no strings attached.*

stroke

—**at a stroke** with a single effort or attempt: *That loan would solve all our financial problems at a stroke.*

—**put (someone) off his** or **her stroke** to hinder or prevent (someone) from proceeding smoothly with an activity: *By laughing at him while he was playing bowls they put him off his*

stroke. <Refers to upsetting the rhythm of someone's rowing>.

strong

—**be (someone's) strong suit** be something at which (someone) is very good: *Organization is not his strong suit.* <Refers to card-playing>.

stubborn

—**stubborn as a mule** see **mule.**

stuck

—**stuck for (something)** in need of (something), unable to go on without (something): *I can't finish the decorating. I'm stuck for wallpaper.*

—**stuck on (someone** or **something)** very fond of (someone or something): *He's stuck on her younger sister.*

—**stuck with (someone** or **something)** burdened with (something): *She's got stuck with the club bore.*

stuff

—**a stuffed shirt** a pompous, over-formal person: *He never seems to enjoy himself. He's a real stuffed shirt.* <Refers to a shop dummy>.

—**do one's stuff** to do something that is necessary and that one either specializes in or does skilfully: *Here's the equipment. Go and do your stuff.*

—**get stuffed** an angry expression used in refusing someone's request, opinion, etc: *You want me to go and get your slippers? Get stuffed!*

—**knock the stuffing out of (someone)** (1) to beat (someone) severely: *The older boy knocked the stuffing out of the bully.* (2) to discourage (someone) completely, to deprive (someone) of vitality: *It knocked the stuffing out of him when he was declared redundant.* <Refers to stuffed animals>.

—**know one's stuff** to be knowledgeable about one's subject, job, etc: *Our neighbour works in computers and he really knows his stuff.*

stumbling

—**a stumbling block** something that hinders or prevents progress: *The cost of the venture is the main stumbling block.* <A biblical reference to Romans 14:13>.

stump

—**stir one's stumps** to hurry up: *You better stir your stumps. Our guests will soon be here.* <Stumps here means legs>.

style

—**cramp (someone's) style** to hinder (someone) from acting in the way that he or she would like or is accustomed to: *His style has been cramped by a wife and two children.*

—**in style** elegantly, luxuriously: *She arrived in style in a chauffeur-driven limousine.*

such

—**such as it is** although it hardly deserves the name: *You are welcome to borrow our wheelbarrow, such as it is.*

suffer

—**not to suffer fools gladly** *see* **fool.**

sugar

—**sugar daddy** an elderly man who has a young girlfriend or mistress to whom he gives expensive presents: *She looks like a Christmas tree wearing all the jewellery her sugar daddy has given her.*

—**sugar the pill** to make something unpleasant more pleasant: *She was told she was losing her job but the boss sugared the pill by offering her some part-time work occasionally.*

suit

—**be (someone's) strong suit** *see* **strong.**

—**one's birthday suit** nakedness: *He ran along the corridor to the bathroom in his birthday suit.*

—**follow suit** *see* **follow.**

—**suit (someone) down to the ground** *see* **ground.**

—**suit oneself** to do as one wishes: *We're all going but you can suit yourself.*

summer

—**an Indian summer** *see* **Indian.**

—**one swallow does not make a summer** *see* **swallow**[1].

sun

—**catch the sun** *see* **catch.**

—**under the sun** in the whole world: *He would like to visit every country under the sun.*

Sunday

—**a month of Sundays** *see* **month.**

—**(someone's) Sunday best** (someone's) smartest, formal clothes, of the kind worn to church on Sundays: *He's wearing his Sunday best because he's going for a job interview.*

sundry

—**all and sundry** *see* **all.**

sure

—**be** *or* **feel sure of oneself** to be confident, to have self-confidence: *He's not very good at his job but he's very sure of himself.*

—**sure enough** as was expected: *I said the parcel would arrive today, and sure enough it came before lunch.*

—**to be sure** certainly: *To be sure, he seems to be very pleasant but I do not trust him.*

surface

—**scratch the surface of (something)** to deal with only a very small part of (something): *In one term you will only scratch the surface of the history of the period.*

suspicion

—**above suspicion** *see* **above.**

swallow[1]

—**one swallow does not make a summer** a single success, etc, does not mean that a generally successful, etc, time is about to come: *He sold his first car on the first morning in the garage and thinks he's going to be a top-class salesman. We couldn't resist telling him that one swallow does not make a summer.* <Refers to the fact that swallows begin to come to Britain at the start of summer>.

swallow[2]

—**swallow one's pride** *see* **pride.**

swan

—**swan around** to wander about in a leisurely way: *We were all working hard and she was swanning about giving orders.*

—**(someone's) swan song** the last work or performance by a musician, poet, playwright, actor, etc, before his or her death or retirement; by extension also applied to anyone who does anything for the last time: *The theatre was full because everyone wanted to be present at the great actress's swan song. He was not to know that that conference speech was his swan song. He died the next week.* <Refers to an ancient legend that the swan sings as it is dying although it is otherwise silent>.

swear

—**swear by (someone** *or* **something)** to have complete trust and faith in (someone or something), to recommend (someone or something) very highly: *He swears by that make of car.*

—**swear like a trooper** *see* **trooper.**

sweat

—**in a cold sweat** *see* **cold.**

—**no sweat!** no trouble, no problem: *No sweat! I'll get your package there on time.*

—**sweat blood** *see* **blood.**

—**the sweat of one's brow** one's hard work: *She spends all the money that he earns by the sweat of his brow.*

sweep

—**make a clean sweep** *see* **clean.**

—**sweep (someone) off his** *or* **her feet** *see* **feet.**

—**sweep (something) under the carpet** *see* **carpet.**

sweet

—**be all sweetness and light** to seem to be

pleasant and good-tempered: *She's all sweetness and light when she gets what she wants.*

—**be sweet on (someone)** to be fond of (someone): *I think he's sweet on my daughter.*

—**have a sweet tooth** to like sweets, cakes and deserts: *She has a real sweet tooth. She always has a bar of chocolate in her bag.*

—**sweet nothings** affectionate things said to someone with whom one is in love, endearments: *We were embarrassed when he sat and whispered sweet nothings in her ear in our kitchen.*

swim

—**be in the swim** be actively involved in social or business activities: *She was in mourning for a long time but she's back in the social swim now.*

—**leave (someone) to sink or swim** see **sink**.

swing

—**get into the swing of things** to become accustomed to (something) and begin to understand and enjoy it: *I hated the job at first but now I'm into the swing of things I'm quite happy.* <Refers to the swing of a pendulum>.

—**go with a swing** to be very successful: *The opening of the exhibition went with a swing.*

—**in full swing** at the most lively or busy part of something: *He came into the hall when the meeting was in full swing.*

—**not to be enough room to swing a cat** see **cat**.

—**swing the lead** see **lead**[2].

—**what you lose on the swings you gain on the roundabouts** disadvantages in one area of life are usually cancelled out by advantages in another: *I got a parking ticket today but I won a prize in a raffle. What you lose on the swings you gain on the roundabouts.*

swoop

—**at** *or* **in one fell swoop** in one single action or attempt, at the same time: *I threw out all my old clothes in one fell swoop.* <Refers to a quotation from Shakespeare's *Macbeth*, Act 4, scene iii, the reference being to a hawk swooping on poultry>.

sword

—**cross swords with (someone)** to enter into a dispute with (someone): *Those two always cross swords at committee meetings. They never agree.*

—**the sword of Damocles** a threat of something bad that is likely to happen at any time: *Possible redundancy is hanging over her like the sword of Damocles.* <Refers to a legend in which Damocles was forced by Dionysius of Syria to sit through a banquet with a sword hanging by a single hair over his head>.

system

—**all systems go** everything is functioning and active: *It's all systems go here today. We have so much work to get through.* <The phrase is used by the controllers of a space flight to indicate that everything is ready for the spaceship to be launched>.

T

—**to a T** exactly, very well: *That portrait of my aunt is her to a T.* <Perhaps T stands for tittle, a small dot or point>.

tab

—**keep tabs on (someone *or* something)** to keep a check on (someone or something): *He keeps tabs on his wife's spending as she's extravagant.*

—**pick up the tab for (something)** to pay for (something): *He picked up the tab for the whole party of us.* <Tab is an American term for bill>.

table

—**turn the tables on (someone)** to change a situation so that one gains the advantage (over someone) after having been at a disadvantage: *At first they were winning but we soon turned the tables on them.* <From the medieval game of tables, of which backgammon is a form, in which turning the board round would exactly reverse the position of the players>.

tail

—**with one's tail between one's legs** in an ashamed, miserable or defeated state: *The children went home with their tails between their legs after the farmer scolded them for stealing apples.* <From the behaviour of an unhappy dog>.

take

—**be taken with (someone *or* something)** to find (someone or something) attractive: *She was quite taken with the little dog.*

—**take after (someone)** to resemble: *She takes after her father.*

—**take (something) as gospel** *see* **gospel**.

—**take (something) as read** *see* **read**.

—**take one's cue from (someone)** *see* **cue**.

—**take (someone) for a ride** *see* **ride**.

—**take heart** *see* **heart**.

—**take (someone) in** to deceive (someone): *She really took the old lady in by pretending to be a social worker.*

—**take it easy** *see* **easy**.

—**take it from me (that)** you can believe me when I say (that): *You can take it from me that he won't come back.*

—**take it or leave it** either to accept (something) or refuse (something) as one wishes but it will not be alter: *That is my final price. Take it or leave it.*

—**take it out on (someone)** to treat (someone) in an angry or nasty way because one is disappointed, angry, etc, about something: *She turned down his proposal and he took it out on the dog.*

—**take off** suddenly to become successful: *His business has really taken off.* <Refers to the launching of a rocket>.

—**take (someone) off** to mimic (someone): *She was taking off her friend's father when he entered the room.*

—**take sides** *see* **side**.

—**take steps** *see* **step**.

—**take the floor** *see* **floor**.

—**take one's time** *see* **time**.

—**take up arms** *see* **arm**.

—**take (someone) up on (something)** to accept (someone's offer, etc): *I'll take you up on your invitation to dinner.*

—**take up the cudgels** *see* **cudgel**.

—**take (something) up with (someone)** to raise (a matter) with (someone): *You should take your complaint up with the manager.*

tale

—**tell its, etc, own tale** to indicate clearly what took place: *The charred remains told their own tale.*

—**tell tales** to report someone's wrong-doing: *Don't let her see you smoking. She'll tell tales to the teacher.*

—**thereby hangs a tale** there is a story associated with that: *He recognized the woman who came into the room and thereby hangs a tale.* <A pun on tail, used by Shakespeare>.

talk

—**money talks** *see* **money**.

—**straight talking** *see* **straight**.

—**talk about (something)!** that is a good example of (something): *Talk about conceit! He looks at himself in every shop window.*

—**talk down to (someone)** to speak to (someone) in a condescending way as if he or she were inferior: *Adults often talk down to teenagers.*

—**talk one's head off** *see* **head**.

—**talk nineteen to the dozen** to talk a great deal and usually very rapidly: *She and her friend talk nineteen to the dozen when they get together.*

—**talk shop** *see* **shop**.

—**talk through one's hat** *see* **hat**.

—**talk through the back of one's head** *see* **back**.

—**talk turkey** *see* **turkey**.

—**the talk of the town** someone or something that is the subject of general conversation or gossip: *Their sordid affair is the talk of the town.*

tall

—**a tall order** a difficult task: *It's a tall order to get the book for you by tomorrow.*

—**a tall story** a story that is extremely unlikely: *His latest tall story is that he has seen a Martian.*

tan

—**tan (someone's) hide** *see* **hide**.

tangent

—**go** *or* **fly off at a tangent** suddenly to leave the subject being discussed or the task being undertaken and move to a completely different subject or task: *It is difficult to follow the speaker's line of thought. She keeps going off at tangents.*

tap

—**on tap** available, ready for use: *There was coffee on tap all day.*

tape

—**have** *or* **get (someone** *or* **something) taped** to have a full knowledge or understanding of (someone or something): *She thought she could deceive me but I have her taped.* <As if measured with a tape>.

—**red tape** *see* **red**.

tar

—**be tarred with the same brush** to have the same faults: *He and his father are tarred with the same brush. They're both crooks.*

—**spoil the ship for a ha'porth of tar** *see* **ship**.

task

—**take (someone) to task** to reprimand or criticize (someone): *The teacher took the pupil to task for being impertinent.*

taste

—**a taste of one's own medicine** same as **a dose of one's own medicine**—*see* **dose**.

tea

—**a storm in a teacup** *see* **storm**.

—**not be one's cup of tea** *see* **cup**.

—**not for all the tea in China** not for anything at all, certainly not: *I wouldn't work there for all the tea in China.* <For a long time, China was the source of the world's tea>.

teach

—**teach one's grandmother to suck eggs** *see* **egg**.

tear[1]

—**tear a strip off (someone)** to scold (someone) severely: *The boss tore a strip off them for their carelessness.*

—**tear one's hair out** *see* **hair**.

tear[2]

—**crocodile tears** *see* **crocodile**.

teeth

—**armed to the teeth** *see* **arm**.

—**by the skin of one's teeth** *see* **skin**.

—**cut one's teeth on (something)** to practise on or get early experience from (something): *The Everest climber had cut his teeth on the hill behind his home.* <Refers to children being given something to chew on to help their teeth come through>.

—**draw the teeth of (someone** *or* **something)** to make (someone or something) no longer dangerous: *He drew the teeth of the blackmailer by threatening to go the police.* <Refers to pulling out an animal's teeth.>

—**get one's teeth into (something)** to tackle (something) vigorously: *He likes a problem that he can get his teeth into.*

—**give one's eye** *or* **back teeth** to be willing to do anything in order to obtain something: *They'd give their eye teeth to go to Australia.*

—**gnash one's teeth** to be angry and disappointed: *We gnashed our teeth as the bus drove away before we reached it.* <A biblical reference to Matthew 8:12>.

—**grit one's teeth** *see* **grit**.

—**in the teeth of (something)** against (something): *They married in the teeth of much opposition.*

—**lie in** *or* **through one's teeth** *see* **lie**[1].

—**kick (someone) in the teeth** to refuse to help or support (someone) when he or she is in need of it: *She had helped him in the past, but when she was in trouble he kicked her in the teeth.*

—**set one's teeth on edge** to irritate one: *His constant whistling sets my teeth on edge.*

—**show one's teeth** to demonstrate one's fierceness, to show that one can be aggressive: *They withdrew their opposition to our scheme when we showed our teeth.* <Refers to a dog, etc, showing its teeth in anger>.

—**teething troubles** problems occurring at the very beginning of a new project, etc: *Our new factory has recovered from its teething troubles.* <From the pain experienced by babies when teeth are just coming through>.

tell

—**I told you so** I warned you and I was right to do so: *"I've discovered he's a real rogue." "I told you so but you wouldn't listen."*

—**tell its own tale** *see* **tale**.

—**tell tales** *see* **tale**.

—**tell (someone) where to get off** *see* **get**.

—**there's no telling** it is impossible to know: *There's no telling how many people will come.*

—**you never can tell** it is possible: *We might get a heat wave. You never can tell.*

—**you're telling me!** that is definitely the case: *You're telling me he's bad -tempered!*

tender

—**leave (someone or something) to (someone's) tender mercies** to leave (someone or something) in the care of (someone inefficient, etc): *My mother-in-law is so vague that I didn't want to leave the children to her tender mercies.*

tenterhooks

—**be on tenterhooks** be very anxious or agitated waiting for something to happen: *We were on tenterhooks waiting for the exam results to be delivered.* <Tenterhooks were hooks for stretching newly woven cloth>.

term

—**be on speaking terms** *see* **speak**.

—**come to terms with (something)** to accept (something) as unavoidable and try to deal with it as best one can: *She will have to come to terms with her widowhood.*

tether

—**at the end of one's tether** *see* **end**.

thank

—**be thankful for small mercies** *see* **mercy**.

—**have only oneself to thank for (something)** to be the cause of (one's own misfortune): *You've only yourself to thank for the children being cheeky. You spoil them.*

that

—**just like that** immediately, without further consideration, discussion, etc: *When she asked for more money he sacked her — just like that.*

—**that's that** there is no more to be said or done: *He's gone and that's that.*

thick

—**a bit thick** more than can be tolerated: *It was a bit thick for her to invite herself round.*

—**give (someone) a thick ear** to slap (someone) across the ear, to box (someone's) ears: *My big brother will give you a thick ear if you hit me.*

—**lay it on thick** *see* **lay**.

—**the plot thickens** *see* **plot**.

—**thick and fast** in great quantities and at a fast rate: *The replies are coming in thick and fast.*

—**thick as thieves** extremely friendly: *The little girls quarrelled but they're thick as thieves now.*

—**thick as two short planks** extremely stupid: *Don't ask him to be in your quiz team. He's as thick as two short planks.*

—**through thick and thin** whatever difficulties arise: *He will support his leader through thick and thin.*

thief

—**set a thief to catch a thief** the best way to catch or outwit a dishonest or deceitful person is to use the help of another who is dishonest as he or she knows the technique: *The ex-convict has become a police informer and they have made many arrests thanks to him. It's true what they say about setting a thief to catch a thief.*

—**thick as thieves** *see* **thick**.

thin

—**be thin on top** to be balding: *He wears a hat to hide the fact he's thin on top.*

—**have a thin time of it** to have an unpleasant or difficult time, especially because of money difficulties: *They're having a thin time of it since she stopped work to have the baby.*

—**into thin air** *see* **air**.

—**(skate) on thin ice** *see* **ice**.

—**the thin end of the wedge** *see* **wedge**.

—**thin as a rake** extremely thin: *She insists on dieting although she's thin as a rake.*

—**thin on the ground** *see* **ground**.

thing

—**a near thing** *see* **near**.

—**be all things to all men** *see* **all**.

—**do one's (own) thing** to do what one likes to do or what one is good at doing: *At the recreation club we all do our own thing.*

—**first things first** *see* **first**.

—**have a thing about (someone or something)** (1) to be very fond of or be particularly attracted to (someone or something): *He has a thing about small blonde women.* (2) to be scared of, to have a phobia about (someone or something): *She has a thing about spiders.*

—**just one of those things** something that must be accepted: *Our flight has been delayed but that's just one of those things.*

—**know a thing or two** to be astute and sensible : *He wouldn't drink and drive. He knows a thing or two.*

—**make (quite) a thing of (something)** to treat (something) as very important, to make a fuss about (something): *She's making quite a thing of her birthday.*

—**no such thing** something quite different: *He says he's a qualified teacher but he's no such thing.*

—**not to know the first thing about (something)** *see* **first**.

—**see things** to see someone or something that is not there: *She must be seeing things. She said she thought saw a large snake in the bedroom.*

—**the thing is** the most important point or question is: *The thing is how will we get the money.*

—**the very thing** *see* **very**.

think

—**have another think coming** to be quite mistaken: *If you think they'll sleep here you have another think coming. The room is damp.*

—**not to think much of (someone** or **something)** to have a low opinion of (someone or something): *I didn't think much of the play.*

—**put one's thinking cap on** *see* **cap**.

—**think better of (something)** *see* **better**.

—**think nothing of (something)** *see* **nothing**.

—**think nothing of it** *see* **nothing**.

—**think (something) up** to invent (something): *He's thought up a good plot for a play.*

—**think the world of (someone)** *see* **world**.

—**think twice** *see* **twice**.

third

—**give (someone) the third degree** *see* **degree**.

Thomas

—**a doubting Thomas** *see* **doubt**.

thorn

—**a thorn in (someone's) flesh** *see* **flesh**.

thought

—**food for thought** *see* **food**.

—**second thoughts** *see* **thought**.

thread

—**hang by a thread** to be in a very precarious or uncertain state: *Our chances victory are hanging by a thread. We are waiting to hear if two players will be fit.* <Probably a reference to the sword of Damocles (*see*)>.

—**lose the thread** to cease to follow the course or development of an argument, conversation, etc: *The lecturer rambled on and I lost the thread.*

three

—**the three R's** *see* **R**.

throat

—**at each other's throats** quarrelling fiercely: *They're at each other's throats over custody of their child.*

—**cut one's own throat** to cause damage or harm to oneself by one's own action: *The firm says that if the workers insist on having a pay rise they will be cutting their own throats because some of them will have to be declared redundant.*

—**have a frog in one's throat** *see* **frog**.

—**jump down (someone's) throat** to attack (someone) verbally or in an angry or violent manner: *She jumped down my throat when I tried to explain my absence.*

—**ram (something) down (someone's) throat** to try forcefully to make (someone) accept ideas, opinions, etc: *He's always ramming his political views down our throats.*

—**stick in one's throat** *or* **gullet** to be difficult for one to accept or tolerate: *It sticks in my throat the way he treats her.*

throne

—**the power behind the throne** *see* **power**.

throw

—**throw in one's hand** *see* **hand**.

—**throw in the towel** *see* **towel**.

—**throw (someone) over** to leave or abandon (a girlfriend or boyfriend): *She threw him over to go out with someone else.*

—**throw (someone) to the lions** *see* **lion**.

—**throw up** to vomit: *The child threw up in the car.*

—**throw up the sponge** *see* **sponge**.

—**throw one's weight about** *see* **weight**.

thumb

—**rule of thumb** *see* **rule**.

—**stick out like a sore thumb** *see* **sore**.

—**thumb a lift** to ask for (and get) a lift in someone's vehicle by signalling with one's thumb: *Two hikers were standing at the roadside thumbing a lift.*

—**thumb one's nose at (someone or something)** to express defiance or contempt at (someone or something), originally by making the rude gesture of putting one's thumb to one's nose: *The new pupil thought it was clver to thumb her nose at the teachers.*

—**thumbs down** rejection or disapproval: *The proposal got the thumbs down from the council.* <From the method employed by the crowds in ancient Rome to indicate whether they thought the defeated gladiator should live or die after a fight between two gladiators. If the crowds turned their thumbs down the gladia-

tor died. If they turned them up the gladiator lived.>

—**thumbs up** acceptance or approval: *Our dress designs have been given the thumbs up from the manufacturers.* <See above>.

—**twiddle one's thumbs** to do nothing, to be idle: *Friday was so quiet in the office everyone was sitting twiddling their thumbs.* <Literally to rotate one's thumbs round each other, indicating a state of boredom>.

—**under (someone's) thumb** under one's control or domination: *The whole family is under the father's thumb.*

thunder

—**steal (someone's) thunder** to spoil (someone's) attempt at impressing people by doing what he or she intended to do before him or her: *She knew her sister was going to announce her engagement on Christmas Day and she deliberately announced hers on Christmas Eve to steal her thunder.* <John Dennis, a 17th/18th century playwright, invented a machine for simulating thunder in plays. When someone else used a similar device in a rival play Dennis said that he had stolen his thunder>.

tick

—**give (someone) a ticking-off** to scold (someone) sharply: *The teacher gave the boy a ticking-off for bullying.*

—**tick over** to run quietly and smoothly. *Sales aren't brilliant but they're ticking over.* <Used literally of a car engine>.

ticket

—**just the ticket** exactly what is required: *A plate of hot soup is just the ticket on a cold winter's day.*

—**meal ticket** someone who can be relied upon to support one, providing food and so on: *She regards her husband purely as a meal ticket.*

tickle

—**be tickled pink** to be delighted: *She was tickled pink with her birthday present.*

—**tickle one's fancy** *see* **fancy**.

tie

—**be tied up** to be busy or engaged: *I'm afraid you can't see the manager. He's tied up in a meeting.*

—**tie (someone) down** to limit (someone's) freedom: *She feels that children would tie her down.*

—**tie (oneself** *or* **someone) in knots** *see* **knot**.

tight

—**in a tight corner** *or* **spot** in a difficult or dangerous situation: *We were in a tight corner practically surrounded by the enemy.*

—**keep a tight rein on (something)** *see* **rein**.

—**run a tight ship** to run an efficient, well-organized firm etc: *During a recession it is exceptionally important to run a tight ship.*

—**sit tight** to be unwilling to move or take action: *Now is not the time to change jobs. Sit tight for a while.*

—**tighten one's belt** *see* **belt**.

tile

—**a night on the tiles** a celebratory evening spent in a wild and unrestrained manner: *They had a night on the tiles after the exams.* <Refers to roof tiles and to cats sitting on them at night>.

tilt

—**at full tilt** at maximum speed: *The boy ran down the street at full tilt to catch the bus.* <Refers to knights tilting or jousting>.

—**tilt at windmills** *see* **windmill**.

time

—**ahead of one's time** with ideas in advance of one's contemporaries, often not understood: *The philosopher was not highly rated as he was ahead of his time.*

—**all in good time** soon, when it is the right time: *The guests will arrive all in good time.*

—**a stitch in time saves nine** *see* **stitch**.

—**at one time** at a time in the past: *At one time he was quite famous.*

—**be high time** *see* **high**.

—**behind the times** not up-to-date, old-fashioned: *His ideas are behind the times.*

—**bide one's time** *see* **bide**.

—**do time** to be in prison: *He's doing time for murder.*

—**from time immemorial** *see* **immemorial**.

—**gain time** *see* **gain**.

—**half the time** for a good part of the time, frequently: *Half the time she doesn't know where her husband is.*

—**have a thin time of it** *see* **thin**.

—**have a time of it** to have a difficult time: *The family have had a time of it since the father lost his job.*

—**have no time for (someone** *or* **something)** to have a very low opinion of (someone or something) and to wish not to associate with him or her or it: *I have no time for people who are rude to old people.*

—**have the time of one's life** to have a very enjoyable time: *The children had the time of their lives at the fair.*

—**have time on one's hands** to have more free

time than one can usefully fill with work, etc: *I could help you in the shop. I have some time on my hands just now.*

—**in good time** early enough, with time to spare: *You should get to your interview in good time.*

—**in (someone's) own good time** when it is convenient for (someone), at whatever time or speed he or she chooses: *There's no point in rushing him. He'll get there in his own good time.*

—**in the fullness of time** see **full**.

—**in the nick of time** see **nick**.

—**in time** early enough: *If we hurry we'll still get there in time.*

—**keep time** (1) of a clock to show the time accurately: *The grandfather clock keeps excellent time.* (2) to perform an action in the same rhythm as someone else: *She kept time with the musicians by clapping her hands.*

—**kill time** to find something to do to pass some idle time, especially time spent waiting for someone or something: *I'm waiting to see the boss. I'm just killing time by reading a magazine.*

—**make good time** to have as rapid, or more rapid, a journey as one expected: *We made good time on the motorway, but the country roads slowed us up.*

—**mark time** to remain in one's present position without progressing or taking any action: *He's not applying for other jobs which come up. He's marking time until something just right comes up.* <Refers to soldiers moving their feet as if marching but not actually moving forwards>.

—**not before time** not too soon, rather late: *You've arrived? Not before time.*

—**no time at all** a very short time: *It will be no time at all before your mother comes back.*

—**on time** at the right time: *You'll be sent away if you don't get there on time.*

—**pass the time of day with (someone)** to greet (someone) and have a brief conversation, e.g. about the weather: *Whenever I meet the postman in the street, I pass the time of day with him.*

—**play for time** to act so as to delay an action, event, etc, until the time that conditions are better for oneself: *He played for time by saying that he would have to discuss the situation with his wife before reaching a decision.* <In games such as cricket it means to play in such a way as to avoid defeat by playing defensively until the close of the game>.

—**take one's time** not to hurry, to take as much

time as wishes to do something: *Take your time. The bus isn't due for ten minutes.*

—**take time by the forelock** to act quickly and without delay: *If you want to travel the world take time by the forelock and go now.* <Refers to the fact that time was often represented by an old man with no hair except for a forelock, a length of hair over his forehead>.

—**take time off** to take a break from work: *He has taken time off to look after his sick wife.*

—**there's no time like the present** if one has decided on a course of action one should get started on it right away: *If you're going to take up running there's no time like the present.*

—**time and tide wait for no man** time moves on without regard for human beings and therefore opportunities should be grasped as they arise as they may not be there for very long: *If you want to marry her you should ask her now. Time and tide wait for no man.*

—**time and time again** repeatedly: *I've told the child time and time again not to go out of the garden gate.*

—**time flies** time passes very quickly: *Is it that time already? Doesn't time fly?*

—**time is getting on** time is passing, it is growing late: *We had better get home. Time is getting on.*

—**time out of mind** same as **time immemorial**—see **immemorial**.

—**time was** there was a time when: *Time was when he could have climbed that hill but he's old and stiff now.*

tin

—**a little tin god** see **god**.

—**put the tin lid on (something)** see **lid**.

tip

—**be on the tip of one's tongue** to be about to be said: *It was on the tip of my tongue to tell him to leave immediately.*

—**the tip of the iceberg** see **ice**.

—**tip (someone) off** to give (someone) some private or secret information: *She was leaving without saying goodbye but he tipped me off.*

—**tip the scales** see **scale**.

—**tip (someone) the wink** see **wink**.

tit

—**tit for tat** repayment of injury or harm for injury or harm: *Your child hit mine and he hit yours. That was simply tit for tat.* <Perhaps a variation on tip for tap, blow for blow>.

to

—**toing and froing** repeatedly going backwards

and forwards: *There's been a lot of toing and froing between the two board rooms. We think a merger is planned.*

toast

—**warm as toast** very warm and cosy: *The child was warm as toast under her quilt.*

tod

—**on one's tod** alone: *He prefers to go on holiday on his tod.* <From Cockney rhyming slang "on one's Tod Sloan", meaning "on one's own", Tod Sloan having been a famous American jockey>.

toe

—**be on one's toes** to be alert and prepared for action: *You had better all be on your toes today. The school inspector is coming.*

—**toe the line** *see* **line.**

—**tread on (someone's) toes** to offend (someone) by doing or saying (something) that is against his or her beliefs or opinions: *I obviously trod on his toes by criticizing the government.*

toffee

—**not for toffee** not at all: *She can't sing for toffee.*

token

—**by the same token** in addition: *If the firm expands we'll need more staff and by the same token more facilities for them.*

told *see* **tell.**

Tom

—**a peeping Tom** a man who gets sexual enjoyment from secretly watching women undress or women who are naked, especially by looking through the windows of their houses: *The police have arrested the peeping Tom who has been creeping around our gardens.* <From the story of Lady Godiva who is said to have ridden naked through the streets of Coventry as part of a bargain made with her husband, Leofric, Earl of Mercia, to persuade him to lift a tax he had placed on his tenants. Everyone was to stay indoors so as not to see her but a character, later called Peeping Tom, looked out to see her and was struck blind>.

—**every** *or* **any Tom, Dick and Harry** absolutely everyone or anyone, every ordinary person: *The club does not admit every Tom, Dick and Harry.* <From the fact that all three are common English Christian names>.

tongs

—**go at it hammer and tongs** *see* **hammer.**

tongue

—**a slip of the tongue** *see* **slip.**

—**be on the tip of one's tongue** *see* **tip.**

—**have one's tongue in one's cheek** to say something that one does not mean seriously or literally, sometimes to say the opposite of what one means for a joke: *He said that he worked for a very generous company but I could tell that he had his tongue in his cheek.*

—**hold one's tongue** to remain silent or to stop talking: *I wanted to tell him what I thought of his actions but I decided to hold my tongue.*

tooth

—**be** *or* **get long in the tooth** to be or become old: *That actor's getting a bit long in the tooth for that part.*

—**fight tooth and nail** to fight, struggle or argue fiercely and determinedly: *She fought tooth and nail to get her children back.*

—**have a sweet tooth** *see* **sweet.**

top¹

—**be thin on top** *see* **thin.**

—**blow one's top** to lose one's temper: *She blew her top when he came home drunk.*

—**off the top of one's head** without much thought, without research or preparation: *I don't know exactly how far it is, but off the top of my head I'd say 500 miles.*

—**on top of the world** *see* **world.**

—**out of the top drawer** *see* **drawer.**

—**over the top** too much, to too great an extent: *He went completely over the top with his criticism of the play.*

—**top the bill** *see* **bill.**

—**the top brass** *see* **brass.**

—**the top of the ladder** *or* **tree** the highest point in a profession, etc: *The young doctor got to the top of the surgical ladder.*

top²

—**sleep like a top** to sleep very soundly: *We slept like tops after our long walk.* <A pun on the fact that sleep used of a top means "to spin steadily without wobbling">.

torch

—**carry a torch for (someone)** *see* **carry.**

toss

—**argue the toss** to dispute a decision: *There's no point in arguing the toss. The judge's decision is final.* <Refers to arguing about the result of tossing a coin>.

touch

—**a soft touch** *see* **soft**².

—**in touch with (someone)** in communication with (someone): *I tried to get in touch with an old friend.*

—**it's touch and go** it's very uncertain or precarious: *It's touch and go with the invalid's condition.* <Perhaps refers to a ship that touches rocks or the ground but goes on past the danger without being damaged>.

—**lose one's touch** to lose one's usual skill or knack: *He used to be good at getting the children to sleep but he's lost his touch.* <Probably refers to someone's touch on piano keys>.

—**out of touch with (someone)** (1) no longer in contact or communication with (someone): *The two friends have been out of touch for years.* (2) not understanding or sympathetic towards: *She's out of touch with the people in her old neighbourhood.*

—**the common touch** the ability to understand and get on with ordinary people: *The prince has the common touch.*

—**the finishing touches** the final details which complete something: *I'm just putting the finishing touches to my report.*

—**the Midas touch** *see* **Midas.**

—**touch a chord** *see* **chord.**

—**touch (something) off** to cause (something), to give rise to (something): *His remarks sparked off a rebellion.*

—**touch wood** *see* **wood.**

tow

—**have (someone) in tow** to have someone following closely behind one: *She had her three children in tow.*

towel

—**throw in the towel** to give up, to admit defeat: *The student can't cope with his studies and he is throwing in the towel.* <From a method of conceding defeat in boxing>.

tower

—**a tower of strength** someone who is very helpful and supportive: *He was a real tower of strength when her husband died.*

—**live in an ivory tower** *see* **ivory.**

town

—**go out on the town** to go out for a night's entertainment: *We're going out on the town to celebrate their engagement.*

—**go to town** to act or behave without restraint, with great enthusiasm or with great expense: *They've fairly gone to town on decorating the new house.*

—**paint the town red** *see* **paint.**

—**the talk of the town** *see* **talk.**

track

—**cover one's tracks** to hide one's activities or movements: *The bank raiders tried to cover their tracks by changing cars.*

—**keep** *or* **lose track of (someone** *or* **something)** to keep or fail to keep oneself informed about the whereabouts or progress of (someone or something): *He must find it difficult to keep track of all his business interests. I lost track of my university friends years ago.*

—**have a one-track mind** *see* **one.**

—**make tracks (for)** to leave or set out (for): *It's late. We must be making tracks (for home).*

—**off the beaten track** *see* **beat.**

—**on the right** *or* **wrong track** on the right or wrong course to get the correct answer or desired result: *The police think they're on the right track to find the killer.*

—**(someone's) track record** the extent of a person's success or failure in his or her profession or trade: *The salesman has an excellent track record.*

trail

—**blaze a trail** to show or lead the way in some new activity or area of knowledge: *His research blazed a trail in cancer treatment.* <Refers to explorers going along a path and marking the way for those coming after them by stripping sections of bark from trees (blazing)>.

tread

—**tread on (someone's) corns** *see* **corn.**

—**tread on (someone's) toes** *see* **toe.**

—**tread water** *see* **water.**

tree

—**bark up the wrong tree** *see* **bark.**

—**not to be able to see the wood for the trees** *see* **wood.**

—**the top of the tree** *see* **top.**

—**up a gum tree** *see* **gum.**

tremble

—**to be** *or* **go in fear and trembling of (someone** *or* **something)** to be extremely afraid: *The children go in fear and trembling of the school bully.* <A biblical reference to Philippians 2:12>.

trial

—**trial and error** the trying out of various approaches or methods of doing something until one finds the right one: *They found a cure for the skin rash by trial and error.*

—**trials and tribulations** difficulties and hardships: *She was complaining about the trials and tribulations of being a mother.*

triangle

—**the eternal triangle** *see* **eternal.**

trick

—**bag of tricks** see **bag**.

—**confidence trick** see **confidence**.

—**do the trick** to have the desired effect, to achieve the desired result: *It's proved difficult to cure her cough but the doctor said that this would do the trick.*

—**never to miss a trick** never to fail to take advantage of a favourable situation or opportunity to bring advantage to oneself: *He was selling insurance to people in his holiday hotel. He never misses a trick.*

—**up to one's (old) tricks** acting in one's usual (wrong, dishonest or deceitful) way: *The police suspect that the local villain is up to his old tricks.*

trooper

—**swear like a trooper** to swear very frequently or very strongly: *He was shocked to hear the young woman swearing like a trooper.* <A trooper was an ordinary cavalry soldier>.

trot

—**on the trot** (1) one after the other: *He won three years on the trot.* (2) very active and busy: *With three children she's on the trot from morning till night.*

trouble

—**fish in troubled waters** see **fish**.

—**pour oil on troubled waters** see **oil**.

trousers

—**catch (someone) with his** or **her trousers down** see **catch**.

—**wear the trousers** to make all the important decisions in a household: *There's no point in asking him if they need any gardening work done. His wife wears the trousers.*

trowel

—**lay it on with a trowel** see **lay**.

truck

—**have no truck with (someone** or **something)** to have no contact or dealings with (someone or something): *I wouldn't have any truck with them. They're always in trouble with the police.*

true

—**ring true** see **true**.

—**true to form** see **form**.

trump

—**play one's trump card** to use something very advantageous to oneself that one has had in reserve for use when really necessary: *The shop manager refused to exchange the faulty stereo system until he played his trump card and said he wrote about consumers' rights.* <In card

games a trump is the a card of whichever suit has been declared to be higher-ranking than the others>.

—**turn up trumps** to do the right or required thing in a difficult situation, especially unexpectedly: *I didn't think our team member would beat the champion but he turned up trumps.* <See above—refers to drawing a card from the trump suit>.

truth

—**home truth** see **home**.

—**truth will out** the true facts of a situation will not remain hidden or secret forever: *He thought that no one would find out that he had committed bigamy, but his neighbour did. Truth will out.*

try

—**try it on** to act in a bold way in order to find out to what extent it will be tolerated: *He didn't expect to be allowed to go to the all-night party. He was just trying it on.*

tug

—**tug of love** a struggle involving the custody of a child: *No-one has asked the child's opinion in the tug of love.*

tune

—**call the tune** to be the person in control who gives the orders: *It's his deputy who's calling the tune since he's been ill.* <Refers to the saying "He who pays the piper calls the tune">.

—**change one's tune** see **change**.

—**in tune with (something)** in agreement with (something), compatible with (something): *Our ideas on the environment are very much in tune.*

—**to the tune of (something)** to the stated sum of money, usually high or higher than is expected or is reasonable: *Instead of hundreds he had to pay to the tune of thousands for that antique.*

tunnel

—**light at the end of the tunnel** see **light**.

turkey

—**cold turkey** a form of treatment for drug or alcohol abuse involving sudden and complete withdrawal as opposed to gradual withdrawal: *He's having a hard time trying to get off drugs cold turkey.*

—**talk turkey** to talk plainly and honestly: *If you're interested in this business deal let's talk turkey.*

turn

—**a turn-up for the books** something favourable which happens unexpectedly: *He discovered there was a later bus after all. That was a turn-up for the books.* <Referred originally to a horse that unexpectedly won a race, the book meaning the total number of bets on a race>.

—**do (someone) a good turn** to help (someone) in some way: *The boy did the old man a good turn and cut his lawn for him.*

—**do a U-turn** *see* **U.**

—**done to a turn** cooked exactly right, cooked to perfection: *The roast beef was done to a turn.*

—**even the worm turns** *see* **worm.**

—**give (someone) quite a turn** to give (someone) a sudden shock or surprise: *You gave me quite a turn coming up behind me so quietly.*

—**not to turn a hair** *see* **hair.**

—**out of turn** (1) out of the correct order, not at the correct time: *You played out of turn. It was my turn.* (2) at the wrong time, without consideration for the circumstances of the situation, someone's feelings, etc: *I hope I'm not talking out of turn but I think you're doing the wrong thing.*

—**the turn of the year** *or* **century** the end of one year or century and the beginning of the next: *He's changing jobs at the turn of the year.*

—**turn a blind eye to (something)** *see* **eye.**

—**turn (someone's) head** *see* **head.**

—**turn of phrase** a way of expressing something: *The novelist has a fine turn of phrase.*

—**turn (someone) off** to arouse feelings of dislike, disgust, etc in (someone): *The sight of the greasy food turned me right off.*

—**turn one's coat** *see* **coat.**

—**turn one's hand to (something)** *see* **hand.**

—**turn (someone) on** to arouse feelings of excitement, interest or lust in (somone): *Jazz really turns him on.*

—**turn on one's heel** *see* **heel.**

—**turn over a new leaf** *see* **leaf.**

—**turn the corner** *see* **corner.**

—**turn the other cheek** *see* **cheek.**

—**turn the tables on (someone)** *see* **table.**

—**turn turtle** to turn upside down, to capsize: *We were afraid that the boat would turn turtle in the rough seas.* <A turtle is helpless and easy to kill if it is turned over on its back>.

—**turn up one's nose at (something)** *see* **nose.**

—**turn up trumps** *see* **trump.**

turtle

—**turn turtle** *see* **turn.**

twice

—**think twice** to give careful consideration: *She wouldn't think twice about leaving him if someone richer came along.*

twiddle

—**twiddle one's thumbs** *see* **thumb.**

twinkle

—**in the twinkling of an eye** *see* **eye.**

—**when (someone) was just a twinkle in his** *or* **her daddy's eye** before (someone) was born, a long time ago: *You were just a twinkle in your daddy's eye when I first met them.*

twist

—**get one's knickers in a twist** *see* **knickers.**

—**round the twist** insane, very foolish: *She's round the twist to buy the house. It's falling to bits.*

—**twist (someone's) arm** *see* **arm.**

—**twist (someone) round one's little finger** *see* **finger.**

two

—**a bird in the hand is worth two in the bush** *see* **bird.**

—**for two pins** *see* **pin.**

—**in two minds** *see* **mind.**

—**in two shakes of a lamb's tail** *see* **shake.**

—**in two ticks** in a very short time indeed: *I'll attend to it in two ticks.* <Refers to the ticking of a clock>.

—**like as two peas in a pod** *see* **pea.**

—**put two and two together** to come to a (correct) conclusion from what one sees and hears: *Eventually I put two and two together and realized he had been in prison.*

—**there are no two ways about it** *see* **way.**

—**two a penny** *see* **penny.**

—**two of a kind** two people of a very similar type or character: *Don't worry about her treating him badly. They're two of a kind.*

—**two's company, (three's a crowd)** a third person who is with a couple is often unwanted as they want to be alone: *Her mother wouldn't let her go on holiday with her boyfriend unless her sister went too but it was very much a question of two's company.*

—**two wrongs do not make a right** a second wrong action does not lead to good and does not improve a situation: *Don't take revenge by damaging his car because he damaged yours: two wrongs don't make a right.*

tyre

—**spare tyre** *see* **spare.**

U

ugly
—ugly as sin *see* sin.
—ugly duckling *see* duck.

umbrage
—take umbrage to show that one is offended: *She took umbrage at not being asked to join our trip to the beach.* <Originally meant to feel overshadowed—from Latin *umbra*, shade>.

uncle
—Bob's your uncle everything is or will be all right: *Just apologize to him and Bob's your uncle.*
—talk to (someone) like a Dutch uncle *see* Dutch.
—Uncle Sam the United States of America: *Uncle Sam is supplying some of the aid.* <Probably from the Initials "U.S." which were stamped on government supplies, possibly because someone called Uncle Sam was employed in handling such supplies>.

Uriah
—Uriah Heep a sycophant, someone who always fawns over and toadies to others: *He's volunteered to go and get the boss's car. He's a real Uriah Heep.* <Refers to a character in Charles Dickens's novel *David Copperfield*>.

under
—come under the hammer *see* hammer.
—take (someone) under one's wing *see* wing.
—under (someone's) (very) nose *see* nose.
—under one's own steam *see* steam.
—under the influence under the influence of alcohol, drunk: *He was caught driving under the influence.*
—under the weather *see* weather.
—under (someone's) thumb *see* thumb.
—under way *see* way.

unknown
—an unknown quantity *see* quantity.

unsound
—of unsound mind insane, deranged: *He murdered his wife while of unsound mind.*

unstuck
—come unstuck *see* come.

up
—be in (something) up to one's neck *see* neck.
—be one up on (someone) *see* one.

—be on the up-and-up to be making successful progress: *The firm was doing badly but it's on the up-and up now.*
—be right up (someone's) street *see* street.
—be up against it *see* against.
—be (well) up in *or* on (something) to have an extensive knowledge of (something): *He's well up in modern medical techniques.*
—be up in arms *see* arm.
—be up to (someone) it is (someone's) responsibility or duty: *It's up to him whether he joins or not.*
—be up to (something) (1) to be occupied with or in (something, often something dishonest, etc): *What's that crook up to now?* (2) to be good enough, strong enough, etc, to do (something): *She's obviously not up to the job.*
—be up to no good *see* good.
—be up to the mark *see* mark.
—be up with (someone) to be wrong with (someone): *What's up with him?*
—it is all up with (someone) *see* all.
—not up to much *see* much.
—(someone's) number is up *see* number.
—up and about out of bed, after an illness: *He was ill for a time but he's up and about now.*
—up-and-coming likely to be successful, rising in popularity or prominence: *She is an up-and-coming young singer.*
—up and doing active and busy: *I don't like doing nothing. I like to be up and doing.*
—up for grabs *see* grab.
—ups and downs good fortune and bad fortune, successful periods and unsuccessful periods: *Their relationship has had its ups and downs.*
—upstage (someone *or* something) to take attention or interest away from (someone or something): *She tried to upstage the other girls at the ball with a very revealing ball gown.*
—up the wall *see* wall.
—up to a point *see* point.
—up to one's ears in (something) *see* ear.
—up to the minute *see* minute.

upshot
—the upshot the result or outcome: *They quar-*

relled and the upshot was that she left. <Literally the last shot in an archery competition>.

upper
—**have** *or* **get the upper hand (of** *or* **over) (someone)** have or get an advantage or control (over someone): *She has the upper hand in the custody dispute as the child lives with her.*

—**keep a stiff upper lip** *see* **lip.**

—**on one's uppers** very poor: *We can't pay the rent. We're on our uppers.* <Literally with no soles on one's shoes>.

—**upper-crust** of the upper class or aristocracy: *She has an upper-crust accent.* <Refers literally to the upper part of the pastry of a pie above the filling>.

upside
—**be** *or* **get upsides with (someone)** to be or become on a level with or equal with (someone): *She's upsides with you now. She has a new car too.*

—**turn (something) upside down** to put (something) into a state of disorder and confusion: *We turned the house upside down looking for the lost document.*

uptake
—**quick** *or* **slow on the uptake** quick or slow to understand: *She's so slow on the uptake that everything has to be explained several times.*

use
—**come in useful** to be useful in the future: *Don't throw out that box. It might come in useful.*

—**have no use for (someone** *or* **something)** to wish not to be associated with (someone or something), to think little of (someone or something): *He has no use for people who lie.*

—**make use of (someone)** to to use (someone) for one's own gain or benefit, to take advantage of (someone): *She just makes use of her mother. She expects her to look after her children every day.*

—**use one's loaf** *see* **loaf.**

U-turn
—**do a U-turn** to change one's opinion, policy, etc, completely: *The government have done a U-turn on their health policy.* <Refers originally to vehicle drivers making a turn in the shape of the letter U to reverse direction>.

V

vain

—**take (someone's) name in vain** to use (someone's) name disrespectfully, especially to swear using God's name: *They were punished for taking the Lord's name in vain.* <A biblical reference to Exodus 20:7>.

value

—**take (someone *or* something) at face value** *see* **face**.

variety

—**variety is the spice of life** the opportunity to do different things, experience different situations, etc, is what makes life interesting. *I will go to the pop concert although I'm really a jazz fan as variety is the spice of life.* <A quotation from a poem by William Cowper>.

veil

—**draw a veil over (something)** not to discuss (something), to keep (something) hidden or secret: *If I were him I would draw a veil over his part in the affair.*

velvet

—**the iron hand in the velvet glove** *see* **iron**.

vengeance

—**with a vengeance** very strongly, much, etc: *It's snowing with a vengeance now.*

vent

—**vent one's spleen** *see* **spleen**.

venture

—**nothing ventured, nothing gained** *see* **nothing**.

very

—**the very thing** exactly what is required: *That scarf is the very thing for her birthday present.*

vessel

—**empty vessels make most noise** *see* **empty**.

vested

—**a vested interest in (something)** *see* **interest**.

vex

—**a vexed question** a difficult issue or problem that is much discussed without being resolved: *Then there is the vexed question of who is responsible for paying for the repairs.*

vicious

—**vicious circle** *see* **circle**.

victory

—**landslide victory** a victory in an election by a very large number of votes: *We expected a victory but not a landslide one.*

—**Pyrrhic victory** *see* **Pyrrhic**.

view

—**a bird's-eye view of (something)** (1) a view of (something) seen from high above: *We got a marvellous bird's-eye view of the town from the top of the tower.* (2) a brief description, etc, of (something): *The book gives a bird's-eye view of alternative medicine, but you will require something more detailed.*

—**in view of (something)** considering (something), because of (something): *In view of his behaviour he will have to be punished.*

—**take a dim view of (something)** *see* **dim**.

villain

—**the villain of the piece** the person responsible for an act of evil or wrongdoing: *We wondered who had broken the window—the boy next door turned out to be the villain of the piece.* <Refers originally to the villain in a play>.

vine

—**a clinging vine** a possessive person, someone who likes always to be with someone else: *His wife's a real clinging vine.*

—**wither on the vine** to die to come to an end without being used, finished, etc: *The research department has some good ideas but they wither on the vine because the company does not have the money to put them into practice.* <Literally of grapes withering on the vine instead of being picked and eaten or made into wine>.

violet

—**a shrinking violet** a very timid, shy person: *She won't speak in public. She's very much a shrinking violet.*

viper

—**nurse a viper in one's bosom** to be helpful to or supportive of someone who does one harm: *The boy whom they were fostering attacked their son with a knife. They were nursing a viper in their bosom.* <A viper is a poisonous snake>.

vital

—**vital statistics** one's chest, waist and hip measurements: *The announcer at the beauty* contest gave everyone's vital statistics. <Refers originally to statistics dealing with population>.

voice

—**at the top of one's voice** loudly, in a high voice: *The teacher shouted at the children at the top of his voice.*

—**a voice crying in the wilderness** (someone) expressing an opinion or warning that no one takes any notice of: *She told them that the proposed product would not sell but she was a voice crying in the wilderness.* <A biblical reference to John the Baptist in Matthew 3:3>.

—**the still, small voice (of reason)** the expression of a calm, sensible point of view: *The still, small voice of reason told her not to accept a lift*

from the stranger, but she did. <A biblical reference to I Kings 19:12>.

volume

—**speak volumes** to express a great deal of meaning without putting it into words: *She made no reply to his insult but her look spoke volumes.*

vote

—**a vote of confidence** a vote taken to establish whether or not the government, a group of people, a person, etc, is still trusted and supported: *The chairman survived the board's vote of confidence.*

—**vote with one's feet** to leave: *The workers had no confidence in the new management and so they voted with their feet by finding other jobs.*

W

wagon

—**hitch one's wagon to a star** to have noble or high ambitions or aims: *He was born into a very poor family but he had hitched his wagon to a star and was determined to go to university.* <Refers to a quotation from *Society at Solitude* by Ralph Waldo Emerson>.

—**on the wagon** not drinking alcohol: *He's on the wagon for health reasons.* <Refers to a water wagon>.

wait

—**lie in wait** to be on the watch (for someone), to ambush (someone). *The rock star tried to leave by the back exit, but his fans were lying in wait for him.*

—**waiting in the wings** *see* **wing**.

wake

—**in the wake of (something)** immediately following, and often caused by (something): *Disease came in the wake of the flood.* <Refers literally to the strip of water left by the passing of a ship>.

walk

—**cock of the walk** *see* **cock**.

—**walk it** to win or succeed easily: *He was nervous about the match but he walked it.*

—**walk of life** occupation or profession, way of earning a living: *People from all walks of life joined the campaign.*

—**walk on air** *see* **air**.

wall

—**go to the wall** to suffer ruin: *Many small firms went to the wall during the recession.* <Origin uncertain>.

—**have one's back to the wall** *see* **back**.

—**the writing on the wall** *see* **write**.

—**up the wall** very annoyed, irritated, harassed, etc: *These children are driving me up the wall with their noise.*

—**walls have ears** someone may be listening (to a secret conversation): *Be careful what you say in the restaurant. It's not busy but walls have ears.*

—**would like to be a fly on the wall** *see* **fly**.

Walter

—**a Walter Mitty** someone who invents stories about himself to make his life seem more ex-citing: *I was amazed at some of his adventures until I discovered that he was a Walter Mitty.* <Refers to a character in a James Thurber short story>.

war

—**have been in the wars** to have a slight injury: *"You've been in the wars," said the nurse to the little boy who had broken his leg falling off a swing.*

—**on the warpath** very angry: *Look out. Father's discovered the broken window and he's on the warpath.* <An North American Indian expression>.

warm

—**warm as toast** *see* **toast**.

—**warm the cockles of the heart** *see* **heart**.

wart

—**warts and all** including all the faults, disadvantages: *Her husband is a bit irresponsible, but she loves him warts and all.* <Refers to the fact that Oliver Cromwell instructed his portrait painter, Sir Peter Lely, to paint him as he really was, including his warts, rather than try to make him look more handsome>.

wash

—**come out in the wash** to come to a satisfactory end: *Don't worry about making a mistake on your first day. It'll all come out in the wash.* <Used literally of a stain on clothes, etc, that comes out when the article is washed>.

—**wash one's dirty linen in public** *same as* **air one's dirty linen in public**—*see* **air**.

—**washed-out** exhausted: *She felt washed-out after her illness.* <Used literally of garments having lost colour as a result of washing>.

—**washed-up** ruined, finished: *Their relationship is all washed up.* <Refers to a shipwreck>.

—**wash one's hands of (something)** *see* **hand**.

waste

—**lay waste (something)** to destroy or ruin (something) by force: *The invading army laid waste the city.*

—**waste not, want not** if one is careful not to waste anything it is likely that one will never be in want: *Don't throw out that bread. Waste not, want not.*

watch
—the or a watched pot never boils see pot.
—watch (someone) like a hawk see hawk.

water
—be water off a duck's back see duck.
—hold water to be accurate, to be able to be proved true: *Your theory won't hold water.* <From a vessel that is not broken>.
—in deep water see deep.
—like a fish out of water see fish.
- of the first water see first.
—pour oil on troubled waters see oil.
—pour or throw cold water on (something) see cold.
—spend money like water see money.
—still waters run deep see still.
—take to (something) like a duck to water see duck.
—tread water to take very little action: *This is not a time to expand the business. We should tread water for a while.* <Literally to keep oneself afloat in water by moving the legs (and arms) rather than by swimming>.
—water (something) down to make (something) less serious, exciting, etc, than it really was: *We had better water down the account of the accident for my mother or she'll worry.* <Literally to dilute with water>.
—water under the bridge something that is past and cannot be changed and should be forgotten: *Stop worrying about our quarrel. It's water under the bridge.*

Waterloo
—meet one's Waterloo see meet.

wave
—on the same wavelength as (someone) having the same opinions, attitudes, tastes, etc, as (someone): *We'll never be friends. We're just not on the same wavelength.*

way
—get into the way of (something or doing something) to become accustomed to (something or doing something): *She can't get into the way of using the computer.*
—get or have one's own way to do or get what one wants: *We all wanted to go the beach but as usual she got her own way and we went to the cinema.*
—go out of one's way to do more than is really necessary, to make a special effort: *She went out of her way to be kind to the new girl.*
—go the way of all flesh to die or come to an end: *He must have gone the way of all flesh by*

now. *Otherwise he would be over 100 years old.*
—have a way with (someone or something) to have a special knack with (someone or something), to be good at handling (someone or something): *He has a way with words.*
—have everything one's own way to get everything done according to one's wishes: *The boss won't listen to any suggestions. He likes to have everything his own way.*
—have it both ways to have the advantages of two sets of situations, each of which usually excludes the possibility of the other: *She wants a full-time job but she wants to look after her children herself. She's not going to be able to have it both ways.*
—in a bad way very ill, injured, distressed, etc: *The accident victim is in a bad way.*
—lead the way to go first, to be in front: *Which country leads the way in electronics?*
—look the other way see other.
—lose one's way to cease to know where one is or which direction one is going in: *We lost our way in the mist.*
—make one's way to go, to progress: *Make your way to the first floor.*
—make way for (someone or something) to stand aside to leave room for (someone or something): *Older people must retire and make way for the young.*
—mend one's ways to improve one's behaviour: *You'll have to mend your ways if you want to stay with the firm.*
—no way see no.
—one way and another in various ways: *He was made to feel very unwelcome in one way and another.*
—on the way about to happen or arrive: *The food's on its way.*
—pave the way for (something) see pave.
—pay one's own way see pay.
—see one's way to (doing something) to be able and willing to (do something): *Could you see your way to giving me a lift to work?*
—there are no two ways about it no other opinion, attitude, etc, is possible: *He's guilty. There are no two ways about it.*
—under way in progress: *His plans are well under way.*
—ways and means methods, especially unofficial ones: *We don't have the money yet, but there are ways and means of getting it.*

wayside
—fall by the wayside to fail to continue to the

end of something; to give up in the course of doing something: *Not all students graduate. Some fall by the wayside.* <A biblical reference to the parable of the sower in Luke 8:5>.

weak

—**in a weak moment** at a time when one is feeling unusually kind, generous, etc: *In a weak moment I agreed to let her stay at my house.*

wear

—**wear one's heart on one's sleeve** *see* **heart**.

weather

—**keep a weather eye open** *see* **eye**.

—**make heavy weather of (something)** *see* **heavy**.

—**under the weather** unwell: *She left work early feeling under the weather.*

—**weather the storm** *see* **storm**.

wedding

—**shotgun wedding** *see* **shot**.

wedge

—**the thin end of the wedge** a minor event or action which could be the first stage of something major and serious or harmful: *Letting her stay for a week is the thin end of the edge. She'll want to stay permanently.*

weep

—**weep buckets** *see* **bucket**.

weight

—**carry weight** to have influence, to be considered important: *Their opinion won't carry any weight.*

—**pull one's weight** to do one's fair share of work, etc: *We'll finish this in time if we all pull our weight.*

—**throw one's weight about** *or* **around** to use one's power and influence in a bullying way: *The deputy manager is throwing his weight around when the manager is away.*

—**weigh (something) up** to assess (something): *It's difficult to weigh up our chances of success.*

—**worth its** *or* **one's weight in gold** *see* **gold**.

well

—**be well out of (something)** to be fortunate in having got out of (something): *You're well out of that relationship. She's not to be trusted.*

—**well off** (1) having plenty of money, rich: *They're very well off althoug they live very simply.* (2) in a fortunate situation: *He's looking for a new job. He doesn't know when he's well off.*

west

—**go west** to be ruined, to be finished: *Our hopes of victory have gone west.* <Airmen's slang from World War 1>.

wet

—**wet behind the ears** to be young, inexperienced and naive: *You can't expect him to deal with that difficult client. He's wet behind the ears.*

—**wet blanket** *see* **blanket**.

—**wet one's whistle** *see* **whistle**.

whale

—**have a whale of a time** to have an extremely enjoyable time: *The children had a whale of a time at the beach.*

what

—**give (someone) what for** to scold or punish (someone): *You'll get what for for borrowing his bike without permission.*

—**know what's what** to know the details of a situation, to know what is going on: *The accountant is the only person who know's what's what in the firm.*

—**what have you** and similar things: *Put your suitcase and what have you over there.*

—**what of it?** what does it matter?: *So I've annoyed him. What of it?*

wheel

—**oil the wheels** *see* **oil**.

—**put a spoke in (someone's) wheel** *see* **spoke**.

—**put one's shoulder to the wheel** *see* **shoulder**.

—**set the wheels in motion** to start a process off: *If you want to get planning permission you'll have to set the wheels in motion right away.*

—**wheeling and dealing** acting in an astute but sometimes dishonest or immoral way, especially in business: *He made a lot of money from wheeling and dealing in the antiques trade.*

while

—**worth (someone's) while** worth (someone's) time and effort: *If you do the work he'll make it worth your while.*

whip

—**a whipping boy** someone who is blamed and punished for someone else's mistakes: *The young clerk is the whipping boy for the whole department.* <Refers literally to a boy who was punished for any misdeeds a royal prince made, since the tutor was not allowed to strike a member of the royal family>.

—**have the whip hand** to have control or an advantage: *He has the whip hand in that relationship. He makes all the decisions.* <Refers to coach-driving>.

whisker

—**win by a whisker** to win by a very short amount: *The government won the election by a whisker.*

—**the cat's whiskers** *same as* **the cat's pyjamas**— *see* **cat**.

whisper

—**in a stage whisper** *see* **stage**.

whistle

—**blow the whistle on (someone)** *see* **blow**.

—**clean as a whistle** *see* **clean**.

—**wet one's whistle** to have a drink: *It's hot. Let's stop and wet our whistles.*

—**whistle for (something)** to ask for (something) with no hope of getting it: *You may need extra money but you can whistle for it.* <Perhaps from an old sailors' superstition that when a ship is becalmed whistling can summon up a wind>.

white

—**a whited sepulchre** someone who pretends to be moral and virtuous but is in fact bad: *He seems to be a whited sepulchre but I've heard that he beats his wife and children.* <A biblical reference to Matthew 23:27>.

—**a white elephant** *see* **elephant**.

—**show the white feather** *see* **feather**.

—**white as a sheet** *see* **sheet**.

—**white lie** a not very serious lie: *I'd rather tell her a white lie than tell her I don't like her dress.*

whole

—**go the whole hog** *see* **hog**.

—**the whole (bang) shoot** *or* **the whole shooting match** *see* **shoot**.

whoop

—**whoop it up** to celebrate in a noisy, extravagant way: *He really whooped it up before his wedding.*

wick

—**get on (someone's) wick** to annoy or irritate (someone) greatly.

wicket

—**be on a sticky wicket** *see* **stick**.

widow

—**grass widow** *see* **grass**.

wild

—**a wild goose chase** a search or hunt that cannot end in success: *I knew it was a wild goose chase to look for an open restaurant at that time in the morning.*

—**run wild** to behave in an uncontrolled, undisciplined way: *The children run wild while their parents are at work.*

—**sow one's wild oats** to enjoy oneself in a wild and sometimes promiscuous way when one is young: *He's sown his wild oats now and he wants to get married and settle down.*

—**spread like wildfire** to spread extremely rapidly: *The disease spread like wildfire through the small community.* <Wildfire was probably a kind of fire started by lightning>.

—**wild horses would not drag (someone) to something** *or* **somewhere** *see* **horse**.

wilderness

—**a voice crying in the wilderness** *see* **voice**.

will

—**willing horse** *see* **horse**.

—**with a will** enthusiastically and energetically: *The children worked with a will weeding the garden.*

—**with the best will in the world** *see* **best**.

win

—**win the day** *same as* **carry the day**—*see* **day**.

wind

—**a straw in the wind** *see* **straw**.

—**get wind of (something)** to receive information about (something) *indirectly or secretly*: *We got wind of the enemy's plans.* <Referring to the scent of an animal carried by the wind>.

—**in the wind** about to happen, being placed or prepared: *I think major changes are in the wind at work.*

—**get the wind up** to become frightened or nervous: *He got the wind up when he heard the police were after him.*

—**raise the wind** to get enough money to do (something): *They're trying to raise the wind to buy a house.*

—**sail close to the wind** *see* **sail**.

—**see which way the wind blows** *see* **blow**.

—**take the wind out of (someone's) sails** to reduce (someone's) pride in his or her cleverness, abilities, etc: *She was boasting about how many exams she had passed when we took the wind out of her sails by telling her that everyone else had passed more.* <Refers to the fact that a ship takes the wind out of another ship's sails if it passes close to it on the windward side>.

—**throw caution to the (four) winds** to begin to behave recklessly: *She had very little money but she threw caution to the winds and bought a new dress.*

windmill

—**tilt at windmills** to struggle against imaginary opposition: *She thinks everyone in the office is in trying to get rid of her but she is tilting at windmills.* <Refers to an episode in Cervantes's novel *Don Quixote* in which the hero mistakes a row of windmills for giants and attacks them>.

window

—**window-dressing** the presentation of something to show the most favourable parts and hide the rest: *There's a lot of window-dressing in this report. It mentions all the benefits of the scheme but it glosses over the disadvantages.* <Refers literally to the arranging of goods in a shop window to attract customers>.

wing

—**clip (someone's) wings** *see* **clip**.

—**spread one's wings** (1) to leave home: *I like living at home but I think it's time to spread my wings and find a flat.* (2) to try to put into practice one's own ideas, to make use of one's abilities: *So far she has been carrying out the head of department's suggestions but it is time for her to spread her wings.* <Refers to young birds ready to try to fly and leave the nest>.

—**take (someone) under one's wing** to take (someone) under one's protection and guidance: *Someone should take the new girl under her wing. She feels lost in this large firm.* <Refers to the practice of some birds of covering their young with their wings>.

—**waiting in the wings** in a state of readiness to do something, especially to take over someone else's job: *She's afraid to be away from the office for very long because her assistant is just waiting in the wings.* <Literally waiting in the wings of a theatre stage ready to go on>.

wink

—**forty winks** *see* **forty**.

—**tip (someone) the wink** to give (someone) information secretly or privately: *He tipped me the wink that the it was her birthday.*

wipe

—**wipe the floor with (someone)** *see* **floor**.

wire

—**get** *or* **have one's wires crossed** to be involved in a misunderstanding: *I thought it was tomorrow we were meeting. I must have got my wires crossed.* <Refers to telephone wires>.

wise

—**a wise guy** someone who thinks that he is smart, knowledgeable, etc, and acts as if he is: *He's such a wise guy that everybody dislikes him.*

—**be wise after the event** *see* **event**.

—**none the wiser** knowing no more than one did before: *I was none the wiser after his explanation.*

—**put (someone) wise to (something)** to give (someone) information about (something), make (someone) aware of (something): *Her friend put her wise to his police record.*

wish

—**wishful thinking** believing that, or hoping that, something unlikely is true or will happen just because one wishes that it would: *I hoped that we would win but it was just wishful thinking.*

—**wish (someone) joy of (something)** to wish that (something) will be a pleasure or benefit to someone (although one doesn't think it will): *I wish you joy of that car, but I found it unreliable.*

wit

—**at one's wits' end** worried and desperate: *She's at her wits' end about her missing husband.*

—**keep one's wits about one** to be alert and watchful: *Keep your wits about you when doing business with him. People say he is a crook.*

—**live by one's wits** to live by cunning schemes rather than by working: *He hasn't done a day's work in his life. He lives by his wits.*

—**scare (someone) out of his** *or* **her wits** to frighten (someone) very much: *They were scared out of their wits when they saw the man with a gun.*

witch

—**witch-hunt** a search for and persecution of people who are thought to have done something wrong, hold opinions which are thought to be dangerous etc: *The company are conducting a witch-hunt of certain union members.* <Refers historically to organized hunts for people thought to be witches>.

without

—**without rhyme or reason** *see* **rhyme**.

—**without so much as a** *see* **much**.

wolf

—**a lone wolf** *see* **lone**.

—**a wolf in sheep's clothing** someone evil and dangerous who seems to be gentle and harmless: *She trusted him but when he turned nasty she realized that he was a wolf in sheep's clothing.* <A biblical reference to Matthew 7:15>.

—**cry wolf** to give a false warning of danger, to call unnecessarily for help: *She said there was an intruder in the garden but she was only crying wolf.* <Refers to one of Aesop's fables in which a shepherd boy used to amuse himself by calling out that a wolf was coming to attack his sheep and did this so many times when it was not true that no one believed when it was true, and all his sheep were killed>.

—**keep the wolf from the door** to prevent poverty and hunger: *He earns very little but enough to keep the wolf from the door.*

wonder

—**a nine days' wonder** *see* **nine**.

—**no wonder** it is not surprising: *No wonder you're tired. It's very late.*

—**small wonder** *see* **small**.

wood

—**not to be able to see the wood for the trees** not to be able to consider the general nature of a situation, etc, because one is concentrating too much on details: *She's busy worrying about putting the commas in the right place that she doesn't appreciate the quality of the text. She can't see the wood for the trees.*

—**out of the woods** out of danger or difficulties: *The patient is improving but he's not out of the woods yet.*

—**this** *or* **that, etc, neck of the woods** *see* **neck**.

—**touch wood** to touch something made of wood supposedly to keep away bad luck: *None of us is poverty-stricken. Touch wood!* <Refers to a well-known superstition>.

wool

—**pull the wool over (someone's) eyes** to deceive (someone): *He pulled the wool over her eyes by pretending to be in love with her but he was really after her money.*

—**wool-gathering** day-dreaming: *The boss complains about her wool-gathering. She has no concentration.* <Refers to someone wandering around hedges gathering wool left by sheep>.

word

—**a man of his word** *see* **man**.

—**be as good as one's word** *see* **good**.

—**eat one's words** to admit that one was wrong in what one said: *I said he would be last but I was forced to eat my words when he won.*

—**from the word go** *see* **go**.

—**get a word in edgeways** *or* **edgewise** to have difficulty in breaking into a conversation: *The old friends were so busy chatting that their husbands couldn't get a word in edgeways.*

—**hang on (someone's) words** to listen carefully and eagerly to everything that someone says: *The student hangs on the lecturer's words.*

—**have a word in (someone's) ear** to tell (someone) something in private: *She doesn't know he's married. You should have a word in her ear.*

—**have a word with (someone)** to have a short conversation with (someone): *I'd like a word with you before the meeting.*

—**have the last word** *see* **last**.

—**have words** to argue or quarrel: *You can tell from their expressions that they've had words.*

—**in a word** briefly: *In a word I dislike him.*

—**keep one's word** to do as one promised to do: *He said he would be there and he kept his word.*

—**mum's the word** *see* **mum**.

—**put in a good word for (someone)** to say something favourable about (someone), to recommend (someone): *You might get the job if he puts a good word in for you.*

—**say the word** say what you want and your wishes will be carried out: *If you want some food just say the word.*

—**take (someone) at his** *or* **her word** to believe (someone) without question and act accordingly: *He said I could buy goods at a discount, and I took him at his word.*

—**take the words out of (someone's) mouth** to say what (someone) was just about to say: *You took the words right out of my mouth. I was going to suggest a trip to the cinema.*

—**words fail me** I cannot put my feelings into words: *Words fail me when I think of their behaviour.*

work

—**all in a day's work** *see* **day**.

—**all work and no play makes Jack a dull boy** people should take some leisure time and not work all the time: *Take some time off and come swimming. All work and no play makes Jack a dull boy.*

—**a nasty piece of work** *see* **nasty**.

—**give (someone) the works** to give (someone) the complete treatment: *She went to the beauty salon and had the works.* <Originally slang for to kill someone>.

—**gum up the works** *see* **gum**.

—**have one's work cut out** to face a very difficult task: *You'll have your work cut out to get there on time.* <Literally to have a lot of work ready for on>.

—**nasty piece of work** *see* **nasty**.

—**throw a spanner in the works** *see* **spanner**.

—**worked up** agitated, annoyed: *She's all worked up because they're late.*

—**work out** to come to a successful conclusion: *I'm glad things worked out for you.*

world

—**a man of the world** a sophisticated and worldly man: *He won't be shocked by her behaviour. He's a man of the world.*

—**dead to the world** *see* **dead**.

—**for all the world like (someone** *or* **something)** exactly like (someone or something): *She looked for all the world like a witch.*

—**have** *or* **get the best of both worlds** *see* **best.**

—**it's a small world** *see* **small.**

—**it takes all sorts (to make a world)** *see* **sort.**

—**on top of the world** very cheerful and happy: *She's on top of the world with her new baby.*

—**out of this world** remarkably good: *The food was out of this world.*

—**think the world of (someone)** to be extremely fond of (someone): *He thinks the world of his children.*

—**with the best will in the world** *see* **best.**

—**the world is (someone's) oyster** (someone) has a great many possible opportunities or chances: *With those qualifications the world is your oyster.* <Refers to a quotation from Shakespeare's *The Merry Wives of Windsor*, Act 2, scene ii>.

worm

—**(even) the worm turns** even the most humble or meek person will protest if treated badly enough: *He had bullied her for years, so it was no surprise when she eventually left him—even the worm turns.*

worth

—**for all one is worth** using maximum effort: *We ran for all we were worth to catch the last bus.*

—**worth its** *or* **one's weight in gold** *see* **gold.**

—**worth one's salt** *see* **salt.**

—**worth (someone's) while** *see* **while.**

wound

—**rub salt in the wound** *see* **salt.**

wrap

—**keep (something) under wraps** to keep (something) secret or hidden: *We're keeping our new product under wraps until the launch.*

—**wrapped up in (someone** *or* **something)** absorbed in, giving all one's attention to (someone or something): *She's completely wrapped up in her work.*

—**wrap (something) up** to finish (something) completely: *At last the contract is all wrapped up.*

wrist

—**a slap on the wrist** *see* **slap.**

write

—**nothing to write home about** *see* **nothing.**

—**the writing on the wall** something which indicates that something unpleasant, such as failure, unhappiness, disaster, etc, will happen: *She should have seen the writing on the wall when her boss kept complaining about her work.* <A biblical reference to Daniel 5:5-31, in which the coming destruction of the Babylonian empire is made known to Belshazzar at a feast through mysterious writing on a wall>.

wrong

—**be in the wrong** to be blameworthy, to be guilty of error: *You must admit that you were in the wrong.*

—**get hold of the wrong end of the stick** *see* **stick.**

—**get off on the wrong foot** *see* **foot.**

—**get out of bed on the wrong side** *see* **bed.**

—**get on the wrong side of (someone)** to cause (someone) to dislike or be hostile to one: *It's unwise to get on the wrong side of the headmaster.*

—**not to put a foot wrong** not to make a mistake of any kind: *The player didn't put a foot wrong in the whole match.*

—**on the wrong track** *see* **track.**

—**rub (someone) up the wrong way** *see* **rub.**

—**two wrongs do not make a right** *see* **two.**

YZ

yarn

—**spin a yarn** to tell a long story, especially an untrue one that is given as an excuse: *When he was late he spun some yarn about being delayed by a herd of cows.* <Telling a story is compared to spinning a long thread>.

year

—**the year dot** a long time, the beginning of time: *I've known him since the year dot.*

—**years of discretion** an age when one is able to judge between what is right and what is wrong: She can stay out until

yesterday

—**not born yesterday** experienced and not eas- ily fooled: *You don't expect me to believe that! I wasn't born yesterday!*

young

—**you're only young once** one should take ad- vantage of the opportunities that arise when one is young and has the energy, freedom, etc, to enjoy or exploit them: *You should take the job abroad. After all, you're only young once.*

zero

—**zero hour** the time at which something is due to begin: *The party begins at six and it's only two hours until zero hour.* <Originally a military term>.

Eponyms and Abbreviations

Eponyms

ampere the standard metric unit by which an electric current is measured, called after the French physicist André Marie Ampère, (1775–1836).

atlas a book of maps, called after Atlas, in Greek mythology the leader of the Titans who attempted to storm the heavens and for this supreme treason was condemned by Zeus to hold up the vault of heaven on his head and hands for the rest of his life. The geographer Gerardus Mercator (*see* Mercator projection) used the figure of Atlas bearing the globe as a frontispiece in his 16th-century collection of maps and charts.

aubrietia a trailing purple-flowered perennial plant, called after Claude Aubriet (1665–1742), a French painter of animals and flowers.

Bailey bridge a type of temporary military bridge that can be assembled very quickly, called after Sir Donald Bailey (1901–85), the English engineer who invented it.

baud a unit used in measuring telecommunications transmission speed denoting the number of discrete signal elements that can be transmitted per second, called after the French telecommunications pioneer, Jean M. Baudot (1845–1903).

Beaufort scale a international system of measuring of wind speed, from) (calm) to 12 (hurricane), called after Admiral Sir Francis Beaufort (1774–1857), the British surveyor who devised it.

becquerel the standard metric unit of radioactivity, defined as decay per second, called after the French physicist Antoine-Henri Becquerel (1852–1908), who began the study of radioactivity.

begonia a genus of tropical plants cultivated for their showy petalless flowers and ornamental lopsided succulent leaves, called after Michel Begon (1638–1710), a French patron of botany.

Belisha beacon a post surmounted by a flashing light in an orange globe that marks a road crossing for pedestrians, called after the British politician Leslie Hore-Belisha (1893–1957).

Biro™ a type of ball-point pen, called after its Hungarian-born inventor, Laszlo Jozsef Biro (1900–85).

bloomers a women's underpants with full, loose legs gathered at the knee, called after the American social reformer Amelia Jenks Bloomer (1818–94).

bougainvillea a genus of tropical plants with large rosy or purple bracts, called after the French navigator Louis Antoine de Bougainville (1729–1811).

bowdlerize to remove what are considered to be indelicate or indecent words or passages from a book, called after the British doctor, Thomas Bowdler (1754–1825) who produced an expurgated edition of Shakespeare.

bowie knife a type of hunting knife with a long curving blade, called after the American soldier and adventurer James Bowie (1799–1836) who made it popular.

boycott to refuse to deal with or trade with a person, organization, etc, in order to punish or coerce, called after the Irish land agent Captain Charles Cunningham Boycott (1832–97) who was accorded such treatment after refusing to reduce rents.

Boyle's law the scientific principle that a volume of gas varies inversely with the pressure of the gas when the temperature is constant, called after the Irish-born British physicist, Robert Boyle (1627–91), who formulated it.

Braille the system of printing for the blind using a system of raised dots that can be understood by touch, called after the blind French musician, Louis Braille (1809–52), who invented it.

Brownian motion the random movement of minutes particles, which occurs in both gases and liquids, called after the Scottish botanist Robert Brown (1773–1858), who first discovered the phenomenon in 1827.

buddleia a genus of shrubs and trees with lilac or yellowish- white flowers, called after Adam Buddle (d.1715), English clergyman and botanist.

Bunsen burner a burner with an adjustable air inlet that mixes gas and air to produce a smokeless flame of great heat, called after the German scientist, Robert Wilhelm Bunsen (1811–99), who invented it.

camellia a genus of oriental evergreen ornamental shrubs, called after the Moravian Jesuit missionary, George Joseph Kamel (1661–1706), who introduced it into Europe.

cardigan a knitted jacket fastened with buttons, called after James Thomas Brudenell, 7th Earl of Cardigan (1797–1868) who was fond of wearing such a garment and was the British cavalry officer who led the unsuccessful Charge of the Light Brigade during the Crimean War (1854).

Celsius the scale of temperature in which 0° is the freezing point of water and 100° the boiling point, called after Anders Celsius (1701–44), the Swedish astronomer and scientist who invented it.

chauvinism an aggressive patriotism, called after Nicolas Chauvin of Rochefort, 19th-century French soldier in Napoleon's army, and now used to apply to excessive devotion to a belief or case, especially a man's belief in the superiority of men over women.

clerihew a four-line verse consisting of two rhymed couplets of variable length, often encapsulating an unreliable biographical anecdote, called after the English writer, Edmund Clerihew Bentley (1875–1956), who invented it.

coulomb the standard metric unit for measuring electric charge, called after the French physicist, Charles Augustin de Coulomb (1736–1806).

dahlia a genus of half-hardy herbaceous perennial plants of the aster family grown for its colourful blooms, called after the Swedish botanist Anders Dahl (1751–89).

daltonism colour blindness, especially the confusion between green and red, called after the British chemist and physicist, John Dalton (1766–1844), who first described it.

Darwinism the theory of evolution by natural selection, called after the British naturalist Charles Robert Darwin (1809–82), who first described the theory.

Davy lamp a safety lamp used by miners to detect combustible gas, called after the English chemist, Sir Humphry Davy (1778–1829), who invented it.

degauss to neutralize or remove a magnetic field, called after the German mathematician Karl Friedrich Gauss (1777–1855). *See also* GAUSS.

derrick now any crane-like apparatus but formerly a word for a gallows, called after a 17th-century English hangman at Tyburn with the surname of Derrick.

diesel an internal-combustion engine in which ignition is produced by the heat of highly compressed air, called after the German engineer, Rudolf Diesel (1858–1913), who invented it.

Doberman pinscher a breed of dog with a smooth glossy black and tan coat and docked tail, called after the German dog breeder, Ludwig Dobermann (1834–94), who bred it.

Dolby™ an electronic noise-reduction system used in sound recording and playback systems, called after the American engineer, R. Dolby (1933–), who invented it.

Don Quixote a chivalrous or romantic person who tends to be carried away by his ideals and notions, called after Don Quixote, hero of the novel *Don Quixote de la Mancha* by the Spanish novelist Miguel de Cervantes Saavedra (1547–1616). *See also* **quixotic**.

Doppler effect *or* **Doppler shift** a change in the observed frequency of a wave as a result of the relative motion between the wave source and the detector, called after the Austrian physicist, Christian Johann Doppler (1803–53).

draconian an adjective meaning very cruel or severe, called after Draco, the 7th-century BC Athenian statesman who formulated extremely harsh laws.

dunce a person who is stupid or slow to learn, called after the Scottish theologian, John Duns Scotus, Scottish (c.1265–1308).

Earl Grey a blend of Chinese teas flavoured with oil of bergamot, called after the British statesman, Charles, 2nd Earl Grey (1764–1845).

Eiffel Tower the tall tower in the centre of Paris, called after the French engineer, Alexandre Gustave Eiffel (1832–1923, who built it.

einsteinium an artificial radioactive chemical element, called after the German-born American physicist, Albert Einstein (1879–1955).

Everest the highest mountain in the world, called after Sir George Everest (1790–1866), who was Surveyor-General of India.

Fallopian tube either of the two tubes through which the egg cells pass from the ovary to the uterus in female mammals, called after the Italian anatomist, Gabriel Fallopius (1523–62), who first described them.

Fahrenheit the scale of temperatures in which 32° is the freezing point of water and 212° the boiling point, called after the German scientist, Gabriel Daniel Fahrenheit (1686–1736), who invented it.

farad the standard metric unit of capacitance, called after the English physicist and chemist, Michael Faraday (1791–1867), who discovered magnetic induction.

fermi a unit of length employed in nuclear physics, called after the Italian-born American physicist, Enrico Fermi (1901–54).

fermium an artificially produced radioactive element, called after the Italian-born American physicist, Enrico Fermi (1901–54).

forsythia a genus of widely cultivated yellow-flowered ornamental shrubs of the olive family, called after the English botanist, William Forsyth (1737–1804).

Fraunhofer lines dark lines that occur in the continuous spectrum of the sun, called after the German physicist and optician, Joseph von Fraunhofer (1787–1826).

freesia a type of sweet-smelling ornamental flower of the iris family, called after the German physician Friedrich Heinrich Theodor Freese (d. 1876).

fuchsia a genus of decorative shrubs of Central and South America, called after the German botanist and physician, Leonhard Fuchs (1501–66).

Gallup poll a sampling of public opinion, especially to help forecast the outcome of an election, called after the American statistician, George Horace Gallup (1901–84), who devised it.

galvanize to coat one type of metal with another, more reactive metal, e.g. iron or steel coated with zinc, to protect the underlying metal; now also meaning to stimulate into action, called after the Italian physician, Luigi Galvani (1737–98).

gardenia a genus of ornamental tropical trees and shrubs with fragrant white or yellow flowers, called after the Scottish-born American botanist, Dr Alexander Garden (1730–91).

garibaldi a type of biscuit with a layer of currants in it, called after Giuseppe Garibaldi (1807–82), the Italian soldier patriot who is said to have enjoyed such biscuits

gauss a standard unit for measuring magnetic flux density, called after the German mathematician, Karl Friedrich Gauss (1777–1855), who developed the theory of numbers and applied mathematics to electricity, magnetism and astronomy. *See also* **degauss**.

Geiger counter an electronic instrument that can detect and measure radiation, called after the German physicist, Hans Geiger (1882–1945), who developed it.

gerrymander to rearrange the boundaries of a voting district to favour a particular party or candidate, called after the American politician, Elbridge Gerry (1744–1814).

Granny Smith a variety of hard green apple, called after the Australian gardener, Maria Ann Smith, known as Granny Smith (d.1870) who first grew the apple in Sydney in the 1860s.

greengage a type of greenish plum, called after Sir William Gage (1777–1864), who introduced it into Britain from France.

guillotine an instrument for beheading people by allowing a heavy blade to descend between grooved posts, called after the French physician, Joseph Ignace Guillotin (1738–1814), who advocated its use in the French Revolution.

Halley's comet a periodic comet that appears about every 76 years, called after the British astronomer, Edmund Halley (1656–1742), who calculated its orbit.

Heath Robinson of or pertaining to an absurdly complicated design for a simple mechanism, called after the English artist, William Heath Robinson (1872–1944).

henry a metric unit of electric inductance, called after the American physicist, Joseph Henry (1797–1878), who discovered the principle of electromagnetic induction.

Herculean of extraordinary strength, size or difficulty, called after Hercules, the Roman name for Heracles, in Greek mythology the son of Zeus and the most celebrated hero or semi-divine personage, best known for completing twelve difficult tasks known as the labours of Hercules.

Hoover™ a kind of vacuum cleaner, called after the American businessman, William Henry Hoover (1849–1932).

Jacuzzi™ a device that swirls water in a bath and massages the body, called after the Italian-born engineer, Candido Jacuzzi (*c*.1903–86).

JCB™ a mechanical earth-mover that has an hydraulically powered shovel and an excavator arm, called after its English manufacturer, Joseph Cyril Bamford (1916–).

joule the metric unit of all energy measurements, called after the British physicist, James Prescott Joule (1818–89) who investigated the relationship between mechanical, electrical and heat energy.

kelvin the metric unit of thermodynamic temperature, called after the Scottish physicist, William Thomson, 1st Baron Kelvin (1824–1907).

Köchel number a number in a catalogue of the works of Mozart, called after the Austrian scientist, Ludwig Alois Friedrich von Köchel (1800–1877), a great admirer of Mozart, who compiled his catalogue in 1862.

leotard a one-piece, close-fitting garment worn by acrobats and dancers, called after the French acrobat, Jules Leotard (1842–70), who introduced the costume as a circus garment.

listeria a bacterium that causes a serious form of food poisoning, listeriosis, called after the British surgeon, Joseph Lister (1827–1912), who pioneered the use of antiseptics.

lobelia a genus of flowers that produce showy blue, red, yellow or white flowers, called after the Flemish botanist, Matthias de Lobel (1538–1616).

loganberry a hybrid plant developed from the blackberry and the red raspberry that produces large sweet purplish-red berries, called after the American lawyer and horticulturist, James Harvey Logan (1841–1928), who first grew it in 1881.

Luddite an opponent of industrial change or innovation, called after Ned Ludd, the 18th-century British labourer who destroyed industrial machinery.

macadam a road surface composed of successive layers of small stones compacted into a solid mass, called after the Scottish engineer, John Loudon McAdam, (1756–1836), who invented it.

Machiavellian cunning, deceitful, double-dealing, using opportunist methods, called after the Florentine statesman and political theorist, Niccolò Machiavelli (1469–1527), author of *The Prince*.

Mach number the ratio of the speed of a body in a particular medium to the speed of sound in the same medium, called after the Austrian physicist and philosopher, Ernst Mach (1838–1916), who devised it.

mackintosh a type of raincoat, especially one made of rubberized cloth, called after the Scottish chemist, Charles Macintosh (1760–1843), who patented it in the early 1820s.

malapropism the unintentional misuse of a word by confusing it with another and so producing a ridiculous effect (e.g. "She is as headstrong as an allegory on the banks of the Nile"), called after Mrs Malaprop, a character in the play *The Rivals* (1775), by the Irish playwright Richard Brinsley Sheridan (1751–1816).

martinet a person who exerts strong discipline, called after Jean Martinet (d.1672), a French army drill master during the reign of Louis XIV.

maverick a stray animal or an independent-minded or unorthodox person, called after the American rancher in Texas, Samuel Augustus Maverick (1803–70), who refused to brand his cattle.

Melba sauce a sauce that is made from raspberries and served with fruit, peach melba, etc, called after the Australian operatic singer Dame Nellie Melba [Helen Porter Mitchell] (1861–1931), for whom it was made. *See also* **Melba toast, peach melba**.

Melba toast bread that is thinly sliced and toasted, called after the Australian operatic singer Dame Nellie Melba [Helen Porter Mitchell] (1861–1931), for whom it was made. *See also* **Melba sauce, peach melba**.

Mercator projection a type of projection for the drawing of maps two-dimensionally, called after the Flemish geographer, Gerardus Mercator [Gerhard Kremer] (1512–94).

mesmerize to hypnotize or to fascinate or spellbind, called after the Austrian physician and pioneer of hypnotism, Franz Anton Mesmer (1734–1815).

Molotov cocktail a kind of crude incendiary weapon made by filling a bottle with petrol and inserting a short short-delay wick or use, called after the Soviet statesman Vyacheslav Mikhailovich Molotov (1890–1986).

Montessori method a system of educating very young children through play, based on free discipline, with each child developing at his or her own pace, called after Maria Montessori (1870–1952), the Italian physicist and educator who developed it.

Moog synthesizer™ a type of synthesizer for producing music electronically, called after Robert Arthur Moog (b. 1934), the American physicist and engineer who developed it.

Morse code a code in which letters are represented by dots and dashes or long and short sounds and are transmitted by visual or audible signals, called after the American artist and inventor, Samuel Finley Breese Morse (1791–1872), who invented it.

narcissism excessive interest in one's own body or self, self-love, called after Narcissus, a handsome young man in Greek mythology who was punished for his coldness of heart in not returning the love of Echo by being made to fall in love with his own reflection in water and who pined away because he was unable to embrace himself.

newton the standard metric unit of force, called after the British physicist and mathematician, Sir Isaac Newton (1642–1727).

Nobel prize an annual international prize given for distinction in one of six areas: physics, chemistry, physiology and medicine, economics, literature, and promoting peace, called after the Swedish chemist and engineer, Alfred Nobel (1833–96), who founded them.

ohm a metric unit of electrical resistance, called after the German physicist, Georg Simon Ohm (1787–1854).

Pareto principle an economic principle that 80 per cent of the sales may come from 20 per cent of the customers, called after the Italian economist and sociologist, Vilfredo Pareto (1848–1923).

Parkinson's disease a progressive nervous disease resulting in tremor, muscular rigidity, partial paralysis and weakness, called after the British surgeon, James Parkinson (1755–1824), who first described it.

Parkinson's law the law that states that work expands to fill the time available for its completion, called after the British historian and author, Cyril Northcote Parkinson (1909–93), who devised it.

pasteurize to sterilize drink or food by heat or radiation in order to destroy bacteria, called after the French chemist and bacteriologist, Louis Pasteur (1822–95).

pavlova a dessert of meringue cake with a topping of cream and fruit, called after the Russian ballerina, Anna Pavlova (1885–1931), for whom it was made.

peach melba a dessert of peaches, ice cream and Melba sauce, called after the Australian operatic soprano singer, Dame Nellie Melba [Helen Porter Mitchell] (1861–1931), for whom it was made. *See also* **Melba sauce, Melba toast**.

Peter principle the principle that in a hierarchy every employee tends to rise to the level of his or her incompetence, called after the Canadian educator, Laurence J. Peter (1919–90), who formulated it.

Peter's projection a form of projection for depicting the countries of the world two-dimensionally, called after the German history, Dr Arno Peters (1916–), who devised it.

platonic of a close relationship between two people, spiritual and free from physical desire, called after the Greek philosopher, Plato (*c*.427–347 BC).

plimsoll a type of light rubber-soled canvas shoe, called after Samuel Plimsoll (see Plimsoll line) because the upper edge of the rubber was thought to resemble the Plimsoll line.

Plimsoll line the set of markings on the side of a ship that indicate the levels to which the ship may be safely be loaded, called after the English shipping reform leader, Samuel Plimsoll (1824–98).

poinsettia a South American evergreen plant, widely cultivated at Christmas for its red bracts, which resemble petals, called after the American diplomat, Joel Roberts Poinsett (1779–1851), who introduced it into the USA.

praline a type of confectionery made from nuts and sugar, called after Count Plessis-Praslin (1598–1675), a French field marshal, whose chef is said to have been the first person to make the sweet

Pulitzer prize one of a series of prizes that are awarded annually for outstanding achievement in American journalism, literature, and music, called after the Hungarian-born US newspaper publisher, Joseph Pulitzer (1847–1911).

Pullman a railway carriage that offers luxury accommodation, called after the American inventor, George Mortimer Pullman (1831–97), who first manufactured them.

quisling a traitor who aids an invading enemy to regularize its conquest of his or her country, called after the Norwegian politician, Vidkun Abraham Quisling (1887–1945), who collaborated with the Nazis.

quixotic, quixotical of a person, chivalrous or romantic to extravagance, unrealistically idealistic, called after Don Quixote, hero of the novel *Don Quixote de la Mancha* by the Spanish novelist Miguel de Cervantes Saavedra (1547–1616).

rafflesia a genus of parasitic Asian leafless plants, called after the British colonial administrator, Sir Thomas Stamford Raffles (1781–1826), who discovered it.

raglan a type of loose sleeve cut in one piece with the shoulder of a garment, called after the British field marshal,, Fitzroy James Henry Somerset, 1st Baron Raglan (1788-1855).

Richter scale a scale ranging from 1 to 10 for measuring the intensity of an earthquake, called after the American seismologist, Charles Richter (1900–85), who devised it.

Romeo a romantic lover, called after Romeo, the hero of Shakespeare's tragedy *Romeo and Juliet*.

Rorschach test a personality test in which the subject has to interpret a series of unstructured ink blots, called after the Swiss psychiatrist, Hermann Rorschach (1884–1922), who devised it.

Rubik cube *or* **Rubik's cube** a puzzle that consists of a cube of six colours with each face divided into nine small squares, eight of which can rotate around a central square, called after the Hungarian designer, Erno Rubik (1944–), who invented it.

rutherford a unit of radioactivity, called after the British physicist, Ernest Rutherford, 1st Baron Rutherford (1871–1937).

sadism sexual pleasure obtained from inflicting cruelty upon another, called after the French soldier and writer, Count Donatien Alphonse François de Sade, known as Marquis de Sade (1740–1814).

salmonella the bacteria that cause some diseases such as food poisoning, called after Daniel Elmer Salmon (1850–1914), the American veterinary surgeon who identified it

sandwich a snack consisting of two pieces of buttered bread with a filling, called after John Montagu, 4th Earl of Sandwich (1718–92), who was such a compulsive gambler that he would not leave the gaming tables to eat but had some cold beef between two slices of bread brought to him

saxophone a type of keyed brass instrument often used in jazz music, called after Adolphe Sax (1814–94), the Belgian instrument-maker who invented it.

sequoia one of two lofty coniferous Californian trees, called after the American Indian leader and scholar, Sequoya (*c*.1770–1843), also known as George Guess.

shrapnel an explosive projectile that contains bullets or fragments of metal and a charge that is exploded before impact, called after the British army officer, Henry Shrapnel (1761–1842), who invented it.

siemens the standard metric unit of electrical conductance, called after the German engineer and inventor, Ernst Werner von Siemens (1816–92).

silhouette the outline of a shape against light or a lighter background, called after the French politician, Etienne de Silhouette (1709–67).

simony the buying or selling of ecclesiastical benefits or offices, called after the sorcerer Simon Magnus, who lived in the 1st century AD.

sousaphone the large tuba that encircles the body of the player and has a forward-facing bell, called after the American bandmaster and composer, John Philip Sousa (1854–1932), who invented it.

spoonerism the accidental transposition of the initial letters or opening syllables of two or more words, often with an amusing effect (e.g. "queer old dean" for "dear old queen"), called after the British scholar and clergyman, William Archibald Spooner (1844–1930).

stetson a type of wide-brimmed, high-crowned felt hat, called after its designer, the American hat-maker John Batterson Stetson (1830–1906)

tantalize to tease or torment by presenting something greatly desired but keeping it inaccessible, called after Tantalus, the mythical Greek king of Phrygia, who was punished in Hades for his misdeeds by being forced to stand in water that receded when he tried to drink and under fruit that moved away as he tried to eat.

tontine a financial arrangement in which a group of subscribers contribute equally to a prize that is eventually awarded to the last survivor, called after the Italian banker, Lorenzo Tonti (1635–90), who devised it.

tradescantia a genus of flowering plants cultivated for their foliage, called after the English botanist, gardener and plant hunter, John Tradescant (*c*.1570–1638).

trilby a type of soft felt hat with an indented crown, called after *Trilby*, the dramatized version of the novel by the English writer George du Maurier. The heroine of the play, Trilby O'Ferral, wore such a hat.

Turing machine a hypothetical universal computing machine, called after the British mathematician, Alan Mathison Turing (1912–54), who conceived it.

Venn diagram a diagram in which overlapping circles are used to show the mathematical and logical relationships between sets, called after the British mathematician and logician, John Venn (1834–1923).

volt the metric unit of measure of the force of an electrical current, called after the Italian physicist, Count Alessandro Volta (1745–1827).

Wankel engine a kind of four-stroke internal-combustion engine with a triangular-shaped rotating piston within an elliptical combustion chamber, called after the German engineer, Felix Wankel (1902–88), who invented it.

watt a metric unit of electrical power, called after the Scottish engineer and inventor, James Watt (1736–1819).

wellington a waterproof rubber boot with no fastenings that extends to the knee, called after Arthur Wellesley, 1st Duke of Wellington (1769–1852), the British soldier who defeated Napoleon at Waterloo (1815).

wisteria *or* **wistaria** a genus of purple-flowered climbing plants, called after the American anatomist, Caspar Wistar (1761–1818).

Zeppelin a rigid cigar-shaped airship, called after the German general and aeronautical pioneer, Count Ferdinand von Zeppelin (1838–1917), who designed and manufactured them.

Abbreviations

A Adult; alcohol; alto; America; American; ampere; angstrom; anode; answer; April; (*math*) area; (*chem*) argon; Associate; atomic weight; IVR Austria.

Å Angstrom unit.

a acre; are (measure).

a. adjective; alto; ampere; *anno* (*Latin* year); anode; answer; *ante* (*Latin* before); *aqua* (*Latin* water); area.

A1 first class.

AA Alcoholics Anonymous; anti-aircraft; Automobile Association.

AAA Amateur Athletic Association; American Automobile Association.

AAC Amateur Athletic Club; *anno ante Christum* (*Latin* in the year before Christ).

AAM air-to-air missile.

A & A additions and amendments.

A & M Hymns Ancient and Modern.

A & N Army and Navy.

A & R Artist and Repertoire.

AAPO African Peoples' Organization.

aar against all risks; average annual rainfall.

AAU Amateur Athletic Union.

AB able-bodied seaman; *Artium Baccalaureus* (*Latin* Bachelor of Arts).

Ab (*chem*) alabamine.

ABA Amateur Boxing Association.

Abb. Abbess; Abbey; Abbot.

abbr., abbrev. abbreviated; abbreviation.

ABC Advance Booking Charter; American Broadcasting Company; Associated British Cinemas; Audit Bureau of Circulations; automatic binary computer.

abd abdicated abridged.

ab init. *ab initio* (*Latin* from the beginning).

abl. ablative.

ABM anti-ballistic missile.

ABMEWS anti-ballistic missile early warning system.

ABP arterial blood pressure.

Abp Archbishop.

abr. abridged; abridgement.

abs. absence; absent; absolute; abstract.

absol. absolute.

abstr. abstract.

abt about.

ABTA Association of British Travel Agents.

abv. above.

AC Air Command; Air Corps; Aircraftman; Alternating Current; analog computer; Annual Conference; *ante Christum* (*Latin* before Christ); Appeal Case; Appeal Court; Army Corps; Arts Council; Assistant Commissioner; Athletic Club.

A/C account; account current.

Ac (*chem*) actinium.

ac. acre.

a.c. *ante cibum* (*Latin* before meals).

acad. academic; academy.

ACAS Advisory, Conciliation and Arbitration Service.

ACC Army Catering Corps.

acc. acceleration; accent; accepted; accompanied; according; account; accusative.

accel. (*mus*) *accelerando* (*Italian* more quickly).

Accred Accredited.

acct account.

accy accountancy.

ACF Army Cadet Force.

ACG automatic control gear.

ACGB Arts Council of Great Britain.

ack. acknowledge(d).

ackt acknowledgment.

ACLS Automatic Carrier Landing System.

ACM Air Chief Marshal.

ACN *ante Christum natum* (*Latin* before the birth of Christ).

ACOP Association of Chief Officers of Police.

ACORN (*comput*) automatic checkout and recording network.

ACP American College of Physicians.

acpt. acceptance.

ACSIR Advisory Council for Scientific and Industrial Research.

Act. Acting.

act. active.

actg acting.

ACTH adrenocorticotrophic hormone, an anti-rheumatic drug.

ACV actual cash value; air cushion vehicle (hovercraft).

ACW Aircraftwoman; alternating continuous waves.

AD (*milit*) active duty; air defence; *anno Domini* (*Latin* in the year of our Lord).

ad. adverb; advertisement.

ADC Aide-de-Camp; (*comput*) analog to digital converter; automatic digital calculator.

add. addendum; addition; additional; address.

ADF automatic direction finder.

ad fin. *ad finem* (*Latin* near the end).

ad inf. *ad infinitum* (*Latin* to infinity).

ad imt. *ad initium* (*Latin* at the beginning).

ad int. *ad interim* (*Latin* in the meantime).

adj, adj. adjacent; adjective; adjoining; adjourned; adjudged; adjunct; adjustment; adjutant.

Adjt Adjutant.

Adjt-Gen. Adjutant-General.

ad lib. *ad libitum* (*Latin* at will).

ad loc. *ad locum* (*Latin* at the place).

adm. administration; administrative; admitted.

admin. administration.

ADN IVR People's Democratic Republic of Yemen.

ADP automatic data processing.

adv. advance; advent; adverb; adverbial; *adversus* (*Latin* against); advertisement; advisory; advocate.

ad val. *ad valorem* (*Latin* according to the value).

advt advertisement.

ADW Air Defence Warning.

AE Atomic Energy.

AEA Atomic Energy Authority.

AE & P Ambassador Extraordinary and Plenipotentiary.

AEF Amalgamated Union of Engineering and Foundry Workers.

AEI Associated Electrical Industries.

AELTC All England Lawn Tennis Club.

aer. aeronautics; aeroplane.

AERE Atomic Energy Research Establishment.

aeron. aeronautical; aeronautics.

AEU Amalgamated Engineering Union (now AUEW).

AEW airborne early warning.

AF Admiral of the Fleet; Air Force; Anglo-French; audio-frequency.

A/F as found.

AFA Amateur Football Association.

AFC Association Football Club; automatic frequency control.

affil. affiliated.

afft affidavit.

AFG IVR Afghanistan.

AFI American Film Institute.

AFM Air Force Medal.

AFN American Forces Network; Armed Forces Network.

Afr. Africa; African.

Afrik. Afrikaans.

AFS Auxiliary Fire Service.

afsd aforesaid.

AFV armoured fighting vehicle.

AG Adjutant General; Attorney General.

Ag (*chem*) silver.

AGC automatic gain control.

AGCA automatic ground controlled approach.

AGCL automatic ground controlled landing.

agcy agency.

AGM air-to-ground missile; Annual General Meeting.

AGR advanced gas-cooled reactor.

agr., agric. agricultural; agriculture.

agst against.

agt agent; agreement.

a.g.w. actual gross weight.

AH *anno Hegirae* (*Latin* in the year of the Hegira).

AI Amnesty International; artificial insemination.

a.i. *ad interim* (*Latin* in the meantime).

AID acute infectious disease; Army Intelligence Department; artificial insemination by donor.

AIH artificial insemination by husband.

AL IVR Albania; Anglo-Latin.

Al (*chem*) aluminium.

al. alcohol; alcoholic.

ALBM air-launched ballistic missile.

Ald. Alderman.

Alg. Algeria; Algerian.

alg, alg. algebra.

ALGOL (*comput*) algorithmic language.

alk. alkali.

alt. alteration; alternate; alternative; altitude; alto.

alter. alteration.

alum. aluminium.

AM Air Marshal; Air Ministry; Albert Medal; amplitude modulation; *anno mundi* (*Latin* in the year of the world); *ante meridiem* (*Latin* before noon); arithmetic mean; *Artium Magister* (*Latin* Master of Arts); Associate Member.

Am (*chem*) americium.

Am. America; American.

a.m. ante meridiem.

amal. amalgamated.

AMDG *ad majorem Dei gloriam* (*Latin* to the greater glory of God).

Amer. America; American.

AMM anti-missile missile.

amn. amunition.

amp. amperage; ampere; amplifier; amplitude.

AMS Ancient Monuments Society.

amt amount.

AMU atomic mass unit.

AN Anglo-Norman.

An (*chem*) actinon.

an. *anno* (*Latin* in the year); anonymous; *ante* (*Latin* before).

anag. anagram.

anal. analogous; analogy; analysis; analytic.

anat. anatomical; anatomist; anatomy.

ANC African National Congress.

anc. ancient; anciently.

AND IVR Andorra.

and. (*mus*) *andante* (*Italian* moderately slow).

Angl. Anglican; Anglicized.

anim. (*mus*) *animato* (*Italian* animated).

ann. annual; annuity.

anniv. anniversary.

annot. annotated; annotation; annotator.

anon. anonymous.

ANS Army Nursing Service.

ans. answer.

ant. antenna; antiquarian; antique; antonym.

anthol. anthology.

anthrop. anthropological; anthropology.

antiq. antiquarian; antiquity.

ANZAC Australian and New Zealand Army Corps.

a/o account of.

AOB any other business.

AOCB any other competent business.

AOC-in-C Air Officer Commander-in-Chief.

AP *ante prandium* (*Latin* before meals); Associated Press; atmospheric pressure.

Ap. Apostle; April.

ap. apothecary.

APC automatic phase control; automatic pitch control.

APEX Advance Purchase Excursion.

aph. aphorism.

apo. apogee.

Apoc. Apocalypse; Apocrypha.

app. apparatus; apparent; appendix; applied; appointed; apprentice; approved; approximate.

appro. approbation; approval.

approx. approximate; approximately.

apptd appointed.

Apr, Apr. April.

APT advanced passenger train.

apt. apartment.

APWU Amalgamated Postal Workers' Union.

aq. *aqua* (*Latin* water).

AR Autonomous Republic.

Ar (*chem*) argon.

Ar. Arabic; Aramaic.

ar. arrival; arrives.

a.r. *anno regni* (*Latin* in the year of the reign).

ARA Associate of the Royal Academy.

Arab Arabian; Arabic.

arb. arbiter; arbitration.

ARC Aeronautical Research Council; American Red Cross; automatic relay calculator.

Arch. Archbishop; Archdcacon; Archduke; Archipelago; Architecture.

arch. archaic; archaism; archery; archipelago; architect; architecture; archive.

archaeol. archaeology.

Archd. Archdeacon; Archduke.

archit. architecture.

ARCS Australian Red Cross Society.

ARD acute respiratory disease.

Arg. Argentina; Argyll (former county).

arg. *argentum* (*Latin* silver).

arith. arithmetic(al).

Ariz. Arizona.

Ark. Arkansas.

ARM anti-radar missile.

ARP air raid precautions.

ARR *anno regni regis* or *regine* (*Latin* in the year of the king's or queen's reign).

arr. arranged; arrangement; arrival.

art. article; artificial; artillery.

ARTC Air Route Traffic Control.

AS Anglo-Saxon; *anno salutis* (*Latin* in the year of salvation); anti-submarine; Assistant Secretary.

As (*chem*) arsenic.

ASA Advertising Standards Authority.

a.s.a.p. as soon as possible.

ASAT Anti-Satellite.

ASCII (*comput*) American Standard Code for Information Interchange.

ASDIC Allied Submarine Detection Investigation Committee.

ASE American Stock Exchange.

a.s.e. air standard efficiency.

ASH Action on Smoking and Health.

ASI air speed indicator.

ASLEF Associated Society of Locomotive Engineers and Firemen.

ASLIB Association of Special Libraries and Information Bureaux.

ASM air-to-surface missile.

ASN Army Service Number.

ASPCA American Society for the Prevention of Cruelty to Animals.

Ass. Assembly.

ass. assistant; association; assorted.

Asscn., Assn. Association.

Assoc. Associate; Association.

asst assistant.

AST Atlantic Standard Time.

ASTMS Association of Scientific, Technical, and Managerial Staffs.

astr. astronomer; astronomical; astro-nomy.

astrol. astrologer; astrological; astrology.

astron. astronomer; astronomical; astro-nomy.

ASW anti-submarine warfare.

AT alternativetechnology; anti-tank.

At (*chem*) astatine.

at. airtight; atmosphere; atomic.

ATA Atlantic Treaty Association.

ATC Air Traffic Control; Air Training Corps.

Atl. Atlantic.

atm. atmosphere; atmospheric.

at. no. atomic number.

ATS (*comput*) Administrative Terminal System; anti-tetanus serum; Auxiliary Territorial Service (now WRAC).

a.t.s. (*law*) at the suit of.

att. attached; attention; attorney.

attn. attention.

attrib. attribute; attributive.

at. vol. atomic volume.

at. wt. atomic weight.

AU Angstrom unit; astronomical unit.

Au (*chem*) gold.

AUBTW Amalgamated Union of Building Trade Workers.

AUEW Amalgamated Union of Engineering Workers.

Aug. August.

AUM air-to-underwater missile.

AUS IVR Australia.

Aust. Australia; Australian.

Austl. Australasia.

AUT Association of University Teachers.

aut. automatic.

auth. author; authority; authorized.

Auth. Ver. Authorized Version.

auto. automatic; automobile; automotive.

aux. auxiliary.

AV audio-visual; Authorized Version.

Av. Avenue.

av. average; avoirdupois.

a.v. *ad valorem* (*Latin* according to the value).

avdp. avoirdupois.

Ave Avenue.

avg. average.

AVM Air Vice-Marshal.

AVR Army Volunteer Reserve.

a.w. atomic weight.

AWOL absent without official leave.

ax. axiom; axis.

az. azimuth.

B Bachelor; bacillus; Baron; base; (*mus*) bass; IVR Belgium; Bible; Blessed; book; born; (*chem*) boron; bowled (in cricket); breadth; British; Brother.

BA *Baccalaureus Artium* (*Latin* Bachelor of Arts); British Academy; British Airways; Buenos Aires.

Ba (*chem*) barium.

BAA British Airports Authority.

BAAB British Amateur Athletic Board.

Bach. Bachelor.

bact. bacteria; bacteriology; bacterium.

bacteriol. bacteriological; bacteriology.

BAFO British Army Forces Overseas.

BAL (*comput*) basic assembly language.

bal. balance.

ball. ballast; ballistics.

BALPA British Air Line Pilots' Association.

B & B bed and breakfast.

b & s brandy and soda.

b & w black and white.

BAOR British Army of the Rhine.

Bap. Baptist.

bap. baptized.

bar. barometer; barometric; barrel; barrister.

barit. baritone.

barr. barrister.

Bart. Baronet.

BASIC (*comput*) Beginners' All-purpose Symbolic Instruction Code.

bat., batt. battalion; battery.

BB Boys' Brigade; double black (pencils).

bb. books.

BBB triple black (pencils).

BBBG British Boxing Board of Control.

BBC British Broadcasting Corporation.

BBFC British Board of Film Censors.

bbl. barrel.

BC before Christ; British Council.

BCC British Council of Churches.

BCD (*comput*) binary coded decimal notation.

BCG Bacillus Calmette-Guerin, antituberculosis vaccine.

BCh *Baccalaureus Chirurgiae* (*Latin* Bachelor of Surgery).

BD Bachelor of Divinity.

B/D bank draft.

bd. board; bond; bound; bundle.

BDA British Dental Association.

bdl. bundle.

BDS Bachelor of Dental Surgery; IVR Barbados.

BDU Bomb Disposal Unit.

BE Bachelor of Education; Bank of England; Bill of Exchange; British Embassy.

Be (*chem*) beryllium.

BEAB British Electrical Approvals Board.

bec. because.

BEd Bachelor of Education.

Beds. Bedfordshire.

BEF British Expeditionary Force.

bef. before.

beg. begin; beginning.

Belg. Belgian; Belgium.

BEM British Empire Medal.

BEng Bachelor of Engineering.

Beng. Bengal, Bengali.

beq. bequeath; bequeathed.

beqt bequest.

Berks. Berkshire.

bet. between.

BeV billion electron-volts.

B/F brought forward.

b.f. bloody fool; (*print*) bold face; *bona fide* (*Latin* genuine, genuinely).

BFBS British Forces Broadcasting Service.

BFI British Film Institute.

BFN British Forces Network.

BG BrigadierGeneral; IVR Bulgaria.

bg bag.

BH IVR British Honduras.

B'ham Birmingham.

BHC British High Commissioner.

b.h.p. brake horsepower.

Bi (*chem*) bismuth.

Bib. Bible; Biblical.

Bibl. Biblical.

bibliog. bibliographer; bibliography.

bicarb. bicarbonate of soda.

b.i.d. *bis in die* (*Latin* twice daily).

BIM British Institute of Management.

biog. biographical; biographer; biography.

biol. biological; biologist; biology.

BIT (*comput*) binary digit.

Bk (*chem*) berkelium.

bk. bank; bark; block; book; break.

bkcy. bankruptcy.

bkg. banking.

bkpt. bankrupt.

bkt. basket; bracket.

BL Bachelor of Laws; Bachelor of Letters; British Legion (now RBL); British Library.

B/L Bill of Lading.

bldlg. building.

BLit Bachelor of Literature.

BLitt *Baccalaureus Litterarum* (*Latin* Bachelor of Letters).

blk black; block; bulk.

B.LL. Bachelor of Laws.

blvd boulevard.

BM Bachelor of Medicine; *Beatae Memoriae* (*Latin* of blessed memory); bench mark; bowel movement; British Museum.

BMA British Medical Association.

BMC British Medical Council.

BMJ British Medical Journal.

BML British Museum Library.

BMR basal metabolic rate.

BMus Bachelor of Music.

BN banknote.

Bn Baron; Battalion.

BO body odour; Box Office; Broker's Order; Buyer's Option.

b/o brought over.

BOA British Olympic Association.

BOD biochemical oxygen demand.

Boh. Bohemia, Bohemian.

Bol. Bolivia, Bolivian.

bor. borough.

BOT Board of Trade.

bot. botanical; botanist; botany; bottle; bought.

boul. boulevard.

BP British Petroleum; British Pharmacopoeia.

b/p bills payable; blueprint.

bp. baptized; birthplace; bishop.

b.p. below proof; bill of parcels; boiling point.

BPh, BPhil Bachelor of Philosolphy.

bpl. birthplace.

BR IVR BraziI; British RaiI.

B/R bills receivable.

Br (*chem*) bromine.

Br. Breton; Britain; British; Brother.

br. branch; brand; brig; bronze; brother; brown.

Braz. Brazil, Brazilian.

BRCS British Red Cross Society.

BRDC British Research and Development Corporation.

Brig. Brigade; Brigadier.

Brig. Gen. Brigadier General.
Brit. Britain; Britannia; British; Briton.
BRN IVR Bahrain.
bro. brother.
BRU IVR Brunei.
BS Bachelor of Science; Bachelor of Surgery; IVR Bahamas; Balance Sheet; Bill of Sale; Blessed Sacrament; British Standards.
b.s. balance sheet; bill of sale.
BSc *Baccalaureus Scientiae* (*Latin* Bachelor of Science).
BSG British Standard Gauge.
BSI British Standards Institution; Building Societies' Institute.
bskt basket.
BSS British Standards Specification.
BST British Standard Time; British Summer Time.
Bt. Baronet.
BTA British Travel Association.
BTh Bachelor of Theology.
BThU British thermal unit.
btl. bottle.
BTU Board of Trade Unit.
Btu British thermal unit.
bu. bureau; bushel.
Bucks. Buckinghamshire.
BUP British United Press.
BUPA British United Provident Association.
BUR IVR Burma.
Bur. Burma; Burmese.
bus. business.
BV *beata virgo* (*Latin* Blessed Virgin); *bene vale* (*Latin* farewell).
b/w black and white.
bx. box; boxes.
Bz (*chem*) benzene.
C Canon; (*physics*) capacitance; Cape; Captain; (*chem*) carbon; Catechism; Catholic; Celsius; Celtic; Centigrade; Central; Century; Chancellor; Chancery; Chapter; Chief; Church; Circuit; Collected; Commander; Confessor; Confidential; Congregational; Congress; Conservative; Constable; Consul; Contralto; Contrast; Corps; coulomb; Count; County; Court; IVR Cuba; Cubic; (*physics*) heat capacity; 100 (Roman numeral).
c. candle; canon; carat; case; cathode; cent; centavo; centigram; centimetre; central; centre; century; chapter; charge; *circa* (*Latin* about); city; class; college; (*math*) constant; contralto; copyright; cubic; cup; currency; current; cycle; (*physics*) specific heat capacity.

CA Central America; Chartered Accountant; Civil Aviation; Consumers' Association; Court of Appeal; Crown Agent.
C/A Credit Account; Current Account.
Ca (*chem*) calcium.
ca. circa (*Latin* about).
CAA Civil Aviation Authority.
CAB Citizens' Advice Bureau.
CAD (*comput*) computer-aided design.
cad. (*mus*) *cadenza* (*Italian* final flourish).
Caern. Caernarvonshire (former county).
Caith. Caithness (former county).
cal. calendar; calibre; calorie.
Cambs. Cambridgeshire.
Can. Canon; Canto.
can. canal; cancel; cannon; canton.
Canad. Canadian.
canc. cancellation; cancelled.
cand. candidate.
C & W (*mus*) country and western.
Cantab. *Cantabrigiensis* (*Latin* of Cambridge).
CAP Code of Advertising Practice; Common Agricultural Policy (of EC).
cap. capacity; capital; capitalize; captain; *caput* (*Latin* chapter).
caps. capital letters; capsule.
Capt. Captain.
car. carat.
Card. Cardiganshire (former county); Cardinal.
Carms. Carmarthenshire (former county).
carp. carpenter; carpentry.
carr. carriage.
cartog. cartography.
cas. casual; casualty.
CAT College of Advanced Technology.
cat. catalogue; catechism.
Cath. Cathedral; Catholic.
cath. cathode.
caus. causation; causative.
cav. cavalier; cavalry.
CB Cape Breton; Citizens' Band; Companion of the Order of the Bath; (*milit*) confinement to barracks.
Cb (*chem*) columbium.
CBC Canadian Broadcasting Corporation.
c.b.d. cash before delivery.
CBE Commander of the Order of the British Empire.
CBI Central Bureau of Investigation (USA); Confederation of British Industry.
CBS Columbia Broadcasting System.
CBW chemical and biological warfare.
CC carbon copy; Chamber of Commerce; Chief

Clerk; closed circuit; County Council; Cricket Club.

cc cubic centimetre; cubic centimetres.

cc. centuries; chapters; copies.

CCC County Cricket Club.

CCF Combined Cadet Force.

CCP Chinese Communist Party.

CCTV closed circuit television.

c.c.w. counter-clockwise.

CD Civil Defence; contagious disease; Corps Diplomatique; compact disc.

Cd (*chem*) cadmium.

cd candela.

cd. cord; could.

c.d. cash discount.

c/d carried down.

CDC Commonwealth Development Corporation.

CDN IVR Canada.

Cdr Commander; Conductor.

Cdre Commodore.

CDSO Companion of the Distinguished Service Order.

CE Chancellor of the Exchequer; Church of England; Civil Engineer; Council of Europe.

Ce (*chem*) cerium.

Cel. Celsius.

Celt. Celtic.

Cem. Cemetery.

cen. central; centre; century.

cent. centavo; centigrade; centime; centimetre; central; *centum* (*Latin* a hundred; century).

cer. ceramics.

cert. certain; certificate; certification; certified; certify.

CET Central European Time.

CF Chaplain to the Forces.

Cf (*chem*) californium.

cf. *confer* (*Latin* compare).

c/f carried forward.

cfm cubic feet per minute.

cfs cubic feet per second.

cft cubic foot or feet.

CG Coast Guard; Commanding General; Consul General.

cg centigram.

c.g. centre of gravity.

CGI City and Guilds Institute.

CGM Conspicuous Gallantry Medal.

cgm centigram.

cgs centimetre-gram-second.

CH Companion of Honour; IVR Switzerland.

Ch. Chairman; China; Chinese.

ch. chain; champion; chaplain; chapter; check; chemical; chemistry; chief; child; choir; church.

c.h. central heating.

Chal. Chaldaic; Chaldee.

Chanc. Chancellor; Chancery.

Chap. Chapel; Chaplain.

chap. chapter.

char. character.

ChB *Chirurgiae Baccalaureus* (*Latin* Bachelor of Surgery).

chem, chem. chemical; chemist; chemistry.

Ches. Cheshire.

chg. change; charge.

Chin. China; Chinese.

Chm Chairman.

chq. cheque.

Chr. Christ; Christian; Chronicles.

chron. chronicle; chronological.

chs chapters.

CI Channel Islands; Commonwealth Institute; IVR Ivory Coast.

Ci. cirrus; curie.

CIA Central Intelligence Agency (USA).

Cicestr. *Cicestrensis* (*Latin* of Chichester).

CID Criminal Investigation Department.

cif cost, insurance and freight.

C-in-C Commander-in-Chief.

CIS Commonwealth of Independent States.

cit. cited.

ckw clockwise.

CL IVR Sri Lanka.

Cl (*chem*) chlorine.

cl centilitre.

cl. class; classical; classification; clause.

cld. called; cancelled; cleared; coloured; could.

clin. clinical.

Cllr Councillor.

Cm (*chem*) curium.

cm centimetre.

Cmdr Commander.

Cmdre Commodore.

Cmdt Commandant.

CMG Companion of the Order of St Michael and St George.

CMO Chief Medical Officer.

CND Campaign for Nuclear Disarmament.

CNS central nervous system; Chief of Naval Staff.

CO Cash Order; IVR Colombia; Commanding Officer; conscientious objector; Criminal Office; Crown Office.

Co (*chem*) cobalt.

Co. Company; County.

c/o care of; carried over.

COBOL (*comput*) common business oriented language.

COD cash on delivery.

cod. codicil.

coef. coefficient.

C of E Church of England; Council of Europe.

C of I Church of Ireland.

C of S Chief of Staff; Church of Scotland.

c.o.h. cash on hand.

COHSE Confederation of Health Service Employees.

COI Central Office of Information.

COL computer-oriented language.

Col. Colonel; Colorado; (*Scrip*) Colossians; Columbia; Columbian.

col. column.

coll. collateral; colleague; collection; collector; college; collegiate; colloquial.

colloq, colloq. colloquial; colloquialism; colloquially.

comp. companion; comparative; compare; comparison; compensation; competitor; compiled; compilation; complete; composer; composition; compositor; compound; comprehensive; comprising.

compar. comparative; comparison.

compd compound.

compl. complement; complete; compliment; complimentary.

COMSAT Communications Satellite (USA).

con. concentration; concerning; concerto; conclusion; *conjunx* (*Latin* wife); connection; consolidated; *contra* (*Latin* against); convenience.

conc. concentrate; concentrated; concentration; concerning.

conf. *confer* (*Latin* compare); conference.

conj, conj. conjugation; conjunction.

conn. connected; connection; connotation.

Cons. Conservative; Constable.

const. constant.

Cont. Continental.

cont. containing; contents; continent; continental; continued; *contra* (*Latin* against); contract.

contd contained; continued.

contr. contract; contraction; contralto; contrary; contrast; control; controller.

contrib. contribution; contributor.

co-op co-operative.

corr. correct; correction; correspondence; corresponding; corrugated; corruption.

cos (*math*) cosine.

cosec (*math*) cosecant.

cosh (*math*) hyperbolic cosine.

cot, cotan (*math*) cotangent.

Cox. Coxswain.

CP Carriage Paid; Common Prayer; Communist Party.

cp. compare.

CPI consumer price index.

cpi characters per inch.

Cpl. Corporal.

cpm cycles per minute.

CPR Canadian Pacific Railway.

cps characters per second; cycles per second.

CPU (*comput*) central processing unit.

CR IVR Costa Rica.

Cr (*chem*) chromium.

CRE Commission for Racial Equality.

Cres. Crescent.

cres. (*mus*) *crescendo* (*Italian* increasing).

crit. criticism; criticize.

CRO cathode-ray oscillograph; Criminal Records Office.

CRT cathode-ray tube.

cryst. crystalline; crystallized; crystallography.

CS IVR Czechoslovakia.

Cs (*chem*) caesium; (*meteor*) cirrostratus.

csch (*math*) hyperbolic cosecant.

CSE Certificate of Secondary Education.

CSEU Confederation of Shipbuilding and Engineering Unions.

CSM Company Sergeant-Major.

CSU Civil Service Union.

ct. carat; cent; *centum* (*Latin* hundred); certificate; county; court.

Cu (*chem*) copper.

cu. cubic.

Cumb. Cumberland (former county).

CUP Cambridge University Press.

CV Curriculum Vitae.

Cwlth Commonwealth.

c.w.o. cash with order.

cwt. hundredweight.

CY IVR Cyprus.

D Democratic; Department; *Deus* (*Latin* God); (*chem*) deuterium; dimension; Director; *Dominus* (*Latin* Lord); Duchess; Duke; Dutch; IVR Germany; 500 (Roman numeral).

d. date; day; dead; deceased; decree; degree; delete; *denarius* (*Latin* penny); density; departs; deputy; diameter; died.

DA Deposit Account; District Attorney.

Dak. Dakota.

Dan. (*Scrip*) Daniel; Danish.

D & C dilation and curettage.

dat.   dpt

dat. dative.
dB decibel.
d.b.a. doing business as.
DBE Dame Commander of the Order of the British Empire.
D. Bib. Douay Bible.
dbl. double.
DBST Double British Summer Time.
DC Death Certificate; Depth Charge; Diplomatic Corps; direct current; District of Columbia.
d.c. (*mus*) *da capo* (*Italian* repeat from beginning); direct current.
DCB Dame Commander of the Order of the Bath.
DCM Distinguished Conduct Medal.
DCMG Dame Commander of the Order of St Michael and St George.
dct document.
DCVO Dame Commander of the Royal Victorian Order.
DD direct debit; *Divinitatis Doctor* (*Latin* Doctor of Divinity).
DDC Dewey Decimal Classification.
DDR Deutsche Demokratische Republik (German Democratic Republic).
DDT dichlorodiphenyltrichlorethane, an insecticide.
deb. debenture; debit.
Dec. December.
dec. deceased; decimal; decimetre; declaration; declension; declination; decrease; (*mus*) *decrescendo* (*Italian* becoming softer).
decd deceased.
decl. declaration; declension.
def. defective; defence; defendant; deferred; deficit; definite; definition.
deg. degree.
Del. Delaware.
del. delegate; delegation; delete.
Dem. Democratic.
Den. Denmark.
Denb. Denbighshire (former county).
dep. department; departs; departure; deponent; deposed; deposit; depot; deputy.
dept department.
der., deriv. derivation; derivative; derived.
Derbys. Derbyshire.
DERV diesel engined road vehicle.
DES Department of Education and Science.
Det. Detective.
det. detachment; detail.
Det. Con. Detective Constable.

Det. Insp. Detective Inspector.
Det. Sgt. Detective Sergeant.
Deut. (*Scrip*) Deuteronomy.
dev. development; deviation.
DF *Defensor Fidei* (*Latin* Defender of the Faith).
DFC Distinguished Flying Cross.
DFM Diploma in Forensic Medicine.
DG *Dei gratia* (*Latin* by the grace of God); *Deo gratias* (*Latin* thanks to God).
dia. diagram; dialect; diameter.
diag. diagonal; diagram.
dial. dialect; dialogue.
diam. diameter.
dict. dictionary.
diff. difference; different; differential.
dig. digest; digit; digital.
dim. dimension; diminished; (*mus*) *diminuendo* (*Italian* becoming softer).
dimin. (*mus*) *diminuendo* (*Italian* becoming softer); diminutive.
Dioc. Diocesan; Diocese.
Dip. Diploma.
Dir. Director.
dis. discontinued; discount; distance; distant; distribute.
disc. discount; discovered.
disp. dispensary; dispensation.
dist distant; district.
distr. distribute; distributed; distribution; distributor.
div. dividend; division; divorce.
DIY do-it-yourself.
DJ dinner jacket; disc jockey.
DK IVR Denmark.
dlvy delivery.
dly daily.
DM Deutsche Mark.
dm decimetre.
DMZ demilitarized zone.
DNA (*chem*) deoxyribonucleic acid.
do. *ditto* (*Italian* the same).
DOA dead on arrival.
d.o.b. date of birth.
doc. document.
DOE Department of the Environment.
dol. (*mus*) *dolce* (*Italian* sweet); dollar.
DOM *Deo optimo maximo* (*Latin* to God, the best and greatest); IVR Dominican Republic.
doz. dozen.
DP data processing; displaced person.
DPh, DPhil Doctor of Philosophy.
DPP Director of Public Prosecutions.
dpt department; deponent; deposit; depot.

Dr Doctor.

Dr. Drive.

dram. pers. *dramatis personae* (*Latin* characters present in the drama).

DS (*mus*) *dal segno* (*Italian* from the sign); disseminated sclerosis.

DSC Distinguished Service Cross.

DSM Distinguished Service Medal.

DSO Distinguished Service Order.

d.s.p. *decessit sine prole* (*Latin* died without issue).

DST Daylight Saving Time.

DT data transmission; delirium tremens.

DTI Department of Trade and Industry.

Du. Duchy; Duke; Dutch.

Dumb. Dumbarton.

Dumf. Dumfriesshire (former county).

Dunb. Dunbartonshire (former county).

dup. duplicate.

DV defective vision; *Deo volente* (*Latin* God willing); Douay Version (of the Bible).

DY IVR Dahomey.

Dy (*chem*) dysprosium.

DZ IVR Algeria.

dz. dozen.

E East; Easter; Eastern; England; English; IVR Spain.

e. elder; electric.

ea. each.

EAK IVR Kenya.

E & OE errors and omissions excepted.

EAT IVR Tanzania.

EAU IVR Uganda.

EAZ IVR Tanzania.

EC East Central; IVR Ecuador; European Community.

eccles ecclesiastical.

Eccles. (*Scrip*) Ecclesiastes.

ECG electrocardiogram; electrocardiograph.

ecol. ecological; ecology.

econ. economical; ecomics; economy.

ECT electroconvulsive therapy.

ed. edited; edition; editor; education.

EDC (*med*) expected date of confinement.

EDD (*med*) expected date of delivery.

edit. edited; edition; editor.

EDP electronic data processing.

educ. educated; education; educational.

EEC European Economic Community.

EEG electroencephalogram; electroencephalograph.

EEOC Equal Employment Opportunities Commission.

EFL English as a foreign language.

EFT electronic funds transfer.

EFTA European Free Trade Association.

e.g. *exempli gratia* (*Latin* for example).

EHF extremely high frequency.

elect. electric; electrical; electricity.

elem. element; elementary.

elev. elevation.

Eliz. Elizabethan.

ELT English Language Teaching.

EM electromagnetic; electromotive.

EMF, emf electromotive force.

EMI Electrical and Musical Industries.

Emp. Emperor; Empire; Empress.

EMR electronic magnetic resonance.

EMS European Monetary System.

EMU, emu electromagnetic unit; European monetary unit.

enc., encl enclosed; enclosure.

ENE east-northeast.

Eng. England; English.

eng. engine; engineer; engineering; engraved; engraver.

enl. enlarged; enlisted.

Ens. Ensign.

ENSA Entertainments National Services Association.

ENT ear, nose and throat.

entom. entomology.

env. envelope.

EO Executive Officer.

EoC Equal Opportunities Commission.

EP electroplate; extended play (record).

Ep. Epistle.

EPNS electroplated nickel silver.

eq. equal.

ER *Elizabeth Regina* (*Latin* Queen Elizabeth).

Er (*chem*) erbium.

ERNIE Electronic Random Number Indicator Equipment.

Es (*chem*) einsteinium.

ESE east-southeast.

ESL English as a second language.

ESN educationally subnormal.

ESP extrasensory perception.

esp, esp. especially.

Esq. Esquire.

ESRO European Space Research Organization.

Est. Established; Estate.

est. estimated; estuary.

ET IVR Egypt; extra-terrestrial.

ETA estimated time of arrival.

et al. *et alii* (*Latin* and others).

etc, etc. *et cetera* (*Latin* and so on).

ETD estimated time of departure.

ethnol. ethnology.

ETU Electrical Trades Union.

etym. etymological; etymology.

Eu (*chem*) europium.

Eu., Eur. Europe; European.

EV, e.v. electron volt.

ex. examination; excellent; except; exchange; excluding; excursion; executed; executive; exempt; express; export; extra.

exam. examination.

Exe. Excellency.

exch. exchange; exchequer.

excl. exclamation; excluding.

exclam, exclam. exclamation.

exec. executive; executor.

ex lib. *ex libris* (*Latin* from the library of).

ex off. *ex officio* (*Latin* by virtue of office).

ext. extension; exterior; external; extinct; extra; extract; extreme.

F Fahrenheit; farad; Father; fathom; February; Fellow; Finance; (*chem*) fluorine; folio; (*mus*) *forte* (*Italian* loud); IVR France; French; frequency; Friday; function.

f. farad; farthing; fathom; feet; female; feminine; filly; fine; fluid; folio; following; foot; (*mus*) *forte* (*Italian* loud); foul; franc; frequency; from; furlong.

FA Fanny Adams; Football Association.

f.a. free alongside.

Fac. Faculty.

fam. family.

FAO Food and Agriculture Organization.

f.a.s. free alongside ship.

fath. fathom.

FBI Federal Bureau of Investigation (USA).

FC Football Club.

FCI Foreign and Commonwealth Office.

FD *Fidei Defensor* (*Latin* Defender of the Faith).

fd. forward; found; founded.

Fe (*chem*) iron.

Feb, Feb. February.

fec. *fecit* (*Latin* he or she made).

fed. federal; federated; federation.

fem. female; feminine.

ff (*mus*) *fortissimo* (*Italian* very loud).

ff. folios; the following.

fict. fiction; fictitious.

Fid. Def. *Fidei Defensor* (*Latin* Defender of the Faith).

fig. figuratively; figure.

Fin. Finland; Finnish.

fin. final; finance; financial; finish.

Finn. Finnish.

FJI IVR Fiji.

FL Flight Lieutenant; IVR Liechtenstein.

Fl. Flanders; Flemish.

fl. floor; florin; *floruit* (*Latin* flourished); fluid.

Flem. Flemish.

Flor. Florida.

flor. *floruit* (*Latin* flourished).

fl. oz. fluid ounce.

FMD foot and mouth disease.

fn. footnote.

FO Flying Officer; Foreign Office.

fo. folio.

f.o.b. free on board.

FOC (*print*) Father of the Chapel (union official); free of charge.

fol. folio; followed; following.

foll. following.

for. foreign; forestry.

fort, fort. fortification; fortified.

FORTRAN (*comput*) Formula Translation.

FP former pupil; freezing point.

fp (*mus*) *forte piano* (*Italian* loud and then immediately soft).

f.p. freezing point.

FPA Family Planning Association.

f.p.s. feet per second; foot-pound-second; (*photog*) frames per second.

Fr (*chem*) francium.

Fr. Father; France; *frater* (*Latin* brother); French; Friar; Friday.

fr. fragment; franc; frequent; from.

f.r. *folio recto* (*Latin* right-hand page).

FRCP Fellow of the Royal College of Physicians.

FRCS Fellow of the Royal College of Surgeons.

freq. frequent; frequentative; frequently.

Fri. Friday.

front. frontispiece.

FRS Fellow of the Royal Society.

FSH follicle-stimulating hormone.

ft, ft. feet; foot; fort; fortification.

fur. furlong.

fut. future.

f.v. *folio verso* (*Latin* left-hand page).

fwd forward.

f.w.d. four-wheel drive; front-wheel drive.

FYI for your information.

fz (*mus*) *forzando* (*Italian* to be strongly accentuated).

G (*physics*) conductance; gauge; German; giga; grain; gram; grand; (*physics*) gravitational constant; guilder; guinea; gulp; gravity.

g gram, gramme; (*physics*) gravitational acceleration.

g. genitive; guinea.

Ga (*chem*) gallium.

Ga. Georgia.

Gael. Gaelic.

gal., gall. gallon.

galv. galvanic; galvanism.

GATT General Agreement on Tariffs and Trade.

gaz. gazette; gazetteer.

GB IVR Great Britain and Northern Ireland.

GBA IVR Alderney.

GBE Grand Cross of the Order of the British Empire.

GBG IVR Guernsey.

g.b.h. grievous bodily harm.

GBJ IVR Jersey.

GBM IVR Isle of Man.

GBZ IVR Gibraltar.

GC George Cross; Golf Club.

GCA IVR Guatemala.

GCE General Certificate of Education.

GCF greatest common factor.

GCMG Knight *or* Dame Grand Cross of the Order of St Michael and St George.

GCVO Grand Cross of the Royal Victorian Order.

Gd (*chem*) gadolinium.

gd good; guard.

Gdns Gardens.

GDR German Democratic Republic.

gds goods.

Ge (*chem*) germanium.

GEC General Electric Company.

Gen. General; (*Scrip*) Genesis.

gen. gender; general; generally; generator; generic; genetics; genitive; genuine; genus.

gent gentleman.

Geo. Georgia.

geog. geographer; geographic; geographical; geography.

geol. geologic; geological; geologist; geology.

geom. geometric; geometrical; geometrician; geometry.

Ger. German; Germany.

ger. gerund; gerundive.

GeV giga-electronvolts.

GG Girl Guides; Governor General.

GH IVR Ghana.

GHQ General Headquarters.

GI gastrointestinal; general issue; Government Issue.

Gib. Gibraltar.

Gk. Greek.

gl. glass.

g/l grams per litre.

Glam. Glamorganshire (former county).

Glas. Glasgow.

GLC Greater London Council.

Glos. Gloucestershire.

gloss. glossary.

GM Geiger-Müller counter; General Manager; George Medal; Grand Master; Guided Missile.

gm gram.

gm² grames per square metre.

GMB Grand Master of the Order of the Bath.

GMBE Grand Master of the Order of the British Empire.

GMC General Medical Council.

Gmc Germanic.

GMT Greenwich Mean Time.

GMWU National Union of General and Municipal Workers.

GNP Gross National Product.

gns. guineas.

GOC General Officer Commanding.

Goth. Gothic.

Gov. Governor.

Govt Government.

GP Gallup Poll; (*med*) general paresis; (*mus*) general pause; General Practitioner; general purpose; *Gloria Patri* (*Latin* Glory to the Father); Grand Prix.

gp group.

Gp Capt. Group Captain.

GPO General Post Office.

GR *Geogius Rex* (*Latin* King George).

Gr. Grecian; Greece; Greek.

gr. grade; grain; grammar; gravity; great; gross; group.

grad. gradient; graduate.

gram. grammar; grammarian; grammatical.

Gr. Br. Great Britain.

gr. wt. gross weight.

GS General Secretary; General Staff; ground speed.

gs. guineas.

gsm grams per square metre.

GT Grand Tourer.

gtd guaranteed.

GTS Greenwich Time Signal.

GU gastriculcer; genitourinary.

guar. guaranteed.

GUY IVR Guyana.

GW gigawatt.

gym. gymnasium; gymnastics.

gyn. gynaecological; gynaecology.

H hard (pencils); hecto-; (*physics*) henry; heroin; hospital; IVR Hungary; hydrant; (*chem*) hydrogen.

h hour.

h. harbour; hard; height; high; hit; horizontal; (*mus*) horn; hour; hundred; husband.

ha hectare.

hab. habitat.

Haw. Hawaii; Hawaiian.

HB hard black (pencils).

HC House of Commons.

HCF highest common factor.

HCJ High Court Judge.

HD heavy duty.

hd hand; head.

hdbk handbook.

hdqrs headquarters.

HE high explosive; His Eminence; His or Her Excellency.

He (*chem*) helium.

Heb. Hebrew.

her., heral. heraldic; heraldry.

Herts. Hertfordshire.

hex. hexagon; hexagonal.

HF high frequency.

Hf (*chem*) hafnium.

hf half.

HG High German; Horse Guards.

Hg (*chem*) mercury.

hgt. height.

HGV heavy goods vehicle.

HH double hard (pencils); His or Her Highness; His Holiness; His or Her Honour.

Hind. Hindi; Hindu.

hist. histology; historian; historical; history.

HIV human immunodeficiency virus.

HJ *hic jacet* (*Latin* here lies).

HJS *hic jacet sepultus* (*Latin* here lies buried).

HK IVR Hong Kong; House of Keys (Manx Parliament).

HKJ IVR Jordan.

HL Honours List; House of Lords.

hl hectolitre.

HM His or Her Majesty.

HMG Higher Middle German; His or Her Majesty's Government.

HMI His or Her Majesty's Inspector.

HMS His or Her Majesty's Service; His or Her Majesty's Ship.

HMSO His or Her Majesty's Stationery Office.

HMV His Master's Voice.

HNC Higher National Certificate.

HND Higher National Diploma.

HO Home Office.

Ho (*chem*) holmium.

ho. house.

Hon. Honorary; Honourable.

Hons Honours.

Hon. Sec. Honorary Secretary.

hort. horticultural; horticulture.

hosp. hospital.

HP hire purchase; horse power; Houses of Parliament.

HQ Headquarters.

hr hour.

HRH His or Her Royal Highness.

HS *hic sepultus* (*Latin* here is buried); High School; Home Secretary.

HT high tension.

ht. heat; height.

Hung. Hungarian; Hungary.

Hunts. Huntingdonshire (former county).

HV high velocity; high voltage.

hwy highway.

hyd. hydraudics; hydrostatics.

Hz hertz.

I (*physics*) current; incisor; Independence; (*physics*) inertia; Institute; Institution; Interest; International; intransitive; (*chem*) iodine; Island; Isle; (*physics*) isospin; IVR Italy; 1 (Roman numeral).

IABA International Amateur Boxing Association.

IAM Institute of Advanced Motorists.

ib. *ibidem* (*Latin* in the same place).

IBA Independent Broadcasting Authority.

ibid. *ibidem* (*Latin* in the same place).

IC integrated circuit.

i/c in charge; internal combustion.

ICA Institute of Contemporary Art.

ICBM intercontinental ballistic missile.

ICI Imperial Chemical Industries.

icon. iconographic; iconography.

ICU intensive care unit.

ID identification.

id. *idem* (*Latin* the same).

IDP integrated data processing.

i.e. *id est* (*Latin* that is).

IL IVR Israel.

ILEA Inner London Education Authority.

Ill. Illinois.

ill., illus. illustrated; illustration.

ILO International Labour Organization.

ILP Independent Labour Party.

ILTF International Lawn Tennis Federation.

IM Isle of Man.

IMF International Monetary Fund.

imit. imitation; imitative.

imp. imperative; imperfect; imperial; impersonal; implemerlt; import; important; importer; *imprimatur* (*Latin* let it be printed); imprint; improper; improved; improvement.

imper. imperative.

imperf. imperfect.

impers. impersonal.

impf. imperfect.

imp. gall. imperial gallon.

In (*chem*) indium.

in. inch.

Inc. Incorporated.

inc. included; including; inclusive; income; incomplete; increase.

incl. including; inclusive.

incog. incognito.

incor. incorporated.

incr. increase; increased; increasing.

IND IVR India.

Ind. Independent; India; Indian; Indies.

ind. independence; independent; index; indicative; indirect; industrial; industry.

indef. indefinite.

indic. indicating; indicative; indicator.

individ. individual.

Inf. Infantry.

inf. inferior; infinitive; influence; information; *infra* (*Latin* below).

infin. infinitive.

init. initial; *initio* (*Latin* in the beginning).

in loc. cit. *in loco citato* (*Latin* in the place cited).

ins. inches; inspector; insulated; insulation; insurance.

Insp. inspected; inspector.

Inst. Institute.

inst. instant; instantaneous; instrumental.

instr. instructor; instrument; instrumental.

int. interest; interim; interior; interjection; internal; international; interpreter; intransitive.

intens. intensified; intensive.

inter. intermediate.

interj. interjection.

INTERPOL International Criminal Police Commission.

interrog. interrogation; interrogative.

intr., intrans. intransitive.

intro. introduction; introductory.

inv. invented; invention; inventor; invoice.

I/O (*comput*) input/output.

Io (*chem*) ionium.

Io. Iowa.

IOC International Olympic Committee.

IOM Isle of Man.

IOU I owe you.

IOW Isle of Wight.

IPA International Phonetic Alphabet or Association.

IPBM interplanetary ballistic missile.

lQ intelligence quotient.

IR infrared; Inland Revenue; IVR Iran.

Ir (*chem*) iridium.

Ir. Ireland; Irish.

IRA Irish Republican Army.

lRBM intermediate range ballistic missile.

IRC International Red Cross.

IRL IVR Republic of Ireland.

IRQ IVR Iraq.

IS IVR Iceland.

Is. (*Scrip*) Isaiah; Island; Isle.

ISBN International Standard Book Number.

isl. island; isle.

isth. isthmus.

It. Italian; Italic; Italy.

ITA Independent Television Authority; Initial Teaching Alphabet.

Ital. Italian; Italic.

ITN Independent Television News.

ITV Independent Television.

lUD intra-uterine device.

i.v. intravenous.

lVR International Vehicle Registration.

IVS International Voluntary Service.

IW Isle of Wight.

J IVR Japan; (*physics*) joule; Journal; Judge; Justice.

JA IVR Jamaica.

Ja. January.

Jan. January.

Jap. Japan; Japanese.

Jas James.

JATO jet-assisted take-off.

JC Jesus Christ; Jockey Club.

JCB (trademark) Joseph Cyril Bamford (manufacturer of an earth-moving vehicle).

jct. junction.

Jl. July.

Jnr Junior.

JP Justice of the Peace.

Jr Junior.

jt joint.

Ju. June.

Jul. July.

Jun. June; Junior.

junc. junction.

Junr Junior.

Jus. Justice.

juv. juvenile.

Jy July.

K (*elect*) capacity; carat; (*math*) constant; (*physics*) kaon; (*physics*) kelvin; IVR Khmer Republic; kilo; King; knight; knit; kopeck; (*chem*) potassium.

K. (*mus*) Köchel (number) (Mozart catalogue).

KB King's Bench; Knight of the Order of the Bath.

KBE Knight of the Order of the British Empire.

KC Kennel Club; King's Counsel; Knight Commander.

kc kilocycle.

KCB Knight Commander of the Order of the Bath.

KCMG Knight Commander of the Order of St Michael and St Gearge.

KCVC Knight Commander of the Royal Victorian Order.

keV kilo-electronvolt.

KG Knight of the Order of the Garter.

kg kilogram.

KGB Komitet Gosudarstvennoi Bezopasnosti (*Russian* Committee of State Security, former USSR).

KGCB Knight of the Grand Cross of the Order of the Bath.

kHz kilohertz.

KIA killed in action.

kilo kilogram.

kJ kilojoule.

KJV King James Version (of the Bible).

KKK Ku Klux Klan.

kl kilolitre.

km kilometre.

km/h kilometres per hour.

kn (*naut*) knot.

KO knock-out.

Kr (*chem*) krypton.

Kt Knight.

kV kilovolt.

kW kilowatt.

kWh kilowatt-hour.

KWT IVR Kuwait.

L (*elect*) inductance; Lake; Latin; learner driver; Liberal; longitude; IVR Luxembourg; 50 (Roman numeral).

l litre.

l. lake; land; latitude; left; length; *liber* (*Latin* book); *libra* (*Latin* pound); line; lire; low.

LA Los Angeles.

La (*chem*) lanthanum.

Lab. Labour; Labrador.

lab. labial; laboratory.

Lancs. Lancashire.

lang. language.

LAO IVR Laos.

LAR IVR Libya.

Lat. Latin.

lat. latitude.

LB IVR Liberia.

lb. pound.

l.b.w. leg before wicket (in cricket).

LC Lance Corporal.

L/C Letter of Credit.

lc, l.c. *loco citato* (*Latin* in the place cited); (*print*) lower case.

LCC London County Council.

LCD lowest common denominator.

LCM lowest common multiple.

L/Cpl Lance Corporal.

Ld. Lord.

Ldg. Leading.

LEA Local Education Authority.

leg. legal; (*mus*) *legato* (*Italian* smooth).

Leics. Leicestershire.

LEM lunar excursion module.

LEV lunar excursion vehicle.

LF low frequency.

LG Low German.

lg. large.

lgth length.

LH luteinizing hormone.

l.h. left hand.

l.h.d. left hand drive.

Li (*chem*) lithium.

Lib. Liberal.

Lieut, Lieut. Lieutenant.

Lincs. Lincolnshire.

ling. linguistics.

lit. literal; literary; literature; litre.

LL Lord Lieutenant.

ll. lines.

LL.B. *Legum Baccalaureus* (*Latin* Bachelor of Laws).

LL.D. *Legum Doctor* (*Latin* Doctor of Laws).

lm (*physics*) lumen.

LMT local mean time.

LNG liquefied natural gas.

LOA leave of absence.

loc. cit. *loco citato* (*Latin* in the place cited).

log. logarithm.

long. longitude.

loq. *loquitur* (*Latin* he or she speaks).

LP long-playing (record); London Philharmonia.

LPG liquefied petroleum gas.

LPO London Philharmonic Orchestra.

L'pool Liverpool.

Lr (*chem*) lawrencium.

LRBM long range ballistic missile.

LRS Lloyd's Register of Shipping.

LS IVR Lesotho.

LSD *librae, solidi, denarii* (*Latin* pounds, shillings, pence); lysergic acid diethylamide.

LSE London School of Economics.

LSO London Symphony Orchestra.

Lt. Lieutenant.

l.t. local time.

LTA Lawn Tennis Association.

Lt. Col. Lieutenant Colonel.

Lt. Comdr Lieutenant Commander.

Ltd Limited.

Lu (*chem*) lutetium.

LV luncheon voucher.

LW long wave.

Lw (*chem*) lawrencium.

LWM low water mark.

lx (*physics*) lux.

M mach (number); Majesty; IVR Malta; Manitoba; Marquis; Master; (*physics*) maxwell; Medieval; Member; (*mus*) *mezzo* (*Italian* half); Middle; Monday; Monsieur; motorway; Mountain; 1000 (Roman numeral).

m (*physics*) mass; metre.

m. male; married; masculine; medium; meridian; mile; million; minim; minute; modulus; month; moon; morning.

MA *Magister Artium* (*Latin* Master of Arts); IVR Morocco.

mach. machine; machinery; machinist.

mag. magazine; magnetic; magnetism; magnesium; magneto; magnitude.

Maj. Major.

MAL IVR Malaysia.

manuf. manufacture.

MAO (*chem*) monoamine oxidase.

Mar. March.

mar. marine; maritime.

March. Marchioness; margin, marginal.

marg. margin; marginal.

Marq. Marquess; Marquis.

masc. masculine.

Mass. Massachusetts.

math. mathematics.

Matt. Matthew.

max. maximum.

MB *Medicinae Baccalaureus* (*Latin* Bachelor of Medicine).

MC Master of Ceremonies; Medical Corps; Military Cross; IVR Monaco.

mc megacycle; millicurie.

MCC Marylebone Cricket Club.

MCP male chauvinist pig.

MCS missile control system.

MD Managing Director; *Medicinae Doctor* (*Latin* Doctor of Medicine); mentally deficient.

Md (*chem*) mendelevium.

Md. Maryland.

Mdm Madam.

ME myalgic encephalomyelitis.

Me (*chem*) methyl.

Me. Maine.

mech. mechanical; mechanics; mechanism.

Med. Mediterranean.

med. medical; medicine; medieval; medium.

Medit. Mediterranean.

mem. member; *memento* (*Latin* remember); memoir; memorandum; memorial.

MEP Member of the European Parliament.

met. metaphor; metaphysics; meteorological; meteorology; metropolitan.

metal. metallurgical; metallurgy.

metaph. metaphor; metaphysics.

meteor. meteorological; meteorology.

MeV mega-electron-volt; million electron-volts.

MEX IVR Mexico.

MF medium frequency.

mf (*mus*) *mezzo forte* (*Italian* moderately loud).

mfd manufactured.

mfr. manufacture; manufacturer.

Mg (*chem*) magnesium; megagram.

mg milligram.

Mgr Manager.

mgt management.

MHF medium high frequency.

MHG Middle High German.

MHz megahertz.

MI MilitaryIntelligence.

mi. mile.

MI5 Military Intelligence, section 5.

MIA missing in action.

MICR (*comput*) magnetic ink character recognition.

Middx Middlesex (former county).

mil millilitre.

mil., milit military.

Min. Ministry.

min. mineralogical; mineralogy; minim; minimum; mining; minister; ministry; minor; minute.

mineral. mineralogical; mineralogy.

MIRAS mortgage interest relief at source.

MIRV multiple independently targetted re-entry vehicle.

misc. miscellaneous; miscellany.

mk mark.

mks metre-kilogram-second.

mkt market.

ml mile; millilitre.

Mlle Mademoiselle.

MLR minimum lending rate.

MM Military Medal.

mm millimetre.

Mme Madame.

MMR measles, mumps and rubella (combined vaccine against these).

Mn (*chem*) manganese.

MO Medical Officer; *modus operandi* (*Latin* mode of operation); Money Order.

Mo (*chem*) molybdenum.

Mo. Monday.

mo. month.

MOD Ministry of Defence.

mod. moderate; modern; modulus.

mod. cons. modern conveniences.

MOH Medical Officer of Health.

mol (*chem*) mole.

mol. molecular; molecule.

mol. wt. molecular weight.

Mon. Monday; Monmouthshire (former county).

Mont. Montgomeryshire (former county).

MOR middle-of-the-road.

MORI Market and Opinion Research Institute.

morph. morphological; morphology.

MOT Ministry of Transport.

MP Member of Parliament; Metropolitan Police; Military Police; Mounted Police.

mp (*mus*) *mezzo piano* (*Italian* moderately soft).

m.p. melting point.

mph miles per hour.

Mr, Mr. Mister.

MRBM medium range ballistic missile.

MRC Medical Research Council.

MRCP Member of the Royal College of Physicians.

MRCS Member of the Royal College of Surgeons.

MRP Manufacturer's Recommended Price.

Ms a title used before a woman's name instead of Miss or Mrs.

MS manuscript; IVR Mauritius; multiple sclerosis.

ms millisecond.

m/s metres per second.

MSC Manpower Services Commission.

MSc Master of Science.

MSG (*chem*) monosodium glutamate.

Msgr. Monseigneur; Monsignor.

msl mean sea level.

MT mean time.

Mt Mount.

mtg. meeting; mortgage.

mth month.

mtn mountain.

Mt. Rev. Most Reverend.

mun. municipal.

mus. museum; music; musical; musician.

mV millivolt.

m.v. (*mus*) *mezzo voce* (*Italian* half the power of voice); motor vessel.

MW IVR Malawi; medium wave; megawatt.

mW milliwatt.

Mx Middlesex (former county).

MY motor yacht.

mycol. mycological; mycology.

myth. mythological; mythology.

N National; Nationalist; Navy; (*physics*) newton; (*chem*) nitrogen; Norse; North; IVR Norway; November.

n. name; *natus* (*Latin* born); navy; nephew; net; neuter; (*physics*) neutron; new; nominative; noon; note; noun; number.

NA IVR Netherlands Antilles; North America.

Na (*chem*) sodium.

n/a no account; not applicable; not available.

NAAFI Navy, Army and Air Force Institutes.

NALGO National and Local Government Officers' Association.

NASA National Aeronautics and Space Administration (USA).

nat. national; native; natural.

NATO North Atlantic Treaty Organization.

NATSOPA National Society of Operative Printers and Assistants.

naut. nautical.

nav. naval; navigable; navigation; navy.

navig. navigation; navigator.

NB *nota bene* (*Latin* note well).

Nb (*chem*) niobium.

NBC National Broadcasting Corporation (USA).

NCB National Coal Board.

NCCL National Council for Civil Liberties.

NCO Noncommissioned Officer.

ncv no commercial value.

Nd (*chem*) neodymium.

NE northeast.

Ne (*chem*) neon.

NEB New English Bible.

NEC National Executive Committee.

NEDC National Economic Development Council.

neg. negative; negatively.

nem. con. *nemine contradicente* (*Latin* no one opposing).

neurol. neurol. neurology.

neut. neuter; neutral.

NF no funds.

NFT National Film Theatre.

NFU National Farmers' Union.

NHS National Health Service.

NI National Insurance; Northern Ireland.

Ni (*chem*) nickel.

NIC IVR Nicaragua.

NIG IVR Niger.

NL IVR Netherlands.

n.l. new line.

NMR nuclear magnetic resonance.

NNE north-northeast.

NNW north-northwest.

No (*chem*) nobelium.

No. Number.

n.o. not out (in cricket).

nol. pros. *nolle prosequi* (*Latin* do not continue).

nom. nominal; nominative.

noncom. noncommissioned.

non seq. *non sequitur* (*Latin* it does not follow logically).

Nor. Norman; North; Norway; Norwegian.

norm. normal.

Northants. Northamptonshire.

Northumb. Northumberland.

nos. numbers.

Notts. Nottinghamshire.

Nov. November.

NP Notary Public.

Np (*chem*) neptunium.

n.p. new paragraph.

NPT normal pressure and temperature.

nr near.

NRC Nuclear Research Council.

ns nanosecond.

n.s. new style.

NSB National Savings Bank.

n.s.f. not sufficient funds.

NSPCC National Society for the Prevention of Cruelty to Children.

NSU (*med*) non-specific urethritis.

NT National Trust; New Testament.

NTS National Trust for Scotland.

NUGMW National Union of General and Municipal Workers.

NUJ National Union of Journalists.

NUM National Union of Mineworkers.

num. number; numeral.

numis. numismatics.

NUPE National Union of Public Employees.

NUR National Union of Railwaymen.

NUS National Union of Seamen; National Union of Students.

NUT National Union of Teachers.

NV New Version (of the Bible).

n.v.d. no value declared.

NVQ National Vocational Qualification.

NW northwest.

NY New York.

NYC New York City.

NZ IVR New Zealand.

O Ocean; octavo; October; Ohio; Old; Ontario; Oregon; (*chem*) oxygen.

O & M Organization and Methods.

OAP Old Age Pensioner; Old Age Pensioner.

OB outside broadcast.

ob. *obiit* (*Latin* he *or* she died).

obb. (*mus*) *obbligato* (*Italian* obligatory).

OBE Officer of the Order of the British Empire.

obj. object; objection; objective.

obl. obligation; oblique; oblong.

obs. obsolete.

obstet. obstetrics.

obv. obverse.

OC Officer Commanding.

OCR (*comput*) Optical Character Reader; Optical Character Recognition.

Oct. October.

oct. octave; octavo.

OD Officer of the Day; overdose; overdraft.

OE Old English.

OECD Organization for Economic Cooperation and Development.

OED Oxford English Dictionary.

OF Old French.

off. offer; office; office; official.

OFT Office of Fair Trading.

OGM Ordinary General Meeting.

OHG Old High German.

OHMS On His *or* Her Majesty's Service.

OM Order of Merit.

o.n.o. or nearest offer.

Ont. Ontario.

o.p. out of print.

op. cit. *opere citato* (*Latin* in the work cited).

OPEC Organization of Petroleum Exporting Countries.

opp. opposed; opposite.

OR Official Receiver; operational research; other ranks.

orch. orchestra; orchestral.

ord. ordained; order; ordinal; ordinance; ordinary; ordnance.

Ore. Oregon.

org. organic; organization.

orig. origin; original; originally.

ornith. ornithology.

orth. orthography; orthopaedic; orthodox.

OS Old Style; Ordinary Seaman; Ordnance Survey; Outsize.

Os (*chem*) osmium.

o.s. out of stock; outsize.

OT Old Testament.

OU Open University.

OXFAM Oxford Committee for Famine Relief.

Oxon. *Oxoniensis* (*Latin* of Oxford).

oz. ounce.

P (*chem*) phosphorus; IVR Portugal; President.

p. page; paragraph; part; participle; past; penny; per; pint; *post* (*Latin* after); power; *pro* (*Latin* in favour of); purl.

PA IVR Panama; Personal Assistant; Press Agent; Press Association; Public Address.

p.a. per annum.

PAK IVR Pakistan.

P & L Profit and Loss.

P & O Peninsular and Oriental (Steamship Company).

p & p postage and packing.

par. paragraph; parallel; parenthesis.

Parl. Parliament(ary).

part. participial; participle; partner.

partn. partnership.

pass. passage; passenger; *passim* (*Latin* here and there); passive.

pat. patent; patented.

path., pathol. pathological; pathology.

Pat. Off. Patent Office.

pat. pend. patent pending.

patt. pattern.

PAYE Pay As You Earn.

Pb (*chem*) lead.

PBS Public Broadcasting System (US).

PBT President of the Board of Trade.

PC personal computer; Police Constable; political correctness; Privy Council.

p.c. per cent; postcard; *post cibum* (*Latin* after meals).

Pd (*chem*) palladium.

pd paid; passed.

pdq (*colloq*) pretty damn quickly.

PDSA People's Dispensary for Sick Animals.

PE IVR Peru; physical education.

PEI Prince Edward Island.

pen. peninsula; penitentiary.

per. period; person.

perf. perfect.

perm. permanent; permutation.

perp. perpendicular.

per pro. *per procurationem* (*Latin* on behalf of).

pers. person; personal.

PFA Professional Footballers' Association.

PG paying guest; Postgraduate.

pg. page.

PGA Professional Golfers' Association.

pharm. pharmacist; pharmacology; pharmacy.

PhD *Philosophiae Doctor* (*Latin* Doctor of Philosophy).

Phil. Philadelphia; Philharmonic.

phil. philology; philosopher; philosophical; philosophy.

philos. philosopher; philosophical; philosophy.

phon. phonetics; phonology.

phot. photograph; photography.

phr. phrase; phraseology.

phys. physical; physician; physics; physiological; physiology.

PI IVR Philippine Islands.

PIN personal identification number.

pizz. (*mus*) *pizzicato* (*Italian* plucking strings with fingers).

pk. pack; park; peak; peck.

pkg. package; packing.

pkt. packet; pocket.

PL Poet Laureate; IVR Poland.

P/L Profit and Loss.

Pl. Place.

pl. place; plate; platoon; plural.

PLA Port of London Authority.

PLC, plc public limited company.

PLO Palestine Liberation Organization.

PLP Parliamentary Labour Party.

PLR Public Lending Right.

plupf. pluperfect.

plur. plural.

PM *post meridiem* (*Latin* after noon); Post Mortem; Prime Minister.

Pm (*chem*) promethium.

p.m. *post meridiem* (*Latin* after noon).

PMT pre-menstrual tension.

PNdb perceived noise decibel.

PO Personnel Officer; Postal Order; Post Office.

Po (*chem*) polonium.

POD pay on delivery.

poet. poetic; poetical; poetry.

pol. political; politics.

pop. popular; popularly; population.

POS point of sale.

pos. position; positive.

poss. possessive; possible; possibly.

pot. potential.

POW prisoner of war.

PP Past President.

pp *per procurationem* (*Latin* on behalf of); (*mus*) *pianissimo* (*Italian* very soft).

pp. pages.

p.p. past participle; *post prandium* (*Latin* after meals).

PPE Philosophy, Politics and Economics.

PPS Parliamentary Private Secretary; *post postscriptum* (*Latin* additional postscript).

PR Proportional Representation; Public Relations.

Pr (*chem*) praseodymium.

pr. pair; paper; power; preferred; present; price; pronoun.

PRC People's Republic of China.

prec. preceding.

pred. predicate.

pref. preface; prefatory; preference; preferred; prefix.

prelim. preliminary.

prep. preparation; preparatory; preposition.

Pres. Presbyterian; President.

pres. present.

pres. part. present participle.

pret. preterit.

prev. previous; previously.

prim. primary; primitive.

prin. principal; principally; principle.

priv. private; privative.

PRO Public Records Office; Public Relations Officer.

pro. professional; prostitute.

proc. proceedings.

prod. product.

Prof. Professor.

prog. programme; progress; progressive.

prom. promenade.

pron. pronoun; pronounced.

prop. proper ; proprietor.

pros. prosody.

Prot. Protectorate; Protestant.

Prov. (*Scrip*) Proverbs; Province.

prov. proverb; proverbial; province; provincial; provisional.

prox. *proximo* (*Latin* next month).

prs. pairs.

PS Parliamentary Secretary; permanent secretary; postscript; Private Secretary.

Ps. (*Scrip*) Psalms.

PSBR public sector borrowing requirement.

pseud. pseudonym.

psi pounds per square inch.

PSV Public Service Vehicle.

psych. psychological; psychology.

PT Pacific Time; physical training.

Pt (*chem*) platinum.

pt. part; patient; payment; pint; point; port; preterit.

p.t. past tense.

PTA Parent-Teacher Association.

ptg printing.

PTO please turn over.

Pty Proprietary.

Pu (*chem*) plutonium.

pub. public; publication; published; publisher; publishing.

PVC polyvinyl chloride.

PVS post-viral symdrome.

Pvt., Pvte Private.

PW Policewoman; prisoner of war.

PY IVR Paraguay.

Q Quebec; Queen.

q. quart; quarter; quarto; quasi; question.

QB Queen 's Bench.

QC Queen's Counsel.

QED *quod erat demonstrandum* (*Latin* that was to be proved).

q.i.d. *quater in die* (*Latin* four times daily).

qlty quality.

QMG Quartermaster General.

qnty quantity.

qt quart.

q.t. quiet.

qto quarto.

qtr. quarter; quarterly.

qty quantity.

quad. quadrangle; quadrant; quadrilateral.

Quango quasi autonomous non-governmental organization.

quot. quotation.

q.v. *quod vide* (*Latin* which see).

R *Regina* (*Latin* Queen); *Rex* (*Latin* King); (*physics*) roentgen, röntgen; IVR Romania.

r. radius; right; river; road.

RA IVR Argentina; Royal Academician.

Ra (*chem*) radium.

RAC Royal Automobile Club.

RADA Royal Academy of Dramatic Art.

RAF Royal Air Force.

rall. (*mus*) *rallentando* (*Italian* gradually decreasing speed).

R & B (*mus*) rhythm and blues.

R & D research and development.

RB IVR Botswana.

Rb (*chem*) rubidium.

RC IVR China; Red Cross; Roman Catholic.

RCA IVR Central African Republic; Royal College of Art.

RCB IVR Congo.

rcd received.

RCH IVR Republic of Chile.

RCM Royal College of Music.

RCMP Royal Canadian Mounted Police.

rcpt receipt.

R/D Refer to Drawer.

Rd Road.

RDC Rural District Council.

RE (*chem*) rare earth elements; Royal Engineers.

Re (*chem*) rhenium.

rec. receipt; recipe; record; recorded; recorder; recording.

recd received.

recit. (*mus*) *recitativo* (*Italian* recitative).

rect. receipt; rectangle.

ref. refer; referee; reference.

refl. reflection; reflective; reflex.

Reg. Regent; Regiment; *Regina* (*Latin* Queen).

reg. regiment; region; register; registrar; registry; regular; regulation.

regd registered.

Regt Regent; Regiment.

rel. relating; relative; relatively.

relig. religion; religious.

REM rapid eye movement.

REME Royal Electrical and Mechanical Engineers.

Renf. Renfrewshire (former county).

Rep. Repertory; Representative; Republic; Republican.

rep. repeat; report; reported; reporter; representative; reprint.

repro. reproduction.

req. request; required; requisition.

res. research; reserve; residence.

resp. respective; respectively.

ret. retain; retired; return; returned.

Rev. (*Scrip*) Revelation; Reverend.

rev. revenue; reverse; revise; revision; revolution.

Revd Reverend.

RF radio frequency.

rgd registered.

Rgt Regiment.

RH IVR Republic of Haiti; Royal Highness.

Rh rhesus; (*chem*) rhodium.

r.h. right hand.

r.h.d. right hand drive.

rhet. rhetoric; rhetorical.

RHF Royal Highland Fusiliers.

RHG Royal Horse Guards.

RHS Royal Horticultural Society.

RI religious instruction; IVR Republic of Indonesia; Rhode Island.

RIBA Royal Institute of British Architects.

RIM IVR Republic of Mauritania.

RIP *requiescat in pace* (*Latin* may he or she rest in peace).

rit. (*mus*) *ritardando* (*Italian* decrease pace).

RL IVR Republic of Lebanon; Rugby League.

rly railway.

RM IVR Malagasy Republic; Royal Mail.

rm ream; room.

RMA Royal Military Academy.

RMM IVR Republic of Mali.

RN Registered Nurse; Royal Navy.

Rn (*chem*) radon.

RNA ribonucleic acid.

RNIB Royal National Institute for the Blind.

RNID Royal National Institute for the Deaf.

RNLI Royal National Lifeboat Institution.

RNR Royal Naval Reserve; IVR Zambia.

RNVR Royal Naval Volunteer Reserve.

ROC Royal Observer Corps.

ROK IVR Republic of Korea.

Rom. Roman; Romania; (*Scrip*) Romans.

rom. roman (type).

RoSPA Royal Society for the Prevention of Accidents.

RP Received Pronunciation.

RPI retail price index.

rpm revolutions per minute.

rps revolutions per second.

rpt. repeat; report.

RRP recommended retail price.

RS Royal Society.

r.s. right side.

RSA Royal Scottish Academy.

RSFSR Russian Soviet Federated Socialist Republic.

RSM Regimental Sergeant-Major; IVR San Marino.

RSPB Royal Society for the Protection of Birds.

RSPCA Royal Society for the Prevention of Cruelty to Animals.

RSPCC Royal Scottish Society for the Prevention of Cruelty to Children.

RSR IVR Rhodesia.

RSV Revised Standard Version (of the Bible).

RSVP *répondez s'il vous plait* (*French* please reply).

rt right.

Rt Hon. Right Honourable.

Rt Rev. Right Reverend.

RU IVR Burundi; Rugby Union.

Ru (*chem*) ruthenium.

RUC Royal Uster Constabulary.

Russ. Russia; Russian.

RV Revised Version (of the Bible).

RWA IVR Rwanda.

S Saint; Saturday; Saxon; School; Senate; September; Society; South; Southern; (*chem*) sulphur; Sunday; IVR Sweden.

S second.

S. section; series; shilling; signed; singular; soprano.

SA Salvation Army; South Africa; South America; South Australia.

Sab. Sabbath.

SAD seasonal affective disorder.

s.a.e. stamped addressed envelope.

SALT Strategic Arms Limitation Talks.

SAM surface-to-air missile.

Sans., Sansk. Sanskrit.

SARAH Search and Rescue and Homing.

Sat. Saturday; Saturn.

Sax. Saxon; Saxony.

sax. saxophone.

SAYE Save As You Earn.

SB Special Branch.

Sb (*chem*) antimony.

sb. substantive.

SBN Standard Book Number.

Sc (*chem*) scandium.

Sc. Scots; Scottish.

sc. scene; science; *sculpsit* (*Latin* he or she engraved it).

s.c. small capitals.

Scand. Scandinavia; Scandinavian.

SCE Scottish Certificate of Education.

SCF Save the Children Fund.

sci. science; scientific.

sci-fi science fiction.

Scot. Scotland; Scottish.

sculp. *sculpsit* (*Latin* he or she engraved it); sculptor; sculpture.

SD IVR Swazilarld.

sd sound.

s.d. *sine die* (*Latin* without date); standard deviation.

SDLP Social and Democratic Labour Party (Northern Ireland).

SDP Social Democratic Party.

SE southeast.

Se (*chem*) selenium.

SEATO Southeast Asia Treaty Organization.

sec. secant; second; secondary; secretary; section; security.

sect. section.

Secy Secretary.

Selk. Selkirkshire (former county).

SEN State Enrolled Nurse.

Sen. Senate; Senator; Senior.

Sep. September; Septuagint.

sep. separate.

Sept. September; Septuagint.

seq. sequel; *sequens* (*Latin* the following).

ser. serial; series; sermon.

Serg. Sergeant.

SF IVR Finland; San Francisco; Science Fiction; Sinn Fein.

sf. (*mus*) *sforzando* (*Italian* with a strong accent on a single note or chord).

SFA Scottish Football Association; (*colloq*) Sweet Fanny Adams, i.e. nothing.

sgd signed.

SGP IVR Singapore.

Sgt Sergeant.

Sgt Maj. Sergeant Major.

Shak. Shakespeare.

SHAPE Supreme Headquarters Allied Powers Europe.

SHO (*med*) senior house officer.

SI *Système Internationale* (*French* international system).

Si (*chem*) silicon.

SIDS sudden infant death syndrome.

sig. signal; signature.

sing. singular.

sinh (*math*) hyperbolic sine.

SLADE Society of Lithographic Artists, Designers, Engravers and Process Workers.

SLP Socialist Labour Party.

SM Sergeant Major.

Sm (*chem*) samarium.

SME IVR Surinam.

SN IVR Senegal.
Sn (*chem*) tin.
SNP Scottish National Party.
Snr Senior.
SOB (*sl*) son of a bitch.
Soc. Socialist; Society.
SOGAT Society of Graphical and Allied Trades.
Som. Somerset.
SONAR Sound Navigation and Ranging.
sop. soprano.
SOR sale or return.
SoS Save our Souls.
SP starting price.
Sp. Spain; Spaniard; Spanish.
sp. special; species; specific; specimen; spelling; spirit; sport.
s.p. *sine prole* (*Latin* without issue).
spec special; specification; speculation.
sp. gr. specific gravity.
SPQR *Senatus Populusque Romanus* (*Latin* the senate and people of Rome).
Sq. Squadron; Square.
sq. sequence; *sequens* (*Latin* the following); squadron; square.
sq. ft square foot.
sq. in. square inch.
SR self-raising.
Sr (*chem*) strontium.
Sr. Senior; Sister.
SRBM short range ballistic missile.
SRC Science Research Council; Student Representative Council.
SRN State Registered Nurse.
SRO standing room only; Statutory Rules and Orders.
SS Secretary of State; Social Security; steamship; *supra scriptum* (*Latin* written above).
SSE south-southeast.
SSM surface-to-surface missile.
SSPCA Scottish Society for the Prevention of Cruelty to Animals.
SSW south-southwest.
St Saint; Strait; Street.
Sta. Station.
Staffs. Staffordshire.
Stir. Stirlingshire (former county).
STOL short take-off and landing.
str. strait.
STUC Scottish Trades Union Congress.
STV Scottish Television.
sub. subaltern; subeditor; subject; submarine; subscription; substitute; suburb; suburban; subway.

subj. subject; subjective; subjectively; subjunctive.
subst. substantive; substitute.
Suff. Suffolk.
suff. suffix.
SUM surface-to-underwater missile.
Sun. Sunday.
supp., suppl. supplement; supplementary.
Supt Superintendent.
surg. surgeon; surgery; surgical.
surv. survey; surveying; surveyor.
SW shortwave; southwest.
Sw. Sweden; Swedish; Swiss.
SWA IVR South West Africa.
SWG standard wire gauge.
Swit., Switz. Switzerland.
SWAPO South West Africa People's Organization.
Sx Sussex.
SY IVR Seychelles.
syll. syllable; syllabus.
sym. symbol; symmetrical; symphony; symptom.
syn. synonym.
SYR IVR Syria.
T temperature; Testament; IVR Thailand; (*chem*) tritium; Tuesday.
t. tense; ton.
TA TerritorialArmy.
Ta (*chem*) tantalum.
tab. table; tablet.
tan (*math*) tangent.
TB tuberculosis.
Tb (*chem*) terbium.
tbs. tablespoon.
TC Tennis Club; Town Councillor.
Tc (*chem*) technetium.
Te (*chem*) tellurium.
tech. technical.
technol. technological; technology.
telecomm. telecommunications.
teleg. telegram; telegraph.
temp. temperate; temperature; temporary; *tempore* (*Latin* in the time of).
ten. (*mus*) *tenuto* (*Italian* sustained).
Terr. Terrace; Territory.
Test. Testament.
TF Task Force.
TG IVR Togo.
TGWU Transport and General Workers' Union.
Th (*chem*) thorium.
Th. Thursday.
theat. theatrical.

theol. theologian; theological; theology.
theor. theorem.
Thos Thomas.
Thurs. Thursday.
Ti (*chem*) titanium.
t.i.d. *tres in die* (*Latin* three times daily).
tkt ticket.
Tl (*chem*) thallium.
TM trademark; transcendental meditation.
Tm (*chem*) thulium.
TN IVR Tunisia.
tn town.
TNT (*chem*) trinitrotoluene, an explosive.
t.o. turn over.
tog. together.
topog. topographical; topography.
TR IVR Turkey.
tr. transitive; transpose.
trad. traditional.
trans. transaction; transferred; transitive; transpose.
transl. translated; translation; translator.
transp. transport.
TRH Their Royal Highnesses.
trig. trigonometrical; trigonometry.
tripl. triplicate.
TRM trademark.
trs. transfer; transpose.
tsp. teaspoon.
TT teetotal; teetotaller; IVR Trinidad and Tobago; tuberculin tested.
TU Trade Union.
Tu. Tuesday.
TUC Trades Union Congress.
Tues. Tuesday.
TV television.
U (*chem*) uranium; IVR Uruguay.
u. unit; upper.
UAE United Arab Emirates.
UAM underwater-to-air missile.
UAR United Arab Republic.
u.c. upper case.
UCCA Universities Central Council on Admissions.
UDC Urban District Council.
UDI Unilateral Declaration of Independence.
UDR Ulster Defence Regiment.
UEFA Union of European Football Associations.
UFO unidentified flying object.
UGC University Grants Committee.
UHF ultrahigh frequency.
UHT ultra-heat treated.
UK United Kingdom.

UKAEA United Kingdom Atomic Energy Authority.
ult. ultimate; *ultimo* (*Latin* last month).
UN United Nations.
UNA United Nations Association.
UNESCO United Nations Educational, Scientific and Cultural Organization.
UNICEF United Nations International Children's Emergency Fund.
univ. university.
UNO United Nations Organization.
US United States.
USA Union of South Africa; IVR United States of America.
USDAW Union of Shop, Distributive and Allied Workers.
USM underwater-to-surface missile.
USSR Union of Soviet Socialist Republics.
usu. usually.
USW ultrashort waves; ultrasonic waves.
UT Universal Time.
UV ultraviolet.
V 5 (Roman numeral); (*chem*) vanadium; IVR Vatican City; (*math*) vector; velocity; volt.
v. verb; verse; *verso* (*Latin* left-hand page); *versus* (*Latin* against); very; *vice* (*Latin* in the place of); *vide* (*Latin* see); voice; volt; voltage.
vac. vacancy; vacant.
val. valuation; value.
var. variant; variety; various.
VAT Value Added Tax.
Vat. Vatican.
vb verb.
VC Victoria Cross; Viet Cong.
VDU (*comput*) visual display unit.
VE Victory in Europe.
veg. vegetable.
vet. veteran.
VF video frequency; voice frequency.
v.g. very good.
VHF very high frequency.
VI Virgin Islands.
v.i. verb intransitive; *vide infra* (*Latin* see below).
Vic. Victoria.
VIP very important person.
Vis. Viscount.
viz. *videlicit* (*Latin* namely).
VJ Victory in Japan.
VLF very low frequency.
VM Victoria Medal.
VN IVR Vietnam.
vo. *verso* (**Latin** left-hand page).
voc. vocative.

vocab. vocabulary.

vol. volume.

vs. *versus* (*Latin* against).

VSO very superior old; Voluntary Service Overseas.

VSOP very superior old pale.

v.t. verb transitive.

VTOL vertical take-off and landing.

VTR videotape recorder.

vulg. vulgar.

Vulg. Vulgate.

v.v. *viva voce* (*Latin* spoken aloud).

W (*chem*) tungsten; Wales; Wednesday; Welsh; west; western; women's.

w. week; weight; width; with; won.

WA West Africa; Western Australia.

WAAA Women's Amateur Athletic Association.

WAAC Women's Auxiliary Army Corps.

WAAF Women's Auxiliary Air Force.

WAG IVR Gambia.

WAL IVR Sierra Leone.

WAN IVR Nigeria.

War. Warwickshire.

WASP White Anglo-Saxon Protestant.

Wb (*physics*) weber.

WBA World Boxing Association.

WBC World Boxing Council.

WC West Central.

w.c. watercloset.

WCC World Council of Churches.

W/Cdr Wing Commander.

WD IVR Dominica.

wd. ward; word; would.

WEA Workers' Educational Association.

Wed. Wednesday.

w.e.f. with effect from.

w.f. (*print*) wrong fount.

WG IVR Grenada.

w.g. wire gauge.

WHO World Health Organization.

WI Women's Institute.

Wilts. Wiltshire.

wk week; work.

WL IVR St Lucia; wavelength.

WNP Welsh Nationalist Party.

WNW west-northwest.

WO War Office; Warrant Officer.

w/o without.

Worcs. Worcestershire (former county).

WPC Woman Police Constable.

wpm words per minute.

WRAC Women's Royal Army Corps.

WRAF Women's Royal Air Force.

WRI Women's Rural Institute.

WRNS Women's Royal Naval Service.

WRVS Women's Royal Voluntary Service.

WS IVR Western Samoa; West Saxon; Writer to the Signet.

WSW west-southwest.

wt weight.

WV IVR St Vincent.

WVS Women's Voluntary Service.

WWI World War I (First World War).

WWII World War II (Second World War).

WX women's extra large size.

WYSIWYG (*comput*) what you see is what you get.

X 10 (Roman numeral).

Xe (*chem*) xenon.

XL extra large.

Xmas Christmas.

x.ref. cross reference.

xs. expenses.

Y (*chem*) yttrium.

y. year.

YB (*chem*) ytterbium.

yd. yard.

YHA Youth Hostels Association.

YMCA Young Men's Christian Association.

Yorks. Yorkshire.

yr. year; younger; your.

yrs. years; yours.

YTS Youth Training Scheme.

YU IVR Yugoslavia.

YV IVR Venezuela.

YWCA Young Women's Christian Association.

Z (*chem*) atomic number; IVR Zambia.

z. zero; zone.

ZA IVR South Africa.

ZANU Zimbabwe African National Union.

ZAIPU Zimbabwe African People's Union.

Zn (*chem*) zinc.

zool. zoological; zoology.

ZPG zero population growth.

ZR IVR Zaire.

Zr (*chem*) zirconium.